Table of Conter

Islamic Jurisprudence According to the Four Sunni Schools

Volume I

Modes of Islamic Worship

Islamic Jurisprudence According to the Four Sunni Schools

Volume I
Modes of Islamic Worship

by
'Abd al-Raḥmān al-Jazīrī

Translated from the Arabic
by
Nancy Roberts

FONS VITAE

First published in 2009 by
Fons Vitae
49 Mockingbird Valley Drive
Louisville, KY 40207
http://www.fonsvitae.com

Library of Congress Control Number: 2008942942

ISBN 9781887752978

This book was typeset by Neville Blakemore, Jr.

Printed in Canada

On *Zakāh* 795

On the *Ḥajj*, or Greater Pilgrimage 853

A Word from the Publisher

This first English translation of Volume I of the *Fiqh 'ala al-madhāhib al-arb'a* required 30 years of effort begun in Cairo, 1979. At every step of the way we have tried to be impeccable in this monumental project. Due to general human deficiency and the complexity of this task, we beg your forbearance regarding any mistakes which may have escaped our scrutiny.

Included for you here are contributions from two eminent scholars on the Fons Vitae Advisory Board, Shaykh Hamza Yusef Hanson and Maryam Ishaq al-Khalifa Sharief.

The Fiqh according to the Four *Madhāhib*

Sunni Muslims all around the world follow four different schools (*madhāhib*, sing. *madhhab*) of jurisprudence (*fiqh*): the Mālikī, the Ḥanafī, the Shāfi'ī, and the Ḥanbalī. Each of these schools derives its name from the great imam who first set its principles of jurisprudence: Abū Ḥanīfa, Mālik ibn Anas, Muḥammad ibn Idrīs ash-Shāfi'ī and Aḥmad ibn Ḥanbal. Each represents one possible reading of Muslim orthopraxis or of Islamic law (*sharī'ah*), covering such fields as ritual law, family law, inheritance law, as well as laws dealing with economic and political practices.

The *madhāhib* enshrine *ikhtilāf*

Historically, the four schools originated from the slightly differing approaches taken by Companions of the Prophet and their direct disciples, vis-à-vis the authoritative texts of Islam—the Qur'ān and the Traditions of the Prophet—when applied wherever they settled, in different lands of the Abode of Islam. Through these differing approaches, they allowed for a diversity of auxiliary tools and procedures in the formulation of laws. These were later acknowledged by posterity as equally authoritative interpretations of the Sacred Texts.

Principally, the four *madhāhib* enshrine the principle of *ikhtilāf* (disagreement/difference), which permits a Muslim to choose the interpretation of the religious teachings that best suits his own circumstances and causes the least harm. Two famous traditions of the Prophet Muḥammad in favour of *ikhtilāf* are: "Difference of opinion in the Muslim community is a sign of divine favour"; and "It is a mercy of God that the men of knowledge (*'ulamā'*) differ in opinion." One can also say that *ikhtilāf*, within the One *Sharī'ah*, represents a direct translation of the universal Islamic ideal that seeks to combine unity with diversity.

The geographical distribution of the *madhāhib*

The Ḥanafī School was adopted by the Ottoman and Moghul empires, which means that their former subjects, as well as adjacent territories in Central Asia, would normally be Ḥanafī. Thus, present day Turkey, the Central Asian republics, the Balkans, Iraq, Afghanistan, Pakistan, India, and Bangladesh are all Ḥanafī. Syria, Jordan, and Palestine as well as Egypt all adopted Ḥanafī judicial systems during the rule of the Ottomans, who imposed the Ḥanafī rite on all their subjects, but did not insist on any changes in the matters of worship, which remained Shāfi'ī.

The Mālikī School hailed from Medina and took root in North Africa, where it is followed in Algeria, Tunisia, Morocco, Mauritania, Libya, Upper Egypt, and Sudan, as well as in sub-Saharan and West African states, such as Chad, Nigeria, Niger and Senegal. In Arabia itself, certain sectors of Saudi Arabia—the Hejaz and parts of the Eastern Province—are also Mālikī. Mālikism is also the school of Kuwait, Bahrain, Dubai and Abu Dhabi.

The Shāfi'ī School is followed by many in the Hejaz, Egypt, North Yemen, and the Muslims of the East African states of Ethiopia, Eritria, Somalia, Kenya, Tanzania and Uganda. Numerically speaking, however, the greatest concentration of the Shāfi'ī School is in South East Asia, where it is followed in: Indonesia, Malaysia, and by the Muslim minority in the Philippines.

The Ḥanbalī School is concentrated mainly in the Najd area of Saudi Arabia, with extensions in Qatar, the North East of Oman and a good part of the Arab Emirates.

Egypt has traditionally accommodated all the four schools since Mamluk times. Each Mamluk Madrassa in Egypt had four sections that accommodated students of each school. Until Muḥammad 'Alī's time there were four courts as well, but he limited it to Ḥanafī legislation. However, the dominant rite of Egypt remains Shāfi'ī.

Maryam Ishaq al-Khalifa Sharief
Al-Azhar University, Cairo, Egypt
January 2009

Note on the Science of Islamic Jurisprudence

Of all of the sciences of Islam, jurisprudence is the one that by far has engaged the most human labor and intellectual effort. Even the great Qur'ān and *ḥadīth* commentaries of the past are replete with the legal implications of the Qur'ān and *ḥadīth*. Muslim scholars have always recognized the subtlety and ambiguity of language and developed a stunning methodological hermeneutic to insure that all of the linguistic possibilities were exhausted before coming to any conclusions about what a verse or prophetic statement did or did not mean. As a result, not only a tolerance but a genuine desire for difference of opinion arose within the scholastic tradition of Islam. The juristic schools emerged as a result. What many Muslims are unaware of is that not only do the various schools differ among themselves, but within each school there is a vast array of difference. Each school developed a normative tradition generally referred to as the 'dominant' (*mashhūr*) opinion of the school. This position in turn was nuanced by geographical regions, such as the dominant Andalusian opinion of the Mālikī school or the Iraqi position of the Shāfi'ī school. This leads to great confusion when studying the books of various legal schools without a teacher. Moreover, due to the vastness of each of the schools, it is almost impossible in one lifetime to master one school, let alone three others. Ibn Daqiq al-Id is one of the few people in the history of Islam known to have issued *fatwas* in two schools due to his mastery of the Shāfi'ī and Mālikī schools. Anyone today who claims to have mastered even one school with its divergent opinions should be viewed with scepticism. It is quite a challenge and takes years of study to master even the dominant opinion of one of the four Sunni schools, not to mention the Ja'fari school. Hence, it is well-known that books attempting to give us the opinions of all four schools must be viewed with great caution. This wonderful text, painstakingly brought to us by Fons Vitae, is extremely valuable as a tool for assessing the vastness of Islam's legal tradition and how those looking at the same sources often came to very different conclusions based upon their own idiosyncratic methodologies that were rooted in nuanced understandings particular to the respective Imams worthy of sound opinion. But invariably mistakes and less reliable opinions are included in summaries such as this. Infallibility is God's alone. For this reason, it is essential that students rely on legal experts trained within the respective schools for sound opinions regarding those schools. Even the Prophet Muḥammad had the Angel Gabriel as his teacher of Qur'ān and on many occasions waited for his teacher's judgment before giving one. While it was a case of a student being greater than the teacher, the lesson from God is obvious.

Hamza Yusef Hanson
Zaytuna Institute
February 2009

The Publisher

Foreword

It is a gratifying and rare event when an Arabic-language work of Islamic jurisprudence or *al-fiqh al-islamī* emerges in a clear, accurate, painstaking translation into English. The publication of *Islamic Jurisprudence According to the Four Sunni Schools: Volume I—Modes of Islamic Worship*, the translation of Volume One of 'Abd al-Raḥmān al-Jazīrī's *al-Fiqh 'alā al-madhāhib al-arba'a* by Nancy Roberts, is such an event.

Islamic law is far from a monolithic corpus of law. The religion and the law come down from the time of the Prophet in many streams. Some of the distinctions among Muslim belief and practice are termed in English "sectarian," such as that between Sunnis and Shi'is and others, since these distinctions stem from quite basic divergences between the groups about the sources (*uṣūl*) of the faith and of the law. Other distinctions are considered to operate within sects, since they concern divergences on how the fundamental sources are to be interpreted. Among Sunnis these latter distinctions are, as to matters of Islamic law, referred to as *madhāhib*, a term meaning roughly schools of thought, or in this case schools of law. Sunnis are considered to have only four surviving schools of law, the Ḥanafī, Mālikī, Shāfi'ī and Ḥanbalī.

The extraordinary feature of this work by al-Jazīrī (1882-1941) is that it records and juxtaposes for comparison the authoritative views of all four of these Sunni schools. Al-Jazīrī's work is not only ecumenical in this fashion; it is also encyclopedic. It treats almost all the essential *fiqh* issues covered by the old standard school treatises, and does so within the relatively manageable confine of five volumes (he himself published only four in his lifetime, others completing his draft of a fifth volume and adding it to later publications). Given these virtues, al-Jazīrī's book has been, ever since its first publication in 1928-1932, a constant resource for Muslims and non-Muslims. It remains today among the most accessible, commonly-used ways to find one's way through Islamic law's famed diversity of opinion.

One may wish to review and compare the views of all four Sunni schools for many reasons. Among Muslims, individuals not sufficiently learned to determine legal rulings for themselves (i.e., *muqallid, 'āmmī*) have the option, under variously stated moral or legal constraints, to choose, on some particular issue, to adopt the view of a school other than the school they ordinarily follow. Administrators of the law often have needed to know the views of various schools and choose among them according to one or another religious or practical criterion. From time to time throughout Islamic history projects for revivification of Islamic law have argued that scholars, and even non-scholars, should exert effort (called, for scholars, *ijtihād*) to investigate all available scholarly views, including those of all the four schools, and select that view which seems to them to be most in conformity with the ultimate sources of Islamic law, the Qur'ān and the Sunna of the Prophet. The constitutions of many of the modern Muslim nations emerging over the last century have incorporated implicitly or explicitly an old Islamic constitutional norm requiring that state legislation avoid fundamental offense to Islamic law. To be sure to meet this test, legislators often have composed their legislation by adopting rules taken from among extant Sunni views, choosing whichever view best supports public need or responds to present circumstance. Many basic reforms of law and regulation in modern Muslim countries have followed this approach.

Despite these and other practical reasons for a book like al-Jazīrī's, to my knowledge no book like it—a basic, didactic work covering all four Sunni schools equally—appeared before modern times. All traditional basic treatises of Islamic law have the object of laying out the views of one school of law only (though some of them cite the views of one or more other schools for comparison). This was for the sound reason that in those centuries all believers belonged to a single school and needed to know the views only of that school. Only in specialized works for scholars (such as those in the genre of *ikhtilāf,* or divergences of opinion), or by arduous comparisons among four different textual traditions, would anyone gain an equal view of all four schools.

The nature of al-Jazīrī's book—as giving the basic teachings of all four Sunni schools—marks it, therefore, as a modern work. Indeed, the work is characteristic of the time and place of its composition—Egypt in the 1920s and early 1930s. Since the middle of the 19th century the Muslim world had experienced earth-shaking change in Islamic legal thought and practice. Modernization and Westernization by emerging and newly independent Muslim nations greatly undermined the autonomy and authority of the traditional schools of law and the institutions that supported them. More positively, this period sparked many new ideas about Islam and its law, ideas either questioning past teachings or seeking to apply them in a new way. Modern educational systems pervasively altered the way that the public accessed knowledge and information. Egypt during the first decades of the 20th century was a hotbed of ideas and projects for reform of Islamic and Islamic legal thought and practice.

All this gives us a brief glimpse into the significance of the text before us. In view of this history and context, it is clear that Nancy Roberts has done the English-reading public an enormous service in spending years of careful work on her translation of the first volume of al-Jazīrī's treatise. This volume covers the intricate rules of ritual practice, chiefly prayer, fasting, alms-tax and pilgrimage. This work will be a valuable aid to many non-Arabic-speaking Muslims for refining their own daily practice, a ready resource for non-Muslims who wish better to understand many of the most essential teachings of Islam, and a basic teaching text in courses on Islamic law for non-Muslims.

We must express our gratitude also to the Fons Vitae publishing house and its Director Gray Henry for seeing this weighty work through editing and production into a splendidly produced volume. It joins their long list of precious publications produced for the enlightenment of the English-speaking world, Muslim and non-Muslim.

With this new volume, understanding of Islam and its law in the English-speaking world takes a notable step forward.

Frank E. Vogel
December 2008

Translator's Preface

Given the specialized nature of the material contained in the present work, I encountered inevitable translation-related difficulties at times, but as Providence would have it, I was given an invaluable consultant in my husband Amin Odeh, who holds a Ph.D. in Arabic Language and Literature and who took an active interest in the work I was undertaking. He bought me a veritable library of reference materials, including a variety of dictionaries dealing with terms relating to jurisprudence and the like, as well as placing at my disposal his already-existing collection of references. When I came to passages whose meaning was less than apparent, we would sit down with my questions and he would suggest possible ways of interpreting them. In addition, Amin went to the Jordanian University library and made photocopies of other editions of *Al-Fiqh 'Alā al-Madhāhib al-Arba'ah*, and on more than one occasion, it turned out that ambiguities in the text were due to either typographical errors or omission of words or phrases, which we found to be corrected in one or more of the other editions. When even then the text remained elusive, he helped me access further assistance by presenting our questions to a colleague of his at AL al-Bayt University in Mafraq, Jordan, with a specialty in Islamic law. In this connection, I extend special thanks to Dr. Fathallah Akthem Tuffahah of the College of Fiqh and Law, AL al-Bayt University for giving so generously of his time toward a proper understanding of the points in question.

In addition to the persons already mentioned, I'd like to thank Gray Henry for affirming her confidence in me by entrusting me with the task of rendering this demanding work into English, and Dr. Mary Ann Fadae for her important contribution to the translation itself, her valuable input and critical eye in proofreading and editing parts of the text and compilation of the glossary. I extend special gratitude to Eli H. Brown V for the momentous and daunting task of proofreading, as well as to Anne Ogden for her help. Thanks also go to my parents, A. Verne Roberts and Elisabeth Euwer Roberts, for the love of language they instilled in me, and for the freedom they always gave me to pursue what mattered most to me in life; to my siblings, Bob, Jim, Elisabeth and Margaret, for their love, support and encouragement over the years; and to my beautiful, vivacious, bright little girls, Batoul and Salaam, whose arrival in the world gave me the excuse I needed to withdraw sufficiently from other professional commitments to devote myself to the vocation I love most.

* * *

Translator's notes are provided either in the form of separate footnotes or, given the fact that 90 percent of the book is already in footnote form, between square brackets embedded in the text followed by the abbreviation "t.n." to identify them as my own interpolations.

All Qur'anic quotations are taken from Muhammad Asad's *The Message of the Qur'an* (Gibraltar: Dar al-Andalus, 1984).

Nancy Roberts
Amman, Jordan
December, 2007

On the Author

'Abd al-Raḥmān Ibn Muḥammad Awaḍ al-Jazīrī was born on the Egyptian island of Shandawīl in 1882 (1299 AH) and was educated at al-Azhar from 1896-1909; he later became a teacher at al-Azhar. In 1912, al-Jazīrī was appointed inspector for the Ministry of Religious Endowment's Department of Mosques, after which he was promoted to position of the Ministry's chief inspector. He was subsequently appointed as a professor in al-Azhar's College of the Principles of Religion, and before his death in Ḥelwān in 1941 (1360 AH), al-Jazīrī became a member of al-Azhar's Committee of Senior Scholars.

Al- Jazīrī's writings include: *Al-Fiqh 'Alā al-Madhāhib al-Arba'ah* ("Islamic Jurisprudence According to the Four Sunni Schools") in four volumes (Volume I was composed jointly by al-Jazīrī and a committee of scholars, while the remaining volumes were composed by al-Jazīrī alone); *Tawḍīḥ al-'Aqā'id* ("Clarification of Doctrines") on the science of monotheism; *Al-Akhlāq al-Dīniyah wal-Ḥikam al-Shar'iyah* ("Religious Ethics and the Manifestations of Wisdom in the Islamic Law"); *Adillat al-Yaqīn* ("Proofs of Certainty") in response to certain Christian evangelists; and *Dīwān Khuṭab* ("Collected Sermons").*

* The information above was taken from *Al-A'lām: Qāmūs Tarājim li-Ashhar al-Rijāl wal-Nisā' min al-'Arab wal-Musta'ribīn wal-Mustashriqīn*, by Khayr al-Dīn al-Ziriklī, Beirut: Dār al-'Ulūm lil-Malāyīn, Vol. III.

Introduction

It has been said that the only essential function with which no legal system can dispense is the preservation of order. Indeed, the relationship between "law" and "order" seems so intimate that the two terms flow together almost naturally, as if driven by some cosmic attraction. While a legal system's ability to quell disputes and eradicate crime will depend, in part at least, on the power of implementation wielded by the state, its ability to maintain order in the sense of sustained legal discourse will depend on the degree to which its sources, rules and ethos inspire a sense of awe and transcendence, the feeling that its authority is so absolute and its subject matter so rich and expansive that no single generation could hope to contain or exhaust it. This sense of awe and transcendence becomes the ground of a certain 'juristic attitude' that takes legal thinking beyond the purely practical. Law comes to include elements that are at once aesthetic, performative, historic and even 'mystical'.

Anyone familiar with Islamic legal literature will recognize this description of orderly legal discourse. Muslim jurists speak with a simultaneous sense of commitment to the present, past and future. They speak in a voice that is at once defiant and humble, individualistic and corporate, final and provisional, pragmatic and theoretical, indeed, exclusivist and catholic. All of this is underwritten, moreover, by a mutual recognition of an agreed-upon set of 'rules of engagement', the so-called "*usūl al-fiqh*," whose function is not merely to assist jurists in extracting meaning *from* the sources or precedents but also to referee the inevitable tendency to read meaning *into* these. In Islamic law, scripture and precedent, on the one hand, and socio-cultural and historical reality, on the other, negotiate a symbiotic rather than a mutually antagonistic, zero-sum relationship.

In many ways, however, it is precisely this sense of order in Islamic law that is lost on the casual observer. Among the major contributors to this obfuscation is Islamic law's status as a religious law. While pluralism, evolution, indeterminateness and an open acceptance of disagreement are easily identified as features of the modern, secular order, these qualities are not easily associated with a legal system whose structural foundations are pre-modern *and* religious. Even the existence of multiple authoritative and mutually recognized schools of law is prone to being encountered agnostically, its significance being misapprehended, devalued or overlooked. Indeed, the *religious* character of Islamic law may even blind the uninitiated to its *legal* properties, according to which authorities and doctrines have to be negotiated, change and evolution are not absent but disguised and pragmatism and theoretical purity co-exist in perpetual tension. Such oversights are particularly costly in attempting to understand Islamic law. For Islamic law was not the product of the Muslim state, as a result of which there existed no central authority capable of definitively resolving interpretive disputes, as does, e.g., the U.S. Supreme Court. Instead, the legal community would have to develop its own, independent system of interpretive adjudication.

Much of the foregoing might emerge from any serious reading of a standard manual of Islamic law. Islamic law manuals are generally written, however, from the perspective of a single school of law or *madhhab*. As such, conflict and contestation is significantly reduced by the very *raison d'être* of the manuals themselves, namely, to establish the "going opinion" (*mashhūr*, *rājih*, *mu'tamad*) within a given school. A full picture, then, of the nature, value and magnitude Sunni Islam's commitment to intramural order is best highlighted through a bird's eye view that takes in all of the Sunni schools of law.

This is precisely the approach of the celebrated work by 'Abd al-Rahmān al-Jazīrī (1299/1882-1360/1941), *al-Fiqh 'alā al-Madhāhib al-Arba'ah* (*Islamic Jurisprudence According to the Four Sunni Schools*). In this four-volume opus, al-Jazīrī catalogues the going opinions of all four Sunni *madhhab*s on a broad (though not the entire) range of topics formally covered by Islamic law in its classical guise. (The fourth volume ends with "The Book of Divorce" (*Kitāb al-Talāq*), and al-Jazīrī had intended to begin the fifth volume with "The Book of Punitive Sanctions" (*Kitāb al-Hudūd*). Alongside the going opinion on each question, he provides explanatory commentary that enables the reader to bring all four schools into conversation with each other and to compare and contrast the various legal doctrines, precepts, perspectives and applications. To take one example, according to al-Jazīrī, the Shāfi'ī and Hanbalī schools consider the shortening of prayers for reasons of travel to be a simple license, leaving it to the individual's own discretion to shorten the prayer or not. The Hanafī and Mālikī schools, meanwhile, assign a much higher priority to the practice of shortening, to the point that the Mālikīs say that a traveler who cannot find other travelers with whom to pray a shortened prayer should pray alone rather than join a non-traveling congregation.

Of course, the striking feature in all of this is the common body of foundation documents, *viz.*, the Qur'ān and Sunna, from which these legal doctrines are derived, at least in the formative period. While a Mālikī traveler might deem it appropriate to pray alone instead of joining his stationary Shāfi'ī or Hanbalī hosts, all can be recognized as following orthodox interpretations of the sources. Thus, while all jurists attribute the same basic level of authority to the foundational documents themselves, there is mutual recognition that these documents are open to multiple interpretations. And in the absence of a unanimous consensus to the contrary, all such interpretations are recognized, *ceteris paribus*, as orthodox.

This cumulative body of orthodox doctrines comes to constitute the precedents on the basis of which post-formative classical Islamic legal discourse proceeds. One notices in this regard that while al-Jazīrī occasionally cites an actual statement or precedent of the Prophet Muhammad as the basis of a school's doctrine, this is the exception rather than the rule. What *al-Fiqh 'alā al-Madhāhib al-Arba'ah* offers, then, is a presentation of Islamic law in its fully developed, post-formative, classical guise, where the institutionalized understandings of the schools of law are accepted *prima facie* and come to function as the primary prism through which the sources themselves are accessed and deployed.

This brings us to a cautionary note regarding the manner in which *al-Fiqh 'alā al-Madhāhib al-Arba'ah* is read. In many ways, al-Jazīrī's depiction parallels that of the *Hornbook Series* in American Constitutional law. It is essentially the skeletal framework within which Islamic law took and continues to take shape. While the going opinions he cites constitute benchmarks, they are not necessarily the last word on the subjects treated; nor are they necessarily intended, even by the schools themselves, to be binding on posterity for all time to come. Many of these rulings are based on methodological and pragmatic considerations, as well as factual assessments (social, cultural or economic reality) that are subject to change across space and time and from jurist to jurist. Thus, for example, according to al-Jazīrī, the Hanafī's, Mālikīs and Hanbalī's consider the fact that modern paper-money is or is not backed by gold or silver to be the basis upon which to determine whether one must pay alms (*zakāt*) on it. Clearly, however, such considerations are both time-bound and factual (i.e., not based on scripture). As such, another time or place could produce a different basis for such rulings and or a different factual conclusion based on this basis itself, in which case the rulings could either change or remain the same. Moreover, it would be the duty of the present generation to make this factual assessment, rather than defer to the conclusions of a previous generation. In sum, Islamic law in many aspects at least, is an on-going process rather than a fixed code. Any attempt to fix it permanently is bound to distort it.

What we have, then, in *al-Fiqh 'alā al-Madhāhib al-Arba'ah* is a solid, reliable and concrete basis for understanding how Islamic law operated in its post-formative past; a partial explanation for why Islamic law assumes many of the postures and confronts many of the challenges it assumes and confronts today; and a number of valuable insights into what Islamic law might and might not look like as it charts its way into the future.

This translation of Volume One of *al-Fiqh 'alā al-Madhāhib al-Arba'ah* will make an enormously valuable contribution to the study of Islamic law in English. Students and teachers alike will now have at their disposal a rich collage of concrete legal doctrines and explanations with which to gauge and demonstrate the workings of Islamic legal theory, as well as the ethos, pluralism and degree of indeterminateness in Islamic law. For this, we owe a great debt of gratitude to *Fons Vitae Publishing* for the vision reflected in this particular choice. And we owe an even greater debt to Nancy Roberts for the absolutely painstaking task that she has undertaken in producing such a lucid translation of this rich, complex, important and highly technical text.

Sherman A. Jackson
The University of Michigan
December 2008

Ritual Purity

On Ritual Purity

Its Definition

The meaning of the word 'purity' (*ṭahārah*) as it is generally used in the Arabic language is: cleanliness and being free from dirt or filth, whether it be physical or spiritual. According to a sound Prophetic Hadith narrated on the authority of Ibn 'Abbās, may God be pleased with him and his father, whenever the Prophet went to visit someone who was ill, he would say, "Be of good cheer! It will serve as a purifier, God willing." The word translated here as 'purifier', namely, *ṭahūr,* rhymes with *faṭūr*. [It is an intensified, active form meaning that which purifies someone of guilt and sin.] Hence, what the Prophet was saying is, "Illness is something which cleanses the sick person of sins," which are spiritual impurities.

The opposite of *ṭahārah* is *najāsah*, which has the meaning of anything deemed as unclean, whether physically or spiritually. Hence, sinful acts (*āthām*) are described as being a kind of *najāsah* in a spiritual sense. The Arabic verb from which the verbal noun *najāsah* is derived is *najasa* with variants *najisa* and *najusa* and *yanjasu* or *yanjusu* (present tense), while the adjective is *najis* or *najas*. Hence we have the Qur'anic saying, "O ye who believe! Truly the pagans are unclean (*najas*)" (9:28).[1]

With respect to the definitions of *ṭahārah* and *najāsah* as used by scholars of Islamic jurisprudence, there are differences among the four orthodox Islamic schools.[2]

---

1. In a note on his translation of this verse, Muḥammad Asad observes, "The term *najas* occurs in the Qur'ān only in this one instance, and carries an exclusively spiritual meaning (see *Manār X*, 322 ff.). To this day, the Bedouin of Central and Eastern Arabia—who, contrary to modern town-dwellers, have preserved the purity of the Arabic idiom to a high degree—describe a person who is immoral, unfaithful or wicked as *najas*" (Repentance, Note 37). [Translator's note: Henceforth, all translator's notes will either be in a separate footnote or set off from the text by square brackets and conclude with the letters "t.n."]

2. According to the Hanafi school, *ṭahārah* is, legally speaking, the state of being free from ritual impurity (*ḥadath* or *khabath*). They state, "Cleanliness includes whatever a person cleans or whatever gets cleaned by itself such as water falling on the unclean area and removing the impurity." They also say, "*Ḥadath* includes both minor impurity (*al-ḥadath al-aṣghar*), which is what invalidates one's ritual ablutions such as passing wind and the like, and major impurity (*al-ḥadath al-akbar*), which refers to sexual discharge, which necessitates the performance of *ghusl*, or major ablutions." The Hanafis define the term *ḥadath* as a legal description which applies either to some members of the body or to the whole body such that it removes ritual purity. This state is referred to as *najāsah ḥukmiyah*, that is, legal or technical impurity. In other words, the Lawgiver has ruled that *ḥadath* is a state of impurity which prohibits one from performing the ritual prayer just as physi-

Types of Ritual Purity

In our definition of *ṭahārah*, or ritual purity, above, we have given a detailed presentation of the views of the four orthodox Islamic schools which, although they differ in some respects, nevertheless allow us to arrive at an agreed-upon meaning for the term *ṭahārah*, or ritual purity. This definition may be stated as follows: Ritual purity is, legally speaking, a subjective or spiritual attribute which the Lawgiver has specified as a condition for the validity of ritual prayer and the permissibility of handling eating utensils, food, and the like. The Lawgiver has stipulated that, in order for a person's prayer to be valid, his body must have the attribute of ritual purity; that in order for prayer to be valid in a given place, this place must

---

cal impurity (*najāsah muḥassah*) prohibits it. As for *khabath*, in Islamic law it refers to the actual substance which is judged to be unclean, and which the Lawgiver requires us to remove.

Given the foregoing, one will understand that *najāsah* is the opposite of *ṭahārah*, and that it is a term which refers to two realities, namely, *ḥadath* and *khabath*. Linguistically speaking, both *ḥadath* and *khabath* are used to refer to anything which is deemed unclean, be it material, such as blood, urine, stool and the like, or spiritual, such as wrongdoing. However, scholars of Islamic law employ the term *ḥadath* to refer only to abstract matters; as such, it is a legal description which the Lawgiver has ruled applies to the entire body when there has been sexual discharge (major ritual impurity, or *janābah,* [thereby requiring *ghusl* or major ablutions], or to those members of the body which are washed when one performs *wuḍū'* or minor ritual ablutions whenever something has occurred to invalidate one's *wuḍū'*, such as passing wind and the like. As for *khabath*, it is used by Muslim jurisprudents to refer only to those physical substances which are deemed under Islamic law to be unclean, such as blood and so on.

Now, someone may say: This definition invalidates the notion of performing ablutions a second time with the intention of simply drawing near to God, since repeating one's ablutions removes neither *ḥadath* nor *khabath*, given the fact that the person who does so is ritually pure already. In reply to this it may be said: Even though performing one's ablutions a second time with the intention of drawing near to God removes no physical impurities, it does remove minor sins, which are a kind of moral or spiritual uncleanness. As we have seen above, the meaning of the word *khabath* in the Arabic language includes spiritual realities, and although Muslim jurisprudents limit the meaning of *khabath* to concrete realities, they nevertheless say that the removal of spiritual realities may be referred to as *ṭahārah*, that is, a kind of purification. Hence, repeating one's ablutions for the sake of drawing near to God is a form of purification in this sense.

This discussion brings us in turn to a familiar claim, namely, that it makes no sense to consider passing wind, for example, or engaging in sexual contact without ejaculation as events which would invalidate one's ablutions; nor does it make sense for the presence of semen on one's body or clothing to require the performance of major ablutions. The basis given for the first claim is that passing wind and the like involves no observable impurity, while the basis for the second claim is that semen

likewise be characterized by ritual purity; and that in order for the prayer of someone wearing certain clothing to be valid, this clothing must have the attribute of ritual purity. In addition, the Lawgiver requires that in order for us to be permitted to eat something, the food must be ritually pure, and so on.

Hence, the true nature of ritual purity is, in essence, one thing. However, it is divided into different types depending on its relation to either *ḥadath* or *khabath*, or depending on the entity to which it is attributed. Hence, based on the first consideration, ritual purity is classified into two types: namely, purity from *khabath* and purity from *ḥadath*. The Lawgiver requires that the body and clothing of the person who performs the ritual prayer be pure of *khabath*, while his body must be pure of

---

is a ritually pure substance; moreover, supposing that it were impure, it would be no more impure than urine or stool. Hence, it is only reasonable that purification from it should involve no more than washing the place where it is located. In response it may be said: Those who put forward such claims have no understanding of the meaning of worship or its expressions. The purpose of worship is to demonstrate submission to God Almighty with both the heart and the body in the manner which God Himself has defined for us. Hence, it is improper for anyone to transgress the limit that God has set for His servants, nor is it in the interest of the creature to debate over expressions and forms of worship except insofar as they cause him hardship or fatigue. After all, we have the right to ask that we not be burdened with responsibilities greater than what we can bear. However, all other matters pertaining to methods and forms should be left to the Worshipped One alone. This matter is clear and unambiguous even on the level of people's customs of showing mutual respect and veneration. Kings, for example, are not questioned as to the reason for the formalities according to which they receive people so long as they cause no undue hardship. Hence, since the Lawgiver has said, "Do not pray when you are in a state of minor or major ritual impurity," then we must obey without saying to Him, "Why?" Otherwise, we would also have the right to ask, "Why should we pray?" since the two types of question are essentially the same. After all, both ritual ablutions and prayer itself are means by which we worship God and express our submission to Him. Rather, what we have the right to say if, for example, we are unable to perform *wuḍū'* or *ghusl* or prayer, is: What should we do, then? It is in light of such situations that the Lawgiver has instituted practices such as *tayammum,* or sand ablutions, the performance of prayer sitting down or reclining, and the like. Hence, those things which concern us—such as the rules governing social conduct or personal status—we may ask about and discuss, since they are concerned directly with our own lives. We have the right to know the wisdom behind every issue and to discuss every particular; while those matters which are the province of God alone, we should accept without question.

This, I believe, is the most reasonable point of view. There are, however, Muslim scholars and thinkers who hold that every ruling related to Islamic law is based on some divine wisdom which can be discerned through human reason—a wisdom which will be clear to some and hidden from others—and that there is no difference in this respect between the forms of worship and the rules governing social conduct.

ḥadath as well. Hence, He has made ritual purity obligatory in both these respects, and ritual purity is consequently divided into these two types. As for *khabath*, it is those concrete substances which are deemed unclean from the point of view of Islamic law, such as blood, urine and the like and, as we have mentioned, such substances may be found on someone's body, on his clothing, or in a place.

Based on the second consideration noted above (namely, the entity to which purity is attributed), purity from such substances is further divided into two types: (1) intrinsic and (2) incidental. Intrinsic ritual purity is that which inheres in those things which are ritually pure by their very nature, such as water, soil, iron, minerals, and so on. This will be discussed below in the section on ritually pure sub-

---

The first claim above has been answered as follows: The passing of wind is unanimously considered unclean since, although it is not visible to the eye, it is perceived by the sense of smell. Moreover, before coming out of the body, it has been in contact with concrete substances which are impure. Those who say that passing wind does not invalidate one's ablutions and that urine or stool only require that one wash the place where they were present on the body must also say that it is only necessary to perform ritual ablutions once members of the body are exposed to various types of dirt, especially the mouth and the nose, while other benefits are spiritual in nature, such as the value of obedience and submission to God Almighty that help us to remain constantly aware of the majesty of our Creator. This awareness in turn causes us to refrain from any sort of loathsome or shameful deeds, which is for our benefit both in this world and the next. Hence, if one's ablutions never lose their validity and thus never need to be repeated, they have thereby lost both their legitimacy and their usefulness.

As for the second claim above, it has been responded to as follows: It is clearly invalid to draw an analogy between urine and stool on one hand, and semen on the other, because it is agreed that semen comes out of all parts of the body [sic]; moreover, it generally does not come out without the exertion of special effort. Then, once it has been expelled, the body experiences a notable sense of languor. It is self-evident that major ablutions restore the body's energy, help to compensate for some of what has been lost, and remove whatever overflow may have been clinging to the skin. Moreover, the legal obligation to perform major ablutions following sexual discharge is one of the beauties of Islamic law, since men cannot do without women and, once they have had intimate contact, they are obliged to clean their bodies; whereas if, by contrast, major ablutions were not required, people might become lazy, allowing themselves to become unclean and offending others by their odor. How, then, can we draw an analogy between semen and ordinary urine, which comes out of a particular part of the body without the exertion of any effort? Such an analogy is specious in every respect. Be that as it may, the various forms of worship in Islam are to be adhered to for God's sake alone without any thought for worldly advantages which might result therefrom, even though such worship itself is beneficial.

* * *

As for the Malikis, they hold that *ṭahārah*, or ritual purity, is a legal condition which renders it permissible for someone to perform ritual prayer in the clothes he has on and in the place where he intends to pray. Such purity is described as a legal

stances. As for incidental ritual purity, it refers to the state of being free of any sort of ritual impurity which might have been found on these substances. This type of purity is referred to as incidental because it may be brought about by means of cleansing agents such as water, soil, and so forth, which do away with the state of *khabath*. This type of purity will be discussed below in the section on removing ritual impurity.

As for *ḥadath*, it is a subjective or non-material attribute by which the Lawgiver describes a person's entire body when there has been sexual discharge, or some members of the body when something has occurred to invalidate one's ablutions such as passing wind, stool and the like. The first type of *ḥadath* is referred to

---

condition due to the fact that it is a subjective or non-material attribute which the Lawgiver has ordained as a condition for the validity of prayer and other acts of worship. If this attribute inheres in the one praying in that he is free of either major or minor ritual impurity, it makes it permissible for him to perform ritual prayer; if it inheres in the place in which one wishes to pray, it makes prayer permissible in the place concerned; and if it inheres in the clothes one is wearing, it makes it permissible to pray in these clothes. As such, ritual purity is an evaluative, spiritual matter rather than a concrete, observable condition.

There are two conditions which stand in contrast to ritual purity, or *ṭahārah*. The first of these is *najāsah*, or ritual impurity, which is a legal condition that renders ritual prayer impermissible in the clothes one is wearing or the place where one intends to pray. As for the second, it is *ḥadath*, which is likewise a legal state or condition which renders prayer impermissible. In other words, *najāsah* is an evaluative or subjective attribute which sometimes applies to one's clothing, thereby making it impermissible to pray in the clothes one has on, at other times to the place where one intends to pray, thereby making it impermissible to pray there, and at still other times, to the person himself, in which case the person's condition is described as one of *ḥadath* and he is not permitted to pray. In any case, *ḥadath* is the description of this condition ordained by the Lawgiver, and it may also be applied to those events or substances which invalidate one's ritual ablutions, as will be explained. The word *najāsah* may also be applied to a particular substance, such as blood, urine and the like.

* * *

According to the Shafiis, the term *ṭahārah* refers to two things, the first of which is an action by virtue of which one is permitted to perform ritual prayer. Such an action might be *wuḍū'*, or minor ritual ablutions, *ghusl*, or major ablutions, *tayammum*, or sand ablutions, the removal of substances which are ritually impure, and so forth, as well as an action with a similar meaning and form, such as sand ablutions, Sunnah-based major ablutions [that is, the performance of major ablutions when one is not obliged to according to Islamic law, but as a means of emulating the practice of the Prophet – t.n.], or repeating one's minor ritual ablutions for the sake of drawing near to God. What this means is that placing water on one's face and other members of the body with the intention of performing ritual ablutions is referred to as *ṭahārah*, since the word *ṭahārah* is a verbal noun describing someone's action. As for the phrase, "or an action with a similar meaning and form,"

as *al-ḥadath al-akbar*, or major ritual impurity, and one is purified from it by means of major ablutions (*ghusl*) as is also the case after menstruation or childbirth, since the Lawgiver deems these to be conditions which affect the entire body and which preclude ritual prayer and the like. As for the second type of *ḥadath*, it is referred to as *al-ḥadath al-aṣghar*, or minor ritual impurity, and one is purified from it by means of minor ritual ablutions (*wuḍū'*). Both major ablutions and minor ablutions may be replaced by sand ablutions (*tayammum*) in the event that water is unavailable or if one is unable to use water for some reason.

We shall now proceed to a discussion of all matters pertinent to this subject:

---

such as repeating one's ablutions when one is already ritually pure or Sunnah-based major ablutions, it indicates that these actions are also types of legal purification. However, they do not themselves render prayer permissible or valid, since prayer was already permitted based on one's initial ablutions without any additional, Sunnah-based ablutions. After all, what prevents the performance of prayer is *janābah,* or ritual impurity. Thus, major ablutions are a duty, not merely an action by which one adheres to the prophetic Sunnah. Nevertheless, it is necessary for a comprehensive definition of *ṭahārah* to include such actions as well.

The second element included in the Shafiis' definition of *ṭahārah* is the elimination of *ḥadath* or the removal of *najāsah*, that is, ritual impurity, or an action with a similar meaning and form, such as sand ablutions, Sunnah-based major ablutions, etc. *Ṭahārah* is in fact the spiritual condition which results from the action. Ritual impurity is removed through minor or major ablutions; hence, the removal is based on the action of an individual, and this is what is meant by *ṭahārah*. However, when the term *ṭahārah* is thus applied to the action itself, this involves metaphorical speech in which the result, namely, the state of ritual purity, is spoken of by referring to its cause, namely, the action of removing the impurity.

* * *

As for the Hanbalis, they hold that *ṭahārah* in its legal sense is the removal of *ḥadath* and any action bearing the same significance, as well as the removal of *najas* or the condition associated with it. What is meant by the removal of *ḥadath* is the removal of the condition which prevents one from praying and the like, since *ḥadath* is essentially a legal state which affects the entire body or some of its members. Hence, being purified from this condition or state entails its removal. When the Hanbalis speak of "any action bearing the same significance", they mean any action that has the same meaning as the removal of *ḥadath*. An example of this is the act of performing major ablutions on someone who is deceased, since the ritual bathing of a deceased person is done not to remove ritual impurity, but rather as an act of piety and devotion. The same is true of repeating one's ritual ablutions even though one is already in a state of ritual purity or performing major ablutions based on the example of the Prophet. After all, these two practices bear the same significance as obligatory ablutions even though they do not serve to remove any actual impurity.

As for the phrase "the removal of *najas*", it refers to the process by which some impure substance is removed, either by virtue of someone's action, for example, by washing the object which has been contaminated by an impurity, or by virtue of some process involving the substance itself, for example, by wine's turning to vin-

Ritually Pure Substances

As we have seen, ritual purity is divided into two types, namely, purity from *ḥadath* and purity from *khabath.* We have likewise seen that according to Muslim jurisprudents, *khabath* refers to a ritually impure substance. In what follows we shall mention examples of such substances, as well as ritually pure substances which stand in contrast to them. Then we shall give examples of types of impurity which may be disregarded, as well as ways in which impurities can be removed. We shall begin with ritually pure substances, since the basic premise from which we begin is that things are ritually pure unless demonstrated to be otherwise.

There are numerous ritually pure entities, among them human beings, whether living or deceased. As God Almighty declares, "Now, indeed, we have conferred dignity on the children of Adam" (17:70). As for God's declaration, "O ye who believe! Truly the pagans are unclean (*najas*)" (9:28), it refers to a state of spiritual impurity, and it does not mean that one who does not worship God alone is intrinsically impure in the way that swine, for example, are. Pure entities include inanimate substances, among which are all objects which have never been alive and which did not emerge from a living being. Inanimate substances are divided into two types, namely solids and liquids. Solids include all parts of the earth and its minerals, such as gold, silver, copper, iron, lead and so on. Also included among solids are all types of plants, even if they happen to be narcotics. Narcotic plants are referred to by the term *mufsid*, meaning that which corrupts, distorts or weakens. They include those plants like hashish and opium, which rob the person who ingests them of his or her reasoning ability without affecting the physical senses and without causing a sense of euphoria and a feeling of being 'high'. Other plants included among solids are, like *datūrah*[3] and henbane, those which exert a soporific or sedative effect and rob one of both his reasoning ability and his physical senses. Still other plants may be harmful to the body, such as poisonous plants. All such plants are ritually pure, even though it may be forbidden to use what is harmful to the mind, the senses, and the like.

As for liquids, they include water, oils, honey, rose water and other types of water derived from flowers, perfume and vinegar. All of these are included among ritually pure inanimate substances provided that they have not been contaminated by some other substance which would render them impure. Such liquids also include the tears, sweat, saliva and mucous of any living creature with variations in detail among the four orthodox schools.[4]

---

egar. As for the phrase, "or the condition associated with it" [that is, with *najas*], this refers to the nullification of the legal ruling which applies to someone or something that is ritually impure. This can take place even with dirt or sand such as in *tayammum*, by virtue of which someone ceases to be in a condition of ritual impurity which would prevent him from performing ritual prayer.

3. Also known as jimson weed or thorn apple [t.n.].

4. According to the Shafiis, these things are ritually pure if they come from an animal which is ritually pure, whether its flesh may be eaten or not. They also hold that the venom of snakes and scorpions is ritually pure.

* * *

Other ritually pure substances include eggs which have not gone bad and milk, be it human milk or that of animals whose flesh may be lawfully eaten. As for the living organism itself, be it human or non-human, it is ritually pure by its very nature, whereas other things are the subject of differing views by the four orthodox schools.[5]

Other ritually pure substances are phlegm, bile and sputum, as well as the gall of edible animals after they have been slaughtered in accordance with Islamic law (gall being the yellow liquid inside the gall bladder) and the gall bladder itself,[6] since it is part of the animal which has been slaughtered and, as such, subject to the same ruling as the animal itself with respect to ritual purity. Also included among ritually pure creatures are aquatic organisms which have died, even those which spent a good part of their lives on land, such as alligators,[7] frogs and sea turtles, even if they happen to resemble dogs, swine, or human beings. This ruling also applies to such creatures whether they die on land or in the water, and whether they die a natural death or are killed. This is based on the words of the Prophet, "There

---

The Maliki school holds that saliva, which is secreted by the mouth in both the waking and sleeping states, is ritually pure; however, what comes back up from the stomach and returns to the mouth is impure; such impure substances may be recognized by the change in their color and odor, as they tend to be yellowish and foul smelling. The Malikis hold that if such secretions are chronic, they may be disregarded, but that if they are present only on occasion, they may not.

* * *

According to the Hanbalis, tears, sweat, saliva and mucous are all ritually pure whether they come from an animal whose meat may be eaten or from some other animal, provided that the animal be similar to or smaller than a cat, and that it not originate from impurity.

* * *

As for the Hanafis, they hold that the ruling on the sweat and saliva of living creatures is the same as the ruling on *su'r* [that is, water in which an animal has fallen, swum, etc.] with respect to both purity and impurity, a point which will be explained below.

5. According to the Shafiis and the Hanbalis, these "other things" are dogs, swine and their offspring, or the offspring of one of them having mated with something else.

The Hanbalis also include animals larger than a cat whose flesh may not be eaten. The Hanafis hold that the only ritually impure animal is the pig, while according to the Malikis, there is no animal which is intrinsically impure; thus, dogs, pigs and their offspring are all ritually pure.

6. The Shafiis hold that gall is ritually impure and that the gall bladder is rendered impure due to its contact with the gall inside it, although it may be purified by being washed; the same holds true in their view for the stomach of ruminant animals, which is rendered impure by its contents and which may likewise be purified through washing. As for the Hanafis, they hold that the ruling on the gall of an animal will be the same as the ruling on its urine; hence, it is grossly impure in the case of animals whose flesh may not be eaten, and mildly impure in the case of

are two creatures which we have been given permission to eat even if they die of their own accord, and two kinds of blood: fish and locusts, and the liver and the spleen." Other creatures which may be eaten even if they die naturally are terrestrial creatures such as flies, woodworms, locusts, ants and fleas, which do not have blood which flows,[8] as well as wine which has turned to vinegar with differences among the orthodox schools over particular details.[9]

Still other ritually pure substances include the meat of animals whose flesh may be eaten lawfully and which have been slaughtered in accordance with Islamic law, as well as hair, wool, fur, and feathers, whether the creature to which the feathers belong is dead or alive and whether or not its flesh may be eaten according to

---

animals whose flesh may be eaten, while the gall bladder is judged to be pure or impure based on the purity or impurity attributed to its contents.

7. In the view of the Shafiis and Hanbalis, this category does not include alligators, frogs and snakes, which are ritually impure, although they deem all other aquatic creatures to be pure.

8. According to the Shafiis, all the creatures mentioned here are ritually impure except for locusts, while the Hanbalis stipulate that in order for a creature that has died naturally to be ritually pure, it must not reproduce by means of impure substances as do maggots, for example.

9. According to the Malikis, wine is purified if it turns to vinegar or solidifies even if such changes have been brought about deliberately, so long as no impurity fell into it before it became vinegar; they also hold that if such changes take place, the container which was holding the wine is likewise rendered ritually pure.

* * *

As for the Hanafis, they hold that wine is purified and that its container is purified along with it if it turns to vinegar, in which case it loses its wine-like properties, namely, bitterness and the ability to intoxicate. They also hold that it is permissible to turn wine into vinegar even if this requires that someone throw something into it such as salt, water, or fish, or that it be heated over a fire. If wine is mixed with vinegar and becomes sour, it is thereby purified even if it still contains more wine than vinegar. Moreover, if a mouse falls into some juice and is removed before it begins to decompose, and if the juice is left until it turns to wine, after which it turns to vinegar or someone turns it into vinegar, it will be pure.

* * *

According to the Shafiis, wine is only purified if it becomes vinegar by itself, and provided that no impure substance gets into it before this, even if the impurity is removed immediately. It is also necessary that the wine not have been kept in the same container as some pure substance before it became vinegar if the presence of such a substance can easily be avoided, since the pure substance will first have been rendered impure by the wine, after which it, in turn, will render the wine-turned-vinegar impure. As for pure substances whose presence is difficult to avoid, such as a small amount of grape seeds, they will be purified along with the wine, as will its container.

* * *

Islamic law. Moreover, all such substances are ritually pure regardless of whether they are still attached to the animal or have been removed, provided that they were not removed by plucking.[10]

Ritually Impure Substances and the Definition of Ritual Impurity

In the course of defining *ṭahārah*, or ritual purity, we have provided a general definition of *najāsah*, or ritual impurity as it is understood by the four orthodox schools of Islam in order to compare the two concepts. Our aim now will be to present the ritually impure entities which stand in contrast to those which are ritually pure.

As for the Hanbalis, they hold that wine is rendered pure if it becomes vinegar by itself, even if this takes place by its being moved from a sunny location to a shaded one or the reverse, or from one container to another without the intention of such actions being to cause the wine to turn to vinegar. When wine turns to vinegar, its container is purified along with it so long as it is not contaminated by something other than the wine-turned-vinegar, such as additional wine or the like.

* * *

In summary, the Malikis and the Hanafis agree that wine becomes pure if it turns to vinegar, whether the change takes place unassisted or by virtue of someone's action. However, they disagree over situations in which some impurity falls into the wine before it turns to vinegar; in such cases the Malikis hold that the wine is not rendered pure by turning to vinegar, whereas according to the Hanafis, the wine is still rendered pure by becoming vinegar provided that any impurity which may have fallen into it before this was removed before it decomposed.

As for the Shafiis and the Hanbalis, they agree that wine is only rendered pure if it turns to vinegar without any outside intervention, whereas if someone deliberately turns it into vinegar, it is not rendered pure. They likewise agree that if some impurity falls into the wine before it turns to vinegar, it will not be rendered pure by turning sour.

10. The Malikis hold that all the things mentioned here are ritually pure whether the animal from which they come is living or dead, whether or not its meat may be eaten according to Islamic law, even if it happens to be a dog or a pig, and whether or not these substances are still attached to the animal or have been removed by some means other than plucking, such as shearing, shaving, cutting, or depilation with lime or some other depilatory agent. The basis for this ruling is that such things have never been living tissue. If, however, they have been plucked out, their roots will be impure while the remaining parts will be pure. Similarly, they hold that the shafts of feathers from birds which have not been slaughtered are impure, whereas the hairlike down which grows on the shaft is unconditionally pure.

* * *

The Hanafis agree with the Malikis on all the aforementioned points with the exception of the Malikis' ruling on pigs; hence, the Hanafis hold that pigs' hair is impure regardless of whether the animal is living or dead, and regardless of whether

This, in turn, calls for a clarification of the meaning of *najāsah* both as it is commonly used in the Arabic language and as a term related specifically to Islamic law.

The most common use of the term *najāsah* is as a name for things which are deemed unclean; the same is true of the words *najis*, *najas*, and *najus*. Muslim jurisprudents divide *najāsah*, or impurity, into two types: (1) legal or 'technical' impurity and (2) actual, or intrinsic impurity, with differences among the four orthodox schools as to the details of their definitions.[11] However, they reserve the term *najas* for that which is impure in its essence such that it would be invalid to apply it to something affected by a merely temporary state of impurity. As for the

---

the hair is attached to the animal or detached, since they hold that the pig is ritually impure by nature.

* * *

According to the Shafiis, all the things mentioned here are ritually impure if they come from a living creature whose flesh may not be eaten according to Islamic law; the only exception they make to this is human hair, which is pure. Such substances are likewise impure if they come from a dead creature other than a human being. However, if they come from a living creature whose flesh may be eaten according to Islamic law, they are ritually pure unless they have been plucked out and there remains on their roots moisture, blood or a small piece of flesh which was removed unintentionally and which is, therefore, of no practical value; in this latter case, the roots will be impure while the remaining portions will be pure. If, on the other hand, they are plucked and a piece of flesh large enough to be of practical value is removed along with them, then both the roots and all portions are rendered impure.

* * *

As for the Hanbalis, they hold that the aforementioned substances are pure if they come from a creature whose flesh may be eaten according to Islamic law, whether it is living or dead, or from a creature whose flesh may not be eaten according to Islamic law, but which was judged to be ritually pure while it was alive; such an animal must also be no larger than a cat and must not reproduce through contact with an impurity. The roots of such substances are impure as long as they are still implanted in the flesh of a dead animal. The same roots are pure if they are still implanted in the skin of a living, ritually pure animal; however, they become impure if they are plucked out, though their other parts remain pure.

11. The Hanbalis define *al-najāsah al-ḥukmiyah*, translated here as legal or technical impurity, as a state of temporary impurity which affects a place which was ritually pure before it was affected by the impurity in question. As such, it includes impurities that take the form of a concrete, perceptible mass which adheres to something otherwise pure. As for *al-najāsah al-ḥaqīqiyah,* translated above as actual or intrinsic impurity, it is an entity which is impure in and of itself.

* * *

term *najis*, it has a broader application. Consequently, jurisprudents hold that the term *najis* can apply either to that which is impure only incidentally or temporarily, or to that which is impure in its essence. Hence, for example, blood can be referred to as either *najas* (impure in itself) or *najis* (incidentally impure), whereas a garment which has been rendered impure can only be described as *najis*.

Now, there are many entities which are ritually impure in themselves.[12] These include dead terrestrial organisms other than human beings which bleed when wounded. In this respect they differ from dead aquatic organisms, which are deemed ritually pure based on the words of the Prophet, "The water in which they live is not only ritually pure, but may be used for purification; moreover, the flesh of those

---

By contrast, the Shafiis define actual, or intrinsic, impurity as that which is characterized by a concrete mass, a taste, a color, or an odor. As for legal, or technical impurity, they define it as that which is characterized by neither a concrete mass, a taste, a color nor an odor, such as dried urine which can no longer be detected.

* * *

According to the Malikis, *al-najāsah al-'ayniyah* [that is, *al-ḥaqīqiyah*, or actual impurity] is the impurity itself, while *al-najāsah al-ḥukmiyah*, or technical impurity, is the effect of actual or intrinsic impurity on the basis of which a legal ruling is made on the entity affected thereby.

* * *

According to the Hanafis, legal or technical impurity refers to *al-ḥadath al-aṣghar* and *al-ḥadath al-akbar*, that is, minor and major ritual impurity, which are legal states that affect either the entire body or some of its members and by virtue of which one ceases to be ritually pure. Actual impurity, by contrast, refers to *khabath*, that is, every substance which is deemed impure according to Islamic law.

12. According to the Shafiis, all bloodless creatures which die, with the exception of locusts, are ritually impure. However, the matter may be disregarded if some part of such a creature falls by itself into water or some other liquid, since it does not render the liquid impure unless some change occurs in it. However, if a human being or an animal casts such a creature into water or some other liquid, or if the liquid in which the creature fell undergoes a change, then it is rendered impure and it may not be disregarded.

13. According to the Malikis, the parts of the dead body which were once living tissue are the flesh (that is, the meat), skin, bones, nerves and the like. However, they do not include the hair, coarse wool, fur or the down of feathers, since they were never alive to begin with and are thus not ritually impure.

* * *

According to the Shafiis, all parts of a dead animal, including bone, flesh, skin, hair, feathers, fur and so on are impure because, in their view, they were all once alive.

* * *

which die may be eaten." Similarly, human beings who have died are ritually pure, as we have mentioned above, as are terrestrial organisms which do not bleed if wounded, such as locusts.

Other ritually impure substances are the parts of a dead animal which were once living tissue,[13] as well as that which comes out of such an animal such as mucous, eggs, milk and rennet.[14]

As for the Hanafis, they hold that since the flesh and skin of a dead animal were once living tissue, they are therefore impure, but that bones, claws, beak, talons, hooves, horns, cloven hooves and hair are pure with the exception of pigs' hair. They base this view on the words of the Prophet, who stated concerning "Maymūnah's ewe", "It is forbidden to eat it." According to one rendering of this hadith, he said, "Its flesh is forbidden," which indicates that nothing but its flesh was forbidden. [It appears that the ewe in question had died for some reason, the circumstances of which are not mentioned – t.n.] Hence, the Hanafis view as pure all the body parts mentioned above so long as they contain no fatty substances, which would render them impure. With regard to nerves, there are two views: according to the more prevalent view, they are pure, although some claim that it is more correct to treat them as impure.

* * *

According to the Hanbalis, all parts of a dead animal with the exception of wool, hair and fur were once living tissue, as a result of which they are all ritually impure. The Hanbalis judge feathers to be pure based on the following words of God Almighty: "And God has given you . . . [the skill to make] dwellings out of the skins of animals, tents which you find light to carry when you travel and when you camp and [to make] of their wool and their fur and their hair furnishings and comfort for a while" (16:80). The apparent sense of these words is that they include both live and dead animals. As for feathers, they are deemed to be ritually pure based on their similarity to the substances mentioned here.

14. The Hanafis hold that the milk, rennet and eggs—both soft-shelled and hard-shelled—which come out of a dead animal or bird are all ritually pure just as they were when the animal was alive.

* * *

The Hanbalis, by contrast, hold that everything which comes out of a dead animal or bird is ritually impure with the exception of eggs that come out of a dead bird whose flesh may be eaten, provided that their shells have hardened.

* * *

As for the Shafiis, they hold that everything which comes out of a dead animal or bird is impure except for eggs with hard shells, regardless of whether the creature from which the eggs came is one whose flesh may be eaten or not.

* * *

The Malikis hold that everything which comes out of a dead organism is impure.

Impure animals include dogs and pigs[15] and their offspring, even if they happened to have mated with a different species. The evidence on the basis of which dogs are judged to be impure is the prophetic hadith narrated by Muslim according to which the Prophet said, "If a dog laps from a container belonging to one of you, its contents should be poured out and it should be washed seven times." As for why swine are deemed impure, it is based on an analogy drawn between dogs and pigs, since if dogs are impure, then pigs must be even more so given the fact that the Lawgiver has issued a prohibition against acquiring them.

Other substances which are deemed impure include that which is secreted by the dog and the pig by way of saliva, mucous, sweat, and tears,[16] as well as blood of all types except for that found in the liver and the spleen, which are deemed pure. The same is true of a martyr's blood as long as it is still on his body; by 'martyr' we mean someone who died in battle. (We shall have more to say on the subject of martyrs in the section entitled "Funerals" below.) Still other types of blood which are deemed ritually pure include the blood which remains in the flesh or veins of an animal which has been slaughtered according to Islamic law, and the blood of fish, lice, fleas and the *kinān*, a red insect with a powerful sting. All these types of blood are ritually pure, as well as some other types in the view of some of the schools.[17]

---

15. According to the Malikis, every living creature is ritually pure in itself, including dogs and swine. The Hanafis agree that dogs are ritually pure as long as they are alive; however, they hold that a live dog's saliva is impure in the way that its flesh is impure after it dies. Hence, if a dog were to fall into a well and then came out while still alive without its mouth having touched the water, the water would remain pure; similarly, if the dog shook off its water and then touched something, it would not render it impure.

16. The Malikis hold that all these substances are pure based on the principle, "Every living thing, including the substances which it exudes, is pure."

17. According to the Malikis, all blood which has been shed is impure without exception, even that of a fish. As for the meaning of "which has been shed" (*masfūḥ*), it is that which flows out of an animal. This is in contrast to that which remains in the flesh or veins of a ritually pure animal that has been sacrificed in accordance with Islamic law.

* * *

According to the Shafiis, all but four types of blood are impure, these four types being: (1) the milk of an animal whose flesh may be eaten if it comes out blood-colored, (2) semen if it is the color of blood, provided that it comes out in the normal manner, (3) eggs if they turn the color of blood, provided that they are still capable of producing life, and (4) the blood of a ritually pure animal if it turns into a clot or an embryo.

* * *

The Hanafis hold that blood which has not flowed out of a human being or animal is pure, as is blood which has turned into an embryo; however, if it has turned into a clot, it is impure.

Other ritually impure substances include pus which is not mingled with blood, the watery liquid which is secreted by a wound and which is mixed with blood, and the liquid secreted by blisters and sores.[18] Also included are human wastes such as urine and stool, even if they are still in the form of food which has been ingested and even if the person is an infant who does not eat food. Other impure substances include the wastes of animals whose flesh may not be eaten and which have blood which flows, such as donkeys and mules.[19] As for the wastes of animals whose flesh may be eaten, the various schools have differing views on the matter.[20]

---

18. The Hanafis hold that liquids secreted by the body other than pus or suppurative matter are pure if they are not a result of some illness or pathological condition; however, if they do result from such a condition, even if it is not associated with any pain, they are impure. This ruling applies to blisters which have filled with fluid and are ready to burst, as well as fluids secreted by the navel, the ear and the eye. As for fluids secreted by an infected eye, they are impure even if they are not associated with pain, for example, when there is an abnormal, constant, but painless flow of tears from the eyes.

* * *

As for the Shafiis, they hold that fluids secreted by blisters and sores (other than pus and blood) are impure only if their color or odor changes; otherwise, they are pure like sweat.

19. With regard to the wastes of animals whose flesh may not be eaten, the Hanafis hold that if the animal is one that flies in the air such as a crow, its waste products are mildly impure, but that otherwise, they are grossly impure; however, in situations where there are large quantities of waste material in the streets in the form of mules' and donkeys' dung, for example, it may be disregarded due to the hardship entailed by avoiding contact with it.

20. The Shafiis hold that the wastes of animals whose flesh may be eaten are also impure.

* * *

According to the Hanafis, the wastes of animals whose flesh may be eaten are mildly impure; however, they make distinctions among different types of birds, saying: If it is one which drops excrement in the air as do pigeons and sparrows, then its wastes are pure; otherwise, they are mildly impure as are the wastes of chickens, domestic ducks and geese (according to the two companions, namely, Abū Ḥanīfah's two companions and disciples Abū Yūsuf al-Qāḍī and Muḥammad Ibn al-Ḥasan al-Shaybanī), or grossly impure (according to the Imam, namely, Abū Ḥanīfah himself).

* * *

According to the Malikis, the wastes of animals and birds whose flesh may be eaten, such as cows, goats, and sheep, are pure if they have not been accustomed to feeding on impurities; however, if they are known or suspected to be feeding on impurities, then their wastes are impure. If there is some doubt as to whether they have been feeding on impurities or not and if it is customary for them to do so as in the case of chickens, then their wastes are impure, whereas if it is not customary for them to feed on impurity, as in the case of pigeons, then their wastes are pure.

Still other substances which are viewed as ritually impure include the semen of human beings and other creatures,[21] semen being the watery fluid which is secreted by the male during pleasure resulting from sexual intercourse and the like. When the man has completed his ejaculation, this fluid is white and viscous, while the secretion produced by the woman is yellowish and thin. Some have said that the fluid secreted by the woman does not leave the vagina, although traces of it may be left on the man's penis. As for those who deny that the woman produces any secretion comparable to the man's semen, saying that what is observed in the woman's body is nothing but the moistness of the vagina, they are denying the obvious. Also included here is pre-seminal fluid (*al-madhī*), that is, the secretion discharged prior

---

* * *

As for the Hanbalis, they hold that the wastes of animals and birds whose flesh may be eaten are pure even if they graze on impurities so long as such impurities do not constitute the greater part of their diet; otherwise, their wastes are impure and so is their meat. Nevertheless, if such animals or birds are prevented from feeding on impurities for a period of three days, then after the end of the three-day period their wastes become pure, as does their meat.

21. The Shafiis hold that human semen secreted after the age of nine is pure whether the person is dead or alive. It remains pure even if it comes out with the appearance of blood so long as it is secreted through its normal channel; otherwise, it is impure. The evidence in support of viewing semen as ritually pure is the hadith narrated by al-Bayhaqī according to which the Prophet was once asked about semen which has gotten on someone's clothing. He replied, in effect, "It is similar to spittle or mucous." Based on this ruling, the semen of any living animal is likewise deemed to be pure, since it is the source from which a pure animal originates. However, they do not include the semen of dogs and swine or their offspring based on the argument that it is rendered impure by its source.

* * *

According to the Hanbalis, human semen is pure if it comes out through its normal channel in response to sexual pleasure after the age of nine for females, and after the age of ten for males, and even if it comes out with the appearance of blood. They base their view of human semen as ritually pure on the words of 'Ā'ishah, may God be pleased with her, who said, "I used to rub semen off of the Messenger of God's robe, after which he would go to pray in it." As for the semen of non-humans, it is pure if it comes from an animal whose flesh may be eaten; otherwise, it is impure.

22. The Hanbalis uphold the purity of both *al-madhī* and *al-wadī* if they come from animals whose meat may be lawfully eaten.

23. According to the Hanafis, vomit is grossly impure if it fills the mouth and has to be involuntarily expelled even if one vomits only once, and even if the substance vomited is food, water, or coagulated blood; this ruling applies even if the substance in question has not settled in the stomach or is the result of an infant's "burping up" after nursing. Hence, vomit differs from the liquid secreted by the mouth while one is asleep, which is pure. It likewise differs from a situation in

to a man's ejaculation during foreplay and the like, and what is termed in Arabic *al-wadī*, that is, a white viscous fluid which generally comes out following urination.[22]

Other ritually impure substances include vomit and partially digested food or drink that has been regurgitated and returns to the mouth, on both of which there are differing views among the four schools.[23]

---

which one vomits up worms, whether a small or large amount, and whether the worms are small or large, since this is pure also. As for partially digested food or drink which comes back up from the stomach, it is similar to vomit, based on the words of the Prophet, "If anyone should vomit or regurgitate while praying, he should stop praying and do his ablutions again." With regard to phlegm and blood mixed with saliva, the Hanafis say that if phlegm comes out unmixed with anything else, it is pure; if it comes out mixed with food and there is more food than phlegm, it is impure; if, on the other hand, there are equal amounts of phlegm and food, then each substance is to be treated separately. That is, if food alone fills the mouth, then the ruling on it is the same as that on vomit. As for blood mixed with saliva, they say that if there is more saliva than blood with the result that what comes out is yellow in color, then it is pure; if, on the other hand, there is more blood than saliva such that it is a red color, whether the amounts of blood and saliva are equal or the amount of blood is greater, then it is impure even if it does not fill the mouth. Similarly, that which has been ruminated by camels, sheep and goats (their "cud") is impure, whether the amount is small or large.

It should also be noted that if one vomits several times in a row and if the amount of vomit each time is insufficient to fill the mouth even though the total amount would have filled the mouth, it is still impure.

* * *

The Malikis define vomit, which they deem impure, as food which has come back up from the stomach after having settled there for some time. However, it is only impure if it has changed from being in the state of food, even if only by virtue of a slight acidity. Regurgitation, by contrast, is the watery fluid which is expelled by the stomach when it is full, and it is only impure if it has taken on any of the characteristics of stool. As for acidity alone, it is not harmful; hence, if the watery fluid which is forced out of the stomach comes out acidic but is otherwise unchanged, then it is not impure, given the mildness of the acidity and the frequency with which this tends to occur. If such fluid has taken on a yellowish color or has a foul odor when it comes out of the stomach, then it is impure like vomit; however, it may be disregarded if it is a chronic occurrence due to the undue hardship it would otherwise entail.

* * *

According to the Shafiis, vomit is impure even if it is food or water which has come up immediately and has not undergone any change. However, it may only be judged impure if it can be verified that it came out of the stomach; if there is doubt as to whether it came out of the stomach, then it should be assumed to be pure. The Shafiis similarly deem impure the watery fluid which comes out of someone's mouth during sleep if it is a yellowish color or has an unpleasant odor; however, it may be

Another substance judged to be impure is rotten eggs taken from a live bird, with differences among the schools as to specific details.[24]

Also deemed ritually impure are substances which have become separated[25] from a live animal which is deemed impure when dead, excluding those parts which have been shown above to be exceptions to the ruling on dead organisms. Also

---

disregarded in the cases of those who experience it chronically. As for the cud of camels, sheep and goats, it is impure regardless of whether the amount is small or large.

* * *

The Hanbalis state that vomit and regurgitated food and water are all impure without discussing this ruling in any detail.

24. The Malikis define 'rotten' in this context as an egg which has become putrid or blue or which has turned to blood, an embryo, or a dead chick; such an egg is to be contrasted with one in which the white has mingled with the yolk (referred to as *mamrūq*), or which contains an intact drop of blood, both of which are pure. As for the egg of a dead bird, it is impure as we have seen above.

* * *

According to the Shafiis, a rotten egg is one which has changed in such a way that it is no longer capable of producing a living organism; it does not include eggs whose whites have mingled with their yolks even if they have an offensive smell; as for the eggs of a dead bird, the relevant ruling has been mentioned above.

* * *

According to the Hanbalis, a rotten egg is one whose white has mingled with its yolk and which has a foul odor. As for eggs which are ritually impure, they are those which have turned to blood, as well as those which have been laid by a living bird but whose shells have not hardened.

* * *

The Hanafis hold that an egg is rendered impure if it turns to blood; however, if it changes simply by virtue of decay, then it is ritually pure, such as putrid meat.

25. There are two things in the category of "that which has been separated from a live animal which is deemed impure when dead" which the Hanbalis declare pure, namely: (1) eggs whose shells have hardened, and (2) a part which has been separated from an animal which was due to be ritually slaughtered out of necessity [for example, an animal which had fallen off a cliff and would not survive the fall – t.n.], but which died before it could be slaughtered in an Islamically proper manner.

* * *

The Shafiis hold that hair, fur, wool, and feathers which have been separated from a living animal whose flesh may be eaten are pure provided that they are not attached to a piece of flesh which has been removed deliberately, that is, which is judged to be of practical value, in which case such substances are rendered impure along with the piece of flesh. If there is some doubt as to whether a given quantity of hair and the other substances with it are pure or impure, they may be assumed to be pure. Moreover, as was mentioned above, the Shafiis view all parts of a dead animal as impure without exception.

exempted from this ruling are the musk secreted by a live musk deer and its skin, both of which are pure. Other substances judged to be impure are the milk of an animal (other than a human being) whose flesh may not be eaten,[26] the ashes and smoke[27] resulting from burning the body of an impure animal, and intoxicating liquids, whether they have been taken from the juice of grapes or an infusion of raisins, dates, or something else. The reason for this is that God Almighty has declared wine to be *rijs*, that is, "a loathsome evil,"[28] *rijs* being customarily viewed as something impure. As for the practice of viewing all types of intoxicating liquids as being forms of wine (*khamr*), this is based on the Prophetic Hadith narrated by Muslim according to which he stated, "Every intoxicating liquid is *khamr*, and every intoxicant is forbidden." Hence, in addition to prohibiting the drinking of such liquids, the Lawgiver has pronounced them ritually unclean as a means of making them loathsome and repellent to us, thereby deterring us from even going near them.

Types of ritual impurity which may be disregarded

The removal of impurity[29] from the body and clothing of the person who prays and the place where he intends to pray is obligatory except with respect to those types of impurity which are exempted from this requirement because of the undue hard-

---

26. According to the Hanafis, all milk products are pure whether the flesh of the animal from which they derive may be eaten or not and whether the animal is dead or alive; the only exception to this ruling is the milk of the pig, whose milk is impure without exception. In addition, they hold that if something which was impure turns to soil without being burned, it is rendered pure.

27. The Malikis hold that such ashes are pure, but that the smoke is impure according to the best attested evidence.

28. See Qur'ān 5:90 [t.n.].

29. The Malikis cite two well-known views on the removal of impurity: (1) that it is a condition for the validity of ritual prayer, and (2) that it is simply a Sunnah-based practice, i.e., it is based on the emulation of the practices of the Prophet. In order for the removal of impurity to be either obligatory or a practice based on the emulation of the Prophet, the person praying must be (1) aware of the impurity [either on his body, his clothing, or the place where he is praying] and (2) capable of removing it. Hence, if someone prays while in a state of impurity due to forgetfulness or the inability to remove it, his prayer is still valid based on both these views, although it would be commendable for such a person to repeat the noon or mid-afternoon prayer sometime before dusk, or to repeat the sundown or evening prayer sometime before dawn, and the dawn prayer sometime before sunrise. On the other hand, if one prays with full knowledge that he [or his clothing, or the place where he is praying] is impure, or out of ignorance, his prayer is invalid based on the first view but valid based on the second. Hence, since according to the first view his prayer was invalid, he is obliged to repeat it some time later, whereas based on the second view, it would simply be commendable for him to do so.

ship that would be caused by having to remove them. As God Almighty declares, I have "laid no hardship on you in [anything that pertains to] religion."[30] As for the specific types of impurity which one is not required to remove, there are different views on them among the four schools.[31]

---

30. Qur'ān 22:78 [t.n.].

31. The Malikis hold that the following substances may be overlooked with respect to ritual purity or impurity:

(1) Urine or stool which has gotten on the clothing or body of a woman due to contact with an infant she is nursing. This ruling applies even if the nursing infant is not her own child provided that she has done her best to avoid such contamination; however, it is recommended that she prepare other clothing to pray in.

(2) The moisture from hemorrhoids if it contaminates one's body or clothing every day, even if this occurs only once. As for the person's hand, he is obliged to wash it each time unless he has to push the tissues back in place more than twice a day. As for his clothing and his body, it is sufficient to wash them once a day. The reason for this distinction is that unlike having to repeatedly wash one's body and clothing, it causes no hardship to wash one's hand unless it has to be done with great frequency.

(3) Incontinence of urine, stool, pre-seminal fluid (*madhī*), *wadī* [the viscous white substance secreted by a man following urination] or semen if such substances are secreted spontaneously, in which case one is not obliged to wash them off one's body or clothing or one's place if it is not possible to move elsewhere. This exemption applies even if such secretions occur only once a day.

(4) Impurities which get onto the clothing or bodies of butchers, cleaners of latrines, doctors who treat wounds, and so forth, though they are advised to have special clothing in which to pray.

(5) Blood which gets on the clothing or body of someone who is praying or the place in which he is praying, whether it is his own blood or that of someone else, and whether it is human or nonhuman blood, even if it is that of a pig, provided that it does not cover an area larger than "a mule's dirham", that is, the black circle found on the front leg of a mule; as for its weight, it is of no consequence. This ruling applies similarly to pus and other suppurative matter.

(6) The urine or dung of horses, mules or donkeys which gets on the clothing, body or place of someone who engages in pasturing, feeding or restraining such animals or related activities, since to remove such impurities would cause undue hardship.

(7) Tracks left by a fly, mosquito, or small ant which alights on some impure substance which then clings to its leg or mouth, after which it alights on someone's clothing or body, due to the hardship involved in avoiding such occurrences; as for the tracks left by large ants, they may not be overlooked due to the rareness with which this takes place.

(8) Traces of blood left on a site where cupping has been performed after the site has been wiped with a cloth and the like; such traces may be disregarded until the site heals, after which it may be washed.

(9) Rainwater or mud mixed with impurities which get on one's clothing or feet, provided that the rainwater and mud are in the streets, even if the rain happens to have stopped; such impurities may be overlooked on three conditions. First: The impurities mixed with the water or mud must not be greater in quantity than the water or mud itself. Second: The impurities concerned must not have gotten onto the person without being mixed with rainwater or mud. Third: The person concerned must not have contributed to getting such mud or water on himself, for example, by turning off a street free of such water and mud and onto another with mud and water on it. This ruling on rainwater and mud applies likewise to water which has been sprinkled on the roads, as well as to water which has collected in swamps.

(10) The liquid pus which flows from more than one abscess or boil, whether it flows out by itself or as a result of squeezing. This ruling applies even if such squeezing was not absolutely necessary, since the presence of multiple abscesses gives cause for such squeezing. Hence, such pus may be disregarded even if it covers an area larger than the "mule's dirham" mentioned above. As for a single abscess, that which flows from it spontaneously or due to squeezing which was necessary may be disregarded; however, if it was squeezed unnecessarily, then the pus which flows out as a result may only be disregarded if it covers an area no larger than a "mule's dirham."

(11) The droppings of fleas, even if they are present in large amounts, and even if the fleas have fed on spilt blood; such droppings are impure, but they may be disregarded. As for fleas' blood, like other creatures' blood, it may not be overlooked unless it covers an area no larger than a "mule's dirham."

(12) The watery fluid which comes out of the mouth of someone sleeping if it originated in the stomach; although such fluid, which is yellowish and malodorous, is deemed impure, it may be disregarded if it results from a chronic condition.

(13) Dead lice, provided that they number no more than three.

(14) The traces of impurity left on the urethral orifice and the anus after the bulk of the impurity has been removed with stones and the like; such impurity may be disregarded and does not have to be washed off with water as long as it has not spread significantly. If it has spread, it must be washed off with water; water is likewise required for removing impurity from the woman's vaginal area, details concerning which will be presented in the section on abstersion below.

* * *

As for the Hanafis, they divide ritual impurity into two categories, namely, gross and mild. As for gross impurity, Imam Abū Ḥanīfah defines it as an impurity concerning which there is a text [from the Qur'ān or the Prophetic Sunnah] which is not countered by any other text; as for mild impurity, he defines it as an impurity concerning which there is a text which is countered by some other text. An example of the latter is the urine of animals whose flesh may be eaten, since the hadith according to which the Prophet stated, "Keep yourselves free of urine" indicates that all urine is ritually impure, whereas another hadith referred to as "the hadith concerning the 'Uraynis" [next paragraph] indicates that the urine of animals whose flesh may be eaten is pure; hence, given these two conflicting pieces of textual evidence, urine is considered to be a mild impurity.

According to the "hadith of the 'Uraynis", a group of people from the tribe of 'Uraynah once came to Medina and found that the climate did not agree with them, as a result of which they suffered from jaundice and bloated abdomens. Consequently, the Messenger of God instructed them to go out to certain camels which had been given away as charity and to drink their urine and milk. They did as he had told them and recovered.

Among the types of gross impurity which may be disregarded are impurities which occupy an area no larger than a dirham. With respect to gross impurity, one may disregard it if it weighs no more than twenty carats. [A carat equals 200 milligrams; hence, 20 carats are equal to 4 grams – t.n.] With respect to light impurity, it may be disregarded if it occupies an area no greater than the hollow of the palm of the hand. Hence, given that such impurities are pardonable as they pertain to the validity of ritual prayer, then prayer performed with the presence of such impurity is undesirable, but not to the point of being forbidden, since the fact that such impurity is 'pardonable' necessitates that it no longer be viewed as sinful. It is true, of course, that the removal of an amount occupying the area of a dirham takes higher priority over the removal of some lesser amount, and most Hanafis hold that prayer under such circumstances is undesirable to the point of being forbidden.

Another example is the urine and feces of cats and mice in situations where they are unavoidable. If a mouse's droppings fell into some wheat in an amount small enough not to be noticeable, this could be overlooked. Similarly, if a mouse fell into a well and some of its urine got into the water, this could be overlooked due to the impossibility of preventing such an occurrence. However, if such substances got onto someone's clothing or some utensil, for example, this could not be disregarded due to the fact that such an occurrence is avoidable. If, on the other hand, a cat's urine got onto someone's clothing in a manner which was unavoidable, this could be disregarded, in contrast to a situation in which its urine or feces got onto something else, in which case it would not be pardonable.

Other examples of impurities which may be overlooked are the steam and dust particles which are given off by an impure substance; hence, for example, if the wind blew over some dung, then blew onto someone's clothing, this would do no harm even if its odor were then found in the garment concerned; the same ruling would apply if dust blew off some dung or the like, then got onto something. The same ruling also applies to a spray of urine if it is as fine as pin heads and is not visible, even if it covers an entire garment or body; it is viewed as though it did not exist due to the unavoidability of the occurrence. A similar case is that of the blood that gets on a butcher, which is pardonable due to necessity. However, if such a spray got onto a garment, after which the garment fell into a bit of water, the water would be rendered impure due to the non-necessity of the garment's falling into it. Similar to this would be the tracks left by a fly which had fallen onto some impurity, then alighted on the clothing of someone praying, in which case the impurity would be pardonable. Another example is the dirty water that gets on someone washing a corpse and which the washer has no way of avoiding in the course of completing this task; or the mud found in the streets even if it happens to be mixed with a large proportion of impurities, so long as one cannot actually see them.

With respect to mild impurity, one may overlook an amount which covers less than one-fourth of an entire garment or one-fourth of the entire body. However, the mildness of such impurity applies only to non-liquid substances, because when an impurity gets into a liquid, the entire liquid is rendered impure without there being any distinction between gross and mild impurity, nor is any consideration given to weight or area.

One may similarly overlook the dung of camels, sheep and goats if it falls into a well or into a container so long as it is not found in excessive amounts, and so long as it does not disintegrate in such a way that the substance with which it has mingled takes on its coloring. An amount small enough to be overlooked is defined as that amount which appears insignificant to someone who looks at it, while an amount too large to be overlooked is, conversely, that amount which appears to be substantial. As for the dung of donkeys, cattle and elephants, it may be disregarded in cases of necessity and hardship, be it dry or moist.

* * *

As for the impure substances which may be disregarded according to the Shafiis, they include those which are invisible to someone with sound vision even if they are gross impurities. They also include small amounts of smoke which have risen from a fire in which some impurity is being burned. However, steam which has risen from an impure substance without its having been burned is ritually pure. Other substances which may be overlooked are traces of impurity which remain in the spot where one has engaged in abstersion with stones. However, such impurities are excusable only with respect to the person from whom they originated; in other words, if water containing such impurities got on someone else, he would be contaminated by them. Similarly, mud in the streets which is mixed with impurities that are known to be present there may be overlooked, and if one is doubtful as to whether the mud is contaminated, it may be viewed as pure. However, if the mud is known to contain impurities, it may only be overlooked on the following four conditions: (1) that the impurities not be visible, (2) that the person walking through the street take care to avoid being contaminated, for example, by not letting the bottom of his robe or other clothing touch the ground or by allowing himself to be sprayed by a water carrier, (3) that the person be contaminated while walking or riding, whereas if he were to fall on the ground with the result that his clothes were contaminated, such contamination could not be overlooked due to the rareness of such an occurrence, and (4) that the impurities concerned be found on someone's clothing or body.

Other impurities which may be disregarded include bread which has been heated or buried in impure ashes, even if a small amount of these ashes have clung to the bread and even if it would not be difficult to remove them. If such bread is placed in milk or some other similar food and traces of such ashes become visible, or if they get onto someone's clothing, this also may be overlooked. Other such impurities include worms which feed on fruit and cheese if they die while still inside, since their dead bodies are impure but may be overlooked. The same is true of the rennet which is used to manufacture cheese and the impure liquids which are added to medicines and perfumes in the course of their production; the amount required to obtain the proper result may be disregarded based on the similarity observed between these processes and that of making cheese with rennet. Also included here are the impurities that may contaminate clothes hung out to dry on walls constructed with impure ashes due to the difficulty of avoiding such contamination; dead nits (louse eggs); as well as the droppings of flies even if they are found in large amounts, and the droppings of birds which fall on the ground and on mats, rugs, carpets and the like. Such droppings on the ground may be disregarded under the following three conditions: (1) that one not deliberately walk on them, (2) that neither side of them still be moist unless they are found on a wet road or path which one has no choice but to walk on, and (3) that avoiding them be a cause of hardship.

Other impurities which may be disregarded include a small amount of soil from a grave that has been exhumed and a small amount of impure hair provided that it not be that of a dog, a pig, the offspring of a dog and a pig together or the offspring of either of them together with some other species. As for hair from a dog or a pig, be it a small or a large amount, it may only be overlooked in the case of a shearer or a rider due to the hardship which would be caused by attempts to avoid such contamination. Fish dung in water may be disregarded provided that it has caused no change in the water and provided that it has not been placed there arbitrarily. Also included here is the blood which remains on meat or bones; such blood may be disregarded if the meat or the bones have been placed in the pot before the blood has been washed off even if the broth is changed as a result. If, before meat and bones are placed in the pot, they are washed until the water that comes off them runs clear, the water is pure, whereas if the water does not run off clear, then it is impure and this impurity may not be disregarded. However, if some color remains this does no harm, since it cannot be avoided. Hence, meat should be washed as usual, and whatever traces of blood remain after this may be overlooked. [There appears to be a contradiction in the text regarding whether or not the blood which remains on meat and bones may be disregarded; be that as it may, the final sentence of this paragraph may be taken as the summary of the author's intent, namely, that one should wash meat as thoroughly as one can, and not concern himself with traces of blood which happen to remain thereafter – t.n.]

Also included among impure substances that may be overlooked is the saliva of someone who is asleep and which is certain to have come from the stomach due to its yellowish color or its unpleasant odor; such saliva may be disregarded by the person who suffers from it even if it is secreted in large amounts. If it is not clear whether the saliva originated in the stomach, it is considered pure. With regard to the cud of a camel or some other ruminant, it may be disregarded if it gets on someone who is in contact with the animal, as someone who is leading it, for example. Likewise exempted is the dung or urine of large domestic animals if it comes in contact with grain as it is being threshed, as well as mouse droppings that have fallen into basins used for abstersion; such droppings may be disregarded if they are present in small amounts and if they cause no change in the character of the water. As for a chickpea used to treat certain conditions by being placed in a member of the body contaminated by impurities, it may be treated as pure provided that this procedure has been judged to be necessary for treatment. Still other allowable impurities are: (1) that which gets into milk by way of dung from a domestic animal being milked or impurities found on its teat, (2) impurities that get into honey from beehives made of mud mixed with the dung of large domestic animals, (3) impurities from the mouth of an infant when it comes in contact with the breast while nursing, or which come in contact with the mouth of someone who kisses him on the lips, (4) a liquid that has become impure due to a bloodless organism—such as an ant, a wasp, a bee and the like—having fallen into it and died; such a liquid may be ingested along with whatever has fallen into it and died provided that this has caused no change in the liquid and provided that the organism which fell into it and died was simply blown into it by the wind, even if it was blown, for example, off the body of a domestic animal, (5) the mark that remains at the site of a tattoo to which indigo and similar substances have been applied with the result that it has turned green or blue (the meaning of "tattoo" being the insertion of needles into the skin until the blood becomes visible on the surface of the skin). The green or blue mark which remains at the site of the tattoo may be disregarded: (a) if the tattoo was done as a means of achieving some benefit which could not have been achieved by any other means, (b) if, at the time the person received the tattoo, he was too young to be held responsible for his action, or (c) if, although the person concerned was responsible for his action, he was unable to remove the tattoo without inflicting harm by virtue of which he would be allowed to perform sand ablutions; and (6) blood, details concerning which are as follows: a) An amount of blood so small that it cannot by seen by someone with sound vision; such an amount may be disregarded even if it is grossly impure such as the blood of a dog or a pig; b) an amount which is visible to someone with sound vision. If such blood is that of a dog, a pig or some other impure animal, it may not be disregarded under any circumstances. Otherwise, it must either be the person's own blood or from some other source. If it is not his own blood, then a small amount may be disregarded provided that he did not spatter himself with it or expose himself unnecessarily to blood other than his own. An exception to this is the blood of fleas and other organisms which have no "liquid blood." As for the blood of fleas, it may be disregarded even if it is present in large amounts, on the following conditions: First, the blood must not have gotten on the person due to his own actions or those of someone else with his permission, even if the other person was too young to be held responsible; otherwise, no more than a small amount may be overlooked. Second, the person must not have exposed himself to blood other than his own when it would have caused no hardship to avoid such exposure; otherwise, only a small amount may be disregarded. Third, the blood must be found on articles of clothing which the person needs, if even just for adornment.

In the case of one's own blood, it will have come either from the primary orifices, namely, the nose, the ear, or the eye, in which case a small amount may be disregarded, or from sources such as pimples, abscesses, or bloodletting (venesection), in which case even a large amount may be overlooked given the following conditions: (1) The blood flow must not be due to the action of the person himself, as when someone squeezes a boil, since otherwise, only a small amount may be disregarded except in cases of venesection and cupping, in which case a large amount may be disregarded even if it is the person's own doing. (2) The blood must not have spread beyond its point of origin. (3) The blood must not have mingled unnecessarily with any foreign substance [i.e., (a) a fluid other than blood, (b) someone else's blood, or (c) fluid or blood from another member of the same person's body – t.n.], such as water, for example. Moreover, blood may only be treated as pure by the person from whom it originated, whereas if someone else were to touch it or handle something in contact with it, it could not be treated as pure. As for what is meant by "point of origin" here, it refers, for example, to the arm or some other part of the body on which an abscess is located rather than the site of the abscess alone.

As for the meaning of 'large' or 'small' amounts, this is a matter of prevailing custom; hence, if there is some doubt as to whether a given amount is 'small' or 'large', it should be treated as pure.

* * *

As for the impurities which, according to the Hanbalis, may be overlooked, they include a small amount of blood, pus or other suppurative matter. As for what is meant by 'small', it is whatever a person considers to be insignificant when found on his own body or clothing. Such small amounts may be disregarded if they come in contact with something that is neither liquid nor food; however, if they come into contact with something which is liquid or edible, they may not be disregarded even if they come from an animal that is ritually pure while alive and even if they originate from a part of the body other than the genitals or the anus.

If blood, pus or suppurative matter comes in contact with various parts of a garment, the affected areas are to be added together. If the total area is small, it may be overlooked; otherwise, it may not. It is not permissible to add together the affected areas of two or more different garments; rather, each garment is to be considered separately. As for the traces of impurity left on the affected site after one has cleaned himself with stones the required number of times—details concerning which will be discussed below—these may likewise be overlooked. One may also overlook a small degree of urinary incontinence—provided that one has done all one can to overcome it—due to the hardship involved in cleansing oneself repeatedly as a result of such a condition. Also included is the smoke and dust which rise from an impurity so long as they have taken on none of the qualities of the impurity itself [such as its odor, its color, and so forth]; a small amount of water that has been contaminated by an allowable impurity; an impurity that has gotten into someone's eye and which would cause the person harm to wash out; and small amounts of mud from the street even when it is known for certain to be mixed with impurities.

32. According to the Ḥanafis, water which is *ṭāhir*, but not *ṭahūr* is equivalent to water which is *ṭahūr* in its capacity to remove impurity; the same applies to any ritually pure liquid which results from a process of squeezing, such as vinegar and rosewater. Hence, these three types of liquid may be used to cleanse anything—be it a garment, a body or a place—which is contaminated with impurity, be it visible or invisible, including even gross impurities.

The means and manner by which ritual impurity may be removed

Impurity may be removed by a variety of means, including water which is judged to be *ṭahūr*. It is not sufficient to use water which is merely *ṭāhir*.[32] (The concepts of *ṭahūr* and *ṭāhir* are discussed in the following section dealing with types of water.)

As for the process of cleansing the site of an impurity, there are various ways in which it may be carried out.[33]

---

33. According to the Hanafis, a garment contaminated by an impurity is rendered pure by being washed even just once so long as the visible impurity is gone. However, this ruling only applies if the garment is washed in running water or if water is poured over it, whereas if it is washed in a basin or the like, it must be washed three times and it must be wrung out after each washing. If a garment is dyed with an impure substance, it will become pure if the water that runs off it after it has been washed is clear, even if some color or odor remains; in other words, it does no harm for the dye's color or odor to remain at the site of the impurity if it would cause hardship to remove it. As for what is meant by 'hardship' here, it refers to a situation in which, in order to remove the impurity, one must use substances other than water, such as soap and the like.

In the case of those who use henna which is contaminated with impurities, the henna may be considered to have become pure if, after being rinsed, the water that runs off it is clear. Similarly in the case of a tattoo, if the needle is inserted in the hand or lip, for example, until blood appears on the surface, and if dye is then applied to the site of the insertion and the wound heals over it, the dye is rendered impure and its effect may not be removed with water. Hence, it may be purified by washing it until the water runs clear. As for contaminated fat or oil, it does no harm for traces of it to remain; however, this is not the case with the fat of a dead organism, since such fat is considered intrinsically impure. As for visible impurities, they may be considered to have been removed if it seems probable to the person doing the washing that the site affected by them has been cleansed without necessarily counting the times it has been washed. However, for the sake of people who are prone to obsessive doubts and misgivings, the maximum number of washings in such a case has been set at three, with the requirement that one wring out the garment after each washing.

As for a contaminated place (namely, the floor), it may be purified by pouring pure (*ṭāhir*) water over it three times and drying the site each time with a pure rag. If one pours enough water over the site that no trace of impurity remains, it may be considered pure. The ground is also rendered pure by drying, in which case its purification requires no water. As for the body, it becomes pure if one removes visible impurities and if one considers it most likely that all other purities have been removed as well.

As for containers and utensils, they are of three types: (1) earthenware or pottery, (2) wood, and (3) iron and the like. Such objects may be purified in four different ways, namely, by burning, by carving or hewing, by wiping, and by washing. If the object is made of new earthenware or stone and if the impurity has gotten into its various parts, it may be purified by burning, whereas if it is old, it should be purified by washing it in the manner described above. If it is new and made of wood, it may be purified by hewing or carving, whereas if it is old it should be washed. If the object is made of iron, copper, lead or glass and has a smooth, glossy surface, it may be purified by wiping, whereas if it has a rough, unpolished surface, it should be washed.

As for contaminated liquids such as oil and clarified butter, one may purify them by pouring water over them, then removing the water three times; or one may place the contaminated fat in a perforated container, then pour water over it so that the fat rises to the top. One then stirs the contents of the container and opens the perforated bottom, allowing the water to escape. This is the procedure to be followed if the contaminated substance is in liquid form; if it is solid, the contaminated portion may be cut out and discarded. As for honey, it may be purified by pouring water over it and boiling the water off of it three times.

Contaminated water may be purified by causing it to flow, that is, by allowing fresh water to enter from one side and to exit from the other. Hence, for example, if there is a channel of impure water, pure water may be poured into one end of it until it is full and the water flows out the other end, in which case its contents become pure running water. Nor is it necessary for the water that flows out of the channel to be equal in volume to the water that was originally inside it. Similarly, if the contaminated water is in a basin or a large bowl or kettle, pure water may be poured over it until it overflows, at which point the contaminated water may be deemed pure even if the amount which overflowed the sides of the container is less than the amount which was known to be contaminated. As for wells and bathtubs, they may be purified in a similar manner, and the water which they contain subsequently may be used for purification of other substances.

Still other means of purification are as follows:

•Rubbing the contaminated object vigorously against the ground.

•Scratching or scraping off the impurity with the hand or a stick; by these means shoes and sandals may be purified provided that the impurity is characterized by a visible, solid mass even if it was originally moist. This includes such things as dried stool and blood. This ruling is based on the words of the Prophet, "Whenever anyone comes to the mosque, let him turn his sandals over. If they have any impurity [literally, "that which is harmful"] on them, let him rub them against the ground, since the earth will purify them." However, if the impurity is not characterized by a solid mass, it must be washed off even if it has already dried.

•Wiping off the traces of the impurity. It is by this means that one may purify glossy, non-porous surfaces such as swords, mirrors, fingernails, toenails, bones, glass, painted utensils and containers, etc.

•Wiping a site where cupping has been performed with three clean, wet rags.

•Drying by means of the sun or the air. It is by this means that the earth is purified as well as everything that is fixed in the ground, such as trees, grass, pastureland, and so forth, but not objects such as rugs, mats or other movable articles, all of which must be purified by washing. As for the ground, however, it is purified by drying; as the Prophet stated, "The earth is purified by drying." Once this has occurred, one may pray on such ground, but it may not be used for *tayammum*. The reason for this is that something can be ritually pure (*ṭāhir*) without necessarily being capable of rendering other things pure (*ṭahūr*), and in order for soil to be used for *tayammum*, it must qualify as a purifying agent (that is, it must be *ṭahūr*) just as water must be *ṭahūr* in order for one to use it in performing one's ablutions.

•Rubbing, which is the means by which dried human semen may be removed. If the semen is still moist, however, it must be washed off based on the Prophet's statement to 'Ā'ishah, "Wash it out if it is moist, and rub it off if it is dry." The traces which remain after the semen has been rubbed off cause no harm. However, semen is considered to have been removed only if the person rubbing it off has performed abstersion with water rather than with a rock, since a rock cannot remove urine which has spread over the glans of the penis. Nevertheless, if the urine has not spread and if semen has not passed over it [and, in so doing, mingled with it] outside the body, then it is still rendered pure by rubbing, since no harm is done by the semen's passing over the urine while still inside the body. Nor is there any difference between the man's and the woman's 'semen' after it has left the body, since the latter mingles with the former which, according to the hadith quoted above, is purified by being rubbed off. As for non-human semen, it is not purified by being rubbed off, since this concession applies to human semen alone, and cannot be applied by way of analogy to other types of semen.

•Carding or combing, which is the process by which cotton is rendered pure if it has been contaminated.

Some processes, such as cutting out and discarding contaminated solid fat, have been included as means of purification by way of concession, since in reality, such a process is merely an isolation of the contaminated part rather than an act of purification. The same is true of the process of dividing something which is contaminated by separating its impure parts from those parts which are pure, as well as the act of giving something which is contaminated to someone who is unaware of the impurities in it, since giving something away cannot actually be considered to have purified it.

* * *

According to the Malikis, the site of an impurity may be cleansed by washing it with water that is *ṭahūr*, even if only once, provided that the water which runs off the site is pure. There is no harm in the site's being affected by dirt which is ritually pure; however, the taste of all impurity must be removed from the site where it was found, however difficult this proves to be, since if it remains, this is evidence that the impurity has become inseparable from it. It is also necessary for the color and odor of the impurity to be removed if possible; however, if these prove difficult or impossible to remove, as in the case of something which has been dyed with a substance deemed to be impure, the site concerned should be pronounced pure. It is not necessary to heat the water unless one is unable to use cold water, nor is it necessary to wash the site with potash, soap, etc. If the water used to wash the site takes on any of the properties of the impurity being removed [such as its taste, color, odor, etc.], such water is rendered impure as well. However, if such water has been altered by virtue of a dye or simple dirt, it remains pure.

When purifying a garment, a mat, shoes or sandals when it is uncertain whether they have been contaminated or not, it is sufficient to sprinkle them once with water which is *ṭahūr* even if the spot concerned is not entirely covered with the water. As for someone's body or the ground when it is certain that it has been contaminated, it can only be purified by being washed, since sprinkling is not perfectly analogous to washing and is thus limited to the aforementioned objects, namely, garments, mats, shoes and sandals. Although washing such objects with water rather than merely sprinkling them is the ideal, sprinkling causes less hardship. As for a floor or an area of ground which is certain or suspected to have been contaminated by some impurity, it may be purified by pouring liberal amounts of *ṭahūr* water over it until the impurity and its properties are gone. This practice is based on the account related by Muslim and al-Bukhārī of the Bedouin who urinated in the mosque. When some of the Companions shouted at the man, the Prophet commanded them to leave him alone and to pour a pail of water over the place where he had relieved himself.

Contaminated water may be purified by pouring *ṭahūr* water over it until the properties of the impurity are gone; however, if liquids other than water such as oil, clarified butter, and honey are contaminated by even a small amount of impurity, they cannot be purified under any circumstances.

* * *

As for the Hanbalis, they prescribe the following method for purifying substances other than the ground or floor with *ṭahūr* water, namely, to wash the contaminated item thoroughly seven times such that once the seven washings have been completed, no trace remains of the color, taste, or odor of the impurity. This ruling applies even if the impurity is not removed until the seventh washing. If the impurity is from a dog, a pig, or the offspring of a dog and a pig which have mated or of a dog or a pig which has mated with some other species, *ṭahūr* soil or soap must be added to the water during one of the washings, preferably the first one. If, after the seventh washing, there still remains some trace of the impurity, it must be washed a sufficient number of additional times to remove it entirely. If it proves impossible to get rid of its taste, the item is still considered to be impure; however, the impurity may be disregarded. Moreover, if it proves impossible to get rid of either its color or its odor or both, the contaminated site is to be considered pure.

When purifying something which has absorbed an impurity, it must be wrung out each time outside the wash water if it is possible to wring it out at all; however, it should not be wrung out so vigorously as to do harm to the garment. As for those things which do not absorb impurities, such as containers and utensils, they may be purified by allowing water to pass over them and run off seven times. In the case of those things which absorb impurities but which cannot be wrung out, it is sufficient to pound them, place a heavy object on top of them, or turn them over in such as way as to allow the water to run off them after each of the seven washings. As for contaminated floors or stone surfaces such as those of large or small cisterns found inside buildings, it is sufficient in purifying them to pour water over them in liberal amounts until the bulk of the impurity is gone. When purifying something contaminated with the urine or vomit of a nursing infant who has never readily taken food, it should be doused with water even if the water does not run off.

* * *

According to the Shafiis, the manner in which *ṭahūr* water is to be used in the removal of gross impurity—specifically, that which comes from a dog, a pig, the offspring of a dog and a pig which have mated together, or the offspring of a dog or a pig that has mated with some other species—is for the site of the impurity to be washed seven times and for *ṭahūr* soil, that is, soil which is neither impure nor has been used for *tayammum,* to be added to the water during one of these washings. As for what is meant by 'soil' here, it includes earth-colored, yellow, red and white soil as well as clay and that which has been mixed with some other pure substance, such as flour, for example.

The steps in this process may be ordered in three different ways: (1) The water may be mixed with the soil before placing it on the site of the impurity; (2) the water may be placed first on the site of the impurity, followed by the soil; or (3) the soil may be placed on the impurity first, after which water is poured over it. The aforementioned washing process, regardless of which order is followed, is not to be carried out until after the concrete, visible mass of the impurity is gone. If the impurity is not characterized by such a mass and if the site of the impurity is dry, then any of the three orders may be followed. If the site of the impurity is moist, the soil should not be placed on it first lest it become contaminated by the water on the site; however, either of the other two orders may be followed. If a gross impurity is found on ground that contains soil that is not impure in itself, it is sufficient to purify it seven times with nothing but its own soil.

The first of the seven washings is defined as the one by virtue of which the bulk of the impurity is removed, even if additional washings follow. Hence, if the bulk of the impurity is removed by one washing, it is considered a single washing and six more washings must be performed. If the impurity is only removed through six washings, these six washings are counted together as one washing, which must be followed by six more washings; if, on the other hand, it is only removed by seven washings or more, these seven or more washings are counted as one washing, which must then be followed by six more. By contrast, the removal of the taste, color or odor of an impurity does not depend on the number of washings; hence, if they are only removed by seven washings, they are counted as seven washings.

With regard to mild impurity, it is removed by sprinkling the site of the impurity with sufficient water to cover the impurity even if it does not overflow its boundaries. What is meant here by "mild impurity" is, for example, the urine of a male child that is not yet two years old and who has not yet fed on anything but milk in its various forms, including cheese, cream, and butter, and whether it is mother's milk or milk from other sources. However, in the case of a female or a 'problematic' hermaphrodite, the urine must be washed off based on the words of the Prophet, "The urine of a young girl must be washed off, whereas a young boy's urine may be sprinkled," with hermaphrodites being placed in the same category as females. However, if a young boy is more than two years old, his urine must be washed off even if he has not taken any nourishment but milk; it is also necessary to wash off his urine if he has been fed something other than milk even once. However, if he has been given something for purposes other than nutrition, such as medicine, for example, then sprinkling is still allowable. The bulk of the impurity must be removed before the site of the impurity is sprinkled with water, for example, by wringing out or drying a garment. It is also essential that the features of the impurity (taste, color and smell) be removed with the sprinkling. The Shafiis limit their discussion of sprinkling to the removal of urine alone in order to exclude other impure bodily wastes, all of which must be removed through washing.

As for what they term 'intermediate' impurity, which differs from what has been discussed thus far, it is divided into two types: (1) legal, or technical impurity, which is not characterized by a concrete, perceptible mass, a taste, a color, or an odor, such as the urine of someone other than a baby boy once it has dried, and (2) actual, or intrinsic impurity, which is characterized by a concrete, perceptible mass or by a taste, a color or an odor.

Legal, or 'technical' impurity is removed by pouring water over the site of the impurity if even only once and even if it is done unintentionally; as for actual, or intrinsic impurity, it is removed in the same way provided that the bulk of the impurity is removed. As for the specific properties of the impurity, the following rulings apply to them: If only the taste remains, its continued presence is considered harmful if it not difficult to remove it, the criterion for 'difficult' being that it can only be removed through physical separation. Once the impurity has thus been removed, the site remains impure, but its impurity may be overlooked. If it is possible to remove the taste following this, one is obliged to do so; however, it is not necessary to repeat any prayers which have been prayed on the site. Moreover, if it proves difficult to remove the taste, one must make use of soap or some similar substance. The same ruling applies to the color and odor of the impurity if they both remain. However, if the color alone or the odor alone remains due to the difficulty of removing it, the site is considered to have been purified. As for the criterion for 'difficulty', it is that the impurity cannot be removed by scrubbing it with water three times; moreover, even if it is possible after this to remove the color or the odor, the site need not be purified.

In the removal of all three types of impurity, it is necessary for water to be present on the site if the amount of water is small; if the amount of water is small and is poured on the site, it will be contaminated merely by coming into contact with the impurity. If the small amount of water present is impure but appears unaltered, *ṭahūr* water may be added to it until it amounts to 'two pitchers full' (*qullatān*), at which point it will become pure. On the other hand, if the water is both contaminated and altered in its appearance, whether it is a small or a large amount, it will only become pure by adding *ṭahūr* water to it until all the effects of the alteration are gone and the amount of water comes to 'two pitchers full'. The procedure for purifying the ground or a floor which has absorbed an 'intermediate' liquid impurity such as urine or wine is to drench it with water. However, if it has not absorbed the impurity, it must first be dried before water is poured over it, even if only once. In the case of contamination by a solid impurity which has not touched the ground, the impurity may be physically removed, whereas if the impurity is moist and if some of it has gotten on the ground, it must first be physically removed, after which water must be poured over the affected area.

Means by which an impure substance may be purified include the transformation of an impure substance into something else which is not impure, such as wine's turning into vinegar or a musk deer's blood into musk, and burning an impurity with fire.[34] As for the tanning of the skins of dead animals, there are differing views among the schools on whether this serves as a purifying agent or not.[35] Moreover, in order for something to be cleansed of an impurity, it is not necessary that this be brought about intentionally.

---

34. According to the Hanafis, burning an impurity with fire renders it pure. The Shafiis and the Hanbalis do not count burning as a purifying agent; rather, they hold that the ashes and smoke resulting from burning an impurity are themselves impure. As for the Malikis, they hold that fire does not remove the impurity of something; however, most of them make an exception for the ashes of an impurity which has been burned.

35. The Hanafis make no distinction with respect to tanning between that which is 'actual,' such as tanning by means of substances taken from the *qaraẓ* tree, alum, and the like, and that which is merely 'technical', such as tanning through a series of ordered steps or by drying in the sun or the air. The tanner purifies the skins of dead animals if they can tolerate the process of tanning; as for those which could not tolerate it, such as snakeskins, they may not be purified through tanning; nor is it possible to purify the skin of a pig by tanning it. As for the skin of a dog, it may be purified by tanning since, strictly speaking, it is not intrinsically impure; moreover, once it has been purified, a dog's skin may be used to pray on and for other purposes, but it may not be eaten. As for the substances clinging to the skin, such as hair and the like, they are pure as has been mentioned above.

* * *

The Shafiis stipulate that in order for the tanning process to have a purifying effect, it must involve the use of a substance which, when touched to the tongue, produces a burning or biting sensation such that it does away with the moisture in the skin and any bodily wastes which might be clinging to it lest the skin putrefy with time. This stipulation applies even if the substance used in the tanning process is impure, such as bird excrement. A skin which has been tanned with an impure substance is like a contaminated garment, and thus must be washed after it has been tanned. As for the skin of a dog, a pig, the offspring of a dog and a pig which have mated together, or the offspring of either a dog or a pig which has mated with a pure animal, it may not be purified. Similarly, that which clings to the skin by way of coarse wool, fur, hair and feathers may not be purified by tanning. However, al-Nawawī states, "Small amounts of such substances may be overlooked due to the hardship entailed by removing them."

* * *

According to the Malikis, tanning has no purifying effect; rather, they understand the 'purity' referred to in the hadith to mean simple cleanliness. Nevertheless, they make an allowance for the use of tanned articles in contact with substances which are either *ṭahūr* or dry provided that nothing be ground on such a skin and provided that it not be that of a pig, for which no such allowance is made. This

Liquids[36] other than water, such as oil, clarified butter, honey, and so forth, may not be purified once they have become contaminated. As for solids, they may be purified unless some parts of them have absorbed the impurity.[37]

---

concession applies to dry substances because impurities on the hide will not cling to them; it also applies to substances which are *ṭahūr* because, since they are so pure, they have the capacity to repel impurity. As for the wool and similar substances found on such a hide, they are ritually pure because, since they have never been living tissue, they were not rendered impure by the death of the animal of which they were a part, as mentioned above. The view that tanning has no purifying effect is the view most common among the Malikis; however, the more discerning among them hold that it does have a purifying effect.

* * *

The Hanbalis also deny that tanning the hides of dead animals renders them pure; hence, they allow their use after tanning with dry substances only. As for the coarse wool, hair, fur and feathers of a dead animal or bird, they consider them to be pure.

36. According to the Hanafis, the liquids mentioned may all be purified with water. (Note the description of how to purify such substances with water in the section above on purifying agents.)

37. As for the Malikis, they hold that solids which may not be purified due to their having absorbed an impurity include meat if it is cooked together with an impure substance, whereas if an impurity comes in contact with meat after it has been cooked, it may be purified. As for eggs which have been boiled together with an impure substance, olives which have been salted with an impure substance, and earthenware which has had an impurity get deep inside it, they may not be purified.

* * *

The Hanbalis agree with the Maliki view regarding what has been mentioned except with respect to boiled eggs, which they say may be purified since the hardness of their shells prevents them from absorbing an impurity. As for meat, whether cooked [roasted] or boiled, they hold that it cannot be purified under any circumstances.

* * *

The Shafiis hold that solids which have absorbed an impurity may be purified; hence, for example, if meat has been cooked in or with an impurity, if wheat has absorbed an impurity, or if a knife has been dipped into an impure substance, they may be purified in every respect by pouring water over them. However, they make an exception with respect to sun-dried brick which has been kneaded together with a solid impurity, holding that it may not be purified even if it is burned and washed with water. Such brick differs, then, from that which has been contaminated by a liquid impurity, which may be purified by being doused with *ṭahūr* water.

* * *

With respect to solids, the Hanafis hold that if the solid is a container, a utensil or something of this nature, it may be purified in the manner described above in the section on means of purification. If something which may be cooked, such as meat

On Types of Water

Water which may or may not be used in purification is divided into three categories: (1) *ṭahūr*, that is, both ritually pure and usable in removing impurity as part of various expressions of worship, (2) *ṭāhir* only, that is, ritually pure but not *ṭahūr*, and (3) contaminated with impurity. The discussion which follows on *ṭahūr* water deals with the following: (1) the definition of the term *ṭahūr*, (2) the difference between *ṭahūr* and *ṭāhir*, (3) rulings on *ṭahūr* water, (4) those things which do and do not cause water to cease being *ṭahūr*, and (5) those things which render *ṭahūr* water impure.

The section on water which is *ṭāhir* but not *ṭahūr* deals with: (1) the definition of *ṭāhir*, (2) the various types of *ṭāhir* water, and (3) those things which cause water to cease being *ṭāhir*.

As for the section on contaminated water, it sets forth the definition of contaminated water and its types.

Water which may be used for ritual purification (*ṭahūr*)

Ṭahūr water includes all water which has come down from the sky or welled up from the earth and none of whose three fundamental properties—namely, its color, taste and smell—have been altered by any of those things which cause water to cease being *ṭahūr*. Nor may such water have been used before.[38] The things which necessitate the use of *ṭahūr* water and those which rob water of its *ṭahūr* quality will be discussed below.

The difference between water which is *ṭahūr* and that which is only *ṭāhir*

The difference between water which is *ṭahūr* and that which is simply *ṭāhir* is that the former may be used in the various expressions of Islamic worship as well as in routine daily activities; hence, for example, it may be used for the performance of minor ritual ablutions, major ablutions to purify oneself from sexual discharge and

---

or wheat, is contaminated by an impurity and then cooked together with it, it may never be purified after this because its parts will have absorbed the impurity. Hence, for example, if a chicken is boiled before its gut has been split open, it may not be purified under any circumstances due to its parts' having absorbed the impurity. Thus, it is necessary before boiling a chicken to split it open, remove its innards, and purify it by washing it. The same applies to animals' heads and intestines, which may not be purified at all if they have been boiled before being washed and purified.

38. According to the Malikis, the use of water does not cause it to cease being *ṭahūr*. Hence, they hold that it is permissible, albeit undesirable, to perform minor and major ablutions with used water.

menstrual flow, as well as for cleansing the body and clothes of visible dirt and so forth. Water which is simply *ṭāhir*, by contrast, may not be used in activities related to Islamic worship such as minor ablutions, major ablutions and the like, nor may it be used in the removal of impurities.[39] However, it is permissible to use such water for ordinary activities such as drinking, cleaning one's body and clothing, kneading dough, and so forth.

Rulings on *ṭahūr* water

The ruling on *ṭahūr* water is divided into two parts. The first part has to do with the effect on the basis of which the Lawgiver established this ruling, namely, that it removes minor and major ritual impurity with the result that it is permissible to use it in the performance of minor ritual ablutions as well as major ablutions to cleanse oneself of sexual discharge and menstrual flow. In addition, it may be used to remove impurity, both observable and otherwise, and it may be used in the performance of religious obligations, recommended actions, and all other acts by means of which one draws near to God, such as performance of major ablutions for the Friday prayer, the prayers for 'Id al-Fiṭr and 'Id al-Aḍḥā, and so forth. It may also be used for ordinary daily activities such as drinking, cooking, laundry, bathing, watering plants, and the like.

The second part has to do with rulings on its use, that is, whether its use is obligatory, recommended, allowed, undesirable or forbidden. Recommended uses of water include the practices of the Prophet, since that which is recommended and that which is based on the prophetic Sunnah are one and the same according to some Muslim scholars, whereas according to others, they are distinct, as will be seen in the section below on recommended practices associated with ritual ablutions. Situations in which the use of water is obligatory include religious obligations the performance of which requires one to be free of major and minor impurity, such as prayer. As for situations in which the use of water is forbidden, they include, for example; (1) those in which the water in question is owned by someone else who has not given permission for it to be used, or in which the water is in a public fountain which has been reserved for drinking, in which case it is forbidden to use such water for ritual ablutions, and (2) situations in which the use of the water would be harmful, as, for example, if performing minor or major ablutions with the water would make someone ill or exacerbate an already existing illness, a subject which will be taken up in the sections below on *tayammum*, or sand ablutions. The use of water is likewise forbidden if the water is so hot or so cold that it would be harmful to use it, or if the use of the water would mean allowing an animal which it is legally impermissible to destroy to go thirsty. In all such cases, it

---

39. According to the Hanbalis, the condition for its being impermissible to use water to remove major or minor ritual impurity from one's body and clothing is that the person doing so be aware that the water he has used is not *ṭahūr*; however, if someone does his ablutions with such water because he has forgotten that it is not *ṭahūr*, then prays following this, his ablutions and his prayer are both valid. They also hold that it is permissible to use such water for the removal of impurity.

is forbidden to use water for either minor or major ablutions; hence, if someone were to perform his ablutions with the water in a public fountain whose contents had been set aside for drinking or with water needed by an animal which it would be impermissible to allow to die, or if he performed his ablutions while suffering from an illness which would grow worse by virtue of such an act, he would be forbidden to do so. Nevertheless, such ablutions would still be valid, as would be the prayer performed on the basis of them.

Uses of water which are recommended include repeating one's ablutions when one is already in a state of ritual purity and performing major ablutions on Friday; uses of water which are permitted, but neither commendable nor obligatory, include activities such as drinking, kneading, and so forth. As for uses of water which are undesirable, though not forbidden, they include the use of water which is extremely hot or cold, but not to the point of actually being harmful to the body. The basis for this ruling is that in such a case, the person performing his ablutions will be so preoccupied with the discomfort caused by either the extreme heat or the extreme cold, he will be distracted from an attitude of reverent submission to God; such a person may do his ablutions, whether minor or total, in such haste that he fails to perform them in the desired manner.

It is likewise undesirable to perform either minor or major ablutions with water which has been heated by the sun, given two conditions: (1) that the water be placed in a container made of copper, lead or some other metal other than gold and silver—although, if the water is in a gold or silver container, it may be used for such ablutions without any undesirability associated with it; and (2) that the practice be observed in a hot country. Hence, if the water is placed in a copper container (such as a low copper kettle or cauldron) which is then placed in the sun until it gets hot, it is undesirable to perform one's ablutions in it, be they minor or major ablutions.

It is also deemed undesirable to wash a garment in such water, then put it on directly while it is still damp. Some explain the undesirability of this practice based on the notion that the use of water in this manner is harmful to the body. However, this is an unconvincing explanation since, if this practice were actually harmful, it would not be merely undesirable, but forbidden, while as a matter of fact, no harm is apparent unless there is rust in the container holding the water. Some have explained the undesirability of this practice by holding that such water would have the odor of putrid, fatty meat hovering over it, which would inevitably cause people to feel an aversion to it.[40] Hence, if other water is available, the use of such sun-heated water is undesirable, whereas if no other water is at one's disposal, there is no undesirability attached to the practice. The same applies to all other undesirable types of water, the use of which becomes acceptable if no other water is available.

---

40. The Shafiis add a third condition which makes it undesirable to use water heated in the sun, namely, that there be an odor of putrid, fatty meat over the water. If no such odor is present, there is no undesirability associated with the use of such water. Moreover, the Shafii school appears to explain the undesirability of this practice on the basis of the argument mentioned above. The Hanbalis say that it is not undesirable to use water heated by the sun under any circumstances.

Muslim jurisprudents have also mentioned other undesirable practices relating to water, about which the four schools differ over certain details.[41]

That which does not cause water to cease being *ṭahūr*

It is possible for the color, taste and smell of water to be altered and for the water nevertheless to remain fit for use in acts relating to Muslim worship such as minor ablutions, major ablutions and the like. However, it is necessary that the water con-

---

41. The Malikis mention three other undesirable practices associated with water:

One: The use of water which has been mingled with impurity; though not forbidden, it is undesirable to use such water given five conditions: (1) That the impurity not have altered any of the water's fundamental properties, i.e., its taste, color, or smell, since if it has altered any of these, it is not permissible to use the water at all; (2) That the water not be running water; since if it is running water and some impurity gets into it, it does not render it impure, though its use is undesirable; (3) That the water not be subject to increase, as is the case with well water, for although the water in a well is not running water, it is nevertheless subject to increase or decrease without water being added to it from outside; hence, it is not contaminated by an impurity falling into it; (4) That the volume of the impurity be no greater than that of a medium-sized raindrop; if it is less than this amount, it causes no harm and it is not undesirable to use the water into which the impurity fell; (5) That there be other water available in which to perform ablutions; if no other water is available, it is not undesirable to perform ablutions with such water.

Two: The use of used water to perform an action, such as ablutions, which requires water that is *ṭahūr*. If, for example, while someone is performing his ablutions, the water drips down off some part of his body after being used, it is undesirable for him to perform his ablutions in the water again. However, such a practice is only undesirable under certain conditions: (1) that the amount of water be small, for if there is a large amount of water and it mingles with water which drips off the parts of the body affected by one's ablutions, this does no harm; (2) that the person concerned be able to find other water in which to perform his ablutions; if he cannot, then there is no undesirability attached to using the water again; and (3) that the water be used in performing obligatory ablutions; for if someone uses such water to perform voluntary ablutions, such as ablutions before going to sleep and the like (as will be discussed below), then it is not undesirable.

The reason given by the Malikis for the undesirability of performing ablutions with used water is that some imams hold that performing ablutions in used water is prohibited; hence, as a concession to this opposing view, the Malikis state that it is undesirable. In addition, they maintain that because the earliest Muslims did not perform ablutions in previously used water, this indicates that to do so is undesirable.

Three: The performance of ablutions with water from which a dog has lapped, even in passing; hence, if a dog has drunk a small amount of water, it would be undesirable to use it, and the same applies to water from which someone accustomed to imbibing in intoxicants has drunk, as well as water in which someone has washed part of his body. As for performing ablutions in water from which a person who has imbibed in an intoxicant drank earlier, it is only undesirable under the following conditions: (1) That the amount of water concerned be small; if it is a large amount, there is no undesirability attached to it. A clarification of what is meant by 'large' and 'small' will be found below. (2) That there be other water available in which to do one's ablutions. (3) That there be uncertainty as to the purity of the mouth of the person who drank from the water or the bodily member which he washed in it. If there was verifiable impurity on the person's mouth, and if this impurity altered one of the water's fundamental properties, then it is forbidden to perform ablutions in it lest one render himself impure as a result. If, on the other hand, the impurity has not altered any of the properties of the water, then its use is undesirable only. Also included here is water which has been drunk from by animals which do not avoid impurity, such as birds, beasts of prey and chickens. However, if it causes undue hardship to avoid such impurity, as in the case of water which has been drunk from by cats and mice, then it is not undesirable to use the water.

* * *

As for the Hanafis, they add three more situations in which the use of water is undesirable:

One: Performing ablutions in water which has been drunk from by someone who imbibes in intoxicants. Such a person might place the water jug to his mouth and drink from it after having drunk some wine. However, the performance of ablutions with the same water is only undesirable—rather than being entirely forbidden—on one condition, namely, that the person drink from it after enough time has passed for the saliva which was mingled with the wine to have replaced itself. In other words, the person might drink some wine, then either swallow it or spit it out, then drink from a container of water. But if he drinks the rest of the wine and traces of it remain in his mouth due to his having neither swallowed it nor spit it out, after which he drinks from a water jug or pitcher, then the water in it is rendered impure and may not be used whatsoever.

Two: Performing ablutions with water which has been drunk from by birds of prey such as the kite, the crow or other birds belonging to the same category, such as unconfined chickens. The reason given by the Hanafis for the undesirability of using such water for ablutions is that such birds may have touched impurities with their beaks. Contrasted to this is water which has been drunk from by beasts of prey and all animals whose flesh may not be eaten, since the water is [definitively] impure due to its having mingled with the animals' impure saliva. Similarly, the sweat of animals whose flesh may not be eaten is deemed impure; hence, if the sweat of a hyena or some other beast of prey got onto a garment or into a small amount of water, it would render it impure.

Three: Performing ablutions in water which has been drunk from by a domestic cat if the amount of water is small. The reason for the undesirability of using such water is that cats do not avoid impurity. Nevertheless, despite the fact that the cat is an animal whose flesh may not be eaten, the water from which such a cat has drunk is deemed to be not impure, but merely undesirable based on the saying of the Prophet, "They [domestic cats] are not impure since they are among those who make the rounds among you [in other words, they are like your household servants]," which appears to be a concession.

As for water from which a mule or a donkey has drunk, there is uncertainty as to whether it is *ṭahūr* or not; in other words, it is deemed to be pure (*ṭāhir*) without further comment or explanation. Hence, if a donkey or a mule drank from a small amount of water, it would be permissible to use such water for ordinary activities such as washing, drinking and the like without any undesirability attached to it. However, as to whether it is *ṭahūr*, i.e., whether it is fit to be used in the performance of minor or major ablutions, this is uncertain. Hence, it is permissible to use it for minor and major ablutions if no other water is available without its being deemed undesirable; if other water is available, then it may still be used for these purposes, but it is preferable to perform minor and major ablutions with the other water.

* * *

In addition to the aforementioned undesirable uses of water, the Shafiis add the use of water which has been altered by virtue of its proximity to something else, be it a solid or a liquid. An example of a proximate solid is fat; if such a solid is placed in close proximity to water, thereby causing the water to change, it becomes undesirable to use it. As for a proximate liquid, an example would be rosewater and the like. If some liquid is placed close to water and the water is altered as a result, it becomes undesirable to use it, the condition for undesirability being that the solid or liquid not cause the water to cease being water altogether [since in this case, it would be impermissible to use it at all]. If, on the other hand, the water took on the fragrance of the rosewater which had been placed next to it, or if it solidified by virtue of the proximity of some fat close to it such that it lost its fluidity and was no longer truly water, it would not be permissible to use it for either minor or major ablutions.

* * *

The Hanbalis list an additional seven types of water the use of which is viewed as undesirable: (1) water which one considers likely to have been contaminated by an impurity; (2) water which has been heated by means of an impure substance, whether or not the water is used while it is still hot; (3) water which has been used for nonobligatory purification, such as the performance of ablutions which are merely recommended rather than obligatory; (4) water whose properties have been altered as a result of the addition of water-derived salt to it [water-derived salt being salt which was obtained by evaporating salty water, as opposed to salt mined from minerals under the ground – t.n.]; (5) water from a well on land which has been taken from others by force, or which was dug by people who were forced to do so against their wills, even if the well is on land which is still in the possession of its original owners; an example of this would be forcing people to dig a well without remuneration, or paying people to dig the well with money that had been acquired by unlawful means; (6) the water from a well located in a cemetery; and (7) water heated with illegally acquired fuel.

cerned not be a source of harm; hence, if the use of such altered water would cause physical harm to the person using it, it is not permissible for him to perform his ablutions with it. People residing in outlying desert areas might be obliged to use altered water when they have nothing else available to them; hence, Islamic law allows such people to use such water if they are not in danger of harm as a result of it. This is supported by the account narrated by al-Bukhārī according to which, when the Muslims emigrated from Mecca to Medina, many of them came down with a fever. In response, some Muslim thinkers at that time instructed the people to fill in a swamp known as *Buṭḥān*. When the swamp was filled in, the fever disappeared, and 'Ā'ishah, may God be pleased with her, said, "*Buṭḥān* gave off brackish (that is, altered) water." Actions which are required by the interests of people's health, such as laying waterlines or destroying fountains and basins used for ritual ablutions for fear that the water they contain may be polluted or otherwise altered in a harmful way, are consistent with the true intentions of the Islamic religion, since they are based on the goal of serving people's best interests and warding off harm.

Muslim jurisprudents mention the following types of change which do not cause water to cease being *ṭahūr*: (1) For all or some of the water's properties to be altered due to the place in which it has settled—such as old ablution fountains or pools in the desert—or the places through which it has passed, as in the case of water which has flowed over minerals such as salt and sulfur. (2) For water to be altered due to the length of time it has stayed in a given place, such as when water is placed in a water skin or large clay jar and left for such a long time that changes occur in it. (3) For water to be altered due to fish or water moss[42] which has reproduced in it (water moss being a green plant which floats on the surface of the water); such moss causes no harm so long as it is not cooked in the water or thrown into the water after being cooked. (4) For water to change as a result of the substance with which its container was tanned, such as tar, sant tree pods, and the like; hence, if one of the properties of water that has been placed in a tanned water skin undergoes alteration, this causes no harm. (5) For water to change because of something whose presence could not have been avoided, such as dust, straw and tree leaves blown into a well by the wind. (6) For water to be altered due to a substance placed next to it; for example, if a corpse were placed along the shoreline of a body of water and the water were altered by the corpse's odor, this change would not cause the water to cease being *ṭahūr*. The practice of placing such things near water is one of the pernicious habits of ignorant village dwellers, who throw the dead bodies of animals onto beaches, and sometimes into the very water which they use, causing it to give off a stench that reaches a long distance away. Hence, although

---

42. The Hanbalis do not stipulate that the moss be cooked; rather, they say, it is harmful to the water [whether it is cooked or not]. If moss is thrown into water deliberately by a rational human being, it causes the water to cease being *ṭahūr* whether it is cooked or not. However, if it grows spontaneously in the water or is blown into it by the wind or some other non-human force, it causes no harm.

the Lawgiver has given permission for such water to be used for ablutions, both minor and major, He has nevertheless issued a severe warning against this if such water causes harm or offense to those who pass by it or use it for ablutions.

Water which is *ṭāhir* but not *ṭahūr*

As we have seen, water is sometimes described as *ṭahūr*, the definition of which has been given above, while at other times it is described as simply *ṭāhir*. As for the definition of water which is *ṭāhir*, it is previously used water which has not been contaminated by any ritual impurity and which may be used in ordinary routine activities such as drinking, cooking, washing and the like, but which may not be used in acts of Muslim worship such as minor and major ablutions.

Types of water which are *ṭāhir* but not *ṭahūr*

There are three types of water which are considered to be *ṭāhir* but not *ṭahūr*:[43]

Type 1 is *ṭahūr* water which has been mixed with something that is ritually pure; for example, if rosewater, dough or some such thing were added to *ṭahūr* water, this would cause it to cease being *ṭahūr* such that it could still be used for such routine activities as drinking, laundry, etc., but it would no longer be permissible to use it for minor or major ritual ablutions. However, such an event only causes water to cease being *ṭahūr* under two conditions: (1) one of the water's fundamental properties—its taste, its color, or its smell—must have been altered by the substance that has been mixed with it, and (2) the substance which has been mixed with the water must be among those things which rob water of its *ṭahūr* quality.[44]

---

43. According to the Malikis, there is only one type of water which is *ṭāhir* but not *ṭahūr*, namely, Type 1 above, which is water that has been mingled with a pure substance that has altered one of the water's three fundamental properties and which is among those things which cause water to cease being *ṭahūr*. Such water is what the Malikis refer to as "*ṭāhir* but not *ṭahūr*." As for Type 2, namely, a small amount of used water, the Malikis deem it to be *ṭahūr* so long as none of its fundamental properties has been altered by this use. And as for Type 3, namely, water which has come from plants, such as rosewater and watermelon juice, they do not include it among the types of water which may be used for purification, since it is not water in the full sense.

44. The Hanafis divide those things which cause water to cease being *ṭahūr* and to become simply *ṭāhir* into two categories, namely, solid and liquid. As for solids, they cause water to cease being *ṭahūr* in two situations: (1) A situation in which the water is mixed with something which robs it of its clarity and fluidity, as, for example, when clay is placed in the water, thereby causing it to lose its fluid quality, in which case it may not be used for purification. Another example of such water is that which remains in the bottom of cisterns when they dry up after containing water mixed with clay. (2) A situation in which the water becomes mixed with something that is to be cooked in it, in which case it may no longer be used for purification even if it has not lost its fluidity. For example, if some lentils were

placed in some water to cook, after which the water boiled twice such that it was altered by the lentils yet without their being cooked, it would no longer be permissible to use it for purification even if it had not lost its liquid, flowing quality. Such an occurrence might take place in the desert when water is scarce. However, an exception is made if water has been altered by soap and other things used for cleaning purposes; if a substance such as this boils in the water and changes its color, taste or smell, the water nevertheless remains *ṭahūr* unless the substance concerned was actually cooked in it, thereby causing it to cease being a clear, flowing liquid.

As for a liquid which combines with water, it will be one of three types: The first type of liquid is one which has all the same fundamental properties as water, namely, taste, color and smell, such as rosewater which has lost its fragrance, or used water. As for the ruling on water which has been combined with such a liquid, it depends on which of the two (the water or the other liquid) is found in the greater amount. If, for example, the larger proportion of the mixture is water, it remains *ṭahūr*, whereas if the larger proportion is the other liquid, the water is now *ṭāhir*, but no longer *ṭahūr*. The same principle applies in cases where the water and the other liquid are found in equal proportions; hence, for example, if a group of people perform their ritual ablutions in a small basin—such as an ablution fountain—and if the amount of used water which flows back into the basin from their hands, feet and other bodily members affected by such ablutions is smaller than the amount which was not used, no harm is done; if, on the other hand, the amounts of used and unused water are equal or if the amount of used water is greater than the amount which went unused, then all of the water remaining in the basin is considered to have become used.

The second type of liquid which may mix with *ṭahūr* water is one which differs from water in all of its fundamental properties, namely, its color, its taste and its smell. An example of such a liquid is vinegar, whose taste, color and smell are all distinct from those of water. Hence, if some vinegar spilled into some water and the water took on most of the properties of the vinegar, such as its taste and its color together, the water would now be *ṭāhir* but no longer *ṭahūr* and, as a result, it would no longer be permissible to use it in acts relating to Muslim worship, although it could still be used in cooking and so on. If, on the other hand, the water took on only one of the properties of the vinegar, it would still be *ṭahūr*.

The third type of liquid with which *ṭahūr* water might be mixed is one which shares some, but not all, of the fundamental properties of water. An example of such a liquid is milk, which has a particular taste and color but no odor. If, then, some milk were mixed with water, the water would become *ṭāhir* rather than *ṭahūr* by virtue of having taken on only one of the properties of milk. An example of such a situation is what might occur when farmers put milk in containers while they are out on the farm and far from water, after which they put water in the same containers before cleaning them out thoroughly, the result being that traces of the milk appear in the water. If the color of the milk is visible in the water, the water ceases to be *ṭahūr* and becomes simply *ṭāhir*.

* * *

As for the Malikis, they hold that there are only three events capable of robbing water of its *ṭahūr* character and rendering it simply *ṭāhir*. The first of these events is for water to be mixed with something which is *ṭāhir*, or ritually pure, and as a result, for one of its three fundamental properties—namely, its taste, its color, or its smell—to be altered, even if the smell is not detectable in the water. However, such a substance can only cause water to cease being *ṭahūr* under four conditions: (1) The substance concerned must not be a necessary accompaniment of water but rather, be something which is usually not associated with water. (2) The substance must not be derived from the earth. (3) It must not be among those substances with which the container has been tanned. (4) It must not be something that is difficult to avoid.

Examples of such things include soap, which is generally not mixed with water, rosewater and other aromatic liquids, since someone who uses water does not generally need such things. Other examples include the dung of livestock since, even though it might be mixed with water which is used for drinking, this is an occurrence which would not be difficult to avoid; the smoke resulting from something burning even if it is part of the earth; tree leaves if they are near a well or a watering trough which can be covered, as well as dust-like substances such as straw and the pollen from date palm trees; and fish which have died in the water or been thrown into it. All such substances, even though they may be ritually pure, rob water of its *ṭahūr* quality if they become mixed with it given the aforementioned conditions; if any of the water's fundamental properties are altered as a result, it becomes *ṭāhir* only.

The second event which is capable of robbing water of its *ṭahūr* character is for the water to be altered while inside the container in which it is being kept. However, the water will only cease being *ṭahūr* if: (1) the container is made of a substance which is not part of the earth, for example, a container made of leather or wood such that the water is altered by its proximity to the container, and (2) the change in the water is obvious by commonly agreed-upon standards. However, if the water has been placed in an earthenware container or if the change in it is not obvious, then it does no harm. The same ruling applies if the water is altered due to its proximity to a flax or fiber rope; such a change does no harm unless it is obvious by commonly agreed-upon standards.

As for the third event capable of changing *ṭahūr* water into water which is simply *ṭāhir*, it is for the water to be changed because of tar, sant tree pods, and the like; however, such substances only rob water of its *ṭahūr* character if the taste or color of the water is changed. If, on the other hand, only its odor changes, then it remains *ṭahūr.*

* * *

According to the Shafiis, water loses its *ṭahūr* quality and becomes simply *ṭāhir* if it is mixed with something ritually pure given the following conditions: (1) The substance which is mixed with the water must be one which the water can do without. Hence, if the water changes due to the addition of other water without which the original water would no longer remain, or if it changes due to the place from which it wells up, then this change causes no harm. (2) The change in the water must be certain to have taken place, since if there is doubt as to whether there has actually been a change, no harm is done. (3) The change in the water must be due to soil, even if it is soil which was deliberately thrown into it. The same applies to water-derived salt, as well as to anything else which is cast into the water, thereby causing it to change, as, for example, if some saffron, dates or the like fell into the water and caused an obvious change in it. A similar situation would be one in which tree leaves or something else falls into some water or in which water changes due to something which has dissolved in it, such as some flax or licorice root or the like, which has been placed in it. In all such cases, the water will no longer be *ṭahūr,* provided that the change involved is obvious and indisputable as mentioned above.

If water has undergone a verifiable change due to tar, it becomes *ṭāhir* only given two conditions: (1) that the tar be free of all fatty substances, and (2) that the purpose for using the tar not be to repair the water skin, since in this latter case, it causes no harm. Similarly, if the water has been altered by salt which was not derived from evaporated water, like mountain salt, it will become merely *ṭāhir*; however, if the salt is in either a place where the water rests or one over which it passes, it causes no harm.

* * *

According to the Hanbalis, there are three things which rob water of its *ṭahūr* quality. The first of these is for water to be mixed with a ritually pure substance which would not have been difficult to avoid. Such a substance only causes water to cease being *ṭahūr* under two conditions: (1) The substance which has been mixed with the water must have caused a significant change in one of the water's characteristics. If the change is only slight, however, this does no harm. (2) The substance in question must not be at the site being purified. Hence, for example, if there were some saffron on the hand of someone performing his ritual ablutions and he took up some water which was then changed on account of the saffron, this change would cause no harm. Nor does it make any difference in this regard if something has first been cooked in the water, such as lupine or chickpeas. If, on the other hand, it is a substance which it is difficult to keep away from water, such as water moss and tree leaves, then it does not cause it to cease being *ṭahūr* unless it has been thrown deliberately into the water by a human being in full possession of his mental faculties.

The second thing which, according to the Hanbalis, causes water to cease being *ṭahūr* is for it to be mixed with water that has been used. However, the original water only ceases being *ṭahūr* if the water which has been mixed with it had been used to remove major or minor ritual impurity or to cleanse something or someone of an impure substance. Hence, it is not sufficient for the water simply to have come into contact with something, but its contact must have been for the purpose of purification. If, for example, water has passed over someone's hand without his purifying his hand with it, then it is not considered used, nor is it considered used if, when it runs off such a site, it is unchanged, or if it amounts to more than 'two pitchers full'.

As for the third thing which renders *ṭahūr* water *ṭāhir*, it is for water to be mixed with a liquid which has the same properties as *ṭahūr* water, and which is

The second type of water which is deemed *ṭāhir*, but not *ṭahūr*, is a small amount of used water,[45] with 'small' being defined as that which is more than two *raṭls* less than "two pitchers full (*qullatān*)." As for the term 'used', it is defined variously by the different schools.[46]

---

found in a larger proportion than the original, *ṭahūr* water. Examples of such liquids are aromatic extracts such as rosewater, basil water and mint infusions which have lost their fragrance. Hence, these three things are viewed as causing water no longer to be *ṭahūr* given the aforementioned conditions.

45. According to the Malikis, a small amount of water is not harmed by being used, nor does the use of water cause it to cease being *ṭahūr*. Hence, if someone performs ritual ablutions in a small amount of water and this water runs back into the container from which he took it, it is permissible for him to repeat his ablutions with the same water. As for the meaning of 'used' as understood by the Malikis, it will be discussed below.

* * *

According to the Hanafis, the 'small' amount of water the use of which causes it to cease being *ṭahūr* refers to water which has been placed in a receptacle with an area less than 10 x 10 cubits, or which is in a round basin with a circumference of less than 36 cubits. As for the amount of water which is large enough that its use does not cause it to cease being *ṭahūr*, it includes all other quantities, such as the sea, rivers, canals, irrigation ditches, the still water in large square ablution fountains with an area of 10 x 10 cubits or more, and the water that flows off water wheels with circumferences of 36 cubits or more. Nor is it necessary for such receptacles to be extremely deep; rather, it is most common for them to be shallow enough that when using the water contained in them, one can see to the bottom. If someone uses less than this amount of water, however, it becomes 'used.' As for the ruling on used water, it will be discussed below.

46. According to the Malikis, using water does not cause it to lose its *ṭahūr* quality, even if it is a small amount. Hence, it may be used for minor and major ritual ablutions and the like, although the use of water which has been used before is undesirable if other water is available. Moreover, the Malikis divide used water into two types: (1) a small amount of *ṭahūr* water which has been used to remove a state of ritual impurity, whether it be minor or major ritual impurity as, for example, when one uses water to perform minor or major ritual ablutions or to remove an impurity from something, be it material or non-material, as has already been mentioned, and (2) water which has been used for a purpose which requires that the water be *ṭahūr*, whether such an act is obligatory, such as performing major ablutions on a deceased person or the performance of major ablutions by a Christian or Jewish woman married to a Muslim man at the end of her menstrual period or after giving birth in order for her husband to be able to resume sexual relations with her, or non-obligatory, such as repeating one's ritual ablutions even though one is still in a state of ritual purity, performing major ablutions on Fridays, on the Day of Sacrifice and the Day of Fastbreaking, or the second and third washings involved in minor ritual ablutions. If water is used for any of these purposes, it is undesirable to use it again: (1) If the water flows over the bodily member con-

cerned, then continues to drip off after this. This condition applies if the water has been used in minor or major ritual ablutions, whereas if it is used simply for the removal of an impurity, it does not, and (2) if the water has been transferred from where it was to the bodily member to be cleansed; however, if the bodily member was immersed in the water, the water is not considered to be used unless the member concerned was scrubbed or rubbed. Hence, if someone in a state of major ritual impurity immersed himself in a pool of water but did not rub his body while in the water, the water would not be considered used.

* * *

As for the Hanafis, they hold that if *ṭahūr* water is used, it becomes merely *ṭāhir*, as a result of which it may be used in routine activities such as drinking, cooking and so on, but not for acts of worship such as minor and major ritual ablutions. Moreover, they divide used water into four types: (1) that which has been used in preparation to perform acts of piety such as ritual prayer, ritual consecration during the pilgrimage (*iḥrām*), touching the Qur'ān, and the like; (2) that which has been used to remove a state of minor or major ritual impurity such as the performance of ablutions by someone in a state of minor ritual impurity; (3) that which has been used in an act by virtue of which a religious obligation is fulfilled even if it removes no impurity, as, for example, if someone were to wash some, but not all, parts of the body which are normally washed as part of minor ritual ablutions. Hence, if someone washed only his face, the water with which he washed his face would become used even if he had not completed his ablutions. The washing of the face fulfills a religious obligation [since this forms part of ritual ablutions]; however, it has not removed a state of ritual impurity, since the latter depends on the performance of one's ablutions to completion; and (4) that which has been used as a means of reminding oneself of an act of worship, such as a menstruating woman's performance of minor ritual ablutions; it is commendable for such a woman to do her ablutions at the time for each of the five daily prayers as a way of keeping herself mindful of the prayers she is accustomed to performing.

It should be added, however, that water does not become 'used' in any of these situations unless the water flows completely off the bodily member which has been washed; hence, if the water flowed over someone's arm but none flowed off, it would not be considered 'used', of course, since otherwise, it would not be possible to purify the entire portion of the arm washed during ablutions.

* * *

The Shafiis define used water as a small amount of water with which one has performed an act which is necessary—whether in substance or merely in form—such as the removal of a state of ritual impurity perceived by the person using the water, or the removal of an impure substance.

What is meant here by a small amount of water is an amount which is less than the 'two pitchers full' mentioned above; hence, if someone performed minor or major ritual ablutions in a small amount of water and dipped out some of the water to wash his hands after having washed his face with his hand, then the water would be 'used'; however, it would only become used if: (1) it was used in fulfilling the religious obligation to maintain ritual purity; hence, if someone performs ritual ablutions in order to pray a voluntary prayer, touch the Qur'ān, or some other non-obligatory act of piety, then dipping out of the water will not render it 'used'; (2) if the water was used for the first washing; in other words, if someone washed his face once outside the container of water, then placed his hand in the water to wash it a second and third time, the water would still not be 'used'; (3) if the amount of water was small to begin with; in other words, if the water amounts to at least 'two pitchers full' and if it is then distributed among several different containers, it does not become 'used' by being dipped into. Similarly, if one were to collect small amounts of used water until it amounted to "two pitchers full," it would then be considered a large amount and would not be affected by being dipped into; (4) if the water flowed off of the bodily member being washed; hence, if the water flowed over one's hand but did not flow off of it, it would not thereby become 'used.'

Moreover, if someone performed minor or major ritual ablutions in a small amount of water, then uttered the intention to dip out of the same water, it would not be 'used.' As for the point during minor ablutions when one should utter such an intention, it comes before [the text reads 'after'] washing one's face and when one is about to wash one's hands. If someone utters such an intention at the point where he rinses out his mouth or his nostrils or washes his face, this is not acceptable. As for the point during major ablutions at which the intention to dip into the water should be uttered, it is after one has uttered the intention to perform major ablutions and as the water is coming into contact with part of his body. However, if, while performing either minor or major ritual ablutions one utters no intention to dip water out—that is, to move the water from where it is and place it on one's body—then the water will be rendered 'used.'

The meaning of the above phrase, "whether in substance or merely in form" is that it makes no difference whether the person performing the ablutions is someone who fulfills all the religious requirements of Islam and who is therefore actually accountable for performing ritual ablutions, or someone who does not fulfill these requirements and for whom ablutions are only a formality.

As for the phrase, "perceived by the person using the water," it means that if the ablutions performed by an individual are valid according to the rulings of his particular school, then the water with which he performed these ablutions will be deemed 'used' even if these ablutions were not valid according to the Shafii school. Hence, if a Hanafi does his ablutions without first uttering his intention to do so, his ablutions will be valid in the view of the Hanafis, but invalid in the view of the Shafiis; despite this fact, however, the water with which the Hanafi did his ablutions will still be considered 'used' to the Shafiis.

And as for the phrase, "the removal of an impure substance", it means that the water with which an impurity is removed will be deemed used, but not impure. However, in order for such water still to be deemed ritually pure, the following conditions must apply: (1) that when the water runs off after a contaminated article of clothing has been washed, for example, and the site of the impurity has been cleansed, the water is ritually pure in the sense that none of its fundamental properties have been altered by the impure substance; and (2) that after the water absorbed by the item washed has drained off together with the dirt which normally becomes suspended in the water, the water which runs off the contaminated spot does not show any increase in weight; supposing, for example, that a contaminated garment is washed in a container holding ten *ratls* of water and the garment soaks up one-tenth of this amount, i.e., 1 *ratl*, while dirt from the garment weighing 1/4 *ratl* is dissolved in the water, then if the weight of the water which runs off comes to 9 1/4 *ratls* or less, this water may be deemed pure, otherwise, it must be deemed impure; and (3) that the water passed over the impurity at the time it was being cleansed; if the water did not pass over it or become mixed with it, it would not be considered used.

It might be said that there is no need for such a discussion given that we live in an age during which running water has become virtually ubiquitous. In response we say: Islamic law is not restricted to any given time or place. There can be no doubt that these rulings are still a necessity for those adherents of the Shafii school who travel in desert areas and locations in which water is scarce. Hence, any Shafii who finds himself in such a situation will undeniably need these rulings.

* * *

The Hanbalis define used water as a small amount of water by means of which a state of major or minor ritual impurity or an impure substance has been removed, or which runs off pure and unaltered from a site that has been rendered ritually pure by being washed seven times; the water which runs off before the seventh washing is impure, whereas that which runs off after the seventh washing is merely used.

The phrase, "a small amount of water" is meant simply to exclude a 'large' amount, that is, any quantity equal to or more than 'two pitchers full'. As for the phrase, 'water by means of which a state of major or minor ritual impurity or an impure substance has been removed', it serves to exclude water which has been used to wash something that was already ritually pure (*ṭāhir*). And as for the phrase, "which runs off pure and unaltered from a site that has been rendered ritually pure by being washed seven times," it means that if someone washes an impure garment, utensil or container, such an item will only be purified by being washed seven times, since according to the Hanbalis, that which has been contaminated by an impurity can only become pure again by being washed seven times.

The Hanbalis likewise classify as 'used' water which has been used to perform major ablutions on a deceased person or water in which someone has placed his entire hand after waking up in the morning from a sleep which invalidated his ritual ablutions, provided that the person who placed his hand in it is an adult Muslim in full possession of his mental faculties, and provided that he placed his hand in the container before washing it three times with both a statement of intention and utterance of the words, "In the name of God, the Most Gracious, the Most Merciful." The same ruling applies if such a person pours the water over his entire hand without placing his hand in it, or if he has a pitcher or jug from which he pours the water onto his hand, in which case the water that drips off his hand is considered to be used. No judgment may be made on whether water is used or not until after it has flowed off the site at which it was used.

In terms of weight, 'two pitchers full' are equal to 446 3/7 (four hundred forty-six and three-sevenths) Egyptian *ratls*, while the container holding the two pitchers full, if it is square, must occupy a volume equal to a 1 1/4 cubit cube (the cubit being based on the length of a medium-sized person's arm). If the receptacle is round, such as a well, it must be 1 cubit in diameter and 2 1/2 cubits deep, and have a circumference of 3 1/7 cubits. If the receptacle is triangular, its area should be 1 1/2 cubits in width, 1 1/2 cubits in length, and 2 cubits deep.

As for the third type of water which is *ṭāhir* only, it is water which comes from plants, whether it is extracted artificially as in the case of rosewater, or comes out naturally as in the case of watermelon juice.

The Third Type:
Contaminated Water

Contaminated water is that which has been mixed with an impurity, and is divided into two categories: (1) a large amount of *ṭahūr* water, which is not contaminated by an impurity's being mixed with it unless one of its fundamental properties—namely, its color, its taste, or its smell—has been altered; and (2) a small amount of *ṭahūr* water, which is contaminated merely by having an impurity become mixed with it, whether any of its fundamental properties have been altered or not.[47]

---

47. The Malikis hold that *ṭahūr* water is not contaminated by being mixed with an impurity provided that the impurity does not change any of its three fundamental properties; however, they deem it undesirable to use such water as a concession to opposing viewpoints.

48. According to the Hanafis, if an animal with blood which flows like that of a human being, a goat or a rabbit falls into a well, there are three different scenarios which might arise:

In the first scenario, after the animal falls in the water it becomes bloated, decomposes, or loses its hair. The ruling on such a case is that the water in the well, the pail which was dipped into it, and the rope attached to the pail after the animal fell in have all been rendered impure. If it is possible to drain the well and allow it to dry out, it will only be rendered pure by taking such measures. If this is not possible, it can be purified by bailing out 200 pails full, using the pail which is usually dipped into the well. Before the well is drained or some of its water is bailed out, the dead animal must be removed. Once these steps have been taken, however, the well, its walls, its pail, its rope, and the hand of the person who removed the impure water from the well are all deemed pure.

In the second scenario, a similar type of animal dies in the well, but without becoming bloated, decomposing or losing its hair. If this occurs, the situation can take one of three forms: (1) The animal which died is a human being, a ewe or a billy goat, be it large or small, young or old. The ruling on such a situation is the same as that for the first scenario, i.e., that the well water, its walls, its pail and its rope have all been contaminated and will not be rendered pure again unless the well is drained and dried out, if possible, or—if this is not possible—200 hundred pails full are bailed out of the well. (2) The animal which died in the well is a small creature such as a dove, a chicken or a cat. If, for example, a cat falls into the well

Well water

There are special rulings relating to well water; hence, we have devoted a separate section to this topic. Moreover, the four schools offer differing viewpoints on various details pertaining to such rulings.[48]

---

and dies but does not become bloated, decompose or lose its hair, then the water in the well is deemed contaminated, and it will only be purified by bailing 40 pails full out of it. (3) The animal which died in the well water is even smaller, such as a sparrow or a mouse. In this case, the well water is judged to have been contaminated as before, and it will only be purified by bailing 20 pails full out of it.

No distinction is made between large and small with respect to any of these types of animals. However, there are explicit texts which mention cases involving human beings, chickens and mice, whereas for all other types, the ruling for a small animal is based on the ruling for a large one.

In the third scenario, an animal falls into a well and is brought out while it is still alive. If this happens, the event may take one of two forms: (1) The animal which falls into the well is intrinsically impure, such as a pig. The ruling in this case is that the well must be drained entirely if possible, and if this is not possible, 200 pails full must be bailed out of it; in other words, it is subject to the same ruling as that which applies to a case where an animal falls in the well, dies and subsequently becomes bloated, decomposes and loses its hair. (2) The animal which falls into the well is ritually pure, such as a goat or some similar animal. The ruling on this situation is that if the animal is found to have gross impurity—such as feces and the like—on its body, then the well has become impure just as it would be if an intrinsically impure animal had fallen into it. If no such impurity is found on the animal's body, there is no obligation to bail any water out of the well. However, it is recommended that 20 pails full be bailed out in order to set people's minds at rest. If, on the other hand, there is no impurity on the animal's body but there is impurity on its mouth, then the relevant ruling is that which applies to the *su'r* of an impure animal [that is, water in which a ritually impure animal has fallen or swum, or from which it has drunk]; for more detail on this, readers may refer to the relevant section above.

As for creatures which lack blood which flows, such as scorpions, frogs, fish and the like, it does no harm for them to die in well water; nor is any harm done if substances which cannot be avoided, such as animal droppings and the like, fall into such water provided that, in the estimation of the person looking at them, they do not seem to be present in a large amount.

* * *

According to the Malikis, well water becomes impure when an animal dies if: (1) the animal is terrestrial, be it a human being or a dumb beast; since if it is aquatic, such as a fish, it does not render the water impure; (2) the terrestrial animal in question has blood which flows; otherwise, as in the case of a cockroach or a scorpion, the water is not rendered impure; and (3) the well water undergoes a change; for if a terrestrial animal dies in the well and the water is not changed by this event, it is not rendered impure, whether the animal happens to be large or small. However, it is considered commendable in such a case for enough water to be bailed out of the well to set people's minds at rest, the amount not being specified. Moreover, the ruling on well water in a case such as this applies likewise to all still water which has no inflow, such as the water in small ponds which are neither deep nor wide.

* * *

As for the Shafiis, they note that the amount of water in a well will either be small—that is, less than the 'two pitchers full' explained above—or large, i.e., equal to 'two pitchers full' or more. If the amount of water in the well is small and a creature which lacks blood that flows dies in it, the water is rendered impure provided that: (1) the impurity is not among those which may be overlooked, a discussion of which is found above, and (2) no one has deliberately cast the impurity into the water. Hence, if the impurity simply falls into the water or is blown into it by the wind, and if it is an impurity which may be overlooked, then it does no harm. If, on the other hand, someone throws it into the water, it causes the water to be contaminated. If a creature with blood which flows has died in a large amount of water—namely, an amount which exceeds 'two pitchers full'—the water does not become impure unless one of its three fundamental properties is altered. Similarly, if an impurity falls into a well and the amount of water in the well is large, it is not rendered impure unless one of its fundamental properties has been altered; however, if the amount of water in the well is small, then it is contaminated the moment it makes contact with the impurity given the two conditions mentioned above, even if no change occurs in any of its fundamental properties.

* * *

The Hanbalis hold the same view as that of the Shafiis; however, in order for a small amount of water to be rendered impure by the death of an animal in it, they do not stipulate the two conditions set forth by the Shafiis, namely, (1) that the impurity in question not be among those which may be overlooked, and (2) that the impurity have been deliberately thrown into the water.

49. The Hanafis hold that *ṭāhir* water may be used in the removal of impure substances; hence, one may remove impurities from one's clothing, one's body or a place with *ṭāhir* water as well as with any other ritually pure liquid which possesses a fragrance, such as rosewater, sweet basil water and the like. However, this practice is deemed undesirable due to the fact that it leads to the needless expenditure of money. Hence, if someone removes an impurity from a garment with rosewater, this practice is permissible, but undesirable unless the person wishes to sweeten the fragrance of his garment. As for washing an impurity out of a garment with *ṭāhir* water, this is not undesirable in the least.

50. The Hanafis divide contaminated substances into two categories, namely, liquids such as water, blood and other fluids; and solids, such as swine, dead organisms, impure animal dung or bird droppings. As for contaminated water, it is only permissible to use it or benefit from it in two cases: (1) the preparation of potter's clay, plaster of Paris, lime, cement and other such substances, and (2) watering riding animals. However, in order for the use of such water in either of these two situations to be permissible, neither the smell, the color, nor the taste of the water can have changed. As for contaminated solids such as pigs, dead animals, animals

Rulings on water which is ritually pure (*ṭāhir*) and water which is impure (*najis*)

Early in our discussion of the different types of water, we mentioned the ruling on *ṭahūr* water and the relevant meanings of this ruling. What remains now is the rulings on the other two types of water, namely, water which is *ṭāhir* and that which is *najis*. As for water which is *ṭāhir,* it is not permissible to use it in acts relating to Muslim worship such as the performance of minor ritual ablutions or major ablutions for purification from sexual discharge; nor may it be used to remove impurities from one's body, one's clothing, or a place, since it removes neither a state of major or minor ritual impurity nor impure substances.[49]

As for the ruling on contaminated water, it may not be used either in acts of Muslim worship or in routine daily activities. Hence, just as it may not be used for the performance of minor or major ritual ablutions, neither can it be used for cooking, making bread dough and so on. If it is put to any of these uses, it renders impure the person and/or substances with which it comes into contact, and for this reason its use is prohibited. In this sense, then, it may be likened to wine which, being ritually impure, may only be used in cases of dire necessity. For example, if someone were lost in the desert and his life depended on drinking impure water, it would be permissible for him to drink it; similarly, if someone were eating and some food got caught in his throat to the point where he was unable to breathe, it would be permissible for him to remove it with impure water or wine if no *ṭāhir* water were available. According to Sunni schools of law, it is also permissible to make use of contaminated water for certain purposes that are not directly related to human beings.[50]

---

which have been strangled or killed, and so forth, there are explicit texts [see Q. 5:3], which forbid their use altogether. It is likewise forbidden to make use of the skins of such animals unless they have been tanned, the only exception being pigs' skin, which is not rendered pure even by tanning. As for other types of contaminated solids, such as contaminated fat, it may not be eaten, but it may be put to other uses, such as oiling machinery and burning it in lamps, provided that they are not in a mosque. An exception to this ruling is made in the case of the fat of dead animals, the use of which is forbidden entirely. As for the fat of ritually pure animals which has been contaminated by some passing impurity, it may not be used until after it has been purified in the manner described above in the section entitled, "The Means and Manner by Which Ritual Impurity May Be Removed." It is also forbidden to make use of human excrement after it has dried unless it has been mixed with soil, thereby becoming fertilizer. As for animal dung, it may be made into fuel.

It is permissible to sell dogs for use in hunting, as guard dogs, and the like; the same holds true for lions, wolves, elephants and all other animals except the pig, since the preferred view is that dogs, like the other animals mentioned, are not intrinsically impure (but rather, that only their mouths and saliva are impure), and that the skins of all such animals may be used with the exception of the pig's.

* * *

According to the Malikis, it is forbidden to make use of contaminated water for drinking and the like, whereas all other uses are permissible. Others of the same school hold that it is also forbidden to use such water in the construction of mosques. The most commonly held view among them is that it is not permissible to make use of liquids such as oil, honey, clarified butter and vinegar if they have been contaminated since, in their view, it is not possible to purify them once they have been contaminated but rather, they must be destroyed. It is also an accepted view among some Malikis that it is undesirable to allow the visible parts of one's body to be splattered with contaminated water, although some hold that it is forbidden and that one must remove it before performing ritual prayer or any other act which requires ritual purity. There is a dispute among Malikis over whether it is obligatory to remove an impurity, with some of them holding that it is obligatory while others hold that it is merely an emulation of the example of the Prophet. Both views, however, are well recognized. As for impure liquids other than water, such as wine, they may not be used at all. Similarly, there are a number of impure solids which it is impermissible to use, including [substances derived from] the pig and the dung of animals whose flesh may be eaten, whether it is entirely forbidden to eat such meat such as the meat of horses, mules and donkeys, or simply undesirable, as is the case with the meat of beasts of prey, hyenas, foxes, wolves and cats.

Moreover, although the Malikis view dogs as ritually pure, they nevertheless hold that it is forbidden to sell them because the Prophet forbade this practice. Some of them say that the sale of dogs is permissible if they are to be used as guard dogs or hunting dogs; in support of this stance, they argue that the prohibition against selling dogs pertains only to those which are not to be put to such uses. A similar position is held by those who hold that it is permissible to sell dogs.

* * *

The Shafiis hold that contaminated liquids, including water, may only be used for two purposes, namely: (1) putting out fires, such as fires inside of ovens and the like, and (2) watering livestock and crops. [Impure] liquids also include wine and blood which has not coagulated, neither of which may be put to any use whatsoever. As for impure solids, such as human feces and dung, it is impermissible to sell them or to make use of them. If such substances become mixed with a pure substance and it is impossible to separate the pure substance from the impure, one may make use of it; hence, for example, if some ritually pure gypsum is kneaded together with impure water after which someone builds a house with it, it will be still permissible to make use of the house by selling it and the like. Similarly, if someone placed dung on some ground in order to fertilize it or made earthenware containers such as jars, troughs, or jugs with impure ashes, it would still be permissible to use or sell them, while the impurity affecting the containers' liquid contents could be overlooked. If, on the other hand, it is not difficult to separate the impure from the pure, as, for example, if chickpeas become mixed with impure dung and it is possible to separate them out, then it is not permissible to make use of them before they have been isolated from the impurity.

* * *

According to the Hanbalis, impure water may not be used for anything but moistening soil, gypsum or similar substances in order to make them into a paste, provided that the paste is not used to build a mosque or a terrace where prayers are to be performed. Similarly, it is not permissible to make use of impure liquids such as wine or blood, nor of impure solids such as substances derived from swine or impure dung. As for pure substances such as dove or pigeon droppings and cattle dung, it may be sold and put to use. However, it is impermissible to make use of substances derived from dead animals, including their fat. As for the fat of a living, ritually pure animal, such as clarified butter into which an impurity has fallen, it may not be eaten, but it may be put to other uses such as burning it in lamps in places other than a mosque.

On Ritual Ablutions

The matter of ritual ablutions relates to a number of topics, namely: (1) the definition of ritual ablutions, (2) the ruling on ablutions, (3) the conditions which make ablutions necessary and upon which their validity depends, (4) the obligations entailed by ablutions, sometimes referred to as their "pillars" (*arkān*), (5) the Sunnah-based practices associated with ablutions, (6) recommended practices associated with ablutions, (7) undesirable practices associated with ablutions, (8) those events and/or substances which render ablutions invalid, and (9) abstersion, that is, how to purify oneself of secretions which invalidate ablutions. In what follows we shall discuss each of these topics in order.

One: The definition of ritual ablutions

Linguistically speaking, the Arabic word *wuḍū'*, translated here as "ritual ablutions," means beauty or excellence and cleanliness. It is a verbal noun. Its related verb is either *tawaḍḍa'a*, in which case the verbal noun takes the form of *tawaḍḍu'*, or *waḍu'a*, in which case its verbal noun is *wiḍā'ah*.[51] It is said that the verb *waḍu'a* follows the verb pattern *karuma*. Moreover, since *wiḍā' ah* means "to be or become excellent, beautiful, clean and pure", the word *wuḍū'* is thus another name for excellence, beauty, cleanliness and purity. This general meaning encompasses the meaning associated specifically with Islamic law, which has to do with a particular type of cleanliness that results in both physical and spiritual purity. As for its more specific legal sense, *wuḍū'* refers to the use of water on particular members of the body, namely, the face, the hands, and so forth in a specified manner.

Two: The ruling on ritual ablutions as it pertains to touching the Qur'ān and related actions

Based on the foregoing, it will be seen that the ruling on ritual ablutions may refer to the effect which the Lawgiver has caused to result from the action of performing ablutions. And this, in fact, is what we mean here, for the Lawgiver has caused ritual ablutions to remove major and minor ritual impurity such that based on this action one may perform both religious obligations and recommended acts such as ritual prayer, the prostration of recitation, the prostration of thanksgiving (which is recognized by some, though not all, of the four schools), and circumambulation of the Ka'bah, whether this is done to fulfill a religious duty or as an act of voluntary piety.[52] This is based on the saying of the Prophet, "Circumambulating the Ka'bah

---

51. The vowelization of the verbal noun given in *Lisān al-'Arab* is *waḍā'ah* [t.n.].

52. The Hanafis hold that if someone circumambulates the Ka'bah without first performing ritual ablutions, his circumambulation will still be valid. However, such a practice is forbidden since ritual purity is a duty for one who wishes to perform the circumambulation, and whoever neglects such a duty errs, though it is not a condition for its legal validity.

is like prayer, except that in the former you speak. Hence, if anyone should speak while circumambulating the Ka'bah, let him speak of nothing but good."[53] The ritual ablution is an inherent obligation in carrying out these religious acts; thus, it is impermissible for anyone who has not performed ritual ablutions to perform any of the aforementioned actions. Similarly, if anyone wishes to touch the Qur'ān, whether all or part of it, including even a single verse, he must first perform ritual ablutions unless certain detailed conditions are met.[54]

---

53. Narrated by al-Tirmidhī with a good chain of transmission; narrated also by al-Ḥākim.

54. According to the Malikis, one may touch all or part of the Qur'ān without first performing ritual ablutions given the following four conditions: (1) that it be written in a language other than Arabic; if it is written in Arabic, however, it may never be touched without prior performance of ablutions regardless of what script it contains, be it Kufic, Moroccan, or the like; (2) that the words be engraved on a coin or some other object which people use in transactions, lest the ablution requirement cause undue hardship; (3) that part or all of the Qur'ān be used as an amulet, in which case one may pick it up or carry it without first performing ritual ablutions. Some hold that a person may carry part of the Qur'ān as an amulet, but that to carry the entire book for this purpose without first performing ritual ablutions is forbidden. Moreover, one may carry the Qur'ān as an amulet on two conditions: First, the person carrying it must be a Muslim and second, the Qur'ān must be covered with something that prevents dirt from getting on it; (4) that the person touching the Qur'ān be a teacher or a student, in which case they may touch the Qur'ān without first performing ritual ablutions; nor is there any distinction in this regard between an adult Muslim who is accountable for observing all the precepts of Islam, and someone who is not, even if the person concerned is a woman at the time of her menses.

In all other cases, however, it is impermissible for someone who is not in a state of ritual purity to pick up or carry the Qur'ān, even if the book is inside a protective cover or is suspended from a strap; nor is it permissible to pick up that which the Qur'ān has been placed on, such as a chest, a pillow or a stand. If it has been placed among other possessions, it may be carried as part of these. However, if one's intention is to pick up the Qur'ān alone, this is not permissible. As for reciting the Qur'ān without the aid of the book, this may be done without performing ritual ablutions first, although it is preferable to have performed them first.

* * *

The Hanbalis stipulate that in order to pick up or touch the Qur'ān without being in a state of ritual purity, it must be inside a cover which is separate from the book itself. Thus, for example, if the Qur'ān is inside a bag or wrapped in a handkerchief, a scarf or a piece of paper, or if it is placed inside a box or among household effects which one wishes to move—whether one intends specifically to touch the Qur'ān or not—it is permissible to touch it or pick it up. Similarly, it is permissible to use the Qur'ān as an amulet provided that one keeps it inside something which will protect it, such as a ritually pure piece of cloth. Therefore, performing ablutions is a condition for the permissibility of picking up the Qur'ān whether or not the person picking it up is an adult Muslim who is accountable for observing all the precepts of Islam. However, a young child is not himself required to perform ritual ablutions but rather, it is the responsibility of his guardian to instruct him to perform ritual ablutions when the child wants to pick up the Qur'ān.

* * *

The Hanafis stipulate the following conditions for the permissibility of touching part or all of the Qur'ān or writing down words from it: (1) There must be some necessity involved; if, for example, it is feared that the Qur'ān might be submerged in water or burned, one may touch it in order to rescue it from danger; (2) The Qur'ān must be inside a cover which is separate from it, such as a bag, a leather pouch or a piece of paper, or wrapped in a handkerchief, scarf, and the like. In cases such as these, it is permissible to touch or pick it up. As for its binding and everything which is sold along with it—whether or not it has text written on it and even if it is not attached to it—it may not be touched by anyone who is not in a state of ritual purity (this latter ruling being based on a legal opinion issued on this point by a scholar of the Hanafi school); (3) The person touching it must be a minor who is being taught from it, lest the requirement of ritual purity cause undue hardship; however, no adult who is not in a state of ritual purity, including menstruating women, may touch the Qur'ān, even if the person is a teacher or a student of the book; (4) The person concerned must be a Muslim; it is not permissible for a Muslim to allow a non-Muslim to touch the Qur'ān if he is able to prevent it; nevertheless, Muḥammad [Ibn al-Ḥasan al-Shaybānī, a companion of Abū Ḥanīfah's] states that it is permissible for a non-Muslim to touch the Qur'ān if he first performs major ritual ablutions, and that it is likewise permissible to help a non-Muslim to memorize the Qur'ān.

However, barring the fulfillment of the aforementioned conditions, it is not permissible for anyone not in a state of ritual purity to touch the Qur'ān with his hand or any other part of his body. As for the recitation of the Qur'ān without the aid of the book itself, this is permissible for someone in a state of minor ritual purity but forbidden to someone in a state of major ritual impurity or a woman at the time of her menses. Moreover, it is commendable for someone in a state of minor ritual impurity to perform ritual ablutions before such recitation.

With regard to commentaries on the Qur'ān, it is undesirable to touch them without first performing ritual ablutions; as for other books relating to Islamic jurisprudence, hadiths and the like, one is permitted, by way of concession, to touch them without first performing ablutions.

* * *

According to the Shafiis, it is permissible to touch or pick up part or all of the Qur'ān on the following conditions: (1) that the person be using the Qur'ān as an amulet; (2) that the words be written on a dirham, a pound [or some other coin]; (3) that it be part of the Qur'ān recorded in books of learning by way of citation, in which case no distinction is made between short and long passages of the Qur'ān. As for commentaries on the Qur'ān, it is permissible to touch them without first performing ritual ablutions provided that the amount of commentary is greater than the amount of Qur'anic text, whereas if the Qur'anic text occupies a greater portion of the book, then it may not be touched without first performing ritual ablutions; (4) that the Qur'anic verses be written on clothing, such as those which are embroidered onto the *kiswah*, [i.e., the covering placed over the Ka'bah]; and (5) that the person touching the Qur'ān be doing so in order to learn from it. Hence, it is permissible for his guardian to allow him to touch it and pick it up for the purpose of study even if he has already memorized it.

If any of these conditions is violated, it is forbidden to touch even so much as a single verse of the Qur'ān [without first performing ritual ablutions]. This prohibition applies even if there is a barrier which is unattached to the Qur'ān, such as a binding or something else. Hence, if the Qur'ān has been placed in a small box such as those which are made to hold the parts of the Qur'ān, or if it has been placed on a small reading stand, it is not permissible to touch the box or the stand as long as the Qur'ān is placed on or inside them. If, on the other hand, the Qur'ān has been placed inside a large box or bag, it is not forbidden to touch the box or the bag except for the part which is in direct contact with the Qur'ān. In cases where the binding of the Qur'ān becomes detached from the book and no longer contains the Qur'ān itself, it remains forbidden to touch it unless it is made into a binding for some other book. As for those parts which are still associated with the Qur'ān from which they were detached, they may not be touched. Moreover, just as it is forbidden to touch the Qur'ān itself, it is likewise forbidden to touch any part of something upon which the Qur'ān has been written, such as a chalkboard, without first performing ablutions, even if the Qur'anic verses which were written on it have been erased. However, it is permissible for an adult, accountable Muslim in such a state to write words from the Qur'ān on a blackboard or the like provided that he does not touch what he is writing.

Lastly, if the Qur'ān has been placed among household effects such as chests, clothing and the like, it is impermissible to carry these items without first performing ritual ablutions unless one's intention is to move only these items; however, if one intends to move the Qur'ān along with them, or the Qur'ān alone, then this is forbidden without one's having first performed ritual ablutions.

Conditions for ritual ablutions

Conditions for ritual ablutions are divided into three categories. The first category is "conditions of obligation"; the second is "conditions of validity"; and the third is "conditions of obligation and validity together." The first category, namely, "conditions of obligation," refers to conditions which render ritual ablutions obligatory for those healthy, sound-minded adults who are accountable for the performance of the religious obligations of Islam such that in the absence of any or all of these conditions, ablutions cease to be required. The second category, "conditions of validity," refers to those conditions which must be fulfilled in order for one's ritual ablutions to be valid, while the third category, namely, "conditions of obligation and validity together," refers to those conditions which, if they are not fulfilled in their entirety, render ablutions unnecessary and, if they are performed, render them invalid.

Conditions of obligation with respect to ritual ablutions include, first of all, that one has attained puberty. Hence, for those who have not yet reached puberty, whether male or female, ritual ablutions are not required. However, the ablutions performed by a prepubescent boy or girl are nevertheless valid. Consequently, if a prepubescent child were to perform ritual ablutions and, an hour later, reached puberty, he would not need to repeat his ablutions in order to pray. This scenario, unusual as it is, could be of benefit to people who are traveling or who dwell in desert areas where water is sparse. Another such condition is the onset of the time period for one of the five daily prayers. (A description of the times for these prayers—dawn, noon, mid-afternoon, sunset and evening—is found in the section below on "Ritual Prayer.") Thus, for example, once a given prayer period begins, an adult accountable for the performance of the religious rites of Islam must perform whatever prayer is required of him during this period. Moreover, given that the ritual prayer may only be performed after one has performed either the minor ritual ablutions or some other rite which serves as their equivalent, such a person must perform ablutions in order to pray. The obligation to pray once the relevant period of the day has begun involves some latitude as to when one will perform the prayer concerned as well as when to perform the ritual ablutions without which one's prayer will not be valid. The term 'latitude' here refers to the fact that those accountable for the performance of a given prayer may pray at any time from the moment the relevant period of prayer begins [with the *adhān*, or call to prayer] to the moment when the subsequent call to prayer is heard. However, if only a short period of time remains before the next call to prayer, one has no choice but to perform ablutions and pray immediately, in which case the aforementioned 'latitude' ceases to be available, since if he were to delay his ablutions and prayer, he would be guilty of wrongdoing. Moreover, just as ritual ablutions are a requirement for someone who wishes to perform any of the five obligatory prayers of the day, so also are they required for someone who wishes to perform a voluntary prayer. Therefore, whoever decides to perform a voluntary prayer is obliged to perform ablutions promptly, since it is forbidden for him to pray without them.

If the onset of the time of day for a particular prayer is only a condition for ritual ablutions being obligatory, but not a condition for their being valid, it follows that if one performs his ablutions before the time for a given prayer has arrived, his ablutions will still be valid unless the person concerned suffers from a condition such as urinary incontinence,[55] in which case his ablutions will only be valid if they are performed after the time for the prayer concerned has begun. Another condition for ablutions to be obligatory is that the person concerned not already be in a state of ritual purity; hence, if one performs his ablutions for the noon prayer, for example, and if nothing happens to invalidate his ablutions throughout the day, he is under no obligation to repeat his ablutions when the times for subsequent prayers arrive. Another such condition is that the person concerned be capable of performing ritual ablutions; thus, for example, ablutions are not obligatory for someone incapable of using water due to some illness or other condition, or for someone who has no access to water. (This subject will be dealt with in more detail in the section on *tayammum*, or sand ablutions.)

As for those conditions which must be fulfilled in order for ritual ablutions to be valid, they are as follows:

(1) The water used must be *ṭahūr*, the meaning of which was discussed above in the sections on water. However, it is sufficient for the water to be *ṭahūr* in the mind of the person performing the ablutions.

(2) The person performing the ablutions must be discerning; hence, the ablutions performed by a young child who is not yet discerning will not be considered valid. This is a principle which might serve as a response to those who hold that a young child is forbidden to touch the Qur'ān unless he has first performed ritual ablutions.

(3) There must be no barrier which prevents the water from making contact with the part of the body to be washed; hence, if there is something on one's hand, face, foot or head which prevents the water from reaching the skin—such as a rheum, or white secretion in the eye which the water cannot penetrate so as to reach the skin, or a piece of solid fat, wax, dough, and the like on the face or hand—one's ablutions will not be valid.

---

55. According to the Malikis, such a person's ablutions are valid both before and after the onset of the time for a given prayer.

* * *

The Hanafis likewise consider such a person's ablutions to be valid even if they are performed before the onset of the time for a given prayer; hence, if someone performs his ablutions before the time for the noon prayer, for example, after which the time for the noon prayer arrives without his ablutions having been invalidated, it is permissible for him to perform the noon prayer, and these ablutions remain valid until the end of the noon period. However, when the time for the mid-afternoon prayer arrives, they cease to be valid, and he may not perform the mid-afternoon prayer until he has performed his ablutions again. (The reason for this ruling will be clarified in a later section.) As for the views expounded in the body of the text, they are those of the Shafiis and the Hanbalis.

(4) As the person performs ablutions, nothing must happen to invalidate them, such as would occur if something issued from him which is incompatible with ritual purity. If, for example, after washing one's face and hands such a thing happened, one would be obliged to begin his ablutions all over again. The only cases in which this ruling does not apply are those in which the person suffers from a condition which exempts him from this stipulation (such conditions will be discussed in a subsequent section). If, for example, someone suffers from urinary incontinence and a few drops of urine are secreted as he performs his ablutions, he is not obliged to repeat them, as will be seen below.

As for the conditions which must be fulfilled in order for ablutions to be both obligatory and valid, they are as follows:

(1) One must be in full possession of his mental faculties; hence, ritual ablutions are not required of someone who is mentally deranged,[56] epileptic, feeble-minded[57] or unconscious, and in the event that someone in any of these conditions did perform ritual ablutions, they would not be counted as valid. Hence, if a feeble-minded person were to perform ritual ablutions, then a moment later was restored to complete mental functioning, his prayer would not be valid based on these ablutions. The same ruling applies to the mentally deranged. As for those who are feeble-minded, epileptic, or unconscious, one would not expect them to perform ritual ablutions in the first place. However, such situations have been mentioned in order to make clear that God Almighty has exempted these groups of people from accountability in all respects such that if one of them did perform ablutions or some other act of worship, it would not be counted as valid. It is likewise to indicate that, as in the realm of daily transactions, so also in the realm of worship, legally valid conduct requires that one be in full possession of one's mental faculties.

(2) A woman must be free of blood flow resulting from menstruation or recovery from childbirth. Hence, ritual ablutions are not obligatory for a woman who is menstruating or postpartum, nor would her ablutions be valid if she performed them. If a menstruating woman performed ritual ablutions, after which her period came to an end, they would not be counted as valid. It is true, of course, that it is commendable for a menstruating woman to perform ritual ablutions at the time for each of the five daily prayers and to sit in the place where she normally prays, as will be discussed below in the section on men-

56. According to the Hanafis, mental derangement, epilepsy and the like render ritual ablutions invalid; hence, in the Hanafis' view, soundness of mind is required both for ablutions to be required and for them to be counted as valid.

57. The Hanafis define the feeble-minded person as someone whose speech is confused and who copes poorly with life, but who is nevertheless tranquil and neither clashes with others nor abuses them verbally or physically. As in the case of a child, acts of worship performed by such a person are counted as valid, but they are not obligatory. Hence, full mental functioning is required for ritual ablutions to be obligatory, but not for them to be valid.

struation. However, such ablutions are merely symbolic, and she is only asked to perform them in order not to forget prayer during this time of the month.
(3) One must not be asleep or in a state of unawareness. Someone who is asleep is mercifully not held accountable for his actions, nor is someone who is in a state of unawareness; hence, if it happened that ritual ablutions were performed by a person in either of these states, they would be invalid. Some may suppose that what is meant here by 'asleep' is that one is lying down in bed or the like, in which case it is unthinkable that he would perform ritual ablutions. However, what is being referred to here is a sleepwalker who may even leave his house (examples of which I have seen among my own neighbors). If such a person were to perform ablutions while in this state of awareness, his ablutions would have no validity.
(4) One must be a Muslim.[58] Being a Muslim is necessary in order for ritual ablutions to be obligatory, meaning that the non-Muslim is not required to perform ablutions while he or she is still in a state of unbelief. Of course, unbelievers are addressed concerning prayer and the means by which it is performed such that [in the afterlife], they will be punished for failing to perform ritual ablutions. Nevertheless, if they were to perform ritual ablutions while still refusing to enter Islam, they would not be valid.

---

58. According to the Malikis, being a Muslim is required for ablutions to be valid, but not for them to be obligatory. Hence, in the Malikis' view, unbelievers are addressed by all aspects of the divine law such that the various forms of Muslim worship are incumbent upon them and they will be punished for neglecting them. However, such worship will not be counted as valid unless they become Muslims. The reason for this is that in the Malikis' view, the validity of all acts of worship is dependent upon one's intention, and as will be seen below, being a Muslim is one of the conditions for the validity of one's intention.

* * *

As for the Hanafis, they hold—contrary to the Malikis—that being a Muslim is required in order for ablutions to be obligatory, but not for them to be valid. Hence, in the Hanafis' view, unbelievers are not addressed by the various aspects of the divine law and are, therefore, not under obligation to perform ritual ablutions, since as they see it, ritual ablutions do not depend on one's intention because intention is not among the obligations associated with them. In this respect, minor ritual ablutions differ from *tayammum*, or sand ablutions, which are not valid when performed by an unbeliever due to the fact that they are dependent for their validity on one's intention, which is one of the obligations associated with this form of worship.

(5) The person must have received the call from the Prophet,[59] our master Muḥammad Ibn 'Abdullah, and realized that God Almighty has sent him as an apostle to all people, calling them to recognize His perfect unity and to describe Him with the attributes of perfection, and commanding them to worship God Almighty alone. Hence, if someone has not received this call, he is not obliged to perform any ritual ablutions; and if he did perform them, they would not be counted as valid. If such a person performed ritual ablutions, then an hour later received the call to Islam, his ablutions would thus not be valid. Some of the schools have also added other conditions.[60]

Obligations involved in ritual ablutions

As generally used in the Arabic language, the word *farḍ*, rendered here as "obligation", means "to cut" or "to notch" as in, "I cut the rope" (*faraḍtu al-ḥabl*), or "I notched the piece of wood" (*faraḍtu al-khashabah*) when one has cut into it, but not entirely through it. However, as used in the context of Islamic law, the word *farḍ* refers to any act which one merits reward for performing and punishment for neglecting. Muslim jurisprudents generally agree that *farḍ* is the equivalent of *rukn*, usually rendered in English as "pillar," both of which are distinguished from *sharṭ*, or "condition," in that an act which is described as an "obligation" or a "pillar" is an integral part of a given religious rite, whereas a condition is something upon which the rite depends for its existence [or validity], but which is nevertheless not an integral part of it. Thus, for example, the utterance of the words, *Allāhu akbar*, or

---

59. According to the Hanafis, it is not necessary for the call of the Prophet to have reached someone for his ablutions to be valid; hence, if someone performed ritual ablutions prior to receiving this call, after which he in fact received it, his ablutions would be valid. Similarly, the Hanafis do not consider it necessary for someone to have received the call to Islam for ritual ablutions to be obligatory; rather, they content themselves with the stipulation that one must first embrace Islam before ritual ablutions become obligatory, since one can only become a Muslim after this call has reached him. Given the foregoing, one will realize that those who consider it necessary for someone to be a Muslim before ritual ablutions become either obligatory or valid are the Shafiis and the Hanbalis.

60. The Shafiis add three further conditions for the validity of ritual ablutions: (1) One must be aware of how ritual ablutions are to be performed; in other words, one must know that ritual ablutions involve washing the face, the arms up to the elbows, etc. Hence, if someone washes his face, his hands and so on, yet without knowing that these actions are the ritual ablutions for which he is held accountable under the divine law, his ablutions will not be valid. (2) One must distinguish between that which is obligatory and that which is not. However, this condition does not apply to ordinary, uneducated folk; hence, if the person doing the ablutions is an ordinary layperson, what is required is simply that he not believe that an act which is obligatory is a voluntary act of piety. In other words, if such a person believes that everything he is doing is obligatory, his ablutions will be valid. Similarly, if one believes that ritual ablutions include both obligatory acts and those which are based on the prophetic Sunnah, yet without distinguishing those acts

"God is the Most Great," as well as kneeling, prostration, and so on are among the obligations entailed in the performance of ritual prayer, while the commencement of the time of day for a given prayer is one of the conditions for prayer's validity. If, for example, one prays the noon prayer before the time period for the noon prayer has begun, he will have performed a genuine prayer, but viewed from the perspective of Islamic law, his prayer will have no validity since one of the conditions of ritual prayer's validity, namely, the commencement of the appropriate period of the day, has not been fulfilled, as mentioned in the chapter on prayer.

The imams of the four orthodox schools differ over the number of obligations entailed in ritual ablutions; however, those which are recorded in the Book of God Almighty come to four, namely: (1) washing the face, (2) washing the hands up to the elbows, (3) wiping either part or all of the head, and (4) washing the feet up to the ankles. As God Almighty states, "O you who have attained to faith! When you are about to pray, wash your face, and your hands and arms up to the elbows, and pass your [wet] hands lightly over your head, and [wash] your feet up to the ankles ..." (5:6). This much is agreed upon among the four imams, who only differ over how one is to wipe one's head; for example, some of them say that the entire head should be wiped, while others hold that only part of the head must be wiped, as will be seen below. Some of the imams have also added further obligations to these four.

---

which are obligatory from those based on the Sunnah, his ablutions will still be valid. (3) One must intend to perform ritual ablutions as one begins, then continue with the same intention until his ablutions are complete. Hence, if one intended to perform ritual ablutions only while washing his face, then washed his hands with only the intention of cleaning them or cooling them off, his ablutions would not be valid. The Shafiis refer to this as "including the intention as a legal reality" until one's ablutions have been completed. Thus, if one intends to perform ritual ablutions and along with this, intends to maintain personal hygiene, his ablutions will not be invalidated because of the latter.

* * *

The Hanbalis add the following conditions for the validity [but not the necessity] of ritual ablutions: (1) The water used for the ablutions must have been obtained in a legitimate manner, since if someone performed ritual ablutions with water which had been seized by force, these ablutions would not be valid. (2) One must intend to perform ritual ablutions, since for the Hanbalis, one's intention is a condition for ablutions' validity. As for the Hanafis, we have seen that in their view intention is simply an emulation of the Prophet and hence, neither an obligatory part of ritual ablutions nor a condition for their validity. As for the Malikis and the Shafiis, they hold that intention is a "pillar," that is, an obligatory part of ritual ablutions. Hence, it is the Hanbalis alone who consider intention to be a condition; as for the distinction between "condition" and "pillar", this will be explained below in the section on 'intention'. (3) Ritual ablutions must be preceded by cleansing with stones or abstersion, an explanation of which will be found in the section below on abstersion.

Lest the discussion become disjointed and there be difficulty in seeing the issues in a clear, integrated manner, we shall undertake in what follows to list all the obligations entailed in ritual ablutions based on the teachings of each school in turn. This done, we shall then point out those elements which are agreed upon by the various schools.[61]

---

61. According to the Hanafis, the obligations entailed by ritual ablutions are restricted to these four, such that if an adult, accountable Muslim performed them without adding anything thereto, he would be in a state of ritual purity in which he would be able to perform ritual prayers, touch the Qur'ān and engage in any other action requiring that one first perform such ablutions. As for the ruling on those who omit practices based on the prophetic Sunnah, this will be discussed in the section dealing with Sunnah-based practices associated with ritual ablutions.

As for the four obligations included in ritual ablutions according to the Hanafi school, they are as follows:

First: Washing the face, concerning which there are a number of points: (1) A definition of what constitutes the face, both lengthwise and crosswise; (2) What must be washed of those areas on which hair grows, such as beards, moustaches and eyebrows; (3) Which parts of the eyes should and should not be washed; and (4) Which parts of the nose are to be washed.

For those who have no beard, the face extends from one's usual hairline to the bottom of one's chin. The hairline tends to be located at the top of one's forehead; however, there exist unusual cases, such as those who are bald or whose hairline extends down close to the eyebrows. If someone is bald, he is not required to wash all parts of his head which have no hair on them due to his baldness; rather, he has only to wash the area up to the place where one's hairline would normally be located. As for the person whose hairline is located further down on the forehead and, in some cases, even approaches his eyebrows, the same ruling applies as that which applies to the bald man; in other words, he must wash up to slightly beyond the top of the forehead, since this is where most people's hairlines are found. The principle followed in such cases is to conform rulings to the situation of the majority. Hence, if someone has a constitution which differs from that of most people, he is not held accountable for more [or less] than what others are.

As for the horizontal limits of the face, they extend from the front of one ear to the front of the other ("front" here referring to the small cartilaginous protrusion at the front of the ear); the space extending from the chin to the ear is also included within the limits of the face, of course. As a consequence, the Hanafis hold that this area must be washed as well. These, then, are the limits of the face, by length and width, according to the Hanafis.

As for facial hair, the most important parts are the beard and the moustache. As for the beard, one must wash that part of it which extends from the upper face to the bottom of the chin, whereas if it extends beyond these limits, it is not necessary to wash it. For example, there are people who let their beards grow long; however, they are only required to wash the hair which is on the skin of the face and the chin. If the hair is thin enough that water can penetrate through it to the skin beneath it, then it must be parted or combed; otherwise, it is sufficient to wash the outer layer of the hair. As for the ruling on moustaches, there is some disagreement in this regard; some hold that if one's moustache is so thick and bushy that water will not penetrate to the skin beneath it, one's ablutions are rendered invalid, while others hold that it is sufficient for such a person to wash the outside of his moustache as he would do with a thick beard. The foregoing is based on legal opinions connected with minor ritual ablutions; however, if one is performing major ritual ablutions, this practice is not acceptable. Rather, if the moustache is so thick that water cannot penetrate it, one's major ritual ablutions are invalidated. The reason for this ruling may be that the Lawgiver has prohibited the practice of letting one's moustache grow long due to the difficulty of keeping it free of dirt, food, and the like; hence, by issuing this stern warning in connection with major ritual ablutions, people may be deterred from growing out their moustaches to no good purpose.

The remaining type of facial hair to be discussed is the eyebrows, the ruling on which is that if they are sufficiently thin that water can penetrate them, one must part or comb them so as to let the water reach the skin beneath, whereas if they are thick, such parting or combing is not necessary.

As for the outside of the nose, one must wash all parts of it, including the lower part of the cartilaginous partition which separates the nostrils, because it is part of the face, and even if a small part of it is omitted, one's ablutions will be invalid. As for the inside of the nose, washing it is not required in the view of the Hanafis. If one has a deep scar as well as any other grooves or wrinkles on the face, one is required to let the water get inside and/or between them.

Lastly, if one were to perform ablutions, then shave his beard or the hair on his head, his ablutions would remain valid.

Second: Washing the hands and arms up to the elbows, in connection with which there are two matters of concern. Firstly, if someone has an extra finger, he must wash it. If one has an extra hand the same size as his original hand, he must wash it as well. If the extra hand is longer than one's original hand, he must wash that part of it which runs parallel to the original hand, whereas he is not obliged to wash that part of it which extends beyond the original hand, though it is recommended that he do so. Secondly, if some clay, mud or dough is clinging to one's hand or fingernail (that is, the part of the nail which is directly attached to the finger), he must remove it and make certain that the water reaches his fingernail; otherwise, his ablutions will be invalid. If the fingernail is long enough that it extends beyond the end of the finger, it must be washed in order for one's ablutions to be valid. As for dirt which is under the fingernail, the legal opinion issued by the Hanafis on this matter is that it does no harm, whether the person who has performed his ablutions is a city dweller or a villager, the purpose for this ruling being to spare people needless hardship. However, some of the more discerning Hanafis see the necessity of washing off any dirt that may be clinging to the underside of a long fingernail such that if one fails to do so, his ablutions are invalid. Such a view is sound due to the harm which can be caused by the accumulation of dirt under the fingernails. Nevertheless, they make an exception for bakers whose fingernails are long and which have some dough under them given the nature of their profession. Nor is there any harm in the effects left by henna or dyes; however, if there is an actual physical mass of henna on one's hand, it is considered to be harmful since it prevents water from making contact with the skin. Moreover, if part of one's hand has been cut off, one is obliged to wash what remains of it, whereas if the entire bodily member one is required to wash as part of ritual ablutions is gone, the requirement to wash it is negated.

Three: Washing the feet and the ankles—which are the two bones protruding at the base of the leg above the foot. Someone who performs ritual ablutions must take care to wash his ankles with water, and he must do the same with the cracks on the bottoms of his feet. If some or all of one's foot is missing, the same ruling applies here as that which applies to a missing hand as mentioned above. If someone applies a lotion or ointment to his feet or his arms, after which he performs ritual ablutions and finds that they repel the water on account of the fattiness of the lotion or ointment, this causes no harm. Moreover, if one's feet are cracked with the result that he applies an ointment or some similar substance, and if it would be harmful to the person for the water to penetrate the ointment to the skin beneath, there is no need to wash them; otherwise, one is obliged to remove the ointment and wash the area under it. If, on the other hand, one's feet are cracked or chapped to the point where it would be harmful to wash them or even to place them in water and immediately take them out again, then the obligation to wash them is dropped. Instead, such a person should simply wipe his feet with water; if he is unable even to wipe them, he is exempted from this requirement as well, and all he must do is to wash whatever will not be harmed by washing.

Four: Wiping one-fourth of the head with water. The Hanafis estimate one-fourth of the head to be equal to the area of the palm of someone's hand. Hence, what one must do is to wipe an area of his head which is equal to the area of his entire palm. If water gets onto the palm of one's hand, after which he places it on his head, whether from behind, from the front, or any other spot, this is sufficient. However, it is not necessary that the wiping be done with the palm itself; rather, it is sufficient for the water to make contact with one-fourth of the head, regardless of the means by which this takes place. If one wipes his head with his hand, he must do so with at least three fingers in order to ensure that the water makes contact with one-fourth of his head before it dries since, if one wiped his head with only two fingers, the water might dry before he had moved on to wipe the rest of the required area. Moreover, if someone wipes his head with his fingertips and the water drips down, it may reach the required area, in which case the wiping is valid; otherwise, it is not.

In addition, it is required that one wipe his head with new water; thus, for example, if one's hand is wet before he wipes his head, the wiping will be sufficient; however, it is not acceptable to take water from another part of his body. Hence, if someone were to wash his arm, after which his hand dried and he took some water off his arm and used it to wipe his head, this would not be acceptable. As for those who have long hair which comes down over the forehead or neck, if they wipe the hair itself, this is not sufficient, since one's aim is to wipe one-fourth of the head proper. If one's head is shaved, the matter is simple; however, if one's head has hair on it, then one must wipe the hair which is actually growing on the head. If, on the other hand, part of one's head is shaved while another part is not, one may wipe whichever part he chooses provided that it comes to one-fourth of the major area of his head. Moreover, if someone wiped his hair, then shaved it off, his ablutions would still remain valid. If one took a piece of ice and wiped his head with it, this would suffice him; similarly, it would be sufficient for one to wash his head along with his face, although this latter practice is undesirable. As for wiping over a turban or some other headwear, this is only permissible for those with specific extenuating conditions; nor is it permissible for a woman to wipe over a head covering such as a scarf, a headcloth, or the like unless it is thin enough for the water to penetrate through to her hair. Moreover, if a woman has henna or some other type of dye on her hair and wipes over it and if the water remains unaltered, her ablutions are valid; however, if it takes on the color of the dye, thereby ceasing to be *ṭahūr*, her ablutions will not be valid.

These, then, are the obligations entailed by ritual ablutions according to the Hanafis; any practice beyond them is simply done in emulation of the Prophet, a discussion of which will be presented in a later section.

* * *

According to the Malikis there are seven obligations associated with ritual ablutions. The first of these seven obligations is intention, which relates to four specific topics: (1) the definition of intention and how it comes about, (2) its time and place, (3) its conditions, and (4) what renders intention invalid.

As to its definition and particulars, intention is defined as the aim and determination to perform a given action; hence, if someone aims to do such-and-such a thing, he is said to intend it. In relation to ritual ablutions, intention means that someone who is in a state of minor ritual impurity aims to make permissible an action from which he has been prevented by this ritual impurity, or simply to fulfill the religious obligation of ritual ablutions or to remove minor ritual impurity. It is evident that the place where intention resides is the heart. Hence, when one aims to perform ritual ablutions for one of the aforementioned purposes, he has entered the state of intention. One is not required to express this intention in words, nor is it necessary to continue bringing one's intention to mind throughout the performance of one's ablutions. Rather, even if one is distracted from his intention while completing his ablutions, they remain valid. As for the time for intention, it is at the beginning of one's ablutions; thus, if someone washes some of the parts of his body included in ablutions without having entered the state of intention, his ablutions are rendered invalid; however, it is acceptable for one's intention to precede the beginning of his ablutions by what would commonly be viewed as a short period of time. Thus, for example, if someone sits down with the conscious intention of performing ritual ablutions, after which a servant brings a pitcher and pours the water over his hands without his consciously recalling his initial intention, his ablutions remain valid because they were not separated from his intention by a significant pause.

As for the conditions of intention, there are three, namely: (1) that the person intending be a Muslim, (2) discernment, and (3) decisiveness. Hence, if a non-Muslim or a young child who lacks a clear understanding of religious accountability and the meaning of Islam (and who, in this respect, is similar to an insane person) intended to engage in any of the Muslim forms of worship, his intention would not be reckoned as valid. As for a young child with discernment and understanding, his intention would be valid. However, if one wavers in his intention—saying to himself, for example, "I will perform ritual ablutions if I am not in a state of ritual purity"—his intention will not be valid. On the contrary, one must be decisive in one's intention. As for that which invalidates one's intention, it is for the person to reject his intention as he performs the ritual ablutions in the sense that he aims to nullify his ablutions and not to treat them as valid. However, if the person goes back on his intention after performing his ablutions to completion, this does no harm since once they have been completed, ritual ablutions retain their validity, and nothing can invalidate them apart from those events which will be discussed below.

The second obligation involved in ritual ablutions is washing the face. As for the limits of the face lengthwise and crosswise, they are the same for the Malikis as those defined by the Hanafis. However, the Malikis hold that the "white" area immediately above and behind the ears as well as the hair along the temples are not part of the face, but part of the head; therefore, they need not be washed, but should simply be wiped. However, the Hanafis say that it is part of the face and therefore, washing it is a requirement.

With respect to the third obligation entailed in ritual ablutions, namely, washing the hands and arms up to the elbows, the Malikis are in agreement with the Hanafis as to the necessity of washing the grooves in one's fingertips and under long fingernails which cover the fingertips. They also hold that the dirt found under the fingernails may be overlooked unless it is excessive.

The fourth obligation of ritual ablutions according to the Malikis is to wipe the entire head. The head is defined as beginning with the normal hairline in front and extending back to the nape of the neck; it includes the hair on the temples as well as the area behind and above the ears. If someone has long hair, the Malikis hold that he must wipe it, and if someone has braided hair, he must loosen it if it has been bound with three or more strings. If the hair has been braided with one or two strings and if the hair is braided tightly, it must be loosened, whereas if it is bound loosely, it does no harm. The same concession applies to hair which has been braided without any strings at all, whether it is bound tightly or not. The condition relating to loosening one's hair when wiping one's head is based on some village dwellers' habit of tying their hair with strings. As for the practice of gathering one's hair without braiding it—common among the majority of Egyptians—this causes no harm; nor is there any harm in braiding the hair without string.

As has been seen from our discussion of the Hanafi school above, the Hanafis content themselves with wiping one-fourth of the head only; moreover, as we shall see below, the Shafiis are even more lenient, as they hold that: (1) it is sufficient to wipe any part of the head, be it small or large, (2) if one washes one's head, this can take the place of wiping it, although this latter practice is undesirable because God has commanded us not to wash the head, but to wipe it, and (3) if one wipes the hair on his head, then removes the water, it is not necessary for him to wipe it again even if, after wiping his head, he rubs the skin vigorously. This [latter point] is agreed upon. As for the outsides of the ears, it is not necessary to wipe them since they are not part of the head; this latter point is agreed upon [by all the schools] with the exception of the Hanbalis, who hold that the outsides of the ears are part of the head, as will be seen below.

The fifth obligation relating to ritual ablutions is washing the feet and the ankles. (Based on what was mentioned in the Hanafi section, the ankles are the bones protruding at the bottom of the leg, above the foot.) In agreement with the Hanafis, the Malikis hold that one must wash the cracks on the bottoms and tops of one's feet; similarly, they agree with the Hanafis that if the part of the body which one is required to wash is missing, this requirement ceases to apply.

The sixth obligation entailed by ritual ablutions is referred to as 'continuity' or 'immediacy' *(muwālāh)*. What is meant here by 'immediacy' is that the person performing ritual ablutions is required to wash each relevant part of the body before the part which was washed immediately previous to it dries off, since given moderation in the place, the time and the state of health, the time which passes between washing one part of the body and that which follows it will not be long enough for the part of the body washed first to dry. What is meant by "moderation of place" is that one is in a place that is not characterized by excessive heat or cold which would dry out the water. As for "moderation of time," it means that one is doing his ablutions during a season which will not lead to the water's drying more quickly than usual. And as for "moderation of state of health", it means that there is nothing in the nature of the person concerned which would require that the water be dried quickly. The Malikis hold that such continuity is required between all the various parts of the body, whether they have been washed or wiped, as is the head. Hence, for example, one must move promptly from wiping the head to washing the feet, while the period of time required for the head to dry is considered to be the same as that required by any other part of the body.

In order for immediacy to be required, the Malikis stipulate two conditions: (1) The person performing ritual ablutions must be mindful [of what he is doing]; hence, for example, if someone forgets and washes his hands before his face, his ablutions will still be valid. However, if he becomes aware of his error, he must renew his intention once he has completed his ablutions, since his original intention was rendered invalid by his forgetfulness. (2) The person must be incapable of maintaining continuity in his ablutions, and not be guilty of neglect. An example of this would be for someone to bring water with which to perform his ablutions, believing the amount he has brought to be sufficient, after which it becomes apparent that the water he has brought is not, in fact, enough for him to complete his ablutions. Hence, after washing his face and his hands, for example, the water runs out and he needs more. Then [in order to bring the required water], he pauses for a period of time in the course of which the parts of his body which he has washed dry off. In a case such as this, the person is exempted from the requirement of promptness mentioned above. Once the water has been brought, he then completes what he began by wiping his head, washing his feet and so forth, even if the intervening pause was a long one. However, if the person demonstrated neglect from the beginning by bringing an amount of water which he suspected not to be enough for him to complete his ablutions, then if a long time passes while more water is being brought, his ablutions will be rendered invalid. On the other hand, if only a short time passes, his ablutions remain valid and he may either complete what he began or start all over again.

The seventh obligation involved in ritual ablutions is rubbing, or passing one's hand over the parts of the body which are washed. This is required in the same way as parting the hair with one's fingers.

In sum, there are seven obligations involved in ritual ablutions according to the Malikis: (1) intention, (2) washing the face, (3) washing the hands and arms up to the elbows, (4) wiping the entire head, (5) washing the feet and the ankles, (6) 'immediacy' or continuity, and (7) rubbing. As for their counting rubbing as an obligation, this involves an exaggeration for the purpose of emphasizing its importance. Similarly, the fact that rubbing is counted as an integral part of ritual ablutions indicates that for the Malikis, ritual ablutions are more than merely pouring water over the body, but rather, a process which is not complete without rubbing the body as well.

* * *

As for the Shafiis, they hold that there are six obligations entailed in ritual ablutions. The first obligation is intention, and the Shafiis agree with the Malikis on its definition, its conditions and all other pertinent points with the exception of the following two: (1) According to the Malikis, it is not necessary for one's intention to accompany all acts involved in ritual ablutions; rather, it is acceptable for one's intention to precede the commencement of ablutions by what is commonly perceived as a short period of time, whereas the Shafiis hold that one's intention must coincide with the first part of one's ablutions. Hence, since the first obligation involved in ritual ablutions is the washing of the face, one's intention must therefore accompany the washing of the first part of the face. If someone begins to wash his face without consciously intending to perform ritual ablutions, his ablutions will be invalid; if, on the other hand, one's intention coincides with the washing of the first part of his face, after which he becomes distracted, his initial intention will be sufficient, since it is not necessary for it to continue until his entire face has been washed. However, if one's intention coincides with the washing of his hands, rinsing out his mouth, or rinsing out his nose, his intention will not be valid, since these [latter] are not considered to be part of the face, whereas if one's intention accompanies the washing of the outer part of the lips while rinsing out the mouth, this intention will be valid given that one's lips are part of the face. Moreover, if one intends to wash his outer lips due to their being part of the face, he is not obliged to wash them again while washing his face; if, however, one's aim [in washing his outer lips] is simply to perform the Sunnah or if he has no aim at all, then the commonly approved practice is to rewash them. Moreover, if there is a wound on one's face which prevents it from being washed, one's intention should accompany the washing of [the hands and] the arms. (2) In contrast to the Malikis, the Shafiis hold that the intention to remove ritual impurity through ablutions is not valid for all people; rather, it has validity only for the healthy person who suffers from no extenuating condition, such as urinary incontinence. As for people with such a condition, their intention must be to make it permissible for themselves to perform ritual prayer, touch the Qur'ān, or some other action which requires that one be in a state of ritual purity. Their intention might also be simply to fulfill the obligation of ritual ablutions, since such a person's state of ritual impurity is not actually removed through ablutions, even if this is his intention. Rather, the Lawgiver has commanded such an individual to perform ritual ablutions in order for it to become permissible for him to perform ritual prayer or to engage in any other act which depends for its validity on ritual purity.

The second obligation involved in ablutions according to the Shafiis is washing the face. As for the outer limits of the face, the Shafiis define them in the same way as the Hanafis. However, in contrast to all the other three schools, the Shafiis hold that one must wash what is under the chin. At the same time, they agree with the Malikis and the Hanbalis (while disagreeing with the Hanafis) that a long beard is to be considered part of the face, as a result of which one must wash it all the way down to its tip. As mentioned, the Shafiis agree with the Hanafis that the hair on the temples as well as the "white" area above the ears are part of the face and that they must be washed; on this point, these two schools disagree with the Malikis and the Hanbalis. As for the matter of combing or parting one's beard with the fingers, the Shafiis agree with the other three schools that if the beard is so thin that someone who looks at it can see to the skin beneath it, then it must be parted during ritual ablutions in order for the water to make contact with the skin; whereas if the beard is thick, only the outer surface of it must be washed, although parting it is considered an emulation of the prophetic Sunnah. However, the Malikis hold that although it is not obligatory to part thick hair, one must nevertheless move it with one's hand in order to allow the water to pass into it, even if it makes no contact with the skin. As for parting the hair all the way through, this is not necessary. In sum, then, all four schools are in agreement that if hair is thin enough that the skin beneath it is visible, it must be parted; as for thick hair, the Shafiis, Hanbalis and Hanafis content themselves with washing its outer surface; whereas the Malikis add that one must move it with one's hand, not with the intention of bringing the water into contact with the skin, but simply in order to wash as much of the hair as can be washed easily; to do more than this, however, is a mistake.

As for the third obligation included in ritual ablutions, namely, washing one's hands and arms up to the elbows, the Shafiis agree with the Hanafis on all of the details presented in the description of the Hanafis' views above. However, the Shafiis hold that if dirt under a fingernail prevents the water from making contact with the skin of the finger directly beneath it, it must be removed. The only exception to this ruling is made for laborers who work with clay and the like, in whose case it is only necessary to remove such dirt if there is so much of it that it soils the fingertips.

The fourth obligation included in ritual ablutions is wiping part of the head, even if only a small area. Moreover, it is not necessary for the wiping to be done with the hand; hence, if someone sprinkles water on part of his head, this is sufficient. If there is hair on someone's head and he wipes part of it, this is sufficient. However, if the hair is so long that it comes down over the neck and one wipes part of this hair, this is not sufficient, even if the person gathers the hair and ties it over his head. Hence, it is necessary according to the Shafiis that one wipe part of the hair which is in direct contact with his head. In addition, they hold that if someone washes his head in place of wiping it, this is sufficient, albeit a departure from the ideal; thus, unlike the other schools, they do not consider this practice to be undesirable.

With respect to the fifth obligation, namely, washing the feet and the ankles, the Shafiis agree with the Hanafis and others on the aforementioned rulings on this matter.

The sixth obligation in ritual ablutions according to the Shafiis is to wash the four parts of the body involved in ablutions in the same order as that mentioned in the noble Qur'ān. Hence, one should first wash his face, then his hands and arms up to the elbows, then wipe his head, then wash his feet up to the ankles, and if one alters this order in any way, his ablutions are rendered invalid. On this point, the Shafiis are in agreement with the Hanbalis; whereas the Malikis and the Hanafis hold that maintenance of this particular order is not obligatory, but simply a matter of following the Prophetic Sunnah.

In sum, then, the Shafiis specify six obligations involved in ritual ablutions, namely: (1) intention, (2) washing the face, (3) washing the hands and arms up to the elbows, (4) wiping part of the head, (5) washing the feet and the ankles, and (6) maintaining the order mentioned in the Qur'ān.

* * *

According to the Hanbalis, there are six obligations included in ritual ablutions. The first is washing the face. The Hanbalis agree with the Malikis concerning the boundaries of the face, as they hold that the hair on the temples and the "white" area above the ears are not part of the face, but part of the head. Hence, one is obliged not to wash them, but only to wipe them. However, in contrast to all three other schools, the Hanbalis hold that the inside of the mouth and the nose are part of the face and that as a result, one must rinse one's mouth out and snuff water up his nostrils. They also differ with all the other schools in regard to intention, as they hold that rather than being an obligation which is an integral part of ritual ablutions, intention is a condition for the validity of one's ablutions such that if one does not consciously intend to perform ritual ablutions, they will have no validity. As has been noted, the Malikis and the Shafiis hold that intention is an obligation which forms part of ritual ablutions themselves, whereas the Hanafis hold that it is simply a means of conforming to the example of the Prophet.

Second: Washing the hands and the arms up to the elbows. In accordance with the teachings of the Hanafis and others, one is obliged to wash one's hands and forearms up to and beyond the elbow. In addition, one must wash between the fingers and under long fingernails which go beyond the fingertips, although insignificant amounts of dirt under the fingernails may be overlooked.

Third: Wiping the entire head, including the ears. The Hanbalis agree with the Malikis concerning the necessity of wiping the entire head, from the natural hairline above the forehead back to the nape of the neck. If one's hair is long enough that it comes down onto the neck or the shoulders, it is only necessary to wipe the portion which is in direct contact with the head and not what falls below it. On this point, the Hanbalis disagree with the Malikis, who hold that all head hair must be wiped. The Hanbalis likewise differ with the Malikis, as well as the other two schools, by considering the ears to be part of the head. In agreement with the other schools, the Hanbalis hold that one may wash his head instead of wiping it provided that one run his hand over his head, although the practice is viewed as undesirable.

Fourth: Washing the feet with the ankles. The requirements relating to this obligation are the same for the Hanbalis as they are for the other schools presented thus far.

Fifth: Proper order. In other words, one must wash his face before washing his arms and must wash his arms before wiping his head, and one must wipe his head before washing his feet, and if this order is violated, his ablutions will not be valid. The Hanbalis agree on this point with the Shafiis; that is, as has been seen, these two schools consider proper order to be an obligation included in the rite of ritual ablutions. As for the Malikis and the Hanafis, they classify proper order as an emulation of the Sunnah; hence, if someone were to wash his arms before washing his face, his feet before his hands, and the like, his ablutions would still be valid according to the Malikis and the Hanafis. Moreover, whereas the Malikis and the Hanafis view it as merely undesirable to change the order in which one washes the face, hands, etc., the Shafiis and the Hanbalis hold that it renders one's ablutions completely invalid.

Sixth: 'Continuity' *(muwālāh)*. As we saw in the discussion of this obligation as understood by the Malikis, who also refer to it as 'immediacy,' it means for one to wash a given part of the body before the previously washed part of the body dries. As already mentioned, the Malikis have a detailed exposition of immediacy. As for the Shafiis and the Hanafis, they hold that "continuity of action" is an emulation of the Sunnah, not an obligation, since it is undesirable to wash a part of the body after the previously washed part has dried. Rather, if one wishes to emulate the example of the Prophet, he should move quickly from washing his face, for example, to washing his hands, then go on to wipe his head before the water on his arms has dried, and so forth. If, on the other hand, someone were to wash his face, then wait until his face was dry before going on to wash his arms, his ablutions would still be valid, but this practice would be viewed as undesirable. However, the Shafiis hold that a person who suffers from incontinence or some other extenuating condition must be excused from this ruling. For a detailed presentation of this view, see below under "Sunnah-based practices associated with ritual ablutions."

In sum, the Hanbalis count six practices as obligations involved in ritual ablutions: (1) washing the face, including the inside of the mouth and nose, (2) washing the hands and arms up to the elbows, (3) wiping the entire head, including the ears, (4) washing the feet, (5) proper order, and (6) "continuity of action." [As for intention, they hold it to be simply a condition for the validity of the ablutions.]

A summary of the obligations included in ritual ablutions

The imams of all four schools are in agreement on the four obligations involved in ritual ablutions which receive mention in the Qur'ān, namely, washing the face, washing the hands and arms up to the elbows, wiping part or all of the head, and washing the feet up to the ankles. Among the schools, the Hanafis are the only ones who add nothing to these four obligations.

In addition, there is disagreement among the schools as to the exact definition of the face: The Shafiis, the Malikis and the Hanbalis hold that the face begins at the customary hairline and ends at the bottom of the chin for those who have no beard, and for those who do, at the bottom of the beard, regardless of how long it is. The Hanafis, by contrast, hold that the face extends from the hairline to the bottom of the chin, and that if someone has a beard which extends below the chin, he is not obliged to wash it. The Malikis and the Hanbalis agree with the Hanafis that what extends below the chin need not be washed, whereas according to the Shafiis, one is obliged to wash also what extends below the chin. The Shafiis and the Hanafis agree that the "white" area above the ears is part of the face and must therefore be washed, whereas the Malikis and the Hanbalis hold, by contrast, that this area is part of the head and that, as a consequence, it is to be wiped, not washed.

All four schools agree that if one's beard is so thin that one can see the skin beneath it, it must be parted to allow the water to reach the skin, whereas if it is thick, it is only obligatory to wash its outer surface without parting or combing it, though parting or combing it is an emulation of the example of the Prophet. However, the Malikis hold that although it is not obligatory to part thick hair, one must nevertheless move it around with one's hand in order to allow the water to penetrate it, even if it makes no contact with the skin. The Hanbalis alone hold that the ears are part of the face and that, consequently, they must be washed with water rather than merely wiped.

The Hanbalis and the Malikis agree that it is obligatory to wipe the entire head. The Hanafis and the Shafiis, by contrast, agree that one is only obliged to wipe part of the head, although wiping the entire head is an emulation of the Sunnah. However, while the Shafiis hold that one must wipe some of the head, however small an area, the Hanafis hold that one must wipe one-fourth of the head, which they deem to be equivalent to the area of the palm of one's hand.

The Malikis and the Hanafis hold that maintaining the order mentioned in the Qur'ān for washing the various parts of the body involved in ritual ablutions is not obligatory, but simply a matter of emulating the prophetic Sunnah; hence, in their view, it is permissible for one to wash his hands, for example, before washing his face, and so on. The Shafiis and the Hanbalis, however, hold that maintenance of this order is obligatory.

The Malikis and the Shafiis agree that intention is an obligatory part of ritual ablutions, though they differ over the proper time for one's intention. Hence, the Malikis hold that one's intention is valid if it precedes the beginning of one's ablutions by a short period of time, whereas the Shafiis hold that intention must come either as one first begins washing his face or, if one is unable to wash his face for some reason, then when one washes the next part of the body. As for the Hanbalis and Hanafis, each of the two schools holds a distinctive view of intention. According to the Hanbalis, it is not an obligation, but a condition for the validity of ritual ablutions, whereas for the Hanafis, intention is merely a means of imitating the example of the Prophet.

With regard to "continuity" or "immediacy"—that is, washing each part of the body involved in ritual ablutions before the body part washed immediately previous to it has dried—the Shafiis and the Hanafis hold that this is a Sunnah-based practice, whereas according to the Malikis and the Hanbalis, it is an obligatory part of ritual ablutions.

The Sunnah of Ablutions: the definition of Sunnah and what it includes by way of practices that are recommended and desirable

The four schools hold differing views on the meanings of the terms Sunnah, 'recommended' (*mandūb*), 'desirable' (*mustaḥabb*), and 'virtuous' (*faḍīlah*). Thus, there are some who say that they are synonymous, and that all of them refer to acts which one merits reward for performing, but which one does not merit punishment for omitting. There are others who hold that a Sunnah-based act is not the same as one which is merely recommended or desirable, since the former was more emphatically enjoined by the Prophet; nevertheless, they are similar in that both merit reward for those who perform them, while they do not merit punishment for those who omit them. There are still others who hold that Sunnah-based acts differ from those which are merely recommended or desirable. In addition, they divide Sunnah-based practices into two categories, namely: (1) those which are emphatically enjoined (*mu'akkadah*), and (2) those which are not emphatically enjoined (*ghayr mu'akkadah*). According to this latter group, someone who omits a Sunnah-based practice which is emphatically enjoined merits punishment in the form of being deprived of the intercession of the Prophet on the Day of Resurrection, although he or she will not be punished in the hellfire.

Consequently, we have seen fit first to supply a detailed definition of Sunnah according to each of the four schools, after which we provide a comprehensive list of the Sunnah-based practices relating to ritual ablutions based on the teachings of each school. Lastly, in order to make it easier to determine precisely what the various schools teach, we list those points which are agreed upon and those which are the subject of disagreement among them.[62]

---

62. According to the Shafiis, the terms Sunnah, 'recommended', 'desirable', and 'voluntary' (*al-taṭawwu'*) are synonymous and refer to a single reality, namely, that which accountable Muslims are called upon, but not commanded, to do. Hence, if one does these things, he will be rewarded, but if he omits them, he will not be punished.

In addition, the Shafiis divide Sunnah-based practices into two categories: (1) individual Sunnah-based acts, that is, acts which every fully accountable Muslim is asked, but not commanded, to do and which are relevant to each and every individual Muslim regardless of what other Muslims may or may not do; an example is the Sunnah-based practices relating to the obligations of ritual prayer; and (2) collective Sunnah-based practices, that is, practices based on a prophetic example set down for Muslims as a community and which, if they are followed by one or more Muslims in a given situation, cease to be required for others. For example, if a group of people were eating together and only one person uttered the *basmalah*, i.e., the words, "In the name of God, the Most Gracious, the Most Merciful," this would suffice for everyone in the gathering, although this person alone would receive the resulting reward.

* * *

According to the Malikis, Sunnah refers to those actions which the Lawgiver called upon people to perform, a call which the Prophet confirmed, emphasized, and demonstrated publicly in the [Muslim] community. In order for an action to be classified as Sunnah, it must also be one for which there is no evidence that it is obligatory. Such actions merit reward for those who perform them, though they do not merit punishment for those who omit them. Moreover, a Sunnah-based action is distinct from a recommended (*mandūb*) action, the latter being an action which the Lawgiver called upon Muslims to perform, yet without laying stress on it. However, like a Sunnah-based action, a recommended action is one which, by performing it, an accountable person merits reward and which, by omitting it, he merits no punishment. The Malikis sometimes refer to recommended actions as 'virtue' or 'virtuous' (*faḍīlah*), one example of which is praying four units of prayer before the time for the noon prayer and the like. Further examples of 'virtue' will be mentioned below in the section on "Recommended actions associated with ritual prayer."

* * *

As for the Hanafis, they divide Sunnah-based actions into two categories: (1) those which are emphatically enjoined, and (2) those which are not emphatically enjoined.

The Hanafis equate an emphatically enjoined Sunnah practice with a 'duty' (*wājib*), which they judge to be less binding than an 'obligation' (*farḍ*). Such a duty is understood by them to be an action supported by evidence about which there is some uncertainty; it is also referred to as a 'practical obligation' in the sense that it is treated, practically speaking, the same as full obligations such that if someone omits it, he becomes guilty of wrongdoing. With respect to such actions, one must adhere to a specified order and if one omits them for some reason, one must make them up later; however, it is not necessary that one believe them to be obligatory. An example of such a practical obligation is the 'separate prayer' (*witr*), which they count as obligatory on a practical level, but which one is not required to view as obligatory. If someone fails to perform this prayer, he is guilty of wrongdoing, although if he denies its obligatory nature, he does not demonstrate unbelief. Contrasted to the *witr* are the five daily ritual prayers, which are not only a practical obligation, but a rite which one must believe to be obligatory. Therefore, those who neglect them commit wrongdoing, and those who deny their obligatory nature demonstrate unbelief. However, the Hanafis do not hold that those who fail to perform what they term 'practical obligations' are guilty of the same degree of wrongdoing as those who fail to perform the fundamental obligations of Islam. Hence, such individuals will not be punished with hellfire; however, they will be deprived of the

The enumeration of Sunnah-based practices and other recommended actions associated with ablutions

As we have seen, the four schools differ in their definitions of the terms Sunnah, recommended, desirable and virtuous. Hence, some of them consider terms such as Sunnah, recommended, desirable and voluntary to be synonymous, while others distinguish among them. In what follows we shall present the views of each school in turn.[63]

---

intercession of the Messenger of God. Thus it is clear that when the Hanafis state that such-and-such a practice is an emphatically enjoined Sunnah-based practice, what they are referring to is one of the duties mentioned above. One of the rulings on such duties is that those who inadvertently fail to perform them during prayer may compensate for this with the prostration of forgetfulness.

As for those Sunnah-based practices which are not emphatically enjoined, and which the Hanafis refer to as 'recommended' and 'desirable', they are actions which merit reward when performed and which, when not performed, merit no punishment.

* * *

In agreement with the Shafiis, the Hanbalis hold that the terms Sunnah, 'recommended' and 'desirable' are synonymous, all of them referring to actions which merit reward for those who perform them, and which merit no punishment for those who do not. However, they divide Sunnah-based practices into the two categories of "emphatically enjoined" and "not emphatically enjoined." Examples of the former include the *witr* prayer, the two *rak'ahs* which precede the dawn prayer, and the *tarāwīḥ* prayers during Ramaḍān. They hold that omission of an emphatically enjoined Sunnah-based action is undesirable, whereas omission of a Sunnah-based action which is not emphatically enjoined is not.

63. According to the Hanafis, the Sunnah-based practices associated with ritual ablutions include some which are emphatically enjoined and which, as a consequence, merit reward if they are performed and punishment if they are neglected; such acts are referred to as 'duties', which the Hanafis nevertheless distinguish from the fundamental obligations of Islam. The emphatically enjoined Sunnah-based practices associated with ablutions include the following:

One: Utterance of the *basmalah*. This is an unchanging Sunnah-based practice, which remains applicable whether the person performing his ablutions has just awoken from sleep or not. One is to utter the *basmalah* as he begins his ablutions; hence, if someone forgets to utter the name of God as he begins his ablutions and then remembers to do so after washing some of the body parts involved in ablutions, he will not have emulated the Sunnah in this regard. However, even if one forgets the *basmalah* at the beginning of his ablutions, he should utter it at some point before finishing his ablutions lest they be entirely devoid of it. One may also pronounce the *basmalah* before and after engaging in abstersion, provided that it not be at a time when one is not fully clothed or when one is at the actual site of the impurities. Further details on this will be found in the discussion on abstersion below. The *basmalah* which the Prophet is reported to have used is, "In the name of

God Almighty. Praise be to God for the religion of Islam." However, if someone were to begin his ablutions by saying, "There is no god but God," "Praise be to God," or "I testify that there is no god but God," he will also have fulfilled the Sunnah.

Two: Washing one's hands up to the wrists—the wrist being known as the area at the base of the palm—though some of the Hanafis hold that washing one's hands up to the wrists three times before placing them in the container holding the ablution water is obligatory. Doing this before the rest of the procedures associated with the ablution is Sunnah. As for the manner in which one is to wash his hands, the following details are given: First of all, the container which one plans to use for ablutions will either be open at the top such as a cooking pot or bowl or have a narrow opening such as a pitcher. If it is a pitcher, it is desirable for one to hold it in his left hand and pour the water over his right hand three times, then grasp it with his right hand and pour the water over his left hand three times. If it is an open container, then if one has a mug or the like, he may dip the water out and pour it over his left hand three times, then over his right hand in the same manner. If one has nothing with which to dip water out of the container, it is desirable to put the fingers of one's left hand into the water without letting his hand go all the way in, then dip water out with his fingers closed tightly. In other words, he should press his fingers together while keeping his hand open but slightly cupped lest the water run out of it. He should not place his entire hand in the water, since if he does so, the water will become 'used' given that it is only a small amount. However, if it seems to the person doing his ablutions that the water which made contact with his hand represents less than half of the water into which he has dipped, it need not be considered to have become used. If the person wishes to place his hand in a small amount of water while allowing the water to remain *ṭahūr* and unused, he must consciously intend to dip from the water but not to wash. In other words, he must say to himself, "I intend to dip from this water," after which he must use it to wash whichever part of his body he wants to wash. In this manner, the water remains unused, since it is only rendered used if one intends to use it for the performance of his ablutions from the very start. As we have seen above, water is not rendered used unless the use to which it has been put was related to an act of worship.

The aforementioned ruling only applies if there is no verifiable impurity on one's hand, for if there is, and one places his hands in the water, it will be rendered impure whether one has intended to dip out of the water or not. If one is unable to remove water from the container with a cup, a ritually pure cloth, or the like, he may take it out with his mouth, then wash the impurity off his hands. If one is unable to do this, either and if no other water is available, one must forego using water and perform sand ablutions (*tayammum*) instead; moreover, if one does this, there is no need to repeat his ablutions afterwards.

Three: Rinsing out one's mouth and nose, both of which are classified by the Hanafis as emphatically enjoined practices based on the prophetic Sunnah. Hence, they are viewed as duties, that is, acts which are obligatory on the practical level such that if one fails to perform them, one is guilty of wrongdoing. According to the Hanafis, it is not necessary to get new water each time [one rinses one's mouth or one's nose]. However, if someone takes some water in his palm and uses some of it to rinse out his mouth, then rinses out his nose with what remains, this is not acceptable. Similarly, if someone places water in his hand and uses it to rinse out his nose, after which he returns the same water to his hand and uses it to rinse out his mouth, this is not acceptable.

As understood by the Hanafis, rinsing out one's mouth means for one to wash out the entire mouth with water, though it is sufficient for one to place water in one's mouth without swishing it around inside. Hence, if someone placed water in his mouth and then swallowed it rather than spitting it out, this would be an acceptable fulfillment of the Sunnah provided that he fill his mouth three times. However, if someone sucked the water in, this would not be acceptable. As for rinsing out the nose, this involves drawing the water itself inside the nostrils until it reaches the top of the cartilaginous part of the nose. However, the Sunnah does not require one to draw the water any further in than this, nor is one to breathe the water in. It is a Sunnah-based practice for one to exaggerate the actions of rinsing out one's mouth and nose unless one is fasting, in which case it is undesirable to do so lest one swallow some of the water and unintentionally break one's fast. Moreover, as has been mentioned, it is consistent with the prophetic Sunnah for one to rinse out his mouth and nose three separate times. As for the manner in which one is to rinse out his nose, it involves placing the water in the nose with the right hand, then blowing it out forcefully while holding it with the left hand. (The Malikis refer to this action as *istinshāq* [which means, literally, 'to snuff up the nostrils'], and they count it among those Sunnah-based practices which are emphatically enjoined, as will be seen below.)

Four: Parting the fingers and toes, that is, running some of one's fingers between others with dripping water. This is unanimously agreed to be an emphatically enjoined Sunnah-based practice. If the water has already gotten between one's fingers and toes while in their normal position, then parting the fingers and toes is an emulation of the Sunnah; otherwise, however, it is obligatory. The manner of parting is such that one separates the fingers by intertwining them, whereas when parting the toes, one uses the little finger on one's left hand to separate the little toe of the right foot from the others, after which one continues in this fashion until he comes to the little toe of the left foot. This is the preferred method; however, one may part his fingers and toes in any way that proves effective.

Five: Repeating each washing three times. In other words, it is obligatory to perform a single washing of each member of the body included in ritual ablutions. Moreover, each washing must completely cover the body part concerned with water, whereas the second and third washings are practices that are emphatically enjoined by the Prophetic Sunnah. It is required in the first, obligatory washing that the water flow over the member and drip off of it. Hence, if the first washing of a given part of the body does not completely cover it with water, after which one washes it a second and a third time until, by the third washing, it has been completely covered with water, one will have fulfilled his obligation, but he will not have emulated the Sunnah.

Six: Wiping the entire head. Wiping the entire head is an emphatically enjoined Sunnah-based practice. Hence, if one contents himself with wiping only that part of the head which is obligatory and repeats this action, he is guilty of wrongdoing, according to the Hanafis. As for the manner in which one is to wipe the head, it involves placing one's fingers at the front of the head, then passing them over the entire head as far as the nape of the neck. If one's hand is still moist after this, one is enjoined by the Sunnah to continue wiping the head; otherwise, this is not required. On this point, the Hanafis hold the same view as the Malikis.

Seven: Wiping the ears. The manner of doing it is to wipe the insides and backs of the ears with the same water as that used to wipe the head, although if someone gets new water for his ears, this is commendable. Some Hanafis favor wiping the ears with new water even when there is still water left on one's hand after wiping his head; if, on the other hand, the water has dried off, one has no choice but to get new water for his ears. In either case, one is to wipe the outsides of his ears with the insides of his thumbs, and wipe the insides of his ears with his index finger.

Eight: Intention. Specifically, one should consciously intend in his heart to remove ritual impurity, to perform ritual ablutions, to seek ritual purity, or to make ritual prayer permissible. It is preferable for one to say, "I intend to perform ritual ablutions in order to pray as a means of drawing near to God Almighty." Or one might say, "I intend to remove ritual impurity," "I intend to seek ritual purity," or "I intend to make it permissible to perform the ritual prayer." Moreover, although the seat of one's intention is the heart, it is nevertheless considered desirable to voice these words, the time for this being while one is washing his face. (Some Hanafis consider intention to be merely desirable rather than an emphatically enjoined practice based on the prophetic Sunnah, but the soundest view is that it is the latter.)

Nine: Proper order. That is, one must begin performing the obligations of ritual ablutions by washing the face, then the hands and arms up to the elbows, then wipe one-fourth of one's head, then wash the feet up to the ankles. As God Almighty declares, ." . . wash your face and your hands and arms up to the elbows, and pass your [wet] hands lightly over your head, and [wash] your feet up to the ankles" (5:6). Proper order is rightly considered to be among the emphatically enjoined Sunnah-based practices; nevertheless, some Hanafis consider it to be simply desirable.

Ten: 'Immediacy', sometimes referred to as 'continuity' or 'doing something in successive fashion'. The meaning of 'immediacy' is that the water with which a given part of the body has been washed not dry before the following part of the body is washed, provided that the weather is moderate. If the weather is excessively hot or cold, no consideration is given to whether one's body dries quickly or not. However, 'immediacy' is only viewed as a Sunnah-based practice if there is no legitimate excuse not to adhere to it; thus, if one's ablution water runs out after washing one's face, for example, after which one has to wait so long for more water to be brought that one's face dries off before the new water arrives, no harm is done. (The ruling on 'immediacy' was also mentioned in the above section on obligations entailed in ritual ablutions according to the Malikis and others.)

Eleven: Cleaning one's teeth and gums. It is not necessary that this be done with a twig from the *arāk* tree [also known as the *siwāk* tree], though it is preferable that one use a twig from some kind of "bitter tree", since this helps to sweeten the mouth and provides other recognized benefits as well, such as strengthening the gums, cleaning the teeth, and protecting the stomach from impurities that might reach it via the mouth. It is preferable for the twig to be moist and for it to be the width of one's little finger and the length of the span of one's hand. If no such twigs are available, a toothbrush may be used instead, and if no brush is available, one may use his finger or chew gum. If one does have a *siwāk* twig, it is recommended that one hold it in his right hand, keeping his little finger under one end and his thumb under the other, with the rest of the fingers on top. The time to clean one's teeth and gums is when one is rinsing out his mouth. It is undesirable to clean one's teeth and gums while lying down. If one cannot tolerate this practice, however, he may omit it out of necessity.

There are differing views on the following points: (1) holding the container of water with one's right hand when washing the feet, then pouring the water onto the front of the right foot and rubbing it with the left hand (after which these actions are repeated two more times), then pouring the water over the front of the left foot and repeating the same process for the left foot; (2) washing one's hands and feet beginning with the tips of the fingers and toes; (3) wiping one's head from the front; (4) rinsing out the mouth before rinsing out the nose; (5) exaggerating the actions involved in rinsing out the mouth and nose, although it is agreed that this is undesirable if one is fasting; (6) drawing the water into one's nose by breathing it in as far as the top of the nose; (7) taking care not to waste water if one believes that he needs to do more than three washings for his ablutions; otherwise, not wasting water is merely recommended rather then a practice based on the prophetic Sunnah; (8) rewashing one's hands when one washes the arms up to the elbows. Washing the hands before beginning one's ablutions is a Sunnah-based practice, as is washing them again together with the forearms. Hence, if someone washes his hands first, then washes his face, after which he washes his arms from the wrist to the elbow without washing his hands again, he will have fulfilled his religious obligation, but he will not have adhered to the prophetic Sunnah.

These, then, are the Sunnah-based practices associated with ritual ablutions according to the Hanafis.

* * *

According to the Malikis, the emphatically enjoined Sunnah-based actions associated with ritual ablutions, which a fully accountable Muslim merits reward for performing but merits no punishment for omitting, include the following:

One: Washing the hands up to the wrists—the wrist being the joint that attaches the hand [to the arm]. The manner in which one is to wash his hands depends on the amount of water he has available. If the amount of water is small (for the meaning of 'small' as it pertains to amounts of water, see the above sections on "Water") and it is not running water, then if it can be poured out such as water in a bowl, the Sunnah may only be performed by washing one's hands before placing them in this water. If one's hands are ritually pure and free of dirt, then if one places one or both hands in the container before washing them, he has committed an undesirable action and he has failed to perform what is required by the Sunnah. If, on the other hand, the amount of water is large or if it is running water, the Sunnah may be emulated simply by washing one's hands, whether this is done in the ablution water or not. Moreover, if the amount of water is small and it cannot be poured out, as in the case of water in a small cistern, basin or tank, then if one's hands are free of dirt or if the amount of dirt on them is not sufficient to alter the water if they were placed in it, one may perform the Sunnah by dipping water out with one or both hands and washing them outside the container. If, on the other hand, one's hands are not clean and one fears that the water might be altered if he placed them into it, then he should remove water from the container with his mouth or a clean piece of cloth; if neither of these is possible and no other water is available, one should perform sand ablutions instead.

Two: Rinsing out one's mouth. This action is defined by the Malikis as deliberately placing water in one's mouth, then spitting it out again. Hence, if water enters one's mouth unintentionally, if one places water in his mouth but does not swish it around, or if he places water in his mouth and swishes it around but swallows it instead of spitting it out, he will not have emulated the Sunnah. On this point, then, the Malikis differ with the Hanafis, who hold that the Sunnah is emulated simply by water entering one's mouth, even if one neither swishes it around nor spits it out again.

Three: Rinsing out one's nose. This action is defined by the Malikis as breathing water into the nose; moreover, unlike the Hanafis, the Malikis hold that the Sunnah is not emulated unless the water is drawn into the nose in this manner.

Four: Forcing water out of the nose with one's breath. Specifically, one is to grasp the top of his nose with his left thumb and index finger as the water comes out; then, if there is mucous or other solid impurities in the nose, one removes them with the little finger of his left hand.

Five: Wiping the outside and inside of one's ears, including the ear canal.

Six: Using new water to wipe the ears. Unlike the Hanafis, the Malikis deem it insufficient in emulating the Sunnah to wipe one's ears with water remaining on one's hand after wiping the head. The preferred manner of wiping one's ears in the Malikis' view is to place the index fingers inside the ears and the thumbs behind them, then to flex both the index finger and the thumb and move them in a circular motion until the outside and inside of both ears have been wiped. If one wipes his ears in some other manner, this is also acceptable, provided that one wipes them thoroughly.

Seven: Maintaining a fixed order among the parts of the body washed in ritual ablutions. Hence, in agreement with the Hanafis, the Malikis hold that one should wash the face before the hands and arms, the hands and arms before the head, and the head before the feet.

Eight: Wiping the head again if water still remains on one's hand after the first wiping.

Nine: Moving a ring one is wearing in order to allow the water to get under it. On this subject, the Malikis provide a significant amount of detail. They note first of all that the wearing of a ring may be permissible, forbidden, or undesirable. If the ring is one that a man is permitted to wear—which means a single silver ring weighing no more than two dirhams [i.e., approximately 6.24 grams]—it is not necessary to move it regardless of whether it is tight or loose, and regardless of whether the water gets under it or not. This ruling is a general one which applies to both minor and major ablutions. Nevertheless, if someone removes such a ring after completing his ablutions, be they minor or major, he is obliged to wash the area under the ring if it is tight and if he suspects that the water did not touch the skin under it. If, on the other hand, the ring is one which a man is forbidden to wear, such as a ring made of gold, a silver ring weighing more than two dirhams, or more than one ring, then if it is loose, it is sufficient simply to turn the ring on one's finger without rubbing the area beneath it with his hand. However, if it is tight, one must remove it from its place and rub the area under it. As for the ruling on rings which it is undesirable for a man to wear—namely, rings made of copper, lead, or iron—it is the same as that for rings which men are forbidden to wear.

The above ruling applies to men; as for women, they are permitted to wear any jewelry they wish, whether it is made of gold or any other metal. Hence, if a woman wears bracelets or anklets, she is not required to move them even if the water does not get under them as she performs her ablutions, and regardless of whether they are tight or loose. However, if she removes them after completing her minor or major ablutions, she must wash the area under them if they are tight and she suspects that the water did not get under them.

(As for the Hanafis, they hold that moving a loose ring is not a practice based on the Sunnah, but simply one which is recommended, as will be seen in the discussion below on "Recommended Actions." As for a ring which is so tight that it prevents water from getting under it, it is obligatory to move it, regardless of whether the wearing of the ring is permitted or forbidden. For the Hanafis, then, it is unacceptable for a woman to wear rings or bracelets which are so tight that water cannot get under them. However, they do not stipulate that one must rub the area beneath them as do the Malikis.)

These, then, are the emphatically enjoined Sunnah-based actions associated with ritual ablutions according to the Malikis.

* * *

According to the Shafiis, there are numerous Sunnah-based practices associated with ritual ablutions. Moreover, as we have seen, they make no distinction between Sunnah, 'recommended', 'desirable', and the like. The practices associated with minor ablutions, whether Sunnah, 'recommended', 'desirable', or 'virtuous' are many. The following is a list of the practices which they include in these categories [and which, in effect, constitute a single category in their view]:

(1) Appealing to God for protection from evil (*isti'ādhah*). Hence, one might say, "I seek refuge in God from the accursed Satan," or something similar. (2) Uttering the *basmalah* (*tasmiyah*) when beginning one's ablutions, that is, when washing one's hands. The simplest form of the *basmalah* one might use is, "In the name of God," although it is preferable to complete the *basmalah* by saying, "In the name of God, the Most Gracious, the Most Merciful." The Sunnah-based practice of uttering the *basmalah* is only fulfilled by uttering the words, "In the name of God" or, "In the name of God, the Most Gracious, the Most Merciful." Hence, in contrast to the Hanafis, the Shafiis hold that if someone utters words other than these, he will not have conformed to the Sunnah, since the Lawgiver has instructed us to utter the *basmalah* in particular. One is to utter the *basmalah* even if he is in a state of major ritual impurity. Moreover, if one fails to utter it at the beginning of his ablutions, whether this omission is deliberate or not, he should utter it at some other

point before his ablutions have been completed. However, once one has finished his ablutions and gone on to utter the testimony of faith ["I bear witness that there is no god but God, and that Muḥammad is the Messenger of God"] and prayers of supplication, it is too late to utter the *basmalah*; on this point, the Shafiis differ with the Hanafis. (3) Consciously intending in one's heart to adhere to the Sunnah-based practices associated with ablutions when uttering the *basmalah.* This intention is to be distinguished from the intention to remove ritual impurity, which is obligatory, and which must accompany the washing of the face. (4) The verbal utterance of this Sunnah-based intention as one begins washing his face just as one does the obligatory intention. (5) Washing one's hands up to the elbows. One begins washing the hands while uttering the *basmalah* and one's intention to perform the Sunnah-based practices associated with ablutions. The Sunnah is fulfilled by washing the hands three times outside the container of ablution water if the water is in a container which may be poured out of onto one's hands, such as a pitcher and the like. If the container is open and the amount of water is small, it is permissible for one to wash his hands in this water if he is certain that they are ritually pure. If one has doubts as to whether they are pure or not, it is undesirable to wash them by placing them inside the container. Moreover, if one is certain that his hands have ritual impurities on them, one is forbidden to place them in the container, and one must instead wash them three times before placing them in the container. However, this washing is merely in order to remove ritual impurity and does not suffice for the performance of the Sunnah-based washing of the hands. Hence, one must follow this by washing his hands three more times, in doing which he has performed the Sunnah.

(6) Washing the hands before rinsing out the mouth. In other words, if someone were to rinse out his mouth, then wash his hands, he would not have performed the Sunnah-based washing of the hands.

(7) Rinsing out the mouth. This involves placing water in one's mouth before washing out one's nostrils. It is not necessary to swish the water around in the mouth or to spit it out; rather, the Sunnah is performed by merely placing water in the mouth. Hence, if one swallows the water, he will still have performed the Sunnah, although the ideal is to swish the water around in one's mouth, then spit it out. (8) Rinsing out the nose after rinsing out the mouth. The Sunnah here is performed by merely placing water in the nose. The ideal is to draw the water in with one's breath, then force it out again; however, the Sunnah is performed even if one does not do so. As for the best way to rinse out the mouth and the nose, it is to place the water in one's palm, then rinse out the mouth with part of the water and rinse out the nose with what remains. One repeats this action three times by rinsing out the mouth, then the nose with three successive handfuls of water, each handful being used in part to rinse out the mouth, and in part to rinse out the nose. (9) Facing the *qiblah* [that is, in the direction of the sacred Ka'bah] if one is performing his ablutions in a place from which it is possible to do so.

(10) Placing a container with a wide opening at the top to one's right, and any other to one's left.

(11) Uttering the supplications associated with the various actions involved in ritual ablutions. That is, after uttering the *basmalah* and while washing one's hands, one says, "Praise be to God for Islam and its blessing. Praise be to God Who has

made this water capable of removing impurity, and Who has made Islam a light. My Lord, I seek refuge in You from the proddings of the evil ones. I seek protection in You, my Lord, from their presence. O God, keep my hands from committing any act of disobedience to You." While rinsing out the mouth, one says, "O God, help me to remember You, to thank You, and to worship You rightly." While rinsing out the nose, one says, "O God, grant that I might smell the fragrance of Paradise." When washing the face, one says, "O God, make my face white on that day when some faces are made white and others, black." When washing one's right hand one says, "O God, give me my book [the record of my deeds on earth] in my right hand and call me to a merciful account" and while washing the left hand, one says, "O God, do not give me my book in my left hand nor behind my back." While wiping one's head, one says, "O God, keep my hair and my skin far from the hellfire, and grant me shade beneath Your throne on that day when there shall be no shade but Yours." While wiping the ears, one says, "O God, cause me to be among those who give ear to people's words and who follow [only] the best of what they hear." While washing the feet, one says, "O God, fix my feet firmly on the straight path on the day when people's feet are slipping [when temptation strikes]." When one has completed his ablutions, he says, "I testify that there is no god but God alone, who has no partner. I testify that our liegelord Muḥammad is God's servant and messenger. O God, cause me to be among those who turn to You in repentance. Cause me to be among those who have been made pure. Glory be to You, O God, and praise! I testify that there is no god but You. I seek Your forgiveness and come to You in repentance." One utters these words while facing the *qiblah*, lifting his hands and his face heavenward, after which he recites Sūrat al-Qadr (Surah 97). (The Hanafis agree with the Shafiis on parts of these supplications, although they hold that they are not based on the Sunnah but are rather to be considered simply recommended or desirable practices. As for the Malikis, they make no mention of these prayers among either Sunnah-based practices or 'virtues', as will be seen below.) (12) Cleaning one's teeth and gums (*istiyāk*). This involves cleaning one's teeth with any object which is not harmful, whether it is a twig from the well-known *arāk* [*siwāk*] tree, a brush, or something else. However, they hold that cleaning the teeth and gums with one's finger is not sufficient. One should clean the teeth and gums before washing one's hands, in which case there is no need to consciously intend the performance of this action. (13) Saying while cleaning one's teeth and gums, "O God, whiten my teeth hereby, strengthen my gums, and keep my uvula steady [which may be a metaphorical way of asking for health, the ability to speak rightly, etc. (t.n.)]. Bless me in this, O Most Merciful of the merciful!" The way to do this is to first clean the right side of one's mouth, then the left, passing the twig or brush over the tops of the molars, the roof of the mouth, and the surface of the tongue. It is also consistent with the Sunnah to wipe one's teeth with a horizontal motion and to hold the twig in one's right hand, with one's little finger [and thumb] under it and one's index finger, middle finger and ring finger on top. Another Sunnah-based practice in this connection is to wash the twig, brush, etc. three times if it becomes contaminated or if it takes on a different odor, while it is undesirable for it to be longer than the span of one's hand. (14) Beginning with the front or outermost sections of the parts of the body to be washed in ritual ablutions [for example, the tips of the fingers and toes], provided that one is using a container from which he dips the water out himself, such as a pan, an ablution font, or the like. If, by contrast, one is performing his ablutions with water that comes down onto his hands without his dipping into it, as is the case when one uses a faucet or a pitcher or when someone else is pouring the water, then when washing the hands, one begins with the wrists and when washing the feet, one begins with the ankles, which is the reverse of the first situation. (15) Dipping water out with both hands together when washing one's face, and not slapping one's face with the water. (16) Parting one's beard if it is thick.

(17) Wiping the entire head, then wiping the insides and outsides of the ears with new water. (18) Rubbing the parts of the body included in ritual ablutions, always beginning with the right side, as has been mentioned. (19) Washing more than is actually required [for example, by washing one's face slightly beyond the hairline, washing one's arms up beyond the elbow, and washing some of the leg above one's ankles, as previously mentioned; this practice is supported by a sound hadith.] (20) Repeating the various actions and utterances involved in ablutions three times. (21) Being certain to maintain "continuity." This does not apply, however, to those who suffer from conditions such as urinary incontinence, in whose case this practice is categorized not merely as Sunnah but as an obligation. (22) Refraining from speaking unnecessarily while performing ritual ablutions except in order to make mention of God. (23) Not asking others for help in performing one's ablutions unless necessary. (24) Refraining from drying off the parts of the body one has washed as part of ritual ablutions or shaking the water off them except out of necessity. (25) Drinking some of the water that remains after one has completed his ablutions. (26) Moving a loose ring. As for a tight ring which prevents the water from making contact with the skin beneath it, it is obligatory to move it in order to allow the water to get under it. The Shafiis make no distinction here between rings which are permissible and those which are not; in this they agree with the Hanafis and differ with the Malikis.

* * *

As for the Hanbalis, they list the following ablution-related practices as being either Sunnah-based, recommended, or desirable:

One: Facing the *qiblah*.

Two: Cleaning one's teeth at the time one rinses out one's mouth. It is recommended that one clean his teeth with a horizontal motion, and his gums and mouth with an up-and-down motion. Similarly, it is recommended that one use the left hand, and for the twig to be supple enough not to be harmful; it is thus undesirable for one to use a hard, dry twig. Cleaning one's teeth and gums is part of the Sunnah at all times except for the afternoon for someone who is fasting, in which case it is undesirable, regardless of whether the twig used is soft or hard. Before noon, however, it a Sunnah-based practice to clean the teeth and gums with a hard, dry twig, although it is permissible at this time to use a moist, soft twig as well. It is similarly a Sunnah-based practice to clean the teeth and gums at the time for each prayer, and well as when one wakes up, when there is a change in the odor in one's mouth, when one performs ritual ablutions, when one reads or recites the Qur'ān, when one enters the mosque or his home, when one's stomach is empty, and when one's teeth are yellowed. Still other Sunnah-based practices in this regard are for one to begin with the right side of one's mouth and to move from the front teeth back toward the molars. Moreover, it is deemed undesirable for one to clean his teeth and gums with [twigs from] sweet basil, pomegranate plants, reeds, or anything else that would be harmful to the gums.

Three: Washing the hands three times, as mentioned above.

Four: Rinsing out one's mouth and nose before washing one's face.

Five: Exaggerating the actions of rinsing out the mouth and the nose unless one is fasting.

Six: Rubbing any part of the body included in ritual ablutions if it repels the water.

Seven: Using a generous amount of water when washing the face due to the presence of hair, depressions and bumps [which presumably might attract or retain ritual impurities – t.n.].

Eight: Parting a thick beard when washing it.

Nine: Parting the fingers and toes if the water has already gotten between them without it [i.e., without the parting of the fingers and toes]; otherwise, such parting is not merely a Sunnah-based practice, but an obligatory one.

Ten: Using new water to wipe the ears.

Eleven: Washing the right side before the left.

Twelve: Taking care to wash more than the required area of the face, the hands, and the feet.

Thirteen: Washing each relevant part of the body a second and third time if the water has covered it completely with the first washing [since if it has not, the second and third washings cease to be Sunnah and become obligatory].

Fourteen: Keeping one's intention present in one's heart throughout one's ablutions.

Fifteen: Consciously intending to perform the Sunnah-based actions when washing one's hands up to the wrists.

Sixteen: Uttering one's intention silently by moving one's tongue and lips such that one can hear himself, but no one else can hear him; and not seeking others' help in performing one's ablutions.

Seventeen: After the completion of one's ablutions, looking upward and saying, "I testify that there is no god but God alone, who has no partner, and I testify that our liegelord Muḥammad is His servant and messenger. O God, cause me to be among those who turn to You in repentance, who have been purified, and who are Your righteous servants. Glory be to You, O God, and praise. I testify that there is no god but You. I seek Your forgiveness and I turn to You in repentance." Here, the meaning of *ghurrah* is that one extends the obligatory washing of the face to include washing the front part of the head; and the meaning of *taḥjīl* is that one extends the washing of the hands to include washing the area above the elbows; and to go beyond washing the feet means to wash part of one's legs above the ankles. Evidence in favor of these practices may be found in the sound hadiths.

Ablution-related practices which are recommended, desirable and the like

As pointed out above, some of the four schools make no distinction among practices based on the prophetic Sunnah and actions which are simply recommended, desirable, voluntary, supererogatory, and virtuous, whereas others draw a distinction between Sunnah-based practices and those belonging to these other categories. Having presented the ablutions-related practices which are based on the prophetic Sunnah, we shall now proceed to a discussion of the ablutions-related actions belonging to the other aforementioned categories as they are understood by those schools which distinguish between them and Sunnah-based actions.[64]

---

64. According to the Hanbalis and the Shafiis, the terms Sunnah, 'recommended', 'desirable', 'voluntary', and so on all refer to the same thing, namely, actions which a fully accountable person merits reward for performing but which he is not considered blameworthy for neglecting. The Sunnah-based actions associated with ritual ablutions according to these two schools have been discussed above; beyond these, they list no actions as belonging to the categories of 'recommended' or 'desirable'.

* * *

According to the Malikis, there are no practices associated with ritual ablutions other than Sunnah-based actions and 'virtues' (*faḍā'il*), neither of which merits punishment for those who do not perform them. However, the reward for the performance of Sunnah-based actions is greater than that for 'virtues'. The Sunnah-based practices recognized by the Malikis have been presented above; as for those which they term 'virtues', they are as follows:

One: Performing one's ablutions in a ritually pure place. Hence, for example, if one were to perform his ablutions over a toilet, his ablutions would be valid; however, such a practice is undesirable nearly to the point of being unlawful even if the toilet has never been used before and is ritually pure, since the Malikis deem it undesirable to perform ritual ablutions in a place whose purpose is to receive impurities, even if it has never been used.

Two: Minimizing the water one uses to wash each part of one's body such that it flows over it entirely, but without necessarily dripping off of it.

Three: Beginning with the right side and ending with the left, i.e., starting with the right hand or leg.

Four: Placing an open container out of which one can dip water to one's right, and a container with a small opening from which one can pour water to the left.

Five: Beginning with those parts of the body which are customarily considered to merit priority, for example, by washing one's face from the top downward, washing the hands and feet beginning with the fingers and toes, and wiping one's head beginning at the front.

Six: Washing each member of the body a second and a third time, including the feet. The second washing is not counted in this regard unless the first washing covered the entire body part with water; similarly, the third washing is not counted unless the second washing covered the body part with water. Hence, if three washings are required to cover the entire body part with water, then all three washings are to be counted together as one washing, and it is recommended that one then wash the body part concerned two more times.

Seven: Cleaning one's teeth and gums with a twig or comparable object prior to performing ablutions. The finger may also be used if nothing else is available. It is also recommended that one use the right hand and begin from the right side, cleaning the teeth with a horizontal motion and the gums with a vertical motion. The twig one uses should be no longer than the span of one's hand and it should not be held too tightly. It is recommended that one clean one's teeth and gums in this manner before the ritual prayer if a fair amount of time has passed since the last cleaning; it is likewise recommended before reading the Qur'ān, when one wakes up, and whenever there is a change in the taste in one's mouth from eating, drinking, and the like.

Eight: Uttering the *basmalah* as one begins one's ablutions by saying, "In the name of God, the Most Gracious, the Most Merciful," and not speaking unnecessarily except for the mention of God.

Nine: Maintaining the proper order between Sunnah-based practices and obligations. Thus, for example, one should wash one's hands up to the wrists and rinse out one's mouth and nose before washing the face, and one should use new water to wipe the head.

* * *

The Hanafis consider the following ablution-related practices—which they treat as essentially the same as what are referred to as virtues, desirable actions, supererogatory acts of worship, or rules of etiquette—to be recommended: (1) sitting in a place somewhat higher than the source of the water from which one is performing ablutions lest the spray of used water come back on one's body; (2) inserting one's wet little finger inside the ear canal; (3) uttering the two testimonies of faith while cleansing each part of one's body; (4) performing one's ablutions in a ritually pure place; (5) not performing ablutions in water which has been heated by the sun (see earlier section on undesirable practices associated with water); (6) washing the uppermost parts of the body before the lower ones; (7) not allowing the water with which one has rinsed out one's mouth and nose to go back into the container of ablution water; (8) facing the *qiblah* while performing ablutions; (9) moving a ring which the water has gotten under, bearing in mind that if the water has not gotten under the ring, it is obligatory to move it; (10) refraining from seeking others' help in performing one's ablutions, although there is nothing wrong with asking someone else to prepare and pour the water; (11) drinking some of the remaining ablution water while standing up and facing the *qiblah*; (12) taking care to wash more than the actual area required; (13) washing the bottoms of one's feet with the left hand out of respect for the right; (14) wiping off the ablution water with a cloth of some kind, but without rubbing too vigorously and without shaking the ablution water off one's hands; (15) reciting Surah 97 (al-Qadr) of the Qur'ān three times after completing one's ablutions; (16) standing after this with one's face toward the *qiblah* and saying, "I testify that there is no god but God alone, Who has no partner, and I testify that Muḥammad is God's servant and messenger. O God, cause me to be among those who turn to You in repentance and who have been made pure"; (17) not speaking needlessly during ablutions except to make mention of God; (18) combining the intention of one's heart with the verbal utterance of one's tongue; (19) uttering the *basmalah* and one's intention while washing and drying every member of the body; (20) dipping out water with one's right hand to rinse out the mouth and nose; (21) forcing the water out of one's nose with the aid of the left hand; (22) not reserving a particular water container for oneself such that one allows no one else to use it for his or her ablutions; (23) using an ablution vessel which is made of earthenware and the like, and if it has a handle, washing it three times; (24) placing an open container which one can dip out of to one's right, and any others to one's left; (25) taking care to wash the inner corners of one's eyes; (26) praying two *rak'ahs* at a time when prayer is not considered undesirable, the undesirable times being at sunrise and the period immediately preceding it, high noon, sunset, and the time immediately preceding sunset following the mid-afternoon prayer; (27) preparing *ṭahūr* water before doing one's ablutions; (28) not performing one's ablutions with water or soil taken from land which has been obtained by illegitimate means; and (29) uttering the supplications associated with the different parts of the body.

Hence, as one begins ablutions, one says, "In the name of God the Majestic, praise be to God for the religion of Islam." One then utters the testimonies of faith and prays for blessings on the Prophet. When rinsing out one's mouth one says, "O God, help me to recite the Qur'ān, to keep You in remembrance, to thank You, and to worship You rightly." When rinsing out the nose one says, "O God, grant that I might smell the fragrance of Paradise, and not the stench of the hellfire." When washing the face one says, "O God, whiten my face on the day when some faces are whitened and others are blackened." When washing one's right arm one says, "O God, give me the record of my deeds in my right hand, and grant me an easy accounting." When washing the left arm one says, "O God, do not give me my book of deeds in my left hand or behind my back." When wiping the head one says, "O God, grant me shade beneath Your throne on that Day when there shall be no shade but that of Your throne." When wiping one's ears one says, "O God, cause me to be among those who give ear to what is said, and who follow the best of what they hear." When wiping the neck, one says, "O God, deliver my neck from the hellfire." When washing one's right foot one says, "O God, keep my steps firm on the straight path on the day when some people's feet are slipping." When washing the left foot one says, "O God, cause my guilt to be forgiven, cause my striving to be repaid with good that serves to increase my thankfulness, and cause my dealings never to fail"; (30) wiping one's neck with the back of one's hand, since the water on this part of the hand will not have been used up yet (as for wiping the throat, this is an innovation); and (31) beginning with the right side of the body and moving to the left.

Undesirable practices associated with ablutions and the definition of undesirability

As for undesirable practices associated with ablutions, they include such things as pouring out more water than one needs for the purpose of completing one's ablutions. This practice is [merely] undesirable when the water is permitted to or owned by the person doing the ablutions; however, if it is public property which has been designated for use in ritual ablutions such as that made available for ablutions in mosques, it is forbidden.

With regard to the definition of 'undesirable' and the specific practices which are deemed undesirable in connection with ritual ablutions, each of the four schools provides its own detailed views.[65]

---

65. The Hanafis divide undesirability into two categories, namely, (1) undesirability which approaches the lawful (*karāhat tanzīh*), and (2) undesirability which approaches the unlawful (*karāhat taḥrīm*). An example of the second type of undesirability is to neglect to perform a duty which has less force than a full religious obligation, and which the Hanafis term an 'emphatically enjoined Sunnah-based practice'. As for undesirability which approaches the lawful, it includes acts which one merits no punishment for committing, but which one merits some reward for refraining from. It is the opposite of recommended or desirable Sunnah-based practices and the like which are not emphatically enjoined.

Acts associated with ritual ablutions which are undesirable nearly to the point of being forbidden involve the omission of one of the emphatically enjoined Sunnah-based practices, which have already been mentioned. As for those practices which, though undesirable, are close to being lawful, they involve omission of one of the acts listed above as being recommended, desirable, or virtuous. However, some of the Hanafis draw analogies between certain undesirable practices and other acts; then, on the basis of these analogies, they judge these other acts to be likewise undesirable. Such acts include the following: (1) striking one's face violently with the water as one performs ablutions. This practice is prevalent among some common, uneducated folk who take the water in their hands, then hit their faces with it as though they wanted to punish themselves. (2) Rinsing out one's mouth and nose with the left hand and forcing out mucous with the right. (3) Wiping one's head or ears three times with fresh water, whereas what one is required to do is to wipe one's head the first time with fresh water, then wipe it again with whatever water remains on one's hands. One then wipes his ears in the same fashion, i.e., without using fresh water. If one wipes his head more than once with fresh water, he has committed an undesirable action. (4) Reserving a container or a place which one uses for one's own ablutions alone. This is what the Hanafis say in their books; however, the principles which they set forth exempt from this ruling those cases in which someone has reason to fear that he might be infected with an illness if he were to perform his ablutions from the same container or in the same place as others, or in which someone believes that by reserving a special container for his own ablutions, he is protecting himself from ritual impurity or the like. If such legitimate motives are the cause for the practice, it is not considered undesirable at all. In fact, such a practice might even be necessary if one suspects that by doing otherwise, he might bring harm to himself. (5) Washing one's face and hands more than three times. If someone washes his face four or five times, this must either be because he believes this number of times is required of him in performing ritual ablutions, or that it is not required. If one believes that it is required, the practice is undesirable to the point of being unlawful, whereas if one does not believe it to be required but does so simply in order to cool off in hot weather, for reasons of hygiene, and so forth, then the practice is undesirable, but approaches the lawful. The reason for this is that maintaining cleanliness and cooling oneself off are to be done at times other than that reserved for worship. (6) Using water too sparingly when performing ablutions. In other words, just as it is undesirable to waste water when performing ablutions, though to a degree approaching the lawful, the same ruling applies to using insufficient water. As for the definition of 'insufficient', the Hanafis define it here as an amount of water which, when used to wash a given part of the body in ablutions, covers the member concerned but without visibly dripping off of it. On this point the Hanafis differ with the Malikis, as will be seen below. As was noted above, the use of excessive water is undesirable when the water is in one's own possession, whereas if it is public property set aside for use in ablutions, as is the water available in mosques and the like, wasting it is not only undesirable, but unlawful. (7) Performing ablutions in a place contaminated with impurity. This practice is deemed undesirable for fear that one might get some impurity on one's body or clothing due to the water's falling onto the site and being contaminated by it.

* * *

According to the Malikis, undesirable practices associated with ritual ablutions are, first of all, those which involve the omission of one of the Sunnah-based practices mentioned thus far. As we have noted, non-performance of a Sunnah-based action entails no punishment; however, there are some Sunnah-based actions which are emphatically enjoined, and others which are not, the latter category sometimes being referred to as 'virtues'. Be that as it may, with respect to undesirable practices associated with ablutions, the Malikis make no distinction between those which are undesirable to the point of approaching the unlawful and those which, though undesirable, nevertheless approach the lawful. The principle on which they rely in this regard is that anything which is undesirable is to be considered of the type which approaches the lawful, even though this is not the ideal approach.

As for those ablution-related actions which the Malikis consider to be undesirable, they include: (1) Pouring out more water than one needs to perform one's ablutions. This ruling only applies, however, to those cases in which one believes that the additional amount of water is required for his ablutions. If, on the other hand, the additional amount is poured out for purposes of hygiene or in order to cool oneself off, then it is not deemed undesirable so long as the water is not public property set aside for ablutions, in which case excessive use is forbidden. Such use is likewise forbidden if the water belongs to someone else who has not given permission for it to be used, as was seen above in the discussion of undesirable practices relating to water. (2) Wiping one's neck with water based on the notion that this represents the type of extra effort which religion enjoins. In this regard, the Malikis make no distinction between the back and front of the neck. The Malikis differ here with the Hanafis, who hold that wiping the neck after wiping the ears without new water is a Sunnah-based practice; as for wiping the throat, however, the Hanafis view it as an undesirable innovation (*bid'ah*), although they do not state directly that it is undesirable. (3) Performing one's ablutions in a place which is known to be contaminated with impurity, or a place made to receive impurities which is still unused, such as a new toilet before it has been used. (4) Speaking while performing ablutions other than by making mention of God Almighty. This point is agreed upon among the schools; however, the Shafiis hold that speaking while performing ablutions is not undesirable, though it is preferable not to do so.

* * *

According to the Shafiis, an undesirable act is one which the Lawgiver has requested, but not commanded, us to refrain from. Hence, if a fully accountable individual refrains from such an act, he will be rewarded for doing so, but if he commits it he will not be punished. The undesirable acts associated with ritual ablutions according to the Shafiis are limited to the omission of those Sunnah-based actions about which there is disagreement as to whether they are obligatory or not—that is, Sunnah-based practices which are viewed by some as a fundamental obligation, and by others as being based simply on the prophetic Sunnah. This type of disagreement sometimes arises in connection with emphatically enjoined Sunnah-based practices. As for the omission of other actions, it is merely a departure from the ideal.

Those actions which the Shafiis classify as undesirable, though approaching the lawful, are: (1) Using excessive water for one's ablutions, unless the water is public property set aside for ablutions, in which case such excess is positively forbidden so long as it is not in a cistern or ablution fount. In this latter case, such excessive use is not forbidden, but simply undesirable, due to the fact that the water will flow back into the receptacle after it has been used. (2) Speaking when one is performing ablutions, which is a departure from the ideal. (3) Exaggerating the actions involved in rinsing out one's mouth or nose when one is fasting. (4) Performing one's ablutions in a place contaminated with impurity. (As for wiping the back and front of the neck, the Shafiis do not consider it undesirable. On the contrary, some of them classify it as a Sunnah-based practice.) (6) Washing or wiping any part of the body more than three times. The Shafiis hold that both the action of washing and the action of wiping are to be repeated three times when performing ablutions unless one is wearing shoes, since it is deemed undesirable to wipe one's shoes more than once.

* * *

The Hanbalis hold that an undesirable action involves the omission of a practice based on the emphatically enjoined Sunnah, such as the *witr* prayer discussed above, the two *rak'ahs* prayed at dawn, the *tarāwīḥ* prayers, and so forth. As for the omission of other Sunnah-based actions such as those mentioned above, it is judged to be simply a departure from the ideal unless there exists a text which contains a non-categorical prohibition against omitting a given action, in which case its omis-

That which invalidates ritual ablutions

The Arabic word *nāqiḍ* (plural, *nawāqiḍ*), rendered as 'that which invalidates ritual ablutions,' is derived from the Arabic verb *naqaḍa*, which means to corrupt or ruin. Some may object, saying, "The use of this word implies that ritual ablutions are associated from the very start with corruption in some sense, which implies, in turn, that the corruption took place even before the occurrence of the *ḥadath* [that is, the discharge from the body of a substance which invalidates one's ablutions]. If this is true, then ritual prayer based on such ritual ablutions will have no validity even if it is performed prior to the corrupting *ḥadath*." In order to get around this objection, some have chosen instead to refer to events which invalidate ritual ablutions with the Arabic word *ḥadath* (plural, *aḥdāth*).

In reply to this same objection, let us note that what is intended by the term *nāqiḍ* is that one's ablutions are invalidated only after the occurrence of the corrupting *ḥadath*, not that they were invalid to begin with.

The occurrences or substances which invalidate ritual ablutions are divided into two main categories:

First: That which comes out of the urethra, the vagina or the anus for the woman, and for the man, that which comes out of the urethra, the seminal duct or the anus. These substances are further categorized based on whether they are (a) normal, regular secretions, or (b) abnormal or unusual.

Second: That which could lead to secretions from one of the aforementioned orifices. This category is further divided into four types: (a) a loss of full mental functioning, (b) touching a desirable woman or young man, which invalidates ritual ablutions given specific conditions which will be mentioned below, (c) touching the penis without the presence of a barrier between the penis and the hand, which invalidates ritual ablutions according to some, but not all of the schools, and (d) bodily secretions other than those which come out of the urethra, vagina, seminal duct or anus, such as blood. Hence the *nawāqiḍ*, that is, events and substances which invalidate ritual ablutions, consist of six different types, each of which will be discussed in what follows:

Type One includes substances which are regularly secreted by the urethra, vagina, seminal duct or anus. Some of these substances simply invalidate ritual ablu-

---

sion is undesirable. Actions which are considered to be a mere departure from the ideal thus include: (1) Pouring out more water than is needed for one's ablutions if the person performing the ablutions has legitimate access to the water in question; if it is public property set aside for use in ablutions, such excess is forbidden. (2) Washing any part of the body more than three times, or wiping any part more than once. (However, the Hanbalis provide here that if one increases the number of washings or wipings for reasons of hygiene or in order to cool oneself off, the practice is not undesirable.) (3) Wiping the neck with water. (4) Exaggerating the action of rinsing out one's mouth if one is fasting. (5) Performing one's ablutions in a place which is ritually impure. (6) Speaking while performing one's ablutions for any purpose other than to make mention of God.

tions, thereby requiring the person to perform them again, while others require one to perform major ablutions (*ghusl*). As for those substances which merely require one to repeat one's minor ritual ablutions, they include urine, *madhī*, or pre-seminal fluid (that is, the thin, yellowish liquid which tends to be secreted when a man experiences sexual pleasure), *wadī* (a thick white liquid resembling semen which tends to be secreted from the penis following urination), *al-wadi al-hādī* (a white liquid which is secreted from a pregnant woman's vagina prior to childbirth), as well as *manī* (semen) which is secreted without being accompanied by sexual pleasure.[66] As is well-known, all these things are secreted from the anterior orifices. As for substances which are discharged through the anus, they include fecal matter and 'wind'. For an explanation of the wisdom in the ruling that passing wind invalidates ritual ablutions, the reader may refer back to the beginning of the section on ritual purity. Moreover, there is unanimous agreement among the schools that all the substances mentioned here serve to invalidate ritual ablutions.

Type Two includes substances which are secreted through the vagina, the urethra, the seminal duct or the anus and which tend to be indicative of an abnormal condition, such as stones,[67] worms, blood, pus and other suppurative matter. All such secretions invalidate ritual ablutions.

(The two types mentioned thus far have to do with substances secreted from either the vagina, the urethra, the seminal duct or the anus. The following four types, by contrast, have to do with events that invalidate ablutions but without the secretion of a substance from one of the aforementioned orifices.)

---

66. According to the Malikis, semen which is secreted without the accustomed sexual arousal—for example, if a man were to get into hot water such that he experienced sexual pleasure and had an emission—does not require one to perform major ritual ablutions, but simply to repeat one's minor ablutions. On this point, the Malikis differ with the other three schools.

As for the Shafiis, they hold that an emission of semen requires the person to perform major ritual ablutions whether it is accompanied by sexual arousal or not. Hence, if it becomes apparent that the substance which has been secreted is semen, one must perform major ablutions. Moreover, even though such an emission requires the man to perform major ritual ablutions, it does not invalidate his minor ablutions. A more detailed discussion of the Shafiis' views on this topic will be found below in the section on "Major Ritual Ablutions."

67. According to the Malikis, minor ritual ablutions are only invalidated by the body's usual secretions which come out through their accustomed orifices, provided that this takes place when one is in a state of normal health. Hence, if substances such as pebbles or worms are generated in the stomach, then come out through the vagina, urethra, seminal duct, or anus, they do not invalidate ritual ablutions; otherwise—for example, if someone swallowed a pebble or a worm and it came out of one of these orifices—they would invalidate one's ablutions, since they would be considered to be strange to the body and, thus, not among its "usual secretions."

Type Three involves a loss of complete mental functioning on the part of the person who has performed ritual ablutions, either due to insanity, epilepsy, or fainting, or as a result of having taken a substance such as wine, hashish, an anesthetic or some other, similar substance. Loss of consciousness may also be due to sleep, which invalidates ritual ablutions not in itself,[68] but due to the resulting *ḥadath* to which it may lead.[69]

Type Four involves touching someone who is sexually desirable, be it a woman or a young man. There is general agreement among Muslim jurisprudents that there are two types of touching, each of which has specific rulings associated with it. The first, referred to in Arabic as *lams*, may be either with the hand or with some other

---

68. According to the Hanbalis, unless one's sleep is very light, it invalidates ritual ablutions in and of itself, even if the person who sleeps has placed his buttocks on something which ensures that he will not pass wind.

As for the Shafiis, they hold that sleeping invalidates ritual ablutions in and of itself if the person falls asleep without placing his buttocks against the floor, the ground or some other similar surface, even if it is certain that no *ḥadath* took place while he was sleeping.

69. In contrast to the Shafiis and the Hanbalis, the Hanafis correctly hold that sleep does not invalidate ritual ablutions in and of itself, but rather, it invalidates them only in three specific situations: (1) if someone sleeps lying on his side, (2) if someone sleeps reclining on his back, or (3) if someone sleeps while resting his weight on one hip. The reason for this is that in these positions, the person is not in control of himself due to the relaxation of his joints [and muscles]. If, on the other hand, someone sleeps while sitting up with his buttocks firmly resting on the ground or some similar surface, then he is not required to repeat his ritual ablutions afterwards. Moreover, if a sleeping person is resting on a cushion, pillow or the like, after which the pillow is pulled out from under him while he is still asleep, then if he falls out of position such that his buttocks ceases to be in contact with the ground, his ablutions will be invalidated. If, on the other hand, he remains in a seated position and his buttocks remain in contact with the ground, his ablutions are not invalidated; the same holds true if someone falls asleep while standing up, while in a full bow such as the bow one makes during ritual prayer, or while prostrating himself, since in all these positions he will remain in control of himself. Similarly, if one sleeps lightly enough while lying down that he is able to hear the speech of those around him, his ablutions will not be invalidated; if he cannot hear them, however, his ablutions will be invalidated. Support for the view that sleep invalidates ritual ablutions only if one is in a reclining position may be found in the saying of the Prophet that, "Ritual ablutions are only required of someone who falls asleep lying down, since when one lies down, his joints relax." (This hadith was narrated by Abū Dāwūd, al-Tirmidhī, Aḥmad in his *Musnad*, and al-Ṭabarānī in his *Mu'jam*.) The Hanafis view the reclining position as analogous to two other positions, namely, sleeping while resting the back of one's neck on something, or while resting one's weight on one hip, since the basis for the rulings on such situations is whether the joints [and muscles] in the hips become relaxed. As for people who suffer from urinary incontinence or the inability to prevent themselves from breaking wind,

part of the body, while the second (*mass*) refers specifically to touching with the hand.[70] As for touching (*lams*) someone who is sexually desirable, it invalidates ritual ablutions under specified conditions, the details of which are spelled out by each of the four schools.[71]

---

sleep is not considered to invalidate their ablutions. Since what comes out of such a person because of either condition does not invalidate his ablutions while he is awake, it makes even less sense for them to be seen as doing so while he is asleep.

* * *

As for the Shafiis, they hold that sleep invalidates ritual ablutions if the person sleeping does not have his buttocks firmly in contact with his resting place, for example, by being in an upright seated position or riding without any space separating his buttocks from the surface beneath him. Hence, if someone were to sleep on his back or side, or if there were some space between his buttocks and the surface under him—as might be the case if someone were very thin—his ablutions would be invalidated. However, ablutions are not invalidated by mere drowsiness, which is defined as a heaviness in the head whereby one can hear the speech of those around him, although he might not understand what they are saying.

* * *

According to the Hanbalis, sleep invalidates ritual ablutions under all circumstances unless it is what would be commonly recognized as a light sleep, and unless the person sleeping is seated upright or standing.

* * *

The Malikis hold that sleep invalidates ritual ablutions if it is a heavy, brief sleep, or if it is a prolonged sleep, regardless of whether the person sleeping is lying down, sitting upright, or prostrating. As for a light sleep, it does not invalidate ritual ablutions regardless of whether it is long or short; nevertheless, it is recommended that one repeat his ablutions after a light sleep if it was a prolonged one.

Ritual ablutions will be invalidated by a short, heavy sleep if the person sleeping does not have the relevant orifices blocked off, for example, by rolling up a garment and placing it between one's buttocks, then sitting down on it, after which the person wakes up while still in this position. As for a long heavy sleep, it invalidates ritual ablutions under all circumstances, even if the person sleeping has blocked off the relevant orifices. As for the definition of a heavy sleep, it is one in which the person sleeping cannot hear voices or feel it when he slips out of the position in which he was sitting (supposing he had been sitting with his legs drawn up and wrapped in a garment), when something falls out of his hand, when he drools at the corners of his mouth, and so on.

70. The Shafiis and the Hanbalis combine rulings on *lams* with rulings on *mass*, whereas the Malikis and the Hanafis list rulings on each type of touching separately, with *mass* being restricted to touching with the hand.

71. According to the Shafiis, touching a 'strange' woman [the word 'strange' here refers to any woman who is not a *maḥram*] invalidates ritual ablutions even if it is not accompanied by any physical pleasure. This ruling applies, moreover, even if the man doing the touching is elderly, and even if the woman is elderly and

unattractive. Someone might object to this ruling, saying: Touching an elderly, unattractive woman would not be expected to give someone sexual pleasure. However, the Shafiis' reply to this objection is that as long as a woman lives, there is always someone who might find pleasure in her. Such touching invalidates ritual ablutions provided that there is no barrier between the skin of the person touching and the person being touched. However, even a piece of sheer fabric or a layer of accumulated dirt, but not perspiration, is sufficient to serve as such a barrier. On the other hand, one man's touching another man does not invalidate one's ablutions, even if the one being touched is a handsome, beardless young man, nor does a female's touching another female or a hermaphrodite's touching another hermaphrodite, a man, or a woman. Provided that the people involved have normal sexual inclinations, such touching only invalidates ritual ablutions if the person touching and the person being touched reach the point of experiencing sexual desire.

The Shafiis hold that a woman's hair, teeth and fingernails may be touched without one's ritual ablutions being invalidated even if one experiences pleasure in doing so, since in general, touching these parts of the body does not bring physical pleasure. Someone might object to this ruling, saying: One's teeth are in the mouth, and the teeth, even more than other parts of the body, have been the subject of erotic poetry and a source of pleasure for a number of people. How, then, can it reasonably be claimed that they are not generally a source of pleasure? In response to such an objection the Shafiis say: If one disregards the mouth and touches what surrounds the teeth, they will be found to be nothing but bones which give pleasure to no one. This is what is meant by saying that generally speaking, the teeth are not a source of physical pleasure.

According to the Shafiis, ritual ablutions are invalidated by touching the dead. However, they are not invalidated by touching a *maḥram*, that is, a woman whom it would be permanently unlawful for the person doing the touching to marry due to kinship based on blood ties, marriage, or having nursed from the same woman's breast. However, if it is a woman whom it would not be unlawful to marry under all circumstances, such as one's wife's sister, her paternal aunt or her maternal aunt, then touching her will invalidate a man's ritual ablutions. Similarly, one's ablutions are invalidated by touching with sexual desire the mother or daughter of a woman with whom one has a sexual relationship because, although the man would be definitively prohibited from marrying either of them, this prohibition is nevertheless not based on blood ties, having nursed from the same woman's breast, or relationship by marriage. Moreover, as was noted earlier, the Shafiis make no distinction between rulings on *mass* and on *lams*.

* * *

According to the Hanbalis, a man's ablutions are invalidated by his touching a woman with sexual desire and without the presence of a barrier between his skin and hers. It makes no difference in this regard whether the woman is 'strange' or a *maḥram*, dead or alive, young or old, large or small, so long as she is potentially desirable. Similarly, if a woman touches a man with physical desire and without a barrier between his skin and hers, her ablutions will be invalidated. However, touching only invalidates one's ablutions if what is touched is a part of the body other than the hair, the teeth, the fingernails or the toenails. As for the person who was touched, his or her ablutions are not invalidated even if he or she experienced pleasure as a result of it. If one man touches another, his ablutions are not invalidated even if the one touched is a handsome, beardless young man; similarly, one woman's touching another does not invalidate her ablutions, nor one hermaphrodite's touching another, even if the person doing the touching experienced pleasure in doing so.

From the foregoing one may see that the Hanbalis agree with the Shafiis that a man's touching a woman without a barrier between his skin and hers invalidates his ablutions even if she is an aged, unattractive woman so long as she is potentially desirable, while they disagree with them over whether touching a woman who is a *maḥram* invalidates a man's ablutions. As we have seen, the Hanbalis—unlike the Shafiis—hold that it will invalidate a man's ablutions even to touch his mother or his sister. In addition, these two schools agree that one man's touching another man does not invalidate his ablutions even if the one being touched is an attractive, beardless young man. However, the Shafiis hold that in this latter situation, it is a Sunnah-based practice to repeat one's ablutions. The Hanbalis and the Shafiis similarly agree that touching a woman's hair, fingernails, toenails or teeth will not invalidate a man's ablutions. Hence, they only differ on minor details mentioned by the Shafiis, and it is for this reason that we have chosen to present the views of each school separately.

* * *

According to the Malikis, if a person who has performed ritual ablutions touches someone else with his hand or some other part of his body, his ablutions will be invalidated given certain conditions, some of which apply to the person doing the touching and others of which apply to the person touched. The person doing the touching must be an adult and must either: (1) be seeking physical pleasure or (2) experience it unintentionally. Hence, if the person is seeking pleasure, his ablutions will be invalidated even if he does not, in fact, experience any pleasure in the touch. Similarly, if the person touching was not seeking pleasure but experienced pleasure unexpectedly through the touch, his ablutions will be invalidated. As for the person touched, he/she must be either naked or dressed in a revealing manner; however, if the person is dressed modestly, the ablutions of the person who touched him/her will not be invalidated unless: (1) the touch involved grabbing part of the other person's body, or (2) the person doing the touching was in pursuit of pleasure and/or experienced pleasure in the touch. It is also necessary that the person touched be someone who would normally be viewed as desirable by the person doing the touching. Hence, for example, a person's ablutions will not be invalidated by touching a 5-year-old girl who has not become sexually desirable or by touching an elderly woman whom men no longer find alluring, since rather than feeling desire for her, one would tend to feel repelled by her.

With regard to the hair, the Malikis hold that a man's ablutions are invalidated by touching a woman's hair either if his intention is to seek pleasure or if he experiences such pleasure in the touch. If, on the other hand, a woman touches someone's hand with her hair, her ablutions are not invalidated. Similarly, neither the man's nor the woman's ablutions are invalidated if his hair touches hers or if his fingernail or toenail touches hers due to the lack of sensation in one's hair, fingernails and toenails. As we have seen, the essential point with respect to [such] touching has to do with whether one has deliberately sought out or experienced physical pleasure. It makes no difference whether the person touched is a 'strange' woman, a wife, a beardless youth, or a young man with a new beard who would normally be viewed as a source of pleasure. If the person touched is a *maḥram*, such as a sister, a niece, a paternal aunt or a maternal aunt, and if the person doing the touching is feeling sexual desire and seeking physical pleasure but fails to experience such pleasure, his ablutions will not be invalidated merely by his seeking pleasure; however, if the person touched is a 'strange' woman, the man's ablutions will be invalidated under such conditions.

Touching also includes kissing on the mouth, which invalidates ablutions in all cases, even if the person doing the kissing was not in pursuit of pleasure and/or did not experience it, and even if the kiss was given unwillingly. If the sole purpose of the kiss is to bid someone farewell or show compassion and if the person who gives the kiss experiences no physical pleasure in it, it will not invalidate his ablutions; however, if it does give him physical pleasure, his ablutions will be invalidated.

All of the foregoing has to do with the person who does the touching. As for the person touched, if he is an adult and experiences pleasure in the touch, his ablutions will be invalidated. Moreover, if he seeks pleasure in the touching, he becomes a 'toucher,' and the relevant ruling applies to him as well. Nevertheless, a person's ablutions are not invalidated by merely thinking about or looking at someone else even if, in so doing, he seeks or experiences pleasure or has an erection. Of course, if some pre-seminal fluid is secreted as a result of such thoughts or glances, his ablutions will be invalidated due to this secretion, and if he has an emission of semen, he must perform major ablutions on this account.

* * *

According to the Hanafis, touching does not invalidate one's ritual ablutions regardless of what part of the body it involves, even if the person doing the touching and the person being touched are naked. Hence, if a man performs his ritual ablutions and sleeps in the same bed with his wife, and if both of them are naked and they lie in direct contact with each other, their ablutions will only be invalidated under two conditions: (1) if they have secretions such as pre-seminal fluid and the like, and (2) if the man places his genitals on the woman's, in which case the man's ablutions will be invalidated given the following two conditions: first, that the man have an erection, and second, that there be no barrier preventing the heat of one body from passing to the other. As for the woman's ablutions, they will be invalidated by the mere contact if the man has an erection. If, on the other hand, a woman were to sleep with another woman and their bodies were in the same type of immediate contact, the ablutions of both women would be invalidated merely by their genitals touching one another while they were naked. Still another potential situation is for two men to be in similar contact while both are naked, as might occur in a public bath when it is especially crowded; the ruling here is that their ablutions are not invalidated unless the man who initiated the touching has an erection.

It is thus clear that with regard to this ruling, the Hanafis differ from all the other schools. As for the Malikis, they make the invalidation of ritual ablutions dependent on the deliberate pursuit or experience of physical pleasure. Further-

Type Five: Another type of event that could lead to secretions from one of the aforementioned orifices is touching something or someone with one's hand, the ruling on which involves a fair amount of detail. First of all, such touching must involve either touching oneself or someone else. Hence, if someone were to touch someone else, he would be considered the person who does the touching, the rulings on which have been presented. As for someone who touches himself, it is generally held that one does not derive pleasure from touching parts of one's own body. Nevertheless, in addition to Prophetic hadiths which indicate that touching one's own penis does not invalidate ritual ablutions, there are hadiths which support the opposite ruling. Consequently, there is disagreement among the four schools on this matter. One hadith cited in support of the view that touching one's penis does not invalidate ritual ablutions is narrated by the compilers of all the *sunan* (that is, hadith collections) except for Ibn Mājah, according to which the Prophet was once asked about a man who was touching his penis during prayer. In reply he asked, "Is it not simply a part of you?" This hadith is narrated also by Ibn Ḥabbān in his *Ṣaḥīḥ*. Al-Tirmidhī describes this hadith as being "the best thing which has been narrated on this question."

As for those who hold that touching one's penis does invalidate one's ritual ablutions, they cite numerous hadiths in support of their view. According to one such hadith, the Prophet said, "If anyone touches his own penis, let him repeat his ablutions." The Shafiis, Hanbalis and Malikis agree that if someone touches his own penis, his ablutions will be invalidated, whereas the Hanafis hold that they will not.[72]

---

more, the Malikis differ with the Shafiis and the Hanbalis in their ruling on touching an elderly woman who would not be considered sexually desirable, since the Malikis hold that touching such a woman does not invalidate a man's ablutions, whereas the Shafiis and the Hanbalis hold that it does. Similarly with regard to touching an attractive beardless young man, the Malikis hold that it invalidates one's ablutions, while the Shafiis and the Hanbalis hold that it does not. On the other hand, they are in agreement that touching does not invalidate ritual ablutions unless the person touched is naked or dressed in a revealing garment, although the Malikis hold that if the person touched is wearing non-revealing clothing and the person doing the touching grabs part of the other person's body with his hand, his ablutions will be invalidated. These schools also differ in their rulings on touching hair. According to the Malikis, if a man touches a woman's hair, his ablutions will be invalidated if in so doing he was in pursuit of physical pleasure, or if he received such pleasure [whether he was seeking it or not], the reason being that hair is agreed to be something in which people find physical pleasure. However, the Malikis hold that if a woman touches a man with her hair, her ablutions are not invalidated since hair has no sensation. As for the Hanbalis and the Shafiis, they hold that touching the hair does not invalidate ritual ablutions.

72. According to the Hanafis, touching one's own penis does not invalidate one's ritual ablutions even if it is done with sexual desire and regardless of whether one touches it with the palm of one's hand or one's fingers. They base this ruling on

the fact that a man who appeared to be a Bedouin once came to the Messenger of God and asked him, "O Messenger of God, what do you say about a man who touches his penis during prayer?" The Prophet replied, "Is it not simply a part (or a piece) of you?" Nevertheless, in deference to the opposing views of other Muslim scholars, the Hanafis hold that it is desirable to repeat one's ablutions after doing so, since forms of worship which are agreed upon among the schools are superior to those over which there is disagreement provided that one does not commit an act which his own school judges to be undesirable.

Some Hanafis understand the hadith quoted above, namely, "If anyone touches his own penis, let him repeat his ablutions" to mean that one is simply to wash his hands, since it is recommended that one wash his hands after having engaged in such touching in preparation for ritual prayer. Similarly, one's ablutions are not invalidated by touching any other part of one's own body; thus, if one touched his anus, for example, his ablutions would not thereby be invalidated, and the same ruling applies to a woman if she touches her vagina. However, if someone were to insert his finger or some object like the tip of an enema dispenser into the anus until it disappeared inside, his ablutions would be invalidated, since this would involve something's having gone inside the body and come out again. If one inserts only part of his finger but, upon bringing it out again, it is moist or bears an odor, his ablutions will be invalidated; otherwise, they will not. Similarly, if a woman inserts her finger, a piece of cotton, etc., into her vagina and it comes out moist, her ablutions will be invalidated, whereas if it comes out dry, they will not.

* * *

The Malikis hold that ritual ablutions are invalidated as a result of touching one's penis given the following conditions: (1) that it be one's own penis and not that of someone else, since in the latter case, the rulings listed above on touching someone else would apply; (2) that the person concerned be an adult, even if he is a hermaphrodite, although the ritual ablutions of a boy are not invalidated by touching himself; (3) that there be no physical barrier between one's hand and the penis; and (4) that the touching be done with the center or edge of one's palm or with one's fingers. (They note here that this also applies to an extra finger provided that it possesses the same sensation and motor abilities as one's minor fingers.) However, if one touched his penis with any other part of the body, such as his thigh or his arm, his ablutions would not be invalidated. Hence, if one were to touch his own penis with an object such as a stick, or with some barrier intervening between the penis and one's hand, this would not invalidate his ablutions.

If the above conditions are met, a person's ablutions are invalidated regardless of whether he experiences pleasure or not and whether the touch was intentional or unintentional. However, a woman's ablutions are not invalidated by touching her vagina even if she inserts her finger into it, and even if this gives her pleasure; nor are one's ablutions invalidated by touching one's anus or by inserting one's finger into it, even though this is forbidden if done unnecessarily; nor by a man's touching the place where his penis was cut off, nor by touching one's testicles or one's pubic hair, even if such touching is a source of pleasure. As for touching someone else's buttocks or a woman's vagina, it is subject to the ruling on sexual intercourse.

* * *

Type Six involves bodily secretions which are discharged from locations other than the urethra, vagina, seminal duct or anus, such as the pus or blood exuded by a boil, the blood which comes out of a wound, and the like. All such substances are ritually impure and invalidate one's ritual ablutions with variations in detail among the schools.[73]

According to the Shafiis, one's ablutions are invalidated by touching the penis, whether it is attached to the body or has been cut off, provided that in the latter case, it has remained in one piece such that the term 'penis' still applies to it. One's ablutions are likewise invalidated by touching the 'stump', that is, the place at which it was cut off. [This appears to reflect war conditions in which some people were subject to gruesome varieties of torture and mutilation – t.n.] However, it only invalidates one's ablutions given the following conditions: (1) that there be no barrier between one's hand and the place being touched, and (2) that the touching be done with the center of the palm or the insides of one's fingers—that is, the area of the hand which is concealed when one makes a fist with light pressure; however, one's ablutions are not invalidated if the touch is done by the outer edge of the palm, the fingertips, or the area in between.

Like the Hanbalis, the Shafiis do not restrict the meaning of touching (*mass*) to a person's touching his own penis; rather, they hold that it includes touching someone else's penis as well. Hence, they maintain that touching the penis invalidates ritual ablutions whether the penis touched is one's own or someone else's, including that of a young boy or a deceased man. However, only the ablutions of the person doing the touching are invalidated, not those of the person touched. Similarly, a woman's ablutions are invalidated if she touches her genitals, as are those of anyone else who touches them, of course. As for the anus, it is subject to the same ruling as the vagina, according to the Shafiis, whereas touching the testicles and the pubic hair does not invalidate ritual ablutions.

73. According to the Hanbalis, one's ablutions are invalidated by every ritually impure substance which comes out of the body, including places other than the vagina, the urethra, the seminal duct and the anus, provided that it comes out in a 'large' amount. As for the meaning of 'large' and 'small' in this connection, it depends on the body of the person concerned, that is, on the person's level of strength and physical size. Thus, for example, if a thin person bled and the amount of blood were large with respect to the size of his or her body, his or her ablutions would be invalidated; otherwise, they would not. The Hanbalis apply the same principle to vomit as well.

Ritual ablutions are invalidated by apostasy.[74] Hence, if someone who has performed ritual ablutions renounces the religion of Islam, his ablutions cease to be valid. Such an occurrence is common among ignorant folks who fly into a rage and utter blasphemous words without concern for the consequences, then later regret what they have done. If people who behave in this way are ritually pure at the time of their outburst, they cease to be ritually pure and need to repeat their ablutions. It will be clear that this is one of the least serious penalties associated with apostasy. Moreover, if people were aware that apostasy thwarts people's good actions and renders them of no effect, they would exercise more self-control and keep themselves from uttering words which bring great harm and serve no good purpose.

Ritual ablutions are not invalidated by laughing out loud[75] during ritual prayer or by eating the meat of a slaughter camel, be it full-grown or young or by performing major ablutions on behalf of a deceased person.[76]

Nor are ritual ablutions invalidated by doubts[77] as to whether or not one is in a state of ritual purity. The following are two illustrations of such doubts: (1) After performing one's ablutions with certainty, the person has doubts, thinking: did something happen after that to invalidate my ablutions or not? However, such doubts do not invalidate one's ablutions, because the person has doubted the occurrence of the *ḥadath*, but not the performance of ritual ablutions, of which he is certain, and doubt cannot remove the certainty of one's ritual purity. (2) Someone performs his ritual ablutions with certainty, then has an occurrence of *ḥadath* also with certainty. However, the person wonders: Did I perform my ablutions before the *ḥadath*, which

---

74. According to the Hanafis, ritual ablutions are not invalidated by apostasy, even though apostasy serves to nullify many of an individual's actions, whether their aims be spiritual and religious, or material and practical. Further clarification of this point is found in Part IV of this work, to which readers may refer if they wish. [To date, Part IV only exists in the original Arabic – t.n.]

The Shafiis hold that apostasy does not invalidate ritual ablutions if the person concerned suffers from no type of incontinence; if he does, however, his ablutions will be invalidated by apostasy since, due to the nature of this condition, his ritual purity is deemed 'weak.'

75. The Hanafis hold that laughing out loud during ritual prayer invalidates one's ritual ablutions, a topic concerning which there are a number of hadiths. According to one such hadith, narrated by al-Ṭabarānī on the authority of Abū Mūsā, one day as the Prophet was praying with the community, a certain man with poor eyesight came in and fell into a hole in the mosque. Many of those in the mosque laughed at the sight even though they were in the midst of prayer, and the Messenger of God instructed those who had laughed to repeat both their ablutions and their prayers. Hence, it is ruled that if someone laughs out loud during prayer, his ablutions will be rendered invalid even if he happens to have laughed only briefly.

If, by contrast, someone praying were to laugh to himself such that no one else could hear him, his ablutions would not be invalidated, but the prayer itself would lose its validity. Moreover, laughing out loud only invalidates one's ablutions if the person concerned is an adult, whether man or woman, and whether or not the person is conscious of his behavior. However, if the person is a child, his ablutions will

would mean that my ablutions have been invalidated? Or did I do them after the *ḥadath*, in which case they are still valid?

This second illustration includes two possible scenarios. In the first scenario, the person thinks back to before the ablutions and the *ḥadath* and has doubts about which of them occurred first. Then, if he recalls that he had had an occurrence of *ḥadath* before his ablutions, he can consider himself in a state of ritual purity because he is certain that he performed his ablutions after the first *ḥadath*, while he has doubts regarding the second occurrence of *ḥadath*. For as we have seen, mere doubt does no harm in the view of the Hanafis. For example, suppose that someone is certain that he performed his ablutions after noon; he is also certain that he had an occurrence of *ḥadath*. However, he is doubtful as to whether the *ḥadath* took place first, in which case his ablutions are still valid, or whether he did his ablutions first, in which case they have been invalidated. If such a situation presents itself, the person should think back to before noon. If he recalls that he was in a state of ritual impurity before noon, he may consider himself to be ritually pure since noon. The reason for this is that he is certain about the first *ḥadath* which took place before noon, just as he is certain of the ablutions which he performed after noon, his only doubt being over the second *ḥadath* after noon: did it occur before his ablutions or afterwards? Hence, since doubt does not negate certainty, he may consider himself ritually pure.

In the second scenario, a person remembers that he had performed his ablutions before noon. He performed his ablutions again after noon as well, then had an

---

not be invalidated by laughing out load. In order for laughing out loud to render ablutions invalid, it is also necessary that it take place during a minor ritual prayer involving bowing and prostration. If it takes place while one is performing a prostration of recitation or something similar, his ablutions will not be invalidated, but his prostration itself will no longer be valid.

According to the Hanafis, if someone decides to conclude his ritual prayer with an audible laugh rather than the usual greeting of peace, his ablutions will be invalidated, but his prayer will remain valid, as will be seen below. Nevertheless, if one chooses to conclude ritual prayer in this manner, he will have committed a discourtesy while speaking privately with his Lord and neglected the duty of delivering the greeting of peace, as will be discussed in the section on ritual prayer.

76. According to the Hanbalis, either eating the meat of a slaughter camel or administering major ablutions to a deceased person will invalidate one's ablutions.

77. According to the Malikis, a person's ablutions are invalidated if he suspects that he is not in a state of ritual purity. For example, after performing one's ablutions, one might wonder whether or not he had broken wind or touched his penis. Or, after the occurrence of some type of *ḥadath*, a person might wonder whether he has performed his ritual ablutions since then or not. Similarly, after the occurrence of some *ḥadath* and the performance of one's ablutions, one might wonder which came first—the *ḥadath* or the ablutions. All these situations, according to the Malikis, lead to the invalidation of one's ritual ablutions, since one's religious obligation cannot be fulfilled without complete certainty, and one who doubts has no such certainty.

occurrence of *ḥadath*. Now, if such a person is in the habit of renewing his ablutions after each prayer,[78] then once he prays the noon prayer, he will consider himself with certainty to be ritually impure (in other words, to have had an occurrence of *ḥadath*). After noon, then, he renewed his ablutions and had another occurrence of *ḥadath* but is uncertain as to which came first—his ablutions or the second *ḥadath*—he is not considered to be in doubt about the invalidation of his ablutions, since he is certain that he performed his ablutions [before noon], and he is likewise certain after this to have had an occurrence of *ḥadath* [since he automatically considers himself to have become ritually impure again after each prayer]. Hence, if he repeats his ablutions a second time, they will be viewed as a renewal of the initial ablutions, which he knows that he performed after the *ḥadath* which he is sure about, and as such, they will not be viewed as removing it [since this initial *ḥadath* had already been removed by his first ablutions]. [Consequently, he may consider himself ritually pure based on the same principle stated above, according to which doubts concerning ablutions one has performed with certainty do not undo their effect – t.n.]. If, on the other hand, this person is not in the habit of renewing his ablutions after each prayer, he may consider himself already to be in a state of ritual purity, since the second performance of his ablutions will have removed the *ḥadath* which he has doubts about.

The aforementioned rulings apply to someone who doubts his ablutions after having completed them. On the other hand, if while a person is performing his ablutions, he has doubts concerning a particular part of his body, then all he has to do is redo the part of his body about which he has doubts.

As we hope will be clear to our readers, we make mention of such academic minutiae in view of the benefit they may provide for seekers of knowledge. As for ordinary laypersons, they need not be aware of such particulars unless necessity requires it—unless, for example, they find themselves in a location where water is scarce or find it difficult to repeat their ablutions due to old age, weakness, or cold and, at the same time, are in a condition which does not allow them to perform sand ablutions and the like. Hence, Muslim scholars have spared no effort to clarify all relevant rulings, whether they benefit the general public or only certain individuals.

On Abstersion and the Rules of Conduct Associated with Eliminating Bodily Wastes

As may be seen from our discussion of those events and substances which invalidate ritual ablutions, all of the schools agree that ritual ablutions are rendered invalid by the secretion of urine, feces, *madhī,* or pre-seminal fluid, and *wadī,* or the fluid which is often secreted following a man's urination. When one or more of these substances are secreted by the body, it is not sufficient simply to perform

78. According to the Hanbalis, such a person should act on the assumption that whatever his original state was [for example, that he was originally not ritually pure], he is in the opposite state now [i.e., ritually pure], even if he is in the habit of renewing his ablutions.

ritual ablutions while the site from which they were secreted remains contaminated. Rather, it is necessary to dry and clean the site at which the impure substance was secreted. Consequently, it is only fitting that we should place this section after the discussion of those events and substances which invalidate ritual ablutions, since in fact it forms a part of it.

This process of drying and cleaning, referred to as *istinja',* or 'abstersion', consists of four essential elements, namely: (1) the person engaging in abstersion, (2) the impure substance which has contaminated the vagina, urethra, seminal duct or anus, (3) the materials used to perform abstersion, such as water, stones, etc., and (4) the site being cleaned, specifically, the vagina, the urethra, the seminal duct or the anus. These are the basic elements without which abstersion cannot be carried out.

The following discussion will deal with two main topics, namely, the process of abstersion and the elimination of bodily wastes (relieving nature). In connection with abstersion, we will provide a definition of this process and the various rulings related thereto. As for the elimination of urine or feces, it will be discussed under three subheadings: (1) the ruling on this process, (2) those places in which one is not permitted to eliminate bodily wastes, and (3) those situations in which one is forbidden to do so.

The definition of abstersion (*al-istinjā'*)

Abstersion is the process by which a substance which has come out through the vagina, the urethra, the seminal duct or the anus is removed from the site at which it exited the body, whether with water, stones or some other material. This process is sometimes referred to in Arabic as *istiṭābah,* as it is likewise called *istijmār*, which means, specifically, to clean oneself with stones (derived from the noun *jimār*, meaning small stones). *Istinjā'* is also called *istiṭābah*, which means literally 'to find something pleasant and agreeable' due to the pleasant sense of relief which one experiences in the removal of the impure substances. As for the term *istinjā'* itself, it is derived from the verb *najā/yanjū*, which means to cut, as in "I cut down the tree," since the person who engages in this process is 'cutting off,' or removing, the impurity from the site at which it came out.

Ideally, abstersion is done with water, and performing abstersion with water alone is a practice which was acceptable among bygone nations. It is reported that the first person to have performed abstersion with water was the prophet Abraham—may peace and blessing be both upon him and our prophet Muḥammad. Nevertheless, the munificence and ease of the Islamic religion has led to the allowance of abstersion with stones or with anything that will not bring harm to the body, details on which will be presented below in the description of how to perform abstersion.

The ruling on abstersion

Based on the foregoing definition of abstersion, it is a religious obligation.[79] Hence, one must perform abstersion to remove any and all impure substances secreted by the body—even if a given secretion only occurs rarely—such as blood, pre-seminal fluid and *wadī*. It is also necessary for the substance secreted to have ceased flowing before one commences abstersion; otherwise, one's abstersion will have no validity (according to the Shafiis and the Hanbalis).

---

79. According to the Hanafis, abstersion or *istijmār*, i.e., cleaning oneself with small stones, is an emphatically enjoined Sunnah-based practice for both men and women such that it is deemed undesirable for an accountable individual to neglect it. Specifically, abstersion with water or cleaning oneself with small stones is called for by the Prophetic Sunnah if the impurity has not spread beyond the site of the orifice through which it was secreted, such as the area immediately surrounding the anus which ceases to be visible when one stands up, and the area immediately surrounding the urethra from which urine is eliminated. In this regard, it makes no difference whether the substance secreted is a normal, minor secretion or an abnormal or unusual one, such as blood, pus and the like. Hence, if the impurity spreads beyond the site of the orifice and he sees that it amounts to more than a dirham, removing it is obligatory and water is prescribed. Since the substance is found outside the immediate area surrounding the relevant orifice, its removal is not considered to be part of the process of abstersion, but rather, the simple removal of impurities, which always requires water. Similarly with respect to urine found on the tip of the urethra [that is, on the glans of the penis]: if it amounts to more than one dirham, it is not sufficient to remove it with stones and the like; rather, it must be washed off with water. The same ruling applies to urine found on the foreskin of an uncircumcised man. The view just explained is that of "the two shaykhs" [that is, Abū Ḥanīfah and his companion and disciple Abū Yūsuf al-Qāḍī. The original text reads, "the two companions," which generally refers to Abū Ḥanīfah's companions and disciples Abū Yūsuf al-Qāḍī and Muḥammad ibn al-Ḥasan al-Shaybanī; however, given the reference in what follows to "Muḥammad" as a third party, it seems most probable that "the two shaykhs" is what the writer intended – t.n.]. As for Muḥammad, may God be pleased with him, he holds that if the impurity spreads beyond the site of the orifice, it must be washed off with water whether it amounts to more than a dirham or not. It appears from this view that one is required to wash off everything found on or around the orifice, because the impurity spreads as a result of washing what is found beyond the opening. This, of course, is the most conservative stance, even if the two companions' view is the preferred one. This [stricter view] may be given greater weight in some situations and less in others. For example, where water is plentiful, as in metropolitan areas, the ideal, of course, is to wash and clean the area entirely, thereby removing all impurities as well as any unpleasant odor. However, if water is scarce, as it is in desert areas, or if it is difficult or impossible for a person to use water for whatever reason, the view put forth by the two companions may be given greater weight.

In sum, the Hanafis hold that it is an emphatically enjoined practice based on the Prophetic Sunnah to remove whatever impurities are found on the orifice through which they were secreted, regardless of whether they are normal, regular secretions such as urine and stool, or irregular secretions such as pre-seminal fluid, post-urinary secretions, blood, and so forth; moreover, this ruling applies regardless of whether the substance is removed with water or something else. This process is referred to variously as *istinjā'* (abstersion), *istijmār* (cleaning with small stones) or *istiṭābah* (making agreeable or pleasant). As for that which has spread beyond the opening and the area immediately around it, the process of cleaning it off is obligatory, but it is not referred to as abstersion; rather, it is simply a matter of removing impurity with water. In this regard one might ask: In order for this to be obligatory, is it necessary for the amount of the impurity to be greater than a dirham? As we have seen, there is a difference of opinion between the "two [shaykhs]" on one hand, and Muḥammad, on the other, with Muḥammad stating that such impurity must be washed off with water even if it amounts to less than a dirham, whereas according to the former, water is not required unless the impurity which has spread beyond the opening amounts to more than a dirham. Moreover, no distinction is made here between the man and the woman except with regard to what is referred to as *istibrā'*, that is, expelling whatever urine or stool remains in the opening until one is fairly certain that no more remains. This process is not required of the woman; rather, all she must do is wait briefly after urinating or passing stool, then either perform abstersion, clean herself with small stones, or a combination of the two. If someone cleans himself with small stones and a trace of the impurity still remains, after which his buttocks perspires and his perspiration gets onto his clothing, his clothes will not be considered contaminated even if the impurity which has gotten onto them amounts to more than a dirham. If, on the other hand, the same person gets into a small amount of water, such as a small bathtub, he will contaminate the water. From this it becomes clear that the essence of abstersion—namely, the removal of those impurities found only on the opening through which they were secreted (and not on the area beyond this)—is not [viewed by all as] obligatory, while the removal of what has spread beyond this is not part of abstersion, but rather, the [obligatory] removal of impurity. Abstersion might be viewed as merely desirable; for example, if someone urinates but does not pass stool, it is desirable for him to wash the site from which the urine came out unless the urine has spread beyond the orifice, in which case he is obliged to wash it off with water. Abstersion might also be viewed as a mere innovation, as it is if someone performs abstersion after breaking wind.

When measuring solid impurities, a dirham is estimated at 20 carats, and when measuring liquid impurities, it is estimated at one palmful. As for a carat, it was once estimated to be equal to the weight of five unhusked grains of barley; however, as it is known in our times, a carat is estimated to equal the weight of one medium-sized carob seed, which in turn weighs the same as four grains of locally grown wheat, and one dirham is equal to sixteen carob seeds. Based on these measures, one may estimate amounts with relative accuracy, thereby striving to adhere to the ideal conduct.

* * *

According to the Malikis, abstersion is fundamentally a recommended practice; hence, when someone relieves nature, it is recommended that he remove whatever impurity remains on the relevant orifice with water or stones. However, they hold that in the following situations, the use of water to remove impurity is not merely recommended, but obligatory.

One: When a woman urinates, whether she is a virgin or not. In such a case, she must wash the entire area of her vagina which is visible when she is sitting down, regardless of whether the urine has spread beyond the vaginal area to her buttocks or not. However, if the spread of urine beyond the vaginal area becomes a chronic problem such that it begins to happen at least once a day, it is viewed as a type of incontinence and may be overlooked.

Two: When the impurity spreads so far beyond the orifice from which it came that it contaminates an uncustomarily large area, for example, by the stool's spreading to the outer buttocks, or the urine's covering most of the glans. In such cases, the entire area must be washed with water, and it is not permissible to restrict oneself to washing off that which [only slightly] exceeds the normal amount.

Three: When a man has an emission of pre-seminal fluid as a result of normal sexual pleasure. In the view of the majority of Maliki jurisprudents, this requires that the entire penis be washed with conscious intention. Even so, if someone had such an emission, then washed his entire penis without conscious intention, after which he performed the ritual prayer, his prayer would be valid based on the prevailing Maliki view. If, on the other hand, he washed part of his penis with conscious intention, then prayed, there are some Maliki scholars who hold that his prayer would be valid, whereas others hold that it would not.

Four: When a man has an emission of semen that does not require major ablutions for the removal of major ritual impurity. This situation might take one of two forms: (1) The person is either in a place where there is not enough water to perform major ablutions, or suffers from an illness which prevents him from doing so. In such cases, he is obliged to perform *tayammum*, or sand ablutions, prior to which he must remove the semen from his penis with water, although it is not necessary to wash the entire organ. (2) The person suffers from incontinence of semen to the extent that he has an emission at least once a day. In such a case, the semen may be overlooked and he will not be obliged to perform abstersion with either water or stones. As in situation (1) above, he would normally be required to wash his penis with water; however, if insufficient water is available, he is exempted from this requirement as well.

Five: When a woman has completed her menstrual period or has given birth but suffers from some condition that exempts her from the obligation to perform major ablutions. (Otherwise, she is obliged to wash her entire body as is the case when a man has an emission of semen.) If a woman's menstrual period ends or her postpartum bleeding stops, yet she suffers from an illness which renders her unable to wash with water or if she is in a place where she has insufficient water to bathe herself, she must perform sand ablutions, and if she has enough water with which to perform abstersion, she must do so with water, as it will not suffice to wipe herself with small stones and the like.

Finally, it should be noted that it is considered undesirable to perform abstersion after passing wind.

Rules of conduct associated with eliminating bodily wastes

As we have seen, the Lawgiver has provided rulings with respect to the elimination of bodily wastes, be it urination or other related processes. Some rulings have to do specifically with how to remove impurities once they have been eliminated, for example, the rulings on abstersion (*istinjā'*), which is done with water, and on *istijmār*, which is performed with stones or some other suitable material. Having presented the rulings on abstersion as interpreted by the various schools, we now proceed to a discussion of the rules of conduct associated with the actual elimination of bodily wastes.

There are some who may ask in this connection: Since eliminating bodily wastes is a natural phenomenon which forms a natural part of people's day-to-day lives and which varies according to their particular conditions and circumstances, having to fulfill legal requirements in this regard will oblige people unnecessarily to do things which cause them hardship. However, such protests are no different from other objections raised by those who wish to dodge the responsibilities laid upon them by Islamic law in all aspects of their lives. Otherwise, what difference is there between the restrictions laid down by the Lawgiver in connection with menstruation, sexual intercourse, and so on, and the restrictions to be presented in what follows?

Fortunately, Islamic law provides a degree of cleanliness which is acceptable to the mind, necessary for the health of the body, and required by an ordered social life. Moreover, although Islamic law is not accountable to us for reasons or causes, since—as we indicated in the first chapter on ritual purity—the responsibilities which it lays upon us are specially suited to human beings, and because they involve acts of worship which no human being has the right to protest against unless he is incapable of performing them, it has nevertheless given us something which is eminently reasonable, having legislated for people those forms of worship which suit their social conditions and the requirements of their bodily well-being. After all, who would dare to say that keeping oneself free of bodily impurities is unnecessary?! Who would dare to say that the rules of etiquette to be presented below are of no benefit to people?! For in fact, the entire law of Islam is for the good of society, an expression of kindness toward human beings, and it contains nothing but sensible limitations with which no one could find fault.

In what follows, then, we present those rulings which relate to the elimination of bodily wastes, including an explanation of associated practices which are judged to be obligatory, forbidden, recommended or undesirable.

One: It is obligatory for a person who wishes to perform abstersion first to engage in *istibrā'*, that is, to expel all of the urine or stool which he possibly can in order to make certain that nothing more remains to be eliminated. It is common for some people, after they have urinated, to have some additional urine come out if they walk, rise to a standing position, or make some ordinary movement following this. Hence, when someone wishes to perform abstersion, he needs to engage first in *istibrā'*, since is it not permissible to perform ritual ablutions when one is uncertain as to whether he has finished urinating or not. If someone performs his ablutions while in such a state of uncertainty, and if a drop of urine comes out as he is performing them, his ablutions will have no value. Hence, he is obliged to expel whatever might be present [in the bladder or the bowels] until he is certain that nothing more is left. This point is agreed upon among all of the schools, although some hold that *istibrā'* is only necessary if one is fairly certain[80] that something remains to be expelled, while others hold that it is necessary every time in order that one may be certain that nothing remains; however, the difference between these two views is of little consequence.

Two: It is forbidden to relieve nature on top of a grave,[81] the reason for which is obvious, since a gravesite is a bearer of warnings and admonitions. Consequently, it is discourteous and unseemly for someone to reveal his private parts over such a site and contaminate it with the filth of his bodily wastes.

There are sound hadiths to indicate that the Prophet urged people to visit graves as a means of reminding themselves of the afterlife. Hence, it is a sign of ignorance and foolishness that people would make use of places which are visited as a means of remembering God and taking spiritual lessons to heart as sites on which to urinate and defecate. As for hadiths on this subject, they do not contain an explicit prohibition. We have, for example, a hadith narrated by Muslim, Abū Dāwūd and others according to which the Prophet stated, "It would be better for someone to sit on smoldering embers until they had burned his clothing and through to his skin than to sit on a grave." This hadith has been taken by some scholars as a warning against sitting on a grave in order to relieve nature. However, there is nothing in the text to indicate that this is what is meant. Rather, what the hadith is referring to is sitting on a grave as a place for conversation and diversion as is the custom of some ignorant village dwellers who use certain graveyards as places to sit in the sun or shade and chat; in other words, they gather in graveyards the way city dwellers gather in clubs. There can be no doubt that this practice is inconsistent with the sense of reverence and readiness to receive admonition which is required when one visits a grave, not to mention the lack of respect which it shows for such a place. According to a hadith narrated by Ibn Mājah with a good chain of transmission, the Messenger of God issued a warning of unmistakable severity, saying, "I would rather step on a live coal or scorching earth or patch my sandals with the skin of my own foot than walk over a grave." The severity of the warning is obvious. Indeed, the Prophet of God would have preferred to patch his sandal with the skin of his foot than to walk on a grave. This topic will be dealt with further in the section on funerals, God willing.

---

80. The Shafiis are the only school which holds that *istibrā'* is unnecessary unless one is fairly certain that there remains some impurity to be eliminated.

81. The Hanafis hold that relieving nature on top of a grave is not utterly forbidden, but undesirable to the point of being nearly forbidden, although they agree with the other schools that anyone who engages in such an act is guilty of wrongdoing. The position taken on this matter by the other schools is that it involves serious wrongdoing; moreover, their view is the most intuitively apparent for the reasons we have mentioned.

Three: It is not permissible to relieve nature in standing water. It is narrated by Jābir on the authority of the Messenger of God that he prohibited urination in standing water; the same prohibition is narrated by Muslim, Ibn Mājah, and others. Moreover, if urination in such water is prohibited, then passing stool is as well, since the latter is even more objectionable and, as a consequence, the prohibition against it is more severe. Each school has its own detailed rulings on the prohibition against urination in water.[82]

---

82. According to the Malikis, eliminating bodily wastes in standing water is prohibited if the amount of water is small; however, if it is wide and deep such as that found in sizable cisterns and the ponds located in large gardens, urinating in them is not prohibited unless the water is someone else's property and its owner has not granted permission to use it, or if the owner has granted permission to use it, but not to urinate in it; in these latter cases, urinating in such water is forbidden. On the other hand, if it is running water, it is permissible to urinate in it unless it is someone else's property and the owner has not given permission to urinate in it, or unless it is public property that has been set aside for a specific use [such as the performance of ablutions].

As for the Hanafis, they hold that relieving nature in a small amount of standing water is strictly forbidden, while if the amount of water is large, urination in it is undesirable to the point of being nearly forbidden. In other words, the degree of interdiction is mitigated due to the largeness of the amount. If it is running water, urination in it is undesirable, though closer to being lawful, unless the water is someone else's property and its owner has not granted permission to urinate in it or unless it is public property which has been devoted to a specific use; in these two latter cases, it is forbidden to urinate in the water even if it is a large amount.

According to the Hanbalis, passing stool is forbidden in both standing and running water, regardless of whether it is a small amount or a large one. The only water in which it is not forbidden to pass stool is the sea, given the necessities faced by travelers, as well as the fact that the sea is so vast that the effects of such an action are virtually imperceptible. As for urination, it is undesirable in standing water, but not forbidden; it is likewise undesirable in a large amount of running water, but not in a small amount of running water [the implication being that the latter is positively forbidden – t.n.]. These rulings apply provided that the water concerned is not public property which has been devoted to a particular use, or the property of another individual who has not granted permission for the water to be used by the public; otherwise, using it for the elimination of bodily wastes is strictly forbidden.

The Shafiis hold that urination and defecation in water, be it a small or large amount, is not forbidden, but merely undesirable, unless it is owned by someone else who has not granted permission to use it, or unless it is a channel or rivulet which is neither deep nor wide, since in these latter two cases, it is forbidden. However, the Shafiis issue different rulings on the practice of relieving nature in water depending on whether it takes place by day or by night. Hence, they hold that relieving nature in the daytime in a small amount of water, whether it is standing or running water, is undesirable. At night, by contrast, it is undesirable to urinate in water regardless of whether it is a small amount or a large one.

This is among the most admirable of Islamic legal rulings, and it is confirmed by both science and common sense. After all, the contamination of water which has been designated for general human benefit is one of the most reprehensible acts one might commit, not to mention the danger which it poses of spreading infectious diseases such as schistosomiasis and others. Hence, it is one of the virtues of Islam that it has always made the worship of God dependent on the very things which a person requires for his own well-being.

Four: It is forbidden to relieve nature in water sources [such as springs or wells] and in places where people regularly pass or seek shade.[83] This prohibition is based on the hadith narrated by Muslim and Abū Dāwūd according to which the Prophet said, "Beware of the two accursed ones." When people asked him, "O Messenger of God, what are the 'two accursed ones'?" he replied, "he who relieves himself along the paths that people tread or in the places where they find shade." The phrase rendered "the two accursed ones" may also be understood to refer to the two actions which result in a curse for the one who commits them, since someone who urinates or defecates on a public roadway or path exposes himself to curses and insults by doing such a harmful thing. In a variant of the same hadith, narrated by Abū Dāwūd and Ibn Mājah on the authority of Mu'ādh Ibn Jabal, may God be pleased with him, the Prophet said, "Beware of the three accursed things: feces in water sources, in the middle of the path, and in the shade." The phrase rendered, "the three accursed things" might also be rendered "the three places where curse resides," since a person who relieves himself in these places exposes himself to

---

83. The Shafiis and the Hanafis hold that it is undesirable to relieve nature in all such places provided that they are not public property which has been devoted to use as a walkway or belong to another individual; otherwise, it is not only undesirable but forbidden.

The imams of the four schools agree unanimously on the prohibition against urinating or defecating in public places through which people pass, in water sources, and in places where people seek shade. However, the Shafiis and the Hanafis judge this practice to be undesirable to the point of being nearly prohibited, whereas the Malikis and the Hanbalis prohibit it entirely. Both of these points of view may be based on the effect which results from the practice. Thus, for example, if the practice will cause people serious harm or if it will adversely affect public health, it is unanimously prohibited by all four schools, since bringing harm to people and exposing them to illness is absolutely forbidden. Hence, those who judge this practice to be merely undesirable rather than prohibited may have done so in view of the vast isolated areas where there are no places specifically designated for this purpose, and where its harmful effects would not be severe.

84. According to the Hanafis, it is undesirable nearly to the point of unlawfulness to face directly toward or away from the *qiblah* when passing urine or stool, regardless of whether one is outdoors or indoors. If someone absentmindedly sits down on a toilet facing either directly toward or directly away from the *qiblah*, then realizes what he has done, he should shift to a different position if possible. Otherwise, he should avoid so far as possible sitting down on a toilet which faces in one of the forbidden directions. The same ruling applies to abstersion and cleaning

being cursed by others. As for the phrase rendered "the shade," it refers to the shade to which people have repaired in search of rest and relief from the sun (Maliki, Hanbali).

Five: If someone is outside, he is forbidden to relieve himself while either facing directly toward, or directly away from, the *qiblah*; hence, he should turn instead in some other direction.[84] On the other hand, if the person is inside a building and is using either a private toilet or a public lavatory, the Malikis, the Shafiis and the Hanbalis hold that it is not forbidden. Once he has finished relieving himself and wishes either to perform abstersion or clean himself with small stones or some other material, the Malikis and the Hanbalis hold that it is undesirable, but not forbidden [to face directly toward or away from the *qiblah*].[85]

Six: It is undesirable for someone who is urinating to face into the wind lest a spray of urine come back on him and contaminate his body or clothing. As may be clearly seen, this ruling takes into account what is best for the person concerned, since it is only natural for someone to want to avoid unclean substances which might contaminate his body or clothing. Hence, the Lawgiver has declared this action to be undesirable for the sake of preserving people's well-being and encouraging them to pursue cleanliness.

Seven: It is undesirable to speak while relieving oneself due to the disrespect which this shows for the act of speech, as well as a lack of concern for the possibility that while speaking, one might make mention of the name of God or His Messenger or some other revered person or entity. Speaking in such a situation is only undesirable if there is no need to speak; however, if such a need arises, it is not undesirable, as, for example, if one needs to request a pitcher of water or a rag with which to dry off some impurity. The same holds true for a situation in which one must speak in order to rescue a young child or a blind person from harm, to prevent property from being damaged, and the like.

Eight: It is undesirable while eliminating bodily wastes to directly face the sun or the moon,[86] since they are among the divine 'signs' and blessings from which the entire universe derives benefit. This ruling is based on a principle of Islamic law, namely, respect and appreciation for the blessings of God Almighty.

Nine: The following practices are recommended when eliminating bodily wastes: (a) using the left hand to perform abstersion, since the right hand is the one generally used for eating and so on; (b) wetting the fingers of the left hand before they make contact with the impurity so as to prevent it from sticking to them; (c) follow-

---

oneself with small stones or some other material, both of which are undesirable nearly to the point of being forbidden. The Hanafis base these rulings on the hadith according to which the Prophet said, "When you come to a place designated for 'relieving nature,' face neither toward nor away from the *qiblah* while urinating or passing stool."

85. The Shafiis hold that facing directly toward or away from the *qiblah* is not forbidden when one is performing abstersion or cleaning himself with small stones or other materials, but only when actually eliminating wastes.

86. According to the Malikis, it is not undesirable to face the sun or the moon directly in this situation; however, it is a departure from the ideal.

ing this by washing one's left hand with a cleansing agent; and (d) relaxing somewhat when performing abstersion so as to facilitate the process of removing all impurities.[87]

Conditions for the validity of abstersion and cleansing oneself with stones, water or other materials

The water which must be used in order for abstersion to be valid must fulfill two conditions: First, it must be *ṭahūr*, and not merely *ṭāhir*; *ṭahūr* water is likewise required for the removal of impurity following abstersion.[88] Second, it must be capable of removing the impurity. Hence, if all one has is a small amount of water which is insufficient to remove the impurity from the site in such a way that it is restored to the way it was before it was contaminated, then water should not be used at all.

As for the question of whether one should first wash the front (that is, the vaginal area for the woman, and the penis for the man) or the back (the anus and buttocks), the answer to it varies among the schools.[89]

As for stones and other materials with which one might clean oneself, they serve as an acceptable substitute for water even if it is available; however, it is

---

87. According to the Shafiis, it is not merely recommended, but necessary, that one relax while performing abstersion in order to clean off the required areas of the body. However, the Hanafis hold that it is only recommended that one relax during abstersion if one is not fasting, since one's fast may be broken by the entry of water into the orifices being cleaned; more details on this ruling will be found below in the discussion on fasting.

88. According to the Hanafis, it is not necessary to use water which is *ṭahūr* when performing abstersion; rather, it is sufficient for it to be *ṭāhir* (for the difference between water which is *ṭahūr* and that which is simply *ṭāhir*, see the earlier sections on types of water). Nevertheless, they hold that performing abstersion with *ṭahūr* water is preferable due to the fact that all of the schools agree on the validity of using *ṭahūr* water to remove impurity, since in the Hanafis' view it is preferable to adhere to those practices which are agreed upon among the various schools.

89. According to the Malikis, it is recommended that one first wash the front when removing impurity unless he is someone whose urine tends to trickle out when he touches his buttocks with water, in which case this recommendation does not apply.

As for the Hanafis, they hold two views on this matter. The view which represents the legal opinion based on the words of Imam Abū Ḥanīfah is that one should wash the back before the front, since the impurity which is secreted through the anus is grosser than urine, and because, by rubbing the anus and the area surrounding it, urine may be caused to flow, as a result of which there is no benefit in washing the front first.

The Shafiis hold that if someone wishes to perform abstersion with water, it is recommended that he wash the front before the back, whereas if he intends to clean himself with stones, it is recommended that he do the back before the front.

preferable to use water, and even more preferable to combine the use of water and stones [or some other acceptable material]. Regarding those materials which one is allowed to use in performing *istijmār*, there are differing views among the schools.[90]

The Hanbalis hold that if someone wishes to perform abstersion or clean himself with small stones, it is a Sunnah-based practice to begin with the front if he is a male or a female who is a virgin, whereas a non-virgin female has a choice between starting with the front and starting with the back.

90. According to the Hanafis, it is a Sunnah-based practice to engage in *istijmār* using objects which are ritually pure, including soil, old rags, stones, and clods of dry earth or mud. It is undesirable to the point of unlawfulness to perform *istijmār* with forbidden objects, such as bones and dung, because the Prophet forbade the use of such substances for this purpose. The same applies to food eaten by human beings, materials taken from riding animals, and objects which enjoy respect under Islamic law due to the prohibition—recorded in both Muslim's and al-Bukhārī's collections of sound hadiths—against wasting money [or other valued possessions]. Objects which enjoy such respect include any part of the human body, even if it is that of an unbeliever or someone who has died; paper on which words have been written, even if the writing consists of disconnected letters, since letters themselves enjoy respect; and blank paper, provided that it is suitable for being written on. As for paper that cannot be used to write on, it may be used for *istijmār* without any undesirability attached to the practice. It is undesirable to perform *istijmār* with objects which possess material value and the use of which will damage them or destroy their value, although if washing them or drying them off afterwards will restore them to their former state, there is no undesirability attached to their use. It is also undesirable to perform *istijmār* with burnt bricks, earthenware, glass, coal, and smooth stone. If the use of such materials is harmful, it is undesirable to the point of being nearly unlawful, because it is not permitted to use anything which can harm; whereas if it is not harmful, it is closer to being lawful but remains undesirable because it fails to purify the site, and it is a Sunnah-based practice to cleanse the site entirely. It is undesirable to the point of unlawfulness to perform *istijmār* with material taken from a wall belonging to someone else, since it is not permissible to trespass on someone else's property; as for one's own wall or a wall which is rented property, there is no undesirability attached to its use. Hence, if one were to perform *istijmār* with any of the materials mentioned here, it would fulfill the purpose of *istijmār*, but the practice would remain undesirable to a greater or lesser degree depending on the factors mentioned above.

This being said, we refer the reader back to the beginning of this section for details on the conditions which must be met by water used for abstersion and/or the removal of impurities, and the ways in which one may use stones and other materials.

* * *

The Shafiis specify a number of conditions for materials which may be used in performing abstersion; hence, they stipulate: (1) that the substance be solid and ritually pure; (2) that it be capable of removing the impurity (which rules out smooth or flimsy substances); (3) that it not be wet; for if it is wet with anything other than perspiration, it will not fulfill the purpose of abstersion; and (4) that it not be afforded respect under Islamic law. As for those substances or objects which enjoy such respect, they include bread, bones, and materials which contain writing on the Islamic legal sciences such as jurisprudence and hadiths or the tools of such sciences, including grammar, syntax, arithmetic, medicine, and prosody. As for materials on which other topics are written about, they do not enjoy such reverence, provided that they contain nothing taken from the Qur'ān or any of the aforementioned branches of learning. Also included among such revered materials are those containing the name of some highly respected personage such as Abu Bakr, 'Umar [Ibn al-Khaṭṭāb], and the like. Still other materials which enjoy a special respected status and which therefore cannot be used for *istijmār* are those attached to or associated with a mosque, be it stone, wood or anything else (including materials which have been removed from a mosque after originally being part of it); and parts of the human body. This includes even the body of someone who has been judged worthy of execution, given the uniquely human 'image' which every person bears.

In connection with the impurity which is being removed through *istijmār*, the following conditions apply: (1) it must be dry, since stones and other such materials will be of no use in removing it otherwise; (2) it must not have mingled with some other 'strange' type of impurity, or with any pure substance other than perspiration; (3) if it is stool, it must not have spread beyond the area of the buttocks which draws together when one stands up; and (4) if it is urine, it must not have spread beyond the glans of the penis.

The foregoing applies to a man; as for the woman, her *istijmār* is valid on the following conditions: (1) that she wipe an area that extends beyond what is visible when she sits down if she is a virgin; otherwise, she is required to use water; (2) that she not wipe beyond this toward the inside of her vagina if she is not a virgin; otherwise, she too is required to use water. (Similarly, an uncircumcised man is required to cleanse himself with water if the urine comes down onto the foreskin.)

When performing *istijmār*, one must wipe the required area no fewer than three times and each wiping must cover the entire area, even if this means using three different edges of a single stone. If the area is wiped fewer than three times, it will not suffice, even if it is thoroughly cleansed. If, on the other hand, the area is still not clean after being wiped three times, it must be wiped a sufficient additional number of times to obtain this result; in other words, it must be wiped again until nothing remains of the impurity but a trace which is so small that nothing but water or small shards of pottery would get it off.

* * *

According to the Malikis, the materials used for *istijmār* must meet five criteria: (1) They must be dry, such as stones, cotton, and wool, and be detached from the animal from which they originated; otherwise, it is undesirable to use them. If the material is not dry, such as clay, it is impermissible to use it for *istijmār*, since it will cause the impurity to spread further. Hence, if someone does use such a material for *istijmār*, the site must be washed with water afterwards; if the person performs ritual prayer without doing so, he will have prayed while contaminated with impurity (the ruling on which was discussed above in the section on the removal of impurity). (2) The materials must be ritually pure. Performing *istijmār* is not permissible with ritually impure substances such as the bones of an animal which has died (without being ritually slaughtered) or the dung of an animal whose flesh is forbidden. If someone does perform *istijmār* with such a material, then if it is solid, if none of it has dissolved or disintegrated, and if it has removed the impurity from the site, this means that it has served the purpose of *istijmār*, but the person who used it will be guilty of wrongdoing. (3) They must be capable of removing the impurity. Thus, smooth materials such as glass and reeds may not be used due to the fact that they fail to remove the impurity entirely. (4) They must not be harmful. Hence, it is not permissible to use something which has a sharp edge like a knife, jagged stones or broken glass. (5) They must not enjoy a respected status under Islamic law. Materials which are granted such a place of respect include food eaten by human beings, which in turn includes salt, medicaments and paper (due to the edible starch it may contain). Other materials enjoying a place of special respect are those which possess 'dignity,' such as written materials due to the sanctity of letters and words, and objects which are someone else's property, be it private property or a public endowment. Hence, it is forbidden to perform *istijmār* with [materials taken from] a wall which is public property devoted to some particular purpose or which belongs to some other individual. If the wall belongs to the person who wishes to use it for *istijmār*, however, it is merely undesirable but not forbidden. It is likewise undesirable to perform *istijmār* with bones and dung which are ritually pure, although if the impurity is effectively removed with them, they will have served the purpose; the same ruling applies to all objects or materials which are forbidden or undesirable. As for those situations in which one is required to perform abstersion with water, they are presented above in the section dealing with the ruling on abstersion.

* * *

As for the Hanbalis, they stipulate the following conditions for a material which may be used in performing *istijmār*: (1) It must be ritually pure. (2) It must be lawful to the person who wishes to use it; hence, for example, it is not permissible to perform *istijmār* with something which has been obtained illegally or by force. (3) It must be capable of cleansing the site of the impurity such that nothing remains of the impurity but a trace which is so small that only water will remove it. Consequently, it is not permissible to use smooth materials such as glass and the like. (4) It must be solid. Hence, it is insufficient to use clay. (5) It must not be dung, bones, or food, including even the food of a domestic animal. (6) It must not be something which enjoys special respect under Islamic law, such as paper on which the name of God Almighty is written, or which contains writing about hadiths or the science of Islamic law or lists those things which may lawfully be used; however, if it contains statements about things whose use is forbidden, then it does not enjoy special respect. (7) It must not be part of an animal, such as its paw, for example, nor may it be something which was attached to an animal, such as its wool. (8) It must not be something whose use is forbidden, such as gold and silver.

One must wipe the area three times, and each wiping must cover the area in its entirety; if the area is cleansed of the impurity with fewer than three wipings, it will not suffice. Moreover, the orifice must not be contaminated with any substance

How those who suffer from urinary incontinence and the like can maintain ritual purity

As we have seen, the law of Islam contains texts which explicitly call for the elimination of undue hardship and difficulty from people's lives. As God Almighty declares, He "has laid no hardship on you in [anything that pertains to] religion" (22:78). Hence, Islamic law requires accountable human beings to do nothing which would involve undue hardship or difficulty. It is this principle which governs the rulings of Islamic law on those who suffer from illnesses which do not prevent them from working, such as a weakness in the bladder that results in a steady or nearly steady leakage of urine; the same applies to those with chronic flows of preseminal fluid and/or other bodily secretions. Such conditions are referred to as 'incontinence' (*salas*). Also included in this category are conditions such as chronic diarrhea or intestinal ailments such as [amoebic] dysentery, which cause blood or pus to be secreted [through the anus]. The ruling on people with any of these conditions is that in matters pertaining to ablutions and other practices relating to ritual purity, they are to be afforded special treatment appropriate to their situations.[91]

---

other than the impurity which one is removing, and the impurity must not have spread beyond the usual area, for if it does, one must use water as well. The impurity which has been secreted must also not be the remainder of some type of injection [an enema, for example]; otherwise, one must use water to clean it off. Finally, the secretion being cleaned off must not have dried before one begins performing *istijmār*; otherwise, one must use water as well.

It should be noted here that the Hanbalis consider the inside of a non-virgin woman's vagina as part of that which is visible from the outside; however, they hold that it is not necessary to wash it when performing abstersion, but rather, that the woman need only wash that which is visible when she sits down to relieve herself.

91. The Hanafis discuss this matter under three headings: (1) the definition of incontinence, (2) the ruling on incontinence, and (3) what those who suffer from this condition are required to do.

The Hanafis define incontinence (*salas*) as a pathological condition which results in the involuntary passing of urine or gas, vaginal bleeding between a woman's ordinary periods, chronic diarrhea, and other similar recognized diseases. When someone suffers from such a condition, he or she is exempted from some of the requirements relating to ritual purity. However, this exemption does not take effect from the time the condition first sets in; rather, it must continue for the duration of a time period associated with one of the obligatory ritual prayers [for example, from the noon call to prayer to the mid-afternoon call to prayer]. If the condition does not continue for the duration of at least one such period, the person is granted no exemption. Conversely, the exemption is not considered to be invalidated unless the incontinence stops for the duration of one prayer period at the least. As for the continuing validity of the exemption once it has been established, it requires simply that the incontinence still be present, even if only part of the time. For example, if someone experiences urinary incontinence from the beginning to the end of the period for the noon prayer, he will be exempted [from the usual requirements of ritual purity], and he will continue to be thus exempted until the incontinence disappears for an entire prayer period—for example, from the beginning to the end of the period for the mid-afternoon prayer. Thus, if the incontinence continues from the beginning to the end of the period for the noon prayer with the result that the person is granted an exemption, after which it ceases during part, but not all, of the period for the mid-afternoon prayer, even if only once, the exemption will remain valid.

The Hanafi ruling on incontinence is that the person who suffers from it must repeat his or her ablutions for each ritual prayer. Once the person has performed his ablutions, he may pray as many obligatory and supererogatory prayers as he wishes without having to repeat his ablutions for each one. Then, when the period for a given prayer comes to an end, his ablutions will be invalidated by virtue of whatever *ḥadath* had taken place before his exemption took effect. In other words, if the person had performed ritual ablutions before his exemption took effect [that is, before it was established that he suffers from incontinence of some sort], his ablutions will not be invalidated simply by virtue of the fact that the time period for a given prayer has come to an end, but rather, by the occurrence of some type of *ḥadath* other than the one in relation to which he enjoys an exemption, for example, due to passing wind or a flow of blood from some other part of the body. It follows, therefore, that the condition for the invalidation of his or her ablutions is the termination of the time period for a given obligatory prayer. Supposing, for example, that someone who suffers from some type of incontinence does his ablutions after sunrise in order to perform the prayer for the Day of Sacrifice or the Day of Fastbreaking, his ablutions will not be invalidated when the time period for the noon prayer begins. The reason for this is that the commencement of the time period for the noon prayer does not mark the termination of the time period for an obligatory prayer [since the time period for the obligatory dawn prayer had already ended at sunrise]. Similarly, the termination of the time period for the holiday prayer does not invalidate such a person's ablutions, since the holiday prayer is not obligatory. Hence, this person may perform whatever prayers he wishes based on the ablutions which he performed for the holiday prayer until the time period for the [obligatory] noon prayer runs out, at which point his ablutions will become invalid. If, on the other hand, he performs his ablutions before sunrise, his ablutions will be invalidated by the rising of the sun, since this marks the termination of the time period for the obligatory dawn prayer. Similarly if he performs his ablutions after the noon prayer, the Hanafis rule that once the time period for the mid-afternoon prayer begins, they will be invalidated again due to the termination of the time period for the obligatory noon prayer.

As for what is required of the person with an extenuating condition such as incontinence, he or she should treat the condition or at least minimize it as much as possible. Hence, if it is possible for the person to treat himself for this condition through medical science and he neglects to do so, he will be guilty of wrongdoing. If such measures as binding or wrapping the opening, or the use of sanitary napkins for women with vaginal bleeding between their regular periods, help to prevent or minimize the flow, then one is obliged to make use of them. Similarly, if performing ritual prayer while standing up leads one to have a leakage of urine, a flow of blood, and the like, then the person concerned is instructed to pray while sitting down, and if bowing or prostrating has a similar effect, one should pray without bowing or prostrating but instead, pray with gestures of the head and the hands. (More details on this matter will be presented below.)

If someone's clothes are contaminated by such a flow while in the midst of prayer, it is not necessary to wash one's clothes if one believes that if he did so, they would simply be soiled again in the same manner before he has completed the prayer he wishes to perform; however, if the person believes that his clothes will not become ritually impure again before he finishes praying, he must wash them out.

* * *

According to the Hanbalis, if someone suffers a chronic flow of urine or pre-seminal fluid, an inability to hold in intestinal gases, and so forth, his ablutions will not be invalidated by such secretions given three conditions:

One: The person must wash the site of the secretion and bind it with a cloth or something similar, or stuff the opening with cotton or some other material which will prevent the flow to the greatest extent possible. One should do everything in his power to minimize the flow of the impurity concerned, for if he neglects to do so, his ablutions will be invalidated by this flow. Moreover, once one has washed the site and bound it securely, he need not do so again for every prayer.

Two: The flow of the impurity must be chronic in the sense that it does not stop long enough during the time period for any of the daily prayers for the person to purify himself and pray. Hence, if it is customary for the flow to stop long enough for one to perform ritual ablutions and pray, he is obliged to do so during this period of time. Moreover, if the person is not accustomed to having the flow stop long enough to purify himself and pray but such a stoppage happens to occur, his ablutions will become invalid.

Three: The time period for the prayer one intends to pray must have begun. Thus, if one performs his ablutions before the beginning of the time period for the prayer he wishes to pray, his ablutions will not be valid unless he has done his ablutions in order to make up for some prayer he has missed or for a funeral prayer. If the person experiences a secretion of the impurity with the chronic flow, he must repeat his ablutions for every prayer he performs; however, if no such secretion occurs, his ablutions remain valid unless they are invalidated by some other type of *ḥadath*. Once such a person has performed his ablutions, he may pray as many obligatory and voluntary prayers as he wishes. If, during prayer, standing up causes a flow of the impurity, he should pray sitting down. However, if bowing and prostrating also cause the flow to occur, he must continue to bow and prostrate, since it is insufficient to pray merely with gestures of the hands and head.

* * *

As for the Malikis, they hold that the flow of an impurity resulting from urinary or similar incontinence does not invalidate a person's ablutions given the following conditions:

One: The incontinent flow must continue for at least half of the time period for a given prayer. Thus, for example, if someone has urinary incontinence in the morning, and two hours later the flow stops, this person will not be exempted [from the requirement to perform his ablutions and pray while in a state of ritual purity]. Rather, he must wait until the flow of urine stops, then do his ablutions for the performance of the noon prayer. Similarly in the case of someone who suffers from the inability to control the passing of intestinal gas or from diarrhea, if this condition continues for at least half of the time period for the prayer he intends to pray, he is exempted from the requirements of ritual purity; otherwise, he is not.

Two: The incontinent flow must come at times which the person is unable to control or predict. If the person is able to specify the times at which the incontinent flow stops, he should do his ablutions at that time. For example, if one knows that the flow stops toward the end of the time period for the noon prayer, he is obliged to wait until the end of the relevant time period, then do his ablutions and pray. Similarly, if one knows that the flow stops at the beginning of the time period for the noon prayer, he must make a point of praying at this time, and he must not delay praying till the end of the time period as he might if he were free of such a condition. If, on the other hand, the incontinence regularly continues for the entire time period for the noon prayer and most of the time period for the mid-afternoon prayer, the person should delay the noon prayer until this period of time, then perform a delayed combination of the noon and the mid-afternoon prayers while the flow is absent. Conversely, if the incontinence regularly lasts for the entire time period for the mid-afternoon prayer and stops toward the end of the time period for the noon prayer, the person should perform an advance combination of the noon and mid-afternoon prayers at this time.

Three: The person suffering from such a condition must not be able to overcome it through treatment, marriage, and the like. For if the person is able to overcome the condition and does not do so, he will no longer be excused from the regular requirements pertaining to ritual purity. On the contrary, he will be guilty of wrongdoing for not receiving treatment. However, once such a person commences treatment for his condition, he will be forgiven [for whatever lapses he may suffer relating to acts of worship during] the period of treatment.

A man who suffers from incontinence of pre-seminal fluid is not considered exempt from the regular requirements of ritual purity unless he suffers from a pathological condition, and unless the emission of pre-seminal fluid occurs without his experiencing sexual pleasure. However, if he suffers from no pathological condition but simply finds that he regularly has such emissions accompanied by sexual pleasure due to not having married or as a result of looking at or thinking about some object of sexual desire, his ablutions will indeed be invalidated every time, even if it occurs regularly.

In conclusion, it should be noted that the view that the secretion of impurities due to incontinence invalidates one's ablutions unless the aforementioned conditions are met is the most widely accepted view among the Malikis. However, there is another Maliki view which, although it is less widely accepted among them, places less of a burden on those who suffer from this condition. According to this alternative view, impurities secreted due to incontinence do not invalidate ritual ablutions even if the conditions listed above are not met. It is desirable for such persons to perform ablutions if the incontinence is present part of the time. However, if it is present all the time, it is not desirable to do so. This is a view which those suffering from incontinence may legitimately adopt if they are faced with undue hardship and difficulty. After all, though this view is not widely held, it may nevertheless be suited to the circumstances of many people, and there is no reason why they should not benefit from it.

* * *

As for the Shafiis, they hold that a person suffering from incontinence should take measures to prevent the flow of the resulting secretions by stuffing or binding the relevant orifice. If he does so and then performs ritual ablutions, after which he experiences additional flow of such secretions, they will have no effect on the validity of prayer and other forms of worship. However, in order for acts of worship to be permissible to such a person without repeating his ablutions, the following conditions must be met:

One: The person must perform abstersion prior to his ablutions.

Two: He must perform abstersion, the necessary binding of the relevant opening, and ablutions in immediate succession. In other words, immediately after performing abstersion, the person should bind the site from which the impurity is secreted, be it urine, stool or whatever else, with a clean cloth or the like, provided that it is not harmful to him in any way—similar to a bandage that a doctor uses. Then, before any more time has passed and without allowing himself to be delayed by work or procrastination, he must proceed directly to his ablutions, such that there is no separation between the binding and the ablutions, nor between the abstersion and the binding.

Three: The same immediate succession should be maintained when performing the actions involved in the ablutions themselves, so that one washes the face first, then washes the hands without delay.

Four: The person should avoid initiating any activities between completing his ablutions and praying, since otherwise, his ablutions will be invalidated. However, it is permissible to take the time necessary for actions which are directly related to prayer, such as going to the mosque. Hence, if someone does his ablutions at home, then goes to the mosque and prays there, this is acceptable; in other words, the time it takes for him to walk there will not invalidate his ablutions. The same ruling applies if one does his ablutions in the manner mentioned above and then waits till it is time for a congregational prayer or a Friday prayer.

Five: All of the aforementioned actions must be performed after the beginning of the time period for the prayer one intends to pray; if they are performed before this, they will have no validity.

In addition, once his ablutions have been performed in the manner described above, the person suffering from incontinence is only permitted to pray a single obligatory prayer. In other words, he must repeat his ablutions in the prescribed manner before every obligatory prayer. As for supererogatory prayers (*nawafil*), he may pray as many as he wishes based on a single performance of ablutions, whether he performs such additional prayers before or after the obligatory prayer he is permitted to pray.

Major ablutions (*ghusl*)

The performance of major ablutions will be discussed under six headings: (1) the definition of the term *ghusl*, both in terms of its usage generally in the Arabic language and as it pertains specifically to Islamic law, (2) those events or conditions which make major ablutions necessary, (3) the conditions relating to major ablutions, (4) the obligations entailed by major ablutions, sometimes referred to as their pillars, (5) Sunnah-related practices associated with major ablutions, and (6) those actions which are forbidden to someone who is in a state of major ritual impurity.

The definition of *ghusl*

As generally used in the Arabic language, the word *ghusl* refers to the action of pouring water over and rubbing one's body and so forth; the same word may also be used to refer to the water with which something is washed. The related word *ghisl* is a noun which refers to any substance used when washing, such as soap and the like. As for *ghasl*, it is used to refer to the water with which the washing is done. Hence, if you use the word *ghusl*, you are speaking of the familiar action of bathing oneself; if you use the word *ghisl*, you are speaking of something used as an aid in washing such as soap; and if you use the word *ghasl*, you are talking about the water with which the washing takes place. As for the meaning of *ghusl* as it is used in the context of Islamic law, it refers to the use of *ṭahūr* water to wash the entire body in a specified manner. By saying "the entire body" here, we are excluding the performance of minor ablutions, which entails washing only certain parts of the body, as has been explained.

It is hoped that readers will have no difficulty understanding the meaning of the term *ghusl* either in its general usage or in the context of Islamic law. This book is intended for use both by the general populace and those engaging in the specialized study of Islamic law, and its purpose is to enable each person to take from it what he or she finds necessary and useful. Hence, it is not necessary that everyone understand such technical terms; rather, all they need to do is to note the obligations, the Sunnah-based practices, and the other recommended actions relating to *ghusl* and commit them to memory.

As was noted in the section on intention, when a person with such a condition performs his ablutions, he must consciously intend by means of them to make prayer permissible for himself; thus, for example, he might say to himself, "I seek by means of these ablutions to be permitted by the Lawgiver to perform ritual prayer." The reason for this is that given this person's condition, his ablutions are, strictly speaking, not 'real', since they are invalidated by the chronic flow of impurities from which he suffers, be it urine or whatever else. However, the munificence of the Islamic religion makes it possible for him to engage in ritual prayer based on these ablutions lest he be deprived of the reward which such prayer brings. After all, the Islamic law is based on an all-embracing concern for people's well-being both in this world and the next.

That which renders major ablutions necessary

There are six situations in which accountable Muslims are required to perform *ghusl*, or major ablutions:

One: If the glans of a man's penis enters someone's vagina or anus. The mere occurrence of such entry suffices for major ablutions to be required even if no emission of semen takes place. Moreover, each of the four schools sets forth specific conditions which must be fulfilled in order for such entry to necessitate major ablutions.[92]

Two: An emission of sexual discharge on the part of either the man or the woman. This is based on the recognition that the woman too has 'semen' [that is, semen-like vaginal secretions – t.n.], although it tends to remain inside the vagina. As for those who deny this fact, they are simply closing their eyes to the empirically obvious. The emission of semen may take place either while one is awake or while one is asleep. As for emissions which take place while one is awake and in situations other than sexual intercourse, they are sometimes brought on by sexual pleasure, while at other times they might result from illness or pain. As for seminal emissions which take place in response to physical pleasure resulting from fondling, caressing, kissing, embracing, looking at an object of sexual desire, memories, and the like, they require one to perform *ghusl* regardless of whether they came about due to pleasure or memories, or whether they took place only after the pleasure had passed. If someone caresses or kisses his wife without experiencing physical pleasure at the time, after which he has an emission of semen, he is required to perform

---

92. According to the Hanafis, if the glans of the penis or its equivalent [that is, an area at the end of the penis equal in size to the glans] disappears inside the vagina or anus of someone with whom the person could have sexual intercourse, and if it takes place without the presence of a barrier thick enough to prevent heat from being passed between their bodies, it is necessary for both persons to perform major ablutions whether an emission of semen takes place or not. This ruling applies if both people are adults; however, if one of them is an adult while the other is not, only the adult is required to perform major ablutions. For example, if a ten-year-old boy entered a grown woman, only she would be required to perform major ablutions. As for the boy, he would be instructed to perform major ablutions in order for him to get accustomed to this discipline just as he would be instructed to pray at this age. The same ruling applies in reverse to a situation in which a young girl is one of the two parties. If an adult male inserts his penis into the vagina of a domestic animal or a woman who has died, he is not required to perform major ablutions. Similarly, if an adult male enters the vagina of a 'problematic' hermaphrodite, it is required of neither the man nor the hermaphrodite to perform major ablutions. If a hermaphrodite with a male organ enters someone's vagina or anus, neither of the parties is required to perform major ablutions; however, if a man enters the anus of a hermaphrodite, the one who is an adult must do so.

* * *

The Shafiis hold that if the glans of the penis—or the equivalent portion of a penis which has been cut off—enters the vagina or anus, both parties involved are

major ablutions. As for an emission which occurs due to illness, a severe blow to the loins, or some other trauma, it does not require one to perform major ablutions. The aforementioned rulings differ in detail from one school to another.[93]

---

required to perform *ghusl* whether both are adults or not. If one of them is not an adult, his guardian must instruct him to perform *ghusl*; if he does so, it will suffice; otherwise, he must do so after he comes of age regardless of whether or not the person he entered was capable of tolerating sexual intercourse, regardless of whether there was a barrier over the boy's penis which would block his body heat, and regardless of whether the recipient of the act was human or nonhuman, dead or alive. He is likewise required to perform *ghusl* after he comes of age if the recipient was a 'problematic' hermaphrodite and if the entry took place in the anus. However, if it took place in the vagina of a hermaphrodite, neither of the two parties is required to perform *ghusl*, nor is it required of either party if a hermaphrodite enters someone else's anus or vagina. Moreover, if the entry is in the vagina, the penetration must be complete; thus, if the penis simply disappears between the labia, the two parties are not required to perform major ablutions unless there was an emission of semen.

* * *

According to the Malikis, one enters a state of major ritual impurity requiring *ghusl* if the glans of the penis enters the vagina or the anus regardless of whether the one entered is male, female or hermaphrodite, human or nonhuman, dead or alive. If the person who was entered is physically capable of tolerating such entry and if the person who engaged in entry is an accountable adult, he must perform *ghusl*. Moreover, if the person who was entered is an accountable adult, she must perform *ghusl* if the one who entered her is likewise an accountable adult. Hence, if an adult woman is entered by a young boy, she is not required to perform *ghusl* unless she has an emission of vaginal secretions. In order for an adult to enter a state of major ritual impurity, it is also necessary that there not be a barrier on the glans of the penis to prevent the experience of sexual pleasure even if the penis penetrates as far as the woman's clitoris. This is based on the hadith according to which, "If the glans of the man's penis penetrates the woman's vagina as far as the clitoris, then major ablutions are required."

* * *

As for the Hanbalis, they hold that if the glans of the penis disappears inside the vagina or anus of someone capable of tolerating sexual relations, and if it takes place without the presence of a barrier (noting that even a sheer barrier will suffice), both parties must perform *ghusl* provided that the male is at least ten years old and the female is at least nine years old. Moreover, major ablutions are required given the entry of the glans of the penis even if the one entered is a domestic animal or a deceased female. If a hermaphrodite inserts his penis into someone else's vagina or anus, neither party is obliged to perform major ablutions, and the same ruling applies if someone else inserts his penis into a hermaphrodite's vagina. However, if a male inserts his penis into a hermaphrodite's anus, both parties must perform major ablutions due to the fact that with regard to the one who performed the entry, there is no doubt as to his gender.

Three: An emission of semen which takes place while one is asleep, that is, a "wet dream". Hence, if someone wakes up to find that his clothes, his penis, or the front part of his body is moist, he must perform major ablutions unless it becomes clear that the moisture is not semen. Moreover, if the person is uncertain whether

---

That said, let me state here that there is little benefit in discussing such matters, since the aforementioned situations occur only rarely, and I would have preferred to omit this section entirely. However, there might arise a need for it in connection with certain rulings or in particular countries.

93. According to the Shafiis, the emission of semen through its normal channel makes major ablutions necessary on one condition, namely, that one verify that it is semen after it has come out. This ruling applies regardless of whether the emission was pleasurable or not, and regardless of whether it was due to an ordinary cause or an extraordinary cause, for example, having received a blow to one's loins or suffering from an illness which causes such emissions. Consequently, they hold that if a man has intercourse with his wife but does not ejaculate, after which he performs major ablutions and then has an emission without experiencing any pleasure, he must perform them again; hence, the decisive factor in determining the necessity of major ablutions is the emission of semen. Their ruling with regard to the woman is that if she performs major ablutions, after which she experiences the flow of some secretion from her vagina, then if she had already experienced such a flow before performing *ghusl* [assuming that this flow is a result of her own vaginal lubrication], she must perform major ablutions again due to the mixing of her vaginal secretions with the man's semen. On the other hand, if she had experienced no flow from her vagina prior to performing major ablutions [assuming that this indicates that she did not lubricate during intercourse], then she is not required to perform them again, since the flow which she experienced following her major ablutions would be the man's semen alone, which has no effect on the validity of her *ghusl.*

* * *

According to the Hanbalis, the necessity of performing major ablutions is not dependent on the actual flow of semen outside the body; rather, the condition for their necessity is that the man feel the semen leaving his loins and for the woman, that she feel the flow of her vaginal lubrication leaving her thorax [sic], which is the bones of the chest upon which a woman wears a necklace or piece of jewelry. Therefore, in the Hanbalis' view, major ablutions become necessary from the moment at which the man's semen or the woman's vaginal lubrication leaves its point of origin, even if the secretion does not come out of the body. Hence, if a man has intercourse with his wife without ejaculating, after which he performs major ablutions, and if he has an emission of semen after he has completed his *ghusl*, then if the emission is accompanied by sexual pleasure, he must perform major ablutions again; whereas if it is not accompanied by pleasure, it simply invalidates his minor ablutions without requiring him to perform major ablutions again. Moreover, the same ruling applies if the emission occurs as a result of a blow or an illness.

Hence, it may be seen that the Hanbalis stipulate that in order for *ghusl* to be required following an emission of semen that occurs outside of actual intercourse, it must be accompanied by physical pleasure. At the same time, they hold that *ghusl* is necessary even if the man's semen or the woman's vaginal lubrication has simply left its point of origin yet without reaching the penis or the vaginal opening respectively, which is a recognized occurrence. (The Shafiis, by contrast, hold that the experience of physical pleasure is not a criterion for the necessity of major ablutions, but rather, the presence of semen on the tip of the penis and its entry into the woman's vagina, as well as the certainty that the substance is, in fact, semen.)

* * *

As for the Hanafis, they note that an emission of semen due to causes of pleasure other than intercourse may take place in two situations. In the first situation, the semen becomes visible on the genitals in response to sexual arousal and ejaculation. If a man embraces his wife and has an emission of semen without entering her, he must perform major ablutions (although if he enters his wife without ejaculating, he is likewise required to perform them). Moreover, if the semen leaves its point of origin [inside the man's body] accompanied by a feeling of physical pleasure but he holds it in, after which he has an emission of semen unaccompanied by pleasure, he must still perform major ablutions. In other words, in order for the *ghusl* to be obligatory, the semen must leave its point of origin and exit the penis. Consequently, if it leaves its point of origin but does not leave the body, it does not call for the performance of major ablutions.

As for the second situation, it involves a partial ejaculation in response to intercourse or some other stimulus, after which the man performs major ablutions before urinating or allowing the passage of sufficient time to ensure that all of his semen has come out. Then, after he has completed his *ghusl*, what remains of his semen comes out, either with or without a sense of physical pleasure. According to Abū Ḥanīfah and Muḥammad [Ibn al-Ḥasan al-Shaybānī], he is obliged in this case to repeat his *ghusl*, whereas according to Abū Yūsuf [al-Qāḍī], he is not required to do so. However, Abū Ḥanīfah and Muḥammad hold that such a person must perform *ghusl* again only if, before performing it the first time, he did not urinate, walk around, or wait a period of time after his initial emission. If the person did any of these things before performing major ablutions the first time, and if he has a further emission of semen following such ablutions, it is agreed upon unanimously that he is not required to perform them a second time.

The Hanafis likewise hold, in the case of the woman, that if she performs major ablutions following intercourse with her husband, after which some semen flows out of her vagina, she is not required to perform them again. As for a man's emissions of semen which occur not in response to physical pleasure but, rather, due to a blow to one's loins or some illness, they do not render major ablutions necessary.

One may see from the foregoing that the Hanafis differ in this ruling with both the Shafiis and the Hanbalis. First of all, the Hanafis stipulate that in order for major ablutions to be necessary, a man's semen [or a woman's vaginal secretions] must actually exit the body, whereas according to the Hanbalis, major ablutions are required only if the man's semen or the woman's vaginal lubrication leaves its point of origin inside the body, regardless of whether it comes out or not. In addition, the Hanbalis stipulate that this process must be accompanied by physical plea-the cause of the wetness is semen, pre-seminal fluid or something else, he must perform major ablutions regardless of whether or not he recalls having experienced sexual pleasure in his sleep.[94]

Four: Vaginal bleeding due to menstruation or childbirth. This point is agreed upon by all four schools. Therefore, if a woman experiences such bleeding due to menstruation or having given birth, she is required to perform major ablutions when the bleeding stops. [Theoretically speaking], even a bloodless childbirth[95] would

---

sure, even if the pleasure does not last long enough for the semen [or vaginal secretion] to exit the body. As for the Shafiis, they stipulate that the semen [or vaginal secretion] must leave the body, whether it is accompanied by physical pleasure or not. Hence, the Hanafis agree with the Shafiis that the semen must actually exit the body in order for *ghusl* to be required, while they differ with the Hanbalis' insistence that *ghusl* is required by the mere departure of the semen from its point of origin regardless of whether or not it is actually expelled from the body. At the same time, the Hanafis and the Hanbalis agree that in order for *ghusl* to be necessary, the secretion must be accompanied by physical pleasure, whereas the Shafiis do not make this stipulation.

* * *

As for the Malikis, they hold that if someone has an emission of semen following an experience of sexual pleasure but without intercourse, he must perform major ablutions regardless of whether he had performed them before the emission or not. However, if the physical pleasure is a response to intercourse, for example, by the man's entering the woman but not having an ejaculation, only to have an emission after the pleasure is gone, then the man is not required to perform major ablutions if he had already done so prior to the emission.

94. The Shafiis hold that if the person is uncertain whether the wetness resulted from semen or pre-seminal fluid, he is not necessarily obliged to perform *ghusl*; rather, he can either take it to be semen and perform major ablutions, or he can take it to be pre-seminal fluid, wash off the affected area, then perform minor ablutions. In the event that the person's interpretation changes, he should take whatever measures are required by his latest interpretation; however, he is not required to repeat actions he performed on the basis of his initial interpretation, be it ritual prayer or anything else.

As for the Hanbalis, they hold that if someone is uncertain after waking up as to whether the wetness is due to semen or to pre-seminal fluid and if he recalls experiencing something before going to sleep that might bring on sexual arousal, such as thinking about or looking at an object of sexual desire, he is not required to perform *ghusl*. Rather, he should take the wetness to be the result of mere pre-seminal fluid; however, if his sleep was not preceded by such an experience, he must perform major ablutions.

95. According to the Hanbalis, a bloodless birth would not require the mother to perform major ablutions.

96. According to the Hanafis, major ablutions are not to be administered to a deceased Muslim if he was a *bāghin* [plural, *bughāh*], that is, someone who, either as an individual or as a member of a group, had disavowed obedience to the rightful

require the mother to perform major ablutions; thus, supposing that the woman who has given birth did not bleed, she will still be required to perform major ablutions simply by virtue of having given birth.

Five: The death of a Muslim.[96] In the case of a Muslim's death, the deceased must be administered major ablutions unless he or she died as a martyr. As for the meaning of 'martyr' and associated rulings, these topics will be discussed below in the section dealing with funerals.

Six: The embracing of Islam by an unbeliever if he is in a state of major ritual impurity.[97] However, supposing that the person who embraced Islam was not in such a state, it would simply be recommended that he or she perform major ablutions.

Conditions associated with major ablutions

The conditions associated with major ablutions are of three types: (1) Conditions for their necessity alone; major ablutions for the purpose of purifying oneself from major ritual impurity are [only] required of someone who would also be required to perform minor ablutions. (2) Conditions for their validity alone; in order for major ablutions to be valid, they must be performed by someone for whom regular ablutions would be valid as well. (3) Conditions for their necessity and validity together. The conditions for the necessity and validity of minor ablutions are discussed above in the section on "conditions associated with ritual ablutions." Hence, seekers of knowledge who wish to acquaint themselves with this topic are advised to review that section.

Some of the conditions associated with major ablutions may differ from those associated with minor ablutions. It is not necessary, for example, for a woman to be a Muslim in order to perform major ablutions which are deemed valid, since a

---

Imam, or Muslim leader, and the Muslim community, their purpose being to overthrow the existing social system and replace it with one answering to their own whims. Given this definition adopted by the Hanafis, any group which possesses sufficient power to achieve such a purpose and which wages an armed struggle against an upstanding Muslim community is included among the *bughāh*. Consequently, if a band of thieves overpowered a village, for example, they would not be classified as *bughāh* in this sense, and if any of them died, he would need to be administered major ablutions.

97. According to the Hanbalis, any unbeliever who embraces Islam is required to perform major ablutions whether he or she is in a state of major ritual impurity or not.

Muslim man who marries a Jewish or Christian woman is not permitted to have sexual relations with her[98] after her menstrual period has ended or after the cessation of her vaginal bleeding after childbirth until she performs major ablutions. Thus, the performance of major ablutions for such a woman, despite her not being a Muslim, is legally prescribed. Some of the schools also include other conditions in connection with major ablutions which differ from those associated with minor ablutions.[99]

Obligations associated with major ablutions, including rulings on hair, a bride's adornment, the wearing of jewels, and so forth

With regard to the obligations associated with major ablutions, we have chosen to list them according to the views held by each school in turn. We then point out which obligations are agreed upon among the schools and which ones are the sub-

---

98. According to the Hanafis, the maximum duration of a woman's menstrual period is ten days, while the maximum duration of a woman's postpartum vaginal bleeding is forty days. Hence, if a woman's menstrual period ends after ten days or if her postpartum vaginal bleeding stops forty days after she gives birth, her husband may have sexual relations with her even if she has not performed major ablutions; this applies whether she is a Muslim, a Jew, or a Christian. However, if her menstrual bleeding stops, for example, in seven days rather than ten, or if her postpartum bleeding stops thirty days after childbirth rather than forty, her husband may not have sexual relations with her until either: (a) she has performed major ablutions, or (b) a complete time period for a given obligatory prayer has passed since her bleeding stopped. For example, if her bleeding stops after the beginning of the time period for the noon prayer, he may not have relations with her until this entire time period has passed and the performance of the noon prayer has become a 'debt' which she owes, so to speak. If, on the other hand, her bleeding stops toward the end of the time period for the noon prayer, then if enough time remains of this period for her to perform major ablutions and utter the words, *Allāhu akbar* as one does at the commencement of ritual prayer, he may have relations with her when this period comes to an end. However, if when her bleeding stops there is not enough time left in the noon prayer period for her to perform such actions, he may not have relations with her unless either: (a) she performs major ablutions, or (b) the entire time period for the mid-afternoon prayer has passed without her having any more bleeding. This ruling applies whether the woman is a Muslim, a Jew or a Christian.

99. According to the Hanbalis, it is not necessary to perform abstersion or *istijmār* before performing major ablutions as it is before minor ablutions.

As for the Shafiis, they hold that minor ablutions are not valid unless the person performing them is fully discerning; hence, if, for example, an insane woman lacking powers of discernment performed minor ablutions, they would have no validity. However, this is not true for major ablutions. Consequently, if such a woman came to the end of her menstrual period and performed major ablutions while still irrational, her husband would be permitted to have sexual relations with her [based on the validity of the major ablutions she had performed].

ject of disagreement, since this makes the information easier to retain and understand.[100]

Sunnah-based practices associated with major ablutions and those practices which are desirable and undesirable

In the section above on minor ritual ablutions, we presented the definitions given by the various schools for such terms as Sunnah-based, recommended, undesirable, and the like, to which readers may refer again if they wish. In this section we shall

---

100. The Hanafis hold that there are three obligations involved in the performance of major ablutions: (1) rinsing out the mouth, (2) rinsing out the nose, and (3) washing the entire body with water. Each of these obligations has specific rulings associated with it. Rinsing out the mouth, for example, involves simply placing *ṭahūr* water in one's mouth, without necessarily swishing it around inside or spitting it out afterwards. Hence, if one places *ṭahūr* water in his mouth, then swallows it, he has fulfilled this obligation with respect to major ablutions provided that the water has made contact with his entire mouth from the inside. If the person's teeth have deep grooves in them such that some food remains lodged in them, his *ghusl* is not invalidated, but it is preferable to remove any food lodged between the teeth or clinging to the gums in order to allow the water to make contact with them.

As for rinsing out the nose, it involves placing water inside the nose in the manner described above in the section on obligations involved in minor ablutions. If there is hardened, dry mucous or dirt inside one's nose, one's major ablutions are not valid unless it is removed. Perhaps this observation will spur Muslims to strive for cleanliness at all times, since the necessity of removing such impurities and washing the area beneath them is clear evidence of the Lawgiver's concern for cleanliness, which is of such great benefit to our bodies both inwardly and outwardly.

As for washing the entire body with water, it is a legally binding, agreed-upon part of cleansing oneself of major ritual impurity such that if even the most insignificant part of the body remains unwashed, one's major ablutions will be invalid. Hence, when one intends to perform *ghusl*, he or she must remove from his or her body everything which might prevent the water from making contact with it. For example, if there are impurities under one's fingernails which prevent the water from making contact with the skin beneath them, one's major ablutions are rendered invalid regardless of whether one is a city dweller or a village dweller. However, mere soil or clay found under the fingernails may be overlooked and does not invalidate one's *ghusl*. With regard to the traces of substances left under the fingernails of those who practice professions such as baking and dyeing—in whose cases it is a necessity that they work constantly with dough and dyes which cling to their hands and which are difficult to remove—there are differing views among the schools, with some holding that major ablutions are invalidated by such substances, and others holding that they are not. The reason given for this latter view is that such substances remain on the hands out of necessity, whereas Islamic law makes exceptions for cases involving necessity; hence, no hardship should be laid upon such people. This view is consistent with the principles of our equitable, merciful law.

A woman who has braided hair is not required to loosen her braids in order to perform major ablutions; rather, all she is required to do is to ensure that the water reaches the roots of her hair. Moreover, if she has locks of hair which come down over her temples, she is not required to wash them. If, on the other hand, her hair is not braided, she must ensure that the water gets between the strands of hair even if it does not penetrate to her scalp. If the woman has applied a thick, perfumed oil to her head which blocks the water from reaching the roots of her hair, she must remove it, and if she is wearing tight bracelets, earrings or rings, she must rotate them in such a way that the water gets under them. If the water does not get under them in this manner, they must be removed, and if she has pierced ears without earrings in them, the water must get inside the holes in her ears. Thus, if the water enters the holes of its own accord, well and good; otherwise, the water must be made to get inside them with whatever object makes this possible. A woman is not required to place her finger inside her vagina when performing *ghusl*.

As for the man, he must ensure that the water gets in between the hairs of his beard and makes contact with their roots whether the hair is braided or not. Moreover, one must insert a finger into depressions in the body such as the navel so as to ensure that the water gets inside them. An uncircumcised male need not ensure that the water gets inside his foreskin; nevertheless, it is desirable for him to do so.

* * *

The Malikis specify five obligations involved in major ritual ablutions: (1) intention, (2) covering the entire body with water, (3) rubbing the entire body, either during or after the pouring of the water, and before the water dries, (4) continuity (*al-muwālāh*) and (5) ensuring that the water penetrates any and all hair on the body.

First: Intention. The rulings on intention as they pertain to minor ritual ablutions have been discussed above. Moreover, just as intention is an obligatory part of minor ablutions, it is likewise obligatory in major ablutions according to the Malikis. The point at which one is to consciously intend the performance of major ablutions is during the washing of the first part of the body which one washes; however, one's ablutions are still valid even if one's conscious intention is delayed by what is customarily agreed to be a 'short time.' As we saw above in the presentation on the obligations involved in minor ritual ablutions, the Hanafis view intention as an emphatically enjoined practice based on the prophetic Sunnah, according to the Hanbalis, it is a condition for the validity of major ablutions without being an integral part of the ablutions themselves. Their views will be presented below. As for the Shafiis, they agree with the Malikis that intention forms an obligatory part of ablutions, and they hold that it is never permissible to allow one's intention to be delayed beyond the beginning of one's ablutions.

Second: Covering the entire body with water. According to the Malikis, the mouth, the nose, the ear canal and the eyes are not included in 'the body'; rather, what is required, in their view, is that one wash the outside of the entire body. As for washing the interior of those parts of the body which have an interior, such as rinsing out the mouth and the nose, this is not obligatory, but simply a Sunnah-based practice, as will be seen, although wherever one finds folds or 'depressions' in the body, one must ensure that the water gets into them.

Third: continuity [though listed fourth above, the author lists it here as third], also referred to as 'immediacy'. In other words, one must wash each member of the body immediately upon finishing with the one prior to it and before it dries, provided that one is mindful of what one is doing and that one is capable of washing one part after the other in immediate succession. For further detail on this obligation, see the earlier section entitled, "Obligations Involved in Ablutions."

Fourth: Rubbing the entire body with water. It is not necessary that the rubbing be done while one is pouring water over the body; it may also be done after the water has been poured and is dripping off the part of the body concerned, but before it has dried. Nor is it necessary according to the Malikis that the rubbing be done with the hand; hence, if someone rubbed part of his body with his arm, or rubbed one of his feet with the other, this would suffice as well. It is also a recognized view of the Malikis that one may perform such rubbing with a towel, a piece of cloth, a rag, etc. For example, someone might take one end of a towel in his left hand and the other end in his right, then use it to rub his back and the rest of his body provided that his body has not already dried off; this practice is acceptable even if the person would have been able to rub himself with his hand. Still another way one could perform the rubbing would be to take a sack in one palm and rub with it. All such methods are unanimously recognized as valid, since they involve the use of the hand. In the case of someone who is incapable of rubbing part or all of his body with his hand or even with a rag, this requirement is dropped, and there is no need for him to ask someone else to perform this task for him.

Fifth: Parting the hair. If a man's beard is thick, there are some Malikis who hold that it is obligatory to run the fingers through it, while others hold that it is simply recommended to do so. As for the hair on other parts of the body, including the eyelashes and eyebrows, underarm hair, pubic hair, and so forth, it is agreed upon that it must be parted regardless of whether it is thin or thick; this ruling applies equally to men and to women. If the hair has been braided, it will have been braided either with strings around the outside, or without strings. If it has been braided with three or more strings, it must be loosened; if it has been braided with fewer than three strings, loosening it is not required unless it has been braided so tightly that it is difficult or impossible to allow the water to reach the scalp. In sum, then, hair which has been braided with three or more strings must always be loosened, since braiding in this way tends to make the braids so tight that water is prevented from making contact with the person's scalp. Moreover, as we have noted, if the hair is braided very tightly, it must be loosened regardless of the number of strings it has been tied with, whereas if it is braided loosely, it does not need to be let down. However, an exception to this ruling is made for a bride who has adorned her hair or applied perfume to it or something similar. She is not required to wash her hair in this situation due to the waste of money [which it would involve to remove the substances which prevent the water from making contact with her skin]. Hence, all a bride is required to do is to bathe her body and wipe her head with her hand in such a way that it does her no harm. Moreover, if a bride has perfume all over her body and fears that by performing major ablutions it will be lost, she is exempted from this requirement and is allowed instead to perform sand ablutions.

As for tight and loose rings, the same ruling cited earlier in the discussion of minor ritual ablutions applies here as well. Hence, if the ring is one which it is permissible for the person to wear, it is not necessary to remove it even if the water does not get under it, and it is sufficient to wash the ring itself.

* * *

The Shafiis hold that there are only two obligations associated with major ritual ablutions, namely: (1) intention, and (2) covering the outside of the body entirely with water.

As for intention, it must take place as one is first beginning to bathe; if it comes before the beginning of one's *ghusl*, it will be invalidated. As we have seen, the Shafiis apply the same principle to minor ritual ablutions.

As for covering the outside of the body with water, this includes the hair on the body, which must be washed from its ends to its roots regardless of whether it is thin or thick. However, if the hair is so thick that water will not penetrate through to the skin, all one is obliged to do is to ensure that the water gets between the strands of hair. If one's hair is braided, it must be loosened if it prevents the water from penetrating the hair; this is true for both men and women. Moreover, if one's hair is naturally nappy, one may forego trying to get the water to penetrate it.

At the same time, however, it is necessary for the water to make contact with every possible part of the outside of the body, provided that this does not cause undue hardship. If even a small part of the body which could have been touched by the water is left dry, one's *ghusl* is invalid. It is also necessary for the water to get inside depressions in the body such as the navel, deep scars, and the like. However, one is not asked to use an instrument such as a tube to achieve this purpose; rather, all that is required is that one exert every reasonable effort to ensure that water reaches the entire outside of the body without undue hardship. One must also remove anything which would serve as a barrier preventing the water from getting beneath it, such as dough, wax, a rheum or some other foreign body in one's eye, and tight rings. If a woman is wearing tight earrings, she must rotate them in her ears so as to allow the water to touch the skin under them; however, if she has pierced ears but is not wearing earrings, she is not required to get the water to go inside the holes in her ears, since what is required according to the Shafiis is simply to wash the outside of the body, whereas such a hole is considered to be internal rather than external. It is also necessary to wash the visible part of the ear, that is, the opening leading into the ear; however, it is not necessary to wash inside the ears.

According to the Shafiis, an uncircumcised man must ensure that the water gets under his foreskin—the foreskin being the loose outer skin which is removed from the penis in circumcision. If this can only be done by pulling it back, then this must be done. If this proves difficult, the ruling in such a case will be the same as that which applies to someone who has neither *ṭahūr* water nor *ṭahūr* soil with which to perform sand ablutions, sometimes referred as "the one deprived of both purifying agents." When an uncircumcised male dies, he is to be buried without being prayed over according to the majority Shafii view. However, some hold that someone may administer sand ablutions to such a person when he dies, then pray over him. From this one may see that circumcision is held by the Shafiis to be obligatory. It also bears noting that in our time, circumcision has become a virtual health necessity, and anyone who fails to be circumcised is simply ignorant and unsanitary.

* * *

As for the Hanbalis, they hold that there is only one obligation involved in major ablutions, that is, covering the entire body with water. In their view, this includes the inside of both the mouth and the nose, which must be rinsed out during *ghusl* just as they are during minor ablutions. Also included is the hair on the body, which must be washed in such a way as to allow the water to penetrate it, even if it does not reach the skin beneath in the case of hair which is thick. If a man has braided hair, he must loosen it when performing major ablutions. As for the woman, however, she is not required to loosen braided hair when performing major ablutions for purification from sexual discharge due to the hardship this would entail; rather, all she must do is part her hair so as to allow the water to get to its roots, whereas it is only recommended that she loosen her braids.

The foregoing applies to major ablutions after sexual intercourse. However, when a woman is performing major ablutions for the purpose of purification following her menstrual period, she is required to loosen her braids, since this occasion does not occur as often and consequently, does not entail undue hardship.

According to the Hanbalis, the outside of the body also includes the area beneath the foreskin. As we have seen, one is required to ensure that water gets under the foreskin if it is not difficult to pull it back; otherwise, this requirement does not apply. It is likewise necessary to ensure that water gets under any rings and the like that one is wearing.

Lastly, in a ruling adhered to only by the Hanbalis, they hold that uttering the *basmalah* as part of performing major ablutions is obligatory given two conditions: (1) that the person performing them be knowledgeable rather than ignorant, and (2) that the person be mindful of what he or she is doing.

A summary of points of agreement and disagreement among the schools regarding the obligations involved in major ablutions:

There is agreement among all four schools that covering the entire body with water is an obligatory part of major ablutions, whereas they differ over whether the inside of the mouth and nose are included in this. Thus, the Hanbalis and the Hanafis hold that the insides of the mouth and the nose are included in "the entire body," and that it is therefore obligatory to rinse out the mouth and the nose when performing *ghusl*. However, whereas the Hanbalis classify these two steps as obligatory when one performs minor ritual ablutions as well, the Hanafis do not. As for the Shafiis and the Malikis, they hold that all that is required in major ablutions is to wash the entire outside of the body and that, as a result, one is not required to rinse out the mouth or the nose as part of either minor or major ritual ablutions. The four schools agree on the necessity of bringing the water into contact with as many parts of the body as possible, including depressions such as the navel and deep scars from surgical operations. Nevertheless, they also agree that one is not required to go to ridiculous lengths to get water into deep depressions in the body, for example, by using instruments such as tubes or pumps. Hence, if someone were hit by a bullet which left a deep gash in his body, all four schools agree that he would simply be required to wash as much of the depressed area as he could without discomfort or undue hardship. Moreover, the Shafiis consider the holes in the ears in which earrings are inserted to be internal and not part of the outside of the body and that, as a result, one is not required to ensure that the water gets inside them even if it would be possible to do so.

It is agreed upon among the four schools that one must remove from one's body anything which might serve as a barrier preventing water from making contact with the skin beneath it, such as dough, wax, a rheum or mucous discharge in the eye, etc. However, the Hanafis differ from the other three schools by allowing that if such substances cling to the fingertips and the skin under the fingernails as a result of one's profession [such as bread baking, dyeing, and the like] and if they would be difficult to remove, they may be overlooked lest such people be subjected to undue hardship.

Another point on which all four schools agree is the necessity of parting the hair on the body if it is thin enough to allow the water to penetrate it to the skin beneath. The Malikis hold that thick hair must also be parted in order for the water to reach the underlying skin. As for the other three schools, however, they hold that although one must allow the water to get in between the strands of hair—for example, by washing the outside of the hair while parting it to allow the water to penetrate it—it is not required that the water make contact with the skin under the hair.

Regarding braided hair, each of the four schools has a different view. According to the Hanafis, it is not necessary to loosen braided hair; rather, one must simply ensure that the water reaches the roots. Similarly if the hair is not braided, it must be rearranged in such a way that the water gets in between the strands of hair. However, no concession will be allowed to a woman who has perfume on her hair which prevents water from making contact with it; rather she is required to remove it first even if she is a bride. This ruling is agreed upon by the Hanafis, the Hanbalis, and the Shafiis. However, the Malikis hold that it is permissible for a new bride not to wash her head, but to leave her perfume and ornaments in place; this, it might be added, is a laudable concession on their part.

The Shafiis hold that braided hair must be loosened if this is the only way to ensure that the water gets between the strands of hair; otherwise, it is not necessary. The Hanbalis hold that if a man has braids in his hair, they must always be loosened before performing *ghusl* [regardless of whether the water would penetrate the hair otherwise]. As for the woman, however, she is only required to loosen her braids when performing *ghusl* for purification from her menstrual period or postpartum bleeding, but not for purification from sexual discharge, since to require it in the latter situation would entail undue hardship. As we have seen, the Malikis are alone in enumerating five different obligations associated with major ablutions. However, both the Malikis and the Shafiis agree that conscious intention is an obligatory part of major ablutions. According to the Hanbalis, intention is not part of ablutions [whether minor or major] but simply a condition for their validity, as was presented in the section on ablutions, while for the Hanafis, it is a practice based on the prophetic Sunnah.

give a detailed presentation of the Sunnah-based and recommended practices associated with major ablutions. As for undesirable practices, they involve the omission of one or more of the practices based on the prophetic Sunnah. Below are the detailed explanations of each school.[101]

Situations in which major ablutions are dictated by the Sunnah, or are at least desirable

As we have seen, there are situations in which it becomes an obligation to perform major ritual ablutions. In addition, there are situations in which major ablutions are not obligatory, but consistent with the prophetic Sunnah or, at the very least, recommended. These situations are explained in detailed below, according to each school.[102]

As for the additional obligations listed by the Malikis, they are classified by the other three schools as practices based on the Sunnah.

101. The Hanbalis enumerate the Sunnah-based practices associated with major ablutions as follows: (1) preceding major ablutions with the performance of minor ablutions, bearing in mind that rinsing out the mouth and the nose is obligatory for them; (2) removing any impurities which are on the body; (3) washing each member of the body three times; (4) washing the right side before the left; (5) maintaining continuity, that is, washing each part of the body before the one before it has dried; (6) rubbing the parts of the body one washes: (7) rewashing the feet in a place other than the one where one performed *ghusl*. In other words, if the person was standing in a basin with his feet submerged in water, it is recommended that he wash them again outside the basin.

As for the utterance of the *basmalah* at the beginning of one's *ghusl*, it is obligatory if the person concerned is informed of the rulings on major ablutions and related matters and is mindful of what he is doing. This requirement does not apply to those who are ignorant or forgetful; consequently, no mention of it is made among the obligations involved in minor ritual ablutions.

Moreover, as we saw in our discussion of minor ritual ablutions, neither the Shafiis nor the Hanbalis recognize any distinction between that which is recommended and that which is based on the prophetic Sunnah.

102. The Hanafis list the following as Sunnah-based practices associated with major ablutions: (1) beginning with a conscious intention in one's heart; (2) saying out loud something like, "I intend to perform major ritual ablutions for the removal of major ritual impurity"; (3) uttering the *basmalah* at the beginning; (4) washing one's hands up to the wrists three times; (5) washing one's genital area after this even if it has no impurity on it; (6) removing any impurities from the body before commencing *ghusl*; (7) performing minor ritual ablutions such as those performed before ritual prayer; (8) delaying the washing of one's feet until one has completed the *ghusl* if one is standing in a place where the water will collect around one's feet, such as a small basin. However, if one is standing on top of a rock, for example, or is wearing clogs, it is not necessary to delay washing his feet. The reason for this ruling is that in the first situation, one would be standing in the same water which is running off one's body, as a result of which it would be likely to contain some

impurities; hence, it is an emulation of the Prophet's example to delay washing the feet till last in such a situation; (9) beginning by washing one's head three times before washing one's body, in which case the first washing is obligatory while the second and the third are based on the prophetic Sunnah; (10) rubbing as one washes; (11) washing the right side before the left, and washing each side three times; (12) and maintaining the temporal order described here.

All practices that are classified as 'Sunnah-based' for minor ritual ablutions (and that have been presented earlier) are classified similarly with respect to *ghusl*.

As for recommended practices associated with *ghusl*, they include all those actions which are recommended in association with minor ritual ablutions; the only exception to this is the traditional prayer or supplication, the use of which is recommended with minor ritual ablutions, but not with the *ghusl*; the reason for this is that when one performs *ghusl*, one tends to be standing in 'used' water, which is likely to be contaminated by impurities.

* * *

As for the Shafiis, they list the following as Sunnah-based practices associated with major ablutions: (1) Utterance of the *basmalah* as one consciously intends the performance of *ghusl*; (2) Washing the hands up to the wrists as one does in minor ablutions; (3) Performance of minor ablutions before commencing *ghusl*, including the rinsing out of the mouth and the nose. If someone performs minor ablutions, then has an occurrence of *ḥadath*, he is not required to repeat them since despite the invalidation of his ablutions, he has successfully emulated the Sunnah in this regard. However, there are some Shafiis who hold that if one's minor ablutions are invalidated before one begins major ablutions, is it necessary to repeat them; (4) Rubbing every part of the body which one washes with his hands; (5) Maintaining continuity; (6) Washing the head before the rest of the body; (7) Washing the right side before the left; (8) Removing any dirt or impurities which would not prevent water from making contact with the skin [since if they would prevent such contact, removing them would be obligatory]; (9) Covering one's private parts even if one is alone; (10) Washing each part of the body three times; (11) Parting the hair, the fingers and the toes [so that water flows in-between]; (12) Refraining from shaving one's hair or trimming one's fingernails and toenails before performing major ablutions; (13) Uttering the *dhikr* [that is, particular phrases which are repeated as a means of invoking the remembrance of God] associated with minor ablutions; (14) Refraining from asking for someone else's help without good reason; (15) Facing the *qiblah*; (16) Washing in a place where one will not be exposed to a spray of water; (17) Refraining from shaking the water off one's body; (18) Refraining from unnecessary speech; (19) In the case of the woman, inserting into her vagina a piece of cotton soaked in musk or some other pleasant fragrance if it is available—provided that she is not in a state of *iḥrām*, fasting, or in mourning for a deceased husband; otherwise, she should not do so; (20) Washing the higher parts of the body before the lower ones with the exception of the genital area, because it is a Sunnah-based practice to wash this area before performing minor ablutions lest they be invalidated by touching it. When washing the genitals, one should consciously intend the removal of *ḥadath* from them. Lastly, as noted earlier, the Shafiis make no distinction between practices that are Sunnah-based and those that are recommended.

* * *

As for the Malikis, they list only four Sunnah-based practices associated with major ablutions, namely: (1) washing one's hands up to the wrists as one does before minor ablutions, (2) rinsing out one's mouth, (3) rinsing out one's nose and expelling the water afterwards (*istinshāq*) and (4) wiping the ear canal.

As for recommended practices connected with major ablutions, the Malikis include the following ten: (1) Uttering the *basmalah* as one begins; (2) beginning by removing impurities from one's genital area and the rest of the body, as well as any dirt which would not hinder the water from making contact with the skin (bearing in mind that if it would hinder such contact, its removal would be obligatory); (3) performing *ghusl* in a ritually pure place; (4) beginning by washing each of the parts of the body involved in regular ablutions three times; (5) washing the higher parts of the body before the lower ones with the exception of the genitals, as it is considered desirable to wash this area before everything else lest one's minor ablutions be invalidated by having touched it; this same ruling applies to both the man and the woman even if the woman's ablutions would not be invalidated by her touching her vagina; (6) washing the head three times and ensuring that the water covers it entirely each time; (7) first covering the right side of one's body with water, back and front, ensuring that the water covers the arm down to the elbow [below which is not necessary since by this time, one will already have performed regular ablutions, which include washing both hands and arms up to the elbows], then doing the same on the left side; (8) using as much water as one needs to wash the various parts of one's body, and no more; (9) keeping in mind one's intention until one's ablutions are completed; and (10) only speaking in order to make mention of God or to say something which needs to be said.

As for those situations in which it is a Sunnah-based practice to perform *ghusl*, the Malikis list the following three: (1) On Friday for someone who intends to pray the congregational prayer, even if one is not actually in need of a bath. The time during which this *ghusl* may be performed extends from daybreak to the time soon before one leaves for the mosque. Hence, if one performs this *ghusl* before daybreak or at a time other than when he intends to leave for the mosque, he will not have emulated the Sunnah, and he must repeat his major ablutions if he wishes to do so. (2) On the two holidays, the Day of Fast-breaking and the Day of Sacrifice. The practice of performing major ablutions on these two days is most preferably classified as Sunnah-based, even though the prevailing view is that it is simply recommended. The time period for this *ghusl* begins with the final sixth of the night, although it is recommended that one perform it after daybreak. Moreover, it is not necessary for it to be performed in direct connection with one's going to the place where the holiday prayer will be prayed, since this *ghusl* is performed not for the sake of the prayer, but for the sake of the day itself. Hence, one is called upon to perform it even if one does not go out for the prayer. (3) When one enters a state of *iḥrām*, in which case it is considered to be an emulation of the Sunnah even for women who are menstruating or still having postpartum bleeding.

Lastly, the Malikis specify eight situations in which it is recommended that one perform major ablutions, namely: (1) when one has administered major ablutions to someone who has died; (2) when one enters Mecca to perform the circumambulation of the Ka'bah (in which case it is not recommended for women who are menstruating or postpartum); (3) when one is about to perform the standing at Mt. 'Arafah, in which case it is also desirable for women who are menstruating and postpartum; (4) when one is about to enter the city of Medina (may abundant blessings and peace be upon its inhabitants); (5) when one first embraces Islam without being in a state of major ritual impurity; (6) in the case of a young girl who has been instructed to perform ritual prayer and who has had sexual relations with an adult man; (7) in the case of a young boy who has been instructed to perform ritual prayer and who has had sexual relations with a female capable of tolerating intercourse; and (8) when a woman who has had chronic vaginal bleeding is cured of this condition.

* * *

According to the Hanafis, there are four situations in which it is an emulation of the prophetic Sunnah to perform major ablutions: (1) On Friday when one intends to pray the congregational prayer. This *ghusl* is for the sake of the prayer, not the day as such; hence, if someone performed major ablutions following the dawn prayer, after which he had an occurrence of *ḥadath* and performed regular ablutions, then prayed the Friday prayer, he would not have emulated the Sunnah. (2) On the two holidays, the Day of Fastbreaking and the Day of Sacrifice. Like the Friday *ghusl*, this is performed for the sake of the prayer, not the day itself. (3) When one is in a state of ritual consecration (*iḥrām*) for the performance of the greater or lesser pilgrimage. (4) When one is about to perform the standing on Mt. 'Arafah.

As for those situations in which it is recommended that one perform major ablutions, they are as follows: (1) When someone returns to full mental functioning after either suffering from insanity, a loss of consciousness, or drunkenness, provided that one finds no wetness on his body or clothing; if one does find such wetness and is certain that it is semen or suspects that it might be either semen or pre-seminal fluid, he is obliged to perform *ghusl*. On the other hand, if he only suspects that it is either pre-seminal fluid or *wadī*, the secretion which sometimes follows urination, he is not obliged to do so, as in the case of someone who has awakened from sleep. (2) After undergoing cupping. (3) On the night before the day which marks the midpoint of the month of Sha'bān. (4) On the night before one stands on Mt. 'Arafah. (5) On the "Night of Power" (Laylat al-Qadr) [traditionally considered the 27th of Ramaḍān]. (6) When one stands at Muzdalifah on the morning of the Day of Sacrifice. (7) Upon entering Minā on the Day of Sacrifice to throw pebbles at the three stone pillars. (8) When entering Mecca to circumambulate the Ka'bah on the Day of Sacrifice [10 Dhū al-Ḥijjah]. (9) Before performing the prayers for solar and lunar eclipses and the prayer for rain. (10) When someone experiences a fright, or when the night is particularly dark or the wind is particularly strong. (11) When entering Medina, the city of the Prophet. (12) Before attending a gathering of people. (13) When one wears a new garment. (14) After administering major ablutions to someone who has died. (15) When one has repented of a sin. (16) After returning from a trip. (17) When a woman who has had chronic vaginal bleeding finds that her flow of blood has stopped. (18) When someone embraces Islam without having been in a state of major ritual impurity; otherwise, a new believer is obliged to perform *ghusl.*

In addition, some Hanafis add a further category, that of 'duty'. Those situations in which it is a duty to perform major ablutions are as follows: (1) Administering major ablutions to a dead person (although the more correct view is that this rite is a collective obligation for Muslims; that is, if one Muslim performs this task, it is not required of everyone else). (2) The performance of major ablutions by someone who has embraced Islam when in a state of major ritual impurity or who reaches puberty by having a 'wet dream' [rather than simply by reaching a particular age], although in reality, major ablutions are obligatory in both these situations. As for a woman who becomes a Muslim after the termination of her menstrual period, it is recommended, but not obligatory, that she perform major ablutions. The reason for this is that whereas the major ritual impurity resulting from sexual discharge is not removed by someone's becoming a Muslim, that resulting from menstruation will have been removed before her conversion [by virtue of her flow having stopped and the subsequent passage of time].

* * *

As for the Shafiis, they hold that all situations in which it is not obligatory to perform *ghusl* are classified as Sunnah, as they make no distinction between Sunnah-based practices and those which are merely recommended. As for those situations in which performing major ablutions is considered an emulation of the prophetic Sunnah, they list nineteen: (1) On Fridays for those who intend to perform the congregational prayer. The time period for this *ghusl* begins with the call to the dawn prayer and ends when the imam leading the Friday prayer has concluded his greetings. It is not a Sunnah-based practice to repeat this *ghusl*, even if after performing it one has an occurrence of *ḥadath.* (2) After one has administered major ablutions to someone who has died, regardless of whether the person who performed them is ritually pure or not. The time period for this *ghusl* begins when one finishes performing major ablutions on behalf of the deceased, and ends when or if the person concerned decides not to perform this *ghusl.* The same ruling applies if one has administered sand ablutions to the deceased. (3) On the two holidays, the Day of Fastbreaking ('Īd al-Fiṭr) and the Day of Sacrifice ('Īd al-Aḍḥā), even if one does not intend to perform the feast day prayer, since the purpose for this *ghusl* is simply to make oneself more presentable. The time period for *ghusl* begins at midnight before the day itself, and ends at sundown. (4) When someone becomes a Muslim without being in a state of major ritual impurity. If the person who embraces Islam is in a state of major ritual impurity, however, the performance of *ghusl* is obligatory even if he or she had performed *ghusl* while still an unbeliever, since such an instance of *ghusl* would lack validity. The time period for this *ghusl* begins when one embraces Islam and ends either with one's rejecting Islam or by virtue of the passage of time. (5) Before praying the prayer for rain or the prayers for the eclipse of the sun or the moon. This ruling applies to anyone who intends to pray one of these prayers even if at home. In relation to the prayer for rain, the time period for this *ghusl* begins when one decides to recite the prayer if the intention is to pray alone, and when people have gathered for the prayer if one's intention is to pray with others. As for the prayers for the solar and lunar eclipses, the time period for the performance of *ghusl* begins when the sun or the moon starts to change, and it ends once the eclipse is fully past. (6) When one has regained full mental functioning after having suffered insanity or a loss of consciousness. This *ghusl* may be performed in emulation of the prophetic Sunnah as early as one moment after regaining one's mental faculties provided that no emission of semen has taken place; otherwise, *ghusl* is obligatory. (7) Before one performs the standing on Mt. 'Arafah. The time period for this *ghusl* begins at dawn on the Day of 'Arafah and it ends at sundown of the same day. (8) Before one stands at Muzdalifah, provided that one has not performed *ghusl* before standing on Mt. 'Arafah, since in the latter case, the first *ghusl* is sufficient. The time period for this *ghusl* begins at sundown. (9) Before standing at the sacred *ḥajj* station at Muzdalifah, an explanation of which will be found in the section on the greater pilgrimage. (10) Before casting pebbles at the three stone pillars at Minā [which stand as a symbol of evil] if one intends to do so on a day other than the Day of Sacrifice [10 Dhū al-Ḥijjah, known variously as *'Īd al-Aḍḥā* and *Yawm al-Naḥr*]. (11) When one's body gives off an unpleasant odor on account of perspiration, dirt, and the like. (12) Before one leaves to attend a gathering devoted to worship or edifying conversation. This ruling is a lovely feature of the Islamic law, since it would not be fitting for someone to be a cause of offense to others due to the disagreeable odor he gives off. (13) After one has undergone cupping and venesection, since the performance of major ablutions restores the body's vitality, thereby helping to compensate for the loss of blood. (14) Before secluding oneself for the sake of contemplation and worship, since it is only fitting that someone who wishes to devote himself to intimate conversation with his Lord should wish to be clean. (15) Before entering the city of the Prophet, that is, Medina. (16) Every night during the month of Ramaḍān. (17) When a young boy reaches puberty by virtue of his age; whereas if he reaches puberty by having a "wet dream," *ghusl* is obligatory, as previously mentioned. (18) When a nearby riverbed begins to flow again due to rainfall or during the season when the Nile floods its banks, since *ghusl* in this situation is a way of expressing one's thanks to God Almighty. (19) When a woman [who has been divorced or widowed] completes her *'iddah*, or waiting period, since from this time on a suitor might approach her, in which case it most fitting for her to be clean and presentable.

* * *

As for the Hanbalis, they list sixteen occasions on which it is an emulation of the prophetic Sunnah to perform major ablutions: (1) On Friday for those who intend to participate in the congregational prayers, provided that they actually perform the congregational prayer. (2) On the major religious holidays [such as the Day of Fastbreaking and the Day of Sacrifice] if the person concerned attends the congregational prayers and actually performs them. Because this *ghusl* is performed not for the sake of the day itself, but for the sake of the prayer, it will not suffice for one to perform it before dawn or after the prayer is past. (3) Before praying the prayers for the solar and lunar eclipses. (4) Before praying the prayer for rain. (5) After administering major ablutions to someone who has died. (6) After regaining full mental functioning if one has suffered from insanity and after regaining consciousness after fainting, provided that no major ritual impurity occurred while in either state. (7) Before each ritual prayer for a woman who suffers from chronic

What must not be done by someone in a state of major ritual impurity before performing major ablutions in preparation to enter a mosque, read the Qur'ān, and the like

Someone in a state of major ritual impurity is forbidden to undertake any act whose permissibility is dependent on the prior performance of minor ritual ablutions. Hence, a person in a state of major ritual impurity is not allowed to perform any obligatory or supererogatory prayers unless he has no water available to him or is unable to use water due to illness or some other cause, the details concerning which will be discussed below in the section on *tayammum* or sand ablutions. As for fasting, be it obligatory or supererogatory, it is valid even if the person fasting is in a state of major ritual impurity. Thus, for example, if a man has sexual relations with his wife before dawn during Ramaḍān and does not perform *ghusl* before daybreak, his fasting will still be valid, as will be mentioned in the section below on fasting.

Acts of piety which are forbidden to those in a state of major ritual impurity include the recitation of the Qur'ān, and even more, the touching of the Qur'ān. After all, even someone in a state of minor ritual impurity is forbidden to touch the written Qur'ān; hence, this is all the more true for someone in a state of major ritual impurity. Such acts also include entering a mosque. Nevertheless, the Lawgiver has provided conditions under which someone in a state of major ritual impurity may recite brief passages from the Qur'ān and/or enter a mosque. Detailed rulings concerning these conditions are given below for each of the four schools.[103]

---

vaginal bleeding. (8) When one is in a state of ritual consecration (*iḥrām*) for the greater or lesser pilgrimage. (9) When entering the sacred precincts of the Ka'bah. (10) When entering Mecca. (11) Before one stands on Mt. 'Arafah. (12) Before standing at Muzdalifah. (13) Before casting pebbles at the three stone pillars at Minā. (14) Before circumambulating the Ka'bah on the 10th of Dhū al-Ḥijjah, which is a pillar of the greater pilgrimage. (15) Before performing the circumambulation of farewell [at the conclusion of the greater pilgrimage].

103 According to the Malikis, those in a state of major ritual impurity are only allowed to recite one or two verses of the Qur'ān, and provided that they do so in one of two situations: (1) when the person is reciting from the Qur'ān with the intention of seeking protection against an enemy or some other danger, and (2) when the person is citing textual support from the Qur'ān for a given legal ruling. Apart from these two situations, no one in a state of major ritual impurity is allowed to recite any of the Qur'ān, be it a large or a small amount.

As for entering a mosque, it is forbidden for a person in a state of major ritual impurity to do so in order to spend the night inside or simply to pass through the mosque on his way to some other place. However, such a person is allowed to enter a mosque in two situations: In the first situation, the person can find no water with which to bathe himself anywhere except inside the mosque. At such times he is permitted to go the mosque to wash. A similar situation would be for the only pail or rope with which water is drawn to be inside the mosque such that the person has no choice but to go in the mosque in order to fetch them. This type of situation used to be quite common in villages which had no running water. Now, however, with running water available virtually everywhere, there no longer exist fountains or basins set aside specifically for ritual ablutions. Rather, what we have are water faucets to which one gains access by going in through a door that does not lead directly into the mosque. Hence, the person in a state of major ritual impurity must enter through such a door and not enter the mosque. Nevertheless, in the event that he finds a mosque which lacks running water and which has no separate room for the performance of ablutions such that the only water available is inside the mosque itself, he may go inside the mosque to bathe himself, but before doing so he must first perform sand ablutions.

In the second situation, the person has reason to fear that he is in danger and has no place to seek refuge but the mosque; in such a case, the person may perform sand ablutions, then go inside the mosque and spend the night there while he waits for the danger to pass. This ruling applies if the person is a local resident and is in good health. However, if he is a traveler or is both in a state of major ritual impurity and ill and unable to use water, he may perform sand ablutions, enter the mosque and pray inside based on these sand ablutions. However, he may not spend the night there unless it is a necessity; if he spends the night there and has a "wet dream," he should leave the mosque promptly, and if he is able to perform sand ablutions quickly as he leaves, this is commendable.

In sum, then, it is not permissible for a person in a state of major ritual impurity to enter a mosque without some clear necessity.

* * *

According to the Hanafis, someone in a state of major ritual impurity is forbidden to recite the Qur'ān, regardless of how long or short the passage happens to be, in all but two situations: (1) when uttering the *basmalah* ("In the name of God, the Most Gracious, the Most Merciful") before initiating some important action, despite the fact that it contains words from the Qur'ān, and (2) when reciting a short verse from the Qur'ān as a means of praying for God's blessing on someone or to praise someone by it, for example, by saying, "O my Sustainer! Grant Thy forgiveness unto me and unto my parents" (71:28) or, "[may they be] firm and unyielding towards all deniers of the truth, [yet] full of mercy towards one another " (48:29).

The Hanafis also hold that those in a state of major ritual impurity are forbidden to enter a mosque unless required to do so by necessity. As for the meaning of 'necessity' in this context, it is determined by the circumstances. For example, it might involve a situation in which someone can find no water with which to bathe himself anywhere but inside the mosque, as is the case in some locations. If this is the case, the person may pass through the mosque in order to reach the place where the water is located in order to bathe. However, he must perform sand ablutions before passing through. Like the Malikis, the Hanafis recognize that someone might be obliged to go into a mosque for fear of some danger, in which case he must perform sand ablutions before entering.

In short, the performance of sand ablutions by someone who needs to enter a mosque but is in a state of major ritual impurity is sometimes a duty, and at other times, simply recommended. It is a duty in the following two situations: (1) when someone enters a state of major ritual impurity while outside the mosque, after which he is obliged to enter the mosque for some reason, and (2) when someone goes to sleep in a mosque while in a state of ritual purity, then has a 'wet dream', after which he is obliged to stay for a period of time in the mosque for fear of some harm which might otherwise come to him.

In other situations, it is not obligatory but recommended that a person in a state of major ritual impurity perform sand ablutions. For example, if someone enters a state of major ritual impurity while inside the mosque [yet without being obliged to stay for a prolonged period], it is recommended that he perform sand ablutions when he wishes to leave. Similarly, if someone in a state of major ritual impurity is obliged for some reason to go into a mosque without being able to perform sand ablutions first, after which the necessity ceases to exist and he comes out again, it is recommended that he perform sand ablutions so that, at the very least, he will have performed sand ablutions before he passes through the mosque again. Nevertheless, when sand ablutions are performed in this type of situation, one is not allowed to recite the Qur'ān or pray on the basis of them.

As for the roof of a mosque, it is subject in such situations to the same rulings which apply to a mosque's interior, although someone in a state of major ritual impurity is permitted to enter the mosque's outer courtyard without performing sand ablutions. The same ruling as that which applies to the mosque's interior likewise applies to the prayer rooms or tents erected for prayers to be performed on the Day of Fastbreaking, the Day of Sacrifice, and/or a funeral, as well as the prayer rooms (*khāniqāh*) used by Sufi orders. As for mosques attached to schools, if they are public in the sense that no one is forbidden to come and pray in them, or if, when they are closed, a group of the school's residents gather inside them, they are subject to the same rulings as all other mosques; otherwise, they are not.

* * *

As for the Shafiis, they hold that it is forbidden for someone in a state of major ritual impurity to recite even a single word of the Qur'ān if his intention in doing so is to chant it; however, if one's intention is simply to keep God in remembrance, or if he utters words from the Qur'ān unintentionally, it is allowed. Examples of the utterance of words from the Qur'ān as a means of keeping God in remembrance are for someone who is about to eat to say, "In the name of God, the Most Gracious, the Most Merciful," or for someone mounting a riding animal to say, "Limitless in His glory is He who has made [all] this subservient to our use—since [but for Him], we would not have been able to attain to it" (42:13).

If someone has no access to either *ṭahūr* water or *ṭahūr* soil, he may recite the Qur'ān as part of the obligatory prayers which he is allowed to perform under such circumstances; the same applies to a woman whose menstrual cycle has ended or who has had postpartum bleeding and needs to perform a *ghusl* but has no access to water or soil which is *ṭahūr*. As for passing through a mosque, it is permissible for someone in a state of major ritual impurity as well as a menstruating woman or a woman with postpartum bleeding provided that they do not linger there for any period of time, and provided that there is no danger of them contaminating the mosque with impurities. Hence, such a person may come in through one door of the mosque and leave through another. However, he or she may not enter and leave through the same door, since it indicates that he or she lingered inside. On the other hand, if the person's original intention was to leave through a door other than the one through which he entered, after which it became apparent that he would have to leave through the same door, this is not forbidden.

In case of necessity, a person in a state of major ritual impurity may stay the night inside a mosque; if, for example, someone goes to sleep in a mosque [while in a state of ritual purity], then has a 'wet dream' but faces difficulty in leaving because the doors are locked or out of fear for himself or his possessions, he may stay. However, such a person must perform sand ablutions with soil other than that connected with the mosque if he can find no water, but if he finds sufficient water to perform minor ritual ablutions, he must do this.

* * *

According to the Hanbalis, someone in a state of major ritual impurity may recite a passage from the Qur'ān which amounts to less than a short verse or the equivalent amount of a long verse, but he is forbidden to recite more than this. It is also permissible for such a person to invoke the remembrance of God by uttering phrases which contain wording from the Qur'ān, such as uttering the *basmalah* before partaking of food or saying when about to set off on a mount, "Limitless in His glory is He who has made [all] this subservient to our use—since [but for Him], we would not have been able to attain to it" (43:13).

As for passing through a mosque and lingering there without staying the night, it is permissible to someone in a state of major ritual impurity, as well as to a woman who is menstruating or experiencing postpartum bleeding provided that there is no danger of contaminating the mosque with impurity. It is also permissible for someone in a state of major ritual impurity to stay the night in a mosque, even when there is no urgent necessity involved, if he has performed minor ritual ablutions. As for a woman who is menstruating or having postpartum bleeding, she is not allowed to stay the night in a mosque based on the performance of minor ritual ablutions unless her bleeding has stopped.

On Menstruation

The subject of menstruation will be discussed under three main headings: (1) the definition of menstruation, which encompasses topics such as how blood is determined to be menstrual flow and the colors which such blood may have, the amount of blood required in order for a woman to be considered to be menstruating, the age range within which girls or women may correctly be said to be menstruating, the question of whether a pregnant girl or woman can be said to menstruate, and other matters pertinent to such a definition; (2) how long menstruation tends to last and conversely, the number of days out of each month during which a girl or woman remains free of menstrual flow; and (3) the meaning of *istiḥāḍah*, i.e., a condition characterized by chronic vaginal bleeding.

The definition of 'menstruation'

As used generally in the Arabic language, the word rendered 'menstruation' here, that is, *al-ḥayḍ*, means 'flow'. Hence, one might say, *ḥāḍa al-wādī*, meaning, "Water flowed through the riverbed," or *ḥāḍat al-shajarah*, that is, "The tree gave off red resin." The same verb is used with respect to a woman whose menstrual blood has begun to flow. Other Arabic words used to refer to menstruation include *al-ṭamth, al-ḍaḥk,* and *al- i'ṣār*.

As for the meaning of *al-ḥayḍ* as it is used in the context of Islamic jurisprudence, the following footnote includes a detailed presentation of the views of the four schools. The aim of this presentation is to help readers commit the information to memory and to gain a good understanding of matters such as what menstrual blood is, whether a pregnant girl or woman may be said to menstruate, the age range within which menstruation is possible, and the amount of blood required in order for the flow to be classified as menstruation.[104]

---

104. The Malikis define menstrual flow as "blood which flows spontaneously out of a woman's vagina during those years in which she would normally conceive, even if it takes place in a single gush." In what follows we shall offer explanations for each term of this definition.

As used by the Malikis here, the word 'blood' refers to blood which is bright red, or which is yellow or dark brown. In the Malikis' view, menstrual blood can be any of these colors, although the most widely accepted Maliki view is that menstrual flow is, specifically, that blood which is pure red. Hence, if a woman who is within the age range for menstruation has a vaginal flow of a yellowish or brownish liquid, she is considered to be menstruating just as she would be if she had a flow of red blood. Some Malikis hold that menstrual flow is restricted to red blood and does not include secretions which are yellow or dark brown, whereas others hold that if yellowish or brownish vaginal secretions occur during the time of the month in which the woman concerned would normally menstruate, then they, too, are classified as menstrual flow; otherwise, they are not. Moreover, some more discerning thinkers [among the Malikis] hold that this latter view is the most valid one.

As for the phrase, "which flows spontaneously out of a woman's vagina", it means that actual menstrual flow takes place of its own accord. Hence, if the blood flows out of the vagina due to childbirth, it is not menstrual flow, but postpartum vaginal bleeding, which will be discussed below. Similarly, if the flow of blood takes place due to perforation of the hymen, it is clearly not menstrual flow but rather, is like that which flows from someone's hand, nose or any other part of the body which is wounded; hence, all the woman is required to do in such a situation is to cleanse the area which was contaminated with blood.

If vaginal bleeding occurs at some time other than the woman's regular menstrual period due to a medication she has taken, the Malikis do not refer to it as menstrual flow; hence, if such a flow occurs, the woman must fast and pray as she would otherwise. Yet, despite the fact that the days on which such flow occurs are not counted toward the completion of her menstrual period, she must do a compensatory fast later due to the possibility that it may have been actual menstrual flow. If, by contrast, she takes medication which prevents vaginal bleeding at times other than her regular period, she is then considered not to be menstruating, and these days on which she has no vaginal flow are counted toward the fulfillment of the minimum number of ritually pure days she is to have each month. However, it is not permissible for a woman either to prevent her periods from coming or to hasten their onset if this is harmful to her health, since the preservation of one's health is a duty. In sum, then, menstrual flow must come out of a woman's vagina; in other words, if it came out of the anus or any other part of her body, it would not be menstrual flow. In addition, it must come out spontaneously rather than due to some extraneous cause.

As for the phrase, "during those years in which she would normally conceive," it means that if a girl who is still too young to menstruate or an older, post-menopausal woman experiences vaginal bleeding, this is not to be considered menstrual flow. In the Maliki view, then, if a girl who is younger than nine years old experiences vaginal bleeding, it may not be considered menstrual flow; if the girl is nine years of age, experienced women or a reliable physician are to be consulted about the matter. If their judgment is that the girl's flow of blood is a result of menstruation, so be it; otherwise, it is assumed not to be. And the same holds true for girls ten to thirteen years of age. Once a girl reaches the age of fourteen, she is considered an adolescent and no such consultation is required if she experiences vaginal bleeding. As for an older woman, if she is fifty years old and she has a flow of blood from her vagina, the event should likewise be brought before those with expertise in such matters and she should act on the basis of their judgment. This ruling applies to women between fifty and seventy years of age. However, if a woman seventy years old or more has vaginal bleeding, it can in no way be considered menstrual flow. In such a case, the Malikis refer to the flow as *istiḥāḍah*, or chronic vaginal bleeding, whereas they view vaginal bleeding on the part of a young girl less than nine years old as due to pathology and dysfunction. On this point, then, the Malikis differ with the Hanafis, who use the term *istiḥāḍah* to refer to vaginal bleeding on the part of either an elderly woman or a young girl less than nine years old.

In addition, the Malikis hold that a pregnant woman menstruates; hence, if a pregnant woman experiences vaginal bleeding two months after conception—two months being the period of time in which it generally becomes apparent that a woman is pregnant—her menstrual period is estimated to be twenty days long. This estimation continues to be valid until the sixth month of pregnancy if she continues to have vaginal bleeding; if, at this point, the woman goes on having vaginal bleeding, her menstrual period is estimated to be thirty days long. This estimation remains in effect until she gives birth. If, on the other hand, a pregnant woman has vaginal bleeding during the first or second month after conception, her menstrual period will be estimated at its usual length. This topic will be further clarified below in the sections entitled, "The period during which menstruation takes place" and "The period during which a woman is ritually pure." [The view that a pregnant woman is capable of menstruating appears to be based on the state of medical knowledge prevalent at the time this book was written – t.n.].

As for the phrase, "even if it takes place in a single 'gush'", it indicates a flow of blood which takes place over a very short period of time. What this means is that even if only an insignificant amount of blood is passed, a woman is still considered to be menstruating, the result being that she is not allowed to perform ritual prayer until she has been purified of such vaginal bleeding. Similarly, if she is fasting, her fasting ceases to be valid and she is required to make it up later. However, in the case of a woman who was recently divorced or widowed, such a small amount of blood cannot be counted as one of the four menstrual periods which must pass before her waiting period (*'iddah*) is complete; rather, in order to be considered menstruation, the flow must continue for an entire day or part of a day.

* * *

As for the Hanafis, they hold that menstruation may be considered either as a type of *ḥadath* such as the passing of wind, or as a ritually impure substance such as urine. In the former case, they define it as a legal state in which the woman is said to be as a result of her vaginal bleeding, and because of which she is forbidden to have sexual relations, to perform ritual prayer and to fast, as well as to engage in other activities which will be mentioned in the section below dealing with the things that a woman who is menstruating is not allowed to do. In the latter case, menstruation is defined as "a flow of blood from the womb of a woman who is not pregnant, and who is neither [too] young to conceive nor old enough to be post-menopausal"; in addition, they stipulate that the flow of blood must not be a result of either childbirth or illness.

The word 'blood' as used in this definition includes blood of six different colors, namely: red, brown, green, soil-color, yellow and black. Hence, if the liquid which flows out of the woman's womb is one of these colors, it is considered to be menstrual flow provided that it reach the visible portion of her vagina, that is, the portion of her vagina which is visible when she is in a sitting position. If she becomes aware of a flow of blood internally and places a piece of cotton or some similar material in the opening, thereby preventing the blood from reaching the visible portion of her vagina, she will not be considered to be menstruating; similarly, if she is fasting and senses that menstrual flow has begun internally, and if she then inserts a piece of cotton, cloth, etc. in the opening to keep it from reaching the outer part of the vaginal area, her fasting will remain valid. The Hanafis also hold that once the woman's menstrual flow has reached the outside of the vagina, she is thereby considered to be menstruating even if the blood is not flowing at a given moment. In other words, she might experience a visible flow of blood, after which the flow stops before the time when her period customarily ends, then begins to flow again. In such a case, she is still considered to be menstruating even during the period of time in which the flow has stopped. Hence, one may not say that menstruation is the blood itself; otherwise, how could a woman be considered to be menstruating even during the cessation of her blood flow? Rather, the Hanafis hold that in this type of situation, a woman is declared, legally speaking, to be menstruating in the sense that the Lawgiver has declared her to be in this state even if no blood is actually flowing.

By adding the phrase, "a woman who is not pregnant", the Hanafis assert that vaginal bleeding experienced by a pregnant woman is not to be classified as menstrual flow. As for the phrase, "who is neither [too] young to conceive nor old enough to be post-menopausal", it excludes from the category of "menstrual flow" any vaginal bleeding experienced either by a young girl who is less than seven years old or by a woman over fifty-five years old, sometimes described as "in despair of menstruating again." This is the most widely held view among the Hanafis; however, if a woman who is over fifty-five years old has heavy vaginal bleeding similar to menstruation, it is [not] considered to be menstrual flow.

In sum, the Hanafis hold that vaginal bleeding which is experienced by a pregnant woman, by a young girl less than seven years old, or by a woman who has gone through menopause is not to be referred to as menstrual flow, but rather, as *istiḥāḍah*, or chronic vaginal bleeding. As for bleeding which results from the perforation of the hymen, the ruling on it is self-evident since it does not originate in the womb; hence, it is commonly agreed not to be menstrual flow.

It may also be noted that there are some who define menstrual flow simply as "blood which has flowed from a woman's womb." The basis for this is that [the notion that] the blood which flows in cases of *istiḥāḍah* does not originate in the womb, which serves as a 'container' for an unborn child but that rather, it originates in the vagina itself. Perhaps this painstaking analysis should be left to medical specialists; after all, since scholars of Islamic jurisprudence have specified the age range within which a female is generally capable of menstruating and defined a maximum and minimum length of time for a woman's menstrual period, anything beyond this may be seen as a type of scrutiny which need not be engaged in by anyone but medical experts who are capable of providing a practical definition of the difference between regular menstrual flow and chronic vaginal bleeding and determining whether they originate in the same place or not.

* * *

According to the Shafiis, menstrual flow is defined as "a flow of blood from the vagina of a woman who is free from any illness which would cause such a flow, who is at least nine years old, and whose flow of blood is not due to childbirth."

The word 'blood' as used in this definition refers to any vaginal secretion which has one or more of the colors of blood, namely, (1) black, which is the darkest of the possible colors of blood, (2) dark red, (3) light red, (4) brown, or (5) yellow. There are some who hold that 'yellow' as used here refers to a color which is bolder than 'soil-colored', while others hold the opposite. Be that as it may, all such colors are included in the description of menstrual flow. As for the phrase, "from the vagina of a woman", it refers to the outermost portion of the uterus or womb; hence, according to the Shafiis, the blood flows from a 'vein' in the outermost portion of the womb, whether the woman is pregnant or not, since according to both the Shafiis and the Malikis—in contrast to the Hanafis and the Hanbalis—a pregnant woman is capable of menstruation. As for the length of the pregnant woman's menstrual period, it is judged to be the same as it would be if she were not pregnant.

Blood which flows from a source other than the womb is not considered menstrual flow, regardless of whether it comes out of the vagina—as in the case of a perforated hymen—or from the anus or any other part of the body. As for the phrase, "who is free from any illness which would cause such a flow", it serves to exclude any flow of blood from the womb which is due to a pathological condition, the latter of which is referred to as *istiḥāḍah*.

The phrase, "who is at least nine years old" excludes from the definition any flow of blood experienced by a young girl who is less than nine years of age, in which case it is referred to by the Shafiis not as menstrual flow, but as *istiḥāḍah*. On this point, then, the Shafiis concur with the Hanafis and differ with the Malikis, who hold that vaginal bleeding on the part of a young girl less than nine years old is not to be referred to as *istiḥāḍah*, but rather, as "bleeding due to pathology and dysfunction."

The Shafiis recognize no upper age limit for menstruation; rather, in disagreement with all the other schools, they hold that a woman could theoretically go on menstruating till the end of her lifetime. Hence, although it is most common for a woman's periods to end by the age of 62 years, a woman might still experience vaginal bleeding after this age, and if this occurs, the Shafiis consider her to be menstruating.

Finally, the phrase, "not due to childbirth" excludes from the definition of menstruation the vaginal bleeding which occurs during the postpartum phase, a discussion of which will be found below.

* * *

The Hanbalis define menstruation as "a natural flow of blood from inside the female's uterus when she is in a state of good health; it occurs when the girl or woman is not pregnant, and at regular intervals, and it is not caused by childbirth."

The word 'blood' as used in this definition most likely refers to blood which is black, red, or soil-colored. The word 'natural' means that it is a regular part of a woman's normal bodily functioning; moreover, this element of the definition is agreed upon by all four schools. As for the phrase, "from inside the female's uterus", it excludes blood which flows from any other part of the body. By using the phrase, "when the girl or woman is not pregnant," the Hanbalis express the view that menstrual flow does not include vaginal bleeding on the part of someone who is pregnant. On this point, then, the Hanbalis agree with the Hanafis and differ with both the Shafiis and the Malikis.

As for the phrase, "at regular intervals", it indicates that vaginal bleeding experienced by a girl less than nine years old or a woman who is post-menopausal (which, according to the Hanbalis, includes all women over fifty years of age) is not to be considered menstrual flow. If a woman this age experiences vaginal bleeding, however heavy, she is not considered to be menstruating.

Lastly, their use of the phrase, "is not caused by childbirth" indicates that vaginal bleeding which occurs postpartum is not to be considered menstrual flow.

The length of menstrual periods

What is meant here by "the length of menstrual periods" is the number of days during which a woman may be considered to be menstruating [within a given month]; hence, if the time which the flow of blood lasts exceeds or falls short of the given time range, it is not to be classified as menstrual flow.

The minimum length of time for a menstrual period is one day and one night, provided that the blood is flowing as it usually does during one's menstrual period so that if the woman placed a piece of cotton [in her vagina], it would come out with blood stains on it. What is meant by "one day and one night" is a 24-hour period. Hence, if the woman notes the commencement of a flow of blood and it stops before 24 hours have passed, she is not considered to have menstruated. At the same time, however, it is not necessary for her to experience the flow of blood from the beginning of the day and have it continue all day long and all night long as well; rather, all that is required is that it continue for 24 hours from the time it began [even if the flow is intermittent].

As for the maximum length of time for a menstrual period, it is fifteen days and nights. Hence, if a woman continued to experienced vaginal bleeding for sixteen days, she would be considered on the 16th day no longer to be menstruating. This estimate is not based on the usual length of a woman's period. Rather, if she is accustomed to having her period last for three, four, or five days, for example, after which the length of her period changes and she begins to have vaginal bleeding for a longer period of time, her vaginal bleeding will continue to be considered menstrual flow [rather than *istiḥāḍah*] up to a maximum of fifteen days.

This is the view adopted by the Shafiis and the Hanbalis, in support of which a significant number of prophetic hadiths are cited. However, none of these hadiths is sound. An example of such hadiths is a well-known saying cited in books of jurisprudence according to which the Prophet said, "Women are deficient in both reason and piety." When asked, "And what is deficient in their piety?" he replied, "They spend half their lives not praying." In other words, they spend half the month menstruating. However, this hadith is invalid. First of all, we have the words of Ibn al-Jawzī, who stated, "This is an unknown hadith," and of al-Bayhaqī, who declared, "I have not found it [this hadith] in any of the collections of prophetic hadiths." Not only so, but others also have declared that it has nothing to support it. Moreover, the fact of the matter is that it makes no sense, because the Lawgiver Himself is the One who has prevented women from performing the ritual prayers while they are menstruating! This being the case, on what basis should they be described in this unjust manner? The only support which the Shafiis and the Hanbalis have for the above estimate, then, is the well-attested statement by 'Alī, may God be pleased with him: "Anything beyond fifteen days [of vaginal bleeding] is *istiḥāḍah*." As for the views of the Malikis and the Hanafis, they are presented in the footnote below.[105]

---

105. According to the Hanafis, the minimum length of a menstrual period is three days and nights, while the maximum is ten days and nights. Hence, if a woman has been menstruating regularly and her period lasts longer than usual but without exceeding ten days and nights, the 'extra' days are still counted as days of men-

strual flow. Moreover, if the usual length of her period is three days, for example, and it lasts for four days, the 'usual' length of her period becomes four days rather than three; similarly, if the usual length of her period is four days and in a given month it lasts five days instead, the 'usual' length becomes five days; and so forth up to ten days. The reason for this is that the 'usual' length of a woman's period is established by a single instance. However, if her period were to last for more than ten days, the flow on all days beyond the tenth would be classified as *istiḥāḍah* rather than as menstrual flow, and the 'usual' length of her period would be set at the maximum ten days and nights.

As for the Malikis, they hold that as far as the validity of acts of worship [such as prayer and fasting] is concerned, there is no minimum for a woman's menstrual period with regard either to the amount of blood flow or the period of time it lasts. Hence, if a woman has a flow of blood which comes all at once and stops within moments, she will be ritually impure. However, in the case of a newly divorced or widowed woman for whom there is a need to make certain that she is not pregnant, they hold that the minimum is one day or part of a day. With regard to the amount of blood flow, there is no upper limit; thus, for example, it is not limited to a *raṭl* or more or less. As for the maximum length of a menstrual period, it is estimated at fifteen days for a girl or woman who has just begun to menstruate and who is not pregnant. Within the limits of this 15-day maximum, the length of her period is estimated to be three days longer than her usual blood flow, the purpose for this being to ensure that the flow has stopped fully [before she performs *ghusl*]. Hence, if her first period lasts five days, after which she has a second period, she should wait three additional days the second month [before performing *ghusl*]; if she then has a third period, her 'usual' length is considered to be eight days since, as we have seen, the 'usual' length of a woman's period is established on the basis of a single instance, and beyond these eight days she must wait an additional three [that is, a total of 11 days] before considering her period to be over. If she then has a fourth period, she waits fourteen days [before performing *ghusl*]. If she continues to have periods after this, she should not wait for more than fifteen days before considering her period to have ended. If any vaginal bleeding occurs beyond these fifteen days—or after the three-day waiting period following the cessation of her menstrual flow if it lasted less than fifteen days—then such bleeding should be viewed as *istiḥāḍah*.

The number of days out of each month during which a woman is considered to be ritually pure with respect to menstrual flow

The minimum period out of each month during which a woman may be considered ritually pure of menstrual flow is fifteen days.[106] Hence, if a woman's menstrual period began and continued for three days, after which her blood flow stopped, then resumed up to fourteen days later, this latter flow of blood would not be considered menstrual flow regardless of whether the time period during which there was no vaginal bleeding fell between two menstrual periods (such that, for example, her period began, after which her blood flow stopped, after which it began again a maximum of fourteen days later), or between postpartum bleeding and a menstrual period (such that, for example, fourteen or fewer days after the cessation of postpartum bleeding, the woman began to menstruate).[107]

As for the maximum length of time during which a woman may be ritually pure of menstrual flow, there is none. Thus, supposing that a woman's menstrual flow stopped and she remained free of it for the rest of her life, she would be considered ritually pure. On the other hand, the Shafiis and the Hanafis hold that if a woman observes vaginal bleeding on one day, after which the bleeding stops, and if it then resumes on another day, she will be considered to be menstruating during the days in between the discontinuation of her vaginal bleeding and its subsequent resumption.[108]

---

106. According to the Hanbalis, the minimum number of days between menstrual periods during which a woman is judged to be ritually pure is thirteen.

107. In agreement with both the Hanafis and the Malikis, the Shafiis hold that the [minimum] time period during which a woman is ritually pure of menstrual flow is fifteen days out of each month. However, they stipulate that this period of time must fall between two menstrual periods, whereas if it falls between the end of a woman's postpartum bleeding and the beginning of menstrual flow, there is no minimum to how long it may last. Thus, for example, if a woman's postpartum bleeding stopped only one day before she had further vaginal bleeding, this latter could still be considered menstrual flow.

108. According to the Malikis, if a woman has a momentary flow of vaginal blood, after which the flow stops, she is to be considered ritually pure until or unless she has a further flow of blood. Hence, until or unless the flow resumes, she is to engage in whatever activities are permitted and/or required of a woman who is in a state of ritual purity.

As for the Hanbalis, they agree with the Malikis that during the period of time which falls between two different flows of blood [be they menstrual flow or postpartum bleeding], a woman is to be considered ritually pure. However, as we have seen, the minimum length of time which a menstrual period may last in the Hanbalis' view is one day and one night; hence, if a woman has vaginal bleeding for one day or less, she is not considered to be menstruating in the first place.

Istiḥāḍah, or chronic vaginal bleeding

Chronic vaginal bleeding (Arabic, *istiḥāḍah*) is defined as a flow of blood from the uterus which takes place at a time other than that for one's menstrual period or postpartum bleeding. All vaginal bleeding which occurs beyond the maximum time period for a woman's menstrual flow, which lasts less than the minimum time period for such flow, or which occurs before a girl has reached the aforementioned age for menstruation, is considered *istiḥāḍah*. Hence, if vaginal bleeding is experienced by a girl less than seven or nine years of age (depending on which school's viewpoint one is referring to), it is to be classified as chronic vaginal bleeding (*istiḥāḍah*).

Like those who suffer from urinary incontinence, chronic diarrhea, etc., a girl or woman who suffers from chronic vaginal bleeding is granted an exemption from certain requirements pertaining to ritual purity. The ruling on *istiḥāḍah* is that the person who suffers from this condition is allowed to engage in activities which would be forbidden to a woman who is menstruating or postpartum, such as reciting the Qur'ān, entering a mosque, touching the written Qur'ān, going on a spiritual retreat to devote herself to worship and contemplation, circumambulating the Ka'bah, and so on. All that is required of a woman suffering from *istiḥāḍah* when she wishes to engage in such acts of worship is that she perform minor ritual ablutions.

As for the determination of the time period taken up by *istiḥāḍah*, this differs among the various schools.[109]

---

109. The Shafiis hold that if a girl or woman who has newly begun to experience chronic vaginal bleeding is able to distinguish between a heavier flow and a lighter one, then her menstrual flow is the heavy flow provided that it neither lasts a shorter time than the minimum for one's menstrual period nor a longer time than the maximum. As for the lighter flow, it is classified as *istiḥāḍah* and hence, during this phase she is to be deemed ritually pure on two conditions: (1) that the number of days of light flow are no fewer than the minimum period out of each month during which a woman is to be considered ritually pure of menstrual discharge, and (2) that the flow is consistent from day to day. For example, if the blood she observes one day is red, while another day it is black, she lacks one condition for distinguishing [between] menstrual flow and *istiḥāḍah*. If neither of these two conditions is met, she is to count her actual menstrual period as one day and one night such that the rest of the month, she is free of menstrual flow just as if she were a young girl unable to distinguish between a heavy or light flow.

As for a girl or woman has suffered from *istiḥāḍah* for some time and is able to distinguish between her light and heavy flows, her menstrual period will be represented by the days of heavy flow. If, on the other hand, she is unable to distinguish light from heavy flow but she knows approximately how long her period generally lasts and how much flow it involves, she is to rely on this.

* * *

According to the Hanbalis, a girl or woman suffering from *istiḥāḍah* will either have had previous experiences of menstruation and postpartum bleeding, or be new to such types of vaginal blood flow. In the case of someone who has previously experienced menstruation and/or postpartum bleeding, she should act on the basis of the customary length of her menstrual periods even if she is able to distinguish between heavy and light flow. If she is new to the experience of vaginal bleeding but is able to distinguish heavy from light flow, she should act on the basis of her own discernment provided that the heavier flow meets the conditions for being classified as menstrual flow, i.e., (1) that it lasts no less than one day and one night, and (2) that it lasts no longer than fifteen days. If she is unable to make this distinction, her menstrual period should be estimated to last one day and one night, after which she should perform *ghusl* and engage in all activities which are required of and/or permitted for women in a state of ritual purity. She should follow these guidelines for the first three months of her menstrual flow; then in the fourth month, she is to begin estimating the length of her period as six or seven days, which is the usual length of women's menstrual periods, relying on her own personal judgments and inquiries.

* * *

As for the Malikis, they hold that if a girl or woman with chronic vaginal bleeding is able to determine that the blood which is flowing at a given time is menstrual flow based on its odor, its color, its consistency or the pain that accompanies it, it is to be considered menstrual flow provided that it has been preceded by the requisite number of days in which she was considered ritually pure, namely, fifteen days. If she is not able to determine for certain that the bleeding she observes is menstrual flow, or if the blood which she determines to be her menstrual flow comes before she has had the minimum number of ritually pure days, it should be considered *istiḥāḍah*; in other words, she should consider herself still to be ritually pure. Theoretically speaking, a woman could continue to be ritually pure in this sense for her entire life. As for someone in a state of uncertainty, the length of her menstrual period is to be estimated at one "white year" [I have not been able to ascertain what the term "white year" refers to – t.n.]. In the case of a girl or woman who is able to distinguish her light from her heavy flow, she should not wait three days beyond the maximum length of her usual menstrual period as a means of ensuring that it has really ended; rather, she should restrict herself to the number of days which her period generally lasts provided that the blood flow which she has determined to be her menstrual period does not continue longer than this; however, if it does continue, she should wait until the flow has stopped completely.

* * *

According to the Hanafis, a girl or woman who suffers from *istiḥāḍah* will be one of three types: (1) a 'beginner', that is, someone who has just had her first experience of menstruation or postpartum bleeding, after which her blood flow continues, (2) 'seasoned', that is, someone who has previously experienced menstruation and/or postpartum bleeding followed by a period of valid ritual purity, or (3) 'perplexed', that is, someone who has previously experienced menstruation and/or childbirth followed by a normal transition to ritual purity, but who now has a chronic vaginal flow and has forgotten how long her menstrual periods used to last.

If the beginner's flow of blood continues, the length of her periods should be estimated at ten days, and the time during which she is ritually pure should be estimated at twenty days out of each month; as for the length of her postpartum bleeding, it should be estimated at forty days, while the phase following this during which she is ritually pure again should be estimated at twenty days, after which her menstrual periods should be estimated at ten days out of each month, and so on.

As for the seasoned girl or woman, she should rely on her memory of how long her menstrual periods used to be and the number of days out of each month she used to spend in a state of ritual purity. However, if the usual length of time she used to remain free of menstrual flow was half the year, that is, a full fifteen days out of each month, and if she is newly divorced or widowed and is calculating the length of her *'iddah*, she should subtract one hour from this [that is, from 15 days] to arrive at the length of her menstrual periods [four of which must pass before her *'iddah* ends]. With regard to matters not pertaining to the *'iddah*, she should refer to the length of her normal menstrual cycle.

As for the girl or woman who is 'perplexed', the Hanafis' ruling on her situation is quite stringent and detailed; hence, anyone who wishes to know their rulings in this connection should refer to some book other than this one.

Postpartum bleeding and its definition

Postpartum bleeding is defined as blood which is shed [by the uterus] slightly before, during or following childbirth.[110] If a woman has had a Caesarian section, the vaginal bleeding which takes place following this is not classified as postpartum bleeding; nevertheless, in the case of a woman who is newly divorced or widowed, her required waiting period (*'iddah*) is brought to completion simply by her having given birth.

As for an aborted fetus, if some of its human features are apparent,[111] such as fingers, fingernails, hair, etc., the blood which is shed following the miscarriage is classified as postpartum bleeding. If, on the other hand, no such human features are apparent, as is the case when what is aborted is a blood clot or an embryo, then if the subsequent flow of blood coincides with the time for the woman's menstrual period, it is to be classified as menstrual flow; otherwise, it is considered to be due to pathology and dysfunction.

If a woman gives birth to twins, the phase of her postpartum bleeding is considered to begin with the delivery of the first twin rather than the second. Hence, if some time passes between the delivery of the first twin and the delivery of the second—even supposing that it is longer than the postpartum phase itself—the woman's postpartum bleeding is considered to begin with the birth of the first child.[112] Thus, supposing that the second twin is not born until forty days after the first, the flow of blood which follows the second birth is considered bleeding due to pathology and dysfunction rather than postpartum bleeding.

---

110. According to the Malikis, the blood shed during or following childbirth is to be classified as postpartum bleeding; this includes blood which is shed during or after the birth of the first of twins or before the birth of the second twin. As for blood which is shed before delivery takes place, the Malikis classify it as menstrual flow.

According to the Hanbalis, the blood which is shed two or three days before delivery along with signs that labor is about to begin, as well as the blood which is shed during delivery, is to be considered postpartum bleeding.

As for the Shafiis, they hold that in order for blood flow to be classified as postpartum bleeding, it must occur after the infant has come entirely out of the uterus. Thus, for example, if bleeding occurs while the birth is still taking place, it is not to be classified as postpartum bleeding. In addition, the Shafiis stipulate that in order for the flow of blood to be postpartum bleeding, it must take place no more than 14 days following delivery. If it takes place after this, it is viewed as menstrual flow. As for the blood which is shed while the infant is being born and/or before labor begins, it is not to be viewed as postpartum bleeding; rather, it is to be viewed as menstrual flow if the woman was, in fact, menstruating [since, as we have seen, the Malikis hold that it is possible for a pregnant woman to menstruate – t.n.]. If she was not, in fact, menstruating, such a blood flow is categorized as 'putrid' (*fāsid*).

The Hanafis hold that postpartum bleeding includes all blood flow which takes place from the time the birth is halfway complete. As for the blood which is shed either before delivery begins or when the delivery is less than half complete, it is

Unlike menstrual flow, there is no minimum length of time set for postpartum bleeding; hence, if a woman gives birth and her bleeding stops immediately or very soon thereafter, or even supposing that she gives birth without any flow of blood at all, her postpartum bleeding will be viewed as having ended and she must engage in all activities required of a woman who is in a state of ritual purity. The maximum length of time set for postpartum bleeding is forty days.[113] As for the intermittent periods during the postpartum phase when there is no flow of blood—for example, when a woman has bleeding one day and not the next—the various schools offer different rulings in this regard.[114]

---

classified as 'putrid blood', as a result of which the mother is to engage in all activities which are permitted to a woman who is in a state of ritual purity.

111. According to the Shafiis, it is not necessary for any of the fetus's human features to be apparent in order for the associated flow of blood to be classified as postpartum bleeding. Rather, if the midwives [nurses, physicians, etc.] attending the event affirm that what was aborted was the beginning of a human life, then the flow of blood following the miscarriage is considered to be postpartum bleeding even if what was aborted was nothing but a blood clot or an embryo.

112. According to the Shafiis, if a woman gives birth to twins, her postpartum bleeding is considered to begin with the delivery of the second child. As for the blood flow which occurs after the first child is born, it is not regarded as postpartum bleeding; rather, if the bleeding coincides with the time for the woman's menstrual period, it is regarded as menstrual flow, and otherwise it is judged to be "bleeding due to pathology and dysfunction."

As for the Malikis, they hold that if a woman gives birth to twins and the second child is delivered sixty days after the first—sixty days being the maximum length of the postpartum period in their view—then each delivery is considered to be followed by a separate postpartum phase. However, if a shorter time period separates the births, there is only one postpartum phase, which is considered to begin with the birth of the first twin.

113. The maximum length of time which the Shafiis recognize for postpartum bleeding is sixty days, although it generally lasts no more than forty days.

As for the Malikis, they set sixty days as the maximum for postpartum bleeding.

114. The Hanafis hold that during the intermittent periods of the postpartum phase when there is no flow of blood, the woman continues to be in a state of major ritual impurity, even if such periods last fifteen days or more.

As for the Shafiis, they hold that during such intermittent periods in which no blood flow occurs, the woman is to be considered ritually pure if the lack of flow lasts fifteen days or more. The blood flow which preceded such an interruption is to be regarded as postpartum bleeding, while that which follows it is regarded as menstrual flow. If the interruption of blood flow lasts fourteen days or less, however, the woman is still considered to be having postpartum bleeding. If no bleeding occurs immediately following delivery and if none occurs within fifteen days thereafter, the woman is considered to be ritually pure, and any blood flow which takes places following this is regarded as menstrual flow. In a case such as this, the woman, in effect, does not experience the 'postpartum' phase.

Activities which are forbidden to a woman who is menstruating or experiencing postpartum bleeding until her flow of blood stops

A woman who is menstruating or experiencing postpartum bleeding is forbidden to engage in the activities which are forbidden to someone, male or female, who is in a state of major ritual impurity, such as ritual prayer, touching the written Qur'ān, Qur'anic recitation, etc. However, in addition to these activities, the menstruating or postpartum woman is likewise forbidden to embark on any type of fast, be it obligatory or voluntary. If a woman in either of these states does fast, her fasting will have no validity; not only so, but if she should do so during the month of Ramaḍān, she is guilty of wrongdoing for which she is liable for severe chastisement, and she shows herself to be shamefully ignorant.

A menstruating or postpartum woman is required to make up any fasting days which she missed during Ramaḍān; however, she is not required to make up prayers which she did not perform during such days. The reason for this is that the obligatory ritual prayers recur every day, hence, making up for them [along with the performance of the prayers she would be required to perform anyway] would cause her undue hardship, whereas God has relieved us of such oppressive burdens. As God declares in His revelation, He "has laid no hardship on you in [anything that pertains to] religion" (22:78).

Another act of worship which is invalid if performed by a woman who is menstruating or postpartum is seclusion for the sake of worship and contemplation.

Still another ruling pertaining to a woman who is menstruating or postpartum is that her husband is forbidden to divorce her when she is in either of these conditions. However, although it is forbidden, it occurs, and when it does, the husband should be commanded to take her back if at all possible. (Those who wish to learn

---

As for the Malikis, they hold that if, during the postpartum phase, a woman experiences no vaginal bleeding for two weeks, she is to be considered ritually pure, and whatever vaginal bleeding occurs after this is to be considered menstrual flow. However, if the interruption in her vaginal bleeding lasts for less than two weeks, then any blood flow occurring thereafter is still to be viewed as postpartum bleeding. Furthermore, the Malikis add together the days on which the woman has had vaginal bleeding, omitting the days on which there was no blood flow, until they add up to sixty days, at which point her postpartum phase is declared to be over; meanwhile, during the days on which there is no blood flow she is to go about her affairs as though she were ritually pure: praying, fasting, and so forth.

The Hanbalis hold that on the days when a woman in the postpartum phase has no vaginal bleeding, she is obliged to engage in all activities which are permitted and/or required of a woman who is ritually pure.

(It bears noting here that the Malikis hold that in order for a flow of blood to be described as *istiḥāḍah*, the girl or woman who experiences it must be within the age range in which she would be capable of menstruation; however, it cannot simultaneously be chronic vaginal bleeding and regular menstrual flow or postpartum bleeding. As for the flow of blood which might be experienced by a very young girl, the Malikis describe it as "resulting from pathology and dysfunction.")

more about the ruling forbidding divorce in the case of a woman who is menstruating or postpartum, as well as the various types of divorce—including those consistent with the prophetic Sunnah, the 'innovative' or heretical, the allowable and the forbidden—may refer to Volume IV of this work.)

A woman who is menstruating or postpartum is forbidden to allow her husband to have sexual relations with her until her flow of blood has stopped and she has performed *ghusl*.[115] If she is unable to perform *ghusl*, she must perform sand ablutions before she comes together with her husband. Included here is the prohibition against [the man's] fondling [the woman] in the area between the navel and the knee; a woman must not allow her husband to fondle or caress this area while she is menstruating or postpartum, nor must he force her to allow him to do so.[116] This activity is only permitted under such circumstances if either the man or the woman wears a garment which covers the genitals as well as the area extending down to the knee and up to the navel. In order for such a garment to achieve its purpose, it must

115. As we have seen, the Hanafis hold that a man may have sexual relations with his wife once her menstrual flow or postpartum bleeding has stopped; he may also have sexual relations with his wife once the maximum time period for each of these phases has passed—the maximum for a menstrual period being ten days and ten nights, and the maximum period for postpartum bleeding being forty days—even if she has not performed *ghusl*.

116. The Hanbalis hold that it is permissible for a man to enjoy all parts of his wife's body during the time when she is menstruating or having postpartum bleeding without any barrier between his skin and hers; the only thing which is not permitted is full sexual intercourse, which is itself not classified as a major sin by the Hanbali school. If someone does commit this sin, he is to atone for his guilt by donating in charity the amount of one dinar or half a dinar if he is able. Otherwise, he is exempted from this requirement. In either case, however, he is required to repent for what he has done. This ruling applies provided that no illness or severe harm will result from the infraction he has committed; otherwise, it is not simply a minor sin, but a serious infraction which is strictly, utterly forbidden by the unanimous agreement of all four schools.

be thick enough to prevent the exchange of their body heat if they come in contact with each other. As for all other parts of the body,[117] it is agreed that they may be touched and enjoyed however the two spouses please. As for actual sexual intercourse before the woman's menstrual flow or postpartum bleeding has stopped, however, this is forbidden even if a barrier is used—such as a condom, for example. If a man should have sexual intercourse with his wife while her flow of blood is still occurring, he is guilty of wrongdoing and should repent without delay; the wife is likewise guilty of wrongdoing for allowing him to do so, and it is a practice based on the prophetic Sunnah for them to give a dinar or half a dinar as charity [in expression of their repentance]. As for the value of a 'dinar', this is clarified in the section on *zakāh* below (Hanafi, Shafii).

---

117. It is agreed upon among the Malikis that a menstruating or postpartum woman is forbidden to have sexual relations as long as her blood flow continues. The question then arises: Is it permissible for her husband to fondle and caress the area between her navel and her knees without a barrier between his skin and hers? There are some Malikis who, like the Hanbalis, rule that it is permissible. However, the prevailing view among the Malikis is that it is forbidden even with a physical barrier due to the danger that, if the husband becomes highly aroused, he might not be able to restrain himself from going on to full intercourse. This ruling is consistent with the fact that the Malikis base their rulings on the principle known as *sadd al-dharā'i'*, that is, of closing the door, as it were, to any situation which might lead to that which is forbidden.

This being said, it should be clear that there are benefits to be found in the prohibition against having sexual relations with a woman while she is menstruating, since there is unanimous agreement among physicians that such a practice is extremely harmful to the reproductive organs. [Such statements no doubt reflect an earlier state of medical awareness – t.n.]. Nevertheless, there are rulings by some of the schools which might remove this restriction. The Hanafis, for example, allow the woman to have sexual relations if her blood flow ceases and if it continues to be absent for the entire time period for one ritual prayer—between the call to the noon prayer and the mid-afternoon prayer, for example—even if she has not performed *ghusl*. Given the fact that there are many women whose flow is intermittent during their menstrual periods, the Malikis also allow a woman to have sexual intercourse immediately after her blood flow stops, provided that she perform *ghusl* first.

In addition, the Malikis hold that if a woman causes her vaginal bleeding to stop, if even by means of medication, it is permissible for her to have sexual relations. Hence, it is not necessary for her vaginal bleeding to have stopped spontaneously. Based on the foregoing, people with particularly robust sex drives who find it difficult to go long periods of time without intercourse are free to reach their own judgments on this matter and to act accordingly.

On Wiping One's Shoes as Part of Ritual Ablutions

The discussion of the practice of wiping one's shoes as part of ritual ablutions will include the following ten topics: (1) the definition of "wiping one's shoes", (2) the definition of the type of shoe which it is permissible to wipe as part of ritual ablutions, (3) the ruling on this practice, (4) the evidence in favor of this practice, (5) the conditions associated with wiping one's shoes as part of ritual ablutions, (6) how much of the shoe is to be wiped, (7) the manner in which the shoes are to be wiped in emulation of the prophetic Sunnah, (8) undesirable practices associated with wiping one's shoes, (9) how long one is allowed to wipe one's shoes as part of ritual ablutions before having to take them off and wash one's feet, and (10) that which invalidates the act of wiping one's shoes.

The definition of "wiping one's shoes"

As used generally in the Arabic language, the word *masḥ* (rendered as 'wiping' here) means to pass one's hand over something. As for its meaning in the context of Islamic law, it refers to the process of wetting a particular type of shoe—the required specifications for which will be explained below—at a specified time.

As for the ruling on this practice, it is a concession which the Lawgiver has granted to accountable men and women, both those who are traveling and those who are settled in one place. As generally used in the Arabic language, the word 'concession' (*rukhṣah*) means 'ease' or 'facility'; as for its meaning in the context of Islamic law, it is defined as a practice which goes against a given piece of legal evidence or legal principle based on additional, opposed legal evidence [which calls for one to act in opposition to the original piece of evidence]. As for a practice which is based on legal evidence without the existence of any opposing texts, it is referred to as a "divinely enjoined duty" (*'azīmah*).[118]

118. The word *'azīmah* also conveys the meaning of 'resolve' or 'determination'. Hence, there are situations in which a divinely granted concession is available to someone—for example, the ruling that if one is traveling during Ramaḍān, he or she is not required to fast. In such a situation, the person may or may not choose to take advantage of this concession, depending on his or her personal resolve in the matter [t.n.].

However, the practice of wiping one's shoes as part of ritual ablutions is sometimes a 'duty' (*wājib*).[119] Examples of situations in which wiping one's shoes rather than washing one's feet becomes obligatory are: (1) when someone fears that if he takes off his shoes and washes his feet, he will miss a given obligatory prayer, (2) when someone fears that he may miss the opportunity to perform some other obligatory act of worship, such as standing on Mt. 'Arafah, and (3) when the person lacks sufficient water to wash his feet. In all other situations, however, it is simply a concession, that is, a practice which one is allowed to adopt under specific circumstances even though washing one's feet would be preferable to wiping one's shoes.[120]

The definition of the type of shoe one may wipe as part of ritual ablutions

The type of shoe that may be wiped as part of ritual ablutions is one which is worn on the feet and which extends up to the ankles. It may be made of leather, wool, hair, camel's hair, linen, or other such materials.[121] As for footwear that is not made of leather, it is referred to as a stocking; a stocking may in some cases be referred to as a 'shoe', but only if it meets the following three conditions. It must: (1) be thick enough to prevent water from penetrating to the skin beneath, (2) stay on the foot by itself without being tied on, and (3) not be transparent such that one can see the person's foot through it. Hence, even if stockings are thick enough to prevent water from soaking through them to one's feet and, in addition, stay on one's feet by themselves, they may not be considered shoes if one can see through them. In sum, then, 'stockings' which meet the three conditions mentioned here—whether they are made of wool, leather, or anything else, and even if they have no soles—may be classified in terms of Islamic law as 'shoes'.

---

119. In other words, there are situations in which, in order to obey some other aspect of Islamic law, one has no choice but to take advantage of this divinely granted concession [t.n.].

120. Nevertheless, the Hanbalis hold that wiping one's shoes is preferable to taking them off and washing one's feet. Their reason for holding this position is that God desires for people to take advantage of the concessions He has granted them, since in this way they become aware of His graciousness toward them, which in turn leads them to be grateful to Him. There are also some Hanafis who share this view.

121. According to the Malikis, it is not permissible to wipe shoes which are made of anything but leather, although their sides might be made of wool, linen, etc., while the upper and lower parts are made of leather as in the case of some shoes which have soles, thick cloth sides, and a leather top. They also stipulate that leather used in shoes must have been bored with an awl; hence, if the pieces are held in place by some sort of material [glue, for example] without having been pierced [and stitched together], then they may not be classified as 'shoes'.

Evidence in support of wiping one's shoes as part of ritual ablutions

The practice of wiping one's shoes is supported by numerous sound prophetic hadiths which have been handed down through so many distinct chains of transmission that there is virtually no doubt as to their reliability. Ibn 'Abd al-Barr [d. 1071 AD/463 AH] tells us in his book entitled, *Al-Istidhkār* that approximately forty of the Prophet's companions relate narratives on the Prophet's authority according to which he himself use to wipe his shoes as part of ritual ablutions. Ḥasan states, "I was told by seventy of the Prophet's companions that he used to wipe his shoes as part of his ritual ablutions." Among the sound prophetic hadiths on this subject is one concerning Jarīr Ibn 'Abdullah al-Bajalī,[122] and related by all six imams.[123] It is narrated by al-A'mash on the authority of Ibrāhīm, on the authority of Hammām, on the authority of Jarīr, that Jarīr once urinated, then performed his ablutions and wiped his shoes rather than washing his feet. "Do you do *that*?!" someone asked him. In reply, he said, "Yes, I do. I have seen the Messenger of God urinate, then perform his ablutions and wipe his shoes rather than wash his feet."

This same point is mentioned by ['Abdullah Ibn Yūsuf] al-Zayla'ī [d. 1360 AD/762 AH] in his book entitled, *Naṣb al-Rāyah*, where he states, "This hadith used to be pleasing to them, because Jarīr's conversion to Islam took place subsequent to the revelation of Sūrat al-Mā'idah,[124] that is, the chapter of the Qur'ān which contains the verse concerning the manner in which ritual ablutions are to be performed, namely, "O you who have attained to faith! When you are about to pray, wash your face, and your hands and arms up to the elbows, and pass your [wet] hands lightly over your head, and [wash] your feet up to the ankles..."[125] This verse explicitly confirms the necessity of washing one's feet with water. Nevertheless, it is opposed by a large number of sound prophetic hadiths which have been passed down through so many distinct chains of transmission that there can be no doubt as to the accuracy of their import; not only so, but it is an established fact that they are later than the verse quoted above. Hence, what one may conclude is that God has commanded us to wash our feet as part of our ritual ablutions if we are not wearing shoes, whereas if we are wearing shoes, all we are required to do is to wipe our shoes rather than wash our feet.

Further evidence in favor of this practice may be found in a prophetic hadith included by al-Bukhārī on the authority of al-Mughīrah Ibn Shu'bah. According to this account, the Prophet once went out to relieve himself and was followed by al-Mughīrah, who came carrying a container of water. When he was finished, al-Mughīrah poured water over him and he performed his ablutions, but instead of washing his feet, he simply wiped his shoes. In another hadith included by al-Bukhārī

122. Jarīr Ibn 'Abdullah al-Bajalī [d. 51 or 54 AH], a lord of the Yemeni tribe of Bajīlah, embraced Islam in the year 10 AH [t.n.].

123. The "six imams" refer to Muslim, al-Bukhārī, Ibn Dāwūd, Ibn Mājah, al-Tirmidhī and al-Nasā'ī, each of whom has a compilation of sound hadiths to his name [t.n.].

124. Surah 5, The Repast.

125. Surah 5:6.

on the authority of al-Mughīrah, he states, "Once when I was accompanying the Prophet on a journey, I reached down to take off his shoes [in order for him to wash them in completion of his ablutions]. But he said, 'Leave them on. When I put them on, they were ritually pure,' after which he proceeded to wipe them." These, then, are two of the accounts to this effect narrated by al-Bukhārī, Muslim, and other compilers of sound prophetic hadiths.

Conditions associated with wiping one's shoes as part of ritual ablutions

As we have seen, the word 'shoe' may be applied to anything worn on the foot regardless of whether it is made of leather, wool or any other material, provided that it meets the three conditions described in the section above. Anything which may be referred to as a 'shoe' in this sense may be wiped in lieu of washing one's feet when performing ritual ablutions, given the following conditions:

(1) The shoes must cover the feet, including the heels; as for that which is above the heel, it need not be covered, nor must the shoe be made of one piece. It is also permissible for them to open at the top and to close with buttons, buckles, shoelaces, etc. Hence, the basic condition here is that they cover the feet, whether they are closed to begin with or are partially open, but with buttons, clasps or some other means by which they are drawn closed after being put on.

(2) They must not be even slightly open at the heel. Thus, for example, if they have holes through which part of the foot is visible, it is not permissible to wipe them in place of washing one's feet. The reason for this is that [when one performs ritual ablutions], it is necessary to wash the entire foot including the heel such that if even a small area remained unwashed, one's ablutions would be invalid. Hence, given that the same ruling applies to the shoe which covers the foot, then if part of the shoe is missing, it cannot serve as a substitute for the foot, as it were. (This is the view of the Hanbalis and the Shafiis.)[126]

---

126. The Hanafis hold that if a shoe fails to cover all of the foot and the heel—as is the case if there are holes in one of the shoes through which parts of the foot can be seen—then if these holes cover an area no greater than the size of three small toes, it does no harm, and the shoes may be wiped even with such holes in them. However, if they amount to an area larger than this, one must wash his feet rather than wiping his shoes.

If there are holes in both shoes, one should add up the areas of the holes in each shoe separately; if the holes in one of the shoes amount to more than the size of one's three smallest toes, it is no longer valid to wipe them as part of one's ablutions. Otherwise, one can wipe them as usual even if the other shoe has holes in it which, if their area were added to those in the first shoe, would amount to more than the size of one's three smallest toes.

As for the Malikis, they hold that if one of the shoes has holes in it which cover one-third or more of the area of the shoe, it is not permissible to wipe the shoes as part of ritual ablutions; however, if the holes amount to less than this area, it is permitted. Hence, the Hanafis and the Malikis agree that even if one's shoes have holes in them through which parts of one's feet are visible, one may still wipe them

(3) That one be able to walk a good distance while wearing the shoes. It is permissible for the shoes to be loose enough for the top, or most of the top, of the foot to show, so long as it is possible to keep walking in them (Hanafi, Shafii).[127]

(4) That the shoes be one's own legitimate possession. If they have been stolen or taken from someone by force, or if there is some doubt as to the legitimacy of one's ownership of them, it is not permissible to wipe them as part of one's ablutions. (This is the view of the Hanbalis and the Malikis.)[128]

(5) That the shoes be ritually pure. If one wears shoes which have impurities on some part of them, it is not permissible to wipe them as part of ritual ablutions. However, the various schools hold differing views on this point.[129]

---

as part of ritual ablutions. However, they differ in their rulings on the area that such holes may cover; that is, the Malikis hold that the holes may amount to one-third of the area of the foot, while according to the Hanafis, the maximum allowable area for such holes is the size of one's three smallest toes.

127. According to the Malikis, if one's shoe is loose enough that some or all of the foot shows, this does no harm; rather, what is not acceptable is for it to be so loose that one's foot does not fill it and, as a result, slips out of place. If this is the case, it is not permissible to wipe such shoes as part of one's ritual ablutions even if one is able to walk some distance in them.

According to the Hanbalis, if one's shoes are loose enough that they make visible a part of the foot which must be washed during ritual ablutions, it is not permissible to wipe them rather than wash one's feet.

128. As for the Hanafis and the Shafiis, they hold that even if the shoes have been stolen or taken by force (in which case it is unlawful to own or wear them), it is nevertheless permissible to wipe them as part of one's ritual ablutions. In other words, the unlawfulness of wearing or owning the shoes does not negate the validity of wiping them as part of one's ablutions. A counterpart to this is the ruling according to which one may use water which has been stolen or taken by force in the performance of ritual ablutions provided that it is *ṭahūr*, although the person who does so is guilty of wrongdoing.

It may be noted in this regard that those who maintain that it is forbidden to use anything which has been stolen or taken by force in the performance of acts of worship whose purpose is to help us draw near to God Almighty have the soundest reasoning on their side.

129. According to the Malikis, it is not permissible to wipe shoes as part of ritual ablutions unless they are ritually pure. Hence, if they have been contaminated by ritual impurity, it is not valid to wipe them as part of one's ablutions despite the view that the removal of impurities from one's clothing is [not obligatory, but rather] an emulation of the prophetic Sunnah. In other words, the Malikis maintain that shoes are subject to their own special ruling, and that impurities which get on them may not be overlooked under any circumstances.

The Shafiis maintain that if a pair of shoes is contaminated by a type of ritual impurity which may be overlooked, it remains permissible to wipe them as part of

(6) That one not have put the shoes on until after performing a complete set of ritual ablutions. Hence, if someone were to wash his feet first, then put the shoes on, then complete his ritual ablutions, it would have no validity. This point is agreed upon by the Malikis, the Shafiis, and the Hanbalis.[130]

---

one's ritual ablutions (note earlier section entitled, "Types of ritual purity which may be overlooked"). However, if they are contaminated by a type of impurity which may not be overlooked, it is not permissible to wipe the shoes as part of one's ablutions before they have been cleaned off.

As for the Hanafis, they hold that shoes may be wiped as part of one's ritual ablutions even if they are not ritually pure; however, although one's wiping of them may be permitted, a ritual prayer performed on the basis of such wiping will not be valid unless the ritual impurity contaminating them is of the type which may be overlooked. As for the amounts of the various sorts of impurities which may be overlooked, this is discussed in the earlier sections entitled, "Types of ritual impurity which may be overlooked" and "Abstersion." The Hanafis also stipulate that if a shoe has some ritual impurity on it, one must wipe the part of the shoe which is uncontaminated.

According to the Hanbalis, shoes contaminated by ritual impurity may be wiped as part of ritual ablutions on two conditions: (1) That the impurity be either on the soles, which come into contact with the ground, or inside the shoes. However, if it is on the top or sides of the shoes, it is not permissible to wipe them. (2) That it be impossible for the person to remove the impurity without taking the shoes off. If the person is able to wash off the impurity while still wearing the shoes, and without damaging the shoes in any way, he must do so. On the other hand, if it would be possible to remove the impurity while keeping the shoes on but the person has nothing with which to remove it, he may go ahead and pray, touch the Qur'ān, and perform other acts of worship which require that he be in a state of ritual purity.

130. As for the Hanafis, however, they hold that performing a complete set of ritual ablutions [before putting the shoes on] is not a necessary precondition for the act of wiping one's shoes to be valid. Rather, if one washed his feet as in ritual ablutions, then put on his shoes without having any occurrence of *ḥadath*, then completed his ritual ablutions, this would be valid provided that one's ablutions had been performed with water, and provided that the water used had made contact with all parts of the body requiring washing or wiping during ritual ablutions.

(7) That one have performed ritual ablutions using water rather than having performed sand ablutions. This applies whether sand ablutions were performed due to a lack of water or on account of an illness which would prevent the person from using water. This condition is agreed upon by all the schools but the Shafiis.[131]

---

131. According to the Shafiis, it is permissible to wipe shoes which one has put on after performing sand ablutions provided that the sand ablutions were performed due to illness, and not due to a lack of water. In other words, if someone performed sand ablutions due to a lack of water, then put on his shoes, after which water became available, he would not be permitted to wipe his shoes as part of his next set of ablutions; rather, in this situation, he would be obliged to take off his shoes and perform a complete set of ritual ablutions. If, on the other hand, someone had performed sand ablutions due to an illness which prevented him from using water, then put on his shoes, after which the illness was cured, this person would be free to perform ritual ablutions and wipe his shoes.

Hence, it may not be said that the feet bear no connection to sand ablutions [simply] because one is not required to wipe one's feet when performing sand ablutions (as will be seen in the section below on sand ablutions).

(8) That there be nothing on the area to be wiped which might prevent the water from making contact with the shoe—such as dough or anything else which, if it were placed on someone's foot, would keep the water from touching the skin.
(9) That the shoes fit well enough that one can walk a certain distance in them (the estimation of this distance varying from one school to another). Hence, if the shoes fall off someone's feet when he walks in them, or if the person wearing them is unable to keep on walking until he has covered this distance, he may not wipe them as part of his ritual ablutions.[132]

Some of the schools also cite further conditions associated with the validity of wiping one's shoes.[133]

---

132. According to the Hanafis, it is not permissible to wipe shoes unless the person wearing them is able to walk the distance of at least one parasang, which is equal to three miles, or 12,000 steps, in them. In other words, they must be sturdy enough to allow someone to walk this distance in them without having to wear anything else, such as boots or shoes, over them.

* * *

The Shafiis hold that if the person wearing the shoes is on a journey, then in order for it to be permissible to wipe the shoes as part of his ritual ablutions, they must be sturdy enough for him to walk in them for three days and three nights without wearing anything else over them. What is meant here is not, of course, that the person has to walk for three days and three nights continuously, but rather that during this period, he will stop to rest here and there along the way. In the case of someone who is resident in one place, it is only permissible to wipe the shoes when performing ritual ablutions if the shoes would be sturdy enough for a traveler to make do with them for one day and one night. In other words, the criterion for judging the sturdiness of a pair of shoes is based on the situation of a traveler, even if the person who wishes to wipe them as part of ritual ablutions is resident in one place. Hence, if the person wearing the shoes is actually a traveler, their sturdiness is determined by whether they will hold up for three days and nights of traveling, including both rest stops and actual travel, whereas if the person wearing the shoes is resident in one place, their sturdiness is determined based on the same criterion as for a traveler; however, unlike the traveler, he is only allowed to continue wiping them as part of ritual ablutions for one day and one night.

* * *

The Malikis do not stipulate that one must be able to walk in shoes for a particular period of time; instead, they stipulate that the shoes must be made of leather, which is suited by its very nature to walking. In addition, the Malikis hold that in order for it to be permissible to wipe shoes as part of ritual ablutions, they must be neither so loose that one's feet do not properly fill them, nor so tight that the person wearing them is not able to walk comfortably.

* * *

As for the Hanbalis, they stipulate simply that one must be able to walk when wearing the pair of shoes, but without specifying a particular distance. Instead they say that the criterion in this regard should be determined by prevailing practice and custom, and that if a person can walk a reasonable distance in the shoes based on this criterion, it is permissible to wipe them as part of ritual ablutions.

133. The Hanafis stipulate the following conditions: (1) The shoes must not have holes in them of a size which would make it invalid to wipe them as part of one's ablutions. (As we have seen, they set the maximum area for such holes as the size of three small toes.) (2) The area wiped must be the size of three little fingers, and this area must be on the top of the shoe. Hence, if one were to wipe the sole of the shoe, the inside of the shoe, the sides, the heel, or the part that extends up beyond the ankle, it would have no validity. (3) One must wipe the shoes with three fingers. It is not permissible to wipe them with a single finger for fear that the others might dry off before one has finished wiping the required area. However, if one were to use a single finger to wipe three separate places on each shoe, using fresh water each time, this would be valid. It is also acceptable to wipe the required area with one's fingertips, and with the water dripping off of them. If the water is not dripping off them, however, the wiping will not be valid. (It should be noted here that it is not necessary for the wiping to be done with one's hand; thus, if the required area of the shoe were 'wiped' by means of rain falling on it, or if water were poured over it, this would suffice.) (4) The part of the shoe which is wiped must be directly over the foot. Thus, for example, if one were wearing shoes which were so long that part of the shoe remained empty, it would not be valid to wipe this part. (5) In the case of someone whose foot has been cut off, at least three toes' length of his foot must remain. Thus, if someone's foot has been cut off and what remains of it is less than this amount, it will not be permissible to wipe one's shoes; if, however, the foot has been cut off above the ankle and the other foot remains, it is permissible to wipe the shoe worn on the remaining foot.

* * *

The conditions set down by the Shafiis are as follows: (1) One must not have put the shoes on over a cast or splint; hence, if someone with a cast on his foot wiped the cast while performing ablutions, then put his shoes on over it, it would not be permissible to wipe them as part of further ablutions. (2) One's feet and the socks one is wearing under the shoes must be ritually pure. (3) The shoes must be thick and sturdy enough to prevent water from soaking through to one's feet if water were poured over them, although water which comes through holes borne with an awl [either for purposes of stitching or for the placement of shoelaces] may be overlooked.

* * *

As for the Malikis, the conditions they add are as follows: (1) The shoes must be made entirely of leather. (2) They must have holes bored in them with an awl. (3) The person who wishes to wipe the shoes as part of ritual ablutions must not be wearing them simply for the sake of adornment and comfort, but rather, in order to emulate the prophetic Sunnah or to protect his feet from heat, cold, thorns, scorpions, or the like. However, if he is simply wearing them in order to protect his feet from fleas, to avoid having to wash them, to protect the henna he has put on them, etc., it is not permissible to wipe them as part of his ritual ablutions, since the purposes for which they are being worn are indicative of a lifestyle of luxury and ease. However, none of the other schools agrees with the Malikis on this condition.

How much of the shoes must be wiped as part of ritual ablutions

Despite the fact that the practice of wiping one's shoes as part of ritual ablutions is a symbolic substitute for washing one's feet, and despite the fact that when performing minor ritual ablutions one must wash the feet in their entirety, the Lawgiver does not require that we wash the entire shoe covering each foot. The reason for this is that this practice represents a special dispensation, as it were, a concession in which God has granted us great latitude as a means of demonstrating His mercy toward us. As for the area of each shoe which must be wiped, there are differing views among the various schools.[134]

What to do when wearing one pair of shoes over another

If someone is wearing a pair of shoes over stockings which are thick enough to fulfill the conditions for being referred to as 'shoes', or if he is wearing one pair of shoes over another, such as two pairs of shoes made of soft leather, or something like galoshes or boots designed to protect shoes from water or mud, it is sufficient to wipe what is being worn on the outside given certain conditions.[135]

---

134. According to the Malikis, one is required to cover the entire top of the shoe; as for the sole of the shoe, that is, the part which comes into direct contact with the ground, it is desirable to wipe this as well. There are those who hold that this latter practice is obligatory; hence, in deference to this view, the Malikis hold that if someone fails to wipe the soles of his shoes, he should repeat whatever prayer he performed [on the basis of the wiping in which he failed to wipe the sole of his shoe] at a time of his choosing. (The time referred to here will be clarified further in the section below on prayer times.) As for the inside of the shoe, it is considered undesirable to wipe it even if the shoes are loose enough that one could get his hand inside them.

* * *

The Hanafis hold that one must wipe a part of the top of each shoe equal to the length and breadth of three little fingers, provided that the part wiped be directly over the foot.

* * *

As for the Shafiis, they hold that one is required to wipe any part of the top of the shoe, and that this may be done even by touching it with a single wet finger rather than actually passing the finger over the area; this ruling is based on the analogy of wiping the head. However, it is not valid to wipe some other part of the shoe, for example, the areas along the edges of the shoe, the heel, the upper rim, the soles or the sides. However, they hold that it is permissible to wipe the part of the shoe which is parallel to the ankles. If there is hair on the surface of the shoe which prevents the water from making contact with the leather beneath it, the wiping will not be valid. Nor is it valid if someone intends only to wipe the hair rather than the leather itself, even if the water comes in contact with the leather.

* * *

As for the Hanbalis, they maintain that one is obliged to wipe most of the top of each shoe, while it is desirable to wipe the sole as well. If one neglects to wipe the sole out of forgetfulness, he should come back and wipe this part alone without repeating his ablutions, even if more time has passed than that allowed between washing one part of the body and another in accordance with the principle of continuity (*muwālāh*). If someone has deliberately neglected to wipe the soles, he should come back and wipe them separately if only a short time has passed, whereas if more than the time allowed for continuity in ablutions has passed, it is recommended that he repeat his ablutions from the beginning and redo the prayer which he prayed performed before wiping his soles if sufficient time remains in the time period for the prayer concerned.

135. The Hanafis specify three conditions for the validity of wiping an outer pair of shoes, namely: (1) The outer pair of shoes must be made of leather. If they are not made of leather and the water penetrates to the shoes beneath them, the wiping is still valid, whereas if it does not reach the shoes beneath, it is not. (2) The outer pair of shoes must be sturdy enough to be walked on if worn alone; otherwise, the wiping is invalid unless the water penetrates to the shoes beneath. (3) The outer pair of shoes must be put on when the person is in the same state of ritual purity he was in when he put on the inner pair; in other words, the outer pair must be put on before any *ḥadath* has occurred and before the inner pair has been wiped.

* * *

As for the Shafiis, they hold that if both the outer and the inner shoes are so flimsy that it would not be permissible to wipe them if worn alone, one must wash his feet in order to complete his ablutions, and wiping will not be valid. If only the inner pair is too flimsy to be wiped if worn alone, the ruling is based on the outer one, and the inner pair is not to be considered a 'shoe'. On the other hand, if the inner shoes are sturdy while the outer ones are flimsy, or if both are sturdy, it is permissible to wipe the outer pair provided that the water is sure to penetrate to the inner one and provided that when doing the wiping, the person concerned has the conscious intention of either wiping the inner shoe through the outer one, or of wiping them both. The same ruling applies if one simply intends to wipe his shoes without specifying which pair. However, if the person intends only to wipe the outer pair, or if he intends to wipe the inner pair but the water does not soak through to the inner pair, the wiping will not be valid.

According to the Hanbalis, if someone puts on one pair of shoes over another before having an occurrence of *ḥadath*, he may wipe the outer pair even if one of the two pairs has holes in it (but not if both of them do, even if, when worn together, they conceal the entire foot). Moreover, if someone places his hand inside the outer pair and wipes the inner one, the wiping is valid so long as the inner pair is sound [free of holes]. They also hold that if someone wipes the outer pair of shoes and then takes them off, he must take off the inner pair as well and wash his feet.

* * *

As for the Malikis, the ruling on wiping in this situation depends on the condition of the outer pair of shoes. Hence, if someone takes off the outer pair, he is obliged to wipe the inner pair immediately in order to maintain the required continuity in the performance of ritual ablutions along with the necessary presence of mind and the ability to maintain such continuity.

The manner in which shoes must be wiped based on the prophetic Sunnah[136]

The Sunnah-based procedure for wiping one's shoes is to place one's right fingers at the tip of one's right shoe while placing the fingers of one's left hand at the tip of one's left shoe, then passing both hands over both shoes up to the upper, innermost edge of each shoe and beyond it to the ankles.

How long one may continue wiping one's shoes before having to remove them and wash one's feet

Someone who is resident in one place may continue to wipe his shoes as part of ritual ablutions for one day and one night,[137] whereas a traveler is allowed to do so for three days and three nights; moreover, this period of time applies to the traveler regardless of whether or not he is on a legitimate journey which is long enough to justify the shortening of ritual prayers,[138] and regardless of whether or not the person concerned suffers from incontinence of some type.[139] This ruling is based on the hadith narrated by Muslim on the authority of Shurayḥ Ibn Hāni', who said, "I once asked 'Ā'ishah, may God be pleased with her, about wiping one's shoes as part of ritual ablutions, and she said, 'Ask 'Alī, since he used to travel with the Prophet.' So I asked 'Alī, and he said, 'The Messenger of God used to allow three days and three nights for travelers, and one and day and one night for those settled in one place.'"

---

136. According to the Malikis, the manner in which one is to wipe one's shoes is simply recommended rather being based on the prophetic Sunnah. As for the recommended procedure in their view, it consists in placing one's right hand over the tips of one's right toes while placing the left hand under them, then passing both hands over the right shoe as far as the ankles. For the left foot one repeats the same process in reverse, that is, by placing one's left hand over the tips of one's left toes and the right hand under them, then passing both hands over the shoes as far as the ankles.

* * *

The Shafiis hold that the Sunnah-based procedure for wiping one's shoes is as follows: The parted fingertips of the left hand are placed under the [right] heel while the parted fingertips of the right hand are placed on top of the [right] toes, after which one draws the right hand as far as the upper, innermost edge of the shoe, while the left hand is drawn up to the tips of the toes from beneath, the result being that one wipes in parallel lines up and down the shoes.

137. The Hanbalis and the Shafiis restrict travel in this context to a legitimate journey which is long enough to justify the shortening of ritual prayers. Thus, if someone went on a journey which was shorter than this, or if the journey were one which involved some sort of disobedience to God's commands, then the period of time allowed for wiping his shoes would be only one day and one night, that is, the same as for someone settled in one place. In addition, the Shafiis stipulate that the journey must be a purposeful one; thus, if someone simply took off and wandered about aimlessly without having any particular destination in mind, he would only be allowed to continue wiping his feet as part of ritual ablutions for one day and one night.

The period of three days and three nights, or one day and one night, is calculated from the time when the person first has an occurrence of *ḥadath* after putting the shoes on.[140] For example, if someone performed ritual ablutions and put on a pair of shoes at noon, after which he remained in a state of ritual purity until time for the evening prayer, at which point he had an occurrence of *ḥadath*, then the period which he would be allowed to continue wiping his shoes as part of his ritual ablutions would be calculated from the moment when he had the occurrence of *ḥadath*, not from the time he put the shoes on.

---

138. According to the Malikis, there is no set limit to the period of time during which one is allowed to continue wiping his shoes as part of ritual ablutions; rather, one need not remove the shoes unless there is a need to perform major ablutions. Nevertheless, it is recommended that those who wish to attend the Friday congregational prayer remove them before the Friday prayer even if they do not intend to perform the Sunnah-based *ghusl* for the Friday prayer. Moreover, if someone does not take off his shoes on Friday, it is recommended that he remove them one week after he first put them on, and on the same day each week thereafter.

139. According to the Hanafis, these periods of time apply only to those who do not suffer from incontinence of any kind. As for those who do, if they perform ritual ablutions, then put on shoes at a time when there is no flow of the substance in respect to which they suffer from the incontinence, they are subject to the same ruling that applies to others; in other words, their wiping of their shoes is not rendered invalid until the maximum period of time has elapsed [that is, either three days and three nights, or one day and one night]. However, if they have a recurrence of their incontinence, or if, when they put the shoes on, the incontinent flow was occurring, the wiping of their shoes will be invalidated with the termination of the time period for each of the five obligatory prayers; if this is the case, they must take off their shoes and—unless their ablutions have been invalidated by something other than a flow of the substance in relation to which they suffer from incontinence—all they need to do is wash their feet.

* * *

As for the Shafiis, they hold that the maximum periods of three days and three nights and one day and one night do not apply to someone who suffers from some sort of incontinence; rather, such a person is required to take off his shoes and perform complete ritual ablutions for every obligatory prayer, although it is permissible for him to wipe his shoes rather than wash his feet for supererogatory prayers.

140. In a more detailed version of this ruling, the Shafiis state that if the *ḥadath* is of the type which occurs by one's own choice—such as touching someone of the opposite sex [given the conditions cited above in the section on "that which renders ritual ablutions invalid" – t.n.] or going to sleep—then the period of time during which one may continue to wipe one's shoes before washing his feet again should be calculated to start from the moment the *ḥadath* begins, whereas if it is of the type over which one has little control—such as relieving oneself of stool or urine, having an involuntary emission of semen, etc.—then the period is calculated to start from when the *ḥadath* ends.

Undesirable practices associated with wiping one's shoes

The following practices associated with wiping one's shoes are considered undesirable, though not to the point of approaching the unlawful: (1) wiping the shoes more than once, and (2) washing the shoes rather than simply wiping them. This practice is undesirable only if what one intends to do by washing the shoes is to remove a state of ritual impurity (*ḥadath*). However, if one washes them simply for purposes of cleanliness, or to remove physical impurities from them, then it is not undesirable to do so, although at the same time, it does not take the place of wiping them. Rather, after the shoes have been washed, they must be wiped as well.[141]

That which nullifies the effectiveness of wiping one's shoes

Events which invalidate the act of wiping one's shoes as part of ritual ablutions include the following: (1) an occurrence which renders it necessary to perform *ghusl*, such as sexual discharge, menstrual flow, postpartum bleeding, and so on, (2) taking the shoes off, even if this only means pulling the feet out as far as the shoes' upper rims,[142] (3) getting a hole in them,[143] and (4) the lapsing of the time period allowed, even if one only suspects that it may have elapsed.[144]

---

141. The Hanafis hold that washing one's shoes, even if it is done without the intention of wiping them—as, for example, if someone washed them for the sake of cleanliness, or even without any intention at all—serves as an acceptable substitute for wiping them. Even so, the practice of washing them is still considered undesirable.

142. The Hanafis hold that properly speaking, the effect of wiping one's shoes as part of ritual ablutions is not invalidated unless more than half the foot comes out of the shoe.

* * *

According to the Malikis, the most trustworthy view is that the effect of wiping one's shoes is only invalidated if the entire foot comes out of the shoe. If this happens, and if the person proceeds immediately to wash his feet, his ritual ablutions will remain valid. If not, and if the reason for his not washing his feet right away is that he forgot to do so, he should wash his feet with the conscious intention of completing his ablutions regardless of how much time has passed since he took off his shoes. If, on the other hand, he deliberately neglected to wash his feet after removing the shoes, he should complete his ablutions in the aforementioned manner only if a short time has passed since he last performed them; [otherwise, he should perform them again from the very beginning].

143. The Shafiis hold that if someone gets a hole in one of his shoes through which one can see a part of the foot which must be washed as part of ritual ablutions—even if it is covered by a sock or a bandage—then the effect of his wiping his shoes is invalidated. If the hole appears when the person is in a state of ritual

purity, all he is required to do is to wash his feet with the intention of completing his ablutions rather than doing them all over again. If the hole appears while he is praying, his prayer becomes invalid, but all he has to do is wash his feet, then begin his prayer again.

* * *

The Hanbalis hold that if one's shoes have a hole in them through which one can see part of the foot, however small, and even if the opening is located where a hole has been bored with an awl for the purposes of stitching, it is no longer permissible to wipe them as part of one's ablutions unless, while one is walking, the hole closes up in such a way as to conceal the part of the foot [which must be washed as part of ritual ablutions and] which was exposed. Moreover, anytime something happens to invalidate the effect of wiping one's shoes—be it a hole, the passage of the maximum period of time during which one may wipe one's shoes, sexual discharge, the occurrence of something which would invalidate an extenuating condition such as incontinence, etc.—he must take off his shoes and repeat his ablutions from the beginning rather than just wash his feet. The reason given for this ruling is that wiping one's shoes has the effect of removing a state of ritual impurity (*ḥadath*) such that when this effect has been invalidated, the state of ritual impurity returns in its entirety, since as the Hanbalis see it, such a state is 'indivisible' as it were [in other words, the matter of *ḥadath* is an all-or-nothing proposition in the sense that either one is in a state of ritual impurity, in which case it is necessary to perform a complete set of ritual ablutions, or one is not – t.n.].

* * *

According to the Malikis, the wiping of one's shoes is rendered invalid by a hole or holes if they cover an area equal to or greater than one-third of the foot. If a hole develops in the shoes after the person has wiped them and when he or she is still in a state of ritual purity, the effect of his wiping the shoes will be invalidated, but not that of his ablutions. Consequently, he should remove the shoes right away and wash his feet so as to maintain the required continuity in the performance of ablutions. If one delays taking off his shoes and washing his feet due either to forgetfulness or to inability, his original ablutions are not invalidated and all he has to do is wash his feet. If someone deliberately puts off removing his shoes and washing his feet and if there has been a long delay, his ablutions are invalidated, whereas if only a short time has passed, only the wiping of his feet is invalidated, and he is only obliged to wash his feet. If, on the other hand, the hole develops while he is praying, he should stop praying, take off his shoes immediately and wash his feet in the manner described above.

* * *

As for the Hanafis, they hold that if the holes in one's shoes amount to an area equaling the size of three little toes, it is invalid to wipe the shoes as part of one's ritual ablutions. However, a hole will only invalidate the wiping of one's shoes if it is so wide open that when the person wearing the shoes starts to walk, the hole will open up and get larger, causing an area equal to the size of three little toes to become visible. If, on the other hand, the hole is long and narrow such that it does not open up when one walks, it has no effect on the validity of the wiping of one's shoes. If the shoes are lined with leather or with a piece of cloth, even a thin one, which has been sewn into the shoes, and if an area of the shoe's lining equaling the size of three small toes becomes visible, it will not invalidate one's wiping of the shoes. However, if the shoes are lined with something other than leather [or cloth], or if what is inside them is not actually sewn into them, such as socks or a bandage, and if a hole in the shoe exposes an area of such a lining or inner layer equal to the size of three small toes, the wiping of one's shoe is invalidated. The aforementioned ruling applies whether the hole is in the sole, the top of the shoe, or the heel; however, if it is near the upper rim above the ankles, it has no effect on the validity of wiping the shoes. If there are a number of holes in one of the shoes, they do not make it invalid to wipe the shoes as part of ritual ablutions unless, when added together, they amount to the size of three small toes or more. If, on the other hand, there are a number of holes in both shoes such that, for example, one shoe has a hole the size of one little finger while the other shoe has a hole the size of two little fingers, this does not make it invalid to wipe the shoes. As for the types of holes which must be counted when adding them together, they include only those holes which one could insert a large needle into, whereas anything smaller than this may be overlooked. Hence, it is permissible to wipe shoes containing holes which may be overlooked provided that what one wipes is the shoe itself rather than anything which is visible through the holes.

If, after wiping one's shoes, a hole the size of three small fingers develops in the manner described above while one's last ablutions are still valid, only the wiping of one's shoes is rendered invalid and all that is required is to wash one's feet. The same requirement applies if some other event [besides a hole in one's shoe] occurs to invalidate the wiping of one's feet, even if one is praying; thus, if the wiping of one's feet is rendered invalid for some reason while one is praying, one should wash one's feet (though consciously intending the completion of one's ablutions is not necessary according to the Hanafis), then repeat the prayer concerned.

144. As we have seen, the Malikis do not recognize any maximum for the period of time one is allowed to wipe one's shoes without having to take them off and wash one's feet.

On Sand Ablutions (*Tayammum*)

Sand ablutions (*tayammum*) will be discussed under the following eight subtopics: (1) their definition, the evidence in support of the practice, and the wisdom behind it, (2) types of sand ablutions, (3) conditions associated with sand ablutions, (4) situations in which sand ablutions are allowed, (5) the pillars or obligations involved in the performance of sand ablutions, (6) Sunnah-based practices associated with sand ablutions, (7) recommended and undesirable practices associated with sand ablutions, and (8) that which invalidates sand ablutions.

The definition of sand ablutions, evidence in their support, and the wisdom in their legitimacy

The meaning of the word *tayammum* as generally used in the Arabic language is 'aiming' or 'intending.' As God Almighty declares, "and choose not [*lā tayammamu*] for your spending the bad things..." (2: 267).[145]

As for the meaning of *tayammum* in the context of Islamic law, it refers to the act of wiping one's face and hands with "purifying dust" in a specified manner.[146] It does not mean begriming one's face and hands with dirt; rather, what it means is that one places one's hand on "purifying dust" (*ṣa'īd ṭayyib*), rocks, or any of a number of other substances to be mentioned below. This practice may be resorted to when water is unavailable or when one is unable to use water for legitimate reasons. (Those reasons which are considered legitimate will be presented shortly.)

The legitimacy of the practice of sand ablutions has been established based on the Qur'ān, the prophetic Sunnah, and the consensus of the Muslim community. As God Almighty says, " ... but if you are ill, or are traveling, or have just satisfied a want of nature or have cohabited with a woman, and can find no water—then resort to pure dust [*ṣa'īdan ṭayyiban*], passing therewith lightly over your face and your hands. God does not want to impose any hardship on you, but wants to make you pure, and to bestow upon you the full measure of His blessings, so that you might have cause to be grateful" (5:6). These gracious words indicate that *tayammum* has been legislated for people when water is not available or when they are unable for some reason to make use of water.

---

145. The entire verse from which this command is taken reads as follows, "O you who have attained to faith! Spend on others out of the good things which you may have acquired, and out of that which We bring forth for you from the earth; and choose not for your spending the bad things which you yourselves would not accept without averting your eyes in disdain. And know that God is self-sufficient, ever to be praised" [t.n.].

146. The Malikis and the Shafiis add to this definition the words "with conscious intention", since they view such intention as an integral part of the rite of sand ablutions.

As for the wisdom behind the legitimacy of this practice, it lies in the fact that God, may He be praised and adored, has relieved Muslims from undue hardship in those acts of worship for which He holds them accountable. Someone might object, saying: "Relieving people of undue hardship means that they should not be required to perform sand ablutions when they lack water or are unable to use it, since sand ablutions themselves are a kind of hardship." However, this is a groundless objection, because the meaning of "relieving people of undue hardship" is holding them accountable only for what they are capable of. Hence, if someone is unable to perform minor or major ritual ablutions but is able to perform sand ablutions, then he is required to obey God's commands by doing the latter, and not to ask God about anything but how such ablutions are to be performed. After all, the purpose behind all acts of worship is to help people learn to obey God's commands, to give them an inward sense of His majesty, and to instill in them the awareness that He alone is the One to whom worship should be devoted.

Some of the means by which God has commanded us to worship Him—such as major and minor ritual ablutions, the physical movements in ritual prayer, not indulging in worldly pleasures while fasting, as well as other practices which are good for the body—provide us with clearly visible benefits, while others provide us with inward benefits, that is, the benefits resulting from the purity of heart achieved through obeying His precepts. Inward benefits such as these lead in turn to outward gains, since the person who holds his Lord in awe and demonstrates this fact by doing His bidding enjoys positive relationships with others, who have no reason to fear he would do them harm but rather, on the contrary, benefit from all the good he does. Such are the goals people strive for in their earthly lives. Thus, obedience to the divine precepts serves the best interests of human society under all circumstances; moreover, there can be no doubt that when one performs sand ablutions, one only does so in surrender to God's decrees. As such, sand ablutions are among the means by which we demonstrate our obedience to God and which lead, in turn, to inward contentment.

Now, some people who lack an understanding of the true aims of the Islamic law, obedience to which results in happiness for society and the refinement of people's morals, might suppose that the soil with which sand ablutions are performed is contaminated with harmful microbes such that wiping one's face with it would be anything but beneficial. However, those who make such claims do not understand the meaning or purpose of sand ablutions, because the Lawgiver stipulates that the soil used be both clean and ritually pure. Moreover, we are not directed simply to take the soil and place it on our faces; rather, we are given a specific manner in which to perform sand ablutions, which make it possible for us to engage in the same acts of worship which are based on the performance of minor and major ritual ablutions. Someone who says that placing one's hand on clean sand, smooth stones, pebbles and the like will transfer harmful microbes to the person who does so might just as well stop putting his hands on bread, fruit or vegetables! He might as well forbid people to work in mines, tan hides, make shoes, or work as carpenters. In fact, he might as well stop putting his hand on anything at all for fear of the microbes that might be clinging to it. Such claims are made by people who would like to shirk their divinely given responsibilities so that they can remain free to pursue the kinds of whims and lusts that captivate corrupt souls, thereby leading them to death and destruction. Otherwise, what are we to say about workers who fertilize the ground with manure and rid crops of disease and pests, and who enjoy better health and happier existences than those who mock the teachings of their religion? Why is it that microbes haven't been the death of them?! The fact is that the Islamic religion urges its followers to maintain both ritual purity and good hygiene by avoiding filth and that which leads to illness. Consequently, Islamic law requires that the soil on which one places one's hands when performing *tayammum* be ritually pure and clean just as if it were a clean garment or handkerchief; hence, if it were contaminated or dirty, it would not be permissible to use it in *tayammum*.

One other question which needs to be dealt with in this regard is: Why do sand ablutions involve only two of the parts of the body normally washed when one performs minor ritual ablutions, namely, the face and the hands? The answer is that the purpose for sand ablutions is to alleviate hardship; hence, it is sufficient when performing them to simulate minor ritual ablutions in a partial manner. The two parts of the body which must always be washed during ritual ablutions are the face and the hands, whereas the head, for example, is to be wiped; as for the feet, they are sometimes washed and sometimes wiped depending on whether one is wearing shoes or not. Hence, God has required that sand ablutions include only those two parts of the body which must always be washed in ritual ablutions, a fact which clearly involves an alleviation of hardship.

As for the legitimacy of sand ablutions, it is supported by numerous prophetic hadiths. One such hadith, narrated by al-Bukhārī and Muslim on the authority of 'Imrān Ibn Ḥuṣayn, tells us that when the Messenger of God once saw a man who remained isolated from others and did not take part in communal prayers, he asked him, "What is it that keeps you from praying with others?" The man replied, "O Messenger of God, I am in a state of major ritual impurity and I have no water." "What you need to use is 'pure dust', then, and it will suffice you," the Prophet told him.

Muslims are in unanimous agreement that sand ablutions serve as a legitimate substitute for both minor and major ritual ablutions, although they hold different opinions on what specific situations call for sand ablutions and what types of earth may be used when performing them.

Types of sand ablutions

Sand ablutions are of two types,[147] namely, obligatory and recommended. Given certain conditions, they are obligatory prior to the performance of any action that must be preceded by minor or major ritual ablutions, such as ritual prayer, touching the Qur'ān, etc., and given the same conditions, they are recommended prior to performing any action before which minor or major ritual ablutions are recommended. Thus, for example, if someone wishes to pray a voluntary prayer and has no water to perform ablutions with, he may perform sand ablutions instead. This is because just as voluntary prayers are recommended, it is likewise recommended that one perform sand ablutions before praying such prayers. In other words, the reward one receives for performing sand ablutions is the reward received for performing a recommended action even though, [in the absence of water], the prayer would have no validity if one failed to perform them. Hence, despite the fact that sand ablutions are recommended rather than obligatory, they are nevertheless a condition for the validity of ritual prayer in such a situation. At the same time, if someone performs neither the sand ablutions nor the voluntary prayer that would have followed them, this will not be held against him.

Conditions associated with sand ablutions

In order for sand ablutions to be valid, the following conditions must be met:

(1) The time period for the ritual prayer for which one is performing them must already have begun.[148]
(2) One must consciously intend[149] to perform sand ablutions.
(3) The person performing them must be a Muslim.
(4) The person must have searched for water when it was unavailable.
(5) There must not be anything on either the face or the hands, be it grease, wax, or anything else, that would form a barrier between the skin and the "purifying dust" used in sand ablutions.
(6) A woman intending to perform sand ablutions must not be menstruating or experiencing postpartum bleeding.

---

147. The Hanafis add a third type as well, namely "sand ablutions as a 'duty.'" As we saw earlier in the section on Sunnah-based practices associated with minor ablutions, the Hanafis hold that a 'duty' [*wājib*] in this sense is less binding than an 'obligation' [*farḍ*]. For example, it is a 'duty' to perform sand ablutions before circumambulating the Ka'bah such that if someone performed this rite without preceding it with either minor ritual ablutions or sand ablutions, his circumambulation would be valid, but he would be guilty of a sin less serious than that of neglecting to perform an obligatory action, or *farḍ*. For a more complete explanation of this point, see the earlier section entitled, "On Ritual Ablutions."

148. According to the Hanafis, sand ablutions performed before this time period has begun are also valid.

149. As we have seen above, the Malikis and the Shafiis view such conscious intention as an integral part of the rite of ritual ablutions (and hence, sand ablutions as well), not simply a condition for their validity.

(7) There must be a sufficient justification for the performance of sand ablutions rather than minor or major ritual ablutions. (Which situations represent such a justification will be discussed below.)

In addition, as in the case of minor and major ritual ablutions, there are conditions which must be met in order for sand ablutions to be obligatory.[150]

---

150. According to the Malikis, there are three types of conditions connected with sand ablutions: (1) those which must be fulfilled in order for sand ablutions to be *obligatory but not necessarily valid*, (2) those which must be fulfilled in order for sand ablutions to be *valid but not necessarily obligatory*, and (3) those which must be fulfilled in order for them to be *both obligatory and valid*.

In order for sand ablutions to be *obligatory*, the following conditions must be met: (1) that one be an adult; (2) that one not have been forced to refrain from this practice; (3) that one be able to make use of the soil to be used in sand ablutions (since if one is unable to do so, sand ablutions cease to be obligatory); and (4) that one's ablutions have been invalidated for some reason.

In order for sand ablutions to be *valid but not necessarily obligatory*, the following three conditions must be met: (1) that one be a Muslim, (2) that there not be any barrier between the skin and the soil to be used, and (3) that nothing take place to invalidate the sand ablutions while they are being performed.

Finally, in order for sand ablutions to be *both obligatory and valid*, the following six conditions apply: (1) that the time period for the ritual prayer for which one is performing them have already begun; (2) that one be in full possession of one's mental faculties; (3) that one have received the message that God Almighty has sent a Messenger; (4) that a woman intending to perform them not be menstruating or having postpartum bleeding; (5) that one be both awake and mindful of what one is doing; and (6) that 'purifying dust' be available.

The Malikis do not include the search for water among the above conditions, although they do affirm its necessity in certain situations to be discussed below. Nor do they mention the existence of a justification as a condition for the performance of sand ablutions; rather, they content themselves with including it among the situations which make sand ablutions necessary. The aforementioned conditions are the same as those given by the Malikis for minor ritual ablutions; the only exception is that, with respect to sand ablutions, the stipulation that the time period for the prayer one intends to pray must already have begun is a condition for both their necessity and their validity, whereas with respect to minor ritual ablutions, this is a condition for their necessity, but not for their validity.

* * *

The Hanafis restrict themselves to mentioning conditions for the *validity* of sand ablutions (as they do also for minor ritual ablutions). As we noted in our earlier discussion of minor ritual ablutions, there is nothing to prevent one from dividing such conditions into the three categories mentioned by the Malikis, namely, (1) conditions for *necessity* alone [that is, for sand ablutions' being obligatory], (2) conditions for *validity* alone, and (3) conditions for *necessity and validity together*. The reasonableness of this classification may be illustrated on the basis of two different considerations, namely, menstruation and postpartum bleeding. The absence of these two physical conditions is a requisite for the *necessity* [of ritual ablutions], since neither the menstruating woman nor the woman with postpartum vaginal bleeding is held accountable for their performance. However, it is also a condition for the *validity* of ritual ablutions with respect to the actual fulfillment of one's religious duty. In other words, the ablutions done by a menstruating woman do not lead to the performance of the action in preparation for which ablutions are generally performed, namely, ritual prayer and other acts of worship. The validity [of sand ablutions] requires that the purpose for which one does them, the performance of ritual prayer, for example—actually be fulfilled—that is, by one's performing the prayer. It is true, of course, that it is considered desirable for a menstruating woman or new mother to perform ritual ablutions as a means of keeping herself mindful of her custom of praying; however, such ablutions are not deemed valid as a prelude to the performance of those acts of worship in preparation for which ablutions were established. Given this consideration, conditions for sand ablutions may be divided into the following three groups:

First, conditions for *necessity alone* are: (1) that one be an adult, (2) that one be capable of using 'purifying dust', and (3) that there have occurred some *ḥadath* which places one in a state of ritual impurity, and/or that the time period for the ritual prayer one intends to pray have begun. As for the beginning of the time period for a given prayer, it is a condition for the necessity of the actual *performance* of sand ablutions, though not for their *necessity per se*. In other words, as a means of relieving hardship, one is not obliged to perform sand ablutions [or minor ablutions, for that matter] until the time period for the prayer concerned actually begins, although the necessity of performing them, legally speaking, may have already existed before this. Moreover, at the beginning of this time period one has more choice as to when to perform sand ablutions, whereas as the time draws to an end, one has less choice in this respect (as is the case in connection with minor and major ritual ablutions).

Second, conditions for *validity alone* include the following seven stipulations: (1) that one consciously intend to perform sand ablutions, (2) that water not be available or that one not be able to use water for some legitimate reason, (3) that there not be any barrier on either the face or the hands, such as oil, wax, and the like, (4) that nothing take place to invalidate the sand ablutions as they are being performed, (5) that one do the wiping with at least three fingers if one is wiping with one's hand (although it is not required that one do all the wiping with the hand itself, as will be explained further in what follows), (6) that one have gone looking for water if he had reason to believe that it could be found, and (7) that one wipe one's entire face and hands.

Third, as for the conditions for both the *necessity and validity* of sand ablutions, they are as follows: (1) that one be a Muslim (since the non-believer is not held accountable for their performance, and since even if he did perform them they would lack validity since the non-believer is not capable of consciously intending to perform such an act of worship), (2) that one not be menstruating or experiencing postpartum bleeding, (3) that one be in full possession of one's mental faculties, and (4) that 'purifying dust' be available. Someone who has no 'purifying dust' at his disposal is not required to perform sand ablutions, and if he did perform them they would not be valid even if the soil used were *ṭāhir*, such as ground which was once contaminated with ritual impurity but then dried out. Such ground is fit to be prayed on (that is, *ṭāhir*); however, it is not considered a purifying agent (*ṭahūr*), and consequently, one would not be allowed to use it in performing sand ablutions as was noted earlier in the section entitled, "The means and manner by which ritual impurity may be removed."

* * *

The Shafiis do not divide the conditions relating to sand ablutions into categories. Rather, they simply list the following eight: (1) that there be a justification for the performance of sand ablutions, such as the unavailability of water or the inability to use it, (2) that the person concerned be aware that the time period for the prayer he intends to pray has begun (since before this, one's sand ablutions will have no validity), (3) that any impurity on one's body be removed unless it is of a type which may be overlooked (since otherwise, one's sand ablutions will not be valid), (4) that the person intending to do the sand ablutions be a Muslim (an exception being a Christian or Jewish woman married to a Muslim man who, when her menstrual period or postpartum bleeding ends, needs to perform *ghusl* before they can resume sexual relations, and who may be unable to do so for some reason), (5) if the person intending to perform sand ablutions is a woman, that she not be menstruating or having postpartum bleeding (the exception to this being cases in which a menstruating or postpartum woman is in a state of ritual consecration for the minor or major pilgrimage, in which case she may perform sand ablutions if she is unable to perform the Sunnah-based *ghusl* prescribed for those who are entering a state of *iḥrām*), (6) that one possess full discretional faculties (an exception being made for a woman who is unbalanced and who performs sand ablutions in order for her husband to be able to have sexual relations with her), (7) the absence of any barrier between the soil used and the person's skin, and (8) that the person concerned look for water before performing sand ablutions (with more details to follow on this condition).

* * *

Like the Shafiis, the Hanbalis make no distinction between conditions for necessity and conditions for validity. The conditions which they list are as follows: (1) The time for the prayer one intends to perform must have begun. This condition applies whether the prayer is obligatory or not so long as it is a prayer which is associated with a particular time, such as the funeral prayer, the time for which begins once either major ablutions or sand ablutions [have been administered to the deceased]. Hence, if someone performed sand ablutions before this, they would not be valid. (2) It must be impossible or very difficult to use water for one of the reasons to be listed below. (3) Purifying soil which has not been burned must be available, provided that it is of the type which will cling to the part of the body being wiped, as will be explained below. (4) One must consciously intend to perform sand ablutions. (5) One must be in full possession of one's mental faculties. (6) One must have reached the age of discernment. (7) One must be a Muslim. (8) There must be no barrier preventing the soil from making contact with the part of the body being wiped. (9) The person must not perform any action which is incompatible with the performance of sand ablutions. (10) One must have performed abstersion before performing sand ablutions.

Situations in which sand ablutions are permissible

Situations in which sand ablutions are permissible fall into two categories: (1) Those in which there is either no water whatsoever, or in which the water available is insufficient to achieve ritual purity.[151] (2) Those in which water is available but one is unable to use it for some reason, or the water is needed for drinking or other vital purposes (details concerning which will be discussed below). In the case of those who have no water available, they are to perform sand ablutions in preparation for any act of worship that requires ritual purity, be it daily ritual prayers, a funeral prayer,[152] a Friday congregational prayer, a prayer for the Day of Sacrifice or the Day of Fastbreaking, circumambulation of the Ka'bah, or a voluntary prayer, even if one wishes to perform such a prayer by itself, that is, unassociated with an obligatory prayer.[153] Moreover, it makes no difference whether the person who has no water with which to perform minor ablutions is healthy or ill, resident or traveling, or—if he is traveler—whether the journey is long enough to warrant the shortening of obligatory prayers, or whether it is based on or leads to disobedience to God's commands.[154]

As for someone who has water available to him but who is unable to use it for some legitimate reason, he is subject to the same ruling which applies to someone who has no water; in other words, he is to perform sand ablutions in preparation for any act of worship that requires ritual purity. As for the situations in which someone might not be able to use water, they include the following:

---

151. The Shafiis and the Hanbalis hold that if the water available is not sufficient for the achievement of ritual purity, one must use a portion of the water to perform partial ritual ablutions, then finish by performing *tayammum.*

152. According to the Malikis, someone who has no water available is not to perform sand ablutions for a funeral prayer if he is resident in a place (that is, not a traveler) and in good health unless he is obliged to perform the prayer due to the fact that there is no one else in a state of ritual purity who could perform it on his behalf. However, if such a person has performed sand ablutions in preparation to perform an obligatory prayer, he may pray the funeral prayer based on the same sand ablutions he had performed for the sake of the obligatory prayer. As for someone who is traveling and/or ill, he may perform sand ablutions specifically for a funeral prayer even if he is not required to perform it.

153. As we noted above, the Malikis hold that unless the person who has no water available is a traveler and/or ill, he may not perform sand ablutions in order to pray a voluntary prayer unless it is associated with one of the obligatory prayers.

154. According to the Shafiis, if someone is committing an act of disobedience by going on a particular journey and if water becomes completely unavailable, he should perform sand ablutions and pray [while on the journey], then repeat the prayer later. However, if this same person is unable to use water due to an illness or some other cause, he may not perform sand ablutions unless he repents of the disobedience he has committed, after which he may perform sand ablutions and pray without having to repeat the prayer later.

(1) When one has good reason to believe that the use of the water available would cause illness, exacerbate an already existing illness, or cause a delay in one's recovery from an illness. In making such a judgment, one may rely on one's own experience as well as on the opinion of a skilled Muslim physician.[155]

(2) When there is an enemy—be it a human being or a wild animal—preventing one from reaching the water and one fears for himself, his possessions, or family members under his protection.

(3) When one needs the water for other vital purposes, be they immediate or more remote; thus, for example, if, based on a well-founded belief rather than a mere suspicion, one fears that by using the water at his disposal he would expose himself, some other human being, or an animal which it would be unlawful to kill (including even a rapacious dog)[156] to thirst that would threaten their lives or well-being, he should perform sand ablutions in order to save the water for drinking. The same ruling applies if the water is needed for making bread or cooking, or in order to remove impurities that may not be overlooked from one's body or clothing.[157]

---

155. According to the Malikis, one may rely in such matters on the opinion of a non-Muslim physician in the event that one knows of no Muslim physicians to consult; similarly, they hold that one may rely on everyday types of evidence such as one's personal experience or the experiences of someone else if he or she has a similar constitution to one's own.

* * *

Similarly, the Shafiis hold that it is sufficient for the physician consulted to be skilled and knowledgeable, whether he or she is a Muslim or not, the only stipulation being that the person concerned be convinced of the physician's reliability. As for personal experience, however, it is preferable not to depend on this alone. If the person concerned is knowledgeable in the area of medicine or is a physician, he may rely on his own judgment in such a situation; however, if he is neither a doctor nor knowledgeable in the field of medicine [and has no access to a physician], he may perform sand ablutions, then repeat his prayers after recovering from his illness.

156. The Hanbalis hold that with respect to black dogs, like rapacious dogs given to biting, one should not save water for them even if they die of thirst.

157. According to the Shafiis, the impurity must be on one's body. If it is on one's clothes, one should perform minor ritual ablutions with water rather than sand ablutions. Then, if one can find no uncontaminated garment to pray in, he should pray naked, and if he does so, he is not required to repeat the prayer later.

(4) If the instrument with which one gains access to water has been lost, such as the rope or the pail with which one draws water from a well.[158]

(5) When the water is so cold that one has reason to fear that it would be harmful to perform ablutions with it; this applies, of course, only if one has no way to heat it.[159]

Thus, in all the aforementioned situations one is to perform sand ablutions. As for the requirement that one go in search of water when it is not available, the various schools offer differing points of view on this matter.[160]

Regarding someone who has water and is able to use it but who fears that if he uses the water for regular minor ablutions rather than sand ablutions, the time period for the prayer he intends to pray will run out, the various schools offer differing opinions as to the validity or lack of validity of sand ablutions.[161]

---

158. According to the Malikis, someone who has lost the instrument with which he gets water, or the person who brings him the water, should not perform sand ablutions unless he is certain, or has good reason to believe, that he will not be able to find other water before the time period for the prayer concerned runs out.

159. According to the Hanafis, one may not perform sand ablutions for fear that the water is too cold unless one is in a state of major ritual impurity, since only someone who is obliged to cover himself all over with such water [as one must do in performing *ghusl*] has good reason to fear such harm; as for someone who is simply in a state of minor ritual impurity, he should not perform sand ablutions unless it is ascertained with complete certainty that such harm would occur.

160. According to the Malikis, if a person without water is certain, or has good reason to believe, that there is water two or more miles away, he is not required to go in search of it. If he is certain, has good reason to believe, or suspects that there is water in a place less than two miles away, he is required to go in search of it provided that such a journey will not cause him undue hardship. However, if it would cause hardship, then even if the distance involved is less than two miles and even if he is riding an animal, he is not required to go in search of the water. At the same time, if he is fairly certain, has good reason to believe, suspects, or even simply imagines that his companions would give him water, he is required to ask them for it. If someone is fairly certain or has good reason to believe that his companions would give him water but he fails to ask them for water, then performs sand ablutions and prays, he must go ask them for water, and if they give it to him, he must repeat the prayer later, regardless of how much time has passed since the original time period for the prayer concerned. If he merely suspects that they would give him water, and if, rather than asking them for it, he performs sand ablutions and prays, he is likewise required to go ask them, and if he does obtain water, he is to repeat his prayer before the time period for the prayer concerned ends. However, if it becomes apparent that he only imagined that they would give him water, he is not required to repeat the prayer. In other words, the factor which determines whether one is required to repeat the prayer or not is whether or not one's travel companions have water [and are willing to give one some of it]; if the person finds out that they do have water [and will give him some], he is required to repeat his prayer given the conditions explained above, whereas if he finds out that they have none, he is not

required to repeat it. However, in the latter case he should seek to purchase water if the price is low enough not to cause him deprivation; and if he intends to stay a relatively long time in the village where he is located, he should borrow money if necessary in order to pay for the water.

* * *

The Hanbalis hold that someone who has no water must search for it in and around his saddlebag and other travel supplies, and he must ask his companions for water unless he is certain that they have none. If someone performs sand ablutions and prays before going in search of water or asking others for it, his sand ablutions will not be valid. However, if the water is far away, one is not required to go after it; as for what is meant by 'far away', this is to be determined by prevailing standards.

* * *

The Hanafis hold that if someone who has no water available to him is in an urban area, he is to go in search of water before performing sand ablutions regardless of whether he has good reason to believe that there is water nearby or not. In the case of a traveler who has good reason to believe that there is water less than a mile away, he must go in search of it provided that he has no reason to fear for his personal safety or his possessions, whereas if he has good reason to believe that the nearest water is a mile or more away, he is not required to go in search of it at all. Moreover, it makes no difference whether the person searches for the water himself or sends someone else to do so for him. If the person has traveling companions, he must ask them for water if he has good reason to believe that if he asked them, they would give it to him, and if he performs sand ablutions before asking, they will have no validity. If someone suspects that his companions might give him water if he requested it of them, and if this person performs sand ablutions and prays, then asks them later and they give it to him, he must repeat his prayer. If, on the other hand, they refuse his request before he starts to pray, then after he has finished praying, they change their minds and give it to him, he is not required to repeat the prayer. If the people from whom he requests water will only give it to him in return for a price reflecting its value in the nearest location where water is available, but scarce, or at a slightly inflated price, then he must buy it from them if he is able, that is, if the price is not so high that by buying it he is deprived of basic necessities. However, if they demand an outrageously inflated price, he is not obliged to buy it, and instead, he may perform sand ablutions.

* * *

According to the Shafiis, someone who has no water available must look for water before performing sand ablutions, either by searching among his own provisions or requesting it from others traveling with him; however, he must not search for the water until after the time period for the prayer he intends to pray has already begun. When seeking to obtain water from his travel companions, he should call upon each one of them—either in person or through a mediator whom he trusts—unless the time period for the prayer he intends to pray is about to run out; if this is the case, he is to perform sand ablutions and pray without trying to request water from each and every one of them due to the lack of time. If the person is obliged to go ahead and perform sand ablutions and pray before having asked everyone for water, he is to repeat the prayer later if it is likely that there is water available somewhere nearby; otherwise, he is not required to repeat it. If, after continuing his search, he still finds no water, he will be in one of three situations: (a) Near enough to call for help, in other words, in a place where, if he called out to his companions for assistance, they would be close enough to come to his aid despite their being occupied with their various tasks. Specifically, this distance is set by the Shafiis at the farthest point that is visible to someone with sound vision, and from which he can see people and distinguish them from one another, (b) Near enough to reach water without assistance, that is, at a distance of no more than half a parasang (or 6,000 steps), (c) Far from the water, that is, with more than 6,000 steps away.

If someone in situation (a) above is certain that there is water to be found, he must go in search of it provided that he is assured of his personal safety and that of his money and other possessions. As long as the person is certain that there is water in the vicinity, it is not necessary that he be assured of finding it before the time period for the prayer he intends to pray runs out. If, by contrast, one is uncertain whether there is water to be found, one must go in search of it if he is assured of his personal safety and that of his money, belongings and anything else under his protection—even if he is not permitted to own it due to its ritual impurity, such as dung; however, such a person must be assured that he will not become separated from his travel companions and that the time period for the prayer he intends to pray will not run out.

Someone in situation (b) above is not required to go in search of water unless he is certain that it can be found and unless he is assured that neither his life, his well-being nor his money is in danger. If the area where he is located is likely to have water in it, it is not necessary to be assured that the water will be found before the time for the prayer he intends to pray runs out; if it is not likely, however, there is no need to go in search of it if there is the added possibility that the time for the prayer intended will run out before water is found.

As for someone in situation (c), he need not go in search of water even if he is certain of its existence due to the distance he would have to travel to reach it.

161. The Shafiis hold that as long as water is available, one should never perform sand ablutions simply because one is afraid that the time period for the prayer one intends to pray will run out, since by doing so one would be violating one of the conditions for the validity of sand ablutions, namely, the absence of water.

* * *

As for the Hanbalis, they hold that one may not perform sand ablutions for fear that the time period for the prayer one intends to pray will run out unless one is traveling and knows that there is water in a place not far away but fears that, if he goes to get the water and performs minor ablutions with it, the time will run out. In this case, he may perform sand ablutions and pray without being required to repeat the prayer later. Similarly, if a traveler has reached a place where water is available but finds that it is being distributed to people by turns, and if he knows that the time will run out before his turn comes, he may perform sand ablutions and pray without being required to repeat the prayer later.

* * *

The Hanafis divide prayer in such circumstances into three categories, namely: (a) prayers for which there is no set time period, such as voluntary prayers that are not tied to a given obligatory prayer, (b) prayers for which there is a set time period but which there is no way to compensate for later, such as funeral prayers and the prayers prayed in honor of the Day of Sacrifice and the Day of Fastbreaking, and (c) prayers that have a set time period and that may be made up later, such as the Friday congregational prayer and the other daily obligatory prayers, since the Friday congregational prayer may be made up by simply praying the Friday noon prayer, while all of the other obligatory prayers may be made up at some later time.

As for prayers belonging to category (a), that is, voluntary prayers, one should not perform sand ablutions for them when water is available unless they happen to be the Sunnah-based prayers performed after the noon prayer, the sunset prayer and the evening prayer. In other words, if performing minor ritual ablutions would delay them so much that the set time period for them would run out, one is permitted to perform sand ablutions in order to perform them on time. In the case of prayers in category (b), that is, funeral and holiday prayers, one may perform sand ablutions for them even when water is available if there is reason to fear that one would miss them by performing minor ablutions. As for prayers in category (c), such as the Friday congregational prayer, one should not perform sand ablutions for them as long as water is available simply for fear that the time will run out; rather, one should let the time run out, then perform minor ablutions and perform the noon prayer instead. Similarly with respect to all other daily obligatory prayers, if one performs sand ablutions and performs them [simply due to the time factor], one must repeat them again later.

* * *

As for the Malikis, they hold that if one fears that one will miss the prayer one intends to pray by using water on the four parts of the body involved in minor ritual ablutions, or by covering the body with water as one does when performing *ghusl*, then one may perform sand ablutions and pray without being required to repeat the prayer later. With regard to the Friday congregational prayer, the prevailing Maliki view is that one should not perform sand ablutions for it so long as water is available, whereas in the case of a funeral prayer, one should not perform sand ablutions for it unless: (1) one has no water and (2) one is obliged to perform it, as we saw above.

The pillars of sand ablutions

The four pillars of sand ablutions are as follows:

(1) Conscious intention,[162] on which various rulings are given by the different schools.[163] The time when one is to express such an intention[164] is when one places one's hand on whatever substance is being used for the ablutions.

---

162. The Hanafis and Hanbalis view conscious intention as a condition for the validity of both minor ritual ablutions and sand ablutions rather than as an integral part of these rites.

163. The Malikis hold that when performing sand ablutions, one's intention should be to make it permissible either to perform ritual prayer, touch the Qur'ān, or engage in some other act of worship which requires ritual purity; one may also intend to make permissible that which has been prevented by a state of *ḥadath*, that is, major or minor ritual impurity, or simply to fulfill the obligation of sand ablutions. However, if someone intends only to remove the state of *ḥadath*, his sand ablutions will be invalid, since in the view of the Malikis, sand ablutions do not remove *ḥadath*. In addition, if one's intention is to be able to perform ritual prayer or some other act which one has been prevented from performing by a state of *ḥadath*, one must distinguish in one's intention between major and minor ritual impurity. Thus, for example, if someone is in a state of major ritual impurity due to sexual discharge and consciously intends to make it permissible to engage in some act which he has been forbidden to perform due to this state of ritual impurity, but without specifying that it is *major* ritual impurity (*al-ḥadath al-akbar*), his sand ablutions will not fulfill their purpose and he will be required to repeat whatever prayer he prays on this basis. On the other hand, if someone intends simply to perform the obligation of sand ablutions, this will suffice even if he has not specified whether the impurity concerned is major (*al-ḥadath al-akbar*) or minor (*al-ḥadath al-aṣghar*), since the intention to perform this obligation covers states of both major and minor ritual impurity.

The Malikis also hold that if someone performs sand ablutions with the intention of praying an obligatory prayer, he may, on the basis of these ablutions, perform a single obligatory prayer in addition to as many Sunnah-based and recommended prayers as he wishes; he may also perform a non-obligatory circumambulation of the Ka'bah, perform the two *rak'ahs* associated with the non-obligatory circumambulation, touch the Qur'ān and recite the Qur'ān (even if he has been in a state of major ritual impurity due to sexual discharge). However, if the person concerned is in good health and is not a traveler, and if he or she performs a second obligatory prayer based on the same set of sand ablutions, the second will have no validity even if the two prayers are being prayed jointly, as when one combines the noon and mid-afternoon prayers under certain circumstances. Hence, when one performs sand ablutions in order to perform a voluntary prayer associated with a given obligatory prayer, he must pray the obligatory prayer first, since if he were to perform the voluntary prayer first, the voluntary prayer would be valid, but not the obligatory prayer performed after this; rather, he would have to perform sand ablutions again in order to pray the obligatory prayer. However, if someone performs sand ablutions specifically in order to perform a voluntary or Sunnah-based prayer on its own, he may touch and recite the Qur'ān (even after having been in a state of major ritual impurity due to sexual discharge), in addition to doing other things which require a state of ritual purity; however, he may not pray an obligatory prayer based on these same sand ablutions. This last ruling applies to those who are ill and/or traveling; as for those who are in good health and settled in one place, they are not allowed to perform sand ablutions in order to pray a voluntary prayer on its own, that is, unassociated with an obligatory prayer.

Finally, if one's conscious intention in performing sand ablutions is to be able to recite the Qur'ān, enter the presence of a sultan, or some other act which does not require a state of ritual purity, then he may not, based on these same sand ablutions, perform acts which do require ritual purity.

* * *

The Hanafis stipulate that in order for the intention associated with sand ablutions to be a valid basis for ritual prayer, one must intend one of the following: (1) to be purified of the state of *ḥadath* which he is in, though it is not necessary to specify whether it is major or minor ritual impurity; thus, if someone is in a state of major ritual impurity and intends to be purified of minor ritual impurity, his sand ablutions will still achieve their purpose, (2) to make it permissible to perform ritual prayer or remove a state of ritual impurity (*ḥadath*), given that according to the Hanafis, sand ablutions are capable of removing *ḥadath*, or (3) to perform an act of worship which is not valid without ritual purity, such as ritual prayer or a "prostration of recitation." Hence, if someone simply intends to perform sand ablutions without noting that his purpose is to make it permissible to perform ritual prayer or to remove the state of *ḥadath* which he is in, his prayer will not be valid based on these sand ablutions. Similarly, if one intends an action which is not, strictly speaking, an act of worship, or an act of worship which does not require that one be in a state of ritual purity, then any prayer prayed on the basis of such sand ablutions will lack validity. For example, if someone performs sand ablutions with the intention of touching the Qur'ān—given that touching the Qur'ān is not in itself an act of worship or an act by which one draws near to God, the real act of worship here being the chanting of the Qur'ān—and if the person later prays on the basis of these sand ablutions, his prayer will not be valid. Similarly, if someone does sand ablutions with the intention of issuing the call to prayer (*adhān*) or the announcement that prayer has begun following the *adhān* (the *iqāmah*)—given that the *adhān* and the *iqāmah* are not specifically intended as acts of worship, their fundamental purpose being simply to convey an announcement, not to mention the fact that they are valid without one's being ritually pure—then any prayer prayed on the basis of these sand ablutions will lack validity. In keeping with this same principle, the Hanafis hold that if someone performs sand ablutions in order to greet others or to respond to their greetings [given that such actions do not require ritual purity, nor are they intended as acts of worship], or if someone in a state of minor ritual impurity does sand ablutions with the intention of reciting the Qur'ān—bearing in mind that although recitation of the Qur'ān is specifically intended as an act of worship, one may nevertheless engage in it while in a state of minor ritual impurity—then any prayer performed on the basis of such sand ablutions will be invalid.

* * *

According to the Shafiis, someone who performs sand ablutions must intend to make permissible the performance of ritual prayer and the like. One may not intend to remove *ḥadath*, since in the Shafiis' view, sand ablutions do not remove *ḥadath*; nor is it permissible to intend simply to perform sand ablutions or to fulfill the obligation of sand ablutions, since sand ablutions represent a kind of "emergency purity measure" as it were; in other words, they were established not as a means of purification in their own right but rather, as a substitute for other means of purification.

As for the person who intends through sand ablutions to make it permissible to perform ritual prayer or some other religious obligation, his intention will be to make it permissible to do one of the following: (1) to perform an *obligatory* rite, such as one of the five daily prayers, the obligatory circumambulation of the Ka'bah, or delivery of the Friday sermon, (2) to perform a *voluntary* act of worship, such as a voluntary prayer, a non-obligatory circumambulation of the Ka'bah, a funeral prayer, etc., or (3) to perform a prostration of recitation or thanksgiving, touch the Qur'ān, or recite the Qur'ān while in a state of major ritual impurity.

If one performs sand ablutions with intention (1), one may perform a single religious obligation on the basis of these ablutions—if the obligatory act is performed before anything else, and even if one changes one's intention—in addition to as many voluntary acts of worship as one desires. Moreover, on the basis of intention (1), one may engage in all actions requiring ritual purity mentioned under intentions (2) and (3) as well.

If someone performs sand ablutions on the basis of intention (2), he or she may engage in all actions requiring ritual purity mentioned under intentions (2) and (3), but not intention (1). In other words, one may pray as many voluntary prayers as he or she wishes and touch the Qur'ān, but he may not perform an obligatory ritual prayer, deliver a Friday sermon, or perform an obligatory circumambulation of the Ka'bah.

As for sand ablutions based on intention (3), they allow the person to engage only in those actions mentioned under intention (3), but not those included under intentions (1) and (2), even if one has changed his intention at some point.

Finally, the Shafiis hold that it is not necessary for the intention associated with sand ablutions to specify either major or minor ritual impurity; hence, if someone in a state of major ritual impurity were to say, "I intend to make it permissible to perform ritual prayer which I have been prevented from performing by minor ritual impurity," based on the belief that he is only in a state of minor ritual impurity, after which he discovers his error, his sand ablutions will still achieve their purpose. However, if this sort of inaccuracy were deliberate, the ablutions would be invalid due to the dishonesty involved.

* * *

As for the Hanbalis, they hold that conscious intention is a condition for the validity of sand ablutions [rather than an integral part of them]. When performing sand ablutions, then, one is to intend to make permissible whatever act in preparation for which one is performing them, be it ritual prayer or circumambulation of the Ka'bah, be it obligatory or voluntary, and regardless of whether one is performing the ablutions due to minor or major ritual impurity or some impurity on one's body. According to the Hanbalis, one may perform sand ablutions to remove the effect of impurity on one's body, but only after having removed as much of it as possible; as for impurities on one's clothes or in the place where one is, they do not provide a basis for sand ablutions. Thus, if someone performed sand ablutions in order to remove a state of *ḥadath*, the ablutions would not achieve their purpose, since in the Hanbalis' view, such ablutions make certain acts permissible, but they do not actually remove a state of impurity.

In addition, the Hanbalis hold that it is not sufficient for one to perform sand ablutions with the intention of performing an act of worship despite only one of the following, that is (1) minor ritual impurity, (2) major ritual impurity, or (3) impurity on one's body. That is to say, if someone in a state of major ritual impurity intends by means of sand ablutions to make it permissible to perform the noon prayer despite his *major* ritual impurity, for example, yet without intending to make it permissible to do so despite his *minor* ritual impurity, he may not pray a ritual prayer on this basis, since he will have negated the effect of his major ritual impurity such that he may recite the Qur'ān, for example; but he will not have negated the effect of his minor ritual impurity. Similarly, if someone intends to make it permissible to perform some act which he has been prevented from performing by minor ritual impurity alone, yet without including the effect of major ritual impurity, his sand ablutions will not negate the effect of his major ritual impurity. However, if someone intends by means of sand ablutions to make it permissible to perform ritual prayer despite the effects of both major and minor ritual impurity as well as the effect of impurity on his body, this intention will achieve all three purposes at once.

Finally, the Hanbalis hold that if someone intends to make it permissible to do a particular thing, he may do whatever it is on the basis of these sand ablutions, as well as other actions belonging to the same category and any action belonging to a 'lesser' category. For example, the weightiest type of action one may perform based on sand ablutions is an obligatory act, while other acts permitted on the basis of sand ablutions in descending order of weightiness, as it were, are: the making or fulfillment of a vow, performing a collective duty [such as administering major ablutions to a deceased person, which, once it has been done, ceases to be the duty of the rest of the community], voluntary acts of worship, a voluntary circumambulation of the Ka'bah, touching the Qur'ān, reciting the Qur'ān or staying in a mosque while in a state of major ritual impurity, and having sexual relations with one's wife after her menstrual flow has stopped. This being the case, someone who does sand ablutions with nothing but a general intention, such as, "to perform ritual prayer" or "to perform a circumambulation of the Ka'bah" may perform nothing but voluntary forms of these actions.

164. According to the Shafiis, it is not sufficient for the intention to coincide with placing one's hand on the 'purifying dust'; rather, it should coincide with the act of lifting the hand with the soil on it and wiping part of the face, since the face is the first part of the body to be wiped.

As for the Hanbalis, they hold that it is not necessary for the intention to coincide with any particular phase of sand ablutions; rather, it is acceptable for it to precede the act of wiping by a short time, as is the case with the intention associated with any other act of worship.

(2) The use of "purifying dust", that is, soil which has never been contaminated by ritual impurity. If it has been thus contaminated, it is not permissible to use it in sand ablutions even if the main bulk of the impurity has been removed along with any remaining traces. As for what is meant by "purifying dust", the various schools offer different interpretations.[165]

---

165. The Shafiis define 'purifying dust' (*ṣa'īd ṭayyib*) as soil which contains dust-like particles; it also includes sand if it contains such particles. However, if the substance does not contain such particles, it is not permissible to perform sand ablutions with it. It makes no difference whether the substance has been burned unless it has turned to ashes; nor does it make any difference whether it is suitable for growing plants in or whether it is briny soil in which nothing will grow. The Shafiis also classify pulverized potter's clay as a kind of 'purifying dust.' However, if the soil or sand is mixed with some other substance, such as brick dust or flour, then even if the amount of the other substance is less than the amount of soil or sand, it is no longer permissible to use it for sand ablutions. In addition, the Shafiis stipulate that soil fit for sand ablutions must not be 'used', that is, soil or sand remaining on the face or hands of someone who has previously performed sand ablutions, or which has dispersed into the air during the process of wiping.

* * *

According to the Hanbalis, 'purifying dust' refers simply to soil which is *ṭahūr*. In order for the soil to fit this definition, however, they stipulate that it must meet the following conditions: (1) It must not have been taken by force such that its use is not legitimate. (2) It must not have been burned or pulverized, as is done sometimes with pottery and the like, since its previous use in cooking causes it no longer to be 'soil' in the strict sense. (3) It must contain particles which will cling to one's skin.

In the event that the soil becomes mixed with some other substance which also contains dust-like particles, such as gypsum or lime, the ruling on it is based on the same principle which governs the ruling on *ṭahūr* water if it becomes mixed with water that is simply *ṭāhir*. In other words, if soil represents the larger percentage of the mixture, it may be used for sand ablutions, whereas if the other substance represents the larger proportion of the mixture and if this other substance does not contain dust-like particles—as is the case with wheat and barley—then it is not permissible to use it for sand ablutions even if such substances are available in large quantities. Nor is it permissible to perform sand ablutions with clay which one has not been able to dry out. If the time period for the prayer one intends to pray is about to run out and the undried clay is the only thing available, it is permissible to use it for sand ablutions. Once the time has run out, however, one must wait until it has dried out thoroughly before performing sand ablutions with it.

* * *

The Hanafis define 'purifying dust' as anything which has its origin in the earth; hence, it is permissible to perform sand ablutions using dirt, sand, small pebbles and rocks, including smooth ones, as well as on dried out briny soil and burnt brick. As for ice, however, it is not permissible to perform sand ablutions with it since it is not a part of the earth, nor is it permissible to use trees, glass, or movable metals. As for metals which are still in their place of origin, that is, in the ground, one may perform sand ablutions with the soil that lies on top of them, but not with the metals themselves. Similarly, one may not perform sand ablutions with pearls, even if they have been pulverized, nor with flour, ashes, lime, arsenic, red ocher, antimony, sulfur, or turquoise. It is not permissible to perform sand ablutions with soil and the like if it has become mixed with something that is not part of the earth and which represents more than half the mixture; however, if the other substance represents half or less of the mixture, one may still use it for sand ablutions.

* * *

Given that the term 'dust' (*ṣa'īd*) has its origin in the verb *ṣa'ida*, meaning 'to ascend', the Malikis hold that it refers to that which has risen, in other words, those parts of the earth which appear on the surface. As such, the word 'dust' here includes soil, which is the most preferable substance whenever it is available, as well as sand, rocks, and ice—the latter of which, although it is frozen water, is nevertheless similar to rocks which are also themselves part of the earth. Also included is fine clay, although when using clay, one must either touch it very lightly or dry it before wiping one's face and hands so as to avoid contaminating other parts of one's body. Other substances which may be used in sand ablutions include gypsum, which they define as a type of rock which, when it is burned, turns to lime; however, once it has been burned, gypsum may not be used for sand ablutions. As for metals, they may be used for sand ablutions with the exception of gold, silver and other precious metals. It is likewise impermissible to perform sand ablutions using metals that have been removed from the earth, such as alum and salt, as well as on burnt bricks. As for unburnt bricks, one may perform sand ablutions with them provided that they are not mixed with an impure substance or even with a large amount of a ritually pure substance, such as straw. As for what is meant by 'a large amount of a ritually pure substance,' it is any quantity that makes up more than half the mixture. Thus, for example, if straw is present in the same amount as clay, it does no harm. If a substance is not a part of the earth, such as wood, grass and the like, it may not be used for sand ablutions even if the time period for the prayer one intends to pray is about to run out and one can find no acceptable substitute; however, some Maliki scholars rule that such substances may be used for sand ablutions given the two aforementioned conditions, namely, shortness of time and unavailability of any suitable substitute.

Finally, the use of 'dust'—that is, the act of placing one's palms on top of it—constitutes 'the first strike' (to be explained below).

(3) Wiping the entire face,[166] if even with just one hand or one finger. The face includes the beard, even if it is long,[167] as well as the bridge of the nose, the sunken area of one's eyelids, and the area extending downward from the ears to the chin.

(4) Wiping the hands up to the elbows.[168] In so doing, one must remove objects which cover any part of this area, such as rings or bracelets, and wipe the skin under them. It is not sufficient simply to rotate them when performing sand ablutions[169] as it is when doing minor ritual ablutions. Moreover, some of the schools include other obligations as well.[170]

---

166. The Hanafis hold that if the wiping is done with one's hand, one must wipe with the entire hand or with most of it, although the basic requirement is the wiping itself, regardless of whether it is done with the hand or with something else. As for covering the face and hands with whatever substance is used in sand ablutions, this is a condition for their validity, but not an integral part of the rite itself. Moreover, based on a hadith according to which, "Sand ablutions [are to consist of] two 'strikes'", the wiping should take the form of "two strikes" or their equivalent. Hence, if dust got onto someone's face, after which he placed his hand on his face and wiped it, this would be considered the first strike. The "two strikes" referred to here are thus one of the pillars of sand ablutions despite the fact that they are not mentioned in the Qur'anic verse describing this rite.

167. According to the Hanafis, all one is required to wipe is the hair that must be washed as part of minor ritual ablutions, namely, whatever grows directly over the face itself; it is not necessary in their view to wipe any part of the beard that extends below this.

168. According to the Malikis and the Hanbalis, one is obliged to wipe one's hands up to the wrists only, whereas wiping them all the way up to the elbows is not obligatory, but an emulation of the prophetic Sunnah, as will be seen below.

169. In the Hanafis' view, it is sufficient when performing sand ablutions simply to rotate tight-fitting rings or bracelets, since such rotation serves to rub the area under them, and since what is obligatory is not that the dust actually make contact with the skin, but rather, the act of wiping or rubbing itself.

170. The Malikis add the stipulation that when performing sand ablutions one must maintain continuity, not only between the various actions included in the sand ablutions themselves, but also between the sand ablutions and whatever acts of worship are performed on the basis of them. Hence, if someone allowed enough time to pass between such events that the required continuity was broken, even if this occurred simply out of forgetfulness, the ablutions would not be valid. Thus, there are, according to the Malikis, four obligations involved in sand ablutions, namely: (1) the conscious intention to use 'purifying dust', (2) wiping the entire face, (3) wiping the hands up to the wrists, and (4) observing continuity.

* * *

As for the Hanbalis, they add two obligations associated with sand ablutions, namely, (1) maintaining the proper order among the actions involved in this rite and (2) continuity provided that the sand ablutions are being performed due to minor ritual impurity. However, if they are being done due to major ritual impurity or impurity on one's body, neither proper order nor continuity is required in their view. Hence, the Hanbalis list the following four obligations as part of sand ablutions: (1) wiping the entire face, not including the inside of the mouth or ears or the skin beneath thin hair, (2) wiping the hands up to the wrists, (3) maintaining proper order, and (4) continuity (the latter two applying only in cases of minor ritual impurity).

* * *

The Shafiis add a number of obligations associated with sand ablutions. These include: (1) maintaining the proper order among the actions involved in sand ablutions, i.e., first the face, then the hands, regardless of whether one is performing them on account of minor or major ritual impurity; (2) placing the dust on one's face and hands. Hence, if some dust simply blew onto one's face or hands, after which one moved the dust around on them with the intention of performing sand ablutions, this would not be sufficient; (3) the use of *ṭahūr* soil which contains dust-like particles; and (4) transferring the dust in a deliberate manner to the parts of the body involved in sand ablutions, the stipulation here being that the transfer take place in the form of "two strikes."

Hence, the Shafiis list seven obligations as part of sand ablutions: (1) conscious intention, (2) wiping the face, (3) wiping the hands up to the elbows, (4) maintaining the proper order among the actions involved in sand ablutions, (5) transferring the dust used to the parts of the body included in sand ablutions, (6) the use of *ṭahūr* soil containing dust-like particles, and (7) transferring the dust to the face and the hands in a deliberate manner.

* * *

The Hanafis, by contrast, list no additional obligations in connection with sand ablutions, since the pillars of sand ablutions, in their view, are restricted to two elements, namely: (1) wiping, and (2) the "two strikes." As for wiping, it is an integral part of sand ablutions based on the Qur'anic verse which describes this rite, whereas the "two strikes" are included on the basis of the aforementioned hadith. All actions beyond these are to be classified as conditions which, although they are essential, are nevertheless not an integral part of this rite.

Sunnah-based practices associated with sand ablutions

As for the Sunnah-based practices associated with sand ablutions, they include utterance of the *basmalah*,[171] maintenance of proper order among the various steps involved,[172] and others, the details of which vary from one to school to another.[173]

---

171. According to the Hanbalis, utterance of the *basmalah* is a 'duty' [which means that, despite its importance, it remains less binding than the established obligations of Islam–t.n.]. Hence, if someone deliberately neglects to utter the *basmalah*, his sand ablutions lose their validity; however, if he omits it out of inattention or ignorance, they remain valid.

* * *

According to the Malikis, the *basmalah* is recommended, but is not based on the prophetic Sunnah.

* * *

The Shafiis hold that the *basmalah* is based on the prophetic Sunnah, but that if the person doing the sand ablutions is in a state of major ritual impurity, it is not permissible to utter it if his or her intention in doing so is to recite the Qur'ān as part of worship. Hence, the intention should be restricted simply to holding God in remembrance; otherwise, one's sand ablutions should not be accompanied by any intention at all.

* * *

The Hanafis, by contrast, hold that the *basmalah* as part of sand ablutions is based on the prophetic Sunnah regardless of whether one's intention in uttering it is to hold God in remembrance, to recite the Qur'ān as an expression of worship, or nothing at all.

172. As noted earlier, the Shafiis and the Hanbalis view the maintenance of proper order as obligatory in sand ablutions.

173. The Hanafis list the following actions as based on the prophetic Sunnah when performing sand ablutions: (1) striking [the 'dust'] with the palms of one's hands; (2) moving one's hands toward the front, then the back; (3) shaking the dust off one's hands; (4) holding one's fingers apart; (5) uttering the *basmalah*; (6) maintaining proper order among the actions involved in sand ablutions; (7) maintaining continuity; (8) parting one's beard and fingers; (9) rotating any rings one is wearing; (10) doing the right side of one's body before the left; (11) striking the 'dust' in such a way that it gets between one's fingers; (12) wiping one's face and hands in the proper manner, the proper manner being as follows: One strikes the 'dust' with his hands, then shakes it off of them and moves them first forward, then back. Following this, one wipes one's entire face with both hands. One then strikes the 'dust' a second time, shakes it off one's hands as before, and wipes one's hands and arms up to the elbows; and (13) cleaning one's teeth and gums with a *miswāk*.

* * *

The following are the Sunnah-based actions connected with sand ablutions listed by the Shafiis: (1) beginning with an utterance of the *basmalah*; (2) cleaning one's teeth and gums with a *miswāk* after uttering the *basmalah* and before transferring the 'dust' to one's face and hands; (3) shaking or blowing excess dust off one 's hands; (4) wiping one's right hand before the left; (5) facing in the direction of the *qiblah*; (6) wiping one's face from the top down and one's hands from the fingertips inward. Specifically, one is to place the fingers of one's left hand [not including the thumb] on top of the fingers of one's right hand [not including the thumb], positioning them in such a way that the right fingertips do not extend beyond the left index finger. One then passes the left hand over the right as far as the wrist, at which point one passes the fingertips of his left hand over the outside of his right arm as far as the elbow. Then, placing the palm of one's left hand along the inside of one's right arm at the elbow, one draws the fingertips of the left hand down the right arm as far as the wrist, keeping the thumb lifted up, after which the left thumb is drawn over the back of the right thumb. This process is then repeated for the left hand and arm. Finally, it is recommended that one wipe each hand with the other; (7) maintaining continuity between the wiping of one's face and hands if one is in good health (whereas if the person concerned suffers from some sort of incontinence, the maintenance of continuity is not merely an emulation of the prophetic Sunnah, but an obligatory act, as it is in minor ablutions); (8) holding one's fingers apart at the beginning of each 'strike'; (9) removing one's ring(s) during the first 'strike' (whereas during the second 'strike', this is obligatory); (10) parting one's fingers after wiping one's hands if one already did so during the second 'strike' (otherwise, this is obligatory); (11) wiping more than the area actually required; (12) not lifting one's hand off the part of the body being wiped until the wiping has been completed; (13) reciting the *dhikr* associated with wiping the face and the hands; and (14) concluding sand ablutions with a recitation of the *dhikr* mentioned earlier in connection with minor ritual ablutions.

* * *

The Malikis list only four Sunnah-based actions in connection with sand ablutions, namely: (1) maintaining the proper order by beginning with the face, then wiping the hands. If someone reverses this order and wipes his hands first, he should wipe them again after the face provided that he has not already prayed when he remembers having done so; if he has already prayed by the time he remembers, however, no harm is done; (2) wiping one's arms from the wrists to the elbows; (3) performing an additional second 'strike' for one's hands; and (4) transferring the dust which is clinging to one's hands to the part of the body one intends to wipe (that is, to one's hands and face) without wiping anything else first.

* * *

As for the Hanbalis, the only Sunnah-based action which they list in connection with sand ablutions is for one to postpone sand ablutions to near the end of the time period for the prayer one intends to pray on the basis of them if one knows, or has good reason to believe, that water can be found before the time runs out, or even if there is a 50-50 chance of finding water during this time. However, if one performs sand ablutions near the beginning of the time period and prays on this basis, his prayer will still be valid, and he will not be required to repeat it later even if he happens to find water before the time period for this prayer runs out.

Recommended practices associated with sand ablutions

Each of the four schools offers a particular view on the matter of recommended practices in connection with the rite of sand ablutions.[174]

Undesirable practices associated with sand ablutions

Similarly, the various schools offer listings of those practices which are undesirable in connection with sand ablutions.[175]

---

174. Neither the Hanbalis nor the Shafiis make any distinction between Sunnah-based and recommended practices associated with sand ablutions; hence, they hold that all of the Sunnah-based actions mentioned thus far may be referred to equally as 'Sunnah', 'recommended' and 'desirable.'

* * *

The Malikis list the following as recommended practices when performing sand ablutions: (1) uttering the *basmalah*; (2) cleaning one's teeth and gums with a *miswāk*; (3) remaining silent except in order to make mention of God; (4) facing the *qiblah*; (5) commencing sand ablutions by wiping the back of one's right hand with the palm of one's left. Specifically, one is to place one's left palm over the fingers of one's right hand; one then passes the left hand over the right hand and arm up to the right elbow. After this, one wipes the inside of the right arm by passing one's left palm over it, beginning at the right elbow and ending with the fingers of the right hand. The right hand is then used to wipe the left hand and arm in the same manner; (6) performing sand ablutions near the beginning of the 'elective' phase of the time period for the prayer one intends to pray if there is no hope that one will find water or that whatever condition is preventing one from using water will pass before the end of this time period. In the case of someone who is uncertain whether water will be found or whether the condition preventing him from using water will pass, it is recommended that he perform sand ablutions at the midpoint between the beginning and the end of this prayer period; this practice represents a type of compromise between the virtue of praying early in the time period for the prayer concerned, and the virtue of achieving ritual purity through the use of water. If, by contrast, the person is hopeful that he will find water or that the condition preventing him from using water will pass during the 'elective' phase of the time period for the prayer concerned, it is recommended that he not perform sand ablutions until this phase is drawing to a close; however, one should not postpone sand ablutions until the 'imperative' phase. [The terms 'elective' and 'imperative' as they pertain to the times for ritual prayer will be discussed below in the section on "The times of the required prayers" – t.n.] This ruling, like the one before it, is based on the fact that ritual purity achieved through the use of water is preferable to that achieved through sand ablutions. However, despite the desirability of ritual purity based on the use of water, postponing sand ablutions until the 'imperative' time phase for the prayer concerned is forbidden.

* * *

As for the Hanafis, they hold that if the person concerned thinks it likely that he will find water [soon], it is recommended that he postpone sand ablutions until close to the end of the most desirable phase of the time period for the prayer he intends to pray. However, if someone has promised to bring him water, he is required to postpone sand ablutions even if he is fearful that the time period for the prayer he intends to pray might run out.

175. The Hanbalis list the following four actions as undesirable: (1) repeating the action of wiping; (2) allowing soil to get inside the mouth or the nose; (3) engaging in more than two 'strikes'; and (4) blowing on the soil if it is present in an amount which is large enough that blowing will not get rid of it. On the other hand, if blowing gets rid of it so effectively that no dust-like particles are left and one then wipes with it, the entire 'strike' must be repeated.

* * *

The Shafiis likewise list four actions which are undesirable in association with sand ablutions, namely: (1) getting an excessive amount of 'dust' or soil on one's hands (since, as we have seen, the purpose of sand ablutions is simply to obey the Lawgiver's command by placing one's hand on it); (2) wiping any part of the body more than once; (3) renewing sand ablutions, even if one has performed a prayer since the last time sand ablutions were performed; and (4) shaking the dust off one's hands after completing sand ablutions.

* * *

The Malikis list the following practices as undesirable in connection with sand ablutions: (1) Wiping more than once; (2) speaking unnecessarily rather than speaking only to make mention of God; and (3) wiping the area above the elbows.

* * *

As for the Hanafis, they list the following two: (1) Repeating the action of wiping, and (2) neglecting to perform any of the aforementioned Sunnah-based practices.

That which invalidates *tayammum*

The events which invalidate sand ablutions are the same as those which invalidate minor ritual ablutions, and the only events which cause someone who was in a state of major ritual impurity when he performed sand ablutions to revert to such a state are those which themselves bring about a state of major ritual impurity and, as a result, require one to perform *ghusl*, or major ablutions. Hence, if someone performs sand ablutions to remove a state of major ritual impurity, after which his or her sand ablutions are invalidated, he will not revert to a state of major ritual impurity, but will simply be in a state of minor ritual impurity again. As a result, such a person may do such things as read or recite the Qur'ān, enter a mosque, and even spend the night in a mosque.[176]

Nevertheless, there is an additional type of event which invalidates sand ablutions, but not minor ritual ablutions, namely, the passing of the condition which made sand ablutions necessary in the first place, for example, by one's finding water after having none,[177] or becoming able to use water after not being able to.[178]

---

176. According to the Malikis, if someone who has performed sand ablutions due to a state of major ritual impurity has an occurrence of minor ritual impurity, his sand ablutions will be invalidated for both minor and major ritual impurity. Hence, they hold that even though the events which invalidate minor ritual ablutions do not invalidate *ghusl*, or major ablutions, they do invalidate sand ablutions which have been performed in lieu of *ghusl*; as a result, such a person is forbidden to engage in those acts which are forbidden to someone in a state of major ritual impurity until he or she performs sand ablutions again.

177. According to the Malikis, the availability of water or the ability to use it invalidates sand ablutions only if the person has not begun to pray yet; moreover, in order for either of these two things to invalidate one's sand ablutions, there must be enough time left for the person to perform minor ablutions and begin performing a *rak'ah* before the time period for the prayer concerned runs out. Hence, if water becomes available after the person has already begun praying, his sand ablutions are not invalidated; rather, he should keep on praying even if there would have been enough time for him to perform minor ablutions and begin his prayer again before the end of the time period for the prayer he is praying. This ruling applies provided that the person has not forgotten about water among his travel provisions. Thus, supposing someone performs sand ablutions and starts to pray, then remembers that there is some water in his saddlebag. In this situation, if there is enough time remaining for the person to perform minor ablutions and begin praying again, the prayer he is praying will be invalidated; otherwise, it will not. If, on the other hand, the person remembers the water after he has finished praying, he must repeat the prayer he just prayed due to the negligence suggested by such forgetfulness, but only if the time period for the prayer concerned has not ended yet.

178. The Hanbalis list two other events which also invalidate sand ablutions, namely: (1) The end of the time period for the prayer in preparation for which one originally performed the sand ablutions; once this happens, one's sand ablutions are rendered invalid regardless of whether one performed them due to major ritual impurity, impurity on one's body, etc. The only prayer to which this ruling does not apply is the Friday congregational prayer. (2) Removing one's shoes if one performed sand ablutions by wiping one's shoes, regardless of whether one had wiped them before that or not.

* * *

As for the Shafiis, they add another two events to those which invalidate sand ablutions: (1) apostasy, even if only in outward appearance, such as that of a young boy [who might utter blasphemous statements without comprehending their import, for example], and (2) the passing of the condition which made it necessary for the person to perform sand ablutions [such as the lack of water or the inability to use it].

This second condition stipulated by the Shafiis applies provided that at the time when one either gains access to water or regains the ability to use it, one has not begun to pray by uttering the words, *Allāhu akbar*. If one regains access to water or the ability to use it after one has begun praying, and if the prayer is of the type it is not necessary to make up later [such as a voluntary, rather than an obligatory, prayer], one's prayer will be valid and one's sand ablutions will remain valid until the prayer has been completed; however, if one is performing a prayer of the type which must be made up later [that is, an obligatory prayer], then both the prayer and one's ablutions will become invalid.

Concerning those who are unable to perform either minor ablutions or sand ablutions (referred to as "those who lack both purifying substances")

If someone is unable to perform either minor ritual ablutions or sand ablutions as a result of some severe ailment, or due to being imprisoned in a place where there is nothing which he could legitimately use for sand ablutions, it is still necessary for him or her to pray at the time for each of the five daily ritual prayers without having performed ablutions of any kind. As for those who are unable to stand up for prayer, they are to pray sitting down, and if they are unable even to sit up, they are to pray with gestures (a topic which will be dealt with below in the section on ritual prayer).

As for the purpose behind such concessions, it is simply to allow people to demonstrate reverence and submission to God Almighty at all times and under all circumstances. After all, as long as we are able to express such reverence in some fashion, we are obliged to do so. Moreover, those who pray under such circumstances receive no less of a reward than those who are strong and healthy; in fact, their reward may be even greater, since those whose hearts are surrendered to their Sustainer, and whose bodily members express this submission even when they are ill and infirm, have exerted an effort which draws them near to God and brings them into the divine grace and favor.

As for the manner in which someone who has no access either to water or to substances suitable for use in sand ablutions may achieve ritual purity and perform ritual prayer, it is subject to rulings which differ from school to school.[179]

---

179. According to the Hanafis, someone who has access to neither of the "two purifying agents", namely, *ṭahūr* water and soil, is to perform a symbolic prayer (*ṣalāh ṣuwariyah*). One does this by prostrating and standing while facing the *qiblah* but without reciting the Qur'ān or uttering expressions of praise to God or any of the testimonies or supplications which form part of the daily ritual prayer. The intention of someone who prays in this manner should not be to perform ritual prayer, regardless of whether he or she is in a state of major or minor ritual impurity. Moreover, this type of symbolic prayer does not exempt the person from the obligation of ritual prayer in the full sense; rather, it serves to "keep the covenant alive" between the person and God until water can be obtained for minor ritual ablutions, or until he or she has access to 'purifying dust' with which to perform sand ablutions.

* * *

The Malikis hold that when someone has no access to *ṭahūr* water or soil, he or she is exempted entirely from the obligation to perform ritual prayer; hence, he or she is neither to perform ritual prayer under such circumstances nor to make up such prayers later.

The basis for this ruling on their part might be the following hadith: "God does not accept prayer without a purifying agent," which makes no mention of the repetition of prayers. However, the Hanafis do not say that ritual prayer without a purifying agent is acceptable; rather, they simply say that it must be repeated.

* * *

As for the Shafiis, they hold that if the person who lacks both purifying agents is in a state of minor ritual impurity, he is to pray a genuine prayer including the intention to pray and a complete Qur'anic recitation. The same ruling applies to someone who is in a state of major ritual impurity except that the latter must restrict his Qur'anic recitation to the *Fātiḥah* alone. In both cases, however, the person must repeat the prayer once water is found. When the person who has been in a state of major ritual impurity finds water, he must perform both major and minor ritual ablutions, then repeat the prayer which he prayed earlier without the benefit of either regular or sand ablutions. As for the person in a state of minor ritual impurity, he is obliged upon finding water to perform minor ritual ablutions, then repeat the prayer which he prayed earlier. However, if either of these two persons finds *ṭahūr* soil or dust with which to perform sand ablutions, he should not perform sand ablutions in order to repeat his earlier prayer unless he thinks it likely that he is in a place where he will find no water, or unless he has no evidence to indicate whether water is likely to be found or not.

* * *

Finally, the Hanbalis hold that the person who has no access to *ṭahūr* water or soil is to pray a genuine ritual prayer without being obliged to repeat it later, the only stipulation being that he restrict himself to obligatory prayers and abide by all conditions without which ritual prayer loses its validity.

Splints and their definition

The term 'splint' (*jabīrah*) as used by Muslim jurisprudents refers to the piece of cloth which is tied around an ailing part of the body, or the medicine which has been applied to such a part. It is not necessary that the splint be held in place by pieces of wood, palm branches, etc., nor is it necessary that the part of the body which has been wrapped be broken; rather, the criterion by which one determines whether it is a 'splint' is that the part of the body on which it has been placed be ailing in some way, be it a broken bone, a bruise, an area affected by rheumatic pain, etc. Hence, the word 'splint' as employed by Muslim jurisprudents refers either to something which has been tied around an ailing part of the body, or to the medicine which has been applied to it.

When a splint prevents someone from using water

Suppose that someone who is held accountable for the performance of ritual ablutions has a 'splint' in the sense described above on some part of his or her body. Now, if the part of the body affected is one which must be washed as part of either minor or major ablutions, and if washing this part of the body would be harmful or painful, then he or she should wipe either the bandage or the medicine, as the case may be, which has been placed on the area concerned. If it would be harmful to wipe the area with medicine on it, the person should wrap the area concerned in a clean cloth and wipe the cloth instead.

This ruling is agreed upon by the Malikis, the Hanbalis and some of the Hanafis.[180]

---

180. As for the Shafiis, they hold that if the ailing part of the body is wrapped, the person must do the following three things: (1) Wash the unaffected part around the wound or ailing area. (2) Wipe the splint or bandage itself. This wiping takes the place of washing the unaffected area which surrounds the wound and which is concealed by the bandage. However, if the bandage covers nothing but the affected area alone, or if one is able to wash the sound area which is concealed by the bandage, the bandage need not be wiped. (3) Perform sand ablutions in lieu of washing the ailing area.

If the person concerned is in a state of major ritual impurity, it is not necessary to maintain any specific order among these three steps, namely: (1) washing the adjacent, unaffected area, (2) wiping the splint, bandage, etc. and (3) performing sand ablutions. In other words, such a person may begin with whichever of these three steps he or she chooses. However, if the person is not in a state of major ritual impurity, he must make certain to perform Step (1) before Step (3). Thus, he must wash the adjacent, unaffected area before performing sand ablutions. As for Step (2), that of wiping the splint, bandage, etc., it may be performed before either Step (1) or Step (3) [or, as we have seen, it may be omitted entirely].

If the person has multiple wounds, sores, etc., he must perform sand ablutions once for each wound or ailing area. However, if the effects of the ailment are found all over the body, it is sufficient to perform sand ablutions just once for all the ailing areas; the same ruling applies if the ailment affects two entire areas which are washed in succession when performing ablutions, such as the face and the arms. In other words, after one has washed the adjacent, unaffected sites and wiped the splints [if necessary], one may perform sand ablutions just once for both areas.

The ruling discussed above applies to an area of the body which is wrapped in a bandage, splint, etc. If it is not wrapped, one is required to wash those parts of the body which are sound and to perform sand ablutions in place of washing the part which is ailing. One is not to wipe the ailing area with water, however, since wiping is not allowed in the Shafiis' view unless it is done in place of washing an unaffected part concealed by a bandage wrapped around the ailing area; in this latter case, the wiping is similar to the act of wiping one's shoes as part of ritual ablutions. If the ailing area is exposed but cannot be washed, it is meaningless to wipe it; hence, one is to perform sand ablutions in place of washing it. Moreover, if the ailment affects the face or the hands/arms, that is, those parts of the body wiped in sand ablutions, such that it would be impossible or harmful to wipe them with the soil used in sand ablutions, one must not wipe them at all; instead, one is simply required to repeat the prayers missed after the affected area has healed.

* * *

As for the Hanafis, there are two rulings in circulation among them on the practice of wiping a splint. According to the first ruling, wiping a splint is a duty rather than a fully binding obligation. (For the difference between 'duty' [*wājib*] and 'obligation' [*farḍ*] in the Hanafis' view, see the earlier discussion of this in the section on Ritual Ablutions.) Given this ruling, if someone fails to wipe an ailing part of the body and then prays, his prayer will be valid but he should repeat it later, since otherwise, he will have deprived himself of the intercession of the Prophet on the Day of Judgment, albeit without actually being punished for this omission.

According to the second ruling—which is in agreement with the views of the Malikis and the Hanbalis—it is a binding obligation (*farḍ*) to wipe a splint over an ailing part of the body. Hence, if someone neglects to do so, his prayer will not be valid.

Both of these rulings are recognized as valid by the Hanafis; hence, the person who finds himself in such circumstances may adopt whichever of the two he finds most suitable.

Conditions associated with wiping a splint

In order for it to be permissible to wipe a splint, be it a bandage, medicine, etc., the following conditions must be met: (1) It must be harmful to wash the ailing part such that one fears that washing it would cause greater pain, cause it to heal less rapidly, etc. If the ailing part has medicine on it but is not wrapped and if it would be harmful to wipe it, one must wrap it in something which will not harm it, then wipe the wrapping, as we have mentioned. (2) The entire splint must be wiped; in other words, the sound area surrounding the splint should be washed, after which the ailing part [that is, the splint itself] should be wiped.

However, if the splint covers an area larger than the ailing part itself due to the necessity of wrapping it properly, the entire splint must be wiped, including both the parts of it which cover the ailing area and the parts which cover the surrounding, unaffected area.[181] [In other words, if the sound parts around the ailing area are covered by the splint, they should not be washed, but wiped only.]

Moreover, if the ailing area is one which is normally wiped anyway, such as the head, for example, the various schools offer different rulings in this regard.[182]

---

181. The Hanafis hold that it is not necessary to wipe the entire splint; rather, it is sufficient to wipe most of it. Thus, if one's entire hand is covered with wounds and one has put a bandage on it, it is sufficient to wipe more than half of the area which has been wrapped.

The Hanafis hold that if the wrapping covers more than the actual area which is ailing or wounded and if it would not be harmful to unwrap the affected area, one must unwrap it and wash it if washing it will do no harm. If washing it would be harmful, one must wipe the affected area and wash the unaffected area surrounding it. If even wiping the area would be harmful, one is to wash the area around it, then put the wrapping back on and wipe the wrapping.

If, on the other hand, it would be harmful to unwrap the ailing area, one must wipe the bandage without removing it even if it would have been possible to wash or wipe what was beneath it; moreover, one must wipe the greater part of the bandage, including those parts of it which cover the surrounding, unaffected area.

* * *

According to the Hanbalis, if the splint was put on when the person concerned was in a state of ritual purity and if it covers more than the affected area, he or she is to wipe with water [the part of the splint covering the ailing area] and perform sand ablutions in place of the rest. If the splint was put on when the person concerned in was not in a state of ritual purity, he or she must perform sand ablutions only and dispense with the wiping, which would not be valid. They also hold that if there are a number of ailing areas, one must perform sand ablutions for each of these areas unless they include all parts of the body which are washed in minor or major ritual ablutions, in which case one is required to perform sand ablutions only once for all of them. Finally, as mentioned above, the Hanbalis stipulate that someone in a state of minor ritual impurity must observe the proper temporal order and continuity among the steps involved.

182. The Malikis hold that if there are wounds all over the head, the ruling on it is the same as that which applies to parts of the body which are washed [rather than wiped]. If the wounds do not cover the head and if it poses no difficulty to wipe some of the head, one is to wipe part of the head and complete the wiping on top of the turban [wrapped around the wounds]. If such wiping would pose difficulty, however, the ruling on it is the same as that which applies to someone whose head is covered with wounds.

* * *

According to the Shafiis, if part of the head is unwounded, it must be wiped; otherwise, one is to perform sand ablutions in lieu of wiping it.

* * *

The Hanafis hold that if part of the head is unwounded and if the unwounded part amounts to one-fourth of the area of the head—i.e., the area which, according to the Hanafis, must be wiped as part of ritual ablutions—one must wipe it. If this is done, there is no need to wipe the splint as well. If, on the other hand, the wounds cover the entire head, the ruling which applies is the same as that which applies to parts of the body which are washed [rather than wiped]; that is, one must wipe it if wiping will cause no harm; otherwise, one need only wipe the splint itself.

* * *

As for the Hanbalis, they hold that if wounds cover the entire head and if it is impossible to wipe it, one is to wipe the entire bandage which covers it; moreover, if the bandage was put on when the person was in a state of ritual impurity, he is to perform sand ablutions as well. If, on the other hand, the head is not covered with wounds, one is to wipe whatever parts are unwounded, then wipe the bandage, since the bandage serves as a symbol for the head itself in such a situation.

That which renders wiping a splint invalid

The act of wiping a splint loses its validity when it either falls off or is removed.[183]

---

183. According to the Malikis, if a splint falls off after the wound or ailment has healed, the effect of wiping it loses its validity and one is required to resume the normal manner of cleansing the area, be it washing or wiping. If this occurs when the person is in a state of ritual purity and he or she wishes to maintain this state, he or she must act promptly to wash or wipe the area under the splint so as not to disrupt the required continuity. However, if a long time passes between the splint's falling off and the person's washing or wiping the area and if the cause of the delay was mere forgetfulness, he or she will remain ritually pure.

Similarly, if the splint falls off before the wound is healed, the person should put it back on and proceed without delay to wipe it lest the required continuity be broken. If the splint should fall off during ritual prayer after the wound has healed, the prayer becomes invalid and it must be repeated after the person has cleansed the area which was under it; if the same thing happens before the wound heals, the same ruling applies, but all one must do before repeating the prayer is to put it back on and wipe the splint itself.

* * *

According to the Shafiis, if a splint falls off during ritual prayer after the wound has healed, both one's prayer and one's ritual purity are rendered invalid. If it falls off before the wound heals, the prayer is invalidated, but not one's ritual purity; hence, all one must do is put the splint back on and wipe it after cleansing whatever parts of the body come after the one on which the splint had been placed [i.e., according to the order in which parts of the body are washed in ritual ablutions].

* * *

The Hanafis hold that if a splint falls off before healing has occurred, the act of wiping it is not invalidated regardless of whether it falls off during ritual prayer or at some other time. If it should fall off during ritual prayer after healing has taken place, and if it happens before the final 'sitting' during which one prays for blessings upon the Prophet, one's prayer will be invalidated; in this case, one must simply cleanse the site of the splint and repeat the prayer. If it falls off during prayer, but after, rather than before the final 'sitting', one's prayer is invalidated according to Imam Abū Ḥanīfah, but not according to the "two companions" [Abū Yūsuf al-Qāḍī and Muḥammad Ibn al-Ḥasan al-Shaybānī], since in this case, one's prayer will have been completed, and the falling off of a splint will be no different from someone speaking or having an occurrence of *ḥadath* after he has finished praying.

* * *

As for the Hanbalis, they hold that if a splint falls off, one's entire ablutions are invalidated regardless of whether it falls off before or after healing has occurred. However, if it falls off after healing is complete, all one has to do is repeat one's ablutions, whereas if it falls off before this, one must perform both regular ablutions and sand ablutions again.

The prayer of someone who has done ablutions by wiping a splint

A prayer performed on the basis of wiping a splint which meets the aforementioned conditions is valid, and there is no need for it to be repeated later after the wound or other condition has healed.[184]

184. According to the Shafiis, there are three situations in which such a prayer must be repeated: (1) when the splint is on either the face or the hands/arms, that is, the parts of the body included in sand ablutions, (2) when the splint is on a part of the body not affected by sand ablutions, and when it conceals a sound area of the body greater than that required for the splint to cling properly, and (3) when the splint is on a part of the body not affected by sand ablutions and conceals only the area required for it to cling properly, but was put on while the person concerned was in a state of ritual impurity.

Ritual Prayer

On Ritual Prayer

The wisdom in the establishment of ritual prayer

All that has preceded this chapter by way of explanation of various aspects of ritual purity was simply an introduction to the subject of ritual prayer. As we have seen, all of the rulings pertaining to ritual purity—which is itself a basis and condition for ritual prayer—are sources of benefit to human society, since they depend upon such things as maintaining bodily cleanliness and keeping places of worship free of those types of filth which generate disease and unpleasant odors. It is true, of course, that some rulings relating to ritual purity do not have a direct bearing on these matters in particular; however, this fact likewise reflects a clearly discernible truth, namely, that the aim of every act of worship in Islam is to demonstrate human submission to God, may He be praised and glorified, through obedience to His commands and avoidance of those acts which He has forbidden.

As for ritual prayer, it is the most important of all the pillars of the Islamic religion. God has ordained ritual prayer for His servants in order that they might worship Him alone and not associate with Him any created being. As God Almighty declares, "Verily, for all believers prayer is indeed a sacred duty linked to particular times [of day]" (4:103). In other words, it is an obligatory act the performance of which is limited to particular time periods that we are required to adhere to faithfully. The Messenger of God states, "Five prayers [per day] have been ordained by God for His servants. Those who perform all of them, not missing a single one out of disdain for their true value, God promises to usher into Paradise." There are numerous prophetic hadiths which stress the importance of ritual prayer, urging us to perform it regularly at its appointed times and warning us not to make light of it or to allow laziness to keep us from it. According to one such hadith, the Prophet says, "The five daily prayers may be likened to an overflowing river of sweet water which flows by someone's door and rushes into the house five times a day. How much filth do you think it will leave in that house?" In response, his listeners replied, "None." "Thus it is," he told them, "that the five daily prayers wash away sins just as water washes away dirt and filth." In other words, the five daily ritual prayers purify people's souls, cleansing them of guilt and sin just as bathing with pure water five times a day would purify and cleanse one's body.

The Messenger of God was once asked, "What is the most virtuous act a person can perform?" He replied, "To pray at the appointed times." Hence, the performance of ritual prayer is the most virtuous, the most sublime, and the most significant single thing a Muslim can do. What more compelling argument could there be in favor of performing prayer at its ordained times each day?

As for warning and inspiring fear in those who neglect prayer, the following words of the Messenger of God should suffice to achieve this end: "Those who do not pray have no share in Islam," and, "The only thing that stands between a Muslim and unbelief is the neglect of prayer." These prophetic hadiths contain a severe reprimand for Muslims who allow sloth to get the better of them by leading them to abandon ritual prayer, the very thing that distinguishes them from those who reject faith. In fact, some Maliki imams hold that the person who deliberately neglects ritual prayer has rejected faith. Be that as it may, all the four schools agree that prayer is one of the pillars of Islam and that those who abandon it have, in effect, destroyed one of the religion's most solid underpinnings.

What people need to realize is that the essential purpose of ritual prayer is to fill our hearts with an awareness of the majesty of God the Creator such that, as a result of prayer, our hearts tremble with awe in God's presence and we seek both to obey His commands and to avoid whatever He forbids. When this takes place, it can only bring benefit to the human race, since those who seek to act righteously and avoid evil bring others nothing but goodness and blessing. As for those who pray while their hearts are unmindful of their Lord, preoccupied instead with personal desires and ambitions and physical pleasures, their prayer might fulfill their legal obligation according to some schools, but even so, it will have failed to produce its intended result. Prayer which is complete is that which God describes thus: "Truly, to a happy state shall attain the believers: those who humble themselves in their prayer..." (Qur'ān 23:1-2).

The most fundamental purpose of ritual prayer, then, is to magnify the Divine, the Creator of the heavens and the earth, by coming before Him in humility and in submission to His eternal glory and everlasting power. We will not have prayed truly unless our hearts are fully present and filled with reverence for God alone. When we are praying in the true sense, we do not become distracted from our intimate communion with God by delusive or harmful thoughts. On the contrary, when we stand in the presence of our Maker with our hearts in a state of lowliness, surrender and awe before the majesty of this all-powerful, invincible Creator, the One Whose authority knows no bounds and Whose will cannot be frustrated, we will, as a consequence, be remorseful for any guilt in our lives and anxious to return to our Sustainer in repentance. When this happens, both our outward actions and our inward intentions will be set aright, our relationship with our Lord will be strengthened, and we will relate with integrity to other human beings, respecting the limits set down for us by our religion and turning away from what has been forbidden to us by the Sustainer of the worlds. As God says, ". . . prayer restrains [people] from loathsome deeds and from all that runs counter to reason" (29:45). When we live in accordance with these realities, we will have become true Muslims.

The prayer which "restrains from loathsome deeds and from all that runs counter to reason" is one in which we are magnifying our Lord, full of reverence for Him and hopeful of experiencing His mercy. Hence, the benefit we receive from our prayers is directly proportionate to the degree to which we fear God and hold Him in awe on the level of our hearts, that is, our inward beings. After all, God looks not at our outward appearances, but at our hearts; hence, He says, " . . . worship Me alone, and be constant in prayer, so as to remember Me!" (20:14). It goes without saying that if our hearts are not mindful of God, we are not remembering Him, nor will we be praying a genuine prayer. As the Prophet declared, "God has no regard for the prayer of someone whose heart is not present together with his body."

This, then, is ritual prayer as understood in Islam. Moreover, prayer in this sense has the effect of refining people's souls and reforming their morals, since every part of it serves to train us in moral virtue and imbue us with praiseworthy traits. What follows is a listing of some of the actions involved in ritual prayer and the ways in which they help in the refinement of our souls:

First: *Intention*, namely, the heartfelt determination to obey God's command to perform prayer as perfectly as possible and with an attitude of loving devotion to God alone. If we were to pray in this manner five times every day, there is no doubt that such loving devotion would be imprinted in our souls, becoming a permanent trait in our characters and yielding the loveliest of fruits in our lives both individually and collectively. After all, there is nothing more beneficial to human society than sincerity and loving devotion in all one says and does. If people demonstrated this sort of attitude toward one another in all they said and did, they would experience contentment and well-being both in this world and the next.

Second: *Standing in the presence of God Most High*. When praying, we stand both physically and spiritually before our Maker, bowing our heads in reverence and speaking with Him in intimate conversation. As we do so, God is closer to us than our very jugular veins, hearing all we have to say and knowing the intentions of our hearts. There can be no doubt that if we do this numerous times a day, our hearts will be molded by our Creator in such a way that we desire to obey His commands and to refrain from anything He has forbidden to us. This being the case, we would never violate other people's sacred rights, commit aggression against another, rob anyone of material possessions, or bring harm to others in connection with their religion or their honor.

Third: *Qur'anic recitation* (the various schools' rulings on which will be mentioned below). It is essential when reciting the Qur'ān that we not move our lips, merely mouthing the words, as it were, while our hearts and minds are elsewhere. Rather, we should ponder the meaning of the words we are reciting so as to take to heart the lessons which they have to offer. When the mention of God our Creator passes over our lips, our hearts should be filled with reverence and awe at God's majesty and sovereignty. As He declares, "Believers are only they whose hearts tremble with awe whenever God is mentioned, and whose faith is strengthened whenever His messages are conveyed to them" (8:2). When God's gracious attributes of mercy and righteousness are mentioned, we must teach ourselves how to take on these same divine attributes, since the Prophet said, "Adorn yourselves with the attributes of God, Who is gracious, ever ready to forgive and pardon, and treats all people with perfect justice." Human beings are held accountable before God for whether they have striven to take on these moral qualities. If as we pray we recite Qur'anic verses which speak of these gracious divine attributes with an understanding of their import, and if we repeat such recitations numerous times each day, our souls are bound to be influenced in such a way that we develop the longing to take on such qualities ourselves, which in turn serves to refine our souls and our morals.

Four: *Bowing and prostrating*, both of which are means of expressing adoration for the King of kings, Creator of the heavens, the earth, and all that lies between them. When we bow in the presence of our Sovereign, it is not enough simply to bend our torsos in the proper manner; rather, we must have a heartfelt awareness that we are humble servants bowing before the majesty of a lofty, glorious Deity, whose might knows no limit and whose greatness knows no end. If these truths are impressed on our hearts as we pray repeatedly throughout the day and night, our hearts will be in a constant state of godly fear that leads us to do only that which is pleasing to Him. Likewise, when we prostrate ourselves before our Creator, placing our foreheads on the ground in declaration of our servanthood and experiencing a sense of our lowly station together with the greatness of our Master and Maker, it goes without saying that we will learn to fear and revere Him. When these things take place, our souls are set on the right path and we abstain "from loathsome deeds and from all that runs counter to reason."

In addition, there are specific aspects of ritual prayer which offer social benefits of great significance. One of these is *community*, that is, communal prayer. The Prophet urges us to take part in communal prayer, saying, "Prayer performed in community is superior to individual prayer by twenty-seven degrees." By gathering as a group to perform ritual prayer in straight, uniform rows, we have the opportunity to become acquainted as human beings. Communal prayer can serve to join hearts which have been alienated, removing hatred and resentments. This is one of the most sublime elements in the unity which God Most High has commanded us to pursue and preserve in His precious book, saying, "And hold fast, all together, unto the bond with God, and do not draw apart from one another" (3:103). As such, coming together for communal prayer serves as a reminder of the brotherhood of which God speaks, saying, "All believers are but brethren" (49:10). Hence, believers who gather to worship a single Lord should not forget that they are brothers and sisters. On the contrary, the greatest among them should be merciful toward the least among them; those who are young should respect and honor their elders; the wealthy among them should come to the aid of those who are indigent; the strong among them should assist the weak; and those who are in good health should visit those who are ill. In so doing, they act in accordance with the words of the Prophet, who said, "Muslims are brothers and sisters to one another; hence, none of them would wrong or dishonor another. Whoever helps his brother in a time of need will himself be helped by God in a time of need; if anyone delivers a [fellow] Muslim from distress in this world, God will deliver him from distress on the Day of Resurrection; and anyone who protects a Muslim [in this world] will be protected by God on the Day of Resurrection."[1] If we were to mention all the benefits prayer provides, we could go on for pages on end; hence, contenting ourselves with what has

1. The Arabic verb *satara*, rendered here as 'protect', and which also means 'cover, conceal, guard, or shield', bears the additional meaning of 'forgive'. Hence, this statement could possibly have been translated, "anyone who *forgives* a Muslim [in this world] will be *forgiven* by God on the Day of Resurrection." In either case, it is interesting to note the connection between shielding, covering, protecting, etc. and the act of forgiveness, which involves a conscious decision to treat an offense as if it were "invisible", so to speak [t.n.].

been said, we ask God for grace to live faithfully by the noble religion He has given us, knowing that He hears our plea.

The definition of ritual prayer

As used generally in the Arabic language, the word rendered "ritual prayer", that is, *al-ṣalāh*, means "an invocation of blessing." As God says [to the Prophet], "…and pray for them: behold, thy prayer will be [a source of] comfort to them..." (9:103). In other words, the Prophet is instructed to invoke blessing on the people and to show mercy to them.

As used by Muslim jurisprudents, the word *al-ṣalāh* refers to words and actions which are introduced by the phrase, *Allāhu akbar*, that is, "God is greatest", and concluded with an invocation of peace and mercy—*Al-salāmu 'alaykum wa raḥmat Allah*—that is, "May peace and the mercy of God be upon you." In order to meet the definition of *al-ṣalāh*, such words and actions must also fulfill a number of conditions, the details of which differ from school to school. This definition includes every ritual prayer which is opened with the utterance of *Allāhu akbar* (also referred to as *takbīrat al-iḥrām*) and concluded with the invocation of peace mentioned above. However, according to the Hanafis and the Shafiis, this definition does not include what is referred to as the "prostration of recitation",[2] that is, a single prostration which is performed when one hears a verse from the Qur'ān the contents of which call for such a prostration, but without the initial "God is greatest" or the final "May peace and the mercy of God be upon you."

Types of ritual prayer

Each of the four schools lists various types of ritual prayer.[3]

Conditions associated with ritual prayer

Associated with ritual prayer there are conditions, some of which must be fulfilled in order for prayer to be *valid*, and some of which must be fulfilled in order for it to be *required*. The various schools use different terms to describe these conditions; they also differ over the exact number of conditions belonging to each type.[4]

---

2. The Malikis and the Hanbalis define ritual prayer as "a physical act by which one draws near to God, which is begun with the utterance of *Allāhu akbar* and concluded with an invocation of peace." They include in this definition a single prostration as well. The phrase "a physical act" refers to such movements as bowing and prostrating, movements of the tongue such as those which are involved in recitation of the Qur'ān and praise to God, and an attitude of the heart characterized by humility and submission.

The Hanafis and the Shafiis do not disagree with this definition; however, there is a difference between them and the two other schools over whether the act of prostration alone may be referred as *ṣalāh*, or ritual prayer, in the full legal sense.

3. The Hanafis divide ritual prayer into four types: (1) Obligatory prayers which are required of every individual Muslim, such as the five daily prayers; (2) Obligatory prayers which are required of the Muslim community as a whole—the funeral prayer, for example—such that if even one Muslim performs it on behalf of all others, the requirement is fulfilled; (3) Prayer which is a 'duty', namely, the *witr*

prayer consisting of three *rak'ahs* [which follows the final evening prayer], voluntary prayers that are being repeated because something happened to invalidate them after they had been begun, and the prayers performed on the Day of Fastbreaking and the Day of Sacrifice; and (4) all voluntary prayers, whether they are based on the prophetic Sunnah or are simply recommended. As for the "prostration of recitation", it is not classified by the Hanafis as ritual prayer, as we have noted above.

* * *

The Malikis divide ritual prayer into two main categories, each of which is further divided into subcategories. The two main categories are: (1) prayer which includes bowing, prostrating, Qur'anic recitation, the opening *Allāhu akbar* and the concluding *Al-salāmu 'alaykum wa raḥmat Allāh*, and (2) prayer which does not include all of these elements.

Prayers belonging to category (1) above are divided into three subcategories, namely, (a) the five daily obligatory prayers, (b) voluntary and Sunnah-based prayers, and (c) *al-raghībah* (literally, "the object of desire"), which refers to the two *rak'ahs* performed before the dawn prayer.

As for category (2), it consists of the following two subcategories, namely: (a) prayers which include nothing but prostration, specifically, the "prostration of recitation", and (b) prayers—like the funeral prayer—which include the opening *Allāhu akbar*, [recitation,] and the concluding *Al-salāmu 'alaykum wa raḥmat Allāh*, but not bowing or prostration.

* * *

According to the Shafiis, ritual prayer consists of two types: (1) prayers which include bowing, prostrating and Qur'anic recitation; this type includes the five daily obligatory prayers and voluntary prayers; and (2) prayers which lack bowing and prostration but which include the opening *Allāhu akbar*, Qur'anic recitation, and the concluding *Al-salāmu 'alaykum wa raḥmat Allāh*. This type comprises only the funeral prayer.

Unlike the Hanafis, the Shafiis do not recognize the category of prayer as 'duty', and unlike the Malikis, they do not have a separate subcategory for the two *rak'ahs* performed before the dawn prayer; nor do they consider the "prostration of recitation" to be ritual prayer.

* * *

As for the Hanbalis, they divide ritual prayer into three main categories: (1) Prayer which includes bowing, prostrating, the opening *Allāhu akbar* and the concluding *Al-salāmu 'alaykum wa raḥmat Allāh*. This category includes both the five daily obligatory prayers and the Sunnah-based prayers. (2) Prayer which includes the opening *Allāhu akbar*, Qur'anic recitation and the concluding *Al-salāmu 'alaykum wa raḥmat Allāh*, but without bowing or prostration. This category includes only the funeral prayer; and (3) Prayer which includes nothing but prostration, namely, the "prostration of recitation." (Thus, like the Malikis, the Hanbalis recognize the "prostration of recitation" as ritual prayer.)

4. The Malikis divide the conditions associated with ritual prayer into three categories: (1) conditions for its *necessity alone*; (2) conditions for its *validity alone*; and (3) conditions for *both its necessity and its validity*.

Category (1) includes two conditions. First: The person concerned must have reached puberty. Hence, ritual prayer is not required of a young boy or girl; however, a child seven years of age may be instructed to pray, while a child ten years old may be spanked lightly for neglecting to pray. The reason for this is that, although the legal responsibilities which Islam lays upon us are based entirely on the goal of serving people's best interests and warding off harm, and despite the fact that people with a sound understanding of things do not find it burdensome to fulfill these responsibilities once they have reached the age of accountability, it is also true that habit has a role to play in such matters. Consequently, although someone may know enough about the material and spiritual benefits of prayer to be motivated to pray, he may nevertheless neglect prayer if the habit of performing it has never been instilled in him.

Second: The person concerned must not be under compulsion to abandon prayer. For example, someone may have been ordered by an unjust superior to stop praying, and he or she may have been threatened that unless such orders are obeyed, he or she will be beaten, killed, placed in shackles, or humiliated by being slapped in the face in public. The Malikis hold that someone who stops praying under duress is not guilty of wrongdoing; rather, such a person is exempted from the obligation to pray as long as such duress continues. As the Prophet declared, "My people are not held accountable for unintentional error, forgetfulness, or that which they have been forced to do." However, that which we are exempted from when we are under duress is prayer which is outwardly visible; otherwise, whenever we have the opportunity to perform ablutions and pray, we are required to do all we can, including conscious intention, uttering the *Allāhu akbar* with which prayer is commenced, Qur'anic recitation, bodily gestures, and so on. Hence, like the sick person with limited capacities, we are obliged to do whatever we are capable of, trusting that we are exempted from anything beyond this.

Category (2), namely, conditions for prayer's *validity alone*, includes the following: (1) the person concerned must be free of *ḥadath* [that is, a state of minor or major ritual impurity]; (2) he or she must be free of *khabath* [that is, physical impurities on his or her person, clothing, or prayer spot]; (3) the person concerned must be a Muslim; (4) he or she must face in the direction of the *qiblah*; and (5) one's private parts must be concealed.

And as for Category (3), namely, conditions for *both the necessity and the validity* of ritual prayer, they include the following: (1) the person concerned must have received the message of Islam, since otherwise, prayer is not required of him or her, and even if such a person did happen to pray, it would not be valid under such circumstances; (2) one must be in full possession of his mental faculties; (3) the time period for the prayer one intends to pray must have begun; (4) he must have access to at least one of the "two purifying agents", that is, *ṭahūr* water or soil; (5) one must not be asleep or unaware of what one is doing; and (6) one must not be menstruating or experiencing postpartum bleeding.

Based on the foregoing, it may be seen that the Malikis have added a condition for the *validity* of ritual prayer, namely, that one be a Muslim, while at the same time, they do not count this as a condition for prayer's *necessity.* In other words, in contrast to other schools, the Malikis hold that non-Muslims are held accountable for not praying, although even if they did pray, it would not be valid until they had entered Islam. In addition, the Malikis alone distinguish between two types of ritual purity, namely, (1) purity from *ḥadath*, and (2) purity from *khabath*, and they add to the list of conditions for prayer's necessity that one not be under compulsion to refrain from praying.

* * *

The Shafiis divide the conditions associated with ritual prayer into only two categories, namely, conditions for its *necessity*, and conditions for its *validity.* The conditions for prayer's necessity are as follows: (1) The message of the Prophet must have reached the person concerned. (2) The person concerned must be a Muslim. Hence, according to the Shafiis, non-Muslims are not required to pray. Nevertheless, they hold that non-Muslims will be punished in the afterlife for neglecting prayer over and above the punishment for their unbelief. As for those who renounce Islam, they are still held accountable for prayer based on their former state. (3) One must have full possession of his or her mental capacities. (4) One must have reached puberty. (5) One must not be menstruating or having postpartum bleeding; and (6) One's physical senses must be sound, even if one has nothing but hearing or sight.

As for the conditions for prayer's validity, they include the following seven: (1) One's body must be free of both minor and major ritual impurity. (2) One's body, clothing, and the place where one is praying must be free of *khabath*, that is, impure substances. (3) One's private parts must be concealed. (4) One must be facing the *qiblah*. (5) One must know, or have good reason to believe, that the time period for the prayer one intends to pray has begun. In this regard, the Shafiis distinguish among three levels of 'knowledge': (a) Knowledge based on one's own reliable information, or based on a report received by a trusted source who knows that the time has begun based either on an accurate timepiece or by having heard the call to prayer from a muezzin who has access to an accurate timekeeping device, such as muezzins inside of mosques in which clocks are kept. (b) Knowledge based on an informed judgment derived from available facts, for example, based on observation of the sun, the shadow it casts, etc. (c) Knowledge based on imitation of someone who has arrived at a judgment such as that spoken of in (b) above. If the person concerned is blessed with sight, he or she must seek to arrive at a judgment independently; however, if he or she is blind, it is permissible to imitate someone else who has reached such an independent judgment. (6) One must be aware of how prayer is performed; and (7) Nothing must happen during one's prayer to invalidate it.

Hence, it may be seen that the Shafiis list three conditions for the validity of prayer which are not included by the Malikis, namely: (1) That one be aware of how prayer is performed. In other words, regardless of whether the person praying is an unlearned individual or someone who has studied the religion sufficiently to know such things, he or she does not mistakenly think that some obligatory actions are simply based on the Sunnah but rather, is able to distinguish between them; (2) That nothing happen during one's prayer to invalidate it; and (3) That one know that the time period for the prayer intended has begun (provided that the prayer is one which is bound to a particular time period).

The Shafiis have also added the condition that one be a Muslim in order for prayer to be required. In other words, they hold that prayer is not required of someone who has never been a Muslim; or rather, it is not required of the person in this life, but in the life to come, he or she will be punished for neglecting it over and above the punishment for his or her unbelief, as we have noted above. As for the apostate, they hold that prayer is required of him in this world and that in addition, he will be punished for its neglect in the afterlife. At the same time, they say that if a non-Muslim prays, his or her prayer will be invalid, which means that they list being a Muslim as a condition for prayer's validity as well.

* * *

Like the Shafiis, the Hanafis divide the conditions for prayer into two types: (1) conditions for its necessity, and (2) conditions for its validity.

As for the conditions for prayer's *necessity*, the Hanafis list the following five: (1) One must have received the Prophet's call to Islam (although many Hanafis do not include this condition, since they consider it to be included in condition #2); (2) One must be a Muslim; (3) One must be in full possession of his or her mental faculties; (4) One must have reached puberty; and (5) One must be free of menstrual flow and/or postpartum bleeding.

As for the conditions for prayer's *validity*, they include the following six: (1) One's body must be free of both minor and major ritual impurity (*ḥadath*) and impure substances (*khabath*); (2) One's clothing must be free of impure substances; (3) The place where one intends to pray must be free of impure substances; (4) One's private parts must be concealed; (5) One must consciously intend to perform ritual prayer; and (6) One must be facing the *qiblah*.

Hence, the Hanafis have added to the conditions for the necessity of ritual prayer that of being a Muslim. On this point the Hanafis agree with the Shafiis; however, the Hanafis hold that non-Muslims are not punished for neglecting prayer over and above the punishment which they will receive for their unbelief. (It may be noted here that the issue of whether non-Muslims are to be punished over and above the punishment due them for their unbelief is merely a theoretical question with no practical value, since the punishment due to someone for having rejected faith is already the most terrible of all punishments, and any torment one could imagine remains less grievous. Hence, any chastisement one might think of will either be included in, or less than, the chastisement for the rejection of faith!)

In addition, they add to the conditions for the validity of prayer that of conscious intention. They hold that ritual prayer has no validity without such intention based on the words of the Prophet, "[The value and meaning of an] action inhere in the intention on which it is based." It is by virtue of one's intention that acts of worship are distinguished from other habitual actions; similarly, acts of worship are distinguished from one another on the basis of one's conscious intention. The Hanbalis agree with the Hanafis that intention is to be viewed as a condition [for the

Evidence for the obligatory nature of prayer and the number of daily prayers required

The five daily obligatory prayers were established in Mecca on the night of the Prophet's "nocturnal journey"[5] one year before his emigration to Medina. The times for the prayers which were revealed to the Prophet on this occasion were the times which are recognized to this day, namely: noon, mid-afternoon, sundown, evening, and [early] morning. The first obligatory prayer to be performed by the Prophet was the noon prayer.

---

validity of ritual prayer], while the Shafiis and the majority of Malikis count it as a pillar of prayer. In our earlier discussion of conscious intention, we pointed out the difference between a condition and a pillar, namely, that although the validity of a given action depends on a condition just as it does on a pillar, a condition is nevertheless not included in the definition of the action itself, whereas a pillar is. Hence, all four schools agree that ritual prayer is only valid when accompanied by conscious intention. As for whether such intention is simply an external condition upon which the validity of prayer depends, or a pillar which is not only required for prayer's validity, but forms an integral part of the prayer itself, this is an issue of concern only to those seekers of knowledge who wish to delve into the intricacies of theoretical questions.

The Hanafis make no mention of the commencement of the time period for the prayer one intends to pray as a condition for either the necessity or the validity of ritual prayer. The reason for this is that they hold that while this is a condition for the necessity of *performing* prayer, it is not a condition for the necessity of prayer as such, as was mentioned earlier in our discussion of sand ablutions. For more detail on this matter, see the discussion below on commencement of the time period for a given obligatory prayer.

* * *

As for the Hanbalis, they part ways with the other schools by not dividing the conditions associated with ritual prayer into conditions for its necessity and conditions for it validity. Rather, they simply list the following nine conditions: (1) that one be a Muslim; (2) that one be in full possession of his or her mental faculties; (3) that one have reached the "age of discretion"; (4) that one be free of both major and minor ritual impurity and that one be capable of performing ritual prayer; (5) that one's private parts be concealed; (6) that one do everything possible to avoid the presence of ritual impurity on one's body, one's clothing, and the place where one intends to pray; (7) that one consciously intend to perform ritual prayer; (8) that one face the *qiblah*; and (9) that the time period for the prayer one intends to pray have begun. The Hanbalis hold that all these conditions are conditions for the validity of ritual prayer.

5. God speaks of this event in Surah 17:1, saying, "Limitless in His glory is He who transported His servant by night from the Inviolable House of Worship [at Mecca] to the Remote House of Worship [at Jerusalem]—the environs of which We had blessed—so that We might show him some of Our symbols: for verily, He alone is all-hearing, all-seeing." [t.n.]

As for prayer's being an obligatory practice without which one may not be considered a Muslim, this is supported clearly by the Qur'ān, the prophetic Sunnah, and the consensus of those most knowledgeable concerning the religion of Islam. Hence, anyone who denies that ritual prayer is a requirement in Islam is judged unanimously to be an apostate. As God Almighty declares, "Verily, for all believers prayer is indeed a sacred duty linked to particular times [of day]" (4:103). Hence, ritual prayer is required of all Muslims at recognized times of the day, as revealed through the Messenger whom God commanded to make clear to people what he had received from his Lord. Moreover, God Most High commands believers to perform ritual prayer in many other verses of the Qur'ān as well.

Now, someone might object here, saying: The only thing which is clearly established in the Book of God is the obligatory nature of ritual prayer. As for there being five prayers each day, to be performed in a specified manner, there is no evidence for this in the Qur'ān. In answer to this objection, it may be noted that the Qur'ān commanded the Prophet to make clear to people what had been revealed to them; in addition, it commanded the people to follow the revelation which the Apostle had brought them. God says, "...accept [willingly] whatever the Apostle gives you [thereof] and refrain from [demanding] anything that he withholds from you..." (59:107).[6] Thus, everything delivered to us from God by the Apostle is, in this sense, clearly established in the Qur'ān itself.

As for the sound prophetic hadiths through which we know of the practices of the Prophet himself and which provide evidence that the number of daily required prayers is five, they are so numerous and have been passed down through so many separate chains of transmission that their reliability is beyond doubt. One such hadith, narrated by al-Bukhārī, Muslim, al-Tirmidhi, and al-Nasā'ī, conveys the following words of the Prophet, "If there were a river at someone's door in which he bathed five times a day, do you suppose any dirt would remain on him?" His listeners replied, "No, none!" "So it is," he continued, "that by means of the five daily prayers, God washes away sins." This hadith states explicitly, then, that there are five prayers required daily of Muslims. In another such hadith, narrated by Muslim, al-Tirmidhī and others on the authority of Abū Hurayrah, may God be pleased with him, we read that the Prophet stated, "The five daily prayers and the Friday congregational

6. The situational context of these words has to do with "[spoils taken] from the people of those villages which God has turned over to His Apostle" (59:107). The literal import of this command has to do with material goods which the Prophet had been given authority to distribute among his people as he saw fit, and the people were being commanded to trust his judgment and be content with whatever he apportioned them of the spoils mentioned. Hence, the author is inducing a spiritual principle from this down-to-earth mandate, namely, that whatever truths we have been given through the Prophet are to be accepted willingly, with gratitude and contentment [t.n.].

prayer serve as an atonement for sins committed at times in between, provided that they are not major sins."[7] In still another such hadith, narrated by Muslim on the authority of Jābir, may God be pleased with him, we read, "The Messenger of God said, 'The five ritual prayers may be likened to a copious river flowing by someone's door in which he bathes five times a day.'"

Hence, it is unanimously agreed upon by the leading Muslim scholars that the number of daily required prayers is five, namely: noon, mid-afternoon, sundown, evening, and morning. However, they differ over how these times are to be determined. For example, there are some (namely, the Malikis) who hold that the time period for a given prayer is divided into 'elective' and 'imperative' phases, while others do not. Similarly, there are some who maintain that the time period for the noon prayer ends when objects' shadows become equal in length to the objects themselves, while others maintain that this time period does not end until the shadows of things are twice the length of the things themselves. Concerning such differences we shall have more to say shortly.

---

7. A relevant verse of the Qur'ān reads, "If you avoid the great sins which you have been enjoined to shun, We shall efface your [minor] bad deeds, and shall cause you to enter an abode of glory" (4:31). [t.n.]

Prayer times

The times of the required prayers

As we have seen in our discussion of the conditions for ritual prayer, the commencement of the time period for the prayer one intends to pray is one condition for the necessity of prayer; in other words, one is not required to pray until after the time period for the prayer concerned has begun. (We have noted, however, that the Hanafis do not consider this to be a condition for either the necessity or the validity of prayer; rather, they hold that the commencement of the time period for the prayer concerned is a condition only for the *performance* of prayer, that is to say, that one's performance of ritual prayer has no validity unless the relevant time period has begun. This distinction is of no real significance, however, since the Hanafis agree with the other schools that one is not required to pray until the relevant time period has begun.)

Once this time period has begun, the Lawgiver addresses each of us with the responsibility to perform the prayer concerned, but with a stretch of time before us in which to choose exactly when we will pray. Hence, if we should perform the prayer at the beginning of the relevant time period, our prayer will be valid and we will have fulfilled our responsibility in this regard. If, on the other hand, we do not pray at the beginning of the relevant time period, we are not guilty of wrongdoing unless we wait until there is so little time left that it is only sufficient for us to perform ablutions (either minor ablutions or, if we are in a state of major ritual impurity, major ablutions, or *ghusl*), but not to pray. If, after becoming ritually pure, we are able to perform the prayer to completion before the relevant time period ends, we will have performed it in the manner required of us and fulfilled our responsibility in this regard just as though we had prayed at the beginning or in the middle of the time period. If, by contrast, we pray the entire prayer after the relevant time has ended, our prayer will be valid, but we will be guilty of serious wrongdoing for having delayed prayer past its appointed time. As for someone who prays part of the prayer before the time period ends and completes it after this, some imams hold that he or she is guilty of wrongdoing, while others do not. (Hence, it becomes apparent that performing a prayer on time does not preclude guilt according to some imams.) However, there is agreement among the various schools that if we perform part of the prayer on time, it will be counted as having been performed at its appointed time rather than being a compensatory prayer.[8]

---

8. According to the Malikis, if someone completes one *rak'ah* of the prayer intended during the 'elective' phase, after which the time period runs out and he completes the prayer during the 'imperative' phase, he is not guilty of wrongdoing. However, if he fails to perform an entire *rak'ah* during the 'elective' phase, he will be guilty of wrongdoing even if he goes on to complete the prayer during the 'imperative' phase. As for the terms 'elective' and 'imperative', their meanings will be explained below.

* * *

As for the times at which the periods for the five prayers start and end according to the various schools, a discussion of this will follow, beginning with the noon prayer which begins immediately after "high noon."

How the times for prayer may be determined

There are five means by which the prayer times may be determined:

(1) By the use of precisely calibrated astronomical clocks, which are now widely available in many cities and villages and which are relied upon in determining the times for prayer.

(2) By examining the shadow cast by some object after the sun reaches its zenith. This method helps in determining the time for the noon and the mid-afternoon prayers.

Unlike the Malikis, the Hanafis do not divide the time period for prayer into 'elective' and 'imperative' phases. Moreover, they hold that if someone performs part of a prayer before the relevant time period ends, even if it is no more than the introductory *Allāhu akbar*, his or her prayer is considered to have been prayed on time rather than as a compensatory prayer; nevertheless, the person will be guilty of minor wrongdoing.

* * *

The Shafiis hold that unless someone completes an entire *rak'ah* of the prayer concerned before its appointed time ends, the prayer will not be counted as having been performed on time, but rather as a compensatory prayer. They also hold that someone who fails to perform a prayer in its entirety before its appointed time ends is guilty of wrongdoing, although it is less serious than the wrongdoing of someone who performs the entire prayer after its appointed time has ended. Thus, the Shafiis agree with the Hanafis on the necessity of performing the entire prayer before its appointed time ends and on not dividing time periods for prayer into 'elective' and 'imperative' phases, while they agree with the Malikis that a prayer is not considered to have been performed on time unless the person concerned completes an entire *rak'ah* before the appointed time runs out.

* * *

As for the Hanbalis, they agree with the Hanafis that even if one only utters the introductory *Allāhu akbar* before the appointed time for the prayer one is praying ends, one is still considered to have performed the prayer on time. Hence, if someone rises to pray at the very end of the relevant time period and utters the introductory *Allāhu akbar*, after which the time period ends before he is able to go any further in his prayer, he will still be considered to have prayed on time. However, unlike the Hanafis, the Hanbalis hold that such a person is not guilty of any wrongdoing since he is considered to have prayed the prayer on time.

It is hoped that this summary gives a clear, accurate presentation of the points of agreement and disagreement on this matter among the various schools.

(3) By observing the setting of the sun, on the basis of which the time for the sundown prayer may be determined.

(4) By noting the disappearance of the red or white twilight 'glow', on the basis of which one knows that the time period for the evening prayer has begun.

(5) By observing the 'whiteness' that appears on the horizon and on the basis of which the time for the morning [dawn] prayer is determined.

The times for the five daily prayers are referred to in a sound prophetic hadith narrated by al-Tirmidhī and al-Nasā'ī on the authority of Jābir Ibn 'Abdullah, who said,

> [The angel] Gabriel came to the Prophet when the sun had reached its zenith and said, "Rise, Muḥammad, and pray the noon prayer (*al-ẓuhr*)." Then, after the sun began descending from its zenith, he waited until the time when the length of a man's shadow is equal to his height, then said, "Rise, Muḥammad, and pray the mid-afternoon prayer (*al-'aṣr*)." Then, after waiting until the sun had set, he came again and said, "Rise, Muḥammad, and pray the sundown prayer (*al-maghrib*)." So he rose and prayed the sundown prayer. Then, after waiting until the twilight glow had disappeared, Gabriel came again and said, "Rise and pray the evening prayer (*al-'ishā'*)." So he did. Finally, after waiting until dawn had broken the next morning, Gabriel returned and said, "Rise, Muḥammad, and pray the morning prayer (*al-ṣubḥ*)."

This portion of the hadith tells us when the time period for each prayer begins; it then goes on to speak of the end of each of these prayer times: Gabriel came to the Prophet again the following day and instructed him to pray the noon prayer when objects' shadows had become equal in length to the objects themselves; then he commanded him to pray the mid-afternoon prayer when things' shadows had become twice as long as the things themselves. After this, he instructed him to pray the sundown prayer soon after the sun had set, and to pray the evening prayer after the first third of the night had passed. Finally, he had him pray the morning, or dawn, prayer when there was a bright glow in the sky. Then he said to him, "All that lies between these two [i.e., the beginning and the end of the prayer time] is time [when one may pray]."[9]

This and other similar prophetic hadiths define the times for the five daily prayers based on natural signs such as those which form the basis for the astronomical calendar, sundials, and the like. We shall now proceed to give a detailed presenta-

---

9. In other words, from the beginning of the period for the noon prayer until the time for the mid-afternoon prayer begins, one may perform the noon prayer; from the moment when the mid-afternoon prayer time begins to the moment when the sun goes down one may pray the mid-afternoon prayer, and so on [t.n.].

tion of the views of the four schools on the times for the five daily prayers, bearing in mind that some of them divide prayer times into 'elective' and 'imperative' phases, while others do not.[10]

The time period for the noon prayer (*al-ẓuhr*)

The time period for the noon prayer commences immediately after the sun reaches its zenith ("high noon"). In other words, as the sun begins to descend from its zenith, the time period for the noon prayer begins,[11] then continues until the shadows of things become equal in length to the things themselves. In order to determine when this has taken place, a wooden stick or similar object may be inserted in level ground such that it stands straight up. (This is to be done before noon, and in a sunny spot.) The stick will cast a shadow, of course, and this shadow will gradually diminish in size until hardly anything is left of it; the shadow may even disappear momentarily. If any of the shadow remains, a marker is placed in the ground at the point where it ends; otherwise, the starting point for observation is the stick itself, as is the case in equatorial regions. When the shadow disappears or reaches its minimum, this is "the meridian hour", that is, midday. When the shadow begins to lengthen again, one knows that noon has past, i.e., that the sun is descending from its zenith, and this is the beginning of the time period for the noon prayer. Then, once the stick's shadow becomes the same length as the stick plus the length of the shadow that was present at midday, this means that the noon prayer period has ended.

---

10. The Malikis divide prayer times into what they term an 'elective' phase, namely, the period during which the choice of when to pray is up to the individual held accountable for prayer, and an 'imperative' phase, namely, the time subsequent to the 'elective' phase. It is referred to as 'imperative' because it pertains to individuals who are bound by special constraints, such as difficulty maintaining mental presence, menstrual flow, loss of consciousness, insanity, etc. No one who suffers any of these conditions is held to be guilty for performing prayer during the 'imperative' phase; as for others, however, they are guilty of wrongdoing if they perform ritual prayer during the 'imperative' phase unless they have managed to complete an entire *rak'ah* during the 'elective' phase.

* * *

The Hanbalis divide the time period for the mid-afternoon prayer into 'imperative' and 'elective' phases. The 'elective' phase ends when the shadows of things become twice as long as the things themselves, while the 'imperative' phase begins at the point just described and lasts until sundown. According to the Hanbalis, one is forbidden to pray the mid-afternoon prayer during this 'imperative' phase even though it is being performed before the time for the sundown prayer. They make a similar division between 'imperative' and 'elective' phases during the period for the evening prayer, details concerning which will be mentioned below.

11. According to the Malikis, it is at this point that the 'elective' phase of the noon prayer time begins; as for the 'imperative' phase of this period, it commences with the beginning of the time period for the mid-afternoon prayer and continues until sundown.

The time period for the mid-afternoon prayer (*al-'aṣr*)

The time period for the mid-afternoon prayer begins when an object's shadow becomes longer than the object itself, but without taking account of the length of its shadow at midday, and it ends at sundown.[12]

---

12. According to the Malikis, the mid-afternoon prayer time is divided into 'elective' and 'imperative' phases. The 'elective' phase begins from the time when objects' shadows become longer than the objects themselves and lasts until the time when sunlight takes on a yellowish hue when reflected off the ground and walls (though the sun itself does not take on such a hue until sunset). As for the 'imperative' phase, it begins at the moment when the 'elective' phase ends and continues until sundown. The most widely accepted point of view among the Malikis is that there is a 'shared' time period between the noon and mid-afternoon prayer times, and that the length of this period is judged to be the amount of time required to complete four *rak'ahs* in urban areas, and two *rak'ahs* for those traveling [through sparsely inhabited areas]. The question then arises: Is this 'shared' time at the end of the period for the noon prayer such that a portion of the time for the mid-afternoon prayer is included in the period for the noon prayer, but not vice-versa? Or is it at the beginning of the period for the mid-afternoon prayer such that a portion of the time for the noon prayer is included in the period for the mid-afternoon prayer, but not vice-versa? According to the former view, if someone prays the mid-afternoon prayer at the end of the period for the noon prayer and completes this prayer at the time when the shadows of things are equal in length to the things themselves, his prayer will be valid, whereas if he prays the noon prayer at the beginning of the period for the mid-afternoon prayer, he will be guilty of wrongdoing for having delayed his prayer past the 'elective' phase. According to the latter view, if someone prays the mid-afternoon prayer at the end of the period for the noon prayer and completes this prayer at the time when the shadows of things are equal in length to the things themselves, his prayer will be invalid, whereas if he prays the noon prayer at the beginning of the period for the mid-afternoon prayer, he is not guilty of any wrongdoing, since he has performed the prayer during the 'shared' time between the noon and mid-afternoon prayer periods.

The Hanbalis likewise claim that the time period for the mid-afternoon prayer includes both an 'elective' and an 'imperative' phase.

The time period for the sundown and evening prayers (*al-maghrib* and *al-'ishā'*)

The time period for the sundown prayer begins when the sun has disappeared entirely over the horizon, and it ends with the disappearance of the red twilight glow.[13]

As for the evening prayer period, it begins from the time when the twilight glow disappears and it continues until the break of "true dawn."[14]

---

13. According to the Hanafis, the Western horizon goes through three successive stages after sundown, namely, (1) red, (2) white, and (3) black. The "twilight glow" as Abū Ḥanīfah defines it is the "white phase" such that when the "black phase" begins, the period for the sundown prayer is over. As for the "two companions", they define the "twilight glow" as the "red phase", in agreement with the other three schools.

* * *

According to the Malikis, there is no extension to the 'elective' phase of the sundown prayer time; rather, it is restricted, being estimated to last only as long as is required to perform the sundown prayer and to fulfill the requisite conditions [for its validity], such as purity from both *ḥadath* and *khabath* and covering one's private parts. In addition to these conditions, the Malikis add that of [having heard] the call to prayer and the announcement that prayer in the mosque has commenced (the *iqāmah*). It is permissible for someone to postpone performing the sundown prayer until he or she is able to fulfill the aforementioned conditions. As for the estimated time required for such a process, it is based on an assumption of moderation; hence, for example, it does not allow for the slowness of someone prone to obsessive-compulsive doubts and repetitions, nor does it allow for the 'shortcuts' that might be taken by someone prone to undue haste. As for the 'imperative' phase of the time period for the sundown prayer, it follows the 'elective' phase and continues until daybreak.

Astronomers say that clocks are set based on a commonly agreed upon time. Hence, if someone prays before the astronomical time shown by the clock [coincides with other indications that the time period for the relevant prayer has begun], his prayer will be invalid. In any case, the preferable course of action is for one to delay prayer at least until this time.

14. The Hanbalis hold that the time period for the evening prayer, like that for the mid-afternoon prayer, includes both an 'elective' phase and an 'imperative' phase. The 'elective' phase lasts from the time when the twilight glow disappears from the sky until the end of the first third of the night, while the 'imperative' phase lasts from the beginning of the second third of the night until "true dawn." According to the Malikis, anyone who prays during this 'imperative' phase is guilty of wrongdoing, even though his or her prayer was performed during the time period for the evening prayer. As for the time periods for the morning, noon, and sundown prayers, they do not divide them into 'elective' and 'imperative' phases, as we have seen.

* * *

The time period for the morning prayer (*al-ṣubḥ*)

The time period for the morning prayer begins with the break of "true dawn"—that is, the pre-dawn sunlight which appears in the East, then continues to expand both horizontally and vertically—and it ends at sunrise.[15] As for "false dawn", which is not to be relied upon, it is a light which does not spread; it emerges as a thin rectangle moving skyward but which, rather than continuing to spread, remains flanked on either side by darkness. This "false dawn" resembles the tail of the black wolf, which is white in the center and black along the sides.

On initiating prayer soon after commencement of the time period for the prayer concerned, and the times at which prayer is not permitted

The various schools provide detailed rulings relating to the performance of prayer at its aforementioned times, judging some practices to be desirable, others undesirable, and so forth.[16]

The Malikis hold that the 'elective' phase of the time period for the evening prayer begins at the moment when the red twilight glow disappears and lasts until the end of the first third of the night, while its 'imperative' phase extends from the beginning of the second third of the night till daybreak. Whoever prays the evening prayer during this 'imperative' phase is guilty of wrongdoing unless he or she suffers from some type of incontinence [which might require one to postpone prayer until this time, for example].

15. The Malikis divide the time period for the morning prayer into 'elective' and 'imperative' phases. The 'elective' phase, which begins at "true dawn", continues until there is full daylight, that is, the time when people's faces are clearly distinguishable by someone with average eyesight in a place not covered by a roof, and when the stars cease to be visible. As for the 'imperative' phase, it begins with the end of the 'elective' phase and continues until sunrise. This view is the most widely held among the Malikis, although there is another, less well supported Maliki view according to which the morning prayer period is not divided into 'elective' and 'imperative' phases.

16. The Malikis hold that the best time to pray is the beginning of the time period for the prayer concerned. They base this position on the words of the Prophet, "The beginning of the time [for a given prayer] is the time of God's good pleasure," and "The best work anyone can perform is to pray at the beginning of the relevant time period." Hence, it is recommended that we give prayer priority by performing it at the beginning of the 'elective' phase of the relevant time period once we are certain that it has actually begun. This ruling applies both in summer and winter, regardless of which of the five daily prayers it is, and whether we intend to pray alone or in community. However, when we speak of "giving priority" to prayer, we do not mean that one should rush to pray early simply in order to pray early; rather, what we mean is that one should not delay prayer unnecessarily once it has become certain that the time period for the prayer concerned has, in fact, begun. Hence, this ruling is not in conflict with the recommendation that we first perform the voluntary prayers which are associated with a given obligatory prayer [such as the two

rak'ahs that precede the dawn prayer and the noon prayer, for example – t.n.]. It is also recommended, both in summer and in winter, that the communal noon prayer be delayed until objects' shadows become one-fourth the length of the objects themselves (while, if the heat is particularly severe, the 'one-fourth' is increased to 'one-half').

* * *

According to the Hanafis, it is desirable to pray the noon prayer after the intense noon heat has broken and walls have begun casting shadows such that it is easier to walk to the mosque. This ruling is based on the words of the Prophet, "Pray the noon prayer after the weather has cooled down, for intense heat is like the breath of Hell." In the winter, by contrast, it is preferable to pray as close as possible to the beginning of the time period for the noon prayer unless the weather is overcast, making it difficult to be certain whether it is past high noon or not. In the latter case, it is preferable to delay the noon prayer for fear of performing it before the proper time period has begun. There is a trend in mosques now to pray the noon prayer as soon as possible after the noon prayer period begins both in winter and in summer; this being the case, one should follow the lead of the imam in one's own mosque lest one miss the communal prayer, despite the fact that the imam may not be following the most desirable practice.

As for the mid-afternoon prayer, the Hanafis hold that it is desirable to delay it somewhat past the beginning of the relevant time period, but not so much that one prays at the time when a change becomes visible in the appearance of the sun, which they judge to be undesirable to the point of being forbidden. This ruling applies if the weather is not overcast; however, if there are clouds covering the sun, it is desirable to pray the mid-afternoon prayer early for fear of delaying it until the time in which its performance would be highly undesirable.

When it comes to the sundown prayer, it is always desirable to perform it as promptly as possible based on the words of the Prophet, "My people will come to no harm so long as they do not—in imitation of the Jews—delay the sundown prayer until there are so many stars in the sky that they seem to blend into one another." However, if there are clouds in the sky, it is desirable to delay it somewhat so as to make certain that the sun has really set.

As for the evening prayer, it is deemed desirable to delay it until slightly before the end of the first third of the night. As the Prophet stated, "If I were not fearful for my people [lest they not get sufficient rest], I would delay the evening prayer until the end of the first third of the night, or even till the end of the first half." Nevertheless, it is preferable to perform the evening prayer early if delaying it would cause one to miss the communal prayer.

As for the dawn prayer, it is desirable to delay it until daylight has appeared; however, one should allow enough time before sunrise that, if it should become apparent that one's first prayer was invalid, one will have enough time left to repeat it after performing a new set of ablutions in the manner consistent with the prophetic Sunnah. This ruling is based on the words of the Prophet, "Perform the dawn prayer after daylight has appeared, for in so doing you merit a greater reward."

As for the times at which the Hanafis deem it undesirable to pray, they are as follows: (1) As the sun is rising. (2) Close enough to sunrise that there is not enough time remaining to pray before the sun comes up; in other words, they hold that if the sun comes up while someone is still praying the morning prayer, it will be invalidated. (3) At high noon. (4) As the sun is setting. (5) Between the mid-afternoon prayer and sundown. In other words, the Hanafis hold that once someone has prayed the mid-afternoon prayer, it is undesirable to the point of being forbidden to pray after this. However, during the period between the beginning of the time for the mid-afternoon prayer and actually performing this prayer, one is free to perform any other prayers one wishes until the sunlight takes on a different hue, since at this time visibility may be reduced.

* * *

The Shafiis divide the times for prayer into eight phases:

(1) The "time of virtue." This time extends from the beginning of the period for the prayer concerned until sufficient time has passed for one to have made all the necessary preparations to pray and to have performed the prayer itself, including all related Sunnah-based and other desirable and/or recommended practices. This time is estimated to last three quarters of an hour, and it is referred to as the "time of virtue" because prayer performed at this time is more virtuous than that performed later. This phase forms part of the time period for every one of the five daily prayers.

(2) The "time of choice." This phase begins when the "time of virtue" ends and lasts until there is just enough time left to pray, and no more. Prayer performed during this time is more virtuous than that performed later, and less virtuous than that performed earlier. As for its being referred to as the "time of choice", it is so called due to its superiority to the time which comes after it. During the time period for the noon prayer, the 'time of choice' ends when there is no time left to do anything but pray. During the time period for the mid-afternoon prayer, it ends when objects' shadows become twice as long as the objects themselves. During the time period for the sundown prayer, it is conterminous with the "time of virtue." During the time period for the evening prayer, it ends at the conclusion of the first third of the night; and during the time period for the morning prayer, it ends with the appearance of daylight.

(3) The "time of permissibility without undesirability." This phase is equal to the "time of choice", and the same rulings which apply to the latter apply to the former. However, during the time period for the mid-afternoon prayer, this phase lasts until sunlight takes on a yellowish hue when reflected off walls and the like; during the time period for the evening prayer, it lasts until the "false dawn"; and during the period for the morning prayer, it lasts until the sky takes on a reddish hue.

(4) The "time of prohibition." This phase represents the very last part of the time period for the prayer concerned, when so little time remains that it is insufficient to perform the prayer to completion.

(5) The "time of necessity." This phase represents the very end of the time period for someone who was subject to a condition which prevented him or her from praying earlier (such as menstrual flow, postpartum bleeding, insanity, and the like), and it includes the period during which there is just enough time to utter the opening *Allāhu akbar* of the prayer concerned. At this time, one is obliged to make up the prayer concerned after its time period has ended. If one's restricting

condition passes while there is still sufficient time to utter the opening *Allāhu akbar*, one must pray both the prayer associated with the time period about to end and the prayer prior to it provided that they are prayers which may be joined, such as the noon and mid-afternoon prayers or the sundown and evening prayers. This ruling applies provided that the passing of the restricting condition—be it menstrual flow, postpartum bleeding, etc.—continues long enough for the person to perform the required ablutions and to pray all the prayers concerned; for example, if a woman has a cessation of menstrual flow at the very end of the time period for the mid-afternoon prayer, she should pray both the noon prayer and the mid-afternoon prayer during the time period for the sundown prayer provided that the absence of menstrual flow lasts long enough for her to complete the necessary ablutions and to pray the noon, mid-afternoon and sundown prayers before the time period for the sundown prayer runs out.

(6) The "time of accountability." This phase falls between the beginning of the time period for a given prayer and the moment when a restricting condition has its onset. For example, suppose that sufficient time during the period for the noon prayer has passed for a certain woman to have performed ablutions and prayed, at which point her menstrual flow begins before she has prayed. In such a case, the woman concerned is accountable for the noon prayer which she could have prayed while she was still free of menstrual flow; consequently, she is now obliged to make up for this missed prayer.

(7) The "time of exemption." This term refers to the time during which one may combine either the noon and the mid-afternoon prayers or the sundown and the evening prayers (whether by performing them in advance, or performing them later), when one is traveling, for example.

(8) The "time of permissibility with undesirability." This phase does not exist in the time period for the noon prayer. In the period for the mid-afternoon prayer, it begins when the sunlight takes on a yellowish hue and continues until there is just enough time left in this period to perform the mid-afternoon prayer to completion. During the period for the sundown prayer, this phase begins 45 minutes after the beginning of this period and continues until there is just enough time remaining to perform the entire prayer. During the time period for the evening prayer, it begins at "false dawn" and continues until there is just enough time left to complete the evening prayer; finally, during the time period for the morning prayer, it begins at the point when the sky takes on a reddish hue and continues until just enough time remains to perform the prayer.

There are certain situations, however, in which it is not desirable to pray during the "time of virtue": (1) When it is the noon prayer and one is in a hot climate. In such a case, it is recommended that prayer be delayed until the sun has descended sufficiently from its zenith that walls cast a shadow in which walking will be more comfortable for those who wish to pray in community, or who simply wish to pray in a mosque by themselves. This ruling applies if the nearest mosque is far enough away that it cannot be reached during the "time of virtue" without suffering so much hardship that by the time one gets there, it will be difficult to pray in a spirit of mindfulness and reverence. (2) When one is waiting for the gathering of a group, or when one has no water with which to perform ritual ablutions at the beginning of the time period for the prayer concerned. In such situations, it is recommended that prayer be postponed. In fact, it may be necessary to let the entire time period pass without praying if there is reason to fear that one will miss the opportunity to depart on the major pilgrimage, that a corpse which needs to be disposed of will burst, that someone about to drown will not be saved in time, etc.

* * *

According to the Hanbalis, it is preferable to pray the noon prayer as soon as possible after the relevant time period has begun except in the following three situations: (1) When the weather is exceptionally hot. In this case, it is an emulation of the Sunnah to delay prayer until the heat has broken. This applies regardless of whether one intends to pray with a group or by oneself, in the mosque or at home. (2) When it is cloudy. When this is the case, it is a Sunnah-based practice to postpone the noon prayer until close to the beginning of the time period for the mid-afternoon prayer, then perform the two prayers in close succession. (3) When one is on the major pilgrimage and wishes to perform the stone-throwing ceremony at Minā, in which case it is a Sunnah-based practice to delay the noon prayer until after completing this ceremony.

These rulings apply provided that it is not time for the Friday congregational prayer, since it is an emulation of the prophetic Sunnah to perform this prayer as early as possible under any and all circumstances. Similarly, it is always preferable to perform the mid-afternoon prayer as close as possible to the beginning of the 'elective' phase of this period. As for the sundown prayer, it is preferable to perform it as close as possible to the beginning of the relevant time period except in the following situations: (1) When the sky is overcast. In such a case, it is a Sunnah-based practice for those who wish to pray this prayer in community to delay it until close to the time for the evening prayer, then pray both prayers in close succession. (2) When one is in a situation in which it is permissible to combine the sundown and evening prayers, in which case one may delay the sundown prayer, then combine it later with the evening prayer if this proves more suitable. (3) When one is on the major pilgrimage and traveling toward Muzdalifah, and when one is in a situation in which it is permissible to combine the sundown and evening prayers. If, when the time period for the sundown prayer begins, one still has not reached Muzdalifah, it is an emulation of the prophetic Sunnah to delay the sundown prayer. If, on the other hand, one reaches Muzdalifah before sundown, one should pray the sundown prayer promptly. As for the evening prayer, it is preferable to delay its performance until the end of the first third of the night provided that one has not delayed the sundown prayer as well, in which case it is preferable to perform the evening prayer promptly in order to pray the combined sundown-evening prayer early in the time period for the evening prayer. Moreover, it is undesirable to delay the evening prayer if this will cause hardship for some of those who will be praying [in a group]. Similarly in the case of the morning prayer, it is always better to pray it as close as possible to the beginning of the relevant time period.

In addition, there may be situations in which one is obliged to delay one of the obligatory prayers until just enough time remains to perform it before the time runs out. For example, someone's father might instruct him to postpone his prayer in order to pray with a group, in which case he must do so. However, if the father

The parts of the body which must be concealed during prayer

The second condition for the validity of prayer is that one conceal those parts of one's body which are judged to be private (*'awrah*). In other words, prayer is not valid if performed by someone who has failed to conceal those parts of his or her body which the Lawgiver has instructed us to conceal during prayer unless he or she is unable to do so.[17] The definition of what constitutes the private parts of the body differs according to whether the person is a man, a free woman, or a bondmaid.[18] Moreover, it is necessary for one to keep such parts of one's body concealed from the moment the prayer is begun until it is complete.[19]

---

instructs him to delay his prayer for some other reason, he should not comply. It is also preferable to delay an obligatory prayer in order to eat first if one is especially hungry, and in order to pray the prayer for the solar and/or lunar eclipse if there is no danger that time will run out by one's doing so.

17. The Malikis add a further condition, namely, 'mindfulness'. In other words, they hold that if someone reveals such private parts unintentionally, his or her prayer will still be valid.

18. According to the Hanafis, the parts of a man's body which must be concealed during prayer include the area which extends from the navel to the knee, with the knee included as a private part but not the navel. The private parts for a bondmaid are the same as those for a man except that in addition, her abdomen, her back and the sides of her torso are included as well. As for a free woman, her private parts consist of her entire body, including even the hair on her head which falls below her ears. This ruling is based on the words of the Prophet, "The woman in her entirety requires concealment" [literally, "The woman is a 'private part'"]. However, the Hanafis exclude from a free woman's private parts the tops of her feet and the palms of her hands.

* * *

According to the Shafiis, the private area of a man's body and that of a bond woman includes everything between, but not including, the navel and the knee. However, although the navel and the knee are not included in what constitutes their private parts, the Shafiis stipulate that part of them should also be covered as a mean of ensuring that the entire private area is concealed. As for a free woman, her private area comprises her entire body, including even the hair on her head that falls below her ears; the only exceptions are the face and the hands.

* * *

The Hanbalis agree with the ruling of the Shafiis in this regard, the only difference being that unlike the Shafiis, the Hanbalis exclude nothing but the face alone from a free woman's private parts.

* * *

As for the Malikis, they divide the private parts for the man and the woman into two types, that is, what might be termed "highly unpresentable" and "mildly unpresentable." Each of these two types has particular rulings associated with it. The highly unpresentable parts for the man include nothing but his penis, his testicles and his buttocks; as for his mildly unpresentable parts, they consist of everything else between the navel and the knee. The highly unpresentable parts for the free woman consist of her entire body except for her extremities, her chest and her upper back, whereas her mildly unpresentable parts include her chest and upper back [repetition in original text – t.n.], her arms, her neck, her head [not including the face], and the area extending from her knee to the end of her foot. As for her face and her hands, they are not included in her private parts. As for a bond woman, her mildly unpresentable parts are the same as those for a man; however, unlike the man, her buttocks is categorized as highly unpresentable, as are her vulva and pubic hair.

If someone knowingly prays with his or her highly unpresentable parts exposed, whether partially or entirely, and even if the exposure only lasts a short time, then—provided that the person concerned would have been able to cover up the exposed areas, if even by buying or borrowing a suitable covering or accepting someone else's offer to lend one to him or her—his or her prayer is rendered invalid, and he or she is required to repeat it later, either during or following the time period for the prayer concerned. As for one's mildly unpresentable parts, their exposure in full or in part does not invalidate one's prayer despite the fact that such exposure is undesirable or even forbidden during ritual prayer and although it is forbidden to look at such parts. If someone prays with his or her mildly unpresentable parts exposed, it is desirable for him or her to repeat the prayer with proper concealment before the time period for the prayer concerned has run out. Specifically, if while a free woman prays, her head [not including the face], her neck, her shoulder, her arm, her chest, her breast, her upper back, her knee, or her calf down to the top of her foot is exposed (even though the bottom of a woman's foot is, according to the Malikis, also included among such a woman's mildly unpresentable parts), she should repeat the prayer before the relevant time period runs out. As for a man, if he prays with his genitals or his buttocks exposed, he must repeat the prayer before the relevant time period runs out; however, no such repetition is required if he has simply exposed his thighs, the area between the pubic hair and the navel, or his lower back above the buttocks.

19. The Hanbalis hold that if some portion of one's private parts is exposed unintentionally as one prays and if the exposure does not last long, one's prayer is not invalidated. If, for example, someone's private parts are exposed partially or even completely by a gust of wind, after which the person moves immediately to conceal them again, the prayer is not invalidated provided that his or her covering these parts up again did not require excessive movement irrelevant to the prayer itself. However, if the exposure lasts what is commonly considered to be a long time, the prayer is invalidated. If, on the other hand, the person exposes such parts deliberately during prayer, the prayer is invalidated regardless of other factors.

* * *

The Hanafis hold that if there occurs an unintentional exposure of one-quarter of an area included within one's highly unpresentable parts (which include the genitals, the buttocks and the surrounding area) or one's mildly unpresentable parts (which include the rest of the body for both the woman and the man), and if this

Regarding the garment with which one conceals one's private parts, it must be sufficiently thick. In other words, it should not be thin enough to reveal the color of one's skin, regardless of whether one's private parts may be seen through it at a single glance or whether others would have to look closely in order to see what is underneath.[20] However, it does no harm for it to cling to one's private parts such that their contours can be distinguished.

---

exposure lasts long enough for one to perform an entire pillar of the prayer—for example, by a gust of wind that blows one's robe up—one's prayer will be invalidated. If such exposure occurs intentionally, one's prayer is invalidated immediately even if the area exposed is less than one-quarter of some area included among one's unpresentable parts. As for a situation in which such exposure takes place before one has begun to pray, it simply means that one cannot begin to pray until after concealing the exposed area.

* * *

According to the Malikis, the exposure of one's highly unpresentable parts during prayer invalidates the prayer without regard for any other factors, even if the person concerned was fully covered when he or she began to pray. If this should occur, the most widely accepted view among the Malikis is that the person concerned must repeat the prayer later, either during the time period for the prayer concerned or after it has ended.

* * *

As for the Shafiis, they hold that if someone's private parts are exposed during prayer when the person would have been capable of keeping them concealed, the prayer is invalidated; however, if such exposure occurs due to a gust of wind and if the person acts immediately to conceal the area again—though without so much movement that the prayer is interrupted—the prayer remains valid; the same ruling applies if some private part is exposed unintentionally and the person conceals it again right away. However, if the exposure takes place due to some cause other than the wind—even if it happens to be something like the movement of a domestic animal or a young child who has no understanding of such matters—the prayer is invalidated.

20. According to the Malikis, the skin beneath one's garment should not be visible at first glance. However, if it becomes visible only after someone has looked closely, this does no harm; rather, it is simply undesirable to pray in such a garment, and it is recommended that one repeat the prayer before the time period for the next prayer begins.

As for someone who has nothing with which to cover his private parts,[21] he may pray naked and his prayer will still be valid.[22] Similarly, if one finds something with which to cover oneself but discovers either that it is made of a ritually impure substance (such as pig's skin, for example) or that it has been contaminated with a kind of ritual impurity that cannot be overlooked, he should pray naked.[23] If, on the other hand, one finds something with which to cover himself but which he would be forbidden to wear, such as silk,[24] for example, he may put it on out of necessity and pray without being required to repeat the prayer later. And finally, if someone finds something that will conceal some, but not all, of his private parts, he should go ahead and use it, giving priority to his genitals and buttocks. However, if nothing at all is available with which to cover oneself, it is not necessary to resort to the cover of darkness.[25]

---

21. The Malikis hold that if one prays while wearing a garment which—even without getting wet or being pressed against the body by a gust of wind—reveals the outlines of one's private parts to a degree that is forbidden or even just undesirable, one must repeat the prayer before the time period for the next prayer begins. As for someone who has prayed in a garment which reveals the outlines of his private parts because of a gust of wind that has blown up or due to its having become wet from rainfall, for example, he is not required to repeat such a prayer, and no undesirability is attached to it.

22. The Hanafis and the Hanbalis hold that in this type of situation, it is preferable to pray sitting down, to replace the regular bowing and prostrating with subtle gestures, and to hold one's thighs close together. The Hanafis likewise add that [rather than sitting, as one normally would in prayer, with the lower legs folded under the thighs], one should sit with one's buttocks directly on the floor and extend one's legs toward the *qiblah* as a way of making extra certain that one's private parts are concealed to the greatest extent possible.

23. According to the Malikis, a person in this situation should go ahead and pray if the only available garment is either made of ritually impure materials, contaminated with impurities, or made of silk. Moreover, if someone has prayed under such circumstances, no repetition of the prayer is required later. However, if the person should find something ritually pure to pray in before the time period for the prayer concerned is over, it is recommended that he perform the prayer again.

* * *

The Hanbalis hold that if the only garment available is contaminated with ritual impurity, he should go ahead and pray in it, but repeat the prayer later; however, if the only garment available is made of a ritually impure material, he should pray naked, in which case no repetition of the prayer is required.

24. According to one hadith, men are not to wear silk [t.n.].

25. According to the Malikis, one must resort to a dark place in such a situation, since they consider darkness to be an acceptable substitute for a concealing garment if none is available. Hence, if someone goes ahead and prays in the light when a dark place is available, his prayer remains valid, but he is guilty of wrongdoing, and it is recommended that he repeat it later.

If someone has no concealing garment available but hopes to obtain one before the time period for the prayer concerned runs out, it is recommended that he or she postpone praying until the end of the time period.[26] When putting on a garment, one is to conceal one's private parts beginning from the top and sides of one's body rather than the bottom; moreover, one is to conceal such parts both from oneself[27] and from others. Thus, for example, if someone has a tear near the top or on the side of his robe such that either he or someone else would be able to see through it to his private parts, his prayer will be invalidated even if no one, in fact, has seen anything. However, if something has become visible from beneath his robe, this does no harm.

The parts of the body which must be concealed when one is not praying

When not praying, a fully accountable Muslim is to conceal his or her private parts both from himself or herself[28] and from others who would not be permitted to look at these parts unless some necessity, such as medical treatment, required it. It is permissible to expose such parts of one's body to the extent required for such purposes, as well as to perform abstersion, to bathe, to eliminate bodily wastes, and the like if one is alone and the exposed parts are visible to no one but oneself.

The private parts of a free woman when she is not praying include the area extending from her navel to her knee if she is alone or in the presence of her *maḥārim*[29] or other Muslim women[30]; in other words, in these situations she is free to expose all other parts of her body. However, if she is in the presence of a strange

---

26. According to the Shafiis, it is not simply recommended, but required that one postpone prayer in such a situation.

27. According to the Hanafis and the Malikis, it is not necessary to conceal them from oneself; hence, although it would be undesirable, for example, for someone to see his own private parts through the neck of his robe while praying, this would not invalidate his prayer.

28. The Malikis hold that if someone is alone, it is undesirable for him or her to expose his or her private parts unless some necessity requires it. As for what constitutes private parts when one is alone, the Malikis judge them to include the genitals, the pubic hair and the buttocks, although they do not consider it undesirable for either a man or a woman to expose the thighs when alone, or for a woman to expose her stomach.

As for the Shafiis, they hold that it is undesirable to look at one's own private parts unnecessarily.

29. The Malikis hold that in the presence of a woman's *maḥārim* who are grown men, her private parts include her entire body with the exception of her head, neck, hands and legs.

As for the Hanbalis, they hold that a woman's private parts in the presence of *maḥārim* who are grown men include her whole body except for her head, her neck, her hands, her feet and her lower legs.

30. The Hanbalis, unlike the other schools, make no distinction in this regard between a Muslim woman and a non-Muslim woman; hence, a Muslim woman may expose any part of her body other than the area between her navel and her knee in the presence of a non-Muslim woman.

man[31] or a non-Muslim woman, her private parts include her entire body except for her face and her hands,[32] the latter of which may be looked at provided that they do not constitute a source of temptation for the other person.[33]

---

31. That is to say, any man whom she would be eligible to marry. More specifically, the word translated here as 'strange' (*ajnabī*, plural, *ajānib*) is used in opposition to the Arabic term *maḥram* (plural *maḥārim*), which refers to male relatives whom it would be unlawful for a woman to marry. Exactly which male relatives this refers to is clarified in the following Qur'anic injunction: "And let them [i.e., the believing women] not display [more of] their charms to any but their husbands, or their fathers, or their husbands' fathers, or their sons, or their husbands' sons, or their brothers, or their brothers' sons, or their sisters' sons..." (24:31).

32. The Shafiis hold that when in the presence of a strange man, a woman's private parts include even her face and her hands. However, when she is in the presence of a non-Muslim woman (or a Muslim woman of corrupt morals), she may expose her face and hands as well as those parts of her body which are visible when she performs household tasks, such as her neck and arms.

33. Of central importance in connection with this issue is the Qur'anic verse which reads, "And tell the believing women to lower their gaze and to be mindful of their chastity, and not to display their charms [in public] beyond what may [decently] be apparent thereof; hence, let them draw their head-coverings over their bosoms" (24:31) The importance of these injunctions (not to mention the potential they hold for differing interpretations) may be seen in the following comments offered by Muḥammad Asad, who states, "My interpolation of the word 'decently' reflects the interpretation of the phrase *illā mā ẓahara minhā* by several of the earliest Islamic scholars, and particularly by al-Qiffāl (quoted by al-Rāzī), as 'that which a human being may openly show in accordance with prevailing custom' (*al-'ādah al-jāriyah*). Although the traditional exponents of Islamic law have for centuries been inclined to restrict the definition of 'what may [decently] be apparent' to a woman's face, hands and feet—and sometimes even less than that—we may safely assume that the meaning of *illā mā ẓahara minhā* is much wider, and that the deliberate vagueness of this phrase is meant to allow for all the time-bound changes that are necessary for man's moral and social growth. The pivotal clause in the above injunction is the demand, addressed in identical terms to men as well as to women, to 'lower their gaze and be mindful of their chastity', and this determines the extent of what, at any given time, may legitimately—i.e., in consonance with the Qur'anic principles of social morality—be considered 'decent' or 'indecent' in a person's outward appearance" (*The Message of the Qur'ān*, Note 37 on Surah 24).

No less enlightening in this regard is what Asad has to say in explanation of the phrase translated, "let them draw their head-coverings over their bosoms" (*wa liyaḍrubnā bi khumurihinna 'ala juyūbihinna*). He notes, "The noun *khimār* (of which *khumur* is the plural) denotes the head-covering customarily used by Arabian women before and after the advent of Islam. According to most of the classical commentators, it was worn in pre-Islamic times more or less as an ornament and

As for a man's private parts when he is not in prayer,[34] they include the area between the navel and the knee; hence, it is permissible to look at any other part of his body provided that this does not constitute a source of temptation. It is forbidden to look at the private parts of a man or a woman regardless of whether they are still attached to their bodies or not; thus, supposing that a woman's hair or arm was cut off, or a man's pubic hair or thigh, it would still be forbidden to look at them.[35]

As for a woman's voice, it is not necessary for it to be concealed, because the wives of the Prophet used to address the Companions, who listened to them as they issued religious rulings. However, it is forbidden to listen to a woman's voice if there is reason to fear that this will be a cause of temptation, even if she is reciting the Qur'ān.

It is likewise forbidden to look at a beardless young man if he is particularly handsome—something which depends, of course, on the person doing the looking—and if one's intention in so doing is to experience pleasure by taking in his physical beauty. However, looking at such a young man without hedonistic intentions is permissible provided that it is not a source of temptation.

---

was let down loosely over the wearer's back; and since, in accordance with the fashion prevalent at the time, the upper part of a woman's tunic had a wide opening in the front, her breasts were left bare. Hence, the injunction to cover the bosom by means of a *khimār* (a term so familiar to the contemporaries of the Prophet) does not necessarily relate to the use of a *khimār* as such but is, rather, meant to make it clear that a woman's breasts are *not* included in the concept of 'what may decently be apparent' of her body and should not, therefore, be displayed" (italics in the original). (*The Message of the Qur'ān*, Note 38 on Surah 24) [t.n.]

34. The Malikis and the Shafiis hold that when a man is not praying, his private parts vary according to who is looking at him. Hence, when he is in the presence of close [female] relatives whom it would not be lawful for him to marry and other men, his private parts include the area between his navel and his knees. If, by contrast, he is in the presence of a strange woman, his private parts include his entire body, although the Malikis make an exception for his head, his hands, and his legs; specifically, a strange woman may look at these parts of a Muslim man's body provided that she does not derive pleasure from doing so. The Shafiis, by contrast, hold that a strange woman is forbidden to look at such parts of a Muslim man's body under any circumstances.

35. The Hanbalis hold that once a person's private parts are no longer attached to his or her body, they lose their taboo character and it thus becomes permissible to look at them.

As for the Malikis, they hold that if the person from whom the private parts have been removed is still alive, it is permissible to look at them, whereas if he or she is no longer alive, it is forbidden.

With regard to the private parts of young children, detailed rulings on this matter are given by all four schools.[36]

Finally, let it be noted that everything which one is forbidden to look at, one is likewise forbidden to touch without some sort of barrier [between the skin of the person touching and the person being touched], even if such touching is done without physical desire.

---

36. According to the Shafiis, the private parts of a child during prayer, whether male or female, adolescent or pre-adolescent, are the same as that of an accountable adult. In the case of an adolescent, whether male or female, the soundest view is that his or her private parts when not praying are the same as those for an adult. If a pre-adolescent boy is able to give an accurate description of private parts which he sees without feeling physical desire, his private parts are judged to be the same as they are when he is in the presence of his *maḥārim*, whereas if he is able to give such a description and feels physical desire when doing so, his private parts are the same as they would be for an adult. However, if he is not able even to give such a description, then he is judged not to have any private parts as such, although it is forbidden for others to look at his genitals or his buttocks unless they are responsible for his care and upbringing. As for a pre-adolescent female who is sexually desirable to those with healthy inclinations, her private parts are the same as they would be for an adult woman; otherwise, they are not, but only those responsible for her care and upbringing are permitted to look at her vagina.

* * *

According to the Malikis, what constitutes a child's private parts varies according to the child's gender and age. For example, a boy who is eight years old or younger has no private parts, hence, it is permissible for a woman to look at his entire body when he is living and to bathe him if he should die. If the boy is between the ages of 9 and 12, a woman may look at his whole body, but she is not permitted to bathe him. Once the boy reaches the age of 13, however, his private parts are the same as they would be for a full-grown man.

As for girls, the Malikis hold that a girl aged 2 years and 8 months has no private parts. A girl between the ages of three and four years likewise has no private parts, at least where being looked at is concerned. Hence, one may look at any part of her body, but her private parts with respect to being touched are the same as those for a grown woman, as a result of which a man may not bathe her. As for a girl six years of age who has a desirable appearance, her private parts are the same as those for an adult woman. Consequently, a man is not permitted either to look at her or bathe her.

As for the private parts of a male child during prayer, they are his genitals, his pubic hair and his buttocks; hence, it is recommended that he conceal these parts. In the case of a female child, her private parts during prayer are the area between her navel and her knees, and it is simply recommended that she conceal this area; however, her guardian should instruct her to conceal it just as he or she instructs her to pray [despite the fact that, legally speaking, neither is actually required of her yet].

Similarly, the concealment of anything beyond this area of her body during prayer is simply recommended rather than required.

* * *

According to the Hanafis, boys and girls up to and including four years of age have no private parts; hence, it is permissible to look at and/or touch any part of their bodies. As for a child who is more than four years old, his or her private parts are restricted to the genitals and the buttocks provided that the child concerned has not yet become physically desirable. However, once the child reaches the age at which he or she begins to experience sexual desire, his or her private parts become the same as those for full-grown men and women, both during prayer and at other times.

* * *

As for the Hanbalis, they hold that children up to seven years of age have no private parts; hence, it is permissible to look at and/or touch any part of their bodies. Between the ages of seven and nine, a boy's private parts include his genitals and his buttocks both while praying and at other times as well. As for a girl of this age, her private parts extend from the navel to the knee while she is praying; at other times, her private parts when in the presence of her *maḥārim* are the same as they are during prayer, and when she is in the presence of strange men, they include her entire body with the exception of her head, her hands and forearms, her lower legs and her feet.

The *qiblah*

On praying toward the *qiblah*

As was mentioned in the beginning of this section, the conditions for the performance of ritual prayer are as follows: (1) The time period for the prayer one intends to perform must have already begun. (2) One must conceal one's private parts. (3) One must face the *qiblah*. Having set forth the rulings on the first two conditions, we will turn now to the rulings on the third condition, namely, facing the *qiblah*. There are five topics to be dealt with here: (1) the definition of the *qiblah*, (2) evidence for the necessity of facing the *qiblah* during prayer, (3) the means by which one can determine the direction of the *qiblah*, (4) the situations in which prayer is still valid even though one is not facing the *qiblah*, and (5) praying inside the Ka'bah.

The definition of the *qiblah*

The word *qiblah* refers either to the direction in which the Ka'bah is located, or to the Ka'bah itself. For those who are living in or near Mecca, ritual prayer is not valid unless they are facing the Ka'bah exactly, so far as such precision is possible. If it is not possible, one must arrive at an independent judgment as to the Ka'bah's location, since as long as someone is inside Mecca, it is not sufficient simply to face in the general direction of the Ka'bah. However, it is permissible for someone to stand facing the atmosphere surrounding it from above or below. For example, if someone in Mecca is standing on a mountain elevated above the Ka'bah, or in a house so tall that it is not possible to face the Ka'bah itself, it is sufficient for him or her to be facing the atmosphere surrounding it. Similarly, someone who is standing on a spot which is lower than the Ka'bah may simply face the atmosphere which comes in contact with the Ka'bah. Three of the four schools agree that facing the atmosphere which comes in contact with the Ka'bah from above or below is the same as facing its actual physical structure; the school which disagrees with this view is that of the Malikis.[37]

People who are in the city of the Prophet, that is, Medina, must face the *miḥrāb* (that is, the recess in one of the walls indicating the direction of prayer) in the Prophet's Mosque. Facing this *miḥrāb* is tantamount to facing the actual Ka'bah, since it was placed where it is based on divine revelation. As for people who are a long distance from Mecca, the condition which applies to them is that they face in the direction in which the Ka'bah is located without being required to face the

---

37. According to the Malikis, those who are in or near Mecca must stand opposite the actual physical structure of the Ka'bah. Thus, they hold that it is not sufficient simply to stand facing the air surrounding it. However, they grant that if someone prays on Mt. Abū Qubays, his or her prayer will be valid based on the view that it is enough simply to face the atmosphere surrounding the Ka'bah (even though they believe this view to have less in its favor).

Ka'bah precisely. Rather, it is permissible for such people to deviate slightly to the right or left of the Ka'bah; in fact, one may even deviate slightly from the direction of the Ka'bah without any harm being done, since the condition which applies here is that part of one's face be directed toward it (or the direction in which it is located). For example, if someone praying in Egypt faces straight east without turning slightly to the right, this does no harm since he or she will still be facing the *qiblah* in an overall sense. Hence, what matters with respect to facing in the direction of the Ka'bah is for part of one's face to be directed toward it. This is the view of all the schools except that of the Shafiis.[38]

The Ka'bah includes neither the *ḥijr* nor the *shādharwān*, both of which are familiar to people who know Mecca, and a further discussion of which will be presented later in our discussion of the *ḥajj*, or greater pilgrimage. Three of the four schools hold that facing either the *ḥijr* or the *shādharwān* will invalidate one's prayer; the only school to differ with this view is that of the Hanbalis.[39]

Evidence for the necessity of praying in the direction of the *qiblah*

Facing the *qiblah* is a condition for the validity of ritual prayer based on the Qur'ān, the prophetic Sunnah, and the consensus of the Muslim community. As God declares in the Holy Qur'ān, "We have seen thee [O Prophet] often turn thy face towards heaven [for guidance]: and now We shall indeed make thee turn in prayer in a direction which will fulfill thy desire. Turn, then, thy face towards the Inviolable House of Worship; and wherever you all may be, turn your faces towards it [in prayer]" (2:144). There are also numerous hadiths which provide evidence of the necessity of turning toward the *qiblah* in prayer. According to one such hadith, narrated by al-Bukhārī and Muslim on the authority of Mālik, on the authority of 'Abdullah Ibn Dīnār, on the authority of 'Abdullah Ibn 'Umar, "One day when the

---

38. According to the Shafiis, both those who are near the Ka'bah and those who are distant from it must pray facing the Ka'bah itself or the atmosphere adjacent to it [and not simply the general direction in which it is located]. However, those who are near the Ka'bah must face either the actual Ka'bah or the atmosphere surrounding it based on certainty—for example, based on seeing it, touching it, etc.—whereas in the case of those who are distant from it, the most widely agreed upon view is that they must face the Ka'bah based on reliable evidence concerning its location in relation to where they are. In addition, the Shafiis hold that if someone is praying while standing or seated, even a slight turning away from the *qiblah* will invalidate his prayer if it takes place in the chest area, whereas if the person concerned turns away from the *qiblah* with his face alone, his prayer is not invalidated. If someone is praying while lying on his right side, a turning away from the *qiblah* with his chest or his face will invalidate his prayer, whereas if he is lying on his back, his prayer will be invalidated if he turns away from the *qiblah* either with his face or the bottoms of his feet.

39. According to the Hanbalis, the *shādharwān* and a little more than six cubits of Ishmael's precinct are part of the Ka'bah; hence, prayers performed while facing these are valid.

people were performing the morning prayer at Qubā', someone came to them and said, 'The Messenger of God received a revelation last night, and he has instructed us to face the Ka'bah [when we pray].' When this announcement was made, everyone had been facing in the direction of Syria [and hence, in the direction of Jerusalem], but when they heard these words, they turned and faced the Ka'bah instead."

In another hadith, narrated by Muslim on the authority of Anas, the Messenger of God had been praying toward Jerusalem when he received the words, "We have seen thee [O Prophet] often turn thy face towards heaven [for guidance]: and now We shall indeed make thee turn in prayer in a direction which will fulfill thy desire. Turn, then, thy face towards the Inviolable House of Worship." Following this, a man of the tribe of Banū Salamah passed by a group of worshipers who were bowing during the dawn prayer. When the man passed by, they had completed only one *rak'ah*. Even so, he called out to them, "The *qiblah* has been changed!" In response, they shifted themselves to face the new *qiblah* even though they were in the midst of prayer.

As we have mentioned, there are numerous other sound prophetic hadiths to this effect. In short, Muslims are in unanimous agreement that facing the Ka'bah is a condition for the validity of ritual prayer.

How the direction of the *qiblah* may be determined

Each school details a number of ways in which one can determine where the *qiblah* is located. In order to make it easier for readers to familiarize themselves with these and commit them to memory without difficulty, I have listed them separately for each school, noting the points on which the various schools agree and disagree.[40]

---

40. The Hanafis point out that if we wish to determine where the *qiblah* lies, we will be in one of two situations: (1) We will be in a town or village inhabited by Muslims, or (2) we will be in a desert or some other outlying area where there are no Muslims. Each of these two situations has specific rulings associated with it.

If someone is in a location where Muslims reside and does not know where the *qiblah* lies, he will be in one of three situations: In the first situation, the locale where the person is has mosques containing old prayer niches which were placed there by the Companions or the Successors as a means of indicating the direction of the *qiblah*. Examples of such mosques are the Umayyad Mosque in Damascus and the Mosque of 'Amr Ibn al-'Āṣ in Egypt. If someone is in the vicinity of a mosque such as these, he must pray toward these old prayer niches. As long as such recognized markers are available—including other mosques with prayer niches whose placement is based on those put in by the Companions and the Successors—we are not permitted to go in search of the *qiblah* and pray in some other direction, and if we do so, our prayer will not be valid. (This view contrasts with that of the Shafiis, who hold that even when such markers are available, we must search for the *qiblah* by means of the north star and other indicators. However, it is in agreement with the view of the Malikis, which will be detailed below.)

In the second situation, we are in a place which contains no old mosques with prayer niches that can serve as reliable indications of the direction of the *qiblah*. When this happens, we must ask someone where the *qiblah* is. However, in order for our inquiry to be effective, three conditions must be fulfilled. One: There must be someone near enough that if we called out to him, he would be able to hear us. In other words, we must not be in a situation where we have to go in search of someone to ask. Two: The person we ask must have knowledge of where the *qiblah* is located; otherwise, there is no use in asking. Three: The person asked must be someone whose testimony can be accepted; hence, it will not do to ask a Muslim living in disobedience to the teachings of Islam, a non-Muslim, or a young boy, since the testimonies of such individuals cannot be accepted. What such persons say about where the *qiblah* lies should not be accepted unless the person asking has good reason to believe that their words are reliable. However, once we have a reliable person to ask, we should be content with this one person's answer and not go on inquiring.

As for the third situation, it is one in which there are no old mosques nearby with reliable prayer niches in them, nor people to ask. In this case, we must find out where the *qiblah* is by the use of informed logic, as it were, then pray in the direction which we think most likely to be that of the *qiblah*. Once we have done this, our prayer will be considered valid no matter which direction we have chosen to face.

The foregoing applies to someone who is in a city or village. However, if the person is traveling through the desert or some outlying area where there are no Muslim inhabitants, and if he is knowledgeable concerning the stars, the sun, the moon, etc. and is able to determine the direction of the *qiblah* by means of them, he may do so. If, on the other hand, he is not knowledgeable about such things and if he finds someone who knows where the *qiblah* is, he must ask this person. If someone asks another person and receives no reply, he must do his best to arrive at an independent judgment in this regard, then pray. Once someone has done this, he is not required to repeat the prayer later even if the person he asked originally and from whom he received no reply decides to answer his question after all.

* * *

The Malikis hold that if someone who wishes to pray is in a place where he does not know the direction of the *qiblah* but where there is a mosque with an old prayer niche, he must pray in the direction of this prayer niche. There are only four mosques which contain such old prayer niches, namely: The Mosque of the Prophet in Medina, the Umayyad Mosque in Syria, the Mosque of 'Amr Ibn al-'Āṣ in Egypt, and the Qayrawān Mosque in Tunisia. If a person in the vicinity of any of these mosques relies on his own judgment concerning where the *qiblah* lies and prays in a direction other than that indicated by one of these mosques, his prayer will be invalid. As for other prayer niches, the Malikis rule that if they are in metropolitan areas and have been located based on sound principles approved by those knowledgeable in such matters, someone who is qualified to reach his own judgment on where the *qiblah* lies is permitted, but not required, to pray toward them. However, those who are not thus qualified are required to pray toward them. As for the prayer niches of mosques located in small towns and villages, one is not permitted to pray toward them if he is qualified to investigate the matter and arrive at his own judgment; rather, such a person is obliged to investigate where the *qiblah* lies before praying. However, if he is not qualified to do this, he should pray toward such prayer niches unless he finds someone else capable of undertaking an independent investigation and conforms to this other person's judgment.

In sum, then, the Malikis divide prayer niches into three categories: (1) those found in the four mosques mentioned above, (2) those found in urban mosques which have been constructed on the basis of sound principles, and (3) those found in the mosques located in villages. In the case of prayer niches belonging to category (1), one must pray in their direction if he or she is uncertain where the *qiblah* is. With respect to prayer niches in category (2), those who are qualified to make their own judgments concerning where the *qiblah* lies are permitted, but not obliged, to pray toward them. And as for prayer niches belonging to category (3), i.e., those found in small villages, it is not permissible for someone qualified to reach an independent judgment on where the *qiblah* lies to pray toward them; however, someone who is not thus qualified and does not know where the *qiblah* is obliged to pray toward them.

The rulings just presented apply to people who are in places where prayer niches are located. If, on the other hand, one finds himself in a place where no prayer niches are to be found, and if the person is capable of determining the direction of the *qiblah* based on his own investigation, he must not ask anyone where the *qiblah* is, but arrive at his own conclusions based on available information, landmarks, etc. If one is unable to see the landmarks showing the direction of the *qiblah*, he must ask a responsible, trustworthy adult who has a good understanding of what constitutes evidence for the location of the *qiblah* even if the person asked happens to be a female or a slave.

The ruling just described applies to someone who is qualified to engage in independent investigation and to reach a personal judgment on this basis. Otherwise, he must ask a responsible, trustworthy adult who knows where the *qiblah* is. If this is not possible, he may pray in any direction he chooses and his prayer will be valid.

It may be seen from the foregoing that the Malikis agree with the Hanafis on the necessity of praying toward old prayer niches, but that the Malikis limit the category of "old mosques" to the four we have mentioned, whereas the Hanafis hold that all prayer niches built by the Companions and the Successors are to be given priority over other signs indicating where the *qiblah* lies. The Malikis also disagree with the Hanafis over the matter of asking others vs. investigating for oneself. The Hanafis hold that if one finds no prayer niches to pray toward, he must first ask someone where the *qiblah* is, but that if there is one to ask, he must investigate the matter himself. As for the Malikis, they hold that someone who is qualified to investigate where the *qiblah* is must do this rather than ask someone else unless the signs which would have aided in his investigation are not observable.

* * *

The Shafiis hold that there are four different 'grades' of knowledge concerning where the qiblah lies. The first is knowledge which one has gained by oneself. If it is possible to determine where the *qiblah* is without anyone else's help, one should do so and ask no one for the answer. Thus, for example, if a blind man in a mosque is able to find the prayer niche by running his hand over the mosque wall so to as determine where the *qiblah* is, he should do so and not ask anyone.

The second grade of knowledge in this regard is that which has been gained by asking a trustworthy person who knows where the *qiblah* lies. As we have mentioned, the step of asking such a person comes only when one is unable to find out by oneself, since otherwise, it is not permissible to ask. The act of asking a trustworthy informant may be replaced by the use of a compass and/or other means by which the *qiblah* can be ascertained, such as the north star, the sun, the moon, and either the prayer niches found in a large Muslim community or those found in a small town or village but which many people pray toward. In sum, this second grade of knowledge includes the knowledge gained through asking a trustworthy person or consulting a compass, the north star, or prayer niches, be they the ones found in the old mosques in which they were placed by the Companions and the Successors, or other prayer niches which are often prayed to. As for the prayer niches found in the small prayer rooms used by some people along roadsides, on farms, and elsewhere, they cannot be relied on.

The third degree of knowledge is that gained through the process of reaching one's own independent judgment on where the *qiblah* is located. One is not permitted to rely on one's own independent judgment unless he has not been able to find a trustworthy person to ask, a means by which to determine the *qiblah*, or a prayer niche either in a large mosque or in a small mosque in which many people pray. If none of these aids is available, one is to rely on his or her own informed judgment, and whatever conclusion one's thinking leads to is one's *qiblah*. Suppose, for example, that someone relies on his own judgment as to where the *qiblah* lies for the noon prayer. If, by the time for the mid-afternoon prayer, he has forgotten where he concluded that the *qiblah* was earlier, he may simply go through the same thinking process again.

As for the fourth degree of knowledge, it involves imitating someone else who has arrived at an informed judgment concerning where the *qiblah* is located. In other words, if we have not been able to determine where the *qiblah* is by asking a trustworthy person, by locating a prayer niche, or by any other means, we may pray in the same direction as someone else who has reached an independent judgment concerning where the *qiblah* lies and is praying in a given direction based on this judgment. In sum, the Shafiis disagree with both the Malikis and the Hanafis regarding the prayer niches found in the mosques built by the Companions and the Successors: The Malikis view some of these prayer niches as primary points of reference such that as long as they are available, no other means of determining the *qiblah* should be used, whereas the Hanafis view all of them as primary points of reference. As for the Shafiis, they hold that all prayer niches are to be viewed as equal to other means by which one may locate the *qiblah*, such as compasses, the north star, etc. The Shafiis and the Hanafis agree that if someone does not know where the *qiblah* is, he must first ask and that if he finds no one to ask, he must engage in an independent investigation and reach a personal judgment on this basis; however, the Shafiis include an additional step in the process of determining where the *qiblah* is, namely, imitation of someone else who has reached an independent judgment on this question.

* * *

The Hanbalis hold that if someone does not know where the *qiblah* lies and is in a town where there are prayer niches which were constructed by Muslims as indicators of the direction of the *qiblah*, he must find them and pray toward them as soon as he learns of their existence. Such a person is not permitted to pray in any other direction under any circumstances; in fact, he is not even allowed to deviate slightly to the right or the left. If, on the other hand, someone finds a prayer niche in a town containing a dilapidated structure and/or ancient ruins [of a mosque], he must not pray toward it unless he verifies that it is, in fact, a mosque which was built by Muslims. If he finds no prayer niches, he must ask where the *qiblah* lies, even if this means knocking on people's doors in search of someone to ask. However, he should only rely on someone who is trustworthy, be it a man, a woman, or a slave. If the person who answers his question is certain where the *qiblah* lies, the person asking must pray in the direction indicated by the person's answer rather than undertaking his own independent investigation. If the person answers the question based on the probability that the *qiblah* lies in a given direction and if this person is knowledgeable of the types of signs that indicate the location of the *qiblah*, one should adopt his or her judgment provided that there is not enough time left to search further; otherwise, the person asking the question must reach his own judgement on the matter. If someone is on a journey and cannot find anyone to ask about the *qiblah* and if he is knowledgeable concerning the signs indicating the direction of the *qiblah*, he must seek to locate it by noting such signs and base his judgement on these. Once this has been done, he should pray in the direction which he believes most likely to be that of the *qiblah*, and his prayer will be valid. However, if he should pray in a direction other than the one which he believes most likely to be the *qiblah*, his prayer will have no validity even if it becomes clear later that he did, in fact, pray toward the *qiblah*. This ruling conveys the sublimity of the practice of *ijtihād*, i.e., arrival at one's own independent judgments; in fact, Muslims recognize the value of this practice in all of life's affairs. Hence, if someone is unable to reach his own judgment on this matter due to an eye inflammation or some other cause and if he cannot determine where the *qiblah* is through other means, he may pray in any direction he chooses without there being any need for him to repeat the prayer later.

From the foregoing we derive the following steps: When one seeks to determine the direction of the *qiblah*, he should (1) rely on prayer niches if they are available. If no prayer niches are available, he must (2) ask someone who knows where the *qiblah* is. If he finds no one to ask, then he must (3) reach his own judgment on the matter if he is capable of doing so, or follow the lead of someone else who has been able to reach such a judgment. If this is also not possible, he must (4) investigate the direction of the *qiblah* to the best of his ability and pray based on whatever conclusion he has reached. If this order of steps is violated, one's prayer will be invalid and must be repeated, even if it becomes apparent later that the direction in which one prayed originally was, in fact, the *qiblah*.

As we have seen, the four schools agree on the following signs as indicators of the direction of the *qiblah*: (1) the prayer niches found in mosques, (2) information provided by a trustworthy person when no prayer niches are available, and (3) undertaking a personal investigation and reaching an independent judgment concerning where the *qiblah* lies when there is no trustworthy person to ask. (As we saw in Footnote 40 above, there are some who hold that personal investigation into the direction of the *qiblah* comes before asking someone else.)

At this point, a number of questions arise: (1) What is the ruling on someone who has investigated the matter of where the *qiblah* lies, but who is still unable to say for certain where it is? (2) What is the ruling on someone whose examination of the evidence led him originally to the conclusion that the *qiblah* lay in such-and-such a direction and who, either while praying or after completing his prayer, realizes, or perhaps only suspects, that he was mistaken? (3) What is the ruling on someone who, even though he could have investigated where the *qiblah* lies and formed his own judgment on this matter, goes ahead and prays without doing so? (4) What is the ruling on someone who, even though he is capable of forming his own judgment on the location of the *qiblah*, instead relies on the judgment of someone else? The answer to the first question is that someone who investigates where the *qiblah* lies but is unable to reach a clear conclusion has done all he can; hence, his prayer will be valid whichever direction he turns. Three of the four schools agree that in such a case, one is not required to repeat the prayer later.[41]

In answer to the second question, it may be said that if someone prays in a direction to which he was led through thought and investigation, after which he realizes as he prays that he was—or may have been—wrong in his judgment, all he has to do is shift to the direction which he now knows or believes to be that of the *qiblah*. When this happens, the person concerned is not required to begin praying all over again; rather, he may simply continue his prayer to completion in the new direction. For example, if someone completes one *rak'ah* of the noon prayer in a direction which previous investigation led him to believe was the *qiblah*, at which point he comes to believe that the *qiblah* lies in a different direction, he should shift to the new direction and build on the *rak'ah* he has already prayed. (This ruling is agreed upon by the Hanafis and the Hanbalis; however, it differs from that of the Shafiis and the Malikis.[42]) If, on the other hand, someone seeks to locate the *qiblah* and prays, after which he realizes, or at least suspects, that he prayed in the wrong

---

41. In agreement with the other schools, the Shafiis hold that if someone seeks to determine where the *qiblah* lies but is unable to reach any certainty about the matter, he may pray in any direction he chooses; however, unlike the other three schools, the Shafiis insist that such a person must repeat the prayer later.

42. According to the Malikis, if someone prays in a direction which his investigation has led him to believe is the *qiblah*, then realizes while praying that his judgment was mistaken, he must discontinue his prayer if: (1) the person is sighted rather than blind, and (2) there is a major difference between the *qiblah* and the direction in which he or she is praying. Regarding the first condition cited here, the Malikis note that all a blind person is required to do is to turn toward the [new] *qiblah* and build on what he has already performed of his prayer and that if he fails

direction, his prayer remains valid and he is not required to repeat it. This is the view of all the schools except the Shafiis, with the Malikis likewise take exception to certain aspects of it.[43]

---

to do so, his prayer will be invalidated. (Thus, the four schools are in agreement with respect to a blind person, but in disagreement in their ruling on someone who is sighted.) As for the second condition, they hold that if there is little difference between the actual *qiblah* and the direction in which the person is praying, his or her prayer remains valid regardless of whether he or she is sighted or blind. Suppose, then, that the person concerned is blind and that there is little difference between the direction in which he is praying and the actual *qiblah*. In such a case, the person should shift toward the actual *qiblah* while still praying; otherwise, his prayer will still be valid, but he will be guilty of wrongdoing.

* * *

As for the Shafiis, they hold that if it becomes clear to someone while he is praying that he is not praying toward the *qiblah*, his prayer becomes invalid; hence, he must stop praying and start all over again. Moreover, the Shafiis apply this ruling equally to sighted and blind persons. For example, if someone begins praying after seeking to determine the direction of the *qiblah* and if he is then informed by a trustworthy person who knows where the *qiblah* is that he is praying in the wrong direction, his prayer is thereby invalidated and his previous judgment is nullified regardless of whether he is sighted or blind. As for someone who, while he is praying, comes to suspect [but not know for certain] that he was in error regarding the *qiblah*, his prayer remains valid and he need not stop praying and start all over again.

Hence, the Shafiis differ with the Malikis, who distinguish between sighted and blind persons; they also differ with the Hanafis and the Hanbalis over whether it is acceptable simply to turn, while still in prayer, in the direction which one now knows or believes to be the *qiblah*.

43. The Shafiis hold that if someone seeks to locate the *qiblah*, then prays to completion, after which he becomes certain that he prayed in a direction other than that of the *qiblah*, his prayer is invalidated and he must repeat it. However, if the person merely suspects that he did not pray toward the actual *qiblah*, no harm is done.

As for the Malikis, they hold that if someone seeks to locate the *qiblah*, then prays, after which it becomes apparent that he prayed in the wrong direction, his prayer will remain valid regardless of whether he is certain that he was in error or merely suspects that he was. However, unlike the Hanafis and the Hanbalis, the Malikis hold that if the person is sighted and sufficient time remains in the relevant prayer period, it is recommended that he repeat the prayer concerned.

In reply to the third question above, we say that if someone neglects to investigate where the *qiblah* lies even though he would have been able to do so —either by praying in the same direction as someone else who has reached an independent judgment concerning the *qiblah* or by simply praying alone without knowing where the *qiblah* is—his prayer will be invalid even if it becomes clear in the end that he did, in fact, pray toward the *qiblah*. This ruling is agreed upon by all the schools except that of the Hanafis.[44]

As for the fourth question, the answer to it may be seen in the rulings which we mentioned earlier in our discussion of ways in which the *qiblah* may be located. Specifically, one is not permitted to imitate someone else who has reached an independent judgment concerning the *qiblah* so long as one is capable of reaching such a judgment oneself. However, if someone is truly incapable of engaging in an investigation into where the *qiblah* lies and forming a judgment on this basis, he is permitted to follow the lead of someone else who has reached an informed judgment on the matter. Otherwise, he may simply pray in any direction he chooses without being required to repeat the prayer later. This is the view adopted by the Hanafis and the Hanbalis.[45]

---

44. According to the Hanafis, if someone is capable of determining where the *qiblah* lies but simply prays in a direction which he believes to be the *qiblah* without verifying this belief, and if it later becomes apparent that the direction in which he prayed was, in fact, the *qiblah*, his prayer remains valid. However, if it becomes clear to him—either during or after praying—that he was mistaken, his prayer is invalidated and he must repeat it.

45. The Malikis hold that if we are unable to determine the direction of the *qiblah* due to conflicting evidence, we must simply choose a direction in which to pray rather than imitating someone else who has formed his own judgment on this matter unless it becomes clear to us that this other person's judgment is correct, in which case we should follow this person's lead without question just as we would if we were in a state of uncertainty and did not have enough time to verify matters on our own. Similarly, if we are unable to locate the *qiblah* due to the fact that the indicators required are not visible to us—for example, due to clouds in the sky, imprisonment, etc.—we must follow the lead of someone who has reached a judgment on where the *qiblah* lies, pray toward a prayer niche, etc. If this is not possible, we may pray in any direction we choose and our prayer will be valid.

As for the Shafiis, they hold that if we find ourselves in this situation, we should postpone praying until the end of the time period for the prayer concerned if we believe that our inability to locate the *qiblah* will pass before this time. Otherwise, we should pray at the beginning of the time period, realizing that we will be required to repeat the prayer later. Similarly, if when we pray at the end of the time period we still have not determined where the *qiblah* lies, we must repeat the prayer at a later time.

How the sun or the north star may be used to locate the *qiblah*

There are some who may imagine that the subject of locating the *qiblah* by means of the sun or the north star has nothing to do with questions of Islamic jurisprudence. However, our ability to determine where the *qiblah* lies may depend on our ability to make proper use of such natural landmarks. There are some who hold that the ability to locate the *qiblah* by means of the sun or north star is not necessary, but simply a means of emulating the prophetic Sunnah, since there are numerous other means by which one could arrive at the same conclusion. However, others hold that such an ability is essential for people traveling by sea and who have no other way to determine where the *qiblah* lies. In either case, the law of Islam—in its rulings connected to forms of worship, human relations, day-to-day transactions, and all other areas of life—is connected in reality to all branches of learning which hold benefit for human society.

As you may be aware, the sun and the stars are included among the signs which indicate the location of the *qiblah*. We can find our way to the *qiblah* by means of the sun since it enables us to identify each of the four directions: The direction in which it rises is the east and the direction in which it sets is the west, and once we have identified east and west, we know where north and south are as well. Once these things are known, it should be easy for people in any location to know where their *qiblah* lies. People in Egypt, for example, turn east and slightly south in order to face the *qiblah*, since the Ka'bah with respect to Egypt is located between the east and the south, but closer to the east.

As for the north star, it is a small star which forms part of the constellation known as Ursa Minor, and like the sun, it may be used to identify the *qiblah* in whichever direction one happens to be located. If we are in Cairo, for example, we should pray with the north star slightly behind our left ear; the same goes for people praying in Asyut, Fuwah, Rashid, Dumyat, and Alexandria, as well as Tunis and Andalusia. If we are praying in Iraq and "Beyond the River",[46] we should pray with the north star behind our right ear; in Medina, Jerusalem, Gaza, Ba'albek[47] and Tartus,[48] one should pray with this star at an angle from his left shoulder. If we are between the Tigris and Euphrates rivers, or in Armenia[49] or Mosul, we should pray with this star directly behind us; if we are in Baghdad, Kufa, Khawarizm,[50] al-

46. "Beyond the River" is a literal translation of the Arabic *mā warā' al-nahr*, which refers to the area of present-day Turkmenistan and Uzbekistan, to the southeast of the Aral Sea (see *Al-Aṭlas al-Tārikh al-'Arabi al-Islāmī*, Fourth Edition, Damascus: Dār al-Fikr, 1996, p. 37) [t.n.].

47. Ancient Heliopolis, northeast of Beirut (*The American College Dictionary*, Random House, n.d.) [t.n.].

48. A city along the Mediterranean coast in northern Syria (*Collins Concise Atlas of the World*, Glasgow: William Collins Sons & Co. Ltd., 1984) [t.n.].

49. The Armenia referred to here corresponds to an area northwest of Tabriz in Iran (*Al-Aṭlas al-Tārikhi al-Islāmī*, p. 67) [t.n.].

50. Khawarizm is also in the area of Uzbekistan (*Ibid.*, p. 48) [t.n.].

Rayy, or Hulwan,[51] we should pray with it above our right cheek. If we are in Basra, Esfahan, Faris, Karman[52] and other places in their vicinity, it should be above our right ear; if we are in Ta'if, ‘Arafat, Muzdalifah or Mina, we should pray with it above our right shoulder. If we are in Yemen, it should be in front of us toward our left side; if we are in Syria, it should be behind us toward our left side, and if someone is in Najran,[53] he should pray with it behind his back. Another means of identifying the directions is by using a properly calibrated compass.

In sum, the direction of the *qiblah* varies according to one's location, and it is determined from wherever one happens to be by reliance on principles of geometry and arithmetic. Specifically, one determines the distance between Mecca and the equator, as well as between the equator and the country in which one is located. One also determines the distance between the longitudes of Mecca and one's one location (that is, how far they are from one another along an east-west line). These figures are then correlated on the basis of the relevant principles to determine the direction of the *qiblah*.

We only mention these final points as a type of supplement to this section. Hence, if any of the lay people reading this find it difficult to comprehend, they are free to bypass it and rely instead on prayer niches which are familiar to them or on any other of the available indicators.

Conditions for the necessity of praying toward the *qiblah*

Everyone who performs ritual prayer must do so facing the *qiblah* on two conditions: (1) that he or she be able to do so, and (2) that doing so not pose danger to the person praying or to his or her possessions.[54] Thus, if someone is unable to pray facing the *qiblah* due to some infirmity and can find no one to turn him in this direction, this requirement ceases to apply, and the person may pray in whatever direction he is able to.[55] Similarly, if we have reason to fear that an enemy, either human or otherwise, might do harm to us or our possessions if we faced in the direction of the *qiblah*, we are permitted to pray in whichever direction is safe. Moreover, in neither of these situations are we required to repeat the prayer later.

---

51. To the northeast of Baghdad, somewhere between Kirkuk in Iraq and Kermanshah in Iran (*Ibid.*) [t.n.].

52. Esfahan, Faris and Karman are all in Iran (*Ibid.*) [t.n.].

53. In the southeastern region of the Arabian Peninsula, immediately north of the Saudi Arabian-Yemeni border (*Collins Concise Atlas of the World*, p. 45) [t.n.].

54. The Malikis add a third condition for the necessity of praying toward the Ka‘bah, namely, that of mindfulness. Thus, they hold that if someone prays unintentionally in a direction other than that of the *qiblah*, his prayer will still be valid, although it is recommended, once he realizes his error, that he repeat the prayer (if it was obligatory) before the time period for the prayer concerned runs out.

55. According to the Hanafis, the requirement that one pray facing the *qiblah* does not apply to someone who is physically unable to place himself in the proper position even if there is someone else who would be able to position him properly.

Prayer inside the Ka'bah

As we have seen from the foregoing, the Ka'bah is the site to which Muslims must direct themselves in prayer. However, this does not mean that a particular direction is held sacred; rather, what it means is that we are called upon to worship God alone in the manner in which He has commanded us to do so. Hence, God declares, "The weak-minded among people will say, 'What has turned them away from the direction of prayer which they have hitherto observed?' Say, 'God's is the east and the west; He guides whom He wills onto a straight way'" (2:142).[56] Hence, the purpose behind turning toward a specific place [during prayer] is simply to express humble submission to God Almighty through obedience to His command. Whoever wishes to understand the wisdom in this may easily perceive that this direction is that of the Ka'bah, the place to which God has instructed people to turn due to the overall benefits which this was, and is, capable of bringing to pass: by training people's souls in obedience to God, teaching them to hold Him in awe and reverence, and bringing sustenance and relief to the inhabits of the area, who [at that time] were bereft of either agricultural produce or other natural resources. As God declares, speaking on the lips of Abraham, "O our Sustainer! Behold, I have settled some of my offspring in a valley in which there is no arable land,[57] close to Thy sanctified Temple, so that, O our Sustainer, they might devote themselves to prayer. Cause

---

56. In an explanatory note on this verse, Asad points out that "prior to his call to prophethood, and during the Meccan period of his ministry, the Prophet—and his community with him—used to turn in prayer towards the Ka'bah. This was not prompted by any specific revelation, but was obviously due to the fact that the Ka'bah—although it had in the meantime been filled with various idols to which the pre-Islamic Arabs paid homage—was always regarded as the first temple ever dedicated to the One God (cf. 3: 96). Since he was aware of the sanctity of Jerusalem—the other holy center of the unitarian faith—the Prophet prayed, as a rule, before the southern wall of the Ka'bah, towards the north, so as to face both the Ka'bah and Jerusalem. After the exodus to Medina he continued to pray northwards, with only Jerusalem as his *qiblah* (direction of prayer). About sixteen months after his arrival at Medina, however, he received a revelation (verses 142-150 of this surah) which definitively established the Ka'bah as the *qiblah* of the followers of the Qur'ān. This 'abandonment' of Jerusalem obviously displeased the Jews of Medina, who must have felt gratified when they saw the Muslims praying towards their holy city; and it is to them that the opening sentence of this passage refers. If one considers the matter from a historical point of view, there had never been any *change* in the divine commandments relating to the *qiblah*; there had simply been no ordinance whatever in this respect before verses 142-148 were revealed" (*The Message of the Qur'ān*, pp. 29-30, Note 116 on Surah 2) [t.n.].

57. Asad notes that this is a reference to "the narrow desert valley of Mecca, which is enclosed by barren, rocky hills" (Note 52 on Surah 14, p 378, *The Message of the Qur'ān*) [t.n.].

Thou, therefore, people's hearts to incline towards them[58] and grant them fruitful sustenance, so that they might have cause to be grateful" (14:37).

This spot has also been rendered holy by the fact that it was here that the Prophet of prophets and Messenger of messengers appeared, bringing to people that which would redound to their spiritual and material good and doing away with the worship of idols in this same region. God Almighty chose to declare His approval of him by turning people's faces and hearts toward the Ka'bah after they had been praying toward Jerusalem. Nevertheless, the sole purpose behind worship in Islam is that we should glorify and reverence God alone above and beyond any and all creatures, no matter how powerful or exalted they might be. As God says, "And God's is the east and the west: and wherever you turn, there is God's countenance. Behold, God is infinite, all-knowing" (2:115).

It becomes clear from the foregoing that God has commanded us to direct ourselves toward the *qiblah*, that is, in the direction of the Ka'bah. Hence, with respect to prayers performed inside the Ka'bah, be they obligatory or voluntary, it must be noted that although one is facing the *qiblah* sufficiently for such prayers to be valid, one is still not facing it completely. Consequently, the various schools hold differing views on the matter of praying inside the Ka'bah.[59]

---

58. That is, "to be desirous of visiting them—namely, on pilgrimage to Mecca—and thus help them to maintain themselves in the holy but barren land" (Asad, Note 53 on Surah 14) [t.n.].

59. According to the Hanbalis, it is not permissible to perform an obligatory prayer either inside the Ka'bah or on its roof unless the person praying either stands so close to one of its walls that virtually none of it remains behind him or her, or stands outside of it and performs prostrations inside. As for voluntary prayers and prayers performed in fulfillment of a vow, they may be legitimately performed either inside the Ka'bah or on its roof provided that one does not perform prostrations along one of its walls or edges; if one does so, the prayer ceases to be valid because in this situation, one is no longer facing the Ka'bah. [The assumption here seems to be that one is facing outward, rather than inward – t.n.]

* * *

According to the Malikis, an obligatory prayer performed inside the Ka'bah is valid; however, it is considered highly undesirable and it is recommended that one repeat the prayer before the end of the time period for the prayer concerned. As for voluntary prayers, if the prayer is not an emphatically enjoined Sunnah-based practice, it is recommended that one perform it inside the Ka'bah, whereas if it is emphatically enjoined, it is undesirable to do so, but there is no need to repeat it. As for prayers performed on the roof of the Ka'bah, they are invalid if they are obligatory prayers, but valid if they are Sunnah-based prayers that are not emphatically enjoined. As for Sunnah-based prayers which are emphatically enjoined, some Malikis hold that they are valid when performed on the roof of the Ka'bah, while others hold that they are invalid, with both views supported by evidence of equal weight.

* * *

Performing obligatory prayers when on a ship, riding an animal and the like

If someone is riding an animal and is unable to dismount due to fear for his safety or that of his possessions or for fear that harm might come to him[60] were he to be separated from the caravan he is traveling with, or if he suffers from some condition on account of which, if he dismounted, he would not be able to get back on the animal, he or she may pray the obligatory prayers while still riding, facing in whichever direction he or she is able to. Someone who prays under these circumstances is exempted from the pillars of prayer which he or she is unable to perform, and no repetition of the prayer is required.

As for performing an obligatory prayer while riding an animal[61] when there is no danger involved in dismounting, it is invalid unless one manages to perform the prayer in its entirety as if it were being performed on the ground. If someone is able to do this, the prayer will be valid even if the animal is moving.

The Shafiis hold that prayers performed inside the Ka'bah are valid whether they are obligatory or voluntary; however, if one prays facing its door when the door is open, one's prayer is invalid. As for prayers performed on its roof, they are valid provided that some part of the Ka'bah with a height of 2/3 of a cubit is located in front of the person praying (a cubit here being measured by the length of a human arm).

* * *

As for the Hanafis, they hold that prayers performed both inside the Ka'bah and on its roof are valid without specifying any particular conditions for their validity; however, they consider praying on its roof undesirable since it suggests a lack of reverence for the Ka'bah.

60. According to the Malikis, merely being afraid of potential harm is not sufficient justification for praying an obligatory prayer while riding an animal. Rather, they hold that it is only permissible to perform an obligatory prayer while riding an animal and with subtle gestures rather than full prostration, genuflection, etc., in the following situations: (1) when one is engaged in an all-out war with infidels or some other type of enemy, such as a thief, for example, (2) when one is fearful of being harmed by a predatory animal, (3) when one suffers from an illness that makes it impossible to dismount, (4) when one is riding through tar or some similar substance which it would be intolerable to step into, or (5) when one is fearful that if he dismounts, the time period for the prayer he intends to pray will run out. In all the aforementioned situations it is permissible to pray an obligatory prayer: (a) while mounted on an animal, (b) with mere gestures rather than the full range of movements normally involved in prayer, and (c) facing in a direction other than the *qiblah*. Once the restricting circumstance has passed, however, it is recommended that one repeat the prayer concerned before its time period runs out.

61. According to the Shafiis, it is not permissible to perform an obligatory prayer while riding an animal unless it is standing up and/or moving, unless its reins are in the hand of someone with full powers of discretion, and unless the prayer meets all the conditions for validity which apply to prayers performed on the ground. The

Someone who wishes to perform ritual prayer, be it obligatory or voluntary,[62] while traveling on a ship must face the *qiblah* to the extent that he or she is able. Hence, for example, if the ship changes course while one is praying, one should shift one's position to accommodate this change. If this is not possible, one should simply pray in whichever direction one is able to; similarly, one is exempted from the requirement to perform prostrations if this is not possible. All such rulings apply to someone who fears that the time period for the prayer in question will run out before the ship—or whatever means of transportation it happens to be, including steam engines, airplanes, and the like—reaches a place where it will be possible to pray normally. If someone does pray in such circumstances, no repetition is required later.

Shafiis hold that this ruling applies equally to those who are safe and able to dismount and to those who are in danger and incapable of dismounting; however, someone who has reason to fear harm if he dismounts may simply pray however he or she is able to, though the prayer must be repeated later.

As for the Hanafis, they hold that an obligatory prayer performed while riding an animal is invalid without a legitimate excuse, even if the prayer has fulfilled all other conditions for its validity and regardless of whether the animal is standing still or moving. They make an exception to this ruling, however, if the person prays on top of a camel-borne litter placed on a riding animal which is standing still. They also stipulate that the litter must have stakes fixed in the ground. As for someone with a condition such as incontinence, he or she is to pray according to his or her ability using gestures, since this is the form which his or her obligatory prayer would have taken in any case. If the person is able to stop the animal, any prayer prayed while the animal is still moving will be invalid. Moreover, the same ruling which applies to obligatory prayers applies similarly to the various types of prayer classified as 'duty.'

62. The Shafiis hold that if someone performs a voluntary prayer on a ship, he must face the *qiblah*, and if this is not possible, he should abandon the attempt to perform such a prayer altogether. This ruling, however, applies to people other than the seamen themselves, who must seek to face the *qiblah* to the best of their ability; if they cannot, they must simply pray in whichever direction they are able to. As for the obligatory prayers, one must perform them while facing the *qiblah* without any exceptions.

Obligations associated with prayer

Our discussion of the duties associated with prayer will include the following subtopics: (1) an explanation of the meanings of the Arabic terms *farḍ* and *rukn*, (2) a listing of the duties associated with prayer according to each of the four schools, (3) an explanation of the duties associated with prayer, as well as the points on which the various schools agree and disagree, and (4) a discussion of the meaning of the Arabic term *wājib* (translated as 'duty') and how it differs from both *farḍ* (obligation) and *rukn* (pillar), as well as an enumeration of the actions classified as *wājib*.

Readers need to grasp these concepts clearly so that they can determine which of the four schools they wish to follow.

The meanings of *farḍ*, or obligation, and *rukn*, or pillar

The meanings of the Arabic terms, *farḍ* and *rukn* were mentioned in our earlier discussion of the obligations associated with ritual ablutions, and as we have seen, these two terms refer essentially to the same reality, namely, an element of an act of worship which the Lawgiver has commanded us to perform, and without which this act of worship will be incomplete. With respect to ritual prayer, its obligations or pillars are those elements without which prayer cannot properly be said to have been performed; consequently, if any of these obligations or pillars is missing, the act of worship which one has performed cannot be referred to as prayer (*al-ṣalāh*). For example, if we say that the opening utterance of the words, *Allāhu akbar*, i.e., "God is greatest" is an obligation, or pillar, of prayer, what this means is that if you do not utter these words as you begin to pray, you will not have prayed [no matter how complete the rest of this act of worship happens to have been].

The words *farḍ* and *rukn* include all parts of obligatory prayer which an accountable Muslim is rewarded for performing and punished for neglecting, as well as all parts of voluntary prayer. Hence, even though a given prayer might be voluntary, these elements must still be present in their entirety in order for it to be described as prayer.

The definition of *farḍ* or 'obligation' is "that which someone merits reward for performing and punishment for neglecting," especially those things about which the Lawgiver has given us a clear command. The word *farḍ* can refer either to part of a more inclusive action or to the wider action itself; for example, the performance of the five daily prayers at their appointed times is an obligation the fulfillment of which merits reward and the neglect of which merits punishment. In addition, the Lawgiver has caused each prayer to be composed of parts, each of which must be present in order for the prayer to have been performed completely. Each of these parts, then, is likewise referred to both as a *farḍ*, or obligation, and as a *rukn*, or pillar; as for prayer itself, it is referred to as a *farḍ* and also as a *rukn*, that is, as an obligation and as one of the pillars of Islam, the other four pillars being the testimony that, "There is no god but God, and Muḥammad is the Messenger of God," fasting the month of Ramaḍān, paying *zakāh*, and performing the greater pilgrimage to Mecca.

An enumeration of the obligations, or pillars, of prayer

As we have seen, what is meant by *farḍ*, in this context, is each of the parts which must be present in their entirety in order for prayer to have been truly performed. An enumeration of these obligations as understood by each of the four schools may be found in the footnote below.[63]

---

63. The Hanafis divide pillars into two types: (1) primary pillars, and (2) auxiliary pillars. A primary pillar is one from which we are completely exempted when we are unable to perform it; in other words, there is no obligation to perform any other action in its place. As for the auxiliary pillars, they are obligations from which we are exempted in certain situations even though we may be capable of performing them. For example, the recitation of the Qur'ān, which the Hanafis consider to be one of the pillars of prayer, is an obligation from which we are exempted if we are being led by someone else in prayer; in fact, the Lawgiver has forbidden us to recite the Qur'ān in this particular situation.

From this it may be seen that those things which are essential for prayer's validity include some elements which are integral parts of prayer, such as the four mentioned below in addition to the final sitting during which one prays for blessings upon the Prophet Abraham and upon the Prophet Muḥammad and his descendents, may peace be upon them all. They also include elements which, even though they are performed during prayer, are nevertheless not integral parts of it; an example of this is the act of reciting from the Qur'ān while standing up (which some classify as a condition for prayer's continuance). And finally, they include elements which are external to prayer and which are classified as conditions for the validity of prayer.

There are four pillars of prayer on which the Hanafis are in agreement, namely: (1) standing, (2) bowing, (3) prostration, and (4) recitation of the Qur'ān, with the first three being considered primary pillars, and the last one auxiliary. These four pillars comprise the essence of prayer in the sense that if the person praying omits any of them when he would have been capable of performing it, he may not be said to have prayed.

As for those elements upon which the validity of prayer depends but which are not included in the essence of prayer, they are divided into two categories: (1) Elements that are external to the act of prayer, such as being free of both *ḥadath* and *khabath*, concealing one's private parts, facing the *qiblah*, waiting until the time period for the prayer intended has begun, intention, and utterance of the opening *Allāhu akbar*. These elements, among others, must be present as one starts to pray. (2) Elements which are included in the act of praying but which still do not form part of prayer's essence. These include, for example, reciting the Qur'ān while standing, bowing after standing, and prostrating after bowing. The Hanafis sometimes refer to these as obligations of prayer, but what they actually mean is that they are conditions for prayer's validity. As for the final sitting during which one asks for blessing upon the Prophet Abraham, the Prophet Muḥammad and their descendents, may peace be upon them all, they agree unanimously that it is an obligation of prayer; however, they differ as to whether it should be classified as a primary pillar or as an auxiliary one. Most of them hold that it is most likely to be an auxiliary pillar, since one may pray to completion without it. As for terminating one's prayer by means of some action which is inconsistent with prayer, such as utterance of the words, *Al-salāmu 'alaykum wa raḥmat Allāh*, speaking, or the like, some consider this to be an obligation. However, the most sound view is that it is not a fundamental obligation (*farḍ*), but rather, a 'duty' (*wājib*).

* * *

The Malikis list the following fifteen obligations associated with ritual prayer: (1) Conscious intention; (2) The opening utterance of *Allāhu akbar*; (3) Standing while uttering the phrase *Allāhu akbar* when performing an obligatory prayer (although, when performing a voluntary prayer, one may utter this phrase while seated even if one would have been able to stand up); (4) Recitation of the *Fātiḥah*; (5) Standing up while reciting the *Fātiḥah* for obligatory prayers; (6) Bowing; (7) Rising again to a standing position; (8) Prostration; (9) Rising again to a sitting position after prostrating; (10) Uttering the greeting, *Al-salāmu 'alaykum wa raḥmat Allāh*; (11) Sitting down for those who are able to do so; (12) Pausing between movements such as bowing, prostrating, rising again, etc.; (13) Rising to a fully upright standing position after bowing, prostrating, and so on; (14) Performing the various parts of prayer in the proper order; and (15) Consciously intending to follow the imam when one is praying in community.

From the foregoing we can see that the Malikis and the Hanafis agree on four of these fifteen obligations, namely, standing up for those who are able, bowing, prostrating, and recitation of the Qur'ān; however, whereas the Hanafis hold that any part of the Qur'ān may be recited and not necessarily the *Fātiḥah*, the Malikis hold that one must recite the *Fātiḥah* in particular and that if one deliberately neglects to do so, he will not have prayed. As will be seen in more detail below, the Malikis agree on this point with the Shafiis and the Hanbalis.

* * *

The Shafiis list thirteen obligations associated with ritual prayer, five of which involve spoken utterances and eight of which are actions. The five which involve spoken utterances are: (1) saying *Allāhu akbar* as one commences prayer (*takbīrat al-iḥrām*), (2) reciting the *Fātiḥah*, (3) uttering the words "I testify that there is no god but God, and that Muḥammad is His servant and His Messenger" (referred to as 'the final testimony of faith' or (*al-tashahhud al-akhīr*), (4) following the final testimony of faith with a prayer for blessings on the Prophet, and (5) the first utterance of the greeting, *Al-salāmu 'alaykum wa raḥmat Allāh*. As for the eight actions, they are: (1) conscious intention, (2) standing up for obligatory prayers if one is able, (3) bowing, (4) standing up straight again after bowing, (5) the first and second prostrations, (6) sitting up between the two prostrations, (7) the final 'sitting', and (8) maintaining the proper order in the actions and words involved in prayer. As for the act of pausing and allowing one's limbs to remain still momentarily between the performance of the various actions involved in prayer (*al-ṭuma'nīnah*), the Shafiis view it as a condition for the completeness of one's bowing, returning to a standing position, prostrating and sitting up; as such, it is essential to prayer even if it is not an auxiliary pillar based on the most compelling evidence.

* * *

As for the Hanbalis, they list fourteen obligations associated with ritual prayer: (1) standing up for obligatory prayers, (2) uttering *Allāhu akbar* as one enters prayer, (3) recitation of the *Fātiḥah*, (4) bowing, (5) rising after one's bow, (6) standing fully upright after bowing, (7), prostrating, (8) rising from the position of prostration, (9) sitting up between the two prostrations, (10) uttering the final testimony of faith (*al-tashahhud al-akhīr*), (11) sitting down for the final testimony of faith and for the two utterances of the greeting, *Al-salāmu 'alaykum wa raḥmat Allāh*, (12) pausing and allowing one's limbs to remain still momentarily after the performance of every action-based pillar (*al-ṭuma'nīnah*), (13) performing the obligations involved in prayer in the proper order, and (14) the two utterances of the greeting, *Al-salāmu 'alaykum wa raḥmat Allāh*.

An explanation of the obligations associated with prayer in their proper order

The subject of 'intention' (*niyyah*) as it pertains to ritual prayer will be discussed under the following subheadings: (1) the meaning of 'intention', (2) the ruling on intention in obligatory prayer, (3) the form to be taken by intention in obligatory prayer, (4) the ruling on intention and the form it is to take in non-obligatory prayer, (5) the proper time for intention, (6) the ruling on conjuring a mental image of the prayer one intends to pray and the conditions for intention, and (7) the intention of someone praying communally to follow the leadership of his imam and the intention of the imam to lead others in prayer.

The first obligation: intention

As for the meaning of intention, it may be defined as "a heartfelt determination or firm resolve to perform an act of worship for the sake of drawing near to God alone." Someone who utters the words involved in ritual prayer without intending to pray from the heart is not really praying. In other words, if someone prays for some worldly motive—for example, in order to be praised by other people such that if no one else commended him for praying, he would stop doing so—then his prayer has no validity. The same goes for the prayer performed by someone who only does so in order to gain wealth or social status or to fulfill some personal desire. This is a fact which we need to understand well; we must realize that the prayer which is performed simply to achieve some worldly aim is null and void, as it were. Far from achieving the worldly goal we are striving for, we will suffer the chastisement reserved for wicked pretenders. As God declares, "And withal, they were not enjoined aught but that they should worship God, sincere in their faith in Him alone, turning away from all that is false" (98:5).[64]

---

64. The Hanafis hold that conscious intention is a unanimously agreed-upon condition [for the validity of prayer]. However, they do not base the necessity of intention on the words, "And withal, they were not enjoined aught but that they should worship God, sincere in their faith in Him alone" (98:5), since they understand 'worship' in this verse to refer simply to belief in the oneness of the Divine. Nor do they base it on the hadith, "[The value and meaning of an] action inhere in the intention on which it is based," since they hold that this statement has relevance to the *reward* one will receive for his actions, whereas it says nothing about the *validity* of such actions.

In fact, however, the texts cited here bear both the interpretation given by the Hanafis and the interpretation offered by others. In the Qur'anic verse quoted above, the reference to the worship of God is not limited only to belief in God's oneness; rather, the meaning which most strongly suggests itself is that of sincerity in one's intention to worship God alone. After all, some of the polytheists used to worship God together with other, created beings, especially the People of the Book [notably the Christians], who are mentioned together with the polytheists in the verse due to the fact that, together with God, they worshiped some of God's prophets.

As for the hadith cited here, it must be remembered that if there is no reward for one's works, they cease to hold any benefit [at least to the person who performed them]. Hence, it makes no sense for the Hanafis to say that an action can be valid

Hence, if we are not sincere in our desire to pray to God alone, we will have disobeyed God's command and our prayer will have no validity even if we have gone through the proper motions. This aspect of the meaning of intention is agreed upon. As for the private thoughts which go through our heads as we pray—for example, if we pray at a time when our minds and hearts are preoccupied with some worldly concern—these do not invalidate prayer. However, those who hold their Lord in awe and reverence must do all they can while praying to resist such preoccupations and to think about nothing but humble submission to God Almighty. If we are still unable to rid our minds of worldly concerns as we stand before our Sustainer, this will not be held against us; however, we must continue to wage war on such futile distractions in the hope of receiving the reward promised to those who serve God faithfully.

In sum, then, we have focused here on two points: (1) the desire to pray and the determination to do so for God's sake alone rather than for some cause which is inconsistent with total devotion to God, and (2) the presence of the heart during prayer rather than preoccupation with thoughts about this or that mundane concern. As we have said, the first is a necessary prerequisite for valid prayer; as for the second, it is not a condition for the validity of prayer, but when we stand before our Maker, we must seek to empty ourselves of anything which is unrelated to prayer. If we still fail to achieve this aim, the reward we receive for our prayer will not be diminished, since we will have done all we were able to do, and God does not hold us accountable for more than this.

The ruling on intention in obligatory prayer

All four schools are in agreement that ritual prayer is not valid without intention. However, some of them say that intention is a pillar of prayer, which means that if someone fails to consciously intend to perform prayer, he cannot be said to have prayed at all, whereas others hold that it is a condition for the validity of prayer, which means that if someone does not consciously intend to pray, he is said to have performed an invalid prayer. Such a dispute, however, is not of much benefit to someone who simply wants to know what is necessary in order for prayer to be valid without legal hairsplitting, as it were; for such a person, it is sufficient to understand that conscious intention is a necessary aspect of prayer and that if it is neglected, one's prayer will lack validity. This much is agreed upon by all four schools and there is no difference, essentially, between its being a condition for prayer's validity or an integral part of prayer itself.

As for seekers of knowledge who wish to be familiar with the terminology used by the various schools, they should know that according to the Shafiis and the Malikis,

---

even though it merits no reward. They might, of course, say that the benefit of such an action is that it removes punishment [even though it brings no reward]. However, this statement finds no support in this hadith; on the contrary, the readily apparent meaning of this text is that conscious, sincere intention is a condition for both the validity of an action and for the reward it merits. As for the claim that it has to do only with the reward merited by one's actions, it is groundless.

intention is a pillar of prayer such that if someone fails to consciously intend to pray, he cannot be said to have prayed at all, whereas in the view of the Hanafis and the Hanbalis, intention is a condition for the validity of prayer, the result being that if someone neglects to conjure a conscious intention to pray, he is said to have prayed a prayer without validity. In sum, then, intention is an obligation or a necessary condition for valid prayer.

The form which intention should take in obligatory prayer

Every ritual prayer will be one of the following: (1) An individual obligation, such as the five daily prayers, (2) A collective obligation such as the funeral prayer and prayers performed in fulfillment of a vow, (3) An emphatically enjoined practice based on the prophetic Sunnah, or (4) A Sunnah-based practice which is not emphatically enjoined.

With regard to the intention associated with obligatory prayers, each of the four schools offers detailed rulings.[65]

---

65. The Hanafis discuss the matter of intention in relation to several different subtopics. The first of these has to do with the fact that every accountable Muslim should know that God has ordained five daily obligatory prayers. If someone is ignorant concerning the obligatory prayers, his prayers will not be valid even if he is performing them at their appointed times, the only exception to this being a prayer in which the person consciously intends to follow an imam. If such a person knows that he is accountable for an obligatory prayer but does not how to distinguish between that which is obligatory, that which is a 'duty', and that which is an emulation of the Sunnah, and if he performs all of these with the intention of performing an obligatory prayer, his prayer will be valid. This is the situation of many lay people. Even though their prayers are valid when they perform them in this way, it is nevertheless essential that they learn the difference between obligatory prayers and others and that they not continue in their ignorance concerning matters pertaining to their religion in this day and age when it would be quite easy for them to attend lessons on Islamic jurisprudence in mosques or elsewhere.

As for the second subtopic, it pertains to the form taken by one's intention to pray. When performing an obligatory prayer, the person praying should be inwardly aware of which of the five daily prayers he is about to perform, be it morning, noon, mid-afternoon, sundown, or evening. This awareness suffices as a valid intention to pray. If one is performing the prayer on time, it is enough to specify which prayer is intended, as we have mentioned, without adding anything further. For example, if one intends to pray the noon prayer, the mid-afternoon prayer, or any of the other five daily obligatory prayers, his prayer will be valid without specifying, for example, that it is "*today's* noon prayer", or "the noon prayer on time." However, some Hanafis hold that it is necessary to add this type of specification, since one day's time period for the noon prayer, for example, could be used to perform a compensatory noon prayer from some other day on which one missed the noon prayer; hence, if someone intends simply to pray the noon prayer, this might mean that he wishes to perform today's noon prayer, or that he wishes to compensate for the noon prayer from some day on which he missed it. Both of these views are sound; however, it is preferable to consciously intend *today's* noon prayer, *today's* mid-afternoon prayer, etc.

The rulings just cited are relevant to daily prayers performed on time. If the person praying is not aware that the time period for the prayer he is performing has run out, it is sufficient for him or her to intend to pray the noon prayer, the mid-afternoon prayer, etc., without further detail. On the other hand, if he or she knows that the relevant time period has run out, there are some who say that it is sufficient for him or her simply to intend to pray the noon prayer, the mid-afternoon prayer, etc., while others hold that this is not sufficient. In any case, as we have noted, it is preferable to specify which day's prayer one intends to perform; for example, one might say, "today's noon prayer", or "today's mid-afternoon prayer." If someone intends to perform an obligatory prayer without thus specifying the day, he or she must at least specify the time—that is, whether it is the morning, noon, mid-afternoon, sundown, or evening prayer.

If someone explicitly intends to perform a given ritual prayer on time, it will be valid provided that it is, in fact, performed on time. Hence, if someone prays a given obligatory prayer after its time period has run out, yet specifies that his intention is to perform it on time, the prayer will not be valid even if he is unaware that the time period for the prayer intended has run out. In other words, one's intention must include a correct specification of the time period of the prayer one intends to perform. As we have seen, however, there are some who hold that such specification is not enough but rather, that one must specify not only which of the five prayer periods, but the day as well, by saying, "today's sundown prayer," "today's evening prayer," and so on. However, there are also those who hold that when we are performing a given obligatory prayer whose time has run out, it makes no difference whether we are aware that its time period has run out or not, and all we need to do is specify that we intend to pray the noon prayer, the mid-afternoon prayer, etc. without any further specification. Finally, it is agreed unanimously that if someone specifies neither the time nor the day for the prayer he or she intends to perform but rather, simply intends to pray an obligatory prayer, this is not sufficient.

As for the third subtopic relating to intention in prayer, it has to do with intention related to performance of the funeral prayer and what the Hanafis term 'duty' prayers. In both cases, the Hanafis hold that intention is a condition for prayer's validity just as it is when performing obligatory prayers. As for the funeral prayer, it is sufficient for one to intend to perform the funeral prayer; however, as will be seen below in the section on funerals, it is better to intend not only to perform the funeral prayer, but to pray for the deceased as well. When performing the Friday congregational prayer, one should simply intend to perform this particular prayer. Moreover, just as conscious intention is a condition for the validity of obligatory prayers, it is likewise a condition for the validity of 'duty' prayers such as the *witr*, or the two *rak'ahs* which accompany the performance of circumambulation around the Ka'bah. Finally, the Hanafis hold that intention is a condition for the validity of a voluntary prayer which was invalidated after the person began to perform it; the reason for this is that if one is performing two voluntary *rak'ahs* which are then invalidated midway through, it becomes a 'duty' to repeat them; and since intention is required for 'duty' prayers, it is likewise required when repeating a voluntary prayer that was invalidated while in progress.

In summary, then, intention is necessary for prayers which are obligatory, both individual and collective, as well as for prayers which are classified by the Hanafis as 'duty' and those which are performed in fulfillment of a vow. As for voluntary prayers, however, they need not be accompanied by conscious intention.

* * *

According to the Malikis, the intention which accompanies performance of an obligatory prayer must include a specification of the time of the prayer, for example, noon, mid-afternoon, and so forth. If someone fails to specify which obligatory prayer he or she intends to perform, the resulting prayer will not be valid. As for the ruling on voluntary prayers, it will be discussed below.

* * *

The Shafiis specify the following four conditions which must be fulfilled in the intention which accompanies an obligatory prayer: (1) It must specify that the prayer intended is obligatory rather than voluntary. (2) It must express the determination to perform the actions included in ritual prayer; this determination is expressed by conjuring a mental image of the actions entailed by prayer, even if only a general one, and consciously determining to carry them out. In this way, the act of prayer on which one is embarking is distinguished from other acts. (3) It must specify which of the five daily prayers is intended, be it noon, mid-afternoon, or some other. (4) The elements listed in (1), (2) and (3) above must all coincide with one's utterance of the opening phrase, *Allāhu akbar*.

If any of these conditions is unfulfilled, both one's intention and one's prayer will be invalid. The reason for this is that intention is one of the obligations of prayer in the Shafiis' view. Some people may find difficulty understanding this; however, the fact is that it is not fitting for us to enter into intimate communion with and worship of our Maker without being fully aware of what we are doing and how we are doing it. Consequently, our first obligation is to consciously intend to perform whatever obligatory prayer we are about to perform, since in this way, prayer is distinguished in our minds [from other actions] from the very start. Secondly, we should conjure a mental image of the prayer we wish to perform. However, in contrast to the view held by some Shafiis, it is not necessary to imagine all parts of the prayer, since this imposes undue hardship, but rather, it is sufficient to imagine an act of prayer involving bowing, prostration, standing, sitting, and Qur'anic recitation. Being conscious from the very beginning that we are fulfilling a duty toward God can help us to enter into a state of reverent submission to our Lord. And as for the stipulation that these thoughts occur simultaneously with the utterance of the opening phrase, *Allāhu akbar*, the reason for this is easy to understand, since in this way, our minds are better prepared to commence prayer in a spirit of submission and humility.

Lastly, the Shafiis hold that if someone performs a given prayer alone, then wishes to repeat the same prayer together with a group, he should specify which prayer he intends to perform in the manner described above.

* * *

The ruling on conjuring a mental image of an intended prayer and the conditions for the validity of intention

As we mentioned in our discussion of the way in which intention is to express itself, three of the four schools agree that conjuring a mental image of prayer—including the actions of standing, Qur'anic recitation, bowing, and prostrating—as one intends to perform the prayer is not a condition for prayer's validity. As we have seen, however, the Shafiis hold that one's intention to pray must be accompanied by a mental image of at least some, if not all, parts of the prayer to be performed.

If, while someone is still praying, he intends to terminate the prayer, thereby canceling out his original intention to begin praying, his prayer will be invalidated even if he happens to complete it. The reason for this is that in this case, the person concerned will have prayed without intention. For example, if someone begins to pray with a sound intention, after which someone else calls to him and the person praying intends to cut off his prayer in order to respond to the other person's call, his prayer is thereby invalidated even if he does not, in fact, terminate his prayer early. This is because one of the conditions for the validity of intention is that the person praying not do anything which is inconsistent with this intention, and it is clear that the intention to terminate one's prayer is inconsistent with the intention to enter prayer.

The conditions for the validity of intention which are agreed upon by all four schools are: (1) that one be a Muslim, (2) that one have reached the age of discretion, and (3) that one be firmly resolved to do what one intends. However, the Shafiis add further conditions; with respect to the intention to pray, for example, they add the determination to perform the acts involved in prayer and the intention to perform a prayer which is obligatory [as opposed to the various types of voluntary prayer]. With respect to the intention to perform ritual ablutions, the Shafiis add the condition that one's intention be simultaneous with washing the first part of the body included in ablutions. As for the condition that one be a Muslim, all of the schools agree on this since, as we saw in the section on conditions for prayer, prayer is not valid if the person who performs it is not a Muslim.

The ruling on the verbal utterance of intention and the intention to perform an obligatory prayer or a compensatory prayer for one that was missed

It is consistent with the example set by the Prophet to voice one's intention aloud. For example, we might say, "I intend to pray the obligatory noon prayer," since in doing so, we increase our own inward awareness of what we are doing. However, if someone has the inner intention of performing the noon prayer but instead says,

---

According to the Hanbalis, the intention that accompanies an obligatory prayer must include a specification of the particular prayer to be performed—noon, mid-afternoon, sundown, Friday congregational, etc. Hence, it is not sufficient merely to intend "an obligatory prayer"; however, once the prayer one intends to pray has been specified, nothing more needs to be added.

"I intend to pray the mid-afternoon prayer," this does no harm since, as we have seen, what counts as far as intention is concerned is the heart. Uttering something with one's tongue is not in itself an intention; rather, it simply helps to awaken the intention already present in the heart. Consequently, a slip of the tongue does no harm so long as the intention of the heart is sound. This ruling is agreed upon by the Shafiis and the Hanbalis.[66]

As for the intention to perform an obligatory prayer on time or a compensatory prayer at a later time, as well as the number of *rak'ahs* these involve, we shall discuss these topics in more detail below.

The intention to perform an obligatory prayer on time, or a compensatory prayer at a later time

It is not necessary for someone who prays to specify whether he intends to perform the prayer on time or as compensation for an earlier prayer which was missed. If someone performs the noon prayer on time, for example, it is not necessary to specify that his intention is to perform this prayer on time. Similarly, if someone prays the noon prayer after the time period for this prayer has run out, there is no need to specify that he intends to perform it in compensation for an earlier prayer missed. So long as one's intention corresponds to outward reality, then regardless of whether the intention is entirely inward or is expressed in words as well, the prayer will be valid. If, on the other hand: (1) the person's intention does not correspond to the outward situation—as would be the case, for example, if someone intended to pray the noon prayer on time when, in fact, the time period for the noon prayer had run out, (2) the person knows that the time period for this prayer has run out or (3) he or she is deliberately defying reality, as it were, his or her prayer will be invalid since it involves a kind of blatant dishonesty.

The Shafiis and the Hanbalis hold that if someone intends to perform four *rak'ahs* for the sundown prayer or five *rak'ahs* for the evening prayer [the actual number of *rak'ahs* in these prayers being five and nine respectively – t.n.], this person's prayer will be invalid even if he or she is merely mistaken rather than engaging in deliberate manipulation.[67]

---

66. The Hanafis hold that voicing one's intention aloud is an illegitimate innovation in prayer, but that it may be approved to stave off obsessive doubts and misgivings if one is prone to such thoughts. As for the Malikis, they maintain that voicing one's intention aloud is a departure from the ideal for those who are not prone to obsessive doubts and misgivings but that for those who are thus prone, it is recommended.

67. According to the Hanafis, if someone intends to perform five, or perhaps three *rak'ahs* for the noon prayer, rather than the actual four *rak'ahs* which make up the noon prayer, and if he or she goes ahead and performs four *rak'ahs*, his or her prayer will be valid and the intention to perform five or three *rak'ahs* will be nullified.

As for the Malikis, they hold that a prayer is not invalidated unless one deliberately intends to perform an incorrect number of *rak'ahs*. Thus, if someone mistakenly intended to perform five *rak'ahs* for the noon prayer, his prayer would still be valid.

The ruling on intention in non-obligatory prayers and how it is expressed

Concerning intention in the performance of voluntary prayers, each of the four schools offers its own detailed rulings.[68]

---

68. According to the Hanafis, it is not necessary to specify exactly what type of prayer one intends to perform when the prayer is of a voluntary nature, regardless of whether it is included in the prophetic Sunnah or not; rather, it is sufficient to intend simply to perform ritual prayer. At the same time, however, it is preferable when performing prayers based on the prophetic Sunnah to specify which of them one intends to pray, since this is what the Messenger of God used to do. Similarly, when performing the *tarāwīḥ* prayers, the Sunnah-based prayers associated with each of the five obligatory daily prayers, and voluntary prayers in the night hours, it is preferable to specify this in one's intention.

If someone comes upon a group praying together and he wishes to join them but is unsure as to whether they are performing an obligatory prayer or the *tarāwīḥ* prayers, he should intend to pray the obligatory prayer. If it then turns out that they were praying the obligatory prayer, his prayer will be valid, and if it turns out that they were praying the *tarāwīḥ* prayers, his prayer will likewise be effective.

* * *

The Hanbalis hold that when performing the *tarāwīḥ* prayers one should specify this in one's intention. However, no such specification is required when performing the Sunnah-based prayers associated with each of the five daily prayers, nor when performing a voluntary prayer which is not associated with any particular occasion.

* * *

With respect to intention in voluntary prayers, the Shafiis distinguish between the following: (1) prayers associated with a particular time, such as the Sunnah-based prayers connected to each of the five daily prayers, and the mid-morning prayer (*al-ḍuḥā*), (2) prayers not connected to a particular time but performed for a specific reason, such as the prayer for rain, and (3) prayers which have neither a specific time nor a specific reason.

If the voluntary prayer one intends to perform has a particular time or reason [Types 1 and 2], one should specify which prayer is intended, for example, the noon Sunnah-based prayer. One should indicate in this case whether it is the Sunnah-based prayer which precedes the obligatory prayer, or that which follows it, and one's conscious intention and specification must coincide with the utterance of the opening *Allāhu akbar* just as they do in obligatory ritual prayers. Moreover, it is desirable, but not necessary to specify that the prayer one intends to pray is voluntary.

In connection with voluntary prayers not associated with any particular time or reason [Type 3], all that is required when performing them is that one intend to perform ritual prayer without any further specification, and that one's intention coincide with the utterance of the opening *Allāhu akbar*. This same ruling applies to voluntary prayers which are inspired by a particular cause, but the purpose for which could be fulfilled by some other prayer; an example of this type is the prayer

The time for expressing intention in prayer

Three of the schools, namely, the Malikis, the Hanafis and Hanbalis, agree that it is acceptable for one's intention to precede the utterance of the opening *Allāhu akbar* by a short period of time. As for the Shafiis, however, they maintain that intention must coincide with one's utterance of *Allāhu akbar* as prayer is commenced, and that if one finishes saying *Allāhu akbar* without having consciously intended prayer yet, one's prayer will be invalid. [In other words, one's intention must neither precede nor follow the words, *Allāhu akbar* according to the Shafiis.]

Details concerning each school's position on this matter are presented in the footnote below.[69]

---

referred to as "the mosque greeting," a Sunnah-based prayer which is elicited by a particular cause, namely, entering the mosque, but whose function could be fulfilled by any prayer one performs after coming into the mosque.

* * *

As for the Malikis, they divide voluntary prayers into three categories, namely:

(1) Emphatically enjoined Sunnah-based prayers, i.e., the *witr* that follows the evening prayer, the prayers performed on the occasion of the Day of Fastbreaking and the Day of Sacrifice, the prayer performed when there is a solar eclipse, and the prayer for rain. When performing any of these, one should specify which prayer he or she intends to perform, such as the *witr*, the prayer for the Day of Fastbreaking, and so on.

(2) The *raghībah* prayer, which refers in Maliki terminology to the two *rak'ahs* performed before the dawn prayer. When performing this also, one should specify that one's intention is to perform the dawn prayer.

(3) Recommended prayers, such as the Sunnah-based prayers associated with each of the five daily prayers, the mid-morning prayer, the *tarāwīḥ* prayers, and the night prayer. In contrast to the first two types, these prayers need not be specified in one's intention; rather, it is enough simply to intend to perform ritual prayer without further specification, since the time at which each of them is performed suffices to identify it.

69. The Hanafis hold that intention may precede one's utterance of *Allāhu akbar* (*takbīrat al-iḥrām*) provided that the two actions are not separated by some other action which is extraneous to prayer, such as eating, drinking, and speaking of things that have nothing to do with praying. If they are separated by activities such as walking to a mosque, performing ritual ablutions, etc., this does no harm. For example, if someone intends to perform the noon prayer, then proceeds to perform ritual ablutions, after which he walks to the mosque and begins to pray without bringing his intention to mind again, his prayer will still be valid. As we have seen above, intention is defined as the desire to perform ritual prayer for God's sake alone without allowing any worldly concerns to enter in. Once a person has this intention and begins to pray without any extraneous action intervening between his intention and his prayer, he will have done what is required of him. Suppose now that Person A begins praying based on this type of sound intention; after this, Person B comes into the room and "A" goes on praying for a long time so as to impress

B with his piety. This in itself does not invalidate prayer; however, A will receive no reward for the lengthiness of his prayer. Rather, he will simply receive the reward for the basic prayer he intended to perform originally. The reason for this is that A's intention as he began was pure; this is what is meant by the statement made by some Hanafis, "Prayer admits of no eye service." What they mean to say here is that a pure intention is sufficient to render prayer valid even if it is tainted by some momentary hypocrisy—granting, of course, the agreed-upon fact that hypocrisy is an evil from which no benefit can derive.

One might also ask whether an intention to perform ritual prayer is valid before the beginning of the time period for the prayer in question. Suppose, for example, that someone intends to perform a particular obligatory prayer before the period of time associated with this prayer has begun. Shortly before the relevant time period begins, he or she performs ritual ablutions, walks to the mosque without saying anything irrelevant to prayer, sits in the mosque until the relevant time period has begun, then prays. Was this person's intention valid? According to statements handed down from Abū Ḥanīfah, the intention to perform a given obligatory prayer is not valid until the time period for this prayer has begun. Some say, however, that such an intention is valid since, according to the Hanafi school, intention is a condition for the validity of prayer, and the condition for something precedes that which it is a condition for; hence, it is only natural that one's intention to pray should precede the prayer.

Be this as it may, Hanafi scholars agree that it is preferable for one's intention to coincide with the utterance of the opening *Allāhu akbar*; hence, those who follow the Hanafi school are advised to act in accordance with this ruling because of its preferability and because, by doing so, they remove a cause for disputation.

* * *

In agreement with the views of Abū Ḥanīfah, the Hanbalis hold that it is acceptable for one's intention to pray to precede the utterance of the opening *Allāhu akbar* by a short space of time provided that it takes place after the beginning of the time period for the prayer concerned. The reason for this is that, like the Hanafis, the Hanbalis hold that intention is a condition for the validity of prayer and that as a consequence, it does no harm for it to precede one's utterance of *Allāhu akbar* [provided that the relevant time period has begun]. However, unlike the Hanafis, the Hanbalis hold that speech which is extraneous to prayer does not invalidate one's intention; hence, if someone intended to perform a given prayer, then said things that had nothing to do with prayer, after which he uttered the opening *Allāhu akbar*, his prayer would still be valid.

In sum, then, the Hanbalis stipulate only that one's intention must follow the commencement of the time period for the prayer intended; in do doing, they seek to circumvent a dispute with those who hold that intention is a pillar of prayer [in which case, it must be simultaneous with the prayer itself]. Hence, in agreement with the Hanafis, the Hanbalis consider it preferable for one's intention to accompany the utterance of the words *Allāhu akbar* as prayer commences.

* * *

As for the Malikis, they hold that the intention to pray may precede the utterance of *Allāhu akbar* by a space of time which is considered to be short by com-

The intention of the prayer leader (*imam*) and those being led in prayer

A prayer performed by someone who is being led by an imam will only be valid if he or she intends from the very beginning of the prayer to follow the imam's lead. Hence, if someone commences prayer alone, then finds an imam while still in the process of praying and consciously intends to follow the imam, his or her prayer will be invalid according the Hanafis and the Malikis.[70]

As for the imam, it is not necessary for him to intend to lead others in prayer except in certain situations.[71]

---

monly held standards. Hence, if someone intends to pray in a place near the mosque, then proceeds to utter *Allāh akbar* in the mosque without remembering to repeat his intention, his initial intention remains valid. Some Malikis maintain that it is not acceptable for intention to precede the utterance of *Allāhu akbar* whatsoever, and that if this occurs, one's intention is invalidated; however, the former view appears to be the one most widely held among them. At the same time, they agree that if intention precedes prayer by what would commonly be viewed as a long period of time, it loses its validity.

Those looking into this matter will realize that the Malikis recognize the importance of simultaneity between one's intention to pray and the utterance of the opening *Allāhu akbar*. As a consequence, this practice should not be unnecessarily neglected out of forgetfulness and the like.

* * *

The Shafiis, as we have already noted, hold that intention must coincide exactly with the utterance of the opening *Allāhu akbar*, and that if it either precedes or follows this, one's prayer will be invalid.

70. As for the positions of the Shafiis and the Hanbalis, they are as follows:

The Shafiis hold that if someone intends to follow an imam in the middle of a prayer that he or she is performing, the prayer will still be valid unless it happens to be one of the following: (1) the Friday prayer, (2) a prayer being joined with another in advance because a rainstorm is about to break out, or (3) a prayer that is being repeated. In these situations, a person must intend to follow the imam's lead from the very beginning.

* * *

The Hanbalis maintain that in order for the prayer of someone being led by an imam to be valid, he or she must intend to follow the imam except in two situations: (1) When there are other individuals who arrived and began praying before him or her. In this case, he or she may follow the lead of someone else who began to pray before he or she did provided that it is not the Friday prayer. (2) When someone residing in a given location (Person A) follows the lead of someone who is a traveler (Person B) and who is shortening prayer as a result. In this case, A may follow B's lead in what remains of the prayer after the imam has finished.

71. According to the Hanbalis, the imam must consciously intend to lead others in prayer every time he does so, and this intention must coincide with the beginning of the prayer except in the two situations mentioned in connection with the ruling described above in Footnote 70.

* * *

According to the Malikis, the imam's conscious intention to lead others in prayer is required in all prayers whose validity depends on their being performed communally, namely, (1) the Friday prayer, (2) the sundown and evening prayers when they are being joined in advance in anticipation of rain, (3) the prayer of fear, and (4) the "prayer of delegated leadership", i.e., a prayer during which the imam has to step aside for some reason and allow one of the worshipers being led in prayer to step forward to take his place.

If the imam fails consciously to intend to lead others in situation (1) above, that is, the Friday prayer, the prayer becomes invalid both for the imam and for those he is leading. If it occurs in situation (2), that is, a combined performance of the sundown and evening prayers in advance, then the second prayer, that is, the evening prayer, is invalidated. If it happens in situation (3), the prayer of fear, the prayer is invalidated only for the first group of those being led, while it remains valid for the imam and the second group. The reason for this is that as the prayer of fear was begun—the beginning of a prayer being the appropriate time for intention—the imam failed to intend to lead the group, thereby invalidating both his prayer and theirs; with the second group, however, the time for intention will already have passed, hence, the requirement of intention for the validity of his prayer and theirs no longer applies. [The prayer of fear consists of two *rak'ahs* performed in a time of war first by one regiment, then by another, for fear that they would not be able to fend off an attack by the enemy if they were all praying at the same time – t.n.] As for situation (4), the " prayer of delegated leadership", if the stand-in imam intends to lead the prayer, it will be valid both for him and for those being led who began to pray before he stepped in as imam, whereas if he fails to consciously intend to lead the prayer, it remains valid for him but is invalidated for all those being led.

* * *

According to the Hanafis, there is only one situation in which it is necessary for an imam to consciously intend to lead others in prayer, namely, a situation in which a man is leading women in prayer. In such a case, the imam's intention to lead is required for the validity of the women's emulation of him due to the 'corruption' which inevitably results from men and women praying side by side, a situation which will be discussed in more detail below.

* * *

As for the Shafiis, they maintain that it is only necessary for the imam to consciously intend to lead others in the following four situations: (1) At the Friday prayer; (2) When two prayers are being joined in advance—either the noon and mid-afternoon prayers or the sundown and evening prayers—due to rain. In this case, the imam only needs to consciously intend to lead others in the second of the two prayers, since the first prayer, unlike the second, is being performed during its appointed time period; (3) When a prayer is being repeated in community during its appointed time period, and (4) When it is a prayer that the imam has vowed to perform in community, in which case he must consciously intend to lead others in order to be released from his vow. If he neglects this intention, the prayer performed will be valid, but he will be guilty of wrongdoing until he repeats the prayer again in community and consciously intends to lead others in it.

The second obligation of prayer: *takbīrat al-iḥrām*, or 'the opening utterance of praise to God'

What is referred to as *takbīrat al-iḥrām* will be discussed under the following subheadings: (1) the ruling on *takbīrat al-iḥrām* and its definition, (2) the evidence for its necessity, (3) its characteristics, and (4) conditions relating to *takbīrat al-iḥrām*. As for the ruling on *takbīrat al-iḥrām*, it is an obligation of prayer according to the Hanbalis, the Malikis and the Shafiis; as for the Hanafis, they view it as a condition for prayer's validity.[72] In either case, however, ritual prayer is not valid without it, a point on which all four schools agree.

As for the meaning of *takbīrat al-iḥrām*, it is defined as "the utterance of words in praise of God by virtue of which one enters into the sanctity of prayer." In other words, once we have uttered these words in glorification of God, we are forbidden to do anything which would be inconsonant with the act of praying. A person in this situation is said to have entered into a state of inviolable consecration (*iḥrām*).[73] According to all the schools accept the Hanafi, *takbīrat al-iḥrām* involves uttering the words, *Allāhu akbar* ("God is greatest") given certain conditions to be discussed shortly. As for the Hanafis, they maintain that it is not necessary to utter these words in particular.

---

72. According to the Hanafis, *takbīrat al-iḥrām* is not, properly speaking, a pillar of prayer, but rather, a condition for its validity. One might respond to this by noting that in order for *takbīrat al-iḥrām* to be valid, the same conditions apply as those which apply to prayer itself, such as ritual purity, covering one's private parts, etc., and that if it were merely a condition for the validity of prayer rather than an integral part of prayer itself, such conditions would not apply to it. (We might also note that, in contrast to *takbīrat al-iḥrām*, an intention to pray—which is agreed to be a condition for the validity of prayer—is valid even if the person doing the intending is not yet in a state of ritual purity or has not covered his or her private parts.) To those who hold that *takbīrat al-iḥrām* is simply a condition for prayer's validity rather than a pillar of prayer, we may reply that it is connected to the act of standing up for prayer, which is one of prayer's pillars; this is why the same conditions required for the validity of prayer apply to *takbīrat al-iḥrām* as well. As readers will be aware, however, such debates belong to the realm of legal philosophy and hold no practical benefit for anyone but seekers of knowledge who might be able to employ them as a basis for precise rulings on this or that question. As for other people, it is sufficient to understand that *takbīrat al-iḥrām* is agreed by all to be necessary for the validity of ritual prayer.

73. The Arabic verb used to describe this action, namely, *aḥrama*, is the same word used to describe someone who is preparing to undertake the pilgrimage to Mecca [t.n.].

Evidence for the necessity of *takbīrat al-iḥrām*

There is unanimous agreement among Muslims that ritual prayer must be opened by the mention of the name of God Almighty, and that if this element is lacking, the prayer will not be valid. This consensus is supported by sound prophetic hadiths. According to one such hadith, narrated by Abū Dāwūd, al-Tirmidhī, and Ibn Mājah, the Prophet declared, "We open the way for prayer by cleansing ourselves of ritual impurity; we render it inviolable by the glorification of God (*al-takbīr*); and we conclude it with a greeting of peace [i.e., the words, *al-salāmu 'alaykum wa raḥmat Allāh*]."

Some find evidence for the obligatory nature of *takbīrat al-iḥrām* in God's command, "And Thy Sustainer's greatness glorify!" (74:3). Moreover, given the consensus among Muslims that the utterance of the phrase, *Allāhu akbar* is not required in any situation other than ritual prayer, this indicates that *takbīrat al-iḥrām* is an obligation, or pillar, of prayer.

As we have already noted, there is no disagreement among Muslim scholars concerning the necessity of *takbīrat al-iḥrām* for the validity of ritual prayer, regardless of whether it is classified as an obligation of prayer or as a condition for its validity.

Characteristics of *takbīrat al-iḥrām*

As we have seen, all the schools except that of the Hanafis agree that *takbīrat al-iḥrām* consists of the words, *Allāhu akbar* and no others, the result being that if someone opened prayer with any words other than these, his prayer would be invalid.[74]

---

74. As for the Hanafis, they deny the necessity of opening ritual prayer with the specific words, *Allāhu akbar*. Rather, they maintain that opening prayer with this statement is a 'duty' the omission of which does not, in and of itself, invalidate prayer. As we have seen earlier, a 'duty' is less binding than a full religious obligation; the Hanafis hold that those who neglect to perform such 'duties' are guilty of wrongdoing and will be punished by being deprived of intercession by the Prophet on the Day of Judgment. Needless to say, this alone should be sufficient chastisement for those who are believers. Be that as it may, we can see from the foregoing that, similar to the other three schools, the Hanafis deem it necessary to open ritual prayer in this manner. The only point of disagreement is that, whereas the other schools maintain that failure to open ritual prayer with such an utterance renders the prayer invalid, the Hanafis hold that it simply obliges the person to repeat the prayer later. If such a person neglects to repeat the prayer, he or she will have fulfilled his or her basic obligation to perform the prayer concerned, but will be guilty of wrongdoing.

As for the particular wording upon which the validity of one's prayer depends, the Hanafis hold that it can be any words which serve to glorify God Almighty alone without the inclusion of any sort of petition. Provided that the formulation fulfills these two specifications, it may be used to open prayer. For example, we might say, "Glory be to God!" (*subḥān Allāh!*), "Praise God!" (*al-ḥamdu lillāh*), "There is no god but God" (*lā ilāha illā Allāh*), or things like, "God is merciful"

Conditions for the validity of *takbīrat al-iḥrām*

The followers of the various schools may find it helpful to memorize the conditions for the validity of *takbīrat al-iḥrām* for each school separately.[75]

(*Allāhu raḥīm*), "God is gracious" (*Allāhu karīm*), or any other phrase which serves to extol and magnify the Divine, glorious and majestic is He. Hence, if we were to say, "May God forgive me," "May God be my refuge," or "There is no power or might but through God," our prayer will not be valid, since phrases such as these include elements other than pure praise of the Divine, namely, pleas for forgiveness, protection, and so on.

In addition, it is necessary to join the mention of the divine attributes with some name or title which refers to the Divine Being itself. Thus, if we were to say nothing but "Gracious", "Merciful," or something of this nature, our prayer would not be valid. If, on the other hand, we use only a name which points to the Divine Persona, by saying, "God", "The Merciful One" (i.e., *al-Raḥmān*), or "Lord" (*al-rabb*) without adding any qualifier, then according to Abū Ḥanīfah, our prayer will be valid, whereas according to his two companions [i.e., Abū Yūsuf al-Qāḍī and Muḥammad Ibn al-Ḥasan al-Shaybānī], it will not be. As for the evidence cited here, it supports the first view. After all, the divine command, "And Thy Sustainer's greatness glorify!" (74:3) does not mean that we are obliged to say, *Allāhu akbar* and nothing else. Rather, what it means is simply that we are to glorify our Sustainer using whatever words or expressions convey the appropriate meanings; the same interpretation applies to the word *takbīr* used in the hadith cited above. At the same time, however, the Hanafis hold that utterance of the words *Allāhu akbar* in particular is a 'duty' due to the fact that the Prophet made it a regular practice.

This, then, is the view of the Hanafis. As for the other three schools, they interpret the same evidence to mean that the words *Allāhu akbar* in particular are to be used when commencing prayer, citing the practice of the Prophet as additional support for this view.

75. The Shafiis list the following fourteen conditions associated with *takbīrat al-iḥrām*, every one of which must be fulfilled in order for one's prayer to be valid:

(1) It must be spoken in the Arabic language if possible; if, however, we cannot articulate it in Arabic and are unable to learn how to do so, then we may express it in whatever language we can.

(2) It must be uttered while one is standing if the prayer involved is obligatory and if one is capable of standing. If it is a voluntary prayer, one may utter it while seated (since in this case, even the entire prayer may be performed seated). If one utters it in an obligatory prayer while in the process of bending forward and if one is in a position which is closer to upright, his prayer will be valid, whereas if he is closer to a bow, it will not. (On this point, the Shafiis agree with the Hanafis and the Hanbalis, but disagree with the Malikis. The Malikis hold that it is permissible to utter *takbīrat al-iḥrām* while bending forward in one situation only, namely, when the person concerned is following the lead of an imam who began to pray before he arrived. According to the Shafiis, however, it is not necessary when praying in community [supposing one has arrived late] to begin following the imam while he is

bowing; rather, if the imam began his bow before the person following him and if, after this, the person following the imam bows by himself, this is acceptable.)

(3) The name *Allāh* must be uttered together with the word *akbar*.

(4) The initial 'A' in the word *Allāh* must not be lengthened, since this would change the meaning of the words, *Allāhu akbar* from, "God is greatest!" to a question, "Is God greatest?"

(5) The final 'a' in the word *akbar* must not be lengthened; the reason for this is that if one pronounced it *akbār*, one would be saying the Arabic word for "large drums" (singular, *kabar*), whereas if one pronounced it, *ikbār*, one would be uttering an Arabic word meaning 'menstruation'. Hence, someone who deliberately distorted the pronunciation in this way would be insulting his God and renouncing his religion.

(6) The 'b' sound in the word *akbar* must not be doubled.

(7) An extra 'u' sound must not be added between the word *Allāh* and the word *akbar*.

(8) No 'u' sound must be pronounced before *Allāhu akbar*, saying, *wa'Allāh abkar*.

(9) One must not pause between the words, *Allāh* and *akbar*. Thus, if someone said, *Allāh*, then after a silence, said, *akbar*, his prayer would not be valid. However, it is acceptable to add the definite article before *akbar*, by saying, for example, *Allāh al-akbar* (meaning, "God the greatest"). It is also acceptable to describe God with a fitting qualifier before pronouncing the word *akbar*. For example, one could say, *Allāh al-'aẓīm akbar* (that is, the mighty God is greatest"), or, *Allāh al-raḥmān al-raḥīm akbar* (i.e., "God the Merciful, the Dispenser of Mercy, is greatest"). However, the use of more than two intervening adjectives invalidates *takbīrat al-iḥrām*—by saying, for example, *Allāh al-'aẓīm al-karīm al-raḥim akbar* ("The mighty, gracious, merciful God is greatest"). *Takbīrat al-iḥrām* will likewise be invalidated if one interpolates a pronoun or a vocative particle between the words *Allāh* and *akbar*, by saying, for example, *Allāh huwa akbar*, or *Allāh yā Raḥmān, akbar*.

(10) One must voice *takbīrat al-iḥrām* loudly enough to be able to hear it oneself. Exceptions to this condition are made for people who are deaf or mute, or who are praying in a place where there is so much noise and commotion that they cannot hear themselves. At the same time, however, someone who is mute, deaf, etc. should do his best to utter *takbīrat al-iḥrām* audibly; for example, if the muteness is a temporary condition and the person is able to move his lips to form the words, *Allāhu akbar*, then he should do so.

(11) The time period for the prayer concerned must have already begun. (This ruling applies only if the prayer being prayed is either an obligatory prayer or a voluntary prayer associated with a particular time or occasion.)

(12) One must utter *takbīrat al-iḥrām* while facing the *qiblah* unless one is in circumstances in which the requirement to face the *qiblah* does not apply.

(13) If the prayer is being performed in community, one must not utter *takbīrat al-iḥrām* until after the imam has done so.

(14) One must utter *takbīrat al-iḥrām* in a place where it would be permissible to recite the Qur'ān. (Conditions for recitation of the Qur'ān will be discussed below.)

* * *

The Hanafis list the following twenty conditions for the validity of *takbīrat al-iḥrām*:

(1) The time for the obligatory prayer concerned must have begun.

(2) The person concerned must believe, or have good reason to believe, that the time period for the prayer concerned has begun; if he or she is uncertain whether it has begun or not but utters *takbīrat al-iḥrām* anyway, it will be invalid even if it turns out later that the time for the prayer had, in fact, begun.

(3) The parts of one's body which are deemed 'private' for prayer must be concealed; if someone utters *takbīrat al-iḥrām* while such parts of his body are exposed, his prayer will not be valid even if he conceals them afterwards.

(4) The person who intends to pray must have cleansed himself or herself of all minor and major ritual impurity, and his clothing, his body and the place in which he utters *takbīrat al-iḥrām* must be free of any type of impurity which may not be overlooked. (See our listing of the types of impurity which may be overlooked in the section above on "Ritual Purity.") If someone utters *takbīrat al-iḥrām* even though he suspects that he or she might not be ritually pure, it will be invalid even if it becomes apparent later that he or she was ritually pure.

(5) One must utter *takbīrat al-iḥrām* while standing up if the prayer one is performing is obligatory, a 'duty', or the Sunnah-based prayer associated with the dawn prayer. In all other voluntary prayers, *takbīrat al-iḥrām* may be uttered while sitting down. If one utters *takbīrat al-iḥrām* while bending forward and if one is closer to a standing position, *takbīrat al-iḥrām* will be valid, whereas if one is closer to a bow, it will be invalid. (This condition, of course, applies to those who are capable of standing up.) If someone who is being led in prayer begins following the imam while the latter is bowing and utters *takbīrat al-iḥrām* after him while still standing, it will be valid, whereas if he says, *Allāhu* while standing and *akbar* while bowing, his prayer will not be valid. Prayer is also invalidated if someone begins following the imam from the very beginning of the prayer, but says *Allāhu* before the imam has finished saying it.

(6) One must intend to perform ritual prayer.

(7) One must specify which of the obligatory prayers one intends to perform, e.g., noon, mid-afternoon, etc. If someone utters *takbīrat al-iḥrām* without such specification, it will not be valid.

(8) In cases where one intends to perform a 'duty' prayer—such as the two *rak'ahs* associated with the circumambulation of the Ka'bah, the prayers performed on the Days of Fastbreaking and Sacrifice, the *witr* following the evening prayer, prayers performed in fulfillment of a vow, and a prayer to compensate for a voluntary prayer which was invalidated after it was begun—one should specify which of these prayers one intends while uttering *takbīrat al-iḥrām*. As we have noted, however, such specification is not required for other voluntary prayers.

(9) One must utter *takbīrat al-iḥrām* loudly enough to hear himself. Thus, if someone whispers it or simply 'thinks' it, it will not be valid. The same condition applies to all utterances included in prayer, be they words of praise, pleas for protection, utterances of the name of God, Qur'anic recitation, prayers for blessings on the Prophet, etc. Hence, similar to things such as pronouncements of divorce, oaths,

etc., *takbīrat al-iḥrām* has no validity or effectiveness as far as the Hanafis are concerned unless one has pronounced it loudly enough to hear himself speak.

(10) One must utter an entire phrase containing the mention of God, by saying, for example, *Allāhu akbar*, *Subḥān Allāh*, or *Al-ḥamdu lillāh*. Thus, as we saw earlier, the utterance of a single word is not valid.

(11) One's mention of God must be for sake of the Divine alone. Hence, *takbīrat al-iḥrām* will not be valid if one's words contain the mention of one's own needs or requests.

(12) One's words must not be *bismillāh al-raḥmān al-raḥīm* ("In the name of God, the most Gracious, the Most Merciful"), since properly speaking, it is not valid to open prayer with these words.

(13) One must not omit the final 'h' sound from the word *Allāh*.

(14) One must be certain to lengthen the vowel in the second syllable of *Allāh*; otherwise, there are differing opinions as to whether one's *takbīrat al-iḥrām* is valid, whether the meat one has slaughtered by pronouncing the name of God is permissible for Muslims to eat, and so on. Given this disagreement, it is best to make certain that one has pronounced the lengthened *ā* sound properly.

(15) One must not lengthen the initial *a* sound in *Allāh* or in *akbar*. If someone says, *Āllāh akbar* unintentionally, for example, his prayer will not be valid since the lengthening of this vowel turns the statement, "God is greatest" into a question, namely, "Is God greatest?" In fact, someone who uses this pronunciation deliberately will have renounced his or her religion. Hence, to lengthen the initial *a* in *Allāh* is a serious error due to the misunderstanding to which it can lead, even if one's intention is to use the vocative case, that is, by saying, "O God…" Whatever one's intention may be, the lengthening of this vowel invalidates prayer. (As we have seen, the Shafiis agree with this view.)

(16) One must not lengthen the vowel following the *b* sound in the word *akbar*; for as we have seen, if it is pronounced *akbār*, it means 'drums', while if it is pronounced, *ikbār*, it becomes a word referring to menstruation, and whoever deliberately uses it in this sense will be guilty of blasphemy. However, such pronunciations invalidate prayer regardless of what one's motive is.

(17) One must not allow his or her intention to be separated from *takbīrat al-iḥrām* by actions or words which are extraneous to prayer. For example, if someone intends to perform a given prayer, after which he or she does something which has nothing to do with prayer—such as speaking, clearing his throat unnecessarily, drinking, or eating (even if the food had been caught between his or her teeth prior to this, provided that it amounts to the size of a chickpea)—then utters *takbīrat al-iḥrām* without renewing his or her intention, the resulting prayer will have no validity. However, if what intervenes between one's intention and one's prayer is something like walking silently to the mosque without doing anything 'extra' along the way, the prayer will be valid.

(18) One's utterance of *takbīrat al-iḥrām* must not precede one's intention to pray. If someone utters *takbīrat al-iḥrām*, then intends to pray, it will be invalid, and if *takbīrat al-iḥrām* is invalidated, so is the prayer which it introduces.

(19) One must be aware of the distinction between what is obligatory and what is not.

(20) The person concerned must believe that he or she is free of *ḥadath* and *khabath*.

It should be noted here that the Hanafis do not stipulate that *takbīrat al-iḥrām* be said in Arabic. Rather, they allow that one may say it in some other language even if he or she would have been able to say it in Arabic, and one's prayer will still be valid. At the same time, however, they rule that if someone is able to voice it in Arabic, it is undesirable to the point of being forbidden to say it in any other language.

* * *

The Malikis stipulate the following ten conditions for the validity of *takbīrat al-iḥrām*:

One: It must be uttered in the Arabic language if the person concerned is capable of this; if he or she is unable to say it in Arabic, as might be the case with some non-Arabs, the requirement of *takbīrat al-iḥrām* is dropped and the person may enter prayer based on his or her intention alone. At the same time, however, some Malikis allow that if *takbīrat al-iḥrām* is translated into a language the person knows, his or her prayer will remain valid. As for people who are able to use Arabic, they must utter the words, *Allāh akbar* in particular; in this situation, no other expression will serve as a substitute even if it is in Arabic and even if it conveys the same meaning. On this point, the Malikis differ with both the Shafiis and the Hanafis. The Shafiis, as we have seen, allow for a separation between the word *Allāh* and the word *akbar* such that someone might say, *Allāh al-raḥmān akbar*; in addition, they retain the requirement of *takbīrat al-iḥrām* for those who are unable to utter it in Arabic by allowing for it to be uttered in some other language. As for the Hanafis, they allow someone who does not know Arabic to utter *takbīrat al-iḥrām* in some other language without attaching any undesirability to this practice; nevertheless, if one could have used Arabic, it is undesirable to the point of being forbidden to use some other language for *takbīrat al-iḥrām* even though one's prayer will still be valid.

Two: When performing an obligatory prayer, one must utter *takbīrat al-iḥrām* while standing up if he or she is able. If someone utters *takbīrat al-iḥrām* while bending forward, it is invalid regardless of whether he or she is closer to a standing posture or to a bow. The only exception to this ruling is a situation in which someone wishes to follow an imam who, when the person following entered prayer, had already finished the first Qur'anic recitation and bowed. Thus, wanting to catch up with the imam, this person utters *takbīrat al-iḥrām* while bending forward and bows before the imam rises from his own bow; in this situation, the person's *takbīrat al-iḥrām* is valid even though he is not standing up. However, the *rak'ah* in which this took place is not counted, so once the imam has finished praying, the person following him must repeat this *rak'ah* in order to complete his prayer. If, by contrast, this same person begins *takbīrat al-iḥrām* while standing before the imam rises from his bow, then completes it while he is bowing or while bending forward on his way into a bow, the entire *rak'ah* will be counted (based on one of two well-attested views). In such a case, the person's intention in uttering *takbīrat al-iḥrām* must simply be to consecrate himself to prayer, or to consecrate himself to prayer and to bow as well; if, on the other hand, his intention is simply to bow, his prayer will be invalid. However, it is not permissible for such a person in this situation to terminate his or her prayer even if it becomes invalid; rather, he or she must complete the prayer out of respect for the imam, then repeat it later.

Three: The word *Allāh* must come before the word *akbar*. Hence, it would not be acceptable to say, *Akbar Allāh*, for example. On this point, all the schools agree.

Four: One must not lengthen the initial *a* sound in the name *Allāh* with the intention of turning the statement, *Allāhu akbar* (meaning, "God is greatest") into the question, *Āllāhu akbar?* ("Is God greatest?"). However, if one pronounces it in this way without intending to make it into a question, or without any intention at all, one's prayer will remain valid.

Five: One should not lengthen the vowel sound *a* following the *b* in *akbar*, thereby turning the word into the plural for 'large drum', since by doing so, one would be speaking ill of one's God. However, if one mistakenly pronounces *takbīrat al-iḥrām* in this way, the lengthening of the *a* here makes no difference. On these two points (that is, Conditions 4 and 5), the Malikis part ways with the other three schools, all of which hold that such variations in the pronunciation of *takbīrat al-iḥrām* render it invalid regardless of the intention of the person praying.

Six: One should draw out the vowel sounds in the name *Allāh* in a natural way; this is a condition on which all the schools agree.

Seven: One should not omit the *h* sound at the end of the name, *Allāh*, by saying, *Allā akbar*. This, likewise, is agreed upon by all the schools. However, if one draws out the *h* sound in such a way that it leads naturally to the pronunciation of the final *u* [as an *ū*], this is acceptable according to the Hanafis and the Malikis, but not according to the Shafiis and the Hanbalis. According to the Shafiis, the pronunciation of the final *u* sound [as an *ū*] at the end of Allāh is forgivable if one is a simple lay person; otherwise, it is not, and doing so will invalidate *takbirat al-iḥrām*; as for the Hanbalis, they hold that this practice invalidates *takbīrat al-iḥrām* regardless of who it is that is praying.

Eight: One should not allow the word *Allāh* to be separated from the word *akbar* by what would commonly be considered a long silence; however, if the silence would be judged by prevailing standards to be short, no harm is done. It is agreed upon by all the schools that it is harmful to allow more than a very brief temporal separation between the utterance of the word *Allāh* and the utterance of the word *akbar*. The Malikis leave it to custom to determine what constitutes a 'brief' length of time. According to the Shafiis, a 'brief', and therefore pardonable, pause is one which lasts just long enough to breath between utterances, or one which results from faltering speech. As for the Hanafis and the Hanbalis, they hold that in order to be harmful, a pause has to be long enough to allow someone to speak, even if only briefly.

Nine: One should not allow the word *Allāh* and the word *akbar* to be separated by speech, even if it amounts to no more than a single letter. This ruling is agreed upon by the Hanbalis and the Malikis. As for the Hanafis, they allow for a separation by means of the definite article such that it would be permissible to say either, *Allāhu akbar* or *Allāh al-kabīr*, for example. The Hanafis also allow one to say, *Allāhu kabīr* rather than *Allāhu akbar*. And as for the Shafiis, we have seen that they allow the words *Allāh* and *akbar* to be separated by up to two qualifiers; hence, one might say, *Allāh al-raḥmān al-raḥīm akbar* ("God, the Merciful and the Dispenser of Mercy, is greatest").

Ten: One must move his or her lips when uttering *takbīrat al-iḥrām*. As for saying it loudly enough to hear oneself, this is not necessary; someone who is mute, for example, is exempted from *takbīrat al-iḥrām*, and he or she may simply begin prayer with intention. On this point, the Malikis differ with the other three schools, all of which hold that *takbīrat al-iḥrām* must be uttered loudly enough that the person saying it can hear himself, and that if all one does is move his lips, his prayer will be invalid. As for the mute, the Hanbalis and the Hanafis exempt them from *takbīrat al-iḥrām* altogether, whereas the Shafiis hold that they must move their tongues and lips when saying it to the best of their ability.

Finally, the Malikis hold that all conditions which must be fulfilled for the validity of ritual prayer—such as facing the *qiblah*, covering one's private parts, ritual purity, and so forth—apply equally to the validity of *takbīrat al-iḥrām*.

* * *

As for the Hanbalis, they stipulate the following nine conditions for the validity of *takbīrat al-iḥrām*:

One: *Takbīrat al-iḥrām* must consist of the two words, *Allāh* and *akbar*. If it consists of any other combination, it will be invalid. The Malikis and the Hanbalis agree that this is the only valid formulation for *takbīrat al-iḥrām*; consequently, if one were to say, *Akbar Allāh*, *Allāh al-akbar*, *Allāh al-kabīr* or *Allāh al-jalīl* or if one used any other expression of praise to the Divine, one's *takbīrat al-iḥrām* would lack validity. The same is true even if one simply utters the name *Allāh*. However, if someone says, *Allāhu akbar*, then follows this with some fitting qualifier, by saying, for example, *Allāhu akbar wa a'ẓam* ("God is greater and more magnificent"), *Allāhu akbar wa ajall* ("God is greater and more majestic"), or *Allāhu akbar kabīran* ("God is greater by far"), one's prayer will be valid, although they consider this undesirable. (As we have seen, the Shafiis approve the interpolation of up to two qualifiers between *Allāh* and *akbar*. Hence, one may say, *Allāh al-raḥmān al-raḥim akbar*, while the Hanafis allow the interpolation of the definite article, such that we could say, *Allāh al-akbar* as well as something like, *Allāh kabir*.)

Three: One should not lengthen the initial *a* sound in the name *Allāh*.

Four: One should not lengthen the *a* sound following the *b* in the word *akbar*, the meaning of which has been discussed.

Five: *Takbīrat al-iḥrām* must be in the Arabic language. However, like the Shafiis, the Hanbalis hold that someone who is unable to say *takbīrat al-iḥrām* in Arabic may use any language he or she knows. If someone who does not know Arabic fails to utter *takbīrat al-iḥrām* in the language he or she does know, his prayer will be invalid for having neglected what is required of him. (On this point, the Hanbalis disagree with the Malikis, who hold that for someone who is unable to utter *takbīrat al-iḥrām* either in Arabic or in any other language, it ceases to be a requirement just as it does for someone who is mute.) If someone is able to utter the word *Allāh* by itself or the word *akbar* by itself, he should do whatever he is capable of. Moreover, unlike the Shafiis, the Hanbalis do not consider it necessary for

The third obligation of prayer: standing

All four schools agree that standing is required in every *rak'ah* of obligatory ritual prayer provided that the person praying is capable of doing so. If someone is not able to stand due to illness or some other cause, this requirement is waived and he or she may pray in whatever position he or she is capable of. (Details on this matter will be discussed below in the section dealing with prayer performed by someone who is ill.)

In prayers which are recommended, emulations of the Sunnah, and so on, standing is not required; rather, they may be performed from a seated position even if the person praying is able to stand. This ruling is also agreed upon among the schools; however, the Hanafis offer additional details in connection with some of the voluntary prayers.[76]

Standing is required for the duration of the time when the worshiper is engaged in an obligatory, Sunnah-based or recommended recitation of the Qur'ān. This ruling is agreed upon by the Shafiis and the Hanbalis; for the views of the Hanafis and the Malikis, see the footnote below.[77]

---

a mute person to move his tongue, since the Lawgiver has not required this of him and his attempt to do so would be futile.

Six: One should not draw out the *h* sound in *Allāh* such that one pronounces the final *u*; if one does so, his or her *takbīrat al-iḥrām* will be invalid.

Seven: One should not omit the *h* in Allāh, saying, *Allā abkar*.

Eight: One should not pronounce an *ū* sound between the words *Allāh* and *akbar*.

Nine: One should not allow the words *Allāh* and *akbar* to be separated by a silence that would be long enough to allow for other speech, however insignificant.

Finally, all conditions pertaining to the validity of prayer pertain similarly to the validity of *takbīrat al-iḥrām*.

76. According to the Hanafis, standing is required not only in the five daily obligatory prayers but also in the following voluntary prayers: (1) the *witr*, (2) prayers performed in fulfillment of a vow, and (3) the two *rak'ahs* which precede the dawn prayer.

77. According to the Hanafis, one must remain standing as long as it takes to complete the obligatory Qur'anic recitation, which amounts to one long verse of the Qur'ān or three short ones. (This will be explained below in the section on recitation of the *Fātiḥah*.) Beyond this, however, one's standing is considered either a 'duty' (for example, if what one is doing while standing is classified as a 'duty', such as recitation of the *Fātiḥah*) or recommended (as when what one is doing while standing is simply recommended). However, this ruling applies solely to the period of time prior to one's Qur'anic recitation; once the recitation has begun, it becomes obligatory to go on standing until it is completed, even if one happens to recite the entire Qur'ān, since it is not permissible to recite one verse while standing, for example, then sit down for the remainder of the recitation. As for the difference of opinion on this matter among the Hanafis, the Shafiis and the Hanbalis, it holds no benefit except insofar as it pertains to how much reward is merited by this or that action. For example, the Shafiis and the Hanbalis hold that if

The fourth obligation of prayer: recitation of the *Fātiḥah*

In relation to the recitation of the *Fātiḥah* in ritual prayer, five questions present themselves:

(1) Do all the schools agree that the recitation of the *Fātiḥah* is an obligatory part of ritual prayer?

(2) Is this practice obligatory in every *rak'ah* regardless of whether the prayer being performed is obligatory or voluntary?

(3) Is this practice obligatory for all those who perform ritual prayer regardless of whether they are praying individually, as imams, or in community following an imam?

(4) What is the ruling on those who are unable to recite the *Fātiḥah*?

(5) Is it necessary for those who recite the *Fātiḥah* to speak loudly enough that they can hear themselves, or will their prayer be valid even if they move their lips without being able to hear what they are saying?

The first two questions may be answered as follows: All of the schools with the exception of the Hanafis agree that it is obligatory to recite the *Fātiḥah* in every *rak'ah* that one performs regardless of whether the prayer is obligatory or voluntary, and that if someone deliberately fails to recite it in any given *rak'ah*, his or her prayer will be invalid. On the other hand, if someone simply forgets to recite the

---

someone does a long recitation, he will simply receive the reward for performing an obligatory prayer; however, someone who stands for a shorter period of time due to omission of a Sunnah-based practice associated with prayer will be chastised for shortening the time he remained standing in prayer despite the fact that omitting a Sunnah-based practice is not punishable. As for the Hanafis, they say that if we remain standing for as long as we are required to, we merit the reward for performance of an obligatory prayer; if, on the other hand, we shorten the time we remain standing by omitting this or that Sunnah-based practice, we merit no punishment. If the Shafiis, the Hanbalis and the Hanafis agree on this view, then there is no essential dispute among them.

* * *

The Malikis hold that when performing an obligatory prayer, one is required to stand up while: (1) uttering *takbīrat al-iḥrām*, (2) reciting the *Fātiḥah*, and (3) bending forward into a bow. As for standing while reciting a further passage from the Qur'ān, this is not obligatory, but a practice based on the prophetic Sunnah. Hence, if someone leans on something for support while reciting a Qur'anic passage other than the *Fātiḥah* such that, if this object were removed, he would fall down, his prayer will still be valid. However, if someone leans on something for support while reciting the *Fātiḥah* or while bending forward in preparation to bow, his prayer will be invalidated. At the same time, however, the Malikis agree with the other three schools that if someone actually sits all the way down while reciting a passage from the Qur'ān, his or her prayer will be invalidated, since the act of sitting down in this situation offends against the attitude proper to prayer.

Fātiḥah in a given *rak'ah*, he or she must perform this *rak'ah* later in the manner which will be described below in our discussion of the prostration of forgetfulness. As for the Hanafis, they maintain that the recitation of the *Fātiḥah* in ritual prayer is not obligatory, but rather, a 'duty'. We might also say that it is an emphatically enjoined Sunnah-based practice; this being the case, one may omit it intentionally without invalidating one's prayer.[78] Evidence in favor of the view that the recitation of the *Fātiḥah* is obligatory may be found in the hadith narrated by both Muslim and al-Bukhārī according to which the Prophet stated, "Whoever has not recited the *Fātiḥah* has not prayed."

For the answer to the third question above, that is, whether a person being led by an imam in prayer is required to recite the *Fātiḥah*, please refer to the footnote below.[79]

In answer to the fourth question concerning the ruling on those who are unable to recite the *Fātiḥah*, we noted the following: According to the Shafiis and the Hanbalis, someone who is unable to recite the *Fātiḥah* in prayer but who is able to recite some other passage from the Qur'ān which contains the same number of verses and words as the *Fātiḥah* should recite this other passage. If, on the other hand, the person has memorized one or more verses but not enough to equal the length of the *Fātiḥah*, he must repeat whatever he has memorized a sufficient num-

---

78. Specifically, the Hanafis hold that what is required in ritual prayer is that one recite from the Qur'ān, whether the passage recited happens to be the *Fātiḥah* or some other part of the Qur'ān. They base this position on the command, "Recite, then, as much of the Qur'ān as you may do with ease" (73:20), where the recitation referred to is that which forms part of ritual prayer. The Hanafis base this ruling on a hadith narrated by both Muslim and al-Bukhārī in which the Prophet states, "As you prepare to pray, perform your ablutions properly, face the *qiblah*, then recite 'as much of the Qur'ān as you may do with ease'." They also cite the following words of the Prophet, "There is no such thing as ritual prayer without Qur'anic recitation."

The Hanafis hold that Qur'anic recitation is required in the first two *rak'ahs* of each obligatory prayer and that it should consist of the *Fātiḥah* in particular. If someone fails to recite the *Fātiḥah* in the first two *rak'ahs* of a four-*rak'ah* obligatory prayer, it may be recited in the two *rak'ahs* following this and the prayer will still be valid, but the person concerned will have neglected what the Hanafis term a 'duty'. If the person has omitted the recitation of the *Fātiḥah* during the first two *rak'ahs* unintentionally, he must conclude the prayer with a prostration of forgetfulness. As for someone who either fails to perform this extra prostration or deliberately neglected to recite the *Fātiḥah* in the first two *rak'ahs*, he must repeat the entire prayer. If the person does not repeat the prayer, the prayer will remain valid, but he or she will be guilty of wrongdoing. When performing the remaining *rak'ahs* of an obligatory prayer, one is not required to recite the *Fātiḥah*, but doing so is an emulation of the prophetic Sunnah. When performing voluntary prayers, however, the recitation of the *Fātiḥah* is a 'duty' in every *rak'ah*; the reason for this is that two *rak'ahs* make up a single, self-contained instance of voluntary prayer even if someone happens to perform several sets of two *rak'ahs* in succession (as when someone prays four voluntary *rak'ahs* followed by a single greeting of peace at the end). The Hanafis classify the *witr* as a voluntary prayer; consequently, it is a 'duty' to recite the *Fātiḥah* in all three of its *rak'ahs*. According to the Hanafis, a complete obligatory recitation of the Qur'ān consists of three short verses or one long verse which equals the length of three short ones, the latter of which is preferable.

79. According to the Shafiis, someone who is being led in communal prayer must recite the *Fātiḥah* behind the imam unless he or she joined the prayer late and missed all or part of the *Fātiḥah*. In this case, the imam's recitation exempts the person being led from whatever part of the *Fātiḥah* he or she missed. This ruling applies, of course, provided that the imam is qualified to do a valid recitation (meaning that there is no reason to believe that he is not in a state of ritual purity or that the person being led walked in while the imam was performing a *rak'ah* not included in the obligatory prayer).

* * *

According to the Hanafis, it is undesirable to the point of being forbidden for a person being led in prayer to recite the *Fātiḥah*—either silently or aloud—behind the imam. They base this ruling on a hadith which has been passed down through a number of distinct chains of transmission and according to which the Messenger of God said, "The imam's recitation will serve as that of the person he is leading." In addition, prohibitions against the recitation of the *Fātiḥah* for those being led in communal prayer have been passed down on the authority of eighty of the Prophet's most prominent Companions, including al-Murtaḍā and al-'Abādilah. [According to scholars of Islamic jurisprudence, the name 'al-'Abādilah', that is, "the 'Abdullahs", refers to 'Abdullah Ibn Mas'ūd, 'Abdullah Ibn 'Abbās and 'Abdullah Ibn 'Umar Ibn al-Khaṭṭāb, whereas hadith scholars hold that it refers to 'Abdullah Ibn Mas'ūd, 'Abdullah Ibn 'Umar Ibn al- Khaṭṭāb, 'Abdullah Ibn 'Abbās and 'Abdullah Ibn al-Zubayr; hadith scholars sometimes substitute 'Abdullah Ibn 'Amr Ibn al-'Aṣ for 'Abdullah Ibn Mas'ūd (al-Qal'aji) – t.n.] We also have reports narrated on the authority of several of the Companions according to which, if a person being led in prayer recites the *Fātiḥah* behind the imam, his or her prayer will be invalidated. However, these reports are not reliable; rather, the strictest view we have on this practice is that it is undesirable to the point of being prohibited.

* * *

According to the Malikis, recitation of the *Fātiḥah* behind the imam is recommended if it is done silently, but undesirable if it is done aloud unless one is doing so out of deference for those with differing viewpoints on this matter, in which case audible recitation behind the imam is likewise recommended.

* * *

As for the Hanbalis, they hold that it is desirable to recite the *Fātiḥah* behind the imam when the prayer is being performed silently, as well as during pauses in the imam's recitation when the prayer is being performed aloud; however, it is undesirable to do so while the imam himself is reciting during a prayer being performed aloud.

ber of times to bring it up to the length of the *Fātiḥah.* If someone is unable to recite any of the Qur'ān at all, he or she must engage in the mention of God by saying, for example, *Allāh, Allāh...* a sufficient number of times to equal the length of the *Fātiḥah*. And as for someone who is unable even to engage in the mention of God, he or she must stand in silence for as long as it would have taken to recite the *Fātiḥah*. If someone fails to do any of these things, his or her prayer will be invalid. However, these two schools also hold that if the *Fātiḥah* is recited, it must be recited in Arabic and that otherwise, one's prayer will be invalid.[80]

As for the answer to the fifth question, that is, whether it is necessary for the person reciting the *Fātiḥah* to hear himself, all the schools with the exception of the Malikis hold that if one does not hear himself as he recites the *Fātiḥah*, it is as if he had not recited it. According to the Malikis, it is sufficient simply to move one's lips and tongue even if one cannot hear oneself; however, in deference to opposing viewpoints, they grant that it is preferable to recite it audibly. Of course, as we have seen, the Hanafis do not view recitation of the *Fātiḥah* as obligatory in ritual prayer; this means that even if someone does not hear himself as he recites it, his prayer will still be valid, but he will have neglected a 'duty'.

The fifth obligation of prayer: bowing

Bowing is agreed to be obligatory in all ritual prayer for those who are capable of it, and the obligatory nature of this practice has been definitively established. The only point on which the various schools differ in this regard has to do with how much bending of the body is required in order for one's prayer to be valid.[81]

---

80. As for the views of the Hanafis and the Malikis on this matter, they are as follows:

According to the Hanafis, those who are unable to recite in Arabic may recite in any other language they know, and their prayer will be valid.

According to the Malikis, anyone who does not know how to recite the *Fātiḥah* should learn to do so if possible. If not, he or she must follow the lead of someone who does know how to recite it. If no such person is available, it is recommended that between uttering *takbīrat al-iḥrām* and bowing [in other words, during the interval when one would normally be reciting the *Fātiḥah* – t.n.], he or she engage in the mention of God Almighty. These rulings only apply, of course, to those able to hear and speak; those who are mute are exempt from such requirements.

81. According to the Hanafis, the bowing required for someone who is standing up consists in tilting one's head toward the front and bending one's torso forward. This much is sufficient for one's prayer to be valid. As for a full bow, it involves bending at the hip until one's head is level with one's buttocks. For those praying while seated, the required movement involves bowing one's head and leaning forward; this movement is not considered complete unless one's forehead is parallel with [the floor or ground] in front of one's knees.

* * *

According to the Hanbalis, the bow that suffices for someone standing up is to bend forward to the point where a person with arms of an ordinary length can touch his knees with his hands. For someone whose arms are unusually long or short, a

The sixth obligation of prayer: prostration and its conditions

Prostration is an agreed-upon obligation of prayer; in the course of performing ritual prayer, one is required to prostrate twice during each *rak'ah*. However, the exact manner in which one is required to prostrate in order for one's prayer to be valid is subject to different rulings by the various schools.[82]

---

sufficient bow consists in bending forward to the point where, if his arms were an ordinary length, he would be able to touch his knees with his hands. As for a complete bow, it involves bending from the hip until one's back is parallel with the ground and one's head is on a level with one's back. For someone sitting down, a sufficient bow consists in leaning forward to the point where one's face is parallel to the ground or floor in front of his or her knees, whereas a full bow involves bringing one's face as close as possible to the floor or ground in front of the knees.

* * *

According to the Shafiis, the minimum bow one may perform from a standing position is to bend forward to the point where a medium-sized person can touch his hands to his knees without placing himself in an awkward position —for example, by lowering the buttocks, raising the head, bringing the chest forward, and the like. They also stipulate that one's intention must be, in fact, to bow. As for a full bow from a standing position, it involves bending deeply enough that one's back and neck are in a straight line. For someone sitting down, the minimum bow consists in bending forward to the point where one's forehead is parallel with the floor or ground in front of one's knees, while a complete bow involves bending forward to the point where one's forehead is parallel with the spot where one performs prostration, yet without actually touching it.

* * *

According to the Malikis, the required bow consists of bending forward until the hands of someone with medium-length arms are close to his knees; in other words, if the person praying let his hands rest, they would rest on the ends of the thighs closest to his knees. They also recommend that one place one's hands firmly on one's knees with one's back straight.

82. According to the Malikis, the minimum prostration involves placing part of one's forehead, however small, on the ground or floor on which one is praying; if someone prostrated by placing one side of his head to the ground, for example, this would not be sufficient. It is also recommended that one bring one's entire forehead into firm contact with the ground, floor, etc. The Malikis hold that it is recommended that one touch his nose to the ground as well, and that if someone neglects to do this, he or she should repeat the prayer before the end of the time period for the prayer concerned out of deference for the view that touching one's nose to the ground is obligatory. (The time period for the noon and mid-afternoon prayers lasts until the sunlight takes on a yellow hue; hence, after this point one should not repeat either of these prayers. As for the sundown, evening, and dawn prayers, they may be repeated until sunrise.) However, if someone prostrates by touching his nose to the ground but not his forehead, this is not sufficient. As for prostrating with

In order for one's prostration to be valid, it must be done on a surface which is solid enough that one's forehead will not sink down into it, such as a mat or a carpet. As for substances such as cotton, straw, rice, corn, and the like, it is not permissible to prostrate on them unless they form a surface which is firm enough that one's forehead will rest on top of it.

It is also necessary when prostrating that one not put one's forehead on top of one's hand. According to the Malikis, the Hanbalis, and the Shafiis, prayer will be invalidated if someone places his forehead on top of his hand while prostrating; only the Hanafis hold that it does no harm, although they consider it undesirable. If the forehead rests on a garment or on some object which dangles from one's body and moves when one's body moves, one's prayer remains valid; however, it is nevertheless considered undesirable by all of the schools with the exception of the Shafiis.[83] As for prostrating on part of one's turban that comes down over the forehead, it does no harm; hence, if someone is wearing a turban with a large *kaffiyeh* on top of it which comes down over part of his forehead, he may let his forehead rest on the kaffiyeh according to all the schools except the Shafiis.[84]

Lastly, when prostrating, one's forehead should not be higher than one's knees. Concerning how high one's head can be during prostration without one's prayer being invalidated, the various schools offer differing rulings.[85]

---

one's hands, knees and toes to the ground, this is a practice based on the prophetic Sunnah, but it is not required.

* * *

According to the Hanafis, the minimum prostration required for a valid prayer involves placing even the most minimal part of one's forehead on a surface on which prostration is allowed. Placing part of one's nose alone on the ground, floor, etc., is not sufficient unless one has a viable excuse. As for prostrating on nothing but one's cheek or chin, this is never acceptable, with or without an excuse. In addition, it is necessary to place at least one hand, one knee and part of the end of one foot—even if it is nothing but a single toe—on a surface on which prostration is valid. As for prostrating on most of the forehead, this practice is a 'duty'. And as for a complete prostration, it involves placing both hands, both knees, the ends of both feet, the forehead and the nose on a surface on which it is permissible to prostrate.

* * *

According to the Shafiis and the Hanbalis, prostration must involve placing part of each of seven different members of the body on the floor, ground, etc. These parts of the body are listed in the following hadith, where the Messenger of God states, "I have been commanded to prostrate on seven 'bones', namely, the forehead, the hands, the knees, and the toes." The Hanbalis hold that prostration is not complete unless one also places part of the nose on the ground, floor, etc. As for the Shafiis, they stipulate that when prostrating, one should place the palms of one's hands and the bottoms of one's toes on the ground, floor, etc.

83. According to the Shafiis, one's prayer will be invalidated if, while prostrating, the forehead rests on something one is wearing. However, they make an exception to this ruling if one remains for a long time in prostration without such an object moving as a result of his movements. They also consider it acceptable to rest one's forehead on a handkerchief or scarf in one's hand, since it is separate from one's body.

84. As for the Shafiis, they hold that prayer is only valid if one prostrates on one's bare forehead. If, for example, one is wearing a turban or headband that covers the forehead, one's prayer will be invalid if one prostrates on top of such an object without a valid excuse (for example, due to a head injury that requires one to wear a headband the removal of which might cause serious hardship). In this type of situation, one's prayer will still be valid even though one's forehead is covered.

85. According to the Hanafis, one's prayer will remain valid unless one's forehead rests on a surface which is more than half a cubit [approximately 23 cm – t.n.] high. However, they make an exception to this ruling in a situation where, due to crowded conditions, the person praying has to prostrate on someone else's back. Prostrating on someone else's back is valid given three conditions: (1) that there not be any empty spot on the ground or floor to rest one's forehead on, (2) that it be done in a single prayer, and (3) that one's knees be on the ground. If any of these conditions is violated, one's prayer will be invalid.

* * *

According to the Hanbalis, prayer will only be invalidated if the elevation of the head during prostration is sufficient to make it look as if one is not praying.

* * *

According to the Shafiis, prayer is invalid if one's forehead rests during prostration on a surface which is higher than one's knees, unless one raises his buttocks over his head and his shoulders. The critical point for the Shafiis is that during prostration, the parts of the body which are normally lower should be elevated above the parts which are normally higher. They make an exception to this ruling, however, for a pregnant woman, who is not required to elevate her buttocks above her head and shoulders if she fears that this might do her harm.

* * *

As for the Malikis, they hold that if one's forehead rests on something which is elevated significantly above the ground or floor, one's prayer will not be valid, but that if it is on top of something small like a key, a wallet, etc., one's prostration will be valid even though it represents a departure from the ideal.

The seventh obligation of prayer: rising after a bow

The eighth obligation: rising after prostration

The ninth obligation: rising to a fully upright standing position

The tenth: *Al-Ṭuma'nīnah*

These four obligations of prayer are interrelated, and three of the four schools—namely, the Shafiis, the Malikis and the Hanbalis—agree on their necessity. As for the Hanafis, they hold that rising after a bow, rising to a fully upright standing position, and *al-ṭuma'nīnah* are not obligatory but rather, 'duties' such that if someone did not perform these particular actions, his or her prayer would remain valid. However, they hold that rising after a prostration is obligatory.

For detailed rulings on these practices by each of the four schools, see the footnote below.[86]

---

86. As we have seen, the Hanafis classify rising after a bow, rising to a fully standing position, and *ṭuma'nīnah* as 'duties', rather than obligations, of prayer. Even so, they offer detailed rulings on each of these practices. *Al-ṭuma'nīnah* is defined by the Hanafis as "a quieting of the limbs until the joints are relaxed and each part of the body 'settles' into position." This relaxed pose, which is to be held long enough for someone to utter the words, *Subḥān Allāh* at least once, is a 'duty' in relation to both bowing and prostrating as well as every other pillar of prayer. When rising after a bow, one simply needs to raise oneself sufficiently that it is clear one has changed positions. However, the movement in which one goes on to a fully upright position—referred to by the Hanafis as *i'tidāl*—is most commonly viewed not as obligatory, but as a practice based on the prophetic Sunnah. As for the act of rising from a prostration, this is obligatory. The minimum requirement here is that one come up into what is close to a sitting position, whereas pulling oneself all the way up to a sitting posture is not obligatory, but based on the prophetic Sunnah.

* * *

The Shafiis define rising from a bow as a return to the same position one was in before bowing, whether this is a standing position or a sitting position. In addition, one must hold still for a moment or two between rising from the bow and going down into a prostration; it is this which the Shafiis refer as *i'tidāl*. When rising from one's first prostration, one sits up straight and pauses until each part of one's body 'settles' into position; if one does not assume a fully upright sitting position at this point, one's prayer will be invalidated. At the same time, however, one must not pause too long in the upright position after rising from a bow or a prostration. Specifically, if one pauses long enough to recite the phrases associated with the standing position [that is, "God hears those who praise Him. To You, O Lord, praise belongs!"], the *Fātiḥah*, the words uttered when one is seated [that is, *rabbī ighfirlī wa li wālidayya*, "My Lord, forgive me and my mother and father"], as well as any part of the greetings and supplications associated with the conclusion of the first

The eleventh obligation of prayer: the final 'sitting'

It is agreed by all four schools that the final 'sitting' is an obligatory part of prayer; however, they differ concerning exactly what this action involves.[87]

---

two *rak'ahs* and/or the final two *rak'ahs*, one's prayer will be invalidated. The Shafiis stipulate that when one rises from either a bow or a prostration, one's intention should be exactly this—i.e., to rise from a bow or a prostration—and nothing else. For example, if someone rises from a bowing position out of fright or alarm, this action will not be valid; consequently, the person praying must return to his or her bow or prostration—but without pausing if he or she already did so the first time—then rise again to an upright position.

* * *

According to the Malikis, rising from a bow involves the act of straightening one's back and adopting an upright position, while rising from a prostration involves simply lifting one's forehead off the ground or floor even if one's hands remain where they are. As for *i'tidāl*, that is, returning to the position one was in before bowing or prostrating, it constitutes a pillar in its own right; it also serves to separate the other pillars one from another. As such, *i'tidāl* is obligatory after bowing, after prostrating, when one is concluding prayer with a final greeting of peace, and when one utters *takbīrat al-iḥrām*. As for *ṭuma'nīnah*, which is likewise an independent pillar of prayer, it involves allowing all parts of the body to rest for a short period of time beyond what is required for adopting the obligatory upright position or bending.

* * *

As for the Hanbalis, they hold that rising from a bow involves simply removing one's hands from one's knees, while *i'tidāl* following a bow involves adopting a fully upright position such that every part of the body returns to the position it was in before. Rising from a prostration involves lifting one's forehead off the ground or floor, while *i'tidāl* following prostration involves sitting up straight afterwards and allowing all parts of one's body to return to their former positions. As we have seen, the Malikis and the Shafiis agree that rising after a bow, rising after a prostration, *ṭuma'nīnah* and *i'tidāl* are all obligatory components of prayer.

87. According to the Hanafis, the final 'sitting' consists, properly speaking, of remaining in a seated position for the duration of the time required to recite the testimony [to be discussed in detail below]. This ruling is based on a hadith narrated on the authority of 'Abdullah Ibn 'Amr Ibn al-'Āṣ, may God be pleased with him. According to this hadith, 'Abdullah Ibn 'Amr Ibn al-'Āṣ was told by the Prophet, "Once you have raised your head after the final prostration and remained seated long enough to recite the testimony, your prayer will be complete."

* * *

According to the Malikis, remaining seated in a fully upright position long enough to recite the required greeting of peace is obligatory, and it is an emulation of the Sunnah to remain in this position long enough to recite the testimony as well. It is recommended, properly speaking, that one remain seated long enough to pray

The twelfth obligation of prayer: the final testimony (*al-tashahhud al-akhīr*)

According to the Shafiis, the final testimony is obligatory; the Hanafis hold that it is a 'duty'; and the Malikis view it as an emulation of the prophetic Sunnah. Each of the four schools offers its own characterization of the testimony.[88]

---

for blessings upon the Prophet, as well as to recite the recommended prayer of supplication. But as for supplications uttered in a communal prayer after the imam has finished praying, they are considered undesirable.

* * *

According to the Shafiis, one must remain in the final seated position long enough to: (1) recite the testimony, (2) pray for blessings on the Prophet, and (3) utter the first of the two final greetings of peace. The reason that it is obligatory to sit for this length of time is simply that it provides an 'environment' conducive to the fulfillment of these three obligatory utterances. In this respect, then, it is similar to the obligation to remain standing for as long as it takes to recite the *Fātiḥah*. As for sitting longer than this (for example, long enough to utter prayers of supplication and the second greeting of peace), this is simply recommended.

* * *

As for the Hanbalis, they hold simply that one must remain seated long enough to recite the testimony and to utter the two greetings of peace.

88. The Hanafis use the following version of the testimony: "Greetings to God, prayers, and good things! May peace be upon you, O Prophet, and God's mercy and blessings. May peace be upon us and upon God's righteous servants. I bear witness that there is no god but God, and I bear witness that Muḥammad is God's Servant and Messenger." (*al-taḥiyyāt lillāh wal-ṣalawāt wal-ṭayyibāt. Al-salāmu 'alayka ayyuhā al-nabī wa raḥmat Allāhi wa barakātuhu. Al-salāmu 'alaynā wa 'alā 'ibād Allāhi al-ṣāliḥīn. Ashhadu an lā ilāha illā Allāh, wa ashhadu anna Muḥammadan 'abduhu wa rasūluhu.*) This is the version received through 'Abdullah Ibn Mas'ūd, which is preferable to the version passed down by Ibn 'Abbās, may God be pleased with them both.

* * *

The version of the testimony adopted by the Malikis is as follows: "Greetings to God—blessed greetings without blemish! Acceptable prayers to God! May peace be upon you, O Prophet, and God's mercy and blessings. May peace be upon us and upon God's righteous servants. I bear witness that there is no god but God alone, who has no partner, and I bear witness that Muḥammad is God's servant and messenger." (Arabic: *Al-taḥiyyāt lillāh, al-zākiyāt lillāh, al-ṭayyibāt al-ṣalawātu lillāh. Al-salāmu 'alayka ayyuhā al-nabī wa raḥmat Allāhi wa barakātuhu. Al-salāmu 'alaynā wa 'alā 'ibād Allāhi al-ṣāliḥīn. Ashhadu an lā ilāha illā Allāh waḥdahu lā sharīka lahu, wa ashhadu anna Muḥammadan 'abduhu wa rasūluhu.*) The use of this particular version is merely recommended; hence, if someone uses another version, he or she will still have emulated the prophetic Sunnah.

* * *

The wording of the testimony adopted by the Shafiis is as follows: "Blessed greetings and acceptable prayers to God! May peace be upon you, O Prophet, and God's mercy and blessings. May peace be upon us and upon God's righteous servants. I bear witness that there is no god but God, and I bear witness that our master, Muḥammad, is God's messenger." (Arabic: *Al-taḥiyyāt al-mubārakāt al-ṣalawāt al-ṭayyibāt lillāh. Al-salāmu 'alayka ayyuhā al-nabī wa raḥmat Allāhi wa barakātuhu. Al-salāmu 'alaynā wa 'alā 'ibād Allāh al-ṣāliḥīn. Ashhadu an lā ilāha illā Allāh, wa ashhadu anna sayyidanā Muḥammadan rasūl Allāh.*) The Shafiis hold that in order to fulfill what is obligatory in this regard it is sufficient to say, "Greetings to God! May peace be upon you, O Prophet, and God's mercy and blessings. May peace be upon us and upon God's righteous servants. I bear witness that there is no god but God, and I bear witness that our master, Muḥammad, is God's messenger." However, it is closer to the ideal to use the first, longer formula.

In addition, the Shafiis stipulate a number of conditions for the validity of the obligatory testimony: (1) It must be expressed in Arabic if one is able to do so. (2) It must be spoken loudly enough that one can hear himself or herself (provided that there is nothing to prevent this, such as noise, deafness, etc.). (3) One should order the words in such a way that they retain their original meaning. Thus, if someone intentionally changes the order of the words in such a way that their meaning is altered, his or her prayer will be invalid; if the change was unintentional, however, no harm is done.

As for the prayer for blessings upon the Prophet following the final testimony, the Shafiis hold that it is a pillar of prayer in its own right and that the minimum one may say in fulfillment of this pillar is, "O God, send down your blessings upon Muḥammad (or, the Prophet)." (Arabic: *Allāhumma, ṣalli 'alā Muḥammad [aw al-nabī].*)

From the foregoing it may be seen that the utterance of at least part of this formula is obligatory in the view of the Shafiis. This contrasts with the ruling of the Malikis, who hold that it is simply an emulation of the prophetic Sunnah; hence, if someone remains seated at the end of his or her prayer long enough to utter these words yet without actually saying anything, his or her prayer will still be valid (though the Malikis view this practice as undesirable). As for the Hanafis, they maintain that if someone omits the testimony, his or her prayer will be valid, but such an omission is undesirable to the point of being forbidden.

* * *

According to the Hanbalis, the wording to be used for the final testimony is as follows: "Greetings to God, prayers, and good things! May peace be upon you, O Prophet, and God's mercy and blessings. May peace be upon us, and upon God's righteous servants. I bear witness that there is no god but God alone, who has no partner, and I bear witness that Muḥammad is God's Servant and Messenger. O God, send Your blessings down upon Muḥammad." (Arabic: *Al-taḥiyyāt lillāh wal-ṣalawāt wal-ṭayyibāt. Al-salāmu 'alayka ayyuhā al-nabī wa raḥmat Allāhi wa barakātuhu. Al-salāmu 'alaynā wa 'alā 'ibād Allāhi al-ṣāliḥīn. Ashhadu an lā ilāha illā Allāh waḥdahu lā sharīka lahu, wa ashhadu anna Muḥammadan 'abduhu wa rasūluhu. Allāhumma, ṣalli 'alā Muḥammad.*) However, the prayer for blessings on the Prophet does not have to be worded in this particular way.

The thirteenth obligation: the greeting of peace

The fourteenth obligation: maintaining the order of the pillars

The Shafiis, the Hanbalis, and the Malikis all agree that in order to terminate one's prayer it is necessary to utter the word, 'Peace' (*al-salām*) and that if one fails to do so, the prayer will be invalid. As for the Hanafis, they hold that one may terminate one's prayer in a valid sense by doing anything which is inconsistent with praying, including even some event that invalidates one's ablutions. However, they do grant that utterance of the word *al-salām* is a 'duty'. As for the form to be taken by this final greeting of peace, each school offers its own detailed ruling in this regard.[89]

As for the maintenance of a particular order in the performance of the various pillars of prayer—for example, standing before bowing, bowing before prostrating, etc.—it is necessary for prayer's validity. Thus, it is an agreed upon principle that if someone prostrated before bowing, bowed before standing and the like, his or her prayer would be invalid. The Hanafis refer to this requirement not as an obligation, but as a condition for the validity of prayer; however, as we have seen, this distinction makes no material difference. We have also seen that, in contrast to the other three schools, the Hanafis do not classify recitation of the *Fātiḥah* as a pillar of prayer; consequently, the *Fātiḥah* has a special ruling associated with it in connection with the order in which the pillars are to be performed.[90]

---

89. According to the Hanafis, it is not obligatory to terminate a ritual prayer with the word, 'peace' (*al-salām*), although they do classify it as a duty. They base this ruling on the fact that when the Prophet was teaching Ibn Mas'ūd about the testimony, he said to him, "Once you have said this, you have completed your prayer. If you wish, you may get up, and if you wish, you may remain seated." The Hanafis note in his regard that the Prophet did not instruct Ibn Mas'ūd to terminate his prayer with the word, 'peace'. Hence, the Hanafis hold that one may legitimately terminate a ritual prayer without the word 'peace', or with the word 'peace' alone unaccompanied by the phrase "be upon you." Hence, if someone terminates his or her prayer without any greeting of peace—even if it is terminated by an occurrence of *ḥadath*—the prayer will still be valid. However, the person concerned will be guilty of wrongdoing until, or unless, he or she repeats the prayer in which this omission took place.

* * *

According to the Hanbalis, ritual prayer must be terminated with a repetition of the phrase, "May peace and the mercy of God be upon you" (*Al-salāmu 'alaykum wa raḥmat Allāh*). If either the words or their order is modified, the person's prayer will be invalidated.

* * *

According to the Shafiis, the order of the words in this phrase is not essential. Hence, someone might say, "Upon you be peace" (*'alaykum al-salām*), and his or her prayer would still be valid, although such a modification is considered undesirable.

* * *

The fifteenth obligation of prayer: sitting upright between the two prostrations

It is agreed upon by the Shafiis, the Malikis and the Hanbalis that sitting upright between every two prostrations is obligatory in ritual prayer. Hence, if someone prostrates once, then raises his head without actually sitting up, then prostrates a second time, his prayer will not be valid. However, the Hanafis hold that sitting upright between every two prostrations is not obligatory.[91] Those who maintain the necessity of sitting upright between each pair of prostrations—as well as the necessity of other practices discussed thus far—base their position on a prophetic hadith narrated by both al-Bukhārī and Muslim according to which, when the Prophet once saw a man praying an incomplete prayer, he taught him how to pray correctly, saying, "When you enter ritual prayer, first utter praises to God, then recite whatever words from the Qur'ān you are able to recite without difficulty (while some versions read, "Recite the 'mother of the Qur'an'" [an expression referring to the *Fātiḥah*]). After this, make a bow and remain there until the various parts of your body have 'settled' into position. Rise after this to a fully upright posture, then prostrate and remain in this position until you have 'settled' into it. Then rise again to a fully upright position. Moreover, do these things every time you pray."

As we have seen, the Hanafis differ with the other three schools' view that sitting upright between the two prostrations and reciting the *Fātiḥah* are obligatory parts of ritual prayer. Specifically, they argue that this prophetic hadith provides no evidence that these actions are obligatory; rather, they say, it simply indicates that

---

As for the Malikis, they hold that the exact phrase, *Al-salāmu 'alaykum* is required for the valid termination of ritual prayer, with no modification in either the words or their order. This obligation is fulfilled by uttering this phrase only once, rather than twice; moreover, it is agreed that this requirement is dropped entirely for those who are unable to speak for some reason.

90. The Hanafis view the maintenance of the above order for the pillars of prayer not as an obligation, but as a condition for prayer's validity. In either case, of course, it remains a necessity. However, they hold that if someone bows before standing up, then prostrates and stands up again, the bow he or she performed will not count [since it was out of the proper order]. If, after the negation of the first bow, this person then bows again and prostrates, and if the original bowing out of order was unintentional, the *rak'ah* will be counted, but he or she must perform a prostration of forgetfulness. However, if it was intentional, his or her prayer will be invalid. On the other hand, if someone stands up without doing any Qur'anic recitation, then bows, his or her prayer will be valid, since Qur'anic recitation is not obligatory in all *rak'ahs*, but rather, in only two of them. Hence, if someone performs two *rak'ahs* without Qur'anic recitation, he or she must follow the correct order in the remaining two *rak'ahs*.

91. Some hold that this practice is a 'duty'—which is what the evidence indicates—while others maintain that it is simply an emulation of the Sunnah which has not been emphatically enjoined.

the Prophet wished to teach this man how to perform a complete prayer that included prayer's obligations, 'duties', and Sunnah-based practices. Since the situation did not allow for an exhaustive explanation, he made no mention of such things as intention and the final 'sitting' despite the fact these are both agreed to be obligatory. Similarly, the hadith makes no mention of the final testimony, which some of the schools view as obligatory, nor of many other parts of ritual prayer, such as utterance of the words, "I seek refuge in God from the accursed Satan", and others.

What all of this suggests [according to the Hanafis] is that the Prophet's purpose here was simply to teach the man how to perform ritual prayer on the practical level such that, at some future time, he could learn which of the actions involved in prayer are obligatory, which of them are 'duty', and which are based on the prophetic Sunnah. As for the other three schools, they reply to this by saying that the mere fact that the Prophet instructed the man to engage in these actions is evidence of their necessity. As for the other obligatory actions involved in prayer, he did not mention them simply because the man was already performing them.

This latter view is acceptable if there is evidence to support it in the hadith. However, where is the evidence? Be that as it may, it is more prudent to adopt this point of view (that is, the view supported by the Shafiis, the Malikis and the Hanbalis), especially given the fact that according to the Hanafis, these actions are 'duty'—in other words, although ritual prayer is valid without them, the person who omits them will nevertheless be guilty of wrongdoing.

The 'Duties' of Ritual Prayer

As we have mentioned on more than one occasion, the Malikis and the Shafiis agree that the terms *wājib* (duty) and *farḍ* (obligation) refer to the same thing, and that there is no distinction between them except in the context of the greater pilgrimage to Mecca, where an obligation is something which, if it is omitted, causes one's pilgrimage to be invalidated, whereas it is not invalidated by the omission of an act classified as a duty, although someone who omits a duty is required to sacrifice an animal in compensation for the omission. Consequently, neither the Malikis nor the Shafiis list duties in connection with prayer; rather, acts associated with prayer are either obligations or acts based on the prophetic Sunnah. (Obligations of prayer have been discussed already, while Sunnah-based acts associated with prayer will be discussed below.) For a treatment of the 'duties' associated with prayer according to the Hanafis and the Hanbalis, see the footnote below.[92]

---

92. As we have seen, the Hanafis classify some acts as 'duties', the omission of which does not invalidate prayer. If a 'duty' is omitted unintentionally, one should perform a prostration of forgetfulness after the final greeting of peace. If it is omitted intentionally, the person praying must repeat the prayer; if he or she does not repeat it, the original prayer will remain valid, but the person concerned will be guilty of wrongdoing. The Hanafis base their ruling that certain acts are to be classified as 'duties' on the fact that the Prophet performed such acts on a regular basis.

The Hanafis list the following seventeen actions as 'duties' associated with ritual prayer:

(1) Recitation of the *Fātiḥah* in all *rak'ahs* of voluntary prayers, and in the first two *rak'ahs* of obligatory prayers; the recitation of the *Fātiḥah* should precede the recitation of some other passage from the Qur'ān, and if this order is reversed, the person praying should perform the prostration of forgetfulness.

(2) Following the *Fātiḥah* with the recitation of some other passage from the Qur'ān in all *rak'ahs* of voluntary prayers and the *witr* prayer, as well as the first two *rak'ahs* of each obligatory prayer. In order to fulfill one's 'duty' in this regard, it is sufficient to recite one of the shorter surahs of the Qur'ān or its equivalent, such as three short verses or one long verse. The three short verses could be something like the Arabic, *thumma naẓara, thumma 'abasa wa basara, thumma adbara w'astakbar* (English, " ...and then he looks [around for new arguments], and then he frowns and glares, and in the end he turns his back [on Our message], and glories in his arrogance" (Qur'ān 74:21-23). This passage consists of ten Arabic words, or 30 letters of the alphabet, counting one with a *shaddah* over it as two letters. Hence, if someone recited this much of a single verse in a given *rak'ah*, it would be sufficient for the fulfillment of his or her 'duty'. For example, it would be enough to recite the following words from the Throne Verse: *Allāhu, lā ilāha illā huwā, al-ḥayy al-qayyūm. Lā ta'khudhuhu sinatun wa lā nawm...* (English, "God—there is no deity save Him, the Ever-Living, the Self-Sufficient Fount of All Being. Neither slumber overtakes Him, nor sleep" (2:255).

(3) Not performing more than the required number of each type of action, for example, by prostrating more than twice in a single *rak'ah*. If someone does this accidentally, the extra prostration will not be counted, and the person praying should perform a prostration of forgetfulness.

(4) Practicing *ṭuma'nīnah* in all basic pillars, such as bowing, prostrating, and the like. This involves allowing one's limbs to remain still until all parts of the body are 'settled' into place, so to speak, and maintaining this stillness for as long as it takes to utter the words, *Subḥan Allāh* at least once.

(5) Performing the first 'sitting' in all prayers, both obligatory and voluntary.

(6) Recitation of the testimony passed down by Ibn Mas'ūd. Following this, one must rise immediately to perform the third *rak'ah*. If someone accidentally goes on to recite the prayer for the Prophet, he or she should perform the prostration of forgetfulness [at the end of the prayer]; if this was intentional, the prayer should be repeated, even though if it is not repeated, it will remain valid.

(7) Utterance of the final greeting of peace twice at the conclusion of the prayer.

(8) Recitation of what is referred to as *du'ā' al-qunūt*, or "the prayer of obedience" following the recitation of the *Fātiḥah* and some other passage from the Qur'ān in the third *rak'ah* of the *witr*. The words of this prayer are as follows: "O God, guide me with those You have guided, grant me wholeness with those to whom You have granted wholeness, watch over me with those You have watched over, bless me in that which You have given, and protect me from the evil of what You have decreed, for You alone are the One who decrees and disposes. No one to whom You grant your succor will be disgraced, nor will anyone whom You oppose enjoy honor and glory. Blessed are You, O Lord, and exalted!" (*Allāhumma ihdinī fī man hadayt, wa 'āfinī fī man 'āfayt, wa tawwalanī fī man tawwallayt, wa bārik lī fī mā*

a'ṭayt, wa qinī sharra mā qaḍayt. Fa'innak taqḍī wa lā yuqḍā 'alayka, wa innahu lā yudhallu man wālayt, wa lā ya'izzu man 'ādayt. Tabārakta rabbanā wa ta'ālayt.)

(9) Uttering the words, *Allāh akbar* three times in each *rak'ah* of the prayers performed on the Day of Fastbreaking and the Day of Sacrifice (details concerning which will be discussed in a later section).

(10) Recitation aloud by the imam in the following prayers: (a) the dawn prayer; (b) the prayers performed on the Day of Fastbreaking and the Day of Sacrifice; (c) the Friday prayer; (d) the *tarāwīḥ* prayers; (e) the *witr* during Ramaḍān; and (f) the first two *rak'ahs* of the sundown and evening prayers. Someone who is praying alone has a choice between reciting silently and reciting aloud in all prayers; however, it is preferable for one to recite aloud in those situations where the imam should recite aloud, and to recite silently in those situations where the imam should recite silently.

(11) Silent recitation—for both the imam and someone praying alone—in the following prayers: (a) voluntary prayers performed during the day; (b) the obligatory noon and mid-afternoon prayers; (c) the third *rak'ah* of the sundown prayer; (d) the last two *rak'ahs* of the evening prayer; (e) the solar and lunar eclipse prayers; and (f) the prayer for rain.

(12) Not reciting anything at all when one is being led in prayer and the imam is standing up.

(13) Placing one's nose on the ground or floor along with the forehead when prostrating.

(14) Opening prayer with the words, *Allāh akbar* unless one is unable to do so or does not pronounce it well, in which case one may open it with one of the names of God.

(15) Uttering *takbīrat al-iḥrām* associated with bowing during the second *rak'ah* of the prayers for the Day of Fastbreaking and the Day of Sacrifice; this is classified as a 'duty' due to its association with the other instances of *takbīrat al-iḥrām* in the holiday prayers and which are likewise classified as 'duties'.

(16) Following the imam in movements which, [although the person led in prayer might not be accustomed to them], are subject to a variety of interpretations. (A further discussion of this topic is found in the section on *imāmah*, or prayer leadership.)

(17) Rising from each bow, and allowing the various parts of one's body to 'settle' into position after bowing, prostrating, and standing up.

* * *

According to the Hanbalis, a 'duty' of prayer is less binding than an obligation; hence, if it is omitted inadvertently or out of ignorance, one's prayer is not invalidated, although one should perform the prostration of forgetfulness at the prayer's conclusion; if it is omitted knowingly and deliberately, however, one's prayer is invalidated. The Hanbalis list the following eight 'duties' of prayer: (1) Including all the utterances of *Allāh akbar* in ritual prayer; as for the utterance of *Allāh akbar* in *takbīrat al-iḥrām*, it is obligatory, while the *Allāh akbar* uttered during a bow by someone who arrives late for a communal prayer and begins following the imam in a bowing position is an emulation of the prophetic Sunnah. (2) Utterance of the words, *sami'a Allāhu li man ḥamidah* ("God hears those who praise Him") by both the imam and those who pray alone. (3) Utterance of the words, *rabbanā wa laka al-ḥamd* ("Our Lord, and to You praise belongs") by everyone who prays. As for when one is to utter the words *Allāhu akbar* (other than at the beginning of one's prayer) and the phrases *sami'a Allāhu li man ḥamidah* and *rabbanā wa laka al-ḥamd*, they are only to be spoken during the transitions between one pillar of prayer and another. (4) Saying, *Subḥān rabbī al-'aẓīm* ("Glory be to my great Lord") once while bowing. (5) Saying, *Subḥān rabbī al-a'lā* ("Glory be to my Lord most exalted") once while prostrating. (6) Saying, *Rabbī ighfir lī* ("My Lord, forgive me") once while seated between the two prostrations of each *rak'ah*. (7) Reciting the first part of the testimony, that is, the entire testimony except for the prayer for blessings on the Prophet. (8) Remaining seated while uttering the testimony. However, if someone's imam absentmindedly gets up right away for the third *rak'ah* rather than reciting the testimony, the person being led in prayer should simply follow his or her imam, and the requirement relating to the testimony and remaining seated for it is dropped.

Sunnah-based Practices Associated with Ritual Prayer

In discussing the Sunnah-based practices associated with ritual prayer, we shall deal with the following subtopics: (1) the definition of 'Sunnah', (2) an enumeration of the Sunnah-based practices included in the act of ritual prayer, with a separate listing for each of the four schools, (3) an explanation of those practices which require clarification, and (4) a presentation of the Sunnah-based practices which, though associated with ritual prayer, are not integral parts of it.

The definition of 'Sunnah'

As noted earlier, the Hanbalis and the Shafiis hold that the terms 'Sunnah', 'recommended', 'desirable', and 'voluntary' all refer to the same reality, namely, an action which an accountable Muslim will be rewarded for performing, but whose omission merits no blame. Hence, If someone omits all or some of the Sunnah-based practices associated with prayer, God will not take him or her to task for this; at the same time, however, he or she will be deprived of the reward which such actions might have entailed. The Malikis agree with this view; however, they draw a distinction between 'Sunnah' and other voluntary practices.

Muslims must never make light of Sunnah-based practices related to prayer. After all, the whole purpose of ritual prayer is to draw near to God the Creator. This act of drawing near to the Divine is of undoubted benefit, since it involves fleeing from torment and seeking out the enjoyment of God's grace and blessings. This being the case, it would make no sense for us to disregard any Sunnah-based practice, since such neglect deprives us of the reward due to those who pursue such practices. Moreover, this deprivation entails a punishment which no reasonable person can fail to perceive, namely, a diminishment of the divine grace and blessings which we will be able to enjoy. Hence, it is of the greatest importance that we be concerned to perform all those actions which the Lawgiver has instructed us to perform, regardless of whether they are obligatory or simply emulations of the prophetic Sunnah. Someone might ask in this regard: Then why has the Lawgiver made some actions binding obligations, but not others? The answer to this question is that God Almighty desires to lighten the burden borne by His servants and to give them a choice concerning whether to perform certain actions, since in this way, He can reward them all the more abundantly when they do choose to pursue such actions. If we choose of our own accord to neglect them, we will be deprived of the reward that their performance would have brought, but without meriting any sort of punishment. This, then, is one of the virtues of the Islamic law, which spares us undue hardship in the fulfillment of what God requires, while at the same time awakening our desire for divine reward.

An enumeration of the Sunnah-based practices related to prayer

In order to help readers commit these points to memory, we shall list the Sunnah-based practices associated with ritual prayer according to each of the four schools.[93]

---

93. The Hanafis list the following Sunnah-based practices in connection with ritual prayer:

1) Raising the hands while uttering *takbīrat al-iḥrām* such that, for a man or a bondwoman, they are next to one's ears while for a free woman, they are next to her shoulders.

2) Leaving one's fingers in a natural position, that is, neither parting them nor closing them tightly together. This does not apply, however, when bowing, as will be seen below.

3) For the man, placing the right hand over the left and holding them under his navel, and for the woman, placing her hands on her chest.

4) Opening prayer with the "prayer of praise" (*al-thanā'*), the words to which are as follows: "Glory be to You, O God, and praise! May Your name be blessed and Your majesty exalted! There is no god but You!" (*Subḥānuk Allāhumma wa biḥamdika, wa tabārak ismuk wa ta'ālā jadduk wa lā ilāha ghayruk*)

5) Uttering the words, "I seek refuge in God from the accursed Satan" (*a'ūdhu billāhi min al-shayṭān al-rajīm*) before commencing any Qur'anic recitation.

6) Silently uttering the words, "In the name of God, the Most Gracious, the Most Merciful" (*bismillāh al-raḥmān al-raḥīm*) at the beginning of each *rak'ah* before reciting the *Fātiḥah*.

7) Saying the word, "Amen" (*āmīn*).

8) Uttering the words, "Our Lord, to You praise belongs" (*Rabbanā wa laka al-ḥamd*).

9) Reciting the prayer of praise and uttering the words *Āmīn* and *rabbanā wa laka al-ḥamd* silently.

10) Remaining in a still, upright position from the beginning to the end of *takbīrat al-iḥrām*.

11) For the imam, uttering the words *Allāhu akbar, sami'a Allāhu li man ḥamidah* and *rabbanā wa laka al-ḥamd* aloud.

12) When standing, holding one's feet at least one foot apart.

13) Making certain that one's Qur'anic recitation is taken from the final seventh of the Qur'ān [which begins with Surat 'Qāf'].

14) Uttering the words *Allāhu akbar* when bowing and prostrating.

15) Uttering the words *subḥān rabbī al-'aẓīm* three times when bowing.

16) Uttering the words *subḥān rabbī al-a'lā* three times when prostrating.

17) Placing one's hands on one's knees when bowing.

18) For the man, spreading one's fingers while placing the hands on the knees during a bow.

19) Keeping one's legs and back straight, and holding one's head on a level with one's buttocks while bowing.

20) Rising to a full standing position after bowing.

21) Rising to a fully upright sitting posture after prostrating.

22) When going down into a prostration, placing first one's hands, then one's knees, then one's face on the floor or ground; and when rising from a prostration, following the reverse order.

23) When prostrating, holding one's hands parallel either with one's head or one's shoulders.

24) During a man's prostration: a) keeping one's abdomen away from one's thighs, b) holding one's elbows away from one's sides, and c) keeping one's arms off the ground or floor.

25) During a woman's prostration, allowing her abdomen to come in contact with her thighs.

26) Sitting up between the two prostrations of each *rak'ah.*

27) Placing one's hands on one's thighs while sitting between prostrations and reciting the testimony.

28) When sitting for the recitation of the testimony, for the man to sit with his calves and feet under his thighs while holding the right foot perpendicular to the floor or ground and pointing the toes of the right foot toward the *qiblah.*

29) For the woman to sit on her buttocks with her right thigh over her left and her left foot extending out from underneath her right hip.

30) Pointing with one's index finger when reciting the words, "I bear witness that there is no god but God, and I bear witness that Muḥammad is God's Servant and Messenger."

31) Reciting the *Fātiḥah* not only in the first two *rak'ahs*, but in subsequent *rak'ahs* as well.

32) Praying for blessings on the Prophet during the final 'sitting'.

33) Following one's prayer for blessings on the Prophet with supplications using words similar to those in the Qur'ān and the Sunnah.

34) Turning to one's right, then to one's left when uttering the concluding greetings of peace.

35) For the imam leading a prayer to address his final greetings of peace to those praying behind him, to the guardian angels, and to the righteous *jinn*, or unseen beings.

36) For someone being led in prayer to address the final greetings of peace to his or her imam if the imam is to the person's right or left. If the imam is directly in front of the person praying, then he or she should address these greetings to the imam, to the other people praying in the same place, to the guardian angels, and to the righteous *jinn.*

37) For someone who is praying alone to address the final greetings of peace to the angels only.

38) To utter the final greetings of peace in a low voice.

39) For someone who arrived late for a communal prayer to wait until the imam has finished his second greeting of peace in order to make certain that he [the imam] does not need to perform a prostration of forgetfulness.

* * *

The Malikis list the following 14 Sunnah-based practices connected with ritual prayer: (1) Following the recitation of the *Fātiḥah* with some other passage of the

Qur'ān in the first two *rak'ahs* of each obligatory prayer, provided that sufficient time remains in the time period for the prayer concerned. (2) Standing up for Qur'anic recitation when performing obligatory prayers. (3) Reciting aloud in those situations in which recitation should be aloud. (4) Reciting silently in those situations in which, based on our discussion above, recitation should be silent. (5) Utterance of all the instances of *Allāhu akbar* other than *takbīrat al-iḥrām*, the latter of which is obligatory. (6) Uttering every instance of the words, *sami'a Allāhu li man ḥamidah*. (7) Uttering every instance of the testimony. (8) Adopting a seated position every time one utters the testimony. (9) Praying for blessings on the Prophet following the final testimony. (10) When prostrating, placing one's knees and the balls of one's feet on the floor or ground. (11) For someone being led in prayer to return the imam's greeting of peace and to extend a similar greeting to the person on his left if there is someone to his left who participated with him in praying at least one *rak'ah* with the imam. (12) Uttering the concluding greeting of peace aloud. (13) For the person being led in prayer to listen to the imam when he is reciting aloud. (14) Allowing one's limbs to 'rest' in position (be it a bow, a prostration, etc.)—beyond what is actually required (*ṭuma'nīnah*).

* * *

The Shafiis divide the Sunnah-based practices associated with prayer into two categories. The first category they refer to as 'forms' (*al-hay'āt*), and the second they term 'parts' (*al-ab'āḍ*). They do not specify a particular number of 'forms'; rather, they say that everything which is neither a pillar of prayer nor part of such a pillar is to be classified as a 'form'. With regard to the Sunnah-based practices classified as 'parts' of prayer, a list of which follows, the Shafiis hold that if someone omits one of them deliberately, he or she should perform a prostration of forgetfulness. (1) Recitation of the prayer of obedience when standing up during the last *rak'ah* of the dawn prayer and when standing up for the *witr* prayer during the second half of Ramaḍān. As for the recitation of the prayer of obedience when one has suffered some tragedy or trial, but not in the context of one of the prayers mentioned here, it is not classified as a 'part' even though it is an emulation of the Sunnah. (2) Standing for the recitation of the prayer of obedience. (3) Following the prayer of obedience with a prayer for blessings on the Prophet. (4) Standing up for the prayer for blessings on the Prophet. (5) Following this prayer with a greeting of peace to the Prophet. (6) Standing up for the greeting of peace to the Prophet. (7) Praying for blessings on the Prophet's family. (8) Standing up for the prayer for blessings on the Prophet's family. (9) Praying for blessings on the Prophet's Companions. (10) Standing up for the prayer for blessings on the Prophet's Companions. (11) Addressing a further greeting of peace to the Prophet. (12) Standing up for this additional greeting. (13) Addressing a greeting of peace to the Companions. (14) Standing up for this greeting. (15) Reciting the first testimony in prayers consisting of three or four *rak'ahs*. (16) Sitting for this testimony. (17) Following this testimony with a prayer for blessings on the Prophet. (18) Sitting for this prayer. (19) Following the final testimony with a prayer for blessings on the Prophet's family. (20) Sitting for the final testimony.

These, then, are the Sunnah-based practices of prayer which the Shafiis classify as 'parts', and which they liken to the pillars of prayer, the unintentional omission of any of which necessitates that it be repeated and that one perform a prostration of forgetfulness. As for the other prayer-related practices belonging to the Sunnah and which the Shafiis refer to as 'forms', they include the following:

(1) For a man to say, *subḥān Allāh,* if something occurs that he wants to draw others' attention to. However, he must not intend simply to alert others [that is, he must also intend the meaning of the words themselves, namely, "Glory be to God"), since otherwise, his prayer will be invalidated.

(2) For a woman who wishes to alert others to something to clap her hands. However, her intention must not be mere amusement, but to announce something. It is permissible for her to clap more than three times in close succession, but she must hold her hands close together while clapping; otherwise, her prayer will be invalidated.

(3) To maintain an attitude of humble reverence, presence of heart and physical calm throughout prayer, constantly aware that one is in the presence of the Divine and that the Divine sees us as we pray.

(4) For those who are praying from a standing position to remain seated briefly between the first and second *rak'ahs* and between the third and fourth *rak'ahs* [since one already remains sitting between the second and third *rak'ahs* in order to recite the testimony]. It is consistent with the prophetic Sunnah to remain seated long enough for the parts of one's body to 'settle' into position (*ṭuma'nīnah*), and it is acceptable to remain in this position longer [between *rak'ahs*] than one does between the two prostrations. This action is to be performed by someone being led in prayer even if the imam does not do so.

(5) To intend to terminate one's prayer from the time one commences the first of the two final greetings of peace. If one's intention precedes this, one's prayer will be invalid, whereas if one's intention is present during or after this first greeting of peace, one's prayer will still be valid, but one will not have emulated the Sunnah.

(6) To place one's right palm over the back of one's left hand while holding onto the left wrist and part of the left forearm. This is the recognized practice among the Shafiis [while standing during prayer – t.n.], although if someone prays with his hands to his sides instead (as the Malikis do), this is acceptable as well. The Shafiis consider the former position to be more desirable, however, since it symbolizes the act of 'holding onto one's heart', as it were. After all, when we fear for something, we tend to protect it with our hands.

(7) To follow *takbīrat al-iḥrām* with a recitation of the prayer of commencement (*du'ā' al-iftitāḥ*), the words to which are as follows: "I turn my face with a pure heart and in full surrender toward the One who created the heavens and the earth, and I am not among those who associate created beings with the Divine. My prayer, my devotion, my life and my death belong to God, the Sustainer of the worlds, who has no partner. Thus have I been commanded, and I am among those who surrender themselves to God." (*Wajjahtu wajhī lilladhī faṭara al-samawāti wal-arḍa ḥanīfan musliman, wa mā anā min al-mushrikīn. Inna ṣalāti wa naskī wa maḥyāyā wa mamātī lillāhi rabb al-'ālamīn, lā sharīka lah. Wa bi dhalika umirtu*

wa anā min al-muslimīn.) The utterance of this prayer is desirable in both obligatory and voluntary prayers for those praying alone, for the imam, and for those being led in communal prayer even if their imam has already begun reciting the *Fātiḥah*. However, one should only recite this prayer given the following five conditions: 1—That the prayer being performed not be the funeral prayer, in which case one should go directly to the prayer for divine protection (*a'ūdhu billāhi min al-shayṭān al-rajīm*). 2—That one not have reason to fear that the time for the performance of the prayer concerned is about to run out. For example, if there is just enough time left to perform one *rak'ah* without reciting this prayer, one should not recite it. 3—That someone being led in communal prayer not have reason to fear that he or she might miss part of the *Fātiḥah*. 4—That the person praying in community not have joined the imam while the imam was pausing in a standing position. 5—That one not have already begun reciting the prayer for protection and the *Fātiḥah*. Once one has begun one of these, whether intentionally or absentmindedly, he or she should not go back to recite the prayer of commencement.

(8) To pray for divine protection against evil during each *rak'ah*; specifically, one should utter the prayer for divine protection between the prayer of commencement and one's recitation of the *Fātiḥah*. Such a prayer for protection may consist of any words which convey a plea to God for protection from evil; however, it is preferable to say, "I seek refuge in God from the accursed Satan" (*a'ūdhu billāhi min al-shayṭān al-rajīm*), while the Sunnah also includes the addition of the words, "the One who hears and knows all" to the description of God (by saying, "I seek refuge in God, the One who hears and knows all, from the accursed Satan" (*a'ūdhu billāh al-samī' al-'alīm min al-shayṭān al-rajīm*).

(9) To do Qur'anic recitation aloud if one is leading others in prayer or praying alone. As for those being led in communal prayer, the Sunnah dictates that they should recite silently. In the case of a woman or a hermaphrodite, it is a Sunnah-based practice for them to recite aloud unless a 'strange' person is present and able to hear their voices, in which case they should recite silently. According to the Shafiis, silent recitation involves reciting in a voice which is low enough that we can hear ourselves, but others cannot hear us. Moreover, one should recite aloud only in the first two *rak'ahs* of any given prayer when praying alone. As for those who arrive late for a communal prayer, the relevant ruling will be mentioned below.

(10) To say *Āmīn* ('Amen') after the recitation of the *Fātiḥah*. If the person praying goes ahead and bows or begins reciting some other passage from the Qur'ān without first saying, *Āmīn*, even if this is done absentmindedly, he or she should simply leave the *Āmīn* unsaid. However, an exception to this ruling is made if the person goes on to say, *Rabbī, ighfir lī* ("My Lord, forgive me"), since the Prophet used to say the *Āmīn* after this. Moreover, if someone recites the *Fātiḥah* and then remains silent for a few moments, the *Āmīn* should still be said after this. In the case of someone being led in prayer, it is an emulation of the prophetic Sunnah to say *Āmīn* together with the imam if the prayer is being performed aloud; otherwise, it is not. If someone being led in a prayer being performed aloud does not say *Āmīn*, or if he or she delays the *Āmīn* until past its recommended time—namely, together with the imam—he or she should say it alone. This ruling is based on the words of the Prophet, "When the imam says *Āmīn*, you also say *Āmīn*," which means that

once it is time for the imam to say *Āmīn*, all those being led in prayer should say it even if the imam does not do so, or even if he delays it past its usual time.

(11) To recite some passage from the Qur'ān following the *Fātiḥah*. This passage may be less than a complete surah, although according to the Shafiis, a complete surah is preferable (the minimum equivalent of a surah being three verses). In some cases, of course, a complete surah of the Qur'ān amounts to less than this or that long verse. For example, the recitation of Surah 2:285, which begins, "The Apostle, and the believers with him, believe in what has been bestowed upon him from on high by his Sustainer..." (*āmana al-rasūlu bi mā unzila ilayhi min rabbihi wal-mu'minūn...*) is preferable to the recitation of an entire surah such as Surah 106 (Quraysh), Surah 105 (Al-Fīl) or Surah 112 (Al-Ikhlaṣ), since the verse mentioned is longer than any of these entire surahs. This is the view approved by the majority of Shafiis; however, some of them hold that a short surah is still preferable to part of a surah [even if the 'part' would have been longer]. In general, then, the Shafiis consider it preferable to recite more rather than less, and they recommend that one make the Qur'anic recitation following the *Fātiḥah* in the first *rak'ah* longer than that in the second. An exception to this is made, however, when the person praying is the prayer leader, or imam, and when there are numerous people being led in prayer in crowded conditions, such as the Friday prayer or the prayer for the Day of Fastbreaking or the Day of Sacrifice. In this case, it is an emulation of the prophetic Sunnah for the imam to make the Qur'anic recitation in the second *rak'ah* longer than that in the first in anticipation of the arrival of more people to join him in prayer. Lastly, the Shafiis hold that in order for the Sunnah to be fulfilled in this connection, such Qur'anic recitation must follow rather than precede the *Fātiḥah* regardless of whether one is the imam or someone praying alone. Thus, if someone recites a passage from the Qur'ān, then recites the *Fātiḥah* after this, the first passage recited will not be counted, and in order to fulfill the Sunnah, he or she must repeat it again after reciting the *Fātiḥah*.

(12) For the imam leading a prayer being performed aloud to remain silent after the *Fātiḥah* long enough to allow those being led in prayer to recite it after him. The ideal practice is for the imam to spend this silent time in inward supplication or recitation. The Shafiis also make mention of other silences which they consider desirable, but which are very brief. Referred to as "reverent pauses" (*saktāt laṭīfah*), they come in the following places in prayer: 1—Between *takbīrat al-iḥrām* and the prayer which begins, "I turn my face with a pure heart and in full surrender toward the One who created the heavens and the earth..." 2—Between this prayer and the utterance of the words, "I seek refuge in God from the accursed Satan" (*a'ūdhu billāh...*) or whatever other phrases one uses with the same meaning. 3—Between the aforementioned prayer for divine protection and the words, "In the name of God, the Most Gracious, the Most Merciful" (*bismillāh al-raḥmān al-raḥīm*). 4—Between the words, "In the name of God..." and the recitation of the *Fātiḥah*. 5—Between the *Fātiḥah* and the word *Āmīn*. 6—Between the word *Āmīn* and the recitation of some other passage from the Qur'ān. 7—Between the Qur'anic recitation and utterance of the words *Allāhu akbar* as one bows. If we add these pauses to the [longer] pause made by the imam after reciting the *Fātiḥah* [for the purpose of allowing those being led in prayer to recite the *Fātiḥah* after him], their number

comes to eight; however, the number generally recognized by the Shafiis is six. The reason for this is that they count pauses number 1 and number 2 above as a single pause; in addition, they count the pause by the imam and those being led in prayer between the *Fātiḥah* and the recitation of some other passage of the Qur'ān as a single pause.

(13) To utter *Allāhu akbar* when going down into a bow or a prostration. Such utterances of *Allāhu akbar*, which the Shafiis classify as part of the prophetic Sunnah, are to be drawn out until one is fully in the bowing or prostrating posture. Moreover, the imam should always utter these words aloud so that those who are being led in prayer can hear them; the same applies to someone who is a *muballigh* (a term which will be explained shortly).

(14) To say *sami'a Allaḥu li man ḥamidah* while lifting one's head after a bow. This applies equally to the imam, those being led in prayer, and those praying alone. The imam, however, should utter these words aloud, whereas those being led in prayer should utter them silently.

(15) To say *rabbanā wa laka al-ḥamd* as one finishes coming up into a standing position. This applies equally to the imam, those being led in prayer, and those praying alone. As for those who are praying from a sitting position, they should utter these words after sitting upright following a bow or prostration. However, it is an emulation of the prophetic Sunnah for the imam, those being led in prayer, and those praying alone to say *rabbanā wa laka al-ḥamd* silently even if the person being led in prayer is a *muballigh*; if someone does utter these words aloud, he or she is simply ignorant.

(16) To praise God when bowing by saying *subḥān rabbī al-'aẓīm* ("Glory be to my great Lord"). This is classified by the Shafiis as an emphatically enjoined Sunnah-based practice; there are even some who hold that those who consistently omit it are apostates. One should utter these words at least once in order to fulfill the Sunnah in a minimal fashion; however, if one wishes to fulfill it perfectly, one must utter them three times regardless of whether he is an imam, someone being led in prayer, or someone praying alone. If one is praying alone or leading a group of worshipers who are content to pray for a longer time, it is an emulation of the prophetic Sunnah to utter this phrase eleven times, but no more. In the case of those praying alone, it is an emulation of the Sunnah to utter the following prayer: "O God, to You do I bow, in You have I believed, and to You have I surrendered. May my hearing, my sight, my marrow, my bones, my nerves, my hair, and my skin all be in humble submission to You. All that my feet carry belongs to God, the Sustainer of the Worlds" (*Allāhumma, laka raka'tu wa bika āmantu wa laka aslamt. Khashi'a laka sam'ī wa baṣarī wa mukhkhī wa 'aẓamī wa 'aṣabī wa sha'rī wa basharī. Wa mā istallaqat bihi qadamī lillāhi rabb al-'ālamīn*). Similarly, it is an emulation of the Sunnah to utter this prayer while bowing if one is an imam leading a small number of people who are content to prolong their prayer.

(17) To utter praise to God while prostrating by saying *subḥān rabbī al-a'lā*. The minimum degree of the Sunnah is fulfilled by saying these words only once; however, in order to fulfill it more completely, one should say them three times, and if one wishes to emulate the Sunnah to the most perfect degree, one should say them eleven times, as when bowing. If the person praying is an imam leading a

small number of worshipers, it is also an emulation of the Sunnah to follow these words of praise with, "O God, to You have I prostrated, in You have I believed, and to You have I surrendered. I touch my face to the ground in awe of the One who created and formed it, who opened up my hearing and my sight. Blessed be God, the Best of all creators" (*Allāhumma, laka sajadtu wa bika āmantu, wa laka aslamtu. Sajada wajhī lilladhī khalaqahu wa ṣawwarahu, wa shaqqa sam'ahu wa baṣarahu. Tabāraka Allāhu, aḥsan al-khāliqīn*). In addition, it is an emulation of the prophetic Sunnah to pray for blessings for oneself and others when prostrating. This is based on the hadith narrated by Muslim according to which the Prophet said, "God's servants are never closer to Him than when they are prostrating. Therefore, offer much supplication [from this position]."

(18) To place one's hands on one's thighs when seated for the first and final testimonies.

(19) When seated, to spread one's left hand in such a way that its fingertips are over one's left knee.

(20) When seated and uttering the words, *Lā ilāha illā Allāh…*, to close one's right hand into a fist, leaving one's index finger extended toward the *qiblah*. It is undesirable to move one's index finger; in fact, some hold that moving it at this time will invalidate one's prayer since such a movement is extraneous to prayer. However, this view is weak since such a movement, properly speaking, would be too subtle to render prayer invalid.

(21) When seated at any time during prayer, to sit on top of one's left calf and heel with the top of the left foot downward, while holding the right foot perpendicular to the ground or floor and pointing one's toes toward the *qiblah*. This ruling applies, of course, only to those who suffer from no physical condition that would prevent them from sitting in this fashion; otherwise—for example, if someone is too overweight to sit in this position—he may adopt whatever seated posture he is capable of.

(22) To utter the second concluding greeting of peace.

* * *

As for the Hanbalis, they divide the Sunnah-based practices associated with ritual prayer into two types, namely, verbal and physical. The verbal Sunnah-based practices are as follows: (1) Utterance of the prayer of commencement quoted above. (2) Praying for divine protection and uttering the words, *bismillāh al-raḥmān al-raḥīm* before commencing Qur'anic recitation. (3) Utterance of the word *Āmīn*. (4) Reciting some other Qur'anic passage following the *Fātiḥah*. (5) In the case of the imam, doing Qur'anic recitation aloud (whereas this practice is undesirable for those being led in prayer). (6) Following the words, "Our Lord, and to You does praise belong" (*rabbanā wa laka al-ḥamd*) with the words, "Our Lord, and to You we owe praise enough to fill the heavens and the earth, as well as all that You might desire beyond this" (*mil' al-samāwāti wa mil' al-arḍi wa mil'u mā shi'ta min shay'in ba'd*). (7) Repeating the words of praise to God associated with bowing (that is, *subḥān rabbī al-'aẓīm*) and prostrating (that is, *subḥān rabbī al-a'lā*) beyond the minimum of a single time, but not more than eleven times. (8) Repeating the words, "My Lord, forgive me" (*rabbī ighfir lī*) more than once, but not more than eleven times when seated between the two prostrations of each *rak'ah*. (9) Praying for the family and descendants of the Prophet when reciting the final testimony. (10) Calling down blessings upon the Prophet and his family during the final testimony, as well as uttering the prayer of obedience in the *witr* prayer.

As for the physical Sunnah-based practices associated with prayer—also referred to as 'forms'—they are as follows: (1) Lifting one's hands when uttering *takbīrat al-iḥrām*, and keeping them open with the fingers together. (2) Lifting one's hands when coming up from a bow, then lowering them again. (3) Placing the right hand over the left and both hands under one's navel when standing for Qur'anic recitation. (4) When in a standing position, keeping one's eyes fixed on the spot where one's head touches the ground or floor during prostration. (5) Uttering *takbīrat al-iḥrām* aloud. (6) During Qur'anic recitation, chanting in a melodious voice. (7) Not prolonging one's prayer if leading others in worship. (8) Making the first *rak'ah* longer than the second. (9) Holding one's feet slightly apart when standing up. (10) Placing one's hands on one's knees when bowing, with one's fingers spread. (11) When bowing, to hold one's back straight and parallel to the ground or floor, and one's head parallel with one's back. (12) Holding one's upper arms away from one's sides when bowing. (13) When coming down into a prostration, to place one's knees on the ground or floor, followed by one's hands and ending with one's forehead and nose; then to keep the knees, hands, forehead and nose in close contact with the floor or ground. (14) During prostration, to hold one's forearms away from one's sides and one's abdomen away from one's thighs. (15) During prostration, to keep one's thighs away from one's calves, to hold one's knees apart, and to hold one's feet perpendicular to the ground while spreading the toes and placing the balls of the feet on the ground. (16) When prostrating, to place one's hands flat on the ground alongside one's shoulders while keeping one's fingers together and pointing them toward the *qiblah*. (17) When rising after the second prostration of the first, second, and third *rak'ahs* in preparation for the next *rak'ah*, to lift one's hands [and head] off the ground first, then to rise onto the balls of one's feet while resting one's hands on one's knees. (18) When seated between the two prostrations of each prayer and when seated for the recitation of the first testimony, to sit with one's thighs over one's calves and the tops of one's feet toward the ground. (19) When seated for the final testimony, to sit with one's right hip over one's right leg and one's left hip on the ground. (20) When seated for the first testimony, to lay one's hands flat on top of one's thighs. (21) When seated for the first testimony, the final testimony, and between the two prostrations in each *rak'ah*, to hold one's fingers close together. (22) While reciting the testimony, to keep the little finger and the ring finger of one's right hand folded inward while bringing the right thumb and middle finger together; then, when uttering the name of the Divine, to point forward with one's index finger. (23) During the testimony, to hold the fingers of one's left hand together while pointing them toward the *qiblah*. (24) When beginning the final greetings of peace, to direct one's face toward the *qiblah*, then to turn toward the right, then toward the left with the intention of ending the prayer. (25) During the final greetings of peace, to turn farther toward the right than one does toward the left. (26) To maintain an attitude of humility and reverence throughout prayer.

An explanation of some Sunnah-based practices associated with prayer, including a discussion of those that are agreed upon and those about which there is disagreement

All four schools agree that it is an emulation of the prophetic Sunnah to raise one's hands when commencing ritual prayer; however, there is disagreement over the exact manner in which they are to be raised.[94]

[The number of verbal Sunnah-based practices given in the Arabic is 12, while the original number of physical Sunnah-based practices is 56. However, in an attempt to highlight the logical connections between the various steps for the reader, I have grouped some of them together—for example, those connected with prostration, those connected with the testimony, etc., thereby consolidating the list somewhat – t.n.]

All the aforementioned Sunnah-based practices apply equally to men and women with the exception of certain ones having to do with one's posture when bowing, prostrating and sitting down. Specifically, the Sunnah-based practice for a woman is to keep her limbs close to her body when bowing and prostrating and, when she is seated, to sit with her buttocks on the floor or ground and her legs out to her right side. In addition, a woman must do recitation silently if she will be heard by a strange man. The same rulings apply to 'problematic' hermaphrodites.

94. According to the Hanafis, a man emulates the prophetic Sunnah by raising his hands when uttering *takbīrat al-iḥrām* and holding them alongside his ears with his fingers parted; the same applies to a female bondservant. As for a free woman, however, she is to hold her hands to her shoulders. Moreover, just as one should raise one's hands for *takbīrat al-iḥrām*, one should also do so for the utterances of *Allāhu akbar* associated with the prayers performed for the Day of Fastbreaking and the Day of Sacrifice and with recitation of the prayer of obedience.

* * *

According to the Shafiis, both men and women emulate the prophetic Sunnah most perfectly by raising their hands in the following situations: (1) when uttering *takbīrat al-iḥrām*, (2) when bowing and rising from a bow, and (3) when rising after the first testimony. One should hold one's raised hands in such a way that the fingertips are alongside the tops of one's ears and one's thumbs are across from one's earlobes. Raising one's hands in this manner represents the most complete emulation of the Sunnah; however, the Sunnah is minimally fulfilled by doing even part of this.

* * *

In the Malikis' view, it is recommended that one hold one's hands to one's shoulders when uttering *takbīrat al-iḥrām*, but that it is undesirable to do more than this. The most widely recognized view among them is that one's hands should remain open, with the backs upward and the palms downward.

* * *

As for the Hanbalis, they hold that both men and women emulate the prophetic Sunnah by raising their hands to their shoulders when uttering *takbīrat al-iḥrām*, when bowing, and when coming up from a bow.

The ruling on saying, *Āmīn* ('Amen')

It is an emulation of the prophetic Sunnah to utter the word, *Āmīn* ('Amen') after completing the recitation of the *Fātiḥah*, provided that one does not pause very long after the *Fātiḥah* or speak other than to engage in supplication. It is agreed upon by three of the schools—namely, the Shafiis, the Hanbalis and the Hanafis—that the utterance of the word *Āmīn* is a Sunnah-based practice for the prayer leader (imam), for those being led in prayer, and for those praying alone. As for the Malikis, they hold that this practice is simply recommended. According to the Shafiis and the Hanbalis, the word *Āmīn* should be uttered silently in prayer which is being performed silently, and aloud in prayer which is being performed aloud. Thus, for example, after one finishes reciting the *Fātiḥah* aloud in the first two *rak'ahs* of the dawn prayer, the sundown prayer or the evening prayer, he or she should utter the word *Āmīn* aloud as well. However, in the remaining *rak'ahs* of such prayers (all of which involve silent recitation of the *Fātiḥah*) as well as in other prayers which likewise involve silent recitation (namely, the noon prayer and the mid-afternoon prayer), it should be uttered silently.[95]

Holding one's right hand over one's left above or below the navel

According to all the schools except the Malikis, it is an emulation of the prophetic Sunnah to hold one's right hand over one's left either above or below the navel. As for the Malikis, they hold that it is simply recommended.[96]

---

95. As for the views of the Malikis and the Hanafis, they are as follows:

According to the Hanafis, one should utter the word *Āmīn* silently regardless of whether the prayer is being performed silently or aloud; this also applies whether one has recited the *Fātiḥah* oneself, or has heard someone else—such as the imam or someone nearby—utter the final phrase of the *Fātiḥah*, even if the other person was reciting it silently.

According to the Malikis, the utterance of the word *Āmīn* is recommended for both those praying alone and those being led in prayer regardless of whether the prayer is being performed silently or aloud. As for the imam, it is recommended that he utter it only when he has been reciting silently. Those being led in a prayer being performed aloud should say *Āmīn* when they hear the imam utter the final words of the *Fātiḥah*, namely, *wa lā al-ḍāllīn* ("nor of those who go astray"); as for those being led in a prayer being performed silently, they should say *Āmīn* when they hear themselves utter the final words of the *Fātiḥah*.

96. With regard to the manner in which one is to hold one's hands during ritual prayer, each of the four schools offers its own specific rulings:

According to the Malikis, it is recommended, though not necessarily part of the Sunnah, to hold the right hand over the left between one's navel and one's chest when performing an obligatory prayer. However, this action is only recommended if one's intention in performing it is to follow the example of the Prophet, whereas if one's intention is simply to support oneself physically, it is undesirable regardless of exactly how it is done. If, on the other hand, one simply holds one's hands in this way for no particular reason, most Malikis appear not to consider it undesir-

Al-tasmīʿ (uttering the words, *samiʿa Allāhu li man ḥamidah*) and *al-taḥmīd* (saying, *rabbanā wa laka al-ḥamd*)

The practices referred to as *al-tasmīʿ*, that is, utterance of the words, *samiʿa Allāhu li man ḥamidah* ("God hears those who praise Him"), and *al-tahmīd*, saying, *Allāhumma rabbanā wa laka al-ḥamd* ("O God, our Lord, and to You does praise belong"), are emulations of the prophetic Sunnah when one is coming up from a bow. This much is agreed upon by the four schools; however, they differ over the exact wording of these statements.[97]

---

able, but even recommended. When performing voluntary prayers as well, this practice is recommended by the Malikis without the addition of specific conditions relating to intention.

* * *

According to the Hanafis, the manner in which we should hold our hands during prayer varies according to whether we are men or women. A man should place the palm of his right hand on top of the back of his left, then place both hands under his navel with his right little finger and his thumb around his left wrist, whereas a woman should simply place both hands on her chest.

* * *

According to the Hanbalis, both the man and the woman should place the right palm over the back of the left hand, then hold both hands under the navel.

* * *

As for the Shafiis, they hold that it is an emulation of the prophetic Sunnah for both the man and the woman to place the palm of the right hand over the back of the left hand, then hold both hands between the navel and the chest and toward the left side of one's body. In addition, one may either hold the fingers of one's right hand flat on top of the left wrist, or spread them upward and outward over the left forearm.

97. According to the Hanafis, the imam utters the words *samiʿ Allāhu li man ḥamidah* as he comes up from a bow, then adds nothing further. Following this, those being led in prayer say *Allāhumma rabbanā wa laka al-ḥamd*. Those being led in prayer might also emulate the Sunnah by saying simply *rabbanā wa laka al-ḥamd* ("Our Lord, and to You praise belongs") or *rabbanā, laka al-ḥamd* ("Our Lord, to You praise belongs"). However, the first version mentioned here is the preferable one, which is then followed by a double repetition of the phrase *rabbanā wa laka al-ḥamd*. As for those praying alone, they join the two utterances, saying, *samiʿ Allāhu li man ḥamidah, Allāhumma rabbanā wa laka al-ḥamd* (or, *rabbanā, laka al-ḥamd*), followed by two more repetitions of the last phrase. As we have mentioned, the Hanafis view these utterances as part of the prophetic Sunnah.

* * *

According to the Malikis, utterance of the words *samiʿa Allāhu li man ḥamidah* is enjoined by the prophetic Sunnah for the imam, those being led in prayer, and those praying alone. As for the utterance of the words *Allāhumma rabbanā wa laka al-ḥamd*, it is recommended, but not Sunnah, for those being led in prayer and

The imam's utterance of the words *Allāhu akbar* and *sami'a Allāhu li man ḥamidah* in an audible voice

The Shafiis, the Hanbalis and the Hanafis all agree that it is consistent with the prophetic Sunnah for the imam to utter the words, *Allāhu akbar* and *sami'a Allāhu li man ḥamidah* in an audible voice. As for the Malikis, they hold that this is merely recommended.

Al-tablīgh by someone behind the prayer leader

The term *al-tablīgh* [literally, 'notification'] as used in this context refers to one of two practices: (1) the imam's raising his voice so that he can be heard by those being led in prayer, or (2) the repetition of the imam's *takbīrat al-iḥrām* in a loud voice by one of the worshipers being led in prayer in order to ensure that the others

---

those praying alone. In the case of the imam, or prayer leader, he is enjoined by the Sunnah only to say *sami'a Allāhu li man ḥamidah* without adding anything further, just as those being led in prayer say only *Allāhumma rabbanā wa laka al-ḥamd* or *rabbanā wa laka al-ḥamd* (the former wording being the preferable one).

* * *

According to the Shafiis, the prophetic Sunnah enjoins the imam, those being led in prayer, and those praying alone to utter both the words *sami'a Allāhu li man ḥamidah* and *rabbanā laka al-ḥamd*. However, the imam must utter the words *sami'a Allāhu li man ḥamidah* in an audible voice, whereas someone being led in prayer is not to utter them audibly unless he is serving as a *muballigh*, that is, someone who repeats the imam's words in a loud voice in order to make certain that the other worshipers heard what he said. As for the words, *rabbanā laka al-ḥamd*, all three—the imam, those being led in prayer, and those praying alone—are enjoined by the Sunnah to utter them silently, including even someone being led in prayer who is serving as a *muballigh*.

* * *

The Hanbalis hold that the prayer leader and those praying alone are to utter both statements: *sami'a Allāhu li man ḥamidah* and *rabbanā wa laka al-ḥamd*. They also maintain that this particular order of words is required; hence, if someone were to say, for example, *man ḥamida Allāha sami'a lahu* ("whenever someone praises God, God hears him"), this would not be acceptable. When the imam or the person praying alone has stood up fully following the bow, he or she says *rabbanā wa laka al-ḥamd*. As for those being led in prayer, they are to say *rabbanā wa laka al-ḥamd* or *rabbanā laka al-ḥamd* without adding anything further as they rise from a bow. The first of these two versions is preferable, and even more preferable is for one to say *Allāhumma rabbanā laka al-ḥamd* (without the word *wa*, that is, "and"). It is also a Sunnah-related practice to utter the following, more complete, formula: *rabbanā wa laka al-ḥamd: mil' al-samāwāti wa mil' al-arḍi wa mil'u mā shi'ta min shay'in ba'd* ("Our Lord, and to You do we owe praise enough to fill the heavens and the earth, as well as all that You might desire beyond this").

have heard it. This practice is allowed provided that the intention of the person raising his or her voice is to enter into ritual prayer by means of *takbīrat al-iḥrām*. It is agreed upon among the four schools that if the person's intention is simply to notify others that prayer is commencing, his or her own prayer will not be valid; however, if the intention is to enter ritual prayer *and* to notify others that the prayer is commencing, no harm is done. If someone raises his or her voice when uttering the other instances of the words *Allāhu akbar* which recur throughout ritual prayer, and if such a person's intention in doing so is simply to make the words heard by the other worshipers, his or her prayer is not invalidated, but he or she will miss the reward for uttering them.[98]

---

98. The Shafiis hold if the intention of someone who raises his or her voice when uttering *tabkīrat al-iḥrām* is simply to notify others that the prayer has begun, or if this person does so without any intention in particular, his or her prayer will be invalidated. However, if this person's intention is both to enter into ritual prayer himself and to inform others that the prayer is beginning, or simply to enter into ritual prayer, his prayer will be valid. Similarly in the case of other instances of the phrase *Allāhu akbar* throughout ritual prayer, if the person uttering them in a loud voice does so simply in order to let others hear it, or if he or she has no intention in particular, his or her prayer will be invalidated, whereas if the intention is both to let others hear and to keep God in remembrance, his or her prayer will be valid. The only exception to this is a case in which the person raising his voice is an uninformed layperson, for if this type of person raises his voice when uttering *Allāhu akbar* simply in order for others to hear, his prayer will remain valid.

* * *

According to the Hanafis, it is an emulation of the prophetic Sunnah for the imam to utter the words *Allāhu akbar*—whether it is *takbīrat al-iḥrām* or other instances of the words *Allāhu akbar* which recur throughout the prayer—loudly enough for those praying behind him to hear him. However, it is undesirable for him or her to speak too loudly. Moreover, if the imam or some worshiper praying behind him raises his voice when uttering *takbīrat al-iḥrām* simply in order for others to hear him and not also to enter into ritual prayer himself, his prayer will be invalid; in fact, the prayers of those who hear him will likewise be invalidated if

Sunnah-based utterances of *Allāhu akbar* in prayer

In addition to the utterance of the words *Allāhu akbar* when commencing prayer (that is, *takbīrat al-iḥrām*), there are other points in the course of ritual prayer at which it is an emulation of the prophetic Sunnah to utter this phrase, namely: (1) when bowing, (2) when prostrating, (3) when coming up from a prostration, and (4) when rising to a standing position. The Malikis and the Shafiis agree that the utterance of *Allāhu akbar* at these points is part of the Sunnah. As for the Hanafis and the Hanbalis, their views are presented below.[99]

---

they know that his intention was simply for them to hear his words. However, as long as the intention is both to inform others and to enter into the consecration of ritual prayer, one's prayer remains valid; in fact, this double intention is what is called for.

With regard to the other repetitions of the phrase *Allāhu akbar*, the Hanafis' ruling is that even if someone utters them in a loud voice simply in order to let others hear him, his prayer will remain valid; the same applies to the various utterances of the phrases *sami'a Allāhu li man ḥamidah* and *rabbanā wa laka al-ḥamd* provided that in speaking loudly, the person is not trying to impress others with his melodious chanting voice.

99. According to the Hanbalis, all these utterances of *Allāhu akbar* are obligatory such that without any of them, one's prayer will not be valid. The only exception made to this ruling is in the case of someone who arrives late for a communal prayer and who joins the imam in a bowing position; in this situation, the utterance of *Allāhu akbar* associated with this person's bow is not obligatory, but simply Sunnah. Hence, if he utters *takbīrat al-iḥrām* and bows immediately without an additional utterance of *Allāhu akbar*, his prayer will still be valid.

* * *

As for the Hanafis, they agree with the Malikis and the Shafiis that all the aforementioned utterances of *Allāhu akbar* are based on the Sunnah rather than being obligatory. However, they classify the utterance of *Allāhu akbar* associated with the bow in the second *rak'ah* of the prayers performed on the Day of Fastbreaking and the Day of Sacrifice as 'duty', or as an emphatically enjoined practice based on the Sunnah (bearing in mind that for the Hanafis, the term 'duty' describes an action which is only slightly less binding than an obligation, or *farḍ*, and more binding than a practice which is simply in emulation of the Sunnah).

Recitation of a surah of the Qur'ān or some comparable passage after the *Fātiḥah*

All four schools agree that one should recite some passage from the Qur'ān after reciting the *Fātiḥah* in the first two *rak'ahs* of the noon prayer, the sundown prayer and the evening prayer, and in the two *rak'ahs* of the obligatory dawn prayer. However, they differ over details of the ruling on this recitation. For example, the Shafiis, the Malikis and the Hanbalis all hold that this practice is based on the prophetic Sunnah.[100]

Similarly with respect to how much of the Qur'ān should be recited, there are differing views among the schools. According to the Shafiis and the Malikis, it is sufficient to recite a small surah, a verse, or even part of a verse, and a worshiper who recites this much following the *Fātiḥah* has fulfilled the Sunnah completely; as for the Hanafis and the Hanbalis, they view the matter differently.[101]

According to the Shafiis and the Hanbalis, recitation of some other passage of the Qur'ān after the *Fātiḥah* in obligatory prayers is a Sunnah-based practice for the imam, for those praying alone, and for those being led in prayer who did not hear the imam's recitation.[102] In voluntary prayers, by contrast, the recitation of some passage from the Qur'ān following the *Fātiḥah* is required in every *rak'ah*, regardless of whether one performs only two *rak'ahs*, four *rak'ahs* with a single greeting of peace at the end, or more than this. However, each of the four schools offers its own details in connection with this ruling.[103]

---

100. According to the Hanafis, the recitation of a surah, three short verses, or one long verse is a 'duty' in the first two *rak'ahs* of every obligatory prayer (bearing in mind that a 'duty' is more binding than a simple Sunnah-based practice, though less binding than a full obligation).

101. According to the Hanafis, one's 'duty' is not fulfilled in this regard unless one recites a short surah, three short verses, or one long verse of the Qur'ān.

As for the Hanbalis, they stipulate that one must recite a verse which can stand independently, as it were, that is, whose meaning is comprehensible without reference to what precedes or follows it. Hence, for example, it would not be acceptable to recite a passage such as, ... *mudhāmmatān*... ("...two gardens of the deepest green...") (55:64) or, ... *thumma naẓara*... ("...and then he looks...") (74:21).

102. The Hanafis hold that someone being led in prayer must never recite behind his or her imam. As for the imam or someone praying alone, the ruling concerning them has been mentioned.

As for the Malikis, they hold that recitation is undesirable for someone being led in a communal prayer being performed aloud, even if the person concerned did not hear the imam or if the imam remained silent.

103. According to the Malikis, the recitation of an additional passage of the Qur'ān following the *Fātiḥah* in a voluntary prayer is simply recommended rather than being a Sunnah-based practice. Moreover, this ruling applies whether one performs only two *rak'ahs* or more.

* * *

The Prayer of Commencement (*du'ā' al-iftitāḥ*), Also Known as the "Prayer of Praise" (*al-thanā'*)

The prayer of commencement is an emulation of the prophetic Sunnah according to the Shafiis, the Hanafis and the Hanbalis; the most common view among the Malikis is that its use is undesirable, although some Malikis hold that it is recommended. As for the wording of this prayer, various views have been expressed.[104]

The Hanafis hold that when performing a voluntary prayer, it is neither merely recommended nor a Sunnah-based practice to recite an additional passage of the Qur'ān after the Fātiḥah, but rather, a 'duty'; moreover, it is a 'duty' in all *rak'ahs* of such a prayer.

* * *

According to the Shafiis, if someone performs a voluntary prayer consisting of more than two *rak'ahs*, it becomes subject to the same ruling that applies to an obligatory four-*rak'ah* prayer, in which the Sunnah-based practice is to recite an additional passage of the Qur'ān after the *Fātiḥah* in the first two *rak'ahs* only; hence, when performing additional *rak'ahs*, one recites only the *Fātiḥah*.

* * *

As for the Hanbalis, they hold that following the *Fātiḥah* with the recitation of either a small surah or a verse with a meaning that stands alone without reference to what precedes it or follows it is a Sunnah-based practice in every *rak'ah* of a voluntary prayer, regardless of whether one performs just two *rak'ahs* or more than this.

104. According to the Hanafis, the wording to be used for this prayer is as follows: "Glory be to You, O God, and praise! May Your name be blessed and Your majesty exalted! There is no god but You!" (*subḥānuk Allāhumma wa biḥamdika, wa tabāraka ismuk wa ta'āla jadduk wa lā ilāha ghayruk*). The Arabic phrase, *subḥanuk Allāhumma*, rendered here as, "Glory be to You, O God!" is also a way of saying, "I declare You, O God, to be free of all imperfection, as befits Your glory and majesty." As for the phrase, *wa biḥamdika* (rendered, "and praise..."), it could also be understood to mean, "I have extolled You in every way that befits who You are and I have sung Your praises." And as for the phrase, *tabāraka ismuka wa ta'āla jadduk*, rendered above as "May Your name be blessed and Your majesty exalted", its fuller meaning is, "May the blessing and goodness of Your name endure, and may Your majesty be exalted and Your splendor be lifted up [for all to behold]." The Hanafis classify this prayer as a Sunnah-based practice in both obligatory and voluntary prayers for the imam, for those being led in prayer, and for those praying alone. The only exception to this is when someone is praying behind an imam and the imam has already gone on to the Qur'anic recitation; in this case the person following the imam should not utter this prayer. If, on the other hand, someone misses the first *rak'ah* but catches up with the imam in the second *rak'ah*, he or she should utter this prayer before the imam begins the Qur'anic recitation; once the imam has begun Qur'anic recitation, however, the worshiper should not utter this prayer, regardless of whether the imam is reciting aloud or silently. Lastly, if the worshiper joins communal prayer as the imam is bowing or prostrating and if he

Prayers for divine protection

The utterance of a prayer for divine protection is a Sunnah-based practice according to all of the schools except the Malikis. For each of the schools' rulings on this matter, see below.[105]

---

has reason to believe that he can finish uttering this prayer before the imam rises from his bow or his prostration, he should go ahead and recite it; otherwise, he should not.

* * *

The prayer of commencement used by the Shafiis is as follows: "I turn my face with a pure heart and in full surrender toward the One who created the heavens and the earth, and I am not among those who associate created beings with the Divine. My prayer, my devotion, my life and my death belong to God, the Sustainer of the worlds, who has no partner. Thus have I been commanded, and I am among those who surrender themselves to God" (*wajjahtu wajhī lilladhī faṭara al-samawāti wal-arḍa ḥanīfan musliman, wa mā anā min al-mushrikīn. Inna ṣalāti wa naskī wa maḥyāyā wa mamātī lillāhi rabb al-'ālamīn, lā sharīka lah, wa bi dhalika umirtu wa anā min al-muslimīn.*) (The Hanafis hold that this particular prayer is to be uttered before or after one's intention in obligatory prayers, and before or after *takbīrat al-iḥrām* in voluntary prayers.) As noted earlier in our discussion of Sunnah-based practices associated with prayer, the Shafiis stipulate five conditions for the use of this prayer. To review these conditions, see the section above which deals with the Sunnah-based practices associated with ritual prayer.

* * *

The wording which the Hanbalis generally use for the prayer of commencement is the same as that adopted by the Hanafis; however, they hold that it is also acceptable to use the Shafiis' version. In fact, the Hanbalis hold that the ideal practice is to use the Hanafi version on some occasions, and the Shafii version on others.

* * *

As for the Malikis, the most widely held view among them is that it is undesirable to recite the prayer of commencement; they base this view on the fact that the Companions tended not to use it. Even though the hadith quoted earlier in this connection is sound, they nevertheless hold to a saying passed down from Mālik, may God be pleased with him, according to which its use is simply recommended rather than based on the Sunnah. As for the wording of the prayer of commencement, it consists of a combination of the Hanafi and Shafii versions. In sum, then, the Malikis tend to view the use of this prayer as undesirable, although some of them view its use as recommended.

105. According to the Hanafis, praying for divine protection is based on the prophetic Sunnah; specifically, one should say, "I seek refuge in God from the accursed Satan" (*a'ūdhu billāhi min al-shayṭān al-rajīm*). This prayer is to be uttered once only, in the first *rak'ah* following *takbīrat al-iḥrām* and the prayer of commencement discussed above. Moreover, it should be used regardless of whether

Utterance of the *basmalah*, i.e., "In the name of God, the Most Gracious, the Most Merciful" in prayer

According to the Hanafis and the Hanbalis, the utterance of the *basmalah* in every *rak'ah* before recitation of the *Fātiḥah* is a practice based on the prophetic Sunnah. The Shafiis hold that it is obligatory, while the Malikis, by contrast, consider it undesirable.[106]

---

one is leading others in prayer, being led in prayer, or praying alone. However, if someone being led in communal prayer arrives so late that he does not join the imam until after he has begun the Qur'anic recitation, he or she should omit this prayer, since in the Malikis' view, the prayer for divine protection must be tied specifically to Qur'anic recitation.

* * *

As we have seen, the Shafiis view the prayer for divine protection as a Sunnah-based practice in every *rak'ah*; the wording which they prefer is, *a'ūdhu billāhi min al-shayṭān al-rajīm*. (For more details concerning their ruling on this point, see the enumeration of Sunnah-based practices for each school presented earlier.)

* * *

The Malikis view the utterance of a prayer for divine protection as undesirable in obligatory prayers, regardless of whether it is recited silently or aloud; in voluntary prayers, by contrast, they allow it if it is uttered silently, but they consider its utterance aloud to be undesirable.

* * *

As for the Hanbalis, they classify the prayer for divine protection as a Sunnah-based practice in the first *rak'ah*. The wording they use is, "I seek refuge in God, the One who hears and knows all, from the accursed Satan" (*a'ūdhu billāh al-samī' al-'alīm min al-shayṭān al-rajīm*).

106. According to the Hanafis, prayer leaders and those praying alone should utter the *basmalah* silently at the beginning of each *rak'ah* regardless of whether the prayer itself is being performed silently or aloud. As for those being led in communal prayer, they do not utter the *basmalah*, of course, since in the Hanafi view, those being led in prayer are forbidden to do any sort of recitation. The point in prayer at which one utters the *basmalah* falls between the prayer for divine protection and the recitation of the *Fātiḥah*. If the worshiper forgets to recite the prayer for divine protection and goes ahead to utter the *basmalah*, he or she should go back and recite the prayer for protection again, then repeat the *basmalah*. However, if he or she forgets to utter the *basmalah* and begins reciting the *Fātiḥah* without it, he or she should continue reciting the *Fātiḥah*. As for uttering the *basmalah* between the *Fātiḥah* and the following Qur'anic recitation, it is not considered undesirable, but it is preferable not to do so regardless of whether the prayer is being performed silently or aloud. Lastly, the Hanafis do not consider the *basmalah* to be an integral part of the *Fātiḥah* or of any surah of the Qur'ān, even though it is, itself, part of the Qur'ān.

* * *

Prolonged Qur'anic recitation

The subject of prolonged Qur'anic recitation in prayer includes the matter of reciting particular surahs of the Qur'ān of varying lengths at specified times of the day.[107] It is an emulation of the prophetic Sunnah to prolong one's Qur'anic recitation when the person praying is settled in a particular place and is praying alone; if the person is on a journey, three of the four schools hold that it is not a Sunnah-based practice to prolong one's recitation, although the Malikis hold a different view.[108] As for imams, it is an emulation of the Sunnah for them to prolong Qur'anic recitation under specified conditions, the details of which differ from one school to another.[109]

According to the Malikis, it is undesirable to utter the *basmalah* in obligatory prayers regardless of whether they are being performed silently or aloud. They make an exception to this ruling if the person concerned is uttering the *basmalah* out of deference for opposing viewpoints, in which case it is recommended that he or she utter it silently right before reciting the *Fātiḥah*; however, to utter it aloud in this case is undesirable. In voluntary prayers, by contrast, it is acceptable to utter the *basmalah* when preparing to recite the *Fātiḥah*.

* * *

According to the Shafiis, the *basmalah* is an integral part of the *Fātiḥah*; hence, its utterance is not simply an emulation of the Sunnah, but an obligation. This being the case, the *basmalah* is subject to the same ruling which applies to the *Fātiḥah* such that in a prayer being performed aloud, one must recite both the *basmalah* and the [rest of the] *Fātiḥah* aloud as well, and if one fails to do so, his or her prayer will be invalidated.

* * *

As for the Hanbalis, they view the silent utterance of the *basmalah* in every *rak'ah* as an emulation of the prophetic Sunnah although, like the Malikis and the Hanafis, they do not consider the *basmalah* to be part of the *Fātiḥah* itself. Moreover, if someone utters the *basmalah* before saying a prayer for divine protection, the requirement that one utter a prayer for protection is dropped and one need not go back to it; similarly, if someone omits the *basmalah* and begins reciting the *Fātiḥah*, there is no need to go back to the *basmalah*.

107. According to the Hanafis, the longer surahs of the section of the Qur'ān referred to as *al-Mufaṣṣal* begin with Surah 49 and extend up to Surah 85. The medium-length surahs extend from Surah 85 to Surah 98, while the short surahs extend from Surah 98 to the end of the Qur'ān. The Hanafis hold that one should recite from the group of long surahs mentioned here during the dawn and noon prayers, although the prophetic Sunnah dictates that one's recitation during the noon prayer should be shorter than the recitation during the dawn prayer. When performing the mid-afternoon and evening prayers, one should recite from the medium-length surahs, and during the sundown prayer, from the short surahs.

* * *

According to the Shafiis, the long surahs of *al-Mufaṣṣal* begin with Surah 49 and extend up to Surah 78; the medium-length surahs extend from Surah 78 as far as Surah 93, while the short surahs extend from Surah 93 to the end of the Qur'ān. During the dawn and noon prayers one is to recite from the long chapters, though it is consistent with the Sunnah to recite less in the noon prayer than in the dawn prayer; however, during the Friday dawn prayer, the first *rak'ah* should include a recitation from Surah 32 even though it does not belong to *al-Mufaṣṣal*, and the second *rak'ah* should include a recitation from Surah 76. During the mid-afternoon and evening prayers one should recite from the medium-length surahs, and during the sundown prayer, one should recite from the short surahs.

* * *

According to the Malikis, the long surahs of *al-Mufaṣṣal* begin with Surah 49 and extend up to the end of Surah 79; the medium-size surahs extend from the end of Surah 79 to Surah 93, while the short surahs begin with the end of Surah 93 and extend to the end of the Qur'ān. It is recommended, though not based on the Sunnah necessarily, to recite from the long surahs during the dawn and noon prayers, from the short surahs during the mid-afternoon and sundown prayers, and from the medium-size surahs during the evening prayer.

* * *

As for the Hanbalis, they divide *al-Mufaṣṣal* as follows: Its long surahs begin with Surah 50 and extend up to Surah 78; its medium-sized surahs end with Surah 93; and its short surahs extend up to the end of the Qur'ān. According to the Hanbalis, one should recite from the long surahs during the dawn prayer only and from the short ones during the sundown prayer only; as for the medium-length surahs, they are to be recited in the noon prayer, the mid-afternoon prayer, and the evening prayer. The Hanbalis hold that it is undesirable to recite more than this during the dawn prayer and other prayers if one has a valid excuse, such as being on a journey, illness, etc; and if no such excuse exists, it is undesirable only during the dawn prayer.

108. According to the Malikis, it is recommended that people praying alone prolong their Qur'anic recitation regardless of whether they are settled or on a journey.

109. The Shafiis hold that it is a Sunnah-based practice for the imam to prolong Qur'anic recitation if he is leading a small group of worshipers who have explicitly stated that they are content for him to do so; however, they make an exception for the Friday dawn prayer, during which it is a Sunnah-based practice for the imam to recite all of Surah 32 and Surah 76, even if those being led in prayer have not given their consent.

* * *

According to the Malikis, it is an emulation of the prophetic Sunnah for the imam to prolong his Qur'anic recitation given the following four conditions: (1) that he be leading a small group of worshipers, (2) that the worshipers request that he prolong the recitation, either explicitly or by way of suggestion, (3) that he know, or have good reason to believe, that those being led in prayer can tolerate a long recitation, and (4) that the imam know or have good reason to believe that none of those being led in prayer suffers some condition that would excuse him or her from

Prolonging Qur'anic recitation in the first *rak'ah* more than in the second, and holding one's feet apart when standing

Another Sunnah-based practice is to prolong one's Qur'anic recitation in the first *rak'ah* more than in the second, regardless of which prayer one is performing. If the worshiper recites the same amount in the first and second *rak'ahs*, he or she will not have emulated the Sunnah; and the recitation of more in the second *rak'ah* than in the first is considered undesirable. An exception to this ruling is made for the Friday congregational prayer, the prayers performed for the Day of Fastbreaking and the Day of Sacrifice, and situations in which there are crowded conditions where the worshipers are gathered to pray; in these three situations, it is a Sunnah-based practice to recite more in the second *rak'ah* than in the first. This ruling is agreed upon by the Hanafis and the Shafiis, but not by the Malikis and the Hanbalis.[110]

As for the position of one's feet when standing in prayer, one should neither hold them too close together nor too far apart, though if someone suffers from obesity or some other physical condition, he or she might be obliged to part the legs more than others would.[111]

---

a long recitation. If any of these conditions is unfulfilled, it is preferable to keep the recitation short.

* * *

According to the Hanafis, it is an emulation of the Sunnah for the imam to prolong Qur'anic recitation if he is certain that this will pose no hardship for those being led in prayer; however, if he knows that a long recitation will pose hardship on some, it is undesirable to prolong it. This ruling is based on the fact that the Prophet once performed the dawn prayer with a recitation of the two shortest surahs in the Qur'ān, namely, Surah 113 and Surah 114. When he finished, someone said to him, "Why did you make the recitation so brief?" He replied, "I heard a baby crying, so I feared that his mother might be tempted to abandon her prayer and that others who are weak, ill or needy might fall prey to the same temptation if they saw what she had done."

* * *

As for the Hanbalis, they state simply that the Sunnah-based practice is for the imam to adjust the length of his Qur'anic recitation according to the condition of those being led in prayer.

110. According to the Malikis and the Hanbalis, it is recommended that one make the Qur'anic recitation in the second *rak'ah* shorter time-wise than in the first *rak'ah*, even if one happens to recite more verses in the second. Making both recitations the same length or making the recitation in the second *rak'ah* longer than in the first is a departure from the ideal. Moreover, they make no distinction in this ruling between the Friday congregational prayer and any other prayer. However, the Malikis draw a distinction between what is recommended and what belongs to the prophetic Sunnah, whereas the Hanbalis and the Shafiis do not.

111. The Hanafis estimate the ideal distance between one's feet while standing in prayer as approximately the width of four fingers; they consider it undesirable for the distance between them to be either more or less than this.

* * *

Praising God while bowing and prostrating

It is an emulation of the Sunnah to praise God when bowing with the words, *subḥān rabbī al-'aẓīm* ("Glory be to my great Lord"),[112] and when prostrating, with the words, *subḥān rabbī al-a'lā* ("Glory be to my Lord most high"). As for the number of times one should repeat these words, it varies among the schools.[113]

According to the Shafiis, it is undesirable either to stand with one's feet directly touching or to allow the distance between them to exceed the span of one's hand. They also consider it undesirable to place one foot ahead of the other.

* * *

According to the Malikis, it is recommended, though not part of the Sunnah, that one hold one's feet apart when standing in prayer; as for the recommended position, it is simply to maintain moderation by neither standing with one's feet touching nor holding them so far apart that one's posture would be considered indecent by commonly accepted standards. The Hanbalis agree with the Malikis on this point, although unlike the Malikis, the Hanbalis recognize no distinction between what is 'recommended' and what is 'Sunnah'.

112. According to the Malikis, praising God when bowing and prostrating is not an emulation of the Sunnah as such, although it is recommended; moreover, they hold that there is no specific wording one must use when thus praising God, although it is preferable to use the wording mentioned above.

113. According to the Hanafis, one has not emulated the Sunnah unless one utters these words of praise at least three times.

* * *

According to the Hanbalis, uttering the words of praise mentioned above [once] is obligatory, while uttering them more than once is an emulation of the Sunnah.

* * *

According to the Shafiis, one fulfills the Sunnah by uttering any formula of praise one wishes, although the most preferable is the formula mentioned above. As for further repetitions of such words up to eleven times, this is a more complete emulation of the Sunnah. The imam repeats these words three times under all circumstances, and only adds further repetitions if those being led in prayer tell him explicitly that they wish for him to do so.

* * *

As for the Malikis, they specify no particular number of repetitions for such phrases.

Placing one's hands on one's knees

Another Sunnah-based practice is to place one's hands on one's knees when bowing with the fingers parted. The man emulates the Sunnah by holding his upper arms away from his sides based on the words of the Prophet to Anas, may God be pleased with him, "When you bow, place your hands on your knees and spread your fingers, keeping your arms away from your sides." As for the woman, she is to hold her arms close to her sides, since this posture is more unobtrusive. This ruling is agreed upon by all of the schools with the exception of the Malikis.[114]

Keeping one's back and neck straight while bowing

It is agreed by all four schools that when bowing, one should hold one's back horizontally, with one's neck parallel to one's back. This is based on the fact that when the Prophet bowed, he used to hold his back so level that if water was poured on top of it, it would not spill off; he also held his head even with his buttocks.

How to come down into and rise from a prostration

One emulates the Sunnah by coming down into a prostration by placing one's knees on the floor first, then one's hands, then one's face; when coming up, the reverse order is followed, that is, one first lifts one's face off the floor, then one's hands, then one's knees. This ruling is agreed upon by the Hanafis and the Hanbalis; as for the Shafiis and the Malikis, see their rulings below.[115]

---

114. According to the Malikis, the practice of placing one's hands on one's knees and keeping one's upper arms away from one's sides is recommended, but not based on the Sunnah. As for whether to part one's fingers or hold them close together, this is up to the individual worshiper unless one or the other position is necessary to allow the person to hold onto his or her knees firmly.

115. According to the Shafiis, the Sunnah-based practice when rising from a prostration is to lift one's knees off the floor first, then stand up leaning on one's hands, regardless of whether the worshiper is weak or strong, a man or a woman.

* * *

According to the Malikis, the recommended practice when going down into a prostration is to place one's hands on the floor before one's knees, and when rising for the next *rak'ah*, to lift one's knees off the floor first, then one's hands.

116. According to the Malikis, one should hold one's hands alongside or near one's ears when prostrating, with the fingers closed and the fingertips pointing toward the *qiblah*.

* * *

The Hanafis hold that the ideal position is to have one's face between one's hands, although they acknowledge that placing one's hands alongside one's shoulders likewise fulfills the Sunnah.

117. According to the Malikis, it is recommended that a man maintain a moderate distance between his abdomen and his thighs, between his elbows and his knees, and between his upper arms and his sides when prostrating.

Someone who is physically weak, is wearing shoes, or suffers from a condition that would make it impossible to come down into and rise from a prostration in the manner described above should do so in whatever manner he or she is capable of.

How to place one's hands while prostrating and related matters

When prostrating, we are to place our hands alongside our shoulders with our fingers close together and pointing toward the *qiblah*. This ruling is agreed upon by the Shafiis and the Hanbalis; as for the Malikis and the Hanafis, see their views below.[116]

When a man prostrates he should keep his abdomen away from his thighs, his elbows away from his sides and his arms off the floor, provided that none of these movements will be harmful to those praying on either side of him; otherwise, such movements are forbidden. The basis for this ruling is that when the Prophet prostrated, he used to hold his abdomen away from his thighs. As for the woman, she emulates the prophetic Sunnah by bringing her abdomen into contact with her thighs when prostrating, since this is considered more modest. This ruling is agreed upon by all the schools with the exception of the Malikis.[117] Lastly, all the schools agree that it is a Sunnah-based practice for the woman to allow her body to 'settle' into position when sitting, bowing, prostrating, standing, etc., for longer than she is actually required to.

Recitation aloud

According to the Malikis and the Shafiis, it is an emulation of the prophetic Sunnah to recite the Qur'ān aloud in the first two *rak'ahs* of the sundown and evening prayers, as well as the two *rak'ahs* of the dawn prayer and the two *rak'ahs* of the Friday congregational prayer. For the views of the Hanafis and the Hanbalis, see below.[118]

---

118. According to the Hanafis, recitation aloud is obligatory for the imam and an emulation of the Sunnah for someone praying alone. Moreover, someone praying alone has the option of reciting either silently or aloud in prayers which are performed aloud, although reciting aloud in such a case is preferable. If, for example, someone has arrived late for the Friday prayer being performed aloud (or a communal dawn prayer, evening prayer or sundown prayer) and wishes to make up the *rak'ah* which he missed behind the imam, he or she has the option of performing this *rak'ah* either silently or aloud. Properly speaking, a prayer which is to be performed aloud should be performed in an audible voice regardless of whether one is praying it on time or making up for it later; however, someone praying alone may perform it either silently or aloud. Thus, for example, someone who misses the evening prayer (which is classified as an audible prayer [*ṣalāh jahriyah*]) and wishes to perform a compensatory prayer at a later time may perform it either aloud or silently. As for a prayer that is to be performed silently (*ṣalāh sirriyyah*), those performing it alone have no choice but to perform it silently. Thus, if someone praying alone performs the noon or mid-afternoon prayer (both of which are classified as 'silent') aloud, he or she will have neglected a 'duty' and will be obliged to perform the prostration of forgetfulness at the end of the prayer. As for those being

On what it means to pray aloud or silently

According to all of the schools with the exception of the Malikis, it is an emulation of the Sunnah to pray silently in all other *rak'ahs* of the five daily prayers [that is, in all *rak'ahs* other than those listed in the section above on "Recitation Aloud"], whereas according to the Malikis, this practice is merely recommended.

Regarding whether to pray aloud or silently in non-obligatory prayers, such as the *witr* and others, the various schools offer differing points of view.[119] Similarly with respect to what constitutes "praying aloud" or "praying silently" for men and for women, differing rulings are offered by the various schools.[120]

---

led in a communal prayer, they must not recite aloud under any circumstances, as we have seen.

* * *

As for the Hanbalis, they likewise hold that those praying alone have a choice between reciting aloud or silently when praying prayers that are performed aloud.

119. According to the Malikis, it is recommended that one recite aloud in all voluntary prayers performed at night, and silently in voluntary prayers performed during the day. Exceptions to this latter category, however, are daytime voluntary prayers which include a sermon, such as the prayers performed on the Day of Fastbreaking and the Day of Sacrifice and the prayer for rain, in which it is recommended that one recite aloud.

* * *

According to the Hanbalis, the Sunnah-based practice is to recite aloud in the prayers performed on the Day of Fastbreaking and the Day of Sacrifice, the prayer for rain, the prayer for the solar eclipse, the *tarāwīḥ* prayers, and the *witr* following the *tarāwīḥ*; in all other voluntary prayers, however, the Sunnah-based practice it to recite silently.

* * *

According to the Shafiis, it is an emulation of the Sunnah to recite aloud in the prayers performed for the Day of Fastbreaking and the Day of Sacrifice, the prayer for the lunar eclipse, the prayer for rain, the *tarāwīḥ* prayers, the *witr* during Ramaḍān, and the two *rak'ahs* performed when circumambulating the Ka'bah either at night or in the early morning; in all other voluntary prayers one should recite silently with the exception of nighttime voluntary prayers which are associated with no particular occasion, in which one should alternate between reciting aloud and reciting silently.

* * *

As for the Hanafis, they hold that it is obligatory for the imam to recite aloud in all *rak'ahs* of the *witr* during Ramaḍān, in the prayers performed on the Day of Sacrifice and the Day of Fastbreaking and the *tarāwīḥ* prayers, whereas it is obligatory for the imam and those praying alone to recite silently in the prayer for the solar eclipse, the prayer for rain, and daytime voluntary prayers. As for nighttime voluntary prayers, they may be performed either silently or aloud.

120. According to the Malikis, audible recitation for a man requires that he be heard at least by those next to him. As for silent recitation, it ranges from mere movement of the tongue to a voice loud enough that he can hear himself, but which no one else can hear. In the case of a woman, audible recitation involves speaking loudly enough that she can hear herself, but not loud enough for others to hear her, while the most commonly recognized view is that silent recitation for a woman involves nothing more than movement of the tongue.

* * *

According to the Shafiis, audible recitation for both men and women involves speaking loudly enough that they can be heard by at least one other person nearby. However, a woman should not recite aloud if she is in the presence of a strange man. As for silent recitation, it involves speaking softly enough that under reasonably quiet conditions, the person speaking can hear himself or herself, but no one else can hear him or her.

* * *

According to the Hanbalis, audible recitation involves speaking in a voice loud enough that at least one other person can hear the speaker, while silent recitation involves speaking loudly enough that one can hear oneself. As for the woman in particular, it is not an emulation of the Sunnah for her to recite aloud; however, she may do so provided that no strange man will hear her.

* * *

As for the Hanafis, they hold that audible recitation [for the man] involves speaking loudly enough that others can hear him without being right next to him, for example, the worshipers in the front row. Thus, if the speaker is heard by only one or two other men, he has not recited loudly enough; as for an upper limit for audible recitation, there is none. As for silent recitation, it involves speaking loudly enough that the speaker can be heard by himself or by one or two other men nearby. In contrast to the other schools, the Hanafis do not consider mere movement of the tongue sufficient in silent recitation even if one clearly enunciates the words. As for the woman, we saw earlier that according to the most commonly recognized view, it is not necessary for her to conceal her voice and that as a consequence, the same ruling with regard to reciting aloud in prayer applies equally to men and women. However, the woman may only engage in audible recitation provided that her voice is not characterized by a melodiousness, smoothness, or protracted quality which, if men were to hear her, would cause their desires to be inflamed. If a woman's voice is of this type, it should be concealed and her audible recitation is to be considered to have a 'corrupting' influence on prayer. It is for this reason that women are not allowed to deliver the call to prayer.

The worshiper's posture while seated during prayer

According to the Shafiis and the Hanafis, it is an emulation of the prophetic Sunnah to place one's hands on one's thighs while seated during prayer, with one's fingertips on one's knees and pointing toward the *qiblah*.[121] As for the position in which one is to sit, the various schools offer different rulings on this point.[122]

Pointing with the forefinger during the testimony and how to utter the greeting of peace

Given differences in detail among the four schools, it is agreed that part of the Sunnah in ritual prayer is to point with one's index finger while uttering the testimony.[123]

Another Sunnah-based practice, which is agreed upon by all three schools except the Malikis, is for the worshiper to turn toward the right when uttering the first greeting of peace, and toward the left when uttering the second.[124]

---

121. According to the Malikis, placing one's hands on one's thighs in simply recommended. As for the Hanbalis, they hold that the Sunnah is acceptably emulated by placing one's hands on one's thighs without necessarily having one's fingertips on one's knees.

122. According to the Malikis, it is recommended that both the man and the woman adopt a sitting position which they refer to as *al-ifḍā'*. In this position, one sits with the left leg and the left side of one's buttocks on the floor with the left foot pointing toward one's right thigh, the right foot held vertically, and the underside of one's right big toe on the floor.

* * *

According to the Hanafis, the Sunnah-based posture for the man when seated is to sit on his calves with his left foot spread out flat and his right foot perpendicular to the floor such that the undersides of his right toes are on the floor and their tips are pointing toward the qiblah so far as is possible. As for the woman, she emulates the Sunnah by sitting with her buttocks on the floor, her right thigh over her left thigh, and her feet resting on the floor alongside her right hip.

* * *

According to the Shafiis, the Sunnah-based posture for the man when seated is like that described by the Hanafis above; however, when seated for the last time, that is, for the recitation of the final testimony, it is an emulation of the Sunnah for him to rest his left hip and left leg on the floor with his left foot resting comfortably on the floor and his right foot perpendicular to the floor. This ruling applies unless he intends to perform a prostration of forgetfulness, in which case he should adopt the same posture for the final testimony as he does in all other 'sittings' during prayer.

* * *

According to the Hanbalis, the Sunnah-based practice when one is seated between the two prostrations of each *rak'ah* and while seated for the first testimony is to adopt the first posture described above in connection with the views of the Hanafis and the Shafiis—that is, to spread one's left foot on the floor and sit on it while holding the right foot perpendicular to the floor and bending the right toes in such a way that their tips point toward the *qiblah*. However, when seated for the final testimony in prayers consisting of three or four *rak'ahs*, one should sit with one's buttocks on the floor, one's left leg and foot on the floor [with the left foot pointing toward the right leg] and one's right foot upright and out to one's right side.

123. The Malikis hold that when the worshiper is seated for the testimony, it is recommended that he or she make a fist with the right hand while leaving the forefinger and the thumb extended, then move the right forefinger back and forth in a continuous, moderate fashion.

* * *

The Hanafis specify, first of all, that the pointing during the testimony should be done with the right index finger only such that, if this finger is defective, ailing or weak, one must not point with some other finger instead. As for the manner in which such pointing is to be done, the Hanafis hold that when denying the divinity of any being other than God Almighty in the words, *lā ilāha...* ("there is no god..."), one should raise the index finger, and when affirming the divinity of God alone in the words, *illā Allāh* ("...but God"), one should lower one's finger again. Hence, raising one's finger signals negation, while lowering it signals affirmation.

* * *

According to the Hanbalis, one should fold one's right little finger and ring finger under while leaving one's middle finger, index finger and thumb free. Then, whenever one utters the Divine name during the testimony and any associated supplications, one points the right index finger but without moving it.

* * *

According to the Shafiis, one should make a fist with one's right hand, leaving the index finger extended and holding one's thumb up against the side of one's hand. Then, when uttering the phrase, *illā Allāh...* ("but God..."), one should point with the right index finger and keep it lifted up and motionless until it is time to stand up after the first testimony, and until one utters the greetings of peace after the final testimony. One should also keep looking at the right index finger as long as one continues pointing.

124. According to the Malikis, it is recommended that someone being led in communal prayer turn first toward the right when uttering the concluding greeting of peace by means of which one ends a ritual prayer. As for such a person's greeting of peace to the imam, this is not merely recommended, but an emulation of the Sunnah, and in this greeting one faces in the direction of the *qiblah* [that is, straight ahead]. It is also an emulation of the Sunnah for such a person to greet other worshipers on his left with whom he has prayed one or more *rak'ahs*. As for the imam and those praying alone, they are only to utter one greeting, namely, the initial concluding greeting mentioned above; it is recommended that they commence this greeting facing the *qiblah* and then—as they utter the syllable, *kum* in *al-salāmu 'alaykum* (that is, the 'you' in "May peace be upon you")—turn toward the right such that those behind them can see their faces. When uttering a greeting of peace other than the one with which someone concludes a prayer, it is sufficient simply to say, 'Peace be upon you [all], and upon you [singular] be peace" (that is, *salām*

Addressing one's greeting of peace to those on one's right and one's left

It is an emulation of the prophetic Sunnah to address one's first greeting of peace to those on one's right and the second to those on one's left, details concerning which vary from one school to another.[125]

'alaykum, wa 'alayka al-salām); it is preferable, in the view of the Malikis, not to add the words, "and God's mercy and blessings" (*wa raḥmat Allāhi wa barakātuhu*) unless one does so in order to show deference for the opposing view of the Hanbalis, in which case one may add the words, "and the mercy of God" (*wa raḥmat Allāh*), reciting them as one turns toward the right, then the left.

125. According to the Hanafis, the Sunnah-based practice in connection with the greeting of peace is to turn in the first greeting to one's right and in the second to one's left until one can see the 'white' part of his right cheek, then his left. If someone forgets and directs his greeting first to the left, we should simply complete it by directing the second one to the right, without repeating the greeting to the left after this. If someone begins the greeting of peace while looking straight ahead, he or she should then direct his or her greetings to the right and the left. The Sunnah-based wording for this greeting is, "May peace and God's mercy be upon you" (*Al-salāmu 'alaykum wa raḥmat Allāh*). Moreover, the second greeting should be voiced more softly than the first. In the case of the imam, he should address his greeting to those who have prayed with him, including other people, the *jinn* and the angels. In the case of someone being led in communal prayer, he or she should address the greeting to his or her imam and the others with whom he or she has prayed, whereas someone who has prayed alone should address it to the guardian angels.

* * *

According to the Shafiis, our intention should be to address our greetings of peace to the angels and believing humans and *jinn* who have not greeted us, and to reply to those who have greeted us, including our imam and others who have been led in prayer together with us. In doing so, we should begin from the center (facing ahead), then turn fully to the right, then fully to the left.

* * *

According to the Hanbalis, the Sunnah-based practice in this connection is to utter the greeting of peace with the intention of concluding our prayer, not with the intention of greeting the angels and those who have prayed with us. However, if our intention is both to conclude our prayer and to greet the guardian angels and those with whom we have prayed, this is acceptable.

* * *

According to the Malikis, it is recommended that, when uttering the first greeting of peace, those who are not leading prayer should intend both to conclude their prayer and to greet the angels. In the case of a prayer leader, his or her intention should be to conclude his or her prayer and to greet those who have been led in prayer. However, unlike those being led in prayer, the prayer leader and someone praying alone are required to utter only one greeting of peace, namely, the initial greeting by means of which they intend to conclude their prayer, as mentioned previously.

Praying for the Prophet in the final testimony

It is agreed upon among the various schools that it is an emulation of the prophetic Sunnah to pray for blessings on the Prophet as part of the final testimony. The preferred version of this prayer is as follows: "O God, send down Your blessings upon Muḥammad and his household just as You sent them down upon Abraham and his household in all the worlds. You are worthy of all praise, full of glory!" (Arabic: *Allāhumma, ṣalli 'alā Muḥammad wa 'alā Āl Muḥammad kamā ṣallayta 'alā Ibrāhīm wa 'alā Āl Ibrāhīm, wa bārik 'alā Muḥammad wa 'alā Āl Muḥammad kamā bārakta 'alā Ibrāhīm wa 'alā Āl Ibrāhīm fīl-'ālamīn. Innaka ḥamīdun majīd.*) According to the Malikis and the Hanafis, this particular wording is part of the Sunnah; for the view of the Shafiis and the Hanbalis, see below.[126]

Supplication during the final testimony

In connection with supplication during the final testimony, each of the schools offers its own ruling.[127]

---

126. As we saw above in our listing of the obligations associated with prayer according to each of the four schools, the Shafiis and the Hanbalis hold that the prayer for blessing upon the Prophet during the final testimony is obligatory. The wording favored by the Hanbalis is this: "O God, send Your blessings down upon Muḥammad and his household just as You sent them down upon Abraham. You are worthy of all praise, full of glory" (*Allāhumma, ṣalli 'alā Muḥammad wa 'alā Āl Muḥammad kamā ṣallayta 'alā Ibrāhīm. Innaka ḥamīdun majīd*). Modern-day adherents of the Shafii school have also added the words, "our master..." (*sayyidinā*) before the names of both Muḥammad and Abraham such that the prayer reads, "O Lord, send Your blessings down upon our master Muḥammad...just as You sent them down upon our master Abraham..."

127. According to the Hanafis, it is an emulation of the Sunnah to utter supplications in words inspired by or similar to those found in the Qur'ān, e.g., "O our sustainer! Let not our hearts swerve from the truth..." (3:8), and the Sunnah, by saying, for example, "O God, I have done myself grave injustice, and no one forgives sins but You alone. Grant me Your forgiveness, then, and Your mercy and compassion, for You are the All-Forgiving, the Most Merciful." It is not acceptable, however, to utter supplications relating to mundane affairs, by saying, for example, "O God, let me marry so-and-so," or, "Please give me such-and-such", be it gold, silver, a worldly position, etc. They hold that if such a request precedes one's sitting down by sufficient time in which to utter the testimony, it will invalidate one's prayer, and that if it comes after it, but before the greeting of peace, one will have failed to fulfill a 'duty'.

* * *

According to the Malikis, it is recommended that one utter prayers of supplication while seated for the final testimony and after praying for blessings upon the Prophet. We may ask for any good we wish, whether in this world or the next, although the preferable practice is to utter such prayers as the following: "O God, grant Your assured forgiveness to us, our parents, our imams, and those who have preceded us in the faith. O God, forgive us for the transgressions we have committed thus far and for those we have yet to commit, for that which we have kept hidden and that which we have made known to others, for we are no less mindful of our transgressions than You yourself are. O our Sustainer! Grant us that which is good in this life and the next, and protect us from the torment of the Fire!"

* * *

According to the Shafiis, it is an emulation of the Sunnah to utter prayers of supplication after praying for the Prophet and before the final greeting of peace, requesting that which is good for one's faith and one's earthly existence. However, if one prays for something that is forbidden, impossible, or 'conditional', that is, something that involves a kind of bargaining with God, his or her prayer will be invalidated. The ideal practice when uttering such supplications is to use words which have been passed down from the Prophet, such as the following supplication narrated by Muslim: "O God, forgive me for the transgressions I have already committed and for those which I have yet to commit, for that which I have kept hidden and that which I have made known to others, and for any excess of which I have been guilty, for I am no less mindful of my transgressions than You yourself are. You alone cause events to come to pass when You will, and there is no deity but You." Moreover, it is a Sunnah-based practice for the imam not to let the length of his supplication exceed that of the final testimony and the prayer for blessings on the Prophet combined.

* * *

As for the Hanbalis, they hold that it is a Sunnah-based practice following the prayer for blessings on the Prophet for the worshiper to say, "I seek refuge in God from the torment of Hell and the torment of the grave, from temptation both in this life and after death, and from the temptation to follow the Anti-Christ [when he comes]." One may utter supplications which have been handed down from others or make requests concerning matters pertaining to the next life even if the words do not resemble those found in traditional supplications. It is permissible to pray for someone else provided that one does not address the person directly; for example, rather than saying, "May God cause you to enter Paradise, father!" (in which case, one's prayer will be invalidated), one should say, "O God, cause my father to enter Paradise!" As for requests for merely worldly pleasures—for example, by asking God for a beautiful slave girl, sumptuous food, and the like—they will invalidate one's prayer. Finally, the Hanbalis hold that it is acceptable to utter lengthy supplications provided that they cause no hardship for those being led in communal prayer.

Recommended practices during prayer

As we have seen, the Shafiis and the Hanbalis make no distinction between the terms 'recommended', 'Sunnah', and 'desirable'; rather, they consider all three terms synonymous. We have already presented the Sunnah-based practices associated with prayer (and which, in the view of the Shafiis and the Hanbalis, may likewise be referred to as either recommended or desirable). As for those who distinguish between the terms 'Sunnah' and 'recommended'—namely, the Malikis and the Hanafis—we have listed the practices which they classify as recommended below.[128]

---

128. The Malikis list the following as recommended actions associated with ritual prayer: (1) Consciously intending either to perform a given prayer on time or to perform it as a compensatory prayer depending on the situation; (2) Consciously intending a specific number of *rak'ahs*; (3) Praying with an attitude of humble reverence, that is, with a constant mindfulness of God's majesty and splendor and with the awareness that one is worshipping God alone; (4) Raising one's hands to one's shoulders when uttering *takbīrat al-iḥrām*, then bringing them gently down to one's sides; (5) Reciting the *Fātiḥah* in its entirety; (6) Lengthening one's Qur'anic recitation in the dawn and noon prayers, bearing in mind that the noon recitation should be shorter than the dawn recitation; (7) Shortening the Qur'anic recitation in the mid-afternoon and sundown prayers; (8) Doing a medium-length recitation in the evening prayer; (9) Making certain that the second *rak'ah* is shorter time-wise than the first; (10) Reciting just loudly enough to be able to hear oneself in silent prayers; (11) For those being led in communal prayer to recite to themselves in silent prayers; (12) For those being led in prayer and for those praying alone to utter the word *Āmīn* both in silent and audible prayers; (13) For the imam to utter the word *Āmīn* only in silent prayers; (14) Uttering the word *Āmīn* silently; (15) Holding one's back straight when bowing; (16) Holding one's hands on one's knees while bowing; (17) Holding one's fingers firmly over one's knees when bowing; (18) Holding one's knees straight while bowing; (19) Praising God when bowing with the words, "Glory be to my great Lord" (*subḥān rabbī al-'aẓīm*); (20) For a man to hold his elbows away from his sides when bowing; (21) For those being led in prayer and those praying alone to say, "Our Lord, and to You praise belongs" (*rabbanā wa laka al-ḥamd*); (22) Uttering the words *Allāhu akbar* when coming down into, or up from, a bow or prostration except when one is standing up after the second of two *rak'ahs*, in which case one waits until he or she is in a fully upright position before uttering it. As for those being led in prayer, they are not to rise after the first two *rak'ahs* until after the imam has stood up; (23) Holding one's forehead firmly to the floor when prostrating; (24) Placing one's hands on the floor before one's knees when coming down into a prostration; (25) Lifting one's knees off the floor, then one's hands when coming up after a prostration; (26) Placing one's hands across from or near one's ears when prostrating; (27) Holding one's fingers

together when prostrating; (28) Pointing one's fingertips toward the *qiblah* when prostrating; (29) For a man to maintain a moderate distance between his elbows and his knees, his abdomen and his thighs, and his upper arms and his sides when prostrating; (30) For a woman to hold her limbs close to her body when prostrating; (31) Lifting one's buttocks in the air when prostrating; (32) Uttering words of praise to God and offering prayers of supplication when prostrating; (33) When seated during prayer, to adopt the posture known as *al-ifḍā'*, in which one sits with the left leg and the left side of one's buttocks on the floor and the left foot pointing toward the right thigh; the right knee is on the floor and the right foot is held perpendicular to the floor, with the underside of one's right big toe on the floor; (34) Placing one's hands on one's thighs (near the knees) when seated; (35) Leaving a space between one's thighs when seated; (36) When seated for the testimony, to fold in all the fingers of one's right hand with the exception of the forefinger and the thumb, and to extend the forefinger and thumb while moving the forefinger back and forth; (37) Reciting the prayer of obedience, particularly during the dawn prayer, and prior to bowing for the second *rak'ah*; as for the text of this prayer, it is as follows: "O God, we seek Your aid and Your forgiveness, placing in You our faith and full confidence. We submit ourselves to You and refuse to follow those who deny Your truth. O God, You alone do we worship. To You do we pray and before You do we prostrate ourselves. It is You for whose sake we strive and We make haste to do Your bidding. We hope to receive Your mercy and we fear Your grievous chastisement; indeed, Your chastisement will overtake those who deny Your truth" (*Allāhumma innā nasta'īnuk wa nastaghfiruk wa nu'minu bika wa natawakkalu 'alayka and nakhḍa'u laka wa nakhla'u, wa natruku man yakfuruk. Allāhumma iyyāka na'budu wa laka nuṣallī wa nasjud, wa ilayka nas'ā wa naḥfud. Narjū raḥmataka wa nakhāfu 'adhābaka al-jidd. Inna 'adhābaka bil-kāfirīna mulḥiq.*) This wording is based on the version passed down by Imam Mālik; (38) Uttering silent supplication before the greeting of peace; (39) Uttering the testimony silently; (40) Wording one's supplication in general rather than specific terms; and (41) Turning toward the right only for the concluding greeting of peace.

* * *

The Hanafis consider the terms 'recommended' (*mandūb*) and 'desirable' (*mustaḥabb*) to be synonymous; in connection with ritual prayer, the Hanafis make use of an additional term which they likewise equate with these two, namely, "rules of etiquette" (*ādāb*). The "rules of etiquette" for prayer are as follows: (1) The worshiper should not look at anything which would distract him or her from prayer. This includes such things as reading something written on a wall, staring at wall inscriptions, etc. Rather, while standing, one should look at the spot on the floor where he places his head when prostrating; while bowing, one is to look at the backs of one's feet; while prostrating, one is to look at the bridge of one's nose; while seated, one should look at his lap; and while uttering the greeting of peace, one should look at his shoulders. (2) When praying, we should do everything in our power to suppress a cough; as for coughing intentionally, for which there is no excuse, it invalidates prayer if it involves letting out a 'belching' sound like that produced by a burp. (3) We should likewise suppress yawns. This is based on the

The worshiper's *sutrah*

The term *sutrah* [literally, a shield or screen] refers to some object which the worshiper places in front of him—be it a chair, a stick, a wall, a bed, etc.—in order to prevent anyone from passing in front of him as he prays. According to the Malikis, the Hanbalis and the Hanafis, this barrier may be either a stationary object such as a wall or a post, or something the person places in front of him; for the Shafiis' ruling on this point, see below.[129]

It is agreed by all four schools that the use of a *sutrah* is recommended. As we have seen, the Shafiis and the Hanbalis make no distinction between that which is recommended and that which is Sunnah; hence, they hold that the use of a *sutrah* is both recommended and an emulation of the Sunnah. The Hanafis and the Malikis, by contrast, restrict the use of a *sutrah* to the category of recommended, which is less binding than a practice based on the Sunnah. Nevertheless, the Hanafis and the

---

statement of the Prophet, "Yawning during prayer is from Satan." Hence, if someone yawns, he or she should suppress it, for example, by forcibly keeping the mouth closed; if this is not possible, he should cover his mouth with his sleeve or the back of his left hand. (4) One should recite the *basmalah* between the *Fātiḥah* and any subsequent Qur'anic recitation. (5) A man should bring his hands out of his sleeves when uttering *takbīrat al-iḥrām*; however, it is more conducive to the woman's modesty not to do so. (6) When we hear the muezzin call out, "Come to prayer!" (*ḥayya 'alā al-ṣalāh!*), we should stand up. (7) When the *muballigh* utters the words, "Prayer has commenced!" (*qad qāmat al-ṣalāh*), the imam should commence the prayer in order for the words of the *muballigh* to reflect the actual fact, as it were. (8) If someone passes in front of someone who is praying, the person praying should make a slight gesture to this person to get out of his or her way.

129. The Shafiis list four types of 'barriers' in descending order of preferability, stipulating that it is not permissible to replace a type higher on the list with a type lower on the list unless it proves too difficult to use the former. The types of barriers are as follows: (1) Stationary, ritually pure objects such as walls and pillars; (2) Sticks inserted in the ground or articles of furniture which one has piled up to the required height; (3) The object on top of which one prays, such as a prayer rug, a cloak, etc., provided that it is not the rug or mat on the floor of the mosque; and (4) A line drawn in the ground either lengthwise or crosswise, though it is preferable for the line to be lengthwise.

In connection with types (1) and (2), they stipulate that the barrier must be at least two-thirds of a cubit [about 31 cm, or 1 foot – t.n.] in height; as for the distance between the barrier and the person praying, it must not be more than 3 cubits [about 1.4 m or 4.6 feet – t.n.] away from the tips of the person's toes when he is standing, or from his knees when he is seated.

In connection with types (3) and (4), they stipulate that the barrier should extend at least two-thirds of a cubit in the direction of the *qiblah*, while the distance between the tips of the worshiper's toes and the end of the barrier closest to the *qiblah* should be no more than 3 cubits [1.4 m, or 4.6 feet].

Malikis hold that if someone prays in a place where people are passing by without using a *sutrah*, and if someone does, in fact, walk in front of the person praying, he or she will be guilty of wrongdoing for not having taken the required precautions in this situation. As for the Shafiis and the Hanbalis, they hold that such an occurrence involves no guilt but that it is simply undesirable. In sum, then, all the schools agree that not using a *sutrah* involves no wrongdoing [if, in fact, no one passes in front of the person praying], but that it is recommended that both the prayer leader and someone praying alone use a *sutrah*; as for those being led in prayer, their imam's *sutrah* serves as their *sutrah* as well.

There are particular conditions relating to the use of a *sutrah* which vary from school to school.[130]

---

130. The Hanafis stipulate the following conditions for the use of a *sutrah*: (1) The *sutrah* must be at least one cubit [47 cm, or 18.5 inches] long; as for its thickness, there is no minimum in this regard; hence, it could be as thin as a pencil and still be acceptable. (2) It must be straight rather than crooked. (3) The distance between the *sutrah* and the worshiper's foot must be 3 cubits [1.4 m or 4.6 feet].

If someone finds an object which would be acceptable as a *sutrah* but is unable to drive it into the ground because it is too hard, he may simply place it on the ground either lengthwise or crosswise, although placing it crosswise is preferable. If no suitable *sutrah* is available, a crescent-shaped line may be drawn on the ground. (A straight or crooked line may also be used, but the first type is preferable.) According to the Hanafis, it is acceptable to use someone else's back as a *sutrah*, but not his or her face; moreover, if the person is a non-Muslim or a strange woman, neither his/her back nor his/her face can serve as a *sutrah*. Finally, if the only *sutrah* a person has available is an object that is ritually impure or has been obtained illegally, he or she may still use it despite the prohibition against stealing or taking things by force.

* * *

The Shafiis stipulate the following conditions relating to a *sutrah*:

1) It must be at least two-thirds of a cubit [about 31 cm, or 1 foot] long, whereas they stipulate no minimum for its thickness; on this point, they agree with the Hanafis and the Hanbalis, while they disagree with the Malikis.

2) The object used must be flat and straight; on this point also, they agree with the Hanafis and the Hanbalis;

3) There should be a distance of three cubits [1.4 m or 4.6 feet] between the *sutrah* and the ends of the worshiper's feet; on this, the Shafiis agree with the Hanafis and Hanbalis and disagree with the Malikis, who hold that the distance need be no more than is necessary for a ewe to pass, plus the space taken up when the person bows and/or prostrates; in fact, [some] Malikis hold that the space need be no greater than that required for a cat to pass through it.

4) The use of a *sutrah* is an emulation of the Sunnah regardless of whether the worshiper has reason to be concerned that someone will pass in front of him or not; on this point, the Shafiis agree with the Hanbalis but disagree with the Malikis and the Hanafis.

5) If someone finds an object fit to serve as a *sutrah* but is unable to drive it into the ground due to its being too hard, he should place it in front of him either crosswise or lengthwise, although placing it crosswise is preferable. On this point, the Shafiis are in agreement with the Hanafis and the Hanbalis but in disagreement with the Malikis, who hold that the sutrah must be placed upright and not flat on the ground, whether lengthwise or crosswise.

6) If someone finds nothing at all to serve as a *sutrah*, he should draw a straight line in the ground in front of him, either lengthwise or crosswise, although lengthwise is preferable. On this point, the Shafiis differ with all the other schools, who hold that it is preferable for such a line to be in the shape of a crescent moon.

7) It is not acceptable to use another person's back or face as one's *sutrah*. On this point, the Shafiis differ with both the Malikis and the Hanafis, who hold that one may use someone else's back, but not his or her face, as one's *sutrah*, and with the Hanbalis, who hold that either a person's face or back may be used as a *sutrah*.

8) It is acceptable to use as one's *sutrah* something which has been obtained by illegitimate means; on this point, the Shafiis agree with the Hanafis and the Malikis and disagree with the Hanbalis, who hold that it is impermissible to use something which has been obtained illegitimately as a *sutrah*, and that it is undesirable to pray toward it.

9) It is acceptable to use a ritually impure object as a *sutrah*; on this point, the Shafiis agree with the Hanafis and the Hanbalis and disagree with the Malikis, who hold that neither a ritually impure object nor a contaminated object may be used for a *sutrah*.

* * *

The Malikis stipulate the following conditions with respect to a *sutrah*: (1) It must be at least one cubit [about 47 cm, or 18.5 inches] in length, and as thick as a spear. (2) The distance between the *sutrah* and the worshiper should be large enough to allow a cat or a ewe to pass between them, in addition to the space taken up when the person bows and/or prostrates. (3) The *sutrah* must be upright; hence, if the ground is too hard for the object to be driven into it, it is not acceptable to place it crosswise or lengthwise in front of the worshiper. (4) It is permissible to use another person's back as one's *sutrah*, but not his or her face. Moreover, if the person is a non-Muslim or a strange woman, neither his/her back nor his/her face may be used in this manner. (5) An object which was obtained by illegitimate means may be used as a *sutrah* despite the impermissibility of theft and extortion. (6) It is not permissible to use something which is ritually impure as a *sutrah*. (7) If nothing acceptable for use as a *sutrah* is available, one should draw a line on the ground, preferably in the shape of a crescent moon. (8) It is equally acceptable to use as one's *sutrah* a wall, a table, a stick, etc. This point is agreed upon by all of the schools.

For a presentation of the points on which the various schools agree and disagree with respect to the use of a *sutrah*, refer to our presentation of the Shafiis' conditions above.

* * *

The ruling on passing in front of someone who is praying

It is forbidden to pass in front of someone who is praying, even if the person praying failed to make use of a *sutrah* without a valid excuse. Similarly, a worshiper is forbidden to expose himself to the possibility that people will pass in front of him while he is praying, for example, by praying without a *sutrah* in a place filled with people passing back and forth. If someone does, in fact, pass in front of the person praying, the person praying becomes guilty of wrongdoing, not due to having failed to make use of a *sutrah*, but rather, due to the fact that someone passed in front of him/her during his/her prayer. It follows, then, that if no one passes in front of the person praying, he or she will incur no guilt, since the use of a *sutrah*, in and of itself, is not obligatory.

If someone passes in front of someone praying in a situation where: (a) the person praying has not made use of a *sutrah* and (b) the person who passed in front of him/her could have avoided doing so, then both parties are guilty of wrongdoing.

As for the Hanbalis, they stipulate the following in this connection: (1) A *sutrah* must be at least one cubit [47 cm or 18.5 inches] long, whereas there is no upper or lower limit to its thickness; on this point, the Hanbalis agree with the Hanafis and the Shafiis. (2) It must be flat and straight. (3) There must be a distance of three cubits [1.4 m or 4.6 feet] between the *sutrah* and the worshiper's feet. (4) If the ground is too hard for the object to be driven into it, it should be placed on the ground crosswise in front of the worshiper, which is preferable to placing it lengthwise. (5) If nothing acceptable is available for use as a *sutrah*, one should draw a line in the ground, preferably in the shape of a crescent moon. (6) One may use someone else's back or face as one's *sutrah*, provided that the person is a Muslim and is not a strange woman. (7) An object obtained by illegitimate means may not be used as a *sutrah*. (8) An object which is ritually impure is acceptable for use as a *sutrah*.

131. According to the Shafiis, it is not forbidden to pass in front of someone who is praying unless the latter has made use of a *sutrah* in accordance with the aforementioned conditions. If the person has made use of a *sutrah*, it is neither forbidden nor even undesirable, although it remains a departure from the ideal. Thus, if someone praying makes no use of a *sutrah* and someone passes in front of him during his prayer, neither of them is guilty of wrongdoing. Nevertheless, it is undesirable for someone to pray in a place so full of people that someone might pass in front of him during his prayer, whether anyone actually passes in front of him or not.

* * *

In agreement with the Shafiis, the Hanbalis hold that it is undesirable for someone to pray in a place where it is necessary for people to be passing back and forth, regardless of whether anyone actually passes in front of him or not. However, the undesirability attaches specifically to the person praying; as for the person who passed in front of him, he or she is only guilty of wrongdoing if he or she could have avoided doing so.

Conversely, if (a) the person praying has used a *sutrah* and (b) the person who passed in front of him/her had no alternative but to do so, neither the person praying nor the person who passed in front of him/her during prayer is guilty of wrongdoing. Moreover, if only one of the two parties has shown negligence in this regard, he or she alone becomes guilty of wrongdoing. These rulings are agreed upon by the Hanafis and the Malikis; for the views of the Shafiis and the Hanbalis, see below.[131]

It is permissible to pass in front of someone who is praying in order to fill a gap in a row of worshipers in communal prayer. This ruling applies regardless of whether the person who passes in front was present with the other worshipers before prayer was commenced or came in as the prayer was beginning. This ruling is agreed upon by all the schools except the Malikis.[132] In addition, it is permissible for someone who is circumambulating the Ka'bah to pass in front of someone praying.[133] As for

---

132. According to the Malikis, someone who has joined the communal prayer late is not permitted to pass in front of someone who is praying even if his purpose is to fill a gap in one of the lines of worshipers unless there is a clear path for him in front of the person praying.

133. According to the Malikis, it is permissible to pass in front of someone praying in the Sacred Mosque [in Mecca] if the worshiper has not made use of a *sutrah*; however, if the person praying has made use of a *sutrah*, it is not permissible. Similarly, it is undesirable for someone circumambulating the Ka'bah to pass in front of someone praying if the latter is making use of a *sutrah*; otherwise, there is no undesirability attached to the practice.

* * *

According to the Hanafis, it is permissible for someone circumambulating the Ka'bah to pass in front of someone who is praying; similarly, it is permissible to pass in front of someone praying inside the Ka'bah or behind the "station of Abraham" even if there is no *sutrah* between the person passing by and the person praying.

* * *

According to the Hanbalis, it is not forbidden to pass in front of someone who is praying in any part of Mecca or its sacred precinct.

* * *

As for the Shafiis, they hold that someone circumambulating the Ka'bah may pass in front of someone who is praying regardless of whether the latter has used a *sutrah* or not.

the boundaries of the space one is forbidden to enter in front of a worshiper, each school offers its own rulings in this regard.[134]

It is also a Sunnah-based practice for someone praying to indicate with a gesture of the eye, the hand or the head that people passing in front of him or her should get out of the way. If this doesn't work, the person might try some other tactic, provided that it does not involve so much movement that his or her prayer will be invalidated. This ruling is agreed upon by the Shafiis and the Hanbalis; for the views of the Hanafis and the Malikis, see below.[135]

---

134. According to the Hanafis, if someone is praying in a large mosque or in the open desert, it is forbidden to pass through the space between his feet and the spot where he places his forehead when prostrating. If he is praying in a small mosque, it is forbidden to pass between his feet and the wall of the mosque facing the *qiblah*, a distance estimated at approximately 40 cubits [18.8 meters, or 21 yards].

* * *

According to the Malikis, if someone is praying toward a *sutrah*, it is forbidden to pass between the person praying and the *sutrah*; however, it is permissible to pass behind it. If the person is praying without a *sutrah*, it is only forbidden to pass through the space in which the person bows and prostrates.

* * *

According to the Shafiis, the space which one is forbidden to pass through between someone praying and his or her *sutrah* is three cubits [1.4 m or 4.6 feet] or less. [In other words, if the distance between the person praying and his/her sutrah is three cubits or less, it is forbidden to pass between them.]

* * *

As for the Hanbalis, they hold that if someone is praying with the use of a *sutrah*, one must not pass between the person praying and his/her *sutrah* no matter how great the distance is between them. If the person praying has not made use of a *sutrah*, it is forbidden to pass through a space of up to three cubits [1.4 m or 4.6 feet] from his or her feet.

135. The Hanafis allow that a person praying is given license to do this although they do not consider it to be based on the Sunnah; moreover, it is not permissible to go beyond a gesture of the eye or head or a louder-than-usual utterance of *subḥān Allāh*, etc. As for the woman in this situation, she may clap once or twice.

* * *

The Malikis hold that it is merely recommended that one seek to urge people out of one's way when praying.

Undesirable practices during prayer

Fiddling with one's clothing, beard and the like

Movements such as fiddling needlessly with one's clothing, beard, etc. are undesirable during prayer; however, if a given movement is necessary, for example, in order to wipe the sweat off one's face or to brush off some dirt, it is acceptable.

Cracking one's knuckles or crossing one's fingers

Cracking one's knuckles during prayer is undesirable based on the saying of the Prophet passed down by Ibn Mājah, "Do not make noises with your fingers while in prayer." As for crossing one's fingers, it is considered undesirable due to the fact that when the Prophet once saw a man crossing his fingers while in prayer, he came and parted them for him.[136]

Placing one's hand on one's waist and turning

It is undesirable for someone praying to place his hand on his waist or to turn unnecessarily to the right or left.[137]

---

136. This report is narrated by al-Tirmidhī and Ibn Mājah.

137. According to the Hanafis, it is undesirable to turn to the left or right with one's neck; however, it is acceptable simply to look to the right or left while facing straight ahead. As for turning with one's chest in a direction other than the *qiblah*, it invalidates one's prayer if the change in position lasts long enough for one to perform a complete pillar of prayer.

* * *

According to the Shafiis, it is undesirable to turn one's face while praying, but it does not invalidate prayer; as for turning with one's chest, it invalidates prayer under all circumstances, since it entails turning away from the *qiblah*.

* * *

According to the Malikis, it is simply undesirable to turn during prayer even if one turns one's entire body; however, as long as one's feet are still pointed in the direction of the *qiblah*, it will not invalidate one's prayer.

* * *

As for the Hanbalis, they hold that turning one's face, chest, etc. during prayer is merely undesirable. However, turning one's entire body or turning one's back to the *qiblah* will invalidate prayer unless the person praying is inside the Ka'bah or in a state of panic.

Placing one's buttocks on the floor and holding one's knees up in the air

Another undesirable practice during prayer is to place one's buttocks on the floor with the legs bent and the knees held up in the air. This is based on the report passed down by Abū Hurayrah, may God be pleased with him, who said, "The Messenger of God forbade me to 'peck' like a rooster,[138] to crouch like a dog, and to turn like a fox." This ruling is agreed upon among the schools with the exception of the Malikis.[139]

Spreading one's arms on the floor and rolling up one's sleeves

Still other undesirable practices during prayer include spreading one's forearms on the floor or ground the way beasts of prey do, and rolling up one's sleeves to expose one's arms. This ruling is agreed upon by all the schools with the exception of the Malikis.[140]

Gesturing during prayer

It is undesirable to gesture with one's eye, eyebrow, hand, etc. during prayer unless there is some need to do so, for example, in order to return someone's greeting. This ruling is agreed upon by the Shafiis and the Hanbalis, but not by the Hanafis and the Malikis.[141]

---

138. The 'pecking' referred to here is the practice of performing one's prostrations so hastily that there is insufficient time to utter the Sunnah-based words of praise to God [t.n.].

139. According to the Malikis, this 'crouching' position is forbidden, although the most widely accepted view among them is that it does not actually invalidate prayer. As for what they consider undesirable, it involves placing the undersides of one's toes on the floor with one's feet perpendicular to the floor and one's buttocks resting on one's heels, or to sit on one's feet with their upper sides on the floor.

140. According to the Malikis, rolling up one's sleeves is only undesirable if one does so specifically in order to pray. However, if someone already has his sleeves rolled up for some other reason, then enters prayer this way, there is no undesirability attached to it.

141. According to the Hanafis, it is undesirable to gesture during prayer for any reason, even to return someone's greeting. The only exception they make to this ruling is a situation in which the person praying is trying to urge people passing in front of him to get out of his way.

* * *

The Malikis hold that it is permissible to gesture during prayer in response to any legitimate need, including that of initiating a greeting, provided that the movement involved is subtle. In fact, they rule that it is obligatory to gesture with one's hand or head to return someone's greeting when one is praying. However, it is undesirable to gesture in response to someone who has uttered a prayer for blessing

Pulling one's hair back before or after commencing prayer

It is undesirable to tie one's hair back before praying; as for doing so during prayer, it invalidates the prayer if it involves too much movement. This ruling is agreed upon by all schools with the exception of the Malikis.[142]

Raising one's robe from the back or the front

It is undesirable for someone who is praying to lift his or her robe either from the front or the back; this is based on the saying of the Prophet, "I have been commanded to prostrate on seven vital parts, and not to gather either my hair or my garments."[143]

Wrapping oneself in a robe or blanket in such a way that there is no opening for the hands

It is undesirable to wrap oneself in a blanket or the like in such a way that there is no opening for one's hands. If someone who is about to pray has only one garment [that is, no undergarment] to wear, let him wrap himself in it, but not in the manner of the Jews, which is undesirable according to the Malikis and the Hanafis; for the views of the Hanbalis and the Shafiis, see below.[144]

Allowing one's garment to hang loosely about the shoulders

It is undesirable to allow one's outer cloak—or, if relevant, the blanket or sheet one has wrapped around oneself—to hang loosely over one's shoulders without bringing one end of it back up over one shoulder. It is also undesirable for a man to cover his mouth while praying unless he has an acceptable excuse for doing so.

---

on the person praying due to his or her having sneezed. [It is a Sunnah-based practice in Islam to respond to someone who sneezes by saying, "May God's mercy be upon you!" (*yarḥamuka Allāh!*) and for the person who sneezed to respond by saying, "May God reward both you and us" (*athābanā wa athābakum Allāh*) – t.n.]

142. The Malikis hold that pulling one's hair back precisely for the purpose of prayer is undesirable, but that if it is done for some other reason, it is acceptable.

143. This hadith is narrated by both Muslim and al-Bukhārī.

144. According to the Hanbalis, the type of 'wrapping' which is undesirable involves wearing one's robe in such a way that its center is under one's right armpit while its ends are over one's left shoulder without wearing another robe underneath. If another robe is worn underneath, this practice is not undesirable.

* * *

As for the Shafiis, they list no such custom among the undesirable practices associated with prayer.

According to the Hanafis and the Hanbalis, it is undesirable to wear one's garment in prayer in such a way that it passes under the right armpit and over the left shoulder, leaving the right shoulder exposed.[145]

Completing the recitation of a surah of the Qur'ān while bowing

It is undesirable to complete one's Qur'anic recitation when in the bowing position; as for completing the recitation of the *Fātiḥah* while bowing, it invalidates one's prayer in a situation where the *Fātiḥah* is obligatory. This ruling is agreed upon by all the schools with the exception of the Hanafis.[146]

Uttering the words *Allāhu akbar* and the like at the wrong time

It is undesirable to utter the various words of divine remembrance (*dhikr*) associated with the transitions between one pillar of prayer and another at the wrong times. This is because the Sunnah dictates that such words should only be said between the end of one pillar and the beginning of the next. For example, it is undesirable to say *sami'a Allāhu li man ḥamidah* ("God hears those who praise Him") after one has risen fully from a bow; rather, it should be said after the bow [one pillar of prayer] is completed and as one rises into a standing position [the next pillar]. This ruling is agreed upon by the Hanafis and the Shafiis; for the views of the Malikis and the Hanbalis, see below.[147]

---

145. According to the Malikis, it is recommended that one let one's cloak or robe hang loosely over one's shoulders; in fact, it is an emphatically enjoined Sunnah-based practice for the mosque's imam. It is also recommended that such a robe, cloak, etc. be 6 cubits [approximately 9 feet – t.n.] long and 3 cubits [approx. 4 1/2 feet – t.n.] wide if possible. An equivalent to such a garment is the burnoose, or hooded cloak.

146. According to the Hanafis, completing the recitation of the *Fātiḥah* while bowing is undesirable just as it is to complete the recitation of some other passage of the Qur'ān while in this position; however, it does not invalidate one's prayer, since in their view, the recitation of the *Fātiḥah* is not obligatory, as we have seen. Nevertheless, the Hanafis rule that completing the recitation of the *Fātiḥah* while bowing is undesirable to the point of being forbidden, whereas the completion of some other Qur'anic passage in this position is not.

147. According to the Hanbalis, uttering the words of divine remembrance associated with the transitions between one pillar of prayer and another at some other time invalidates one's prayer entirely if it is done deliberately, whereas if it is unintentional, it simply requires that one perform a prostration of forgetfulness before the concluding greeting of peace. The reason for this is that according to the Hanbalis, it is obligatory to utter such transitional phrases during the transitions themselves, and at no other time.

* * *

As for the Malikis, they hold that it is simply a departure from what is recommended to utter such transitional phrases at a time other than the actual transition.

Closing one's eyes and looking upward

All four schools agree that it is undesirable to close one's eyes during prayer unless this serves a specific purpose, for example, helping one to avoid distractions. It is likewise undesirable to look upward while praying; this is based on the following prophetic hadith, narrated by al-Bukhārī, according to which the Prophet said, "Why is it that some people look up at the sky while in prayer? If they persist in doing so, their very sight will be lost to them." According to the Hanafis and the Shafiis, this practice is undesirable under all circumstances; for the rulings of the Malikis and the Hanbalis, see below.[148]

Reciting more in the second *rak'ah* than in the first

It is undesirable to recite more in the second *rak'ah* than in the first; for example, by reciting Surah 94 in the first *rak'ah*, and Surah 93 in the second, or by reciting the verse which reads, *qad aflaḥa man zakkāhā* ("To a happy state indeed shall attain he who causes this [self] to grow in purity" (91:9)) in the first *rak'ah*, and all of Surah 91 in the second.

As for repeating the same passage twice in the same *rak'ah* or in two different *rak'ah*s of the same prayer, it is undesirable if one has memorized other passages as well; this ruling, which applies whether one is performing an obligatory or a voluntary prayer, is agreed upon by the Malikis and the Shafiis. For the rulings of the Hanafis and the Hanbalis, see below.[149]

---

148. According to the Malikis, if one looks up in order to contemplate the divine 'signs' revealed in the heavens, it is not undesirable. As for the Hanbalis, they make an exception in the case of someone who burps while in communal prayer, in which case it is acceptable to raise one's head [presumably as a means of directing any unpleasant odor away from the other worshipers – t.n.].

149. According to the Hanafis, this ruling applies only to obligatory prayers, whereas in voluntary prayers, repetition of the same Qur'anic passage more than once is acceptable.

As for the Hanbalis, they hold that what is undesirable is to repeat the *Fātiḥah* more than once in a single *rak'ah*, or to recite the entire Qur'ān in a single obligatory prayer. However, they do not deem it undesirable to recite the entire Qur'ān in a voluntary prayer.

Praying in front of an oven or stove

It is undesirable to pray in front of an oven or a stove with live embers in it due to the similarity which this bears to the Mazdians' practice of fire worship. The only school which makes no mention of this practice as undesirable is that of the Shafiis.

Praying in a place where there is a picture

According to the Shafiis and the Malikis, it is undesirable to pray facing something which might distract the worshiper, such as a picture of an animal or something else; however, if it causes no distraction, there is no undesirability attached to facing it when in prayer.[150]

Praying behind a row of worshipers that has a gap in it

According to all the schools with the exception of the Hanbalis, it is undesirable to pray behind a row of worshipers that has a gap in it. As for the Hanbalis, they hold that if someone is praying alone behind a row of worshipers with a gap in it, his prayer will be invalidated, whereas if he is together with others, it is merely undesirable.

---

150. According to the Hanafis, it is undesirable to pray facing the picture of an animal under any circumstances even if it causes no distraction to the person praying; moreover, it is undesirable regardless of whether the picture is over the worshiper's head, in front of him, behind him, to his right or to his left. However, there are degrees of undesirability in this regard. If these positions were ordered from the most undesirable to the least, they would be as follows: in front of the person praying, then above his head, then to his right, then to his left, then behind him. The only exception to this ruling is a case in which the picture is so small that it can only be seen clearly on careful examination, such as the images on coins. Hence, if someone prayed near some coins with raised images on them, this would be acceptable; it is also acceptable to pray toward a large picture if it has no head. As for pictures of trees, it is only undesirable to pray toward them if they will be a source of distraction.

* * *

As for the Hanbalis, they hold that it is undesirable to pray toward a picture which stands upright even if it is so small that it only becomes visible on close examination. However, this ruling does not apply if the picture is lying down, or if it is behind, above, or to one side of the person praying.

Praying on the open road, in a garbage dump, and the like

It is undesirable to pray in a garbage dump, a butcher shop or slaughterhouse, the open road, a public bath, and the spots where camels are brought to drink, kneel down, then drink again even if the person praying is assured that he or she is not in contact with any ritual impurity. This ruling is agreed upon by the Shafiis and the Hanafis; for the views of the Malikis and the Hanbalis, see below.[151]

---

151. According to the Malikis, there is no undesirability attached to praying in a garbage dump, a butcher shop or a slaughterhouse or in the middle of a road provided that the person praying is assured that he or she will not be contaminated by any ritual impurity. If the person praying is certain or has good reason to believe that he or she has come in contact with some ritual impurity, his or her prayer will be invalid, whereas if he or she only suspects this, the prayer remains valid, but should be repeated before the time period for the prayer in question has run out. (If someone prays on the road due to the mosque's being too crowded and has some doubt as to his ritual purity, he is not required to repeat the prayer.) However, the Malikis hold that praying in the spots where camels are brought to kneel down and drink is undesirable even if the person praying is assured that he or she has not come into contact with any ritual impurity; hence, they hold that such a prayer should be repeated before the time period for the prayer concerned runs out. As for prayer in the places where camels halt to rest and sleep, the most widely accepted view is that this is not undesirable if the person praying is assured that he or she has not come into contact with any ritual impurity.

* * *

As for the Hanbalis, they rule that prayer performed in a garbage dump, a butcher shop or slaughterhouse, the open road, a public bath, and places where camels stop to kneel down and drink is both forbidden and invalid unless someone has a legitimate excuse, such as having been confined to such a place against his or her will. The same applies to the roofs of such places; however, an exception is made for the funeral prayer, which may be performed in a graveyard, in a tomb or on top of a tomb.

Praying in a cemetery

Similarly, it is undesirable to pray in a graveyard, with differences of detail provided by the various schools.[152]

---

152. According to the Hanafis, it is undesirable to pray in a cemetery if there is a grave directly in front of the person praying such that, if he or she looks down reverently, he or she will look directly at it. However, if the tomb is behind, above, or below the spot where the worshiper is standing, there is no undesirability attached to the prayer. Moreover, if the cemetery contains a place which has been specially set aside for prayer and which, consequently, is kept free of dirt and ritual impurity, praying in the cemetery is not undesirable. It must also be noted that no undesirability attaches to prayer at the gravesites of the prophets, may peace be upon them.

* * *

According to the Hanbalis, prayer in a cemetery (which they define as a spot where at least three tombs are located on land which has been set side as a religious endowment for burial) is invalid under all circumstances. However, if the spot contains fewer than three tombs, prayers performed there are valid and have no undesirability attached to them provided that one does not pray facing one of the tombs; in this case, the prayer will be valid, but undesirable.

* * *

According to the Shafiis, it is undesirable to pray in a cemetery in which the graves have not been dug up, regardless of whether they are behind, in front of, or to the left or right of the worshiper. As for the graves of martyrs and prophets, praying at them is not undesirable provided that one's intention in doing so is not to venerate the people buried there; if this is the intention, however, it is forbidden. As for prayer in a cemetery containing graves which have been dug up, and without any sort of barrier between such graves and the person praying, it is invalid due to the ritual impurity which is bound to be present.

* * *

As for the Malikis, they hold that prayer in a cemetery is permissible and has no undesirability attached to it provided that the person praying is assured that he or she has not come into contact with any ritual impurity. Otherwise, the ruling relevant to prayer in a garbage dump and other similar places applies here as well.

An overview of undesirable practices associated with prayer

In the footnote below, we have provided a complete listing of those practices associated with prayer which are considered undesirable by each of the four schools.[153]

---

153. The Hanafis list the following practices as being undesirable in association with ritual prayer: (1) Deliberately neglecting to perform a 'duty' or an emphatically enjoined Sunnah-based practice; this is undesirable to the point of being forbidden, although the guilt resulting from neglect of a 'duty' is more serious than that resulting from neglect of an emphatically enjoined Sunnah-based practice; (2) Fiddling with one's clothes or one's body; (3) Removing small stones from in front of where one is praying, unless it is done when preparing to prostrate; (4) Cracking one's knuckles; (5) Crossing one's fingers; (6) Turning one's head away from the *qiblah* (as opposed to merely looking to the side, which is acceptable, and as opposed to turning with one's chest, which invalidates prayer); (7) Crouching [that is, sitting with one's buttocks on the floor, one's legs bent and one's knees up]; (8) Spreading one's arms on the floor; (9) Rolling up one's sleeves to expose one's arms; (10) Praying in nothing but trousers when one could have put on a shirt as well; (11) Returning someone's greeting with a gesture; (12) Sitting cross-legged without a legitimate excuse; (13) Braiding one's hair; (14) Tying a scarf around one's head while leaving the crown exposed; (15) Lifting one's garment up in the front or the back when preparing to prostrate; (16) Allowing one's *izār* to drag on the floor [the *izār* being a garment consisting of a piece of fabric that wraps around a man's waist and comes down to the ankles – t.n.]; (17) Wrapping oneself in one's robe, etc., in such a way that there is no opening for one's hands; (18) Passing the center of one's garment under the right armpit and draping its ends over the left shoulder, or vice-versa; (19) Completing a Qur'anic recitation when one is not standing up; (20) Prolonging the first of every pair of *rak'ahs* in a voluntary prayer, unless there is support for such a practice which is attributed either to the Prophet or one of his Companions, for example, by the recitation of Surah 87, then Surah 109, then Surah 112 in the *witr*, since the rulings which apply to voluntary prayers in connection with Qur'anic recitation apply likewise to the *witr*; (21) Making the second *rak'ah* longer than the first (bearing in mind that all four schools agree on the desirability of reciting three or more verses in all obligatory prayers and, properly speaking, in voluntary prayers as well); (22) Reciting the same passage from the Qur'ān twice in a single *rak'ah* or in two consecutive *rak'ahs* in an obligatory prayer; in voluntary prayers, however, such repetition is acceptable; (23) Reciting, in two consecutive *rak'ahs*, two different surahs of the Qur'ān which are separated by a single surah (for example, by reciting Surah 112 in the first *rak'ah*, and in the second, Surah 114 while leaving out Surah 113), since this gives the impression that one prefers some passages of the Qur'ān over others and thus deliberately leaves some of them out; (24) Deliberately smelling some perfume; (25) Fanning oneself once or twice with a fan, one's robe, etc.; if it is done three or more times, one's prayer will be invalidated; (26) Pointing the tips of one's fingers or toes away from the *qiblah* while prostrating ; (27) Neglecting to place one's hands on one's knees while bowing; (28) Neglecting to place one's hands on one's thighs while seated between the two prostrations of a given *rak'ah* and while seated for the

testimony; (29) Failing to hold one's right hand over one's left in the manner described above while standing; (30) Yawning; if one cannot resist a yawn, one should suppress it as much as possible, for example, by placing the back of one's right hand or one's sleeve over one's mouth while standing, and the back of one's left hand while in some other position; (31) Closing one's eyes, unless closing them serves some good purpose; (32) Looking upward; (33) Stretching; (34) Engaging in movements which are inconsistent with the act of praying unless they contribute toward prayer in some way such as moving one's fingers; for example, if an insect is biting the worshiper so much that he or she cannot concentrate on his/her prayer, it is not undesirable to kill it, though one should take care not to come in contact with its blood; (35) Covering one's nose and mouth; (36) Placing something which does not dissolve in one's mouth if the object will distract one from completing the Sunnah-based recitations or otherwise occupy one's thoughts; (37) Prostrating on part of one's turban; (38) Prostrating on nothing but one's forehead [that is, not placing one's nose on the floor as well] unless one has some excuse, such as a nose ailment of some sort; without such an excuse, this practice is undesirable to the point of being forbidden; (39) Praying on the road, in a public bath, in the bathroom, or in a cemetery; (40) Praying on someone else's property without its owner's permission; (41) Praying in a place located close to ritual impurity of some kind; (41) Praying when one needs badly to urinate, defecate or pass wind; if someone begins praying in such a state, it is recommended that he or she cut off the prayer [in order to "relieve nature" and repeat his or her ablutions, then begin again – t.n.] unless he has reason to fear that the time period for the prayer concerned is about to run out, or that he will miss a communal prayer; (43) Praying in worn-out, everyday clothes that have not been kept away from dirt and impurities; (44) Praying with one's head uncovered out of mere laziness; however, if one leaves one's head bare as an expression of humility and entreaty to God, there is no undesirability attached to it; (45) Praying in the presence of food which one has a particular predilection for, unless one is concerned that the time period for the prayer concerned might run out; (46) Praying in the presence of anything that might cause distraction or detract from one's sense of reverence, such as entertainment, play, and the like. It is for this reason that there is a prohibition against approaching prayer in a hurry; rather, one emulates the Sunnah by coming to prayer in a calm, decorous manner; (47) Counting the number of verses one has recited and/or the number of times one has said *subḥān Allāh* on one's hands; (48) In the case of the imam, standing with his entire body inside the *miḥrāb* rather than standing outside and prostrating inside; however, if there is so little space in the mosque that he has no choice but to stand entirely inside the *miḥrāb*, there is no undesirability attached to it; (49) For the imam to stand in a place which is at least one cubit [18.5 inches] higher than where those behind him are standing, or for him to stand on the floor or ground while those behind him stand on a spot that is raised above him; (50) Reserving for oneself a particular spot in the mosque such that it becomes a habit to pray there and nowhere else; (51) Standing behind a row of worshipers that has a gap in it; (52) Praying in a garment with figures on it; (53) Praying in the presence of a picture, regardless of whether it is above one's head, behind, in front, or to the side; however, this does not apply if the picture is quite small, has the head cut off, or represents an inanimate object; (54) Praying toward a stove or oven with live embers inside it; however, there is no undesirability attached to praying toward a lamp or light; (55) Praying in the presence of people who are asleep; (56) Wiping one's forehead with harmless soil during prayer; and (57) Limiting all one's recitation to a single surah of the Qur'ān simply to make things easy on oneself.

* * *

The Shafiis list the following practices associated with prayer as undesirable: (1) Needlessly turning one's face away from the *qiblah* when praying from a standing position; for someone obliged to pray from a reclining position, turning even his face will invalidate his prayer; (2) For a man to keep his hands inside his sleeves while uttering *takbīrat al-iḥrām*, while bowing, while prostrating, while seated for the first testimony and rising afterwards, and while seated for the final testimony; (3) Gesturing needlessly with one's eye, eyebrow, etc., even if one happens to be mute. If the gesture serves a specific need, for example, responding to someone's greeting, it is not undesirable provided that it is not done in jest, in which case one's prayer is invalidated; (4) Praying aloud in a situation where one should be praying silently and vice-versa unless there is some need to do so; (5) Praying aloud behind one's imam except in order to say *Āmīn*; (6) Placing one's hand on one's waist for no particular reason; (7) Rushing through one's prayer, yet still performing all obligatory actions; if one also fails to perform some obligatory action as a result, one's prayer will be invalidated; (8) For a man who is fully clothed during prayer to hold his upper arms close to his sides and his abdomen close to his thighs while bowing or prostrating; however, in the case of a female or a man who is wearing little, this practice is desirable; (9) Crouching; (10) Striking the floor or ground with one's forehead while prostrating; if one then allows the forehead to rest on the floor while uttering the relevant words of praise to God, this practice is merely undesirable. However, if, in addition to striking the floor with one's forehead, one rises again in haste, one's prayer is invalidated; (11) Spreading one's forearms on the floor while prostrating the way beasts of prey do, unless there is some need to do so; (12) Always praying in a particular spot in the mosque. This does not apply, however, to the imam, for whom it is not undesirable for him always to pray in the *miḥrāb*; (13) Lowering one's head excessively while bowing; (14) Prolonging the first or last testimony, even if one does so by uttering phrases that are recommended in prayer. In the case of the imam, this practice is not undesirable; (15) Passing the middle section of one's robe under one armpit and its ends over the opposite shoulder, leaving one shoulder bare; (16) Crossing one's fingers; (17) Cracking one's knuckles; (18) Letting one's garment drag on the floor; (19) Closing one's eyes unnecessarily. However, this may be necessary if someone is praying behind a row of scantily clad worshipers or in front of a wall with inscriptions on it; (20) Looking upward (bearing in mind that it is an emulation of the Sunnah to look skyward immediately after completing one's ablutions); (21) Gathering up one's hair or robe; (22) Covering one's mouth with one's hand or something else for no reason, although if one needs to do so in order to suppress a yawn, for example, it is not undesirable; (23) Spitting in front of oneself or to one's right side, but not to one's left; (24) Praying while one has to suppress the need to defecate, urinate or pass wind; (25)

Praying in the presence of some food or drink that one craves; (26) Praying in a place where there are many people passing by, such as the open road or the area where people circumambulate the Ka'bah; (27) Praying in a place where acts of disobedience take place, such as a public bath and the like; (28) Praying in a church; (29) Praying in a place where one is likely to come in contact with ritual impurity, such as a garbage dump, a slaughterhouse or butchery, a place where camels come to kneel and drink, etc.; (30) Praying in the direction of a grave; (31) Praying while standing on one foot; (32) Praying with one's feet touching; (33) Praying when one is very drowsy; (34) Praying separately from the row of worshipers as a communal prayer is being performed unless there is some reason for one not to pray communally [for example, when one worshiper is combining two obligatory prayers and others praying in the same place are not – t.n.].

The above rulings apply provided that there is sufficient time to avoid practices that would be undesirable; if there is not enough time, they are acceptable.

* * *

The Malikis list the following actions as undesirable in association with ritual prayer: (1) Uttering a prayer for divine protection in obligatory prayers; (2) Uttering the *basmalah* before either the *Fātiḥah* or some other passage of the Qur'ān. In voluntary prayers, including those being performed in fulfillment of a vow, the Malikis consider it ideal to leave off both the prayer for divine protection and the *basmalah*. However, if one wishes to show deference for those with opposing viewpoints, it is best to include both these supplications in all prayers; (3) Uttering prayers of supplication before or during Qur'anic recitation; (4) Uttering supplications while bowing; (5) Uttering supplications before or after the first testimony, or after the final testimony; (7) For someone being led in prayer to utter supplications after his imam has completed his prayer; (8) Uttering obligatory prayers of supplication aloud; (9) Uttering the testimony aloud; (11) Prostrating on a garment one is wearing; (12) Prostrating on part of one's turban. If it is thin, one is not required to repeat the prayer; however, if it is thick, one must repeat the prayer before the time period for the prayer concerned has run out; (13) Prostrating on a garment not being worn by the person praying; (14) Prostrating on a rug or a soft mat provided that it is not the carpet in a mosque, in which case there is no undesirability attached to it; (15) Reciting from the Qur'ān while bowing or prostrating unless one does so as part of a supplication; (16) Relying constantly on a single set of phrases for one's supplications; (17) Turning while in prayer without there being a clear need to do so; (18) Crossing one's fingers or cracking one's knuckles; (19) Crouching; (20) Placing one's hand on one's waist; (21) Closing one's eyes unless one does so out of fear; (22) Looking toward the sky for some reason other than to ponder the divine 'signs' found there; (23) Praying on one foot, unless there is some clear reason to do so; (24) Placing one foot on top of the other; (25) Standing with one's feet touching; (26) Thinking about mundane matters while in prayer; (27) Holding something in one's sleeve or one's mouth. If the object in one's mouth does not interfere with one's enunciation, it is simply undesirable, whereas if it does interfere, it invalidates one's prayer; (28) Fiddling with one's beard or something else; (29) Uttering a prayer for blessing on someone who has sneezed (for example, by saying, *yarḥamuka Allāh*); (30) Gesturing with one's hand or head in response to someone who has uttered such a prayer for blessing due to one's having sneezed while praying; (31) Scratching one's body slightly without a clear need. If there is a need, it is permissible, but if the scratching is excessive, it invalidates one's prayer; (32) Smiling voluntarily. If it is only a slight smile by commonly accepted standards, it is only undesirable, whereas if it goes beyond this, it invalidates prayer even if it was involuntary; (33) Deliberately omitting a minor Sunnah-based practice, such as a single utterance of *Allāhu akbar* or *sami'a Allāhu li man ḥamidah*. Neglecting an emphatically enjoined Sunnah-based practice, however, is forbidden; (34) Reciting a passage from the Qur'ān in some *rak'ah* of an obligatory prayer other than the first two; (35) Clapping due to a need relating to prayer; (36) Uttering the phrase *subḥān Allāh* without a need to do so; (37) Wrapping one's cloak, blanket, etc. around one's body in such a way that no opening is left for the hands; (38) Passing the middle of one's robe, blanket, etc. under one armpit while draping its ends over the opposite shoulder and leaving one shoulder bare; (39) For someone praying with mere gestures [due to some physical ailment, limitation, etc.] to remove something in front of him that he has been prostrating on, whether the object is in contact with the floor/ground or not; (40) Moving small stones out of the shade or the sun in order to prostrate on them; and (41) Uttering a prayer of supplication in some language other than Arabic if one could have done so in Arabic.

* * *

The Hanbalis list the following practices as undesirable in association with prayer: (1) Praying in a place where God once caused the earth to cave in; (2) Praying in a spot where a great chastisement was brought down, such as Babylon; (3) Praying inside a mill or on its roof; (4) Praying in a salt marsh; however, it is not undesirable to pray in a monastery or a church even if there are pictures in the place, provided that they are not set upright in front of the person praying; (5) Allowing one's garment to drag on the floor/ground; (6) Passing the middle section of one's robe under one armpit and its ends over the opposite shoulder and leaving one shoulder bare; (7) Covering one's mouth, nose, or face; (8) Rolling up one's sleeves for no reason; (9) Binding one's midsection with a cloth waistband, etc. This includes a man's or a woman's binding his or her tunic from the outside with something such as a scarf. As for a leather belt over something like a kaftan, this is acceptable; (10) Praying the prayer of obedience in any prayer other than the *witr* except in the event of some great misfortune. However, it is an emulation of the Sunnah for the "greater imam" [this may be a reference to the imam of the Sacred Mosque at Mecca – t.n.] to utter this supplication during all prayers with the exception of the Friday congregational prayer; (11) Turning slightly for no reason, either with one's face only or with one's chest as well. Moreover, if one turns enough that he or she is facing away from the *qiblah* entirely, his or her prayer will be invalidated unless he or she is in the Ka'bah or in a state of panic, in which cases the prayer remains valid; (12) Looking upward. If, however, someone burps while praying in community and looks up in order to spare others whatever odor the burp may have produced, this practice is acceptable; (13) Praying toward a picture set upright in front of the person praying; (14) Prostrating onto a picture; (15) Praying while having on one's person something that contains an image, such as the images found on currency; (16) Praying toward an animal or toward someone's face; (17) Praying toward something that will distract or preoccupy the person praying; (18) Praying toward something which contains fire, including even a lamp or a lit candle; (19) Sticking out one's tongue; (20) Holding one's mouth open; (21) Placing something in one's mouth; (22) Praying toward a place where people have gathered to talk; (23) Praying toward someone who is asleep; (24) Praying toward someone who is not a Muslim; (25) Leaning lightly on something for support such that if it were withdrawn, one would remain upright. If one is leaning so heavily that the object's withdrawal would cause one to fall, however, one's prayer will be invalidated; (26) Praying under conditions which would make it difficult or impossible to perform in the best manner, such as extreme hot or cold; (27) Spreading one's arms on the floor or ground the way beasts of prey do; (28) Crouching; (29) Praying while in urgent need to expel urine, stool, or intestinal gas; (30) Praying when one is extremely hungry, thirsty, or desirous of sexual intercourse; (31) Turning over small stones or pebbles; (32) Fiddling with this or that; (33) Placing one's hand on one's waist; (34) Fanning oneself unless there is some need to do so; if one does so excessively, one's prayer will be invalidated; (35) Resting one's weight first on one foot, then on the other; (36) Cracking one's knuckles; (37) Crossing one's fingers; (38) Leaning on one's hand while seated; (39) Praying with one's arms folded over one's chest; (40) Braiding one's hair; (41) Gathering up one's hair or robe; (42) Pulling one's robe up with one's hand before prostrating; (43) Designating a particular object on which to place one's forehead while prostrating; (44) Hanging an object in the direction of the *qiblah*, such as a sword or a copy of the Qur'ān; (45) Smoothing out the place where one is going to prostrate, unless one has a legitimate excuse for doing so; (46) Repeating the *Fātiḥah* in a single *rak'ah*. As for reciting more than one surah of the Qur'ān in a single *rak'ah*, even if it is an obligatory prayer, this is not undesirable; and (47) Reciting the entire Qur'ān in a single obligatory prayer.

Actions Which are Desirable and Undesirable in a Mosque

Passing through a mosque

It is undesirable to use a mosque as a pathway by which to reach some other destination, with each school offering its own rulings in this regard.[154]

---

154. According to the Hanafis, it is undesirable to the point of being forbidden to use a mosque as a path to reach some other destination without a legitimate excuse, although given such an excuse, it is permissible. If someone passes through a mosque more than once in a single day under such circumstances, it is sufficient for him or her to pray a two-*rak'ah* "mosque greeting" only once during the day. If someone makes a habit of passing through a mosque without a legitimate excuse, he or she incurs serious guilt; however, it is excusable to pass through it once or twice under such circumstances. Moreover, any guilt which may have been incurred can be counteracted by the intention to seclude oneself in the mosque for prayer and worship, even if the person does not stay overnight.

* * *

According to the Malikis, it is permissible to pass through a mosque if it is not done frequently; if it does occur frequently, it is undesirable if the mosque building was already in existence before there arose a need for a passageway between the place from which the person is coming and his or her destination. However, if there was once a roadway in existence on the spot where the mosque was constructed, this practice is not deemed undesirable. As for the performance of the two-*rak'ah* "mosque greeting", the Malikis hold that it is not required of someone who is merely passing through a mosque.

* * *

According to the Shafiis, it is permissible to pass through a mosque whether one is ritually pure or not; as for a menstruating woman, it is undesirable for her to pass through a mosque, although she may do so if she is certain not to contaminate it with any ritual impurity; if she is not certain of this, it is forbidden. Moreover, it is an emulation of the prophetic Sunnah for someone passing through a mosque to perform a two-*rak'ah* "mosque greeting" whenever he or she comes in provided that he or she is ritually pure or that it is possible to perform ritual ablutions somewhere nearby.

* * *

As for the Hanbalis, they hold that it is undesirable to use a mosque as a path to reach some other destination regardless of whether one is ritually pure or not unless there is a need to do so. As for staying the night there without being in a state of ritual purity, it is completely forbidden. It is also undesirable for a woman who is menstruating or postpartum to pass through a mosque unnecessarily even if she is

Eating and drinking in a mosque

Each of the four schools offers its own rulings on the undesirability of sleeping in a mosque.[155] As for eating in a mosque, it is undesirable for everyone but those who are secluding themselves there for prayer and worship, although on this matter as well, the schools' rulings differ in detail.[156]

---

assured that she will not contaminate it. However, if the need to pass through the mosque exists—for example, in a situation where it represents the shortest path to a given destination—it is acceptable for all the groups mentioned above.

155. According to the Hanafis, it is undesirable to sleep in a mosque for anyone but a sojourner or someone intending to seclude himself there for the purpose of worship and prayer. Someone who wishes to sleep in a mosque may intend to practice seclusion there; having settled on this intention, he must proceed to perform the required acts of obedience, after which he may sleep in the mosque without any undesirability attached to this.

* * *

According to the Shafiis, there is no undesirability attached to sleeping in a mosque unless it results in disturbance or distraction for those praying there, for example, due to a person's loud snoring.

* * *

According to the Hanbalis, sleeping in a mosque is permissible both for those who wish to seclude themselves there for worship and prayer, and for others as well. However, those who do sleep in a mosque must not sleep in front of those who are praying, since it is undesirable to pray toward someone who is sleeping, and if necessary, the worshipers may remove such a person elsewhere.

* * *

As for the Malikis, they hold that it is permissible to sleep in a mosque during the afternoon hours when people tend to take a nap regardless of whether the mosque is in an outlying area or in a city. As for sleeping in a mosque at night, it is permissible to do so in a rural mosque. If the mosque is located in a city, it is permissible, albeit undesirable, to sleep there at night if one has no house or will find it difficult to reach home in the dark. As for living in a mosque on a permanent basis, this is impermissible except for a man who has devoted his entire life to worship; for a woman, it is forbidden to live permanently in a mosque.

156. According to the Hanafis, eating foods which have no offensive odor in a mosque is mildly undesirable, whereas eating foods that do have such an odor, such as garlic and onions, is undesirable to the point of being forbidden; in fact, those who have recently eaten such foods are forbidden to enter a mosque. The same applies to someone who has such bad breath that he would cause offense to other worshipers, as well as to anyone who might cause others offense or harm, even if only with his tongue [presumably by what he says to others – t.n.].

* * *

According to the Malikis, it is permissible for strangers who have nowhere to stay but the mosque to take refuge there and eat there as well, provided that what they eat is a type of food that does not soil the place, such as dates. They may also

Raising one's voice in a mosque

It is undesirable to raise one's voice in a mosque, whether in regular speech or in the remembrance of the Divine; for further details, see below.[157]

---

eat foods which have the potential of soiling the mosque if they make sure not to do so, for example, by spreading out a mat or cloth on which to place the food. These rulings apply only to those foods which do not have an unpleasant odor, whereas foods such as these are forbidden in the mosque.

* * *

According to the Shafiis, it is permissible to eat in a mosque provided that the food is not liable to soil the place as is honey, ghee and other fatty food; otherwise, it is forbidden even if the food itself is ritually pure. As for eating foods which would litter the mosque but not necessarily get it dirty, such as fava beans and the like, it is undesirable.

* * *

As for the Hanbalis, they hold that those who are secluding themselves in the mosque for the purpose of prayer and worship may eat any type of food there provided that they do not get the place dirty or throw bones and the like here and there; if they do, they are required to clean up after themselves. If the food has an unpleasant odor, however, such as onions and garlic, it is undesirable to eat it in the mosque. Similarly, it is undesirable for someone who has eaten such foods or who suffers from halitosis to come into a mosque, and if such a person does come in, it is considered desirable to have him leave in order to avoid offense. For the same reason, it is undesirable to pass wind inside a mosque.

157. According to the Hanafis, it is undesirable to raise one's voice in a mosque when engaging in *dhikr*, that is, when uttering words and phrases in remembrance of God, if this causes distraction or disturbance to those praying or if it wakens those who are asleep; otherwise, however, it is acceptable. In fact, it may be desirable if it awakens the heart of the person doing the *dhikr*, thereby helping him overcome drowsiness and energizing him for acts of obedience. As for raising one's voice when engaged in regular speech, the Hanafis rule that if it involves talking about things which it is not permissible to speak of, it is undesirable to the point of being forbidden. However, if it involves the discussion of things which it is permissible to speak of, it is only undesirable if it causes distraction or disturbance to someone who is praying. These rulings apply to someone who has come into the mosque for the purpose of worship; otherwise, however, raising one's voice is undesirable under all circumstances.

* * *

According to the Shafiis, it is undesirable to raise one's voice in a mosque when engaging in *dhikr* if it causes distraction or disturbance to someone who is praying, teaching, reciting the Qur'ān, reading, or sleeping (provided that the person sleeping is one who, according to the Sunnah, shouldn't be woken up); otherwise, there is no undesirability attached to it. As for raising one's voice in regular speech, the Shafiis rule that if it involves speaking of things which are not permis-

Buying and selling in a mosque

Given differences in detail among the various schools' rulings, they agree that it is undesirable to conclude trade agreements in a mosque.[158]

---

sible, such as reciting spurious hadiths and the like, it is totally forbidden; if, on the other hand, it involves legitimate concerns, it is only undesirable if it causes disturbance or distraction.

* * *

According to the Malikis, it is undesirable to raise one's voice in a mosque even when engaging in *dhikr* and the pursuit of knowledge given the following exceptions: (1) If a teacher needs to raise his voice in order to make himself heard by his students, it is acceptable. (2) If the raising of one's voice causes disturbance or distraction for someone praying, it is forbidden. (3) Raising one's voice when uttering the *talbiyah* [a formula of praise to God used during the pilgrimage] in the Sacred Mosque at Mecca or in the Prophet's Mosque in Medina is acceptable. (4) It is acceptable for someone who has been secluding himself in the mosque for prayer and worship to raise his voice when uttering *takbīrat al-iḥrām* and the like.

* * *

As for the Hanbalis, they hold that raising one's voice in a mosque when engaging in *dhikr* is permissible unless it causes disturbance or distraction to those praying. As for raising one's voice in a mosque when speaking normally, it is acceptable if it involves the discussion of legitimate concerns and causes no disturbance to others; however, if it involves the discussion of matters which are not legitimate or if it causes disturbance to others, it is undesirable.

158. According to the Hanafis, it is undesirable to conclude exchange agreements involving purchase, sale or rent in a mosque; as for agreements concerning the giving of gifts, donations and the like, this is acceptable. In fact, it is desirable to conclude marriage contracts in a mosque. In addition, someone who is secluded in a mosque to devote himself to prayer and worship may conclude various sorts of contracts in the mosque, provided that: (1) they concern him or his children, (2) they do not involve bringing any sort of merchandise to the mosque itself, and (3) they are not actual business contracts.

* * *

According to the Malikis, it is undesirable to engage in purchase, sale, and the like in a mosque if this involves handling and examination of merchandise by potential buyers; otherwise, it is acceptable. However, selling in a mosque through a broker is forbidden. As for agreements concerning the giving of gifts, donations, etc. and marriage, they are acceptable; in fact, the conclusion of marriage contracts in a mosque is recommended. What is meant here by a marriage contract, however, is simply the conclusion of the basic agreement without going into detail or discussing conditions which have no bearing on its validity.

* * *

Making inscriptions on a mosque and bringing ritually impure objects inside it

It is considered undesirable to place inscriptions and ornamentation on a mosque with substances other than silver and gold, and if silver or gold is used, the practice is completely forbidden. This ruling is agreed upon by the Shafiis and the Hanbalis; for the views of the Malikis and the Hanafis, see below.[159]

It is forbidden to bring into a mosque anything which is ritually impure in itself or which has been contaminated with ritual impurity, even if it is dry. Hence, it is not permissible to use contaminated oil or fat in a lamp which is to be placed in a mosque, to plaster it with a substance which is ritually impure or to expel bodily wastes of any kind, even if it is done into a container, unless necessity requires it. An exception is made for entering a mosque wearing contaminated sandals or shoes,

---

According to the Hanbalis, buying, selling and renting in a mosque are forbidden, and any agreement concerning such matters concluded in a mosque is null and void. However, it is consistent with the prophetic Sunnah to conclude marriage contracts there.

* * *

As for the Shafiis, they hold that it is forbidden to use a mosque as a place for buying and selling if such activities rob it of its sanctity; otherwise, it is still undesirable unless it is necessary for some reason, and if it causes disturbance to someone praying there, it is forbidden. As for the conclusion of marriage contracts, it is permissible for those secluded in a mosque for purposes of worship and devotion.

159. According to the Malikis, it is undesirable, though not forbidden, to place inscriptions and ornamentation on a mosque regardless of whether the material is gold, silver, or something else, and regardless of whether it is done in its prayer niche (*miḥrāb*), on its ceiling, or on its walls; as for the construction and plastering of mosques, it is recommended.

* * *

According to the Hanafis, it is undesirable to place inscriptions in the *miḥrāb* or on the walls of the mosque's dome using paint containing actual gold if the money used to finance it was legitimately obtained and was not set aside as a religious endowment; however, if the money used to finance the inscriptions was obtained by illegitimate means or had been set aside as a religious endowment, it is forbidden. It is acceptable to place inscriptions on the mosque's ceiling and other walls provided that the money used to fund them is the legitimate possession of some individual; otherwise, it is forbidden. However, it is acceptable to fund the placement of inscriptions on a mosque with money that has been set aside as a religious endowment under any of the following conditions: (1) It is feared that the money might fall into the hands of unjust people; (2) The inscriptions will help to maintain the mosque's physical structure, or (3) The party who set aside the money as a religious endowment has decided to use it for such inscriptions.

which may be done if necessary provided that one is careful not to contaminate the mosque with anything that might fall off them. This ruling is agreed upon by the Malikis and the Shafiis; for the views of the Hanafis and the Hanbalis, see below.[160]

Bringing young children and the mentally deranged into a mosque

It is undesirable to bring young children or the mentally deranged into a mosque, though each school offers its own particular rulings in this regard.[161]

---

160. According to the Hanafis, all the practices mentioned above—including bringing into a mosque substances that are ritually impure in themselves or contaminated with such impurity, using lamps that burn impure oil or fat in a mosque, building a mosque with impure substances, urinating, etc. inside a mosque—are undesirable to the point of being forbidden.

* * *

According to the Hanbalis, it is completely forbidden to bring into a mosque that which is ritually impure or contaminated with such impurity if this will lead to some of it spilling or falling onto the mosque floor; otherwise, it is not forbidden. As for using impure oil or fat in a lamp placed in the mosque or urinating there, even if it is done into a container, it is forbidden. As for constructing or plastering a mosque with a ritually impure substance, it is simply undesirable.

161. According to the Hanafis, bringing young children or the mentally deranged into a mosque is undesirable to the point of being forbidden if there is some reason to believe that they might do something to contaminate the mosque with ritual impurity; otherwise, it is undesirable, but permitted.

* * *

According to the Malikis, it is permissible to bring a young child into a mosque if he or she will not be unruly or if he or she will remain quiet if forbidden to play; otherwise, it is forbidden. It is also forbidden to bring young children or the mentally deranged into a mosque if this will cause the mosque to be contaminated with ritual impurity.

* * *

According to the Shafiis, it is permissible to bring young children who have not yet reached the age of discernment or those who are mentally deranged into a mosque if one is assured that they will not contaminate the mosque with ritual impurity, inflict harm on those inside, or expose their private parts. As for a child who has reached the age of discernment, he may be brought into the mosque provided that he does not come in simply to play; otherwise, it is forbidden.

* * *

As for the Hanbalis, they hold that it is undesirable to bring a child who has not reached the age of discernment into a mosque without there being a need to do so; however, if such a need exists—for example, in order to give writing lessons—it is acceptable to bring both young children and the mentally deranged into a mosque.

Other matters relating to mosques

Spittle and mucous in a mosque

It is undesirable to allow spitting or the expulsion of mucous in a mosque; for the various schools' rulings on this matter, see below.[162]

Searching for lost items in a mosque

It is undesirable to search in a mosque for an item one has lost; this ruling is based on the hadith according to which the Prophet said, "If you see someone searching in a mosque for something he has lost, say to him, 'May God not restore it to you!'" All four schools agree on this ruling, although the Shafiis offer some specific details not mentioned by the others.[163]

---

162. According to the Shafiis, if someone first digs a hole in which to spit, then buries the spittle in the dirt, he commits no wrongdoing; if, on the other hand, he spits before digging a hole, he commits wrongdoing to begin with, but if he then buries the spittle, he will remove whatever guilt he may have incurred. Similarly, if someone spits on the tile floor of a mosque, he removes whatever guilt he may have incurred by wiping it up completely. However, if he spits on the floor and simply leaves it, he will have committed a forbidden action.

* * *

According to the Hanbalis, spitting in the mosque is forbidden. If the mosque has a dirt floor or a floor covered with gravel, someone who buries his spittle will remove his guilt after having spit, whereas if it has a tile floor, he must wipe it up rather than simply covering it up with a mat or the like even if no one sees it. Moreover, if someone sees spittle on the mosque floor, he has an obligation to remove it, wipe it up, bury it, etc.

* * *

According to the Malikis, it is undesirable to leave a small amount of spittle on a tile floor, while a large amount is forbidden. However, if it has a gravel floor, spitting is acceptable.

* * *

As for the Hanafis, they rule that leaving spittle, mucous or phlegm anywhere in the mosque, be it the floor, the walls, on top of a map or under a mat, is undesirable to the point of being forbidden, and anyone who does deposit such a substance there is duty bound to remove it. Moreover, it makes no difference whether the floor of the mosque is dirt, tile, covered with mats, or anything else.

163. According to the Shafiis, it is undesirable to look for a lost item in a mosque if it causes no disturbance or distraction for people who are praying or sleeping; if it does cause such disturbance, however, it is forbidden. This ruling applies to all mosques except the Sacred Mosque in Mecca where, because it is a gathering place for people, it is acceptable to search for something one has lost.

Reciting poetry in a mosque

With regard to the recitation of poetry in a mosque, each of the four schools offers its own rulings.[164]

Begging or teaching in a mosque

It is impermissible either to beg or to give a beggar charity in a mosque.[165]

All four schools agree that as for the impartation of knowledge through instruction, Qur'anic recitation, moral admonitions and wise sayings, it is permissible, though care must be taken not to cause distraction or disturbance to those praying. Moreover, the same rulings that apply to the inside of a mosque apply to its roof as well; hence, whatever is undesirable or forbidden inside a mosque is undesirable or forbidden on its roof as well. As for residences located over a mosque, they are not subject to the same rulings.

---

164. According to the Hanafis, if the poetry concerned contains moral admonitions and wise aphorisms and makes mention of God's grace and the qualities of those who are conscious of the Divine, its recitation in the mosque is a good thing. If it contains mention of abandoned campsites and the days of yore, the history of nations and peoples, and so forth, it is permissible. However, if it contains satire and fatuousness, it is forbidden; moreover, if it contains descriptions of cheeks, physical forms, hair, waists, etc., it is undesirable if it does not arouse people's passions, whereas if it does, it is forbidden.

* * *

According to the Hanbalis, poetry which contains words in praise of the Prophet and similar themes which are neither forbidden nor undesirable may be recited in a mosque.

* * *

According to the Malikis, the recitation of poetry which speaks in praise of God or His Messenger or which urges the pursuit of goodness is to be encouraged; if it does not contain such themes, however, it is not permissible.

* * *

As for the Shafiis, they hold that if the poetry concerned contains wise aphorisms, moral admonitions and other themes which are consistent with the principles of Islam and if it causes no disturbance or distraction to others, it is permissible; otherwise, it is forbidden.

165. According to the Hanbalis, it is undesirable to ask for charity in a mosque or to give charity to someone who asks for it; however, it is permissible to give charity to someone who does not ask for it.

* * *

According to the Shafiis, begging in a mosque is permissible but undesirable if it causes no disturbance to others; if it does disturb others, however, it is forbidden.

* * *

According to the Malikis, both begging and giving to a beggar in a mosque are forbidden; however, offering someone charity there is permissible.

* * *

Writing on mosque walls, performing ritual ablutions in a mosque, and closing a mosque except at prayer times

For the various schools' rulings on writing on mosque walls, see below.[166]

According to the Shafiis and the Hanbalis, it is permissible to perform ritual ablutions inside a mosque provided that one takes care not to soil it with spittle or mucous; otherwise, it is forbidden. As for the Malikis and the Hanafis, they hold that is undesirable to perform ablutions in a mosque under any circumstances.

As for keeping a mosque closed except at prayer times, this is deemed permissible by all of the schools except the Hanafis, who hold that it is undesirable unless there is reason to fear for property inside the building.

The preferability of praying in some mosques over others

Islamic law does not arbitrarily deem any location superior to any other. Rather, if it attributes superiority to this or that location, it is due to some distinctive spiritual attribute that sets it apart from other places. Consequently, it may be preferable to pray in mosque 'A' rather than mosque 'B' due to the religiously significant events that once took place in mosque 'A'. For example, the Sacred Mosque in Mecca is the site of the Ka'bah, the spot where we have been commanded by God to worship Him in a specified manner. Similarly, the Prophet's Mosque in Medina enjoys a special status which reflects the momentous spiritual events which took place there, such as the descent of revelation on the Prophet Muḥammad and the fact that it served as the center where scholars and leaders of Islam received the religion's

---

As for the Hanafis, they hold that begging in a mosque is forbidden, whereas giving to a beggar in a mosque is merely undesirable.

166. According to the Malikis, if the writing is on the wall of the mosque that faces the *qiblah*, it is undesirable because it will cause distraction to those praying regardless of whether what has been written is a Qur'anic passage or something else; as for writing on the mosque's other three walls, it is acceptable.

* * *

According to the Shafiis, it is undesirable to write anything from the Qur'ān on the walls or ceiling of a mosque, and if something from the Qur'ān has been written on a wall, it is forbidden to lean one's back against it.

* * *

According to the Hanbalis, it is undesirable to write anything on the walls or ceiling of a mosque; moreover, if this has been done with money set aside as a religious endowment, it is forbidden. In such a case, it is necessary to have the person who undertook such writing give the money back; however, if it is being done with his own money, he may be allowed to pursue the work.

* * *

As for the Hanafis, they hold that no writing should be placed on the walls of a mosque for fear that it might fall off and be desecrated by people's stepping on it.

fundamental tenets through the Messenger of God. Thus, scholars of jurisprudence have given preference to certain mosques over others based on their distinctive religious features.[167]

---

167. The Hanafis rank mosques as follows, in descending order of superiority: (1) the Sacred Mosque in Mecca, (2) the Prophet's mosque in Medina, (3) al-Aqṣā Mosque in Jerusalem, (4) the Qubā' Mosque, (5) the most ancient mosques wherever they happen to be found, (6) mosques which occupy the largest area, and (7) mosques located nearest to the worshiper. They add, however, that praying in a mosque in which religious lessons are offered is preferable to praying in a mosque which happens to be older, larger, or closer. Moreover, one's neighborhood mosque is preferable to a mosque where more people gather to worship, since one's neighborhood mosque possesses a right, as it were, to the participation and support of those who live near it. In sum, then, those who pray in a mosque should choose where they will pray based on the aforementioned considerations.

* * *

According to the Shafiis, the best of all mosques is the Sacred Mosque in Mecca, followed by the Prophet's mosque in Medina, al-Aqsā Mosque in Jerusalem, then those in which the largest number of worshipers gather (unless the imam of such a mosque is one whom it would be undesirable to follow, in which case a mosque with a smaller number of worshipers is preferable). Similarly, if a particular person's praying in a better attended mosque would cause a less well attended mosque to falter due to his being its imam, or due to his having a positive influence on attendance there, it is preferable for him to pray at the mosque that is less well attended.

* * *

According to the Malikis, the best of all mosques is the Prophet's mosque in Medina, followed by the Sacred Mosque in Mecca and al-Aqṣā Mosque in Jerusalem. Beyond these three, the Malikis deem all mosques to be equal, although neighborhood mosques have a special claim to our loyal participation.

* * *

As for the Hanbalis, they place mosques in the following order of preference: (1) the Sacred Mosque in Mecca; (2) the Prophet's mosque in Medina; (3) al-Aqṣā Mosque in Jerusalem; (4) mosques in general. However, they hold that it is preferable to pray in a mosque whose communal prayer depends on our presence; similarly, if our absence will have a demoralizing influence on the mosque's imam and its congregation, this is where we should pray; (5) old mosques; (6) mosques where larger numbers of worshipers pray; and (7) mosques which are more distant.

Actions, Events, etc. That Invalidate Ritual Prayer

After listing those events, actions, etc. which invalidate prayer according to each of the four schools, we shall present an explanation of those points on which they agree and those on which they differ in this regard.[168]

---

168. The Shafiis list the following as invalidating ritual prayer: (1) The occurrence of *ḥadath*, that is, major or minor ritual impurity; (2) Speaking in the middle of prayer; (3) Weeping and wailing; (4) Engaging in excessive movement, either movement unrelated to prayer itself, or the addition of movements pertaining to prayer itself [e.g., deliberately praying five *rak'ahs* in a four-*rak'ah* prayer – t.n.]; (5) Moving a hand up and down or from right to left three times. If the upward and downward movements are in immediate succession, they count as 'one', whereas if they are separated in time, each movement counts as one time. In the case of one's foot, a movement in a single direction counts as one time; (6) Doubting whether one consciously intended to perform ritual prayer, doubting the fulfillment of some condition for prayer's validity, or wondering which prayer one actually intended (e.g., was it the noon or the mid-afternoon prayer that I intended?). If such a doubt persists for the duration of an entire pillar of prayer, the prayer will be invalidated. However, if the doubt persists for less time than this, one's prayer remains valid; (7) Intending to cut off one's prayer before it is complete; (8) Hesitating over whether to cut off one's prayer or carry on with it; (9) Linking the intention to cut off one's prayer with some mundane event; for example, by saying to oneself, "If Zayd comes, I'll cut my prayer short." However, if one links it to some sort of mental event, such as two irreconcilable opposites meeting, no harm is done; (10) Shifting one's intention from one prayer to another unless the prayer to which one is shifting is obligatory. Thus, someone praying alone can shift his intention from the prayer he is praying [thereby invalidating this prayer] to another, voluntary, prayer if he sees a group praying such a prayer communally and he wishes to join them; (11) Suddenly renouncing one's faith or suffering an attack of insanity while in prayer; (12) Allowing one's private parts to be revealed during prayer even though one would have been able to conceal them; (13) Finding something with which to cover oneself if one has been praying naked; (14) Having one's body or clothing come in contact with ritual impurity that cannot be overlooked. This applies even if the ritual impurity gets, for example, inside one's eyes; however, if the substance comes out quickly of its own accord, one's prayer remains valid; (15) Prolonging the action of rising from a bow or the time one remains seated between the two prostrations in a given *rak'ah*. Practically speaking, prolonging the action of rising from a bow means that once one has finished uttering the required words of praise to God, one takes as long to rise to a standing position as it would take to recite the *Fātiḥah*; as for prolonging one's 'sitting' between prostrations, it means remaining seated

long enough not only to utter the prayer of supplication uttered at this time, but the obligatory portion of the final testimony as well. An exception to this ruling is allowed when rising during one's final *rak'ah*, and when seated between the two prostrations in the *tarāwīḥ* prayers; (16) Praying two or more pillars ahead of or behind one's imam without a legitimate excuse; (17) Deliberately uttering the concluding greeting of peace before it is time to do so; (18) Repeating *takbīrat al-iḥrām* with the intention of beginning one's prayer a second time; (19) Deliberately neglecting to perform some pillar of prayer even if it is merely verbal in nature; (20) The expiration of the time period allowed for one to wipe one's shoes rather than wash one's feet during ritual ablutions while one is in the middle of prayer, or the exposure of part of one's foot or sock from inside the shoe one has been wiping; (21) Following the prayer leadership of someone who should not be followed due to unbelief or some other cause; (22) Deliberately repeating some pillar of prayer that involves bodily movements; (23) Allowing something to go down into one's stomach that would cause one's fast to be broken, even if the substance was not actually eaten (a ruling which applies only to someone who is fasting); (24) Turning away from the *qiblah* with one's chest; and (25) Deliberately altering the order of pillars of prayer which involve bodily movements.

* * *

The Malikis list the following as invalidating ritual prayer: (1) Deliberately neglecting some pillar of prayer. (2) Unintentionally neglecting some pillar of prayer and not remembering this until a relatively long time has passed since one's having uttered the concluding greeting of peace with the belief that the prayer was completed properly. However, if someone mistakenly omits a pillar of prayer, utters the concluding "greeting of peace," then realizes the omission soon thereafter, he or she should cancel the *rak'ah* in which the omission occurred, then build on whatever he or she had prayed before this until the prayer is complete. If the person has not yet uttered the concluding greeting of peace or has uttered it by mistake and if the omission occurred in the prayer's final *rak'ah*, he or she should simply perform the omitted pillar, then bring the prayer to a close. If the omission occurred in some earlier *rak'ah*, he or should likewise perform the omitted pillar provided that he or she has not yet risen fully from the bow of the *rak'ah* following the one in which the omission occurred. If the worshiper has already risen to a full standing position from the bow in the *rak'ah* following the one containing the omission and remained still for a moment, he or she should cancel the *rak'ah* in which the omission occurred and not perform the omitted pillar. (However, in the event that the pillar omitted was the bow, the condition for canceling the *rak'ah* containing the omission will be that one has simply begun to go down into a bow in the following *rak'ah*.) (3) Retracting one's initial intention to perform prayer. (4) Deliberately performing a pillar twice, for example, by bowing twice in a row, prostrating twice in a row, etc. (5) Deliberately adding an extra testimony while seated following the first or third *rak'ah* [the usual place for the testimony being after the second and fourth *rak'ahs* – t.n.]. (6) Laughing out loud, whether intentionally or unintentionally. (7) Eating or drinking. (8) Speaking for some reason other than to correct an error in one's imam's prayer. If one does speak with this intention, one's prayer will remain valid provided that one does not speak excessively. (9) Deliberately raising one's voice. (10) Deliberately blowing out of one's mouth. (11) Deliberately vomiting. (12) Uttering the concluding greeting of peace when one is doubtful as to whether the prayer is complete or not. (13) The occurrence of something that would invalidate one's ablutions. (14) The exposure of any portion of one's highly private parts. (15) The event of some ritual impurity coming in contact with the person praying or his/her clothing during prayer. (16) Trying to correct or guide some other worshiper with whom one is being led in a communal prayer. (17) Engaging in excessive movement which is not part of the actual prayer. (18) Interruption by an event or a thought that prevents completion of one's prayer, for example, by realizing one is so preoccupied by the need to expel urine that it is not possible to concentrate, or by remembering a previous obligatory prayer that one forgot to perform. If, for example, someone praying the mid-afternoon prayer suddenly realizes that he or she forgot to perform the noon prayer, there are some who hold that one's mid-afternoon prayer is invalidated, while others hold that it remains valid and that one should simply pray a compensatory prayer for the one missed in accordance with the details presented below on making up missed prayers in the proper order. (19) Unintentionally adding four additional *rak'ahs* to a four-*rak'ah* prayer even if one is on a journey, or to a three-*rak'ah* prayer (a *witr*), adding two *rak'ahs* to a two-*rak'ah* prayer or a *witr*, or adding a number of *rak'ahs* equal to those performed in a voluntary prayer which is associated with a particular occasion such as the Day of Sacrifice. (20) For someone who arrives late for a communal prayer and has not yet performed a *rak'ah* with the imam to perform the prostration required of his imam before getting up to perform the parts of the prayer he has missed. This action invalidates such a person's prayer regardless of whether the prostration is one that precedes or follows the concluding greeting of peace. If, on the other hand, this person has performed an entire *rak'ah* with the imam, he should go ahead and prostrate with the imam. If the prostration [of forgetfulness] precedes the concluding greeting of peace, such a worshiper should perform it with the imam before rising to perform the parts of the prayer he missed at the beginning; however, if the prostration is one that follows the final greeting of peace, the worshiper must postpone it until after he has performed all parts of the prayer he missed in the beginning, and if he performs such a prostration before making up for what he missed, his entire prayer will be invalidated. (The prostration [of forgetfulness] that precedes the final greeting of peace is required of someone who omits a minor Sunnah-based action, such as a single utterance of *Allāhu akbar* or of the words *sami'a Allāhu li man ḥamidah*, or a desirable action, such as utterance of the prayer of obedience.) (21) Unintentionally omitting three Sunnah-based practices associated with prayer, then failing to perform a prostration of forgetfulness on this account and not realizing this until what would commonly be judged to be a 'long' time has passed since concluding one's prayer.

* * *

The following is a listing of those events, actions, etc. which the Hanbalis consider to invalidate ritual prayer. (1) Engaging in excessive, unnecessary movement which is not an integral part of prayer. (2) Getting some type of ritual impurity which may not be overlooked on one's body or clothing and having it remain rather than come off quickly of its own accord. (3) Turning one's back to the *qiblah*; (4) The occurrence of some event that invalidates one's ritual ablutions. (5) Deliberately exposing some portion of one's private parts (as opposed to its being exposed by the wind, for example, after which one immediately covers it up again). (6) Leaning heavily on something without having a legitimate excuse for doing so such that, if the object were removed, one would fall down. (7) Going back deliberately to the first testimony if one forgot to utter it and began reciting the *Fātiḥah* for the following *rak'ah*. (8) Deliberately adding an extra pillar that involves physical movement, such as an extra bow. (9) Deliberately changing the order in which one performs the pillars of prayer. (10) Deliberately uttering the concluding greeting of peace before one's prayer has been completed. (11) Mispronouncing words in one's recitation in such a way that its meaning is changed and not attempting to correct them. (12) Nullifying one's initial intention to pray by intending to cut off one's prayer. (13) Hesitating over whether to nullify one's original intention or not. (14) Determining to nullify one's original intention, even if one does not actually do so. (15) Doubting whether one consciously intended to pray as one commenced prayer and performing some action, such as a bow or a prostration, with this doubt present in one's mind. (16) Doubting whether one actually uttered *takbīrat al-iḥrām*. (17) Asking God for some worldly pleasure while in prayer. (18) Addressing someone other than God or His Messenger Muḥammad while in prayer. (19) Laughing out loud. (20) Saying something that is not an actual part of the prayer. (21) Getting ahead of one's imam. (22) The invalidation of the prayer being performed by one's imam, unless the imam prays forgetting that he is not in a state of ritual purity (a matter to be discussed below in the section on *imāmah*). (23) Deliberately uttering the concluding greeting of peace before one's imam. (24) Absentmindedly uttering the concluding greeting of peace [early], then not repeating it after the imam has uttered it as well. (25) Eating and drinking, unless it is an insignificant amount taken in by someone who does so absentmindedly or out of ignorance. However, voluntary prayers are not invalidated even if one drinks a small amount deliberately while performing them. (26) Swallowing something like sugar which dissolves [in the mouth], unless one does so inadvertently or out of ignorance. (27) Needlessly clearing one's throat. (28) Blowing out in such a way that it produces a speech-like sound. (29) Weeping for some reason other than brokenness before God if it involves the production of audible sounds; however, one's prayer is not invalidated if one's tears are beyond one's control. The same goes for coughing, sneezing or yawning even if it results in an audible sound. (30) Talking in one's sleep when one is neither sitting nor standing up. However, if one only dozes off for a short time and if one is sitting or standing up, one's prayer remains valid.

* * *

As for the Hanafis, they list the following as invalidating ritual prayer: (1) Uttering clear, audible speech which is unrelated to prayer, whether it is spoken absentmindedly, deliberately, by mistake, or out of ignorance. (2) Making mundane requests such as, "O God, give me something new to wear," "O God, pay off my debt", or "Let me marry so-and-so." (3) Uttering the words, "Peace be upon you" (*'Alaykum al-salām*) even if one says them absentmindedly or without the intention of greeting someone. (4) Returning someone's greeting verbally, even if one does so absentmindedly, since it falls under the category of "mundane speech", or returning such a greeting with a handshake. (5) Engaging in excessive movement which is unrelated to prayer. (6) Turning one's chest area away from the *qiblah*. (7) Eating or drinking something that was not already in one's mouth. (8) Eating something caught between one's teeth if it is as large as a chickpea. (9) Clearing one's throat unnecessarily due to the sound it produces. (10) Saying "Uff" or some such thing in expression of frustration, displeasure, etc. (11) Moaning. (12) Weeping out loud due to physical pain or some calamity one has suffered, such as the loss of a loved one or the loss of material wealth. (13) Saying *yarḥamuka Allāh* to someone who has sneezed. (14) Replying to someone inquiring about the uniqueness of God by saying *lā ilāha illā Allāh* ("There is no god but God!"). (15) Saying *innā lillāhi wa innā ilayhi rāji'ūn* ("Verily, unto God do we belong and, verily, unto Him we shall return" [Qur'ān 2:156]) in response to a piece of bad news. (16) Remembering an earlier prayer that one missed, provided that the person praying is among those who believe in the necessity of praying all prayers in their original order and if there is sufficient time [to cut off one's current prayer and make up the missed prayer first]. However, one's current prayer is only invalidated if one has performed fewer than five prayers since the one that was missed and if, when performing these prayers, one was aware of the prayer/s he had missed. (For more details on this point, see the section entitled, "Compensation for Prayers Missed.") (17) Saying "Praise God!" (*al-ḥamdu lillāh*) upon hearing some good news. (18) Saying "Glory be to God!" (*subḥān Allāh*) or "There is no god but God!" (*lā ilāha illā Allāh*) in expression of amazement at something. (19) The recitation of a passage from the Qur'ān as a response to something someone else has said, for example, by saying, "O John! Hold fast unto the divine writ with all thy strength" (19:12) in response to someone who comes to take a book or some such thing, saying, "Bring us our midday meal" (18:62) in response to someone asking for clarification concerning something he is to bring, or, "These are the bounds set by God. Do not, then, offend against them" (2:187) to someone who has requested permission to take something. However, if one recites such words simply in order to make it known that one is praying [for example, if someone knocks on the door and the person praying cannot answer], one's prayer will remain valid. (20) For someone praying on the basis of sand ablutions to see water that he or she could use for minor ablutions, provided that he or she sees it before he or she has been seated long enough to utter the testimony. The same applies to someone who performed minor ritual ablutions but who is praying behind an imam who performed sand ablutions, in which case his or her prayer, if it is an obligatory one, is invalidated as an obligatory prayer and turns into a voluntary one [with the result that the obligatory prayer will need to be repeated – t.n.]. (21) The expiration of the period during which one is allowed to wipe his shoes as part of ritual ablutions, or the person's removing his/her shoes, before he/she has been seated long enough to utter the testimony. (22) For an illiterate person praying to learn a new verse from the Qur'ān—whether by hearing it from someone else or by recalling it—provided that the person concerned is not following someone else's recitation. In order for the prayer to be invalidated, the learning must occur before the person has been seated long enough to utter the testimony; beyond this point, however, learning a verse by hearing it from someone else does not invalidate prayer. (23) For someone who has been obliged to pray with only gestures to regain the ability to bow and prostrate, since it would not be fitting to complete that which is 'weak' with that which is 'strong'. (24) Allowing someone to take over for the prayer leader when the person appointed is not fit for this task, for example, due to being unlettered or having a condition which exempts him from the usual requirements of ritual purity. (25) Seeing the sun come up as one is praying the dawn prayer. (In this connection, it is sufficient to see the sun's rays rather than the actual sphere.). (26) For the sun to go down as one is performing the prayer for either the Day of Fastbreaking or the Day of Sacrifice. (27) For the time period for the mid-afternoon prayer to begin while one is still performing the Friday congregational prayer. (28) For a splint to fall off due to the wound beneath it having healed over. (29) The termination of an exemption from the requirement of ritual purity [such as urinary incontinence, for example] by the occurrence of some kind of *ḥadath* not included in this exemption [for example, by one's passing gas when one has a recognized exemption from ritual purity on account of urinary incontinence – t.n.], or by the expiration of the time period for one prayer and the beginning of the next when one has such an exemption. (30) Deliberately bringing on an occurrence of *ḥadath* [such as passing gas and the like – t.n.]. (31) Fainting. (32) Suffering a sudden loss of sanity. (33) Entering a state of major ritual impurity (*janābah*) by means of a 'wet dream' or by looking at something that causes sexual arousal. (34) Praying alongside a woman while being led in communal prayer. (35) The exposure of some portion of one's private parts, even if this takes place due to one's performing ritual ablutions (since a woman, for example, must reveal her arms in order to perform ablutions). (36) For someone who had an occurrence of ritual impurity while praying to engage in Qur'anic recitation either as he is on his way to perform ritual ablutions, or on his way back from doing so. [According to the Hanafis, an occurrence of *ḥadath* during prayer invalidates not the prayer itself, but one's ablutions. Hence, in the case of such an occurrence, one may interrupt one's prayer to go perform ablutions, then resume one's prayer to completion – t.n.] (37) In the case of someone who has an occurrence of *ḥadath* during prayer, to postpone the required ablutions as long as it would take to perform one pillar of prayer. However, if one has an excuse for the postponement, such as being in a crowded place or needing to stop a nosebleed, one's prayer will remain valid. (38) Bypassing water that is nearby for water that is further away by a distance equal to two rows [of worshipers]. (39) Leaving the mosque because one suspects that he has had an occurrence of ritual impurity, since such a movement is counter to prayer. However, if he or she remains in the mosque in such a situation, his or her prayer will remain valid. (40) Leaving the spot where one is praying because one suspects that he or she did not perform ritual ablutions, that the period allowed for wiping his shoes has run out, that he has a missed prayer to make up, or that some ritual impurity has gotten on him, even if the person concerned does not actually leave the mosque. (41) For someone being led in prayer to turn unnecessarily toward another worshiper to teach him, correct him, etc. However, saying something to help correct the imam himself is allowed. (42) Receiving correction or instruction from some other person being led in the same communal prayer. (43)

Uttering *takbīrat al-iḥrām* with the intention of switching from one prayer to another. This applies, for example, to situations in which someone praying alone wishes to begin following someone else's lead in prayer, or vice-versa, or to switch from one obligatory prayer to another, from an obligatory prayer to a voluntary prayer, or from a voluntary prayer to an obligatory one. Any of the above 'switches' will invalidate one's prayer if it takes place before one has been seated long enough to utter the final testimony; otherwise, the original prayer remains valid. (44) Drawing out the initial *a* in the phrase, *Allāhu akbar.* (45) Reciting a passage of the Qur'ān which one has not memorized, or teaching such a passage to someone else through recitation. (46) Performing an entire pillar of prayer, or allowing the passage of enough time to perform such, while a portion of one's private parts is exposed or while one is in contact with ritual impurity which would preclude the performance of ritual prayer. (47) Being at least one entire pillar of prayer ahead of one's prayer leader. (48) For someone who arrived late for a communal prayer to perform a prostration of forgetfulness along with his imam even though he knows that this prostration is meant for the imam alone and not for anyone else. (This applies to a situation in which, for example, someone being led in prayer gets up either before or after the imam's final greeting of peace after having remained seated long enough to utter the testimony and completes his *rak'ah* with a prostration, after which the imam remembers that he needs to perform a prostration of forgetfulness, and the person being led in prayer performs the prostration of forgetfulness together with the imam.) (49) Failing to repeat the final 'sitting' after performing either a prostration which is an integral part of obligatory prayer or a prostration of recitation which one only remembered after performing the final 'sitting' for the first time. (50) Failing to repeat a pillar of prayer that one performed the first time in one's sleep; (51) Laughing out loud by the prayer leader or someone who arrived late for the communal prayer, even if the laugh was unintentional. (52) Mistakenly uttering the concluding greeting of peace after the first two *rak'ahs* of a four-*rak'ah* prayer. This might occur, for example, when someone praying the regular noon prayer thinks that he is praying the Friday congregational prayer [which consists of only two *rak'ahs* – t.n.]. (53) For someone being led in prayer to stand with one or both feet ahead of the prayer leader; as for standing parallel with the prayer leader, which does not invalidate prayer, it will be discussed below in the section dealing with prayer leadership (*imāmah*).

A woman's praying next to or in front of a man while being led by an imam

It is agreed upon by all of the schools except the Hanafis that if a woman being led by an imam prays beside or in front of a man, her prayer will not be invalidated, nor will the prayers of those to her right or left.[169]

---

169. As for the Hanafis, they hold that if a sexually desirable woman prays beside or in front of a man while being led by an imam, her prayer will be invalidated given the following nine conditions: (1) The woman must be sexually desirable; hence, her prayer will not be invalidated if she is a prepubescent girl, for example. (2) The woman's calf and ankle must be directly across from a man; however, if her calf and ankle are slightly behind him, her prayer remains valid. (3) The woman must be standing directly across from a man for the duration of an entire pillar of prayer. Hence, if she utters *takbīrat al-iḥrām* while standing next to a man, after which she steps back, her prayer will remain valid, since *takbīrat al-iḥrām* is neither considered to be a pillar of prayer nor to take as much time as the performance of one pillar would require. (4) The prayer being performed must not be the funeral prayer or any other prayer which lacks bowing and prostrating. Hence, the funeral prayer and other prayers lacking bowing and prostration may be performed with the woman next to a man and remain valid. (5) The man that the woman is standing next to must either be acting as her imam or be praying with her behind the same imam. In other words, if the woman is praying behind one imam and the man she is standing beside is praying behind another imam, no harm is done. (6) The man and the woman must be standing beside each other without an 18-inch barrier between them, or without being separated by a space large enough for a man to stand in. (7) The man must not have indicated that the woman should step back. However, if he does indicate that she should step back and she fails to do so, his prayer remains valid. (8) The man must have the intention of leading the woman in prayer. If he does not have this intention, her prayer will be valid. [The text reads, *fa'inna ṣalātahā lā taṣaḥḥu*, that is, "her prayer will not be valid"; but due to the contradiction this poses with what has just been stated, I opted to omit the negative – t.n.] (9) The man and the woman must be standing on the same level. However, if the woman is praying on a surface higher than the one the man is praying on, they are no longer considered to be beside each other, and her prayer is valid.

Deliberately uttering words unrelated to prayer

Deliberately uttering words which are irrelevant to prayer causes one's prayer to be invalidated. This ruling is agreed upon by all of the schools based on the words of the Prophet, "Mundane speech has no part in this prayer. Rather, it should include nothing but praise and glorification of God and the recitation of the Qur'ān."[170]

In order to invalidate prayer, speech must consist of at least two letters of the alphabet, even if they communicate no meaning, or one letter (or syllable) if it does communicate a meaning. For example, if someone says, *'i.* this is only one syllable, but it communicates meaning in the Arabic language, since it is a command meaning, "Be aware! 'Know!', or 'Remember!' If, on the other hand, one were to utter a single meaningless letter or syllable, such as the Arabic letter *jīm*, this would not invalidate one's prayer. Moreover, uttering a single letter without diacritical points[171] which communicates no meaning is similar to uttering incomprehensible sounds. (This ruling is agreed upon by all of the schools except the Malikis.[172]) In sum, the utterance of a single letter without diacritical points which communicates no meaning or a sound which contains no discernible letters or syllables has no effect on the validity of one's prayer.

Uttering irrelevant speech during prayer either absent-mindedly or out of ignorance

According to the Hanafis and the Hanbalis, uttering speech irrelevant to prayer causes prayer to be invalidated even if it is spoken out of forgetfulness.[173] The Hanafis, the Hanbalis and the Malikis agree that speaking during prayer out of ignorance causes prayer to be invalidated even if the person concerned was raised

170. Narrated by Muslim.

171. The undotted consonants in Arabic include letters such as *ḥā*, *dāl*, *rā*, *sīn*, *ṣād*, *ṭā*, *'ayn*, *lām*, *mīm*, *nūn* and *wāw* [t.n.].

172. The Malikis define speech which invalidates prayer as that which consists of one or more meaningful words; there are some Malikis, however, who hold that any sound extraneous to prayer, even if it communicates no meaning, will invalidate one's prayer.

173. The Shafiis hold that if someone speaks during prayer out of forgetfulness, this will not invalidate his prayer provided that he speaks only briefly. (In order for speech to be deemed 'brief', it must consist of no more than six commonly recognized words.) This ruling applies regardless of whether the speech is uttered before or after the concluding greeting of peace.

* * *

The Malikis hold that prayer is not invalidated by speaking absent-mindedly provided that it is brief; as for what is to be considered 'brief' or 'lengthy', this is determined by commonly accepted standards. Moreover, the same ruling applies whether the speech occurred before or after the concluding greeting of peace.

in a non-Islamic environment where there were no Muslim scholars to consult, or where it was difficult to gain access to them.[174]

All four schools agree that the prayer of someone who has been forced by others to speak while praying is invalidated. The Shafiis, the Malikis and the Hanafis agree that if someone dozes off while in prayer, but not deeply enough for his or her ablutions to be invalidated and if he or she speaks while asleep, his or her prayer will be invalidated; the Hanbalis, by contrast, maintain that such a person's prayer remains valid. However, the most intuitively appealing view is that such an occurrence invalidates ritual prayer; after all, someone who falls asleep while praying and, while in this state, utters things that have nothing to do with prayer, is totally oblivious to his Lord at such a time. Of what value, then, is a prayer performed by someone who behaves in this way?

---

174. As for the Shafiis, they hold that if someone speaks during prayer out of ignorance, his or her prayer will remain valid provided that the speech was brief and that the person concerned is still new to Islam or was raised so far from Muslim scholars that he or she was unable to reach them due to fear, lack of sufficient funds, etc. Otherwise, however, prayer is invalidated by such speech, and ignorance is not deemed an acceptable excuse.

175. As for the Malikis, they hold that speaking to correct someone else's prayer does not invalidate the prayer of the person who spoke regardless of whether this occurred before or after the final greeting of peace, and regardless of whether the correction came from the imam or someone being led in prayer. If the correction comes from someone being led in prayer, his or her prayer remains valid given the following two conditions: (1) That he or she not speak so much that he or she is sidetracked from prayer itself; and (2) That the imam not have understood what the person was trying to communicate to him by uttering the phrase, *subḥan Allāh*.

Hence, if the person seeking to correct the imam's prayer speaks excessively, or if the imam would have understood if this person had simply alerted him to his error by saying, *subḥān Allāh*, the prayer of the person who made the correction is invalidated. For example, if the imam mistakenly utters the concluding greeting of peace after the second *rak'ah* of a four-*rak'ah* prayer or, after completing the fourth *rak'ah* of such a prayer, he rises to perform a fifth *rak'ah*, and if he does not perceive the purpose behind the person's corrective *subḥān Allāh*, it is permissible for the latter to tell the imam something like, "You said the concluding 'greeting of peace' after only two *rak'ahs*," or, "You got up to pray a fifth *rak'ah*."

Speaking deliberately to correct someone else's prayer

All the schools with the exception of the Malikis agree that if the imam forgets part of a prayer and one of the worshipers he is leading says to him, "You forgot such-and-such," the prayer of the person who thus spoke will be invalidated.[175] However, it does not invalidate prayer for someone to utter the final greeting of peace out of forgetfulness; for example, if someone absent-mindedly utters the final greeting of peace after the second *rak'ah* of the four-*rak'ah* noon prayer, his or her prayer will remain valid.

Speaking during prayer to rescue a blind person and speaking by mistake

It is agreed upon by all four schools that speaking in order to rescue a blind person from danger of some sort invalidates ritual prayer; hence, if someone praying finds himself or herself in such a situation, he or she should simply cut off his or her prayer, then begin again. As for someone who speaks mistakenly, that is, who has a slip of the tongue and says something unrelated to prayer as a result, three of the four schools hold that his or her prayer remains valid; however, according to the Hanafis, speaking mistakenly invalidates ritual prayer.

The foregoing applies to a situation in which something is said during prayer by a worshiper being led by an imam. If the person to speak is the imam, his prayer remains valid given three conditions. (1) That he not speak excessively; (2) that he speak only when other means of communicating, such as the utterance of *subḥān Allāh*, have not been understood; and (3) that the imam not have any doubts about the correctness of his prayer, whether on his own or in response to words spoken by those praying behind him. If the imam does doubt any part of his prayer, he must cancel whatever part he suspects that he either omitted or failed to perform correctly, then resume his prayer, building on what he is certain that he performed correctly the first time. However, he must not ask anyone else about this matter, since if he does, his prayer will be invalidated. [In clarification of the second two conditions, suppose, for example, that someone being led in prayer thinks that the imam has made a mistake in his prayer and says *subḥān Allāh!* to alert the imam to the error. The imam, however, is certain that he has not, in fact, erred in his prayer and simply continues praying. The person being led in prayer repeats *subḥān Allāh!* and again, the imam simply keeps praying. If the misunderstanding continues, the imam may legitimately say something to correct matters, for example, "I've prayed two *rak'ahs*", or the like, without his prayer being invalidated – t.n.]

Clearing one's throat during prayer

If it involves the production of two or more syllable-like sounds, clearing one's throat invalidates ritual prayer. However, if it is necessary to clear one's throat, for example, in order to be able to pronounce the words in one's recitation clearly and correctly, in order to alert one's imam to an error he needs to correct, etc., it does not invalidate prayer. According to the Hanafis and the Hanbalis, clearing one's throat during prayer is also acceptable if it arises out of a spontaneous need. For the views of the Malikis and the Shafiis, see below.[176]

Moaning and sighing during prayer

Moaning, sighing, muttering in complaint, and weeping invalidate ritual prayer if they result in the production of audible, speech-like sounds unless they are an expression of humble brokenness before God Almighty or result from a pathological condition such that they are not under one's control. This ruling is agreed upon by the Hanafis and the Hanbalis; for the views of the Malikis and the Shafiis, see below.[177]

---

176. The Malikis hold that clearing one's throat does not invalidate prayer even if it involves the production of syllable-like sounds and even if one does not actually need to do so, provided that it is not excessive or done in jest.

* * *

As for the Shafiis, they hold that one may be excused for clearing one's throat slightly if it cannot be helped. Moreover, if someone suffers a chronic condition that makes it impossible to go without clearing his or her throat for the duration of a single prayer, a larger amount is excusable as well. Similarly, it is permissible to engage in a great deal of throat-clearing if it is required for one to be able to perform a pillar of prayer that involves speech, such as the recitation of the *Fātiḥah*. However, if the words involved are not a pillar of prayer, but simply an emulation of the Sunnah, it is not permissible to clear one's throat a great deal in order to be able to say them.

177. According to the Malikis, if moaning, sighing, weeping and the like are due to physical pain or if they are an expression of reverence before God, they do not invalidate prayer. However, moaning from pain does invalidate prayer if it is excessive; otherwise, it is subject to the same rulings that apply to speech during prayer. In other words, if someone moans in pain unintentionally, it will not invalidate his or her prayer unless it becomes excessive. If, on the other hand, the person praying moans, mutters, weeps, etc. intentionally, such sounds will invalidate his prayer unless they are associated with some other purpose, such as alerting someone else to an error in his or her prayer.

* * *

As for the Shafiis, they specify three scenarios associated with moaning, sighing, muttering and the like which result in the production of two or more syllable-like utterances: (1) Such expressions overcome the person praying to the point where he/she is unable to hold them back. In this case, the person praying is excused for what would generally be considered a moderate amount; however, no such excuse is granted to someone who carries them to excess, even if they happen to result

Supplication during prayer in a manner which resembles mundane speech

Ritual prayer is rendered invalid by uttering supplications which resemble ordinary speech, although the various schools differ in their particular rulings in this regard.[178]

---

from one's fear of the afterlife. (2) Such expressions are within the person's control, in which case he or she is not excused even for a slight amount even if they result from a fear of the afterlife. (3) Such expressions are excessive according to commonly accepted standards. In this case, they are only excused if they become a chronic condition, in which case they are judged by necessity not to invalidate prayer. The same ruling applies to yawning, sneezing and burping, each of which will be discussed below.

178. According to the Hanafis, ritual prayer is invalidated by uttering supplications which resemble ordinary speech. In order for a given supplication to be acceptable as part of ritual prayer, it must meet the following conditions: (1) It must consist of words and phrases taken from the Qur'ān and the prophetic Sunnah, and (2) it must be a request that could not be fulfilled by a mere creature. Hence, one may request anything one wishes if such requests are found in the Qur'ān or the Sunnah; as for requests not found in either the Qur'ān or the Sunnah, they are permissible provided that they are things that could not be asked of finite creatures but, rather, must be sought from God alone, such as assurance of one's daily sustenance, blessing on one's wealth, children, and the like. As for requests that might be made of other creatures, such as, "O God, give me an apple to eat" or, "O God, marry me to so-and-so!", these invalidate one's prayer.

* * *

According to the Malikis, prayer is not invalidated by making supplication for that which is good in this life and the next; rather, one may even ask God for things that would not be impossible for some mere creature to provide, by saying, for example, "O God, feed me an apple," and the like.

* * *

According to the Shafiis, supplications which invalidate prayer are those which involve a request for something that is forbidden, impossible, or conditional on the occurrence of something else. Beyond these, however, someone in prayer may ask for any and all good in this world and the next provided that in doing so, he or she addresses only God or His Messenger, for if someone in prayer addresses any but these two, his or her prayer will be invalidated regardless of whether the entity being addressed is a rational being (for example, if one were to say to someone who had sneezed, *yarḥamuka Allāh*, that is, "God bless you"), or inanimate (for example, by addressing the earth, saying, "God is my Lord and yours. I seek refuge in God from your evil and the evil of all that live upon you!").

* * *

As for the Hanbalis, they hold that supplications which invalidate prayer are those which are not found in either the Qur'ān or the prophetic Sunnah, and/or those which do not pertain to the afterlife. Hence, if one were to ask God for the provision of earthly needs and/or pleasures—by saying, for example, "O God, grant

Other Prayer-related matters

Guiding someone else being led in communal prayer

One's ritual prayer will be invalidated if someone being led in communal prayer does or says something to guide someone other than the imam whom he is praying behind. For example, if person 'A' is praying behind an imam while person 'B' beside him is himself serving as an imam but recites something incorrectly or is unable to recite at all, it is not permissible for 'A' to seek to aid or guide 'B', since he is bound to keep following his own imam and is not to concern himself with some other worshiper. For the detailed rulings of the various schools in this regard, see below.[179]

---

me a beautiful slave girl, a sumptuous palace, beautiful clothes," etc.—one's prayer would be invalidated. However, it is permissible to pray for another person provided that in doing so, one addresses God and not this other person. Thus, one might pray saying, "O God, have mercy on so-and-so"; however, if one were to say, "May God have mercy on you, so-and-so," one's prayer would be invalidated.

179. According to the Hanafis, if the imam forgets a verse of the Qur'anic passage he is reciting and pauses or hesitates, it is permissible for someone praying behind him to help him; however, in doing so, his conscious intention must be to help the imam and not to engage in actual recitation, which in the Hanafi view, is undesirable to the point of being forbidden.

It is undesirable for someone being led in prayer to take the initiative to help the imam in such a situation; it is likewise undesirable for the imam to encourage someone being led in prayer to help him. Instead, he should continue by reciting the minimum number of verses required from some other surah of the Qur'ān or another entire surah; if, on the other hand, he has already recited enough to fulfill what is obligatory in this regard, he may simply go ahead and bow.

As for a worshiper's providing assistance to someone other than his imam, such as another worshiper being led in prayer with him, an imam other than his own, someone praying alone, or someone not praying at all, this will invalidate his prayer unless his intention is simply to recite the Qur'ān rather than to guide someone. In the latter case, however, he will still have engaged in an undesirable act, since according to the Hanafis, it is undesirable to the point of being forbidden for someone being led in prayer to engage in Qur'anic recitation. Similarly, if someone praying accepts the guidance or assistance offered by someone else, his or her prayer will be invalidated (although, as we have mentioned, an imam may accept guidance from someone praying behind him). Hence, if someone being led in prayer or praying alone forgets a verse and is corrected by someone else and if he or she acts on this correction or guidance, his or her prayer will be invalidated unless he or she remembers the correct passage of his or her own accord. Moreover, just as ritual prayer is invalidated by following someone else's instructions with regard to Qur'anic recitation, it is likewise invalidated by following someone else's lead in a particular action. For example, if someone being led in prayer is instructed to fill a gap in a row of worshipers and he carries out this instruction, his prayer will be invalidated. What a person in this situation should do is to wait some time before doing anything, then fill the gap of his own accord.

* * *

According to the Malikis, it does not invalidate ritual prayer for someone being led by an imam to help the imam in his recitation or in some other aspect of prayer. However, the person being led in prayer should only offer such assistance if the imam stops his recitation and requests such assistance by hesitating. If, on the other hand, the imam stops his recitation but does not hesitate [that is, if he simply goes on to the next pillar of prayer – t.n.], it is undesirable to offer him such correction or assistance. In the first case described above—that is, when the imam stops reciting and hesitates—it is *obligatory* for someone being led in prayer to offer help if this is necessary in order for an obligatory recitation to be completed (for example, in order to complete the *Fātiḥah)*; it is *an emulation of the Sunnah* to offer such help if this aids towards correcting the Qur'anic passage following the *Fātiḥah*; and it is *recommended* that one offer such help if it will aid toward the completion of the surah being recited after the *Fātiḥah* (since recitation of an entire surah is recommended at this point). As for offering assistance to someone other than one's imam, whether such a person is praying or not, it invalidates the prayer of the person who does so.

* * *

According to the Shafiis, it is permissible for someone being led in prayer to offer assistance to his imam if the imam has fallen completely silent. However, if he is simply hesitating, he should not be offered any assistance, and if he is offered such, the continuity in his recitation will be broken and he will have to commence his recitation all over again. Moreover, if someone does offer assistance to his or her imam, his or her conscious intention in doing so must be either to engage in recitation alone or to engage in recitation and to correct the imam as well. However, if his or her intention is to simply correct the imam or if he or she has no particular intention at all, his or her prayer will be invalidated based on the prevailing view among the Shafiis. As for offering assistance to someone other than one's imam, whether this person is also being led in prayer or not, this interrupts the continuity in one's recitation; if, in this situation, the person's intention is to engage in the remembrance of God alone or to engage in the remembrance of God and communicate to the other worshiper as well, he should start his recitation over again. Otherwise (that is, if the intention is not to engage in the remembrance of God), this person's prayer will be invalidated altogether.

* * *

As for the Hanbalis, they hold that it is permissible for a worshiper to offer assistance to his or her imam if the imam has been prevented from reciting for some reason or has committed an error. Moreover, if the imam has been prevented from completing his recitation or has made a mistake in it and if the recitation concerned is necessary in order for his prayer to be valid, it becomes obligatory for the person

Saying *Subḥan Allāh* to alert the prayer leader to an error or to alert others to the fact that one is in prayer

Ritual prayer is not invalidated by one's uttering the phrase *subḥān Allāh* to let others know that one is in prayer [for example, if someone is knocking on the door and needs to know why no one is answering – t.n.] or to alert one's prayer leader to the need to correct some error he has made. As for uttering the words *subḥān Allāh*, repeating the phrase *lā ilāha illā Allāh* and other words of divine remembrance other than those which form part of ritual prayer, or reciting a verse of the Qur'ān simply in order to communicate something to someone, the various schools hold differing views on whether and when this invalidates ritual prayer.[180]

---

being led in prayer to provide such assistance. As for offering such assistance to someone other than one's imam, whether this person is taking part in the communal prayer or not, it is undesirable insofar as it is unnecessary; however, it does not invalidate one's prayer.

180. According to the Hanafis, if someone who is praying says *subḥān Allāh* or *lā ilāha illā Allāh*, utters words of praise when mentioning God's name by saying, for example, *jalla jalāluhu* ("May His majesty be exalted"), prays for blessings on the Prophet when making mention of him, says *ṣadaqa Allāh al-'aẓīm* ("Truly has Almighty God spoken") when a reciter has completed a recitation of the Qur'ān, repeats after the muezzin when he gives the call to prayer, etc., either with the intention of responding to something which has been said or done or with no intention at all, his or her prayer will be invalidated. If, on the other hand, one's intention in saying such words is to praise God, keep God in remembrance, or chant the Qur'ān, the prayer remains valid. Similarly, if someone recites a verse of the Qur'ān simply in order to communicate something to someone—for example, by addressing someone by the name of Yaḥyā (John) who wishes to take a certain book with the words, "O John! Hold fast unto the divine writ with all thy strength" (19:12) or to reply to someone who has asked him, "What wealth do you own?" with the words, "...horses and mules and asses for you to ride..." (16:8)—his prayer will be invalidated. Similarly, prayer is invalidated if: (1) after hearing a piece of unwelcome news while praying, one says *lā ḥawla wa lā quwwata illā billāh* ("There is no power or might but through God"), (2) after seeing something pleasing while in prayer, one says *subḥān Allāh* ("Glory be to God!"), (3) after the occurrence of something frightening, one says *bismillāh* ("In the name of God"), or (4) while praying one calls down blessings or curses upon someone. However, if one's intention in saying such things is simply to praise God or keep God in remembrance, one's prayer will remain valid.

Still another speech-related initiative that invalidates prayer is raising one's voice while saying *subḥān Allāh* or *lā ilāha illā Allāh* in order to restrain someone from doing something. However, if someone raises his or her voice in Qur'anic recitation in order to restrain someone, not by means of the recitation as such, but by means of raising one's voice, this will not invalidate one's prayer. Moreover, an exemption to all such rulings is made if one utters the words *subḥān Allāh* in order to announce to someone else that one is in prayer or to alert one's imam to an error he has made in his prayer. This is based on the hadith according to which the Prophet said, "If any of you encounters an error in prayer, let him say, *subḥān Allāh*."

* * *

According to the Malikis, prayer is not invalidated by reciting words from the Qur'ān with the intention of communicating something to someone provided that it is done at the appropriate point in one's prayer. Suppose, for example, that while someone is praying, someone else comes along and requests permission to enter. If this request for permission to enter coincides with the transition between reciting the *Fātiḥah* and reciting some other passage from the Qur'ān, the person praying may say, "Enter here in peace, secure!" (15:46) in response. If, on the other hand, the request coincides with some other part of prayer, for example, bowing, prostrating, or recitation of the *Fātiḥah*, it will invalidate the person's prayer to interrupt one of these pillars in order to recite words from the Qur'ān in response to such a request. However, if the person praying responds simply by saying *subḥān Allāh*, *lā ilāha illā Allāh*, or *lā ḥawla wa lā quwwata illā billāh*, his or her prayer will remain valid, since phrases such as these may be uttered at any point during prayer without invalidating it.

* * *

According to the Hanbalis, prayer is not invalidated by uttering the words *subḥān Allāh*, *lā ilāha illā Allāh* or any other words of divine remembrance even if they are spoken in response to a particular event. Thus, for example, if someone who is praying sees something pleasant and says, *subḥān Allāh!*; if he or she is stricken with some calamity and says, *lā ḥawla wa lā quwwata illā billāh*; if he or she suffers pain and says, *bismillāh*, etc., his or her prayer will remain valid, although such interruptions to the flow of prayer are undesirable. As for praying for blessings on the Prophet when mentioning him, this is desirable only during voluntary prayers, whereas when performing obligatory prayers, this practice is neither required nor does it invalidate prayer. Nor is prayer invalidated by one's reciting a verse of the Qur'ān in order to achieve some purpose, for example, by responding to someone requesting permission to come in with the words, "Enter here in peace, secure!" (15:6), or by addressing someone named John with the words, "O John! Hold fast unto the divine writ with all thy strength" (19:12). However, if one simply uses a single word from the Qur'ān which is indistinguishable from ordinary speech, for example, by addressing someone by the name of Abraham with the words, "O Abraham!", this will invalidate one's prayer.

* * *

As for the Shafiis, they hold that if someone praying utters a verse from the Qur'ān with the sole intention of communicating something to someone else or with no intention at all, his or her prayer will be invalidated. However, if the intention is both to communicate and to recite the Qur'ān, one's prayer remains valid. Similarly, one's prayer remains valid in the following situations if one's intention is to engage in divine remembrance, even if this is combined with some other intention: (1) if someone requests permission of someone who is praying [to enter the room, take an object, etc.] and the latter responds by saying, *subḥān Allāh*; (2) if

Invoking blessing on someone who has sneezed

According to the Shafiis and the Hanbalis, prayer is invalidated if someone who is praying invokes blessing on someone who has sneezed, by saying, for example, *yarḥamuka Allāh* ("May God have mercy on you!"), that is, by addressing the person who sneezed directly. However, if the person praying says something like, *yarḥumuhu Allāh* ("May God have mercy on him") or *yarḥamunā Allāh* ("May God have mercy on us!"), the prayer will remain valid.[181]

---

someone being led in prayer says, *subḥān Allāh* in order to alert his imam to an error in his prayer; or (3) if someone praying says, *Allāh* in response to some alarming event. However, if the intention to engage in divine remembrance is lacking in any of these situations, one's prayer will be invalidated. As for the utterance of the words, *ṣadaqa Allāh al-'aẓīm* after hearing a verse from the Qur'ān or saying, *lā ḥawla wa lā quwwata illā billāh* when hearing a piece of bad news, neither of these invalidates prayer under any circumstances, since they involve nothing but praise to God Almighty; however, they do interrupt the continuity of one's recitation if they occur while one is reciting the Qur'ān, in which case one must resume one's recitation from the beginning. The same applies if someone responds to the words of the muezzin. As for someone being led in prayer who repeats the words, "You alone do we worship, and to You alone do we turn for aid" (verse 5 of the *Fātiḥah*) in imitation of the imam, or if he or she says, "We have turned to God for aid" (*ista'annā billāh*) or "We turn to God for aid" (*nasta'īnu billāh*), this person's prayer will be invalidated unless his intention in saying such words is to recite the Qur'ān or bring a supplication before God; if such an intention is present, his or her prayer will remain valid even though this practice is viewed as a forbidden innovation. As for praying for blessings on the Prophet when he is mentioned, the Shafiis hold that if the supplication includes the Prophet's name, it interrupts one's continuity but does not invalidate one's prayer, whereas if it includes only the personal pronoun [for example, by saying, "May blessings and peace be upon him..." rather than "May blessings and peace be upon Muḥammad" – t.n.], it neither invalidates prayer nor interrupts its continuity.

181. According to the Hanafis, the prayer of someone who invokes blessing on someone who has sneezed is invalidated under all circumstances, regardless of whether the person says, *yarḥamuka Allāh* (that is, addressing the person directly), or *yarḥamuhu Allāh* (that is, asking God to bless the person as if the person weren't present). However, if the person praying is the one who sneezes, and if he or she says to himself or herself, *yarḥamunī Allāh* (that is, "May God have mercy on me!") or, addresses himself or herself with the pronoun 'you', saying, *yarḥamuk Allāh* ("May God have mercy on you!"), his or her prayer will remain valid.

* * *

As for the Malikis, they hold that uttering words during prayer to invoke blessing on someone who has sneezed invalidates prayer under all circumstances.

Returning someone's greeting of peace while in prayer

It is agreed upon by all four schools that if, as we are praying, someone greets us, we will invalidate our prayer if we return the greeting verbally, whereas if we merely respond with a gesture, our prayer will remain valid. Unlike the other schools, however, the Malikis hold that we are actually required to respond to someone's greeting with a gesture.

Yawning, sneezing and coughing while in prayer

According to the Malikis and the Hanbalis, yawning, sneezing, coughing and burping do not invalidate prayer even if they involve the production of speech-like sounds out of necessity. For the views of the Shafiis and the Hanafis, see below.[182]

Excessive movement which is not part of prayer itself

According to the Malikis and the Hanbalis, prayer is invalidated by engaging in excessive movement which is not an integral part of prayer itself, where "excessive movement" is defined as movement which, if we were to look at the person praying, we would think that he or she was not praying. For the views of the Shafiis and the Hanafis, see below.[183]

---

182. According to the Hanafis, prayer is not invalidated by yawning, sneezing, coughing or burping provided that one does not deliberately produce additional sounds which go beyond what is natural, for example, by letting out an audible "Aah" sound while yawning, or sneezing more loudly than would have been necessary.

* * *

As for the Shafiis, they hold that the actions of yawning, sneezing, coughing and burping are subject to the same ruling that applies to moaning and groaning. That is, if they come over the person praying such that he or she cannot hold them back, he or she is excused for producing what would commonly be considered a moderate amount of noise. However, if the person could have held it back but did not, his or her prayer will be invalidated.

183. The Shafiis define 'excessive movement' as three successive steps or their equivalent, such as one large leap. As for the term 'successive', they define it here as meaning that when the movements are performed, the person observing them would not see them as separate actions. Moreover, 'excessive movement' only invalidates prayer if it is performed without a valid excuse, for example, due to an illness which prevents one from remaining still long enough to perform a prayer to completion. In the absence of such an excuse, excessive movement renders prayer invalid.

* * *

The Hanafis define 'excessive movement' as that which, if we look at the person praying, we will feel certain that the person is not actually praying. As long as some doubt remains, however, the movement is classified, properly speaking, as 'moderate' rather than 'excessive'.

'Excessive' movement invalidates ritual prayer regardless of whether it occurs absent-mindedly or deliberately. As for moderate movement, it does not invalidate prayer according to three of the schools. The Malikis, however, classify movement which is less than excessive into two categories: (1) Moderate. This includes such things as leaving the spot where one is praying, which invalidates prayer only if it is intentional; and (2) Slight. This includes such things as gesturing or scratching one's skin, which does not invalidate prayer even if it is intentional.

As for the addition of extra movements of the same type as those that make up prayer itself, such as performing additional bows or prostrations, this invalidates prayer if it is intentional, even if the addition is only a minor one. However, if the addition takes place unintentionally, it does not invalidate prayer even if it is a major one. Similarly, additions to the verbal pillars of prayer, such as repetition of the *Fātiḥah*, do not invalidate prayer even if they are deliberate; rather, one simply performs a prostration of forgetfulness once one's prayer is complete. This ruling is agreed upon by all the schools with the exception of the Malikis.[184]

Turning away from the *qiblah* and eating or drinking while in prayer

Turning away from the *qiblah* invalidates ritual prayer, although the details of this ruling differ from one school to the next.[185]

As for eating and drinking while in prayer, they likewise invalidate prayer, with details that differ from school to school.[186]

---

184. The Malikis hold that prayer is invalidated even by the unintentional addition of movements which belong to the same type as those that make up prayer if they are 'excessive'. By 'excessive', they mean additions which equal the number of *rak'ahs* included in a two-*rak'ah* or four-*rak'ah* prayer—for example, praying eight *rak'ahs* instead of four for the noon prayer or four *rak'ahs* instead of two for the dawn prayer. Praying four *rak'ahs* instead of three for a three-*rak'ah* prayer [such as the obligatory sundown prayer] is likewise considered 'excessive', as is a number of *rak'ahs* equal to those included in a voluntary prayer associated with a particular occasion such as the Day of Sacrifice or the Day of Fastbreaking and the Sunnah-based two-*rak'ah* prayer connected with the dawn prayer. In the case of the *witr*, which is likewise associated with particular times, it is not invalidated by the addition of just one *rak'ah* [as would be the obligatory three-*rak'ah* prayer at sundown]; rather, two or more *rak'ahs* must be added to it in order for it to be invalidated. As for prayers which are not linked to a specific time [or occasion], such as voluntary prayers consisting of an even number of *rak'ahs*, they are not invalidated by any addition whatsoever. Moreover, if the extra *rak'ahs* are not 'excessive'—such as the addition of two or three *rak'ahs* to a four-*rak'ah* prayer—the original prayer is not invalidated.

185. According to the Malikis, turning away from the *qiblah* does not invalidate prayer so long as one's feet are still pointed toward it.

* * *

Similarly, the Hanbalis hold that turning away from the *qiblah* only invalidates prayer if one's entire body turns away from it.

* * *

The Hanafis hold that if someone turns away from the *qiblah* with his or her chest area under compulsion, it does not invalidate prayer unless the person stays in this position for the duration of an entire pillar of prayer. If it is done voluntarily, turning away from the *qiblah* with one's chest invalidates prayer if there is no excuse for doing so; if such an excuse exists, however, one's prayer remains valid regardless of whether the change in position lasts for a shorter or a longer time period of time.

* * *

As for the Shafiis, they hold that turning away from the *qiblah* with one's chest area invalidates prayer even if the person praying has been forced to do so by someone else and even if he or she quickly returns to his or her original position. However, if the person turns away out of ignorance or forgetfulness and quickly returns to his or her original position, his or her prayer will remain valid.

186. According to the Hanafis, eating or drinking invalidates ritual prayer regardless of whether the amount eaten or drunk is large or small, and regardless of whether it is done intentionally or unintentionally. Hence, prayer would be invalidated even by eating a sesame seed or swallowing a raindrop that had fallen into one's mouth. If, on the other hand, the person eats before beginning to pray and finds that food amounting to less than the size of a chickpea has clung to his teeth, his prayer will not be invalidated by his swallowing what was clinging to his teeth. However, if the person praying chews such food three or more times in a row, his or her prayer will be invalidated. Prayer is likewise invalidated by one's swallowing sugar or some other sweet that has dissolved in one's mouth, provided that it actually reaches the person's stomach.

* * *

According to the Malikis, ritual prayer is invalidated by one's eating a large amount or by drinking deliberately, where a 'large amount' is defined as that which amounts to an entire bite. If the food is caught between one's teeth, however, it does not invalidate prayer to swallow it even if one chews it up, since chewing in such a case does not require sufficient movement to invalidate prayer. Similarly, if one picks up a small piece of food off the floor and swallows it without chewing it, this will not invalidate one's prayer. As for eating or drinking absent-mindedly, this does not invalidate prayer although, as prayer is being concluded, one should perform a prostration of forgetfulness. However, if one has both eaten and drunk during prayer, or if one of these occurs unintentionally during the final greeting of peace, one's prayer will be invalidated.

* * *

According to the Shafiis, all food or drink that reaches the stomach of someone in prayer, even if no chewing takes place and even if the amount is very small, will render the person's prayer invalid if it takes place deliberately, with full knowledge that eating and drinking during prayer is forbidden and that one is, in fact, in prayer. However, if the person praying eats or drinks out of absent-mindedness or ignorance, he or she is excused; similarly, if the person has forgotten that he or she is praying and eats a small amount, this is excusable, but if the amount is large, one's prayer is invalidated. As for chewing something without swallowing it, it invalidates prayer only if a large amount of movement is involved. In the case of sugar or

If something happens during prayer to invalidate one's ablutions

The Shafiis, the Malikis and the Hanbalis agree that ritual prayer is invalidated if something happens before the final greeting of peace to invalidate the person's ritual ablutions, be they minor ablutions or major ablutions, sand ablutions, or wiping one's shoes, a cast or a bandage of some sort.[187]

According to the Malikis and the Hanbalis, prayer is likewise invalidated by laughing loudly enough to hear oneself, regardless of how long it lasts. Moreover, prayer is invalidated by laughter regardless of whether it was intentional or unintentional, whether or not one could have suppressed it, and whether or not it results in the production of speech-like sounds. For the views of the Hanafis and the Shafiis, see below.[188]

---

other foods that have dissolved in one's mouth, it invalidates prayer for them to reach one's stomach; however, it does no harm to swallow food which is caught between one's teeth if it simply goes down with one's saliva such that it is not possible to distinguish it as food and spit it out.

* * *

As for the Hanbalis, they hold that eating or drinking a large amount invalidates prayer, whereas a small amount only invalidates prayer if it is taken in deliberately. Swallowing something caught between one's teeth does not invalidate prayer if it is not chewed up. As for what constitutes a 'large' or a 'small' amount, this is determined by commonly prevailing standards. Moreover, in the case of sugar or sweets that have dissolved in one's mouth, swallowing them invalidates prayer unless it is only a small amount and one has swallowed them out of forgetfulness.

187. As for the Hanafis, they hold that this sort of event invalidates ritual prayer if it occurs before one has been seated long enough to recite the final testimony. If it occurs after this, even if one has not yet uttered the final greeting of peace, one's prayer remains valid according to the most strongly attested point of view.

188. According to the Hanafis, prayer is only invalidated by laughter if it occurs before one has been seated long enough to utter the final testimony; if it occurs after this, however, one's prayer remains valid even if the laughter has invalidated one's ablutions, since in the Hanafis' view, prayer is complete with the conclusion of the final testimony.

* * *

As for the Shafiis, they hold that voluntary laughter does not invalidate prayer unless it involves the production of at least two speech-like sounds that carry no meaning, or one such sound that does communicate a meaning. Hence, what invalidates prayer in this situation is not the laughter itself, but the sounds that result from it. However, if the person is so overcome with laughter that he or she cannot restrain it, brief laughter will have no effect on prayer, whereas laughing for a longer time will invalidate it.

If someone being led in prayer gets ahead of the imam by an entire pillar

According to the Malikis and the Hanbalis, if someone being led in prayer deliberately gets an entire pillar ahead of his imam—for example, by bowing and rising again before his imam has bowed—his prayer is invalidated, whereas if this occurs unintentionally and he then rejoins the imam, his prayer remains valid. For the views of the Hanafis and the Shafiis, see below.[189]

Prayer is likewise invalidated if, while in prayer, someone who is praying on the basis of sand ablutions finds water that he could use to perform regular ablutions.[190] Similarly, if someone who is praying 'naked' finds a garment with which to cover himself and if, in addition, he is able to put it on without engaging in so

---

189. According to the Hanafis, getting an entire pillar ahead of one's imam will invalidate one's prayer regardless of whether it was intentional or not. However, if the person concerned repeats the pillar either with the imam or after him, and if he or she then utters the concluding greeting of peace with the imam, his or her prayer will remain valid. (For more details on this point, see the section below entitled, "Communal Prayer.")

* * *

As for the Shafiis, they hold that the prayer of someone being led by an imam is only invalidated by his or her deliberately getting at least two entire pillars ahead of or behind the imam. However, if there is an excuse, such as absent-mindedness or slowness in one's recitation, his or her prayer remains valid.

190. According to the Hanafis, this event only invalidates prayer if the water is found before the person has been seated long enough to utter the final testimony, whereas if it happens after this, his or her prayer remains valid due to the fact that with the utterance of the final testimony, one's prayer is complete.

* * *

According to the Shafiis, finding water during prayer by someone who has done sand ablutions will only invalidate prayer if the prayer being performed is one that will have to be made up later [that is, an obligatory prayer], as was seen earlier in our discussion of sand ablutions.

* * *

According to the Malikis, if someone who has done sand ablutions finds water while in prayer, his or her prayer is not invalidated; however, if the person remembers that he has water in his possession that he had forgotten about at the time he performed sand ablutions, his prayer is invalidated provided that he has enough time to do minor ablutions and compete one *rak'ah* before the time period for the prayer he is praying runs out.

* * *

As for the Hanbalis, they state simply that if someone who has done sand ablutions finds water while praying, and if he would be able to use the water for minor ablutions, his prayer is invalidated.

much extra movement that his prayer would be invalidated thereby, he should simply put the garment on and continue his prayer to completion. If, on the other hand, putting on the garment would require so much movement that it would invalidate his prayer, his prayer ceases to be valid.[191]

If someone praying the mid-afternoon prayer remembers that he did not pray the noon prayer

The Hanafis and the Hanbalis hold that if, while praying the mid-afternoon prayer, someone remembers that he or she missed the noon prayer, the mid-afternoon prayer will be invalidated provided that the person concerned is among those who believe in the obligatory nature of praying all prayers in their original order. (More details on this subject may be found below in the section on "Compensating for Prayers Missed".) For the views of the Malikis and the Shafiis, see below.[192]

---

191. According to the Malikis, if someone praying 'naked' finds, while in prayer, something he could use to cover himself and if the garment is nearby (that is, no more than approximately two rows of worshipers away), he should take it and cover himself with it, and if he fails to do so, he should repeat the prayer before its time period runs out. If, on the other hand, the garment is far away (that is, more than two rows of worshipers away), he should simply complete his prayer without covering himself with the garment, then repeat the prayer before its time period runs out.

* * *

According to the Hanafis, if someone praying 'naked' finds a garment that he could cover himself with, his prayer will be invalidated unless the entire garment he finds is ritually impure, in which case he has a choice of whether to continue praying naked or to put on the impure garment. If, on the other hand, one-fourth of the garment is ritually pure, he is obliged to cover himself with it, since its presence causes his prayer to be invalidated.

192. The Malikis hold that if, while praying, someone who is praying alone or leading others in prayer remembers that he or she missed an earlier obligatory prayer, if the number of prayers missed is four or fewer, and if the person remembers the missed prayer or prayers before completing a full *rak'ah*, he must cut off his current prayer. If the person is being led in prayer, he should cut off his prayer only if his imam does so, after which it is recommended that he repeat the prayer before its time period has run out. If the person remembers the missed prayer or prayers after completing one full *rak'ah*, he should add one more *rak'ah* to the first one, then utter the concluding greeting of peace, at which point the prayer he is performing becomes a supererogatory prayer rather than an obligatory one. If, on the other hand, the person remembers the missed prayer or prayers after completing two full *rak'ahs* of the sundown prayer or three *rak'ahs* of a four-*rak'ah* prayer, he should carry on until the prayer is complete, and the prayer thus completed will be considered fully valid. However, if the missed prayers number five or more, one should not cut off a current prayer under any circumstances.

* * *

If someone learns a new verse while in prayer

According to the Hanafis and the Hanbalis, it invalidates prayer for an illiterate person to learn a new verse of the Qur'ān while praying, provided that the person is not being led in prayer by someone else who is reciting. For the views of the Malikis and the Shafiis, see below.[193]

Deliberately uttering the concluding greeting of peace before one's prayer is complete

Ritual prayer is invalidated by deliberately uttering the concluding greeting of peace before the prayer is complete. However, if one utters this greeting by mistake, thinking momentarily that one's prayer is finished, this does not invalidate the prayer provided that one does not engage in excessive movement or begin saying things that are extraneous to prayer.

As for the Shafiis, they hold that remembering an earlier prayer that one missed does not invalidate the prayer one is currently performing regardless of whether the performance of prayers in their original order is deemed to be simply an emulation of the prophetic Sunnah (as is the case if the earlier prayer was missed due to a legitimate excuse) or is obligatory (as is the case if the prayer was missed without a valid excuse).

193. According to the Malikis, if such a person is being led in prayer by someone else who is doing the reciting, it is sufficient for him or her simply to follow the other person's lead. If, on the other hand, the person is not being led in prayer by someone else and he learns the *Fātiḥah* while praying, he should simply build on what he has prayed thus far, and his prayer will remain valid due to his having begun it in a legitimate manner.

* * *

As for the Shafiis, they hold that if an illiterate person learns some recitation while in prayer, he should simply build on what he has prayed thus far by reciting what he has learned.

The *Adhān*, or Call to Prayer

As we have seen, the *adhān* is a Sunnah-based practice which is associated with ritual prayer, but which does not form an integral part of it. The *adhān* will be discussed under the following seven headings: (1) its definition, (2) the basis for its legitimacy and the evidence in support of it, (3) the words of which it consists, (4) the ruling pertaining to it, (5) its conditions, (6) Sunnah-based and other recommended practices associated with the *adhān*, and (7) undesirable practices associated with the *adhān*.

The meaning of the term *adhān*

The Arabic term rendered as "call to prayer" (*adhān*) means simply, "an announcement" or "an act of informing". God Almighty declares, "And a proclamation (*adhān*) from God and His Apostle" (9:3). He also says, "Hence, [O Muḥammad], proclaim thou [*adhdhin*] unto all people the [duty of] pilgrimage" (22:27); that is, inform them of their obligation to perform the pilgrimage. In the context of Islamic law, the term *adhān* is used to refer to the announcement that the time period for one of the five daily ritual prayers has begun.

The legitimacy of the call to prayer finds its basis in the Qur'ān, the prophetic Sunnah, and the consensus of the Islamic community. God Almighty said, "O you who have attained to faith! When the call to prayer is sounded on the day of congregation, hasten to the remembrance of God and leave all worldly commerce. This is for your own good if you but knew it" (62:9) and, "...when you call to prayer, they mock at it and make a jest of it..." (5:58).

The Prophet once stated, "When the time period for a given prayer begins, let one of you announce it to the others."[194] As for the way in which the call to prayer is to be delivered and the words of which it consists, these are mentioned in other prophetic hadiths.

When and why the *adhān* was instituted, and its merit

The call to prayer was instituted in the first year after the Hijrah (1 AH) in the city of Medina. It is an element of the religion whose legitimacy every believer must acknowledge; hence, a denial of its legitimacy is tantamount to a declaration of unbelief.

The reason for the institution of the *adhān* lies in the fact that when the Prophet came to Medina, it was difficult for people to know when the prayer times were. When they consulted together about the matter, some suggested that they use a bell to announce the prayer times. In response, the Prophet said, "That is what the Christians use." Some suggested that they use a horn, but the Prophet said, "That is what the Jews use." Some suggested the use of a tambourine, but the Prophet objected, "That is what the Byzantines use." Some suggested that a fire be lit, but the Prophet, "That is what the Magians use." Finally, some proposed that they raise a banner

---

194. Narrated by al-Bukhārī and Muslim.

such that whoever saw it could inform others. However, none of these proposals met with the Prophet's approval, and nothing was agreed upon. After this the Prophet rose [and withdrew], preoccupied with the matter.

That night, 'Abdullāh Ibn Zayd went to sleep pondering the Prophet's concern and had a dream in which he saw an angel who taught him the *adhān* as well as the announcement of prayer's having commenced (the *iqāmah*). The next day, 'Abdullāh Ibn Zayd told the Prophet about his night vision, which turned out to be in agreement with a revelation that the Prophet had received. Hence, he gave instructions for the *adhān* and the *iqāmah* to be instituted in the Muslim community.[195]

According to a hadith recorded by Muslim and al-Bukhārī on the authority of Anas, when the Muslim community began to grow larger, the people suggested that they decide on some means by which they could be alerted to the prayer times. Some suggested that they light a fire or that they set up a gong. The Prophet then instructed Bilāl to utter the call to prayer (the *adhān*) an even number of times, and to announce the commencement of prayer (the *iqāmah*) an odd number of times.

As for the merit in the call to prayer, it is spoken of in numerous sound hadiths. According to one such hadith, passed down on the authority of Abū Hurayrah, the Prophet said, "If people realized the true value of the call [to prayer] and of standing in the front row of worshipers, they would vie with each other to be the first to respond to it."[196] According to another such hadith, narrated on the authority of Mu'āwiyah, the Prophet said, "Muezzins will, of all people, have the longest necks[197] on the Day of Resurrection."[198]

The words of the *adhān*

The words of the call to prayer are as follows: "God is greatest! God is greatest! God is greatest! God is greatest! I testify that there is no god but God! I testify that there is no god but God! I testify that Muḥammad is God's Messenger. I testify that Muḥammad is God's Messenger. Come to prayer! Come to prayer! Come to salvation! Come to salvation! God is greatest! God is greatest! There is no god but God" (*Allāhu akbar, Allāhu akbar, Allāhu akbar, Allāhu akbar! ashhadu an lā ilāh illā Allāh. ashhadu an lā ilāh illā Allāh. ashhadu anna Muḥammadan rasūl Allāh. ashhadu anna Muḥammadan rasūl Allāh. ḥayya 'alā al-ṣalāh, ḥayya 'alā al-ṣalāh.*

---

195. This is the gist of a hadith narrated by Aḥmad, Abū Dāwūd and Ibn Mājah; part of it is mentioned by al-Tirmidhī, who describes the account as a well-attested hadith.

196. This is an agreed-upon hadith.

197. This reference to the length of muezzins' necks on the Day of Judgment is reflective of the elevated status they have earned through their performance of the task of summoning people to prayer. Given the fact that the use of their voices in the performance of this service was associated with their necks (or more specifically, with anatomical parts located within the neck), this statement by the Prophet is likewise an affirmation of the Qur'anic principle that on the Day of Resurrection, people's bodies will "bear witness", as it were, to the actions they committed during their earthly lives [t.n.].

198. Narrated by Muslim.

ḥayya 'ala al-falāḥ, ḥayya 'alā al-falāḥ. Allāhu akbar, Allāhu akbar. la ilāha illā Allāh). This wording is agreed upon by the Shafiis, the Hanbalis and the Hanafis; as for the Malikis, they hold that it should begin with only two, rather than four, repetitions of the phrase, "God is greatest."

In the dawn prayer following the phrase, "Come to salvation (*ḥayya 'alā al-falāḥ*)!" it is recommended that the muezzin add, "Prayer is better than sleep! Prayer is better than sleep (*al-ṣalātu khayrun min al-nawm*)!" All four schools agree that it is undesirable to leave this addition out.

Tarji', or the repetition of the two confessions of faith in the call to prayer

According to the Hanafis and the Hanbalis, nothing is to be added to the wording mentioned above; as for the Malikis and the Shafiis, they hold that it is an emulation of the prophetic Sunnah first to utter the two confessions of faith in a low, but audible voice, and then in a loud voice. The Malikis refer to the repetition of the two confessions in a loud voice as *tarjī'*, whereas the Shafiis use the term *tarjī'* to refer to their initial utterance in a low voice.

The explanation of this difference may be that the Malikis look at the matter from a linguistic point of view, since the word *tarjī'* means, literally speaking, 'repetition', and since the muezzin first utters the two confessions in a soft voice, then repeats them in a louder voice. As such, referring to the louder utterance as *tarjī'*, that is, 'repetition' is consistent with this term's linguistic meaning. As for the Shafiis, they base their terminology on the fact that the essential element in the call to prayer involves the utterance of the two confessions aloud; as such, it is more fitting to refer to their utterance before this in a low voice as *tarjī'* or 'repetition', since it represents a 'mirroring' of what comes after it.

Be that as it may, both the Shafiis and the Malikis hold that the wording of the *adhān* following the utterance of "God is greatest!" is as follows: "I testify that there is no god but God! I testify that there is no god but God!" in a low voice, followed by, "I testify that there is no god but God! I testify that there is no god but God!" in a loud voice; then, "I testify that Muḥammad is God's Messenger! I testify that Muḥammad is God's Messenger!" in a soft voice, following by, "I testify that Muḥammad is God's Messenger! I testify that Muḥammad is God's Messenger!" in a loud voice. Lastly, the muezzin repeats the words, "Come to prayer!" twice in a loud voice, then, "Come to salvation!" twice in a loud voice. He then ends the call to prayer with, "God is greatest! God is greatest! There is no god but God!"

The only exception to this wording, as we have noted, is that in the dawn call to prayer, it is recommended that the muezzzin add, "Prayer is better than sleep! Prayer is better than sleep!" following the second utterance of the words, "Come to salvation!" It is undesirable to leave out this addition; however, even with its omission the call to prayer will be valid. Similarly, it is undesirable to omit *tarjī'*, but its omission will not invalidate the call to prayer.

In sum, then, the Shafiis and the Malikis agree on the wording of the *adhān* except in regard to the phrase, "God is greatest", with the Shafiis holding that it should be uttered four times and the Malikis holding that it should be uttered only twice.

The ruling on the *adhān*

The Shafiis, the Malikis and the Hanafis are in agreement that the call to prayer is an emphatically enjoined Sunnah-based practice, though not obligatory; as for the Hanbalis, they hold that it is a collective obligation, which means that if one member of the community issues the call, the obligation has thereby been fulfilled for all other members as well. The four schools also differ on specific details of the ruling on the call to prayer.[199]

---

199. According to the Shafiis, the call to prayer is a collective Sunnah-based practice for those praying communally, and an individual Sunnah-based practice for someone praying alone if he or she has not already heard someone else deliver it. If an individual hears the *adhān* and responds by going to pray with a group, he or she will have emulated the Sunnah in so doing, whereas if he or she hears the call to prayer but does not go to pray communally, or if he or she goes to join a group but does not pray, he/she will not have emulated the Sunnah. Uttering the call to prayer is an emulation of the Sunnah for the five obligatory prayers whether one is traveling or settled in one place, and even if one is engaged in a compensatory performance of prayers missed; however, if someone is making up a number of missed prayers in succession, it is sufficient to utter the call to prayer just once. Similarly, when one wishes to join the noon and mid-afternoon prayers or the sundown and evening prayers when traveling, one may begin with a single utterance of the call to prayer. When performing the funeral prayer, prayers which are in fulfillment of a vow, and other voluntary prayers, it is not an emulation of the Sunnah to begin them with the *adhān*.

* * *

According to the Hanafis, utterance of the call to prayer is an emphatically enjoined, collective Sunnah-based practice for residents of a single neighborhood. Moreover, as in the case of other practices which the Hanafis classify as 'duty', one incurs guilt by omitting the call to prayer. The Hanafis hold that the call to prayer is an emulation of the Sunnah when performing the five daily prayers whether one is traveling or settled, whether one is praying communally or alone, and whether one is performing the prayer on time or compensating for a prayer missed. However, it is not considered undesirable to omit the call to prayer if one is praying at home in an urban area, since the call to prayer issued for the neighborhood as a whole suffices, as we have mentioned. The call to prayer is not an emulation of the Sunnah when performing the funeral prayer, the prayers for the Day of Fastbreaking and the Day of Sacrifice, a solar eclipse, prayers for rain, the *tarāwīḥ* prayers, or the Sunnah-based prayers associated with the dawn, noon, sundown and evening prayers. When praying the *witr*, the Hanafis hold that utterance of the *adhān* is not an emulation of the Sunnah despite the fact that they classify the *witr* as a 'duty'; rather, they say that the *adhān* preceding the evening prayer suffices for the *witr* as well.

* * *

According to the Malikis, utterance of the *adhān* is a collective Sunnah-based practice for a group which is waiting for someone who is expected to pray with them in a location in which it is customary for people to gather for prayer; similarly,

Conditions associated with the *adhān*

There are five conditions associated with the *adhān*:

One: Intention. If the muezzin delivers the call to prayer using the wording given above, yet without consciously intending it as a call to prayer, it will not be valid according to the Malikis and the Hanbalis. As for the Shafiis and the Hanafis, they do not stipulate intention as a condition for the validity of the *adhān*.

Two: Utterance of the words of the call to prayer in close succession such that they are not interrupted by a long silence or by many words unrelated to the call to prayer. As for interrupting a call to prayer with an insignificant amount of speech, this does not invalidate it[200] regardless of the specific nature of the words spoken. This ruling is agreed upon by all of the schools except the Hanbalis, who hold that interrupting a call to prayer with an insignificant amount of speech, even if it is nothing but a single word, invalidates the call to prayer if it involves the utterance of

---

it is a collective Sunnah-based practice for each individual mosque, even if there are several mosques adjoining one another or located one on top of another. The *adhān* for prayers which are obligatory for every individual [such as the five daily prayers] should be uttered during the 'elective phase', even if the time is judged to fall within this phase in a purely judicial sense, as might be the case, for example, when prayers are being joined and performed either in advance of or later than their specified time. However, when performing voluntary prayers, compensating for prayers missed, performing prayers which are a collective duty (such as the funeral prayer), or praying during the 'imperative phase', it is undesirable to utter the call to prayer.

At the same time, utterance of the call to prayer is not undesirable for a group which is not waiting for anyone else to join them, nor is it undesirable for someone praying alone in an isolated area; on the contrary, utterance of the *adhān* is recommended in such cases. In populated areas, by contrast (that is, areas where sufficient numbers of people live for there to be communal Friday prayers), the call to prayer is a collective duty such that if it is neglected, the area's residents should be opposed with force for this omission.

* * *

As for the Hanbalis, they hold that utterance of the *adhān* is a collective duty for free men resident in villages and urban areas and who are performing the five daily obligatory prayers in a group. However, there is no need to utter the call to prayer when performing a funeral prayer, a prayer for a special religious holiday, voluntary prayers, or prayers which are in fulfillment of a vow. When making up for a prayer which was missed and when praying as an individual, whether as a resident or as a traveler, utterance of the call to prayer is an emulation of the Sunnah; it is also an emulation of the Sunnah for someone who is traveling, whether he or she is praying alone or communally.

200. The Arabic text here actually reads, "this invalidates the call to prayer ..."; however, it seems sufficiently clear from the context that it should read in the negative rather than the affirmative [t.n.].

something which would not be permissible under Islamic law. Thus, for example, the Hanbalis hold that if someone issuing the *adhān* interrupts it in order to curse someone, if even with a single word, it will cease to be valid.

Three: Issuance of the call to prayer in the Arabic language, unless the muezzin is a non-Arab and wishes to deliver the *adhān* to himself or to a group of people who are likewise non-Arabs. If, on the other hand, he is issuing the call to prayer to a group of people who do not know his language, it will be invalid, of course, since they will not understand what he is saying. This ruling is agreed upon by all of the schools except that of the Hanbalis, who hold that no call to prayer is valid unless it is in Arabic.

Four: Issuance of the call to prayer after the time period for the prayer concerned has begun. All four schools agree that if the call to prayer is issued before the commencement of the time period for the noon, mid-afternoon, sundown or evening prayer, it will be invalid. As for the dawn call to prayer, the Shafiis, the Malikis and the Hanbalis hold that given certain conditions, it may be issued before the time period for this prayer has begun; for the Hanafis' view on this matter, see below.[201]

---

201. According to the Hanafis, a call to prayer which is delivered before the time period for the dawn prayer has begun is invalid and, properly speaking, it is undesirable to the point of being forbidden. As for the view that it is permissible to issue the dawn *adhān* before the time period for this prayer has begun, this applies to the utterance of phrases in praise of God, such as *subḥān Allāh*, in order to wake people who are still asleep.

* * *

According to the Hanbalis, it is permissible to issue the dawn *adhān* from midnight onwards, since this is when the "elective phase" of the evening prayer runs out. It is not desirable to issue the dawn call to prayer too long before the time period has actually begun; on the other hand, it is desirable to deliver such a pre-dawn call to prayer at the same time every night since in this way the call to prayer is something people can rely on. Moreover, it is only to be repeated during the month of Ramaḍān, during which time it is undesirable for there to be only one pre-dawn *adhān*.

* * *

According to the Shafiis, the *adhān* is invalid if it is issued before the time period for the prayer concerned has begun, and it is forbidden entirely if it causes people confusion [for example, by leading them to believe that the time period for the prayer concerned has begun when it has not], or if the intention behind it is simply to engage in personal worship. However, this does not apply to the dawn call to prayer, which may be issued from midnight onwards since it is an emulation of the Sunnah for there to be two dawn calls to prayer: the first some time after midnight, and the second after the break of dawn.

* * *

As for the Malikis, they also hold that the *adhān* is invalid if it is issued before the beginning of the time period for the prayer concerned, and that it is forbidden

Five: Utterance of the words of the call to prayer in the proper order. Thus, for example, if the person issuing the call says, "Come to salvation!" before saying, "Come to prayer!" he must repeat the phrases which were spoken out of order, for example, by saying, "Come to prayer! Come to salvation!" or the like. If such phrases are not repeated in their proper order, the call to prayer will be invalidated. This ruling is agreed upon by the Shafiis, the Malikis and the Hanbalis; as for the Hanafis, they hold that a call to prayer in which the phrases are not ordered properly is valid, but undesirable. Hence, whoever issues the *adhān* should go back and repeat whatever phrases were not spoken in the right order.

The choral *adhān*

Another agreed-upon condition for the validity of the call to prayer is that it should be issued by a single person. Hence, if one muezzin delivered part of the call to prayer and someone else finished it, this would not be valid. Similarly, the call to prayer will not be valid if two or more people utter the various parts of the call to prayer by turns such that each person utters a different phrase. This practice, referred to by some people as a 'choral' call to prayer, is based on ignorance and those who engage in it violate the Sunnah associated with the call to prayer. It is true, of course, that if each person repeats precisely the phrases uttered by the other such that each of them ends up delivering a complete call to prayer, it will be valid and the Sunnah associated with the call to prayer will have been fulfilled. However, it is still an unnecessary innovation and may be impermissible if it is restricted to a single musical mode. On the other hand, there is nothing in the prophetic Sunnah

---

entirely if it will cause people confusion, except in the case of the dawn call to prayer, since it is recommended that a call to the dawn prayer be issued during the final sixth of the night in order to wake people up and that, in accordance with the Sunnah, another call to the dawn prayer be issued after dawn has broken.

202. According to the Hanafis, the three conditions mentioned above in connection with the muezzin are not necessary for the validity of the call to prayer. Rather, a call to prayer issued by a woman, a hermaphrodite, a non-Muslim, or by someone who is insane or inebriated will still be valid and will serve to remove from the community whatever guilt it might have incurred if no call to prayer had been issued. At the same time, however, the Hanafis hold that it is not valid to depend on the report given by a non-Muslim, someone who is insane, or a *fāsiq* in determining whether the time period for the prayer concerned has begun. Rather, in order for such a report to be credible, the person who supplies it must be a Muslim: (1) whose reports are known to be accurate and reliable, be the person a man or a woman, and (2) who is in full possession of his mental faculties and capable of distinguishing among the time periods for the five daily prayers. Hence, if a person who does not meet these requirements issues a call to prayer, the call to prayer will be valid in itself, but it will not be a valid indicator that the time period for the

which expressly forbids this practice, nor do the general rules associated with the call to prayer preclude it since a call to prayer issued by two or more people in a single place is tantamount to their having issued calls to prayer in several different places. However, the spirit of the Islamic law requires that we adhere to the limits set by the religion in connection with acts of worship; hence, given that such a practice is not specifically mentioned anywhere in the prophetic Sunnah, it is preferable that it not be adopted.

Conditions applicable to the muezzin

According to the Shafiis, the Malikis and the Hanbalis, the muezzin must be (1) a Muslim, (2) in full possession of his mental faculties (such that the call to prayer issued by someone who is insane, inebriated or who has fainted would not be valid), and (3) male (such that a call to prayer issued by a female or a hermaphrodite would not be valid). For the conditions specified by the Hanafis, see below.[202]

However, it is not necessary for the muezzin to be an adult. Rather, according to the Shafiis, the Hanbalis and the Hanafis, the call to prayer issued by a boy who has reached the age of discernment is valid regardless of whether he issues the call by himself or relies on an adult muezzin; for the Malikis' view, see below.[203]

Lastly, it is not necessary for the validity of the call to prayer that each phrase or statement contained in the call be devoid of inflectional endings. Hence, if someone were to say, "Come to prayer, come to prayer!" (i.e., without any appreciable pause between the two phrases, in which case the first instance of the word 'prayer' would contain inflectional endings in Arabic), this would be valid according to the

---

prayer concerned has actually begun. It is thus considered undesirable for someone who fails to meet these requirements to issue the call to prayer, just as it is for someone who is *fāsiq* or who is in a state of major ritual impurity. If such a person issues the call to prayer in place of the regular muezzin, it is recommended that it be repeated. However, if such a person issues the call to prayer to a group of people who already know that the time period for the relevant prayer has begun and if this call to prayer is not serving to replace that of the regular muezzin, there is no need for it to be repeated. As for a boy who has not reached the age of discernment, his call to prayer will not be valid, nor will it serve to alleviate the neighborhood residents of the guilt they would incur if no call to prayer were issued. And as for the call to prayer issued by a woman, it is disallowed if the sound of her voice is likely to arouse physical desire on the part of those who hear her, as we saw in our earlier discussion of audible recitation during prayer.

203. According to the Malikis, the muezzin must be an adult; hence, if a boy who has reached the age of discernment issues the call to prayer, it will not be valid unless he relies on an adult either in the call to prayer itself or in regard to whether the time period for the prayer concerned has begun. The call to prayer is valid if it is issued by someone whose reports are known to be accurate and reliable, whereas if issued by a *fāsiq*, it will only be valid if the person relies on the call to prayer issued by someone else.

Shafiis and the Hanafis, although they hold that it is an emulation of the prophetic Sunnah for the muezzin to pause at the end of each such phrase. For the views of the Hanbalis and the Malikis, see below.[204]

Sunnah-based and other desirable practices associated with the *adhān*

It is recommended that the muezzin: (1) be free of both major and minor ritual purity when he issues the call to prayer, (2) have a strong, pleasant-sounding voice, (3) issue the call to prayer from an elevated spot, such as a minaret or mosque rooftop, (4) issue the call to prayer from a standing position unless there is some legitimate reason for him to be seated, such as illness or some other cause, and (5) face the *qiblah* when issuing the call to prayer unless it is necessary to turn away from it in order to make himself heard, in which case it is permissible to turn his back to the *qiblah*.[205]

The sixth recommended practice associated with the call to prayer is for the muezzin to turn toward his right when saying, "Come to prayer!" and toward his left when saying, "Come to salvation!" According to the Shafiis, the Hanafis and the Hanbalis, he should maintain his *qiblah*-oriented position by turning only with his face and the front of his neck rather than with his chest area and his feet. The Malikis maintain that these acts of turning are not recommended, while the Hanbalis differ with the other three schools on the manner in which the muezzin is to turn; in their view, the muezzin may turn with his chest area as well as his face and neck without losing his *qiblah*-oriented position as long as he is still facing the *qiblah* with the rest of his body.

---

204. According to the Hanbalis, the *adhān* will only be valid if each component phrase is concluded without inflectional endings, and if someone does supply such endings, the only part which will be valid is the phrase, "God is greatest!" (*Allāhu akbar*) with which the call begins. Hence, the Hanbalis agree with the Malikis that leaving off concluding inflectional endings is recommended. The Hanbalis also hold that it is impermissible for someone other than the regular muezzin to issue the call to prayer without his permission unless it is done for fear that the time period for issuing the call will pass before he arrives. If the regular muezzin arrives after this, it is an emulation of the Sunnah for him to issue the call to prayer again. The Hanbalis also stipulate that in order for the call to prayer to be valid, it must not be mispronounced in a way which would alter its meaning. Finally, they hold that raising one's voice when issuing the call to prayer is a 'pillar' unless it is being issued to someone who is present, in which case all that is required is that it be loud enough for the other person to hear it. This ruling on the raising of one's voice is agreed upon by the Hanbalis and the Shafiis.

* * *

As for the Malikis, they hold that for the call to prayer to be valid, the muezzin must pause after each of its component statements with the exception of the initial "God is greatest!", after which such a pause is only recommended. Thus, if someone were to say, "God is greatest God is greatest", without any intervening pause, it would still be valid, albeit a departure from the recommended practice.

As for the seventh and final recommended practice associated with the call to prayer, it is for the muezzin to pause at the end of every sentence that makes up the call to prayer; however, rather than pausing after each separate utterance of, "God is greatest!" (*Allāhu akbar*), he is to pause only at the end of each pair of such utterances.[206]

Responding to the muezzin

Responding to the muezzin is a practice which is recommended for everyone who hears it, even if he or she is in a state of major ritual impurity, and even if the person who hears it is a woman who is menstruating or who is experiencing post-partum bleeding. Specifically, the recommended practice is for the person to repeat whatever the muezzin says except the phrase, "Come to prayer! Come to salvation!" at which point the person is to say, "There is no might or power but through God" (*lā ḥawla wa lā quwwata illā billāh*). This ruling is agreed upon by all of the schools except the Hanafis, who hold that it is not recommended that a menstruating woman or a woman experiencing post-partum bleeding respond to the muezzin. In addition, the Hanbalis stipulate that if someone has already performed the prayer for

---

205. According to the Malikis, it is recommended that the muezzin rotate in a circle while issuing the call to prayer even if it becomes necessary for him to turn his back to the *qiblah* in order to enable people to hear him; however, he should begin the call to prayer facing the *qiblah*.

* * *

According to the Shafiis, it is an emulation of the prophetic Sunnah for the muezzin to remain facing the *qiblah* if the village in which he is located is small by commonly accepted standards, that is, if it is small enough that people can hear his voice without his rotating as he issues the call. If, on the other hand, the village is larger than this, it is an emulation of the Sunnah for him to rotate in a circle as he speaks. They likewise judge it to be a Sunnah-based practice for him to face toward the village and away from the *qiblah* if the minaret is situated between the village and the *qiblah*.

* * *

According to the Hanafis, it is an emulation of the Sunnah for the muezzin to face the *qiblah* while delivering the call to prayer unless he is delivering it from a minaret, in which case the Sunnah calls for him to rotate as he speaks so that people can hear him from all directions. If he delivers the call to prayer while riding an animal (as opposed to walking), the Sunnah likewise does not require him to face the *qiblah*.

* * *

As for the Hanbalis, they hold that the Sunnah-based practice is for the muezzin to remain facing the *qiblah* throughout the entire call to prayer even if he is delivering it from a minaret or some similar spot.

206. For the difference among the schools concerning this last point see Note 204 above in the subsection entitled, "Conditions applicable to the muezzin."

which the *adhān* is being issued, it is not recommended that he or she respond to the muezzin.[207] Similarly, when the dawn call to prayer is being sounded and the muezzin says, "Prayer is better than sleep", one should respond by saying, "You have spoken truthfully and righteously" (*ṣadaqta wa barart*). If the *adhān* is associated with an obligatory prayer,[208] it is recommended that one respond to the muezzin; otherwise, however, no response is required. This ruling is agreed upon by the Shafiis, the Hanafis and the Hanbalis; for the Malikis' view, see below.[209]

---

207. According to the Hanbalis, it is recommended that someone who has not performed the prayer concerned in community respond to the muezzin in the manner described above; if he has, however, he should not respond since he is not being addressed by this call to prayer.

* * *

As for the Hanafis, they hold that neither a menstruating woman nor a woman experiencing post-partum bleeding is required to respond to the muezzin since, given that they are not eligible to respond to the call to prayer in action, they are likewise not eligible to respond to it in words.

208. That is, if it is associated with one of the five obligatory prayers for each day, as opposed to calls to prayer associated with other occasions, such as issuing the call to prayer in the ear of a newborn or an epileptic, at a time of war, and so on [t.n.].

209. According to the Malikis, the listener is not to repeat the muezzin's utterance of, "Prayer is better than sleep", nor is he or she to respond to it with the phrase, "You have spoken truthfully and righteously." Rather, according to the best attested views among them, one should only repeat the phrases of the call to prayer up to the end of the two testimonies [i.e., "I testify that there is no god but God, and I testify that Muḥammad is the Messenger of God"].

Someone who is engaged in prayer, even if he is performing a voluntary prayer or a funeral prayer, is not required to respond verbally to the call to prayer; rather, it is undesirable for people who are already praying to speak in response to the call to prayer. In fact, such a person's prayer will be invalidated by responding to the *adhān* by saying, "You have spoken truthfully and righteously", "Come to prayer!" or "Prayer is better than sleep." If, on the other hand, the person responds by saying, "There is no power or might but through God", "God has spoken truly", or "The Messenger of God has spoken truly," this will not invalidate the prayer he or she is performing.

Someone who is having sexual relations with his spouse or who is eliminating bodily wastes is not required to answer the call to prayer since such situations are incompatible with speaking the divine name; nor is it required of someone who is listening to a sermon. These rulings are agreed upon by the Shafiis and the Hanbalis; as for the Malikis and the Hanafis, their views may be seen below.[210] As for teachers and students, they are required to respond to the call to prayer according to the Malikis, the Shafiis and the Hanbalis; as for the Hanafis, they hold that it is not required of someone teaching or learning the sciences related to Islamic law to respond to the call to prayer while engaged in teaching or learning, whereas it is agreed upon by all four schools that someone who is reading or reciting the Qur'ān or engaged in the verbal remembrance of God is required to do so. The Malikis and the Hanbalis agree that someone who is eating is required to repeat after the muezzin when the call to prayer is issued, whereas the Shafiis and the Hanafis hold that he/she is not so required. The Malikis and the Shafiis who advocate the practice of *tarjī'* (that is, the repetition of the two confessions of faith in a low voice, then in a loud voice while issuing the call to prayer) hold that one should repeat after the

---

210. According to the Malikis, responding to the *adhān* is recommended for someone who is praying a voluntary prayer; however, if such a person wishes to complete the prayer he or she is performing, he/she should respond to the words, "Come to prayer!" and "Come to salvation!" by saying, "There is no power or might but through God" (*lā ḥawla wa lā quwwata illā billāh*). If, on the other hand, the person praying repeats the phrases, "Come to prayer!" and "Come to salvation!" as they were spoken by the muezzin either deliberately or out of ignorance, his or her prayer will be invalidated. As for someone who is busy performing a required prayer, even if it is a prayer which is being performed in fulfillment of a vow, it is undesirable to repeat the words of the *adhān* at this time; however, it is recommended that he or she do so once he or she has finished praying.

* * *

As for the Hanafis, they hold that whether the prayer one is performing is required or voluntary, it will be invalidated if the person praying responds to a muezzin issuing a call to prayer. Such a person's prayer will be invalidated regardless of whether he or she intended to respond to the call to prayer or intended nothing at all; however, if his or her intention was simply to praise God and His Messenger, his or her prayer will remain valid.

muezzin when he is engaged in *tarjīʿ*; however, whereas the Shafiis say that the recommended practice is to repeat the *tarjīʿ* twice, the Malikis maintain that the recommended practice is to repeat it only once, and that if several muezzins issue several successive calls to prayer, it is recommended that one respond verbally to each one separately.

Lastly, it is recommended that after responding to the *adhān*, one pray for blessings upon the Prophet, then say, "O God, the One who has issued this perfect call and established the prayers we perform, grant Muḥammad the means [to accomplish his mission] and the virtue [which he has merited], and resurrect him to the position of honor which You have promised him" (*Allāhumma rabba hādhihi al-daʿwati al-tāmmah wal-ṣalāti al-qāʾimah, āti Muḥammadan al-wasīlata wal-faḍīlah, wabʿathhu maqāman maḥmūdan alladhī waʿadtah*).

Issuing the *adhān* for prayers that have been missed

It is an emulation of the prophetic Sunnah to utter the *adhān* aloud for a prayer missed earlier if one is praying with a group, whether the person praying is at home or in the open desert. If, on the other hand, the person is praying by himself at home, he is not to raise his voice. When making up a prayer that was missed earlier in a mosque, one should not utter the *adhān* at all; this ruling is agreed upon by the Shafiis, the Hanbalis and the Hanafis; for the Malikis' view, see below.[211]

If someone has numerous prayers to make up and wishes to make them up in a single session, he should utter the call to prayer for the first one only, and he is free to choose whether to repeat it for the prayers which follow. This ruling is agreed upon by the Hanafis and the Hanbalis; as for the Malikis, we have seen that they consider it undesirable to utter the *adhān* for prayers one is making up regardless of the circumstances. As for the Shafiis, they hold that it is forbidden to utter the *adhān* for any but the first of a group of prayers one is making up in a single session; however, if one wishes to make up each missed prayer in a separate session, one may utter the *adhān* for each one.

---

211. According to the Malikis, it is always undesirable to utter the *adhān* when making up a prayer missed earlier, regardless of whether the person praying is at home or in the desert, with a group or alone. Moreover, this ruling applies whether one is making up one's missed prayers in a single session or in more than one session, and whether one has many prayers to make up or just a few.

Issuing the call to prayer slowly and deliberately

The Arabic term which conveys the sense of slowness and deliberateness here, namely, *tarassul*, means that the muezzin enunciates each phrase of the call to prayer separately from every other. However, scholars of jurisprudence differ on certain points relating to the meaning of *tarassul*.[212]

As for the ruling on *tarassul*, the Hanafis and the Malikis hold that it is a practice based on the prophetic Sunnah and that it is undesirable to neglect it, whereas the Shafiis and the Hanbalis hold that *tarassul* is simply recommended and that, consequently, neglecting it is merely a departure from the ideal.

As for the definition of *tarassul* given above, two of the four schools have added additional qualifications to it.[213]

---

212. According to the Hanafis, the term *tarassul* means that between each two phrases, the muezzin pauses long enough for someone to repeat what he just said; however, in the case of the words, *Allāhu akbar*, a pause is to be placed not between each two instances of this phrase, but rather, between each two *pairs* of the phrase. (In other words, the muezzin says, *Allāhu akbar Allāhu akbar*, pauses, then repeats, *Allāhu akbar Allāhu akbar*.)

* * *

According to the Malikis, the term *tarassul* means not prolonging the words in the call to prayer as one would do if he were singing or chanting. If such prolongation is not excessive, it is permissible but undesirable, however, if it is excessive by commonly accepted standards, it is forbidden altogether. From this it may be seen that delivering the call to prayer in a voice which resembles modern-day popular songs is forbidden according to the Malikis, who in this way make known their condemnation of people who perform such songs.

213. The Shafiis define *tarassul* as a slow, deliberate delivery in which the muezzin enunciates each phrase separately from every other; the only exception to this ruling is the words *Allāhu akbar* with which the call to prayer begins and ends, and which are to be repeated twice as a single phrase.

* * *

As for the Hanbalis, they define *tarussul* simply as an unhurried, deliberate delivery of the call to prayer.

Undesirable practices associated with the *adhān*: Its issuance by someone who is corrupt (*fāsiq*)

One undesirable practice associated with the call to prayer is for it to be issued by someone who is *fāsiq*, that is, living in disobedience to the teachings of Islam. According to the Shafiis and the Hanafis, a call to prayer issued by a *fāsiq* is valid, but undesirable. The Malikis, by contrast, hold that a call to prayer issued by a *fāsiq* will only be valid if he relies on a call to prayer delivered by someone else, while according to the Hanbalis, no call to prayer issued by a *fāsiq* is valid.

Not facing the *qiblah* when issuing the call to prayer, and a call to prayer issued by someone who is not in a state of ritual purity

It is undesirable to issue the call to prayer while facing in a direction other than the *qiblah* unless this is done in order to ensure that people can hear the muezzin.

It is likewise undesirable for the call to prayer to be issued by someone who is in a state of ritual impurity, especially if it is a state of major ritual impurity. This ruling is agreed upon by the Malikis and the Shafiis; for the Ḥanafis' and Hanbalis' views, see below.[214]

The call to women's prayers

According to the Malikis, the Hanbalis and the Hanafis, it is undesirable to issue the *adhān* for prayers to be performed by women, including both prayers to be prayed on time and those to be made up. As for the Shafiis, they hold that if the call to women's prayers is issued by a man, there is no undesirability attached to it but that if such a call to prayer is issued by one of the women concerned, it has no validity and if, by delivering such a call women are seeking to emulate men, it is forbidden altogether. If this is not the intention behind women's call to prayer, it is to be viewed simply as a means of holding God in remembrance, and no undesirability attaches to it if it involves no raising of the voice.

---

214. According to the Hanbalis and the Hanafis, a call to prayer issued by someone in a state of major ritual impurity is undesirable, but valid nevertheless. As for a call to prayer issued by someone in a state of minor ritual impurity, there is no undesirability attached to it. The Hanafis also add that it is recommended that a call to prayer issued by someone in a state of major ritual impurity be repeated.

Speaking while issuing the call to prayer

While issuing the call to prayer, it is undesirable to say anything which is not legitimately required; as for speech which is necessary, such as a response to someone's greeting of peace or an invocation of God's blessing on someone who has sneezed, the schools offer varying rulings on the matter.[215]

Speaking while delivering the call to prayer is undesirable unless one speaks in order to protect a blind person from some danger or for some similar purpose; however, if the muezzin does face such a situation, it is not only desirable, but obligatory to speak before the call to prayer has been completed. If the muezzin has spoken only briefly, he may simply resume the call to prayer where he left off, whereas if he has spoken more than this, he must start again from the beginning.

It is also considered undesirable to issue the *adhān* while seated or riding unless one is on a journey or has some other legitimate reason for doing so. If a muezzin is on a journey, it is not undesirable for him to issue the call to prayer while seated even if he has no other excuse for doing so. This ruling is agreed upon by the Shafiis, the Hanbalis and the Hanafis; as for the Malikis, the most widely recognized view among them is that a call to prayer issued while the muezzin is riding [an animal or some other means of transport] is not undesirable.

---

215. According to the Hanafis, a muezzin is not required to respond to someone's greeting or to invoke blessing on someone who has sneezed, even silently, either during or after his issuance of the call to prayer; consequently, even this amount of extraneous speech on his part is undesirable. Hence, if a muezzin does speak during his issuance of the call to prayer, he should repeat it.

* * *

According to the Shafiis, speaking briefly to respond to someone's greeting and/or invoke blessings on someone who has sneezed during the call to prayer is not undesirable but rather, simply a departure from the ideal. Once the muezzin finishes delivering the *adhān*, he is obliged to respond to any greetings he may have received during the *adhān*, while it is an emulation of the Sunnah for him to invoke blessings on someone who sneezed while he was delivering it; moreover, these rulings apply even if a relatively long period of time passes between the end of the call to prayer and the muezzin's fulfillment of this duty or Sunnah-based practice.

* * *

According to the Hanbalis, it is permissible to return someone's greeting and/or invoke blessings on someone who has sneezed while delivering the call to prayer, although the muezzin is under no obligation to make such a response either during or after the call to prayer. In addition, the Hanbalis hold that it is permissible to speak briefly while delivering the call to prayer even if it is in response to a mundane event, such as answering someone who has called one's name.

* * *

As for the Malikis, they hold that it is undesirable to interrupt the call to prayer in order to respond to someone's greeting or to invoke blessings on someone who has sneezed; however, these same verbal responses are obligatory for the muezzin once he has finished delivering the call to prayer.

Issuing the call to prayer in a melodious voice

Issuing the call to prayer in a chanting, sing-song voice as is prevalent today is not sanctioned by Islamic law; the reason for this is that the call to prayer is a form of worship which is intended to awaken a sense of humble reverence before God Almighty [rather than draw attention to human qualities or abilities – t.n.]. Nevertheless, the various schools offer differing rulings on this point.[216]

A call to prayer issued by a boy who has reached the age of discernment or by someone who is blind is not considered undesirable by the Hanafis and the Hanbalis if the person concerned has someone to help him determine what time it is; for the views of the Malikis and the Shafiis, see below.[217]

---

216. According to the Shafiis, delivering the call to prayer in a melodious voice involves moving back and forth among various musical tones or notes, whereas the practice supported by the prophetic Sunnah is for the muezzin to maintain a single tone throughout the call to prayer.

* * *

According to the Hanbalis, delivering the call to prayer in a melodious voice involves making music in a manner that produces delight and rapture, which they consider undesirable.

* * *

The Hanafis, by contrast, hold that issuing the call to prayer in a chanting, melodious voice is good unless it leads to a change in the words of the call to prayer by the addition of a vowel or consonant. Producing such a change is forbidden; it is likewise forbidden to listen to a call to prayer in which such a change has been produced.

* * *

As for the Malikis, their ruling is that creating a moderate musical effect when delivering the call to prayer is undesirable due to its incompatibility with humble reverence before God, and that if the musical effect is excessive by commonly accepted standards, it is completely forbidden.

217. As we have seen, the Shafiis consider it undesirable for a boy who has reached the age of discernment to issue the call to prayer.

* * *

As for the Malikis, they hold that if a young boy who has reached the age of discernment relies on an adult either in his issuance of the call to prayer or in determining what time it is, his call to prayer will be valid; otherwise, it will not.

The *iqāmah*:

Its definition and description

The *iqāmah* is the announcement that prayer has commenced, and its wording is as follows: "God is greatest! God is greatest! I testify that there is no god but God. I testify that Muḥammad is God's Messenger. Come to prayer! Come to salvation! Prayer has now begun. Prayer has now begun. God is greatest! God is greatest! There is no god but God" (*Allāhu akbar Allāhu akbar! ashhadu an lā ilāh illā Allāh. ashhadu anna Muḥammadan rasūl Allāh. ḥayya 'alā al-ṣalāh, ḥayya 'alā al-falāḥ. qad qāmat al-ṣalātu qad qāmat al-ṣalāh. Allāhu akbar, Allāhu akbar. la ilāha illā Allāh)*. This wording is agreed upon by the Shafiis and the Hanbalis; for the views of the Hanafis and the Malikis, see below.[218]

The ruling on the *iqāmah*

According to the Shafiis, the Hanbalis and the Hanafis, the ruling on the *iqāmah* is the same as that which applies to the *adhān*. As for the Malikis, they hold that unlike the *adhān*, utterance of the *iqāmah* is an individual Sunnah-based practice for grown males, and a collective Sunnah-based practice for a group of adult males praying in community. For children and for women, utterance of the *iqāmah* is recommended as an individual practice; however, if they are in the company of one or more grown men, it is not recommended, since the *iqāmah* issued by the adult male who is with them will suffice.

---

218. According to the Hanafis, the *iqāmah* should contain four repetitions of "God is greatest!" at the beginning rather than just two, and two repetitions at the end, while all the other phrases should be repeated twice. Hence, the wording of the *iqāmah* is as follows: "God is greatest! God is greatest! God is greatest! God is greatest! I testify that there is no god but God. I testify that there is no god but God. I testify that Muḥammad is God's Messenger. I testify that Muḥammad is God's Messenger. Come to prayer! Come to prayer! Come to salvation! Come to salvation! Prayer has now begun. Prayer has now begun. God is greatest! God is greatest! There is no god but God."

* * *

As for the Malikis, they hold that all the phrases that make up the *iqāmah* are to be pronounced once only with the exception of the words, *Allāhu akbar* ("God is greatest"), which is uttered twice in the beginning and twice at the end. The wording of the *iqāmah* is thus as follows: "God is greatest! God is greatest! I testify that there is no god but God. I testify that Muḥammad is God's Messenger. Come to prayer! Come to salvation! Prayer has begun. God is greatest! God is greatest! There is no god but God."

Conditions for the *iqāmah*

The conditions which apply to the *iqāmah* are the same as those which apply to the *adhān* with two exceptions: The first exception has to do with gender. Unlike the call to prayer, which must be issued by a male, the *iqāmah* is valid whether it is issued by a man or a woman.[219] If it is issued by a woman, however, she must utter the *iqāmah* for herself only, whereas if she is praying in community with men, her *iqāmah* will not be valid according to the Shafiis and the Malikis. As for the Hanafis and the Hanbalis, their views may be seen below.[220]

The second exception consists in the fact that unlike the *adhān* [which is required by Islamic law to be temporally associated with prayer], the *iqāmah* is temporally associated with prayer only on the basis of commonly recognized custom. Thus, if someone announces the commencement of prayer, then proceeds to speak at length, eat, drink, etc., and prays after this without repeating the *iqāmah*, his announcement will still be valid because he has fulfilled the Sunnah connected with this practice. This ruling is agreed upon by the Shafiis, the Malikis and the Hanbalis. As for the Hanafis, they hold that the *iqāmah* should be repeated if it is separated from the prayer by lengthy speech or action, such as eating and the like. However, they also say that if the muezzin issues the *iqāmah*, after which the imam prays the two [Sunnah-based] *rak'ahs* of the dawn prayer, there is no need for the *iqāmah* to be repeated again [before the obligatory dawn prayer].[221]

---

219. As was seen earlier, however, the Hanafis hold that an *adhān* issued by a woman will be valid [t.n.].

220. According to the Hanafis, the conditions mentioned above for the *adhān* are not conditions for its validity but rather, for its perfection. Hence, it is undesirable for any of these conditions not to be fulfilled, but this does not invalidate the *adhān*. The *iqāmah* is similar to the call to prayer in this respect except that in cases where any of the conditions associated with the call to prayer are unfulfilled, it is recommended that it be repeated, whereas if any of the conditions associated with the *iqāmah* are unfulfilled, there is no need for it to be repeated. Hence, if a woman announces the commencement of prayer for men, her announcement is valid according to the Hanafis despite its undesirability.

* * *

As for the Hanbalis, they hold that maleness is a condition for the validity of both the *adhān* and the *iqāmah*. Hence, a woman should not be asked to issue either of them.

221. This is presumably due to the fact that the performance of these *rak'ahs* (as opposed to the utterance of speech extraneous to the call to prayer or the *iqāmah*) is a form of worship and as such, it does not necessitate a repetition of the *iqāmah* before the obligatory prayer is performed [t.n.].

When a person being led in prayer should rise for prayer after the *iqāmah* is issued

The four schools offer differing views on when a person being led in prayer should rise for prayer after hearing the *iqāmah*.[222]

Sunnah-based and other desirable practices associated with the *iqāmah*

The Sunnah-based practices associated with the *iqāmah* are the same as those associated with the *adhān* with the following differences: (1) According to the Shafiis, the Hanafis and the Malikis, it is an emulation of the Sunnah for the *adhān* to be delivered from an elevated spot, whereas this does not apply to the *iqāmah*. For the Hanbalis' view, see below.[223] (2) According to those schools which favor the practice of *tarjī'*, that is, the Malikis and the Shafiis, *tarjī'* is recommended in the *adhān* but not in the *iqāmah*. As for the Hanbalis and the Hanafis, they support *tarjī'* in neither the *adhān* nor the *iqāmah*. (3) According to the Shafiis, the Hanafis and the Hanbalis, it is an emulation of the Sunnah to deliver the call to prayer slowly and deliberately, and to deliver the *iqāmah* at a brisk pace. As for the Malikis, they hold

---

222. According to the Malikis, it is permissible for those who wish to pray (other than the person issuing the *iqāmah*) to get up while the *iqāmah* is still being issued, or as soon as they are able thereafter without any time restrictions. As for the person who issues the *iqāmah*, he should rise from the time when the *iqāmah* first begins.

* * *

According to the Shafiis, it is an emulation of the Sunnah to rise for prayer immediately after the conclusion of the *iqāmah*.

* * *

According to the Hanbalis, it is an emulation of the Sunnah to rise for prayer when the person issuing the *iqāmah* says, "Prayer has now begun" (*qad qāmat al-ṣalāh*) if he or she sees that the imam has risen. Otherwise, he or she should wait until the imam has stood up.

* * *

As for the Hanafis, they hold that those being led in prayer should rise when they hear the phrase, "Come to salvation!" (*ḥayya 'alā al-falāḥ*).

223. According to the Hanbalis, it is an emulation of the Sunnah for the *iqāmah* to be issued from an elevated spot just as it is for the call to prayer unless this would be a cause of hardship.

that both the call to prayer and the *iqāmah* should be delivered slowly and deliberately. (4) According to the Hanbalis and the Shafiis, it is an emulation of the Sunnah for the muezzin to place his forefingers in his ears as he delivers the *adhān*. For the views of the Malikis and the Hanafis, see below.[224]

Uttering the *adhān* when making up earlier prayers missed

It is an emulation of the prophetic Sunnah to utter the call to prayer for only the first of the missed prayers one is making up; in the case of the *iqāmah*, by contrast, the Shafiis, Hanafis and Hanbalis rule that it is consistent with the Sunnah to utter it before each compensatory prayer one performs. As for the Malikis, they hold that it is undesirable to utter the *adhān* for any compensatory prayer; however, in the case of the *iqāmah*, they hold that it should be uttered for every missed prayer one makes up.

According to the Shafiis, the Malikis and Hanafis, the *adhān* is required of only men and not women, whereas the *iqāmah* is required of both men and women.[225]

The time period separating the *adhān* and the *iqāmah*

It is an emulation of the Sunnah for the muezzin to sit down between the *adhān* and the *iqāmah* for as long as it takes for regular worshipers to arrive at the mosque, though not so long that the "time of virtue" is allowed to pass. In the case of the sundown prayer, however, the muezzin should not delay it; rather, he should allow only enough time to pass between the *adhān* and the *iqāmah* for three verses of the Qur'ān to be recited. This ruling is agreed on by the Shafiis and the Hanafis; for the view of the Malikis and the Hanbalis, see below.[226]

---

224. According to the Hanafis, placing one's forefingers in one's ears is recommended when delivering the call to prayer, but not when delivering the *iqāmah*. Hence, although it is better to follow this practice during the *iqāmah*, it is nevertheless not undesirable to omit it.

* * *

According to the Malikis, placing one's fingers in one's ears while delivering the *adhān* in order to help other people hear is permissible, though not an emulation of the Sunnah.

225. As for the Hanbalis, they hold that neither the *adhān* nor the *iqāmah* is required of the woman but that, on the contrary, it is undesirable for a woman to issue either of them.

226. According to the Malikis, if a group of worshipers are waiting for others to join them, it is preferable for them to pray as soon as possible after the beginning of the time period for the prayer concerned after performing whatever Sunnah-based prayers precede the obligatory prayer. However, they make an exception to this rule for the noon prayer, in which case it is preferable to delay the prayer until the sun has descended sufficiently from its zenith to cast a shadow equal to one-fourth of a person's height; this waiting period is lengthened further if the weather is particularly hot, in which case it is recommended that prayer be delayed until the middle of the time period. As for someone praying alone or a group of worshipers who are not waiting for anyone to join them, it is preferable that they proceed as soon as

Accepting remuneration for issuing the *adhān* and the like

According to the Hanafis and the Shafiis, it is permissible to accept remuneration for issuing the call to prayer and related functions, such as serving as imam and teaching [the Qur'ān]; however, the Hanbalis and the Malikis differ with this point of view.[227]

Uttering the *adhān* in the ear of a newborn or epileptic, as well as in the event of fire, war, and the like

It is recommended that the *adhān* be uttered in an infant's right ear soon after it is born, and that the *iqāmah* be uttered in the baby's left ear. It is likewise recommended that the call to prayer be delivered when there is a fire or a war, when someone departs on a journey, and in the ear of someone who is care-worn or afflicted with epilepsy.

Praying for the Prophet before issuing the *adhān*, and uttering praise to God during the night before the *adhān*

Praying for blessings on the Prophet following the *adhān* is agreed by all schools to be a legitimate practice, whether on the part of the muezzin or someone else. This is based on the prophetic hadith narrated by Muslim according to which the Prophet said, "When you hear the muezzin, repeat what he says after him, then pray for me." His saying, "then pray for me" is a general command which includes both the muezzin and those who have heard him. The Prophet's statement does not specify

---

possible to perform whatever Sunnah-based prayers precede the obligatory prayer, then perform the obligatory prayer as soon as possible thereafter.

* * *

As for the Hanbalis, they hold that between the time he finishes the *adhān* and the time he utters the *iqāmah*, the muezzin should sit down and remain seated long enough for someone who is eliminating bodily wastes or doing his ablutions to finish what he is doing and perform two *rak'ahs*. They make an exception to this ruling for the sundown prayer, however, in which case it is recommended that the muezzin remain seated for what would generally be considered a short period of time between the *adhān* and the *iqāmah*.

227. According to the Malikis, it is permissible to accept remuneration for delivering the *adhān* and the *iqāmah* and for serving as an imam if the function of imam is simply that of delivering the *adhān* or the *iqāmah*. As for accepting payment for fulfilling the function of a regular imam who has been appointed to serve a particular mosque, this is undesirable if his remuneration is supplied by the worshipers themselves. However, if the payment is derived from a religious endowment or from the public treasury, there is no undesirability attached to it.

* * *

As for the Hanbalis, they hold that it is forbidden to receive remuneration for delivering the *adhān* and the *iqāmah* if there is someone who would be willing to volunteer these services. Otherwise, whoever is charged with oversight of such matters should pay the person who performs these functions out of the public treasury given the Muslims' need for such services.

whether we are to pray for him silently or aloud. Hence, there is nothing to prevent the muezzin from praying aloud for the Prophet as a way of reminding people of the command contained in this hadith. However, care must be taken when engaging in this practice not to go beyond the act of praying for blessings and peace in a spirit of worship to the act of chanting and making music by singing songs which have the effect of shifting people's inward orientation from worship and devotion to the mere enjoyment of music. This is what is done by some muezzins of our day; however, it is one of the worst types of innovation and, as such, should be abandoned. The Shafiis and the Hanbalis state openly that this practice is based on the prophetic Sunnah; however, in so saying, perhaps they are speaking of it in the sense mentioned above, [namely, a simple invocation of blessings on the Prophet].

As for words of praise and pleas for divine assistance during the night before the dawn call to prayer, there are some who hold that they are not permissible due to the fact that they might disturb people who are asleep and who are not accountable to God for waking at this time. Others, however, hold that this practice is permissible due to the fact that it might serve to help others wake up [for the dawn prayer as well as other, voluntary acts of worship]. In other words, even though this practice is not enjoined by any ruling or precept in Islam and is not, therefore, based on the Sunnah or even recommended, it remains true that waking others for the purpose of worship is legitimate in and of itself provided that it does not cause harm to anyone. Even so, it is preferable to eliminate this practice unless its purpose is to waken people before dawn during the month of Ramaḍān since during this month in particular, it is a practice which holds clear benefits.

Voluntary Prayer

Voluntary prayer: its definitions and types

Voluntary ritual prayer is prayer that accountable Muslims are encouraged to engage in over and above that which is required [namely, the five daily obligatory prayers]. The two primary types of voluntary prayer are: (1) prayers not associated with any of the five daily obligatory prayers, such as the prayer for rain, the prayers performed for the solar and lunar eclipses, and the *tarāwīḥ* prayers performed during Ramaḍān, and (2) prayers which are to be performed either directly before or directly after one of the five daily prayers. This second category of voluntary prayers is further divided into prayers which are based on the prophetic Sunnah, those which are simply recommended, and those that are referred to as *raghībah*.[228]

---

228. The Hanbalis divide the voluntary prayers which are associated with the five obligatory prayers into two categories: The first category, referred to in Arabic as *rātibah*, consists of a total of ten *rak'ahs*, namely: (a) two *rak'ahs* before the noon prayer and two after it, (b) two *rak'ahs* after the sundown prayer, (c) two *rak'ahs* after the evening prayer, and (d) two *rak'ahs* before the dawn prayer. These are based on the hadith passed down from Ibn 'Umar, may God be pleased with him, in which he states, "I memorized ten *rak'ahs* which I learned from the Prophet," after which he went on to list the ten mentioned here. These ten *rak'ahs* are classified as an emphatically enjoined Sunnah-based practice, which means that if one misses them, one should make them up later; however, if one misses them along with the obligatory prayers themselves, and if a large number of prayers have been missed for one reason or another, it is considered preferable not to make them up lest doing so be a cause of undue hardship. The only exception to this last ruling is the two *rak'ahs* preceding the dawn prayer, which should be made up even if a large number of obligatory prayers have been missed. Moreover, if someone does not perform the *rak'ahs* which precede the obligatory prayer until after the obligatory prayer, this is considered to be a compensatory performance even if these *rak'ahs* were performed during the time period for the obligatory prayer concerned.

As for the second category of voluntary prayers tied to the five obligatory prayers, they consist of twenty more *rak'ahs*: (a) four *rak'ahs* before the noon prayer and four after it, (b) four *rak'ahs* before the mid-afternoon prayer, (c) four *rak'ahs* after the sundown prayer, and (d) four *rak'ahs* after the evening prayer. It is also permissible to perform two *rak'ahs* between the sundown call to prayer and the sundown prayer itself based on the following hadith passed down on the authority of Anas, who said, "During the days when the Prophet was among us, we used to pray two *rak'ahs* after sunset." When asked whether the Messenger of God used to perform these two *rak'ahs* as well, Anas replied, "He used to see us praying them, but he neither commanded nor forbade us to do so." It is also permissible to pray two *rak'ahs* from a seated position following the *witr*, and it is considered preferable to perform at home the *rātibah* prayers, the *witr*, and any other prayers which Islamic law does not specify that we should pray in community. It is an emulation of the prophetic Sunnah for the Sunnah-based *rak'ahs* to be separated from the obligatory prayers by an act of rising to one's feet or speaking. With respect to the Friday congregational prayer, there is a Sunnah-based prayer following it which consists of a minimum of two *rak'ahs* and a maximum of six. It is also considered an emulation of the Sunnah to pray four more *rak'ahs* prior to the Friday congregational prayer; however, these *rak'ahs* are not classified as *rātibah* [i.e., emphatically enjoined Sunnah-based practices], since there are no emphatically enjoined Sunnah-based *rak'ahs* prior to the Friday congregational prayer.

* * *

The Hanafis divide the voluntary prayers associated with the five daily obligatory prayers into two categories, namely, (1) Sunnah-based, and (2) recommended. The first category consists of the following five prayers: (a) Two *rak'ahs* before the dawn prayer. These two *rak'ahs* are the most binding of all the Sunnah-based voluntary prayers; consequently, it is not permissible to perform them from a seated position or while riding an animal without a legitimate excuse. The time period for their performance, as we have seen, is the same as that for the dawn prayer. Once this time period has passed, they may only be made up in connection with the dawn prayer itself. Thus, for example, if someone sleeps until after sunrise, he should first make up these two *rak'ahs*, then make up the dawn prayer afterwards. As for the time period during which these two *rak'ahs* may be made up, it extends up till noon, after which they may no longer be made up. If, on the other hand, the time period for these two *rak'ahs* in particular runs out (by, for example, one's praying the dawn prayer without performing these two *rak'ahs* first), they may no longer be made up, whether before or after sunrise. The Sunnah-based practice in connection with these two *rak'ahs* is for them to be performed at home at the beginning of the time period for the dawn prayer; in the first *rak'ah* one is to recite Surah 109 and in the second, Surah 112. If the commencement of the communal dawn prayer is announced before one has prayed these two *rak'ahs* and if there is enough time to pray the dawn prayer with the community after performing them, one should go ahead and perform them first; otherwise, one should forego them in order to pray the communal prayer on time, after which they are not to be made up. Lastly, it should be noted that the two *rak'ahs* which precede the dawn prayer are the only voluntary prayer which it is permissible to perform after the communal prayer has been announced. (b) A set of four *rak'ahs* which are to be performed as a single unit before the noon prayer, and which are the second most binding of all voluntary prayers after the two *rak'ahs* preceding the dawn prayer. (c) Two *rak'ahs* to be performed after the noon prayer on all days but Friday; on Fridays, by contrast, the Sunnah-based practice is to perform four *rak'ahs* after the noon prayer, and four *rak'ahs* before it as well. (d) Two *rak'ahs* after the sundown prayer. (e) Two *rak'ahs* after the evening prayer.

As for the second category of voluntary prayers connected with the obligatory prayers, namely, those which are simply recommended, they consist of four prayers: (a) Four *rak'ahs* (or, if one wishes, two) before the mid-afternoon prayer, (b) Six *rak'ahs* after the sundown prayer, (c) Four *rak'ahs* before the evening prayer, and (d) Four *rak'ahs* after the evening prayer. These four *rak'ahs* are based on a hadith passed down on the authority of 'Ā'ishah, may God be pleased with her, who said, "The Messenger of God used to perform four *rak'ahs* before the evening prayer and four after it, then lie down on his side."

In addition to the prayers already listed, one is free to perform as many other voluntary prayers as one wishes. For voluntary prayers performed during the daytime, the Sunnah-based practice is to utter the final greeting of peace after completing four *rak'ahs*, provided that one does not perform them during times when their performance would be undesirable. Thus, for example, if someone utters the final greetings of peace after performing only two *rak'ahs*, he will not have emulated the Sunnah. As for the voluntary *rak'ahs* which follow the sundown prayer, one may either perform them all with a single utterance of the final greeting of peace, or utter the final greeting of peace after every two *rak'ahs*. In the case of the evening prayer, the voluntary portion consists of four *rak'ahs* before the obligatory prayer, and four more afterwards. It is also a Sunnah-based practice to separate the obligatory evening prayer from the voluntary prayer which follows it either with the words, "O God, You are peace and from You does peace proceed. Blessed art Thou, O Majestic and Honorable One" (*Allāhumma anta al-salāmu wa minka al-salām, tabārakta yā dhā al-jalāli wal-ikrām*), or with any other traditional words and phrases whose purpose is to invoke the remembrance of the Divine.

* * *

The Shafiis divide the voluntary prayers associated with the five obligatory prayers into two categories: (1) emphatically enjoined, and (2) non-emphatically enjoined. The first category consists of the following: (a) Two *rak'ahs* before the dawn prayer, to be performed sometime between "true dawn" and sunrise. It is an emulation of the Sunnah to perform these two *rak'ahs* before the dawn prayer provided that one has no reason to fear that by doing so, one would be late performing the dawn prayer or would miss the opportunity to perform it in community. If there is reason to fear either of these two possibilities, one should pray the obligatory dawn prayer first and the two voluntary *rak'ahs* after this; if one does so, there is no undesirability attached thereto. If, by sunrise, one has still not prayed the dawn prayer, one may make up these two *rak'ahs* by praying them later. It is also an emulation of the Sunnah to follow one's recitation of the *Fātiḥah* with Surah 2:136 in the first *rak'ah* and Surah 3:64 in the second *rak'ah*. Lastly, it is an emulation of the Sunnah to separate the obligatory dawn prayer from these two voluntary *rak'ahs* by an action such as lying down, turning to one side, or speaking (provided that one does not speak of worldly matters). (b) Two *rak'ahs* before the noon prayer or the Friday congregational prayer. (c) Two *rak'ahs* following the noon prayer or the Friday congregational prayer. (It is an emulation of the Sunnah to perform two *rak'ahs* after the Friday congregational prayer only if one did not follow this by praying the noon prayer as well. If one prays the noon prayer after the Friday congregational prayer, it is not an emulation of the Sunnah to perform these two *rak'ahs* as well.) (d) Two *rak'ahs* after the sundown prayer, in which case one is encouraged to recite Surah 109 in the first *rak'ah* and Surah 112 in the second. (e) Two *rak'ahs* after the evening prayer. [All of the aforementioned voluntary prayers are referred to in Arabic as *rawātib* (singular, *rātibah*), which means, simply, 'regular', due to their regular association with the daily obligatory prayers – t.n.] (f) The *witr*, which must consist of at least one *rak'ah*. In order to achieve the minimum degree of perfection, one must perform three *rak'ahs*, while the maximum is eleven, and it is preferable to utter the concluding greeting of peace after each pair of *rak'ahs*, as well as after the final *rak'ah*. The time for the *witr* is following the evening prayer even if it is being joined with the sundown prayer and performed in advance. The time period during which the *witr* may be performed lasts until sunrise, after which it must be performed as a compensatory prayer.

As for the second category, namely, voluntary prayers which are not emphatically enjoined, they come to a total of twelve *rak'ahs*: (a) two *rak'ahs* before the noon prayer or the Friday congregational prayer over and above those already mentioned; (b) two *rak'ahs* after the noon prayer or the Friday congregational prayer in addition to those already mentioned; (c) four *rak'ahs* before the mid-afternoon prayer; (d) two *rak'ahs* before the sundown prayer (which, in accordance with the Sunnah, may be performed quickly after one responds to the muezzin; this practice is based on the Prophet's statement, "Between every two *adhāns* there is a prayer", where the first of the two *adhāns* refers to the call to prayer, and the second to the *iqāmah*); and (e) two *rak'ahs* before the evening prayer.

* * *

As for the Malikis, they divide the voluntary prayers associated with the five obligatory prayers into two categories: (1) *rawātib*, and (2) others. Category (1) includes prayers performed at the following times: (a) between the commencement of the time period for the noon prayer and the performance of the noon prayer itself, (b) after the noon prayer, (c) between the commencement of the time period for the mid-afternoon prayer and the performance of the mid-afternoon prayer, and (d) after the sundown prayer. Unlike the other schools, the Malikis do not specify how many *rak'ahs* such prayers should consist of; however, they hold that the preferred numbers are those which are commended in certain hadiths, namely: (a) four *rak'ahs* before the noon prayer, (b) four *rak'ahs* after the noon prayer, (c) four *rak'ahs* before the mid-afternoon prayer, and (d) six *rak'ahs* after the sundown prayer.

The ruling on these voluntary prayers is that they are emphatically recommended. As for the performance of voluntary prayers before the sundown prayer (after its time period has commenced), it is undesirable due to the shortness of the time available. And as for performing voluntary prayers before the evening prayer, there is no explicit text in Islamic law which deals with this matter, although it may be inferred from the hadith quoted above, namely, "Between every two *adhāns* [i.e., between each *adhān* and its associated *iqāmah*] there is a prayer," that this is a desirable practice.

As for Category (2) above, it includes: (a) two *rak'ahs* before the dawn prayer, the ruling on which is that they occupy a position somewhere between desirable practices and those based on the Sunnah. The time for these two *rak'ahs* is between "true dawn" and sunrise. If they are performed between sunrise and noon, they are considered to be a compensatory prayer; after noon, however, they may no longer be made up. If someone prays the dawn prayer before performing these two *rak'ahs*, it is undesirable to perform them until the time at which voluntary prayers become permissible, namely, the time at which the sun is elevated the length of one spear (i.e., the length of twelve medium-sized hand-spans) above the horizon. If the sun

The *dhikr* following prayer

Islamic law contains a number of specific phrases that are to be uttered after one concludes each obligatory prayer. They include such phrases as, "Glory be to God!" (*subḥān Allāh*) (33 times), "Praise be to God!" (*al-ḥamdu lillāh*) (33 times) and "God is greatest!" (*Allāhu akbar*) (33 times). These, as well as numerous others, are to be uttered after one concludes the dawn and noon prayers.

One question relating to such phrases of divine remembrance and worship is: Is it an emulation of the prophetic Sunnah to utter such phrases before or after a voluntary prayer? For example, when someone concludes the noon prayer, should he or she go on to utter these phrases directly, then pray the Sunnah-based voluntary prayer that follows the noon prayer? Or should he/she first go on to the Sunnah-based voluntary prayer, then conclude everything with the utterance of such phrases of divine remembrance?[229]

---

rises before one has prayed the dawn prayer, one should perform the obligatory dawn prayer first (based on the officially recognized view among the Malikis). Moreover, it is recommended that one recite nothing but the *Fātiḥah* during these two *rak'ahs* without reciting any other passage from the Qur'ān, whereas the *Fātiḥah* is obligatory, as we have seen. (b) The *shaf'* (meaning "even number"), which consists of a minimum of two *rak'ahs* and has no maximum. It is recommended that one recite Surah 87 in the first *rak'ah* and Surah 109 in the second. The *shaf'*, which is simply recommended, is performed between the evening prayer and the *witr*. (c) The *witr*, which is the most emphatically enjoined of all voluntary prayers other than the two *rak'ahs* associated with the circumambulation of the Ka'bah, is to be performed after the evening prayer provided that the latter was performed after the evening 'glow' disappeared from the sky; the so-called elective phase for the *witr* extends from the appearance of the evening glow referred to here until dawn, while its imperative phase extends from the break of dawn to the time for the dawn prayer. It is undesirable to postpone the *witr* until the imperative phase without a legitimate excuse. If someone remembers the *witr* while performing the dawn prayer, it is recommended that he cut off his prayer to perform the *witr* unless he is being led in prayer by an imam. It is thus permissible to cut off the dawn prayer in order to perform the *witr* provided that there is no reason to fear that by doing so, one will delay the dawn prayer past its designated time period. It is recommended when performing the *witr* that one recite Surah 112 in the first *rak'ah*, and in the second, Surah 113 and Surah 114, which are generally referred to in Arabic as *al-mu'awwidhatān*, or "the two pleas for divine protection."

Lastly, it should be noted that when praying any voluntary prayer, it is an emulation of the Sunnah to utter the concluding greeting of peace after each pair of *rak'ahs*. This is based on an application of the Prophet's statement, "[Voluntary] nighttime prayers should be performed two by two" to daytime voluntary prayers as well, since there is essentially no difference between them.

229. The Hanafis view it as undesirable, though not to the point of being forbidden, to separate one's obligatory prayer from its associated Sunnah-based prayer by more than the time required to say, "O God, You are peace and from You does

peace proceed. Blessed art Thou, O Majestic and Honorable One!" (*Allāhumma, anta al-salāmu wa minka al-salāmu, tabārakta yā dhā al-jalāli wal-ikrām.*) As for the hadiths which deal with the matter of *adhkār* (the plural of *dhikr*), they do not conflict with this ruling, since the Sunnah-based voluntary prayers are not extraneous to, but rather, extensions of the obligatory prayers. It is desirable to ask for divine forgiveness (by saying, *astaghfir Allāh*) three times following the Sunnah-based prayer, to recite the Throne Verse (2:255) and Surahs 113 and 114 of the Qur'ān, then to say, *subḥān Allāh, al-ḥamdu lillāh* and *Allāhu akbar*, each 33 times. In addition, it is desirable to repeat the following 100 times: "There is no god but God alone, who has no partner. To Him belong dominion and praise, and He is capable of all things" (*lā ilāha illā Allāhu waḥdahu lā sharīka lah. Lahu al-mulk wa lahu al-ḥamd wa huwa 'ala kulli shay'in qadīr*). Then one says, "O God, no one can withhold what You have given, nor can anyone give what You have withheld, and no one will benefit from riches or good fortune except to the extent that he offers them to others in righteous action" (*Allāhumma lā māni'a limā a'ṭayt, wa lā mu'ṭin li mā mana't, wa lā yanfa'u dhā al-jaddi minka al-jadd*). Finally, one may offer supplications and conclude by saying, "Glory be to your Lord, the Possessor of all glory, honor and strength, who is far above all that they attribute to Him" (*subḥān rabbika, rabb al-'izzah, 'ammā yaṣifūn*).

* * *

According to the Malikis, it is preferable for the Sunnah-based prayer that follows an obligatory prayer to be performed after, rather than before, the phrases of divine remembrance associated with the obligatory prayer. Such phrases include, as we have seen, recitation of the Throne Verse (2:255) and Surah 112, and utterance of the phrases *subḥān Allāh, al-ḥamdu lillāh* and *Allāhu akbar* 33 times followed by a single repetition of the words, "There is no god but God alone, who has no partner. To Him belong dominion and praise, and He is capable of all things" (*lā ilāha illā Allāhu waḥdahu lā sharīka lah. Lahu al-mulk wa lahu al-ḥamd wa huwa 'alā kulli shay'in qadīr*).

* * *

In a view similar to that of the Malikis, the Shafiis hold that it is an emulation of the Sunnah for the obligatory prayer to be separated from its corresponding Sunnah-based prayer by the phrases of divine remembrance which we have discussed. Hence, after completing the obligatory prayer and before commencing the following Sunnah-based prayer, one should ask God's forgiveness three times and say, "O God, You are peace and from You does peace proceed. Blessed art Thou, O Majestic and Honorable One!" One should then say *subḥān Allāh, al-ḥamdu lillāh* and *Allāhu akbar* 33 times each, then conclude with the words, "There is no god but God alone, who has no partner. To Him belong dominion and praise, and He is capable of all things. O God, no one can withhold what You have given, nor can anyone give what You have withheld, and no one will benefit from riches or good fortune but to the extent that he offers them to others in righteous action."

* * *

As for the Hanbalis, they hold that one should utter the phrases of divine remembrance that follow the obligatory prayer before going on to perform the Sunnah-

Performing voluntary prayers in the place where one has prayed with a group

If someone prays an obligatory prayer in community and then wishes to pray an additional voluntary prayer, should he/she perform the voluntary prayer in the same place in which he/she prayed with the group, or is one required to move elsewhere? The rulings on this question differ in detail among the four schools.[230]

---

based prayers. One begins by saying, *astaghfir Allāh* three times. One then says, "O God, You are peace, from You does peace proceed, and to You we bring greetings of peace. Blessed art Thou and exalted, O Majestic and Honorable One! There is no god but God alone, who has no partner. To Him belongs dominion and praise, and He is capable of all things. There is no power or might but through God. There is no god but God, and we worship none but Him. He is the Gracious, Munificent One, and to Him belongs the most perfect praise (*lā ilāha illā Allāhu wa lā na'budu illā iyyāh, lahu al-ni'matu wa lahu al-faḍlu wa lahu al-thanā' al-ḥasan*). There is no god but God, and to Him we offer ourselves in sincere devotion even if this is hateful to those who deny the truth (*lā ilāha illā Allāhu, mukhliṣīn lahu al-dīn wa law kariha al-kāfirūn*). There is no god but God alone, Who has no partner. To Him belongs all dominion and all praise, and He is capable of all things. O God, there is no one who can withhold what You have given, and no one will benefit from riches or good fortune but to the extent that he offers them to others in righteous action." After this one should say *subḥān Allāh, al-ḥamdu lillāh* and *Allāhu akbar* 33 times each. It is also preferable that one conclude this *dhikr* by saying 100 times, "There is no god but God alone, Who has no partner. To Him belongs dominion and praise, and He is capable of all things."

230. The Hanafis hold that if someone performs an obligatory prayer as an imam, it is undesirable for him to move elsewhere for the voluntary prayer. As for someone who is being led by an imam, he may either perform the voluntary prayer in the same place where he prayed the obligatory prayer, or he may move elsewhere; however, it is preferable for such a person to move elsewhere before going on to the voluntary prayer.

* * *

According to the Shafiis, it is a Sunnah-based practice for someone who has prayed an obligatory prayer to move to another spot before performing the associated voluntary prayer. If one is unable to move because the room is too crowded or for some other reason, the Sunnah dictates that he speak, by saying, for example, "I have completed the obligatory prayer" or some such thing, then proceed to perform whatever voluntary prayers he wishes.

* * *

According to the Malikis, if someone is praying the *rātibah* voluntary prayers, that is, the Sunnah-based prayers associated with the obligatory prayers, it is preferable to perform them in the mosque, whether in the same spot where he performed the obligatory prayer or elsewhere in the mosque. If, by contrast, the person is praying a voluntary prayer which is not connected to an obligatory prayer, such as the forenoon prayer, it is preferable to perform it at home. An exception to this

The forenoon prayer (*al-ḍuḥā*)

According to the Shafiis, the Hanbalis and the Hanafis, the forenoon prayer is based on the prophetic Sunnah; as for the Malikis, they hold that it is emphatically recommended, but not part of the Sunnah.

The period during which the forenoon prayer is to be performed is from the moment when the sun is elevated one spear's length [above the horizon] until high noon. According to the Shafiis, the Hanafis and the Hanbalis, it is best to begin it after one-fourth of the daylight hours have passed; for the Malikis' view, see below.[231]

The forenoon prayer consists of a minimum of two and a maximum of eight *rak'ah*s. If one knowingly and deliberately performs the forenoon prayer in more than eight *rak'ahs*, the extra *rak'ahs* will have no validity; however, if one does so out of forgetfulness or ignorance, the extra *rak'ahs* will count as an unqualified voluntary prayer according to the Shafiis and the Hanbalis; for the Malikis' and Hanafis' views, see below.[232]

According to the Shafiis and the Hanbalis, it is an emulation of the Sunnah to make up the forenoon prayer if its time has run out; for the views of the Malikis and the Hanafis, see below.[233]

The "mosque greeting" (*taḥiyyat al-masjid*)

Upon entering a mosque, it is a Sunnah-based practice to perform two *rak'ahs* as a "mosque greeting." According to the Shafiis and the Hanbalis, one may pray as

---

ruling arises when the person concerned is in the Prophet's mosque in Medina, since it is recommended that anyone in Medina perform voluntary prayers in the place where the Prophet used to pray, namely, in front of the prayer niche located beside the pulpit in the center of the mosque.

* * *

As for the Hanbalis, they hold that the Sunnah-based prayers connected with the various obligatory prayers as well as all other voluntary prayers with the exception of those which Islamic law stipulates should be performed in community, are best performed at home. If someone does perform such a prayer in the mosque, he may either perform it in the spot where he prayed the obligatory prayer or move to another spot. (As we have noted, the Shafiis agree that voluntary prayers are best performed at home.)

231. According to the Malikis, it is preferable to postpone the forenoon prayer until as much time has passed since sunrise as passes between the beginning of the time period for the mid-afternoon prayer and sunset.

232. According to the Hanafis, the maximum number of *rak'ahs* for the forenoon prayer is sixteen. If someone performs more than this number and intends to perform the entire number with a single concluding greeting of peace, all the *rak'ahs* the person performed with the intention of praying the forenoon prayer will be valid, while any extras will be counted as an unqualified voluntary prayer. (However, it is undesirable to perform more than four *rak'ahs* with a single concluding greeting of peace in a daytime voluntary prayer.) If, on the other hand, one per-

many *rak'ahs* as one wishes with this intention. As for the Malikis and the Hanafis, their views are presented below.[234]

There are a number of conditions associated with the mosque greeting:

(1) One must enter the mosque at a time other than those during which it is forbidden to perform voluntary prayers there, such as sunrise and the period following the mid-afternoon prayer. (These times will be listed in full and discussed later in this work.) However, it is not necessary that one intend to stay in the mosque for a period of time; hence, even if someone enters the mosque with the intention of simply passing through it to reach another destination, he or she is asked to perform the mosque greeting according to the Shafiis, the Hanbalis and the Hanafis. As for the Malikis, they hold that the mosque greeting is only required of someone who enters the mosque with the intention of remaining there.

(2) One must be in a state of ritual purity when entering the mosque. According to the Malikis, the Hanbalis and the Hanafis, the mosque greeting is not required of someone who enters the mosque while in a state of ritual impurity. As for the Shafiis, they hold that if someone enters the mosque while in a state of ritual impurity and if it would be possible to perform ritual ablutions in a short period of time, the mosque greeting is required of such a person; otherwise, it is not.

(3) One must not have entered the mosque at a time when a communal prayer is being performed. If one enters and finds the imam leading a group in prayer, one should not perform the mosque greeting according to the Shafiis, the Hanbalis and the Hanafis. The Malikis, by contrast, hold that if someone enters the mosque while the regular imam is leading a group in prayer, he should not perform the mosque

---

forms more than sixteen *rak'ahs* for the forenoon prayer and performs them in successive units of two or four *rak'ahs*, there will be no undesirability attached to the performance of the additional *rak'ahs*.

* * *

As for the Malikis, they hold that if one performs more than eight *rak'ahs* for the forenoon prayer, the extra *rak'ahs* will be valid without any undesirability attached to them, properly speaking.

233. The Malikis and the Hanafis hold that voluntary prayers may not be made up once their designated time period runs out, the only exception to this being the two *rak'ahs* preceding the dawn prayer, which may be made up any time until noon.

234. According to the Hanafis, the mosque greeting consists of either two or four *rak'ahs*, with four being the preferred number; however, no additional *rak'ahs* may be performed with the intention of praying the mosque greeting.

* * *

As for the Malikis, they hold that the mosque greeting consists of only two *rak'ahs*, with no additions allowed. Based on the best attested views, the mosque greeting is no more than an emphatically recommended practice, although some Malikis hold that it is based on the prophetic Sunnah. Such a difference, however, causes no difficulty.

greeting, whereas if one enters while a communal prayer is being led by someone other than the regular imam, one may perform the mosque greeting if he wishes.

(4) One must not have entered the mosque after the speaker has come out to deliver the sermon for the Friday congregational prayer, the sermons for the Day of Sacrifice and the Day of Fastbreaking, and the like. If one enters the mosque at this time, one should not perform the mosque greeting according to the Malikis and the Hanafis; as for the Shafiis and the Hanbalis, they hold that if someone comes into the mosque while the imam is behind the pulpit, it is an emulation of the Sunnah to perform two brief *rak'ah*s before sitting down. One should not, however, perform more than two *rak'ah*s, and if one sits down before performing the mosque greeting in such a situation, one should not get up again in order to do so.

An exception to such rulings is made for the Sacred Mosque at Mecca, whose mosque greeting has special rulings which apply to it specifically.[235]

---

235. According to the Malikis, if someone enters the Sacred Mosque in Mecca and is under obligation to perform a circumambulation of the Ka'bah (even if only as a recommended practice or in fulfillment of a personal intention), his or her mosque greeting consists in circumambulating the Ka'bah. If someone enters Mecca in order to see the Ka'bah, for example, yet without being under any obligation to perform a circumambulation, and if such a person is a resident of Mecca, his/her mosque greeting consists of two *rak'ahs*, whereas if he or she is not a resident of Mecca, his/her mosque greeting consists in a circumambulation of the Ka'bah.

* * *

The Hanafis hold that, properly speaking, the mosque greeting for someone who enters the Sacred Mosque in Mecca consists in the performance of two *rak'ahs*. However, if someone enters the Sacred Mosque with either an obligation or an intention to perform a circumambulation of the Ka'bah, he/she should first perform the circumambulation, then perform the two *rak'ahs* associated with the circumambulation, in which case these two *rak'ahs* serve as his/her mosque greeting.

* * *

According to the Shafiis, if someone enters the Sacred Mosque and wishes to perform a circumambulation of the Ka'bah, he or she is required to offer two greetings: a greeting to the Ka'bah, which takes the form of circumambulation, and a greeting to the mosque, which takes the form of prayer. It is preferable that one first circumambulate the Ka'bah, then pray the two *rak'ahs* associated with circumambulation; these two *rak'ahs* then serve as one's mosque greeting. It is also possible for one to perform four *rak'ahs* after circumambulating the Ka'bah, intending the first pair of *rak'ahs* as a mosque greeting and the second pair as the Sunnah-based prayer associated with circumambulation; however, this particular order must be followed since otherwise, one's prayer will not be valid. If, on the other hand, someone enters the Sacred Mosque without wishing to perform circumambulation, he or she is only required to perform a mosque greeting in the form of prayer.

* * *

As for the Hanbalis, they hold that the greeting to the Sacred Mosque must take the form of circumambulating the Ka'bah, even if one has not entered the mosque for this purpose.

In the event that someone is unable to perform a mosque greeting because he/she is not in a state of ritual purity or for some other reason, it is recommended that he/she repeat four times, "Glory be to God! Praise be to God! There is no god but God! God is greatest!" (*subhān Allāh wal-ḥamdu lillāh wa lā ilāha illā Allāh wa Allāhu akbar*). This ruling is agreed upon by the Shafiis, the Hanafis and the Malikis; the Hanbalis, however, do not recommend this practice.

In addition, the mosque greeting may be replaced by some other prayer which consists of bowing and prostrating when one first comes in. If, for example, after entering the mosque, someone performs a prayer which he had missed earlier, this compensatory prayer serves as his/her mosque greeting provided that he/she consciously intends, in performing this compensatory prayer, to offer the mosque greeting as well. According to the Hanafis and the Shafiis, one receives the reward for performing the mosque greeting [even] if one did not consciously intend to perform it [by way of some other prayer, e.g., a compensatory prayer for one missed earlier – t.n.], whereas if one consciously intends *not* to perform it, one misses out on both the performance of the mosque greeting and its corresponding reward.

Lastly, although the Hanafis and the Malikis hold that it is undesirable to sit down immediately after entering the mosque before performing the mosque greeting, this does not necessarily mean that one must not get up and perform it after this. By contrast, the Shafiis hold that if someone deliberately sits down before performing the mosque greeting, he or she loses any opportunity to perform it after this. Similarly, if one sits down out of forgetfulness or ignorance and remains seated long enough to have performed two *rak'ah*s, one's chance of performing the mosque greeting is forfeited; however, if one remains seated for a shorter time, one may still get up and perform it. As for the Hanbalis, they hold that one loses the opportunity to perform the mosque greeting if one sits down after entering the mosque and remains seated for what would be considered a 'long' time by commonly accepted standards.

Performing two *rak'ah*s immediately after completing one's ablutions and when departing on or returning from a journey

It is recommended that one perform two *rak'ah*s immediately after completing one's ritual ablutions, before setting out on a journey, and when one returns from a journey. This recommendation is based on the Prophet's statement, "There is nothing better that one can leave with his family than two *rak'ah*s that one has performed among them when he intends to travel somewhere,"[236] and on the statement by Ka'b Ibn Mālik, "The Messenger of God always returned from his journeys during the forenoon hours, and when he arrived he would first go to the mosque, perform two *rak'ahs*, then remain seated there for a while."[237]

236. Narrated by al-Ṭabarānī.
237. Narrated by Muslim.

Keeping night prayer vigils (*al-tahajjud*) and the performance of two *rak'ahs* in a request for divine guidance (*ṣalāt al-istikhārah*)

It is recommended that one keep night prayer vigils based on the Prophet's saying, "Every believer should pray by night, even if only as long as it would take to milk a ewe."[238] Prayer performed by night is considered superior to that performed by day based on the Prophet's words, "The best prayer one can perform apart from the obligatory prayers is one performed at night."[239]

Another recommended practice is that of performing two *rak'ahs* in a petition for divine guidance (*ṣalāt al-istikhārah*). This recommendation is based on the hadith traced back to Jābir Ibn 'Abdullāh, may God be pleased with him, who said, "The Messenger of God used to teach us to seek God's guidance in all our affairs just the way he used to teach us surahs of the Qur'ān. The words he taught us to say are as follows: "O God, I seek sound guidance through reliance on Your knowledge, I ask You for strength through reliance on Your power, and I request Your great bounty. For You are capable while I am not, You know while I know not, and You are fully aware of all that is hidden from human perception. O God, if You know that this undertaking would be beneficial for my spiritual condition, my earthly existence and my life in the hereafter, then give me the ability to pursue it, facilitate it for me, and bless me in it. However, if You know that it would be harmful to my spiritual condition, my earthly existence and my life in the hereafter, then put it away from me, help me to pursue that which is good wherever it may lie, and enable me to find contentment therein." (*Allāhumma, innī astakhīruka bi 'ilmika wa astaqdiruka bi qudratika, wa as'aluka min faḍlika al-'aẓīm. fa innaka taqdir wa lā aqdiru, wa ta'lamu wa lā a'lam, wa anta 'allām al-ghuyūb. Allāhumma, in kunta ta'lamu anna hādha al-amra khayrun lī fī dīnī wa ma'āshī wa 'āqibati amrī, fa aqdirhu lī wa yassirhu lī, thumma bārik lī fīhi. wa'in kunta ta'lam anna hādha al-amra sharrun lī fī dīnī wa ma'āshī wa 'āqibati amrī, faṣrifhu 'annī waṣrifnī 'anhu, wa aqdir lī al-khayra ḥaythu kāna, thumma arḍinī fīhi.*) The person praying then mentions his or her specific concern."[240]

Prayer performed for the fulfillment of a need (*ṣalāt qaḍā' al-ḥawā'ij*)

It is recommended that someone with a legitimate need perform two *rak'ahs* based on the Prophet's statement, "If someone has a need which only God can meet, or a need which he perceives could be met by another human being, then let him perform ritual ablutions in the most careful, thorough manner, then perform two *rak'ahs*, utter words of praise to God Almighty, pray for blessings on the Prophet and say, 'There is no god but God, the Forbearing and Most Bountiful. Glory be to God, Lord of the mighty throne. Praise be to God, Sustainer of the worlds. I ask You to grant me Your mercy, forgiveness, righteousness, and safety from all iniquity. Leave

---

238. Narrated by al-Ṭabarānī with a chain of transmission traceable back to the Prophet.

239. Narrated by Muslim.

240. Recorded by all the compilers of sound hadiths with the exception of Muslim.

no sin of mine unforgiven, no anxiety unrelieved, and no need of mine unmet, O Most Merciful of the merciful!'" (*lā ilāha illā Allāh al-Ḥalīm al-Karīm. subḥān Allāh, rabb al-'arsh al-'aẓīm. al-ḥamdu lillāhi rabb al-'ālamīn. as'aluka mūjibāti raḥmatika wa 'azā'ima maghfiratika wal-ghanīmah min kulli birr wal-salāmata min kulli ithm. Lā tada' lī dhanban illā ghafartahu wa lā hamman illā farrajtahu wa lā ḥājatan hiyā li riḍan illā qaḍaytahā, yā arḥama al-rāḥimīn.*)[241]

The *witr* and the "prayer of obedience" that forms part of the *witr* and other prayers

According to the Shafiis, the Malikis and the Hanbalis, the *witr* is an emulation of the prophetic Sunnah, whereas according to the Hanafis, it is classified as a 'duty' (*wājib*); as we have seen, a 'duty' within the Hanafi framework is more binding than a Sunnah-based practice and less binding than a full obligation, or *farḍ*. Hence, they hold that omitting a 'duty', although it does not subject us to punishment in the afterlife as would the neglect of a full obligation, nevertheless deprives us of the intercession of the Prophet—a consequence which, for believers who cherish the intercession of the Chosen One, is sufficient punishment in itself. For each school's detailed rulings on the *witr*, see below.[242]

---

241. Narrated by al-Tirmidhī on the authority of 'Abdullāh Ibn Abī Awfā.

242. The Hanafis, as we have seen, classify the *witr* as a 'duty'. The *witr* consists of three *rak'ahs* concluded by a single greeting of peace. In each *rak'ah* one is to recite the *Fātiḥah* followed by another surah of the Qur'ān or some passage which would amount to the length of a short surah. It is recorded in a hadith that the Prophet used to recite Surah 87 in the first *rak'ah*, Surah 109 in the second, and in the third, Surah 112.

Once the worshiper has finished his or her recitation in the third *rak'ah*, he/she should raise his/her hands and utter the words *Allāhu akbar* as one does when commencing ritual prayer; however, rather than reciting the prayer of commencement, namely, "Glory be to You, O God, and praise! May Your name be blessed and Your majesty exalted! There is no god but You!" (*subhānuk Allāhumma wa biḥamdika, wa tabāraka ismuk wa ta'ālā jadduk wa lā ilāha ghayruk*), one recites what is referred to as a prayer of obedience (*qunūt*) which, in its most basic definition, is any speech which contains praise to God and supplication. However, the Sunnah-based practice in this respect is for the worshiper to recite the words which have been passed down on the authority of Ibn Mas'ūd, may God be pleased with him: "O God, we seek Your aid, Your guidance and Your forgiveness. We place our faith in You and rely on You in all our affairs, and to You we offer the highest praise. We thank You rather than denying You, and we declare ourselves in disobedience to all who refuse to walk in Your ways. O God, You alone do we worship, to You do we pray and bow down, and toward You do we strive in all haste, hoping for Your mercy and fearing Your chastisement; indeed, Your grave chastisement shall overtake those who deny the truth." After reciting this prayer, the worshiper prays for blessings and peace on the Prophet and his descendents.

The time period for the utterance of the prayer of obedience extends from the time the sunset glow disappears from the sky up to the break of dawn. If someone fails to recite this prayer either deliberately or out of forgetfulness, he or she should make it up later, even if a long time has passed. The prayer of obedience should not be uttered until after the evening prayer in order to maintain the obligatory order in one's prayers; however, if someone utters it before the evening prayer out of mere forgetfulness, it will still be valid; the same ruling applies if one performs all prayers in the proper order, then discovers that his/her evening prayer was invalid for some reason. In other words, such a person's prayer of obedience will still be valid in this situation, and it is only necessary to repeat the evening prayer, since the required temporal order for prayers is dropped in this type of situation.

It is not permissible to pray the *witr* from a seated position if one is capable of standing, nor is it permissible to pray it while riding without a legitimate excuse. Recitation of the prayer of obedience as part of the *witr* is a 'duty', whereas it is an emulation of the Sunnah to recite it silently, whether one is a prayer leader, someone being led in prayer, or praying alone. As for those who are not able to recite the prayer of obedience, they may say, "O our Sustainer! Grant us good in this world and good in the life to come, and protect us from suffering through the fire" (2:201). Or one might say, "O God, forgive us!" three times. If someone forgets to recite the prayer of obedience, then remembers while bowing, he/she should not recite it during the bow or rise again to a standing position; rather, one should simply complete one's prayer, then perform a prostration of forgetfulness after the concluding greeting of peace. If the worshiper returns to a standing position from the bow in order to recite the prayer of obedience and if, after this, he or she does not repeat the bow, his or her prayer will remain valid. If, on the other hand, someone inadvertently bows before reciting either a passage from the Qur'ān or the prayer of obedience, he or she should lift his/her head to recite them both, then repeat the bow; then, after completing the entire prayer, he/she should perform a prostration of forgetfulness. Lastly, if someone inadvertently bows without having recited the *Fātiḥah*, a further passage from the Qur'ān, or the prayer of obedience, he or she should lift his/her head and recite all three, then repeat the bow; however, if one does not repeat the bow, one's prayer will still be valid. In all such cases, one should conclude one's prayer with a prostration of forgetfulness.

The prayer of obedience is not to be recited in any prayer other than the *witr* unless one is facing exceptional suffering and tribulation. In this latter case, the most widely acknowledged view is that it is an emulation of the Sunnah to utter the prayer of obedience during the dawn prayer after rising from one's bow. In this respect, then, the manner of reciting the prayer of obedience during the dawn prayer differs from its manner of recitation during the *witr*. The Sunnah-based practice is for the prayer of obedience during times of tribulation to be recited by an imam rather than by someone praying alone; as for those being led in communal prayer, they are to recite it silently along with their imam unless he is reciting it aloud, in which case they are to say *Āmīn* following his recitation.

Lastly, Islamic law calls for the *witr* to be prayed communally only during the month of Ramaḍān, at which time its performance in a group is considered desirable. The reason for this is that, in some respects, the *witr* is similar to purely voluntary prayers [which, in general, it is judged desirable to perform alone] despite the fact that the Hanafis classify it as a 'duty'. As for praying the *witr* communally during times other than Ramaḍān, it is viewed as undesirable if the purpose in doing so is to call people to gather; however, if one person follows another in praying the *witr*, or if even two or three individuals follow another person's lead, this is acceptable since it involves no call for people to gather as a group.

* * *

According to the Hanbalis, the *witr* is an emphatically enjoined Sunnah-based practice. The *witr* consists of a minimum of one *rak'ah* and a maximum of eleven *rak'ahs*, although performing just one *rak'ah* is not considered undesirable. The minimum number of *rak'ahs* to perform if one strives for perfection in the *witr* is three; one may also choose to perform five, seven, nine or eleven *rak'ahs*. (a) If one performs eleven *rak'ahs*, one may utter the greeting of peace after each pair of *rak'ahs*, then perform the last *rak'ah* by itself, which is considered preferable. However, one may also perform the entire *witr* with a single greeting of peace, either with two testimonies of faith or with one. For example, one might pray ten *rak'ahs* and utter only the testimony, then rise for the eleventh *rak'ah* and conclude with the testimony and the final greeting of peace. Alternatively, one might pray the entire eleven *rak'ahs* at a single stretch, then utter the testimony at the very end, followed by the final greeting of peace. (b) If one performs nine *rak'ahs*, one may pray the *witr* with a single greeting of peace and two testimonies. For example, one may pray eight *rak'ahs*, then sit and utter the testimony, then perform the ninth *rak'ah* followed by a second utterance of the testimony and the final greeting of peace, which is considered preferable. Alternatively, one might pray all nine *rak'ahs* at a single stretch, then utter the testimony and the final greeting of peace. A third way would be to utter the greeting of peace after each pair of *rak'ahs*, then perform the ninth *rak'ah* and utter the final greeting of peace. (c) If one performs seven or five *rak'ahs*, it is preferable to pray the *witr* with a single testimony and a single greeting of peace, although one may perform it with two testimonies by sitting down after the sixth or fourth *rak'ah* and uttering the testimony but not the greeting of peace, then rising and performing the final *rak'ah*, then uttering the testimony again and the final greeting of peace. It is also possible in this case to utter the greeting of peace after every pair of *rak'ahs*. (d) If one performs three *rak'ahs*, it is preferable to recite Surah 87 in the first *rak'ah*, Surah 109 in the second *rak'ah*, then utter a greeting of peace, then recite Surah 112 in the third *rak'ah* followed by the testimony and the final greeting of peace. One may also simply perform all three *rak'ahs* in succession, then utter the testimony followed by the final greeting of peace. Lastly, one might perform the *witr* with two testimonies and a single greeting of peace, as in the sundown prayer, although this is the least preferable way.

It is an emulation of the Sunnah to utter the prayer of obedience after rising from one's bow in the final *rak'ah* of the *witr*, both during Ramaḍān and all other months of the year. When uttering this prayer, it is preferable to rely on the wording which has been passed down through prophetic hadiths, namely, "O God, we seek Your aid, Your guidance and Your forgiveness. We come to You in repentance, we place our faith in You, we rely on You in all our affairs. To You we offer the highest praise, and we thank You rather than denying You. O God, You alone do we worship and toward You do we strive in all haste, hoping for Your mercy and fearing Your chastisement; indeed, Your grave chastisement shall overtake those who deny the truth." (*Allāhumma innā nasta'īnuk wa nastaghfiruk wa nu'minu bika wa natawakkalu 'alayka and nakhḍa'u laka wa nakhla'u, wa natruku man yakfuruk. Allāhumma iyyāka na'budu wa laka nuṣallī wa nasjud, wa ilayka nas'ā wa naḥfud. Narjū raḥmataka wa nakhāfu 'adhābaka al-jidd. Inna 'adhābaka bil-kāfirīna mulḥiq.*) "O God, guide us with those You have guided, grant us wholeness with those to whom You have granted wholeness, watch over us with those You have watched over, bless us in that which You have given, and protect us from the evil of what You have decreed, for You alone are the One who decrees and disposes. No one to whom You grant your succor will be disgraced, nor will anyone whom You oppose enjoy honor and glory. Blessed are You, O our Lord, and exalted!" (*Allāhumma ihdinā fīman hadayt, wa 'āfinā fīman 'āfayt, wa tawallinā fīman tawallayt, wa bārik lanā fīmā a'ṭayt, waqinā sharra mā qaḍayt, innaka subḥānuka taqḍī wa lā yuqḍā 'alayka, innahu lā yadhillu man wālayt, wa lā ya'izzu man 'ādayt, tabārakta rabbanā wa ta'ālayt*). "O God, we seek refuge from Your displeasure in Your favor, we seek refuge from Your chastisement in Your pardon, and we seek refuge from You in You! To You do we offer boundless praise, for Yours are all the praiseworthy attributes with which You have described Yourself" (*Allāhumma na'ūdhu bi riḍāka min sukhṭika, wa bi 'afwika min 'uqūbatika, wa bika minka, wa lā nuḥṣī thanā'an 'alayka, anta kamā athnayt 'ala nafsik*). Following this, one is to pray for blessings upon the Prophet, and one may pray for blessings upon his family and descendents as well. It is acceptable as part of one's prayer of obedience to ask for anything one wishes in addition to the petitions included in the words above, although the traditional petitions are considered to be preferable.

It is an emulation of the prophetic Sunnah to utter the prayer of obedience aloud if one is an imam or praying alone; as for those being led in prayer, they are to say *Āmīn* aloud in response to the prayer of obedience uttered by their imam. It is a Sunnah-based practice for someone praying alone to change the first person plural pronouns to first person singular, for example, by saying, "Guide me" rather than "guide us", whereas in the case of an imam, he/she should use the first person plural pronouns contained in the traditional versions of the prayer.

After completing the *witr* with the final greeting of peace, the worshiper may emulate the prophetic Sunnah by saying, "Glory be to the Sovereign Supreme, the Holy" (*subḥān al-malik al-quddūs*) three times, repeating this phrase more loudly the third time. However, it is undesirable to utter the prayer of obedience in any prayer other than the *witr* unless the Muslims are afflicted by some tribulation or misfortune other than the plague. In the event of such a tribulation, it is a Sunnah-based practice for the sultan and his deputy to utter the prayer of obedience during all of the five daily prayers—with the exception of the Friday congregational prayer—using phases and petitions which are appropriate to the trial being faced by the people. As for the plague, it is not to be responded to with the prayer of obedience. However, if someone other than the sultan and his deputy utters the prayer of obedience in response to a time of trial, the prayer will not be invalid regardless of whether the person who does so is an imam or someone praying alone; as for someone who is being led by an imam in the dawn prayer, he/she should follow the imam in his prayer of obedience, saying *Āmīn* in response to the imam's petitions if they are audible and, if they are not, making his or her own petitions. During the final *rak'ah* of the *witr*, a worshiper may say *Allāhu akbar,* raise his hands and recite the prayer of obedience before bowing. However, it is preferable to do so after one's bow, as mentioned earlier. It is also a Sunnah-based practice when uttering the prayer of obedience to raise one's hands to the level of one's chest with one's palms upwards, then wipe one's face with one's hands after finishing the prayer. The time during which this prayer may be uttered extends from after the evening prayer until the full break of dawn. It is preferable to utter this prayer toward the end of the night if one is confident of being able to wake up in time for it; otherwise, it is best to perform the *witr* before going to bed, and if one misses the *witr*, the Sunnah-based practice is to make it up together with the *shaf'*. During Ramaḍān, the Sunnah dictates that the *witr* be performed in community, although it is permissible to perform the *witr* communally during the rest of the year as well.

* * *

According to the Shafiis, the *witr* is the most emphatically enjoined of all Sunnah-based voluntary prayers. The *witr* consists of a minimum of a single *rak'ah* and a maximum of eleven *rak'ahs*. If someone knowingly, deliberately performs more than eleven *rak'ahs* when praying the *witr*, the extra *rak'ahs* will not count. However, if one does so out of ignorance or forgetfulness, the extra *rak'ahs* are simply counted as an unspecified voluntary prayer. As for performing only one *rak'ah* for the *witr*, it is considered a departure from the ideal.

It is permissible for someone praying the *witr* in more than a single *rak'ah* to do so in one of two ways, referred to as 'connected' and 'disconnected' (the latter being the most preferable). If one prays the *witr* in its connected form, this means that the final *rak'ah* is continuous with those which come before it, whereas if one prays it in its disconnected form, the final *rak'ah* is isolated from those which precede it. If someone prays the *witr* in five *rak'ahs*, for example, he or she may perform two *rak'ahs* with a single greeting of peace, then three more *rak'ahs* with another greeting of peace. Alternatively, one may perform the final *rak'ah* in isolation from those which precede it, whether one prays the first four *rak'ahs* in two pairs (with each pair followed by a greeting of peace), or all four in succession. If one performs the *witr* in the connected form, one may not utter the testimony more than twice; moreover, as has been mentioned, praying it in its disconnected form is considered preferable.

The time period during which the *witr* is to be performed lasts from the end of the evening prayer (even if it has been joined with the sundown prayer and performed ahead of time) to the break of true dawn. It is an emulation of the Sunnah to delay the *witr* until the latter part of the night if one is confident of being able to wake up for it; similarly, one emulates the Sunnah by postponing the *witr* until after the night prayer in order to conclude with the *witr*. It is a Sunnah-based practice to perform the *witr* in community during the month of Ramaḍān, and to utter the prayer of obedience during the final *rak'ah* of the *witr* during the last half of this month. One also emulates the Sunnah by reciting the prayer of obedience after rising from one's bow in the second *rak'ah* of the dawn prayer every day.

The prayer of obedience, essentially, is any speech which contains words of praise to God and supplication; however, it is an emulation of the Sunnah to rely on the wording passed down on the authority of the Messenger of God, namely, "O

God, guide me with those You have guided, grant me wholeness with those to whom You have granted wholeness, watch over me with those You have watched over, bless me in that which You have given, and protect me from the evil of what You have decreed, for You alone are the One who decrees and disposes. No one to whom You grant your succor will be disgraced, nor will anyone whom You oppose enjoy honor and glory. Blessed are You, O our Lord, and exalted! Praise be to You for what You have decreed. I seek Your forgiveness and I turn to You in repentance. May God's blessings and peace be upon our master Muḥammad, the unlettered prophet, and on his descendants and companions." This version of the prayer of obedience, which is expressed in the first person singular ("Guide me... Grant me wholeness...", etc.), is to be used by someone who is praying alone. However, the phrase, "our Lord" as in "Blessed are You, O our Lord" should be kept in the plural rather than changed to "my Lord." As for the imam, he should employ the first person plural pronouns, saying, "Guide us...", "Grant us wholeness...", etc. The Sunnah-based practice for the imam is to utter the prayer of obedience aloud, whereas someone praying alone is to utter it silently, whether he/she is performing the prayer on time or in compensation for a prayer missed. As for those being led in prayer, they are to say *Āmīn* in response to the imam's petitions. Someone who leaves out part of the prayer of obedience should perform the prostration of forgetfulness at the end of his/her prayer. If the time for the *witr* passes without one's having performed it, one emulates the Sunnah by making it up later; the same applies to all voluntary prayers which are associated with a particular time of day.

Lastly, during times of severe tribulation, it is an emulation of the Sunnah to utter the prayer of obedience at all prayer times and for both the imam and those praying alone to utter it aloud even if the prayer they are performing is one which is generally performed silently. As for those being led in prayer, they are to say *Āmīn* after the imam's petitions, although if they miss some part of his prayer, they are not to perform a prostration of forgetfulness.

* * *

As for the Malikis, they hold that the *witr* is an emphatically enjoined Sunnah-based practice. According to the Malikis, the four most emphatically enjoined voluntary prayers are, in descending order, as follows: (1) the two *rak'ahs* associated with the obligatory circumambulation of the Ka'bah, (2) the two *rak'ahs* associated with the non-obligatory circumambulation of the Ka'bah, (3) the two *rak'ahs* associated with the *'umrah*, or minor pilgrimage, and (4) the *witr*.

The *witr* consists of a single *rak'ah*, and it is undesirable to join it with the *shaf'* [that is, to perform the *shaf'* and the *witr* as part of a single prayer]. It is recommended when praying the *witr* that one follow the recitation of the *Fātiḥah* with Surah 112 and Surahs 113 and 114. It is an emphatically enjoined practice to recite the last two surahs aloud. If someone adds an additional *rak'ah*, the *witr* remains valid, properly speaking; however, if one adds two extra *rak'ahs*, it is invalidated.

There are two time periods for the *witr* prayer: (1) an 'elective' phase and (2) an 'imperative' phase. The 'elective' phase begins immediately after the evening prayer (that is, from the time when a valid evening prayer has been performed following the disappearance of the red twilight 'glow' from the sky). Hence, if someone performs the *witr* after the evening prayer, then discovers that his/her evening prayer was not valid for some reason, he/she should repeat the *witr* after performing the evening prayer again. If someone joins the evening prayer with the sundown prayer and performs them both ahead of time on account of rain (a situation the details of which will be dealt with in a later section), he/she should postpone the *witr* until after the red twilight glow has disappeared from the sky, since otherwise, it will not be valid. The 'elective' time then extends up to the true break of dawn. (2) As for the 'imperative' phase, it extends from the break of dawn to the time when the dawn prayer is actually performed. Hence, if an imam or someone praying alone remembers, while performing the dawn prayer, that he did not perform the *witr*, it is recommended that he cut off the dawn prayer in order to perform it. If an imam cuts off his dawn prayer in such a situation, he should appoint someone else to take his place (provided that he has no reason to fear that the time for the dawn prayer will run out as a result of his cutting it off to perform the *witr*). As for someone being led in prayer, he may either cut off his dawn prayer or carry on to the end of it. If he chooses to cut off the dawn prayer in order to perform the *witr*, he should pray the *shaf'* before the *witr*, then repeat the Sunnah-based pair of *rak'ahs* which precede the dawn prayer, followed by the dawn prayer itself. One should be aware, however, that it is undesirable to delay the *witr* to the 'imperative' phase without a legitimate excuse. If, on the other hand, such a person goes ahead and completes the dawn prayer, he should not make up the *witr* since, apart from the two *rak'ahs* which precede the dawn prayer, voluntary prayers may not be made up in the Malikis' view.

According to the Malikis, the prayer of obedience is not prayed during the *witr* but rather, as we have seen, is recommended only during the dawn prayer. Moreover, it is recommended that the prayer of obedience be uttered before one bows; if someone forgets to utter it before bowing and then remembers it in the midst of the bow, he/she should not stand back up in order to utter it (and if one does stand back up, his/her prayer will be invalidated). Rather, one should simply utter the prayer of obedience after bowing. In this way, one fulfills the recommendation that one utter the prayer of obedience even though one has failed to fulfill the recommendation that one utter it before bowing. (In other words, the Malikis consider these to be two separate recommendations.)

According to the officially recognized Maliki view, it is permissible, albeit not desirable, to perform the *witr* from a seated position when one would have been able to stand. As for performing the *witr* while lying on one's side, this is not permitted if one has the ability to sit up. It is permissible, when riding an animal, to perform the *witr* by simply bowing and prostrating; moreover, if the journey is long enough to justify the shortening of ritual prayers, one may perform the *witr* with mere gestures, in which case the worshiper will be facing in whichever direction he or she is traveling. One condition for the most perfect performance of the *witr* is that one precede it with the *shaf'* [i.e., an even number of *rak'ahs*]; conversely, it is undesirable to perform the *witr* without performing the *shaf'* first. It is recommended that the *witr* be delayed until the final hours of the night by those who are in the habit of waking up at this time, since in this way, one complies with the Prophet's exhortation, "Let the last of your night prayers be the *witr*." However, if someone performs the *witr* immediately after the evening prayer, then gets up in the final

The *Tarāwīḥ* Prayers

The *tarāwīḥ* prayers are an emphatically enjoined emulation of the Sunnah for individuals, both men and women, according to the Shafiis, the Hanafis and the Hanbalis; for the view of the Malikis, see below.[243] In addition, the Sunnah dictates that each individual perform the *tarāwīḥ* prayers communally such that if they are performed by one group of worshipers, this does not exempt other individuals from performing them with a group as well. Thus, for example, if a particular man performs the *tarāwīḥ* in his home, it is an emulation of the Sunnah for him to pray together with others in his household, and if he performs them alone, he will miss out on the reward for following the Sunnah with respect to performing them in community. This ruling is agreed upon by the Shafiis and the Hanbalis; for the views of the Malikis and the Hanafis, see below.[244]

---

hours of the night to perform voluntary prayers, it is undesirable to repeat the *witr* at this time based on the Prophet's prohibition, "No one should pray the *witr* twice in a single night." The basis for this ruling is that whenever there is a conflict between a prohibition and an allowance, the former takes priority over the latter.

The Malikis offer the following rulings with regard to night prayers: (1) If, when someone wakes up in the morning, there is just enough time left before sunrise to complete one's ablutions and perform two *rak'ahs*, one should omit the *witr*, perform the dawn prayer, and delay the two Sunnah-based *rak'ahs* which normally precede the dawn prayer until the sun is a spear's length above the horizon, at which time he or she may make them up. (2) If, when someone wakes up, there is only enough time left before sunrise to perform three *rak'ahs*, one should perform the *witr* and the dawn prayer, omitting the *shaf'*, and postpone the two pre-dawn Sunnah-based *rak'ahs*, as explained under (1) above. (3) If, when one wakes up, enough time remains before sunrise to perform five *rak'ahs*, one should perform the *shaf'*, the *witr* and the dawn prayer, postponing the two Sunnah-based pre-dawn *rak'ahs* as explained above. (4) If, when one wakes up, there remains sufficient time before sunrise to perform seven *rak'ahs*, one should perform everything in its ideal order [i.e., the *shaf'*, followed by the *witr*, followed by the two Sunnah-based pre-dawn *rak'ahs* and concluding with the dawn prayer itself – t.n.].

Lastly, it should be noted that it is recommended that the *shaf'* and the *witr* be performed communally only during the month of Ramaḍān, at which time the *tarāwīḥ* prayers are recommended as well.

243. According to the Malikis, the *tarāwīḥ* prayers are emphatically recommended for all worshipers, both men and women.

244. According to the Malikis, praying the *tarāwīḥ* communally is simply recommended, while according to the Hanafis, praying them in a group is a collective Sunnah-based practice for residents of a given neighborhood. Hence, if some of the residents perform the *tarāwīḥ* in a group, others in the neighborhood will be exempted from this responsibility.

The fact that the performance of the *tarāwīḥ* in community is a Sunnah-based practice is confirmed by the action of the Prophet. It is recorded by both Muslim and al-Bukhārī that he went out on three separate nights during Ramaḍān, namely, the third, the fifth, and the twenty-seventh; on these nights the Prophet prayed in the mosque and the people followed him in his prayer. On these occasions he would perform eight *rak'ahs* with the people, after which they would complete the prayers in their homes, where the sound of their prayers was like the droning of bees.

On this basis, we know that the Prophet established the practice of performing the *tarāwīḥ* in community. However, he did not lead the people in twenty *rak'ahs* as has been the custom since the era of the Companions. Rather, the Prophet did not go out to the people again lest, as he stated directly in some accounts of the hadith mentioned above, such prayers be taken as an obligation for which they would now be held accountable. It is likewise apparent from this hadith that the number of *rak'ahs* performed in the *tarāwīḥ* is not restricted to the eight which he performed with them, since the people are said to have completed the prayers in their own homes.

The practice followed by 'Umar [Ibn al-Khaṭṭāb], may God be pleased with him, was to gather the people and pray twenty *rak'ahs* with them in the mosque; moreover, the other Companions agreed with this practice, and among the rightly guided caliphs who succeeded 'Umar, none expressed any disagreement with it. The Prophet once declared, "You are to cling steadfastly to my example and to that of the rightly guided caliphs."[245] When Abū Ḥanīfah was asked once about what 'Umar had done, he replied, "The *tarāwīḥ* prayers are an emphatically enjoined Sunnah-based practice. Hence, what 'Umar did was not to introduce a practice which he had invented or innovated on his own; rather, his orders pertaining to these prayers had their origin in a covenant from the Messenger of God." It is true, of course, that during the era of 'Umar Ibn 'Abd al-'Azīz, may God be pleased with him, additions were made to this practice, in that the number of *rak'ahs* prayed during the *tarāwīḥ* was increased to thirty-six. However, the purpose behind this increase was to allow those people who pray outside Mecca to attain merit equal to that attained by the people of Mecca. The people of Mecca would circumambulate the Ka'bah after every four *rak'ahs* of the *tarāwīḥ*; hence, 'Umar, may God be pleased with him, introduced the practice of having the people outside Mecca pray an additional four *rak'ahs* in place of every circumambulation of the Ka'bah performed by worshipers in Mecca.

This development serves as evidence of the validity of scholars' support for additions to legitimate, recognized forms of Islamic worship. After all, there is no doubt that it is permissible to perform as many voluntary prayers as one is able to both during the day and at night except during those times when there is a prohibition against the performance of such prayers. As for whether the *rak'ahs* which are performed over and above the number passed down in the Sunnah are to be classified as part of the *tarāwiḥ*, this depends on how inclusive the term *tarāwiḥ* is judged to be. Be that as it may, it is preferable that one apply the term *tarāwīḥ* only to what

245. Narrated by Abū Dāwūd.

was explicitly approved by the Prophet and those of his Companions who were qualified to issue independent judgments.

It has thus been established that the *tarāwīḥ* prayers consist of twenty *rak'ahs* in addition to the concluding *witr*.[246] As for the time at which the *tarāwīḥ* prayers are to be performed, the Shafiis, the Hanbalis and the Hanafis hold that it begins after the evening prayer, even if one has combined the evening and sundown prayers by performing them ahead of time.[247] The Malikis, however, hold that if the evening and sundown prayers are combined and performed ahead of time (by those who hold that it is permissible for someone on a short journey and the like to combine such prayers in accordance with the conditions to be discussed below in the section on joining prayers), the *tarāwīḥ* prayers must be postponed until after the twilight glow has disappeared from the sky. The reason for this, according to the Malikis, is that if they are performed before this time, they will be classified simply as an unspecified voluntary prayer rather than the *tarāwīḥ*; however, their performance will still be required.

The time period for performing the *tarāwīḥ* prayers ends with the break of dawn. According to the Shafiis, the Hanbalis and Hanafis, the *tarāwīḥ* are valid and have no desirability attached to them whether they are performed before or after the *witr*, although it is preferable to perform them before the *witr*. The Malikis, by contrast, hold that the *tarāwīḥ* are to be performed between the evening prayer and the *witr*, and that it is undesirable to postpone them until after the *witr* based on the Prophet's injunction, "Let the last of your night prayers be the *witr*." The Hanafis, the Hanbalis and the Malikis hold that once the time period for the *tarāwīḥ* prayers runs out, they may not be made up regardless of whether only the *tarāwīḥ* have been missed, or the *tarāwīḥ* along with the evening prayer. As for the Shafiis, they hold that the *tarāwīḥ* may be made up under any and all circumstances.

Recommended practices associated with the *tarāwīḥ* prayers

It is recommended that one utter both parts of the testimony and the final greeting of peace at the end of each pair of *rak'ahs* performed as part of the *tarāwīḥ* prayers. The Malikis, the Hanafis and the Hanbalis hold that if one simply sits down [and utters the testimony] at the end of each pair of *rak'ahs*, then utters the final greeting of peace once at the very end, one's *tarāwīḥ* will be valid, although this practice is

---

246 According to the Malikis, the *tarāwīḥ* prayers consist of twenty *rak'ahs* in addition to both the *shaf'* and the *witr*.

247. This applies, of course, to those schools which approve the practice of joining prayers on the part of people who are on journeys of a minimum length; for a further discussion of this point and the conditions associated with the joining of prayers, see below under the heading, "Combining Two Consecutive Prayers, Either by Praying Both at an Earlier time, or by Praying Both of Them Later."

248. The Hanafis hold that if someone prays four *rak'ahs* of the *tarāwīḥ* prayers with only one greeting of peace at the end, they will count as two *rak'ahs* rather than four. However, if one prays more than four *rak'ahs* with only one greeting of peace, opinion on the matter is divided, with some saying that they count as two *rak'ahs* of the *tarāwīḥ,* and with others saying that they are invalid.

* * *

undesirable; for the Shafiis' view, see the footnote below.[248] If, on the other hand, the worshiper does not sit down after each pair of *rak'ahs*, the various schools offer different rulings on this situation. It is also recommended that someone praying the *tarāwīḥ* sit down simply to rest [at intervals].[249] This is the practice which was followed by the Prophet's Companions, may God be pleased with them, and it is for this reason that this set of prayers was first referred to as *tarāwīḥ*.[250]

According to the Hanbalis, such *rak'ahs* will be valid, and if the worshiper has performed twenty *rak'ahs* with just one final greeting of peace, they will count as twenty *rak'ahs*; however, this practice is undesirable.

* * *

In agreement with the Hanbalis, the Malikis hold that such *rak'ahs* will still be valid, and if the worshiper has performed twenty *rak'ahs* with just one final greeting of peace, they will count as twenty *rak'ahs*. However, he or she will have neglected the Sunnah-based practice of uttering both the testimony and the final greeting of peace at the conclusion of each pair of *rak'ahs*, which is undesirable.

* * *

As for the Shafiis, their ruling is that the *rak'ahs* performed in the *tarāwīḥ* prayers will only be valid if one utters the final greeting of peace at the end of each pair; moreover, this ruling holds regardless of whether one sits down after each two *rak'ahs* or not.

249. According to the Hanafis, the act of sitting for a while after each pair of *rak'ahs* is recommended. According to this view, one may remain seated for as long as it would take to perform four *rak'ahs*, during which time one may occupy oneself with words and phrases of divine remembrance and praise, or one may simply remain silent.

* * *

The Malikis hold that if the worshiper has spent a long time standing while performing a given pair of *rak'ahs*, it is recommended that he/she sit down to rest in emulation of the Prophet's Companions; otherwise, it is not recommended that one sit down.

* * *

According to the Hanbalis, remaining seated for a period of time between pairs of *rak'ahs* is recommended, though omitting this practice is not undesirable. As for making supplication while one is seated, this is considered a departure from the ideal.

* * *

As for the Shafiis, they hold that this act of sitting is recommended as an emulation of the worthy ancestors [*al-salaf*, namely, the Companions, their followers, and their followers' followers – t.n.], although there is no mention of it [in relevant Islamic texts].

250. The word *tarāwīḥ* is the plural of the verbal noun *tarwīḥ*, meaning "to provide comfort or rest to" [t.n.].

The ruling on recitation of the entire Qur'ān in the *tarāwīḥ* prayers, the ruling on the intention to do so, and related matters

It is an emulation of the Sunnah to recite the Qur'ān in its entirety during the *tarāwīḥ* prayers such that one finishes reciting it on the last day of Ramaḍān. However, if those being led in prayer are harmed in some way by such long recitations every day, it is preferable to take their condition into consideration provided that the imam does not recite so quickly that it detracts from the quality of the prayer. This ruling is agreed upon by the Shafiis, the Hanbalis and the Hanafis; as for the Malikis, they hold that the imam's recitation of the entire Qur'ān during the month of Ramaḍān is merely recommended, while neglecting to do so is a departure from the ideal unless the imam has not memorized the Qur'ān and there is no one else available who knows the Qur'ān by heart, or unless there is someone who has memorized the Qur'ān, but who is not otherwise qualified to serve in this capacity.

Each pair of *rak'ahs* is considered to be an independent unit of the *tarāwīḥ* prayers; hence, at the beginning of each pair, one makes the conscious intention to pray, utters the opening *Allāhu akbar* (*takbīrat al-iḥrām*), recites the prayer of commencement, and recites from the Qur'ān; this is the ruling of the Shafiis, the Hanafis and the Hanbalis. As for the Malikis, they hold that it is undesirable to utter the prayer of commencement between *takbīrat al-iḥrām* and the Qur'anic recitation.

After uttering the testimony, one prays for blessings upon the Prophet. It is preferable to pray the *tarāwīḥ* from a standing position provided that one is able to stand; however, one's prayer will be valid even if one performs the *tarāwīḥ* from a seated position, although this is considered a departure from the ideal. It is also considered undesirable for someone being led in prayer to delay standing up until the time when the imam bows due to the appearance of laziness which this involves. Lastly, the Shafiis, the Hanbalis and the Hanafis hold that it is preferable to perform the *tarāwīḥ* prayers in the mosque, since all forms of worship which may legitimately be performed in community are best performed in a mosque; for the Malikis' view, see below.[251]

---

251. According to the Malikis, it is recommended that the *tarāwīḥ* prayers be performed in one's home even if they are prayed in a group, since praying them at home is less likely to encourage hypocrisy [that is, the performance of voluntary prayers in public for the sake of mere appearance – t.n.]. However, they should only be performed at home given the following three conditions: (1) That one be conscientious about performing them at home; (2) that one not be present either in Mecca or Medina when one is a resident of some place other than these two cities; and (3) that one's performance of the *tarāwīḥ* at home not discourage people from praying in the mosque. If one fails to meet any of the aforementioned conditions for praying the *tarāwīḥ* at home, they should be performed in the mosque.

The prayers performed on Īd al-Fiṭr, the Day of Fastbreaking, and 'Īd al-Aḍḥā, the Day of Sacrifice

The subject of the prayers performed on the Days of Fastbreaking and Sacrifice will be discussed under the following headings: (1) The ruling on these prayers and the time periods during which they are to be performed, (2) the evidence for these prayers' legitimacy, (3) how they are performed, (4) the ruling on whether the holiday prayers are to be performed in community and making them up if they are missed, (5) rulings on the sermons delivered on these two days: their pillars and conditions, (6) the ruling on the *adhān* and the *iqāmah* in relation to the holiday prayers, (7) Sunnah-based and other recommended practices associated with the Day of Fastbreaking and the Day of Sacrifice, (8) spending the night prior to these two days in prayer and worship, (9) where the holiday prayers are to be performed, and (10) what is referred to as *takbīr al-tashrīq*, namely, the utterance of *Allāhu akbar* following the five daily prayers during the holidays.

The ruling on the prayers performed on these two days and the times when they are performed

The four schools offer various rulings on the prayers performed on the Day of Fastbreaking and the Day of Sacrifice, as well as on the time periods during which they are to be performed.[252]

---

252. According to the Shafiis, the holiday prayers are an emphatically enjoined emulation of the Sunnah for each individual Muslim who is held accountable for performing ritual prayer; it is also an emulation of the Sunnah to perform them in community for all worshipers other than those who are performing the *ḥajj*, or greater pilgrimage, in whose case the Sunnah dictates that they should be performed individually.

* * *

According to the Malikis, the holiday prayers are an emphatically enjoined Sunnah-based practice which is second only in importance to the *witr*. These prayers are an emulation of the Sunnah for all those who are required to perform the Friday congregational prayer provided that they are performed with an imam; for those who miss performing them with the imam, they are merely recommended, in which case recitation should be silent. The holiday prayers are also recommended for those who are not required to perform the Friday congregational prayer, such as young boys and slaves. An exception to this ruling is made for those performing the greater pilgrimage, who are not asked to perform the holiday prayers since their standing at the pilgrimage station at Muzdalifah (east of Mecca) is considered to take their place. At the same time, it is recommended that residents of Minā who are not on the pilgrimage perform the holiday prayers individually rather than communally, lest their performing them communally lead to the pilgrims' praying with them.

* * *

According to the Hanafis, the two holiday prayers are a 'duty', properly speaking, for those who are obliged to perform the Friday congregational prayer; moreover, the conditions which apply to the Friday congregational prayer apply likewise to the holiday prayer, be they conditions for its necessity or conditions for its validity. However, an exception is made for the condition which applies to the sermon, which precedes the prayer in the Friday congregational worship but follows it in the holiday gathering for worship. Another exception is made for the condition which applies to the number of worshipers required for a communal prayer, since the quorum for the holiday prayers, unlike the Friday congregational prayer, is one worshiper with the imam. Similarly with respect to the condition relating to whether the prayer is to be performed in community or not, we find that performance of the holiday prayers communally is obligatory in the sense that if one prays them individually, one incurs guilt; however, they still remain valid. The Friday congregational prayer, by contrast, is only valid if performed in community.

* * *

As for the Hanbalis, they rule that the holiday prayers are a collective obligation for those who are required to perform the Friday congregational prayer; moreover, the holiday prayers are only to be performed where the Friday congregational prayer is performed. However, the sermon is merely an emulation of the Sunnah on the Day of Fastbreaking and the Day of Sacrifice, whereas during the Friday congregational worship it is a condition for the prayer's validity. In addition, the holiday prayer may be an emulation of the Sunnah for those who missed performing it with the imam, in which case it may be performed at any time one chooses in the manner described below (under the heading, "How the Holiday Prayers are to be Performed").

* * *

As for the matter of the time period during which the holiday prayers are to be performed, the views of the four schools are as follows:

According to the Shafiis, the time during which the two holiday prayers are to be performed extends from sunrise to noon, after which they may be made up at any time. Moreover, it is an emulation of the Sunnah not to perform them until the sun is one spear's length above the horizon.

According to the Malikis, the holiday prayers may be performed between the time when the sun is one spear's length above the horizon and noon, and it is an emulation of the Sunnah to perform them as soon as possible after the beginning of this time period.

According to the Hanbalis, the holiday prayers may be performed from the time when the sun is one spear's length above the horizon until just before noon. If one misses them on the holiday itself, they are to be made up the following day even if it would have been possible to make them up on the same day. The holiday prayers can also be made up even if several days have passed, and whether one has an excuse for having missed them or not.

As for the Hanafis, they hold that the holiday prayers may be performed from the time when the sun is one spear's length above the horizon until noon. If the noon hour passes while the holiday prayers are being performed and before one has been seated long enough to utter the testimony, they are counted as nothing but an unspecified voluntary prayer. As for making them up, the ruling on this will be presented below.

Evidence for the legitimacy of the prayers associated with the Day of Fastbreaking and the Day of Sacrifice

The prayers associated with the Day of Fastbreaking and the Day of Sacrifice were established in the year 1 A.H. We read in a hadith narrated by Abū Dāwūd on the authority of Anas, "When the Messenger of God came to Medina, the people had been celebrating and amusing themselves for two days. 'What are these two days?' he asked, and they replied, 'They are days that we used to celebrate during the time before the coming of Islam.' And he said to them, 'God has given you two other holidays which are better: the Day of Fastbreaking and the Day of Sacrifice.'"

How the holiday prayers are to be performed

Each of the four schools offers its own detailed rulings on how the two holiday prayers are to be performed.[253]

---

253. According to the Hanafis, one begins both holiday prayers with a conscious intention of the heart as well as with the words, "I am praying the holiday prayer for God Almighty." If one is being led in a communal prayer, one also consciously intends to follow one's imam, then utters *takbīrat al-iḥrām*, placing one's hands on one's abdomen beneath the navel. The imam and those being led in prayer then recite the prayer of commencement together, after which the imam utters the words *Allāhu akbar* three additional times (that is, three times in addition to *takbīrat al-iḥrām* and the utterance of *Allāhu akbar* when going down into a bow) and is followed by those being led in prayer. After each utterance of *Allāhu akbar*, the imam is to remain silent for the duration of three instances of *Allāhu akbar*. It is not an emulation of the Sunnah to engage in *dhikr* during this silence; however, one may say *subḥān Allāh wa al-ḥamdu lillāh wa lā ilāha illā Allāh wa Allāhu akbar*. It is an emulation of the Sunnah for both the imam and those being led in prayer to lift their hands every time they say *Allāhu akbar*. The imam utters the words, "I seek refuge in God from the accursed Satan" (*a'ūdhu billāhi min al-shayṭān al-rajīm*) and silently utters the *basmalah*, after which he recites the *Fātiḥah* aloud followed by some other surah of the Qur'ān (the recommended surah being Surah 87). The imam then bows and prostrates and is followed by those being led in prayer. When the imam stands up for the second *rak'ah*, he begins with the *basmalah*, followed by the *Fātiḥah* and some other passage from the Qur'ān (the recommended passage being Surah 88). After reciting the additional passage from the Qur'ān, the imam and those being led in prayer join in uttering three more instances of *Allāhu akbar*, raising their hands each time, after which the imam brings the prayer to its conclusion.

Performing the holiday prayers in the manner just described is preferable to uttering more than three instances of *Allāhu akbar*; it is also preferable to placing the extra utterances of *Allāhu akbar* before the Qur'ānic recitation in the second *rak'ah*, although it is permissible to do so. If the imam utters the words *Allāhu akbar* more than three times, those being led in prayer should follow him in doing so up to a maximum of 16 times. If someone being led in prayer arrives after the imam has completed some utterances of *Allāhu akbar* and is still standing, he or she should complete the additional utterances of *Allāhu akbar* on his/her own while continuing to stand. If, on the other hand, the imam performs an entire *rak'ah* before the person being led in prayer joins him, and if the person being led in prayer rises after the imam has finished praying in order to complete his own prayer, he/she should first do the Qur'anic recitation, then utter the additional instances of *Allāhu akbar*, then bow. As for someone who joins the imam when the latter is bowing, he/she should utter the *takbīrat al-iḥrām*, then utter the additional instances of *Allāhu akbar* while still standing if he/she is assured that there will be enough time left to bow with the imam; otherwise, he should utter *takbīrat al-iḥrām* while standing, then bow, then utter the additional instances of *Allāhu akbar* while bowing without raising his hands. Moreover, he should not wait for the imam to finish praying before he makes up the additional instances of *Allāhu akbar* which he has missed, since any phrases of divine remembrance one misses must be made up before the imam has finished his prayer. (In the case of physical movements, by contrast, they are to be made up after the imam has finished praying.) Hence, if the imam raises his head before the person being led in prayer has uttered all the additional instances of *Allāhu akbar*, he or she is exempted from any which have not been uttered yet since, if he/she went on to complete them, he/she would miss the obligatory action of following the imam in rising from the bow. Lastly, if someone being led in prayer joins the imam after he has risen from the bow, he/she should not utter any of the additional instances of *Allāhu akbar*; rather, after the imam has completed his prayer, he or she should make up the missed *rak'ah* along with the additional utterances of *Allāhu akbar*.

* * *

The Shafiis hold that the holiday prayers, like other voluntary prayers, consist of two *rak'ahs*, except that when performing the holiday prayers, it is recommended that during the first *rak'ah*, one add seven utterances of *Allāhu akbar* after *takbīrat al-iḥrām* and the prayer of commencement and before the utterance of the words, *a'ūdhu billāhi min al-shayṭān al-rajīm* ("I seek refuge in God from the accursed Satan") and the Qur'anic recitation. One raises one's hands to shoulder height with every utterance of *Allāhu akbar*; moreover, it is an emulation of the Sunnah to pause after each utterance of *Allāhu akbar* for the length of time it would take to recite a medium-length verse from the Qur'ān while placing one's right hand over one's left below one's chest. It is desirable to say silently, *subḥān Allāh wa al-ḥamdu lillāh wa lā ilāha illā Allāh wa Allāhu akbar* during this same pause. During the second *rak'ah*, it is an emulation of the Sunnah to utter *Allāhu akbar* five additional times after the opening utterance of this phrase, pausing after each utterance while placing one's right hand over one's left under one's chest as in the first *rak'ah*.

These additional utterances of *Allāhu akbar* are a practice based on the prophetic Sunnah and are referred to as a *hay'ah*, meaning 'form'; if any of them is omitted it is not necessary to perform the prostration of forgetfulness, even though such an omission is undesirable. If the worshiper is uncertain as to how many such utterances he has completed thus far, he should assume that he has completed a lesser rather than a greater number.

It is desirable, but not necessary, to complete these utterances of *Allāhu akbar* before saying, *a'ūdhu billāhi min al-shayṭān al-rajīm*; however, uttering them before the Qur'anic recitation is a condition of the prayer's validity. Hence, if one begins the Qur'anic recitation without having first completed these utterances of *Allāhu akbar*, one may not utter them at all, since their proper position in the prayer will have passed.

All the rulings mentioned thus far apply equally to the imam and to those being led in prayer. However, if someone being led in prayer joins the imam while the imam is performing the second *rak'ah*, he or she should utter the words *Allāhu akbar* five times in addition to *takbīrat al-iḥrām*, whereas if the imam utters them more than five times, he or she should not to follow his lead; then, when he or she is making up the *rak'ah* he missed after the imam has completed his prayer, he or she should utter the phrase *Allāhu akbar* five times in addition to the opening utterance of this phrase.

If the imam omits the additional utterances of *Allāhu akbar*, those being led in prayer should omit them as well. If someone being led in prayer performs these utterances when his/her imam has omitted them, his/her prayer will be invalidated if he/she lifts his/her hands three times in a row during the process (since they constitute movement which is excessive enough to invalidate prayer); otherwise, however, his/her prayer will still be valid. Moreover, if someone is praying behind an imam who makes fewer than five utterances of *Allāhu akbar*, he/she should follow the imam's example.

Qur'anic recitation in the holiday prayers is to be performed aloud by both the imam and those praying alone, whereas the Sunnah dictates that all worshipers—the imam, those praying alone, and those being led in prayer—are to utter the phrase *Allāhu akbar* aloud. Lastly, the prophetic Sunnah dictates that in the first *rak'ah* one follow the recitation of the *Fātiḥah* with Surah 50, Surah 87, or Surah 109 and that in the second *rak'ah*, one follow the *Fātiḥah* with either Surah 54, Surah 88, or Surah 112.

* * *

According to the Hanbalis, someone who wishes to pray the holiday prayer should consciously intend to perform two *rak'ahs* as a communal obligation. It is then recommended that both the imam and those being led in prayer recite the prayer of commencement and utter *Allāhu akbar* six times, raising their hands with each utterance of this phrase. It is also recommended that between each two utterances of *Allāhu akbar* one say silently, "God is greatest indeed, may God be praised often, glory to be God morning and evening, and may God's blessings and abundant peace be upon the Prophet and his descendents" (*Allāhu akbaru kabīran walḥamdu lillāhi kathīran wa subḥān Allāh bukratan wa aṣīlan, wa ṣallā Allāh 'alā al-nabī wa ālihi wa sallama taslīman*). It is not necessary, however, that these words in particular be spoken; rather, one may use any words of divine remembrance one so chooses, since the recommended practice is simply to utter any words or phrases which invoke the remembrance of God; however, no *dhikr* is permitted after one has completed all the aforementioned additional utterances of *Allāhu akbar*. One then seeks divine protection from evil, saying, *a'ūdhu billāhi min al-shayṭān al-rajīm*, utters the *basmalah*, recites the *Fātiḥah* and Surah 87, then bows and completes the *rak'ah*. One then rises to perform the second *rak'ah*, uttering *Allāhu akbar* five times in addition to the utterance of this phrase with which one rises for a new *rak'ah*. In between each two utterances of *Allāhu akbar*, one utters the same phrases mentioned above in connection with the first *rak'ah*; moreover, as in the first *rak'ah*, one is not to engage in any *dhikr* after completing all the aforementioned additional utterances of *Allāhu akbar*. It is then recommended that one utter the *basmalah* followed by the *Fātiḥah* and Surah 88, after which one bows and concludes one's prayer.

If someone being led in prayer does not join the imam until after he has completed some or all of the additional utterances of *Allāhu akbar*, he or she should not perform them at all since they are a Sunnah-based practice whose proper time has passed. Similarly, if someone forgets some or all of the additional utterances of *Allāhu akbar* until after he/she has begun the Qur'anic recitation, he/she should not perform them since their time has passed; in this respect, the additional utterances of *Allāhu akbar* are similar to the prayer of commencement and the utterance of *a'ūdhu billāhi min al-shayṭān al-rajīm* in that, if one recites the *Fātiḥah* before uttering either of them, one should not go back to make them up.

* * *

As for the Malikis, they hold that the holiday prayer consists of two *rak'ahs* as do other voluntary prayers. However, the holiday prayer is distinguished by the fact that in the first *rak'ah* one is to utter the words *Allāhu akbar* an additional six times between *takbīrat al-iḥrām* and the Qur'anic recitation, while in the second *rak'ah*, one is to say *Allāhu akbar* an additional five times between the opening utterance of *Allāhu akbar* and the subsequent Qur'anic recitation. The practice of uttering these instances of *Allāhu akbar* before one's Qur'anic recitation is merely recommended; hence, if one delays it until after the recitation, one's prayer will still be valid. If someone being led in prayer is following an imam who utters the words *Allāhu akbar* a greater or lesser number of times than those mentioned or who delays doing so until after the Qur'anic recitation, he or she should not follow the imam's lead in this. Moreover, it is recommended for those being led in prayer and for those praying alone that they complete all utterances of *Allāhu akbar* in uninterrupted succession; as for the imam, however, he is to wait silently after each utterance until those being led in prayer have repeated the phrase after him, and it is undesirable for him to utter words of praise and the like during this pause.

Each of the additional utterances of *Allāhu akbar* is an emphatically enjoined Sunnah-based practice; hence, if the worshiper forgets any of them, then remembers it before bowing, he or she should make it up, and if the worshiper is either an imam or praying alone, it is recommended that he or she repeat the Qur'anic recitation, then perform the prostration of forgetfulness after the final greeting of peace for having added to the first recitation. If, on the other hand, the worshiper remembers after bowing, he or he should not go back or make it up during the bow; if the person does go back or make up the forgotten *Allāhu akbar* while bowing, his or her prayer will be invalidated. If the worshiper does not go back, he or she should perform a prostration of forgetfulness before the final greeting of peace for not having completed all the additional utterances of *Allāhu akbar*, even if only one such utterance was left out. This ruling does not apply, however, to those being led in communal prayer since in this case, the person responsible for making up for the omission is the imam.

The ruling on performing the prayers for the Day of Fastbreaking and the Day of Sacrifice in community, and on making them up if their time period has passed

For the four schools' rulings on performing the holiday prayers in community and on making them up if one has not performed them with the imam, see below.[254]

If someone being led in communal prayer does not hear the imam utter the words *Allāhu akbar* on this or that occasion, he or she should seek to determine whether the imam did utter them [for example, by observing the responses and gestures of other worshipers – t.n.] and utter the phrase *Allāhu akbar*. If someone being led in prayer joins the imam while the latter is saying *Allāhu akbar*, he or she should utter whatever is left of the phrase with the imam, then make up whatever part he/she missed after the imam has completed his utterance. If, on the other hand, the person being led in prayer joins the imam while the latter is reciting from the Qur'ān, he or she should make up the *Allāhu akbar* that he or she missed following *takbīrat al-iḥrām* regardless of whether he or she joined the imam during the first or the second *rak'ah*. If the worshiper joined the imam during the first *rak'ah*, he or she should complete six additional utterances of *Allāhu akbar*, whereas if he/she joined the imam during the second *rak'ah*, he or she should complete five such utterances, then, after the imam's final greeting of peace, complete six additional utterances of *Allāhu akbar* in the *rak'ah* being made up. If, on the other hand, the person being led in prayer joins the imam so late that he or she gets to perform less than one *rak'ah* with the imam, he or she should stand up after the imam has finished praying in order to make up what he or she missed, then utter six instances of *Allāhu akbar* during the first *rak'ah* in addition to the opening utterance of *Allāhu akbar*.

According to the Malikis, it is undesirable to raise one's hands while completing the additional utterances of *Allāhu akbar*; rather, they hold that it is recommended that one raise one's hands only during *takbīrat al-iḥrām*, just as in all other ritual prayers. It is recommended that one complete one's Qur'anic recitation aloud in the holiday prayer; similarly, it is recommended that after reciting the *Fātiḥah* in the first *rak'ah*, one recite Surah 87, and in the second *rak'ah*, Surah 91.

254. According to the Hanafis, performing the holiday prayers in community is a condition for their validity; if someone fails to perform them with the imam, he or she is required to make them up before the time period for the holiday prayers runs out, whereas after this, they may not be made up. If one wishes to make them up individually, one may perform four *rak'ahs* without the additional utterances of *Allāhu akbar*. In such a case, one is to recite Surah 87 after the *Fātiḥah* in the first *rak'ah*, Surah 93 in the second, Surah 94 in the third, and Surah 95 in the fourth.

* * *

According to the Hanbalis, performing the holiday prayer in community is a condition for its validity just as it is for the validity of the Friday congregational prayer; however, for those who missed performing the holiday prayer with the imam,

Sunnah-based and other desirable practices related to the two holiday prayers

One of the Sunnah-based practices associated with the two holiday prayers is the preaching of sermons. (As we have seen, the Malikis hold that the two sermons delivered on these occasions are merely recommended.) It is recommended that those listening to the sermons preached in connection with the two holiday prayers repeat the phrase *Allāhu akbar* after the imam; in this respect, the holiday prayers differ from the Friday congregational prayer, during which (according to the Malikis and the Hanbalis) it is forbidden for those being led in prayer to speak even by uttering words of divine remembrance. The Shafiis hold that speaking during any of these sermons (those preached during the holiday prayers and those preached during Friday congregational prayers) is undesirable, including words or phrases of divine remembrance. As for the Hanafis, they hold that properly speaking, uttering words or phrases of divine remembrance during these sermons is acceptable, but that any other sort of speech on such occasions is forbidden.

It is recommended that one express one's obedience to God by spending the nights before the Day of Fastbreaking and the Day of Sacrifice in *dhikr* (divine remembrance), prayer, Qur'anic recitation, and the like based on the words of the Prophet, "If someone spends the nights before the Day of Fastbreaking and the Day of Sacrifice in worship out of the desire for a reward not from people, but from God, his or her heart will not perish on that day when hearts perish."[255] One may be considered to have spent these nights in worship if one performed both the evening prayer and the dawn prayer in community.

Someone might object here, saying, "The reward mentioned in this saying of the Prophet is incommensurate with this practice being [merely] recommended

---

it is an emulation of the Sunnah to make it up at any time they wish in the prescribed manner.

* * *

According to the Shafiis, performing the holiday prayer in community is an emulation of the Sunnah for everyone except those performing the greater pilgrimage. As for those who missed performing it with an imam, they emulate the Sunnah by making it up at any time they wish in the prescribed manner. If someone makes up the prayer before noon, he is considered to have performed it on time, whereas if he/she makes it up after noon, it is considered a compensatory prayer.

* * *

As for the Malikis, their ruling is that performance of the holiday prayer in community is a condition for its being an emulation of the Sunnah; hence, the holiday prayer is only judged to be an emulation of the Sunnah for those who intend to perform it with a group. If someone misses performing the holiday prayer with an imam, he/she may perform it [alone] until noon; once noon is past, however, it may not be made up.

255. Narrated by al-Ṭabarānī.

[rather than an emulation of the Sunnah], since the meaning of someone's heart 'living' on the Day of Resurrection is that he or she has attained the favor of God Almighty, after which one has no need to fear God's wrath." In reply to this objection we say: Islamic law holds people responsible for the fulfillment of certain duties, and whoever fulfills such duties in the manner prescribed indisputably merits God's favor, while those who neglect to do so merit God's disfavor. As for other acts of virtue, Islamic law encourages people to perform them by letting them know that such acts bring a goodly reward, although those who do not perform such acts are not subject to any sort of punishment. However, it goes without saying that the reward promised to those who engage in acts of virtue is only available to those who have also fulfilled their duties. Hence, if someone who is held accountable under Islamic law for fasting the month of Ramaḍān neglects to fast, and if someone who is able to perform the greater pilgrimage fails to perform it and does not give the charity required of him or her, and if such a person spends the entire night before the Day of Fastbreaking or the Day of Sacrifice in prayer, *dhikr*, Qur'anic recitation and the like, he or she will have gained nothing at all. If, on the other hand, such a person's motivation for spending the night in worship and devotion is a sincere desire to repent and be released from guilt, it will most certainly have a great effect, since it is an agreed-upon principle of Islam that genuine repentance blots out the guilt associated even with major sins.

According to the Shafiis, the Malikis and the Hanbalis, it is recommended that one perform major ablutions (*ghusl*) for both these holidays in the manner described in the section above on this topic; as for the Hanafis, they hold that it is an emulation of the prophetic Sunnah.

It is recommended that men dress up and put on cologne on the Days of Fastbreaking and Sacrifice; as for women, it is not recommended that they do so if they go out to perform the holiday prayers in community lest by so doing they cause others temptation. Otherwise, however, women also are encouraged to dress up and put on cologne for these days. This practice is also recommended for men who have not performed the holiday prayer, since it is agreed upon that such adornment is for the sake of the holiday itself, not for the sake of the prayer; however, the Hanafis hold that this practice is not merely recommended, but an emulation of the Sunnah.

Similarly, it is recommended that both men and women wear the best clothes they have for these two holidays, be they new or used, white or some other color. However, the Malikis hold that it is recommended that one wear something new, even if some other garment is actually better, while according to the Hanafis, wearing something new is not merely recommended, but an emulation of the Sunnah.

It is recommended that one eat before going out to the place where the holiday prayer will be performed on the Day of Fastbreaking, and that the food one partakes of be three or five dates; on the Day of Sacrifice, however, it is recommended that one delay eating until one returns from praying. According to the Hanbalis and the Hanafis, it is recommended that one eat some of the meat one has sacrificed [before going out to pray] if one has slaughtered a sacrificial offering, whereas if one has not slaughtered an offering, one has the choice between eating before or after the prayer. As for the Malikis and the Shafiis, they hold that it is recommended that one delay eating on the Day of Sacrifice until after one has prayed regardless of whether one has slaughtered a sacrificial animal or not.

According to the Shafiis, the Hanbalis and the Hanafis, it is recommended that worshipers other than the imam leave for the place where the holiday prayer is to be performed immediately after performing the dawn prayer, even if this means going out before sunrise; the Malikis, by contrast, hold that it is recommended that worshipers other than the imam leave after sunrise if their houses are near the site where the prayer will be performed, and that otherwise, they should leave just long enough before the *iqāmah* to arrive on time to pray with the imam. As for the imam himself, it is recommended that he delay leaving for the prayer site such that he arrives just on time to commence the prayer.

It is recommended on the Days of Fastbreaking and Sacrifice that one enhance one's appearance by trimming one's fingernails, trimming one's hair, and washing. However, the Hanbalis note that this recommendation holds for everyone who is accountable for ritual prayer even if it is not one of these two holidays.

It is recommended that one go out to the prayer site on foot, that one say *Allāhu akbar* aloud upon leaving one's house, and that one continue uttering these words until the prayer commences. This ruling is agreed upon by all the schools except the Hanafis, who hold that it is preferable to utter the words *Allāhu akbar* silently.[256] According to the Malikis, one should continue saying *Allāhu akbar* either until the arrival of the imam or until he rises for prayer even if the prayer has not actually

---

256. Specifically, the Hanafis rule that one emulates the Sunnah by saying *Allāhu akbar* regardless of whether one says it aloud or silently, but that its silent utterance is preferable.

257. According to the Malikis, it is recommended, albeit not an emulation of the Sunnah, that the holiday prayers be performed outdoors; it is undesirable to perform them in the mosque without a legitimate excuse unless one is in Mecca, where it is preferable to perform them in the Sacred Mosque due to the honorable nature of the site, and in order to view the Ka'bah.

* * *

According to the Hanbalis, it is an emulation of the Sunnah to perform the holiday prayers outdoors provided that the site is close to the mosque by commonly accepted standards; if they are performed in a site which would commonly be agreed to be far from the mosque, they will be invalid. It is undesirable to perform them in the mosque without a legitimate excuse except for those who are in Mecca, where they are to be performed in the Sacred Mosque; on this point, then, the Hanbalis agree with the Malikis.

* * *

According to the Shafiis, by contrast, it is preferable to perform the holiday prayers in the mosque due to the honorable nature of this place unless there is a reason not to do so, such as its being too small. In a case such as this, it is undesirable to perform them there due to its being too crowded, and the Sunnah dictates that they be performed outdoors.

* * *

begun; as for the imam, he is to continue saying *Allāhu akbar* until he enters the *miḥrāb* [that is, until he takes his place facing the *qiblah* to lead the prayer].

It is recommended that if one reaches the prayer site by one route, one should leave by another. In addition, it is recommended that one show a friendly, joyful demeanor to the believers one meets, that one give as much voluntary charity as one is able, and on the Day of Fastbreaking, that one distribute one's zakah funds between the dawn prayer and the holiday prayer.

The place where the two holiday prayers are to be performed

The holiday prayers are performed out of doors; it is undesirable to perform them in a mosque without a legitimate excuse.[257]

When the imam goes out to lead the holiday prayer, it is recommended that he appoint someone else to lead prayer for those worshipers who would be harmed by praying outdoors, since it is permissible for the holiday prayers to be performed in more than one place.[258]

As for the Hanafis, they hold that it is undesirable to perform the holiday prayers in any mosque, including the Sacred Mosque in Mecca; on all other points, however, they agree with the Hanbalis and the Malikis.

258. According to the Malikis, it is not recommended that the imam appoint someone else to lead the holiday prayer inside the mosque. As for those who are unable to take part in the holiday prayer out of doors, they may perform it, but they are not to recite aloud, and they are to pray without a sermon. As in the case of the Friday congregational prayer, the holiday prayer is to be performed in one place, namely, the place where the imam is leading the prayer for those who are able to come out for it. Those who perform the holiday prayer before the imam does have not emulated the Sunnah; hence, in order to emulate the Sunnah, they should perform it with the imam as well; as for those who miss the holiday prayer with the imam, it is recommended that they perform it later, as has been mentioned.

Undesirable practices associated with the two holiday prayers

It is undesirable for either the imam or those being led in prayer to perform voluntary prayers before or after the holiday prayer.[259]

There are, in addition, other recommended and undesirable practices associated with the holiday prayer mentioned by the Malikis, the Shafiis, and the Hanafis.[260]

Disallowance of the *adhān* and the *iqāmah* in connection with the prayers on the Day of Fastbreaking and the Day of Sacrifice

There is to be no *adhān* for the holiday prayers, nor any *iqāmah*. However, the Shafiis, the Hanafis and the Hanbalis hold that it is recommended that people be called together with the words, "Prayer is gathering [the worshipers]" (*al-ṣalātu jāmi'ah*). Most Malikis judge this practice to be undesirable, or at least a departure from the ideal, although some of them hold that this type of announcement is only undesirable if it is believed that this practice is required. Otherwise, it is acceptable.

---

259. According to the Malikis, it is undesirable to perform voluntary prayers either before or after the holiday prayer if it has been performed out of doors in accordance with the Sunnah. However, if it has been performed in the mosque, it is not undesirable to perform voluntary prayers either before or after the holiday prayer.

* * *

According to the Hanbalis, it is undesirable to perform voluntary prayers before or after the holiday prayers in the same spot where the holiday prayer was performed, whether in the mosque or outside.

* * *

According to the Shafiis, it is undesirable for the imam to perform voluntary prayers either before or after the holiday prayer, whether out of doors or elsewhere. As for those being led in communal prayer, it is acceptable for them to perform voluntary prayers before the holiday prayer under all circumstances; and following the holiday prayer, they may engage in voluntary prayers if they did not hear the sermon due to deafness, because they were too far from the imam, etc.

* * *

As for the Hanafis, they hold that it is undesirable to perform voluntary prayers before the holiday prayer whether one is in the mosque or elsewhere. Following the holiday prayer, they consider it undesirable to do so only in the mosque, whereas at home, it is acceptable.

260. According to the Malikis, it is recommended that one sit down during the first sermon and between the two sermons for the holiday prayers, whereas for the Friday congregational prayer, this practice is an emulation of the Sunnah. Moreover, if [the imam] becomes ritually impure during the holiday prayer sermons, he should proceed to the end without appointing anyone to take his place, whereas if this happens while he is delivering the sermons for the Friday congregational prayer, he is to appoint a replacement for himself.

* * *

The ruling on the holiday prayer sermon

The two sermons preached on the Day of Fastbreaking and the Day of Sacrifice are agreed by the Shafiis, the Hanbalis and the Hanafis to be an emulation of the Sunnah, whereas the Malikis hold them to be simply recommended. As has been mentioned, the Hanbalis and the Shafiis make no distinction between that which is 'recommended' and that which is 'Sunnah'; hence, they agree with the Malikis who say that these two sermons are 'recommended', as well as with the Hanafis, who say that they are 'Sunnah.' Nevertheless, there are certain pillars and conditions associated with these two sermons just as there are with the sermons preached for the Friday congregational prayer.

Pillars associated with the two holiday sermons

The two holiday sermons can only be said to have "taken effect", so to speak, if their associated pillars are fulfilled. These pillars are the same as those of the two sermons preached during the Friday congregational prayer with the exception of the manner in which they are opened: The Sunnah-based practice with regard to the holiday sermons is for them to be opened with the utterance of *Allāhu akbar*, which is then followed by the specified number of additional utterances of this phrase, whereas the sermon associated with the Friday congregational prayer is opened with words of praise to God. For the pillars of the holiday sermons according to each of the four schools, see below.[261]

According to the Shafiis, it is necessary during the two sermons delivered for the Friday congregational prayer that the imam be standing, that he be ritually pure, and that he have all his private parts concealed; he is also required to sit down briefly between the two sermons. However, in connection with the sermons delivered for the holiday prayer, these practices are merely desirable.

* * *

As for the Hanafis, they hold that it is undesirable for the imam to sit down before commencing the first sermon of the holiday prayer, whereas before the first sermon of the Friday congregational prayer, it is an emulation of the Sunnah for the imam to sit down briefly.

261. According to the Hanafis, both the holiday sermon and the sermon preached during the Friday congregational prayer have a single pillar, namely, that they must contain words of divine remembrance. These words may be chosen by the speaker and they may be either lengthy or brief. Hence, it is sufficient for the speaker to utter any word of praise, glorification or affirmation of God's oneness (such as *al-ḥamdu lillāh, subḥān Allāh, lā ilāha illā Allāh*, etc.) in order for the sermon to be valid. However, it is undesirable, though not to the point of being forbidden, for the speaker to limit his words to such phrases. As for the second sermon, the Hanafis do not consider it to be obligatory; rather, they hold it to be an emulation of the Sunnah as will be seen below in the discussion of the Friday congregational prayer.

* * *

According to the Malikis, both the holiday sermon and the sermon preached for the Friday congregational prayer have a single pillar, namely, that they must contain either a warning or encouragement.

* * *

According to the Hanbalis, the holiday sermon has three pillars: (1) prayer for blessings and peace upon the Prophet; (2) the recitation of a verse from the Qur'ān which either conveys a complete thought or contains a particular ruling (thereby excluding a phrase such as, "...two gardens of deepest green..." (55:64); and (3) exhortation to be conscious of God. The minimum one should say in this connection would be something like, "Be conscious of God and beware of disobeying His commands." Opening the holiday sermon with the utterance of *Allāhu akbar* is an emulation of the Sunnah, whereas opening the sermon for the Friday congregational prayer with words of praise to God is a pillar.

* * *

The Shafiis list the following four pillars for the two holiday sermons:

(1) The speaker must pray for peace and blessings upon the Prophet in each of the two sermons, specifically using the word *ṣallā Allāhu 'alā...* ("May God bestow blessings upon..."). It is not necessary to use the name 'Muḥammad'; however, the speaker must use one of his epithets [for example, *al-Muṣṭafā*, i.e., "the Chosen One"], and refrain from the use of the pronoun 'him'.

(2) The speaker must urge his listeners to be conscious of God in both sermons, even if he does so without using this specific phrasing; hence, it is sufficient to say something like, "And obey God." However, it is not sufficient simply to warn people against the fleeting world and its temptations but rather, he must urge his listeners to be obedient.

(3) The speaker must recite a verse from the Qur'ān in one of the two sermons, preferably the first. The verse recited must be complete if it is short, whereas if it is long, it will suffice to recite only part of it. Moreover, the verse must contain a promise, a threat, a ruling, a story, a parable, or a report; hence, this pillar will not be fulfilled if he says, "...and then he looks..." (74:2).

(4) The speaker must pray for believers, both male and female, in the second sermon; the prayer should be for something non-temporal, such as forgiveness, although if he has not memorized any prayers of this nature, it will suffice to pray for them pertaining to some worldly concern, e.g., by saying, "O God, provide for the material needs of all of the male and female believers" or some such thing. In addition, the speaker's supplication must include those present with him; hence, if he intends only other people in his prayer, his sermon will be invalid. The two holiday sermons are to be opened with the utterance of *Allāhu akbar* as mentioned in connection with the holiday prayers. In this respect, then, the holiday sermon differs from the sermon issued for the Friday congregational prayer, one pillar of which is that it must be opened with words of praise to God, e.g., *al-ḥamdu lillāh* or *aḥmadu Allāh* ("I praise God").

Conditions associated with the holiday sermons

See the footnote below for a summary of the conditions associated with the holiday sermons according to each of the four schools.[262]

---

262. According to the Malikis, the two holiday sermons must be in the Arabic language even if the people who listen to them are foreigners who do not know the language. In the case of the Friday congregational prayer, if there is no one present who would be capable of delivering a sermon, the obligation to perform the congregational prayer is dropped for the group of people concerned. These two sermons are to be delivered following the prayer; hence, if they are delivered before the prayer, it is an emulation of the Sunnah for them to be repeated after the prayer if not too much time has passed according to commonly accepted standards.

* * *

According to the Hanafis, the holiday sermon will only be valid if at least one person comes to hear it, provided that it be someone who may validly perform the Friday congregational prayer. (For more details concerning who belongs in this category, see the section on the Friday congregational prayer). It is not necessary, however, for the person actually to hear the sermon; hence, if he is deaf, too far away to hear it, etc., the sermon will still be valid. It is sufficient for it to be attended by someone who is ill or on a journey; however, it will not suffice for those attending the sermon to be women or young boys. The Hanafis do not stipulate that the holiday sermons be in Arabic or that they be delivered after the prayer. Rather, it is simply an emulation of the Sunnah to postpone the holiday sermons until after the prayer; hence, if they are delivered before the prayer, it is not necessary that they be repeated afterwards.

* * *

According to the Shafiis, both the holiday sermons and those preached for the Friday congregational prayer will be valid only if forty people are in attendance to hear them, and only if the person delivering the sermons utters the pillars aloud, with the term 'aloud' being defined here as speaking loudly enough for forty people to hear his voice. However, it is not necessary that they actually hear the speaker; rather, it is only required that they all be close enough to the speaker and in sufficiently sound physical condition that if they listen, they will hear him. It does no harm if some of them daydream or are otherwise distracted during part of the sermon; however, if they are actually unable to hear due to deafness, being asleep, or being too far away, the sermons will not be valid. It is likewise stipulated that the sermons come after the prayer; hence, if the speaker delivers them before the prayer, they are not to be counted, and it is recommended that they be repeated after the prayer even if a long time has passed.

* * *

According to the Hanbalis, neither the holiday prayers nor those preached for the Friday congregational prayer will be valid unless the speaker utters them loudly enough to make himself heard by the number of people who make up a quorum for the prayer concerned. In agreement with the Shafiis, the Hanbalis set this quorum

The utterance of *Allāhu akbar* following the five prayers during the days following the Day of Sacrifice

The Shafiis and the Hanbalis agree that the utterance of *Allāhu akbar* following the five daily prayers during the days subsequent to the Day of Sacrifice is an emulation of the Sunnah. According to the Hanafis, this practice is a 'duty', whereas according to the Malikis, it is simply recommended. It has become customary to refer to this practice as *takbīr al-tashrīq*, where the word *takbīr* refers, as we have seen, to the utterance of the words *Allāhu akbar*, while the word *tashrīq* refers to the process of cutting the meat of the sacrificial animals into strips and drying it in the sun during the three days following the Day of Sacrifice in Minā. For the wisdom in this practice as well as the detailed manner in which it is to be carried out according to each of the four schools, see below.[263]

---

at forty people. If those in attendance have failed to hear the pillars of the two sermons due, not to sleep, inattention, or deafness but rather, because the speaker's voice is too low or because they are too far away, the sermon will not be valid. The Hanbalis also stipulate that the two sermons be delivered after the prayer, as has been mentioned [the text reads "before" the prayer here; however, in light of what the author has stated earlier, I have rendered it as "after" – t.n.].

263. According to the Hanafis, the utterance of *takbīr al-tashrīq* is a 'duty' given the following four conditions: (1) One must have performed an obligatory prayer in community; if one performed it alone, or if it was not an obligatory prayer, the utterance of *takbīr al-tashrīq* is not a 'duty'. (2) The group with which the prayer was performed must have been composed of men; hence, if women have performed the prayer in community behind a woman, *takbīr al-tashrīq* is not required of them. If, on the other hand, women have prayed in community behind a man, they are required to utter *takbīr al-tashrīq* silently, but not aloud. As for the imam and the men praying behind him, they are to utter it aloud. (3) The worshiper must be resident in a given place rather than on a journey. (4) The worshiper must be in a metropolis rather than in a small village or town.

The time during which *takbīr al-tashrīq* is required begins immediately following the dawn prayer on the Day of 'Arafah and ends immediately after the mid-afternoon prayer on the fourth day of the holiday, that is, three days later. The wording of *takbīr al-tashrīq* is as follows: *Allāhu akbar, Allāhu akbar, lā ilāha illā Allāh, wa Allāhu akbar, Allāhu akbar, wa lillāhi al-ḥamd*; one may also add, *Allāhu akbar kabīran wal-ḥamdu lillāhi kathīran...*"

The utterance of *takbīr al-tashrīq* must follow immediately upon the prayer's final greeting of peace; hence, if someone deliberately speaks or allows an occurrence of ritual impurity after the final greeting of peace, he/she will miss the opportunity to utter *takbīr al-tashrīq* and will be guilty of wrongdoing. If, on the other hand, one has an unintentional occurrence of ritual impurity before having the chance to utter *takbīr al-tashrīq*, one may either utter it immediately given the fact that its utterance is not conditional on being ritually pure, or one may repeat ritual ablutions before uttering it.

Takbīr al-tashrīq is not to be uttered after the *witr* or the holiday prayers; however, if one misses one of the prayers after which *takbīr al-tashrīq* is required, one should make up *takbīr al-tashrīq* along with this prayer even if one makes the prayer up at some time other than the three days following the Day of Sacrifice. If, on the other hand, one makes up a prayer after which *takbīr al-tashrīq* is not required, one should not utter it even if the prayer is being made up during the three days following the Day of Sacrifice. If the imam omits *takbīr al-tashrīq*, those following him in prayer should utter it anyway; however, they should only do so after the imam has done something which would create a 'break' following the end of his prayer—by leaving the mosque, deliberately allowing an occurrence of ritual impurity, speaking, etc.—such that it would no longer be possible for others to build on the prayer he performed. Thus, if the imam, after omitting *takbīr al-tashrīq*, remains in the spot where he prayed without either speaking or having an occurrence of ritual impurity, those who were led in prayer should likewise not utter *takbīr al-tashrīq*.

* * *

According to the Hanbalis, it is an emulation of the Sunnah to utter *takbīr al-tashrīq* after every obligatory prayer performed in community during the period which begins immediately after the dawn prayer on the Day of 'Arafah if the worshiper is not in a state of ritual consecration (or from noon on the Day of Sacrifice if the worshiper is in a state of ritual consecration), and which ends mid-afternoon on the fourth day after the Day of Sacrifice. This ruling applies equally to those who are resident in one place and to those who are traveling, to males and females, and to prayers which are being performed on time and those which are being made up during the three days following the Day of Sacrifice, provided that they are obligatory prayers being performed in community. (Hence, it is not an emulation of the Sunnah to utter *takbīr al-tashrīq* after voluntary prayers or after obligatory prayers which were performed alone.) As for the wording of *takbīr al-tashrīq*, it is as follows: *Allāhu akbar Allāhu akbar, lā ilāha illā Allāh, wa Allāhu akbar Allāhu akbar, wa lillāhi al-ḥamd.*

One emulates the Sunnah by saying these words once, and if one repeats them three times, this is acceptable as well. If someone misses one of the prayers after which *takbīr al-tashrīq* is required and if he/she makes this prayer up after the three days following the holiday have passed, he/she should not follow the compensatory prayer with *takbīr al-tashrīq*. If the imam forgets to utter *takbīr al-tashrīq*, those who are following him in prayer should utter it anyway. As for someone who needs to perform a prostration of forgetfulness after the final greeting of peace, he should postpone *takbīr al-tashrīq* until after the prostration. Someone who arrives late for a communal prayer should utter *takbīr al-tashrīq* after making up for whatever parts of the prayer he missed at the beginning and after the final greeting of peace. This particular *takbīr al-tashrīq* is referred to as 'restricted', while they also have what they refer to as an 'unrestricted' utterance of the same. For the Day of Fastbreaking, the time for uttering the unrestricted *takbīr al-tashrīq* lasts from the beginning of the night before the holiday and until the end of the holiday sermon, whereas for the Day of Sacrifice the time for uttering it lasts from the beginning of 10 Dhū al-Ḥijjah until the two holiday sermons have been preached. Moreover, it is an emulation of the Sunnah for males, but not for females, to utter *takbīr al-tashrīq* aloud, be it the restricted or the unrestricted type.

* * *

According to the Malikis, it is recommended that all worshipers, including travelers, young boys and women, utter *takbīr al-tashrīq* after fifteen obligatory prayers, regardless of whether they have been performed alone or in community and regardless of whether the worshiper is from a metropolitan area or elsewhere. The time for the utterance of *takbīr al-tashrīq* begins after the noon prayer on the holiday itself and ends with the dawn prayer on the fourth day after the holiday. It is undesirable to utter *takbīr al-tashrīq* after voluntary prayers or after prayers which are being made up, regardless of whether they were missed during the three days since the holiday or at some other time.

Takbīr al-tashrīq should be uttered immediately after one has prayed; hence, it should be placed before any words of divine remembrance which come after the prayer, such as recitation of the Throne Verse (2:255), words of praise, and the like. However, if someone is due to perform a prostration of forgetfulness after the prayer, he should postpone *takbīr al-tashrīq* until after the prostration, which is considered to be an auxiliary part of the prayer itself. If someone omits *takbīr al-tashrīq* either intentionally or unintentionally, he or she should go back and make it up if not too much time has passed by commonly accepted standards, and if the imam omits *takbīr al-tashrīq*, those being led in prayer should utter it anyway. As for the wording of *takbīr al-tashrīq*, it is simply, *Allāhu akbar, Allāhu akbar, Allāhu akbar*. When women utter it, they should say it just loudly enough to be able to hear themselves, whereas when men utter it, they should say it loudly enough that those on either side and in front of them can hear it as well.

* * *

According to the Shafiis, *takbīr al-tashrīq* is an emulation of the Sunnah following all obligatory prayers [during the three days following the holiday], whether these prayers have been performed in community or not, and whether the imam has uttered it or not; it is likewise an emulation of the Sunnah to utter *takbīr al-tashrīq* after voluntary prayers, after the funeral prayer, and after obligatory prayers which are made up during the three days following the holiday. For those who are not on the major pilgrimage, the time period during which *takbīr al-tashrīq* is to be uttered lasts from dawn on the Day of ʻArafah until sunset on the fourth day after the holiday; for those who are performing the major pilgrimage, the time for utterance of *takbīr al-tashrīq* lasts from noon on the Day of Sacrifice until sunset three days later.

According to the Shafiis, it is not necessary that *takbīr al-tashrīq* be directly subsequent to the final greeting of peace; hence, if someone does something else in between the conclusion of the prayer and uttering *takbīr al-tashrīq*, whether intentionally or unintentionally, and even if a long time passes between the two events, the worshiper may still utter *takbīr al-tashrīq*.

The preferred wording for *takbīr al-tashrīq* is as follows: "God is greatest, God is greatest, God is greatest. There is no god but God. God is greatest, God is greatest, and to Him belongs all praise. God is greatest by far, and to Him much praise is

The prayer for rain

The prayer for rain will be discussed under the following four headings: (1) the definition and basis of the prayer for rain (*'istisqā'*), (2) how the prayer for rain is performed, (3) the ruling on the prayer for rain and the time at which it is to be performed, and (4) desirable actions on the part of the imam before the prayer for rain.

The definition and basis of the prayer for rain

The meaning of the Arabic word *istisqā'* is a request for water either of God or of some other person. If someone is in need of water and requests it of someone else, this request is referred to as ' *istisqā'*'. As for the meaning of this term as used in Islamic jurisprudence, it refers specifically to a request for rain made by human beings of God Almighty when they are in need of water, for example, when they are in a location where there are insufficient rivers, wells and the like from which they can drink, water their crops and livestock, etc.

---

due, and glory to be to God in the morning and the evening. There is no god but God alone. His promise has proven true. He has given succor to His servant, granted strength to His soldiers, and defeated the confederates single-handedly. There is no god but God, and we worship none but Him, sincere in our faith in Him alone, however hateful this may be to those who deny the Truth. O God, grant Your blessings to our master Muhammad, his family, his companions, his helpers and his descendents, and grant them Your abundant peace." *(Allāhu akbar, Allāhu akbar, Allāhu akbar, lā ilāha illā Allāh, wa Allāhu akbar, Allāhu akbar, wa lillāhi al-ḥamd. Allāhu akbar kabīran wal-ḥamdu lillāhi kathīran, wa subḥān Allāh bukratan wa aṣīlan. lā ilāha illā Allāh waḥdahu, ṣadaqa wa'dahu wa naṣara 'abdahu wa a'azza jundahu wa hazama al-aḥzāba waḥdahu. lā ilāha illā Allāhu wa lā na'budu illā iyyāh, mukhliṣīn lahu al-dīn wa law kariha al-kāfirūn. Allāhumma ṣalli 'alā sayyidinā Muḥammad wa 'alā āli sayyidinā Muḥammad, wa 'alā aṣḥāb sayyidinā Muḥammad, wa 'alā anṣār sayyidinā Muḥammad wa 'alā dhurriyat sayyidinā Muḥammad, wa sallim taslīman kathīra.)*

The utterance of *takbīr al-tashrīq* following one's prayers using the formula above is referred to as 'restricted'. It is also an emulation of the Sunnah to utter *takbīr al-tashrīq* aloud in one's home, in the marketplace, in the streets and elsewhere using the same formula from sundown on the days preceding the Day of Fastbreaking and the Day of Sacrifice until the time when the imam commences the holiday prayer. If someone prays alone, he/she should continue uttering *takbīr al-tashrīq* until uttering the opening *Allāḥu akbar* of the holiday prayer. If, on the other hand, he/she does not perform the holiday prayer, he/she should continue uttering *takbīr al-tashrīq* until noon. This ruling applies to both men and women; however, a woman should not raise her voice when uttering *takbīr al-tashrīq* if she is in the presence of men who are not her next of kin. This type of *takbīr al-tashrīq* is referred as 'unrestricted'. And whereas the 'restricted' utterance of *takbīr al-tashrīq* should be uttered before the words of divine remembrance which follow one's prayer, the 'unrestricted' type should be delayed until after such words or phrases of divine remembrance.

How the prayer for rain is to be performed

If people are in need of water in the sense described above, Muslims are asked to perform the prayer for rain in a manner whose details differ somewhat from one school to another.[264]

---

264. According to the Shafiis, the prayer for rain consists of two *rak'ahs* which are to be performed in community. They also stipulate that the imam for this prayer must be the Muslims' supreme ruler or his proxy; if neither of these is available, the prayer may be led by some other influential, authoritative Muslim leader.

The manner in which the prayer for rain is to be performed is like that of the holiday prayers. Hence, in the first *rak'ah*, the imam and those praying behind him utter the words *Allāhu akbar* seven times in addition to *takbīrat al-iḥrām*; in the second *rak'ah*, they utter *Allāhu akbar* five times in addition to the utterance of *Allāhu akbar* with which the second *rak'ah* begins. The imam raises his hands to shoulder level with each utterance, then seeks divine protection, saying, *a'ūdhu billāh min al-shayṭān al-rajīm*, after which he utters the prayer of commencement. It is desirable between each two utterances of *Allāhu akbar* to pause for as long as it would take to recite a medium-length verse of the Qur'ān, then to utter silently some words or phrases of divine remembrance followed by recitation aloud. During the first *rak'ah*, it is desirable after reciting the *Fātiḥah* to recite Surah 50 or Surah 87, and in the second *rak'ah*, either Surah 54 or Surah 88 analogously to what is recited in the holiday prayers.

After the two *rak'ahs* of the prayer for rain have been performed, it is recommended that the imam deliver two sermons like those delivered on the Days of Fastbreaking and Sacrifice. However, the imam does not utter *Allāhu akbar* during the sermon following the prayer for rain; rather, he prays for God's forgiveness nine times before commencing the first sermon, then does so nine more times during the second sermon. The wording for this prayer for divine forgiveness is as follows: "I seek forgiveness from the majestic God, apart from whom there is no other deity, the Ever-Living, the Self-subsistent Fount of Being, and I turn to Him in repentance" (*astaghfir Allāh al-'aẓīm alladhi lā ilāha illā Allāh, al-ḥayy al-qayyūm wa atūbu ilayhi*). However, if one says nothing but *astaghfir Allāh*, this is sufficient.

It is recommended, once the speaker has finished one-third of the second sermon, that he face the *qiblah* and reverse his outer garment (such as a cloak, robe, etc.) by grasping its lower left edge with his right hand and bringing it up over his right shoulder, and by grasping its lower right edge with his left hand and bringing it up over his left shoulder. It is undesirable for the imam to omit this gesture. When the imam thus reverses his garment, the worshipers being led in prayer emulate the Sunnah by doing the same to their outer garments while seated.

It is an emulation of the Sunnah for the imam to engage in a great deal of supplication, both silently and aloud, during the prayer for rain, and to open his supplication by uttering the "prayer of distress", the wording of which is as follows: "There is no deity but God, the Majestic, the All-Forbearing. There is no deity but God, Lord of the great throne. There is no deity but God, Lord of the heavens, Lord of the earth, and Lord of the noble throne" (*lā ilāha illā Allāh, al-*

'aẓīm al-ḥalīm, lā ilāha illā Allāh rabb al-'arsh al-'aẓīm, lā ilāha illā Allāh rabb al-samāwāti wa rabb al-arḍi wa rabb al-'arsh al-karīm).

It is an emulation of the Sunnah for the speaker to spend a great deal of time praying for God's forgiveness and for him to recite the Qur'anic words, "Ask your Sustainer to forgive you your sins—for verily, He is all-forgiving! He will shower upon you heavenly blessings, and will aid you with worldly goods and children, and will bestow upon you gardens, and bestow upon you running waters" (71:10-11). In addition, he is to include in his sermon the prayer of the Prophet, the wording of which is as follows: "O God, cause it [the rain] to be a mercy, and not a draught of suffering, destruction, tribulation or flooding. O God, cause it to fall on the rolling hills, on the places where trees grow, and in the dry riverbeds. O God, [cause the rain to be poured out] round about us, not upon us. O God, grant us rain that brings succor, relief, and deliverance from adversity. Grant us rain that brings wholeness, health, and fertility. Grant us pouring rain that showers the earth. O God, grant us rain and do not cause us to be among those who despair. O God, your servants and their lands have suffered strain, hunger and distress of which we complain to You alone. Cause what we have planted to bring forth vegetation and let udders overflow. May the heavens' blessings descend upon us, and may the blessings of the earth spring forth. O God, relieve our affliction as none but You can. O God, we seek Your forgiveness, for indeed, You are the All-Forgiving. Open up the heavens and cause them to pour forth upon us in abundance."

* * *

There is disagreement among the Hanafis as to how the prayer for rain is to be performed. According to some of them, it consists simply of supplication and pleas for divine forgiveness without ritual prayer; hence, the imam utters supplications while standing and facing the *qiblah*, raising his hands as the other people sit facing the *qiblah* and say *Āmīn* in response to his supplications. Such a supplication might be the prayer mentioned earlier, namely, "O God, grant us rain that brings succor, relief, and deliverance from adversity. Grant us rain that brings wholeness, health, and fertility. Grant us pouring rain that showers the earth," or other words uttered either aloud or silently. However, this view is not well supported; rather, the best supported view is that the prayer for rain involves the performance of two *rak'ahs*, in agreement with the other schools. As in the case of the holiday prayers, there are some who say that the prayer for rain is simply recommended, while others hold that it is based on the prophetic Sunnah. However, unlike the holiday prayers, the prayer for rain does not involve additional utterances of *Allāhu akbar*. As in the case of the holiday prayer, two sermons are preached following the prayer for rain either by the imam or by his proxy; however, in the case of the prayer for rain, the imam stands holding a bow, a sword or a stick in his hand, then reverses his outer garment after completing part of the first sermon. If the garment is square, he turns it upside down; if it is round, he brings its right side over to the left and its left side over to the right; and if it is lined, as in the case of an overcoat, he turns it wrong side out. However, it is agreed that the worshipers who are praying behind him do not reverse their outer garments along with the imam.

* * *

According to the Hanbalis, the prayer for rain is performed in exactly the same way as the holiday prayer: In the first *rak'ah*, the imam utters the words *Allāhu akbar* seven times and in the second *rak'ah*, five times. In the first *rak'ah* he recites Surah 87 and in the second, Surah 88; alternatively, he might recite Surah 71 in the first *rak'ah* and whatever passage of the Qur'ān he chooses in the second. The imam sits down to rest briefly, then mounts the pulpit and delivers one sermon rather than two; like the holiday sermon, the sermon for the prayer for rain is opened with nine utterances of *Allāhu akbar*. During the sermon, the imam is to offer many prayers for the Prophet as well as prayers for divine forgiveness, uttering the verse, "Ask your Sustainer to forgive you your sins—for verily, He is all-forgiving! He will shower upon you heavenly blessings, and will aid you with worldly goods and children, and will bestow upon you gardens, and bestow upon you running waters" (71:10-11).

As the imam is offering prayers of supplication, it is an emulation of the Sunnah for him to raise his hands high enough that his armpits are visible, holding his palms downward. Those being led in prayer utter the word *Āmīn* in response to the imam's supplications, raising their hands like the imam but remaining seated. The imam's supplications are valid whatever he chooses to say; however, it is preferable to rely on traditional prayers such as, "O God, grant us abundant rain that brings benefit and delivers us from distress, rain that brings wholeness, health and fertility, pouring down blessing over the entire land. Soon, O God, grant rain to Your creatures, both man and beast, and spread abroad Your mercy, restoring life to Your dead land. O God, grant us rain and do not cause us to be among those who despair. O God, cause it [the rain] to be a mercy, and not a draught of suffering, destruction, tribulation or flooding. O God, your servants and their lands have suffered adversity, hunger and distress of which we complain to You alone. Cause what we have planted to bring forth vegetation and let udders overflow. O God, give us to drink of the blessings of heaven, and cause Your blessings to descend upon us. O God, remove hunger, hardship and nakedness from among us, relieving our affliction as none but You can. O God, we seek Your forgiveness, for indeed, You are the All-Forgiving. Open up the heavens and cause them to pour forth upon us in abundance!"

When the imam utters a supplication, those listening respond by saying *Āmīn*. It is desirable for the imam to face the *qiblah* during the sermon, then turn his outer garment inside out; those being led in prayer do likewise, then leave their outer garments reversed in this way until they take them off. On this occasion the imam faces the *qiblah* while praying silently, "O God, You have commanded us to call upon You and You have promised to answer. We have called upon You as You commanded us, so answer us as You have promised, for surely, You do not break Your promises." Once the imam has said this, he turns and faces his listeners again, urging them to give charity and to do good. He then prays for blessing upon the Prophet and for believers, both men and women, recites from the Qur'ān, and says, "I seek God's forgiveness for myself, for you, and for all Muslims." With this, the imam concludes his sermon.

The Hanbalis do not stipulate that an *adhān* is required for the prayer for rain, nor is it required for the associated sermon. However, people can be called to take part in this prayer with the words, *al-ṣalātu jāmi'ah* (i.e., "Prayer is gathering [people]"). The prayer for rain is also to be performed by those who are traveling and those who live in villages, in which case any one among them may deliver the associated sermon.

* * *

According to the Malikis, the prayer for rain is performed in the same manner as the holiday prayers with the exception that unlike the holiday prayers, the prayer for rain does not involve any additional utterances of the phrase *Allāhu akbar*. On this point, the Malikis are in agreement with the Hanafis and in disagreement with the Shafiis and the Hanbalis.

The imam is to deliver two sermons as part of the prayer for rain; when he finishes the second sermon, it is recommended that he face the *qiblah* with his back to the people, then turn his outer garment inside out [or wear it backwards]; however, he is not to turn it upside down. It is recommended that men who are praying behind the imam reverse their outer garments while seated; however, it is not recommended for women. The imam then prays extensively for God to lift whatever affliction has befallen the people; here, it is recommended that the imam rely on traditional prayers of supplication, including the one found in [Imam Mālik's] *Al-Muwaṭṭa'*, namely, the prayer which was used by the Prophet when he prayed for rain: "O God, grant Your servants rain, both man and beast, spread abroad Your mercy, and restore life to Your dead land."

The Malikis agree with the Shafiis and the Hanbalis that performance of the prayer for rain is a Sunnah-based practice for men which is second only to the holiday prayer in importance if it is performed in community; however, for those who missed performing it with the imam, it is only recommended. It is likewise only recommended for boys who have reached the age of discernment and for elderly women. As for young women, it is undesirable for them to go out for the prayer for rain, and if it is feared that their going out will cause others temptation, it is forbidden.

The ruling on the prayer for rain and the time when it is performed

The prayer for rain is an emphatically enjoined Sunnah-based practice when there is a need for water. Hence, when people are in need of water, it is an emulation of the Sunnah for them to perform the prayer for rain in one of the ways we have mentioned thus far, any and all of which will be valid. It is thus not necessary to perform the prayer for rain in the manner prescribed by any one school, since the accounts concerning this prayer have been a subject of disagreement among the various schools; for example, the Hanafis who hold that the prayer for rain does not include additional utterances of *Allāhu akbar* also quote some of their own imams as saying that the prayer for rain does include such utterances, similar to the holiday prayer, and so on. Hence, we have mentioned the manner in which the prayer for rain is to be performed according to each of the four schools in order to make it easy for people to familiarize themselves with all of them without confusion. As for its being an emphatically enjoined Sunnah-based practice, this is agreed upon by all the schools except the Hanafis.[265]

---

265. According to the Hanafis, the prayer for rain is merely recommended. It is true, of course, that it is mentioned in both the Qur'ān and the Sunnah; however, what is clearly based on these two sources includes [only] pleas for divine forgiveness, praise to God, and other petitions. As for ritual prayer, it is not mentioned in any authentic hadiths in connection with the prayer for rain. Be that as it may, the Hanafis are agreed that ritual prayer [in connection with the prayer for rain] may legitimately be performed alone rather than just in community since it is an unspecified voluntary prayer. As for the mention of the prayer for rain in the Qur'ān, it is in the passage which reads, "Ask your Sustainer to forgive you your sins—for verily, He is all-forgiving! He will shower upon you heavenly blessings" (71:10). And that which was a law for those who preceded us [Muslims] is also a law for us so long as God and His Messenger make mention of it without condemnation. There are authentic hadiths according to which the Prophet prayed to God Almighty for rain. It bears noting in this context that a prayer for rain was made through him when he was a boy. We read, for example, that the people of Mecca were once suffering a drought, so the Qurayshites said, "Abū Ṭālib, the riverbed has gone dry and our families are afflicted with drought. So come, pray for rain!" Abū Ṭālib then brought out a boy [i.e., the Prophet] who was so beautiful, it was as if he were a sun that had just been revealed by the parting of a dark cloud. Around him there were other young boys as well. Abū Ṭālib took the boy and had him stand with his back to the Ka'bah, and he clung to his [Abū Ṭālib's] finger. There had not been even so much as scattered clouds in the sky, but [not long after this] clouds began to appear here and there. Then they poured down copious rain, causing the riverbed to overflow and turning the entire land green and fertile. It was in reference to this event that Abū Ṭālib uttered the following line of poetry:

A fair-skinned [lad] by whose face the clouds are entreated for rain,
A refuge for orphans and a protector of widows. (Recorded by Ibn 'Asākir)

As for the time at which the prayer for rain is to be performed, the Hanafis and the Hanbalis hold that it includes any time at which it is permissible to perform voluntary prayers; for the views of the Malikis and the Shafiis, see below.[266]

The Shafiis, the Hanbalis and the Malikis hold that if rain is delayed in coming, it is an emulation of the Sunnah to repeat the prayer for rain until the rain comes. According to the Hanafis, repetition of the prayer for rain is merely recommended, and it should not be repeated on more than three consecutive days.

Desirable practices for the imam before going out to perform the prayer for rain

The following five practices are desirable for an imam before he goes out to lead the people in the prayer for rain: (1) It is agreed upon by all four schools that the imam should command the people to repent, give charity and abandon all forms of injustice. (2) According to all schools except the Malikis, the imam should instruct the people to be reconciled with their enemies. (3) According to the Hanafis and the Shafiis, the imam should instruct the people to fast for three days before the prayer for rain; then, on the fourth, he is to lead them out by foot to the place where the prayer will be performed. For the views of the Malikis and the Hanbalis, see below.[267] (4) According to the Malikis, the Hanafis and the Shafiis, it is desirable for the imam to go out with the people wearing clothing indicative of an attitude of humble submission and self-abasement; the Hanbalis, however, hold that the people should go out for the prayer for rain wearing their finest attire, as they would for the holiday prayers. (5) According to the Hanafis and the Shafiis, it is desirable for the imam to instruct the people to bring out their young children, their elderly, and their animals and to keep infants away from their mothers in order to cause them to cry and scream, the idea being that in this way the people's cries are more likely to kindle God's compassion; for the views of the Malikis and the Hanbalis, see below.[268]

---

266. According to the Malikis, the time at which the prayer for rain may be performed, like the time for the holiday prayers, lasts from the moment when the sun is one spear's length above the horizon until noon; as for the Shafiis, they hold that the prayer for rain is valid at any time, including those times when other voluntary prayers are forbidden, since it is tied to a specific cause.

267. According to the Hanbalis, it is not recommended that the imam take the people out on the fourth day; rather, it is simply recommended that they go out on whatever day the imam specifies. As for the Malikis, they hold that it is recommended that the people go out during mid-morning on the fourth day unless their houses are far from the prayer site, in which case they are to go out at whatever time is necessary in order to arrive on time to pray with the imam.

268. According to the Malikis, the recommended practice is to bring out young boys who have reached the age of discernment and who are thus able to perform valid ritual prayer; as for other children, however, it is undesirable to bring them out, just as it is undesirable to bring out livestock.

* * *

In agreement with the Malikis, the Hanbalis hold that it is an emulation of the Sunnah for boys who have reached the age of discernment to come out for the prayer for rain; as for livestock and the elderly, it is permissible for them to come out.

The prayer performed during a solar eclipse

The prayer associated with the solar eclipse will be discussed under the following headings: (1) the ruling on this prayer, the evidence in support of it and the wisdom in its establishment; (2) how the prayer for the solar eclipse is to be performed, (3) the obligatory and Sunnah-based practices associated with this prayer; and (4) the ruling on the sermon associated with the prayer for the solar eclipse.

The ruling on the prayer for the solar eclipse, the evidence in its favor, and the wisdom in its establishment

The prayer for the solar eclipse is an emphatically enjoined Sunnah-based practice. It has its origins in the statement of the Prophet, "The sun and the moon are two of God's signs, and neither of them is eclipsed due to anyone's birth or death. If you see either of them in eclipse, perform ritual prayer and call upon God in supplication until the event passes."[269] It has been established based on a hadith narrated by both Muslim and al-Bukhārī that the Prophet performed prayers for both the solar and the lunar eclipses.

As for the wisdom to be found in this prayer, it lies in the fact that the sun is one of the greatest blessings that God Almighty has bestowed upon us, and on it creatures' very lives depend. Hence, a solar eclipse is an indication that the sun is subject to annihilation; in fact, it serves as a sign that the entire world is under the control of an all-powerful Deity who, at any moment, could cause it simply to pass out of existence. Thus, praying at this time is an expression of total humility and subjection to this powerful, eternal God. This is one of the virtues of Islam, which urges us to acknowledge God's perfect oneness and to abandon the worship of false deities, be they the sun, the moon or anything else.

How the prayer for the solar eclipse is to be performed

According to the Shafiis, the Hanbalis and the Malikis, the prayer performed for the solar eclipse consists of only two *rak'ahs*. If one completes these two *rak'ahs* before the eclipse is over, one is to utter supplications to God until it has passed. Moreover, each *rak'ah* of this prayer is to consist of two bows and two returns to a standing position rather than the usual one bow and one return to a standing position. For the Hanafis' view, see below.[270] As for those who differ with the Hanafis, they say that one may also validly perform the prayer for the solar eclipse without doing it in this manner. Hence, for example, if someone simply performs two *rak'ahs* as in the case of other voluntary prayers, this is acceptable. The point of disagree-

---

269. Narrated by both Muslim and al-Bukhārī.

270. The Hanafis, by contrast, hold that the prayer for the solar eclipse is not valid if each *rak'ah* contains two bows and two returns to a standing position; rather, they insist that each *rak'ah* should be restricted to a single bow and a single return to a standing position just as in other voluntary prayers. In addition, they hold that the prayer for the solar eclipse consists of a minimum of two *rak'ahs* and that one may perform four *rak'ahs* or more if one wishes, whereas the most preferable practice is to perform four *rak'ahs* with either one or two final greetings of peace.

ment, then, between the Hanafis and others is that whereas the Hanafis hold that each *rak'ah* of this prayer must consist of only one bow and one return to a standing position, others hold that it may be validly performed either way. As for those who hold that each *rak'ah* can include two bows and two returns to a standing position, they consider that the first bow and rising is the obligatory one, while the second is merely recommended.

Sunnah-based practices associated with the prayer for the solar eclipse

It is an emulation of the Sunnah to prolong the Qur'anic recitation in the prayer for the solar eclipse. Thus, in the first 'standing' of the first *rak'ah* one might recite Surah 2 in its entirety (or some comparable passage) following the *Fātiḥah*, while in the second one might recite Surah 3 following the *Fātiḥah*; in the second *rak'ah* one might follow the *Fātiḥah* with a passage comparable to Surah 4 during the first 'standing', and during the second 'standing' follow the *Fātiḥah* with a passage comparable to Surah 5. This approach is agreed upon by all the schools other than the Hanafis.[271]

It is an emulation of the Sunnah to prolong one's bows and prostrations in both *rak'ahs*, though the degree of such prolongation varies from one school to the next.[272]

---

271. According to the Hanafis, it is an emulation of the Sunnah to prolong the Qur'anic recitation in the first *rak'ah* by reciting something like Surah 2, and in the second *rak'ah* by reciting something comparable to Surah 3. However, if one shortens these two recitations and lengthens one's supplications, one has also emulated the Sunnah, since in the Hanafis' view, the essential requirement of the Sunnah in this regard is that one spend the entire time taken up by the eclipse in prayer and supplication. Thus, if one of these two components is reduced, the other should be lengthened in order to maintain an attitude of humble reverence and fear until the eclipse has passed.

272. According to the Hanafis, it is an emulation of the Sunnah to prolong one's bows and prostrations in both *rak'ahs* without any specified limit.

* * *

According to the Hanbalis, one is to prolong both bows in both *rak'ahs* without any specified limit. However, one is to utter words of praise to God in the first bow of the first *rak'ah* for as long as it would take to recite one hundred verses of the Qur'ān and in the second bow of the first *rak'ah*, as long as it would take to recite seventy verses. The same ruling applies to the second *rak'ah* except that it should be kept shorter than the first *rak'ah*. As for prostrations, they should be prolonged in both *rak'ahs* to the degree consistent with prevailing custom.

* * *

According to the Shafiis, one should prolong the first bow of the first *rak'ah* for as long as it would take to recite one hundred verses of Surah 2, and the second bow for as long as it would take to recite eighty verses of the same surah. One should prolong the first bow of the second *rak'ah* for as long as it would take to recite seventy verses of the same surah, and the second bow for as long as it would take to recite fifty verses of this surah. As for prostrations, one should hold the first pros-

Moreover, a *rak'ah* will not count if one joins the imam on the second bow or the second rise to a standing position of the *rak'ah* concerned.[273]

In the prayer for the solar eclipse, the preferences of those being led in prayer are not to be taken into consideration; hence, it is legitimate to prolong the various postures and recitations in this prayer even if those being led in prayer would prefer not to do so. This ruling is agreed upon by the Shafiis, the Hanafis and the Hanbalis, whereas according to the Malikis, it is only legitimate to prolong the various components of this prayer if it causes no hardship to those being led in prayer, and if there is no reason to fear that the time period allowed for this prayer (namely, from the time when the morning sun is one spear's length above the horizon until noon) will run out.

There is no *adhān* or *iqāmah* for this prayer; rather, it is simply recommended that people be invited to take part in it with the words, *al-ṣalātu jāmi'ah*, i.e., "Prayer is gathering [the people]." According to the Shafiis, the Hanafis and the Malikis, it is recommended that Qur'anic recitation in this prayer be done silently, although the Hanbalis hold that it should be done aloud. It is also recommended that the prayer for the solar eclipse be performed in community. According to the Shafiis, the Malikis and the Hanbalis, it is not required that the imam who leads it be the same one who leads the Friday congregational prayer or be authorized to perform this function by the political powers of the day;[274] however, the Hanafis hold a different view.[275]

---

tration of each *rak'ah* for as long as one held the first bow, and hold the second prostration of each *rak'ah* for as long as one held the second bow.

* * *

According to the Malikis, one is to hold each bow for about as long as it took to recite the surah of the Qur'ān which was recited immediately prior to it. Hence, one holds the first bow for approximately as long as it took to recite Surah 2, the second bow for as long as it took to recite Surah 3 and so on. As for the prostration in each *rak'ah*, it is recommended that one hold it as long as the bow which preceded it, with the second prostration somewhat shorter than the first. It is also recommended that one utter the phrase *subḥān Allāh* while both bowing and prostrating.

273. All the schools but the Malikis agree on this ruling; as for the Malikis, they hold that it is the second bow and the second rise to a standing position which are the obligatory components of each *rak'ah*, whereas the first bow and the first rise to a standing position of each *rak'ah* are simply in emulation of the Sunnah, the consequence being that if someone joins the imam on the second bow or the second rise to an upright position within a given *rak'ah*, he or she will have realized the entire *rak'ah*.

274. Literally, the sultan [t.n.].

275. According to the Hanafis, the person to lead the prayer for the solar eclipse must be the imam who leads the Friday congregational prayer; if he is not available, the ruler of the land must authorize someone to fulfill this function, and if this is also not possible, the prayer should be performed individually in people's homes.

According to the Shafiis, the Hanbalis and the Hanafis, it is recommended that this prayer be performed in the mosque; the Malikis, however, rule that this practice is only recommended if the prayer is being performed communally, whereas if it is being performed individually, one may perform it wherever he or she chooses.

When the prayer for the solar eclipse is to be performed

The time when the prayer for the solar eclipse is to be performed begins with the commencement of the eclipse and ends when the sun has fully reappeared, provided that the eclipse does not occur during a time when it is forbidden to perform voluntary prayers. If this happens, one should restrict oneself simply to prayers of supplication and not perform any ritual prayer according to the Hanafis and the Hanbalis; for the views of the Shafiis and the Malikis, see below.[276]

The sermon delivered at the prayer for the solar eclipse

[According to the Hanafis, the Hanbalis and the Malikis,] it is not permissible to deliver a sermon during the prayer for the solar eclipse; for the Shafiis' view, see below.[277] If the eclipse ends while the prayer is still being performed, it should be concluded normally, and if the sun sets while still in eclipse, there ceases to be any basis for the prayer.

---

276. According to the Shafiis, it is an emulation of the Sunnah to perform this prayer as soon as it is ascertained that a solar eclipse is taking place even if it is at a time when voluntary prayers would otherwise be forbidden, since this prayer is a response to a particular cause. As for the Malikis, they hold that the only time during which the prayer for the solar eclipse may be performed is that which extends from the moment when the morning sun is one spear's length above the horizon until noon.

277. According to the Shafiis, it is an emulation of the Sunnah to deliver two sermons following the prayer for the solar eclipse when it is being performed by men in community; in this respect, their ruling on this prayer is similar to that on the holiday prayers; moreover, the sermons are to be delivered even if the eclipse has come to an end. Unlike the holiday prayers, however, the utterances of *Allāhu akbar* are replaced with prayers for divine forgiveness, since this is more appropriate to the occasion. Of the conditions for validity which apply to the sermons delivered for the Friday congregational prayer, the only ones which likewise apply to the prayer for the solar eclipse are: (1) that people actually hear the sermons, (2) that the sermons be in the Arabic language, and (3) that the speaker be male.

* * *

According to the Malikis, if the eclipse comes to an end before a complete *rak'ah* has been performed with both its prostrations, the prayer should be concluded as if it were a regular voluntary prayer, without performing an additional bow and an additional return to a standing position in each *rak'ah*, and without prolonging one's Qur'anic recitations. However, if the eclipse ends after a complete *rak'ah* with both its prostrations has been performed, there are some who hold that the prayer should be concluded with the additional bow and rising, though without prolonging the Qur'anic recitation, while according to others, it is to be completed as if it were a regular voluntary prayer. Both these views are equally valid.

The prayer for the lunar eclipse and the prayer of fear

With the exception of specific details that vary from one school to another, the ruling on the prayer for a solar eclipse and the manner in which it is performed is the same as that which applies to the prayer for the solar eclipse.[278]

As for the prayer of fear, it is simply recommended. In other words, it is recommended that two *rak'ahs* be performed when one feels fearful on account of earthquakes, lightning bolts, extreme darkness, strong winds, plague, or the like. The reason for this is that such phenomena are signs by means of which God alarms His servants in order to move them to abandon disobedience and return to Him in repentance. Hence, when such events occur, we must return to God with the worship that serves as the basis for our happiness both in this life and the next.

As in the case of unspecified voluntary prayers, the prayer of fear is not to be prayed in a group and has no sermon connected with it, nor is it an emulation of the Sunnah to perform it in the mosque. Rather, it is considered preferable to perform this prayer in one's home. This ruling is agreed upon by the Malikis and the Hanafis; the Hanbalis rule that it is not recommended that one perform a ritual prayer in response to any of the aforementioned events with the exception of earthquakes if they continue, in which case one should perform two *rak'ahs* like those performed for the solar eclipse. As for the Shafiis, they make no mention of ritual prayer being recommended in response to any of the events mentioned here.

---

278. According to the Hanafis, the prayer for the lunar eclipse is the same as that for the solar eclipse except that the prayer for the lunar eclipse is merely recommended rather than based on the Sunnah. Moreover, it is not legitimate to perform the prayer for the lunar eclipse in community and it is not an emulation of the Sunnah to perform it in the mosque; rather, it is to be performed individually in people's homes.

* * *

According to the Shafiis, the prayer for the lunar eclipse is like that for the solar eclipse with two exceptions: (1) In the prayer for the lunar eclipse one is to perform Qur'anic recitations aloud, whereas in the prayer for the solar eclipse they are to be performed silently. (2) The prayer for the solar eclipse ceases to be relevant if the sun sets while still in eclipse, whereas even if the moon sets while still in eclipse, the prayer for the lunar eclipse may still be performed until sunrise. If someone misses either of these two prayers, they are not to be made up.

* * *

According to the Malikis, the prayer for the lunar eclipse is merely recommended based on the most widely recognized point of view, whereas the prayer for the solar eclipse is an emulation of the prophetic Sunnah, as we have seen. The prayer for the lunar eclipse is to be performed in the same way as other voluntary prayers, without prolongation of the Qur'anic recitations or the performance of an additional bow and return to a standing position in each *rak'ah*. It is recommended that one perform recitations aloud in the prayer for the lunar eclipse, while the time during which it may be performed lasts from the time when the eclipse begins until

Times at which prayer is forbidden

In our earlier discussion of the five daily obligatory prayers, it became clear that there are specific times during which such prayers are to be performed, and that if the worshiper performs such prayers during times when they are forbidden, he or she will be guilty of wrongdoing, while if he/she performs them during times when they are undesirable, he/she will have committed an undesirable act.

According to the Shafiis, the Malikis and the Hanbalis, an obligatory prayer will be valid if it is performed after its specified time period has begun; however, the Hanafis hold that there are three particular times during which obligatory prayers will not be counted.[279]

---

the time when the moon reappears. It is forbidden to perform this prayer during those times when voluntary prayers are forbidden, and one may fulfill the recommended practice by performing two *rak'ahs*. It is recommended that the prayer for the lunar eclipse be repeated until the moon either reappears or sets, or until dawn breaks. (In this respect, it differs from the prayer for the solar eclipse, which is not to be repeated unless the sun reappears and is eclipsed again.) Lastly, it is undesirable to perform the prayer for the lunar eclipse in the mosque or in a group.

* * *

According to the Hanbalis, the prayers for the solar and lunar eclipses are the same except that if the moon disappears by night while still in eclipse, the prayer for the lunar eclipse is still to be performed, whereas if the sun sets while still in eclipse, there is no more need for the prayer for the solar eclipse to be performed.

279. According to the Hanafis, there are three times at which obligatory prayers are not valid:

(1) From sunup until the sun begins to ascend through the sky. Hence, if someone begins to perform the dawn prayer before sunup and if the sun comes up while he is still praying, his prayer will be invalid unless he is performing the final *rak'ah* and has been seated long enough to utter the testimony. In this latter case, some Hanafis hold that the person's prayer will be invalid, while others hold that it will remain valid.

(2) Between the time when the sun reaches its zenith and the time when it begins to descend.

(3) The period between the time when the sun takes on a reddish hue and the time when it sets. This ruling does not apply to the mid-afternoon prayer of the same day; rather, this prayer may be validly performed after the sun has taken on a reddish hue prior to setting, although it is considered undesirable to the point of being forbidden. The ruling which applies to obligatory prayers in this regard applies likewise to the prostration of recitation (*sajdat al-tilāwah*). However, the prostration of recitation will only be invalid if it became necessary before such a time of proscription has commenced—as, for example, when someone hears a verse of the Qur'ān that calls for a prostration of recitation before sunrise and is still prostrating as the sun rises. If, on the other hand, someone hears such a verse of the Qur'ān after a time of proscription has already commenced and prostrates in response, the prostration will be valid. Thus, if someone hears a verse which calls for a prostra-

As for the times during which it is forbidden to perform voluntary prayers, there is some disagreement concerning them among the four schools.[280]

---

tion of recitation as the sun is rising, when the sun is at its zenith, or when the sun has taken on a reddish hue prior to setting and if the person prostrates in response, his/her prostration will be valid. However, it is preferable to postpone such a prostration until the time when ritual prayer would be valid.

Lastly, the ruling which applies to the prostration of recitation applies likewise to the funeral prayer; hence, if the body of the deceased is brought before one of the times of proscription begins and if it has not yet been prayed over, it is not valid to pray over it once this time period has begun. If, however, the body is brought after such a time period has already begun, it may validly be prayed over; in fact, it is considered undesirable to delay the funeral prayer until a time during which ritual prayer would be valid.

280. According to the Hanafis, it is undesirable to the point of being forbidden to perform voluntary prayers during the following times: (1) Between dawn and the dawn prayer; an exception is made here, however, for the two *rak'ahs* which are prayed before the dawn prayer in emulation of the Sunnah. (2) Between the dawn prayer and the time when the sun comes up; during this period, not even the two-*rak'ah* pre-dawn Sunnah may be performed (e.g., if it was missed, since if one misses these two *rak'ahs*, the requirement that one perform them is dropped and they may not be made up, as mentioned previously). (3) Between the mid-afternoon prayer and sundown. (4) After the speaker has come out to deliver a sermon for a communal prayer, be it for the Friday congregational prayer, one of the holiday prayers, or a prayer on the occasion of the greater pilgrimage, a marriage, a solar eclipse or a prayer for rain. (5) When the muezzin is uttering the *iqāmah* for one of the obligatory prayers; this does not apply, however, to the two-*rak'ah* pre-dawn Sunnah-based prayer provided that there is no reason to fear that by performing it, one will miss the opportunity to perform the dawn prayer in community. (6) Before and after the holiday prayer. (7) Between the noon and mid-afternoon prayers if they are being combined at 'Arafah and performed ahead of time, even if it happens to be the Sunnah-based *rak'ahs* associated with the noon prayer. (8) Between the sundown and evening prayers when they are being combined at Muzdalifah and performed late, even if the voluntary prayer concerned is the Sunnah-based *rak'ahs* associated with the sundown prayer. (9) When there is very little time left in the designated period for a given obligatory prayer. If a voluntary prayer is performed during any of these time periods, it will be valid, but undesirable to the point of being forbidden; hence, one should discontinue such a prayer and postpone it until a time when such prayers are allowed.

* * *

According to the Hanbalis, voluntary prayers are both invalid and forbidden, even if they are performed due to a particular cause, at the following three times:

(1) From the break of dawn to the time when the sun is one spear's length above the horizon. An exception to this ruling is made, however, for the two-*rak'ah*

Sunnah-based prayer performed before the dawn prayer. These two *rak'ahs* are valid at this time if they are performed before the dawn prayer; after this, however, they are both invalid and disallowed.

(2) Between the mid-afternoon prayer, even if it has been combined with the noon prayer and performed early, and sunset. An exception to this ruling is the Sunnah-based *rak'ahs* connected with the noon prayer, which may be performed following the mid-afternoon prayer when it is combined with the noon prayer.

(3) Between the time when the sun reaches its zenith and the time when it begins to descend.

An exception to all these times of proscription is made for the following voluntary prayers: (a) the two *rak'ahs* performed on the occasion of circumambulating the Ka'bah, which are valid at all the aforementioned times despite their being voluntary, (b) prayers which are being repeated, provided that the communal prayer commenced when the person concerned was in the mosque, since it is a valid practice to repeat a prayer one has prayed in community even if it is counted as voluntary, (c) the two *rak'ahs* performed as a mosque greeting if the person concerned enters the mosque while the imam is delivering a sermon and the sun happens to be at its zenith.

If one of these times of proscription begins while someone is performing a voluntary prayer, one is forbidden to complete the prayer even if up to this point it was valid. As for the funeral prayer, it is forbidden and invalid at the time when the sun is at its zenith, from the time the sun begins to set until it has set completely, and from the time it begins to rise until it has fully risen (unless there is a valid excuse for performing the funeral prayer at one of these times).

* * *

According to the Shafiis, all voluntary prayers not associated with a particular cause are undesirable to the point of being forbidden and deemed invalid if they are performed at any of the following five times:

(1) Between the performance of the dawn prayer on time and the sun's ascending through the sky.

(2) From the time the sun rises until the time when it is one spear's length above the horizon.

(3) After performing the mid-afternoon prayer on time, even if it has been combined with the noon prayer.

(4) From the time the sun takes on a yellowish hue and until it sets.

(5) From the time the sun reaches its zenith and until it begins its afternoon descent.

With regard to prayers performed in response to a prior cause, such as the mosque greeting, the two Sunnah-based *rak'ahs* performed immediately after one's ritual ablutions, and the two *rak'ahs* performed on the occasion of circumambulating the Ka'bah, they may be prayed validly and without any undesirability attached to them during the aforementioned times due to the temporal priority of their causes, namely, entering the mosque, performing one's ablutions, and circumambulation of the Ka'bah respectively. The same applies to prayers which are performed in response to a simultaneous cause, such as the prayer for rain and the prayer for the solar eclipse, both of which remain valid and fully acceptable [even during the aforementioned times] on account of their simultaneous causes, namely, drought and the absence of the sun respectively. However, voluntary prayers which are performed in response to a subsequent cause, such as the prayer for divine guidance (*ṣalāt al-istikhārah*) and the prayer of repentance, they lack validity due to the delayed nature of their causes. Lastly, an exception to this ruling is made for [voluntary] prayers performed in Mecca, which are valid, albeit a departure from the ideal, when performed during the times mentioned above. In connection with the time when the sun is at its zenith, an exception is made for Fridays, since on this day it is not forbidden to pray when the sun is at its zenith. It is true, of course, that it is categorically forbidden to perform any prayer but the mosque greeting once the speaker has ascended the pulpit on Friday; as for the mosque greeting in this situation, it is an emulation of the Sunnah provided that it does not exceed two *rak'ahs*. (If someone rises for a third *rak'ah* in the mosque greeting in this situation, his/her prayer will be invalidated.)

As for sermons other than the Friday sermon, it is undesirable to perform prayer during them, though not to the point of being forbidden; it is likewise undesirable to perform voluntary prayers during the *iqāmah* for obligatory prayers other than the Friday congregational prayer. As for the Friday congregational prayer, it is forbidden to perform voluntary prayers during its *iqāmah* if doing so would involve missing the performance of its second bow with the imam; if there is a danger of missing this bow on account of a voluntary prayer being performed, the latter should be terminated. If someone is still performing a voluntary prayer when the *iqāmah* is uttered, he/she should pray the prayer to the end provided that there is no concern that in doing so, he will miss the chance to perform the [Friday] prayer in community with the imam's concluding greeting of peace; otherwise, it is recommended that one cut off the voluntary prayer if one does not have good reason to believe that he will be able to perform the same prayer with another group.

* * *

According to the Malikis, it is forbidden to perform voluntary prayers (which are defined as all prayers other than the five obligatory prayers each day) such as the funeral prayer when there is no reason to fear that the body might undergo change if it is not performed immediately, the prostration of recitation and the prostration of forgetfulness, during the following seven periods of time: (1) between the beginning and completion of sunrise, (2) between the beginning and completion of sunset, (3) during the Friday sermon and, based on the most well-attested view, during the holiday sermons as well, (4) when the imam is coming out to deliver the sermon, (5) when very little remains of either the 'elective' or the 'imperative' phase for obligatory prayers, (6) when one remembers a prayer that one missed and needs to make up (with the exception of the *witr* due to its 'lightness') based on the words of the Prophet, "If someone forgets a prayer, let him/her perform it as soon as he/she remembers it, as this is the only atonement for it [i.e., forgetting]," and (7) when the regular imam is uttering the *iqāmah* for prayer, based on the words of the Prophet, "Once the commencement of prayer [i.e., the *iqāmah*] is announced, none but obligatory prayers are to be performed."

It is undesirable to perform voluntary prayers and other forms of voluntary worship such as those mentioned above during the following times:

(1) From the break of dawn until immediately before the sun rises. Exceptions to this include the following: (a) the Sunnah-based two *rak'ahs* preceding the dawn prayer, since these are undesirable following the dawn prayer, but not before it, and (b) the *witr*, which a person obliges himself/herself to perform by undertaking night prayers. Thus, it is not undesirable to perform the *witr* after the break of dawn; in fact, it is recommended given the following conditions:

*That one perform it before both the dawn prayer and the Sunnah-based two *rak'ahs* which precede it, since once the dawn prayer has been performed, it is too late to make up the *witr*. If, while praying the two pre-dawn *rak'ahs*, someone remembers that he/she did not perform the *witr*, he/she should interrupt them and go back to make up the *witr* first. If, after finishing the two pre-dawn *rak'ahs*, someone remembers not performing the *witr*, he/she should make up the *witr*, then repeat the two pre-dawn *rak'ahs* since, as has been stated, the opportunity to perform the *witr* only passes once the dawn prayer has been performed.

* That one perform the *witr* before the appearance of full daylight, since it is undesirable to perform it after this.

* That one be accustomed to praying the *witr*, since if one has not been in the habit of performing voluntary night prayers, it is undesirable to perform voluntary prayers after the break of dawn.

* That the reason for delaying the *witr* be that the person fell asleep toward the end of the night, since if the delay was due simply to laziness, it is undesirable to perform it after dawn.

* That there be no reason to fear that by praying the *witr* at this time, one will miss the opportunity to perform the dawn prayer in community. If there is reason for such a concern, it is undesirable to perform the *witr* at this time if one is outside the mosque, and it is forbidden entirely if one is in the mosque and the communal prayer is being led by the regular imam.

Another exception to the ruling on the undesirability of the *witr* at the time mentioned here is the *shaf'* and *witr* prayers if one has not performed them before the break of dawn. If one has not delayed the dawn prayer so long that there is only enough time left before sunrise to perform the dawn prayer and nothing else, one is required to perform both the *shaf'* and the *witr* as well; however, if one has delayed the dawn prayer until so late that no time remains for any other prayers, one should omit the *shaf'* and the *witr* and perform the dawn prayer alone. Another exception is made for the funeral prayer and for the prostration of recitation if they are performed before full daylight even if it is after the dawn prayer; once there is full daylight, however, it is undesirable to perform either the funeral prayer or the prostration of recitation unless, in the case of the funeral prayer, it is feared that if it is delayed, some change will take place in the corpse.

(2) From the time the sun has fully risen until it is one spear's length (or twelve medium-sized hand spans) above the horizon.

(3) From the time when the mid-afternoon prayer is performed until immediately before sundown. An exception in this regard is made for the funeral prayer and for the prostration of recitation, which may be performed without any undesirability attached to them before the sun takes on a yellowish hue; after this time,

Making up for a voluntary prayer if its time has passed or if it lost its validity after it was begun

No voluntary prayers that have been missed are to be made up with the exception of the two Sunnah-based *rak'ahs* performed before the dawn prayer. As we have seen, these two *rak'ahs* may be made up once the morning sun has risen one spear's length above the horizon according to the Hanafis and the Malikis. For the views of the Shafiis and the Hanbalis, see below.[281] The Shafiis and the Hanbalis hold that if someone begins a voluntary prayer which is then invalidated while in progress, there is no obligation to make it up since there was no obligation to perform it in the first place; for the views of the Malikis and the Hanafis, see below.[282]

---

however, they are undesirable unless, in the case of the funeral prayer, it is feared that if the prayer is delayed, some change will take place in the corpse.

(4) Between sundown and the performance of the sundown prayer.

(5) Before or after the holiday prayer at the site where the holiday prayer will be (or was) performed, in accordance with the details presented earlier in this connection.

Voluntary prayers are forbidden at all of the aforementioned times (including both the times when such prayers are forbidden and the times when they are merely undesirable) if they are deliberately intended as such. Hence, if someone consciously intends to perform a voluntary prayer at one of these times, it is either undesirable or entirely forbidden even if it is being performed in fulfillment of a vow or as a way of making up for a voluntary prayer which was invalidated while in progress. However, if the prayer was not consciously intended to be voluntary—as, for example, if someone begins to perform an obligatory prayer during one of the times when voluntary prayer is forbidden, and if, after performing a complete *rak'ah* of this prayer, he/she remembers a prayer that he/she needs to make up—it is recommended that he/she add another *rak'ah* to the prayer and make it into a voluntary prayer, which is not considered undesirable. If someone utters *takbīrat al-iḥrām* for a voluntary prayer during a time when such prayers are forbidden, he/she must cut the prayer off. As for someone who comes into the mosque while the imam is delivering a sermon and, out of ignorance or forgetfulness, begins to perform a voluntary prayer, he/she should not cut the prayer off. Similarly, if the speaker comes out to the pulpit after the person has begun a voluntary prayer, he/she should perform the prayer to completion even if, by the time the speaker comes out, he or she has performed less than a single *rak'ah* of the prayer in question. As for voluntary prayers commenced during the times when such prayers are undesirable, it is recommended that they be cut off; moreover, whether voluntary prayers are forbidden or merely undesirable during the time period concerned, they may not be made up later.

281. According to the Shafiis, it is recommended that one make up voluntary prayers associated with a particular time, such as those which are connected with the five daily prayers as well as the two holiday prayers and the mid-morning prayer. As for voluntary prayers not associated with any particular time, they are not to be

Whether voluntary prayers are to be performed at home or in a mosque

It is considered better to perform voluntary prayers at home based on the saying of the Prophet, "O people, pray in your homes, since apart from the obligatory prayers, the best prayer a person can perform is one that he or she performs at home."[283] However, exceptions to this ruling are made for those voluntary prayers that were established as communal prayers, such as the *tarāwīḥ*, which are better performed in a mosque as we saw in detail in our earlier discussion of these prayers.

Voluntary prayers performed while riding an animal

It is permissible to perform voluntary prayers while riding an animal without any particular justification for doing so; however, details on this ruling differ from one school to another.[284]

---

made up regardless of whether they have a specific cause, such as the prayer for the solar eclipse, or are unspecified voluntary prayers.

* * *

According to the Hanbalis, it is not recommended that one make up any voluntary prayers other than the Sunnah-based *rak'ahs* associated with the five obligatory prayers and the *witr*.

282. According to the Hanafis, if someone begins performing a voluntary prayer after which it is invalidated, he or she must make it up. Hence, if someone consciously intends to perform two *rak'ahs* or does not specify the number of *rak'ahs* which he/she intends to pray, after which the prayer is invalidated, he or she must make up two *rak'ahs*; the same applies if he/she intended originally to perform four *rak'ahs*. If someone begins to perform a voluntary prayer which he or she believes to be required of him or her, and if it becomes apparent while praying that this prayer is not, in fact, required of the person concerned, there is no need to make it up.

* * *

According to the Malikis, one is obliged to make up a voluntary prayer that was invalidated while in progress. Hence, if someone consciously intends to perform two *rak'ahs* or does not specify the number of *rak'ahs* intended, and if the prayer is invalidated while in progress, one must make up two *rak'ahs*. If one consciously intends to perform four *rak'ahs* which are then invalidated, and if the prayer is invalidated before the worshiper has lifted his head from the bow of the third *rak'ah* and maintained this position for a moment or two, he or she must make up two *rak'ahs*; however, if the prayer is invalidated after this point, he/she must make up four *rak'ahs*.

283. Narrated by al-Bukhārī and Muslim.

284. According to the Shafiis, it is permissible to perform a voluntary prayer while riding an animal provided that one faces in the direction in which one is traveling; it is not permissible to face in any other direction unless it is that of the *qiblah*. If the worshiper turns knowingly and deliberately in some direction other than that of the *qiblah*, his or her prayer will be invalidated. Performing a voluntary

prayer while riding an animal is only permitted if one is on a journey, though it need not be a journey which is long enough to justify the shortening of one's prayers.

When performing a voluntary prayer while riding an animal, one is to perform it as a complete prayer, including bowing and prostration, unless this poses undue hardship, in which case one may simply gesture in place of bows and prostrations in such a way that one leans forward farther for the prostration than one does for the bow if this poses no difficulty; otherwise, one is to do whatever he/she is able. It is also necessary to face the *qiblah* if this does not cause undue hardship; if facing the *qiblah* during the entire prayer poses undue hardship, the worshiper must face it when opening the prayer with *takbīrat al-iḥrām*. If this likewise causes difficulty, the requirement that one face the *qiblah* is dropped given six conditions: (1) That one's journey be a permissible one. (2) That the traveler be intending to go to a place where he/she will not hear the call to the Friday congregational prayer. (3) That the journey be for a legitimate purpose, such as business, trade, etc. (4) That the journey last until one has finished performing the prayer that one began; if one cuts off his trip while still praying, it becomes obligatory for him/her to face the *qiblah*. (5) That one keep moving on the animal; hence, if the worshiper dismounts or stops to rest during the prayer, he/she is obliged to face the *qiblah* for as long as he/she is stationary. (6) That one not engage in excessive movement unrelated to the prayer—such as running, jogging, etc., unnecessarily—without a legitimate excuse; however, if there is an actual need for such movement during the prayer, it will do no harm.

When performing a voluntary prayer while riding an animal, the place where one is sitting on the animal must be ritually pure. If the animal urinates, if its mouth bleeds, or if it steps into a moist substance which is ritually impure and if the animal's rein is in one's hand, the prayer is invalidated; however, if the worshiper does not have the rein in either hand, the prayer remains valid. If the impurity into which the animal steps is dry and if it does not cling to its hooves, the prayer will likewise remain valid. However, if the worshiper causes his mount to step into impurity, his/her prayer will be invalidated regardless of the considerations just mentioned. It is permissible for a traveler to perform voluntary prayers while walking; if he is not walking in mud, he must complete both the bows and the prostrations and remain facing the *qiblah* as he does so; he must also face the *qiblah* during *takbīrat al-iḥrām* and when he is seated between the two prostrations. Such a person should only walk during the parts of the prayer which involve standing up, returning to a standing position after a bow, and uttering the testimony and the final greeting of peace. If the worshiper is walking through something like snow, mud or water, he/she may simply engage in gestures symbolizing bows and prostrations; however, when doing so he must be facing the *qiblah*. If such a person deliberately steps into an impure substance, his prayer will be invalidated regardless of the considerations just mentioned; if someone steps accidentally into some ritual impurity and if the impurity is dry and does not cling to him, his prayer will remain valid; otherwise, however, it will be invalidated in this case as well.

* * *

According to the Malikis, someone who is on a journey in which it is permissible to shorten one's prayers may perform voluntary prayers, including even the *witr*, while riding an animal provided that he is riding it in the accustomed manner. He may do so once he has covered a distance sufficient to justify his shortening the daily obligatory prayers. If the traveler is riding in a sedan chair, a mule-born litter or something else which would make it easier to perform bows and prostrations, he should pray with bows and prostrations from a standing position or, if he wishes simply to gesture in place of bowing and prostrating, he may remain seated. In this situation, facing in the direction in which one is traveling takes the place of facing the *qiblah*. If the traveler is riding a she-ass or some similar mount, he should pray using bows and by gesturing in the place of the prostrations, provided that the gesturing is toward the ground and not toward the saddle, and provided that he move his turban back off his forehead. It is not necessary that the ground in the direction of which one gestures be ritually pure, nor that one be facing the *qiblah*; rather, it is sufficient for the person to face in the direction in which he is traveling. However, if he deviates from this direction deliberately and unnecessarily, his prayer will be invalidated unless the deviation is toward the *qiblah*, which is the ideal direction in any case. It is recommended that such a traveler begin his prayer facing the *qiblah*, although it is not obligatory even if it would be easy to do so. As for someone who is walking or on a journey on which it is not allowed to shorten one's obligatory prayers—either because the journey is not long enough or because it has been undertaken for an illegitimate reason—as well as someone who is riding his mount in an unaccustomed manner (e.g., by riding it backwards), his prayer will not be valid unless he faces the *qiblah* and engages in complete bows and prostrations. It is permissible for someone performing a voluntary prayer while riding a mount to do whatever is a necessary part of riding, such as striking the animal with a whip, moving his feet, grasping the rein with his hand, etc.; however, he is not to speak or to turn in either direction. If someone begins to pray while mounted, then comes to a halt, and if he makes it his intention to stay at the site such that the rulings pertaining to travelers cease to apply to him, he should dismount and complete the prayer on the ground with the normal bows and prostrations; otherwise, he should shorten his recitations and complete his prayer while mounted.

As for the performance of an obligatory prayer while riding a mount, even if it is a voluntary prayer being performed in fulfillment of a vow, it is not valid unless it is performed inside a camel litter or something similar; moreover, one must be facing the *qiblah* and perform full bows and prostrations from a standing position. As for prayers performed while riding a she-ass or a similar mount, they are not valid unless they are performed under such conditions out of necessity.

* * *

According to the Hanafis, it is recommended that one pray while riding a mount facing whatever direction the animal is moving in. If the person praying unnecessarily faces in a direction other than that in which his mount is moving, his prayer will be invalid. It is not necessary, in fact, that the person concerned be on a journey; rather, even someone settled in a particular location may perform voluntary prayers whenever he traverses a distance away from the city which would be sufficient for an actual traveler to be permitted to pray in this fashion. When praying while riding a mount, one must gesture in place of actual bowing and prostrating; moreover, if someone prostrates on something which he has placed [on the mount's back] or on the saddle, his prostration will be considered a gesture if it is lower than his bow. It is not necessary that one face the *qiblah* while beginning such a prayer since, given that it is permissible to perform such prayer while facing away from the Ka'bah, it follows that it is permissible to commence such prayer while facing away from the Ka'bah as well; at the same time, of course, it is desirable to open such prayer while facing the Ka'bah if this causes no hardship. It is permissible for someone praying while riding a mount to urge his animal on by means of movement which is not excessive. Similarly, it is permissible to begin one's prayer while mounted, then dismount without excessive movement and complete one's prayer on the ground. However, if one begins praying on the ground, it is not permissible to complete the prayer while mounted. If someone begins praying while outside the city and enters the city before completing the prayer, he should finish it while still mounted. As for obligatory prayers, those which are classified as a 'duty', and the two Sunnah-based *rak'ahs* performed before the dawn prayer, they are not permissible while one is mounted unless there is a clear need to perform them under such conditions—for example, if someone fears that harm would come to his person, his mount or his clothing from a thief, a beast of prey, etc. were he to dismount. Lastly, a prayer performed while one is mounted remains valid even if the mount has a large amount of impurity on it and even if it happens to be on the saddle, the stirrups, etc. As for someone who is walking, he is not permitted to perform voluntary prayers unless he comes to a halt and performs the prayer with full bows and prostrations.

* * *

According to the Hanbalis, it is permissible for someone who is traveling on a permissible journey to a specific place, whether the journey is long enough to merit the shortening of obligatory prayers or not, to perform voluntary prayers while riding a mount, or on the ground if he or she is walking. Someone who is performing a voluntary prayer while riding a mount must bow, prostrate and face the *qiblah* throughout the entire prayer if this can be done without undue hardship. However, if any of this does cause hardship, it is not required. For example, if it is too difficult to face the *qiblah*, he may face in the direction in which he is traveling; if it is too difficult either to bow or to prostrate, one may simply gesture for one or both of these. The gesture which serves as one's prostration must be lower than that which serves as one's bow so long as this poses no hardship. As for someone who is walking, he must open his prayer while facing the *qiblah* and bow and prostrate on the ground toward the *qiblah* as well, performing the other parts of the prayer while walking and facing in the direction in which he is traveling. In the case of someone who is performing a voluntary prayer while mounted and while facing in the direction in which he is traveling, the Hanbalis rule that if the animal shifts direction, taking the traveler with it, or the traveler faces in a direction other than that in which the animal is walking, then if the shift is toward the *qiblah*, his prayer will remain valid. If the shift is in some other direction, the prayer will remain valid if there was a valid excuse for the shift; otherwise, it will be invalidated. Similarly, the prayer will be invalidated if the shift occurred for a valid reason but lasted what would be considered a long time by commonly accepted standards.

The Friday congregational prayer

The Friday congregational prayer will be discussed under the following headings: (1) the ruling on this prayer and the evidence supporting it, (2) the time for the Friday congregational prayer, (3) when one is to set out for the Friday prayer, (4) conditions associated with the Friday prayer, (5) an explanation of some of these conditions, namely: (a) the ruling on women's attending the Friday prayer, (b) the ruling on the existence of a variety of mosques in which the Friday worship is held in a single town, (c) the quorum for the Friday prayer, (d) the Friday sermon (its pillars, the conditions and Sunnah-based practices associated with it, practices which are undesirable in connection with the Friday sermon, speaking during the sermon and when the orator comes out of his private chamber and sits down on the pulpit, and the practice of reciting from the Qur'ān for 'protection' in the presence of the orator), (6) an explanation of what one is not permitted to do on Friday in the mosque or elsewhere, such as passing over people's necks in the mosque and traveling on Friday, (7) whether someone who missed the Friday prayer is permitted to perform the noon prayer before the imam has finished performing the Friday prayer, (8) whether it is permissible for someone who missed the Friday prayer to perform the noon prayer in community, (9) the ruling on someone who performed part of the Friday prayer with the imam, and (10) recommended practices associated with the Friday congregational prayer.

The ruling on the Friday prayer and the evidence in its support

The Friday prayer is obligatory for everyone who fulfills the conditions to be presented below. Moreover, the Friday prayer consists of two *rak'ahs* based on the hadith narrated on the authority of 'Umar, may God be pleased with him, who said, "The Friday prayer consists of two *rak'ahs* in their complete form (i.e., without their being shortened), as your Prophet declared." This hadith was narrated by Aḥmad, al-Nasā'ī, and Ibn Mājah with a good chain of transmission.

The Friday prayer is an individual obligation for every Muslim who is capable of performing it and who fulfills the requirements for being held accountable for the performance of Islamic forms of worship as well as the conditions for being accountable for this particular prayer. The Friday prayer is not a substitute for the noon prayer; however, if someone misses the Friday prayer, he must perform the noon prayer as four *rak'ahs*.

It is necessary when performing voluntary prayers in such a situation for everything under the rider to be ritually pure, including the pack-saddle and the like; however, it is not necessary for the animal itself to be ritually pure. As for someone who travels but without heading for a particular destination, as well as someone who undertakes a journey which is either undesirable or forbidden, he is obliged when praying to face the *qiblah* as well as to fulfill other requirements of regular ritual prayer.

The obligatory nature of the Friday prayer has been established based on the Qur'ān, the Sunnah, and the consensus of the Muslim community. The evidence for its necessity in the Qur'ān may be seen in the words of God Almighty, "O you who have attained to faith! When the call to prayer is sounded on the day of congregation [i.e., on Friday], hasten to the remembrance of God, and leave all worldly commerce…" (62:9). Support in the Sunnah for the necessity of the Friday prayer is found in the Prophet's saying, "I am about to instruct a man to lead the congregation in prayer [in my stead], whereupon I will burn down the houses of men who stay back from the Friday prayer!"[285] Lastly, it is agreed upon unanimously by the Muslim community that the Friday prayer is an individual obligation.

The time for the Friday congregational prayer and the evidence for this

The time for the Friday prayer is the same as that for the noon prayer, namely, from high noon until the length of each object's shadow becomes equal to the object's height, not including the length of the shadow cast at high noon, as was explained earlier in the section on the times for ritual prayer. The Friday prayer is thus not valid before this time, nor is it valid after it has ended according to the Hanafis and the Shafiis; for the views of the Hanbalis and the Malikis, see below.[286]

---

285. Narrated by Muslim.

286. The Hanbalis hold that the time for the Friday prayer begins when the sun has risen one spear's length in the morning sky, and ends when the length of each object's shadow is equal to the object's height, not including the length of the shadow cast at high noon. During the time preceding high noon, it is permissible to perform the noon prayer, whereas during the time following high noon, it is obligatory; moreover, performing it after high noon is preferable to performing it before high noon.

* * *

According to the Malikis, the time for the Friday prayer extends from high noon until sundown such that if someone performs this prayer to completion together with the Friday sermon before sundown, he will have fulfilled his obligation in this regard. If the person concerned knows that the time remaining before sundown is sufficient only to perform one *rak'ah* of the Friday prayer following the sermon, he should not commence it; rather, he should perform the regular noon prayer, and once he has begun the noon prayer, it will be valid.

For the various schools' rulings on a situation in which the time for the Friday congregational prayer runs out while it is still being performed, see below.[287]

The evidence in support of when the Friday prayer is to be performed is found in the hadith narrated by al-Bukhārī in his compilation of authentic hadiths on the authority of Anas, may God be pleased with him, who said, "The Prophet used to perform the Friday prayer when the sun had begun to decline from its zenith." In another hadith narrated by Muslim on the authority of Salamah Ibn al-Akwa', the latter stated, "We used to gather with the Messenger of God [for the Friday prayer] when the sun had reached its zenith, after which we would observe the shadow."

---

287. According to the Hanafis, the Friday prayer will be invalidated if the time runs out before it has been performed to completion, since the condition [that the prayer be performed during its designated time period] will no longer have been fulfilled. This ruling applies even if the time does not run out until the worshipers have been seated long enough at the end of the prayer to utter the testimony.

* * *

The Shafiis hold that if, when a group of worshipers commences the Friday prayer, there is sufficient time remaining for it to be performed to completion and if, in spite of this, they take so long to complete the prayer that the time runs out anyway, what they have prayed thus far will not be invalidated; rather, they are to complete it as a regular noon prayer, building on what they had performed of the original prayer without intending to perform the noon prayer, while the imam is to recite silently in what remains of the prayer. It is forbidden for such a group to cut off their Friday prayer and to begin the noon prayer from the beginning. If, on the other hand, they begin the Friday prayer when there is less than sufficient time to perform it to completion, thinking mistakenly that they have enough time to complete it and if the time runs out while they are still praying, their prayer will be invalidated without its turning into a regular noon prayer.

* * *

The Hanbalis hold that if a group of worshipers begins the Friday prayer toward the end of its designated time period and if, after this, the time runs out while they are still praying, they are simply to perform it to completion as the Friday prayer.

* * *

As for the Malikis, they hold that if the Friday prayer is begun based on the belief that it can be completed during its designated time period and if the sun then sets after one *rak'ah* with both of its prostrations has been performed, it is to be performed to completion as the Friday prayer; if the sun sets before this, it is to be performed to completion as a regular noon prayer.

When one must depart for the Friday prayer, and when selling becomes prohibited: the second *adhān*.

Those who are required to attend the Friday prayer are to set out for the mosque when they are summoned to the prayer by the *adhān* which is sounded in the presence of the orator [who delivers the Friday sermon]. It is at this time that selling becomes forbidden based on the words of God Almighty, "O you who have attained to faith! When the call to prayer is sounded on the day of congregation [i.e., on Friday], hasten to the remembrance of God, and leave all worldly commerce…" (62:9). God Almighty has issued the command to set out for the Friday prayer when one hears the call to prayer. Al-Bukhārī, Abū Dāwūd, al-Nasā'ī and al-Tirmidhī relate that during the days of the Prophet, this was the only *adhān* known; hence, when he ascended the pulpit, the muezzin would sound the call to prayer in his presence. 'Uthmān, may God be pleased with him, later added another call to prayer prior to this when the number of Muslims had increased. It is related on the authority of al-Sā'id Ibn Yazīd that "the call to prayer on Friday was first sounded when the imam had sat down on the pulpit during the days of the Prophet, Abū Bakr and 'Umar. Then during 'Uthmān's caliphate, when the number of Muslims had grown, he added the second call to prayer at al-Zawrā'." This new call to prayer was announced at al-Zawrā', a place in Medina between the Prophet's mosque and the marketplace – t.n.]. In another version of the same hadith it is stated that 'Uthmān added "the third call to prayer"; the reason it is called "the third" is that the *iqāmah* (that is, the announcement that prayer has commenced) may also be referred to as an *adhān*, or a call to prayer. There can be no doubt that the addition of this call to prayer was legitimate, since the aim in so doing was to inform others; in other words, when the number of Muslims had grown, it was necessary to inform them of when the time for prayer had begun, and our master 'Uthmān was among the leading Companions who were qualified to issue independent rulings on legal questions and were acquainted with the principles of the religion, and who passed these down on the authority of the Messenger of God.

The Shafiis, the Malikis and the Hanbalis agree that those who are held accountable for performing the Friday prayer are to set out for the mosque when they hear the call to prayer issued in the presence of the orator, since this, in their view, is the call to prayer which is referred to in the Qur'anic verse quoted above in this connection. However, the Hanafis hold that when those held accountable for performing the Friday prayer hear the call to prayer issued after high noon, it is then that they must set out for the prayer. The Hanafis base this opinion on the fact that the call to prayer known at the present time, which is issued from minarets and the like, is the signal which indicates that one must set out for the Friday prayer. After all, they say, this is a legitimate call to prayer, and the Qur'anic verse cited above is general in its import rather than being restricted in its reference to the call to prayer issued in the presence of the orator as the other three schools claim.

As for selling, the Hanafis and the Shafiis hold that it becomes forbidden at the time of the call to the Friday prayer, even if the transaction being completed is a valid one. However, by the "call to prayer", the Shafiis mean the one which is issued in the presence of the orator, whereas the Hanafis hold that selling is forbidden from the time of the call to prayer which is issued prior to this until the time when the Friday prayer is completed. For the views of the Malikis and the Hanbalis, see below.[288]

The foregoing applies to those who are held accountable for performing the Friday prayer. As for those who are not thus accountable, they are not required to set out for the Friday prayer, nor are they forbidden to engage in selling [once the call to prayer has been issued]. However, if one of the parties to the transaction is obliged to attend the Friday prayer while the other is not, they are both forbidden to complete the transaction; the reason for this is that in such a case, the person not accountable for performing the Friday prayer will have helped the other in committing an act of disobedience.

Based on the foregoing, it will be clear that one is not required to make one's way [to the mosque], nor is selling prohibited, before the aforementioned call to prayer (bearing in mind the difference of opinion noted above concerning exactly which "call to prayer" is referred to). Nevertheless, if someone's home is far from the mosque, he must set out early enough to ensure that he will be able to perform the prayer required of him.

---

288. The Malikis hold that if a sale takes place at the time of the aforementioned call to prayer, it will be invalidated unless the substance of the item being sold undergoes some change, as, for example, when an animal is slaughtered, when some of the animal is eaten, etc., or unless its market changes, as when, for example, the item's price goes down or up. Such events cause the sale not to be invalidated (a point which will be discussed in the second volume of this work). Hence, if any event of this nature takes place, the transaction may proceed; moreover, what must be paid is the value of the item sold on the day when it is collected, not the price specified in the contract.

* * *

As for the Hanbalis, they hold that if a sale is transacted at this time, it will not go into effect immediately.

The conditions associated with the Friday congregational prayer and the definition of 'city' (*miṣr*) and 'village' (*qaryah*)

The conditions associated with the Friday prayer are the same as those associated with the regular noon prayer as well as all other ritual prayers. However, the Friday prayer has additional conditions associated with it as well and which we shall list below in connection with each of the four schools.[289] Following this, we shall present those conditions which are agreed upon among the schools and those concerning which they differ.

---

289. The Hanafis divide the conditions for the Friday prayer which are additional to those associated with other ritual prayers into two types. The first type (conditions of necessity) consists of conditions which must be fulfilled in order for the prayer to be obligatory, while the second type (conditions of validity) consists of conditions which must be fulfilled in order for the prayer to be valid.

The Hanafis list the following six conditions of necessity for the Friday congregational prayer: (1) Maleness. The Friday congregational prayer is not required of females, although if a female attends the prayer and performs it, it will be valid and it will serve as a substitute for her regular noon prayer. (2) Freedom. The Friday prayer is not required of someone who is in bondage, although if a slave were to attend it and perform it, it would be valid. (3) Sound health. The Friday prayer is not required of someone who is ill and who would suffer harm as a result of going to attend it on foot. If someone is incapable of going to the mosque on foot, he will be exempted from the obligation to perform the Friday prayer even if he finds someone to carry him. As for someone who is blind and who is unable to go to attend the prayer by himself, Imam Abū Ḥanīfah holds that he is exempted from the obligation to attend the Friday prayer even if he finds someone willing to guide him to the mosque voluntarily or for a wage which he can afford to pay. The two companions [Abū Yūsuf al-Qāḍī and Muḥammad Ibn al-Ḥasan al-Shaybānī], by contrast, hold that if a blind person is able to go to the Friday prayer, even if he requires the assistance of a volunteer guide and/or even if he must pay a fare which he is able to afford, he is obliged to go. A blind person is free to adopt either of these two opinions; however, it is preferable that one adopt the view of the two companions, especially since all Hanafis agree that the Friday prayer is valid if performed by a blind person. (4) Residence in the location where the Friday prayer is held, in a place adjacent to it. If someone is in a place which is distant from the site where the Friday prayer is held, he is not obliged to perform it. As for what distance is deemed 'far', the Hanafis estimate it at one parasang, that is, three miles (where a mile is equal to 6,000 cubits), 5 kilometers and 40 meters, [or 3 miles]. This is the estimate chosen for use in the legal ruling issued on this question. Others, however, have estimated the distance at 400 cubits [187 meters, or 205 yards], a unit of distance termed a *ghalwah*. Based on the foregoing, then, it may be seen that the Friday prayer is not required of someone who is on a journey unless he intends to remain in a single location for at least fifteen days. (5) Full possession of one's mental faculties. Hence, the Friday prayer is not required of someone who is insane or in a condition comparable thereto. (6) Maturity. Hence, the Friday prayer is not required of a boy who has not reached puberty.

This said, the reader will perceive why full possession of one's mental faculties and maturity are listed as conditions of necessity for the Friday congregational prayer in addition to those listed in connection with regular ritual prayer. That is, in the Hanafis' well-known books, the conditions which they list for ritual prayer include only conditions of permissibility and conditions of validity. Even so, there can be no doubt that maturity is a condition of necessity for ritual prayer, as are ability and sound health, since ritual prayer is not required of someone who is incapable of performing it due to illness or some other cause. However, those who do not include maturity, ability and full possession of one's mental faculties among the conditions of necessity for the Friday prayer—based on the fact that these are already listed as conditions for ritual prayer in general—have good grounds for their point of view.

As for the conditions which must be met in order for the Friday prayer to be valid, the Hanafis list the following six:

One: Residence in a city (*miṣr*). Hence, the Friday prayer is not required of someone who is a resident of a village based on a saying attributed to 'Alī, may God be pleased with him, who said, "There shall be no Friday prayer, no 'days of meat drying', and no prayer for the Day of Fastbreaking or the Day of Sacrifice unless one is in a major city." (This hadith is narrated by Ibn Abī Shaybah in his *al-Muṣannaf* and attributed to 'Alī. It is also narrated by 'Abd al-Rāziq.) The difference between a village and a city is that in the case of a city, its largest mosque will not be large enough to accommodate those of its inhabitants who are accountable for attending the Friday prayer, even if they do not actually attend. This is the legal ruling which has been issued by most Hanafi scholars of jurisprudence. Given this ruling, the Friday prayer will be valid in all Egyptian towns that have mosques in which the Friday prayer is held, since there is no village whose largest mosque will accommodate all those of its inhabitants who are accountable for the Friday prayer. Supposing there were, in fact, a village so small that this condition did not apply to it, the Friday prayer would not be valid on the part of its inhabitants if the village were located one parasang [three miles] or more from the nearest town; otherwise, its inhabitants would be obliged to go to this other town in order to perform the Friday prayer.

However, the most widely accepted ruling among the Hanafis is that a 'city' is a population center which has a mayor and a magistrate capable of carrying out most of the Qur'anically prescribed criminal penalties, even if he does not, in fact, carry them out. Based on this latter ruling, the Friday prayer will not be valid in the mosques of a town to which this condition [i.e., this definition] does not apply. However, given that most Hanafi scholars adopt the first position, it is most prudent to adhere to this position in practice, especially in view of the fact that not all the [four] imams have stipulated this condition [i.e., the definition of 'city' mentioned above]. Moreover, those who abandon the Friday prayer based on the abovementioned definition of 'city' (which has gained popularity among some Hanafis) have not adopted the practice which best preserves the teachings of their religion, especially if their neglect of the Friday prayer causes ordinary believers to doubt [their religion] and to make light of the need to perform their religious obligations. Even so, those who hold to this definition of 'city' find support for their view in the aforementioned hadith narrated by Ibn Abī Shaybah on the authority of 'Alī, may God be pleased with him. In his book, *Naṣb al-Rāyah*, al-Zayla'ī reports that no statement to this effect has been passed down on the authority of the Prophet. However, even assuming that this hadith [attributed to 'Alī] is authentic, we may still ask: Whence comes the definition of 'city' as a population center which has a mayor and a magistrate capable of carrying out the Qur'anically prescribed criminal penalties? Hence, the truth is clear, and reliance upon this hadith is of no benefit whatsoever. Consequently, most researchers into Hanafi thought adopt the view that a 'city' is a population center whose largest mosque would not accommodate all those of its inhabitants who are accountable for the [Friday] prayer, whether or not they actually attend. As for the other imams [i.e., al-Shāfi'ī, Mālik and Aḥmad Ibn Ḥanbal], whose conditions will be presented below, they did not rely on this hadith passed down on the authority of 'Alī, may God bring him honor.

Two: Permission from the sultan or his proxy. Hence, if the imam appoints an orator, this orator may in his turn appoint someone else [as an orator], even if the imam appears not to have granted him permission to appoint someone else. However, some Hanafis hold that the imam must grant permission for someone else to be thus appointed.

Three: The commencement of the requisite time period. Specifically, the Friday payer will not be valid unless the time period for the noon prayer has commenced. As we have seen, the commencement of the time period for any ritual prayer is a condition for its validity as well as for its necessity, be it the Friday prayer or any other ritual prayer. However, the Hanafis have mentioned this as a condition for the validity of the Friday prayer as a concession. If the time period designated for the Friday prayer runs out before it has been performed to completion, it will be invalidated even if the time does not run out until after the worshipers have been seated at the end of the prayer for long enough to recite the testimony. As we have seen, the time period for the Friday prayer is the same as that for the noon prayer, namely, from high noon until the length of each object's shadow becomes equal to the object's height, not including the length of the shadow cast at high noon.

Four: The sermon, details concerning which will be presented below.

Five: Delivery of the sermon before the prayer.

Six: Communal performance of the prayer. The Friday prayer will not be valid if performed alone. In order for the Friday prayer to be considered communal, the Hanafis hold that it must be attended by three worshipers in addition to the imam even if they do not attend the sermon (as will be seen below in the discussion of the quorum for the Friday prayer).

Seven: Public access granted by the imam (the ruler). In other words, the Friday prayer will not be valid in a place to which some worshipers have been denied access. If, for example, the imam holds the Friday prayer in his home with his retinue and his servants, it will be valid, albeit with undesirability attached to it, but only if he opens its doors and allows people to come in. The same ruling applies to a fort or a citadel, although it does no harm to close a fort or a citadel for fear of an enemy; hence, the Friday prayer will still be valid in a fort or a citadel if other worshipers are still allowed to come in. The Friday prayer is also valid when performed in the open air provided that: (1) permission to do so has been granted by the imam, and (2) the place where the prayer is performed is no more than one parasang away from the city or is connected to the city in some way, such as the site which has been prepared for horse races or for burial of the dead, details concerning which will be presented below in the relevant section.

* * *

The Malikis divide the conditions associated with the Friday prayer into two types, namely, conditions of validity and conditions of necessity. Such conditions are the same as those associated with regular ritual prayer, with the following additions: (1) Maleness. The Friday prayer is not required of the woman; however, if she performs this prayer with the community, it will serve as a valid substitute on her behalf for the regular noon prayer. (2) Freedom. The Friday prayer is not required of a slave; however, if he attends and performs it, it will be valid. (These two conditions are agreed upon among all four schools.) (3) The absence of any condition that would exempt one from performing it. The requirement to perform the Friday prayer is thus waived for someone who, due to illness, would be harmed by attending the prayer, whether by riding to the mosque or being carried there. If such a person is capable of reaching the site of the Friday prayer, even if he must pay a fare that is not unduly costly for him, he is required to attend it. If the worshiper is an invalid, he is not required to attend the Friday prayer unless he finds someone who can carry them there and unless he would not be harmed by being thus transported. (4) Sight. The Friday prayer is not required of someone who is blind if it is excessively difficult for him to attend on his own or if he can find no guide. However, if he is able to walk there on his own, or if he finds a guide, he is required to attend. (5) That the person not be so frail and elderly that it would be difficult for him to attend. (6) That the weather not be excessively hot or cold or excessively rainy or muddy. (7) That the person [not] have reason to fear that if he attends the Friday prayer, he will be imprisoned or beaten unjustly by an oppressive ruler; however, if the person deserves to be imprisoned or beaten, such a fear will not exempt him from the obligation to attend the Friday prayer. (8) That the person [not] have reason to fear that if he attends the Friday prayer, his wealth, his family or his own person would be dangered. In order for this condition to apply, however, the wealth for which the person fears must be wealth the loss of which would cause him great harm. (9) That the person be residing in the town in which the Friday prayer is held, or in a village or tent which is [no more than] three and one-third miles away from such a town. This distance is to be calculated from the minaret located at the outermost edge of the town if there is some necessity which renders it permissible for the town to have several different mosques; however, if the presence of several different mosques in the town is disallowed, the distance is to be calculated from the minaret of the mosque in which the Friday prayer has (or has not) been held. Someone who is a resident, or any traveler who intends to remain for four entire days, is required to attend the Friday prayer even though it does not count as a valid prayer for the traveler in such a situation. As for being 'settled' in a place, it refers to residing somewhere with the intention of remaining there permanently. 'Settledness' in this sense is the first condition which must be fulfilled in order for the Friday prayer to be obligatory or valid. Hence, the Friday prayer is only required of people who have taken up residence in a town with the intention of staying there permanently such that it will be possible [for them] to protect the town and defend it against overwhelming, unforeseen dangers. (10) That the person be in a 'settled' town. Hence, if a large group of people stop in a place with the intention of staying there for a month, for example, the Friday prayer will not be required of them, nor will it be valid if they intend to perform it. It is not necessary for the place in which the Friday prayer is held to be a city; rather, it will be valid in a village and even in dwellings built with Persian cane or palm branches stripped of their leaves; as for people who live in tents, however, they are not required to perform the Friday prayer, nor will it be valid if they do perform it (since such people tend to be migratory), unless they are located near a town in which the Friday prayer is held, in which case they are required to perform it by virtue of their association with said town, as we have seen.

As for the conditions of validity associated with the Friday prayer, the Malikis list the following five: (1) A group of people's being 'settled' in a town or some other location in the sense that they are living there on a permanent basis and are capable of defending themselves against compelling, unexpected dangers. Moreover, just as 'settledness' is a condition for the validity [of the Friday prayer], it is likewise a condition for its being obligatory, as we saw earlier in our discussion of the conditions associated with ritual ablutions. (2) Attendance by twelve worshipers in addition to the imam. It is not necessary for all of the town's residents to attend, even on the first Friday on which the Friday prayer is held, properly speaking. However, it is necessary that the residents be present in the town itself, or near enough to the town that they could be called upon for support every Friday. (3) The presence of the imam. The two following conditions must be met by the imam: (a) He must either be a resident or a traveler who intends to stay for four days, and (b) He must be the person who delivers the sermon. Thus, if the person who leads the congregation in prayer is different from the one who delivers the sermon, the prayer will be invalid unless the orator has been prevented from leading the prayer by some circumstance or condition which renders it permissible for him to appoint someone else to replace him as the imam, such as a nosebleed, some event which invalidates his ablutions, etc. Someone else can lead the congregation in prayer if the condition which has prevented the orator from praying is not expected to pass within a short period of time; otherwise, however, the congregation must wait for the orator. As for what is meant by a short period of time, it is estimated as the time required to perform the first two *rak'ahs* of the evening prayer including their Qur'anic recitation. (4) The two sermons, details concerning which have been presented above. (5) The mosque. The Friday congregational prayer will thus not be valid if it is performed in people's homes, for example, or in an uninhabited area.

In connection with the mosque in which the Friday prayer is held, the following four conditions apply: (1) It must be an actual edifice; hence, the Friday prayer will not be valid in a mosque which has simply been walled in with stones or bricks without having been built into a solid structure. (2) The quality of the edifice must be at least equal to that of the buildings to which the town's residents are accustomed. Hence, if most of the homes in the town were made of palm branches stripped of their leaves, it would be permissible to construct the mosque out of Persian cane. (3) The mosque must be either in the town or close enough to it that it is within range of the smoke that comes from the town in which the Friday prayer is held. (4) It must be a single mosque. If there are several mosques in the same town, the Friday prayer will only be valid in the oldest mosque. For more details on this condition, see the earlier discussion of having several different mosques in a single location.

* * *

The Shafiis divide the conditions associated with the Friday congregational prayer into two types, namely, conditions of necessity and conditions of validity. The conditions of necessity which the Shafiis list over and above those which apply to regular ritual prayer include the first ten conditions listed by the Malikis. The Shafiis thus agree with the Malikis that the Friday prayer is not required of someone who is ill, invalid, or blind except given the conditions mentioned by the Malikis in their listing of conditions of necessity. Nor is it required under conditions of severe cold and heat, in agreement with the Malikis, or when there is heavy rain or excessive amounts of mud, or when the person concerned has reason to fear that if he attends the Friday prayer, he will be endangered by an unjust foe or ruler. Nor is it required of someone who has reason to fear that if he attends the Friday prayer he will lose money; however, unlike the Malikis, the Shafiis hold that this exception applies whether the loss of such money would cause the person harm or not. Nor is the Friday prayer required of someone who has reason to fear for his own safety or that of his family. Nor is it required of women or slaves, although if they perform it, it will be valid.

The Hanbalis agree on these conditions as well; however, they hold that the Friday prayer is not required of a blind person unless he finds a guide or something which could serve as a guide, such as a wall which he can lean on until he reaches the mosque, a rope he can hold on to, etc. As we have seen, the Hanafis hold unanimously that the obligation to perform the Friday prayer is waived for a sick person who will be harmed by going to attend the prayer on foot, and that if he is unable to do so, he is exempted from the obligation to perform it even if he finds someone to carry him. With regard to someone who is blind, however, there is a difference of opinion among them. Hence, some Hanafis hold that the obligation to perform the Friday prayer is waived for a blind person even if he finds someone who will volunteer to be his guide, while others hold that if a blind person is able to go to the Friday prayer, he must attend it even if, in order to do so, he must employ the services of a volunteer guide or of one whose services he is able to afford (as we saw earlier in our presentation of the conditions of necessity as listed by the Hanafis). The Hanafis agree with the other three schools that the Friday prayer is not required of someone who fears that by attending the prayer, he will be subject to an assault on his wealth, his family, or his own person, provided (according to the Hanafis, the Malikis and the Hanbalis, but not according to the Shafiis) that the loss of the wealth in question would cause him undue hardship. If, on the other hand, the person concerned is himself a wrongdoer, he will not be exempted from the obligation to attend the Friday prayer based on his fear of just retribution.

The Shafiis also list the following conditions of necessity for the Friday congregational prayer: residence in or near the location where the Friday prayer is held. The other three schools stipulate this condition as well; however, the Shafiis expound it in greater detail. Specifically, they stipulate that those who are resident in a location near the one in which the Friday prayer is held must be able to hear the call to prayer from where they reside. Hence, the Friday prayer is not required of someone who resides in a place which is so far away from the prayer site that he and its other residents are unable to hear the call to prayer unless the number of residents comes to forty. If there are forty or more residents in the location in question, they are under obligation to perform the Friday prayer where they are rather than going to the town which they reside close to. Nor does the obligation to perform the Friday prayer require that people be 'settled' (i.e., residing in a place with the intention of staying there permanently in the sense that they do not leave the site of their residence either in summer or in winter unless some necessity requires it, as is the practice of those residing in a town). However, being 'settled' in the sense mentioned here is a condition that must be fulfilled in order for the Friday prayer to take effect, as it were. Hence, the Friday prayer will only take effect for those who are 'settled'; in other words, if the prayer is attended by fewer than forty worshipers who meet the criteria for being termed 'settled', and if the fortieth person to attend is not 'settled', the prayer will not take effect, nor will it have any validity, nor will it be required of the worshipers concerned.

Another condition of necessity for the Friday prayer is that the worshiper be residing in one place; hence, the Friday prayer is not required of someone who is on a journey unless he intends to stay for four days in a town where the Friday prayer is held. If someone departs on a journey from his own town after dawn on a Friday, he will be obliged to perform the Friday prayer if he reaches his destination in time for this prayer. If, on the other hand, he sets out from his town before dawn on a Friday, he will not be obliged to attend the Friday prayer. This ruling applies whether the journey in question is long or short unless the person concerned wishes to go to a place which is sufficiently close that when he arrives there, he will be able to hear the call to prayer from the town which he left. If, on the other hand, the person can hear the call to prayer from some other town, he will not be obliged to attend the Friday prayer. Hence, if harvesters and laborers set out from their town for their work site before dawn, the Friday prayer will not be required of them unless they are able to hear the town's call to prayer from the work site.

As for the conditions of validity for the Friday prayer, the Shafiis list the following six: (1) The entire Friday prayer, and the two sermons associated with it, must fall with certainty within the time period designated for the noon prayer. (2) The prayer must be performed in a structured 'space' which represents a community, be it a city or a village, a town, a mountain cave, or an underground chamber. Hence, the Friday prayer will not be valid if performed in the desert. The officially recognized criterion for the validity of the Friday prayer in such a 'space' is that if it is a place in which regular ritual prayers may not be shortened—such as an open area inside the town wall—the Friday prayer will be valid there, whereas if it is a place where regular ritual prayers may be shortened, the Friday prayer will not be valid there. (3) It must be performed communally, in conformity with the aforementioned conditions for communal prayer. (4) The number of worshipers who attend the prayer must come to forty given the conditions mentioned previously in this connection. (5) The Friday prayer must be performed prior to other prayers in the same place; details pertaining to this condition will be presented below in the discussion of repeated performances of the Friday prayer. (6) The prayer must be preceded by the two sermons, including the pillars and in accordance with the conditions to be presented below.

* * *

The conditions of necessity which the Hanbalis list over and above those which apply to regular ritual prayer are divided into two types, namely, conditions of necessity, and conditions of validity. The conditions of necessity which fall into this category include those which have been listed above by the Malikis, the Shafiis and the Hanafis; in addition, the include the following: (1) Freedom. Hence, the Friday prayer is not required of slaves. (2) Maleness. The Friday prayer is not required of females, although if they attend it, it will be valid. (3) The absence of any condition which would render it permissible not to perform it; hence, the Friday prayer is not required of someone who is ill and who would be harmed by going to the Friday prayer by riding [an animal] or being carried. However, if such a person is capable of going to the mosque by paying a wage or fare which would not cause him undue hardship, he is required to attend it. The same proviso applies to someone who is an invalid. (4) Sightedness. Hence, the Friday prayer is not required of someone who is blind even if he has found someone who can serve as his guide, unless he is able to hold onto a rope connected with the mosque where the Friday prayer is held. (5) The absence of severe hot or cold, heavy rain or excessive amounts of mud. (6) That one [not] have reason to fear that if he attends the Friday prayer, he will be unjustly imprisoned or otherwise harmed. (7) That one [not] have reason to fear the loss of wealth the loss of which would cause him undue harm, or reason to fear for his family or himself. (8) Residence in an area which is united under a single name, such as Cairo; everyone who resides in the city of Cairo [assuming that they meet all other conditions of necessity – t.n.] is required to attend the Friday prayer even if a distance of many parasangs separates them from the site where the prayer is being held, since it is a single city with a single name. As for areas which have their own separate names, such as New Cairo, al-Zaytūn, Ma'ādī, etc., each of them is treated as an independent residential center with respect to this condition. As a consequence, the Friday prayer is only required of those who are permanent residents of such areas if the Friday prayer is held there. If such a neighborhood contains no mosques in which the Friday prayer is held and if it is adjacent to another neighborhood where the Friday prayer is held, the person concerned must go to the neighborhood in which the Friday prayer is held, provided that the two neighborhoods are no more than one parasang apart from each other. If the two neighborhoods are farther apart than this, however, the Friday prayer is not required of the aforementioned worshiper. The Friday prayer is not required of tent dwellers, nor of the inhabitants of small villages with populations of no more than 40 people; if the population is forty or more, however, the Friday prayer is required of them if they remain settled there both summer and winter. It is also necessary, in order for the Friday prayer to be required, that one be resident in one place; hence, it is not required of someone who is on a journey unless he intends to stay in a single place for more than four days. As for the minimum distance which must have been traversed in order for someone to be deemed a traveler, the Hanbalis hold that in order for the Friday prayer to be required of a traveler, he must be one parasang or less away from the place where the Friday prayer is held; if he is farther from it than this, he is not required to attend it.

As for the conditions of validity associated with the Friday prayer, the Hanbalis list the following four: (1) The commencement of the time period designated for this prayer. Hence, the Friday prayer will not be valid if performed either before its designated time period begins or after it has ended. However, according to the Hanbalis, the time period for the Friday prayer is the same as that for the holiday prayer; hence, once the sun has risen sufficiently in the sky for voluntary prayers to be permissible [i.e., once it has risen one's spear's length in the sky – t.n.], the Hanbalis hold that the Friday prayer may also be performed. (2) That the worshiper be residing in a city or a village as was mentioned before in connection with the conditions of necessity. Hence, the Hanbalis hold that the Friday prayer is not valid in a desert, a tent, or the like. On this point, the Hanbalis differ with the Hanafis, who hold that the Friday is valid in the desert. (3) That it be attended by forty or more worshipers, including the imam, even if some of them are mute. However, if all those in attendance are mute, the prayer will not be valid. (4) Delivery of the two Friday sermons, including all of their pillars and in a manner consistent with the rulings relating thereto.

Women's attendance of the Friday congregational prayer

As we have seen, maleness is a condition of necessity in connection with the Friday prayer; in other words, the Friday prayer is not required of the woman. However, it is valid if she performs it instead of the regular noon prayer. One might ask here: Is it better, then, for the woman to attend the Friday congregational prayer or to perform the regular noon prayer at home? For the various schools' rulings on this question, see below.[290]

---

290. The Hanafis hold that it is preferable for a woman to perform the regular noon prayer in her home whether she is elderly or young, since communal prayer was never legally instituted for the woman.

* * *

The Malikis hold that in the case of an elderly woman whom men no longer find desirable, it is permissible for her to attend the Friday prayer; otherwise, they hold that it is undesirable for her to do so. As for a young woman in whose case there is reason to fear that her attendance might subject men to temptations, either while she is on her way to or from the prayer or while she is in the mosque, she is forbidden to attend the prayer as a means of avoiding corruption.

* * *

According to the Shafiis, it is undesirable for an attractive woman to attend communal prayer under any circumstances, be it the Friday prayer or some other communal prayer. The Shafiis apply this ruling even if the woman is wearing tattered clothing. Similarly in the case of a woman who is not attractive, she is forbidden to attend the Friday prayer if she makes herself up or puts on perfume. As for an elderly woman, she may attend the Friday prayer without any undesirability attaching thereto if she goes out in tattered clothing, puts on no perfume, and attracts no interest on the part of men.

However, the foregoing rulings apply given the following two conditions: (1) The woman must have received permission to attend the prayer by her guardian; this applies whether she is young or old, and if her guardian does not grant her permission to attend, she is forbidden to do so. (2) There must be no reason to fear that her attendance of the communal prayer will cause anyone temptation; otherwise, she is forbidden to do so.

* * *

As for the Hanbalis, they hold that it is permissible for a woman to attend the Friday prayer provided that she is not attractive; if she is attractive, however, it is undesirable for her to attend it under any circumstances.

The existence of a variety of mosques in which the Friday worship is held

The aim behind the Friday congregational prayer is to enable people to gather in a single place in humble reverence for their Lord, thereby strengthening the bonds of friendship and love among them, increasing their capacity for mercy and compassion, and putting to death those forces which would foster hatred, resentment and bitterness. By means of their gathering for this prayer, each worshiper is encouraged to view every other with good will and brotherly affection such that the strong among them come to the aid of the weak, the wealthy among them assist the poor, the elderly among them have mercy upon the young, and the youthful among them revere the elderly, with all of them together perceiving themselves as servants of God alone, aware of Him as the One Who is "truly self-sufficient, the One to Whom all praise is due" (60:6), the Possessor of absolute authority and that majesty which knows no bounds.

These, then, are some of the aims in pursuit of which the Islamic law urges people to gather for worship. There can be no doubt that the unnecessary proliferation of mosques serves to defeat these noble aims, since Muslims are thereby scattered among numerous mosques and, as a consequence, they do not experience the benefit of gathering together or sense the greatness of the Creator Whom they assemble to worship in obedient, humble submission. It is for this reason that some schools of Islamic jurisprudence hold that if numerous mosques are constructed unnecessarily, the Friday prayer will only be valid for those worshipers who performed it earliest. According to this point of view, the Friday prayer will count for those who are known with certainty to have completed the prayer first, while all other worshipers will be considered to have performed a regular noon prayer. For the various schools' views on this point, see below.[291]

---

291. The Shafiis note that the existence of numerous places in which the Friday prayer is held may or may not be based on a need for such proliferation. An example of a need for additional mosques would be a situation in which the existing mosque ceases to accommodate all the people of a given town who attend the Friday prayer. If there is a proliferation of mosques or of other places in which the Friday prayer is held without there being a need for such, the Friday prayer will be valid for those worshipers who performed it first if it has been established with certainty that the congregation which prayed in this particular place uttered *takbīrat al-iḥrām* before any others did. If this is not known with certainty, or if, rather, it is established with certainty that the various congregations prayed at the same time (by uttering *takbīrat al-iḥrām* at the same time), or if there is some doubt as to whether they all uttered *takbīrat al-iḥrām* simultaneously, or whether one congregation uttered it before another, the prayers performed by all of the various congregations will be invalidated. In such a case, all the congregations must gather together and repeat the prayer as a Friday congregational prayer if possible; if this is not possible, they are to perform it as a regular noon prayer.

If, on the other hand, there has been a proliferation of mosques in response to a need for such, the Friday prayer will be valid in all of them, though it is recommended that they perform the noon prayer after the Friday prayer.

* * *

The Malikis hold that if there are several mosques in a single town, the Friday prayer will only be valid in the mosque where it was performed first even if this mosque was constructed later than others. If, for example, a given town contains zawiyahs where the Friday prayer has never been performed, after which a mosque is built where the Friday prayer is performed, after which still another mosque is built in which the Friday prayer is also performed, it will only be valid in the mosque where it was performed first. However, in order for this ruling to apply, the following four conditions must be met: (1) People must not abandon the old mosque in order to pray in the new one without a valid excuse for doing so. (2) The old mosque must be too small to accommodate all those who are likely to attend prayer there even if they are not obliged to do so and it must not be possible to expand it, with the result that people are in need of a new mosque. (3) There must not be reason to fear that if the inhabitants of the town assemble in a single mosque, it will lead to some sort of conflict or wickedness, as when, for example, the town contains two rival families, one of which lives on the west side of the town while the other lives on the east side, in which case it is permissible for each family to have its own mosque. (4) There must not have been a decree by a ruler to the effect that the Friday prayer will be valid in the new mosque.

* * *

The Hanbalis hold that it is permissible to have numerous mosques in a single town in response to a genuine need, as when the mosques which exist in the town are not large enough to accommodate those of its inhabitants who may validly perform the Friday prayer (even if it is not obligatory for them, and even if they do not actually attend); in such a case, the Friday prayer will be valid in all of them. Moreover, they hold that this ruling applies whether the ruler has granted permission for the proliferation or not, and that it is preferable for the noon prayer to be performed after the Friday prayer.

If, on the other hand, the proliferation of mosques has taken place without there being a need for such, the Friday prayer will only be valid in the place in which the ruler permits it to be held. In this case, the Friday prayer will not be valid in any other place even if it was performed there first. If the ruler permits it to be held in numerous different mosques without there being a need to justify this, or if he does not permit it to be held anywhere, the Friday prayer which is valid will be the one whose *takbīrat al-iḥrām* was uttered first. If the Friday prayer is performed in more than one place at the same time (that is, if the worshipers in the various mosques utter *takbīrat al-iḥrām* simultaneously) and if it is demonstrated with certainty that this has occurred, everyone's Friday prayer will be invalidated. If, after this, it is possible for them to repeat the prayer as a Friday prayer, they are to do so; otherwise, they are to perform it as a regular noon prayer. If, on the other, it is not known which of the Friday prayers was performed first, it will be considered to have been valid in one of the mosques, but without specifying which of them; in this case, it is not to be repeated as a Friday prayer, but everyone concerned will be required to perform a regular noon prayer.

* * *

As for the Hanafis, they hold that it does no harm for there to be numerous places where the Friday prayer is held even if the prayer is performed earlier in one place than in another, properly speaking. However, if someone who is performing the Friday prayer in a given mosque learns with certainty that worshipers in other mosques began the prayer before he did, he will be obliged to perform four *rak'ahs* with the intention of performing the most recent noon prayer with a single greeting of peace. It is preferable in such a situation for the person to perform these *rak'ahs* at home lest ordinary, uneducated Muslims think that this prayer is a binding obligation. (As we have seen, a 'duty' [*wājib*] according to the Hanafis is less binding than a full obligation [*farḍ*]; and if one wishes, one might say that a 'duty' is an emphatically enjoined emulation of the Sunnah.) If, on the other hand, such a worshiper is uncertain as to whether or not others began the Friday prayer before him, it is recommended that he pray four *rak'ahs* with the intention of performing the most recent noon prayer only; when doing so, he is to recite a surah or three short verses from the Qur'ān in each *rak'ah* due to the possibility that the prayer he is performing is a voluntary one (bearing in mind that, as we have seen, such Qur'anic recitation is required in every *rak'ah* of a voluntary prayer).

Some might ask: Should this person perform the aforementioned four *rak'ahs* before or after the four *rak'ahs* which are an emulation of the Sunnah on Friday? The answer to this question is that he should perform them after the four Sunnah-based Friday *rak'ahs*, since if he performs them first, he will have departed from the ideal. Given the foregoing, those who perform the Friday prayer are to perform four *rak'ahs* thereafter as an emulation of the Sunnah associated with Friday in particular; following this, they are to perform four *rak'ahs* with the intention of performing the most recent noon prayer, followed by two *rak'ahs* as an emulation of the Sunnah in connection with the regular noon prayer (and which were listed above with the Sunnah-based practices associated with the noon prayer).

Whether the Friday prayers may be performed in the open air

According to the Shafiis, the Hanafis and the Hanbalis, the Friday congregational prayer may validly be performed out of doors; however, the Malikis hold that it is only valid if performed in a mosque.[292]

The quorum for the Friday congregational prayer

All four schools agree that there is a quorum which must be met in order for the Friday prayer to be valid; however, they differ concerning the number which makes up this quorum as well as the specific conditions associated with it.[293]

---

292. According to the Malikis, the Friday congregational prayer is valid neither in people's homes nor out of doors; rather, it must be performed in a mosque.

* * *

According to the Hanbalis, the Friday congregational prayer is valid if performed outside provided that the site where it is performed is close to the mosque by commonly accepted standards; otherwise, it is not. Moreover, if the imam leads the Friday prayer out of doors, he must appoint someone else to lead the prayer in the mosque for those too weak to come out.

* * *

According to the Shafiis, the Friday congregational prayer is valid if performed out of doors if the site is near the mosque, where "near" is defined as no farther from the mosque than a point which, if a traveler reached it, he would not yet be permitted to shorten his ritual prayers. (Details on this issue will be found in the sections below on shortening prayer.) Moreover, the rulings which apply to the out-of-doors apply likewise to trenches such as those found inside some towns' walls.

* * *

The Hanafis do not stipulate that the Friday prayer must be performed in a mosque in order to be valid; rather, it may validly be performed outside provided that the site is no more than one parasang away from the city and that the imam grants permission for it to be performed there as we saw earlier in the discussion of the conditions associated with the Friday prayer.

293. According to the Malikis, the minimum number of worshipers who must be present in order for the Friday prayer to be initially valid is twelve men in addition to the imam. Moreover, these twelve must meet the following conditions: (a) they must be individuals who are required to perform the Friday prayer; hence, it will not be valid if they include a slave, a young boy or a woman; (b) they must be 'settled'; hence, they may not include someone who is residing in the town where the Friday prayer is being held only in order to do business, for example, or a traveler who intends to stay for four days; (c) they must be present from the beginning of the two sermons until the end of the prayer; hence, if the prayer of any of them is invalidated after it begins, even if this takes place after the imam has uttered the final greeting of peace and before the worshiper himself has uttered the final greeting of peace, the Friday prayer will be invalidated for the entire group; (d) they must all be either Malikis or Hanafis. If they are Shafiis or Hanbalis, who set the quorum at forty, the Friday prayer will not have any initial validity unless they imitate Mālik or Abū Ḥanīfah.

When the first Friday prayer is being performed in a given village, it is not necessary that everyone in the village attend; rather, it is sufficient for the minimum twelve to attend based on the most well-attested view. As for the imam, it is necessary that he be among those who are required to perform the Friday prayer, even if he is a traveler who intends to stay for four days; however, his stay must not be with the intention of delivering the sermon, for if it is with the intention of delivering the sermon, it is not valid for him to be an imam.

* * *

The Hanafis set the quorum for the Friday congregational prayer at three people in addition to the imam even if they do not all attend the sermon. Thus, if the prayer leader delivers the sermon with one person in attendance, if this person then leaves before the prayer and three men come to take his place, and if the leader then prays with these three men, the prayer will be valid without his repeating the sermon to them. The Hanafis also stipulate that these three people be men, even if they are slaves, ill, travelers, illiterate, or deaf since they would be fit to lead the Friday prayer, whether for unimpaired worshipers or worshipers who share the same impairment (be it illiteracy, dumbness, etc.), once the sermon has been delivered by someone else. Thus, given that it is not necessary for the speaker to be the imam for the Friday prayer, their fitness to lead the prayer for others belonging to the same group is to be given priority. In the case of women or young children, by contrast, the quorum for the Friday congregational prayer cannot be met by them alone due to the fact that they would not be qualified to lead others like themselves in this prayer. It is also necessary that those present continue with the imam until he has completed his first prostration. If they leave him after this, their own prayers will be invalidated, but the imam may conclude his prayer as the Friday congregational prayer; if, on the other hand, they leave him before he prostrates for the first time, both their prayers and his prayer will be invalidated according to Abū Ḥanīfah. As for the imam, he must be the highest legal authority or someone whom the ruler has given permission to lead the Friday prayer. This is a condition for the validity of the Friday prayer; hence, if the imam is not the highest legal authority or his proxy, the Friday prayer will be invalid from the very beginning and the people will be required to perform it as a regular noon prayer. However, someone who has been granted permission by the imam to lead the Friday prayer may appoint someone else as his proxy and authorize him to carry out this function.

* * *

The Shafiis stipulate the following conditions in connection with the quorum for the Friday congregational prayer: (1) The number of worshipers must be at least forty, including the imam. The Friday prayer will not have any initial validity with a smaller number than this. If the number of worshipers is insufficient to meet the quorum, it is permissible to imitate a school of jurisprudence which does not stipulate this number. However, those who imitate a school other than their own [with regard to the quorum for the Friday prayer] must take care not to engage in "school-splitting" by, for example, following this other school in connection with the requirements for ritual purity as well. (2) Those in attendance must be individuals whose presence lends the Friday prayer its initial validity; in other words, they must be free males who are 'settled' in one place and who are qualified to be held accountable for Muslim acts of worship. Hence, they may not be slaves, women, young children or travelers. (3) They must continue with the imam until the end of the first *rak'ah* in a valid prayer which does not need to be made up later due to some extenuating condition. Once they have entered the second *rak'ah*, however, it is no longer necessary for them to stay together as a group. In other words, if the group intends to part with the imam in the second *rak'ah* and they complete their prayers on their own, their Friday congregational prayer will still be valid; similarly, if the imam intends to part with the group during the second *rak'ah* and completes the prayer on his own, his prayer will be valid as the Friday congregational prayer. However, if the prayer of anyone in the group is invalidated either before or after the imam utters the final greeting of peace, the Friday congregational prayer will be invalidated for everyone because, in order for the Friday prayer to be valid, the full quorum must be present until the very end. If this occurs, then if time permits, they must repeat the prayer together as a Friday congregational prayer; otherwise, they are to perform it as the regular noon prayer. (4) Those being led in prayer must not delay beginning their prayer too long past the imam's commencement of his. Specifically, if they delay the commencement of their prayer for so long that the time between their opening *takbīrat al-iḥrām* and the imam's rise from his first bow is insufficient for them to recite the *Fātiḥah* and go down into a bow, their Friday congregational prayer will have no initial validity. (If the imam is one of the minimum forty worshipers, he must meet the same conditions required of those being led in prayer; if, on the other hand, there are forty or more worshipers besides the imam, it is permissible for him to be a young boy, a slave or a traveler.) (5) The imam must consciously intend to lead the congregational prayer even if he is a young boy, a slave, or a traveler; similarly, those who are being led in prayer must consciously intend to follow the imam. If either of these two intentions is missing, the prayer will start out invalid. (6) The quorum required for the validity of the Friday prayer must continue to be present [in the mosque] from the beginning of the sermon until the end of the prayer.

* * *

The Hanbalis stipulate the following conditions concerning the Friday congregational prayer: (1) The number of worshipers must be at least forty, not including the imam. (2)The worshipers must be individuals for whom the Friday prayer is obligatory, namely, free adult males who are 'settled' in the place where the Friday congregational prayer may validly be held (namely, a community with regular, fixed structures). Hence, the quorum may not include those who are slaves, females, young boys, travelers, or residents who are not permanently settled or who are settled in a location outside the town where the Friday prayer is being held, even if they would otherwise be obliged to attend. (3) All the worshipers who make up the quorum must attend both the sermon and at least part of the prayer. For example, if the minimum forty worshipers are present for the entire sermon and part of the prayer, and if they then leave after the arrival of a sufficient number of other worshipers to make up for their absence, the Friday prayer will still be valid. If, on the other hand, the number of worshipers drops to below forty during the prayer before the arrival of enough other worshipers to bring the number up to forty again, the

The pillars of the Friday sermon. First: opening it with praise to God.

In our earlier discussion of the holiday prayers (i.e., the prayers performed on the Day of Fastbreaking and the Day of Sacrifice), we noted that the pillars of the two sermons delivered with the holiday prayers are the same as those of the Friday sermons with the exception of the way they are opened. The holiday prayers are opened with the utterance of *Allāhu akbar*, whereas the Friday prayer is opened with the words *al-ḥamdu lillāh*.

The pillars of the two sermons delivered with the holiday prayers have been enumerated in detail for each of the four schools; however, whereas according to the Shafiis and the Hanbalis, opening the Friday sermon with the words *al-ḥamdu lillāh* is a pillar, the Malikis and the Hanafis hold that it is not a pillar of either the holiday sermon or the Friday sermon. Consequently, we have chosen to list the pillars for the Friday sermon here as well, presenting each of the four schools in turn.[294]

Friday prayer will be invalidated; if this occurs, it should be repeated as a Friday congregational prayer if possible. An exception to this ruling is made if those being led in prayer believe, based on their particular school, that the Friday prayer will be valid with only twelve worshipers present, for example; if their number then drops below forty until it becomes only twelve, the prayer will remain valid for them. In such a case, the imam must appoint one of the worshipers to finish leading the prayer because, for him personally, the prayer is invalidated if, according to his school, the quorum for the Friday congregational prayer is forty. If, on the other hand, those being led in prayer are of the opinion that a quorum of forty is necessary for the prayer to be valid whereas the imam does not hold this opinion, and if their number falls below forty before the arrival of enough other worshipers to bring their number back up to forty, the prayer will be invalidated for all of them.

294. According to the Hanafis, the Friday sermon has a single pillar, namely, the utterance of words and phrases of divine remembrance; neither the content nor the number of these phrases is specified. Hence, the required sermon will be valid even if the speaker utters only one instance of *al-ḥamdu lillāh*, one instance of *subḥān Allāh*, or one instance of *lā ilāha illā Allāh*. Nevertheless, it is undesirable for the speaker to limit the sermon to only this, as will be seen in the discussion of the Sunnah-based practices connected with the Friday sermon. For the Hanafis, only the first of the two sermons is required, whereas its repetition is an emulation of the Sunnah, as will be seen below.

* * *

The Shafiis stipulate the following five pillars for the Friday prayer: (2) Praise to God. The phrase used here must include, specifically, *al-ḥamdu lillāh*. Hence, it is not sufficient to say, *ashkur Allāh* ("I thank God"), *uthnī 'alayhi* ("I exalt Him"), *al-ḥamdu lil-raḥmān* ("Praise be to the All-Merciful"), etc. However, it is permissible for the speaker to say, *aḥmadu Allāh* or *innī ḥāmid Allāh* ("I praise God"). This pillar is essential in both the first and the second sermons. (2) Prayer for blessings upon the Prophet in both sermons. One must specifically use the term, "Pray…"; hence, it is not sufficient to say, *raḥim Allāhu sayyidanā Muḥammad* ("May God have mercy upon our master Muḥammad"). It is not necessary that one specifically use the name, 'Muḥammad'; rather, one may use any of his epithets. However, it will not suffice to use only the pronoun 'he' even if one of the Prophet's names has been used before this. (3) An exhortation to be conscious of God in each of the two sermons, even if these specific words are not used. Hence, it is sufficient to say something like, "And obey God…."; however, it is not sufficient simply to issue warnings against the world and its temptations without also urging one's listeners to be obedient to God. (4) Recitation of a verse from the Qur'ān in one of the two sermons, preferably the first. The verse recited must be an entire verse or part of a long one. It must also have a comprehensible meaning, for example, in the form of a promise, a threat, a ruling, a story, a parable, or a report. As for a phrase such as, *thumma naẓara…* ("then he looks…."), it will not suffice to fulfill this pillar of the sermon. (5) Supplication for believers, both male and female, in the second sermon. The supplication should be spiritual in nature—a plea for forgiveness, for example—if one has memorized a prayer of this type; otherwise, it is sufficient to make a more mundane request. Moreover, the speaker should not exclude those present by uttering his supplication on behalf of others rather than those in attendance.

* * *

According to the Malikis, the Friday sermon has only one pillar, namely, either a warning or an announcement of good news. Properly speaking, it is not necessary that the speaker use rhymed prose; hence, if he uses poetry or unrhymed prose, the sermon will still be valid, but it is recommended that it be repeated if the prayer has not yet been performed. Once the prayer has been performed, however, the sermon should not be repeated.

* * *

The Hanbalis list four pillars for the Friday sermon; hence, the speaker must: (1) Open each of the two sermons with the words, *al-ḥamdu lillāh*; hence, it is not sufficient to say, for example, *aḥmad Allāh*. (2) Pray for blessings upon the Messenger of God, specifically using the word, "Pray…." (3) Recite a verse from the Book of God. The verse must convey a self-contained meaning or ruling; hence, it would not be sufficient to recite a phrase such as, *mudhāmmatān* ("… two [gardens] of the deepest green") [Qur'ān 55:64]. (4) Exhort his listeners to be conscious of God Almighty; the least that the speaker might say in this regard is, "Be conscious of God" or some such thing.

The conditions for the validity of the two Friday sermons

The following conditions must be met in order for the two Friday sermons to be valid: (1) According to the Shafiis, the Hanafis and the Hanbalis, the sermons must precede the Friday congregational prayer; for the Malikis' ruling, see below.[295] (2) According to the Hanafis and the Hanbalis, the Friday sermon will not be valid if the speaker does not commence it with a conscious intention to deliver the Friday sermon; as for the Malikis and the Shafiis, they hold that intention is not a condition for the sermon's validity. The Shafiis stipulate that the speaker must not allow him-

---

295. According to the Malikis, if the two sermons are delayed until after the prayer, only the prayer should be repeated, while the sermons will remain valid. However, the prayer must be repeated without delay and before one has left the mosque. If it is not repeated before one leaves the mosque, or if what would be considered a 'long' time by commonly accepted standards passes before its repetition, the sermons must be repeated and the prayer must be repeated after them.

296. According to the Hanafis, it is permissible for the sermon to be in a language other than Arabic even if the speaker knows Arabic, and regardless of whether the worshipers are Arabs or not.

* * *

According to the Hanbalis, if the speaker is able to deliver the sermon in Arabic, the sermon will not be valid in any other language. If he is unable to do so, he may say whatever he is able to in some other language [and which is appropriate to the occasion], regardless of whether the listeners are Arabs or not. However, the Qur'anic verse, which is a pillar of the sermon, must be uttered in Arabic; hence, if he is unable to utter it in Arabic, he may utter any other Arabic words of divine remembrance which he is capable of. If he is unable to do this, either, he should simply remain silent for the time it would have taken to utter the verse.

* * *

The Shafiis hold that if the listeners are Arabs, the pillars of the two sermons must be in Arabic if it is possible for the speaker to learn the language; if not, he may preach in some other language. If the listeners are non-Arabs, it is not necessary for the pillars of the sermon to be in Arabic at all even if the speaker could learn the language; however, the Qur'anic verse must be uttered in Arabic. If the speaker is unable to recite the verse in Arabic, he may replace it with a supplication or other words of divine remembrance in Arabic. If he is unable to do this, either, he must stand in silence for the time it would have taken to recite the verse. As for parts of the sermon other than its pillars, it is not necessary for them to be in Arabic; rather, it is simply an emulation of the Sunnah.

* * *

As for the Malikis, they hold that in order to be valid, the Friday sermon must be in Arabic; however, if the listeners are non-Arabs who do not understand the language and if there is no one among them who would be able to deliver the sermon in Arabic, they are exempted from the requirement to perform the Friday congregational prayer.

self to be distracted from the sermon in any way; hence, if he sneezes and says, *al-ḥamdu lillāh*, his sermon will be invalidated; none of the other schools make this stipulation, however. (3) The sermons must be in Arabic, with the various schools offering their own specific rulings in this regard.[296] (4) They must be delivered within the time period for the Friday congregational prayer. All four schools agree that if the sermons are delivered before the time for the Friday congregational prayer begins and if the prayer is performed during the time period, the prayer will not be valid. (5) The speaker must deliver the sermons loudly enough that they can be heard by those in attendance. For differences in detail among the schools' specific rulings, see below.[297]

---

297. The Hanafis stipulate that in order for the Friday sermon to be valid, it must be delivered loudly enough that everyone present can hear it barring the presence of something that would prevent them from doing so, such as deafness, some other physical condition, or being too far from the speaker. The Hanafis hold that the entire sermon can consist of nothing but the words *lā ilāha illā Allāh*, *al-ḥamdu lillāh*, or *subḥān Allāh*. Hence, if the speaker utters one of these phrases aloud, he will have delivered the sermon even if no one heard him. Nevertheless, it is undesirable to restrict the sermon to such a phrase. The two companions [Abū Yūsuf al-Qāḍī and Muḥammad Ibn al-Ḥasan al-Shaybānī] hold that the sermon must consist, at the very least, of a phrase of divine remembrance which is as long as the testimony recited as part of the ritual prayer, specifically, *al-taḥiyyātu lillāh, al-ṣalawātu al-ṭayyibātu lillāhi ta'ālā, al-salāmu 'alayka ahhuya al-nabī wa raḥmat Allāhi wa barakātuhu, al-salāmu 'alaynā wa 'alā 'ibād Allāhi al-ṣāliḥīn. Ashhadu an lā ilāha illā Allāh waḥdahu lā sharīka lah, wa ashhadu anna Muḥammadan 'abduhu wa rasūluh.* Regardless of which of these rulings one follows, at least one person must attend the sermon; moreover, such a person must be someone who may validly perform the Friday congregational prayer, namely, an adult male in full possession of his mental faculties, even if he happens to be excused from the Friday prayer due to being ill or on a journey.

* * *

The Shafiis stipulate that in order for the Friday sermon to be valid, the speaker must utter all the pillars of the sermon loudly enough that they can be heard by the forty who make up the quorum for the Friday prayer. As for their actually hearing him, this is not a condition for the sermon's validity. Rather, it will suffice for them to have heard the speaker potentially; in other words, it is enough for them all to be close enough to the speaker to be able to hear him and willing to hear him when he speaks even though they might be prevented from hearing him in actuality by drowsiness or some other temporary physical condition; however, if they lack even the capacity to hear the speaker, for example, due to being deaf, sound asleep, or too far away, the two sermons will not be valid due to the fact that the audience lacks even the potential to hear them.

* * *

According to the Hanbalis, the speaker must deliver the two sermons loudly enough that the entire number of worshipers who make up the quorum for the Fri-

Whether it is permissible for there to be a 'break' between the two sermons and the prayer

Another condition for the validity of the Friday sermons is that the speaker not allow a long break between the sermons and the Friday prayer; for each school's ruling on what constitutes a 'long' break, see below.[298] For a comprehensive listing of each school's conditions in this regard, see below.[299]

---

day congregational prayer would be able to hear its pillars barring the presence of factors such as sleep, inattention or deafness that would prevent them from doing so. If the aforementioned number of worshipers, or even some of them, do not hear because the speaker's voice is too low or because they are too far away, the sermon will not be valid since the very purpose for the sermon will have been defeated.

* * *

The Malikis stipulate that in order for the Friday sermon to be valid, it must be delivered aloud; however, they do not stipulate that those present must hear it or even be listening, although listening to the sermon is a duty in and of itself.

298. According to the Shafiis, there must be continuity both between the pillars of the two sermons and between the sermons and the Friday prayer. In order for there to be such continuity, any break between the pillars of the two sermons or between the sermons and the Friday prayer must last no longer than the time it would take to perform two *rak'ahs* as quickly as possible. If such a break lasts longer than this, the sermons will be invalidated unless the additional time is devoted to exhorting the people to do good or other edifying speech.

* * *

The Malikis stipulate that in order for the Friday sermons to be valid, they must directly precede the prayer and they must follow upon each other directly as well, although a break between them is acceptable if it is insignificant by commonly accepted standards.

* * *

According to the Hanafis, the speaker must not allow an interruption between the two sermons and the prayer during which he engages in some activity which is unrelated to prayer itself, such as eating and the like. If, on the other hand, the interruption is taken up in an activity relating to prayer itself, such as making up a prayer missed earlier or uttering a voluntary prayer of commencement before the second sermon, this will not invalidate them; it is ideal in such a situation, however, to repeat the sermon again. Similarly, if the Friday prayer itself is invalidated and repeated, the sermons will remain valid.

* * *

The Hanbalis stipulate that in order for the Friday sermons to be valid, there must be continuity among their constituent parts, as well as between the two sermons and the prayer, where continuity is defined as there not being any break between them which is 'long' by commonly accepted standards.

299. The Hanafis list the following conditions for the validity of the Friday sermons: (1) That they precede the prayer. (2) That they be delivered with the intention of delivering a sermon. (3) That they be delivered during the time period for the Friday prayer. (4) That they be attended by at least one person. (5) That this one person be someone who may validly form part of the quorum for the Friday prayer. (6) That there be no interruption between the sermons and the prayer which is taken up by an activity unrelated to worship. (7) That the speaker deliver the sermons loudly enough that those present can hear them, provided that there is nothing to prevent them from doing so [such as deafness, for example]. As for the sermons' being in the Arabic language, Abū Ḥanīfah held that this is not a condition for their validity even if the speaker would be able to deliver them in Arabic, whereas according to the "two companions", delivering the sermons in Arabic is a condition for their validity if the speaker is able to do so. (This ruling is similar to that related to *takbīrat al-iḥrām* and phrases of divine remembrance connected to ritual prayer.)

* * *

The Shafiis stipulate the following conditions for the validity of the Friday sermons: (1) That they precede the prayer. (2) That they be delivered during the time period for the Friday prayer. (3) That the speaker not be distracted from the sermons in any way. (4) That they be in Arabic. (5) That there be continuity between one sermon and the other, and between both sermons and the Friday prayer. (6) That the speaker be ritually pure, i.e., free of both major and minor ritual impurity, as well as impurities on his clothing or body beyond that which may be overlooked. (7) That the speaker have his private parts concealed during both sermons. (8) That the speaker deliver the sermons from a standing position if he is able to do so; if he is unable, the sermons will be valid even from a sitting position. (9) That the speaker sit down between the two sermons for long enough to maintain a brief repose. Thus, if the speaker delivers the first sermon from a seated position due to some extenuating condition, he must remain silent between the first and second sermons for longer than it would take merely to catch his breath. Similarly, he must remain silent between them if he delivers the first sermon from a standing position and is unable to sit down. (10) That the speaker speak loudly enough that the forty who make up the quorum for the Friday prayer can all hear the pillars of the two sermons. (11) That all forty in attendance be at least potentially able to hear the speaker. (12) That both sermons be delivered in a place where the Friday prayer will be valid. (13) That the speaker be male. (14) That the speaker be qualified to serve as the people's imam. (15) When the speaker is learned in the principles of the religion, that he perform pillars as pillars [i.e., with the recognition that they are obligatory rather than simply emulations of the Sunnah – t.n.] and Sunnah-based actions as emulations of the Sunnah; otherwise, he must not believe pillars to be mere emulations of the Sunnah, although the reverse situation (i.e., the belief that a given Sunnah-based action is obligatory) is permissible.

* * *

The Hanbalis list the following conditions for the validity of the Friday sermons: (1) That they be delivered during the time period for the Friday congregational prayer. (2) That the speaker be someone who is himself required to perform

Sunnah-related practices associated with the sermon: Praying during the sermon for blessing upon Muslim imams and those in authority over them

For the Sunnah-based practices associated with the Friday sermons according to each of the four schools, see below.[300]

---

the Friday prayer; hence, the sermons will not be valid if they are delivered by a slave or someone who is traveling, even if he intends to stay for a period which would be long enough to interrupt his journey. (3) That they contain words of praise to God Almighty. (4) That they be in the Arabic language. (5) That each sermon contain an exhortation to be mindful of God Almighty. (6) That the speaker pray for blessings upon the Messenger of God. (7) That the speaker recite an entire verse from the Qur'ān in each of them. (8) That the speaker maintain continuity among the various parts of each sermon, and between the two sermons and the prayer. (9) That the speaker deliver the sermons with the conscious intention of doing so. (10) That the speaker utter the pillars loudly enough that they can be heard by the number of worshipers that make up the quorum required for the Friday prayer where there are no impediments to their being heard such as some of those present being asleep, inattentive, or deaf.

* * *

As for the Malikis, they stipulate that in order for the Friday sermons to be valid, the following conditions must be met: (1) The sermons must precede the Friday prayer. (2) There must be continuity between the sermons and the prayer, and between the various parts of each sermon. (3) They must be in the Arabic language. (4) The speaker must deliver them aloud. (5) They must be delivered inside a mosque. (6) They must fit the definition of what the Arabs have [traditionally] viewed as "a sermon." (7) They must be attended by the quorum which is required for the Friday congregational prayer, namely, twelve men, even if they do not actually hear them. (8) The speaker must deliver them standing up, though some Malikis hold that it is only an emulation of the Sunnah for the speaker to be standing. Both these views are recognized as valid; however, it is preferable to adopt the view that it is required for the speaker to stand when delivering the sermons.

300. The Shafiis list the following Sunnah-based practices associated with the Friday sermon: (1) Ordering the pillars of the sermon as follows: a) Utterance of *al-ḥamdu lillāh*; b) prayer for blessing upon the Prophet; c) exhortation of the people to be mindful of God; d) recitation of a verse from the Qur'ān; e) making supplication for the believers and, in the second sermon, praying for Muslim imams and those in authority over them to live righteously and to be aided in being faithful to the truth. It is also acceptable to pray by name for the king, the sultan, [or whoever else rules over them – t.n.]; f) praying for peace upon the Prophet after praying for blessings upon him; and g) praying for blessings and peace upon the Prophet's family and companions. (2) Listening attentively to the sermon for those who, if they listen, will hear it; as for those who are unable to hear the sermon, it is recommended that they recite words or phrases of divine remembrance, most preferably Surah 18 followed by prayers for blessing upon the Prophet. (3) Delivering the

sermon from a pulpit or from some area which is elevated above the listeners. (4) For the pulpit to be located to the right of those who face the mosque's prayer niche. (5) For the speaker to greet those who are near the pulpit before he ascends it if he has come out of the private chamber customarily reserved for him or, if he enters the mosque from outside, for him to greet everyone he passes, just as other worshipers should do, then to face them once he has ascended the pulpit. (6) For the speaker to sit down on the pulpit before the first sermon and greet the people before sitting down; as for the people's return of his greeting of peace, this is not only an emulation of the Sunnah, but a duty. (7) For a single person, rather than a group, to issue the call to prayer in the presence of the speaker; (for a group to do so is undesirable). As for the call to prayer which is issued before this from the minaret, it is an emulation of the Sunnah if it is required in order for the people to gather for the Friday prayer. (8) For the sermon to be delivered in literary Arabic, but in a style which is easily comprehended by lay people; moreover, it should be neither too short nor too long. (9) For the sermon to be shorter than the prayer. (10) For the speaker to continue facing his listeners during the sermon without turning in either direction. (11) For the speaker to deliver the sermon while holding a sword, if even a wooden one, or a stick in his left hand and while placing his right hand on the edge of the pulpit.

* * *

According to the Hanbalis, the speaker who delivers the Friday sermon emulates the Sunnah by: (1) delivering the sermon from a pulpit or from some other place which is elevated above his listeners, (2) greeting those gathered for communal prayer when he comes out to them, greeting them again after he ascends the pulpit, and turning his face toward them, (3) sitting down until the muezzin delivers the call to prayer in his presence, (4) sitting down between the two sermons for as long as it would take to recite Surah 112, (5) delivering the sermon standing up, (6) leaning during the sermon against a sword, a bow or a stick and facing straight ahead without turning to the right or the left, (7) keeping both sermons brief, but making the first longer than the second, (8) delivering both sermons in as loud a voice as he is able, (9) offering supplications for the believers (with it likewise being permissible for the speaker to pray for a specific individual, such as the ruler, the ruler's son, the ruler's father and the like), and (10) delivering his sermon from written notes before him.

* * *

According to the Malikis, it is an emulation of the Sunnah for the imam to sit down on the pulpit before the first sermon and to remain seated until the muezzin finishes delivering the call to prayer, then to sit down briefly between the two sermons, where some have defined 'briefly' as the time required to recite Surah 112.

It is recommended that the sermon be delivered from a pulpit; however, it is preferable that the speaker not ascend the pulpit all the way unnecessarily; rather, he should go up only as far as is ideal for enabling his listeners to hear him.

Other practices which are emulations of the Sunnah for the imam are as follows: (1) To greet the people as soon as he comes out to deliver the sermon; beginning with a greeting of peace is dictated by the Sunnah, whereas delivering this greeting as soon as the imam comes out is simply recommended. It is undesirable for the imam to delay greeting the people until after he has ascended the pulpit, and if he does, those who hear him are under no obligation to return his greeting. (2) To lean during the sermon on a stick or something similar. (3) To commence each of the two sermons with praise and glorification of God followed by prayers for blessing and peace upon the Messenger of God. (4) To conclude the first sermon with some recitation from the Qur'ān, and to conclude the second sermon with the words, *yaghfir Allāhu lanā wa lakum* ("May God forgive us and you"). In place of this he might also say, *udhkurū Allāha yadhkurkum* ("Remember God and He will remember you"). (5) To ensure that both sermons include an expression of hope that the listeners will be mindful of God, supplications for all Muslims, and prayers for God's favor upon the Prophet's companions. It is desirable for the imam to do the following: 1) to pray for whoever is in authority over the Muslims, that God would grant him victory over enemies and strengthen Islam through him, 2) to be in a state of ritual purity while delivering both sermons, and 3) to ask God during both sermons to pour out abundant blessings, to ward off calamities, to grant victory over enemies, and to provide protection from illness and infirmity. It is also permissible to pray for those in authority to comport themselves in a just, benevolent manner.

Lastly, it is recommended that the imam speak loudly enough to enable all his listeners to hear him, that he speak more loudly in the first sermon than in the second, that he make the first sermon longer than the second, and that he keep both sermons relatively short.

* * *

The Hanafis note that some of the Sunnah-based practices relating to the Friday sermon have to do with the sermon itself, while others have to do with the speaker. The following practices are an emulation of the Sunnah for the speaker: (1) He should be ritually pure, that is, free of both major and minor ritual impurity; if he is not, this is undesirable, but the sermon will still be valid. If the speaker is in a state of major ritual impurity during the sermon, it is recommended that he repeat the sermon provided that he is able to do so before very much time has passed since its first delivery. (2) He should sit down on the pulpit before commencing the sermon. (3) He should deliver the sermon while standing; it is undesirable to deliver it from a seated or reclining position, but if this occurs, the sermon will still be valid. (4) In those countries which were opened to Islam by force, the speaker should deliver the sermon while leaning with his left hand on a sword, whereas in those lands which were opened to Islam through a peace treaty, he should deliver the sermon without a sword. (5) While delivering the sermon, the speaker should continue facing the people without turning either to the right or to the left. (6) The speaker should deliver two sermons, one of which is an emulation of the Sunnah, and the other of which is a condition for the validity of the Friday prayer, as we have seen. (7) He should sit down between the two sermons for as long as it would take to recite three verses (given this school's definition of what a 'verse' consists of); if he neglects to sit down at this time, he will have conducted himself in an unseemly manner. (8) He should begin the first sermon by praying silently for divine protection, followed by praise and glorification of God in a manner which

Undesirable practices associated with the Friday sermon

According to the Hanafis and the Malikis, the meaning of 'undesirable' in this context is the omission of one of the Sunnah-based practices listed in the previous section; for the views of the Shafiis and the Hanbalis, see below.[301]

---

befits His Majesty, utterance of the two testimonies ["I bear witness that there is no deity but God, and I bear witness that Muḥammad is His servant and His messenger"], prayer for blessings and peace upon the Prophet, warnings against disobedience and all acts which would merit God's disfavor and chastisement, and reminders to his listeners of that which will deliver them from harm both in this world and the next followed, lastly, by recitation of a verse from the Qur'ān.

(1) He should begin the second sermon with praise and glorification of God, prayers for blessing and peace upon God's Messenger and prayers for blessing and forgiveness for believers, both men and women. As for offering supplications for the king and the emir to be granted victory, support and success in all that would serve the interests of their subjects and the like, this is recommended based on the fact that Abū Mūsā al-Ash'arī used to pray for the Caliph 'Umar in his sermons and none of the Prophet's companions found fault with him for this.

(2) He should sit in the vicinity of his private chamber.

Lastly, it is undesirable for the imam to greet the people and to pray in the prayer niche before the sermon, or to depart during the two sermons from the themes of instructing the people to do that which is good and to refrain from evil.

301. According to the Shafiis, neglecting the Sunnah-based practices mentioned above is not undesirable in every case; rather, there are some cases in which it is undesirable, and other cases in which it is simply a departure from the ideal. Thus, for example, it is undesirable for someone listening to the sermon to speak while the sermon is being delivered and for a group of people (rather than a single individual) to deliver the call to prayer in the presence of the speaker, whereas it is simply a departure from the ideal for the speaker to close his eyes unnecessarily while delivering the sermon.

* * *

The Hanbalis also hold that omission of the aforementioned Sunnah-based practices is sometimes undesirable and at other times simply a departure from the ideal; examples of undesirable practices include the speaker's turning his back to his listeners while delivering the sermon and raising his hands when making supplication.

Recitation from the Qur'ān for 'protection' in the presence of the speaker who delivers the sermon

There are people who, when in the presence of the speaker who is to deliver the Friday sermon, recite the Qur'anic verse which says, "Verily, God and His angels bless the Prophet: [hence,] O you who have attained to faith, bless him and give yourselves up [to his guidance] in utter self-surrender!" (33:56). They follow this with a long chant (*unshūdah*); then, when the muezzin has finished issuing the call to prayer in the presence of the speaker, they say, "If, while the imam is delivering the Friday sermon, you [even so much as] say to your friend, 'Listen!', you have spoken foolishly."[302] After this they say, "Listen and you will be rewarded."

This practice is a groundless, uncalled-for innovation which exposes the muezzin's ignorance of the meaning of the prophetic hadith just quoted. After all, he commands others to listen and not to speak, after which he himself speaks, saying, "Listen and you will be rewarded." I myself do not know what need there is for this sort of addition, which is neither commanded by the religion nor consistent with its principles. After all, the purpose of the Friday congregational prayer is to demonstrate submission and humble reverence before God Almighty. Hence, any disturbance or speech other than that of the speaker himself is vain prattle. The Malikis and the Hanafis agree, in principle, with this ruling, while each of the four schools offers its own detailed opinion in connection with it.[303]

---

302. A hadith narrated by Abū Dāwūd, Muslim, al-Nasā'ī and Ibn Mājah.

303. The Malikis hold that this practice (referred to in Arabic as *tarqiyah*) is an undesirable innovation unless a request for such is stipulated in writing in a copy of the Qur'ān which someone has given to the mosque as an endowment.

* * *

According to the Hanafis, it is undesirable to the point of being forbidden for anyone to speak from the time the imam emerges from his private chamber until he finishes his prayer. This ruling applies whether the utterances concerned are words of divine remembrance, prayers for blessings and peace upon the Prophet, or mundane speech. This was the view held by Imam Abū Ḥanīfah, and it is the view officially recognized by the Hanafi school. On this view, *tarqiyah* or any other type of speech is undesirable to the point of being forbidden in this situation. As for the "two companions", they held that speaking is only undesirable during the sermon itself. However, after the imam comes out of his private chamber and while he is seated silently on the pulpit, it is not undesirable for those present to speak; rather, it is only undesirable to engage in ritual prayer. On this view, it is not undesirable at this time for someone present to utter words or phrases of divine remembrance or to utter prayers for blessing upon the Prophet provided that in doing so, he causes no disturbance to others. In either case, however, the practice referred to as *tarqiyah* is an undesirable innovation in the Hanafis' view with the result that it is deemed preferable to avoid it.

* * *

Speaking during the Friday sermon

It is not permitted to speak during the Friday sermon, although each of the four schools offers its own detailed ruling in this regard.[304]

Although the *tarqiyah* which is known to be practiced in mosques is an innovation which did not exist during the era of the Prophet or that of his companions, the Shafiis nevertheless view it as a good practice which is not forbidden by the religion since it involves urging people to pray for blessings upon the Prophet and warns against speaking while the imam is delivering the Friday sermon by making mention of the Qur'anic verse and hadith mentioned above. At the same time, it is a certainty that the Shafiis, who hold that the practice of *tarqiyah* is permissible, do not permit the melodious recitation of the well-known chants such as the following: "O God, pray for, grant peace to, honor, glorify and bless the one who was overshadowed by the cloud..." (*Allāhumma, ṣalli wa sallim wa karrim wa majjid wa bārik 'ala man tuẓallilahu al-ghimāmah*), etc., since this type of chanting is agreed to be disallowed.

* * *

According to the Hanbalis, it is not permissible to speak during the two sermons; however, during the time when the speaker is silent either before or after them, speaking is allowed. Speaking is likewise allowed when the speaker has begun making supplications. These rulings thus indicate their ruling on *tarqiyah* as well.

304. According to the most proper view among the Hanafis, it is undesirable to the point of being forbidden for anyone to speak during the Friday sermon regardless of whether he or she is near the speaker; and, according to the most popular view, speaking at this time is unacceptable whether what is said is of a mundane nature or involves the remembrance of God and the like. It is likewise undesirable to speak during the sermon even if the speaker, when making mention of wrongdoers, says foolish things. If someone hears the name of the Prophet during the sermon, he should simply pray for him in his or her heart. If someone listening to the sermon observes something offensive, there is nothing wrong with his gesturing with his hand or head; moreover, just as it is undesirable to speak during the sermon, it is likewise agreed to be undesirable to pray at this time, as we have seen. Abū Ḥanīfah holds that the same ruling applies to the time when the imam emerges from his private chamber, since he maintains that the imam's coming out of his private chamber marks the end of all talking as well as all praying. His two companions [Abū Yūsuf al-Qāḍī and Muḥammad Ibn al-Ḥasan al-Shaybānī], by contrast, hold that it precludes praying, but not speaking. Among the types of speech which are considered undesirable during the Friday sermon is returning someone's greeting of peace both in one's heart and aloud. The imam is not obliged to return other people's greetings of peace either before or after the sermon, since initiating a greeting of peace at this time is not legitimate in the first place; in fact, someone who does so is guilty of wrongdoing, as a result of which others should not reply to his greeting. The same ruling applies to saying *yarḥamukum Allāh* to someone who

has sneezed [during the sermon]. Moreover, it is undesirable for the imam to greet the people. However, it is not undesirable to warn others of a scorpion or a snake which poses danger to them, calling out to protect a blind person from danger, or any other speech which would involve protecting someone from harm.

* * *

According to the Malikis, it is forbidden to speak either during the sermon or while the imam is seated on the pulpit between the two sermons. This ruling applies whether the person concerned is listening to the sermon or not; hence, it is forbidden for anyone at all to speak during these times, even if he is in the mosque courtyard or on a street adjacent to the mosque. However, such speech is not forbidden if the imam should say things which are unfitting during the sermon, for example, by praising someone whom it would be impermissible to praise, or by condemning someone whom it would be impermissible to condemn; if this does happen, the imam's sanctity is lost, so to speak. It is also permissible to speak while the imam is seated on the pulpit before beginning the first sermon and at the end of the second, when the speaker begins making supplication for Muslims, the companions of the Prophet or the caliph.

Specifically, one type of speech that is forbidden during the sermon is to initiate a greeting of peace and/or to respond to such a greeting; another is to speak in order to restrain someone who is talking during the sermon. Moreover, just as it is forbidden to speak during the sermon, it is likewise forbidden to gesture toward someone who is speaking or to throw pebbles at him in order to get him to be quiet. It is also forbidden to drink or to invoke blessing upon someone who has sneezed; however, it is recommended that someone who sneezes while the imam is delivering the sermon praise God silently. Similarly, if the speaker cites a verse from the Qur'ān which mentions divine chastisement in the afterlife, the hell-fire, etc., it is recommended that those present silently utter brief prayers for divine protection, and when the speaker utters a supplication, for those present to utter the word *Āmīn* to themselves. It is undesirable, however, to do so out loud, while it is completely forbidden to say *Āmīn* to excess. The same ruling applies to prayers for divine protection and divine forgiveness, as well as to prayers for blessing upon the Prophet if there is some reason for either of these; if one utters only brief supplications of this nature, it is recommended that they be made silently. As for the performance of voluntary prayers, it is forbidden from the time the imam comes out to deliver the sermon, the ruling being that his coming out precludes all ritual prayer, while his speaking precludes others' speech.

* * *

The Shafiis hold that in the case of someone who is close enough to the speaker that, if he listened, he would hear the sermon, it is undesirable (and, according to some, forbidden) to speak while the speaker is performing the pillars of the sermon even if he does not actually hear them. As for the parts of the sermon which are not actually pillars, it is not undesirable to speak while they are being performed; nor is it undesirable to speak before the first sermon even if the imam has come out of his private chamber, between the two sermons, or between the second sermon and the announcement that the Friday prayer has commenced. Similarly, speaking during the sermon is not undesirable for someone who is so far from the imam that, even if he listened, he would not be able to hear him; in such a person's case, it is an emulation of the Sunnah to occupy himself with divine remembrance.

The Shafiis make the following four exceptions to what they consider to be undesirable speech during the Friday sermon: (1) Invoking blessing upon someone who has sneezed, since this practice is actually recommended; (2) Praying aloud for blessings and peace upon the Prophet when his noble name is mentioned (though without raising one's voice excessively), which is also a recommended practice; (3) Returning someone's greeting of peace, which is obligatory despite the fact that it is undesirable to initiate such a greeting toward someone who is listening to a sermon; and (4) Speaking with the intention of preventing some kind of harm, for example, to rescue a blind person from danger or to warn others of the presence of a scorpion and the like, since to do so is obligatory. As for praying during the sermon, the ruling on this has been mentioned above.

* * *

According to the Hanbalis, it is forbidden for someone who is close enough to the speaker to hear the Friday sermon to say anything while the sermon is being delivered, be it words of divine remembrance or anything else; this ruling applies, moreover, even if the speaker is not a person of good character. As for the speaker himself, he may speak with someone else in order to serve some interest, while it is likewise permissible for someone else to speak with him. It is also permissible for someone listening to the sermon to pray for blessings upon the Prophet when his name is mentioned; however, it is an emulation of the Sunnah to do so silently. It is permissible for someone to utter the word, 'Amen!' in affirmation of the speaker's supplication, to say *al-ḥamdu lillāh* quietly if he sneezes, to say *yarḥamukum Allāh* to someone else who sneezes, and to return someone's greeting in words, though not with a gesture. As for someone who is so far from the speaker that he cannot hear him, he is permitted to speak, and if such a person occupies himself with divine remembrance and Qur'anic recitation, this is preferable to his remaining silent; however, in so doing, he should not raise his voice so as not to distract others from listening to the speaker. According to the Hanbalis, it is not forbidden to speak before the two sermons, during the imam's silence between the two sermons, following the two sermons, or when the speaker begins making supplication, since at this point he will have completed the pillars of the two sermons; hence, the supplication is something which worshipers are not obliged to listen to, and if someone hears someone else speaking, he may not silence him by saying something to him. However, he may gesture to him to be silent by placing his forefinger over his mouth. There are also times when one may be obliged to speak during the sermon, for example, to save a blind person from some danger or to warn someone else of the presence of a snake, a scorpion, fire or the like.

Passing between those seated in order to attend the Friday prayers or cutting into rows

It is not permissible to cut into the rows of those seated to attend the Friday prayer (also referred to as "passing over necks") given detailed conditions which vary from one school to another.[305]

Traveling on Friday

All four schools agree that traveling on Friday is forbidden, although their rulings on the matter differ in detail.[306]

---

305. According to the Hanafis, there is nothing wrong with cutting into the rows of worshipers gathered for the Friday prayer given two conditions: (1) that one not cause offense by doing so, for example, by stepping on someone's robe or touching his body, and (2) that one do so before the imam has begun delivering the sermon; otherwise, it is undesirable to the point of being forbidden. An exception to such conditions is made if someone passes through a row out of necessity, as, for example, when this is the only way he will be able to find a place to sit down.

* * *

According to the Shafiis, "passing over necks" at the time of the Friday congregational prayer is undesirable; they define "passing over necks" as lifting one's leg and passing it over the shoulder of someone who is seated. As for passing between rows, this is not included here. In addition, there are certain situations which are excluded from this ruling, namely: (1) If the person who does the "passing" is one from whom such an action would not be considered offensive, such as a righteous or great man; (2) If the person sees a "gap" which he wants to fill, in which case it is an emulation of the Sunnah for him to pass over others in order to do so; (3) If those who are sitting in the front rows where the listeners can hear the speaker are people whose attendance will not go toward completing the quorum for the Friday prayer (such as young boys), in which case it is obligatory for those whose attendance does go toward completing the quorum to pass over others in order to sit in the front rows; and (4) If the person who does the "passing" is the imam for the Friday prayer, and if he is only able to reach the pulpit by doing so.

* * *

According to the Hanbalis, it is undesirable for anyone but the imam or the muezzin who delivers the call to prayer in the presence of the speaker after he enters the mosque for the Friday prayer to pass over people's necks unless the person sees an opening in the front row and is unable to get to it without doing so. As for the "passing over" which is considered undesirable, it involves lifting one's leg and passing it over the shoulder of someone who is seated.

* * *

According to the Malikis, "passing over necks" is forbidden after the speaker ascends the pulpit even if its purpose is to fill a gap in one of the rows. Before the speaker ascends the pulpit, "passing over necks" is undesirable [rather than forbidden entirely] if it is done for some reason other than to fill a gap in one of the rows and if it causes no offense or harm to someone already seated. If one "passes over necks" to fill a gap in a row, it is acceptable, whereas if it causes harm or offense to any of those seated, it is forbidden. Between the end of the sermon and the beginning of the Friday prayer, "passing over necks" is permissible; as for passing between rows, it is permissible even while the sermon is being delivered.

306. According to the Hanafis, it is undesirable to leave one's city on Friday after the first call to prayer and before one has performed the Friday congregational prayer, properly speaking. As for traveling before noon, it is not undesirable.

* * *

According to the Malikis, it is undesirable to travel after dawn on Friday if the person who does so will not be able to perform the Friday congregational prayer on the way; otherwise, it is acceptable. It is also permissible to travel before dawn; as for traveling after noon, it is forbidden even if it is before the call to prayer unless there is some clear need to do so, for example, if someone has fallen behind travel companions and fears harm to himself or his property as a result. In this case, and if the person knows that he will be able to perform the Friday prayer on the way, it is permissible for him to travel.

* * *

According to the Shafiis, it is forbidden for someone who is accountable for performing the Friday congregational prayer to travel after dawn on Friday unless he has good reason to believe that he will be able to perform the Friday prayer on his way, or unless the journey is being made in fulfillment of a duty (for example, in order to complete the greater pilgrimage before the time period allowed for this runs out) or out of necessity (for example, in order to catch up with travel companions in whose absence one fears one would suffer some kind of harm); however, if it is simply a matter of feeling lonely without them, this will not render the trip permissible. As for traveling before dawn on Friday, it is undesirable.

* * *

According to the Hanbalis, it is forbidden for someone who is obliged to perform the Friday prayer to travel after noon on Friday unless not doing so would cause him harm, for example, by his lagging behind travel companions on a permissible journey. As for traveling before noon, it is undesirable. Specifically, traveling before noon is undesirable or forbidden if the person who does so does not perform the Friday prayer along the way; otherwise, it is permissible.

If someone has missed the Friday congregational prayer without an excuse, he is not permitted to perform the noon prayer before the imam has finished praying

If someone who is accountable for attending the Friday congregational prayer refrains from attending it without a valid excuse, he is not permitted to perform the noon prayer before the imam has finished leading the Friday congregational prayer and uttered the concluding greeting of peace. If such a person performs the noon prayer before this, it will have no validity according to the Shafiis and the Hanbalis; for the views of the Hanafis and the Malikis, see below.[307]

As for individuals who are not accountable for performing the Friday congregational prayer, such as those who are ill and the like, their noon prayer will be valid even if they perform it while the imam is still leading the Friday congregational prayer. Nevertheless, it is recommended that one delay one's noon prayer if there is some hope that the condition which prevented the person from attending the Friday congregational prayer will pass [soon]; otherwise, it is recommended that such a person perform the noon prayer as soon as possible after the relevant time period begins rather than waiting for the imam to conclude the Friday congregational prayer. This view is agreed upon by the Shafiis, the Malikis and the Hanbalis; for the view of the Hanafis, see below.[308]

---

307. The Hanafis hold that if someone who has no excuse for not attending the Friday congregational prayer refrains from attending it, then performs the noon prayer before the imam has concluded his own prayer, his noon prayer will be valid given certain conditions. If this person does not attend the Friday congregational prayer at all, his noon prayer will be valid even though it is forbidden to neglect the Friday congregational prayer. If, on the other hand, he walks to the place where the Friday prayer is being held and the imam has not finished his prayer when he arrives, this person's noon prayer will be invalidated by his walking from his home to the mosque, and it will be counted as a voluntary prayer [the reason being that, by leaving home to go to the mosque, the person has the intention of repeating the noon prayer – t.n.]; in this case, he must join the imam in the Friday congregational prayer, and if he does not join him in time, he must repeat the noon prayer. If, on the other hand, the imam has finished the Friday congregational prayer [by the time the worshiper arrives at the mosque], his noon prayer will not be invalidated by walking. The same ruling applies if the person's walking coincides with the imam's completion of his prayer, or if it precedes the *iqāmah* for the Friday congregational prayer.

* * *

The Malikis hold that if someone is accountable for performing the Friday congregational prayer and has no excuse which would allow him to absent himself from it, and if he performs the noon prayer although he has good reason to believe that if he went to the place where the Friday congregational prayer is being held he would arrive in time to perform one *rak'ah* of it, his noon prayer will be invalid, properly speaking, and he must repeat it. If, on the other hand, he is far enough from the site of the Friday prayer that if he went there he would not arrive in time to

Whether it is permissible for someone who has missed the Friday congregational prayer to perform the noon prayer in community

If someone misses the Friday congregational prayer, with or without an excuse, it is permissible for him to perform the noon prayer in community; however, each school offers its own detailed ruling on this matter.[309]

---

perform one *rak'ah* of it, his noon prayer will be valid. Similarly, the noon prayer will be valid when performed by those who are not accountable for performing the Friday congregational prayer even if they know that if they went to the site of the Friday prayer, they would arrive in time to perform the entire prayer.

308. The Hanafis hold that for someone with a condition that exempts him from attending the Friday congregational prayer, it is an emulation of the Sunnah to delay his noon prayer until after the imam has finished leading the Friday congregational prayer, and that performing the noon prayer before this is undesirable regardless of whether he has reason to hope that his condition will pass or not.

309. According to the Hanafis, if someone misses the Friday congregational prayer with or without an excuse, it is undesirable for him to perform the Friday noon prayer in community if he is in a city. However, in the case of inhabitants of rural areas for whom the Friday congregational prayer is not valid, it is permissible for them to perform the Friday noon prayer with a group without any undesirability attached to it, since for such people, Friday is no different from any other day of the week.

* * *

The Shafiis hold that if someone misses the Friday congregational prayer with or without an excuse, it is an emulation of the Sunnah for him to perform the noon prayer in community. If the condition on account of which he was excused from performing the Friday congregational prayer is apparent to others, such as his being on a journey, he will emulate the Sunnah by openly performing the noon prayer in community, whereas if the condition is unseen, such as severe hunger, it is an emulation of the Sunnah for him to conceal the fact that he is performing the noon prayer in community. Moreover, if someone neglects the Friday congregational prayer without an excuse, he must perform the noon prayer immediately after the imam finishes the Friday congregational prayer.

* * *

The Hanbalis hold that if someone misses the Friday congregational prayer without an excuse or if he refrains from attending it because it is not required of him, it is preferable for him to perform the noon prayer communally in an open manner provided that he does not fear causing others temptation in this way; otherwise, he is required to conceal the fact that he has performed it in community.

* * *

According to the Malikis, someone with a condition which exempts him from attending the Friday congregational prayer (such as insanity, or an illness that renders him unable to walk to the mosque) is required to perform the noon prayer in community; however, it is recommended that such a person conceal the fact that he

The ruling on someone who joins the imam in time to perform one *rak'ah* or less of the Friday prayer

A worshiper who joins the imam in time to perform the second *rak'ah* of the Friday congregational prayer is considered to have made a valid beginning of this prayer, after which it is agreed that he must perform one more *rak'ah*, then utter the concluding greeting of peace. However, if such a person does not join the imam until the final 'sitting' [during which the testimony and the final greeting of peace are uttered], he must perform four *rak'ahs* as the regular noon prayer. In this situation, the worshiper should stand up after the imam has finished praying and perform four *rak'ahs*. According to the Malikis and the Shafiis, such a person will not have performed the Friday congregational prayer; for the views of the Hanafis and the Hanbalis, see below.[310]

---

is performing the noon prayer in community lest he be accused of neglecting the Friday congregational prayer. It is also recommended that such a person delay the noon prayer until after the Friday congregational prayer has been performed. However, in the case of someone who has not taken part in the Friday congregational prayer without a valid excuse, or with an excuse which need not prevent him from attending the prayer—such as fear for his money if he attends—it is undesirable for him to perform the noon prayer in community.

310. According to the Hanafis, someone who joins the imam in time to perform any part of the Friday prayer with him will have made a valid start even if he does not join the imam until he is uttering the testimony as part of a prostration of forgetfulness; then, after the imam has finished praying, the worshiper may complete his own prayer as a valid Friday prayer.

* * *

As for the Hanbalis, they hold that if a worshiper joins the imam in time to perform one complete *rak'ah* of the Friday congregational prayer, he may complete it on his own as the Friday congregational prayer; otherwise, he must complete it as a regular noon prayer. In this case, however, he must have performed the congregational prayer during the time period for the noon prayer, and he must have made it his conscious intention to perform the noon prayer. Otherwise, he must complete it as a simple voluntary prayer, then perform the noon prayer as well.

Recommended practices associated with the Friday congregational prayer

Recommended practices associated with the Friday congregational prayer include the following:

(1) Improving one's appearance by trimming one's fingernails and one's moustache, removing underarm hair, etc.

(2) Bathing and putting on cologne. This practice is based on the prophetic Sunnah according to the Shafiis, the Hanafis and the Hanbalis, whereas the Malikis hold that it is merely recommended.

(3) Reciting or reading Surah 18 both during the day and at night on Friday. For those who have memorized this chapter of the Qur'ān or who can read it, it is recommended that they do so. As for reciting or reading it in the mosque, it is agreed by all schools not to be allowed if raising one's voice would cause disturbance or show a lack of reverence for the mosque's sanctity.

(4) Offering many prayers for blessings and peace upon the Prophet.

(5) Offering extra supplications on this day. This practice is based on the saying of the Prophet, "There is an hour on Friday during which no Muslim asks anything of God Almighty but that God will give it to him," after which he gestured with his hand to indicate the briefness of this period of time.[311]

(6) Going early to the place where the Friday prayer is to be held. This applies to worshipers other than the imam; as for the imam, it is not recommended that he go to the site early. As for the meaning of 'early', it includes any time before the call to prayer.

(7) Walking calmly to the Friday prayer site approximately two hours before it is due to begin. This practice is recommended by the Shafiis, the Hanafis and the Hanbalis; for the Malikis' view, see below.[312]

(8) Dressing up in one's best clothes, the preferable color being white according to the Shafiis and the Hanafis. As for the Malikis and the Hanbalis, their views may be seen below.[313]

---

311. Narrated by Muslim.

312. According to the Malikis, it is recommended that one go to the Friday prayer at midday and that one start out about one hour before high noon. As for going very early, that is, before this time, it is undesirable.

313. According to the Malikis, the recommended practice is to wear white on Fridays. If either the Day of Fastbreaking or the Day of Sacrifice happens to fall on a Friday, one should wear something new in the early part of the day, even if it happens to be black, since the Sunnah-based practice for the holidays is to wear something new regardless of what color it is. Then, when one goes out for the Friday congregational prayer, it is recommended that one wear something white. In this way, one will have dressed in a manner which befits both Friday and the holiday.

* * *

As for the Hanbalis, they hold that the recommended practice on Friday is to wear white and nothing else.

Prayer leadership (*al-imāmah*)

Prayer leadership will be discussed under the following headings:

(1) Its definition and the number of worshipers required to make it valid.

(2) The ruling on prayer leadership and the evidence in its support.

(3) The conditions associated with prayer leadership, which include the following: (a) the ruling on prayer leadership by women; (b) the ruling on prayer leadership by a boy who has reached the age of discernment; (c) the ruling on prayer leadership by someone who neither reads nor writes; (d) the ruling on prayer leadership by someone who has had an occurrence of ritual impurity, then forgotten about it; (e) the ruling on prayer leadership by someone with a lisp or some other speech defect; (f) the worshiper's intention to emulate the prayer leader; (g) the prayer leader's intention to lead the prayer; (h) the situation in which a worshiper performing an obligatory prayer follows an imam who is performing a voluntary prayer; (i) the worshiper's emulation of his imam; and (j) consistency between the obligatory prayer being performed by those being led in prayer and the one being performed by the imam; for example, it is not valid for those being led in prayer to perform the noon prayer behind an imam who is performing the mid-afternoon prayer.

(4) Conditions which cause the requirement to perform a given prayer in community to be dropped.

(5) Those who have the right of priority in prayer leadership.

(6) Undesirable practices associated with prayer leadership.

(7) How the worshiper is to stand with his imam, how the imam is to stand with the worshipers praying behind him, and who is more entitled to stand in the front row.

(8) Keeping the rows even and close together.

(9) The right of someone who has performed an obligatory prayer in community to pray with another group as well.

(10) Repeating a communal prayer in the same mosque in which it was performed the first time.

(11) How much of a prayer must be performed in order for it to be valid as a communal prayer.

(12) The ruling on a worshiper who misses some or all *rak'ahs* with his imam due to a valid excuse, such as overcrowding in the mosque, etc.

(13) The imam's appointment of someone else to take his place.

The definition of prayer leadership and a discussion of the quorum required in order for such leadership to be valid

Prayer leadership (*imāmah*) involves one person's linking his ritual prayer to that of a prayer leader, or imam, who meets all the conditions for this function. (Such conditions will be outlined below.) As a consequence, he follows the imam in his standing, bowing, prostrating, sitting, and so on. This linking, or association, is referred to as prayer leadership, or *imāmah*; however, it will be clear that this association is one-directional in the sense that the person being led in prayer is dependent on the prayer leader, or imam, but not vice-versa, since it consists in the former's following the latter in the actions involved in ritual prayer. Hence, if the prayer of the person following is invalidated, the imam's prayer remains valid, whereas if the imam's prayer is invalidated, so is that of the person following him, since he has linked his prayer to that of the imam.

Prayer leadership is valid given the presence of at least one worshiper in addition to the imam; moreover, all four schools agree that this one worshiper may be either a woman or a man. According to the Hanafis and the Shafiis, the one worshiper may be a young boy who has reached the age of discernment, whereas according to the Malikis and the Hanbalis, he must be joined by at least one other as well in addition to the imam.

The ruling on prayer leadership for the five obligatory prayers and the evidence in its favor

All four schools agree that prayer leadership is desirable in connection with the obligatory prayers; hence, those who are held accountable for such prayers should not pray alone without a valid excuse. However, the Hanbalis hold that prayer leadership is an individual obligation in connection with every one of the five obligatory prayers. None of the other three schools agree with the Hanbalis on this point; however, the Hanbalis—along with other scholars who agree with them—support this position based on the hadith narrated by al-Bukhārī and Abū Hurayrah according to which the Prophet said, "[I swear] by the One Who holds my soul in His hand, I am about to give orders to have firewood brought, to have the prayer performed and the call to prayer sounded, and to assign a man to lead the people in prayer [in my place], then to take issue with [certain] men and burn their houses down! By the One Who holds my soul in His hand, if one of these men knew that he would find a rich piece of meat or a couple of handsome hunting arrows [at the mosque], he would attend the evening prayer!"[314]

This hadith indicates that communal prayer is an obligation, since the punishment of burning with fire would only be for the neglect of a duty or the commission of an offense of the most serious nature. This conclusion does not require that the Prophet actually have burned down the houses of the men mentioned in the hadith; rather, it is sufficient to understand his words as an affirmation of the weighty significance of communal prayer and his earnest concern to promote it. It should also be noted that this saying mentions only the evening prayer (*al-'ishā'*), and none of the other five daily prayers. Thus, if the Hanbalis and those who agree with them on this point have a basis for their inference, it must be limited in its application to the evening prayer alone. As for the other four obligatory prayers, they are not included here.

Scholars of the other three schools have offered a variety of responses to this argument by the Hanbalis. They have noted, for example, that this saying of the

---

314. The editor notes that this hadith is narrated by Abū Dāwūd, Ibn Mājah, al-Tirmidhī, al-Nasā'ī and Muslim as well [t.n.].

Prophet was uttered in the very early days of Islam when the number of Muslims was still small and it was only required that they perform the evening prayer in particular in community, since it was in the evening that they would be finished with their day's labors; later, however, when their numbers had grown, this saying was superceded by another, namely, "Communal prayer is superior to individual prayer by twenty-seven degrees." To speak of one entity as superior to another implies that both entities share in some degree of virtue. Moreover, it follows from the fact that individual prayer is virtuous that it must be permissible, and all four schools agree that the ruling on burning with fire for those who fail to attend communal prayer has been abrogated; hence, there is only a weak basis for citing this hadith as evidence that communal prayer is obligatory.

The Hanbalis also base their view that obligatory prayers must be performed in community on the following Qur'anic verse: "Thus, when you are among the believers and about to lead them in prayer, let [only] part of them stand up with you, retaining their arms. Then, after they have finished their prayer, let them provide you cover while another group, who have not yet prayed, shall come forward and pray with you, being fully prepared against danger and retaining their arms..." (4:102). The basis for the Hanbalis' induction from this passage is that God Almighty held the believers accountable for performance of communal prayer even in times of tribulation and danger. From this they conclude that if communal prayer were not obligatory, God would not have held them accountable for performing it in this manner. However, scholars of the other three schools hold that this passage means simply that communal prayer is permissible, but not that it is an individual obligation. As for the observation that this was a time of fear and tribulation, this is true, of course; however, the reason for which they were taught to pray in this manner may be that it allowed them to be on their guard against danger better than individual prayer would have, since the group standing in the direction of the enemy acted as a guard for the others such that, if the enemy found an opportunity to attack them unawares, the group standing guard could warn the others to discontinue their prayer and resist the enemy, an arrangement that entailed the utmost precision and vigilance. At the same time, this verse is evidence of the great importance placed on communal prayer among the first Muslims, who were aware of the grandeur of the ever-living, eternal Creator of all that exists, who never passes away. They knew that ritual prayer is an expression of humble subservience to their Creator and a demonstration of humble reverence which must not be neglected even in the most critical and perilous situations. In sum, then: All four schools agree that communal prayer is desirable; as for saying that it is an individual obligation for all five of the daily prayers, however, this is not accepted by the majority of them.

For the view of each of the four schools on performing the five daily prayers in community, see below.[315]

---

315. According to the Malikis, there are two valid rulings on performing the five daily obligatory prayers in community. The first of these has the widest popularity, while the second is closer to the most valid position. According to the first

view, performing the obligatory prayers in community is an emphatically enjoined Sunnah-based practice for every worshiper, in every mosque, and in the town where the worshiper is residing. Based on this view, if some residents of the town perform the prayers in community, other residents of the same town need not have arms taken up against them for their neglect of this practice; otherwise, the entire town is to be resisted with arms for having made light of the prophetic Sunnah. As for the second view, it holds that performing the five daily prayers in community is a collective obligation within the town; this means that if everyone in the town neglects this practice, arms must be taken up against them, but if some of them adhere to it, the others in the town are exempted from the obligation. According to this same view, the performance of the five daily prayers in community is an emulation of the Sunnah for men in every mosque, and recommended for each worshiper individually. Adherents of the Maliki school may follow either of these two views. If one adopts the ruling that performing the five daily prayers communally is an emphatically enjoined emulation of the Sunnah for each worshiper and in every mosque, this is considered a valid point of view. Nevertheless, even though it is an emphatically enjoined emulation of the Sunnah for each individual worshiper, it is also true that if some residents of a given town engage in this practice, it is no longer required of the rest of them; hence, they are not to be resisted militarily for neglecting it. In other words, the existence in a town of even one mosque where communal prayers are performed is sufficient to protect the town from having arms taken up against it due to those residents who do not perform the prayers in community. As for those who hold that performing the five daily prayers in community is a collective obligation, they also hold that if some residents of the town engage in this practice, the obligation to do so is dropped for the rest. The Shafiis agree with this view, although they differ with the Malikis over certain details.

* * *

According to the Hanafis, performance of the five daily prayers in community is an emphatically enjoined Sunnah-based practice for each individual worshiper; one might also refer to it as a 'duty', since properly speaking, emphatically enjoined Sunnah-based practices are, in effect, duties. (As we have seen, a 'duty' in the Hanafis' understanding is a practice which is less binding than a full obligation; hence, someone who neglects a 'duty' incurs less guilt than someone who neglects a full obligation.) On this point, the Hanafis agree with those Malikis who hold that performing the five daily prayers is an emphatically enjoined emulation of the Sunnah for each individual. However, they disagree with them over the issue of taking up arms against the people of the town for neglecting this practice; rather, they hold that this practice is an emulation of the Sunnah for free men who are in full possession of their mental faculties, who are fully clothed, and who do not suffer any condition which would exempt them from performing the five daily prayers in community. As for the ruling on communal prayer as it pertains to women and young boys as well as the remaining conditions associated with prayer leadership, these will be discussed below.

* * *

There is more than one view among the Shafiis concerning the ruling on performing the five obligatory prayers in community. The view with the most solid

The ruling on prayer leadership for the Friday congregational prayer, funeral prayers, and voluntary prayers

Having presented the ruling on the performance of the five daily prayers in community, it now remains to present the ruling on the communal performance of other ritual prayers, such as the funeral prayer, the Friday prayer, the two holiday prayers, the prayer for the solar eclipse, the prayer for rain, and other voluntary prayers. For each school's ruling on this matter, see below.[316]

---

support is that it is a collective obligation such that, if some residents of a given community perform the required prayers in community, this obligation is dropped where other residents are concerned. Hence, if a prayer is performed in community in one of the town's mosques, the other residents of the town are not obliged to perform it in community. Another view, which enjoys popularity among the Shafiis, is that it is an emphatically enjoined Sunnah-based practice. Moreover, they apply the same ruling to the funeral prayer; however, they hold that if even one man or one boy who has reached the age of discernment performs the funeral prayer, the obligation to do so is dropped for others (whereas if one woman performs the funeral prayer, this does not exempt others from the obligation.) For more details on this matter, see the section below on the funeral prayer.

The Hanbalis hold that performing the five daily prayers in community is an individual obligation given the conditions to be enumerated below; as for the basis for this ruling, it has been explained in the body of the text.

316. The Malikis' rulings in this regard may be enumerated as follows: (1) With regard to the Friday congregational prayer, its performance in community is a condition for its validity. (2) With respect to the prayer for the solar eclipse, the prayer for rain, and the prayers performed on the Day of Fastbreaking and the Day of Sacrifice, their performance in community is a condition for their being an emulation of the Sunnah; in other words, one misses the reward for emulation of the Sunnah when performing these prayers unless one performs them in community. (3) Performance of the *tarāwīḥ* prayers in community is considered desirable. (4) As for all other voluntary prayers, their performance in community is sometimes considered undesirable and at other times, acceptable. It is undesirable if they are performed in the mosque or with a large group, or if they are performed in a place which is frequented by large numbers of people, whereas it is acceptable if they are performed with a small group, in one's home, or in some place which is not frequented by many people.

* * *

The Hanafis' rulings on this matter are as follows: (1) Communal performance of the Friday prayer and the prayers for the Day of Fastbreaking and the Day of Sacrifice is a condition for their validity. (2) Communal performance of the *tarāwīḥ* prayers and the funeral prayer is a collective emulation of the Sunnah. (3) With regard to unidentified voluntary prayers and the *witr* at times other than Ramaḍān, their communal performance is undesirable if the number of worshipers following the imam is greater than three. As for communal performance of the *witr* during Ramaḍān, there are two views on this which are both recognized as valid: According to the first, it is desirable, and according to the second, it is not desirable, but permissible. The second of these views has the most solid support.

* * *

According to the Shafiis, performance of the first *rak'ah* of the Friday prayer in community is an individual obligation, whereas in the second *rak'ah*, it is an emulation of the Sunnah. Hence, if a worshiper joins the imam in the first *rak'ah* of the Friday prayer, then consciously intends to part with the imam and pray the second *rak'ah* alone, his prayer will be valid. The Shafiis also identify five other situations in which the performance of ritual prayer in community is an individual obligation: (1) In every prayer which is repeated during the time period for the prayer concerned. Thus, for example, if someone prayed the noon prayer on his own or with a group, then wished to perform the prayer again, it would not be permissible for him to do so unless he performed it with a group. (2) In a prayer which is joined with the prayer subsequent to it and performed early on account of rain. In such a case, however, only the second of the two prayers joined must be performed in community. If, for example, it is raining heavily after the commencement of the time period for the noon prayer, one may legitimately join the noon and mid-afternoon prayers by performing them both earlier. However, whereas one may validly pray the noon prayer alone, the mid-afternoon prayer must be performed in community; otherwise, it will not be valid. (3) In a ritual prayer which one has vowed that he will perform in community. (4) In an obligatory prayer which only two people are available to perform. For example, if it happened that there were only two people present in a given place, it would be their duty to perform whatever the prayer happened to be communally. The reason for this is that, properly speaking, the communal performance of the five daily required prayers is a collective duty; hence, if there were only two people available to pray the prayer, this communal performance would be obligatory for both of them. (5) In a situation where a worshiper joins the imam while the latter is bowing and the worshiper knows that if he follows the imam, he will be able to complete one entire *rak'ah* of the prayer during the relevant time period whereas if he performed the prayer on his own, he would miss the *rak'ah*.

As for the prayers for the Day of Fastbreaking and the Day of Sacrifice, the prayer for rain, the prayer for the solar eclipse, the *tarāwīḥ* and the *witr* during Ramaḍān, it is recommended that they be performed in community according to the Shafiis. It is similarly recommended that one perform communally a missed prayer which one needs to make up when the imam is performing the same prayer; for example, if a worshiper needs to make up a noon prayer, it is recommended that he make it up behind an imam who is performing this prayer. Communal performance of prayer is also recommended for someone who missed the Friday congregational prayer due to some valid excuse; for such a person, it is recommended that he perform the noon prayer communally in place of the Friday prayer. In the case of a ritual prayer which someone has vowed to perform, its communal performance is allowed. However, communal performance of prayer is undesirable if: (a) the person being led is performing the prayer on time while the imam is making up for a prayer missed, or vice-versa, (b) the person being led is performing an obligatory

Conditions for prayer leadership

Being a Muslim

In order for communal prayer to be valid, a number of conditions must be met by the imam, or prayer leader, one of which is that he be a Muslim. All four schools agree that the prayer leadership of a non-Muslim is not valid and that if a worshiper prays behind someone who is merely claiming to be a Muslim and discovers this fact after praying, the prayer which he performed behind this person will be invalidated and must be repeated.

Some of my readers might think that such situations rarely occur. In fact, however, the opposite is the case, since non-Muslims frequently make themselves out to be Muslims for material gain, putting on an air of piety in order to achieve their own [worldly] aims.

Being of legal age, and whether a boy who has reached the age of discernment may serve as prayer leader

One of the conditions for the validity of prayer leadership is that the prayer leader be "of age"; hence, if an adult worshiper follows the leadership of a boy who has reached the age of discernment in an obligatory prayer, the prayer will be invalid according to all of the schools with the exception of the Shafiis.[317]

---

prayer while the imam is performing a voluntary prayer, or vice-versa, or (c) if the person being led is performing a *witr* while the imam is performing *tarāwīḥ* or vice-versa.

* * *

As for the Hanbalis, their rulings are as follows: (1) Communal performance of the Friday congregational prayer is required. (2) It is an emulation of the prophetic Sunnah for free, able-bodied men to perform communally any required prayers which they have missed and need to make up. (3) It is an emulation of the Sunnah to perform the funeral prayer in community. (4) As for voluntary prayers, there are some for which it is an emulation of the Sunnah to perform them in community, such as the prayer for rain, the *tarāwīḥ* prayers, and the prayers for the Day of Fastbreaking and the Day of Sacrifice, while there are others which it is simply permissible to perform in community, such as voluntary night prayers and the Sunnah-based *rak'ahs* which are associated with each of the five daily prayers.

317. According to the Shafiis, it is permissible for an adult to follow a boy who has reached the age of discernment in any obligatory prayer except the Friday congregational prayer. In the case of the Friday prayer, the imam must be an adult if he is included in the quorum required for this prayer's validity; however, if the quorum is complete without the imam, he may be a boy who has reached the age of discernment.

In voluntary prayers, by contrast, an adult may follow the leadership of a boy who has reached the age of discernment according to all of the schools except the Hanafis.[318]

As for a boy who has reached the age of discernment acting as imam for another boy of the same age, this is acceptable according to all four schools.

Women's serving as prayer leaders

Another condition for the validity of prayer leadership is confirmed maleness; hence, a woman may not validly serve as the prayer leader, nor may a "problematic hermaphrodite" if those being led in prayer are men. However, if those being led in prayer are women, it is not necessary for the imam to be a male. Rather, it is permissible for a woman to act as imam for other women or for hermaphrodites according to the Shafiis, the Hanafis and the Hanbalis; for the view of the Malikis, see below.[319]

Rationality

Another condition for the validity of prayer leadership is that the imam be fully rational; hence, it is not permissible for someone who is insane to act as prayer leader if he remains in this state at all times. However, if he becomes lucid at times and returns to a state of derangement at others, his prayer leadership will be valid when he is lucid, and invalid when he is not.

A literate person being led in prayer by someone who is illiterate

In order for prayer leadership to be valid, the prayer leader must be literate if the person being led in prayer is literate. Hence, it is not permissible for an illiterate person to lead a literate person in prayer, the fundamental condition for 'literacy' being that the imam is able to recite those words and phrases without which the prayer itself will be invalid. Thus, for example, if the imam of a given village is able

---

318. According to the Hanafis, an adult may never validly follow the leadership of a boy in any prayer, be it obligatory or voluntary.

319. According to the Malikis, it is not permissible for a woman or for a "problematic hermaphrodite" to serve as imam for anyone, man or woman, and regardless of whether the prayer being performed is obligatory or voluntary. Rather, they hold that maleness is always a condition for valid prayer leadership regardless of the gender of those being led in prayer.

to recite those words and phrases without which the prayer would not be valid, it is permissible for an educated person to pray behind him. However, if the imam is illiterate, he may only serve as prayer leader to someone who is illiterate as he is, regardless of whether there is a literate person who would be able to lead them in prayer or not. This is the view of the Shafiis, the Hanafis and the Hanbalis; for the view of the Malikis, see below.[320]

The prayer leader's being free of any condition that would exempt him from leading prayer, such as urinary incontinence

Another condition for the validity of prayer leadership is that the imam must be free of any condition that would exempt him [from the usual requirements of ritual purity and the like], such as urinary incontinence, chronic diarrhea, chronic intestinal gas, nosebleeds, etc. Someone who suffers from one of these conditions may not validly serve as prayer leader for someone who is free of them. If the prayer leader and the person being led in prayer suffer from exactly the same condition, then the prayer leadership will be valid; however, if they have different conditions—for example, with one of them suffering from urinary incontinence and the other from chronic nosebleeds—then neither of them may validly serve as imam for the other. This much is agreed upon by the Hanafis and the Hanbalis; for the views of the Shafiis and the Malikis, see below.[321]

---

320. According to the Malikis, it is not permissible for an illiterate person who is unable to recite the *Fātiḥah* to be led in prayer by someone like him if there is a literate person available; rather, both of them should follow the literate person in prayer and if they fail to do so, their prayer will be invalid. As for someone who is capable of reciting the *Fātiḥah* but who does not do it well, the most proper approach is for him to be forbidden initially to follow in prayer someone who is like him if someone capable of reciting the *Fātiḥah* well is available to serve as imam. Nevertheless, whether or not such a person is available, the illiterate person may validly be led in prayer by someone like himself.

321. According to the Malikis, the validity of prayer leadership does not require that the imam be free of those conditions which may be overlooked; for example, if he suffers from urinary incontinence which may be overlooked due to its chronic nature, even if it only afflicts him half of the time, his prayer leadership will be valid. Similarly, if he suffers from chronic intestinal gas or some other condition which does not invalidate ritual ablutions or ritual prayer, his prayer leadership will continue to be valid. However, it is undesirable for him to lead in prayer someone who does not suffer from the same condition.

* * *

As for the Shafiis, they hold that if the condition from which the imam suffers does not require him to repeat a given prayer, his prayer leadership will be valid even if the person being led in prayer is free from such a condition.

The prayer leader's being free of ritual impurity

Another agreed-upon condition for the validity of prayer leadership is that the imam be free of ritual impurity; hence, if a worshiper prays behind an imam who either has had an occurrence of ritual impurity [be it urination, the passing of gas, etc., without his having repeated his ritual ablutions since then – t.n.] or has some impurity on his body or clothing, his prayer will be invalid, as will be that of the imam, provided that the imam is aware of the impurity and is knowingly performing the prayer despite this fact. If the imam is unaware of the impurity, however, his prayer will be valid. For the various schools' detailed rulings on this point, see below.[322]

---

322. According to the Malikis, the prayer leadership of an imam who has had an occurrence of ritual impurity is invalid if he knows about the impurity and is proceeding with his prayer anyway; the prayers of those following him will be invalid as well. If the imam commences prayer having forgotten the occurrence of ritual impurity or if it take places while he is praying, and if he proceeds to lead the worshipers in prayer after he realizes that he is in a state of ritual impurity or after he has had an occurrence of ritual impurity during the prayer, the prayers of those following him will be invalidated. Similarly, their prayers will be invalidated if they follow the imam after they realize that he is in a state of ritual impurity, even if the imam himself is not aware of it. If the worshipers are not aware of the imam's lack of ritual purity and if the imam is also unaware of it until the prayer has been completed, the prayers of those following the imam will be valid; however, the imam's prayer will be considered invalid in all of the cases described here, since ritual purity is a condition for the validity of prayer. Moreover, the ruling on the prayer of the imam and those being led in prayer if there is some ritually impure substance clinging to the imam's body or clothing is the same as the ruling on their prayers if the imam has had an occurrence of ritual impurity; however, in this case, the imam's prayer will remain valid if he does not learn of the impurity clinging to his body or clothing until after he has completed his prayer, since the presence of impurity on one's body or clothing invalidates prayer only if one is aware of its presence.

* * *

According to the Shafiis, it is not permissible to pray behind an imam who has had an occurrence of ritual impurity if the person being led in prayer knows about this from the very beginning; if he learns of it during the prayer, he must consciously intend to part with the imam and finish praying on his own, and if he does so, his prayer will be valid. If, on the other hand, the person being led in prayer only learns of the ritual impurity associated with the imam after the prayer has been concluded, his prayer will be valid and he will receive the reward for having prayed in community. As for the imam's prayer, it will be invalid in all of the above cases due to the absence of ritual purity which is a condition for the validity of prayer; hence, he must repeat it. It is also impermissible to pray behind an imam who has some ritually impure substance on his person which is not visible, such as dried urine, if the person being led in prayer is aware of it. However, if he is not aware of it, his prayer will be valid unless it is the Friday congregational prayer; moreover,

Prayer leadership by someone who has a lisp or some other speech defect

Another condition of the validity of prayer leadership is that the imam be free of any speech defect that causes him to pronounce one letter as another, for example, by pronouncing the *rā'* sound as a *ghayn*, the *sīn* as a *thā'*, the *dhāl* as a *zāy*, the *shīn* as a *sīn*, or any other such substitution. A person with such a condition should correct his pronunciation and seek to articulate each letter correctly to the best of his ability. If, after making such efforts, he is still unable to pronounce some letters correctly, his prayer leadership will only be valid for someone with the same condition. If such a person makes no effort to correct his pronunciation, even his own prayers will be invalid, not to mention his leadership of others in prayer. This ruling is agreed upon by the Hanafis, the Shafiis, and the Hanbalis; however, the Hanafis hold that if such a person is able to correctly recite a passage from the Qur'ān other than the *Fātiḥah*, and if he does so, his prayer will not be invalidated, since the recitation of the *Fātiḥah* is not obligatory in their view. The Malikis, on the other hand, hold that such a person's prayer leadership is unconditionally valid, as will be seen in the presentation of their school's teaching below.

---

even the Friday congregational prayer will be valid if the quorum for this prayer is complete without the imam. Otherwise, the prayer will be invalidated for everyone due to the fact that the quorum was incomplete. If, on the other hand, there is obvious, visible ritual impurity on the imam's person, it is not permissible to pray behind him under any circumstances even if he is ignorant of his condition.

* * *

According to the Hanbalis, it is not permissible for an imam who is in a state of either major or minor ritual impurity to lead others in prayer; nor is it permissible for an imam who has some ritually impure substance on his person and is aware of this. If, on the other hand, both the imam and those being led in prayer are unaware of the ritual impurity on the imam's person until the prayer is over, the prayer of those being led will be valid, but not that of the imam. This ruling applies whether the prayer concerned is the Friday congregational prayer or some other prayer. However, in order for the Friday congregational prayer to be valid, the quorum—that is, forty worshipers not counting the imam—must be complete; otherwise, the prayer will be invalid for everyone. The prayer will also be invalid if those being led in prayer number exactly forty and if one of them has had an occurrence of ritual impurity or has some ritually impure substance on his person.

* * *

As for the Hanafis, they hold that it is not permissible for someone who has had an occurrence of ritual impurity or who has some ritually impure substance on his person to lead others in prayer due to the fact that his own prayer is invalid. As for the prayers of those being led by him, they are valid provided that they are unaware of the imam's ritual impurity. If, on the other hand, they learn of the imam's ritual impurity through the testimony of reliable witnesses or through the testimony of the imam himself (if he is reliable and trustworthy), their prayers will be invalidated and they must repeat it. If the imam who has informed them of his ritual impurity is not trustworthy and reliable, his report is not to be accepted; however, it is desirable for the worshipers to repeat their prayer just in case.

The same rulings apply to someone who assimilates one letter to another by accident, for example, by turning the *s* sound into a *t* sound when the *s* is followed by the *t*, causing him to pronounce the word *mustaqīm* as *muttaqīm*. Such a person must do his best to correct his pronunciation; if he is unable to correct it, his prayer leadership will be valid for others with the same condition, whereas if he makes no effort, both his own prayers and his leadership of others will be invalidated.

As for those who stutter by repeating the letters *fā'* and *tā'* as they speak, they may serve as imam for other worshipers who have the same condition as well as for those who do not have this condition, although the latter practice is undesirable according to the Shafiis and the Hanbalis. According to the Malikis, the prayer leadership of such individuals is unconditionally valid and has no undesirability associated with it. As for the Hanafis, the prayer leadership of such individuals is like that of someone with another sort of speech defect; hence, their prayer leadership is only valid for those with the same condition, given the same stipulation mentioned above. For the Malikis' view on these matters, see below.[323]

---

323. According to the Malikis, individuals with any or all of the speech defects described above may validly serve as prayer leaders, both for others with the same condition and for individuals who suffer from no speech defect. This ruling applies even if there is someone who could teach the person to pronounce the sounds correctly, and before such teaching has taken place, provided that there is sufficient time for him to complete the prayer concerned. According to the best attested view, such a person is under no obligation to work at correcting his pronunciation. Hence, it may be seen that the Malikis do not stipulate that the imam must be free from all speech defects in order validly to lead others in prayer.

324. According to the Malikis, if someone prays behind someone else who arrived in time to perform one *rak'ah* with the imam, his prayer will be invalid regardless of whether the person following the other arrived late or not. If, on the other hand, one person who arrived late for the prayer imitates the movements of someone else who arrived late and is completing his own prayer after the imam's completion of his, and if he does not consciously intend to follow this person as his imam, his prayer will be valid. Similarly, if someone who arrived late for the prayer manages to perform less than one *rak'ah* with the imam—for example, if he only arrived in time for the final testimony—it is permissible to follow him as one's imam since in this case, he is considered to be praying alone rather than to be praying behind the imam.

* * *

According to the Hanafis, it is not permissible for one worshiper to pray behind another who joined the imam late in a given prayer, whether the latter managed to perform an entire *rak'ah* with his imam or less than this. Hence, if two worshipers arrive late for prayer behind a single imam and if, after the imam finishes his prayer, one of the two makes it his intention to pray behind the other [while they complete their own prayers], the prayer of the worshiper who prays behind the other will be invalidated. However, if one of them simply follows the other's movements as a way of remembering which parts of the prayer he missed yet without intending to

Prayer leadership by someone who is praying behind someone else

Another condition for the validity of an imam's prayer leadership is that he not be himself praying behind another imam. For example, if someone joins the mosque's imam for the last two *rak'ahs* of the mid-afternoon prayer, after which the imam utters the concluding greeting of peace and the worshiper concerned rises to make up the first two *rak'ahs*, and if, after this, someone else comes to the mosque and intends to perform the mid-afternoon prayer behind the person who is making up his two missed *rak'ahs*, will this second person's prayer be valid? And secondly, if the mosque is crowded with worshipers and if someone standing in one of the back rows, unable to hear the imam or see his movements, follows the lead of one of the other worshipers praying behind the same imam, will his prayer be valid? Each of the schools offers its own detailed rulings on such questions.[324]

Praying behind someone who is an adherent of a different school

Another condition for the validity of prayer leadership is that the prayer of the imam must be valid according to the school of the person being led in prayer. Hence, if a Hanafi prays behind a Shafii who, after bleeding, did not repeat his ritual ablutions, or if a Shafiis prays behind a Hanafi who touched a woman [and did not repeat his ablutions afterwards], the prayer of the person following the imam will be invalid because, according to his school, the imam's prayer is invalid. This is the view of the Hanafis and the Shafiis; for the views of the Malikis and the Hanbalis, see below.[325]

---

pray behind him as his imam, both their prayers will be valid based on their association with their previous imam.

* * *

According to the Shafiis, it is not permissible to pray behind another worshiper as long as the latter is himself being led in prayer. However, if one worshiper prays behind another as his imam after the latter's imam has concluded his prayer, or after he has made it his intention to part with his imam—given that the intention to part with one's imam is permissible in the Shafii view—it will be permissible for him to pray behind him as his imam. This ruling applies to all ritual prayers other than the Friday congregational prayer.

* * *

Like the Shafiis, the Hanbalis hold that it is not permissible to pray behind another worshiper who is being led in prayer as long as the latter is himself being led in prayer. However, if this worshiper arrived late for the prayer, it will be permissible for someone else to follow him once his imam has concluded his prayer. The only exception to this ruling is that in the Friday congregational prayer, it is not permissible for one person who arrived late to follow another who arrived late as his imam.

325. According to the Malikis and the Hanbalis, the sole basis for judging the validity of a prayer is the school to which the imam adheres. Hence, if a Maliki or a Hanbali follows a Hanafi or a Shafii in a communal prayer, and if the Hanafi or the Shafii did not wipe his entire head when performing ritual ablutions, the prayer

The person being led in prayer sitting or standing in front of his imam, and his ability to observe what the imam is doing

Another condition for the validity of prayer leadership is that the person being led in prayer not stand or sit in front of his imam; if this happens, both the prayer and the prayer leadership associated with it will be invalid. This ruling is agreed upon by the Shafiis, the Hanafis and the Hanbalis; for the Malikis' view, see below.[326] However, those who hold that the worshipers being led in prayer must not move ahead of their imam make an exception to this ruling if the prayer is being performed around the Ka'bah; in this situation, they hold that it is permissible for someone being led in prayer to move ahead of his imam. However, the Shafiis stipulate specific details in this regard.[327]

If the prayer is being performed from a standing position, the condition for the validity of the prayer of the person following the imam is that the back of his foot not be placed ahead of that of the imam; if it is being performed from a sitting position, the prayer of the person being led is valid provided that his buttocks not be ahead of that of the imam. If, on the other hand, the person being led in prayer is directly across from the imam, the Hanafis, the Hanbalis and the Malikis hold that his prayer will be valid without any undesirability attached to it. As for the Shafiis, they hold that it is undesirable to be sitting or standing parallel with one's imam.

Still another condition for the validity of communal prayer is that those being led in prayer have the ability to perceive the imam's movements, whether by sight, hearing, or even through a *muballigh*. If the person being led in prayer is able to do so, his prayer will be valid unless he and his imam are in two different locations; for detailed rulings on this point, see below.[328]

---

of the person following will still be valid given the fact that the imam's prayer is valid according to his own school. As for the validity of the act of following someone else in prayer, this is judged on the basis of the school to which the follower adheres. Thus, for example, if a Maliki or a Hanbali performing an obligatory prayer follows a Shafii who is performing a voluntary prayer, his prayer will be invalid, since a condition for the validity of one worshiper following another as imam is that they both be performing the same prayer.

326. According to the Malikis, following someone else as one's imam does not require that the person or persons being led in prayer not move ahead of the imam. Rather, even if one or all of those being led in prayer were to move ahead of the imam, their prayer would remain valid according to the most widely acknowledged view among the Malikis. At the same time, however, it is considered undesirable to move ahead of the imam unnecessarily.

327. According to the Shafiis, it is not permissible for someone being led in prayer around the Ka'bah to move ahead of his imam if they are both praying from the same side, whereas if they are praying from different sides, it is permissible. However, it is undesirable to move ahead of one's imam without there being some clear necessity, for example, the mosque's being overcrowded.

328. The Shafiis hold that if the imam and the person being led in prayer are both in the mosque, they are considered to be in the same place even if the distance between them is greater than three hundred cubits [141 meters]. (They consider the mosque courtyard to be part of the mosque as well.) Hence, if the imam is praying at one end of the mosque, while those being led in prayer are praying at the other end, the prayer leadership will be valid so long as there is no barrier between the imam and the person being led in prayer which would prevent the latter from reaching the former, such as a door which was fixed in place before the prayer was commenced. Hence, if the way between them is blocked after the prayer is begun, this does no harm, nor would it do any harm for a door to be closed between them during the prayer. Nor does it make any difference whether the direction the person being led in prayer must move to reach the imam is toward, or away from, the *qiblah*.

If the imam and the person being led in prayer are praying outside the mosque and if the distance between them is no greater than approximately three hundred cubits (measured by a human arm length), the prayer will be valid even if there is a partition between them such as a river down which ships sail or a busy street or thoroughfare, provided that the partition or barrier not be one which would actually prevent the person being led in prayer from reaching the imam if he wished to do so. It is also necessary that the person being led in prayer be able to reach the imam by moving directly toward, rather than away from, the *qiblah*. It makes no difference, if the barrier would in fact prevent such a person from reaching the imam, whether the barrier is a door fixed in place before the commencement of the prayer, a closed door, etc. If, on the other hand, one of the two is outside the mosque while the other is inside and if the distance between the person outside the mosque and the edge of the mosque nearest to him is greater than three hundred cubits, the prayer leadership will be invalidated; otherwise, it will be valid if there is no barrier between them which would prevent the person praying from reaching the imam as described above.

* * *

The Hanafis hold that, properly speaking, if the imam and the person being led in prayer are in two different places, the act of following the imam in prayer will be invalidated regardless of whether the person being led in prayer has difficulty perceiving what the imam is doing and saying or not. Thus, if a man, while in his own home, follows the prayer leadership of the mosque's imam and if his house is separated from the mosque by a road or some similar partition, his following of the imam in prayer will be invalid due to their being in different places. However, if the person's house is adjacent to the mosque such that there is nothing between them but the mosque wall, his prayer as a 'follower' will be valid if he has no difficulty perceiving what the imam is doing and saying; the same ruling applies if someone following the imam's leadership prays on the roof of his house when his roof is contiguous with that of the mosque, since he and the imam are not considered to be in two different places. Hence, as long as the imam and the person being led in prayer are in a single, spacious place, such as a large mosque, the prayer of the one following the imam will be valid provided that he is able to perceive what the imam is doing and saying, whether by hearing or seeing the imam, by hearing the *muballigh* or by seeing other worshipers who are following the same imam. However, it is not permissible to follow the *muballigh* if the latter's intention in uttering *takbīrat al-iḥrām* was simply to inform others [and not also to commence prayer himself], since in this case, the *muballigh*'s own prayer will be invalid, thereby invalidating the prayer of anyone who follows him. The prayer of someone following another as his imam in a large mosque will be valid so long as the imam and the person being led in prayer are not separated by a thoroughfare traveled by wheeled vehicles or a river that would be wide enough for a small boat to pass down it. As for the prayer of someone following someone else as his imam in the desert, it will not be valid if the imam and the person following him are separated by an open area wide enough to hold two rows [of worshipers]; the same ruling applies to very large mosques, such as the Dome of the Rock.

* * *

According to the Malikis, the prayer of someone following someone else as his imam is not invalidated by their being in two different places. Hence, even if the imam and the person following him in prayer are separated by a river, a road or a wall, the prayer of the person following the other as his imam will be valid provided that he is able to observe the imam's actions, even if only through someone else who is able to hear him. However, if someone performs the Friday congregational prayer in a house adjacent to the mosque with the intention of following his imam, his prayer will be invalid, since the validity of the Friday congregational prayer is conditional on its being performed in a mosque.

* * *

As for the Hanbalis, they hold that if the imam and the person following him in prayer are not in the same place, the prayer of the person following the imam will not be valid. Specifically, if the imam and the person being led in prayer are separated by a river down which ships pass, the prayers of both the imam and the person being led in prayer will be invalidated. If they are separated by a road and if the prayer concerned is one which—like the Friday congregational prayer and others that involve large gatherings of worshipers—is not valid if performed on a road when it is crowded, the prayer of the person following the imam will not be valid. If the rows are in contact with the road, the prayer of those being led by the imam will be valid even with the existence of a barrier between the imam and those he is leading; otherwise, however, it will not be valid. If both the imam and those he is leading in prayer are in the mosque, his leadership of them will be valid even if there is a barrier between him and them when *takbīrat al-iḥrām* is heard. If both the imam and those being led in prayer are outside the mosque, or if those being led in prayer are outside the mosque while the imam is inside, the prayer leadership will be valid provided that those being led in prayer can see either the imam or someone who is behind him for the duration of at least part of the prayer; this includes seeing the imam through a window. As long as this condition is fulfilled, the prayer leadership will be valid even if the distance between the imam and the person being led in prayer is greater than three hundred cubits.

The intention of the person being led in prayer to follow the imam, and the imam's intention to lead prayer

Another condition for the validity of prayer leadership is that the person to be led in prayer must consciously intend to follow his imam in all prayers; this ruling is agreed upon by the Shafiis, the Hanbalis and the Malikis.[329] One's intention should come at the beginning of one's prayer such that it coincides with the utterance of *takbīrat al-iḥrām* by the person being led in prayer, whether in a literal sense or in the legal sense, as was seen in the earlier discussion of intention. Thus, if a worshiper commences his prayer with the intention of performing it alone, after which he finds an imam during the prayer and intends to follow him, his prayer will not be valid due to the fact that the intention [to follow the imam] did not come in the beginning of the prayer. Hence, it is not permissible for someone praying alone to switch during the prayer to performing it in community, nor is it permissible for someone who began his prayer communally to switch during the prayer to performing it alone by intending to part with his imam unless there is some clear necessity for doing so—for example, in a case where the imam is taking an excessively long time to pray. These rulings are agreed upon by the Hanafis, the Hanbalis and the Malikis; for the Shafiis' rulings, see below.[330]

---

329. According to the best attested view among the Hanafis, the intention to follow one's imam is not a condition for prayer's validity in the case of the Friday congregational prayer and the holiday prayers, since these prayers are only valid if they are performed in community, as a result of which there is no need for the intention to follow one's imam.

330. According to the Shafiis, the conscious intention to follow the imam does not have to come at the very beginning of the prayer concerned. Thus, if a worshiper consciously intends to follow his imam only after the prayer is in progress, his prayer will still be valid, even though this practice is undesirable. However, in the case of the Friday congregational prayer and other prayers whose validity depends on their being performed in community, the intention to follow one's imam must come at the very beginning of the prayer; that is, it must coincide with the utterance of *takbīrat al-iḥrām*. It is permissible for someone being led in prayer consciously to intend to part with the imam even without an excuse, although it is undesirable to do so; an exception to this ruling is made for prayers which are only valid if they are performed in community, such as the Friday congregational prayer, in which case it is not permissible to intend to part with the imam during the first *rak'ah*. The same applies to a prayer which someone wishes to repeat in community and to prayers which are being joined and performed ahead of time; it is not permissible to intend to part with the imam during any part of them.

* * *

The Hanafis hold that if someone being led in prayer switches from praying communally to praying individually, his prayer will be invalidated unless he engages with the imam in the final 'sitting' for long enough to recite the testimony, after which some necessity presents itself, prompting him to utter the final greeting of peace and part with the imam. If he thus parts with the imam without an excuse, his prayer will be valid, although this practice is undesirable, as will be seen below.

As for the imam's intention to lead the prayer (such as his consciously intending to lead the noon prayer, the mid-afternoon prayer, etc.), this is not a condition for the validity of prayer leadership except in specific situations detailed below.[331]

---

331. According to the Hanbalis, the validity of every prayer by someone who follows an imam is dependent on the imam's intention to lead the prayer. Hence, the prayer of someone being led by an imam will be invalidated if the imam has not consciously intended to lead the prayer.

* * *

According to the Shafiis, the validity of the prayers of those being led by an imam requires that the imam consciously intend to lead the prayer communally in those prayers whose validity depends on their being performed communally, such as the Friday congregational prayer, prayers which are being joined and performed early on account of rain, and prayers which are being repeated.

* * *

According to the Hanafis, the imam's intention to lead others in prayer is required for the validity of the prayer of those being led if they are women. Hence, women's prayer will be invalidated if their imam fails consciously to intend to lead them in prayer. However, the imam's own prayer will remain valid even if a woman has prayed directly across from him.

* * *

According to the Malikis, the imam's intention to lead others in prayer is not a condition for the validity of either the imam's prayer or the prayers of the people he is leading except in specific situations: (1) The Friday congregational prayer; this prayer (for both the imam and those he is leading) will be invalidated if the imam does not consciously intend to lead others. (2) When the sundown and evening prayers are being joined [ahead of time] due to rain. The imam's intention to lead others is necessary at the beginning of each of these two prayers; if it is omitted from either prayer, this prayer will be invalidated for both the imam and those being led in prayer due to the fact that these prayers are only valid if they are performed in community. However, the prayer for which this intention was omitted will only be invalid if the imam neglected this intention in the first of the two prayers, in which case the second prayer will be invalidated as well even if the imam did intend to lead others for this prayer. At the same time, there are some Malikis who hold that the first prayer will not be invalidated under any circumstances due to the fact that the first prayer [unlike the second] was performed at its proper time. (3) The prayer of fear, which is performed as follows: After dividing the army into two groups, the imam performs part of the prayer with each group. If the imam omits the intention to lead the others, the prayer is invalidated for the first group only, whereas it remains valid for the imam and the second group. (4) In the case of someone who has been appointed to take the imam's place for a valid reason, he must consciously intend to lead others in prayer in order for the prayers of those who follow him to be valid; if he fails to make this his conscious intention, the prayers of those who follow him will be invalid, although his own prayer will be valid. In addition, the imam obtains the reward for praying in community without the conscious intention

Someone performing an obligatory prayer following an imam who is performing a voluntary prayer

Another condition for the validity of prayer leadership is that the imam not be in a state which is 'weaker' than that of the person being led in prayer. Thus, it is not permissible for someone performing an obligatory prayer to be led by an imam who is performing a voluntary prayer according to the Hanafis, the Hanbalis and the Malikis; the Shafiis, however, hold that it is permissible, albeit undesirable, for someone performing an obligatory prayer to follow an imam performing a voluntary prayer. Similarly, it is not permissible for someone who is capable of bowing to follow an imam who is unable to bow, nor for someone who is fully clothed to follow an imam who is not fully clothed because he was unable to find anything with which to cover himself according to the Hanafis and the Hanbalis; for the views of the Shafiis and the Malikis, see below.[332] According to the Shafiis, the Hanbalis and the Hanafis, it is not permissible for someone who is ritually pure to pray behind an imam who is ritually impure because he has been unable to achieve ritual purity for some reason; the Malikis, by contrast, hold that it is merely undesirable. Lastly, it is not permissible for someone who is able to read and write to pray behind an imam who is illiterate, as we have seen, although it is permissible for someone who is standing up to pray behind an imam who is unable to stand.[333]

---

to lead others in prayer; hence, if someone led a group in prayer without consciously intending to serve as their imam, he would still merit the reward due to those who pray in community.

Lastly, it should be noted that what is meant by the intention to lead others as being a condition for the validity of prayer in the aforementioned situations is that the imam *not* intend to pray alone.

332. According to the Shafiis and the Malikis, it is permissible for someone who is clothed to pray behind an imam who is not fully clothed because he was unable to find anything with which to cover himself; however, whereas the Malikis hold that this practice is undesirable, the Shafiis do not.

333. According to the Malikis, it is not permissible for someone who is standing to follow an imam who is seated and unable to stand even if the prayer being performed is voluntary rather than obligatory, unless the person being led in prayer chooses to sit down during the voluntary prayer, in which case his prayer will be valid behind an imam who is also seated. In a situation in which the person being led in prayer is unable to perform the pillars of prayer, it is permissible for him to follow an imam who is likewise unable to perform them if their handicap is the same—for example, by their both being unable to stand up. An exemption to this ruling is a situation in which one prays with gestures, in which case it is impermissible for a worshiper to lead someone else who also prays with gestures; the reason for this is that gestures are not subject to 'standardization', as it were; thus, the imam's gestures may be less pronounced than those of the person being led in prayer. Similarly, if the imam is unable, for example, to prostrate while the person being led in prayer is only unable to bow, their handicap is thus unequal, which renders the prayer leadership invalid.

* * *

The person being led in prayer following his imam in the actions of prayer

Another condition for the validity of prayer leadership is that the person praying behind the imam follow his imam in the actions of prayer, with each school offering its own detailed ruling in this regard.[334]

According to the Hanafis, it is permissible for someone who is standing up to follow the prayer leadership of someone who is sitting down and who is able to bow and prostrate. As for someone who is unable to bow and prostrate, it is not permissible for someone who is standing up to pray behind him if the person following him is able to bow and prostrate. If both the imam and the person being led in prayer are unable [to bow and prostrate], and if their prayer is being performed through gestures, the prayer leadership will be valid, whether they are seated, lying on their sides, lying on their backs, or in different positions, provided that the imam be in a 'stronger' position than the person being led in prayer, for example, with the imam seated and the person being led in prayer lying on his side.

* * *

According to the Shafiis, a prayer performed by someone who is standing up behind an imam who is either seated and unable to stand or lying on his side and unable to sit up will be valid; similarly, they hold that a prayer performed by someone who is able to bow and prostrate behind someone who is unable to do so will be valid.

* * *

According to the Hanbalis, someone who is standing up may not validly pray behind an imam who is seated and unable to stand up unless he is the regular imam [of the mosque], and unless his inability to stand up is a condition which it is hoped will pass.

334. The Hanafis divide the process of following one's imam into three types: (1) Simultaneous. In this type, the person being led in prayer engages in each act of prayer simultaneously with his imam; for example, he utters *takbīrat al-iḥrām* at the same time as the imam, he bows with the imam, he utters the final greeting of peace with the imam, etc. Included in this category is the situation in which the person being led in prayer bows before his imam, then remains in the bowing position until his imam has completed his own bow. (2) Immediate. In this type, the person being led in prayer commences each action immediately after the imam does so, then shares with him in the rest of it. (3) Delayed. In this type, the person being led in prayer performs the action concerned after the imam does so and with a slight delay, although he catches up with the imam before he begins the subsequent pillar.

Each of these three categories is considered to be a valid type of following of one's imam in the actions of prayer. Thus, for example, if the imam bows and if the person being led in prayer bows either with him, immediately after him such that he takes part in the bow with the imam, or after the imam has come up from his bow and before he goes down into a prostration, he may be said to have followed the imam in the bow. This act of following, whichever of the three types it happens to be, is obligatory in connection with those actions of prayer which are themselves obligatory, a 'duty' in connection with those actions that are classified as 'duties', and an emulation of the Sunnah in connection with those actions which are emulations of the Sunnah. Thus, for example, if the person being led in prayer bows and comes up from his bow before the imam commences his bow rather than bowing with or after the imam, his prayer will be invalidated due to his not having followed the imam in an obligatory action of prayer. Similarly, if the person being led in prayer bows and prostrates before the imam, the *rak'ah* in which this occurred will be nullified. The second *rak'ah* is then counted as the first, the third *rak'ah* is counted as the second, and the fourth *rak'ah* is counted as the third; then, after the imam utters his concluding greeting of peace, there remains one *rak'ah* which the person must make up, and if he fails to make it up, the prayer he just performed will be invalid. Further clarification of this ruling will be found below in the section, "The prayer of someone who has arrived late for communal prayer." If the person being led in prayer does not follow his imam in the prayer of obedience, he commits wrongdoing for having neglected something which is a 'duty', whereas if he fails to follow the imam in the words of praise to God which are uttered while bowing, for example, he will simply have neglected a practice based on the Sunnah.

In addition, there are four situations in which the person being led in prayer should not follow his imam: (1) If the imam deliberately performs an extra prostration. (2) If the imam utters the phrase *Allāhu akbar* more times than the Prophet's companions, may God be pleased with them, are reported to have done in the holiday prayers. (3) If the imam utters the words *Allāhu akbar* more than five times when performing the funeral prayer. (4) If, after the final 'sitting', the imam absentmindedly gets up to perform a *rak'ah* beyond what is included in one of the obligatory prayers. If, in this last situation, the imam rises after the final 'sitting' to perform an extra *rak'ah* and then confirms this *rak'ah* with a prostration, the person being led in prayer should utter the final greeting of peace on his own. If the imam does not perform the extra *rak'ah* with a prostration but instead, returns to his seated position and utters the final greeting of peace, the person being led in prayer should utter it with the imam. However, if the imam rises to perform the extra *rak'ah* before the final 'sitting', and if he confirms it with a prostration, everyone's prayer will be invalidated.

If the imam omits any of the following nine practices, the person being led in prayer should perform them on his own rather than follow the imam: (1) Raising the hands while uttering *takbīrat al-iḥrām*, (2) Reciting the prayer of commencement, (3) Uttering the instances of *Allāhu akbar* which coincide with bowing, (4) Uttering the instances of *Allāhu akbar* which coincide with prostrating, (5) Uttering the words of praise to God which coincide with bowing and prostrating, (6) Uttering the words *sami'a Allāhu li man ḥamidah* ("God hears those who praise Him"), (7) Reciting the testimony, (8) Uttering the greeting of peace, and (9) Uttering the words *Allāhu akbar* [after each of the five obligatory prayers] during the three days following the Day of Fastbreaking and the Day of Sacrifice.

Lastly, there are five desirable practices which, if the imam omits them, the person being led in prayer should also omit: (1) The instances of *Allāhu akbar* which are uttered in the prayers performed on the Day of Sacrifice and the Day of

Fastbreaking, (2) the first 'sitting', (3) the prostration of recitation, (4) the prostration of forgetfulness, and (5) the prayer of obedience (if he has reason to fear that by reciting it, he would miss the bow; otherwise, he should recite it on his own).

As we have seen, reciting behind one's imam is undesirable to the point of being forbidden; hence, it is not permissible to follow him in this. As for following the imam in the final greeting of peace and *takbīrat al-iḥrām*, these will be discussed in a separate section.

If someone who is being led in prayer misses some or all *rak'ahs* of a prayer, he must still follow the imam in the final greeting of peace once he has finished reciting the testimony. If he completes his testimony before the imam and if he utters the final greeting of peace before the imam as well, his prayer will be valid, even though to do so is undesirable to the point of being forbidden if it takes place without an excuse. The preferred practice with respect to following one's imam in the final greeting of peace is for the person being led in prayer to utter the final greeting neither before nor after the imam, but together with him. We have mentioned the ruling on the situation in which the person being led in prayer utters the final greeting of peace before his imam; as for uttering it after one's imam, this is a departure from the ideal.

If the person being led in prayer utters *takbīrat al-iḥrām* before the imam, his prayer will not be valid, and if he utters it with the imam, his prayer will be valid. [The text reads "not be valid" here, though given the context, one suspects that the word 'not' is an error – t.n.] If he utters it after the imam, however, he will have missed the "time of virtue" for utterance of *takbīrat al-iḥrām*. This topic will be discussed further in the section entitled, "If someone being led in prayer misses some *rak'ahs*."

* * *

According to the Malikis, the process of following one's imam in prayer requires that the action performed by the person being led in prayer come directly after that of the imam; in other words, it should not come before or during the imam's action, nor should there be a delay between the action of the imam and that of the person being led in prayer. This process is divided into four parts:

(1) Following one's imam in *takbīrat al-iḥrām*. The ruling on this aspect of following the imam is that it is a condition for the validity of the prayer of the person following the imam. Specifically, if the person being led in prayer utters *takbīrat al-iḥrām* before or with his imam, his prayer will be invalid; instead, the person being led in prayer must utter *takbīrat al-iḥrām* after his imam has finished doing so; hence, if he utters it after his imam has begun the utterance but finishes before or with the imam, his prayer will likewise be invalid.

(2) Following one's imam in the final greeting of peace. The person being led in prayer, in order for his prayer to be valid, must utter the final greeting of peace after that of his imam. Hence, if he inadvertently utters it before the imam, he must wait until the imam has uttered the greeting, then repeat it after him, in which case his prayer will be valid. If the person being led in prayer begins the final greeting of peace after the imam but finishes with him or after him, his prayer will be valid; however, if he finishes before the imam, his prayer will be invalidated. Consequently,

it is preferred that the imam utter the final greeting of peace promptly lest any of the worshipers praying behind him finish before him, causing their own prayer to be invalidated; the same applies to the utterance of *takbīrat al-iḥrām*. If the imam leaves out the final greeting of peace, and if what would be considered a 'long' time passes after this, everyone's prayer is invalidated, even if those being led in prayer utter it themselves. The reason for this is that, as we have seen, the final greeting is a pillar of prayer for each worshiper; hence, if it is omitted by the imam, his prayer will be invalidated and, as a consequence, so will the prayers of the worshipers following him.

(3) Following the imam in bowing and prostrating. This aspect of following one's imam may take any of three forms: (a) The person being led in prayer bows or prostrates before his imam either absentmindedly or by mistake. In this case, he must wait until his imam bows or prostrates, then participate with him in his bow, allowing his muscles and limbs to remain in a state of repose for a moment, and his prayer will be valid. If the person being led in prayer does not wait for his imam but instead, rises from his bow either deliberately or out of ignorance, his prayer will be invalid. If, on the other hand, he rises from his bow inadvertently, he should go back to sharing with the imam in his bowing and prostrating, in which case his prayer will be valid. (b) The person being led in prayer deliberately bows or prostrates before his imam. In this case, if the worshiper then waits for the imam in order to share in the imam's bowing and prostrating, his prayer will be valid, but he will incur guilt for deliberately going ahead of the imam. If, on the other hand, he does not wait for the imam and instead, deliberately rises from his bow or his prostration before the imam, his prayer will be invalidated, whereas if he does so unintentionally, he must go back to participating with the imam, and his prayer will be valid. (c) The person being led in prayer lags so far behind the imam that the latter finishes an entire pillar without him (for example, by his continuing to stand and recite while his imam bows and rises from his bow). In this situation, the prayer of the person being led by the imam is invalidated given two conditions: First, it must take place in the first *rak'ah* of the prayer; otherwise, the prayer remains valid, but the person concerned becomes guilty of wrongdoing. Second, it must be deliberate; if it is accidental, the person being led in prayer must simply cancel the *rak'ah* in which this took place, then repeat it after the imam has finished his prayer.

(4) Actions in which it is not necessary to follow one's imam. These, in turn, are of two types: The first type includes actions which it is desirable for the person being led in prayer to perform even if the imam does not do so. These include, for example, Sunnah-based practices such as the utterance of *Allāhu akbar* in *takbīrat al-iḥrām* and the testimony, as well as its utterance on the Day of Fastbreaking and the Day of Sacrifice. It is an emulation of the Sunnah for the person being led in prayer to make these utterances even if the imam does not. It also includes actions which are recommended, such as the utterance of *Allāhu akbar* after the five daily required prayers during the three days following the Day of Fastbreaking and the Day of Sacrifice. (This was discussed above in the sections dealing with the Day of Fastbreaking and the Day of Sacrifice.) It is recommended, if the imam omits these, for the person being led in prayer to utter them alone. Also included here is the practice of raising one's hands when uttering *takbīrat al-iḥrām*, which is recom-

mended for both the imam and those being led in prayer, and which it is recommended that those being led in prayer adhere to even if their imam does not. The second type includes actions in which the person being led in prayer is not permitted to follow the imam, as, for example, when the imam engages in some action which is not permitted during prayer, such as additions, omissions, and the like. If the imam inadvertently performs an extra *rak'ah*, prostration, or some other pillar while praying, the person being led in prayer is not to follow him in this; rather, he should utter the words *subḥān Allāh* to alert the imam to his error. If, on the other hand, the imam makes such an addition deliberately, his prayer will be invalidated, and as a matter of course, so will the prayers of those praying behind him. Similarly, the Malikis hold that those being led in prayer must not follow the imam if he adds to the utterances of *Allāhu akbar* which are part of the holiday prayers, as was seen earlier in the discussion of the holiday prayers. Similarly, if the imam utters more than four instances of *Allāhu akbar* as part of the funeral prayer or if he performs an extra pillar (for example, by rising inadvertently after the four *rak'ahs* of the noon prayer to perform a fifth *rak'ah*), those being led in prayer should not do likewise; rather, they should utter the phrase *subḥān Allāh* to alert him to his error. If someone who is being led in prayer deliberately imitates the imam when he has made such an error, his prayer will be invalidated unless it becomes apparent after the conclusion of the prayer that the imam was in the right and that the person being led in prayer was mistaken.

If the imam omits the first 'sitting' and begins to rise for the third *rak'ah* and if he does not lift his hands and his knees off the ground but rather, returns to his original position and performs the first 'sitting', his prayer will remain valid. If, on the other hand, he lifts his hands and his knees off the ground before returning to his original position, his prayer will remain valid properly speaking, but he must perform a prostration of forgetfulness after uttering the final greeting of peace since, properly speaking, he should have returned to his original position before rising and reciting the *Fātiḥah*. Moreover, those being led in prayer should follow the imam in all of the above. (The Hanafis say that if the imam is closer to a standing position than to a sitting position before he lowers himself again for the first 'sitting', his prayer will be invalidated. Those being led in prayer should also follow their imam if he performs a prostration of recitation during the prayer; however, if the imam does not perform such a prostration—as, for example, if he is a Hanafi who holds that the prostration of recitation takes place as part of the bow—those being led in prayer should omit it as well.)

* * *

According to the Hanbalis, following one's imam in prayer requires that the person being led in prayer not get ahead of the imam in the utterance of *takbīrat al-iḥrām* or the final greeting of peace, nor in the performance of any of the actions involved in prayer. If the person being led in prayer utters *takbīrat al-iḥrām* before his imam, his prayer will have no validity regardless of whether he did so intentionally or unintentionally. Similarly, if he utters *takbīrat al-iḥrām* together with the imam, his prayer will have no validity; hence, simultaneous utterance of *takbīrat al-iḥrām* invalidates prayer. However, this ruling does not apply to other pillars of prayer, in which simultaneity is simply undesirable. For example, if someone being led in prayer deliberately utters the final greeting of peace before his imam or if he utters the final greeting of peace before the imam and fails to utter it again after him, his prayer will be invalidated. This, then, is the ruling on someone being led in prayer who utters either *takbīrat al-iḥrām* or the final greeting of peace before his imam.

If, by contrast, the person being led in prayer gets ahead of the imam in some other action, this will involve either bowing, going down into a prostration, prostrating or rising, each of which has its own associated rulings. If a worshiper deliberately bows and comes back up from his bow before his imam does so, his prayer will be invalidated. If the worshiper bows before his imam, then remains in the bowing position until the imam bows also and completes the bow with the imam, his prayer will not be invalidated if he bows again after his imam, or if he bows and comes up from the bow before his imam inadvertently or by mistake; in both these cases, the worshiper must nullify what he did first, then bow and rise from his bow after the imam. Hence, if a worshiper bows and rises from his bow, whether intentionally or unintentionally, before his imam does so, and if he remains standing until the imam has finished bowing and rising from his bow, then goes down with the imam into a prostration, his prayer will be invalidated.

The rulings just described apply to a situation in which a worshiper bows and rises from his bow before his imam. If, by contrast, the imam bows before the person following him and rises from his bow, and if the worshiper deliberately fails to follow the imam in this, his prayer will be invalidated. If, on the other hand, the worshiper lags behind the imam in his bowing and rising out of absentmindedness or with a valid excuse for doing so, his prayer will remain valid. In this latter case, he must bow and rise from the bow by himself provided that there is no reason to fear that he will miss the following *rak'ah* with the imam by doing so; if there is, in fact, reason to fear that by completing these actions by himself he will miss the next *rak'ah* with his imam, he must follow the imam in whatever he does next, cancel the *rak'ah* which he missed with the imam, then make up the missed *rak'ah* after the imam has concluded his own prayer. This ruling applies likewise to other actions of prayer, including prostration, standing up, and others. If a worshiper fails to follow his imam in any of these actions out of inattentiveness or by mistake, he must make it up on his own provided that by doing so, he does not risk missing subsequent actions with his imam; otherwise, he must follow his imam in whatever actions come next, then make up an entire *rak'ah* on his own after the imam has concluded his own prayer.

The aforementioned ruling applies to a situation in which a worshiper does not follow his imam in bowing; a contrasting situation is one in which the worshiper does not follow his imam in going down into a prostration. If, for example, the imam goes down into a prostration while the worshiper is still standing, after which the worshiper goes down into a prostration by himself and catches up with the imam in his prostration, or if he prostrates with the imam but rises before the imam for the subsequent *rak'ah*, his prayer will remain valid; however, he must go back to follow the imam in what he is doing presently. If this takes place inadvertently, no harm is done; however, the worshiper must likewise go back and follow what his imam is doing, canceling out what he did before on his own. If he fails to do so, the *rak'ah* he has performed will not count and he will have to make it up after the conclusion of the imam's prayer.

If a worshiper deliberately fails to follow his imam in two entire pillars of a prayer—for example, if the imam bows, prostrates, and rises from his prostration while the worshiper is still standing—his prayer will be invalidated; however, if it is unintentional, and if the worshiper is able to perform the two missed pillars quickly enough to catch up with the imam and follow him through the rest of the prayer, he should do so. Otherwise, he must cancel the *rak'ah* in which he missed the two pillars and make it up after the conclusion of the imam's prayer. If a worshiper lags behind his imam by an entire *rak'ah* or more based on a valid excuse, such as having dozed off briefly while seated, he must follow the imam in what remains of the prayer after he wakes up, then make up what he missed after the imam has uttered the final greeting of peace since in this case, he is like someone who arrived late for the prayer.

* * *

According to the Shafiis, the worshiper's following of his imam is necessary in situations which some refer to as "conditions for [being an] exemplar." These are as follows: (1) The worshiper must follow his imam in the utterance of *takbīrat al-iḥrām*; if he utters even a single letter of this phrase either before or with his imam, his prayer will have no validity from the start. If the worshiper suspects that he preceded the imam in some part of *takbīrat al-iḥrām*, his prayer will be invalidated if this suspicion occurs to him while he is still praying; however, if it does not occur to him until after his prayer has been concluded, the suspicion will have no effect and he need not repeat the prayer. (2) The worshiper must not utter the final greeting of peace before his imam; if he does so, his prayer will be invalidated. If the worshiper utters the final greeting of peace with his imam, his prayer will be valid, though this practice is undesirable; however, even if he merely suspects that he uttered the final greeting before the imam, his prayer will be invalidated. (3) The worshiper must not get ahead of his imam by an entire two pillars of the prayer. If this occurs, it will happen in one of two ways: (a) the worshiper will have arrived in time to pray with the imam for as long as it would take to recite the *Fātiḥah*, or (b) the worshiper will not have arrived in time to pray with the imam for the aforementioned length of time. If a worshiper in situation (a) gets ahead of his imam by two entire *rak'ahs* (for example, by bowing alone, rising from the bow, and going down for a prostration while the imam is still standing), his prayer will be invalidated given the following three conditions:

1. The worshiper must have gotten ahead of his imam by an entire two *rak'ahs*, as we have seen. Thus, if he gets ahead of the imam by one *rak'ah*, for example by bowing alone while the imam is still standing up and reciting, but without rising from his bow until the imam has bowed. If he then shares with the imam in the bow, his prayer will remain valid. Nevertheless, it is forbidden for a worshiper to get ahead of his imam by an entire action-based *rak'ah* without a valid excuse.

2. The two *rak'ahs* which the worshiper has performed ahead of his imam must both be action-based rather than merely verbal. If the worshiper gets ahead of his imam by two verbal pillars (for example, by reciting the testimony and praying for

blessings upon the Prophet before his imam), this will do no harm regardless of whether it is done deliberately, out of ignorance, or out of forgetfulness. If a worshiper gets ahead of his imam by two pillars, one of which is verbal and the other of which is action-based (for example, by reciting the *Fātiḥah* before his imam, then bowing before him), it is forbidden for him to bow before his imam, whereas no importance is attached to reciting the *Fātiḥah* before him.

3. The worshiper must have deliberately gotten ahead of his imam by two *rak'ahs*. Thus, if a worshiper bows before his imam and rises from the bow out of ignorance or forgetfulness, his prayer will not be invalidated; however, in this case he must, as soon as he realizes what he has done, go back and follow his imam, canceling what he did before on his own. Similarly, if an ignorant person learns something new during prayer, he must go back and follow his imam; otherwise, both his prayer and that of the imam will be invalidated.

This, then, is the ruling on a worshiper who arrived in time to join the imam long enough to recite the *Fātiḥah* and who got ahead of his imam by two action-based pillars either deliberately, out of ignorance, or out of forgetfulness, or who got ahead of his imam by two verbal pillars or by one verbal and one action-based pillar. As for a worshiper who arrived in time to join the imam long enough to recite the *Fātiḥah* and who then lagged behind the imam—for example, if the worshiper is a slow reciter while the imam recites at a medium pace—it is pardonable for the worshiper to lag behind the imam by as many as three 'long' pillars, namely, the bow and the two prostrations. As for (1) holding still for a moment or two between rising from the bow and going down into a prostration or between rising from a prostration and going down again into this position (which the Shafiis refer to as *i'tidāl*), and (2) adopting a sitting position between the two prostrations, these are considered 'short' pillars and are not counted as part of the worshiper's lagging behind the imam. Hence, if the imam gets ahead of the worshiper following him by more than this—for example, if the worshiper does not finish his recitation until after the imam has begun the fourth pillar subsequent to this, he must follow the imam in what he is doing presently, then make up what he missed of the prayer after the imam has finished praying. If the worshiper fails to start following his imam again until he has commenced the fifth pillar subsequent to what the worshiper is doing, his prayer will be invalidated. If the person being led in prayer arrived in time to join the imam long enough to recite the *Fātiḥah*, this ruling applies regardless of whether the worshiper is performing an obligatory recitation or one which is simply an emulation of the Sunnah, such as the prayer of commencement.

The ruling on the person being led in prayer who did not join the imam for enough time to recite the *Fātiḥah* is that it is an emulation of the Sunnah for him not to occupy himself with a Sunnah-based recitation but, rather, with the recitation of the *Fātiḥah*, unless he has good reason to believe that he would be able to catch up with the imam despite his occupation with a Sunnah-based recitation. If the worshiper does not occupy himself with a Sunnah-based recitation, and if his imam then bows while he is still reciting the *Fātiḥah*, he must follow his imam in the bow; in such a case, the worshiper is exempted from the requirement to complete his recitation of the *Fātiḥah*. If, on the other hand, the worshiper does not follow the imam in the bow until the imam rises, he will miss the entire *rak'ah*; however, his prayer will not be invalidated unless he lags behind the imam by two action-based pillars (for example, by his remaining standing and reciting the *Fātiḥah* while the imam bows, rises from his bow, and goes down for a prostration). However, if the worshiper engages in a Sunnah-based recitation such as the prayer of commencement, he must lag behind the imam and recite as much of this supplication as would equal the length of the *Fātiḥah*. Then if, once he has completed this recitation, he joins the imam for the bow, the *rak'ah* will count for him. However, if when he completes his recitation the imam has already risen from his bow, the worshiper should not bow himself, and he will miss the *rak'ah*. Thus, if the worshiper is still completing his recitation when the imam is ready to go down for a prostration, the worshiper must make it his intention to part with his imam and pray on his own; if he does not make this his intention when the imam goes down for a prostration, his prayer will be invalidated regardless of whether he prostrates with the imam or not.

Having presented the ruling on a worshiper who joins the imam late, it remains for us to present a number of concluding points: (1) If a worshiper being led in prayer forgets to recite the *Fātiḥah* but remembers it before the imam bows, he must lag behind the imam to recite the *Fātiḥah*, in which case it is pardonable for him to part with the imam for the duration of three long pillars. However, if he remembers not having recited the *Fātiḥah* only after he bows with the imam, he should not go back to recite it; rather, he must perform an extra *rak'ah* after the imam has concluded his prayer. (2) If a worshiper being led in prayer does not recite the *Fātiḥah* because he is waiting for the imam to pause for a moment of silence after his own recitation, and if the imam, rather than pausing for a moment of silence, bows directly after his recitation of the *Fātiḥah* and before the worshiper following him has recited it, the worshiper will be excused, and should not follow the imam in his bow; rather, he should recite the *Fātiḥah* himself, and it is pardonable for him not to follow the imam for up to three long pillars (i.e., a bow and two prostrations). Moreover, he must complete the prayer behind the imam in accordance with his particular situation regardless of whether he caught up with the imam in all the prayer-related actions or not.

The rulings just mentioned apply to a situation in which the imam recites at a moderate pace; however, if he recites at a rapid pace and if the worshiper following him in prayer bows at the same time as the imam does, the person following should simply recite as much as he can of the *Fātiḥah* and let the imam recite the rest on his behalf. In this case, it is not pardonable for the person being led in prayer to lag behind the imam for as much as three long pillars.

Someone whose back is straight praying behind someone whose back is bowed

Another condition for the validity of prayer leadership is that the imam's back must not be stooped to the point where he looks as though he were performing a bow. If the curvature of his back is this severe, it is not permissible for him to lead in prayer someone whose back is normal. However, he may serve as imam for those with a similar condition. This ruling is agreed upon by the Hanafis, the Hanbalis and the Malikis; the Shafiis, however, hold that it is permissible for a person with a bowed back to serve as imam both for those with a similar condition and for those whose backs are normal, even if he is so stooped that he looks as though he were performing a bow.

Consistency between the obligatory prayers being performed by the imam and the one being led in prayer

Another condition for the validity of prayer leadership is that the imam and the person being led in prayer must be performing the same obligatory prayer; for example, it is not permissible for someone to perform a noon prayer behind an imam who is performing the mid-afternoon prayer, for someone who is performing a noon prayer on time to pray behind an imam who is making up a noon prayer that was missed earlier or vice-versa, or for someone to perform Saturday's noon prayer behind an imam who is performing Sunday's noon prayer, even if both of them are making up a prayer that was missed earlier. This ruling is agreed upon by the Malikis and the Hanafis; as for the Shafiis and the Hanbalis, their views are presented below.[335]

---

335. According to the Shafiis and the Hanbalis, all the situations described above are permissible. However, the Hanbalis hold that it is not permissible to perform a noon prayer behind an imam who is performing a mid-afternoon prayer or vice-versa, and the like. The Shafiis, moreover, stipulate that the prayer being performed by the imam and the prayer being performed by the person following him must be uniform in terms of form. For example, a worshiper may not perform a noon prayer behind an imam who is performing a funeral prayer due to their different forms; similarly, someone performing a dawn prayer may not pray behind an imam who is performing the prayer for a solar eclipse, since the latter includes two acts of standing and two bows in each *rak'ah.*

However, someone performing a voluntary prayer may pray behind an imam who is performing an obligatory prayer; someone who is fulfilling a vow to perform a particular voluntary prayer given the occurrence of a specific event may pray behind an imam who is fulfilling a similar vow; someone fulfilling an unconditional vow to perform a voluntary prayer may pray behind an imam who is fulfilling a similar vow; and someone fulfilling a vow to perform a certain prayer given the occurrence of a specific event may pray behind an imam who is fulfilling an unconditional vow to perform a certain prayer, even if the specific vows involved are different (as, for example, if someone who has vowed to perform two *rak'ahs* after high noon given the occurrence of a particular event prays behind an imam who has made an unconditional vow to perform two *rak'ahs* without specifying the time). Similarly, it is permissible for someone on a journey to pray behind an imam who is a resident of the place concerned, both during the time period for a given prayer and at other times; in this case, however, the prayer must be performed as a complete four *rak'ahs*. These rulings are agreed upon by all but the Hanafis.[336]

Prayer leadership also has other associated conditions which differ from one school to another.[337]

---

336. According to the Hanafis, the person being led in prayer must have made exactly the same vow as the imam; for example, if the person being led in prayer has said, "I pledge to perform the same two *rak'ahs* which so-and-so pledged to pray," it is permissible for him to follow the other in prayer. On the other hand, it is not permissible for someone who has pledged to perform a prayer contingent on the occurrence of a specific event to pray behind an imam who has made an unconditional pledge to pray; however, the reverse situation—i.e., one in which someone who has made an unconditional pledge to pray follows an imam who has made a conditional pledge—is permissible, as is the case when someone who has made an unconditional pledge to pray follows an imam who has made a similar pledge.

In addition, the Hanafis hold that it is not permissible for someone who is on a journey to perform a four-*rak'ah* prayer behind an imam who is resident in the location concerned if the time period for the prayer in question is past. The reason for this is that in this situation, someone on a journey is obliged to perform only two *rak'ahs*; consequently, the first sitting will be obligatory for the traveler, whereas all four *rak'ahs* are obligatory for the imam since he is a resident. Moreover, since the first sitting will be simply an emulation of the Sunnah for the imam whereas it is obligatory for the person he is leading, this will require someone performing an obligatory prayer to pray behind an imam who is performing a voluntary prayer, which is not permissible. For more on this matter, see the section below on rulings pertaining to prayer during a journey.

337. The Hanafis add to the conditions for the validity of following another person as one's imam that the imam and those following him must not be separated

from each other by a row of women. If it is a row of three women, the prayers of three men from each row behind them will be invalidated; if it is a row of two women, the prayers of two of the men in each row behind them will be invalidated; and if it is a single woman, the prayers of the men she was directly adjacent to (i.e., to her right, to her left, and immediately behind her) will be invalidated. (The conditions associated with the invalidation of prayer due to one's being next to a woman are detailed in the section above on "That which invalidates prayer.")

* * *

As for the Hanbalis, they add the following two conditions for the validity of following an imam: (1) If there is only one person being led in prayer, he must stand to the right of the imam; if he stands to the imam's left, or behind him, his prayer will be invalidated if he is a male or a hermaphrodite. In the case of a woman, her prayer will not be invalidated by standing behind the imam or to his right, since this is where she is meant to stand. However, her prayer will be invalidated if she stands to his left. They also stipulate that if someone being led in prayer completes an entire *rak'ah* with the imam while standing in a spot other than the one where he should, his prayer will be invalidated; however, if he performs less than one *rak'ah* with the imam before taking his proper place, his prayer will remain valid. (2) The imam must be an upright, trustworthy person. Hence, the prayer led by a *fāsiq* will not be valid for anyone, including others who are like him in this respect, even if his behavior is concealed from others. If someone prays behind a *fāsiq* without realizing it, and if he then finds out the reality after concluding his prayer, he must repeat the prayer except in the case of the Friday prayer and the prayers for the Day of Fastbreaking and the Day of Sacrifice, which are valid even if performed behind a *fāsiq* if there is no opportunity to perform them behind someone of more upright character.

* * *

As for the Shafiis, they stipulate, firstly, that in order for one person's following another in prayer to be valid, the person being led in prayer must conform to his imam in the performance of three specific Sunnah-based practices in which inconsistency between the imam and those following him tends to be especially conspicuous. These are as follows: (1) The prostration of recitation during the dawn prayer on Friday. Those being led in prayer must follow their imam if he performs this prostration, and similarly, they must follow him if he omits it. (2) The prostration of forgetfulness. Those being led in prayer should follow their imam only if he performs this prostration, whereas if he omits it, it is an emulation of the Sunnah for them not to perform it until after he has concluded his prayer. (3) The first testimony. Those being led in prayer must omit this testimony if it is omitted by the imam, but if he recites it, it is simply an emulation of the Sunnah for them to recite it as well. As for the prayer of obedience, those being led in prayer are not obliged to follow their imam with respect to it, whether he omits it or recites it.

Secondly, the Shafiis stipulate that in order for an imam's prayer leadership to be valid, he must be performing a prayer which will not need to be repeated. Thus, for example, it is not valid to follow an imam who has access to neither water nor soil which is *ṭahūr*, since his prayer is one which will need to be repeated.

* * *

Conditions which cause the obligation to pray in community to be waived

The obligation to perform ritual prayer in community is waived given excuses such as the following: heavy rain, severe cold, mud which is so widespread or in such large amounts that it would cause harm to travel through it, illness, fear of [being harmed by] an unjust ruler as a result of attending prayer in community, fear of being incarcerated for a debt when one is in dire financial straits, blindness (if the blind person is unable to make his way to the mosque on his own and can find no one to lead him to the mosque), as well as other extenuating circumstances.

Who is most entitled to serve as imam

The four schools' rulings on who is most entitled to serve as imam are enumerated in the footnote below.[338]

The Malikis add the following conditions for the validity of prayer leadership: (1) The imam must not be repeating his prayer in order to gain the merit associated with praying in community. The reason for this is that it is not permissible for someone performing an obligatory prayer to pray behind an imam who is repeating a prayer, since a prayer which is being repeated is, by definition, voluntary, and it is not permissible to perform an obligatory prayer behind an imam performing a voluntary prayer. (2) The imam must be aware of how to perform the prayer in the valid manner, as well as its conditions such as the proper performance of minor ablutions, major ablutions, etc., even if he does not distinguish the pillars from other aspects of these rites. (3) The imam must not be guilty of disobedience pertaining to ritual prayer itself, such as negligence in fulfilling its conditions or in performing its obligatory rites. Hence, the prayer leadership of someone who is thought to be praying without having first performed ritual ablutions, who leaves out recitation of the *Fātiḥah*, etc., is not valid; as for someone whose disobedience is not directly related to prayer, such as someone who commits adultery, who imbibes in alcoholic beverages, etc., his prayer leadership will be valid, although according to the best attested view, it is undesirable.

338. According to the Hanafis, the person most entitled to serve as imam is, in order of priority: (1) the most knowledgeable of the rulings on ritual prayer with respect to its validity and/or invalidity, provided that he avoids conspicuous acts of immorality, (2) the most skilled at Qur'anic recitation, (3) the most pious and conscientious, (4) the one who has been a Muslim for the longest time, (5) the oldest (if both (4) and (5) were born into Islam), (6) the one with the best character and temperament, (7) the one with the most pleasing face, (8) the one with the most

noble lineage, then, (9) the one wearing the cleanest clothes. If those present are equal with respect to all these criteria, lots are to be cast if there is competition among them as to who should be imam. Otherwise, those present should put forward whoever they wish. If there is a dispute over the result of the lot that was cast, they may put forward whoever is favored by the majority. If the person chosen by the majority is not the most worthy, they will have acted offensively, but they will incur no guilt as a result. All these rulings apply, however, if there is no 'sultan', that is, no ruler vested with religious authority, and if they are not meeting in a person's house with the owner of the house present, or a regular imam. If a 'sultan' is present, he has first right to serve as imam, followed by the owner of the home in which the prayer is being performed; if it is being performed in a mosque, the right belongs to the regular imam. If, on the other hand, the prayer is being performed in someone's home and if both the owner of the home and its renter are present, priority should go to the renter.

* * *

According to the Shafiis, it is recommended that priority right to serve as imam be granted to: (1) the governor in the domain of his governorship, then (2) the regular mosque imam, then (3) the person residing by right [in the place where the prayer is being performed], if he is qualified to serve as imam. If no one who fits any of these descriptions is present, the following list of criteria is to be used: (1) the most knowledgeable of Islamic jurisprudence, (2) the most skilled reciter, (3) the most ascetic and self-disciplined, (4) the most pious and conscientious, (5) the one who emigrated the longest time ago [this seems to be an anachronism going back to the generation of the Prophet, referring to the original emigration from Mecca to Medina – t.n.], (6) the one who has been a Muslim for the longest time, (7) the one with the most superior family lineage, (8) the one with the most honorable life history, (9) the one with the cleanest clothes, body and occupation, (10) the one with the most pleasant voice, (11) the one with the most attractive appearance, and (12) one who is married. If those present are equal with respect to all these criteria, lots are to be cast among them. It is permissible for the person most entitled to serve as imam to put forward someone else for the task provided that the former is not superior to the latter with respect to a particular personal attribute, for example, his being more knowledgeable of Islamic jurisprudence, in which case he may not do so.

* * *

The Malikis hold that in the case of a group of worshipers every member of which would be qualified to serve as imam, it is recommended that priority be given to the following: (1) the sultan or his proxy, even if someone else is more virtuous and more knowledgeable of Islamic jurisprudence; (2) the regular mosque imam; (3) the owner of the house in which the worshipers are gathered, with a renter being given priority over the actual owner. If the owner of the house is a woman, she has priority right to serve as imam; however, since her prayer leadership would not be valid, she must appoint someone else to take her place; (4) the person most knowledgeable about the rulings on ritual prayer; (5) the person most well-versed in hadiths, both in terms of knowledge of the various narratives and in terms of the number of hadiths he has memorized; (6) the person known to be trustworthy and reliable; (7) the most knowledgeable about Qur'anic recitation; (8) the most given to worship; (9) the one who has been a Muslim for the longest time; (10) the one with the most noble lineage; (11) the one with the most upright character; (12) the one who wears the nicest clothing.

If those gathered are equal with respect to all these criteria, the most pious and God-fearing of them is to be put forward, though it is forbidden to put forward a slave to serve as imam. If they are still equal with respect to all these criteria [assuming, for example, that the most pious and God-fearing among them is a slave, or that all of them are equally pious and God-fearing – t.n], lots are to be cast among them unless they are willing to put forward one of their number. If, on the other hand, they are all vying to be imam out of pride and the desire for ascendancy, they are all thereby disqualified.

* * *

According to the Hanbalis, the criteria for determining who is most entitled to serve as imam are, in descending order of importance: (1) the greatest knowledge of Islamic jurisprudence and superior ability in Qur'anic recitation, (2) good knowledge of Islamic jurisprudence and superior ability in Qur'anic recitation, (3) superior ability in Qur'anic recitation but without knowledge of Islamic jurisprudence, provided that the person is well-versed in the rulings on ritual prayer, (4) knowledge of and adherence to ritual prayer's requirements together with superior knowledge of Islamic jurisprudence, (5) knowledge of and adherence to ritual prayer's requirements together with a good knowledge of Islamic jurisprudence, (6) knowledge of and adherence to prayer's requirements and knowledge of jurisprudence as it relates to ritual prayer, (7) the ability to recite the Qur'ān but without knowledge of jurisprudence as it relates to ritual prayer. If none of the worshipers gathered has the ability to recite, they should put forward the person most knowledgeable of the rulings on ritual prayer; if they all have equal ability to recite and equal knowledge of Islamic jurisprudence, they should put forward the oldest, then the person with the most noble lineage, then the person who emigrated the longest time ago by himself, then the person who has been a Muslim for the longest time, then the most pious and God-fearing. If all of them are equal in all these respects, lots are to be cast. The person most entitled to serve as imam if the worshipers are gathered in a home is the owner of the home provided that he is qualified to be imam, whereas the most entitled to be imam if the worshipers are gathered in a mosque is the mosque's regular imam even if he is a slave among them. However, if someone with religious authority vested in him, such as the sultan, is present, he is to be given priority.

339. According to the Hanbalis, the prayer leadership of a *fāsiq* is invalid even if those whom he leads in prayer are like him in this respect. However, they make an exception to this ruling for the Friday congregational prayer and the prayers

Undesirable practices associated with prayer leadership: Prayer being led by a *fāsiq*, or someone who is blind

According to the Hanafis and the Shafiis, it is undesirable for someone who is *fāsiq* to lead others in prayer unless they are like him in this respect; for the views of the Hanbalis and the Malikis, see below.[339]

It is agreed upon by all four schools that it is undesirable for a heretic to lead others in prayer if the heresy which he originated is one which does not place him outside the pale of believers. [Otherwise, it is entirely forbidden, since this would make the prayer leader a non-believer – t.n.] According to the Malikis, the Hanbalis and the Shafiis, it is undesirable, though not to the point of being forbidden, for the imam to prolong ritual prayer unless those who are being led in prayer consist of a small number of people and unless they have consented to the prayer's being long; for the Hanafis' view, see below.[340]

---

performed on the Day of Fastbreaking and the Day of Sacrifice if it would be impossible for worshipers to pray behind anyone else, in which case it is permissible for such a person to lead others in prayer out of necessity.

* * *

According to the Malikis, the prayer leadership of a *fāsiq* is undesirable even if those being led in prayer are like him in this respect.

340. According to the Hanafis, it is undesirable to the point of being forbidden for the imam to prolong ritual prayer unless he is leading a small group of worshipers who have consented to the prayer's being prolonged. This ruling is based on the saying of the Prophet, "Whoever leads others in prayer should keep it 'light'." However, prolongation of prayer is only undesirable in this sense if the imam engages in practices which go beyond those based on the Sunnah.

341. According to the Shafiis, such practices are valid provided that the imam will not need to repeat the prayer he is performing; thus, for example, if someone wipes a cast or splint and if this wiping is sufficient [the text reads 'insufficient' –

Someone who has performed minor ablutions praying behind someone who has performed sand ablutions, and the like

According to the Hanafis and the Hanbalis, it is permissible and fully acceptable for someone who has performed regular ritual ablutions to follow in prayer someone who has performed sand ablutions, or for someone who has washed his feet to pray behind someone who has merely wiped a shoe or a cast. For the views of the Shafiis and the Malikis, see below.[341]

There are, in addition to those already cited, other undesirable practices associated with prayer leadership according to each of the four schools.[342]

---

t.n.] to make ritual prayer valid without the prayer's being repeated, it is also permissible for this person to be an imam; otherwise, however, it is not.

* * *

According to the Malikis, it is undesirable for someone who has performed regular ritual ablutions to follow an imam who has performed sand ablutions, or for someone who washed his feet to follow an imam who merely wiped his feet through shoes or a splint.

342. The Hanafis list the following as undesirable practices associated with prayer leadership: (1) Prayer leadership by a blind person unless he is superior to all others. (2) Prayer leadership by a person of illegitimate birth. (3) Prayer leadership by someone who is ignorant, be he a Bedouin or a city dweller, if someone more knowledgeable is available. (4) Prayer leadership by a handsome young man, even if he is the most knowledgeable person among the worshipers, if it is feared that his leading the prayer will cause others temptation or distraction. Otherwise, however, prayer leadership by such a person is not considered undesirable. (5) Prayer leadership by a legally incompetent person who does not behave appropriately. (6) Prayer leadership by a hemiplegic or by someone with leprosy which has spread over his body. (7) Prayer leadership by a eunuch, someone with a limp that causes him to stand on just one part of his foot, or someone whose hand is missing. (8) Prayer leadership by someone who serves as imam in return for remuneration, unless someone who has donated a religious endowment has stipulated that such a person should receive such pay, since in this case he is receiving the money as charity and assistance. (9) Prayer leadership by someone who violates the subsidiary rulings of the schools to which those in the congregation adhere if it is suspected that he is showing no consideration for the difference between their respective schools regarding what invalidates prayer or ritual ablutions. However, if it is known that he does show consideration for such differences or that he is unaware of them, it is not undesirable for such a person to serve as imam. (10) The imam's standing in a spot which is elevated one or more cubits above those being led in prayer, or those being led in prayer standing in a spot which is elevated this distance above the imam; if the elevation is less than this, no undesirability is attached to it. In both these situations, the undesirability attaches only to a situation in which the imam is alone at one elevation while those following him are all on another; however, if one or more of those being led in prayer are on the same level as the imam, there is no undesirability attached to it. (12) Prayer leadership by someone who is

disliked by people if he arouses in them an aversion to praying behind him due to some shortcoming or flaw on his part. (13) Women's praying in community, including even the *tarāwīḥ* prayers. An exception to this is made for the funeral prayer, in which case a woman should stand in the midst of the other women, similar to the way prayer is performed by those who are only partially clothed. (14) Women's attendance of communal prayer, including even the Friday congregational prayer, the holiday prayers, and homilies delivered at night, although if the prayer concerned is during the day it is permissible for women to attend it if there is no reason to fear that by their doing so, they would cause others temptation or distraction. (15) A man's leading women in communal prayer in a house where there is neither another man nor a woman who is a close relative of his, such as his wife or his sister.

* * *

According to the Shafiis, it is undesirable for the following people to lead others in prayer: (1) someone who took over the position of imam without meriting it, (2) someone who does not take care to avoid ritual impurity, (3) someone who is employed in a base profession, such as cupping, (4) someone who is disliked by most of the people due to some objectionable characteristic or habit, such as laughing too much, (5) someone of unidentified paternity, (6) someone of illegitimate birth, unless he is leading someone else who is likewise of illegitimate birth, (7) someone who is uncircumcised, even if he is an adult, (8) a young boy, even if he is more well-versed in Islamic jurisprudence than the adults, (9) someone who involuntarily repeats the *f* and *w* sounds in his speech, (10) someone who mispronounces words, though not so severely that their meanings are altered, and (11) someone who violates the subsidiary rulings of the school to which those following him adhere, such as a Hanafi who believes that utterance of the *basmalah* is not obligatory. In addition, it is considered undesirable for the place where the imam stands to be elevated above the place where those being led in prayer are standing, and vice-versa, unless this is due to a clear necessity, for example, due to the mosque's layout, in which case it is not undesirable. They note, in addition, that it is not undesirable for a blind person to lead others in prayer.

* * *

According to the Hanbalis, it is undesirable for the following to lead others in prayer: (1) someone who is blind, deaf, or uncircumcised, even if he is an adult, (2) someone who is missing one or both of his hands or legs if he is able to stand up; if he is unable to stand up, he may only serve as imam to others with the same condition; (3) someone whose nose is missing, (4) someone who has occasional epileptic spells, (5) someone who involuntarily repeats the *f* and *t* sounds when speaking, (6) someone who does not enunciate some letters, (8) someone who mispronounces words, but not to the point of changing their meanings, for example, by pronouncing the letter *dāl* in the phrase *al-ḥamdu lillāh* followed by an *i* sound in place of the *u* sound, and (9) someone who is disliked by most of the people for good reason, for example, due to a shortcoming in his religion or character, although it is not deemed undesirable to imitate such a person's movements in prayer. According to the Hanbalis, it is undesirable for the place where the imam stands to be elevated one cubit or more above the place where those being led in prayer stand; however, it is not undesirable for the place where those being led in prayer are standing to be elevated above that of the imam. In addition, they deem it undesirable for a man to lead one or more women in prayer if they are not blood relatives of his and if there is no other man present.

* * *

The Malikis list the following practices and situations as undesirable in connection with prayer leadership: (1) Prayer leadership by a Bedouin, that is, a desert-dweller, when the person following him is a city-dweller, even if the desert dweller recites more than the city-dweller or is superior to the city-dweller in recitation. The reason for this is that desert-dwellers are known for their harshness and bad manners; moreover, since the imam serves as a kind of intercessor for those praying behind him, he should be a person with a gentle, compassionate disposition. (2) Prayer leadership by someone who is disliked by some people due to negligence on his part toward his religion provided that the people who dislike him are not of distinguished virtue; as for someone who is disliked by most people or by those of distinguished virtue, he is forbidden entirely to lead prayer. (3) It is undesirable for a eunuch, someone who breaks up his speech as women do, or someone of illegitimate birth to be a regular imam. However, such persons may lead prayer without any undesirability attached to it if they are not regular imams. It is also undesirable for a slave to be a regular imam. The undesirability of prayer leadership by someone belonging to any of these categories applies only to those prayers which are either obligatory or emulations of the Sunnah; however, such persons may lead voluntary prayers as regular imams without any undesirability attaching to it. (4) Prayer leadership is undesirable when undertaken by someone who is uncircumcised, by someone about whom it is not known whether he is upright or *fāsiq*, and by someone of unknown paternity. (5) It is undesirable for people who are on the lower deck of a ship to follow the prayer leadership of someone on the upper deck lest the ship turn in such a way that they are no longer able to discern the imam's movements; similarly, it is undesirable for people who are on Mt. Abī Qubays to follow the prayer leadership of someone who is in the Sacred Mosque in Mecca. (6) It is undesirable for a man to pray among women, or for a woman to pray among men. (7) It is undesirable for an imam to pray without a garment to throw over his shoulder if he is in the mosque, to perform a voluntary prayer in his prayer niche, or to sit there in this condition [presumably the condition of not having anything thrown over his shoulder – t.n.] while praying. (8) It is permissible for someone who is blind to lead prayer, although it is preferable that he be sighted. (9) It is likewise permissible for those being led in prayer to be elevated above the place where the imam is standing provided that this is not intended as an expression of arrogance; otherwise, it is forbidden and it will cause their prayer to be invalidated, even if those being led in prayer are on the roof of the mosque. This ruling applies to prayers other than the Friday congregational prayer; as for the Friday prayer, it will be invalid if performed on the roof of the mosque, as we have seen. (10) It is undesirable for the imam to stand in a place which is elevated above those who are being led in prayer unless the elevation is slight (between a hand span and a cubit), or is

How those being led in prayer are to stand with their prayer leader

If the imam is leading either a man or a boy who has reached the age of discernment, the man or the boy being led in prayer should stand to the right of, and slightly behind, the imam; it is undesirable for them to stand directly across from the imam,[343] to the imam's left, or directly behind the imam. If the imam is leading two men or a man and a boy, it is recommended that they stand behind the imam. If the imam is leading a man and a woman, the man should stand to the imam's right while the woman stands behind the man; if he is leading a boy and a woman, the same ruling applies.

If those being led in prayer include men, boys, hermaphrodites and females, the men should stand in front, followed by the boys, followed by the hermaphrodites, followed by the females. These rulings are agreed upon by all four schools; however, the Hanbalis hold that if a single man being led in prayer performs an entire *rak'ah* while standing to the left of the imam, his prayer will be invalidated, and that if a man and a boy are praying together, the man must be to the imam's right, whereas the boy may pray to his right or to his left, but not behind him.

The imam must stand in the center in relation to the group he is leading in prayer; if he stands to their right or to their left, he will have offended by violating the prophetic Sunnah. The 'best' worshipers should stand in the first row so that if anything should prevent the imam from completing the prayer (for example, due to his having had an occurrence of ritual impurity), any one of them would be qualified to step in for him. The first row is considered superior to the second, the second superior to the third, and so on. In addition, it is necessary that someone who steps in to fill a gap in one of the rows be qualified to stand in that row; hence, it would not be permissible for a woman to leave her legitimate place to fill a gap in a row where she would not be allowed to stand. As for boys, they are granted the same status as men; hence, if a given row is lacking, it is recommended that a boy come to complete it if there are no men available to do so. This ruling is agreed upon by the Shafiis, the Hanbalis and the Malikis; as for the Hanafis, they hold that if the congregation of worshipers includes only one boy, he should stand in one of the men's rows, whereas if there are several boys present, they should form a row by themselves, and if any of the men's rows is incomplete, they should not be allowed to complete it.

---

based on a particular necessity, for example, the need to teach people how to perform ritual prayer. (11) It is undesirable for an adult to follow a boy in a voluntary prayer. (12) It is undesirable for someone on a journey to pray behind someone who is resident in a place, and vice-versa; however, the latter practice is more undesirable.

343. According to the Hanafis, it is not undesirable to stand directly across from the imam.

When the worshipers gathered begin to pray, they should line up in neat, tight rows, shoulder to shoulder. If someone arrives late for prayer, he may find the imam bowing or see a gap in one of the rows after he has uttered *takbīrat al-iḥrām*; each of the schools offers its own rulings on what such a worshiper should do in these situations.[344]

---

344. The Hanafis rule that if, when someone arrives for prayer, he finds the imam performing a bow and if there is a gap in the last row, it is undesirable for him to utter *takbīrat al-iḥrām* outside of the row; rather, he should first fill the gap in the row, then utter *takbīrat al-iḥrām* even if this means missing the *rak'ah*. If, on the other hand, there is no gap in the last row but there is a gap in one of the other rows, the worshiper should likewise not utter *takbīrat al-iḥrām* outside the row. If there is no gap in any of the rows, the worshiper who just arrived should utter *takbīrat al-iḥrām* behind the last row; in this case, he may draw one of the worshipers in the last row back toward him so that they form a row of two provided that in doing so, he does not engage in so much movement that it would invalidate his prayer. As for praying alone behind all of the rows, this is considered undesirable.

If, after commencing prayer, a worshiper sees a gap in one of the rows in front of him in the direction of the prayer niche, it is recommended that he walk forward to fill the gap provided that the gap is no more than one row away from him. For example, if he is in the second row and sees a gap in the first row, he may move up to the first row; however, if he is in the third row and the gap is in the first row, he may not walk forward to fill it, and if he does so, his prayer will be invalidated due to the excessive movement involved.

* * *

The Hanbalis rule that if someone arrives for communal prayer when the imam is bowing, and if there is a gap in the last row of worshipers, he may utter *takbīrat al-iḥrām* outside of the row in order not to miss the first *rak'ah*, then walk to where the gap is and fill it. When such a worshiper walks over to fill the gap, he may either do so while still in a bowing position or after rising from the bow if the imam has not yet prostrated. If such a worshiper does not enter the row before the imam prostrates, and if he can find no one to form a separate row with him, his prayer will be invalidated; similarly, if he utters *takbīrat al-iḥrām* behind the row out of fear of missing the first *rak'ah* and does not enter the row until after rising from the prostration, his prayer will be invalid. If a worshiper utters *takbīrat al-iḥrām*, then finds a gap in the row in front of him, it is recommended that he walk forward to fill it if this will not require what is considered to be "excessive movement" by commonly accepted standards; otherwise, his prayer will be invalidated. If someone comes to pray with the community and finds no gap in any of the rows and if he is unable to stand to the right of the imam, he must alert some other man in the row—by speaking to him or clearing his throat, though it is undesirable to do so by tugging on the person even if he happens to be one's slave or one's son— to stand with him behind the row; if such a person performs an entire *rak'ah* behind the row alone, his prayer will be invalidated.

* * *

According to the Malikis, if someone arrives for communal prayer and finds the imam already praying and if he believes that he will be able to perform the *rak'ah* even if he postpones commencing prayer with the imam until after he has entered the row, it is recommended that he postpone *takbīrat al-iḥrām* until he enters the row. However, if the worshiper believes that he will miss the *rak'ah* if he postpones *takbīrat al-iḥrām* until after he has entered the row, it is recommended that he utter it outside the row if he believes that, after uttering *takbīrat al-iḥrām*, he will be able to get into the row before the imam raises his head from bowing. If he does not believe this to be the case, he should postpone *takbīrat al-iḥrām* until he has entered the row even if this means missing the *rak'ah*. However, if the imam is performing the final *rak'ah*, the worshiper should utter *takbīrat al-iḥrām* before entering the row in order not to miss having performed the prayer communally.

If someone walks over to another row during prayer in order to fill a gap in it, he is permitted to walk a distance equal to two rows, not including the row he is leaving or the row he plans to join. If there are several gaps to be filled, the worshiper should go to the one which is closest to him in the direction of the prayer niche provided that the distance involved is no more than the aforementioned (i.e., a distance of two rows, not including the row he is leaving or the row he plans to join). When moving over to the new row, the worshiper should walk in a bowing position during the first *rak'ah* and from a standing position during the second *rak'ah*; however, it is undesirable to walk while rising from a bow, seated or prostrating. [It isn't clear how they think someone could walk while seated or prostrating – t.n.] If someone arrives for communal prayer and does not find a gap in the row, he should utter *takbīrat al-iḥrām* outside the row; however, it is undesirable for him to draw someone out of the row to stand with him, and if he does so, it is undesirable for the other person to comply with him.

* * *

The Shafiis hold that if, when someone arrives for communal prayer, the imam is bowing and there is a gap in the row, it is recommended that he postpone entering prayer with the imam until he has reached the row even if this involves missing the *rak'ah*. If, after commencing prayer, he finds a gap in one of the rows, he may pass through the rows until he reaches the gap provided that this does not require him to take three consecutive steps and provided that he walks from a standing position; otherwise, his prayer will be invalidated. Moreover, one may only walk during prayer to fill a gap in another row if the gap already existed before one began to pray; if the gap comes into being after the person begins to pray, he may not pass through rows to reach it. If someone arrives for prayer and does not find a gap in the row, he should utter *takbīrat al-iḥrām* outside the row; in such a case, it is an emulation of the Sunnah—after he has uttered *takbīrat al-iḥrām* and while standing—for him to draw toward him a free man whom he hopes will agree to stand with him. However, the row from which the man was drawn must contain more than two worshipers; otherwise, it is not in accordance with the Sunnah to draw him out.

Repetition of the congregational prayer

If someone performs the noon prayer, the sundown prayer or the evening prayer by himself, after which he comes upon a group who are performing the same prayer which he already performed, is it permissible for him to repeat the prayer with this group? Each school offers its own ruling on this question.[345]

---

345. It is an emulation of the Sunnah for someone to repeat a prayer during the time period for this same prayer, regardless of whether he performed it alone the first time or with a group, given the following conditions: (1) The entire second prayer must be performed in community. (2) The person concerned must consciously intend to repeat an obligatory prayer. (3) Based on the best attested view, the second prayer must be performed during the time period for the original prayer even if only one *rak'ah* of it is completed before the time runs out. (4) The imam must repeat the prayer with those who believe that the prayer's repetition is recommended and/or permissible. (5) The first prayer must have been either an obligatory prayer or a voluntary prayer which it is an emulation of the Sunnah to perform in community. (6) According to the best attested view, the prayer must be repeated only once. (7) It must not be the funeral prayer. (8) The second prayer must be valid even if it would not serve to make up a prayer that had been missed. (9) At the time when *takbīrat al-iḥrām* is being uttered, the person repeating the prayer must not be standing apart from the row of worshipers if he could have entered the row. If he stands apart from the row under these circumstances, his repetition of the prayer will not be valid; however, if he only stands apart from the row after uttering *takbīrat al-iḥrām*, his prayer will be valid. (10) The second prayer must be performed from a standing position for those able to stand. (11) Performance of the prayer in community must be desirable for the person who is repeating it; thus, for example, if the person is incompletely clothed, he should only repeat the prayer in the dark. Lastly, if any of these conditions is unfulfilled, the repetition of the prayer will be invalid.

* * *

According to the Hanbalis, it is an emulation of the Sunnah for someone who performed an obligatory prayer either alone or in community to repeat this prayer in community if a communal prayer is begun while he is in the mosque; this applies whether the time at which the repetition is performed is a time when prayer is forbidden or not, and whether the person repeating the prayer with him is the regular imam or someone else. However, if a worshiper enters the mosque and finds the communal prayer already being performed and if the time is one when prayer is forbidden, he is forbidden to repeat the prayer and his repetition will not be valid; this ruling applies whether the person concerned went to the mosque with the intention of gaining merit for praying communally or not. If the time is not one in which prayer is forbidden and if the person has gone to the mosque for the express purpose of repeating a prayer, it will not be an emulation of the Sunnah to repeat the prayer, whereas if he did not go there with this intention, repeating the prayer is an emulation of the Sunnah.

The aforementioned rulings do not apply to the sundown prayer; as for the sundown prayer, it is never an emulation of the Sunnah to repeat it.

Lastly, for those who repeat a prayer, the first one is counted as obligatory, while the second is counted as voluntary; hence, one may intend it either as a repeated prayer or as a voluntary prayer.

* * *

The Malikis hold that if someone performs a prayer by himself or if he performs it as the imam for a boy, it is recommended that he repeat the prayer as long as there is time left to do so with another group the initial validity of whose prayer is not dependent on his being part of the quorum (for example, by the group's consisting of two other people). In order for such a person to repeat a prayer with just one other worshiper, the other worshiper must be a regular imam.

Prayers which are not to be repeated include the sundown prayer and the evening prayer once the*witr* has been performed. It is forbidden to repeat either of these two prayers in order to gain merit for having prayed in community. Another exception applies to someone who has prayed alone in one of the following three mosques: (1) the Sacred Mosque in Mecca, (2) the Prophet's Mosque in Medina, and (3) al-Aqṣā Mosque in Jerusalem. If someone has prayed alone in one of these mosques, it is not recommended that he repeat it communally anywhere else; however, it is recommended that such a prayer be repeated communally inside the same mosque. Moreover, if someone who has prayed alone repeats his prayer in order to gain the merit for having prayed communally, he must pray it behind an imam; in other words, it is not permissible for him to be an imam for others who have not performed this prayer.

When someone repeats a prayer, he should make it his intention to perform it as an obligatory prayer, leaving it to God which of the two prayers to accept. The reason for this is that if one repeats a prayer with the intention of performing a voluntary prayer the second time, after which it becomes apparent that the original, obligatory, prayer was invalid, the repeated prayer will not serve to make it up.

As for someone who has performed a given prayer with a group, it is undesirable for him to repeat the prayer with another group unless the first group with whom he prayed was outside any of the three mosques mentioned above, after which he entered one of these mosques; in this latter case, it is recommended that he repeat the prayer in this mosque [i.e., one of the three mosques mentioned above] communally rather than alone.

* * *

The Hanafis hold that if someone prays alone, then repeats the prayer communally with an imam, the second prayer is counted as voluntary. However, the imam himself must be performing an obligatory prayer rather than a voluntary one. The reason for this is that it is not undesirable to perform a voluntary prayer behind an imam who is performing an obligatory prayer; however, it is undesirable to perform a voluntary prayer behind an imam who is likewise performing a voluntary prayer if the group of worshipers consists of more than three people. Hence, if a group prays together, then repeats the same prayer again, this is undesirable if the group consists of more than three worshipers; if it does not, it is not undesirable provided that they repeat the prayer without either an *adhān* or an *iqāmah*. It is undesirable for a group to repeat a prayer communally with an *adhān* regardless of how many people the group consists of.

Repetition of the congregational prayer in the selfsame mosque

It is undesirable for a communal prayer to be repeated in the same mosque, for example, by one group after another performing prayers in it. For each school's ruling on this matter, see below.[346]

Given that the second prayer is categorized as a voluntary prayer, the ruling on voluntary prayers must apply to it during those times when voluntary prayers are undesirable. Hence, it is not permissible to repeat the mid-afternoon prayer, since voluntary prayers are forbidden following the mid-afternoon prayer.

If someone commences an obligatory prayer alone or if the prayer is being performed on time rather than to make up for a missed prayer, to fulfill a vow or as a voluntary prayer, and if the same prayer is then begun communally before the worshiper concerned has prostrated, it is desirable for the person to discontinue his prayer while standing after a single greeting of peace in order to gain the merit for praying in community.

As for repeating a prayer due to some flaw in it—for example, because the worshiper neglected a 'duty' and the like (to be discussed in the section on making up prayers that have been missed)—this is not undesirable; however, if the prayer performed had no flaw in it, it is undesirable to the point of being forbidden to repeat it [on the pretext that it was flawed – t.n.]. Similarly, it is not undesirable under any circumstances to repeat the same communal prayer in a mosque which has a regular imam and a regular group of worshipers who pray in it provided that the repeated prayer is performed without an *adhān* or an *iqāmah*.

346. According to the Hanafis, it is not undesirable for a communal prayer to be repeated in 'roadside mosques', that is, mosques which have no particular imam or congregation associated with them; as for 'way station mosques', that is, mosques which are associated with a particular imam and congregation, it is not undesirable to repeat communal prayers in these either if they are performed in a different manner the second time (for example, by the first prayer's being performed in the prayer niche, but not the second).

* * *

The Hanbalis hold that if the regular imam is leading a group in prayer, it is forbidden for anyone else to lead a group in prayer at the same time. It is likewise forbidden for a group to pray before the regular imam has prayed; in fact, a communal prayer other than that led by the regular imam is invalid in both of these cases if it is performed without his permission. However, if the prayer is performed with the regular imam's permission, it is not forbidden. Similarly, it is not forbidden for someone other than the regular imam to lead a communal prayer if: (1) the imam is late in arriving at the mosque due to some valid excuse, (2) it is believed that he will not arrive, or (3) it is believed that he will arrive, but it is known that he would not object to someone else's leading the prayer in his absence.

As for communal prayers led by someone other than the regular imam once he has finished his prayer, they are permissible without any undesirability attached to them unless they are performed in the Sacred Mosque in Mecca or the Prophet's Mosque in Medina, since repeating communal prayers in either of these two mosques is undesirable unless there is a valid excuse for doing so. If, for example, someone sleeps through the imam's prayer at one of these two mosques, he may pray the same prayer with a group without any undesirability attaching to it. Lastly, it is undesirable for an imam to lead a group twice in the same prayer, for example, by intending the first time as an obligatory prayer being performed on time, and the second as a compensatory prayer.

* * *

According to the Shafiis, it is undesirable under all circumstances for a communal prayer to be performed in a mosque without the regular imam's permission. This ruling applies whether the prayer is performed before, during, or after the imam's own prayer, unless: (1) it is performed in a "roadside mosque" which lacks a regular imam, (2) the mosque is so crowded that not all the worshipers can fit into it at the same time, or (3) it is feared that the time period for the prayer concerned will run out [if they go somewhere else to perform it].

* * *

According to the Malikis, it is undesirable for a communal prayer to be repeated after the regular imam has prayed; this ruling applies to every mosque or location in which it is customary for people to gather and pray and in which there is a regular imam, even if the imam has given his permission. It is likewise undesirable for a communal prayer to be performed before the regular imam has prayed if he will pray at his accustomed time; otherwise, however, it is not undesirable. As for performing a communal prayer alongside the group being led by the regular imam, it is forbidden; the ruling in this regard is that once the communal prayer being led by the regular imam has begun, it is not permissible for any other prayer to be performed, be it obligatory or voluntary, communal or individual, and whoever is present in the mosque must enter with the imam into the prayer he is leading if he has not already performed the prayer being performed or if he has only performed it alone. If, on the other hand, the worshiper concerned has already performed the prayer in community, he must leave the mosque in order not to discredit its imam. If someone who is in the mosque needs to perform an obligatory prayer other than the one the imam intends to perform (if, for example, this worshiper still needs to perform the noon prayer when the regular imam is about to commence the mid-afternoon prayer), he should follow the imam only in appearance; in other words, he should pray behind the imam, but intend the noon prayer as an individual, adhering to the requirements for an individual prayer.

If there are several regular imams in a given mosque, it is forbidden for all of them to pray at the same time due to the confusion which would result. If, on the other hand, they pray in succession, this is undesirable according to the best attested view, but not forbidden.

As for those mosques or other locations in which there is no regular imam, it is not undesirable to repeat communal prayers there, for example, by various groups praying one after another.

How much of a congregational prayer must be performed with the imam in order for it to count as a congregational prayer, and congregational prayer performed in a home

If a worshiper joins his imam in even part of his prayer—for example, if he arrives only in time for the end of the final 'sitting' before the concluding greeting of peace, or utters *takbīrat al-iḥrām* immediately before the imam concludes his prayer and without sitting down with him—the worshiper's prayer will count for him as a congregational prayer. This ruling is agreed upon by the Hanafis, the Hanbalis and the Shafiis; however, the Shafiis make an exception for the Friday congregational prayer, since they hold that in order for this prayer to count as a communal prayer, a worshiper must perform an entire *rak'ah* with his imam. For the Malikis' view, see below.[347]

With regard to the merit attached to communal prayer, no distinction is made between a communal prayer performed in a mosque and one performed in a home; however, it is preferable for women to do so in a home.

---

347. According to the Malikis, a worshiper only gains the merit associated with praying communally by performing an entire *rak'ah* with the imam; specifically, the worshiper must begin his bow before the imam raises his head from his own bow even if he does not pause and allow his limbs to be still during the bow until after the imam has stood up again; he is then to complete both prostrations with the imam. Once a worshiper has completed the *rak'ah* in this manner, he will have gained the merit associated with communal prayer and the rulings pertaining to those being led by an imam will apply to him. In such a case, the worshiper may not serve as imam for this same prayer or repeat it with another group. As has been stated, rulings pertaining to those being led in prayer now apply to such a worshiper; this means, for example, that he must perform the prostration of forgetfulness with the imam if the latter does so, either before or after the final greeting of peace, and he is to greet both the imam and the worshiper to his left.

However, if the aforementioned worshiper only joins the imam after the latter has risen from his bow, or if he performs the bow with the imam but is not able to prostrate with him for some valid reason, such as crowding and the like, he will not gain the merit associated with praying communally, nor will the rulings pertaining to those being led in prayer apply to him. Consequently, it will be permissible for him to serve as imam in this same prayer, and it is deemed desirable for him to repeat it with another group in order to gain the merit for having performed it in community. In this case, the worshiper is not to greet the imam or the worshiper to his left, nor do other rulings pertaining to those being led in prayer apply to him.

Lastly, the Malikis hold that the merit mentioned in the prophetic saying, "Communal prayer is superior to a prayer performed by any of you alone by twenty-seven degrees" requires the worshiper to have performed an entire *rak'ah* with the imam; however, this does not mean that those who do not perform an entire *rak'ah* with the imam are deprived of any merit or reward whatsoever. Rather, someone who only manages to utter the final testimony with the imam likewise receives a reward, even though it does not amount to the degree described in the hadith just quoted.

If someone being led in prayer misses some or all the *rak'ahs* of the prayer performed

If a worshiper fails to share with his imam in part of the prayer which the latter has performed, it will be one of the two following situations: (1) The worshiper misses one or more *rak'ahs* of the prayer due to some valid excuse, such as crowding, etc. after beginning the prayer, or (2) he or she misses part of the prayer before joining the imam, for example, by joining the imam during the second, third or final *rak'ah* of the prayer. Each of the four schools offers its own detailed rulings on these situations.[348]

---

348. According to the Hanafis, the worshiper who finds himself in situation (1) above is referred to as 'on time', while the worshiper in situation (2) is termed tardy. The worshiper described as 'on time' commences prayer with the imam, after which he misses some or all the *rak'ahs* due to a valid excuse, such as crowding, whereas the worshiper described as tardy does not commence prayer with the imam but, rather, joins the imam after the latter has already begun to pray. The ruling which applies to the worshiper who is 'on time' is the same as that which applies to anyone else being led in prayer with regard to parts of prayer that he misses. Hence, he must not recite when making up the *rak'ahs* he has missed [since, according to the Hanafis, someone being led in prayer is forbidden to recite behind his imam], nor should he perform a prostration of forgetfulness for anything he neglects while making up these *rak'ahs*, since a worshiper being led in prayer is not required to perform a prostration of forgetfulness for anything he neglects while praying behind his imam, nor does the number of *rak'ahs* required of him increase from two to four by his intending to stay in one place if he has been on a journey.

A worshiper who is 'on time' should make up what he has missed of the prayer while the imam is still praying, then continue following the imam if he is able to catch up with him; if he is not able to do so, he should proceed with his own prayer to the end but not recite anything while standing as he makes up for what he has missed, since he is still viewed as praying behind the imam.

Moreover, if the imam has a prostration of forgetfulness to perform, the worshiper should not perform it with the imam until he has made up everything he missed. It is also possible that the worshiper in situation (1) above, that is, someone who joins the imam on time then misses part of the prayer, will also find himself in situation (2) by virtue of missing one or more *rak'ahs* before joining the imam. An example of this would be someone who joins the imam during the second *rak'ah*, after which he misses one or more *rak'ahs* while praying behind the imam. In this case, the worshiper should first make up what he missed after joining the imam without performing any recitation; he should then follow the imam in what remains of the prayer if he can catch up with him, then make up what he missed before joining the imam, with recitation. If, in such a case, the imam has a prostration of forgetfulness to perform, the worshiper should perform it after making up what he missed before joining the imam. As for the worshiper who makes up what he missed before joining the imam before making up what he missed after he joined the imam, his prayer will be valid, but he will incur guilt for not having followed the legitimate order.

As for the worshiper who is termed tardy, there are a number of rulings related to his situation: (1) If he joins the imam while the latter is performing a silent *rak'ah*, he should recite the prayer of commencement after uttering *takbīrat al-iḥrām*. If he joins the imam while the latter is performing a *rak'ah* involving recitation aloud, he should not recite the prayer of commencement, properly speaking, with the imam; rather, he should recite it when he is making up those parts of the prayer which he missed. When making up such parts, the worshiper is to utter a prayer for divine protection (by saying, *a'ūdhu billāhi min al-shayṭān al-rajīm*—"I seek refuge in God from the accursed Satan"), then utter the *basmalah* in preparation for his Qur'anic recitation as he would if he were praying alone. If, by contrast, the worshiper joins the imam while the latter is bowing or prostrating, and if he thinks it most likely that he will be able to perform part of the bow or the prostration with the imam even if he recites the prayer of commencement, he should go ahead and recite it; otherwise, however, he should refrain from doing so. If the worshiper joins the imam while the latter is seated, he should not recite the prayer of commencement; rather, he should utter *takbīrat al-iḥrām*, then immediately sit down with the imam. (2) It is undesirable to the point of being forbidden for a tardy worshiper to rise to make up for those parts of the prayer he missed before the imam utters the concluding greeting of peace [even] if he has remained seated long enough to utter the final testimony except in certain situations: (a) when a worshiper who performed his ablutions by wiping his shoes fears that the period of time permitted to pray based on such ablutions will run out if he waits for the imam's final greeting of peace; (b) when the worshiper is subject to an extenuating condition [such as urinary incontinence] and is fearful that if he waits for the imam's final greeting of peace, the time period for the prayer he is performing will run out (since in this person's case, his ablutions automatically become invalid once the time period for a new prayer begins); (c) when it is a Friday and the worshiper fears that if he waits for the imam's final greeting of peace, the time period for the mid-afternoon prayer will begin; (d) when it is either the Day of Fastbreaking or the Day of Sacrifice and the worshiper fears that if he waits for the imam's final greeting of peace, the time for the noon prayer will run out, or the sun will come up; (e) when the worshiper is fearful that he will have an occurrence of ritual impurity; (f) when the worshiper fears that if he waits for the imam's final greeting of peace, people will pass in front of him. In all these situations, the worshiper may rise before his imam utters the final greeting of peace in order to make up what he missed of the prayer concerned if the imam has remained seated long enough to utter the final testimony; however, if the worshiper rises before the imam has been seated long enough for the final testimony, his prayer will be invalidated.

Neither the tardy worshiper nor the worshiper who joined his imam on time is obliged to follow his imam in the greeting of peace if any of these aforementioned conditions applies. If no such extenuating circumstance is present, the person being led in prayer must follow his imam in the greeting of peace if he has completed the testimony. If the imam utters the final greeting of peace before this, the worshiper following him should not utter it with him; rather, he should first finish uttering the testimony for himself, then utter the final greeting of peace. If the person being led in prayer finishes uttering both the testimony and the final greeting of peace before his imam, his prayer will be valid, but this practice is deemed undesirable if none of the aforementioned extenuating conditions is present. The preferred practice with regard to following the imam in the final greeting of peace is for the person being led in prayer to utter the greeting at the same time as the imam rather than before him or after him. If the worshiper utters the final greeting of peace before the imam, his prayer will be invalidated, and if he utters it after him, he will have departed from the ideal. The same ruling applies to following the imam in *takbīrat al-iḥrām*; hence, the preferred practice is for the worshiper to utter *takbīrat al-iḥrām* together with his imam. If he does so before the imam, his prayer will be invalid, and if he does so after the imam, he will have missed the most virtuous time for uttering *takbīrat al-iḥrām*.

Another of the Hanafis' rulings in this connection is that a worshiper being led in prayer must make up the beginning of a prayer with respect to recitation, and the end of it with respect to the testimony. Thus, if he has performed one *rak'ah* [i.e., the final *rak'ah*] of the sundown prayer, he must make up two *rak'ahs* and recite in each of the two the *Fātiḥah* and some other passage of the Qur'ān, since the two *rak'ahs* which he is making up are the first and the second with respect to recitation. He should also sit down following the first *rak'ah* and utter the testimony, since it is the second for him. Hence, he will have performed the sundown prayer in this case with three separate 'sittings'. If a worshiper has performed one *rak'ah* of the mid-afternoon prayer, he must make up one *rak'ah* in which he recites the *Fātiḥah* and an additional passage of the Qur'ān, then utter the testimony; he must then make up another *rak'ah* in which he recites the *Fātiḥah* and an additional passage of the Qur'ān, but without uttering the testimony. He should then rise to make up the final *rak'ah*; in this final *rak'ah* he has the choice of whether to recite or not to recite, although recitation is preferable to no recitation. If he has performed two *rak'ahs* of the mid-afternoon prayer, he should make up two *rak'ahs* in which he recites the *Fātiḥah* and another passage of the Qur'ān, then utter the testimony, and if he neglects the recitation in one of the two *rak'ahs*, his prayer will be invalid.

According to the Hanafis, the rulings which apply to the tardy worshiper with respect to the parts of prayer that he makes up are the same as those which apply to someone who is praying alone except in the following four situations: (1) It is not permissible for a tardy worshiper to follow another tardy worshiper as his imam, nor is it permissible for anyone else to follow him as imam. If one tardy worshiper follows another as his imam, the prayer of the person who did the following will be invalidated, but not that of the person who was followed; and if the person who was thus followed in prayer himself follows someone else as imam, his prayer will be invalidated. (2) If a tardy worshiper utters *takbīrat al-iḥrām* with the intention of commencing a new prayer after discontinuing his original prayer, his new prayer will be valid, whereas this would not be the case for someone praying alone. (3) If the imam forgets some part of his prayer before the tardy worshiper joins him, if the tardy worshiper following the imam then rises to make up some part of the prayer he missed, and if he sees the imam performing a prostration of forgetfulness, he must go back and prostrate with the imam provided that he has not yet confirmed the *rak'ah* which he has risen to make up by means of a prostration. If the worshiper does not join the imam in his prostration of forgetfulness, he should continue his prayer and perform a prostration of forgetfulness after he finishes praying. This ruling, however, does not apply to someone who is praying alone, since someone who is praying alone is not required to perform a prostration of forgetfulness on account of someone else's omission, inattention, etc. (4) If the imam remembers a prostration of recitation which he failed to perform during his prayer and goes back to make it up and if, when he does so, the worshiper following him has risen to make up parts of the prayer which he missed before joining the imam, he must go back to following his imam in making up the prostration of recitation, since following the imam in this case is an obligation. The reason for this is that the imam's going back to make up the prostration of recitation serves to cancel out his final 'sitting' so that he is obliged to repeat it; it is likewise an obligation to follow him in this repetition, and if the worshiper fails to follow his imam in this, his prayer will be invalidated. This ruling applies if the tardy worshiper has not confirmed the *rak'ah* he has risen to make up with a prostration; if he has already confirmed the *rak'ah*, his prayer will be invalidated regardless of whether he goes back to following his imam or not. The same ruling applies if the imam leaves out a basic prostration. However, if the imam does not go back to make up the prostration of recitation that he missed, his prayer and the prayer of the tardy worshiper will both be valid.

* * *

According to the Malikis, someone who is being led in prayer and who misses one or more *rak'ahs* before commencing prayer with the imam is classified as tardy. The ruling on such a person is that he must make up whatever parts of the prayer he missed after the imam utters the final greeting of peace. However, with respect to parts of prayer which involve speech, he will be making up what he missed, whereas with respect to the parts that involve action, he will be building on what he did before. When the Malikis speak of the worshiper making up what he missed before, this means that he begins his prayer with what he missed, performing whatever recitation he missed in exactly the form in which he missed it the first time, for example, by reciting the *Fātiḥah* and some other surah of the Qur'ān, or the *Fātiḥah* alone, either silently or aloud, depending on what he missed. Moreover, when they speak of the worshiper building on what he did before, this means that he begins his prayer with what he has already performed. To clarify this ruling, let us say that a certain worshiper joined the imam during the fourth *rak'ah* of the evening prayer, which means that he missed three *rak'ahs* before beginning to pray. Once the imam has uttered his final greeting of peace, the worshiper referred to here should rise and perform a *rak'ah* in which he recites the *Fātiḥah* and some other passage of the Qur'ān aloud, because this is the beginning of his prayer with respect to recitation. He then sits down for the testimony, since this is the second *rak'ah* for him with respect to sitting. He then rises after the testimony and performs a *rak'ah* in which he recites the *Fātiḥah* and another passage of the Qur'ān aloud, since this is the second *rak'ah* for him with respect to recitation; however, he does not sit down after this for the testimony, since this is the third *rak'ah* for him with respect to sitting. He then rises and performs a *rak'ah* in which he recites the *Fātiḥah* silently without reciting any other passage from the Qur'ān, since this is the third *rak'ah* for him with respect to recitation. He then sits down after this for the testimony, because this is the fourth *rak'ah* for him with respect to actions. Then he utters the final greeting of peace.

Among the utterances which such a worshiper would be making up is the prayer of obedience. Hence, if he commences prayer with the imam in the second *rak'ah* of the dawn prayer, he should utter the prayer of obedience along with his imam. When the imam utters the final greeting of peace, the worshiper should then rise to make up the first *rak'ah* of the dawn prayer, but he should not utter the prayer of obedience in this *rak'ah*, since the *rak'ah* he is making up is the first *rak'ah* of the dawn prayer, which contains no prayer of obedience. Moreover, if the imam has a prostration of forgetfulness to perform and if it is one which is to be performed before the final greeting of peace, the worshiper should perform it with the imam before he rises to make up what he missed; whereas if the prostration of forgetfulness is to be performed after the final greeting of peace, the worshiper should delay performing it until after he has made up whatever he missed of the prayer. If a tardy worshiper has performed either two complete *rak'ahs* or less than one *rak'ah* with the imam, he should make up for what he has missed by uttering *takbīrat al-iḥrām*; otherwise, he is not to utter *takbīrat al-iḥrām* when he rises to make up what he missed of the prayer. Rather, he should simply rise silently.

If a worshiper misses part of the prayer after he begins praying with the imam due to some valid excuse, such as crowding or drowsiness which would not invalidate ritual ablutions, he will be in one of three situations: (1) He will have missed a bow or the rising from a bow. (2) He will have missed one or both prostrations. (3) He will have missed one or more *rak'ahs*.

In situation (1) where the worshiper misses a bow or rising from a bow with his imam, this will happen either in the first *rak'ah* or in some other *rak'ah* of the prayer concerned. If it takes place in the first *rak'ah*, he should follow his imam in whatever part of the prayer he is presently performing and cancel the first *rak'ah* due to (a) his not being considered to be following the imam in prayer any longer if he misses bowing with him and (b) the *rak'ahs* not being 'confirmed' with the imam if a worshiper misses rising from the bow with him. The worshiper concerned must then make up the *rak'ah* that was canceled after the imam utters his final greeting of peace. If, on the other hand, the bow or the rise from the bow is missed in some other *rak'ah* of the prayer and if the worshiper has reason to believe that if he bowed or rose from the bow, he would be able to perform as much as a single prostration with the imam, he should perform whatever actions he has missed in order to catch up with the imam. If the worshiper's expectation is not confirmed—if, for example, it happens that as soon as he bows, the imam raises his head from the second prostration—he should cancel what he has done and follow the imam in whatever he is doing at present, then make up a *rak'ah* after the imam's final greeting of peace. If, however, the worshiper does not expect to be able to perform any prostration with the imam, he should cancel this *rak'ah*, then make it up after the imam's final greeting of peace. Lastly, if the worshiper goes against what he has been instructed and makes up what he missed and if he manages to perform some of the prostration with the imam, his prayer will be valid and the *rak'ah* will count; otherwise, his prayer will be invalidated due to his having violated what he was instructed to do [i.e., having not followed the imam and, instead, making up what he missed – t.n.].

In the case of the worshiper in situation (2), namely, someone who has missed one or two prostrations, the ruling here is that if the worshiper has reason to believe that he can catch up with the imam before he raises his head from the bow of the following *rak'ah*, he should perform what he has missed, then catch up with the imam, in which case the *rak'ah* will be counted for him; otherwise, he should cancel the *rak'ah*, follow the imam in what he is presently doing, then perform a *rak'ah* after the imam has uttered his final greeting of peace. In this situation, the worshiper is not required to perform a prostration [of forgetfulness] after the final greeting of peace on account of the addition of the *rak'ah* which he canceled, since the imam takes responsibility for such actions on his behalf.

As for situation (3), in which the worshiper misses one or more *rak'ahs* after commencing prayer with the imam, the ruling on it is that he should make up what he missed after the imam has uttered his final greeting of peace in the same form in which it was missed with respect to recitation and the prayer of obedience, whereas with respect to actions, he should build on what he did before. A worshiper might miss part of a prayer before commencing the prayer with the imam, after which he misses another *rak'ah* after joining the imam due to crowding or other causes. For example, a worshiper might begin praying with the imam in the second *rak'ah* of a four-*rak'ah* prayer, after which he completes the second and third *rak'ahs* with him, then misses the final *rak'ah* as well. He has now missed two *rak'ahs* of the four-*rak'ah* prayer: one before he began praying with the imam, and one afterwards. The ruling on such a situation is that after the imam has uttered his final greeting of peace, the worshiper should first make up the second *rak'ah* which he missed, which was the imam's fourth *rak'ah*; in making up this *rak'ah*, the worshiper should recite the *Fātiḥah* silently without any other passage from the Qur'ān even if it is a prayer which is to be performed with recitation aloud, then sit down following it because it was the imam's final *rak'ah*. He should then rise to make up the first *rak'ah* which he missed; in so doing, he should recite both the *Fātiḥah* and another passage from the Qur'ān since it is the first *rak'ah* of the prayer, and he should recite aloud if it is a prayer which requires recitation aloud. He should sit down afterwards since it is his own final *rak'ah*, then utter the final greeting of peace.

* * *

According to the Hanbalis, a worshiper is considered 'tardy' if he has missed part of the prayer with his imam, regardless of whether he joined the imam in the very beginning of the prayer or after one or two *rak'ahs*. If someone joins his imam from the beginning of the prayer, then falls behind him by an entire pillar due to some excuse, such as inattention or falling asleep (though not to the degree that would invalidate ritual ablutions), he must perform what he missed whenever the extenuating circumstance passes if he can do so without having reason to fear missing the following *rak'ah* by virtue of his not performing its bow with the imam; in this case, the *rak'ah* will be counted. However, if the worshiper fears missing the following *rak'ah* with the imam, he must follow his imam [in whatever action he is presently performing – t.n.] and cancel the *rak'ah*, then make up the cancelled *rak'ah* after the imam has uttered his final greeting of peace.

If a worshiper falls behind his imam by one or more *rak'ahs* due to any of the aforementioned extenuating circumstances or conditions, he should follow his imam in whatever he is doing presently, then make up whatever parts of the prayer he missed by falling behind after he has completed the prayer [with the imam]. The parts of the prayer which were missed must be made up in their original form. This means that if, for example, what the worshiper missed was the first *rak'ah* of the prayer, he should make it up by reciting those things which are required in the first *rak'ah*, such as the prayer of commencement, the prayer for divine protection, the *Fātiḥah* and some other passage of the Qur'ān. If what the worshiper missed was the second *rak'ah*, he should make it up by reciting another passage of the Qur'ān after the *Fātiḥah*, whereas if it was the third or fourth *rak'ah*, he should recite only the *Fātiḥah*.

If a worshiper commences prayer with his imam and performs the bow of the first *rak'ah* with him, and if, after this, he falls behind the imam such that he misses the prostration with him due to some extenuating circumstance, and if the extenuating circumstance passes after his imam has raised his head from the bow of the second *rak'ah*, he should follow his imam in the prostration for the second *rak'ah*. In this case, the worshiper will have completed a *rak'ah* composed of the bow from the first *rak'ah* and the prostration from the second *rak'ah*; after the imam has uttered his final greeting of peace, the worshiper should then make up what he missed according to the form in which he missed it, as we have seen.

The aforementioned ruling applies if the person being led in prayer joined his imam from the beginning of the prayer. However, if the worshiper joined the imam one or more *rak'ahs* after the beginning of the prayer, he must make up what he missed after the imam finishes his own prayer. When making up what he missed, he should begin with what he missed and end with what he performed with his imam. Hence, if someone joined the imam for the third *rak'ah* of the noon prayer, he must make up the first two *rak'ahs* after the imam has finished praying. In so doing, he utters the prayer of commencement, prays for divine protection and recites the *Fātiḥah* and another passage from the Qur'ān in the first *rak'ah*, then recites the *Fātiḥah* and another Qur'anic passage in the second *rak'ah*. If the prayer is not the Friday congregational prayer (during which it is forbidden for those being led in prayer to utter recitations aloud), the worshiper has a choice of whether to recite aloud or silently.

A tardy worshiper must rise to make up what he has missed of the prayer before the imam utters his second greeting of peace. If he rises during the second greeting of peace without an excuse which would make it permissible to part with his imam, the worshiper must sit back down, then rise again after the greeting; otherwise, his prayer will turn into a voluntary prayer, as a result of which he will need to repeat the obligatory prayer which he performed with the imam. Moreover, what the tardy worshiper makes up is the beginning of his prayer, not including the testimony. Hence, if the worshiper only joins his imam in time to complete one *rak'ah* of a four-*rak'ah* prayer or of the sundown prayer, he should not utter the testimony until after he has made up another *rak'ah* lest he alter the form of the prayer. Moreover, the tardy worshiper must sit with his right hip over his right leg and his left hip on the ground (*tawarruk*) during his imam's final testimony if the prayer is either the sundown prayer or a four-*rak'ah* prayer, in deference to his imam. If the tardy worshiper absent-mindedly utters the final greeting of peace with his imam, he must perform a prostration of forgetfulness at the end of his prayer; similarly, he must perform such a prostration if he becomes distracted while praying with his imam or while making up parts of the prayer on his own. This ruling applies even if the worshiper took part with the imam in the latter's prostration of forgetfulness. If the imam forgets something while praying and does not perform a prostration of forgetfulness afterwards, the tardy worshiper who is following him must himself perform this prostration after making up whatever parts of the prayer he missed.

A tardy worshiper is considered to have joined a communal prayer if he utters *takbīrat al-iḥrām* before the imam utters the first greeting of peace; however, he will not be considered to have performed a given *rak'ah* unless he performs its bow with the imam, even if he does not pause and allow his limbs to be still (*ṭuma'nīnah*) in the bow with the imam. However, if he does not pause with the imam, he must do so on his own, then continue following the imam.

* * *

The Shafiis divide those who are being led in prayer into two categories: (1) 'tardy', that is, those who have not prayed with the imam long enough to recite the *Fātiḥah* at a moderate pace, even if they managed to complete the first *rak'ah*, and (2) 'parallel', that is, those who, after their utterance of *takbīrat al-iḥrām* and before the imam's bow, prayed with the imam long enough to recite the *Fātiḥah*, even if this was during the final *rak'ah* of the prayer. Each of these categories has its own associated rulings:

A worshiper classified as tardy will be in one of three situations: (1) He will have joined the imam while the latter was bowing; (2) He will have joined the imam while the imam was standing but, as soon as he uttered *takbīrat al-iḥrām*, he bowed with the imam; or (3) He will have joined the imam while the latter was standing up but close enough to bowing that the person being led in prayer was only able to recite part of the *Fātiḥah*. In the first two situations described here, the ruling on the worshiper being led in prayer is that he must bow with the imam, but he is exempted from the requirement to recite the *Fātiḥah*. The *rak'ah* will count for him if he pauses with the imam in the bow; otherwise, however, the *rak'ah* will not count and instead, he must perform another *rak'ah* after the imam's final greeting of peace. In the third situation, the worshiper must recite as much as he can of the *Fātiḥah* before the imam's bow, after which he is exempted from reciting any more of it. It is recommended that such a worshiper omit the prayer of commencement and the prayer for divine protection, since if he occupies himself with either of these, he must remain standing until he has recited a portion of the *Fātiḥah* which takes as much time as it took him to recite either the prayer of commencement or the prayer for divine protection. Moreover, if he paused with the imam in the bow, the *rak'ah* will count for him; otherwise, it will not. However, his prayer will be valid and he will not be required to intend to part with the imam unless he continues to be occupied with the recitation required of him until the imam has gone down into his prostration, in which case he must intend to part with the imam; if he does

Appointing a proxy for the imam: its definition and the wisdom in its legitimacy

The Arabic term *istikhlāf*, rendered here as "the appointment of a proxy", is employed by scholars of Islamic jurisprudence to refer to the act by which either the imam or one of the worshipers being led in prayer appoints a man who would be qualified to serve as imam to finish leading the worshipers in prayer in the event that their imam cannot do so. For example, as the imam is leading a congregation in prayer, he may complete one or two *rak'ahs* with them (or more, or less), after which something happens which prevents him from completing the prayer, such as a sudden illness, an occurrence of ritual impurity, etc. In such a case, the imam may choose a man from among the worshipers praying behind him, or someone else who is present, and set him up as imam to finish leading the worshipers in what remains of the prayer being performed. If the imam does not does so, those in the congregation may themselves choose someone from among them and set him up as the imam's proxy without speaking or turning away from the *qiblah*, as will be seen below.

Someone might object here, saying: Why should it be this way? Would it not be easier and more reasonable to say that if something prevents the imam from continuing to pray, his prayer will invalidated, at which point some other upright man can simply step in to take his place? In reply it may be said: Prayer is accorded great sanctity under Islamic law. Hence, when someone commences ritual prayer and stands before his Lord, entrusting his secrets to Him in humility and reverence, he must remain in position until he has concluded his prayer; similarly, if he neglects to perform some action included in prayer, he must perform it [when he becomes

---

not make this his intention, his prayer will be invalidated due to his having lagged behind his imam by two action-based pillars without a valid excuse.

As for the worshiper described above as 'parallel', the rulings which pertain to him were mentioned in the discussion on following one's imam. However, it should be noted here that both the worshiper described as 'tardy' and the one described as 'parallel' in the senses described above may be tardy, that is to say, they may both have missed some *rak'ahs* of the prayer with the imam. The ruling on this is that the beginning of the prayer performed by the worshiper in this case is what he performed with the imam; hence, if he performs only the second *rak'ah* with the imam, then rises to make up what he missed, the *rak'ah* which he performed with the imam will be counted for him as his first even though it was the imam's second *rak'ah*. Hence, it is an emulation of the Sunnah for him to utter the prayer of obedience in the *rak'ah* which he makes up since it is his second, even if he already uttered the prayer of obedience in the *rak'ah* which he performed with the imam. Lastly, the tardy worshiper whose imam did not recite the *Fātiḥah* on his behalf must make certain that his prayer includes a passage of the Qur'ān after the *Fātiḥah*; thus, for example, if the worshiper joins the imam in the third *rak'ah* of the noon prayer and if he then makes up what he missed after the imam has finished praying, it is an emulation of the Sunnah for him to recite a verse or surah of the Qur'ān after the *Fātiḥah* as he makes up what he missed.

aware of the omission] and correct it by means of a prostration of forgetfulness. Similarly, if something happens to the imam which would invalidate the group's prayer, he must discontinue his prayer and appoint someone else to complete it for him. The purpose of all of this is to ensure that ritual prayer is performed to completion once it has been begun, since prayer is an action which is required by Islamic law and which must not be neglected under any circumstances.

The reason for appointing a proxy for the imam

As for the reason for which a proxy might need to be appointed for the imam, the various schools offer their own rulings on this issue.[349]

---

349. According to the Hanafis, the reason a proxy for the imam may be chosen is that the imam has had an involuntary occurrence of ritual impurity whereby, for example, he passes gas, has a flow of blood, etc. If, on the other hand, some impurity gets on his clothing or body such that he cannot continue praying, or if his private parts are revealed for the duration of an entire pillar of prayer, the imam's prayer will be invalidated, as will the prayer of those being led in prayer. In such a case, the Hanafis hold that it is not permissible to appoint a proxy for the imam; they also disallow the appointment of a proxy for the imam if he laughs out loud, goes insane, or loses consciousness. (Such conditions will be discussed further under, "Conditions for the appointment of a proxy for the imam.") However, the Hanafis allow the appointment of a proxy for the imam if he is unable to complete the required amount of recitation. If the imam is unable to bow or prostrate due to the need to urinate or defecate, he is not to appoint a proxy if he is able to pray sitting down, and in this case those being led in prayer should complete their prayer behind him from a standing position. This is the view of Imam Abū Ḥanīfah. Lastly, the Hanafis do not allow the appointment of a proxy for the imam if he fears harm or the loss of money; rather, he should simply discontinue his prayer, while those he was leading should begin their prayers all over again as they are able to do so.

* * *

The Malikis stipulate three situations in which it is permissible to appoint a proxy for the imam: (1) While praying, the imam realizes that there is reason to fear for the safety of someone's money, be it his own or someone else's, in which case he is obliged to discontinue his prayer in order to rescue the money in question. In this situation, it is recommended that the imam appoint someone to take his place. However, in order to cut off prayer out of fear for someone's money, the Malikis stipulate that loss or damage to the money concerned would lead to its owner's either dying or being severely harmed. In a case such as this, the imam has no choice but to cut off his prayer whether it is a large or a small amount of money, and regardless of whether there would be sufficient time left in the time period for the prayer concerned to perform the prayer after going to retrieve the money. If, on the other hand, the imam is not fearful that the money would be lost, but is not confident that it should be left unguarded, it is permissible for him to cut off his prayer given two conditions: (a) That there be enough time left to perform the prayer that he cut off before the time period for the following prayer begins; and (b) that it be a large amount of money—where a 'large amount' is defined as that which has value and importance to its owner. If either of these two conditions is unfulfilled, it is not permissible for the imam to cut off prayer. Moreover, similar to fear for someone's money is the fear for someone's life and/or well-being. Thus, for example, if the imam fears that a blind man might collide with a car or fall into a hole so deep that it would hurt him to fall into it, he is under obligation to cut off his prayer in order to rescue him.

In sum, then, fear for the safety of someone's money or person given the aforementioned conditions makes it obligatory for the imam to cut off his prayer. Having done so, it is then recommended that he appoint someone to finish leading the prayer in his place. As we have seen, the Hanafis hold that where there is reason to fear for someone's money, life, well-being, etc., it is obligatory to discontinue prayer; however, they also hold that it is not permissible for the imam to appoint a proxy. Rather, the imam's prayer and that of the worshipers behind him are invalidated. In this situation, it is permissible for those who were following the imam to appoint two imams and for two groups to complete the prayer, one of them behind one of the two imams, and the other behind the other imam. If, on the other hand, the imam has appointed one person to complete the prayer while those who were following him have appointed someone else, and if two groups complete the prayer—one behind the imam's appointee and the other behind the other appointee—both prayers will be valid; however, if the imam has appointed someone to take his place, those who were following him are, properly speaking, forbidden to set up someone else as their imam.

The aforementioned rulings apply to prayers other than the Friday congregational prayer; if such an occurrence takes place as the imam is leading the Friday prayer without his appointing a replacement and if the worshipers perform the Friday prayer individually, it will be invalidated due to the fact that the Friday congregational prayer must be performed communally in order to be valid. If the imam appoints one substitute while the worshipers he has been leading appoint someone else, their Friday prayer will be valid behind the one who was appointed by the imam, and invalid behind anyone else. If, during the Friday prayer, the imam does not appoint anyone to replace him while those he has been leading in prayer appoint two replacements for him, the prayer will be valid behind whichever of the two precedes the other, but if both of them utter the final greeting of peace at the same time, the prayer will be invalidated for everyone. Consequently, they will have to repeat the Friday prayer if sufficient time remains; otherwise, they are to perform it as a regular noon prayer. (On this point, the Hanafis differ, saying: If the imam does not appoint a replacement for himself and the congregation performs the prayer individually, their prayer will be invalidated regardless of whether it is the Friday prayer or some other prayer.) Similarly, they hold that if the imam appoints someone as his replacement while the congregation appoints someone else, the prayer performed behind the person appointed by the congregation will be invalid. Lastly, if neither the imam nor the congregation appoints a substitute for the imam and if one of the worshipers steps forward on his own to finish leading the others in prayer, the prayer will be valid.

* * *

According to the Shafiis, the reason for appointing a substitute for the imam is that the imam has ceased to be qualified to lead others in prayer due either to the occurrence of some ritual impurity, whether it took place intentionally or unintentionally, or due to his discovering that he was in a state of ritual impurity before he began to pray. However, the Shafiis hold that such causes are not necessary in order for the imam to appoint someone as his replacement. Rather, an imam can appoint someone else to replace him even if no such cause has arisen

The Shafiis hold that if the imam appoints one person as his substitute while the congregation appoints someone else, the prayer will be valid behind either of the two, although preference should be given to the one appointed by the congregation, not to the one appointed by the imam unless he is a regular imam, since prior right to prayer leadership goes to the person who was appointed by the regular imam. If the imam appoints someone as his substitute and if someone comes forward and appoints himself, the prayer will be valid behind either of them; however, priority should be given to the one who was appointed by the imam, be he a regular imam or not. It is apparent, then, that the Shafiis differ with both the Hanafis and the Malikis on such rulings.

* * *

According to the Hanbalis, one reason for appointing a substitute for the imam is that the imam has been afflicted by some illness which is so severe that he is unable to finish leading the prayer, while another is that the imam has become unable to perform a particular verbal pillar of prayer, such as recitation of the *Fātiḥah*, or a verbal 'duty', such as the words of praise uttered while bowing and prostrating. If such an extenuating condition arises, it is permissible for the imam to appoint someone as his replacement, even if this person is not among those praying behind him, to finish leading the congregation in prayer. However, the Hanbalis do not consider an occurrence of ritual impurity to be such an extenuating condition; rather, if the imam's ritual ablutions are invalidated during his prayer, his prayer and the prayer of those praying behind him will be invalidated, and it is not permissible for him to appoint someone else to finish leading the prayer for him. If, on the other hand, a condition presents itself which permits the imam to appoint a replacement for himself and if, despite this, he appoints no one, it is permissible for the congregation to appoint a worshiper from among themselves to finish leading them in prayer; similarly, it is permissible for them to complete the prayer individually without an imam. If, on the other hand, the congregation appoints one person as the imam's replacement while the imam appoints someone else, their prayer will only be valid behind the replacement who was appointed by the imam; on this point, the Hanbalis are in agreement with the Hanafis.

The ruling on appointing a proxy for the imam

Each of the four schools offers its own ruling on the matter of appointing a temporary replacement for the imam.[350]

---

350. According to the Hanafis, appointing a proxy for the imam is preferable; hence, they hold that if neither the imam nor the congregation appoints a proxy and if no one comes forward of his own accord without being appointed, the prayer will be invalidated and the worshipers will have to repeat it from the beginning, in addition to which they will have departed from the ideal practice. This ruling applies if it will be possible for them to repeat the prayer within the time period for the prayer concerned; otherwise, it is not obligatory to appoint a replacement for the imam regardless of whether it is the Friday congregational prayer or some other prayer. If the imam appoints one person to replace him and the congregation appoints someone else, the prayer will only be valid behind the person who was appointed by the imam; however, if one of the worshipers steps forward without being appointed and finishes leading the others in prayer, the prayer will be valid. Lastly, if neither the imam nor the congregation appoints anyone to lead them, if no one steps forward to lead them of his own accord, and if they complete the prayer individually, the prayer will be invalid.

* * *

The Hanbalis' ruling on appointing a proxy for the imam is that it is permissible given the existence of the one of the reasons mentioned above. In such a case, the imam may appoint either one of the worshipers he has been leading in prayer, or someone else, to finish leading the congregation in prayer. If the imam appoints one person as his proxy while the congregation appoints someone else, the prayer will only be valid behind the one who was appointed by the imam; on this point, then, the Hanbalis agree with the Hanafis. However, the Hanbalis hold that it is permissible for the congregation to complete their prayers individually without any proxy for the imam having been appointed, and in this respect, they differ with the Hanafis. Consequently, the Hanbalis do not stipulate that there must be sufficient time left to perform the prayer [before the time period for the subsequent prayer begins – t.n.], since they deem it permissible for the congregation to complete their prayers alone without an imam in such a case. Similarly, they make no distinction between the Friday congregational prayer and other prayers; rather, they hold that worshipers may complete this prayer on their own without an imam.

* * *

The Malikis' ruling on appointing a proxy for the imam is that it is recommended. As we have seen, they hold that it is permissible for those being led in prayer to complete their prayers individually if neither the imam nor the worshipers themselves have appointed anyone. This ruling applies provided that the prayer concerned is not the Friday congregational prayer. As for the Friday prayer, it will be invalidated if they perform it individually; consequently, they must repeat it as the Friday prayer if time permits and if they have not appointed any proxy for the imam to finish leading them in it. Unlike the Shafiis, the Malikis do not stipulate explicitly that appointing someone to replace the imam is obligatory for the Friday congregational prayer; rather, what they appear to teach in this regard is that appointment of a proxy for the imam is recommended in any case, and that it is undesirable for the imam and those being led in prayer not to do so.

* * *

The Shafiis' ruling on appointing someone to replace the imam is that it is recommended provided that the person appointed is qualified to serve as imam for the prayer concerned. During the Friday congregational prayer, however, it is obligatory to appoint someone to take the imam's place if something occurs to warrant it during the first *rak'ah*. If, for example, something happens to the imam during the first *rak'ah* to prevent him from completing the prayer, he is obliged to appoint someone else to finish leading the prayer for him; however, if he has led the congregation through the end of the first *rak'ah*, after which something happens that would prevent him from continuing, it is simply recommended that he appoint someone to lead them through the second *rak'ah*. At this point, worshipers may intend to part with the imam if they so choose and pray the second *rak'ah* individually. In order for the appointment of a proxy for the imam during the Friday prayer to be valid, two conditions must be fulfilled: (1) The person appointed to replace the imam must have been among the worshipers who were following the imam in prayer before the appointment took place; thus, it is not permissible during the Friday prayer to appoint someone to replace the imam unless he was among those following the imam, although this is allowed during other prayers. (2) The appointment must take place immediately. Hence, if the time which passes between the occurrence of the extenuating condition and the appointment of the imam's replacement is long enough to perform a short pillar of prayer (such as bowing, for example), the appointment will cease to be valid. Moreover, if the person appointed to replace the imam during the Friday congregational prayer completed the first *rak'ah* with the imam, the Friday prayer will count for him and for those who are being led in prayer; however, if he only joined the imam for the second *rak'ah* of the Friday prayer, the prayer will count for those being led in prayer, but not for the proxy himself.

The Shafiis do not stipulate any conditions for the validity of appointing a proxy for the imam during prayers other than the Friday congregational prayer, as we have seen. Hence, it is permissible for him to appoint someone who was not following him in prayer before, to appoint someone as his proxy after a long time has passed, and even to appoint someone after he has left the mosque; however, if the person appointed to replace the imam was not following him in prayer before the appointment and if this person's prayer was inconsistent with that of the imam's—for example, by his being on the first *rak'ah* while the imam was on the second—the Shafiis require that this person have had an inward, unspoken intention to follow the imam. Otherwise, they require no intention. Similarly, if the time which passes before the appointment of the proxy is long enough for the performance of at least one pillar of prayer, they require the person to renew his intention [to follow the imam]. Moreover, the proxy must observe the same 'pattern' of prayer as that followed by the imam; such observance is obligatory with respect to obligatory parts of the prayer, and recommended with respect to those parts of prayer which are recommended. If the proxy was tardy, he must indicate to the congregation after they have finished their prayer whether they are to wait for him or part with him, although it is preferable for them to wait. If no one has been appointed to replace the imam during a prayer other than the Friday congregational prayer, the congregation should intend to part with their imam, then finish their prayers individually, in which case they will be valid. Lastly, the Shafiis rule that once the worshipers have completed the first *rak'ah* of the Friday prayer in community, they may intend to part with the imam and perform the second *rak'ah* individually provided that the full quorum remains present until the end of the prayer.

* * *

The Hanafis stipulate the following three conditions for the validity of appointing someone to replace the imam: (1) The imam must not leave the mosque in which he was praying before the appointment took place. If he does leave, the appointment of someone to finish leading the prayer on his behalf will be invalid regardless of whether the person was appointed by the imam himself or by the congregation, since everyone's prayer will be invalidated by his leaving the mosque. (2) The person appointed to take over for the imam must be qualified to serve as an imam himself; hence, if the imam has appointed a boy or someone who is illiterate, everyone's prayer will be invalidated. (The procedure to be followed when appointing someone else to finish leading the prayer is as follows: The imam should step back while stooping over somewhat and placing his hand over his nose as if he were suffering a nosebleed even if he is not, in fact, having a nosebleed. The wisdom in doing this is clearly discernible, since it preserves the orderliness of the prayer and shows respect for rules of general etiquette.) (3) The conditions for the validity of building on what one has already performed of a given prayer must be fulfilled; if these conditions are not fulfilled, the prayer will be invalidated and the appointment of a proxy for the imam will be invalid as well. There are eleven such conditions:

1. The occurrence of ritual impurity must have been involuntary. 2. The ritual impurity must have come from the imam's own body; hence, if it comes in contact with him from outside, as it were, he will not be permitted to build on what he has already prayed. 3. The ritual impurity concerned must not be of the sort which requires the performance of major ablutions (*ghusl*), such as a seminal emission resulting from sexual fantasies. 4. The cause for the imam's having to discontinue his prayer must not be something out of the ordinary, such as laughing out loud, fainting, or loss of sanity. 5. The imam must not have performed a pillar of the prayer after the occurrence of the ritual impurity or walked. 6. The imam must not have performed an action which is incommensurate with prayer, such as deliberately bringing on an occurrence of ritual impurity after an occurrence which was involuntary. 7. The imam must not have done something unnecessary, such as going to a source of water which is far away when another source more nearby is available. 8. The imam must not have fallen behind by the equivalent of an entire pillar of prayer due to crowding and the like. 9. It must not have become apparent that the imam was already in a state of ritual impurity before he began to pray. 10. The imam must not have recalled a prayer that he missed earlier if he is among those who believe that all ritual prayers must be performed in their original order.

11. The person being led in prayer must not complete his prayer anywhere other than where he began it. Thus, for example, if a worshiper, be he the imam or someone following an imam, has an occurrence of ritual impurity, after which he goes to perform ritual ablutions, he must, after completing his ablutions, return to pray with the imam; as for someone praying alone, he has a choice as to whether to finish his prayer in the same place in which he began it or not.

* * *

The Malikis stipulate that in order for the appointment of a proxy for the imam to be valid, the proxy must have performed with the imam part of the *rak'ah* during which the imam became unable to complete the prayer, and that the proxy must have been praying with the imam before the imam raised his head after bowing; hence, it is invalid to appoint as a proxy someone who missed bowing with the imam if the extenuating condition had its onset after this. Similarly, it is invalid to appoint someone who did not begin praying with the imam until after the onset of the condition which rendered the imam unqualified to go on leading the prayer. In addition, the proxy must observe the 'pattern' of the imam's prayer—by, for example, resuming the Qur'anic recitation from the place where the imam left off if he knows where the imam left off and, if he does not know this, by beginning the recitation all over again, by sitting in the same place, etc. If the proxy joined the imam late for the prayer, he should first finish leading the congregation in prayer from the point where the imam left off; this includes his performing a prostration of forgetfulness before the final greeting of peace if the imam would have been required to perform one, and the congregation's performing it along with the proxy. Following this, the proxy should signal to the congregation to wait for him while he rises to make up whatever parts of the prayer he missed. Once the proxy has made up what he missed and utters the final greeting of peace, the congregation should utter it with him; if they utter the final greeting of peace without waiting for him, their prayer will be invalidated. If, on the other hand, the imam would have been obliged to perform a prostration of forgetfulness after [rather than before] the final greeting of peace, the proxy should postpone performing it himself until after he has made up what he missed of the prayer; once he has done this, he should utter the final greeting of peace with the congregation, then perform the imam's prostration of forgetfulness. If there is someone in the congregation who joined the prayer late, he should not rise to make up what he missed of the prayer until the proxy has uttered the final greeting of peace, and if the proxy himself joined the prayer late, the worshiper should wait for the proxy while seated until he has made up what he missed and uttered the final greeting of peace; once the proxy has done this, the worshiper may rise to make up whatever he himself missed of the prayer, and if he does not wait for the proxy, his prayer will be invalidated. For example, if the worshiper being led in prayer joined the imam in the second *rak'ah* while the proxy was appointed during the third, and if both the proxy and the worshiper being led in prayer joined the prayer late, the worshiper being led in prayer should not utter the final greeting of peace before the proxy does; rather, he should wait while seated until the proxy has finished making up whatever he missed and uttered the final greeting of peace. Once the proxy has uttered the final greeting of peace, the worshiper who has been waiting may rise and make up what he himself missed, whereas if he rises to make up what he missed without waiting until the proxy has finished, his prayer will be invalidated.

* * *

The Hanbalis do not stipulate any conditions relating to the imam's proxy other than those which apply to the imam himself; hence, it is not necessary for the proxy to have been among the worshipers who were being led by the imam in prayer. In fact, none of the conditions stipulated by the Hanafis are stipulated by the Hanbalis in this regard. As we have seen, the Hanbalis do not allow for the appointment of a proxy for the imam unless he is unable to perform either a verbal or an action-based pillar of the prayer. As for an imam whose ablutions have been invalidated for some reason, his prayer is invalidated, but he may not appoint someone to finish leading the prayer for him. The Hanbalis hold that the proxy must resume the prayer exactly where the imam left off in order to avoid causing confusion for the congregation. Hence, if the proxy joined the prayer late in the beginning, he should still take up the prayer where the imam left off. Then, before he utters the final greeting of peace, he is to appoint someone to utter this greeting with the congregation while he rises to make up what he missed before he joined the imam in prayer; otherwise, the congregation may either utter the final greeting of peace on their own or wait for the proxy while seated until he has made up what he missed, then let him lead them in the final greeting of peace.

The prostration of forgetfulness (*sujūd al-sahw*):

Its definition, when it is called for, and whether it must be preceded by an intention

The meaning of the Arabic word *sujūd*, rendered in English as 'prostration', is complete, utter submission, whether this is expressed by placing one's forehead on the ground or in some other way, such as obeying God's commands. As for the Arabic term *sahw*, rendered variously as 'inattention', 'distraction', 'oversight', etc., it means to neglect or omit something unknowingly, and there is no essential difference, linguistically speaking, between this term and 'forgetfulness' (*nisyān*).

Scholars of Islamic jurisprudence likewise make no distinction between the Arabic terms *sahw* and *nisyān*. In fact, they make no distinction in meaning among the Arabic terms *sahw* (inattention, absent-mindedness, unintentional omission), *nisyān* (forgetfulness, forgetting) and *shakk* (doubt, uncertainty). However, they do distinguish between these three concepts on one hand, and the concept of *ẓann* (a well-founded suspicion) on the other. Specifically, they define the term *ẓann* as "the recognition of what is most probable", as when, for example, one thinks it most likely that he or she performed a particular action. In this respect, *ẓann* differs from the three concepts mentioned above, since the latter indicate that the person is unable to determine whether he or she is likely to have performed the action in question or not.

This, then, is the meaning of the prostration of forgetfulness in linguistic terms; as for its meaning in the context of Islamic jurisprudence, the situations in which it is to be performed, and its relationship to intention, these matters are discussed below.[351]

---

351. According to the Hanafis, the prostration of forgetfulness refers to the worshiper's performance of two prostrations after delivering the final greeting of peace to his right only. After the two prostrations he is to utter the testimony and another greeting of peace. If the worshiper does not utter the testimony, he will have neglected a 'duty', but his prayer will be valid. After uttering the testimony for the prostration of forgetfulness, the worshiper must utter the greeting of peace; if he does not do so, he will have neglected a 'duty'. It is not sufficient for the worshiper to utter the first greeting of peace by means of which he concluded his prayer, since the prostration of forgetfulness cancels out this first greeting of peace, just as it cancels out the final testimony preceding the final greeting of peace. As for prayers for blessing upon the Prophet and supplications, the worshiper is to utter these during the last testimony prior to the final greeting of peace. According to the most preferred view, one is not to utter them during the prostration of forgetfulness, al-

though some hold that they should also be uttered during the prostration of forgetfulness "just in case."

Once the worshiper has uttered the final greeting of peace both to his right and to his left, he is, properly speaking, exempted from performing the prostration of forgetfulness. If the worshiper deliberately utters both final greetings of peace before performing the prostration of forgetfulness, he will be guilty of wrongdoing for having neglected a duty, but if he does so absented-mindedly, he is exempted from performing the prostration of forgetfulness without incurring any guilt; nor is he required to make up the prostration of forgetfulness, since forgetting to perform the prostration of forgetfulness renders it unnecessary. Similarly, if the worshiper utters speech which is not part of ritual prayer either intentionally or unintentionally, he will be exempted from the prostration of forgetfulness. The prostration of forgetfulness is not required if a worshiper deliberately omits a 'duty' or a pillar of prayer; if someone knowingly omits a 'duty', his prayer will be valid and he will not be required to perform the prostration of forgetfulness, but he will be guilty of wrongdoing. As for someone who deliberately omits a pillar of prayer, his prayer will be invalidated altogether such that the prostration of forgetfulness would do him no good. The reason for this is that in the Hanafis' view, the prostration of forgetfulness is only required if someone has omitted something unintentionally; as for the deliberate omission of some part of prayer, it is not permissible to perform a prostration of forgetfulness in order to correct it.

* * *

According to the Shafiis, the prostration of forgetfulness involves the worshiper's performing two prostrations before the final greeting of peace and after the testimony and prayers for blessing upon the Prophet and his family, with an inward intention. The intention associated with the prostration of forgetfulness should be in one's heart rather than spoken aloud, since uttering it aloud would invalidate one's prayer. As we have seen, the Shafiis hold that the prostration of forgetfulness should precede the final greeting of peace; hence, if one were to speak aloud before performing it, his prayer would be invalidated as a matter of course. If a worshiper knowingly, deliberately performs the prostration of forgetfulness without an intention, his prayer will also be invalidated. However, intention is required only of the imam and someone who is praying alone; as for someone who is being led by an imam, he needs no intention, since it is sufficient for him to have intended to follow his imam.

The Shafiis do not stipulate that the prostration of forgetfulness must be performed only when one has unintentionally omitted some part of prayer; rather, it is to be performed (in the manner to be described below in the section on reasons for performing the prostration of forgetfulness) whether the omission was unintentional or deliberate. The reason for its being referred to as a prostration of forgetfulness is that a person is not likely to neglect some part of ritual prayer on purpose. If the reason for performing such a prostration is, in fact, that the worshiper unintentionally left something out of his prayer, it is good for him to say while prostrating, "Glory be to the One who neither sleeps nor forgets" (*subḥān alladhī lā yanāmu wa lā yashu*). If, on the other hand, the reason for the prostration is that the worshiper left something out deliberately, it is good for him to pray for God's forgiveness during the prostration.

From the foregoing it may be seen, then, that the Hanafis agree with the Shafiis on the necessity of intention when performing a prostration of forgetfulness, while they disagree on other points: The Shafiis hold that this prostration should be performed before the final greeting of peace, whereas the Hanafis hold that it should be performed afterwards, and whereas the Shafiis hold that the prostration of forgetfulness includes only two prostrations and nothing else, the Hanafis hold that it includes a final 'sitting' and an utterance of the testimony.

* * *

According to the Malikis, the prostration of forgetfulness consists of two prostrations followed by the testimony, but without any supplication or prayers for blessing upon the Prophet. They hold that if the prostration of forgetfulness is performed after the final greeting of peace, the worshiper should then utter the testimony and repeat the final greeting of peace, although if he does not repeat the greeting of peace after the prostration, his prayer will still be valid. We have seen what the Shafiis and the Hanafis have to say on this point: According to the Shafiis, the prostration of forgetfulness must always be performed before the final greeting of peace; hence, the greeting of peace follows the two prostrations as a matter of course. As for the Hanafis, they hold that the greeting of peace is a 'duty' in the prostration of forgetfulness; hence, if a worshiper neglects it, the prostration will be valid, but he or she will be guilty of wrongdoing.

In addition, the Malikis hold that if the prostration of forgetfulness precedes the final greeting of peace, it requires no intention. The reason for this is that since the prostration of forgetfulness represents a part of the prayer, one's initial intention to perform ritual prayer suffices for this prostration as well. If, on the other hand, the prostration follows the final greeting of peace, it does require an intention since it may no longer be considered an integral part of the prayer itself. Hence, the Malikis agree with the Hanafis on the necessity of intention for the prostration of forgetfulness if it follows the final greeting of peace, whereas they differ with the Shafiis, as we have seen.

The Malikis hold that if, during the Friday congregational prayer, a worshiper forgets to perform the prostration of forgetfulness due to something he has left out and if he then utters the final greeting of peace, he must utter the prostration of forgetfulness in the same mosque in which he prayed. If, by contrast, the prostration of forgetfulness was due to something he added to his prayer, he may perform the prostration in any mosque he wishes, since it comes after the final greeting of peace. However, such a worshiper's prostration will only count in a mosque where the Friday congregational prayer is performed. If the prostration of forgetfulness is due either to something which the worshiper left out of his prayer only, or to both something which was left out and something which was added, the prostration should be performed prior to the final greeting of peace. If, for example, the worshiper forgets to recite an additional passage of the Qur'ān following the *Fātiḥah* and he fails to realize this until he bends down for a bow, he should not go back to recite the passage, and if he does so, his prayer will be invalidated. If he does not go back, however, he must wait until he has uttered the final testimony, prayed for blessings upon the Prophet and uttered a supplication, then perform two prostrations in which he utters the testimony in emulation of the Sunnah. (However, he should not pray for the Prophet during his testimony or utter any supplication.) Lastly, he should utter the final greeting of peace.

If, by contrast, the prostration of forgetfulness is due only to something which the worshiper added to his prayer, he should perform the prostration after the final greeting of peace; however, it is undesirable to delay the prostration. One is forbidden either deliberately to precede the final greeting of peace with a prostration which was meant to follow it, or deliberately to delay a prostration; if one does either of these things unintentionally, however, it is neither undesirable nor forbidden, nor is the worshiper's prayer invalidated thereby.

* * *

According to the Hanbalis, the prostration of forgetfulness consists in uttering the phrase *Allāhu akbar*, then performing two prostrations. This much is agreed upon. Moreover, it is permissible for the prostration to be performed either before or after the final greeting of peace for any of the reasons to be explained below. If the prostration follows the final greeting of peace, the worshiper should utter the testimony before the final greeting of peace, and if it precedes the final greeting of peace, he or she should not utter the testimony during the prostration of forgetfulness, contenting himself instead with the testimony which he or she uttered before this; on this point, the Hanbalis agree with the Shafiis. However, the Hanbalis hold that it is preferable for the prostration of forgetfulness to precede the final greeting of peace as a matter of course except in the following two situations: (1) When the prostration results from having left out one or more *rak'ahs* of one's prayer; in this case, the worshiper should first make up what he left out, then perform the prostration of forgetfulness after the final greeting of peace. (2) When the imam has an uncertainty concerning some part of his prayer, after which he builds on what he thinks himself most likely to have done, in which case it is preferable for him to perform the prostration of forgetfulness after the final greeting of peace. It is sufficient to perform just one prostration of forgetfulness no matter how many particular parts of the prayer were left out; moreover, if the worshiper is due to perform one prostration before the final greeting of peace and another one after it, he should perform the prostration before it.

* * *

The Hanafis list the following five occasions for the prostration of forgetfulness:

One: The worshiper has either omitted or added one or more *rak'ahs*. If, for example, someone performs four *rak'ahs* in the noon prayer, then rises for a fifth *rak'ah* and realizes what has happened after rising from his bow, he may cut off his prayer by uttering the final greeting of peace before sitting down, or he may sit down, then utter the final greeting of peace, although it is preferable for him to sit down first, then utter the greeting. In either case, the worshiper should conclude with a prostration of forgetfulness. Similarly, if a worshiper leaves out a *rak'ah* (for example, by performing only three *rak'ahs* for the noon prayer, then sitting down) and realizes this after sitting down, he must stand up to perform the fourth *rak'ah*, utter the testimony and pray for blessings upon the Prophet, etc., then perform the prostration of forgetfulness in the manner described above.

If the worshiper is uncertain as to how many *rak'ahs* he has performed, the ruling will depend on whether such uncertainties occur only on occasion or are habitual. If it is unusual for the worshiper to have uncertainties as to how much he has prayed, he should cut off his prayer and start all over again; in such a case, he must cut off the prayer by performing some action which is counter to prayer rather than by merely intending to end the prayer. As we have seen, concluding ritual prayer by uttering the final greeting of peace is a 'duty'. In this case, the worshiper may sit down and utter the final greeting of peace; if he utters the final greeting while standing up, this is permissible, albeit a departure from the ideal, as we have seen. If, on the other hand, the worshiper has a habit of being uncertain how much he has prayed, he should not cut off his prayer; rather, he should simply build on whatever he thinks himself most likely to have prayed thus far. For example, if someone who is praying the noon prayer begins to wonder, during the third *rak'ah*, whether he is performing the third *rak'ah* or the fourth *rak'ah*, he should simply act in accordance with what he thinks is most likely. If he thinks it most probable that he is on the fourth *rak'ah*, he should sit down, utter the testimony, pray for the Prophet, then utter the final greeting of peace and perform the prostration of forgetfulness in the manner described above. If, on the other hand, he thinks it most probable that he is on the third *rak'ah*, he should perform another *rak'ah*, utter the testimony, pray for the Prophet, etc., then utter the final greeting of peace and perform the prostration of forgetfulness afterwards in the manner described above.

The rulings just described apply to a worshiper who is praying alone. As for an imam who has uncertainties about some part of his prayer, the Hanafis rule that if those being led in prayer confirm that he either left something out or added something to his prayer, he must repeat the prayer based on what they have said. However, if those in the congregation are unanimous in their opinion that he prayed only three *rak'ahs* whereas he insists that he performed four, for example, he need not repeat the prayer. Similarly, if at least one of the worshipers agrees with the imam, the imam's opinion will hold sway. If the imam is uncertain [of how many *rak'ahs* he has performed] and if some of the worshipers are certain that he performed the entire prayer while others are certain that he did not, the prayer must be repeated only by those who are uncertain. If, by contrast, the imam is certain that he has not performed the entire prayer, they must [all] repeat the prayer unless they are certain that the prayer has been performed it in its entirety. Lastly, if one of the worshipers is convinced that the prayer was incomplete while both the imam and the rest of the worshipers are uncertain, they should repeat it "just in case" if the time period for the prayer has not yet elapsed; otherwise, however, they should not.

If, after the prayer is concluded, the imam is informed by a reliable individual (even if he is not among those whom he led in prayer) that he performed only three *rak'ahs* for the noon prayer, and if he doubts the person's truthfulness, he should still repeat the prayer "just in case." However, if he is informed by two reliable individuals, he has no choice but to accept what they have said and his own uncertainty is not to be taken into account. If, on the other hand, the person who speaks thus to the imam is not reliable, his statement is not to be taken seriously. If the imam doubts whether he consciously intended to perform the prayer concerned or whether he uttered *takbīrat al-iḥrām*, or if while praying he suspects that he may have had an occurrence of ritual impurity or that some ritual impurity may have gotten on his body or his clothing, the Hanafis' ruling is that if he is having such a doubt for the first time, he should cut off his prayer, verify whether his suspicions are correct, and repeat the prayer. However, if he frequently has such uncertainties, he should give them no credence and, instead, simply proceed with his prayer. Lastly, if such doubts occur after he has completed his prayer, they need not be taken into account.

Two: The worshiper forgot to perform the final, obligatory 'sitting' and stood up. The ruling in this case is that he should sit down again for as long as it would take to utter the testimony, then utter the final greeting of peace and perform the prostration of forgetfulness for having delayed the final 'sitting' past its usual place in the prayer. If the worshiper continues with his prayer and performs the prostration of forgetfulness before sitting down, the prayer will turn [from an obligatory prayer] into a voluntary prayer as soon as he raises his head from the prostration. He then adds a sixth *rak'ah*, even if what he is performing is the mid-afternoon prayer. In this case, he is not to perform a prostration of forgetfulness, properly speaking, since the fact that the prayer has become voluntary cancels out the need for the prostration of forgetfulness; if, by contrast, the prayer was voluntary to begin with, he should perform the prostration of forgetfulness. However, the worshiper is obliged in either case to repeat an obligatory prayer which turned into a voluntary prayer.

Three: The worshiper forgot to perform the first 'sitting' (which is a 'duty' rather than a binding obligation). If a worshiper forgets to perform the first 'sitting' of an obligatory prayer by getting up immediately after the second *rak'ah*, and if he remembers before standing all the way up and sits back down again, his prayer will be valid and there will be no need for him to perform a prostration of forgetfulness. If, on the other hand, the worshiper does not realize his error until after he has stood all the way up, he should not go back to make up the [first] testimony. If the worshiper does go back to utter the testimony, there are some who say that his prayer will be invalidated; the reason for this point of view is that sitting to utter the first testimony is not a binding obligation, whereas standing up is; hence, the worshiper in such a case has busied himself with a voluntary action in place of an obligatory action, and neglecting an obligation for the sake of something voluntary invalidates prayer. However, the most correct point of view is that such a person's prayer is not invalidated, since he did not neglect the obligation to stand up but rather, simply delayed it. A comparable situation would be one in which someone forgets to recite a passage from the Qur'ān [after the *Fātiḥah*] and bows; in such a case, the worshiper is to cancel the bow, stand up again and perform the Qur'anic recitation which he forgot; in such a case, his prayer will be valid, but he will need to perform a prostration of forgetfulness for having delayed a pillar or obligation of prayer past its proper place.

The aforementioned ruling applies to someone who is either an imam or praying alone; in the case of someone being led in prayer, the ruling is that if he stands up and his imam remains seated in order to recite the testimony, he must sit back down again, since this is required of him by virtue of his following the imam.

Four: The worshiper reverses the proper order of either two pillars or a pillar and a 'duty'. An example of the first situation is that someone bows before performing the obligatory recitation; specifically, he might utter *takbīrat al-iḥrām*, recite the prayer of commencement, then get distracted and bow before reciting anything. If he realizes his error, he should go back and recite, bow again, then perform a prostration of forgetfulness in the manner described above; if, on the other hand, he does not realize his error [before completing the bow], this *rak'ah* should be considered void, and in this case he must perform an additional *rak'ah* before uttering the final greeting of peace, then perform a prostration of forgetfulness. As for the second situation mentioned here, namely, that of reversing the proper order of a pillar and a 'duty', an example of this would be for someone to bow before reciting a passage of the Qur'ān after the *Fātiḥah*. The ruling on this situation, as we have seen, is that if the worshiper realizes his error during his bow, he should rise from the bow and recite the Qur'anic passage, then bow again; if he does not realize his error while bowing, he should simply perform a prostration of forgetfulness after the final greeting of peace.

Five: The worshiper neglects one of the following eleven 'duties': (1) Recitation of the *Fātiḥah*. If the worshiper leaves out most or all of the *Fātiḥah* in one of the first two *rak'ahs* of an obligatory prayer, he should perform a prostration of forgetfulness; however, if he leaves out [half or] less than half of the *Fātiḥah*, no prostration of forgetfulness is required, since the ruling on 'most' of something is the same as the ruling on the entire entity. In this respect, there is no difference between an imam and someone praying alone. The prostration of forgetfulness is likewise called for if such a worshiper leaves out all or most of the *Fātiḥah* during any *rak'ah* of a voluntary prayer or the *witr*, since its recitation is obligatory in all *rak'ahs* of such prayers. (2) The recitation of a surah of the Qur'ān, three short verses, or one long verse after the *Fātiḥah*. If the worshiper recites nothing or if he recites a short verse, he must perform a prostration of forgetfulness; however, if he recites two short verses, no prostration of forgetfulness is called for since, as we have noted, the ruling on 'most' of something is the same as the ruling on the entire entity. If the worshiper forgets to recite the *Fātiḥah* or the Qur'anic passage following it and bows, then realizes his error, he should go back and recite what he forgot. If what he forgot is the *Fātiḥah*, he should recite it, then repeat whatever passage he recited the first time; he should then repeat his bow and perform a prostration of forgetfulness. If what he forgot is the prayer of obedience associated with the *witr*, and if after this he bows, then realizes his error, he should not go back to recite it but rather, should simply perform a prostration of forgetfulness. If such a worshiper does go back and recite the prayer of obedience, his bow will be acceptable, but he should perform a prostration of forgetfulness as well. If someone absented-mindedly recites the *Fātiḥah* twice, the prostration of forgetfulness is called for because he delayed the recitation of the Qur'anic passage following the *Fātiḥah* past its proper place in the prayer. If the worshiper reverses the order of Qur'anic passages by, for example, reciting Surah 93 in the first *rak'ah* and Surah 87 in the second, he is not required to perform the prostration of forgetfulness, since observance of the order of surahs as they appear in the Qur'ān is a duty associated with the organization of the Qur'ān, but it is not a duty associated with ritual prayer. Similarly, if a worshiper pauses silently between reciting an additional passage from the Qur'ān and bowing—thereby delaying the bow—he is not required to perform a prostration of forgetfulness; this situation occurs frequently among the Shafiis when someone is praying as an imam. (3) Performing Qur'anic recitation specifically in the first and second *rak'ahs* of obligatory prayers. Hence, if a worshiper performs such recitation only in the last two *rak'ahs*, or in the second and third *rak'ahs* only, a prostration of forgetfulness is called for, whereas if the prayer is voluntary or the *witr*, it is not required. (4) The [proper] order in an action which is repeated in a single *rak'ah*, namely, prostration. Hence, if a worshiper unintentionally performs only one prostration, then rises to perform the next *rak'ah* and completes both of its prostrations, and if he adds to this *rak'ah* the prostration which he left out of the *rak'ah* before it, his prayer will be valid; in this case, he will need to perform a prostration of forgetfulness for having left out this 'duty', but he will not be obliged to repeat the previous *rak'ah*. If a worshiper fails to observe the proper order in actions which are not repeated—for example, by uttering *takbīrat al-iḥrām*, then bowing and rising from the bow, then reciting the *Fātiḥah* and another passage from the Qur'ān, the [first] bow will be void and the worshiper must repeat it after the recitation, then perform the prostration of forgetfulness for having 'added' the first bow. (5) *Ṭuma'nīnah* when both bowing and prostrating. Properly speaking, a worshiper who absentedmindedly neglects this practice should perform a prostration of forgetfulness. (6) The 'sitting' which is classified by the Hanafis as a 'duty' (that is, the sitting which is not the final one), whether in an obligatory or a voluntary prayer. If someone unintentionally misses the 'first sitting' and stands up to perform the next *rak'ah*, he should continue with his prayer, then perform a prostration of forgetfulness for having neglected this 'duty', as we have seen. (7) Utterance of the testimony. If someone neglects the testimony unintentionally, he must perform a prostration of forgetfulness. This ruling applies whether the testimony was left out during the first or second 'sitting', the ruling on which we have seen. (8) Utterance of the prayer of obedience during the *witr*. This prayer is considered to have been neglected if the worshiper bows before uttering it. (9) Utterance of the phrase *Allāhu akbar* associated with the prayer of obedience. A worshiper who leaves this out should perform a prostration of forgetfulness. (10) Utterance of the words *Allāhu akbar* during the bow of the second *rak'ah* in the holiday prayer; this utterance is considered to be a 'duty', in contrast to the utterance of these words during the first *rak'ah*, as we have seen. (11) The imam's recitation aloud in situations which require this, and silently in situations which call for silence. If the imam neglects what is required in this regard, he should perform a prostration of forgetfulness. However, this does not apply to supplications, the prayer of commencement and the like; hence, if the imam recites any of these aloud, he is not required to perform the prostration of forgetfulness.

The aforementioned rulings apply equally to voluntary and obligatory prayers.

* * *

The Malikis specify three reasons for which the prostration of forgetfulness needs to be performed:

One: The worshiper has left out a Sunnah-based practice associated with ritual prayer. This reason is, in turn, divided into three different situations: (1) The Sunnah-based practice which was left out is an integral part of the prayer, such as the recitation of a passage from the Qur'ān following the *Fātiḥah* if someone forgets to include this in its proper place. If this happens, regardless of whether it occurred for certain or is merely suspected to have occurred, it is considered an omission, as a result of which the worshiper is to perform a prostration of forgetfulness before the final greeting of peace. If one is uncertain whether what occurred was an addition or an omission, it should be considered an omission, which means that the prostration of forgetfulness must precede the final greeting of peace.

In order for a prostration of forgetfulness to be required as a result of omitting a Sunnah-based practice, three conditions must be met: (a) The practice omitted must be an emphatically enjoined Sunnah-based practice, as we have seen. Otherwise (for example, if one were unintentionally to omit one of the utterances of *Allāhu akbar* which are made while bowing or prostrating, or a recommended practice such as utterance of the prayer of obedience during the dawn prayer), no prostration of forgetfulness is required. If one performs a prostration of forgetfulness before the final greeting of peace for the omission of a Sunnah-based practice which is not emphatically enjoined, his prayer will be invalidated due to his having added to the prayer something which was not a part of it. If, however, he performs the prostration after the final greeting of peace, his prayer will not be invalidated, since the addition made will have been external to the prayer. (b) The Sunnah-based practice which was omitted must be an integral part of ritual prayer. If someone omits a Sunnah-based practice which is external to prayer, such as the wearing of appropriate attire, he is not to perform a prostration of forgetfulness on this account if it was a result of inattention. (c) The worshiper must have omitted the practice out of forgetfulness. If someone deliberately omits an emphatically enjoined Sunnah-based practice which is an integral part of prayer, there is disagreement as to whether his prayer remains valid or not. Moreover, the same ruling and conditions which apply to emphatically enjoined Sunnah-based practices apply likewise to the two non-emphatically enjoined practices which form an integral part of prayer; hence, if someone omits them by accident, he should perform a prostration of forgetfulness before the final greeting of peace, whereas for someone who omits them deliberately, there is disagreement over whether his prayer is valid or not. However, if someone deliberately omits more than two Sunnah-based practices, his prayer will be invalid based on the best attested view; such a person should pray for God's forgiveness and repeat the prayer.

In sum, the omission of an emphatically enjoined Sunnah-based practice and of the two 'light' Sunnah-based practices may be redressed by performing a prostration of forgetfulness. However, the omission of non-emphatically enjoined Sunnah-based practices and practices which are simply recommended—sometimes referred to as 'virtues'—is not to be redressed by a prostration of forgetfulness; if a worshiper performs a prostration of forgetfulness for such an omission before the final greeting of peace, his prayer will be invalidated, although if he does so after the final greeting of peace, his prayer will remain valid. If, on the other hand, someone omits an obligation of ritual prayer, this may not be redressed by performing a prostration of forgetfulness; rather, the omitted obligation must be made up regardless of whether it was omitted in the final *rak'ah* or in some other *rak'ah* of the prayer. However, if the pillar which was omitted was part of the final *rak'ah*, the worshiper should perform it if he remembers it before uttering the final greeting of peace in the mistaken belief that he has completed his prayer; if he utters the final greeting of peace in this belief and if he then makes up the omitted pillar, cancels the incomplete *rak'ah*, and performs another *rak'ah* in its place, his prayer will be valid and he must perform a prostration of forgetfulness after his final greeting of peace due to his having added a *rak'ah* in place of the one which he canceled. This ruling applies if what is commonly considered to be a short period of time has passed since his final greeting of peace; otherwise, his prayer will be invalidated. If the omitted pillar was part of a *rak'ah* other than the final one, the worshiper should make it up if he has not yet confirmed the bow of the following *rak'ah* (where confirmation of the bow involves raising one's head afterwards and remaining momentarily in a still, upright position). However, if what was accidentally omitted was the bow itself, the confirmation of the following *rak'ah* involves simply bending forward in the bow, even if the worshiper has not risen from it, as we have seen. If a worshiper omits the prostration of the second *rak'ah*, then stands up for the third *rak'ah*, he should make up the omitted prostration if he remembers it before raising his head from the bow of the third *rak'ah* and momentarily maintaining a still, upright posture. If he does not realize his error until he has completed the bow of the third *rak'ah*, he should continue praying and count the third *rak'ah* as his second, sit down, perform two more *rak'ahs*, then perform a prostration of forgetfulness before his final greeting of peace due to the omission of the Qur'anic passage from the second *rak'ah* (which had originally been the third *rak'ah*, and in which he recited only the *Fātiḥah*), and due to the addition of the *rak'ah* which he canceled.

As for the manner in which one is to make up an omission, it is as follows: Someone who omitted a bow should stand up again, and it is recommended that he recite something from the Qur'ān other than the *Fātiḥah* before his bow in order for his bow to follow a Qur'anic recitation. Someone who omitted the act of rising from a bow should go back into a hunched-over position until he is about to complete a full bow, then raise himself up again, while someone who omitted a single prostration is to sit down in order to make up the prostration from a sitting position. As for someone who has omitted two prostrations, he is to make them up by going down from a standing position. An exception to the foregoing is made for the *Fātiḥah* if someone omits it unintentionally and does not realize this until after he bows; in such a case, the worshiper is to continue in his prayer based on the most widely held view, then perform a prostration of forgetfulness before the final greeting of peace regardless of whether the omission occurred in one *rak'ah* or more than one *rak'ah* of the prayer concerned, even if he only recites it in one *rak'ah* of his prayer. The reason for this is that although the officially recognized view among the Malikis is that the *Fātiḥah* is obligatory in every *rak'ah* of a given ritual prayer, it is nevertheless true that if the worshiper utters it in even one *rak'ah* of the prayer and omits it unintentionally in all the others, his prayer will still be valid and that the omission may be redressed by performing a prostration of forgetfulness before the final greeting of peace in deference to the view that the *Fātiḥah* is required in one *rak'ah* only. Even so, it is recommended that such a person repeat the prayer just in case, either before or after the time period for the prayer elapses. If a worshiper omits the prostration of forgetfulness which he should have performed for having omitted the *Fātiḥah* and if the omission was deliberate, his prayer will be invalidated, whereas if it was unintentional, he should make up the prostration if not too much time has passed by commonly accepted standards; otherwise, the prayer will be invalidated. If someone omits the *Fātiḥah*, whether intentionally or unintentionally, and if he realizes this before the bow but does not make it up on the basis of the view that it is not required in every *rak'ah*, his prayer will be invalidated; the basis for this ruling is the widespread acceptance of the view that the *Fātiḥah* is required in all *rak'ahs*.

Two: The worshiper has added an action which is not part of the prayer, such as unintentionally eating a small amount, unintentionally speaking, or adding an action-based pillar such as a bow, a prostration, or a 'part' of prayer such as one or two *rak'ahs* as we saw in the section entitled, "That which invalidates ritual prayer." If what is added is an utterance and if the added utterance is not obligatory—for example, if the person unintentionally adds a passage from the Qur'ān in the last two *rak'ahs* of a four-*rak'ah* prayer—no prostration of forgetfulness is required. Similarly, one's prayer will remain valid if one performs the prostration after the final greeting of peace since, as we have seen, it is an addition which takes place outside of the prayer. If, on the other hand, the utterance is obligatory—for example, if the person unintentionally repeats the *Fātiḥah*—he should perform a prostration of forgetfulness. Any addition beyond what has been mentioned [also] requires a prostration of forgetfulness, even if one is uncertain as to whether it actually occurred. For example, if someone who is performing the noon prayer is uncertain as to whether he performed three or four *rak'ahs*, he should build on what he is certain to have performed, then perform another *rak'ah* and perform a prostration of forgetfulness after the final greeting of peace due to the possibility that the *rak'ah* which he last performed was extra. Similarly, if someone who is performing the *shaf'* is uncertain as to whether he is performing the *shaf'* [which consists of two *rak'ahs*] or the *witr* [which consists of three], he should make what he is praying the *shaf'*, then perform another *rak'ah* to make it a *witr*, then perform a prostration of forgetfulness after the final greeting of peace due to the possibility that he prayed the *shaf'* in three *rak'ahs*, in which case he will have added an extra *rak'ah*. Another type of addition to prayer is for the worshiper to prolong excessively a part of the prayer which may not legitimately be prolonged, such as rising from a bow or sitting between the two prostrations. Excessive prolongation is for the worshiper to spend a noticeably longer time on *ṭuma'nīnah* than is required or consistent with the Sunnah. However, if one prolongs other parts of prayer, such as prostration and the final 'sitting', this is not considered to be an addition; hence, it calls for no prostration of forgetfulness. Another type of addition is for the worshiper to fail to recite the *Fātiḥah* silently, even in a single *rak'ah*, and instead to recite it in a voice which is loud enough that he can be heard not only by those immediately around him, but by others as well. If, on the other hand, the worshiper neglects to recite aloud [something which is meant to be recited aloud] and instead recites with nothing but the movement of his tongue [and lips], this is considered to be an omission from the prayer rather than an addition to it; in this case, he should perform a prostration of forgetfulness before the final greeting of peace if this occurs only in connection with the *Fātiḥah*, or in connection with the *Fātiḥah* and the following passage from the Qur'ān. If it occurs in connection only with the Qur'anic passage following the *Fātiḥah*, the worshiper need not perform a prostration of forgetfulness if it only occurred in one *rak'ah*, since it is considered to be a non-emphatically enjoined Sunnah-based practice; however, if it occurs in two *rak'ahs*, he should perform such a prostration.

If an imam or someone who is praying by himself omits the 'sitting' for the first testimony, he should go back to make it up in emulation of the Sunnah provided that he has not yet lifted his hands and his knees off the floor; otherwise, he should not go back to make it up. If he does go back to make it up, his prayer will not be invalidated even if he does so after reciting part of the *Fātiḥah* [for the third *rak'ah*]; however, if he does so after reciting the *Fātiḥah* in its entirety, his prayer will be invalidated. If the imam goes back to make up the missed 'sitting' before his hands and knees have left the floor, or if he goes back to make it up after leaving the floor and before a complete recitation of the *Fātiḥah*, those being led by him in prayer must follow him in going back to make it up [the text reads, "in bowing" – t.n.]. Similarly, they should follow him in not going back to make it up if his hands and his knees have left the floor; if those being led in prayer diverge from the imam deliberately in any of this and if this divergence is not due to either ignorance or some particular interpretation on their part, their prayer will be invalidated.

Three: The worshiper has both omitted a Sunnah-based practice from the prayer and added something to it (where 'addition' is to be understood in light of the aforementioned explanation of the second reason for performing a prostration of forgetfulness). Hence, if a worshiper neglects to recite aloud the Qur'anic passage following the *Fātiḥah* and if he unintentionally adds a *rak'ah* to the prayer, he has joined an omission and an addition. In such a case, the worshiper should perform a prostration of forgetfulness before the final greeting of peace, thereby giving more weight to the omission than to the addition.

* * *

The Hanbalis list three reasons for which a prostration of forgetfulness needs to be performed, namely: (1) addition, (2) omission, and (3) uncertainty concerning some part of the prayer, provided that the suspected error was unintentional. If the error occurs deliberately, one should not perform a prostration of forgetfulness; rather, the prayer will be invalidated if the part of prayer concerned was an action, though not if it was an utterance which was made out of place.

Omitting part of a prayer unintentionally calls for a prostration of forgetfulness unless the omission occurs in a funeral prayer, a prostration of recitation, a prostration of forgetfulness or a prostration of thanksgiving, all of which are exceptions to such rulings.

With regard to (1) above, namely, additions to prayer, an example of this would be for a worshiper to stand up or sit down an additional time, even if the 'sitting' lasts only as long as what is referred to as the "sitting of repose" which some [jurisprudents] support. Another example would be for the worshiper to recite the *Fātiḥah* with the testimony while seated, or to recite the testimony with the *Fātiḥah* while standing. In such situations, the worshiper is obliged to perform a prostration of forgetfulness for the addition of an action, while it is recommended that he perform such a prostration for the addition of an utterance which he made out of place.

With regard to (2) above, namely, an omission from prayer, an example of this would be for a worshiper unintentionally to omit a bow, a prostration, or the recitation of the *Fātiḥah*. If he realizes his error before commencing the recitation for the subsequent *rak'ah*, he should make up the omission and what follows the omission, then perform a prostration of forgetfulness at the end of his prayer; if he does not realize his error until after having commenced the recitation for the subsequent *rak'ah*, the *rak'ah* in which the omission occurred is canceled and the following *rak'ah* will take its place, after which the worshiper must perform an extra *rak'ah* to compensate for the one that was cancelled, then perform a prostration of forgetfulness. If the worshiper goes back to make up what he missed even after having commenced the recitation of the following *rak'ah*, and if he does so knowing that this is forbidden, his prayer will be invalidated; however, if he does so in the belief that it is permitted, his prayer will remain valid. If the worshiper realizes his error before commencing the recitation for the subsequent *rak'ah* but deliberately fails to go back to make up what he missed, his prayer will be invalidated if he is knowledgeable of the ruling on this matter, whereas if he is not aware of it, only the *rak'ah* concerned will be canceled and the *rak'ah* following it will take its place. Following this, he should perform an extra *rak'ah* to compensate for the one that was cancelled, then perform a prostration of forgetfulness. If the worshiper only realizes his error after uttering the final greeting of peace and if what he omitted was in some *rak'ah* other than the final one, he must make up an entire *rak'ah*; if what he missed was in the final *rak'ah*, he must make up what he missed as well as whatever followed it, then perform a prostration of forgetfulness. This ruling applies if: (1) not very much time has passed since the conclusion of the prayer, and (2) the worshiper has neither spoken nor had an occurrence of ritual impurity; otherwise, his prayer will be invalidated and he will be obliged to repeat it.

As for (3) above, namely, uncertainty as to whether one has erred in the prayer in a way that calls for a prostration of forgetfulness, an example of this would be for a worshiper to suspect that he omitted a pillar of the prayer, or to wonder how many *rak'ahs* he has prayed. In this case, he should build on what he is certain to have done thus far and perform what he is unsure whether he did or not, then conclude his prayer, after which he is obliged to perform a prostration of forgetfulness. If someone joins the imam while the latter is bowing, then wonders whether he bowed with the imam before he raised his head, the *rak'ah* in which this uncertainty occurred will not count; hence, the worshiper concerned must repeat the *rak'ah* when he is making up the other parts of the prayer that he missed, then perform a prostration of forgetfulness. If, on the other hand, a worshiper wonders whether he has omitted a 'duty' of prayer—such as one of the utterances of praise to God which are made while bowing and prostrating—he should not perform a prostration of forgetfulness, since such a prostration is not called for by doubting whether one has performed a 'duty' of prayer but rather, by actually (albeit unintentionally) omitting a 'duty'. If someone completes all *rak'ahs* of a given prayer, then, while uttering the testimony, wonders whether the final *rak'ah* was extra, he should not perform a prostration of forgetfulness; however, if he wonders such a thing before he has uttered the testimony, he should perform it. The same ruling applies if one wonders whether he performed an extra prostration.

It may be seen from the foregoing that uncertainty about some part of one's prayer does not call for a prostration of forgetfulness in all situations; moreover, if someone performs such a prostration in a situation where it is not called for, he must perform another prostration of forgetfulness because of this, since in so doing, he has added to his prayer two prostrations which are not 'legitimate'.

If someone knows that he committed some unintentional error in his prayer but does not know whether such an error calls for the prostration of forgetfulness or not, he should not perform it, since its cause has not been verified, and since the default option, as it were, is not to perform one. If someone commits an error in his prayer and wonders whether he has performed a prostration of forgetfulness on this account, he should perform it as two prostrations only. If someone who is being led by an imam suspects that he has omitted a pillar or a *rak'ah*, he should build on what he is certain to have performed thus far as though he were praying alone rather than relying on what his imam has done. Once his imam has uttered the final greeting of peace, he should make up whatever he suspects that he omitted, then perform a prostration of forgetfulness and utter the final greeting of peace himself. If others are praying with him behind the same imam, the worshiper should rely on what has been performed by his imam and the others in the congregation. If someone has a suspicion of the type which calls for a prostration of forgetfulness and if it then becomes apparent that he did not commit the error which he suspected he had, he should not perform any prostration of forgetfulness on account of the suspicion. Lastly, if someone mispronounces words during prayer, either by mistake or out of ignorance, in such a way that their meaning is changed, he must perform the prostration of forgetfulness, and if he omits a Sunnah-based practice, it is permissible for him to perform it.

* * *

The Shafiis list six situations in which the prostration of forgetfulness is to be performed:

One: The imam or someone who is praying alone omits one of the emphatically enjoined Sunnah-based practices (referred to by the Shafiis as 'parts' of prayer), such as the first testimony or the regular prayer of obedience (as opposed to the prayer of obedience which is uttered at times of distress or tribulation). If he omits one of the non-emphatically enjoined Sunnah-based practices (referred to by the Shafiis as "outward forms"), such as recitation of a Qur'anic passage after the *Fātiḥah*, he should not perform a prostration of forgetfulness on this account regardless of whether the omission was deliberate or not.

If the imam or someone praying alone omits an obligatory part of prayer, such as a prostration or a bow, and if he realizes his error before performing the next such movement in the prayer, he should make it up immediately; if he does not realize his error until after performing another instance of the same action, the second instance will be considered as if it were the first, while anything which was done between the two will be cancelled. For example, if he omits the first bow, then remembers it before performing the second bow, he should make up the bow which he omitted, canceling what he did first, then continue with his prayer to completion and perform a prostration of forgetfulness before uttering the final greeting of peace. If he remembers omitting the first bow after performing the second, the second bow will be considered as if it were the first; hence, what is done later is considered to replace what was done earlier, while whatever came between them is cancelled, provided that the error is realized before the utterance of the final greeting of peace. However, if the worshiper does not realize his error until after uttering the final greeting of peace and if: (1) little time has passed by commonly accepted standards since the conclusion of the prayer, (2) he has not come in contact with ritual impurity of the sort which cannot be overlooked, (3) he has not spoken more than six words, and (4) he has not engaged in excessive movement which would invalidate prayer, he must make up what he forgot. For example, if what the worshiper omitted was a bow, and if he realizes this after performing the final greeting of peace given the aforementioned conditions, he must rise and bow, then perform whatever will complete the prayer, utter the testimony and perform a prostration of forgetfulness before uttering the final greeting of peace [again]. If someone omits an emphatically enjoined Sunnah-based practice such as the first testimony, then rises to a position which is closer to standing than it is to sitting, he should not sit down again, and if he does sit back down deliberately and knowingly, his prayer will be invalidated. If he sits back down out of inattention or ignorance, his prayer will not be invalidated, but it is an emulation of the Sunnah for him to perform the prostration of forgetfulness. If someone omits the regular prayer of obedience (i.e., other than the one which is uttered at times of affliction), then moves to sit down, he should not stand back up again if he has reached a bowing position, and if he does stand up again knowingly and deliberately, his prayer will be invalidated; otherwise, the ruling on this situation is the same as it was for the testimony.

The aforementioned rulings apply to someone who is either an imam or praying alone; as for someone who is being led in prayer, if he deliberately omits the testimony and the prayer of obedience, he may choose between going back to following his imam or waiting until the imam catches up with him, at which point he is to continue with the imam. If someone omits the testimony and the prayer of obedience out of inattention, he must go back to following his imam; otherwise, his prayer will be invalidated unless he makes it his intention to part with his imam, in which case he will be praying alone. If, for example, the imam and the worshiper following him in prayer deliberately omit the first testimony or the prayer of obedience, and if they are closer to a standing position than to a sitting position in the first situation [i.e., that of having omitted the first testimony], or if they have reached a bowing position in the second situation [i.e., that of having omitted the prayer of obedience], and if the imam then returns to his previous position, the worshiper following him in prayer must not do likewise; rather, he must part with the imam with a conscious intention of the heart or wait for him while standing or prostrating.

If the worshiper being led in prayer knowingly, deliberately follows the imam in such a situation, his prayer will be invalidated. Otherwise, however, it will remain valid. Lastly, if the imam omits the first testimony and stands up, the worshiper being led in prayer must get up with the imam, whereas if the imam goes back to his previous position, the worshiper being led in prayer should not do likewise.

Two: The worshiper suspects that he may have added something to the prayer. If he has doubts about the number of *rak'ahs* he has performed, he should build on the number he is certain to have completed, finish the prayer, then perform a prostration of forgetfulness due to the possibility that he prayed more than the required number of *rak'ahs*. In such a situation, the worshiper should not rely simply on what he thinks to be probable, nor on someone else's report, unless the number of people reporting is great enough to preclude all doubt concerning what they are saying.

Three: The worshiper has unintentionally done something that does not invalidate prayer unless it is done deliberately. Examples of such actions include the prolongation of a short pillar, such as remaining still in a standing position, remaining seated momentarily between two prostrations, or speaking briefly out of inattention; in such a case, the worshiper should only perform a prostration of forgetfulness if he is certain to have done such a thing, whereas if he merely suspects it, he should not. As for actions which do not invalidate prayer whether they are performed deliberately or not, such as turning at the neck and walking two steps, they do not call for a prostration of forgetfulness. Lastly, actions which invalidate prayer whether they are performed intentionally or not, such as speaking at length or eating, cannot be rectified by a prostration of forgetfulness due to the invalidity of the prayer which results from them.

Four: Performing a verbal pillar out of place. This includes, for example, repeating the recitation of the *Fātiḥah*, in whole or in part, while sitting down, or performing a verbal Sunnah-based practice, such as the recitation of a passage from the Qur'ān after the *Fātiḥah*, out of place (during the bow, for example, rather than before it). In such a case, the worshiper should perform a prostration of forgetfulness. However, if the additional Qur'anic passage is recited before the *Fātiḥah*, no prostration of forgetfulness is to be performed.

Five: The worshiper suspects that he left out a particular 'part' of prayer [that is, an emphatically enjoined Sunnah-based practice]. For example, he might suspect that he omitted the prayer of obedience for a situation other than a major affliction, or he may be uncertain as to whether he left out part of the prayer of obedience, such as the prayer for blessings upon the Prophet. However, if he simply wonders [in general] whether or not he completed all the 'parts', no prostration of forgetfulness is called for.

Six: The worshiper has prayed behind someone whose prayer has a flaw in it, even if the flaw is only suspected by the person being led in prayer. This includes, for example, following someone who omitted the prayer of obedience in the dawn prayer, or someone who utters the prayer of obedience before bowing; in such cases, the worshiper should perform a prostration of forgetfulness after the imam's final greeting of peace and before his own. The same ruling applies if the worshiper follows someone who omits the prayer for the Prophet in the first testimony.

The ruling on the prostration of forgetfulness

Each of the four schools offers its own detailed ruling on the prostration of forgetfulness.[352]

---

352. According to the Hanafis, the prostration of forgetfulness is a 'duty', properly speaking. Hence, if a worshiper neglects to perform this prostration, he is guilty of wrongdoing, but his prayer will remain valid. Moreover, the prostration of forgetfulness is only required if the time when it is called for is a time when prayer would be valid. Thus, if the sun comes up after someone has completed the dawn prayer and if this person is required to perform a prostration of forgetfulness, this requirement will be dropped due to the invalidity of prayer at this particular time. The same ruling applies in the following situations: (1) if the sun takes on a reddish hue while one is still performing the mid-afternoon prayer before sundown and (2) if, after finishing one's prayer, one performs some action which is contrary to prayer (such as deliberately bringing on an occurrence of ritual impurity, speaking or leaving the mosque), as well as any other action which would make it invalid for a worshiper to build on what he has prayed thus far.

In all the situations mentioned here, the requirement to perform a prostration of forgetfulness is dropped, and there is no need to repeat the prayer unless the requirement was dropped due to some deliberate action contrary to prayer.

The prostration of forgetfulness is only required of someone who is an imam or who is praying alone; as for someone who is being led in prayer, the prostration of forgetfulness is not required of him if its cause arises on his part while he is following the imam. If the cause for the prostration originates with the imam, the worshiper must follow the imam in performing the prostration if the imam himself prostrates; if the imam does not prostrate in such a situation, it is not required of a worshiper following him in prayer to do so regardless of whether he or she joined the imam on time or missed some of the prayer. Hence, if the imam does not perform the prostration, it is not required of those following him in prayer to do so either, nor are they required to repeat the prayer unless the imam's not performing it resulted from his deliberately performing some action contrary to prayer, in which case both the imam and those following him are required to repeat the prayer. Lastly, it is considered preferable for the prostration of forgetfulness to be omitted during the Friday congregational prayer and the two holiday prayers if they are attended by a large congregation, lest its performance cause them confusion.

* * *

According to the Hanbalis, the prostration of forgetfulness is sometimes obligatory, sometimes an emulation of the Sunnah, and sometimes simply permissible depending on what the occasion for it happens to be. This applies to the imam and to someone who is praying alone; as for someone who is being led in prayer, he must follow his imam in performing the prostration even if it is merely permissible in a given situation, and if he fails to perform the prostration with the imam, his prayer will be invalidated.

If the imam or someone who is praying alone omits the prostration of forgetfulness and if it is a situation in which its performance is an emulation of the Sunnah or simply permissible, there is nothing wrong with omitting it. If, on the other hand, the prostration is obligatory and if it would be preferable to perform it before the final greeting of peace—as is the case when the occasion for it was the unintentional omission of some 'duty' of prayer—one's prayer will be invalidated if he deliberately omits the prostration of forgetfulness. However, if he omits it unintentionally, then utters the final greeting of peace, and if he realizes his error before what would commonly be considered a long time has passed, he must make it up; this ruling applies even if the worshiper has spoken or turned away from the *qiblah* since concluding his prayer provided that he has not had an occurrence of ritual impurity or left the mosque, in which case it ceases to be required without there being any need to repeat the prayer. This latter ruling likewise applies if what would commonly be viewed as a long time has passed since the conclusion of the prayer.

If the prostration of forgetfulness is omitted out of ignorance, the worshiper's prayer remains valid. In a situation in which it would be preferable for the prostration of forgetfulness to be performed after the final greeting of peace (as when someone accidentally utters the final greeting of peace before having completed the prayer) and in which the prostration is omitted deliberately, the worshiper will be guilty of wrongdoing, though the prayer will remain valid. If the worshiper realizes the omission before what would commonly be viewed as a long time has passed since the end of the prayer, he must make up the prostration, and if he does not do so, he will be guilty of wrongdoing, though the prayer will remain valid. If what would commonly be considered a long time has passed since the conclusion of the prayer, or if the worshiper has had an occurrence of ritual impurity or left the mosque, the requirement of the prostration of forgetfulness is dropped, and if the worshiper omits it out of ignorance, he incurs no guilt as a result of it and his prayer remains valid.

Lastly, if someone who is being led in prayer makes an unintentional error while praying behind his imam, and if he is 'parallel', that is, someone who, after uttering *takbīrat al-iḥrām* and before the imam's bow, prayed with the imam for long enough to recite the *Fātiḥah* (even if this was during the final *rak'ah* of the prayer), his imam will bear responsibility for this on his behalf, whereas if he is tardy, he must perform the prostration of forgetfulness like someone who is praying alone. Lastly, if the imam neglects an obligatory prostration of forgetfulness, the person being led in prayer must perform it if he despairs of the imam's doing so; if he was tardy, however, he must perform it after he has made up what he missed.

* * *

According to the Malikis, the prostration of forgetfulness is a Sunnah-based practice for the imam and for someone praying alone; as for someone who is being led in prayer, their ruling is that if there comes about a cause for the prostration on such a worshiper's part, the imam bears responsibility for it on his behalf so long as he is praying behind the imam. If the imam himself is required to perform a prostration of forgetfulness, the worshiper should follow him in it even if he does not understand the reason for it, and if he fails to do so, his prayer will be invalidated if it is a situation in which neglect of the prostration of forgetfulness would invalidate prayer; in other situations, however, it will not. (There will be further explanation below of those things the neglect of which invalidates prayer, and those things the neglect of which does not invalidate it.)

If the imam or someone praying alone omits the prostration of forgetfulness, and if it is the type which is to be performed after the final greeting of peace, he may perform the prostration at any time thereafter, including even those times when prayer is generally forbidden. If, on the other hand, it is of the type which is to be performed before the final greeting of peace and if its cause is the omission of three Sunnah-based practices associated with prayer, the deliberate omission of the prostration of forgetfulness will invalidate his prayer. If it was omitted unintentionally and if the worshiper realizes his error before what would commonly be considered a long time has passed since the conclusion of the prayer, he should make up the prostration; if he does so, his prayer will be valid provided that he has performed [no] action contrary to prayer since the final greeting of peace, such as deliberately bringing on an occurrence of ritual impurity, etc. Otherwise, his prayer will be invalidated just as it will be if he does not realize his error until what is considered to be a long time by commonly accepted standards has passed since the end of the prayer.

Lastly, if the cause for the prostration of forgetfulness is the omission of fewer than three Sunnah-based practices, such as two of the Sunnah-based utterances of *Allāhu akbar*, there is nothing wrong with omitting the prostration of forgetfulness even if one does so deliberately. Specifically, if the worshiper omits the prostration of forgetfulness by accident, then utters the final greeting of peace, he should make it up if not much time has passed since the end of the prayer; otherwise, he may leave it unperformed, and his prayer will still be valid.

Lastly, if the imam is due to perform a prostration of forgetfulness, the worshiper following him in prayer is to perform it even if it is omitted by the imam.

* * *

According to the Shafiis, the prostration of forgetfulness is sometimes obligatory and at other times, an emulation of the Sunnah. The prostration of forgetfulness is obligatory for a worshiper who is following an imam in prayer if the imam himself performs such a prostration. If the worshiper deliberately fails to do so, his prayer will be invalidated and he must repeat it unless he had consciously intended to part with the imam before the latter prostrated. If the imam himself fails to perform the prostration of forgetfulness, the worshiper praying behind him is under no obligation to perform it; rather, it is merely recommended that he do so.

As for the imam or someone praying alone, it is an emulation of the Sunnah for him to perform the prostration of forgetfulness for any of the reasons to be mentioned below unless the imam's doing so would cause confusion for those in the congregation. Hence, if it is a large gathering, it is an emulation of the Sunnah for the imam to forgo the prostration of forgetfulness. If either the imam or someone praying alone omits a Sunnah-based prostration of forgetfulness, there is nothing wrong with this and it does not invalidate his prayer.

If someone commits an unintentional error while praying behind his imam, he is not required to perform a prostration of forgetfulness, since the imam will bear this on his behalf provided that he is qualified to do so (by his not being known to have had an occurrence of ritual impurity, for example). However, if he commits an

The prostration of recitation and the evidence in favor of its legitimacy

Muslim and al-Bukhārī relate in their compilations of authentic prophetic hadiths, on the authority of Ibn 'Umar, may God be pleased with him, that, "Whenever the Prophet recited the Qur'ān and had completed a surah in which there is a prostration, he would prostrate and we would prostrate with him until some of us could find nowhere to rest our foreheads." Moreover, the Prophet said, "If someone recites a surah in which there is a prostration and prostrates, Satan will withdraw, weeping, and say, 'Woe betide him! Human beings were commanded to bow down and they did so, so they will enjoy Paradise. As for me, I was commanded to bow down and I disobeyed, so I will suffer the Hellfire!'"[353]

It is unanimously agreed upon by the Muslim community that it is legitimate to prostrate oneself when particular passages of the Qur'ān are read or recited.

The ruling on the prostration of recitation

According to the Shafiis, the Malikis and the Hanbalis, the prostration of recitation is an emulation of the Sunnah for both the reciter/reader and the listener, given certain conditions to be presented below. For the Hanafis' view, see below.[354]

---

error while praying independently from his imam—as, for example, while he is making up what he missed—he will be like someone praying alone, which means that it will be an emulation of the Sunnah for him to perform the prostration of forgetfulness if there is a reason to do so.

353. Narrated by Muslim.

354. According to the Hanafis, the prostration of recitation is a 'duty' for both the reader/reciter and the person who hears it. Hence, if either of the two fails to prostrate when a relevant passage of the Qur'ān has been read or recited, he or she will be guilty of wrongdoing. In some situations there is ample latitude as to when this duty may be performed, whereas in other situations, there is little or no such latitude. For example, if someone recites a passage from the Qur'ān calling for such a prostration when he is not praying, he incurs no guilt for delaying the prostration indefinitely, even if he were to die without having prostrated. Nevertheless, such a delay is deemed undesirable. However, such latitude does not exist if someone recites a passage calling for prostration while performing ritual prayer; in this case, the prostration must be performed immediately, where immediacy is defined as the passage—between the recitation of the Qur'anic verse or verses calling for the prostration and the prostration itself—of a length of time which allows for no more than the recitation of three verses. If more than this length of time passes between the two events, the condition of immediacy will be violated. Moreover, the verse calling for the prostration may be either in the middle of a surah or at the end of it; if it is in the middle of the surah, it is preferable for the worshiper to prostrate directly after its recitation and before completing the surah, then to rise, complete the surah, and bow. If the worshiper does not prostrate and bows before 'immediacy' has run out, and if he intends to perform the prostration of recitation as part of the bow, he may do so. Similarly, the worshiper may prostrate as part of his prayer before 'immediacy' has run out even if he does not intend this prostration to serve as a prostration of recitation. However, even after 'immediacy' has run out,

The conditions for the prostration of recitation

One of the conditions associated with the prostration of recitation is that the person who hears the verse which calls for such a prostration must be consciously intending to listen to it; otherwise, according to the Malikis and the Hanbalis, he or she is not obliged to perform it. For the views of the Shafiis and the Hanafis, see below.[355] The various schools list other conditions associated with the prostration of recitation as well.[356]

---

the obligation to perform the prostration of recitation remains in force even if the worshiper has bowed or prostrated as part of his prayer; hence, it must be made up by means of a special prostration provided that the person has not concluded his prayer yet. Once he has concluded his prayer, he may no longer make up the prostration of recitation unless he concluded the prayer by means of the final greeting of peace, and unless he has performed no actions since ending the prayer which would be contrary thereto; in this case, the worshiper may make up the prostration after the final greeting of peace.

Lastly, if the verse calling for the prostration of recitation comes at the end of the surah, it is preferable for the worshiper to bow and to intend the prostration of recitation as part of the bow. If he prostrates for the verse and does not bow, and if he stands back up, it is recommended that he recite verses from the subsequent surah, then bow and complete his prayer.

355. According to the Hanafis, it is not necessary that the person have deliberately intended to hear the verse; rather, whoever hears it should prostrate regardless of whether he was deliberately listening or not. [The Shafiis' view is not mentioned – t.n.]

356. The Hanafis stipulate that the same conditions which apply to ritual prayer apply likewise to the prostration of recitation. Exceptions to this, however, are *takbīrat al-iḥrām* and the intention to pray a specific ritual prayer, neither of which is a condition for the performance of the prostration of recitation. Nor is *takbīrat al-iḥrām* uttered as part of the prostration of recitation, as will be seen below in its detailed definition. However, the conditions which must be fulfilled in order for the prostration of recitation to be obligatory are those which likewise apply to ritual prayer, for example, that one be a Muslim, that one be of legal age, that one be in full possession of his mental faculties and, in the case of a woman, that she be free of menstrual flow or post-partum bleeding. Hence, the prostration of recitation is not required of someone who is a non-Muslim, a young boy, or insane; nor is it required of a woman who is menstruating or experiencing post-partum bleeding. With respect to these conditions, there is no difference between the person who recites the verse and the person who hears it. As for the person who hears the verse, he must prostrate if he meets the conditions for its being obligatory either at the time when it is heard, or as a compensatory performance at a later time. Hence, the prostration of recitation is required of someone who is inebriated or in a state of major ritual impurity, since both such individuals will meet the conditions for its being obligatory at a later time [i.e., when the former regains his sobriety, and when the latter has performed major ablutions – t.n.]. This ruling applies unless the per-

son who read or recited the verse is insane, in which case those who heard the verse are not required to perform the prostration of recitation. The same exception, moreover, applies if the reader/reciter is a young boy who has not yet reached the age of discernment, since recitation is only valid when performed by someone who has reached this age. Similarly, if someone hears a verse that calls for a prostration of recitation from a non-human being, such as a parrot, or across an electronic medium such as a phonograph record [a cassette tape, or a CD – t.n.], he is not obliged to perform a prostration of recitation, since the recitation was performed by a non-discerning entity and, as such, is not valid.

* * *

With respect to both the reader/reciter and the listener, the Hanbalis stipulate the same conditions that apply to the validity of ritual prayer, such as freedom from any occurrence of ritual impurity, avoidance of impure substances, facing the *qiblah*, conscious intention, and other such conditions which have been presented above. They also stipulate two additional conditions with respect to the listener: (1) The reader/reciter must be qualified to act as the listener's imam, if even only in a voluntary prayer. Thus, if someone hears a verse calling for a prostration recited by a woman, it is not an emulation of the Sunnah for him to prostrate; the same applies if he hears the verse from a non-human, such as a parrot, or through an electronic medium. Nevertheless, if someone hears the verse from someone who is illiterate or someone who is chronically ill or an invalid (and who would therefore be unqualified to serve as his imam), it is an emulation of the Sunnah to perform the prostration of recitation. (2) The reader/reciter must have prostrated; otherwise, it is not an emulation of the Sunnah for the listener to prostrate, either.

The Hanbalis also stipulate that it is not permissible for someone to perform a prostration of recitation in front of, or to the left of, the reader/reciter if the space to his right is free. It is undesirable for the imam to recite a verse which calls for a prostration in a prayer which is meant to be performed in silence, nor is it required of the worshiper being led by this imam to follow the imam if he does prostrate in this situation. However, if the prayer is one which is meant to be performed aloud, the worshiper being led in prayer should follow the imam in the prostration of recitation if he performs one.

Lastly, if such a verse is recited or heard more than once, it is an emulation of the Sunnah to repeat the prostration of recitation.

* * *

The Malikis stipulate, with respect to both the reader/reciter and the listener, the same conditions which apply to the validity of ritual prayer, such as freedom from occurrences of ritual impurity or ritually impure substances, facing the *qiblah*, concealment of one's private parts, and other such conditions listed above. The reader/reciter should perform the prostration even if he or she is not qualified to serve as an imam, such as a woman or a *fāsiq*, and even if his or her intention in doing the recitation is to show others what a beautiful voice he or she has. He or she should also perform the prostration during ritual prayer if he or she recites it at this time, even if it is an obligatory prayer; however, it is undesirable deliberately to recite a verse which calls for prostration while performing an obligatory prayer.

The aforementioned rulings apply to someone who is an imam or praying alone. As for someone who is being led in prayer, he should perform the prostration of recitation by virtue of his following his imam; however, if he does not prostrate [with the imam], his prayer will still be valid since this prostration is not an integral part of ritual prayer. If someone being led in prayer recites a verse which calls for a prostration, and if he recites it alone [that is, without the imam], he should not prostrate, and if he does, his prayer will be invalidated due to his having acted contrary to the imam.

The prostration of recitation is not to be performed during the funeral prayer. Moreover, if a verse calling for a prostration is recited during a Friday sermon or some other sermon, no prostration of recitation is required. However, if such a prostration is performed during either the funeral prayer or a sermon, the prayers will not be invalidated.

The Malikis stipulate three additional conditions in connection with the listener: (1) The reader/reciter must be qualified to serve as the listener's imam for obligatory prayers; hence, he must be male, of legal age, in full possession of his mental faculties, Muslim, and in a state of ritual purity. If the reader/reciter is insane, a non-Muslim, or in a state of ritual impurity, then neither he nor the listener is to perform the prostration of recitation. Moreover, someone who hears a verse which calls for a prostration of recitation but who was not deliberately listening to it should not prostrate. Lastly, if the reader/reciter is a woman or a young boy, he or she should prostrate, but not the listener. (2) The reader/reciter must not be performing the recitation in order to show off the beauty of his/her voice, and if he/she is reciting for this reason, the person who hears the verse is not to prostrate. (3) The hearer's purpose in listening must be to learn from or to teach the reader/reciter about recitation or its rules, such as 'demonstration' (*iẓhār*), 'assimilation' (*idghām*), 'prolongation' (*madd*), 'shortening' (*qaṣr*) and the like, or the various Qur'anic readings such as *warsh* and others.

When the conditions related to the hearer are met, he is to prostrate even if the reader/reciter does not do so unless it is in the middle of a ritual prayer, in which case he is to omit it if the imam omits it. If the reader/reciter is not in a state of ritual purity, he should pass over any verse which calls for a prostration and merely utter it in his heart in such a way that he preserves the order of the recitation; he should likewise pass over it if it is a time at which the prostration of recitation would be forbidden. If a teacher or a student repeats the same verse calling for a prostration more than once, it is an emulation of the Sunnah for both of them to prostrate for it the first time only.

If the reader/reciter goes slightly past the place where the verse calling for a prostration was read/recited—for example, by one or two verses—he should prostrate without reciting the verse again. However, if he goes significantly past the verse, he should repeat the verse, then prostrate, even if he is performing an obligatory prayer. However, one should not perform a prostration of recitation during an obligatory prayer if he has leaned down for a bow; in a voluntary prayer, the worshiper should recite the verse calling for a prostration in the second *rak'ah*, then prostrate if he has not [yet] bowed, but once he has bowed for the second *rak'ah*, he will have missed the prostration of recitation.

* * *

The Shafiis stipulate the following seven conditions for the performance of the prostration of recitation: (1) The recitation must be allowed; if it is disallowed, such as a recitation performed by someone who is in a state of major ritual impurity, or undesirable such as a recitation performed by someone who is praying and engaged in a bow, it is not an emulation of the Sunnah for either the reader/reciter or the hearer to perform a prostration of recitation. (2) The recitation must be deliberate; thus, if it came about without conscious awareness (as in the case of a parrot's reciting a verse that calls for prostration, or such a verse being heard over an electronic medium), one is not to perform a prostration of recitation. (3) What is recited must include the entire verse which calls for the prostration; hence, if only part of it is read or recited, no prostration is called for. (4) The recitation of the verse which calls for a prostration must not be meant to replace the recitation of the *Fātiḥah* in the event that the worshiper is unable to recite the latter; if it is recited for this purpose, no prostration is called for. (5) There must not be a long pause between recitation of the verse which calls for a prostration and the prostration itself; if a long time passes without the person's prostrating, no prostration should be performed. (A 'long time' is defined as more than sufficient time for the performance of two *rak'ahs* with a medium-length Qur'anic recitation.) (6) The verse which calls for a prostration must be read/recited by just one person. Hence, if one person recites part of it while someone else recites the rest, no prostration is called for. (7) The conditions associated with ritual prayer, such as ritual purity, facing the *qiblah*, etc., must also be fulfilled for the performance of the prostration of recitation.

The aforementioned conditions apply generally both to someone who is praying and to others as well. There are, in addition, two conditions which apply only to someone who is praying: (1) The worshiper's intention in reciting the verse which calls for a prostration must not be the prostration itself. Hence, if one recites such a verse precisely in order to prostrate, then deliberately performs a prostration of recitation, his prayer will be invalidated. An exception to this ruling is made for the recitation of Surah 32 (entitled *al-Sajdah,* that is, 'Prostration') in the Friday dawn prayer, which is an emulation of the Sunnah; hence, it is likewise an emulation of the Sunnah to perform the prostration of recitation on this occasion. If someone recites some other surah during the Friday dawn prayer and prostrates, his prayer will be invalidated by the prostration if it is performed deliberately and knowingly [as a prostration of recitation]. Similarly, if someone recited Surah 32 during the Thursday dawn prayer and performed the prostration of recitation at this time, his prayer would be invalidated. Someone who is being led in prayer must prostrate in imitation of his imam if the latter's prostration is permissible, and if he fails to follow the imam deliberately and knowingly, his prayer will be invalidated. (2) The worshiper who is praying must himself be the reciter. Hence, if someone else recites a verse which calls for a prostration and prostrates, the person praying should not do so, and if he does so deliberately and knowingly, his prayer will be invalidated. Lastly, during the funeral prayer, the person delivering the sermon emulates the Sunnah by performing the prostration of recitation, whereas it is forbidden for those in the congregation to do so due to the fact that it would distract them from the sermon.

Reasons for performing the prostration of recitation

Each of the four schools offers its own detailed listing of the reasons for performing the prostration of recitation.[357]

The definition and essential components of the prostration of recitation

Each of the four schools offers a detailed definition of the prostration of recitation and its essential components.[358]

---

357. The Hanafis list three occasions on which the prostration of recitation is to be performed: (1) Recitation. If a verse calling for a prostration is recited, it must be performed by the person who recited it, even if he did not hear himself, such as would be the case if he were deaf. This ruling applies regardless of whether the person is praying or not, or whether he is an imam or praying alone. As for someone who is being led in prayer, he is not obliged to perform the prostration of recitation since [according to the Hanafi view] he is forbidden to recite behind his imam, as a result of which his recitation is not considered to be an occasion for the performance of the prostration of recitation. However, if the person delivering the sermon for the Friday congregational prayer or for either of the two holiday prayers recites a verse calling for a prostration, the prostration must be performed both by the speaker and by those who hear him; in such a case, the speaker is to come down off the pulpit in order to prostrate, and the congregation is to prostrate with him. It is undesirable for the speaker to recite a verse calling for a prostration while he is on the pulpit; as for reciting such a verse while in prayer, it is not undesirable provided that one performs the prostration as part of a bow or regular prostration; however, it is undesirable to perform this prostration by itself during prayer due to the confusion this might cause to those in the congregation. (2) Hearing someone else recite a verse which calls for a prostration. The person who hears the verse may be praying, as well as the person who recited it; if the person who hears the verse is praying and if he is either an imam or praying alone, he must perform the prostration outside of prayer unless he heard it from someone being led in prayer, in which case he is not required to prostrate at all, properly speaking. If a worshiper hears such a verse from his imam and if he joined his imam on time for prayer, he must follow him in his prostration, whereas if he joined the imam late for prayer and before the latter's prostration of recitation, he should perform it with him. If the worshiper joined the imam after the prostration of recitation, but during the same *rak'ah* in which he recited the verse calling for the prostration, he should not prostrate, whereas if he joined the imam in the *rak'ah* after this, he should perform the prostration after the completion of the prayer. (3) Following someone else in prayer. If the imam recites a verse calling for a prostration, it must be performed by those following him in prayer even if they did not hear it.

* * *

According to the Hanbalis, there are two occasions for the performance of the prostration of recitation: (1) Recitation [of a verse calling for a prostration], and (2) Listening to such a verse given the aforementioned conditions, provided that there is not what would commonly be considered to be a long pause between the occasion and the prostration itself. If the reader/reciter or the hearer has had an occurrence of ritual impurity and is not able to use water, he should perform sand ablutions and prostrate; however, if he is able to use water, he is exempted from the prostration of recitation because, if he were to perform ritual ablutions, there would be a long pause between the occasion for the prostration and the prostration itself. As for someone being led in prayer, he should only prostrate in response to a recitation as a means of following his imam.

* * *

The Malikis stipulate only two occasions for the prostration of recitation, namely: (1) Recitation [of a verse calling for a prostration], and (2) Hearing such a recitation with the intention of listening to it, as was seen above in the listing of conditions associated with the prostration of recitation.

* * *

As for the Shafiis, they stipulate the following two occasions for the prostration of recitation: (1) recitation, and (2) hearing, given the conditions explained above.

358. The Hanafis define the prostration of recitation as the performance of a single prostration between two utterances of *Allāhu akbar*, the first of which is uttered when placing one's forehead on the floor in the prostration, and the second of which is uttered as one raises one's forehead again. It does not include an utterance of the testimony or a greeting of peace. As for the two utterances of *Allāhu akbar*, they are emulations of the Sunnah, which means that if someone prostrated without uttering this phrase, the prostration of recitation would still be valid, although such an omission is undesirable. Thus, the prostration of recitation [the text reads, "of forgetfulness" here – t.n.] consists of a single pillar, namely, placing one's forehead on the floor or ground, or an action which would serve in its stead, such as a bow, a regular prostration, or a gesture on the part of someone who is ill or traveling and performing ritual prayer while mounted on an animal, since the Hanafis hold that the prostration of recitation may be performed as part of a bow, a prostration or a gesture meant to signal such a movement. When performing the prostration of recitation the worshiper is to say *subḥān rabbī al-a'lā* three times, or he may utter whatever phrases of praise to the divine he has memorized, such as, "Record it [i.e., this prostration] for me as a basis for reward from You, use it to relieve me of a burden, cause it to be a storehouse [of virtue] in Your sight, and accept it from me as You accepted it from Your servant David" (*Allāhumma, uktub lī bihā 'indaka ajran, wa ḍa' 'annī bihā wizran, waj'alhā lī 'indaka dhukhran, wa taqabbalhā minnī kamā taqabbaltahā min 'abdika dāwūd*). It is desirable for someone who recited the verse that calls for a prostration while seated to stand up and then prostrate. If the worshiper repeats a verse calling for a prostration in a single session, he should prostrate only once; however, if he repeats the verse in more than one session, he should perform the prostration again.

* * *

The Hanbalis define the prostration of recitation as a prostration without *takbīrat al-iḥrām*; however, it should be accompanied by two utterances of *Allāhu akbar*, the first of which is uttered as the worshiper places his forehead on the floor, and the second of which is uttered as he raises his forehead from the floor. The worshiper is not to utter the testimony; however, it is recommended that he sit down if he is not performing a ritual prayer in order to utter a greeting of peace from a seated position. Nevertheless, they say that the two utterances of *Allāhu akbar* are not pillars of the prostration of recitation but rather, 'duties'. As for the pillars of the prostration of recitation, the Hanbalis specify three: (1) prostration, (2) rising from the prostration, and (3) the first greeting of peace. As for the second greeting of peace, it is neither a pillar nor a 'duty', and it is recommended that while prostrating, the worshiper utter the supplication mentioned above in connection with the Hanafis.

* * *

The Malikis define the prostration of recitation as a single prostration accompanied by neither an utterance of *Allāhu akbar* nor a greeting of peace. Rather, it is simply an emulation of the Sunnah to utter the phrase, *Allāhu akbar* as one goes down into the prostration. If the worshiper is standing up, he should go down into the prostration from a standing position regardless of whether he is performing ritual prayer or not. It is not required that the worshiper sit down; rather, he is to prostrate as does someone who has stood up from the bow of a regular ritual prayer regardless of whether he is actually engaged in ritual prayer or not. If the worshiper is mounted on an animal or something else, he should dismount and prostrate on the ground unless he is either on a journey or resident in a place but fulfills the conditions for the performance of a voluntary prayer while mounted on an animal (conditions which were mentioned in an earlier section), in which case he may prostrate from atop the animal by means of gestures. Lastly, it is recommended that while prostrating, the worshiper utter the supplication mentioned above in connection with the Hanafis.

* * *

According to the Shafiis, the prostration of recitation may be performed either by someone praying, or by someone who is not praying. With respect to someone who is not praying, the Shafiis define the prostration of recitation as consisting of the following five pillars: (1) uttering one's intention to perform the prostration; (2) uttering *takbīrat al-iḥrām*; (3) performing a single prostration like those performed as part of ritual prayer; (4) sitting down after the prostration; and (5) uttering a greeting of peace.

Someone who is performing ritual prayer and recites a verse which calls for a prostration should also perform the prostration of recitation. Such a prostration is valid given two conditions: (1) A conscious, silent intention to perform the prostration; if the intention is uttered aloud, the person's prayer will be invalidated; and (2) The performance of one prostration like those performed in ritual prayer. If the person is being led in prayer, the requirement of a conscious intention is dropped, since his imam's intention will suffice. However, someone who is not praying must voice his intention to perform the prostration of recitation along with his utterance of *takbīrat al-iḥrām*, as mentioned earlier. It is an emulation of the Sunnah to raise one's hands when uttering *takbīrat al-iḥrām* and to utter *Allāhu akbar* when going down into the prostration and when coming up from it as well, as well as to utter supplications during the prostration along with the second greeting of peace. It is

The Qur'anic passages which call for the prostration of recitation

There are fourteen Qur'anic passages the recitation of which calls for this prostration:

(1) "Behold, those who are near unto thy Sustainer are never too proud to worship Him; and they extol His limitless glory, and prostrate themselves before Him" (7:206).

(2) "And before God prostrate themselves, willingly or unwillingly, all [things and beings] that are in the heavens and the earth, as do their shadows in the mornings and the evenings" (13:5).

(3) "For before God prostrates itself all that is in the heavens and all that is on earth—every beast that moves, and the angels: [even] these do not bear themselves with false pride. They fear their Sustainer high above them, and do whatever they are bidden to do" (16:49-50).

(4) "And so they fall down upon their faces, weeping, and [their consciousness of God's grace] increases their humility" (17:109).

(5) "...whenever the messages of the Most Gracious were conveyed unto them, they would fall down [before Him], prostrating themselves and weeping" (19:58).

(6) "....for verily, God does what He wills" (22:18).

(7) "O you who have attained to faith! Bow down and prostrate yourselves, and worship your Sustainer [alone], and do good, so that you might attain to a happy state!" (22:77)[359]

(8) "Yet when they [who are bent on denying the truth] are told, 'Prostrate yourselves before the Most Gracious', they are wont to ask, 'And [who and] what is the Most Gracious? Are we to prostrate ourselves before whatever thou biddest us [to worship]?' —and so [thy call] but increases their aversion" (25:60).

(9) "...[for they have come to believe] that they *ought not* to adore God—[although it is He] who brings forth all that is hidden in the heavens and on the earth, and knows all that you would conceal as well as all that you bring into the

---

also an emulation of the Sunnah to utter the supplication mentioned above in connection with the Hanafis.

Lastly, the prostration of recitation may be replaced by anything that would replace the mosque greeting. Hence, if the worshiper does not wish to perform the prostration of recitation, he may recite the following formula four times: *subḥān Allāh wal-ḥamdu lillāh wa lā ilāha illā Allāh wa- Allāhu akbar, wa lā ḥawla wa lā quwwata illā billāh al-'alī al-'aẓīm* ("Glory to be God, praise be to God, there is no deity but God, God is greatest, and there is no power or strength except through God, the Most High, the Almighty"). The recitation of this formula four times will take the place of the prostration of recitation even if the worshiper concerned is in a state of ritual purity [and would, therefore, be permitted to perform the prostration – t.n.].

359. These verses are agreed upon by the Shafiis and the Hanbalis; however, the Malikis [and the Hanafis] do not include this passage among those which call for the prostration of recitation.

open: God, save whom there is no deity—the Sustainer, in awesome almightiness enthroned!" (27:35-36).

(10) "Only they [truly] believe in Our messages who, whenever they are conveyed to them, fall down, prostrating themselves in adoration, and extol their Sustainer's limitless glory and praise: and who are never filled with false pride" (32:15).

(11) "....[hence], adore not the sun or the moon, but prostrate in adoration before God, who has created the—if it is Him whom you [really] worship" (41:37).

(12) "Do you, perchance, find this tiding strange? And so you laugh instead of weeping, and divert yourselves all the while? [Nay,] but prostrate yourselves before God, and worship [Him alone]!" (53:62).

(13) "...and [that], when the Qur'ān is read unto them, they do not fall down in prostration?" (84:21).

(14) "Nay, pay thou no heed to him, but prostrate thyself [before God] and draw near [to Him]!" (96:19).[360]

As for the passage which reads, "And [suddenly] David understood that We had tried him: and so he asked His Sustainer to forgive him his sin, and fell down in prostration, and turned unto Him in repentance" (38:24), it is not included in this grouping by the Shafiis and the Hanbalis, in disagreement with the Malikis and the Hanafis.[361]

All four schools agree that the prostration of recitation is to be performed at the conclusion of each of the passages listed above; however, the Hanafis differ with this view with respect to certain passages.[362]

---

360. These are agreed upon among the Shafiis, the Hanafis and the Hanbalis; as for the Malikis, they do not include Qur'ān 53:59-62, 84:21, or 96:19 among the passages which call for a prostration of recitation.

361. The Hanafis and the Malikis include this verse among those which call for a prostration of recitation; however, the Malikis hold that the prostration is to be performed upon the recitation of the words, "and turned unto Him in repentance", whereas according to the Hanafis, it should be performed upon recitation of 38:25, "And thereupon We forgave him that [sin]; and verily, nearness to Us awaits him [in the life to come], and the most beauteous of all goals!"

From this it may be seen that the number of Qur'anic passages which call for a prostration according to the Hanafis comes to fourteen, in that they exclude Qur'ān 22:77 and add Qur'ān 38:24; as for the Malikis, they recognize twelve [the text reads eleven – t.n.] passages as calling for this prostration in that they exclude 53:59-62, 84:21, and 96:19, while adding 38:24.

362. According to the Hanafis, the prostration should be performed at the end of verse 38 rather than verse 37 of Surah 41, i.e., after the verse which reads, "And though some be too proud [to listen to this call], they who in their hearts are with their Sustainer extol His limitless glory by night and by day, and never grow weary [thereof]."

The prostration of thanksgiving

According to the Shafiis and the Hanbalis, the prostration of thanksgiving is a desirable practice which consists of a single prostration similar to the prostration of recitation; this prostration is to be performed when some blessing has been renewed or received, or when a danger has been averted. The prostration of thanksgiving is to be performed separately from ritual prayer; if someone performs it as part of a ritual prayer, his prayer will be invalidated, and if he intends it to be part of a regular bow or prostration of prayer, it will have no effect. For the views of the Malikis and the Hanafis, see below.[363]

---

363. The Malikis view the prostration of thanksgiving as undesirable and hold that the desirable practice when a blessing is experienced or a danger averted is for the person concerned to perform a two-*rak'ah* prayer of thanksgiving, as we have seen.

Based on a formal legal opinion issued in this regard, the Hanafis hold that the prostration of thanksgiving is desirable, and that if a worshiper intends it as part of the bow or prostration of a ritual prayer, it will be valid. However, they view it as undesirable to perform the prostration of thanksgiving immediately after a ritual prayer lest uninformed worshipers in a congregation take this to mean that it is a 'duty' or a practice based on the Sunnah.

Shortening of prayers

Shortening four-*rak'ah* prayers and the ruling on this practice

It is permissible for someone who fulfills given conditions to shorten the four-*rak'ah* obligatory prayers—that is, the noon prayer, the mid-afternoon prayer and the evening prayer—by performing them as two *rak'ahs* only. According to the Shafiis and the Hanbalis, it is permissible for such a person to pray such prayers to completion, whereas the Malikis and the Hanafis hold that the shortening of prayers is not merely permissible, but required, for those who are on a journey. However, they differ concerning the ruling on this practice: According to the Hanafis, the shortening of prayer is a 'duty', which in their view is less binding that a full obligation and equal in force to an emphatically enjoined Sunnah-based practice. This being the case, it is undesirable for someone on a journey to pray the four-*rak'ah* prayers to completion although if he does, his prayers will still be valid provided that he does not omit the first 'sitting', since it is obligatory in this case.[364] However, the traveler who prays the four-*rak'ah* prayer to completion will have offended by neglecting a 'duty' and, although he will not be punished for it in the hellfire, he will be deprived of the intercession of the Prophet on the Day of Resurrection, as we have seen.

The Malikis hold that the shortening of prayers is an emphatically enjoined Sunnah-based practice which has even greater importance than communal prayer. If a traveler neglects this practice, he will not be punished for doing so; rather, he will be deprived of the reward for performing an emphatically enjoined Sunnah-based practice, but not of the Prophet's intercession on Judgment Day as the Hanafis hold. Hence, the Hanafis and the Malikis agree that the shortening of prayers is an emphatically enjoined emulation of the Sunnah, but they disagree concerning the consequences of neglecting it.

For each school's detailed rulings on this practice, see below.[365]

---

364. The reason for this is that the first 'sitting' in a four-*rak'ah* prayer is optional, whereas the second, or final, 'sitting' is obligatory; thus, when the four-*rak'ah* prayer is shortened to two *rak'ahs*, the first 'sitting' becomes, in effect, the final one and, as such, obligatory [t.n.].

365. According to the Hanafis, the shortening of prayers is a 'duty' in the sense detailed above. If a traveler prays a four-*rak'ah* prayer to completion, he commits an undesirable act by virtue of neglecting a 'duty'. In addition, praying such a prayer to completion involves delaying the obligatory greeting of peace past its proper place in the prayer. The reason for this is that the worshiper is to utter the final greeting of peace after completing the final 'sitting', and the final 'sitting' in a traveler's prayer is, of course, that which follows the two *rak'ahs* which are required of him; hence, if he performs two *rak'ahs* and does not perform a 'sitting'

after this, his prayer will be invalidated since, like the final 'sitting' of a regular four-*rak'ah* prayer, this 'sitting' is obligatory. If the traveler does not utter a greeting of peace after the 'sitting' and rises for a third *rak'ah* [as he would if he were praying the prayer to completion], he will have performed an undesirable act since in so doing, he has delayed the required greeting of peace past its proper place in the prayer.

* * *

According to the Malikis, the shortening of four-*rak'ah* prayers is an emphatically enjoined emulation of the Sunnah, as was mentioned above. Consequently, they hold that if someone neglects this [as a traveler] and prays a four-*rak'ah* prayer to completion, he will be deprived of the reward for performing this Sunnah-based practice. If a traveler finds no other fellow traveler whom he may pray behind as his imam, he should pray a shortened prayer alone. Moreover, it is undesirable for a traveler to pray behind an imam who is not a traveler since, in this case, he is obliged to perform the prayer to completion, thereby missing the opportunity to perform the emphatically enjoined Sunnah practice embodied in the shortening of prayers.

* * *

The Shafiis are in agreement that it is permissible for someone who has traveled a sufficient distance to allow for the shortening of prayers to either shorten four-*rak'ah* prayers to two *rak'ahs* or to pray them to completion. However, shortening prayers is viewed as preferable to praying such prayers to completion provided that the length of the person's journey comes to three 'stages' [72 miles]; otherwise, however, shortening prayers is not preferable. The reason for this is that the minimum distance which must be traveled in order for one to shorten prayers, according to the Shafiis, is two 'stages' [48 miles – t.n.]. If the length of the person's journey is only two 'stages', the traveler may either shorten prayers or pray them to completion; however, if the length of the journey is three or more 'stages' [72 miles or more], it is considered preferable to shorten one's prayers. More specifically, shortening prayers is preferable in this case provided that the traveler is not a navigator, i.e., someone engaged in steering a ship along with his assistants, generally known as sailors. If such individuals are on a journey, it is preferable for them to pray all their prayers to completion even if the length of their journey exceeds three 'stages.'

The Shafiis also hold that if a traveler postpones prayer until so close to the end of its designated time period that there is only enough time left to perform two *rak'ahs*, he must shorten his prayer, and it is not permissible for him to pray the prayer to completion under any circumstances since by performing only two *rak'ahs*, he can perform the entire prayer before its time period runs out. (This ruling is similar to the earlier one pertaining to performing ritual ablutions by wiping one's shoes; that is, the Shafiis hold that if the time period for a given prayer is about to run out, it is obligatory to wipe one's shoes [rather than remove them to wash one's feet] in order to complete the prayer within its designated time period.

* * *

According to the Hanbalis, shortening prayers is permissible. Thus, someone who is covering a distance sufficient to allow for the shortening of prayers may

Evidence for the ruling on shortening prayers

The legitimacy of the practice of shortening prayers is confirmed by the Qur'ān, the Sunnah and the consensus of the Muslim community. God Almighty has said, "And when you go forth [to war] on earth, you will incur no sin by shortening your prayers if you have reason to fear that those who are bent on denying the truth might suddenly fall upon you…." (4:101). This verse indicates that the shortening of prayers is legitimate when one has reason to be afraid. Moreover, although this verse does not indicate that the shortening of prayers is legitimate when one is safe from danger, authentic prophetic hadiths and the consensus of the Muslim community support its legitimacy in times of safety as well. An example of such a hadith is the one narrated on the authority of Ya'lā Ibn Umayyah, who said, "I [once] asked 'Umar, 'Why do we shorten prayers even though we are safe from danger?' He replied, 'I asked the Messenger of God this same question, and he said to me, "It is a gift of charity which God has bestowed upon you; so accept His gracious gift."'"[366] In addition, Ibn 'Umar, may God be pleased with him, said, "When I accompanied the Prophet on a journey, he would only pray two *rak'ahs*. This was likewise the practice of Abū Bakr, 'Umar and 'Uthmān."[367] It is also an established fact that once, following the Hijrah, when the Prophet was leading the people of Mecca in a four-*rak'ah* prayer, he uttered the final greeting of peace after only two *rak'ahs*, then turned and said to them, "Complete your prayers [on your own], since I am on a journey."

Given the above, the Muslim community is in unanimous agreement concerning the legitimacy of shortening prayers.

---

either perform four-*rak'ah* prayers to completion or shorten them without any undesirability attached thereto, although praying them to completion is preferable. An exception to this ruling is made in certain situations to be mentioned in our listing of conditions for shortening prayer. One such exception is made for the navigator (sailor) who has family members with him on the ship, in which case it is not permissible for him to shorten prayers due to his being, legally speaking, 'resident' where he is. The Hanbalis' ruling on this point is thus similar to that of the Shafiis, who rule that praying prayers to completion is preferable only in the case of sailors, whereas the Hanafis and the Malikis make no distinction in connection with this ruling between sailors and other travelers.

366. Narrated by Muslim.

367. An agreed-upon hadith, narrated by Muslim and al-Bukhārī.

368. According to the Hanafis, the minimum distance one must travel in order for the shortening of prayers to be legitimate is to be measured in terms of time; specifically, the journey must take three days measured by the length of the shortest days of the year. Moreover, it is sufficient for the person to travel from morning to noon on each of the three days at a medium pace, that is, at the pace at which a camel travels and/or at which one may walk. Hence, if the traveler rises early on the first day and walks until noon, thereby covering a distance equal to one 'stage' [i.e., 24 miles], then encamps and spends the night at this spot, and if he does the same

The conditions for the validity of shortening prayers: The length of the journey required for the shortening of prayers to be valid

In order for the shortening of prayers to be legitimate, certain conditions must be fulfilled. One such condition is that the distance traveled by the person concerned must be at least sixteen parasangs, one way. A parasang is equal to three miles, while a mile is equal to 6,000 cubits. The minimum distance, then, comes to 80 1/2 kilometers, 140 meters [that is, approximately 50 miles – t.n.]. This is the distance which may be traveled in one day and one night by a burden-bearing camel who is walking at a medium pace.

This estimation of the distance that someone must travel one way in order to legitimately shorten prayers is agreed upon by the Shafiis, the Malikis and the Hanbalis; for the Hanafis' view, see below.[368] The Shafiis estimate this distance at two 'stages', where the 'stage' is defined as eight parasangs [that is, 24 miles]. According to the Hanafis and the Hanbalis, it does no harm for the distance actually traveled to be slightly less than this, by one or two miles, for example. As for the Malikis and the Shafiis, their views are presented below.[369] Moreover, it is not necessary that the distance be covered within the time period specified, that is, one day and one night; hence, if someone were to cover the distance in less than this time—or even in a single moment, as when one is traveling on an aircraft—the shortening of prayers would still be valid. This view is agreed upon.

---

again on the second and third days, he will have covered the minimum distance required for the legitimate shortening of prayers. When this method of estimation is used, there is no need for reference to parasangs based on the view formally recognized by the Hanafis. Nor is it permissible to shorten prayers if the distance traveled is less than the one described here. Some Hanafis do estimate the distance in terms of parasangs; however, they hold that the minimum distance is 24 parasangs, that is, three 'stages' rather than two.

369. The Malikis hold that if the distance traveled is up to eight miles less than the minimum and the traveler goes ahead and shortens his prayers, they will be valid and, based on the most widely accepted Maliki view, he will not be obliged to repeat them. The requirement of a minimum distance is waived for the people of Mecca, Minā, Muzdalifah and al-Muḥaṣṣab if they have gone out during the pilgrimage season in order to stand at 'Arafah. In this case it is an emulation of the Sunnah for them to shorten prayers both when they are going and when they are returning if they still have more pilgrimage rites left, and if such rites are to be performed somewhere other than their country of origin; otherwise, they should perform prayers to completion.

* * *

According to the Shafiis, if the journey takes even slightly less than the minimum period of time specified, it is not permissible to shorten prayers. However, all the Shafiis require for an estimation of the distance is that one be reasonably, rather than absolutely, certain of it.

The intention to undertake a journey

It is agreed upon by all four schools that in order for the shortening of prayers to be valid, one must make it his intention to undertake a journey. However, there are two conditions associated with the intention to travel: (1) The person must intend to traverse the entire distance from the very beginning of the trip. Hence, if someone goes out aimlessly, not knowing where he is headed, he may not validly shorten prayers even if he circles the entire globe, because he did not make it his conscious intention to travel the distance. This ruling is agreed upon by all four schools. Similarly, a traveler may not validly shorten prayers if, despite his having consciously intended to travel the whole distance, he then makes it his intention to stay somewhere along the way for a period of time sufficient to exclude him from the legal category of 'traveler.' (An explanation of what constitutes a stay long enough to make someone no longer a traveler will be found below.) The only school to disagree with this ruling is that of the Hanafis.[370] (2) The intention must have been arrived at independently. Hence, the intention of someone who is subordinate to someone else (such as a wife to her husband, a soldier to his commander, or a servant to his master) is not given any weight apart from the intention of the person to whom he or she is subordinate. If a wife intends to travel a distance sufficient to justify the shortening of prayers without her husband, she may not validly shorten them. The same applies to the soldier, the servant, etc. regardless of whether the person in the subordinate position intends to free himself of the person to whom he is subordinate at the earliest opportunity or not. This ruling is agreed upon by the Malikis, the Hanafis and the Hanbalis; however, the Shafiis hold a different view.[371]

---

370. According to the Hanafis, the intention to stay in a place for a period of time long enough to make the ruling on travelers inapplicable does not invalidate the shortening of prayers unless the intention is actually carried out. Hence, if someone travels from Cairo, for example, with the intention of staying in Asyut for fifteen days or more, he must continue to shorten prayers the entire way until he actually commences his intended stay.

371. The Shafiis add another ruling here, namely, that if the subordinate intends to return from his journey whenever he is able to free himself from his dependent relationship (for example, by a soldier's being discharged from military service, or by a servant's being dismissed from service), he should not shorten his prayers until he has traveled the entire distance required to make this practice legitimate, namely, two 'stages.' If such a person misses a prayer after traveling this distance, he should make it up as a shortened prayer, since it will be considered a prayer missed during a journey.

It is not necessary that the person intending to go on a journey be an adult; hence, if a boy intends to travel a sufficient distance to warrant the shortening of prayers, he may legitimately shorten his prayers. However, the Hanafis disagree with this ruling.[372]

The ruling on shortening prayers during a journey which is either forbidden or religiously undesirable

Another condition for the validity of shortening prayer is that the journey being undertaken must be a legitimate one. Thus, if the trip is being made in order to steal money, to engage in highway robbery, etc., the person making it is not to shorten his prayers, and if he does shorten them, they will have no validity. This view is agreed upon by the Shafiis and the Hanbalis; for the views of the Hanafis and the Malikis, see below.[373] As for a situation in which the journey is deemed undesirable, each school offers its own ruling in this regard.[374] Lastly, if the journey itself is legitimate but the traveler commits some disobedience while traveling, it is still permissible to shorten prayers.

---

372. The Hanafis stipulate that the intention to undertake a journey must be made by an adult; hence, it is not valid if made by a child. Their three conditions for the validity of an intention to undertake a journey are: (1) the intention to traverse the entire distance from the very beginning of the trip, (2) the independence of the intention, and (3) adulthood.

373. The Hanafis and the Malikis do not make this stipulation. According to the Hanafis, every traveler is obliged to shorten prayers even if the journey he is going on is forbidden, although he incurs guilt by virtue of his wrongdoing. As for the Malikis, they hold that if the journey being undertaken is forbidden, it is still permissible to shorten prayers despite the guilt the person incurs [by virtue of the journey itself].

374. According to the Hanafis, shortening prayer during an undesirable journey is obligatory just as it would be on a journey which is desirable.

* * *

According to the Shafiis, it is permissible to shorten prayers on a journey which is deemed undesirable.

* * *

According to the Malikis, it is undesirable to shorten prayers on a journey which is deemed undesirable.

* * *

As for the Hanbalis, they hold that it is not permissible to shorten prayers while on a journey which is deemed undesirable, and if one does shorten prayers on such a journey, the prayers will have no validity just as they would have no validity during a journey that was forbidden.

The place in which the traveler may begin to shorten prayers

A traveler is not permitted to begin shortening prayers until after he has begun his journey and has traveled a particular distance from his place of residence. This distance is specified by each of the four schools in its own way.[375]

---

375. The Shafiis hold that before one may begin shortening prayers on a journey, he must reach a place in which he would, by commonly accepted standards, be considered a traveler. For someone residing in a settlement composed of constructed dwellings, his journey is deemed to begin when he goes beyond a wall connected to the place from which he is traveling if the wall is located on the side of the settlement from which he intends to travel. This ruling applies even if there are, inside the wall, uninhabited areas, farms and houses, since all of this is still considered part of the place the traveler intends to leave. In this regard, no significance is attached to a trench or an archway so long as the wall is present. Moreover, the same ruling that applies to a wall applies likewise to the bridges that residents of a village have built. Hence, if there is no wall but there is an archway or a trench, the traveler must pass beyond the latter. If none of these things is present, what matters is for the person to pass out of the inhabited, built-up area even if it is interspersed with ruins. However, it is not necessary that the traveler pass beyond the ruins that lie at the outskirts of the inhabited area if their walls are no longer standing. Nor is it necessary for him to pass beyond the farms and orchards even if they contain castles or houses which are inhabited during some seasons of the year. However, he must pass beyond the graves which are adjacent to the village if the village has no wall. If the inhabited area has one or two villages which are commonly considered to be connected to it, for example, the Shafiis stipulate that the traveler must pass beyond them if they are not separated by a wall; otherwise, the stipulation is that he pass beyond the wall. If, on the other hand, the two villages are not connected, it is sufficient to pass beyond what is commonly recognized to be the traveler's own village. As for the manors located in the orchards adjacent to the inhabited area, the ruling on them is that if they are lived in throughout the year, they are to be treated like the two villages mentioned above; otherwise, they are not, as we have seen.

As for someone who is a tent dweller, his journey is deemed to begin when he passes beyond the tents and their associated facilities, such as the site where ashes are thrown, the children's playground, and the places where horses are tied. If the person is on a hill, he must pass beyond the site where it joins level ground, and if he is in a low-lying area, he must pass beyond the point at which the land rises. Similarly, he must pass beyond the middle of the valley if that is where he began his journey. These rulings apply provided that the upward and downward slopes involved, as well as the middle of the valley referred to, are moderate in their degree, depth and width. However, if they are excessively steep, deep or wide, it is sufficient merely to pass beyond the dwellings whose inhabitants gather for evening conversation and entertainment, and where they are able to borrow necessities from one another.

As for the traveler who lives neither in a settlement composed of constructed dwellings nor in tents, his journey is deemed to begin once he gets beyond his stopping place and its associated facilities.

The rulings above apply if the journey is on land; however, if it is by sea and if the water is adjacent to a city such as Suez or Jedda, the person's journey is deemed to begin from the time the ship first moves regardless of the presence or location of walls, even if there are walls in the city concerned. This is the view formally adopted by the Hanafis. However, if the ship is moving parallel to the buildings located in the city, the traveler should not begin shortening prayers until the ship has passed beyond them.

* * *

According to the Hanbalis, a traveler is to shorten his prayers once he has departed from the inhabited dwellings on the site where he resides by a sufficient distance that he will be considered, by commonly accepted standards, to have actually departed; this ruling applies regardless of whether these dwellings are inside or outside the 'wall', and regardless of whether they are adjacent to abandoned dwellings or a desert. However, if the abandoned dwellings [he comes across] are adjacent to inhabited dwellings, he must pass beyond both of them in order to shorten his prayers. Similarly, the traveler is not to shorten his prayers if the abandoned area is adjacent to orchards which are inhabited by their owners for summer recreation, for example, until he has passed beyond the orchards.

If the traveler is a tent-dweller, he should not shorten his prayers until he has departed from his tents, and if he resides in a manor or an orchard, he should not shorten them until he has left the place with which the orchards or the manors are commonly associated. Similarly, if the person lives among people who inhabit farmhouses constructed out of corncobs and the like, he should not shorten his prayers until he has departed from the site where his people reside.

* * *

According to the Hanafis, someone who intends to travel a sufficient distance to warrant the shortening of prayers may begin shortening his prayers once he has passed beyond the built-up, populated area of the locale where he resides; this ruling applies regardless of whether he resides in a city or elsewhere. Hence, if someone leaves the city he lives in, he is not to shorten his prayers until he has passed beyond its dwellings on the side from which he is departing, even if there are dwellings located on another side as well. Moreover, such a person must pass beyond all the dwellings, even if they are not immediately adjacent to one another, that form part of the city. Hence, if a group of inhabited dwellings that is now separate once formed part of the city, the traveler must pass beyond it before he may shorten his prayers. However, if such dwellings are in disrepair and no one is living in them, it is not necessary for the traveler to pass beyond them in order to shorten his prayers. The Hanafis also stipulate that the traveler must pass beyond dwellings that surround the city as well as the villages adjacent to them; however, this does not apply to villages adjacent to the *finā'*, that is, the area which has been prepared to serve their inhabitants, nor is it necessary that the homes be out of the traveler's sight.

If a tent-dweller leaves the camp in which he lives, he will not be deemed a traveler until he has passed beyond the tents regardless of whether they are adjacent to another or widely separated. As for someone who resides on water or in an area from which firewood is gathered, he is considered to be a traveler if he leaves the water or the firewood-gathering area provided that the firewood-gathering area is not very extensive or, in the case of a river, that neither its head nor its mouth is very far away; otherwise, the important thing is for the person to pass beyond the populated area. The Hanafis also stipulate that the traveler is to pass beyond the area next to his place of residence which has been prepared to serve the area's inhabitants—such as a place for beasts of burden to run, a place for burial of the dead, a place to throw dirt, etc. If this type of area is separated from the residence site by a farm or an empty space 400 cubits [187 meters or 205 yards] in width, the traveler is not required to pass beyond it before shortening his prayers; nor is it necessary for him to pass beyond orchards, since they are not considered part of the populated area regardless of whether the people of the town inhabit them all year round or just part of the year.

* * *

The Malikis note that a traveler will be journeying either from a settlement composed of constructed dwellings, from tents (as in the case of a Bedouin), or from a place where there are neither buildings nor tents (as in the case of a mountain-dweller). Someone traveling from a town is not to shorten his prayers unless he has passed beyond its buildings, the open space which surrounds it, and the orchards which are inhabited by the town's people, even if they only do so during just part of the year, so long as they are connected to the town either in fact or in a legal sense—for example, by the orchards' inhabitants receiving benefit from the townspeople. If, on the other hand, the orchards are uninhabited for part of the year [as farms are], the traveler is not required to pass beyond them as he would have to pass beyond farms; nor is it necessary to pass beyond them [before shortening one's prayers] if they are separate from the town and if their inhabitants gain no benefit from the townspeople.

Similarly, according to the view officially adopted by the Malikis, it is not required that a traveler traverse three miles from the wall of a town in which the Friday congregational prayer is held. Rather, even if he is coming from a town in which the Friday congregational prayer is performed, what matters is simply for him to pass beyond the aforementioned orchards. As for orchards that are connected to the town he is leaving and whose inhabitants receive some benefit from the townspeople, the traveler must pass beyond them as well. When there are beneficial dealings among the inhabitants of neighboring estates, they are to be treated as a single town; consequently, the traveler is not to shorten his prayers when moving from one to another, but rather, must first pass beyond all of them.

As for a tent-dweller, he is not to shorten his prayers when he travels until he has passed beyond all the tents whose inhabitants are united by a single tribe and family name, or by just a family name. If they are only joined by a single tribe name, or if they belong neither to a single tribe nor a single family but are, nevertheless, joined by mutually beneficial relations, the traveler must still pass beyond all of them before beginning to shorten his prayers. Otherwise, it is sufficient for the traveler to depart from his own tent alone; as for the traveler who is leaving a site containing neither buildings nor tents, he may begin shortening his prayers as soon as he leaves the place where he has been staying.

A traveler's praying behind someone who is resident in a place

Another condition for the validity of shortening prayers is that the traveler who is shortening his prayers must not pray behind someone who is resident in one place, or behind another traveler who is praying his four-*rak'ah* prayers to completion. The reason for this is that if he does, he will likewise be obliged to pray his four-*rak'ah* prayer to completion regardless of whether the prayer is performed during the time period for the prayer concerned or after its time period has run out. This view is agreed upon by the Shafiis, the Malikis and the Hanbalis; for the Hanafis' view, see below.[376]

This ruling is the same whether the person being led in prayer performs the entire prayer with his imam or not, and even if all he performs with the imam is the final testimony; in either case, he is to pray the prayer to completion. This view is agreed upon by the Shafiis, the Hanafis and the Hanbalis; for the Malikis' view, see below.[377]

The only school which deems it undesirable for a traveler to pray behind a 'resident' imam is that of the Malikis, who hold that this practice is undesirable unless the imam is superior in some respect or possesses some specific advantage over the traveler to be led in prayer.

---

376. According to the Hanafis, it is permissible for a traveler to pray behind someone who is resident in one place if he does so during the time period for the prayer concerned, at which time the traveler is obliged to pray four-*rak'ah* prayers to completion anyway. (The reason for this is that the obligatory prayer for the traveler at this time changes from two *rak'ahs* to four *rak'ahs*.) However, once the time period for the prayer concerned has run out, it is no longer permissible for a traveler to pray behind someone who is resident in a single place, since at this time, the obligatory prayer for the traveler is only two *rak'ahs*, and if he prays behind a 'resident', his prayer will be invalidated. The reason for this is that in this case, the first 'sitting' of the prayer for the traveler is obligatory, whereas for his imam, it is not, and the imam should always be in a 'stronger' position than the person following him in prayer, both during the time period for the prayer concerned and after it has run out. As for someone who is 'resident' following a traveler in prayer, this is permissible at any time. What happens in this case is that the 'resident' performs two *rak'ahs* with his imam; then, after his imam [i.e., the traveler] utters the final greeting of peace, the 'resident' gets up and finishes his prayer on his own just as he would if he had arrived two *rak'ahs* late for a communal prayer.

377. The Malikis hold that if a traveler does not perform an entire *rak'ah* with his 'resident' imam, he is not required to perform the prayer to completion; rather, he is to shorten his prayer, since the imam-follower relationship is only confirmed by the latter's performing an entire *rak'ah* with the imam.

The intention to shorten one's prayers

Another condition for the validity of shortening prayers is that one must renew one's intention to do so each time one prays, as explained earlier in the discussion of intention. This view is agreed upon by the Shafiis and the Hanbalis; for the views of the Malikis and the Hanafis, see below.[378]

Conditions which preclude the shortening of prayers: Being resident in a place

One situation which precludes the shortening of prayer is that the person has made it his conscious intention to stay in one place for a period of time; each school offers its own detailed ruling concerning what this intention entails.[379]

---

378. According to the Malikis, the intention to shorten prayer at the beginning of the first prayer shortened during one's journey is sufficient, and there is no need to renew this intention in subsequent prayers. In this respect, it is like the intention to fast the month of Ramaḍān on the eve of the first day of this month, which suffices for the rest of the month.

* * *

According to the Hanafis, what is required is that one consciously intend to undertake a journey before praying; once the intention to undertake the journey has been confirmed, the obligatory number of *rak'ahs* for each prayer becomes two only. Moreover, as we have seen, there is no need for the intention to include a specification of the number of *rak'ahs* to be performed.

379. According to the Hanafis, a traveler may not shorten prayers if he intends to stay in a particular place for fifteen whole consecutive days; if the intention is to stay any less than this, if even by a single hour, he will not be considered 'resident'. A traveler is forbidden to shorten prayers in the following situations: (1) When the person has actually stopped moving; thus, if he intends to stay in a particular place but keeps on moving, he is still not considered to be 'resident', and he must continue to shorten his prayers. (2) When the location where the traveler intends to stay is fit to reside in. Thus, if someone intends to stay in a place such as an uninhabited desert, on an island with nothing but ruins on it, or on a sea, he must continue to shorten his prayers. (3) When the site in which the traveler intends to stay is a single place. Hence, if someone intends to stay in two different towns without specifying which of the two he intends to stay in, he must continue to shorten his prayers. (3) When the decision to stay in a particular place has been made independently. Hence, if a subordinate intends to stay in a given place, his intention will not be valid, and he may not perform his prayers to completion unless he is aware of the intention of the person to whom he is subordinate, as we saw earlier.

If someone intends to travel a distance that can be covered in three days and if he then comes back before completing this distance, he must resume performing his prayers to completion as soon as he makes the decision to return. Similarly, if such a person makes it his intention to stay in a given place before completing the distance he had intended to travel, he must begin performing his prayers to completion in the place at which he has arrived even if it would not be fit to reside in, as will be seen more clearly below.

Lastly, if someone intends to stay in a place for fewer than fifteen days or if he stays in a place but without a conscious intention to do so, he will continue to be deemed a traveler. As such, he must continue to shorten his prayers even if he stays in the place for several years; however, if the person is waiting for the arrival of a caravan, for example, and knows that the caravan will not arrive for at least fifteen days, he is considered to have intended to stay this length of time and must therefore perform his prayers to completion.

* * *

According to the Hanbalis, a traveler may not shorten prayers in the following situations: (1) if he intends to stay indefinitely in a single place, even if it is not fit to be lived in, (2) if he intends to stay in a place for a period of time during which he would be obliged to perform more than twenty prayers [i.e., more than four whole days], and (3) if he intends to stay in a place in order to accomplish a purpose which he has good reason to believe will not be achieved in less than four days (where the four days include the day he arrives and the day he departs).

If, in the course of his journey, someone stays in a particular place in order to accomplish some purpose, yet without consciously intending to stay there, and if he does not know when his purpose will actually be accomplished, he may shorten his prayers even if he happens to stay in this place for years. This ruling applies whether he expects to stay a long or a short time so long as it appears probable to him that the purpose will be accomplished within a period of time which is brief enough that the ruling on travelers will continue to apply. However, if a traveler returns to the place where he began his journey before traversing the entire distance he had intended to cover, he should not shorten his prayers on the way back.

* * *

According to the Malikis, the ruling pertaining to travelers ceases to apply and the shortening of prayers is precluded by the intention to stay somewhere for four days, given two conditions: (1) That the four days are complete; in other words, they must not include the day of arrival if the person arrives after sunrise, or the day of departure if the person departs during the day, and (2) That twenty prayers will be required of the traveler during his stay. Hence, if someone stays in a place for four whole days, then departs after sundown on the fourth day, and if he was intending to do this before actually staying in the place, he should continue to shorten his prayers during his stay due to the fact that fewer than twenty prayers were required of him. Similarly, if the person arrives in the place at noon and is intending to leave during the fourth day (not counting his day of arrival), he must continue to shorten his prayers due to his not having stayed for four entire days.

The intention to stay in a particular place will be formed either at the beginning of one's journey or after the journey has begun. If the intention is formed at the beginning of the person's journey, the distance between the place where the intention originated and the place where the person stays will either be long enough to warrant the shortening of prayers or not. If the distance is long enough to warrant the shortening of prayers, the traveler should shorten his prayers until he actually arrives at the place where he intends to stay; otherwise, he should perform his prayers to completion from the time he consciously intends to stay in the place concerned. If, on the other hand, the intention originates during the person's journey, he should shorten his prayers until he actually arrives at the place where he intends to stay even if the distance between the two points is less than the distance required in order to warrant the shortening of prayers. (This is based on the officially recognized Maliki view.) In addition, it is not necessary for the place in which the person stays to be fit to be resided in; hence, if someone intends to stay in a place where there are no buildings or other residents, he is not to shorten his prayers when he arrives there, as we have seen.

Similar to the intention to stay in a given place is for someone to know that someone like him would customarily stay in a place for four days or more, in which case he should perform his prayers to completion even if he has not made it his intention to stay [this length of time]. If, on the other hand, he wishes to part with custom and intends not to stay for the usual four days, he will continue to be deemed a traveler, legally speaking.

The intention to reside in a given place does not include the intention to camp somewhere out of fear; hence, the latter does not exclude the person concerned from the category of traveler. Similarly, if someone stays in such a place during his journey without a conscious intention to do so, his stay there will likewise not preclude his shortening his prayers even if he stays there for a long period of time. If, on the other hand, he stays without a conscious intention to do so in a place where his journey ends, this stay precludes his shortening prayers unless [the text reads 'if' – t.n.] he knows, or has good reason to believe, that he will leave this place before he has spent enough time there for him to be excluded from the category of traveler.

Lastly, if, after beginning a journey, a person returns to the place from which he originally traveled, regardless of whether this place is a 'homeland' or simply a place where he has been residing, his return trip will be considered a separate journey. If the length of the journey is sufficient to warrant the shortening of prayers, he should shorten them; otherwise, he should not, even if he has no intention to stay in this place, and whether he is returning to retrieve something he forgot or not.

* * *

According to the Shafiis, one may not shorten prayers if he consciously intends to stay in a place for four complete days, not including the day he arrives and the day he departs. If the person's intention is to stay for less than four days or if he intends nothing at all, he may continue to shorten his prayers until he has actually been in the place for four days. This ruling applies if the person has no particular purpose for staying in the place; however, if he does have such a purpose, and if he is certain that this purpose will not be fulfilled within four days, his journey will be deemed to have ended as soon as he settles in the place regardless of whether he intends to stay after his arrival there or not. If, on the other hand, he expects that his purpose may be fulfilled at any time such that he cannot be certain that he will have to stay four whole days, he may continue to shorten his prayers for up to eighteen days.

Conditions which invalidate the shortening of prayer, an explanation of the meaning of "original homeland," and other topics

The shortening of prayer is invalidated by the traveler's returning to the place at which it first became permissible for him to shorten prayer as he started out on his journey, whether this place is his 'homeland' or not. Moreover, the same ruling which applies to an actual return applies likewise to an intention to return. For each school's detailed rulings on such matters, see below.[380]

---

380. The Hanafis hold that if a traveler returns to the place from which he departed and if he does so before traveling the minimum distance required in order for one to shorten prayers, he will no longer be considered a traveler; the same applies if the person merely intends to return, even if he does not return in fact; in both cases, the person is obliged to perform his prayers to completion.

If, on the other hand, the traveler intends to return after covering the minimum distance required in order to shorten prayers, he is not to perform his prayers to completion until he actually does return. In other words, the shortening of prayers in this situation is not invalidated by a mere intention to return, or even by beginning to return.

As for the concept of 'homeland', the Hanafis divide it into two categories: (1) 'original homeland', which includes the place where one was born, where one has a wife, or where one intends to make a living, even if he was not born there or has no wife there; and (2) 'resident homeland', namely, a place which is fit to be resided in for fifteen days or more if one has the intention to stay there. An 'original homeland' is only abrogated by another, comparable, 'homeland'. For example, if someone was born in Asyut, this makes Asyut his 'original homeland'. If this person then moves to Cairo, marries there, or settles there for the purpose of making a living, Cairo will likewise be a 'homeland' to him. In this case, if such a person travels from Cairo to Asyut, where he was born, he must shorten his prayers in Asyut provided that he does not intend to stay there long enough to preclude the shortening of prayers. The reason for this is that even though Asyut is his 'original homeland', it has now been abrogated by another, comparable 'original homeland', namely, Cairo. Moreover, it is not necessary, in order for one such 'homeland' to be abrogated by another, for the two places to be separated by a distance sufficient to warrant the shortening of prayer. Thus, if someone was born in al-Wāsiṭī, for example, after which he moves to Cairo with the intention of settling there or marries there, and if after this he travels to Asyut, passing by or entering al-Wāsiṭī on his way, he is to shorten his prayers; the reason for this ruling is that even though it [al-Wāsiṭī] is this person's 'original homeland', it has nevertheless been superceded by another, comparable 'resident homeland', namely, Cairo, even though the distance between the two sites would not be sufficient to warrant the shortening of prayers.

However, one's 'original homeland' may not be superceded by a 'resident homeland'. Thus, if someone travels from his birthplace, the town in which his wife lives, or the place where he makes a living to a location to which none of these descriptions applies and stays there for fifteen days, and if he then returns to the place from which he came, he must perform his prayers to completion even if it is not his intention to stay, since one's 'resident homeland' may not supercede one's 'original homeland'.

As for a 'resident homeland', it is abrogated by three things:

(1) By one's 'original homeland'. Thus, if someone stays in Mecca, for example, for fifteen days, then travels from there to Minā and marries, and if he then returns to Mecca, he should perform his prayers to completion due to the abrogation of his 'resident homeland', namely, Mecca, by virtue of his having been in his 'original homeland', namely, Minā.

(2) By another 'resident homeland'. Thus, if someone travels a distance which is sufficient to warrant the shortening of prayers to another place which is fit to be resided in and stays there for fifteen days with the conscious intention to do so, then leaves this place for a third location and stays there for the same length of time, then returns to the first place, he must shorten his prayers if he does not intend to stay there for fifteen days. The reason for this is that this person's first 'resident homeland' has been abrogated by the second 'resident homeland'. However, it is not necessary, in order for one 'resident homeland' to be abrogated by another, for the two places to be separated by a distance which is sufficient to warrant the shortening of prayers, as we saw likewise to be the case in connection with the 'original homeland'.

(3) Commencing one's journey from one's 'resident homeland'. If a traveler who is going a distance sufficient to warrant the shortening of prayers stays for fifteen days or more in a place fit to be resided in, and if he then intends to travel to another place, his 'resident homeland' will be abrogated by his having commenced his journey from there. If this person returns to his former 'resident homeland', he may not pray his prayers to completion due to its no longer being his 'resident homeland' on account of his having commenced his journey from there. However, if he commences his journey from some other place, this will not abrogate his 'resident homeland' unless: (a) the traveler does not pass through his 'resident homeland' on his way, and (b) the distance between the place where the person commenced his journey and his 'resident homeland' is sufficient to warrant the shortening of prayers. If the distance is less than this, it is not abrogated as his 'resident homeland'. For example, if two merchants depart, one of them from Asyut and the other from Gergā, and if the first merchant stays in Cairo for fifteen days with the conscious intention of doing so while the second stays at Kafr al-Zayyāt with the same intention, Cairo will now be the 'resident homeland' for the first merchant while Kafr al-Zayyāt will become the 'resident homeland' for the second. The distance between Cairo and Kafr al-Zayyāt is sufficient to warrant the shortening of prayers. Hence, if each of the two merchants goes to Banhā, they should both perform their prayers to completion since the distance between Banhā and each of the other two cities is less than what is required in order for a traveler to shorten his prayers. Moreover, if both merchants stay in Banhā for fifteen days, Banhā will now be the 'resident homeland' for both merchants in place of Cairo or Kafr al-Zayyāt, since a 'resident homeland' is abrogated by another, comparable 'resident homeland'. If these two merchants depart from Banhā and go to Kafr al-Zayyāt with the intention of commencing their journey from Kafr al-Zayyāt to Cairo, and if they stay in Kafr al-Zayyāt for one day, then go to Cairo, they are to perform their prayers to completion in Kafr al-Zayyāt because the distance is less than that required in order to shorten prayers. Similarly, they are to perform their prayers to completion while they are on their way to Cairo if they pass through Banhā because, even though the distance between Kafr al-Zayyāt and Cairo is sufficient to warrant the shortening of prayers, it is nevertheless also the case that because of their having passed through Banhā on their journey, Banhā

is not abrogated as their 'resident homeland'. The reason for this is that a 'resident homeland' is not abrogated by a traveler's commencing his journey from some other place (in this case, Kafr al-Zayyāt) provided that the traveler passes through it, and provided that the distance between it and the place from which the journey was commenced is less than that required to warrant the shortening of prayers.

* * *

The Malikis hold that if someone departs from a town with the intention of traversing the distance required to shorten prayers and if he then returns to this town, this town will either be: (1) his town of origin—that is, the place where he grew up and with which he is associated, (2) another town where he wishes to reside permanently, or (3) a place where he has resided based on a conscious intention for long enough that he is no longer categorized as a traveler. If this person returns either to his town of origin or to the town where he wishes to reside permanently, he is to perform his prayers to completion as soon as he arrives there even if he does not have a conscious intention to stay there for a period of time long enough to exclude him from the category of traveler unless, when he left this town, he was renouncing the notion of living there anymore. In this latter case, his arrival in the town does not preclude his shortening his prayers unless: (1) he has made it his conscious intention to stay there for a period long enough to exclude him from the category of traveler or (2) he has a wife there for whom he has built a home. If he returns to his place of residence, his arrival there does not preclude his shortening of prayers unless he consciously intends to remain there for the aforementioned period of time. This, then, is the ruling which applies in the event of the person's presence in the town from which he departed.

As for a situation in which someone travels back to this town, the ruling thereon depends on the distance. If the distance traveled in returning is sufficient to warrant the shortening of prayers, one should shorten them; otherwise, he should not. If the return distance is not sufficient to warrant the shortening of prayers, one is no longer considered to be a traveler, and one is to perform one's prayers to completion whether one is returning to the town or is present in it, even if it is not one's home town or one's place of permanent residence. If, on the other hand, it is his home town or the town which he had decided while on the way to reside in permanently and if he then enters this town, his mere entry will exclude him from the category of traveler [as a result of which, he must perform his prayers to completion]. The same ruling applies to the town in which one's wife resides if the person concerned has built a residence for her there and if she is not 'unruly'; in other words, his mere entry into the town causes him no longer to be classified as a traveler. If, while still traveling, someone intends to enter such a town, the ruling on this situation depends on the distance between the location where the intention was made and the town mentioned (namely, either one's hometown, the town of one's permanent residence, or the town where one's wife resides). If this distance is sufficient to warrant the shortening of prayers, one should do so as he travels toward the town; otherwise, he should not. However, some Malikis rule that one should shorten one's prayers in either case. Lastly, merely passing through a town does not preclude the shortening of one's prayers, nor is it precluded by the traveler's entering the town where his wife resides if he has not yet had sexual relations with her or if she is 'unruly'.

* * *

According to the Shafiis, one's 'homeland' is the place where one resides on a permanent basis, summer and winter. Any other place is not one's 'homeland'. If someone returns to his homeland after having traveled away from it, his journey will end as soon as he arrives there, whether he returns for a particular purpose or not and whether he intends to stay four days there or not; in such a case, he is to shorten his prayers [during the return journey] until he arrives there.

If someone returns to a place other than his 'homeland', his return will either be for a particular purpose, or without any such purpose. If his return has no particular purpose, his journey will only end by his consciously intending, before his arrival, to stay in this place for long enough to exclude him from the category of traveler, or by his intending to stay there without a specification of the length of his intended stay; moreover, the intention must be formed not while he is moving, but while he is staying in one place [along the way] and it must be formed independently rather than as a subordinate. Given these conditions, the person's journey will end as soon as he arrives. If the person concerned has no intention to make the aforementioned stay, he will only cease to be deemed a traveler in one of two situations: (1) If he actually does stay the length of time mentioned above, or (2) if he forms the intention to stay there for this period of time after he arrives. If, by contrast, the person's return is for a particular purpose and if he is certain that this purpose will not be fulfilled within four days, he will cease to be deemed a traveler as soon as he settles in the town even if he does not intend to stay there. If, on the other hand, he knows that his purpose will be fulfilled within four days, he will continue to be deemed a traveler as long as he stays in the town.

This ruling applies if the traveler does not anticipate that his purpose might be fulfilled at any time; if he expects that it might be fulfilled at any time, he may continue to shorten his prayers for up to eighteen whole days. Moreover, the same ruling which applies to returning to one's homeland applies likewise to the intention to do so. Hence, one's journey is deemed to end as soon as one makes it his intention to return, provided that one does the intending while staying in one place rather than while moving. As for the intention to return to a place other than one's homeland, it causes one's journey to end if one is returning without a particular purpose to fulfill; however, if there is a particular purpose for one's intended return, it does not cause one's journey to be considered over. Lastly, the same ruling that applies to the intention to return applies likewise to hesitation over whether to return.

* * *

The Hanbalis hold that if someone returns to his 'homeland' from which he first commenced his journey or if he intends to return there and if the distance is less than that which warrants the shortening of prayers, he must perform his prayers to completion until he leaves his 'homeland' for a second time or until he goes back on his intention to return. In this case, the traveler is not required to repeat the prayers which he shortened before returning or intending to return. Moreover, it makes no difference whether the person's return is for a particular purpose or is due to his having canceled the journey altogether. If, on the other hand, the distance between the person's 'homeland' and the place in which he made it his intention to return is sufficient to warrant the shortening of prayers, he should shorten them as he returns, since it involves a lengthy journey. If the traveler passes through his 'homeland', he should perform his prayers to completion even if he has no particular purpose for going there other than the fact that it is on his way; similarly, if he passes through a town in which he has married, even if it is not his 'homeland', he should perform his prayers to completion until he leaves it.

Combining consecutive prayers

Combining two consecutive prayers, either by performing both at an earlier time or by performing both of them later, and the definition of this practice

This practice will be discussed under the following headings: (1) its definition, (2) the ruling on it, and (3) the conditions and reasons associated with it.

Its definition

This practice is defined as someone's combining the noon and mid-afternoon prayers either by praying both during the time period for the noon prayer or by postponing the noon prayer and performing it with the mid-afternoon prayer during the time period for the latter. The sundown and evening prayers may be combined in the same two ways described here for the noon and the mid-afternoon prayers. As for the dawn prayer, it may never be combined with any other prayer.

It is not permissible for someone who is qualified to be held accountable for the performance of ritual prayer either to postpone an obligatory prayer past its designated time period or to perform it before its designated time period has begun unless it is for one of the reasons listed below. The reason for this is that God Almighty has commanded us to perform the obligatory ritual prayers during their designated time periods (which were detailed above in the section entitled, "The times of the required prayers"). He says, "Verily, for all believers prayer is indeed a sacred duty linked to particular times [of day]" (4:103). However, Islam is a religion which lays no undue burden on its adherents; hence, it allows ritual prayers to be performed at other than their originally designated times in situations where performing them on time would cause hardship for the person concerned.

The ruling on this practice and the reasons for it

The ruling on this practice is that it is permitted; as for the reasons and conditions associated with it, they differ in detail among the four schools.[381]

---

381. The Malikis specify the following five reasons for combining two prayers: (1) being on a journey, (2) illness, (3) rain and mud together with darkness at the end of the month, and (4) a pilgrim's being at 'Arafah or Muzdalifah. (1) Being on a journey: The term 'journey' here refers to any journey, whether the distance traveled is sufficient to warrant the shortening of four-*rak'ah* prayers or not; however, in order for the combining of prayers to be allowed, the journey must not be one which is forbidden or undesirable. Hence, if someone is on a journey which is legitimate, he may combine the noon and mid-afternoon prayers by performing both during the time period for the noon prayer given two conditions: 1. That the sun reach its zenith while he is staying in the place where he has stopped to rest, and 2. That the traveler intend to depart before the commencement of the time period for the mid-afternoon prayer and not to stop to rest again until after sundown. If the traveler intends to stop before the sun has taken on a yellowish hue, he must per-

form the noon prayer before departing and postpone the mid-afternoon prayer until he stops, since he will be stopping during the 'elective' time for the mid-afternoon prayer, as a result of which there is no need to perform it early. If the traveler performs the mid-afternoon prayer early with the noon prayer, it will be valid, but he will be guilty of wrongdoing, and it is recommended that he perform the mid-afternoon prayer again during its 'elective' time period after he stops. If, on the other hand, the traveler intends to stop after the sun has taken on a yellowish hue before sundown, he should perform the noon prayer before departing. With respect to the mid-afternoon prayer, however, he is free to choose between performing it early and postponing it until he stops. The reason for this is that the mid-afternoon prayer in such a case falls in its 'imperative' time period either way since, if he performs it early, he will perform it during its advance 'imperative' phase for the sake of travel, whereas if he postpones it, he will perform it during its legitimate [i.e., usual] 'imperative' phase. If the time period for the noon prayer commences (by the sun's reaching its zenith) while the person is traveling, and if he intends to stop at or before the time when the sun takes on a yellowish hue, he is permitted to postpone the noon prayer and combine it with the mid-afternoon prayer after he stops. If, on the other hand, he does not intend to stop until after sundown, he may not postpone the noon prayer in order to combine it with the mid-afternoon prayer, nor may he postpone the mid-afternoon prayer until after he stops, since this would involve causing both prayers to be performed outside their designated time periods. Rather, he is to do a 'token' combination of the two prayers, by performing the noon prayer at the end of its 'elective' phrase and the mid-afternoon prayer at the beginning of its 'elective' phase. Moreover, the same rulings which apply to combining the noon and mid-afternoon prayers apply to the combining of the sundown and evening prayers. It should be noted that the beginning of the time period for the sundown prayer, namely, the setting of the sun, is considered parallel to the sun's reaching its zenith with respect to [the time period for the] noon prayer. The [end of the] first third of the night is parallel to the time when the sun takes on a yellowish hue after the mid-afternoon prayer, while the break of dawn is parallel to the setting of the sun with respect to the sundown prayer. Hence, if the time for the sundown prayer commences while the traveler is staying in a particular place, and if he intends to depart before the time period for the evening prayer begins and stop again after the break of dawn, he is to combine the evening prayer with the sundown prayer by performing both of them before his departure; if, on the other hand, he intends to stop before the end of the first third of the night, he is to postpone the evening prayer until he stops. If he intends to stop after the end of the first third of the night, he should perform the sundown prayer before his departure, whereas with respect to the evening prayer, he has a choice [as to when to perform it]. Combining prayer is permissible for travelers; however, it is a departure from the ideal, hence, it is preferable not to do so. Lastly, it is only permissible if the traveler is on land, whereas if he is traveling by sea, it is not permitted, since the concession entailed in the combining of prayers applies only to travel by land. (2) Illness: If someone is so ill that it causes him hardship to rise for each separate prayer or instance of ritual ablutions—such as someone who suffers an intestinal ailment, for example—he may perform a token combination of the noon and mid-afternoon prayers and the sundown and evening prayers, by performing the noon prayer at the end of its elective phase and the mid-afternoon prayer at the beginning of its elective phase, and by performing the sundown prayer immediately before the disappearance of the twilight glow and the evening prayer immediately afterwards. This is not a true combining of prayers due to the fact that each prayer has been performed during its own designated time period; however, it is permissible without any undesirability attached to it. When someone engages in such a token combination of prayers, he earns the same merit as that associated with performing prayer at the beginning of its designated time period, but only if he has a condition which justifies his doing so. If a person does not suffer from such a justifying condition, he is still permitted to engage in a token combination of prayers, but he does not gain the merit associated with performing prayer at the beginning of its time period. Moreover, if a healthy person has reason to fear that he might suffer dizziness that would prevent him from performing a given prayer in the best possible manner, or that he might faint, thereby being prevented from praying at the commencement of the time period for the second prayer (such as the mid-afternoon prayer with respect to the noon prayer, or the evening prayer with respect to the sundown prayer), he may perform both of the prayers during the time period for the first. If he performs both prayers early in this manner and if, after having done so, what he feared would happen fails to take place, it is desirable for him to repeat the second prayer during its designated time period. (3) Rain and mud with darkness, when rain is so heavy that it forces ordinary people to cover their heads or if there is a great deal of mud (where 'a great deal' is defined as enough to oblige ordinary people to take off their shoes): If such conditions exist, it is permissible to combine the evening prayer with the sundown prayer by performing both of them during the time period for the sundown prayer in order to make it possible to perform the evening prayer in community without undue hardship. In such a case, the worshiper goes to the mosque at the time for the sundown prayer and performs both the sundown prayer and the evening prayer at one time. This practice is permissible, but a departure from the ideal; moreover, it is applicable only to prayers performed in the mosque, not to those performed in one's home. As for the manner in which this type of combination is to be carried out, it is as follows: The *adhān* for the sundown prayer is first sounded in a loud voice as usual. It is then recommended that the sundown prayer be postponed past the *adhān* by the length of time it would take to perform three *rak'ahs*. Once the sundown prayer has been performed, it is recommended that the *adhān* for the evening prayer be sounded in a low voice from inside the mosque rather than from the minaret lest people think that the regular time period for the evening prayer has begun. The evening prayer is then performed without any voluntary prayers between it and the sundown prayer. It is likewise undesirable for voluntary prayers to be performed between any other two prayers which are combined, although if one does perform voluntary prayers, this does not preclude the combining of prayers. Nor is one to perform voluntary prayers after the evening prayer and the sundown prayer have been combined on account of rain. As for the *witr*, it is to be delayed until after the twilight glow has disappeared from the sky, since the *witr* is not valid until after this time. If someone is praying on his own in the mosque, he may only combine prayers if he is a regular imam who has a home to which he can depart. Such a person is to combine [prayers] on his own, yet with the intention of both combining prayers and leading others as their imam since [in his capacity as a regular imam], his prayer alone is reckoned as a communal prayer. As for someone who has secluded himself in the mosque to devote himself to prayer and worship, he may combine prayers in imitation of others who are combining prayers in the mosque. Lastly, if the rain stops after the worshiper has begun performing the first of the two prayers, it remains permissible to combine them; however, if it stops before he has begun the first prayer, combining them is no longer permissible. (5) A pilgrim's being at 'Arafah or Muzdalifah: If a pilgrim is at 'Arafah, it is an emulation of the Sunnah for him to combine the noon and the mid-afternoon prayers by performing both during the time period for the noon prayer while at 'Arafah. This ruling applies whether the pilgrim is a native of 'Arafah or of some other city in which pilgrimage rites are performed, such as Minā and Muzdalifah, or is from some other location. Pilgrims who are not natives of 'Arafah emulate the Sunnah by shortening their four-*rak'ah* prayers to two, even if the distance between their homelands and 'Arafah is less than that which warrants the shortening of prayers. As for pilgrims who have come from 'Arafah to Muzdalifah, it is an emulation of the Sunnah for them to postpone the sundown prayer until they reach Muzdalifah, then to combine it with the evening prayer. However, the combining of the sundown and evening prayers in this fashion is only an emulation of the Sunnah for those who stood at 'Arafah with the imam; otherwise, they are to perform each of these prayers during its own designated time period. It is an emulation of the Sunnah to shorten the evening prayer for those who are not natives of Muzdalifah, since the rule is that combining prayers is a Sunnah-based practice for every pilgrim, while the shortening of prayers is only for those who are not natives of either 'Arafah or Muzdalifah.

* * *

According to the Shafiis, it is permissible for someone traveling a distance sufficient to warrant the shortening of prayers to combine the two prayers mentioned either by performing the second prayer during the time period for the first, or by performing the first prayer during the time period for the second given the conditions for classifying one as a traveler. Rain serves as a basis for combining prayers during the time period for the first prayer only, and not during the second; moreover, in order for one to combine prayers by performing both of them during the time period for the first prayer, six conditions must be met: (1) One must maintain the temporal order between the prayers by beginning with the one which is being performed during its own designated time period. Hence, if someone wishes to combine the mid-afternoon prayer with the noon prayer during the time period for the noon prayer, he must begin with the noon prayer. If the order is reversed, the noon prayer will be valid since it was performed during its regular time period, but the mid-afternoon prayer will have no validity either as an obligatory prayer or as a voluntary prayer unless the worshiper concerned needs to make up a mid-afternoon prayer which he missed earlier; if he does need to make up an earlier prayer from this time period, the one which he last performed will serve to make up the one he missed. However, if he has reversed the prayers' order out of forgetfulness or ignorance, the prayer will count as a voluntary prayer [rather than as an obligatory prayer]. (2) One must intend to combine the two prayers during the time period for the first of the two prayers by intending in one's heart to perform the mid-afternoon prayer immediately after completing the noon prayer. In order for such an intention to be valid, it must coincide with some part of the first prayer. In other words, it must neither precede the first prayer's *takbīrat al-iḥrām* nor come after its concluding greeting of peace. (3) There must be continuity between the two prayers. In other words, the two prayers must not be separated by a time lapse greater than that required to perform two *rak'ahs* as quickly as possible. Consequently, one may not perform the voluntary *rak'ahs* regularly associated with such prayers between the first and the second prayer being combined. However, it is permissible to separate the two prayers by uttering the *adhān* and the *iqāmah* and performing ritual ablutions. For example, if someone performs the noon prayer after performing sand ablutions, then wishes to perform the mid-afternoon prayer during the time period for the noon prayer, he may perform sand ablutions again before performing the mid-afternoon prayer, since it is not permissible to combine two prayers based on a single performance of sand ablutions. (4) One must continue to travel until one has begun the second prayer with *takbīrat al-iḥrām* even if one's journey is interrupted after this during the same prayer. If, however, one's journey is discontinued before one begins the second prayer, one is no longer permitted to combine prayers since the reason for doing so no longer exists. (5) The time period for the first prayer must continue for a certainty until the second prayer has been begun. (6) One must have good reason to believe that the first prayer was valid. Thus, for example, if the first prayer is a Friday congregational prayer which has been performed in a place where a number of different mosques have been built unnecessarily, and if there is some doubt regarding which congregation began the prayer first and whether they prayed it simultaneously, it will not be permissible to combine this prayer with the mid-afternoon prayer by performing the mid-afternoon prayer during the time period for the noon prayer.

Given the foregoing, the ideal practice is to refrain from combining prayers since the four schools differ over whether it is permitted or not. However, it is an emulation of the Sunnah to combine prayers when a pilgrim is traveling or when he is in 'Arafah or Muzdalifah; when in 'Arafah, it is preferable for the pilgrim to combine the noon and mid-afternoon prayers by performing the latter during the time period for the former, whereas if he is in Muzdalifah, it is preferable for him to combine the sundown and evening prayers by performing the sundown prayer during the time period for the evening prayer since all four schools agree on the permissibility of combining prayers in these two situations.

It should also be realized that combining prayers may also be a 'duty' or a recommended practice. For example, if there is insufficient time left within the time period for the first prayer [i.e., either the noon prayer or the sundown prayer] to perform the necessary ritual ablutions and to perform the prayer as well, one is obliged to combine this prayer with the prayer which follows it [i.e., either the mid-afternoon prayer or the evening prayer, respectively]; similarly, it is recommended that the pilgrim who is a traveler as described above combine prayers. It is also recommended that one combine prayers if it is necessary in order to perform a given prayer in the most ideal possible manner, for example, in order for one to be able to perform a prayer in community rather than performing it alone by not combining it with another prayer.

In order to combine two prayers by performing the first prayer during the time period for the second while on a journey, two conditions must be met: (1) The intention to perform the first prayer late must be made during the time period for the first prayer, provided that there is still enough time remaining to perform this prayer either to completion or in a shortened form. If the worshiper does not consciously intend to delay the prayer, or if when he makes this his intention, the time remaining in the first prayer's usual time period is insufficient to perform the prayer, he will have committed an act of disobedience; in such a case, the first prayer will either be considered a compensatory prayer, or it will be considered 'on time', but involving the commission of a forbidden act. (2) One must continue traveling until the completion of both prayers to be combined. If the traveler stops somewhere before this, the prayer which he had intended to delay will be considered a compensatory prayer rather than a prayer performed on time.

As for maintaining the temporal order of the prayers and continuity between them when combining two prayers during the time period for the second prayer, they are emulations of the Sunnah, but not conditions for the validity of combining them.

It is permissible, on account of rain, for a person who is 'resident' in a place to combine prayers as one would while traveling, including the combination of the Friday congregational prayer with the mid-afternoon prayer during the time period for the Friday prayer; this ruling applies even if the rain is light enough that it only wets the top of one's garment or the soles of one's shoes, and the same applies to snow or hail which is melting. However, the person who is 'resident' somewhere may only engage in this practice given the following conditions: (1) The rain, hail, or snow must be present when the worshiper utters *takbīrat al-iḥrām* for both prayers and when he utters the final greeting of peace for the first prayer. However, it does no harm for the rain to stop during the first or the second prayer, or after they are both concluded. (2) The original order between the two prayers must be maintained. (3) There must be continuity between the two prayers. (4) The worshiper must consciously have intended to combine the two prayers as we saw above in connection with combining prayers while on a journey. (5) The second prayer must be performed in community, even if this includes only the utterance of *takbīrat al-iḥrām*. However, it is not required that the community remain present until the end of the second prayer based on the best-attested view, even if the worshiper parts with the group and begins praying on his own before completing its first *rak'ah*. (6) The imam must consciously intend both to lead others in prayer and to pray in community. (7) The prayer must be combined in a mosque or some other site set aside for prayer which is far enough away by commonly accepted standards that it would cause hardship for people to get there. An exception to this is made for the regular imam, who may lead the congregation in combining prayers for this reason even if he would not be harmed by the rain.

If any of the conditions listed here remains unfulfilled, it is not permissible for a 'resident' to combine prayers. Moreover, the reasons for which someone who is 'resident' somewhere may combine prayers do not include intense darkness, winds, fear, mud or illness based on the most widely prevalent view, although there are well-attested arguments in favor of the view that it is permissible to combine prayers (both during the time period for the second prayer and during the time period for the first prayer) on account of illness.

* * *

According to the Hanafis, it is not permissible to combine two prayers for any reason during the time period for one of the two prayers whether one is 'resident' or on a journey except in the two following cases: First: It is permissible to combine the noon and the mid-afternoon prayers during the time for the noon prayer given four conditions: (1) It must be the Day of 'Arafah. (2) The worshiper must be in a state of ritual consecration for the major pilgrimage. (3) The worshiper must pray behind the Muslims' imam or someone who has been appointed to take his place. (4) The noon prayer performed by the worshiper concerned must have been valid. If it appears that it was not valid, it must be repeated, and the worshiper will not be permitted to combine it with the mid-afternoon prayer; rather, he must perform the mid-afternoon prayer during its own designated time period. Two: It is permissible to combine the sundown and evening prayers during the time period for the evening prayer given the following two conditions: (1) The worshiper must be in Muzdalifah. (2) He must be in a state of ritual consecration for the major pilgrimage.

When two prayers are combined, only one call to prayer is to be sounded for both of them, although a separate *iqāmah* may be sounded for each. 'Abdullāh Ibn Mas'ūd states, "By the One besides Whom there is no deity, the Messenger of God never performed any prayer outside its designated time period except in two situations, namely, when he combined the noon and the mid-afternoon prayers at 'Arafah, and when he combined the sundown and evening prayers at Muzdalifah. (This hadith is narrated by Muslim and al-Bukhārī.)

* * *

According to the Hanbalis, it is permissible to combine the noon and mid-afternoon prayers or the sundown and evening prayers either during the time period for the first prayer or during the time period for the second, though it is preferable to refrain from this practice. It is an emulation of the Sunnah to combine the noon and the mid-afternoon prayers during the time period for the noon prayer at 'Arafah, and to combine the sundown and evening prayers during the time period for the evening prayer while at Muzdalifah.

In order for it to be permissible to combine prayers, the following conditions must be met: (1) The worshiper must be traveling a distance sufficient to warrant the shortening of prayers. (2) The worshiper must be so ill that it causes him or her undue hardship not to combine prayers. (3) The worshiper must either be a nursing mother or a woman with a chronic menstrual flow. Such a woman is permitted to combine prayers due to the hardship caused by having to reestablish ritual purity again before every prayer. The same applies to someone with a condition such as urinary incontinence, someone who is unable to use water for the purpose of ritual ablutions or to perform sand ablutions for every prayer, those who are unable to determine the times for prayer, such as the blind and those living underground, and those who have reason to fear that harm might come to them, their money, or their families if they refrained from combining prayers. Allowance is made in this regard also for workers who are unable to leave their jobs [at every prayer time].

All these situations make it permissible to combine the noon and mid-afternoon prayers or the sundown and evening prayers, both during the time period for the first prayer and during the time period for the second. It is permissible to combine the sundown and evening prayers in particular on account of snow, hail, ice, mud, powerful, cold winds and rain which gets one's clothing wet and causes undue hardship. This ruling is the same whether the person is going to pray in a mosque or in his home, and even if the path leading [to the mosque] is roofed over. It is preferable, when one intends to combine two prayers, to do it in the manner that would be the easiest, whether this means performing both prayers during the time period for the first prayer, or during the time period for the second. If both ways appear to be equal in this regard, it is preferable to perform both prayers during the time period for the second prayer.

In order for combining prayers in either of the ways mentioned to be valid, the original order of the prayers must be preserved; this requirement is not dropped by virtue of forgetfulness as it is with respect to making up prayers which have been missed.

For the validity of combining prayers during the time period for the first prayer, four conditions must be met: (1) The intention to combine the prayers must coincide with the utterance of *takbīrat al-iḥrām* for the first prayer. (2) The two prayers must not be separated by any more time than it would take to utter the *iqāmah* and to perform ritual ablutions in the most minimal fashion. Moreover, one must not perform a voluntary prayer of the sort that is associated with the five daily prayers between the two. (3) The condition that makes it permissible to combine the prayers must exist at the time when the prayers are commenced, and when the final greeting of peace for the first prayer is being uttered. (4) The condition that makes it permissible to combine the prayers must continue to exist until the second prayer has been completed.

As for the combining of two prayers during the time period for the second prayer, only two conditions must be met: (1) The intention to combine the prayers must be formed during the time period for the first of the two prayers. If there is not enough time left in the time period for the first prayer to perform this prayer, it is not permissible to combine it with the second. (2) The condition which makes it permissible to combine prayers must continue to exist from the moment when one forms his intention to combine the prayers during the time period for the first prayer until the commencement of the time period for the second prayer.

Making Up Prayers

Making up prayers which have been missed

The obligatory prayers are to be performed during their designated time periods. If someone delays such a prayer beyond its designated time period without a valid excuse, he is guilty of a severe offense, as we saw above in the section on, "The times of the required prayers." As for someone who delays such a prayer based on a valid excuse, he is not guilty of any wrongdoing.

In some cases the excuse or condition exempts the worshiper from prayer completely, while in others, it exempts him only temporarily. If someone misses a prayer due to a condition of the latter type, he must still make it up later once the condition which exempted him from prayer has passed.

Conditions which exempt one completely from prayer

The obligation to perform ritual prayer is dropped entirely for a woman who is menstruating or experiencing post-partum bleeding; hence, such a woman is not required to make up prayers which she missed while she was in either of these states. Similarly, the obligation to perform ritual prayer is dropped entirely for someone who is insane, someone who has lost consciousness, or an apostate if he returns to Islam, since he is considered to be like someone who was originally an unbeliever and who, therefore, was not held accountable for ritual prayer before his conversion. This is the ruling of the Malikis and the Hanafis; as for the Shafiis, they differ with respect to the apostate, whom they say is still held accountable for ritual prayer even after committing apostasy. As for the Hanafis, they differ with respect to someone who loses consciousness and the like. All details relating to such matters may be found in the footnote below.[382]

---

382. The obligation to perform ritual prayer is waived entirely for someone who has lost consciousness or who is insane given two conditions: (1) The fainting spell, coma, etc. or the insanity must last through more than five obligatory prayers. If they last through five or fewer prayers, and if the person regains consciousness or sanity following this, he must make up the prayers missed during this time. (2) The person must not have regained consciousness or lucidity at regular intervals during the overall period of unconsciousness or insanity—for example, either by not having regained consciousness or lucidity whatsoever, or by having become conscious or lucid at irregular intervals. If the person becomes lucid at a known time—during the morning, for example—this event marks an end to the period of unconsciousness or insanity and, as a result, he or she must make up the prayers missed.

If someone's mind is clouded due to his having taken an unlawful substance such as alcohol, for example, he must make up whatever prayers he missed while he was intoxicated; based on the best-attested view, the same ruling applies to someone whose mind was affected by a lawful substance such as an anesthetic used for the sake of medical treatment.

If a condition which exempts one from ritual prayer has its onset at the end of the time period for a given prayer when there is only enough time left for *takbīrat al-iḥrām*, one is not obliged to make up this prayer after the condition has passed. However, if such a condition passes when there is still enough time left in the time period for a given prayer to utter *takbīrat al-iḥrām*, it must be made up if it is an obligatory prayer.

If the blood flow of a woman who is menstruating or post-partum ceases and if this cessation lasts for the greater part of the time period specified for menstruation or post-partum bleeding, she must make up the obligatory prayer concerned if there is enough time left [in its designated time period] to utter *takbīrat al-iḥrām*. In this respect, this ruling is the same as that which applies to other conditions that exempt a worshiper from the obligation of ritual prayer. However, if the blood flow stops for less than half of the time period specified for menstruation or post-partum bleeding, she is not required to make up the prayers missed unless the time remaining is sufficient for her to perform major ablutions and to utter *takbīrat al-iḥrām*.

* * *

In addition to those already mentioned, the Malikis include intoxication produced by legal substances among the conditions which exempt one from the obligation to make up obligatory prayers which have been missed. For example, if someone were to drink some fermented milk which he did not expect to intoxicate him but which, in fact, did intoxicate him, he would not be required to make up the prayers he missed on account of this intoxication. If, on the other hand, someone is intoxicated by a forbidden substance, he will not be exempted from the necessity of making up prayers missed due to this intoxication, nor does the intoxication expunge the guilt resulting from having delayed ritual prayer.

According to the Malikis, such conditions may exist in three situations: (1) The condition lasts the entire time period for a given prayer, including both its 'elective' phase and 'imperative' phases, for example, by a fainting spell lasting from high noon until sundown, in which case the person concerned is exempted both from praying during this time and from having to make up the prayer missed after the fainting spell has passed. (2) The condition has its onset during the time period for a given prayer. If it begins when there is still enough time left for both prayers—the noon prayer and the mid-afternoon prayer, for example—the obligation to pray either prayer is waived. If, when the condition has its onset, there is enough time left to perform only the second prayer or a minimum of one *rak'ah* thereof including both its prostrations, the obligation to perform the second prayer is dropped while the obligation to perform the first remains with the result that one must make it up once the condition has passed. (The time which is deemed to suffice for the performance of both prayers is defined as enough time to perform five *rak'ahs* for a 'resident' and three *rak'ahs* for a traveler with respect to the noon and mid-afternoon prayers, as compared to four *rak'ahs* for both a 'resident' and a traveler with respect to the sundown and evening prayers. The reason for this is that the sundown prayer is estimated at three *rak'ahs* even when one is traveling since it is not a prayer that may be shortened, while the evening prayer is estimated at one *rak'ah* since one is considered to have validly begun this prayer if one completes only one *rak'ah* thereof before the time period for this prayer runs out.) If, when the condition has its onset, the time remaining is less than the periods just mentioned, this time is designated for the second prayer; hence, the condition is considered to have begun during the time period for the second prayer only such that the obligation to perform the second prayer is dropped, while the obligation to perform the first remains. (2) The condition passes at the end of the time period for a given prayer. In this case, the person concerned is exempted from those prayers whose time periods passed while the condition was still present. As for the prayer at the end of whose time period the condition passes, the ruling on it is that if, when the condition passes, the time remaining is sufficient to perform both prayers [either the noon and the mid-afternoon prayer or the sundown and evening prayers] after having established ritual purity, they must both be made up. If, when the condition passes, there is enough time remaining to perform only the second prayer or one *rak'ah* thereof after achieving ritual purity, only the second prayer must be made up, whereas the obligation to make up the first prayer is dropped since its designated time period ran out while the condition was still present.

From the foregoing it becomes clear that the achievement of ritual purity is taken into account when determining whether one will be able to perform a given prayer before its time period has run out when such a condition passes, whereas it is not taken into account when determining whether one will be exempted from a given prayer when such a condition initially begins. Thus if, when a condition of this sort passes, there remains enough time to perform one *rak'ah* of the prayer concerned after achieving ritual purity, it must be performed; otherwise, one is not obliged to perform it. If, when such a condition begins, there is enough time left to perform the prayer, if even without achieving ritual purity, the obligation to perform this prayer is dropped, and one is not obliged to make it up after the condition passes.

All such rulings apply only to those prayers which are subject to being combined, namely, the noon and mid-afternoon prayers and the sundown and evening prayers. With respect to the dawn prayer, the ruling is that if a condition of this sort passes when enough of the dawn prayer's 'imperative' phase remains for one to perform one *rak'ah* after achieving ritual purity, one is obliged to perform it; otherwise, one is not, since in order to perform this prayer before its time period runs out, one must complete one *rak'ah*, as we have seen. When performing this *rak'ah*, the worshiper should take care to recite the *Fātiḥah* at a moderate pace and to allow his limbs to remain still momentarily [when rising, bowing, prostrating, etc.]; however, he is not to perform Sunnah-based actions such as the recitation of an additional passage from the Qur'ān following the *Fātiḥah.*

If, when such a condition has its onset, there is enough time left in the time period for the dawn prayer to perform a single *rak'ah*, if even without achieving ritual purity, the obligation to perform it is dropped; otherwise, the worshiper must make the prayer up after the condition passes due to the fact that, legally speaking, its time period ran out before the onset of the condition.

* * *

The Hanbalis hold that if, when a condition of this type has its onset, sufficient time has passed since the beginning of the time period for the prayer concerned to utter *takbīrat al-iḥrām*, this prayer must be made up after the condition passes. Moreover, if, when the condition passes, there is enough time remaining in the time period concerned to utter *takbīrat al-iḥrām*, one must perform the prayer during whose time period the condition passed along with the prayer with which it may be combined, for example, the noon prayer along with the mid-afternoon prayer, or the sundown prayer with the evening prayer.

If a state of insanity lasts the entire time period for a given prayer, it is not necessary to make this prayer up; however, if the state of insanity has it onset long enough after the beginning of the time period for one to utter *takbīrat al-iḥrām*, the prayer must be made up. Moreover, if such a state of insanity passes long enough before the time period runs out to allow one to utter *takbīrat al-iḥrām*, the prayer during whose time period the insanity ended must be made up along with the prayer which preceded it if it is one which may be combined with it. The ruling that applies to someone who has a fit of insanity applies likewise to a young boy who reaches puberty when enough time remains in the time period concerned to utter *takbīrat al-iḥrām*.

The Hanbalis also hold that if someone's mind is clouded due to an intoxicant, be it forbidden or allowed, due to a legitimate type of medication or by some illness other than insanity, one must make up whatever prayers were missed as a result of it.

* * *

According to the Shafiis, if a state of insanity lasts the duration of the time period for a given prayer, the person concerned need not make up the prayer which was missed if his insanity did not lead him to commit any sort of transgression; otherwise, he must make it up. The same ruling applies to drunkenness and a loss of consciousness. If, on the other hand, a state of insanity or some comparable condition (such as menstruation) has its onset long enough after the beginning of the time period to allow for the quickest possible performance of the prayer along with achievement of the required ritual purity, the prayer must be made up. If, when the condition passes, there remains enough time to utter *takbīrat al-iḥrām*, the prayer must be made up along with the prayer that preceded it if it could validly be combined with it, such as the noon prayer with the mid-afternoon prayer. In order for this ruling to apply, however, the condition must remain absent continuously for long enough to achieve ritual purity and perform the two prayers, in addition to the time required for the prayer performed and the achievement of its requisite ritual purity [what the author means by 'the prayer performed' in addition to the other two prayers mentioned isn't clear – t.n.]. This ruling applies if ritual purity is attained by means of regular ritual ablutions (*wuḍū'*). If it is attained through sand ablutions (*tayammum*), the Shafiis stipulate that the period of time mentioned here must be long enough for one to achieve ritual purity twice and to perform prayer twice. If it is only long enough for a single ritual purification and a single prayer, one is not required to perform the preceding prayer. The Shafiis also hold that if someone commits apostasy, he is not exempted from making up the prayers he missed during his time as an apostate; rather, if he returns to Islam, he must make up the prayers he failed to perform while an apostate.

The circumstances which make it permissible to delay a prayer beyond its usual time

As for the circumstances which make it permissible to delay a prayer past its designated time period, some of these were discussed above in the section on combining prayers. Other such circumstances include being asleep, forgetting, and being unaware that the time for the prayer concerned has begun; this ruling applies even if this is a result of negligence. However, the Shafiis disagree with this ruling.[383]

Making up missed prayers, and the ruling on this

Making up a required ritual prayer one has missed is obligatory as soon as one realizes it was missed, whether it was missed due to a condition which does not exempt one from the obligation to make up the prayer, or without any excuse whatsoever. This is the ruling of the Malikis, the Hanbalis and the Hanafis; for the Shafiis' ruling, see below.[384]

It is not permissible to delay making up a prayer which was missed without a valid excuse, such as eating, sleeping and activities which are required to make one's living or to gain knowledge or learning for which there is a material necessity. Moreover, the guilt resulting from delaying a prayer is not erased by merely making it up; rather, it must be accompanied by repentance as well. Nor is the obligation to pray lifted by repentance alone; rather, one must actually make up the prayer, since one of the conditions for the validity of repentance is that one desist from wrongdoing, and the person who repents of having delayed prayer without making the prayer up has not actually desisted from his wrongdoing.

---

383. According to the Shafiis, forgetting is an excuse sufficient to remove the guilt resulting from delaying prayer unless it results from negligence. Hence, if someone forgets to perform a given prayer because he was busy playing backgammon or checkers, for example, he will not be excused on account of having forgotten; rather, he will be guilty of wrongdoing for having delayed it past its designated time period.

384. The Shafiis rule that if the delay occurs without a valid excuse, one must make up the prayer immediately, whereas if it occurs with a valid excuse, it must still be made up, but not necessarily right away. Situations in which it is not necessary that one make up a prayer immediately are the following: (1) If one remembers the prayer which was missed while the Friday sermon is being delivered. In this case, the worshiper must delay making up the prayer until he has performed the Friday congregational prayer. (2) If the time period for the current prayer is insufficient for one to make up the prayer which was missed without an excuse and, in addition, to complete one *rak'ah* of the current prayer. In this case, one must first perform the prayer at hand lest its time period run out. (3) If one remembers the prayer he missed after beginning to perform the current prayer. In this case, one should first complete the prayer he has begun, whether there would have been time to make up the missed prayer first or not.

It is inconsistent with making up missed prayers immediately to occupy oneself with the performance of voluntary prayers; for the various schools' ruling on this point, see below.[385]

385. According to the Hanafis, occupying oneself with the performance of voluntary prayers is not inconsistent with the immediate making up of prayers which have been missed. However, they hold that it is preferable to occupy oneself with making up missed prayers and to omit all voluntary prayers except for those which are associated with the five daily required prayers, the forenoon prayer, the prayer of praise, the mosque greeting, the four *rak'ahs* performed prior to the noon prayer and the six *rak'ahs* performed after the sundown prayer.

* * *

According to the Malikis, someone who has a missed prayer to make up is not permitted to perform any voluntary prayers with the exception of the two *rak'ahs* preceding the dawn prayer, the *shaf'*, the *witr*, and Sunnah-based prayers such as the holiday prayer. If someone performs a voluntary prayer other than these, such as the *tarāwīḥ*, he will be rewarded insofar as prayer, in and of itself, is an act of obedience; however, he will be guilty of wrongdoing due to his having delayed making up a missed prayer. The Malikis nevertheless offer concessions in connection with minor voluntary prayers such as the mosque greeting and the Sunnah-based *rak'ahs* associated with each of the five required prayers.

* * *

According to the Shafiis, if someone has missed prayers he is obliged to make up immediately (those prayers which must be made up immediately have been mentioned above), he is forbidden to occupy himself with any type of voluntary prayers, be they the Sunnah-based *rak'ahs* associated with the five daily required prayers or other voluntary prayers, until he has made up all prayers missed.

* * *

According to the Hanbalis, someone who has missed prayers to make up is not permitted to perform voluntary prayers which are not associated with any particular time or situation, and if he performs such a prayer, it will have no validity. As for voluntary prayers which are tied to particular times or situations, such as the Sunnah-based *rak'ahs* associated with each of the five daily prayers and the *witr*, they may be performed even when one has missed prayers to make up; however, it is preferable to omit them if many prayers have been missed. An exception to this ruling is made for the two Sunnah-based *rak'ahs* that precede the dawn prayer and which, due to their importance and the Lawgiver's stress upon them, one is required to perform even if one has missed many prayers.

How a missed prayer is made up

If someone misses a prayer, he should make it up in the same form in which it was missed. Hence, if someone misses a four-*rak'ah* prayer while traveling a distance sufficient to warrant the shortening of prayers, he should make it up as a two-*rak'ah* prayer even if, when he makes it up, he is not traveling anymore. This ruling is agreed upon by the Hanafis and the Malikis; for the views of the Shafiis and the Hanbalis, see below.[386] Conversely, if someone is 'resident' in a given place when he misses a four-*rak'ah* prayer, he should make it up as a four-*rak'ah* prayer even if, when he makes it up, he is traveling a distance which would warrant the shortening of prayers. By the same token, if someone misses a prayer in which recitation is to be done silently, such as the noon prayer, for example, he should recite silently when making it up even if he makes it up at night; and if someone misses a prayer in which recitation is to be done aloud, such as the sundown prayer, for example, he should recite aloud when making it up even if he makes it up during the day. This ruling is agreed upon by the Hanafis and the Malikis; the views of the Shafiis and the Hanbalis may be seen below.[387]

---

386. The Hanbalis and the Shafiis rule that if someone misses a four-*rak'ah* prayer while traveling a distance that would warrant the shortening of prayers, he should make it up as a two-*rak'ah* prayer if he is still traveling; however, if he is no longer on a journey, he should make it up as a four-*rak'ah* prayer, since the ideal is to perform prayers to completion. Hence, one should return to the ideal when resident in one place.

387. According to the Shafiis, the way in which one does the recitation depends on the time at which one makes up the prayer. Hence, if one makes up a missed noon prayer [in which the recitation would normally be done silently] at night, one should do the recitation aloud, while if someone makes up a missed sundown prayer [in which the recitation would normally be done aloud] during the day, he should do the recitation silently.

* * *

As for the Hanbalis, they hold that if one is making up the prayer during the day, he should do the recitation silently regardless of whether the prayer missed was one in which the recitation is to be done silently or aloud, and regardless of whether the worshiper is an imam or praying alone.

If one is making up the prayer at night, he should do the recitation aloud if the prayer missed was one in which the recitation is to be done aloud and if the worshiper is an imam, due to the consistency between the prayer missed and the time of day during which it is being made up; however, if the prayer missed was one in which recitation is to be done silently, one should make it up silently no matter what time of day it is being made up. Lastly, if the prayer missed was one in which the recitation is to be done aloud and one is praying alone, it should be made up with silent recitation.

Maintaining the order of missed prayers when making them up

It is necessary to observe the correct order among the prayers one is making up. Hence, one must make up the dawn prayer before the noon prayer, the noon prayer before the mid-afternoon prayer, and so on. It is also necessary to observe the correct order between the prayers one has missed and the current prayer, and between the two prayers one is obliged to perform at the present time, such as two prayers which are being combined during a single time period. For the various schools' rulings on these matters, see below.[388]

---

388. According to the Hanafis, the order among the prayers one has missed, as well as between the prayers missed and the current prayer, must be maintained. Hence, it is not permissible to perform the current prayer before making up prayers missed earlier, nor to make up a missed noon prayer before making up a missed dawn prayer. Similarly, one must maintain the proper order between the required prayers and the *witr*; hence, it is not permissible to perform the dawn prayer before making up the previous *witr* if it was missed, nor to perform the *witr* before making up the evening prayer if it was missed. However, maintenance of the order among prayers missed is only required when the number of prayers missed is five or fewer, not including the *witr*. Hence, if someone has missed five or fewer prayers and wishes to make them up, he must make them up in their original order; performing the dawn prayer before the noon prayer, the noon prayer before the mid-afternoon prayer, and so on. If such a person performs the noon prayer before the dawn prayer, the noon prayer will be invalidated, and he must repeat it after making up the dawn prayer that he missed. The same applies if one performs the mid-afternoon prayer before the noon prayer, and so on. Similarly, if someone has five or fewer prayers to make up and wishes to make them up together with the current prayer, he must perform them in order before performing the current prayer unless the time remaining in the time period for the current prayer is about to run out [in which case the current prayer should be performed first]. However, if the number of prayers one has missed comes to six or more in addition to the *witr*, one is no longer required to make them up in their original order. If someone misses a single prayer, then remembers this while performing the prayer immediately after it, and if he completes the second prayer without making up the first, the obligatory character of the second prayer will be provisionally cancelled out. If this same person performs a third prayer after this, the third prayer will be invalidated as well, and likewise the fourth and the fifth. If the time period for the fifth prayer runs out before the person concerned has made up the missed prayer referred to here, all the prayers he has performed since then will become valid again, and all he has to make up is the original prayer he missed. The reason for this is that these prayers have now become like missed prayers the order of which one is no longer obliged to observe, since the observation of the proper order between missed prayers and the prayer due at the present time ceases to be required not only when too many prayers have been missed but, in addition, when too many prayers have been performed during the time intervening.

If, on the other hand, the worshiper makes up the prayer missed before the end of the time period for the fifth required prayer subsequent to it, all the required prayers he has performed are turned, legally speaking, into mere voluntary prayers, as a result of which he must make them up. If, for example, someone misses the dawn prayer, after which he performs the noon prayer even though he remembers that he missed the dawn prayer, the noon prayer will be provisionally invalidated as a required prayer. If, after this, he performs the mid-afternoon prayer without having yet made up the dawn prayer, the mid-afternoon prayer is likewise provisionally invalidated; this continues to apply until the time period for the dawn prayer of the next day has run out. If the person makes up the missed dawn prayer from the previous day before this, the obligatory nature of all the prayers he has performed during this time will be invalidated and they will be deemed merely voluntary, as a result of which he must make them up. Otherwise, these prayers will be valid as obligatory prayers, and all the person is required to do is to make up the dawn prayer he missed the previous day.

If, while performing a prayer on time, someone remembers one or more prayers he missed, the prayer he is performing turns from an obligatory prayer into a voluntary prayer; as a result, he should complete the prayer in just two *rak'ahs*, then make up the prayers he missed, taking care to maintain both the proper order among the missed prayers and between the missed prayers and the prayer he is still due to perform. If someone remembers missing the dawn prayer during the Friday congregational prayer, the ruling is that if he has no reason to fear that the time period for the Friday prayer will run out, he should make up the missed prayer first, then perform the current prayer, either as the Friday congregational prayer or as a regular noon prayer. If, however, he has reason to fear that the time period for the Friday prayer will run out, he should complete the Friday prayer first, then make up the missed dawn prayer.

The obligation to maintain the original order among prayers is thus waived in the following situations: (1) When the number of prayers missed is six or more, not counting the *witr*. (2) When there is insufficient time left in the time period for the current prayer to perform both the current prayer and the prayer(s) missed. (3) When someone has not yet remembered the prayer(s) missed while performing the current prayer. The reason for this is that when a prayer has been missed out of forgetfulness, it has, in essence, no 'time' to speak of; however, it cannot be considered to take priority over the current prayer. As the Prophet said, "My people have been exempted from responsibility for unintentional error, forgetfulness, and that which they have been forced to do against their wills."

* * *

According to the Malikis, one must maintain the original order among missed prayers whether they are numerous or few, given two conditions: (1) The person concerned must remember the previous prayer(s) missed. (2) He must be capable of maintaining the prayers' proper order. In other words, he must not be in a situation in which he is obliged not to maintain this order. This obligation is unconditional; hence, if one violates it, the prayer one prayed improperly before another prayer that should have preceded it remains valid and one need not repeat it due to the fact that its time period is considered to have run out by the mere fact of its having been performed; however, the person who performed the prayer "out of place" will be guilty of wrongdoing.

Given the two aforementioned conditions, one must also preserve the proper order between prayers one has missed (when they number five or fewer) and the current prayer by making them up before performing the current prayer. If the time period for the current prayer is about to run out and one deliberately performs the current prayer before making up the prayers he has missed, the prayer will be valid but he will be guilty of wrongdoing, and it is recommended that he repeat it after making up the prayers he missed if time remains (including even its 'imperative' phase, an explanation of which is found in the section above on "The times of the required prayers"). If, on the other hand, one performs the current prayer first because he has forgotten that he has other prayers to make up, and if he does not remember this until after he has concluded the current prayer, the prayer will be valid and he will be guilty of no wrongdoing; however, it is recommended that he repeat the current prayer. If one remembers missing five or fewer prayers while performing the current prayer, and if one remembers them before completing the first *rak'ah* thereof, one must cut off the current prayer and go back to make up the prayers missed first regardless of whether he is an imam or praying alone, while those being led by him in prayer must likewise cut off their prayer in deference to him as their imam. In the case of someone who is being led in prayer, the ruling is that if, while performing the current prayer, he remembers that he has five or fewer prayers to make up, he should refrain from cutting off his prayer out of deference for his imam; however, it is recommended that he repeat the prayer after making up the prayers he missed if sufficient time remains (including even the 'imperative' phase) of the time period for the current prayer. If, after completing a *rak'ah* of the current prayer with both of its prostrations, one remembers that he has missed earlier prayers, it is recommended that he add one more *rak'ah* to this and make the prayer a voluntary one, then utter the final greeting of peace and go back to make up the prayers he has missed. If one only remembers that he has missed prayers after he has performed two *rak'ahs* of a two-*rak'ah* or a three-*rak'ah* prayer, or after he has performed three *rak'ahs* of a four-*rak'ah* prayer, he should complete the prayer he is performing, then make up the prayers he missed, then repeat the current prayer (though the latter is not required, but only recommended) if sufficient time remains in this prayer's designated time period.

If, while performing a voluntary prayer, one remembers having missed five or fewer prayers, he should complete the voluntary prayer he is performing. However, if he has reason to fear that the time period for the current obligatory prayer will run out (assuming he has not performed it yet) and if he has not yet completed one *rak'ah* of the voluntary prayer, he should cut it off. If the number of prayers missed comes to more than five, it is not necessary to make them up before performing the current prayer; rather, it is recommended that one first perform the current prayer [even] if sufficient time remains in its designated time period [both to perform the current prayer and to make up the prayers missed], whereas if little time remains, it is obligatory to perform the current prayer first.

It is required, given certain conditions, that one maintain the proper order between the two current prayers which are subject to being combined (namely, the noon and the mid-afternoon prayers, and the sundown and evening prayers, respectively) regardless of whether they are actually being combined or not. Thus, for example, one must perform the noon prayer before the mid-afternoon prayer, and the sundown prayer before the evening prayer. If this order is violated, the prayer performed earlier than it should have been will be invalidated unless the person concerned was forced to perform it earlier or unless he did so out of forgetfulness; in this latter case, the prayer will remain valid if the person does not remember having missed the first prayer until after he has completed the second. However, it is recommended that he repeat it after performing the first prayer if sufficient time remains (even if it falls within the 'imperative' phrase of the time period). If, on the other hand, the worshiper remembers having missed the first prayer while performing the second, the ruling is the same as that which applies (based on the officially recognized view) when someone remembers having missed fewer than five prayers while performing the current prayer; in other words, if the worshiper has [not] confirmed the first *rak'ah* of the current prayer, he should cancel his intention to perform the obligatory prayer he is performing. Otherwise, it is recommended that he add another *rak'ah* to this one and make the prayer into a voluntary prayer; further details in this regard are mentioned above.

* * *

According to the Hanbalis, maintaining the original order among prayers missed is obligatory in and of itself regardless of whether they are many or few. If a worshiper violates this order, as, for example, by making up a missed mid-afternoon prayer before making up a missed noon prayer, the prayer which was improperly performed before the other [in this case, the mid-afternoon prayer] will be invalidated if, when praying the second prayer, the worshiper realizes that he has not yet performed the prayer before it. If, on the other hand, the worshiper fails to recall that he has not yet performed the earlier prayer as he performs the later one, and if he only realizes this after finishing the later prayer, the later prayer will be valid.

It is likewise necessary to preserve the original order between missed prayers and the current prayer unless there is reason to fear that the time period for the current prayer will run out, even if this is only the 'elective' phase; in such a case, one must first perform the current prayer, then make up the prayers one has missed and if one does so, the current prayer will be valid. Similarly, the current prayer will be valid even though the worshiper performs it before making up missed prayers if he has forgotten that he has prayers to make up and, as a consequence, does not realize he has prayers to make up until after completing the current prayer.

It is also necessary to preserve the original order between two prayers which could be combined, provided that the person realizes that he has not yet performed the first of the two prayers. If, for example, someone is traveling and wishes to combine the noon and mid-afternoon prayers during the time period for the mid-afternoon prayer, he must perform the noon prayer before the mid-afternoon prayer. If he violates this order with the realization that he is doing so, or if he remembers not having performed the noon prayer yet while performing the mid-afternoon prayer, his mid-afternoon prayer will be invalidated. If, on the other hand, he does not realize until after completing the mid-afternoon prayer that he has not yet performed the noon prayer, the mid-afternoon prayer will be valid.

Lastly, the obligation to preserve the original order among prayers is not waived due to ignorance of this obligation or due to one's fear of missing the opportunity to pray with a group. Rather, if someone misses the dawn prayer [the text reads "and the mid-afternoon prayer" – t.n.], then performs the noon prayer before making up the dawn prayer out of ignorance of the necessity of maintaining their proper order, and if he then performs the mid-afternoon prayer during its designated time period, his mid-afternoon prayer will be valid due to the fact that when he performed it, he was not aware of other prayers he needed to make up. At the same time, however, he will be under obligation to repeat the noon prayer.

* * *

According to the Shafiis, maintaining the original order among prayers that have been missed is, in and of itself, an emulation of the Sunnah whether they are many or few. If someone reverses their order, the prayer that was improperly performed before another prayer that should have preceded it will remain valid, but the worshiper concerned will not have emulated the Sunnah. Hence, it is preferable to repeat this prayer. If someone performs the mid-afternoon prayer before the noon prayer, or performs Thursday's noon prayer before Wednesday's noon prayer, his prayer will likewise be valid. As for maintaining the proper order between missed prayers and the current prayer, this is an emulation of the Sunnah given the following two conditions: (1) that there not be any reason to fear that the time period for the current prayer will run out (i.e., that one will not be able to perform its first *rak'ah* during the designated time period), and (2) that the person concerned remember the prayers he has missed before commencing the current prayer. If he does not remember them until after he has begun to perform the current prayer, he should complete the current prayer rather than interrupting it in order to make up the prayers he has missed even if sufficient time to do so remains in the time period for the current prayer. If, on the other hand, the worshiper begins making up a missed prayer before commencing the current prayer, thinking that there is enough time remaining both to make up what he has missed and to perform the current prayer, and if it then becomes apparent that if he completes the prayer he is making up, the time period for the current prayer will run out, he must either cut off the prayer or complete it in two *rak'ahs* only, thereby turning it into voluntary prayer, then utter the final greeting of peace in order to perform the current prayer, which is preferable.

Lastly, the Shafiis hold that maintenance of the proper order between two current prayers which are being combined during the time period for the earlier prayer is obligatory, whereas if they are being combined during the time period for the later prayer, it is simply an emulation of the Sunnah.

If someone who is legally accountable for his actions has missed prayers but is uncertain how many prayers he has missed

If someone has missed a number of prayers but is uncertain exactly how many, he must continue to make up prayers until he feels completely certain that he has no more "prayer debts outstanding", as it were. This is the ruling of the Shafiis and the Hanbalis. As for the Malikis and the Hanafis, they hold that it is sufficient for the person to be reasonably certain that he has made up all prayers missed. According to the Shafiis, the Malikis and the Hanbalis, it is not necessary, when making up prayers in such a situation, to specify the exact day for which one is making up the prayer; rather, it is sufficient to specify that it is the noon prayer, the mid-afternoon prayer, etc.; as for the Hanafis, they hold that it is necessary to specify that one intends, for example, to make up the first noon prayer whose time period came and went without one's praying it, and so on, or to make up the last noon prayer which he missed in this way, and so forth.

Whether a missed prayer may be made up at a time when voluntary prayers are forbidden

Missed prayers may be made up at any time, including those times when it is forbidden to perform voluntary prayers. For each school's particular ruling on this point, see below.[389]

---

389. According to the Hanafis, it is permissible to make up missed prayers at all but the following times: (1) when the sun is rising, (2) when the sun is at its zenith (high noon), and (3) when the sun is setting. Apart from these three times, missed prayers may be made up at any time, including the time between the mid-afternoon prayer and the sundown prayer.

* * *

The Malikis hold that if one is certain, or has good reason to believe, that he has missed a prayer, he may make it up even during those times when the performance of voluntary prayers is disallowed. Hence, one may make up a missed prayer when the sun is rising or setting, as well as at other times when one is forbidden to perform voluntary prayers. If, on the other hand, one is uncertain whether he has a prayer to make up or not, he should make it up during times other than those at which it is forbidden to perform voluntary prayers. Specifically, making up prayers one is not certain to have missed during times when it is forbidden to perform voluntary prayers is forbidden, while making them up during times when voluntary prayers are undesirable is likewise undesirable.

* * *

According to the Shafiis, it is permissible to make up missed prayers during all times at which it would be forbidden to perform voluntary prayers unless one intends to make them up at these times in particular, in which case it is not permitted, nor will the made-up prayers be valid. It is likewise not permissible to make up missed prayers when the sermon for the Friday congregational prayer is being delivered; from the moment when the orator sits down on the pulpit and until both

How an ill person is to pray

If someone is ill and is unable to perform the required ritual prayers from a standing position, he is to pray from a sitting position. If he is able to stand but finds that standing up causes him to suffer from some other illness, increases symptoms which he already suffers, or delays his recovery, he may pray from a sitting position. If, for example, someone suffers from urinary incontinence and knows that if he prays from a standing position he will be incontinent whereas if he prays from a sitting position he will maintain his ritual purity, he should likewise pray from a sitting position. Similarly, if someone who is otherwise in good health knows from experience that if he prays from a standing position he will faint or get dizzy, he is to pray from a sitting position. Moreover, in all the cases mentioned here, the worshiper must complete the prayer with bows and prostrations.

If a worshiper is unable to stand on his own but can do so by supporting himself on a wall, a cane, etc., he must stand while leaning on something, and he may not pray from a sitting position. This is the view of the Hanafis and the Hanbalis; for the views of the Malikis and the Shafiis, see below.[390]

---

sermons, including their associated parts, are concluded, no compensatory prayer will have any validity.

* * *

As for the Hanbalis, they rule that it is permissible to make up missed prayers during all times when voluntary prayers are forbidden, without going into further detail.

390. According to the Malikis, someone who is able to stand while leaning on something for support is not required to stand; rather, he may remain seated if he is able to sit up without leaning on anything. However, if he is unable to sit up without support, he must stand up while leaning on something.

* * *

According to the Shafiis, if a worshiper is able to stand up while leaning for support on another person, he must stand up if he only needs such a person's support when rising at the beginning of each *rak'ah*. However, if he requires the other person's support throughout the entire time he remains standing, he is not required to stand and may pray from a sitting position instead. Moreover, if the person is able to stand by leaning on a cane, a wall, etc., he must stand even if he requires this support throughout the entire time he is standing.

If someone is able to stand part of the time—even if only long enough to utter *takbīrat al-iḥrām*—he must stand for as long as he is able, then continue the prayer from a sitting position. When praying from a sitting position, one is to sit up without leaning on anything for support if one is able to do so; if, however, one is only able to sit up with support, one must sit up while leaning on something rather than lying on one's side. If, however, one is unable to sit up even with support, one may pray either lying on one side's or on one's back.[391]

The posture to be adopted by someone who is praying from a sitting position

The Malikis and the Hanbalis hold that if someone is praying from a sitting position due to his inability to stand, it is recommended that he sit cross-legged, although the Hanafis and the Shafiis differ with them on this point. Each of the four schools offers its own detailed ruling on this matter.[392]

---

391. According to the Malikis, if someone is unable to sit up even with support, he is to lie on his right side and pray with gestures, facing the *qiblah*. If he is not able to do this, he is to lie down on his left side with his face to the *qiblah*. If he is unable to do this, he is to lie on his back with his feet toward the *qiblah*. The order of priority among these three positions is only recommended; hence, if someone lies on his left side even though he would have been able to lie on his right side, or if he lies on his back even though he would have been able to lie on either his right or his left side, his prayer will still be valid even though he will not have done what is recommended. If someone is unable to lie on his back, he is to lie on his stomach with his head toward the *qiblah*, and to pray by gesturing with his head. However, if someone lies on his stomach when he would have been able to lie on his back, his prayer will be invalid, because the order of priority between these two positions is obligatory.

* * *

According to the Hanafis, it is preferable to pray while lying on one's back and with one's feet toward the *qiblah*, and to keep one's knees straight and one's head slightly raised so that one's face will be toward the *qiblah*. It is acceptable to pray on one's right side or on one's left, although the right side is preferable. All of this applies, of course, if one is able to do it; otherwise, one is to do whatever he is capable of.

* * *

According to the Hanbalis, if someone is unable to sit even by leaning on something for support, one is to pray on his side with his face to the *qiblah*, with the right side being preferable to the left. It is permissible, albeit not desirable, to pray on one's back with one's feet toward the *qiblah* even when one would have been able to pray on one's right side. If one is not able to pray on his side, one may pray on one's back with his feet toward the *qiblah*.

* * *

The Shafiis hold that if someone is unable to sit up at all, he is to pray while lying on his side with his face and his chest toward the *qiblah*. It is an emulation of the Sunnah to lie on one's right side rather than one's left, but if one is not able to lie on his right side, he may lie on his left, bowing and prostrating from a reclining position if he is able to do so. Otherwise, he is to make gestures indicating bows and prostrations. If the worshiper is unable to lie on his side, he is to pray while lying on his back and with the soles of his feet toward the *qiblah*. When lying on one's back, one is to raise one's head with a pillow or some other object in order that one's face may be directed toward the *qiblah*, then gesture with one's head for the bows and prostrations. In this case, the gestures for the prostrations should be more pronounced than the gestures for the bows if one is able to make them thus; otherwise, it is not required. If someone is unable to gesture with his head, he may gesture with his eyelids, in which case it is not required that the gestures for the prostrations be more pronounced than the gestures for the bows. Moreover, if one is unable to do any of this, he may perform the pillars of the prayer in his heart.

392. According to the Malikis, it is recommended that such a person sit cross-legged except when he is prostrating, seated between the two prostrations, and seated to utter the testimony. In these latter three situations, he should sit in the manner described above in the section dealing with recommended and Sunnah-based practices associated with ritual prayer.

* * *

According to the Hanafis, one may sit however he wishes while doing Qur'anic recitation and bowing, although it is preferable to sit as one does while uttering the testimony. While prostrating and uttering the testimony, however, one should sit in the manner described above provided that this causes no discomfort or hardship; otherwise, one may choose whichever posture is easier in all these cases.

* * *

According to the Shafiis, someone praying from a sitting position emulates the Sunnah by sitting with his thighs directly over his calves and the tops of his feet to the floor except in two situations: (1) when he is prostrating, in which case he should place the undersides of his toes on the floor, and (2) when he is sitting down to perform the final testimony, in which case he should place his left hip on the floor while his right hip rests on top of his left leg and foot.

If the person praying is unable to bow and prostrate

If a worshiper is unable to bow and prostrate or is able to perform only one of these actions, he should use gestures in place of that which he is unable to perform. Thus, if he is able to stand up and to prostrate but is unable to bow, he must stand up for *takbīrat al-iḥrām* and the Qur'anic recitation, gesture in place of the bow, then prostrate. If someone is able to stand up but is unable to bow and prostrate, he should utter the opening *Allāhu akbar* and perform the Qur'anic recitation while standing, then gesture for the bow from a standing position and for the prostration from a sitting position; if such a person gestures for the prostration from a standing position or for the bow from a sitting position, his prayer will be invalid according to all of the schools except the Hanafis, whose ruling is found below.[393] If the person is unable to stand, he is to gesture for both the bow and the prostration from a sitting position; in such a case, one's gesture for the prostration must be lower than that for the bow. If the worshiper is able to stand but is unable to sit down, bow or prostrate, he should gesture for both the bow and the prostration from a standing position.

According to the Shafiis, the Malikis and the Hanbalis, the obligation to stand is not waived when one is unable to prostrate; for the view of the Hanafis, see below.[394] When this is the case, one's gestures for prostrations should be lower than one's gestures for bows. If, on the other hand, someone is unable to perform any part of the ritual prayer except by a movement of his eyes or by pondering its actions in his heart, he must do so, and this obligation remains as long as he is mentally alert. Hence, the Shafiis, the Hanbalis and the Malikis hold that if one is able to gesture with his eye, he must do so rather than merely 'conjuring' the actions involved in prayer; for the Hanafis' view, see below.[395]

---

393. According to the Hanafis, gesturing for both the bow and the prostration is valid whether it is done from a standing position or a sitting position; however, gesturing while one is sitting is preferable.

394. The Hanafis hold that if someone is unable to prostrate, whether he is also unable to bow or not, he is, properly speaking, exempted from the obligation to stand up. Instead, he is to pray from a sitting position, gesturing from this position for both bows and prostrations, which is considered preferable to gesturing from a standing position, as we have seen.

395. According to the Hanafis, if someone is only able to gesture with his eye, his eyebrow, or his heart, the obligation to pray is waived, since they do not consider prayer valid if performed in any of these ways regardless of whether the person concerned is in full possession of his mental faculties or not. Nor is such a person required to make up prayers missed while he was ill to this degree if they number more than five; if they number five or fewer, however, they must be made up.

It is undesirable for someone who is required to pray with gestures to place something raised in front of him to prostrate on; if he does so, he will be considered to be gesturing and it will not be permissible for someone who is in a stronger condition than he is to follow him in prayer. This is the view of the Malikis, the Hanbalis and the Hanafis; for the Shafiis' view, see below.[396]

Lastly, if someone recovers from an illness while performing ritual prayer, he should build on what he had already done before his recovery and complete the prayer in the manner in which he is able. This ruling is agreed upon by the Shafiis, the Malikis, and the Hanbalis; for the Hanafis' view, see below.[397]

---

396. According to the Shafiis, it is permissible for someone to be followed in prayer by someone who is in a stronger condition than he is if the prayer of the person being followed is valid in the sense that it exempts him from having to repeat the prayer later.

397. The Hanafis hold that if a worshiper is unable to stand and is praying from a sitting position with both bows and prostrations, and if, while he is praying, he regains the ability to stand, he should simply build on what he has already done and finish the prayer from a standing position even if he does not actually bow or prostrate. If someone who has been praying from a sitting position and gesturing in the place of bows and prostrations becomes able to bow and prostrate again during his prayer, and if this occurs after he has gestured for one entire *rak'ah*, he should complete the prayer by building on what he has already done; otherwise, he should cut off the prayer and start again. The worshiper must also begin a new prayer if, after commencing a prayer while lying on his side and gesturing in place of the bows and prostrations, he becomes able to sit up.

On Funerals

What is to be done with someone who is dying

It is an emulation of the Sunnah for someone who is about to die to be placed on his right side and turned so that he is facing the *qiblah* if this does not cause hardship; otherwise, he may be placed on his back with his legs toward the *qiblah* and with his head raised somewhat so that his face is toward the *qiblah* as well. According to the Malikis, however, this practice is only recommended rather than being an emulation of the Sunnah.

It is desirable for someone who is dying to have the testimony of faith dictated to him in his presence so that he can utter it himself. This is based on the prophetic hadith according to which he said, "Instruct those among you who are approaching death in the saying *lā ilāha illā Allāh*, since there is no Muslim who says this at death but that he is rescued thereby from the Fire." This hadith was narrated by Abū Ḥafṣ Ibn Shāhīn in his section on 'Funerals' on the authority of Ibn 'Umar, with a chain of transmission that is traceable back to the Prophet. Another version of the same hadith, narrated by Muslim on the authority of Abū Hurayrah, reads, "Instruct those among you who are approaching death in the words *lā ilāha illā Allāh*." One is not to tell the dying person, "Say…", since this would give him the opportunity to refuse, in which case he would be thought ill of. Nor should one press the dying person as he utters these words for fear that he might become uneasy or annoyed unless, after saying them, he utters other speech that has nothing to do with the testimony. In the latter case, the testimony should be dictated to the person again in order that it might be the last speech he utters before departing from this world.

It is also desirable to dictate the words of the testimony after the deceased person has been buried and the soil has been arranged over his grave. In this situation, the dictation involves addressing the deceased person with the words, "O so-and-so, son of so-and-so (if his identity is known; otherwise one is to say, "O so-and-so, son of Eve, may be peace be upon her")! Remember the covenant on the basis of which you departed from the world, i.e., the testimony that there is no god but God and that Muḥammad is God's Messenger, that Paradise is a reality, that the Hell-fire is a reality, that the Resurrection is a reality, that the Hour is coming without a doubt, that God will raise the dead from their graves, and that you have contented yourself with God as your Lord, with Islam as your religion, with Muḥammad as your prophet, with the Qur'ān as your guide, with the Ka'bah as your *qiblah*, and with the believers as your brothers and sisters." This dictation is desirable according to the Shafiis and the Hanbalis; for the views of the Malikis and the Hanafis, see below.[398]

---

398. According to the Hanafis, dictation following burial is neither forbidden nor commanded, although the apparent sense of what has been narrated is that it is forbidden.

* * *

According to the Malikis, dictation during and following burial is undesirable; however, it is desirable while the person is dying, as has been mentioned.

It is recommended when someone is dying that the most virtuous of his friends and family be brought in to see him and that much supplication be made for him and for those present. It is also recommended that women who are menstruating or experiencing post-partum bleeding, those who are in a state of major ritual impurity, and anything which is displeasing to the angels—such as instruments of diversion[399]—be kept away from the dying person, that perfume be brought in, and that Surah 36 of the Qur'ān (Yā Sīn, "O Thou Human Being") be recited in his presence based on the hadith narrated by Abū Dāwūd which reads, "There is no ill person in whose presence 'Yā Sīn' is recited but that he will die with his thirst quenched, enter his grave with his thirst quenched, and be gathered on the Day of Resurrection with his thirst quenched." This ruling is agreed upon by the Shafiis, the Hanbalis and the Hanafis; for the Malikis' ruling, see below.[400] Such recitation should be done silently so as not to disturb the dying person; after the person has died, however, all four schools agree that no recitation should be done at all.

It is recommended that someone who is dying should have a positive conception of God Almighty based on the words of the Prophet, "Let no one among you die without having a positive conception of God, by believing that He will show him mercy and pardon him." It is narrated by Muslim and al-Bukhārī that God Almighty said, "I am as My servant believes Me to be." Hence, it is also recommended that those who are present with someone who is dying should encourage him to have a positive conception of God.

It is an emulation of the Sunnah to close the eyes of the deceased and for the person closing his or her eyes to say, "In the name of God, and in accordance with the religion of His Messenger. O God, forgive him, grant him an exalted station among those who are guided aright, and cause him to be succeeded by [the righteous of] those who remain. Forgive both him and us, O Sustainer of the worlds. Clear a space for him in his grave [i.e., let it be a place of tranquility and comfort for him] and grant him light therein." This saying was narrated on the authority of the Prophet, who spoke these words when he closed the eyes of Abū Salamah. This ruling is agreed upon by the Shafiis, the Hanbalis and the Hanafis; as for the Malikis, they hold that closing the deceased's eyes is only recommended rather than being an emulation of the Sunnah, and that the supplication which is uttered when doing

---

399. This seems to refer to musical instruments [t.n.].

400. The Malikis favor the view that it is undesirable to recite anything from the Qur'ān in the presence of someone who is dying because this was not the practice of the righteous ancestors. However, some of them say that it is desirable to recite "Yā Sīn" in such a person's presence.

* * *

According to the Hanafis, it is undesirable to recite aloud from the Qur'ān in the presence of the deceased before major ablutions have been performed on him or her if the reciter is near the body; however, if he is at a distance, there is no undesirability attached to the practice. Nor is it undesirable to recite the Qur'ān near the deceased if his/her entire body is covered by a ritually pure garment.

so (namely, "In the name of God and in accordance with the religion of His Messenger," etc....) is not required.[401]

What is to be done with the deceased before he or she is administered major ablutions

When someone has died, it is recommended that his lower jaw be bound with a broad piece of cloth which is tied above his head, that his joints be gently relaxed, that he be lifted off the floor or ground, and that he be covered with a garment to shield him from people's gazes after the removal of the clothing in which he died. This ruling is agreed upon by the Shafiis, the Hanafis and the Hanbalis; for the Malikis' view, see below.[402]

Before preparing the body for burial, it should be ascertained with certainty that death has actually occurred. After the death has been confirmed, however, the body should be promptly prepared for burial and buried. It is desirable to inform others of the person's death, even if only by calling out to people in the market places for them to attend the person's funeral, though without excessive adulation. The person announcing the death might say, for example, "God's humble servant, so-and-so, son of so-and-so, has died, so come to his funeral." This ruling is agreed upon by the Shafiis, the Malikis and the Hanafis; as for the Hanbalis, they hold that such an announcement is permitted, but that it is undesirable to raise one's voice when delivering it. The Malikis agree with the Hanbalis on the undesirability of raising one's voice when making such an announcement. Hence, it is consistent with the views of these two schools to announce a death by means of the obituary column in the newspapers, as is the custom at the present time.

Performing major ablutions for the deceased and the ruling on this practice

Performing major ablutions on behalf of someone who has died is a collective obligation for the living; hence, if someone undertakes this obligation, it is waived for everyone else. What is required is that the person be washed one time in such a way that water covers his or her entire body; as for the practice of repeating the washing an odd number of times [by washing the body three, five, or seven times, for example], this is an emulation of the Sunnah, as will be seen below. This ruling is agreed upon by the Shafiis, the Hanbalis and the Hanafis; however, the Malikis hold that washing the body an odd number of times is recommended, but not an emulation of the Sunnah.

---

401. According to the Shafiis, the only supplication one should utter when closing the deceased's eyes is the words, "In the name of God, and in accordance with the religion of His Messenger."

402. According to the Malikis, there are two alternative views on removing the clothes in which a person died: (1) They should be partially removed; that is, the person's shirt or tunic should be left on. (2) None of the deceased's clothes should be removed; rather, an additional garment is to be placed over them in order to shield his or her entire body from people's gazes.

Conditions for performing major ablutions for the deceased

In order for the ritual washing of the deceased's body to be a requirement, a number of conditions must be met: (1) The deceased must be a Muslim. In other words, it is not required that major ablutions be performed on behalf of someone who is a non-Muslim; in fact, it is forbidden to do so according to the Malikis, the Hanbalis and the Hanafis. However, the Shafiis hold that it is not forbidden, since it is done in this case for the sake of hygiene and cleanliness rather than as an act of religious devotion. (2) The deceased must not be a miscarried fetus. However, the various schools offer their own detailed rulings on this matter.[403] (3) A certain amount of the deceased's body must be present, even if it is a small amount. This is the ruling of the Shafiis and the Hanbalis; for the views of the Malikis and the Hanafis, see below.[404] (4) The deceased must not have died as a martyr, i.e., have been killed in the course of spreading the word of God, as will be seen in the section below on martyrs. This ruling is based on the saying of the Prophet concerning the Muslims who were slain in the Battle of Uḥud, "Do not wash them, for every wound or place where they have bled will be redolent with musk on the Day of Resurrection. Nor should they be prayed over."[405]

Lastly, sand ablutions will suffice in place of the usual ritual washing of the deceased when no water is available or when major ablutions would not be possible

---

403. According to the Shafiis, if a fetus is miscarried before the pregnancy is, legally speaking, "complete" (that is, before the mother has completed six months and two moments of her term), it will either be known to have been alive, in which case it must be washed as if it were an adult, or it will not be known for certain to have been alive. If it is uncertain whether the fetus had been alive and if its bodily features are recognizable, it must be washed but not prayed over; if its bodily features are not yet recognizable, it is not necessary to wash it. As for a miscarried fetus which is aborted after the time period mentioned above, it must be ritually washed even if it is still-born. In either case, however, it is an emulation of the Sunnah to name the fetus provided that the spirit of life has been breathed into it.

* * *

According to the Hanafis, if a miscarried fetus is known to have been alive by its making an audible sound or an observable movement—even if this takes place before it is miscarried—it must be ritually washed regardless of whether or not the miscarriage took place before the pregnancy was complete in the legal sense (that is, before the mother had completed six months and two moments of her term). If the fetus is still-born but fully formed, it is to be ritually washed; if, on the other hand, it is only partially formed, it is not to be ritually washed in the usual fashion but, instead, water is to be poured over it and it is to be wrapped in a cloth. In any case, however, it should be given a name because it will be gathered on the Day of Resurrection.

* * *

The Hanbalis hold that if a fetus is miscarried before it has been in its mother's womb for four entire months, it must be ritually washed, whereas if it has been in its mother's womb for any less than this, its ritual washing is not required.

* * *

for some other reason, for example, in a situation in which someone died in a fire and it is feared that the body would disintegrate if it were washed and rubbed, or even by pouring water over it without rubbing it. However, if the body is not likely to come apart simply by having water poured over it, sand ablutions should not be performed; rather, major ablutions should be performed on it by pouring water over it, but without rubbing it.

Rulings on looking at and touching the deceased's private parts, women's performing major ablutions for a deceased man, and vice-versa

The private parts of the deceased's body must be covered, since it is impermissible for anyone, including the person who washes the body, to look at them or to touch them. Hence, the person who will be washing the body must wrap a cloth around his hand in order to wash the body's private parts, including both those which are highly unpresentable and those which are mildly unpresentable. As for all other parts of the deceased's body, the person washing it may touch them directly. This ruling is agreed upon by all four schools; however, the Hanbalis hold that it is recommended that the person washing the body wrap his hand in a cloth when washing other parts as well. There is also a well-attested view attributed to the Hanafis according to which it is not forbidden to touch the mildly unpresentable parts of the deceased's body, although it is desirable to conceal them and not to touch them.

A man is not permitted to wash the body of a deceased woman, nor may a woman wash the body of a deceased man unless he or she is the other's spouse; hence, a wife may wash her deceased husband's body and a husband may wash his deceased wife's body unless the wife had been divorced, even if only revocably,[406]

As for the Malikis, they hold that if a miscarried fetus is ascertained to have been alive by some evidence such as its crying and showing clear signs of wanting to nurse—which people of knowledge say only occurs when a child is definitively alive—it must be ritually washed; otherwise, it is undesirable to do so.

404. According to the Hanafis, no ritual washing of the body is required unless most of the body is still present, or unless half of the body is present in addition to the head.

* * *

According to the Malikis, no ritual washing is required unless two-thirds of the body is present, not including the head. If less than this amount is present, it is undesirable to perform a ritual washing.

405. Narrated by Aḥmad Ibn Ḥanbal.

406. A revocable divorce under Islamic law is one in which the words, "I divorce you" have been pronounced only once or twice (but not yet three times) by the husband and in which, once the wife's required waiting period of approximately 3 months has elapsed, a reconciliation may take place [t.n.].

in which case neither of the spouses would be allowed to wash the other's body in the event of his or her death. This ruling is agreed upon by the Shafiis and the Malikis; for the views of the Hanafis and the Hanbalis, see below.[407]

If a woman dies among men without there being other women or a husband present to wash her and if it is impossible to bring a woman to wash her—as, for example, if she died while on a journey in an inaccessible location—each school offers its own detailed ruling on this matter.[408]

If the deceased is a young boy, his body may be washed by women, and if it is a young girl, her body may be washed by men. As for the definition of 'young' in such a context, see the section above on the parts of the body which must be concealed [during prayer and outside of prayer]. Rulings on washing the body of a 'problematic hermaphrodite' also differ among the various schools.[409]

---

407. The Hanafis hold that if a married woman dies, her husband will not be permitted to wash her body due to the fact that death has terminated the marital bond between them; in other words, he has now become a 'strange' man in relation to her. If, on the other hand, a married man dies, his wife may wash his body because, legally speaking, she is still in her "waiting period", as a result of which she is still 'married'; this ruling applies even if, before her husband's death, she had been revocably divorced. However, if she had been irrevocably divorced before his death, she may not wash his body even if her waiting period has not yet elapsed.

* * *

The Hanbalis likewise hold that a wife who had been revocably divorced before her husband's death may wash his body, whereas if she had been irrevocably divorced, she may not.

408. The Malikis hold that if, when a woman dies, she has neither her husband nor other women around her but there is a close (unmarriageable) male relative of hers, he must wash her. When he does so, he is to wrap a thick cloth around his hands so as not to come in direct contact with her body; in addition, he is to hang a partition between himself and the body, then extend his hand inside the partition while closing his eyes. If, on the other hand, there is no one available but 'strange' men, one of them must perform sand ablutions on her, but only up to her wrists rather than wiping up as far as her elbows. If a man dies among women and if his wife is among them, she alone must be the person to wash him. If his wife is not present and if there is another close (unmarriageable) female relative of his, she must wash him. When she does so, however, she must not come in direct contact with his body; hence, she must wrap her hand in a cloth and cover his private parts. If no unmarriageable female relative of his is available, some other woman must perform sand ablutions for him, but up to his wrists only.

* * *

The Hanafis hold that if, when a woman dies, there are no other women to wash her body, and if there is a close (unmarriageable) male relative available, he must perform sand ablutions for her up to her elbows. If there is only a 'strange' man available, he should place a cloth over his hand and perform sand ablutions for her in the same manner, but without looking at her arms. If the woman's husband is present, the same ruling as that for the 'strange' man applies to him as well except that he is not required to look away from her arms. These rulings apply, moreover, whether the deceased woman was young or old. If a man dies among women, if neither his wife nor other men are available, and if there is a prepubescent girl present who is not yet sexually desirable, she is to be instructed by the women in how to perform a ritual washing, after which she is to wash the body. If no girl meeting these criteria is present, the women must perform sand ablutions for the deceased up to his elbows while turning their gazes away from his private parts. Lastly, they hold that if the deceased is washed in a manner that violates any of the aforementioned rulings, the washing will still be valid, although those who committed the violation will be guilty of wrongdoing.

* * *

The Shafiis hold that if a woman dies among men and if they include neither her husband nor a close (unmarriageable) male relative, one of the 'strange' men present is to perform sand ablutions for her up to the elbows, casting his gaze away from her private parts and taking care not to touch her. If a close (unmarriageable) male relative is present but not her husband, he must perform major ablutions for her; if her husband is present, however, he is to be given priority over the other male relative. If a man dies among women who include neither his wife nor a close (unmarriageable) female relative, some other woman is to perform sand ablutions for him with a cloth wrapped around her hand to prevent direct contact with his body and without looking at his private parts. If the man's wife is present, she is to administer major ablutions for him, with or without a barrier between her hand and his body. If his wife is not present but some other close (unmarriageable) female relative is available, such as his daughter, his sister, or his mother, she may wash him, although the wife is given priority over other female relatives.

* * *

As for the Hanbalis, they hold that if a woman dies among men who do not include her husband, one of the 'strange' men present must perform sand ablutions for her with some kind of barrier over his hand, and if a man dies among women who do not include his wife, one of the 'strange' women present must perform sand ablutions for him with a barrier over her hand. It is not permissible for anyone to perform sand ablutions for the deceased person without a barrier over his or her hand unless the person performing them is in a state of ritual consecration for the pilgrimage to Mecca, in which case the sand ablutions may be performed without a barrier.

409. The Malikis hold that if it is possible to provide a female servant for the problematic hermaphrodite, whether at his own expense, at the expense of the public treasury, or at the expense of the Muslim community, she alone should be the one to wash his body.

* * *

The Hanafis hold that problematic hermaphrodites who are held accountable under Islamic law for Islamic religious obligations, as well as adolescents, are not to wash either a man or a woman, nor are they to be washed by a man or a woman; rather, they should be administered sand ablutions through a garment.

* * *

Recommended practices associated with administering major ablutions to the deceased: Repeating the ablutions up to three times

There are a number of practices which are recommended in connection with administering major ablutions to the deceased. One of these is to repeat the ablutions up to three times such that each washing covers the entire body in the manner to be described below. According to the Shafiis, the Malikis and the Hanbalis, one of the three washings which cover the entire body with water is obligatory, while the two washings subsequent to it are recommended. However, the Hanafis hold that the other two washings are not merely recommended, but are in emulation of the Sunnah; the Shafiis and the Hanbalis may, in fact, agree with the Hanafis on this point, since the Shafiis and the Hanbalis make no distinction between the terms 'recommended' and 'Sunnah-based'.

All four schools agree that if the deceased's body is clean after having been washed three times such that each of the three washings covers the body completely with water, it is considered undesirable to perform any further washings; it is likewise undesirable to perform fewer than this even if the body is clean before three washings have been done. However, if the body is still not clean after three

---

According to the Hanbalis, if a problematic hermaphrodite who is at least seven years old dies and has a female servant, she should wash his body; otherwise, he should be administered sand ablutions with the use of a barrier that prevents direct contact with his body. Moreover, a man should be given priority over a woman as the person to administer the sand ablutions.

* * *

The Shafiis hold that either a 'strange' man or a 'strange' woman may perform major ablutions for a deceased adult problematic hermaphrodite if he has no close, unmarriageable relative available, although the person administering the major ablutions must neither look at nor touch the body. Moreover, the person administering the major ablutions should wash the body only once, making certain that the water covers the entire body. As for a hermaphrodite who is still a child, he is to be treated like any other child who dies.

410. The Malikis hold that if the body needs a fourth washing, it should be washed four times. The first time should be with clear water, while the three subsequent washings should be done with some sort of cleansing agent, such as soap. Then a fifth washing should be done in order for the total number of washings to be uneven. If the body is still not clean after the fifth washing, a sixth washing should be done with a cleansing agent (not counting the first washing), after which a seventh washing should be added in order to preserve the uneven number. If the body is still not clean after seven washings, an eighth washing should be done, but no more than this. In all cases, however, the final washing should be done with clear water to which perfume has been added.

* * *

The Hanbalis maintain that if the body of the deceased is still not clean after three washings, further washings should be performed up to seven. If the body is still not clean after the seventh washing, it is preferable (but not obligatory) to

washings, each of which covers the entire body, it is recommended that more washings be performed until the body is clean, provided that the final number of washings is uneven. Hence, if the body is clean after four washings, a fifth washing should be added, and so on. This ruling is agreed upon by the Shafiis and the Hanafis; for the views of the Malikis and the Hanbalis, see below.[410]

Rulings on mixing the ablution water with perfume and the like

A second recommended practice associated with the administration of major ablutions to a deceased person is that camphor or some other perfume be added to the water for the final washing, with camphor being preferable to other perfumes. As for washings other than the final one, it is recommended that they be done with water that contains Christ's-thorn leaves or some other cleansing agent, such as soap.

However, perfume should only be placed in the water if the deceased is not wearing the garb of someone in a state of ritual consecration for the pilgrimage to Mecca; in this case, no perfume should be added, since the person's body is to be treated as if it were alive. This ruling is agreed upon by the Hanbalis and the Shafiis; for the views of the Malikis and the Hanafis, see below.[411]

Heating the water for use in major ablutions

A third recommended practice associated with administering major ablutions to the deceased is that the washing should be done with cold water unless some necessity dictates otherwise, such as extreme cold or the body's being particularly dirty. This ruling is agreed upon by the Shafiis and the Hanbalis; as for the Malikis, they hold that it makes no difference whether the water is cold or hot, whereas the Hanafis hold that hot water is better in all circumstances.

---

continue performing more washings until it is clean, though it is recommended that the total number of washings be uneven.

411. According to the Hanafis and the Malikis, it is recommended that perfume or some other scent be placed in the water used to wash the body of the deceased, whether he or she is dressed as those who are ritually consecrated for the pilgrimage to Mecca or not. The reason for this ruling is that a deceased person is no longer held accountable for performing the rites of Islam; hence, his or her state of ritual consecration for the pilgrimage comes to an end when he or she dies. Thus, unlike someone living who is dressed for the pilgrimage, his or her head is to be covered after death. However, the Malikis hold that the first washing must be done with clear water since, as we saw in the section on types of water, the Malikis also hold that the ritual cleansing property of water is lost if soap, or something similar, is placed in it.

Applying perfume to a deceased person's head and beard

A fourth recommended practice associated with administering major ablutions to the deceased is that perfume (with the exception of saffron, and with the preferred perfume being camphor) be applied to the head and beard after the washing of the body has been completed. The perfume is to be placed on those members of the body on which one prostrates: the forehead, the nose, the hands, the knees and the feet. In addition, it is to be placed in the person's eyes, ears, and armpits.

This ruling applies provided that the deceased is not dressed as those who are in a state of ritual consecration for the major pilgrimage, in which case he or she is not to be perfumed. This ruling is agreed upon by all of the schools except the Malikis, who hold that placing perfume on the person's head and beard is not recommended.

Burning incense near the deceased and removing his or her clothing for the administration of major ablutions

A fifth recommended practice in this situation is that incense be burned near the deceased, with each school offering its own detailed ruling on this point.[412]

According to the Malikis, the Hanbalis and the Hanafis, it is recommended that when the deceased's body is being washed, all of his or her clothing be removed with the exception of that which conceals his or her private parts; for the Shafiis' view on this point, see below.[413]

---

412. According to the Malikis, burning incense is not recommended.

* * *

According to the Hanafis, it is recommended that incense be burned in three situations: (1) At the moment when the person actually dies. When it is ascertained with certainty that the person has died, his or her body is to be placed on a raised surface such as a bed or bench; before this, a censer is to be carried around the bed, bench, etc. three, five or seven times, but no more, after which the deceased is to be placed on it. (2) While the deceased's body is being washed, by passing the censer around the bed or bench in the manner mentioned above. (3) While the body is being wrapped, again in the same manner mentioned above.

* * *

According to the Hanbalis, the site where the washing is taking place should be perfumed with incense until the washing has been completed.

* * *

According to the Shafiis, it is recommended that incense be burned near the deceased from the time he dies until he is prayed over.

413. According to the Shafiis, it is recommended that the body of the deceased be washed in a shirt which is sufficiently sheer to allow water to soak through to the skin. If it is possible for the person doing the washing to place his hand inside the shirt's wide sleeve, he is to do so; otherwise, he is to tear it at the sides.

Whether minor ritual ablutions should be administered to the deceased prior to major ablutions

It is recommended that minor ritual ablutions be performed on behalf of the deceased person in the same manner in which they are performed when one is alive and is about to perform major ablutions for purification from major ritual impurity; however, the actions of rinsing out the mouth and exhaling water which has been drawn into the nostrils are omitted in the case of a deceased person due to the hardship involved, and in order to prevent water from going down into the person's gut, thereby causing the body to decompose more quickly. However, it is considered desirable for the person who is washing the body to wrap a cloth around his index finger, wet the cloth with water, then use it to wipe the deceased person's teeth, gums and nostrils in place of the person's rinsing his or her mouth out and expelling water through his or her nostrils. This ruling is agreed upon by the Hanafis and the Hanbalis; for the views of the Malikis and the Shafiis, see below.[414]

Qualities which are recommended in the person who performs major ablutions for the deceased

It is recommended that the person who washes the body of the deceased be someone who is of trustworthy character and who, as a result, will do a careful, thorough job, concealing whatever he sees that is unbecoming and revealing whatever he sees that is lovely or attractive. For example, if he or she notes an expression of joyful radiance on the deceased's face and a pleasant fragrance coming from his body, it is desirable for him or her to speak of such things to other people. However, if he or she detects an unpleasant odor or sees an unhappy expression on the face of the deceased, it is not permissible for him or her to speak of it. It is also recommended that he or she dry off the body of the deceased after washing it in order to prevent the grave clothes from getting wet.

---

414. According to the Malikis and the Shafiis, minor ritual ablutions performed on behalf of a deceased person should include rinsing out the mouth and expelling water which has been taken up into the nostrils; as for cleaning the deceased person's teeth and nostrils with a cloth, this is desirable, but it is not considered a substitute for the two actions mentioned here.

Undesirable actions relating to the deceased

According to the Malikis, the Hanbalis and the Hanafis, it is undesirable to part the deceased's hair, whether it is the hair on his head or his beard. However, the Shafiis hold that it is an emulation of the Sunnah to part the deceased's hair if it is tangled or matted; otherwise, it is neither undesirable nor an emulation of the Sunnah. It is likewise undesirable to cut the deceased's fingernails or toenails, hair or moustache, or to remove underarm hair or pubic hair. Rather, everything which was originally on the body of the deceased must be buried with him; hence, if anything should fall off, it should be placed back inside the grave clothes in order to be buried with the body. This ruling is agreed upon by the Shafiis and the Hanafis; for the views of the Hanbalis and the Malikis, see below.[415]

If some impurity comes out of the deceased's body after major ablutions have been performed

If, after the body of the deceased has been washed, some impurity comes out and clings either to the body or to the grave clothes, it must be removed, but it is not required that the body be washed again after this. This is the view of the Malikis and the Shafiis; for the views of the Hanbalis and the Hanafis, see below.[416]

How major ablutions are to be performed for the deceased

Each of the four schools provides a detailed description of the manner in which major ablutions are to be administered to the deceased.[417]

---

415. According to the Hanbalis, it is an emulation of the Sunnah to trim the deceased's moustache and the fingernails (unless he was in a state of ritual consecration for the pilgrimage to Mecca) if they have grown long, and to remove the hair under his armpits. However, after the hair and fingernails have been removed, they are to be placed with the deceased inside his grave clothes. As for shaving the deceased's head, it is forbidden, because if the person's hair was long, it was kept this way either as a sign of devotion to God or as physical adornment. As for shaving the deceased's pubic hair, this is forbidden also, since doing so would involve the risk of touching or looking at the person's private parts.

* * *

As for the Malikis, they hold that whatever one is forbidden to do with the hair while alive—such as shaving off the moustache and the beard—is likewise forbidden after death; whereas whatever one is permitted to do with the hair while alive is undesirable after death.

416. According to the Hanafis, no harm is done by an impurity which comes out of the deceased's body, whether it touches the body or the grave clothes. If the impurity comes out before the body has been wrapped in its grave clothes, it is to be washed off for the sake of hygiene, but not as a condition for the validity of praying over it. If it comes out after the body has been wrapped in its grave clothes, it is not to be washed off due to the hardship this would involve. However, if the grave clothes themselves are contaminated with impurity or made of a ritually impure substance, this will invalidate the prayer performed over the deceased.

* * *

The Hanbalis hold that if some impurity comes out of the deceased's body after it has been washed, the impurity must be removed and the body must be washed again up to seven additional times. If further impurity comes out after the seventh washing, all that is required is that it be washed off, but without repeating major ablutions for the body itself. If, on the other hand, the impurity comes out after the body has been wrapped in its grave clothes, the major ablutions are not invalidated, and they need not be repeated again.

417. According to the Hanafis, the deceased's body is to be placed on a raised surface for washing, such as a board designated for this purpose. It is also to be perfumed with incense as it is being washed by passing a censer around the board three, five or seven times, as we have seen. The body is then stripped of its clothing with the exception of the garment which covers its private parts. It is recommended that the only person present be the one who is actually performing the washing, in addition to his or her assistant. The person doing the washing should wrap his hand in a cloth, wet the cloth, and wash the deceased's genitals and buttocks, after which he performs ritual ablutions on the deceased's behalf. When performing minor ablutions, the person performing them should begin with the deceased's face, since the rule of beginning with the hands applies only to the living, who wash themselves and, as a consequence, need to clean their hands, whereas in the case of the deceased, he or she is being washed by someone else. Performing major ablutions on behalf of the deceased does not include the actions of rinsing out the mouth or expelling water which has been taken up into the nostrils; instead, the deceased's teeth and nostrils are cleaned with a cloth, as we have seen, after which the person's head and chin are cleaned with a cleansing agent such as soap if they have hair on them. If they have no hair on them, however, they are not to be washed. The deceased should then be positioned on his left side in order to begin washing his right side; in washing the right side, water is poured over the right side of the body from the head to the feet three times until the water covers its lower portion. It is not permissible to position the deceased on his or her face in order to wash his or her back; rather, the body is simply to be moved from the side until water covers it completely. With this, then, the first washing is completed. If the first washing covers the entire body with water, the collective obligation to wash the deceased's body will have been fulfilled. As for the Sunnah, it is fulfilled by washing the body two additional times. In order to do this, the body is positioned on its right side, after which water is poured over its left side three times in the manner described above. The person doing the washing now places the body in a sitting position; then, while propping the body up, he strokes its abdomen gently and washes off whatever comes out as a result. With this, the second washing is completed. For the third washing, the body is positioned once more on its left side and water is poured over its right side in the manner described above, which completes the third washing.

The first two washings should be done with warm water together with a cleansing agent such as Christ's-thorn leaves and soap; as for the third washing, it should be done with clear water containing some camphor, after which the body is dried and perfumed, as we have seen.

Lastly, the validity of washing the deceased's body does not require an intention, nor is intention required in order to fulfill the collective obligation to wash the dead, properly speaking. However, intention is required in order to obtain the reward for fulfilling this obligation.

* * *

According to the Malikis, a deceased person whose body is to be washed should first be placed on a raised surface; after this, all of his or her clothes should be removed with the exception of those which cover the private parts, both those which are highly unpresentable and those which are only mildly unpresentable. The person performing the major ablutions is first to wash the deceased's hands three times, then press his abdomen gently in order to expel whatever impurities or wastes might be inside lest they come out after the ablutions have been completed. He should then wrap a thick cloth around his left hand and use it to wash the deceased's genitals and anus while water is being poured over them. He is then to wash off whatever impurities might be on the body, rinse out the mouth, and put water up the nostrils while inclining the head gently in the direction of the chest. After this, he is to wipe the teeth and the inside of the nose with a cloth and complete all other actions involved in regular ablutions. The ablutions should be performed three times for every part of the body involved. After this, he is to cover the head with water three times without any intention, since intention is not permissible when performing major ablutions on behalf of the deceased. He should then wash the right side of the body, both back and front, etc., followed by the left side, back and front. This completes the first washing, which is to be done with clear water; once the first washing has been completed, the obligation to wash the deceased's body has been fulfilled.

It is recommended that the body be washed a second and a third time for the sake of cleanliness. The first of these two additional washings should be done with soap or some other cleansing agent; the body should first be scrubbed with soap, after which water should be poured over it. As for the second of the additional washings, it should be done with water to which perfume—preferably camphor—has been added. If the body is clean after these three washings, no additional washings should be done. However, if the body needs a fourth washing, a fourth washing should be done while observing the practices described above in the section entitled, "Recommended practices associated with administering major ablutions to the deceased." Following this, it is recommended that the body be dried and that perfume be placed in "the senses" [apparently a reference to the nose, the eyes, the ears, the mouth, and the hands – t.n.], in those spots on which one prostrates, such as the forehead, the hands, and the feet, and in deep-set areas such as the armpits. Lastly, cotton with some perfume on it is to be placed in the bodily orifices.

* * *

The Shafiis hold that when a deceased person is washed, it is recommended that the body be placed on a raised surface, that the washing be performed in a private place closed to everyone but the person who does the washing and whoever is assisting him or her, and that when the deceased is washed, he or she be wearing a sheer garment that allows water to soak through to the skin. If the person doing the washing is able to place his hand inside the garment's wide sleeve, he should content himself with this, and if he is unable to do so, he should split the garment from the sides. If there is no garment available in which to wash the deceased, his private parts must be concealed. It is desirable that the deceased's face be covered from the time he is placed on the surface where his body is to be washed, and that the washing be performed with cold, salty water unless necessity dictates otherwise (for example, on account of cold weather or the need to remove dirt from the body), in which the water is to be heated slightly.

The person doing the washing then gently places the deceased in a sitting position on top of the raised surface by placing his right hand on the deceased's shoulder and his thumb in the nape of his neck while supporting his back with his right knee. While in this position, the person doing the washing is to stroke the deceased's abdomen with his left hand, then repeat this action with slight pressure in order to expel whatever wastes might be inside. It is also recommended that the person doing the washing have a censer nearby to perfume the area and that he pour plenty of water over the body in order not to allow the odor to be detected from outside the area where he is working.

After this, the person doing the washing is to lay the deceased on his back, wrap a cloth around his left hand, and wash the deceased's genitals, anus and other private parts. He should then dispose of the cloth he just used and wash his own hand with soap and water if it has become contaminated with any substance that came out of the deceased's body. He then wraps another cloth around his left forefinger and cleans the deceased's teeth and nostrils; however, he is not to part the deceased's teeth unless his mouth has some impurity in it, in which case he should part the teeth in order to clean inside the mouth. He then performs minor ritual ablutions on behalf of the deceased by rinsing out his mouth and putting water up his nostrils, then letting it run out again. When doing so, the person doing the washing should consciously intend to perform ablutions by saying, "I intend to perform ritual ablutions on behalf of this deceased person." (This is the officially recognized Shafii view.) As for consciously intending to perform major ablutions, this is simply an emulation of the Sunnah. The person doing the washing then washes the deceased's head and chin whether they have hair on them or not with a cleansing agent such as Christ's-thorn leaves and soap, then parts the hair on the deceased's head and chin with a wide-toothed comb if the hair is matted or tangled (and provided that the deceased was not in a state of ritual consecration for the pilgrimage to Mecca). The parting of the hair must be done gently lest any of it fall out; if any of it does fall out, it is to be placed back inside the deceased's grave clothes.

After this, the person doing the washing washes the deceased's right side from the neck to the foot, both front and back, after which the left side is washed in the same manner. The body is then moved onto its left side so that its right side can be washed from the back of the neck down to the foot; it is then placed on its right side again and the left side is washed in the same manner. (Out of respect for the deceased, it is forbidden to turn him on his face.) Each such washing is to be done with soap or some other cleansing agent. Water is then poured over the deceased from head to foot in order to remove the soap; lastly, the person doing the washing pours over the body clear water to which a small mount of camphor has been added (where the amount of camphor should be small enough not to change the water).

All of the above applies, as we have seen, to a deceased person who was not in a state of ritual consecration for the pilgrimage to Mecca. Moreover, the three washings described are counted as a single washing. The reason for this is that due to the alteration of the water [by the addition of soap] in the first and second washings, only the third washing fulfills the obligation to perform major ablutions on behalf of the deceased. Consequently, the conscious intention to perform major ablutions is to accompany the final washing only, and not those that preceded it. If only these three washings are performed, the collective duty to wash the deceased will have been fulfilled, though it is an emulation of the Sunnah to repeat this process a second and third time, bringing the total number of washings to nine. However, it is recommended that the repetition be in the washing of the head, the face and the chin.

* * *

The Hanbalis hold that when the person who will be performing major ablutions for the deceased begins the washing, he must conceal the deceased's private parts as we have seen, after which it is recommended that he remove whatever other clothing is on the deceased's body. Thus, it is permissible to wash the body in a light shirt with wide sleeves. It is an emulation of the Sunnah for the deceased to be hidden from people's gazes by being placed in a roofed area or a tent. As the washing begins, the deceased's head should be gently raised until he is in a near sitting position if this causes no hardship. After this, the abdomen of the deceased should be pressed gently in order to expel whatever wastes might be inside; however, this does not apply if the deceased is a pregnant woman. When pressing the abdomen, generous amounts of water should be poured over the body in order to wash away whatever wastes come out and in order to get rid of any resulting odor. In addition, the place where the washing is being done should be perfumed with incense for the same purpose.

The person doing the washing should then wrap his hand in a coarse cloth and use it to wash either the genitals or the anus; he should then place another cloth over his hand and wash whichever of these two openings he did not wash the first time. It is also desirable that the person doing the washing not touch any of the rest of the body with anything but a cloth. Then, after having removed all clothes except those which conceal the deceased's private parts and washing both the genitals and the anus in the manner explained above, the person doing the washing should make it his conscious intention to perform major ablutions on behalf of the deceased. (This intention is required for the validity of the major ablutions; hence, if it is omitted, the washing will be invalidated.) The person performing the major ablutions then says, "In the name of God" without either adding to or omitting any of this phrase. He then washes the deceased's palms and removes whatever impurities may be on his body. After this, he wraps a coarse cloth around his forefinger and thumb, wets the cloth with water and wipes the deceased's teeth and nostrils. (The cleaning of the deceased's teeth and nostrils in this manner is considered desirable.)

It is an emulation of the Sunnah for the person doing the washing to perform minor ritual ablutions on behalf of the deceased as part of the first washing. However, the ablutions are not to include rinsing out the mouth or introducing water into

Wrapping the deceased for burial

Wrapping the deceased for burial is a collective duty incumbent upon Muslims such that if one or more of them fulfill this duty, it is not required of anyone else. The wrapping must conceal the entire body of the deceased, be it male or female. If the grave clothes conceal less than the deceased's entire body, the collective duty to wrap the deceased for burial will not have been fulfilled.

The grave clothes in which the deceased is wrapped should be purchased with the deceased's own money provided that it does not belong by right to someone else, such as money which had been deposited (with the deceased) as security. If the deceased had no money of his own, his grave clothes must be provided at the expense of whoever was responsible for his financial support while he was alive. If the deceased is a wife who left money behind, her husband is responsible for providing her grave clothes if he is financially able to do so.[418] If the person who was responsible for the deceased's financial support while he or she was living has no money, the grave clothes are to be provided at the expense of the public treasury if the Muslims have a public treasury and if it is permissible to draw from it. Otherwise, the community of financially able Muslims themselves must provide for the wrapping; the same rulings which apply to the matter of wrapping the deceased for burial apply likewise to the provision of other related requirements, including transportation to the gravesite, the burial itself, etc.

As for the various types of grave clothes and their description, each of the four schools offers its own detailed ruling in this regard.[419]

---

the nostrils to be expelled again. He then washes the deceased's head and chin with Christ's-thorn leaves or some other cleansing agent, after which he washes the rest of the deceased's body with a cleansing agent as well. (In fact, Christ's-thorn leaves or some other cleansing agent should be used in every washing.) He then washes the deceased's right side from head to foot beginning with the side of the neck, from the right hand to the shoulder, the shoulder, the right side of the chest, then the thigh and the calf down to the foot; the left side should be washed in the same manner. With the deceased's right side up, the person performing the ablutions is to wash his back, his hip and his thigh, but without laying him on his face; he should then do the same with the deceased's left side. Lastly, he is to pour clear water over the deceased's entire body. With this, one complete washing has been performed and it is permissible to stop at this point; however, it is an emulation of the Sunnah to repeat the major ablutions in this same manner three times, as we have seen.

418. According to the Malikis and the Hanbalis, the husband is not responsible for providing grave clothes for his deceased wife even if she was poor.

419. According to the Shafiis, it is only permissible for the deceased to be wrapped for burial in materials it would have been permissible for him or her to wear during his or her lifetime. Hence, neither a man nor a hermaphrodite may be wrapped for burial in silk or saffroned fabric if something else is available; if nothing else is available, however, it is permissible out of necessity. It is undesirable for a man or a hermaphrodite to be wrapped for burial in fabric died with safflower (i.e., bright red). As for a young boy, an insane person, or a woman, it is permissible to wrap them in silk or fabric dyed with safflower or embroidered with gold or

silver thread, although such a practice is undesirable. It is preferable for the grave clothes to be white, old, and washed; if such garments are not available, the deceased may be wrapped in anything which is permissible. Hence, if nothing but silk, leather, grass, kneaded henna and clay are available, preference should be given to the silk over the leather, to the leather over the grass, to the grass over the kneaded henna, and to the kneaded henna over the clay.

In addition, the grave clothes must be ritually pure; hence, it is not permissible to wrap the deceased in something which is ritually impure when something ritually pure could have been used, even if the pure material happens to be silk. If nothing ritually pure in which to wrap the deceased is available, the deceased should be prayed over naked, then wrapped in something ritually impure and buried. It is undesirable for the grave clothes to be overly expensive; similarly, it is undesirable for someone to save grave clothes for himself or herself during his or her lifetime unless they are a relic left by righteous ancestors, in which case it is permissible to do so. It is forbidden to write anything from the Qur'ān on the grave clothes, and it is undesirable for the grave clothes to contain any color other than white (such as safflower dye and the like).

The grave clothes are to consist of three robes for both males and females. Each robe should cover the entire body with the exception of the head of a man who was in a state of ritual consecration for the major pilgrimage, and the face of a woman who was in such a state. This ruling applies provided that: (1) the cost of the grave clothes was covered by the deceased's own bequest, (2) he or she did not leave a debt which it took the entire bequest to repay, and (3) the deceased did not stipulate before his death that he was to be wrapped in a single robe. Otherwise, the deceased is to be wrapped in a single robe which covers his entire body provided that he was not in a state of ritual consecration for the major pilgrimage. It is permissible to add other robes if someone has donated them. However, in the case of someone who is wrapped for burial at the expense of the public treasury or with money that has been set aside as a religious endowment to be used to pay for grave clothes, it is forbidden to use more than a single robe unless the person who set the money aside as a religious endowment stipulated that more than one robe be used, in which case his request is to be carried out.

If the deceased is a man, an additional shirt may be placed on the body under the three robes mentioned above, as well as a turban on his head. However, it is preferable that only the three robes be used. Even so, such an addition is permitted if the deceased's heirs do not include a minor or someone who has been declared legally incompetent and, as a result, has been placed under guardianship. If the heirs do include a minor or someone under guardianship, such an addition is forbidden.

If the deceased is a female, the ideal practice is for her grave clothes to consist of five pieces: (1) an *izār*, (2) a tunic, (3) a veil, and (4) two 'wrappers'. The manner in which the body is to be wrapped is as follows: First, the best and largest of the 'wrappers' is laid out and some *ḥanūṭ* or some other scent, such as camphor, is placed on it. The second wrapper is then placed on top of the first, with more *ḥanūṭ*; this is followed by the third wrapper if there is a third. Lastly, the body is placed gently on top of the wrappers, lying on its back with the hands on the chest, either with the right hand on top of the left or with both hands resting alongside the torso. A piece of cotton with some *ḥanūṭ* on it is placed between the buttocks, which are then drawn up tightly with a cloth that has been split at both ends like a bandage until the cloth touches the anus, though without being placed inside it. The wrappers are then drawn around the body one by one as follows: The left edge of each wrapper is brought up over the body toward the right, after which the right edge is brought up toward the left. What remains of the grave clothes is gathered at the head and feet, and in the case of someone who did not die in a state of ritual consecration for the major pilgrimage, the wrappers are tied closed with string or rope lest they come apart when the body is picked up. The bands are then untied again after the body has been placed in the grave in the hope that the deceased will be released from tribulations. Neither the grave clothes nor the body of someone who died in a state of ritual consecration for the major pilgrimage is to be perfumed at all; nor is perfume to be placed in the water used to wash such a person's body, as we have seen. Nor is it permissible to wrap such a person's body in anything he or she would have been forbidden to wear while in such a state of ritual consecration, such as a stitched garment.

* * *

According to the Hanafis, it is preferable for grave clothes to consist of white garments, be they new or worn. Moreover, anything that a man is permitted to wear while alive may also be used to wrap him for burial after death; as for materials he would not have been permitted to wear while alive, it is undesirable to use them to wrap his body after death. Hence, it is undesirable for a deceased man's body to be wrapped in silk, fabric dyed with saffron [yellow], safflower [red], etc. unless nothing else is available. As for a woman who dies, it is permissible to wrap her body for burial in such materials. When choosing what to use to wrap a man's body for burial, one should consider what he used to wear to go out on the Day of Sacrifice and the Day of Fastbreaking. When deciding what to use to wrap a woman's body for burial, one should look to what she used to wear when she went to visit her parents.

Grave clothes are divided by the Hanafis into three types: (1) grave clothes which are in accordance with the prophetic Sunnah, (2) grave clothes 'of sufficiency', and (3) grave clothes 'of necessity'. Each of these three types is further classified in terms of whether it is for a man or a woman. Thus, for example, grave clothes which are in accordance with the prophetic Sunnah for both men and women consist of a tunic, an *izār*, and a wrapper. The tunic should extend from the neck to the feet; the *izār* should extend from the top of the head to the feet, and likewise the wrapper. In the case of a deceased woman, a veil covering her face is also added and a cloth to bind her breasts. The tunic should have neither sleeves nor openings at the bottom, whereas the wrapper should be long enough that it extends beyond both the head and the feet so that it can be tied at the top and the bottom, thereby concealing the entire body. It is also permissible to tie the wrapper at the middle with a band of the same cloth from which the grave clothes are made if it is feared that it might come open.

As for the grave clothes of sufficiency, they consist of either just the *izār* or just the wrapper, or one of these two with the veil and the cloth to bind the breasts for women without the tunic; this is considered sufficient without any undesirability attached to it. And as for the grave clothes of necessity, they consist of whatever is available, even if it is no more than what is required to conceal the deceased's private parts. If nothing at all is available, the body is washed and covered with schoenanthus (an aromatic plant) if any is available, after which a prayer is performed over the deceased's grave. If a deceased woman has braids, they should be placed on her chest between the tunic and the *izār*; it is also recommended that the grave clothes be perfumed with incense, as we have seen. If the deceased had little money and if he has many heirs, or if he was in debt, only the grave clothes of sufficiency should be used.

The body is to be wrapped as follows: The wrapper is laid out, after which the *izār* is laid out on top of it; the deceased is then placed on top of the *izār* and dressed in the tunic. The *izār* is then folded over the deceased, first from the left, then from the right. In the case of a deceased woman, the wrapper and the *izār* are laid down, her body is placed on top of them and she is dressed in the tunic. Her hair is to be plaited into two braids, which are then placed on her chest over the tunic. The veil is placed over the tunic, and the wrapper and the *izār* are folded over the body. Lastly, a cloth is tied around the grave clothes and above the feet.

* * *

According to the Malikis, it is recommended that the grave clothes be placed over a single robe for both men and women. They hold that it is preferable for a man to be wrapped in five items: (1) a tunic with sleeves, (2) an *izār*, (3) a turban with a tassel which is one cubit [about 18 inches] in length and which is cast over his face, and (4) two wrappers. As for the woman, her body is to be wrapped in seven items: (1) an *izār*, (2) a tunic, (3) a veil, and (4) four wrappers. The only thing that should be added to the grave clothes for either the man or the woman is what is referred to as the *ḥifāẓ*, which is a piece of cloth placed over the cotton that has been inserted between the thighs lest any impurity come out of the genital openings or the anus. It is recommended that the grave clothes be white, although it is permissible for them to be made of fabric dyed with saffron or *wars*. It is undesirable, however, for the grave clothes to be made of fabric dyed with safflower [red] or a green color; it is likewise undesirable to use silk or any material which is ritually impure. Such substances are only undesirable if nothing else is available; otherwise, there is no undesirability attached to their use. The deceased should be wrapped for burial in what he used to wear to attend the Friday congregational prayer, even if it is old, and if the deceased's heirs dispute among themselves, with some of them wanting to dress him in what he used to wear to the Friday prayer and others wanting to dress him in something else, the ruling should favor the first point of view. It is recommended that the grave clothes be perfumed with incense and that perfume be placed inside every wrapper, as well as on a piece of cotton which is placed in various orifices such as the nose, the mouth, the eyes, the ears, and the anus. The preferred type of perfume is camphor, as we have seen, and it is recommended that a deceased woman's hair be braided and allowed to fall behind her.

* * *

The Hanbalis distinguish two types of grave clothes: (1) obligatory, and (2) Sunnah-based. The obligatory type of grave clothes consists of a robe that conceals the entire body of the deceased regardless of his or her gender. The robe must be of the same type that may be worn to Friday congregational prayers and to the prayers performed on the Day of Sacrifice and the Day of Fastbreaking unless the deceased left instructions that he should be wrapped in something inferior to this, in which case his instructions must be followed. However, it is undesirable for the deceased to be wrapped in anything more elegant than what would be worn to Friday congregational prayers and the prayers for the Day of Sacrifice and Day of Fastbreaking even if the deceased left instructions that he should be wrapped in such garments.

As for the Sunnah-based type of grave clothes, they differ according to who the deceased is. If the deceased is a man, it is an emulation of the Sunnah for him to be wrapped for burial in three white cotton wrappers. It is undesirable to add anything more than this or to place a turban on the deceased's head. The manner in which the wrapping is to be done is as follows: The wrappers are first laid out on top of each other. They are then scented with incense such as aloe wood or something similar and the body is placed on top of them. It is an emulation of the Sunnah for the outermost wrapper to be the nicest of the three, and for *ḥanūṭ* to be placed between them. A piece of cotton with *ḥanūṭ* on it is then placed between the buttocks, after which a piece of cloth which is split at the ends is tied over it. It is desirable to perfume the entire body. The right edge of the innermost wrapper is then folded over the left side of the body, after which the left edge of the same wrapper is folded over the right side of the body; the same procedure is then followed for the second and third wrappers. Of the extra length of the wrapper, most is to be left at the head; the extra fabric is tied together, then untied again after the body is placed in the grave.

Adult females and hermaphrodites are to be wrapped in five white, cotton items, namely: (1) an *izār*, (2) a veil, (3) a tunic, and (4) two wrappers. When wrapping the body, the two wrappers are to be dealt with as in the description above; the veil is placed on the head and the *izār* around the middle part of the body, after which the deceased is dressed in the tunic. It is an emulation of the Sunnah for a young boy to be wrapped in a single robe and for a young girl to be wrapped in a tunic and two wrappers. It is undesirable for wrapping to be done with [fabric made from] hair or wool, with fabrics dyed with saffron or safflower, or with a cloth which is so sheer that it reveals the contours of the body. As for cloth which is so sheer that what is beneath it shows through, it is insufficient. Wrapping the deceased in leather or silk is forbidden even if the deceased is a woman; the same applies to fabric which is embroidered with gold or silver thread. However, it is permissible to use silk and cloth embroidered with gold or silver thread if nothing else is available.

The funeral prayer and related rulings

The funeral prayer is a collective obligation incumbent upon the living; hence, if even just one person performs it, it is not required of anyone else.

A description of the funeral prayer

We would like to clarify here how the funeral prayer is performed according to each of the four schools; in the process, note will be made of which parts of the prayer are pillars, which are conditions for the prayer's validity, which are emulations of the Sunnah, and which are simply recommended.[420]

---

420. According to the Hanafis, the funeral prayer is performed as follows: The worshiper stands opposite the deceased's chest, then consciously intends to perform the obligatory funeral prayer in adoration of God Almighty. He then utters the phrase *Allāhu akbar* as a way of commencing the prayer while raising his hands. He then recites the prayer of commencement (also known as the prayer of praise). The worshiper then utters the phrase *Allāhu akbar* again without raising his hands and prays for blessing upon the Prophet. He then utters *Allāhu akbar* again without raising his hands. He then utters prayers of supplication on behalf of the deceased and all Muslims, while it is preferable that one use the previously mentioned supplication. He then utters *Allāhu akbar* a fourth time without raising his hands and utters two greetings of peace, the first to his right (in which he addresses those on his right) and the second to his left (in which he addresses those on his left). However, in uttering the greetings of peace, he is not to address the deceased himself. All parts of the prayer are to be performed silently with the exception of the four utterances of *Allāhu akbar*.

* * *

According to the Malikis, the funeral prayer is performed as follows: The worshiper stands parallel to the deceased's waist if he is a man, and parallel to the shoulders if the deceased is a woman. He then consciously intends to perform prayer for all deceased Muslims who are present. He commences the prayer by uttering *Allāhu akbar* while raising his hands; he then utters *Allāhu akbar* a second time without raising his hands. He then utters a prayer of supplication followed by a third utterance of *Allāhu akbar* without raising his hands. He then utters *Allāhu akbar* a fourth time without raising his hands, followed by another prayer of supplication. He then utters a single greeting of peace to his right by which he intends to conclude the prayer (as we saw above in the discussion of ritual prayer); however, the worshiper is not to utter a second greeting of peace even if he is being led in prayer by an imam. It is recommended that all utterances of the prayer be done silently except on the part of the imam, who is to utter the greeting of peace and the phrase *Allāhu akbar* aloud in order for those being led in prayer to hear him, as we have seen. It should also be noted that every supplication should be commenced with the words *al-ḥamdu lillāh* and with a prayer for blessings upon God's Prophet.

* * *

According to the Shafiis, the funeral prayer is to be performed as follows: The imam or someone praying alone stands at the deceased's head in the case of a male, and at the deceased's hips in the case of a female or a hermaphrodite. The worshiper then forms an intention in his heart and states, "I intend to perform four utterances of *Allāhu akbar* over those deceased Muslims who are present here, thereby fulfilling a collective obligation for the sake of God Almighty." He then utters *takbīrat al-iḥrām*. If the worshiper is being led in prayer, he intends to follow his imam, after which he says *a'ūdhu billāhi min al-shayṭān al-rajīm* without uttering the prayer of commencement. He then recites the *Fātiḥah*, but does not follow this with another passage from the Qur'ān. He then utters the second *Allāhu akbar*, after which he says, "O God, send down Your blessings upon our master Muḥammad and his household just as You sent them down upon our master Abraham and his household in all the worlds. You are worthy of all praise, full of glory!" (*Allāhumma, ṣalli 'alā sayyidā Muḥammad wa 'alā Āl sayyidinā Muḥammad kamā ṣallayta 'alā sayyidinā Ibrāhīm wa 'alā Āl sayyidinā Ibrāhīm, wa bārik 'alā sayyidinā Muḥammad wa 'alā Āl sayyidinā Muḥammad kamā bārakta 'alā sayyidinā Ibrāhīm wa 'alā Āl sayyidinā Ibrāhīm fīl-'ālamīn, innaka ḥamīdun majīd*). He then utters the third *Allāhu akbar* followed by a prayer of supplication for the deceased which includes some request relating to the afterlife, although it is preferable that the previously mentioned supplication be used. [This appears to be a reference to the supplication detailed in Footnote 422 in the presentation of the Malikis' and Shafiis' views on the supplication to be offered on behalf of a deceased person – t.n.] Then he utters the fourth *Allāhu akbar* and says, "O God, do not deprive us of his reward, nor lead us into temptation after him." He then utters the following passage from the Qur'ān, "They who bear [within themselves the knowledge of] the throne of [God's] almightiness, as well as all who are near it, extol their Sustainer's limitless glory and praise, and have faith in Him, and ask forgiveness for all others who have attained to faith: 'O our Sustainer! Thou embraceth all things within Thy grace and knowledge. Forgive, then, their sins unto those who repent and follow Thy path, and preserve them from suffering through the blazing fire!" (40:7). He then utters the first greeting of peace addressing those on his right, followed by the second greeting of peace in which he addresses those on his left. The worshiper is to raise his hands while uttering each instance of *Allāhu akbar*, then place them below his chest as he does while performing a regular ritual prayer.

* * *

According to the Hanbalis, the funeral prayer is performed as follows: The worshiper stands parallel with the deceased's chest if he is a male, and with the deceased's waist if she is a female. He then intends to pray over those deceased Muslims who are present, or over this particular deceased person. He utters *takbīrat al-iḥrām* while raising his hands as one does during regular ritual prayer, then prays for divine protection from evil, saying, *a'ūdhu billāhi min al-shayṭān al-rajīm* and the *basmalah*. He then recites the *Fātiḥah* without following it with any other passage from the Qur'ān. He utters a second *Allāhu akbar* while raising his hands, then prays for blessings upon the Prophet as he would in the final testimony. He then utters a third *Allāhu akbar* while raising his hands, after which he utters a prayer of supplication for the deceased, as we have seen, followed by a fourth *Allāhu*

Pillars of the funeral prayer

The funeral prayer consists of pillars without which the prayer cannot be said to have been properly performed; if any of these pillars is missing, the prayer will be invalid and must be repeated. The pillars of the funeral prayer are as follows: (1) Intention. Intention is a pillar according to the Malikis and the Shafiis; as for the Hanafis and the Hanbalis, they hold that it is not a pillar, but rather a condition [for the prayer's validity]. In either case, however, intention is necessary in the funeral prayer just as it is in all other ritual prayers. As for the exact description of this intention, it differs in detail among the four schools.[421] (2) Four utterances of *Allāhu akbar*, including *takbīrat al-iḥrām*. Each of these four utterances, which is considered the equivalent of one *rak'ah*, is agreed to be a pillar by all four schools. (3)

---

akbar while raising his hands again. The worshiper says nothing more after this; rather, after allowing a short silence, he utters a single greeting of peace, though a second greeting of peace may be uttered as well.

421. According to the Hanafis, a silent intention to perform the funeral prayer is sufficient. Some of them, however, say that it is necessary for the worshiper to intend to perform the prayer over either a man, a female, a young boy, or a young girl, and that if the person praying does not know which of these the deceased is, he is to say, "I intend to perform the [funeral] prayer over the deceased person over whom the imam prays." The reason for this is that the deceased person is the cause for the prayer, and the cause must be identified. This is the interpretation of their ruling which appears to be the most correct. Some Hanafis say that, in addition, the person praying must intend to utter a prayer of supplication for the deceased as well.

* * *

According to the Malikis, it is sufficient for the worshiper to intend to perform the prayer "for this deceased person" without knowing whether the deceased is male or female. Hence, if the worshiper believes the deceased to be a male, after which it becomes apparent that it is a female, no harm is done. Nor is it necessary for him to intend the funeral prayer as an obligation, as the Hanafis do.

* * *

According to the Shafiis, the worshiper must intend to perform the obligatory funeral prayer even if he does not state specifically that it is a collective obligation. It is not necessary to specify that one is praying for the deceased person who is actually present; however, if one identifies the deceased, after which it becomes apparent that the deceased was someone else, the prayer will be invalid.

* * *

According to the Hanbalis, the worshiper must intend to pray "over this deceased person" or "over these deceased persons" whether or not he knows their number.

Remaining in a standing position from its beginning to its end; hence, if someone were to perform it from a sitting position without a valid excuse for doing so, it would be invalidated. (4) A prayer of supplication for the deceased; as for the exact description of this prayer, it differs from one school to another.[422] (5) Utterance of a greeting of peace after the fourth utterance of *Allāhu akbar*. This is a pillar of the funeral prayer according to the Shafiis, the Malikis and the Hanbalis. As for the Hanafis, they hold that it is a 'duty', just as it is in all other ritual prayers; hence,

---

422. Based on the formally recognized Maliki view, one must utter a prayer of supplication for the deceased after each of the four utterances of *Allāhu akbar*. When uttering such a prayer, the least one may say is: "O God, forgive him," and the like, whereas the preferred practice is to utter the prayer attributed to Abū Hurayrah, may God be pleased with him. Abū Hurayrah's prayer involves first praising God and praying for blessings upon His Prophet, after which one says, "O God, he is Your servant, the son of Your servant, and the son of Your handmaid. He bore witness that there is no god but You alone and that You have no partner, and that Muḥammad is Your servant and Your Messenger. You are the most knowledgeable of him. O God, if he was a doer of good, then increase his good deeds, and if he was a doer of ill, then overlook his bad deeds. O God, deprive us not of his reward, nor put us to the test after him." If the deceased is a woman, the worshiper is to say, "O God, she is Your handmaid, the daughter of Your servant and the daughter of Your handmaid," then proceed with the aforementioned prayer using the appropriate feminine referents. If the deceased is a male child, the worshiper should say, "O God, he is Your servant and the son of Your servant and You created him and provided for his sustenance. You caused him to die, and it is You who will cause him to live again. O God, cause him to go before his parents and make intercession for them, and let him be a storehouse of blessing and reward for them. Through him, cause their weight of good deeds to be heavy in the balance and cause their reward from You to be great, and do not put us and them to the test after him. O God, cause him to join the ranks of the righteous believers who went before us, and to benefit from the pledge given to Abraham. Grant him an abode better than his former abode and a family better than the family he left behind, and spare him the affliction of the tomb and the torment of Hell."

If the worshiper is praying over a male and a female together, he should use dual masculine referents, saying, "They are Your [two] servants, the [two] sons of Your [two] servants, and the sons of Your [two] handmaids…", etc. Similarly, if he is praying over a group of men and women, he should use masculine plural referents rather than feminine ones, saying, "O God, they are Your servants, the sons of Your servants," etc. If the deceased are a group of women, he should say, "O God, they are Your handmaids, the daughters of Your servants and the daughters of Your handmaids. They bore witness…," etc. Then, following the fourth utterance of *Allāhu akbar*, the worshiper should add, "O God, forgive our forebears, those who have gone ahead of us to make intercession on our behalf, and those who preceded us in faith. O God, those of us to whom You grant life, cause them to live in faith, and those of us whom You cause to die, cause them to die in Islam, and forgive all Muslims, both male and female." In conclusion, he utters a greeting of peace.

* * *

According to the Hanafis, the prayer of supplication for the deceased should follow the third utterance of *Allāhu akbar*. They do not specify any particular formula that must be followed; rather, they stipulate only that the prayer should consist of requests pertaining to the afterlife. Moreover, they consider it preferable for the worshiper to rely on the traditional supplication recorded in the hadith passed down on the authority of 'Awf Ibn Mālik, namely: "O God, forgive him, have mercy upon him, protect him, pardon him, and grant him an honorable abode. Broaden his entryway, wash him with water, snow and hail, and cleanse him of sins as a white robe is cleansed of impurities. Grant him an abode better than the abode he left behind, a family better than the family he left behind, and a spouse better than the one he left behind. Cause him to enter Paradise, and spare him the torment of both the grave and the Fire." This is the wording to be followed if the deceased is a man; if the deceased is a female, the masculine pronoun is replaced with the feminine pronoun and one does not say, "Grant her a spouse better than the one she left behind." If the deceased is a child, the worshiper says, "O God, cause him to go before us and make intercession on our behalf. O God, cause him to be for us a storehouse of blessing and reward. O God, cause him to be for us an intercessor whose intercession is acceptable [to You]." If the worshiper does not know this prayer, however, he may offer any supplication he wishes.

* * *

The Shafiis stipulate that the prayer of supplication be said after the third utterance of *Allāhu akbar*, and that it include a petition for blessing on behalf of the deceased person present. Hence, if the worshiper makes supplication for believers in general without singling out the deceased person whose funeral it is, this will not suffice unless the deceased is a young child, in which case it is sufficient to make supplication for the child's parents. In addition, they stipulate that the petition be for some blessing that pertains to the afterlife, such as forgiveness, mercy, etc.; this applies, moreover, even if the deceased was not held morally accountable under Islamic law, such as a young child or an insane person who had grown up insane and had continued in this state until he died. The worshiper is not restricted in this supplication to a particular formula. However, it is preferred that he use the supplication which is most widely used so long as there is no danger that the body may begin to smell. If there is reason to fear that this may happen, the supplication should be kept to a minimum. The wording of the supplication mentioned here is as follows: "O God, this is Your servant and the son of Your servant. He has departed from the spirit of the world and its spaciousness, from those he loved and those who loved him in the world, to enter the darkness of the tomb and whatever it is that he will meet there. He bore witness that there is no god but You alone and that You have no partner, and that our master Muḥammad is Your servant and Your Messenger. You, however, know him better than we ourselves do. O God, he has taken up his abode with You, and You are the best of all abodes. He is in need of Your mercy, while You have no need to punish him. We have come seeking You and offering intercession on his behalf. O God, if he was a doer of good, increase his good deeds, and if he was a doer of ill, overlook his sin, granting him, instead, Your mercy and Your favor and protecting him from the grave's affliction and torment.

Make his grave spacious, keep the earth from encroaching upon him, and grant him, by your Mercy, safety from Your chastisement until You resurrect him into Your Paradise, O Most Merciful of the merciful!"

Before this, it is desirable to say, "O God, forgive our living and our dead, those of us who are present and those of us who are absent, our young and our old, our males and our females. O God, those of us whom You cause to live, cause them to live in Islam, and those of us whom You cause to die, cause them to die in faith. O God, do not deprive us of his reward."

It is recommended that before these two supplications, one say, "O God, forgive him, have mercy upon him, protect him, pardon him, and grant him an honorable abode. Broaden his entryway and wash him with water, snow and hail, cleansing him of sins as a white robe is cleansed of impurities. Grant him a home better than the home he left behind, a family better than the family he left behind, and a spouse better than the spouse he left behind. Protect him from the grave's torment and affliction, and from the torment of the Fire." It is permissible, when making supplication for a child who has died, to replace the supplication mentioned with the following prayer: "O God, cause him to go ahead of his parents and make intercession for them, and to be a storehouse of blessing and reward for them. Cause him to be an intercessor, an admonition, and a warning. Through him, cause his parents' weight of good deeds to be heavy in the balance, fill their hearts with patient endurance, put them not to the test after him, and deprive them not of his reward."

Lastly, it is an emulation of the Sunnah for the person praying to raise his hands during every utterance of *Allāhu akbar*.

* * *

According to the Hanbalis, the supplication for the deceased is to be made after the third utterance of *Allāhu akbar*, although it is permissible to place it after the fourth utterance. However, it is not acceptable to utter it after the first or second utterance of *Allāhu akbar*. The least one is to say if the deceased is an adult is, "O God, forgive him", and the like, while the minimum if the deceased is a child is to say, "O God, forgive his parents on his account", or the like. It is an emulation of the Sunnah to use a supplication which has been passed down through hadith, one of which follows: "O God, forgive our living and our dead, those of us who are present and those of us who are absent, our young and our old, our males and our females. You know the end we will meet in death and our final place of rest, and You are capable of all things. O God, those of us whom You cause to live, cause them to live as adherents of Islam and the Sunnah, and those of us whom You cause to die, cause them to die likewise as adherents of Islam and the Sunnah. O God, forgive him, have mercy upon him, protect him, pardon him, and grant him an honorable abode. Broaden his entryway and wash him with water, snow and hail, cleansing him of guilt and sin as a white robe is cleansed of that which is impure. Grant him a home better than the one he left behind and a spouse better than the one he left behind. Bring him into Paradise, grant him refuge from the torment of the grave and the torment of the Fire. Cause his tomb to be spacious and filled with light."

they hold that prayer is not invalidated if the greeting of peace is omitted. (6) Prayer for blessings upon the Prophet after the second utterance of *Allāhu akbar*. This is a pillar of the funeral prayer according to the Shafiis and the Hanbalis; the views of the Hanafis and the Malikis are presented below.[423]

As for recitation of the *Fātiḥah*, the various schools hold differing views on its role in the funeral prayer.[424]

Conditions for the funeral prayer

The conditions which must be fulfilled in order for the funeral prayer to be valid are as follows: (1) The deceased must have been a Muslim. It is forbidden to perform the funeral prayer over a non-Muslim based on the words, "And never shalt thou pray over any of them that has died…" (9:84) (2) The deceased must be present. It is thus not permissible to pray over a deceased person who is absent. As for the Prophet's having performed the funeral prayer over the Abyssinian emperor [in his absence], the Hanafis and the Malikis consider it to have been a prerogative unique to him. For the views of the Shafiis and the Hanbalis, see below.[425] (3) The body of the deceased must have been ritually purified. Hence, all four schools agree that it is not permissible to perform the funeral prayer over the deceased's body before major ablutions or sand ablutions have been performed on it. (4) The deceased must be placed in front of the congregation. According to the Shafiis, the Hanbalis

---

This supplication is to be uttered if the deceased is an adult, whether male or female; however, feminine pronouns are to be used if the deceased is a female. If the deceased is a child or someone who grew up insane and continued to be insane until he died, the person praying should say, "O God, cause him to be a storehouse of blessing for his parents and someone who goes ahead to make intercession. Let him be a source of reward for them, and may his intercession for them be heard and answered. O God, through him, cause his parents' weight of good deeds to be heavy in the balance and cause their rewards to be great. O God, cause him to join the ranks of the righteous believers who have gone before us, let him be a beneficiary of the pledge given to Abraham, and protect him by Your mercy from the torment of Hell." This supplication is made for both males and females; however, the pronouns must be made feminine if the deceased is a female.

423. The Hanafis hold that the prayer for blessings upon the Prophet after the second utterance of *Allāhu akbar* is an emulation of the Sunnah, but not a pillar.

* * *

According to the Malikis, the prayer for blessings upon the Prophet is recommended following every utterance of *Allāhu akbar* before commencing the prayer of supplication.

424. According to the Hanafis, the recitation of the *Fātiḥah* with the intention of chanting the Qur'ān is undesirable to the point of being forbidden; however, if it is recited as part of a prayer of supplication, it is permitted.

* * *

According to the Shafiis, recitation of the *Fātiḥah* is a pillar of the funeral prayer. The *Fātiḥah* may be recited after any of the four utterances of *Allāhu akbar*, although it is considered preferable to recite it after the first of these. Once one has

and the Hanafis, it is not permissible to pray over the body if it is placed behind the worshipers. For the Malikis' view, see below.[426] (5) According to the Hanafis and the Hanbalis, the deceased must not be mounted on a riding animal, carried in others' arms, or borne on top of their shoulders at the time when the funeral prayer is being performed. The Malikis and the Shafiis, however, hold that praying for the deceased while the body is borne on an animal, carried in others' arms or on top of their shoulders is permissible. (6) The deceased must not have died as a martyr. (A separate discussion of martyrs will be found below.) According to the Shafiis, the Malikis and the Hanbalis, it is forbidden to pray over the body of a martyr due to the fact that it is not permissible to perform major ablutions on it prior to the prayer. However, the Hanafis hold that even though it is forbidden to wash a martyr's body, it must nevertheless be prayed over. (7) That which is present of the deceased's body must be those parts which have to be washed. (For those parts which must be washed, see the earlier section on performing major ablutions on the deceased.) If the ruling on a miscarried fetus is that it must be washed, it is also obligatory to perform the funeral prayer over it.

As for the conditions associated with the person who performs the funeral payer, they are the same as those that apply to regular ritual prayer, such as intention, ritual purity, facing the *qiblah*, concealment of one's private parts, etc.

---

begun reciting the *Fātiḥah* after any of the utterances of *Allāhu akbar*, one must complete it; it is thus not permissible to cut it off or to postpone it until after the following utterance of *Allāhu akbar*, and if one does so, the prayer will be invalidated. This applies to all worshipers, including those who have arrived late for the funeral prayer.

* * *

According to the Hanbalis, the recitation of the *Fātiḥah* is a pillar of the funeral prayer, and must follow the first utterance of *Allāhu akbar*.

* * *

As for the Malikis, they hold that the recitation of the *Fātiḥah* is undesirable during the funeral prayer.

425. According to the Hanbalis, it is permissible to perform the funeral prayer on behalf of someone who is absent provided that it takes place no more than a month after the person's death.

* * *

According to the Shafiis, the funeral prayer is valid even if it is performed for someone absent from the country without any undesirability attached to it.

426. According to the Malikis, the presence of the deceased is obligatory. As for placing the body in front of the person performing the funeral prayer such that he is standing across from the shoulders of the deceased in the case of a man, or across from the deceased's middle in the case of a woman, this is simply recommended.

Sunnah-based practices related to the funeral prayer: How the imam should stand to pray over the deceased

The Sunnah-based practices associated with the funeral prayer are listed in detail below.[427]

---

427. The Hanafis list the following as Sunnah-based practices in connection with the funeral prayer: (1) Utterance of the prayer of commencement (or the prayer of praise), namely, "Glory be to You, O God, and praise! May Your name be blessed and Your majesty exalted! There is no god but You!" (*subhānuk Allāhumma wa biḥamdika, wa tabāraka ismuk wa ta'ālā jadduk wa lā ilāha ghayruk*) following the first utterance of *Allāhu akbar*. (2) Prayer for blessings upon the Prophet after the second utterance of *Allāhu akbar*. (3) Supplication for the deceased (based on the view that such supplication is not a pillar of the funeral prayer).

In addition, it is recommended that the imam stand across from the deceased's chest, whether the deceased is a male or a female, an adult or a child, and that the worshipers praying for the deceased be divided into three rows. This is based on the saying of the Prophet, "If a deceased person is prayed over by three rows of worshipers, his sins will be forgiven." Hence, if there are seven worshipers taking part in the funeral prayer, one should stand in front [as the imam], followed by a row of three, followed by a row of two, followed by a row of one.

* * *

According to the Malikis, there are no Sunnah-based practices associated with the funeral prayer, but rather, desirable practices. These are as follows: (1) Performing the funeral prayer silently. (2) Raising the hands when uttering the first *Allāhu akbar* only. They should be raised until they are level with one's ears as one does when uttering *takbīrat al-iḥrām* for other ritual prayers. (3) Beginning the prayer of supplication with praise to God Almighty and a prayer for blessings upon the Prophet, as we have seen. (4) For the imam and someone who is praying alone to stand at the deceased's waist if he is a man, and at the deceased's shoulders if she is a woman. The head of the deceased, whether it is a man or a woman, should be to the worshiper's right unless the funeral prayer is being performed in the *Rawḍah*, in which case it should be to the worshiper's left in order for it to be located toward the Prophet's tomb. As for those who are being led in the funeral prayer, they should stand behind the imam as they would in any other ritual prayer, and as we saw earlier in our discussion of communal prayer. (6) For the imam to utter the greeting of peace and the *Allāhu akbar* loud enough to be heard by those behind him; as for other worshipers, however, they are to utter them silently.

* * *

The Hanbalis list the following four Sunnah-based practices in connection with the funeral prayer: (1) That it be performed in community. (2) That the number of worshipers in each row not be less than three if there is a large congregation. If there are six worshipers, the imam should divide them into two rows [of three], and if there are four, he should divide them into two rows of two each. As in other ritual prayers, it is not acceptable for one person to pray alone behind the other rows. (3)

That the imam or someone praying alone stand at the deceased's chest if the deceased is a male, and that he stand at the deceased's middle if the deceased is a female. (4) That recitations and supplications be performed silently.

* * *

As for the Shafiis, they list the following Sunnah-based practices in connection with the funeral prayer: (1) Uttering the prayer for divine protection, *a'ūdhu billāh min al-shayṭān al-rajīm,* before reciting the *Fātiḥah.* (2) Concluding the *Fātiḥah* with the word *Āmīn.* (3) Uttering all parts of the prayer silently, even if it is being performed at night. This applies unless there is a need for the imam or the *muballigh* to speak aloud when uttering the phrase *Allāhu akbar* and the greeting of peace. (4) Performing the funeral prayer in community. (5) Dividing the worshipers into three rows if possible. The minimum size for a given row is two worshipers even if this includes the imam; hence, it is not considered undesirable for one of the worshipers being led in prayer to stand alongside the imam. (6) Uttering the most complete prayer for blessings upon the Prophet, as was mentioned in connection with regular ritual prayer. (7) Praying for blessing upon the Prophet's descendents, but without greeting them, and upon the Prophet. (8) Uttering the phrase *al-ḥamdu lillāh* before praying for blessings upon the Prophet. (9) Uttering a prayer of supplication for all believers, male and female, after the prayer for blessings upon the Prophet. (10) Uttering the traditional prayer of supplication associated with the funeral prayer. (11) Uttering the second greeting of peace. (12) Uttering the words, "O God, do not deprive us of his reward or put us to the test after him" and reciting the verse which reads, "O our Sustainer! Thou embracest all things within Thy grace and knowledge. Forgive, then, their sins unto those who repent and follow Thy path, and preserve them from suffering through the blazing fire!" (40:7) between the fourth utterance of *Allāhu akbar* and the greeting of peace. (13) Standing at the deceased's head if he is a male, and at the deceased's hips in the case of a female or a hermaphrodite. (This is an emulation of the Sunnah for the imam or for someone who is praying alone.) (14) Raising one's hands during each utterance of *Allāhu akbar*, then placing them on one's stomach right under the chest. (15) Not concluding the funeral until those who arrived late have finished performing the prayer. (16) Having different people perform the funeral prayer over the same person; as for repeating the prayer, this is considered undesirable. (17) Omitting the prayer of commencement and the recitation of a passage from the Qur'ān after the *Fātiḥah.*

Lastly, the Shafiis hold that it is undesirable to pray over the deceased before he or she has been wrapped for burial.

Who is most entitled to pray over the deceased

The various schools differ in their rulings on who is most entitled to pray over a deceased person.[428]

---

428. According to the Hanafis, those entitled to pray over a given deceased person are as follows in descending order of priority: (1) the sultan [i.e., head of state] or his proxy, namely, the mayor of the city or village where the prayer is being conducted. (3) the magistrate, (4) the chief of police, (5) the deceased's living imam if he is superior to the deceased's guardian, (6) the deceased's guardian based on the hierarchy of male relatives by marriage (in other words, first priority is given to the deceased's son, then the son's son, grandson, great-grandson, etc., then the father, then the grandfather, great-grandfather, etc., then the full brother, then the half-brother on the father's side, then the full brother's son, and so on, as is detailed in the section on marriage). If the deceased has no guardian, priority is given to the spouse, then the neighbors. If the deceased left instructions that a certain person should pray over him or wash him, such instructions are to be considered null and void and not implemented. Lastly, the person who is most entitled to pray over the deceased may grant permission to someone else to perform the funeral prayer in his stead.

* * *

According to the Hanbalis, those entitled to pray over a given deceased person in the capacity of imam are as follows in descending order of priority: (1) A reliable trustee. In other words, if the deceased left instructions that a particular trustworthy person should pray over his body, this person should be given priority over all others. (2) The sultan [i.e., head of state], then his proxy. (3) The deceased's father, grandfather, great-grandfather, etc. (4) The deceased's son, grandson, great-grandson, and so on, based on the order of priority employed when determining who is to be given shares of an inheritance. (5) Maternal relatives. (6) The deceased's spouse.

If the deceased's guardians have equal degrees of closeness to the deceased, such as brothers, paternal uncles, etc., priority is given to those who best meet the requirements for serving as an imam, and which were listed in our discussion of communal prayer. If they are all equal with respect to all criteria, lots are to be cast among them if there is a dispute. Moreover, if the deceased's guardian appoints someone else to pray in his stead, this person is to be considered his equal and given priority over the person next in rank to him [that is, the deceased's guardian], whereas someone appointed by the trustee is not to be considered his equal.

* * *

According to the Shafiis, the right to pray over the deceased in the capacity of imam is granted first to the deceased's father, grandfather, great-grandfather, etc., then to his son, grandson, etc., then his full brother, then his paternal half-brother, then his full brother's son, then his paternal half-brother's son, and so on in the same order as that which is followed in determining priority rights among heirs. If the deceased has no surviving relatives, priority is given to the person who granted him his freedom [assuming he was once a slave], then to his relatives on his father's side in order of decreasing closeness, then to the chief imam or his proxy, then to the deceased's maternal relatives in order of decreasing closeness. When the candidates are equal in other respects, as in the case of two sons, priority is given to the one who has been a Muslim for a longer time and who is known to be upright and trustworthy, then to the most knowledgeable of Islamic jurisprudence, then to the most skilled in Qur'anic recitation, then to the most pious. However, if the deceased left instructions for someone to pray over him when such a person would not otherwise deserve to be given priority, his or her instructions are not to be implemented.

* * *

According to the Malikis, the right to pray over the deceased is given first to the person whom the deceased left instructions that he should pray over him if these instructions were given in the hope of receiving the blessing of the person to perform the prayer; otherwise, however, such a person is not to be given such priority. Second in order of priority is the caliph; as for his proxy, he has no priority right in this regard unless he is the caliph's proxy in the roles of governing and delivering the sermon. Third in order are the deceased's closest paternal relatives; first in order is the deceased's son, then his son's son, his father, then his brother, then his brother's son, then his grandfather, then his paternal uncle, then his paternal uncle's son, and so on. If there are several such relatives who are equally close to the deceased, priority right is to be given based on their knowledge of Islamic jurisprudence or hadiths, and the like. No one other than the deceased's paternal relatives is to be given priority right unless he is a 'chief' or 'head' [within the clan], in which case he is next in line following the deceased's paternal relations. If the deceased has no surviving paternal relatives and there is no 'chief' available, all outsiders are to be considered equal; however, they are to be ranked according to the same criteria that apply to the right to serve as imam for a communal prayer.

If the imam utters the words *Allāhu akbar* either more than or fewer than four times

First: If the imam utters the phrase *Allāhu akbar* either more than or fewer than four times, the various schools holding differing views on whether those being led in prayer are to follow the imam in this or not and on the resulting validity, or lack thereof, of the funeral prayer.[429]

---

429. According to the Hanafis, if the imam utters the phrase *Allāhu akbar* more than four times, those being led in prayer are not to follow him in this addition; rather, they are to wait, then utter the final greeting of peace with him. If they do this, everyone's prayer will be valid. If the imam utters the words *Allāhu akbar* fewer than four times, everyone's prayer will be invalidated if the omission was deliberate. If the omission was unintentional, the ruling that applies to this situation is the same as that which applies when a *rak'ah* is omitted from ritual prayer; however, no prostration of forgetfulness is to be performed for the funeral prayer. As for the ruling on the omission of a *rak'ah* during ritual prayer, this has been discussed above.

* * *

The Shafiis hold that if the imam includes more than four utterances of *Allāhu akbar*, those being led in prayer are not to follow him in this; rather, they are to intend in their hearts to part with the imam, then utter the final greeting of peace before he does, or wait and perform the final greeting of peace with the imam, the preferred practice being to wait. When this occurs, everyone's prayer will be valid unless, as those being led in prayer wait for the imam, he raises his hands during a succession of three additional utterances of *Allāhu akbar*, in which case the prayer is invalidated both for him and for those being led in prayer. If the imam utters the words *Allāhu akbar* fewer than four times, the prayer will be invalidated both for him and for those being led in prayer if the omission was deliberate. If it was not deliberate, he should simply make up the omission as he would for a regular ritual prayer, but without performing a prostration of forgetfulness.

* * *

As for the Malikis, they hold that if the imam performs more than four utterances of *Allāhu akbar*, whether intentionally or unintentionally, it is undesirable for those being led in prayer to wait for him. Rather, they should utter the final greeting of peace without him, in which case both his and their prayers will be valid. If the imam deliberately performs fewer than four utterances of *Allāhu akbar* because this is what he believes his school of jurisprudence teaches him to do, those being led in prayer should not follow him in this; instead, they should complete four utterances of *Allāhu akbar* and everyone's prayer will be valid. If, on the other hand, the imam deliberately performs fewer than four utterances of *Allāhu akbar* without seeing this as what his school of jurisprudence teaches him to do, both his prayer and the prayer of those following him will be invalidated. If the imam mistakenly omits one or more utterances of *Allāhu akbar*, those being led in prayer should say *subḥān Allāh* to alert him to his error; if he corrects his error promptly and performs all four utterances of *Allāhu akbar*, they are to complete them with him and everyone's prayer will be valid. If, on the other hand, the imam does not correct his error for a long time, those being led in prayer are to complete the four utterances of *Allāhu akbar* themselves, in which case their prayer will be valid, but that of the imam will be invalid.

* * *

The Hanafis hold that if the imam utters the words *Allāhu akbar* more than four times, those being led in prayer are to follow him up to seven times. If he says *Allāhu akbar* more than seven times, they are to alert him to his error; however, they should not utter the final greeting of peace before him and if they adhere to this ruling, everyone's prayer will be valid. If the imam intentionally utters the phrase *Allāhu akbar* fewer than four times, everyone's prayer will be invalidated; if he does so unintentionally, those being led in prayer should not utter the final greeting of peace but rather, alert him to his error. If, after being alerted, the imam quickly makes up what he omitted, everyone's prayer will be valid; however, if a long time passes, or if the imam performs some action which is inconsistent with prayer, the imam's prayer will be invalid. As for the prayer of those being led by the imam, it will remain valid if they make it their intention to part with the imam; if they do not, their prayer will likewise be invalidated.

If a worshiper misses one or more utterances of *Allāhu akbar* with the imam

Each of the four schools offers its own ruling on a situation in which, when a worshiper arrives for the funeral prayer, the imam has already performed one or more utterances of the phrase, *Allāhu akbar*.[430]

430. The Hanafis hold that if, when a worshiper arrives for the funeral prayer, the imam: (1) has completed *takbīrat al-iḥrām* and is uttering the prayer of commencement, (2) has completed the second utterance of *Allāhu akbar* and is praying for blessings upon the Prophet, or (3) has performed the third utterance of *Allāhu akbar* and is uttering a prayer of supplication for the deceased, he should not utter the phrase *Allāhu akbar* right away; instead, he should wait for his imam in order to utter the phrase *Allāhu akbar* with him. If he does not wait for the imam in this situation and goes ahead and says *Allāhu akbar*, his prayer will not be invalidated; however, this utterance of *Allāhu akbar* will not be counted, and after the imam has uttered the final greeting of peace, the worshiper who arrived late should make up the utterances of *Allāhu akbar* that he missed provided that the funeral does not end immediately. If the funeral does end immediately, the worshiper should simply utter the final greeting of peace and not make up the utterances of *Allāhu akbar* which he missed. If, on the other hand, the worshiper arrives after the imam has performed the fourth utterance of *Allāhu akbar* and before he has uttered the final greeting of peace, the correct practice is for him to enter the prayer with the imam, then complete it on his own after the imam has uttered the final greeting of peace in accordance with the detailed description [of the funeral prayer] given above.

* * *

The Malikis hold that if, when a worshiper arrives for the funeral prayer, the imam is uttering a prayer of supplication for the deceased, he should not utter the *Allāhu akbar*; rather, he should wait until the imam does so, then utter it with him. If the worshiper does not wait for the imam to utter *Allāhu akbar* and utters it by himself, his prayer will be valid; however, his opening utterance of *Allāhu akbar* will not be counted whether he waits for the imam or not. Then, when the imam utters the final greeting of peace, the worshiper should rise and make up whichever utterances of *Allāhu akbar* he missed regardless of whether the funeral ends immediately or continues. If the funeral continues, the worshiper should utter a prayer of supplication after every utterance of *Allāhu akbar* he makes up. If, on the other hand, the funeral ends immediately, he should perform the various utterances of *Allāhu akbar* in immediate succession without uttering prayers of supplication between them lest he be praying over someone who is absent, since praying over a deceased person who is absent is forbidden, as we have seen. If a worshiper arrives for the funeral prayer after the imam and those with him have completed the fourth utterance of *Allāhu akbar*, he should not join the imam in the prayer, properly speaking, since by this time, the imam will be ready for the final testimony, and if he joined him at this point, he would be repeating the funeral prayer over the deceased, which is undesirable.

* * *

According to the Hanbalis, if a worshiper arrives for the funeral prayer (1) after the imam has completed the first utterance of *Allāhu akbar* and is performing Qur'anic recitation, (2) after the latter has uttered the second *Allāhu akbar* and is praying for blessings upon the Prophet, or (3) after the latter has uttered the third *Allāhu akbar* and is uttering a prayer of supplication for the deceased, he is to utter *Allāhu akbar* immediately and not wait for the imam to do so. He should then follow the imam in whatever he performs next. After the imam utters the final greeting of peace, he should make up whatever he missed by, for example, reciting the *Fātiḥah* after making up the first *Allāhu akbar*, then by praying for blessings upon the Prophet after making up the second *Allāhu akbar* if he has no reason to fear that the funeral is about to end. If he does have reason to fear that the funeral might end, he should make up all utterances of *Allāhu akbar* which he missed in immediate succession, without intercession and the like between them, then utter the final greeting of peace. The Hanbalis hold that it is permissible for a worshiper to utter the final greeting of peace without making up what he missed; they also hold that one may join the imam following the final utterance of *Allāhu akbar*, after which it is desirable to make up the other three utterances.

* * *

As for the Shafiis, they hold that if, when a worshiper arrives for the funeral prayer, the imam has finished uttering the first *Allāhu akbar* or any of the other four utterances of this phrase and is engaged in what follows it such as recitation, [supplication, etc.], he should join the imam rather than waiting until he utters the subsequent *Allāhu akbar*. However, he should proceed with his prayer based on the same pattern he would follow if he were praying on his own. Hence, after uttering the first *Allāhu akbar*, he should recite as much of the *Fātiḥah* as he can before the imam says *Allāhu akbar* [again], in which case he will be exempted from whatever of the *Fātiḥah* remains. He should then pray for blessings upon the Prophet after the second *Allāhu akbar* and so on. When the imam completes his prayer, the worshiper following him is to complete his own prayer based on the aforementioned pattern whether the funeral has ended or not. Moreover, if the worshiper is unable to utter any of the *Fātiḥah* because the imam said *Allāhu akbar* immediately after he [the person following the imam] uttered the opening *Allāhu akbar*, the worshiper should utter *Allāhu akbar* together with the imam, allowing the imam's recitation of the entire *Fātiḥah* to suffice in his stead.

Whether it is permissible to repeat the prayer over the deceased

It is undesirable to repeat the funeral prayer; hence, it is to be performed only once, since its initial performance was done in community. If, on the other hand, someone first performs the funeral prayer alone, it is recommended that it be performed again in community provided that the burial has not taken place yet. This is the view held by the Hanafis and the Malikis; the views of the Shafiis and the Hanbalis are presented below.[431]

Whether it is permissible to pray over the deceased in a mosque

It is undesirable to pray over the deceased in a mosque even if the deceased is outside the building proper; it is likewise undesirable to bring the deceased into the mosque without praying over him or her according to the Hanafis and the Malikis. As for the Hanbalis and the Shafiis, their views on this matter are presented below.[432]

On those who died as martyrs

The four schools differ in detail concerning the definition of 'martyr', the ruling on martyrs, and the types of martyr.[433]

---

431. According to the Shafiis, it is an emulation of the Sunnah to perform the funeral prayer again for the sake of those who did not pray it before, even if this is done following the burial.

* * *

According to the Hanbalis, it is permissible to repeat the funeral prayer for the sake of those who did not pray it before even if this is done after the burial; however, it is undesirable for the funeral prayer to be repeated by those who prayed it before.

432. According to the Hanbalis, it is permissible to pray over the deceased inside a mosque if there is no reason to fear that this would result in contaminating the mosque with impurities. Otherwise, it is forbidden both to pray over the deceased in the mosque and to bring him or her into the mosque.

* * *

As for the Shafiis, they hold that it is recommended that the prayer over the deceased be performed in a mosque.

433. According to the Hanafis, a martyr is someone who was killed unjustly, whether he was killed in a war or was murdered by an outlaw, a non-Muslim citizen of a non-Muslim state which is making war on Muslims, a highway robber or a thief. Moreover, the definition of 'martyr' applies even if the person was killed through an indirect cause.

The Hanafis identify three types of martyr. First: The 'perfect' martyr, or the martyr in both this world and the next. In order to be a martyr in this sense, the following six conditions must be met: (1) The person must have been in full possession of his mental faculties. (2) The person must have been of full legal age. (3) He or she must have been a Muslim. (4) The deceased must have been free of major ritual impurity, including menstrual flow and post-partum bleeding. (5) He or she must have died immediately from his or her wound, that is, before having eaten, drunk, or slept. In addition, the person must have died without having first been treated or moved from the place where he or she was wounded to his or her tent or home, and he or she must have died from the wound before the time for the subsequent prayer had passed. (6) The person's death must have been such as to require legal retribution, even if such retribution has been rescinded due to some intervening development such as arbitration and the like. If, on the other hand, the death was of the type that calls for monetary compensation (as, for example, when someone is killed unintentionally), the person who was killed may not be considered a 'perfect' martyr. This type of martyr also includes those who were killed while engaged in defending their property, their lives, or the Muslims, or those belonging to a protected religious minority (*ahl al-dhimmah*); however, he or she must have been killed with a sharpened instrument. The ruling with respect to this type of martyr is that he or she is only to be washed if there is some impurity, other than his or her blood, clinging to the body. The body of such a martyr is to be buried in the same clothes that he or she was wearing when he or she died, although if they include materials that would not be permissible as grave clothes, such as tanned leather, stuffing [*al-ḥashw*; it is unclear what is being referred to here – t.n.], his headgear, his shoes, his weapon, and his coat of mail, these should be removed. Trousers, however, need not be removed; nor 'stuffing' nor tanned leather if they are the only materials available. If the clothes the deceased is wearing fall short of the grave clothes prescribed by the Sunnah, they are to be supplemented, and if they exceed this, some of them are to be removed. Once this has been done, the deceased is prayed over and buried with his blood and clothing.

Second: Those who are martyrs in the afterlife only. These include those who fail to fulfill one of the conditions mentioned above, for example, (1) by having been killed unjustly, but while in a state of major ritual impurity, while menstruating, or while experiencing post-partum bleeding, (2) by not having died immediately from their wounds, (3) due to being a child or insane, or (4) by having been killed by accident such that the killing called for monetary compensation. Such people are still martyrs in the afterlife and receive the same reward promised to martyrs on the Day of Resurrection; however, they are not 'perfect' martyrs. As a consequence, they are to be washed and wrapped for burial and prayed over just as others are. Others who are likewise classified as martyrs in the afterlife are those who drowned, who were burned to death, those who died from having walls fall on them, those who died while living in a foreign land, those who died of the plague, dropsy, diarrhea, pleurisy, post-partum bleeding, tuberculosis, epilepsy, fever, or a scorpion sting and the like, as well as those who died while in the pursuit of knowledge and those who died on a Thursday night. Such people are to be washed, wrapped for burial and prayed over even though they have the same reward as martyrs in the hereafter.

Third: Those who are martyrs in this life only, that is, hypocrites who were killed [while fighting] in the Muslim ranks and the like. Such people are not to be washed, they are to be wrapped for burial in the same clothes they were wearing when they died, and they are not to be prayed over, based on what they appeared to be.

* * *

The Hanbalis define a martyr as someone who died in battle as a result of fighting against unbelievers. This definition includes those who died in this manner and who were not held morally accountable under Islamic law, as well as those who kept back some of the spoils of war for themselves, be they men or women. The ruling on martyrs of this type is that it is forbidden to wash them or pray over them and that they must be buried in the same clothing in which they were killed unless they were in need of major ablutions (other than those required when one first enters Islam) before they were killed. In the case of a martyr who was in need of major ablutions at the time of his or death, he or she is to be wrapped for burial, prayed over and buried with the blood which is on him or her unless there is some impurity on his or her body other than blood, in which case [only] the impurity should be washed off. It is necessary to remove from the martyr's body whatever weapons or tanned leather he was wearing or carrying; however, nothing should be taken away from or added to the clothes he was wearing when he was killed. If the person has been despoiled of his clothing, he must be buried in other clothes. Other people who also fall under this category of martyr are those who were killed unjustly, for example, while they were defending their honor, their property, etc.; such martyrs are not to be washed, prayed over, or wrapped for burial; rather, they are to be buried in their clothes. As for those who do not fall within this category, they include those who did not die due to some action committed by an enemy but rather, due to falling off a riding animal while in battle, falling off a high mountain, or having their own arrow come back at them. It also includes those who were found dead outside of battle or who were wounded, then carried away, as a result of which they ate, drank, or got thirsty, or survived their wounds for what would commonly be considered a long time before they died; such people are to be washed, wrapped for burial and prayed over like non-martyrs. Even so, they will be like martyrs on the Day of Resurrection.

The type of martyr described thus far is a martyr in both this world and the next; there is another type of martyr, referred to as a martyr in the afterlife, namely, someone who does not fulfill the previously mentioned conditions. However, authentic sources indicate that such people are, in fact, martyrs on the Day of Resurrection. Such martyrs include those who died from a plague, from a stomach ache or by drowning or choking, those who burned to death, those who died due to a building being razed on top of them, those who died of pleurisy, tuberculosis or facial paralysis, who fell off a mountain or who died while performing some type of obedience or service to God (such as those who died while on the major pilgrimage or in the pursuit of knowledge), those who left home with the sincere intention of fighting in the way of God and being martyred but who died on the way without encountering the enemy, those who died while stationed as guards on an enemy frontier or while serving as God's trustees on earth, that is, as scholars, those who were killed while defending their religion, honor, property, or lives, and those who were killed by beasts of prey and the like.

* * *

The Malikis define a martyr as someone who was killed by a non-Muslim subject of a non-Muslim state which is at war with the Muslims, or who was killed in a battle between Muslims and non-Muslims, whether the fighting took place in the non-Muslims' territory or the Muslims' territory. This definition also applies to someone who was killed by non-Muslims invading Muslim territory. The ruling in connection with this type of martyr is that it is forbidden to wash him or pray over him even if he did not actually fight (as, for example, if he was unaware or asleep and was then killed), or if he was killed by a Muslim who thought he was a non-Muslim, or was trampled by horses, or was killed when his own sword or arrow came back at him, or fell into a well or off a high mountain. In all such cases, it is forbidden to wash or pray over the deceased. This ruling applies equally to someone who was in a state of major ritual impurity and to someone who was not; rather, all that is required is that the person not have been removed from the battlefield while still alive. If he was removed alive, he must be washed and prayed over unless, when he was taken away, he was so overwhelmed that he could neither eat, drink nor speak; such a person is like someone who was taken away from the battle dead and, therefore, must neither be washed nor prayed over. In addition, a martyr of this type must be buried in the same clothes in which he died provided that they are the type of clothes in which it would be permissible to wrap someone for burial. Nothing is to be added to the deceased's clothing so long as it covers his entire body; if it does not, enough should be added to conceal the entire body. Such a person's shoes are not to be removed, nor his head covering, nor his belt or sash if it is of little value; similarly, his rings are not to be removed if the stones they contain are of little value and if the rings are not silver. If they are silver, they should be removed and he should be buried without them. The deceased's fighting gear, such as his sword, his coat of mail, etc., should likewise be removed.

The description above includes: (1) martyrs in this world and the next, that is, those who fought in order to advance the word of God, (2) martyrs in this world only, that is, those who fought for the spoils of war, and (3) martyrs in the next world only, that is, those who died of causes such as an intestinal disorder, those who drowned, those who died in a fire, etc., and those who were killed unjustly (but not while fighting non-Muslim combatants). Such martyrs are to be washed and prayed over just as non-martyrs are, and they are not to be buried in their clothes. Someone who is a martyr in the next life is to receive the reward in the afterlife promised in Islamic law, God willing; as for those who are martyrs in this world alone, they have no reward in the afterlife even though they are given the same treatment as martyrs in this world, as we have seen.

* * *

The Shafiis divide martyrs into the following three categories: (1) Martyrs in this life and in the next. Martyrs in this category are those who fought non-believers in order to advance the word of God without hypocrisy and without taking any of the spoils for themselves before they had been divided among the other fighters. (2)

Martyrs in this life only. Martyrs in this category are those who fought for the spoils of war, even if they also did so in order to advance the word of God, or who fought out of hypocrisy or took some of the spoils before they had been divided. (3) Martyrs in the next life only. Martyrs in this category are those who died due to a building being razed on top of them, who drowned, etc, as well as those who were killed unjustly.

Those belonging to the first and second categories may not be washed or prayed over even if they are in a state of major or minor ritual impurity. This ruling also applies whether the person was killed by the weapon of a non-believer or accidentally by another Muslim. This ruling applies likewise to someone who was killed by his own weapon, who fell off his riding animal and died, or who was trampled by beasts of burden. This ruling also applies equally to someone who died immediately and someone who remained alive for some time after his or her injury, provided that the cause of death occurred before the war came to an end or that, although he or she died after the war's end, there was so little life left in his or her body after the injury that it made no motion but that of a slaughtered animal. Such a martyr must be wrapped for burial, but it is an emulation of the Sunnah for him or her to be wrapped for burial in his or her clothing; if the clothing is insufficient to cover the deceased's body, more clothing must be added to it. It is also recommended that the deceased's fighting gear, such as his coat of mail, shoes, tanned leather pieces, weapons, etc., be removed.

As for martyrs belonging to the third category, they are martyrs only in terms of their reward in the afterlife; with respect to this life, however, they are given the same treatment as non-martyrs in the sense that they must be washed and prayed over. All the aforementioned considerations connected to what covers the deceased must be observed here as well. Lastly, any impurity clinging to the body of someone whom it is forbidden to wash must be removed with the exception of the blood of martyrdom, even if the removal of the impurity results in the removal of the blood as well.

Miscellaneous matters relating to funerals and the visiting of graves

Rulings on carrying the deceased and how this is to be done

Like the washing of the deceased, wrapping the body for burial, and praying over the deceased, carrying the deceased to the grave is likewise a collective duty. Concerning the Sunnah-based manner of carrying the deceased, each of the four schools offers its own detailed rulings.[434]

---

434. According to the Hanafis, the minimum emulation of the Sunnah is achieved by the deceased's being carried by four men in relay fashion, as it were, with the bier being carried ten steps on each side. As for a perfect emulation of the Sunnah, it is achieved as follows: The person carrying the deceased begins with the right front corner of the bier, placing it on his left shoulder [the text reads "right shoulder" – t.n.] for ten steps; he then moves to the right rear of the bier and places it on his left shoulder [text reads "right shoulder" – t.n.] for ten more steps. He then moves to the left front of the bier and carries it on his right shoulder [the text reads, "left shoulder" – t.n.], then moves to the left rear of the bier and places it on his right shoulder [text reads "left shoulder" – t.n.] as well. It is undesirable for the bier to be carried initially on one's shoulder, however. Rather, the Sunnah dictates that one should take hold of the leg of the bier with one's hands, then place it on one's shoulder. It is undesirable to carry the deceased on two poles, with one man carrying it from the front and the other from the back unless it is necessary to do so.

As for a nursing infant, a toddler, or a child somewhat older than this, he or she should be carried by a single man in his arms, then be passed from one person to another, who should also carry the child in his or her arms. It is also acceptable for someone to carry a deceased child in his arms while riding [an animal]. However, it is undesirable to carry a deceased adult on a riding animal or the like unless necessity requires it.

It is recommended that the funeral procession move forward at a brisk pace, but not so brisk as to agitate the deceased on his or her bier. It is recommended that a woman's bier be covered; similarly, her grave should remain covered while burial is in progress until her *lahd* has been completed. The reason for this is that the woman is considered to be 'unpresentable' from head to toe; hence, none of her body should be revealed, and if it is certain that part of it will be revealed, it is obligatory to cover her grave.

* * *

According to the Hanbalis, it is an emulation of the Sunnah for the deceased to be carried by four men such that each of them carries the bier one time by each of its legs. Specifically, one of the men places the left front leg on his right shoulder and walks a distance; he then turns this leg over to someone else and moves to the rear left leg and places it on his right shoulder as well. After carrying this leg for a distance, he turns it over to someone else and places the right front leg on his left shoulder. He then turns this leg over to someone else and moves to the rear right leg and places it on his left shoulder as well. It is acceptable to carry the bier between two of its legs; it is also acceptable to carry a deceased child in one's arms without a bier, or to carry the deceased on a riding animal if this is due to some necessity, such as the graveyard's being a long distance away, etc. It is an emulation of the Sunnah to conceal the woman's bier with a dome-like cover made of wood or palm leaves, and to cover the dome with a robe.

* * *

According to the Malikis, there is no specific manner in which the deceased must be carried. Hence, the deceased may be carried by four people, three people, or two people without any undesirability attached thereto. Nor is it necessary to begin carrying the bier from a particular side; in fact, the Malikis hold that specifying a certain side from which it must be carried first is an [unjustified] innovation. It is recommended that a deceased child be carried in one's arms; in fact, it is undesirable to carry a deceased child on a bier due to the ostentation this suggests. It is recommended that a woman's bier be covered with something like a dome, since this is more conducive to the concealment she requires. It is undesirable to spread silk under the deceased. As for concealing it with silk, this is permissible provided that it is not colored; otherwise, it is undesirable.

* * *

The Shafiis specify two ways of carrying the deceased, the first of which they deem preferable to the second. In the first, three men carry the bier in such a way that the first man is carrying the front end of the bier with one corner on one shoulder, one corner on the other shoulder and his head in the center. The rear end of the bier is then carried by two other men, each of whom places one corner of the bier on one of his shoulders. In the second way, four men carry the deceased, with two carrying the front end of the bier and two others carrying the back end. Those who are walking to the right of the deceased place the edge of the bier on their left shoulders, while those walking to the left of the bier place the left edge of the bier on top of their right shoulders.

The Shafiis stipulate that the deceased person must not be carried in an undignified manner, for example, by an adult's being carried in one's arms or over one's shoulders, whereas such a mode of carrying would be appropriate for a deceased child. In addition, they hold that it is an emulation of the Sunnah for a woman's bier to be concealed by a cover or for something like a dome to be placed over it. They also hold that silk may be placed over the cover of a woman's bier. According to the officially recognized Shafii view, this applies likewise to a child's bier. As for a man's bier, it may not be covered with silk.

Rulings on escorting the deceased to his final resting place and related matters

As for escorting the deceased to the gravesite, this is an emulation of the Sunnah, although according to the Malikis, it is simply recommended. According to the Malikis, the Hanbalis, and the Shafiis, it is recommended that those escorting the deceased to the graveyard be on foot, and it is undesirable for them to ride unless there is a valid excuse for doing so, in which case it is acceptable. As for the Hanafis, they hold that there is nothing objectionable about riding in a funeral procession, although it is preferable to walk. However, if the person escorting the bier is riding, it is undesirable for him to be at the head of the procession because he will disturb those behind him by stirring up dust.

The Malikis and the Hanbalis hold that it is recommended that those escorting the deceased be at the head of the procession if they are on foot, and that they remain behind it if they are riding. For the views of the Hanafis and the Shafiis, see below.[435]

According to the Hanbalis, the Hanafis and the Shafiis, it is recommended that such escorts be close to the procession by commonly accepted standards; as for the Malikis, they hold that this is not recommended. It is recommended that the funeral procession move at a moderately brisk pace, somewhat faster than a regular walk. The Shafiis and the Hanbalis hold that it is undesirable for women to escort funeral processions unless it is feared that they might be a cause of temptation, in which case they are forbidden to do so; for the views of the Hanafis and the Malikis, see below.[436]

It is an emulation of the Sunnah for those escorting the funeral procession to remain silent; hence, it is undesirable for them to raise their voices even in the

---

435. According to the Hanafis, it is preferable for someone escorting the deceased to his or her grave to walk behind the procession, and it is permissible for him or her to walk in front of it as well unless he or she is far away from it or gets ahead of everyone else, in which case it is undesirable to walk in front. As for walking to the right or to the left of the funeral procession, it is a departure from the ideal.

This ruling applies unless there are women behind the procession whom it is feared that the males might mix with, or among whom there is a hired female mourner, in which case it is considered preferable to walk in front of the procession.

* * *

As for the Shafiis, they hold that those who are escorting the deceased to his final resting place are a type of "intercessor", as a result of which it is preferable that they go before the procession regardless of whether they are riding or walking.

436. According to the Malikis, if a woman is elderly she may escort a funeral procession under any and all circumstances; when she does so, she is to walk behind the procession and behind any men who are riding. If she is a young woman and there is no cause to fear that she might cause others temptation, she may escort

remembrance of God, recitation of the Qur'ān, or recitation of other things such as *Al-Burdah*,[437] *Al-Dalā'il*,[438] and the like. If those who are escorting the funeral procession wish to engage in the remembrance of God, they should do so silently. It is also undesirable for the procession to be followed by censers and candles based on the prophetic saying, "Do not come after funeral processions with noise or fire." If the procession is accompanied by things which are forbidden, such as music and hired female mourners, those escorting the procession should do everything they can to prevent such things. If they are unable to do so, the Shafiis, the Malikis and the Hanafis hold that they should not turn back from following the procession; as for the Hanbalis, they hold that if they cannot put a stop to the forbidden practice, those following the funeral procession must withdraw, since to do otherwise would be to condone disobedience.

It is preferable for those escorting the funeral procession to go to the grave, then wait for the burial to be completed; however, according to the Shafiis and the Hanbalis, there is no undesirability attached to turning back before this, whether one leaves before the funeral prayer or after it. For the views of the Malikis and the Hanafis, see below. As for sitting down before the bier has been set on the ground, each school offers its own ruling on this.[439]

Lastly, the Malikis, the Hanbalis and the Hanafis hold that it is undesirable for people to stand up when a funeral procession passes by them if they were originally sitting down; as for the Shafiis, they hold that based on the most preferable view, it is desirable to stand when one sees a funeral procession.

---

the funeral procession of someone who was dear to her, such as a father, a son, a husband or a brother, and when she does so, she is to abide by the same stipulations just mentioned. However, if there is cause to fear that by her going out she will cause others temptation, she may not do so.

* * *

As for the Hanafis, they hold that women's escorting funeral processions is, in all circumstances, undesirable to the point of being forbidden.

437. This is the name of a long ode written in praise of the Prophet by Imam al-Buṣīrī [t.n.].

438. This is a reference to a book entitled *Dalā'il al-Khayrāt*, which is a collection of prayers on behalf of the Prophet written by Imam al-Jazuli [t.n.].

439. According to the Malikis, sitting down before the bier has been set down is permissible without any undesirability attached to it.

* * *

According to the Hanafis, it is undesirable to the point of being forbidden unless it is necessary to do so.

* * *

According to the Hanbalis, this practice is acceptable for someone who is far from the bier, but it is undesirable for someone who is close to it.

* * *

As for the Shafiis, they hold that it is an emulation of the Sunnah not to sit down until after the bier has been set down.

Weeping over the deceased and what follows upon this

Weeping over the deceased with loud wailing and the like is forbidden according to the Malikis and the Hanafis; however, the Shafiis and the Hanbalis hold that it is acceptable. As for the silent shedding of tears, all four schools agree that this is acceptable. Other practices which are forbidden include lamenting the deceased by enumerating his good qualities by saying, for example, "O how handsome he was! What a strong, reliable support he was!" and the like, the actions performed by professional female mourners, dyeing one's face, striking one's cheeks, and tearing one's clothing. These prohibitions are based on the words of the Prophet, who said, "Those who strike their cheeks, rend their clothing and say the things that used to be said in such situations during the days of ignorance [i.e., prior to the advent of Islam] do not belong to us."[440]

The deceased is not tormented by his family's forbidden weeping over him unless he specifically instructed them to weep over him. Moreover, if someone knows that his family will weep over him after he dies and thinks it probable that if he ordered them to refrain from weeping they would obey his instructions, and if, despite this fact, he fails to tell them not to weep over him, their weeping after his death will be a cause of torment for him.

Rulings on burying the deceased and related matters

Burying the deceased is a collective obligation if it is possible to do so. If burial is not possible—as for example, when someone dies on board a ship far from the shore—and if it would be impossible for the ship to anchor in a place where the body could be buried before its odor undergoes a change, the body should be tied to a weighted object and thrown into the water.

When burial is possible, a hole should be dug in the ground which is at least deep enough to prevent the smell of the body from being detectable and to keep beasts of prey from digging it up. As for additional depth, each of the four schools offers its own ruling on this.[441] As for the minimum width and length of the grave, they are equal to whatever size is large enough to hold both the deceased and the

---

440. Narrated by al-Bukhārī and Muslim.

441. According to the Malikis, it is undesirable to make a grave deeper than this unless there is a need to do so.

* * *

According to the Hanafis, it is an emulation of the Sunnah for the depth of the grave to equal, at the least, half the height of a medium-sized man, although it is preferable for it to be deeper than this.

* * *

According to the Shafiis, it is an emulation of the Sunnah to increase the depth of the grave up to what would equal the height of a medium-sized man with his arms pointed upward.

* * *

As for the Hanbalis, they simply state that it is an emulation of the Sunnah to make the grave deep, without specifying any exact depth.

person digging the grave. It is not permissible to place the deceased person on top of the ground and to build over him without digging a hole unless it is not possible to dig. If the ground is firm, it is an emulation of the Sunnah to make a *laḥd*, that is, to dig an opening large enough to hold the deceased into the bottom of the grave in the direction of the *qiblah*. In this regard, the Malikis say that making a *laḥd* in firm soil is desirable, but not based on the Sunnah. If the soil is loose, it is permissible simply to make a furrow, that is, to dig a lengthwise crevice into the center of the bottom of the grave, then to build up its sides with brick. This ruling is agreed upon by the Hanafis and the Hanbalis; for the views of the Malikis and the Shafiis, see below.[442] The brick sides built up from the furrow are then roofed over after the body is placed inside them.

The Shafiis, the Hanbalis and the Hanafis agree that the body of the deceased must be placed in the grave facing the *qiblah*; as for the Malikis, they hold that this is not obligatory, but merely recommended. It is an emulation of the Sunnah for the deceased to be placed in his grave on his right side, and for the person who is placing the body in the grave to say, "In the name of God, and in accordance with the religion of God's Messenger." This is the ruling of the Shafiis, the Hanafis and the Hanbalis; as for the Malikis, they recommend two additional elements here, namely: (1) that the person placing the deceased in the grave place his right hand on the body of the deceased after he is placed in the grave, and (2) that he say, "O God, grant him the most gracious reception." If the person placing the body in the grave omits any of these steps, for example, by not positioning the body facing the *qiblah*, by placing the head where the feet should be, or by placing the body on its back or on its left side and if the dirt has already been piled on top of the grave, the grave should not be dug up again to correct the error. However, if the dirt has not yet been piled on top of the grave, the error must be corrected even if this requires removal of the bricks that have been laid. This ruling is agreed upon by the Hanafis and the Malikis; as for the Shafiis and the Hanbalis, they hold that if the deceased is not positioned facing the *qiblah*, the grave must be dug up again in order to position the body correctly.

It is desirable for the deceased's head and feet to be supported on some dirt or brick inside the grave. However, it is undesirable for the body to be placed inside a coffin unless there is a clear need to do so, for example, on account of the soil's

---

442. According to the Malikis and the Shafiis, forming such a furrow is not only permissible, but desirable when the soil is loose, and is considered preferable to a *laḥd*.

In addition, the Shafiis hold that it is an emulation of the Sunnah for the person placing the body in the grave to say, "In the name of God, the Most Gracious, the Most Merciful, and in accordance with the religion of God's Messenger. O God, open the doors of heaven to his spirit, grant him an honorable abode, broaden his entryway, and make his grave spacious for him" (*bismillāh al-raḥmān al-raḥīm wa 'alā millat rasūl Allāh, ṣallā Allāhu 'alayhi wa sallam. Allāhumma iftaḥ abwāb al-samā' li rūḥihi wa akrim nazlahu wa wassi' madkhalahu wa wassi' lahu fi qabrihi*).

being moist and loose. It is also undesirable to place a pillow, mat or the like with the deceased in his grave; this is the ruling of the Hanafis and the Shafiis. For the views of the Malikis and the Hanbalis, see below.[443]

After the deceased has been buried in the *laḥd* or the furrow and after the grave has been closed with brick and the like, it is desirable for everyone who witnessed the burial to strew soil over the grave three times with both hands in the direction of the deceased's head. While strewing the soil the first time, they are to say, "Out of this [earth] have We created you"; while strewing it the second time, they are to say, "and into it shall We return you", and while strewing it the third time, "and out of it shall We bring you forth once again" (20:55). Then more dirt is piled on top of the deceased until the grave is completely filled in. According to the Malikis and the Hanbalis, however, nothing from the Qur'ān is to be recited while soil is being strewn over the deceased.

According to the Malikis, the Hanbalis and the Hanafis, it is recommended that the dirt on top of the grave be piled up to a height of one *shibr* and be shaped like a camel's hump. The Shafiis, however, hold that it is preferable to make the soil level and evenly distributed. It is undesirable to whiten the grave with gypsum or lime. As for coating the grave with clay, the Shafiis, the Hanbalis and the Hanafis hold that this is acceptable, since it is not intended as adornment; however, the Malikis hold that coating the grave with any substance whatsoever—be it gypsum, clay, or lime—is undesirable. It is likewise undesirable for stones, wood, and the like to be placed on the grave unless there is reason to fear that its markings will disappear, in which case it is permissible to place something on it for identification. However, if such materials are placed on the grave in a show of ostentation, they are forbidden. This ruling is agreed upon by the Malikis, the Hanbalis and the Hanafis; however, the Shafiis hold that it is an emulation of the Sunnah to place a stone or some similar object at the end of the grave for purposes of identification. As for writing on graves, each school offers its own ruling on this practice.[444]

---

443. According to the Hanbalis, it is undesirable under any and all circumstances to place the deceased inside a coffin.

* * *

As for the Malikis, they hold that placing the deceased inside a coffin is merely a departure from the ideal.

444. The Malikis hold that it is forbidden to write anything from the Qur'ān on a tomb; as for writing the person's name and date of death, this is undesirable.

* * *

According to the Hanafis, it is undesirable to the point of being forbidden to write anything on a tomb unless there is reason to fear that its identifying marks may be lost.

* * *

According to the Shafiis, writing on a grave is undesirable regardless of whether what is written is from the Qur'ān or some other source unless it is the grave of a scholar or saint; in this latter case, it is recommended that the person's name be written on the grave as well as whatever will help in the grave's identification.

* * *

Building on top of graves

It is undesirable to build houses, domes, schools, or mosques on top of graves; it is likewise undesirable to build walls around them, forming a kind of courtyard, if this is not done for the sake of ornamentation and ostentation; if it is done for such motives, it is forbidden altogether. This ruling applies if the land is classified as neither *musabbalah*, that is, an area which people have been accustomed to using for burials and which has never been privately owned, nor *mawqūfah*, that is, land which has been set aside by its owner as a religious endowment, such as the Qarāfah in Egypt[445] which was set aside as a religious endowment by our master 'Umar Ibn al-Khaṭṭāb, may God be pleased with him. As for lands which are, in fact, either *musabbalah* or *mawqūfah*, it is forbidden entirely to build on them due to the restrictions and prohibitions which this imposes on people. This ruling is agreed upon by all four schools; however, the Hanbalis hold that building on graves is not forbidden, but rather undesirable under all circumstances, whether the land is *musabbalah* or not, although it is more undesirable if the land is, in fact, *musabbalah*. Based on the foregoing, you will understand the ruling on the various sorts of pomp which people have contrived through building on top of graves, making such structures into palaces and dwellings the likes of which many of the living do not enjoy. It is unfortunate, moreover, that this practice is pursued in connection with the graves of the distinguished and the non-distinguished alike.

Sitting, sleeping, relieving oneself, and walking on graves

It is undesirable to sit or sleep on a grave, whereas urinating or defecating there is completely forbidden, as we saw earlier in the section dealing with the rules of conduct associated with relieving oneself. This ruling is agreed upon by the Shafiis and the Hanbalis; for the views of the Hanafis and the Malikis, see below.[446] It is undesirable to walk on top of graves unless there is some need to do so, as, for example, if one can only reach the grave one is trying to get to by walking over another grave. This ruling is agreed upon by the Shafiis, the Hanbalis and the Hanafis; as for the Malikis, their view may be seen below.[447]

As for the Hanbalis, they hold that it is undesirable to write on graves regardless of whether those buried there are scholars, saints, etc.

These, then, are the views of the four schools on this matter. Given what they have to say, it is to be hoped that people will return to their religion, abandoning the ostentation exhibited by writing gold inscriptions and the like on graves. After all, the tomb of a saint or a righteous person should serve as an admonition and a cause for reflection, not as a cause for boasting and pride.

445. The Qarāfah is a graveyard below the Muqattam Hills near Cairo [t.n.].

446. The Hanafis hold that sitting and sleeping on top of a grave are simply undesirable, whereas urinating, defecating and the like are undesirable to the point of being forbidden.

* * *

As for the Malikis, they hold that it is acceptable to sit or sleep on a grave, whereas urinating, etc. is forbidden.

Moving the deceased from the location where the death took place

Each of the four schools offers its own detailed rulings on moving the deceased from the place where the death took place, before and after burial.[448]

---

447. According to the Malikis, it is undesirable to walk on a grave if the soil on top of it is in the shape of a camel's hump and if it is not in one's path; otherwise, it is permissible. It is likewise permissible to walk on a grave if no part of the deceased is visible anymore, even if it is shaped like a camel's hump.

448. According to the Malikis, it is permissible to transfer the deceased to another location before or after burial given three conditions: (1) That the body not burst open upon being moved. (2) That the body's sacredness not be desecrated by, for example, its being moved in a degrading manner. (3) That it be transferred in order to serve a particular interest, for example, because there is reason to fear that seawater will flood the grave, because there is a desire to move the body to a place of particular value or to a spot close to his family, or in order to facilitate family visits to the grave. If any of these three conditions is unfulfilled, it is forbidden to transfer the body.

* * *

According to the Hanafis, it is desirable for the deceased to be buried in the same place where he or she died, although it is acceptable for the body to be moved to another location before burial provided that there is no reason to fear that its odor will change during the transfer. After the burial has taken place, however, it is forbidden to dig the body up and move it unless the land in which the body was buried turns out to have been taken illegally, or unless the land is taken by right of preemption.

* * *

According to the Shafiis, it is forbidden to transfer the deceased before burial from the place where he died to be buried elsewhere even if there is no danger of the body's odor changing, unless the prevailing custom of the community is to bury their dead outside their own town. An exception to this ruling is made for someone who died near Mecca, Medina or Jerusalem, or near a cemetery where righteous individuals are known to be buried, in which case it is an emulation of the Sunnah to move the body there provided that there is no reason to fear that its odor may change; if this fear is present, however, it is forbidden to move the body. All such rulings, moreover, apply only if the body has been ritually washed, wrapped for burial, and prayed over in the place where the death occurred. Until these things have been done, it is forbidden to transfer the body under any circumstances. It is likewise forbidden to transfer the body after burial unless it is necessary to do so, as, for example, if someone was buried on land that had been taken illegally, in which case it is permissible to move the body if the proprietor demands his land back.

* * *

According to the Hanbalis, there is nothing wrong with transferring the deceased from the place where the death took place to another, distant location provided that the transfer is made for a legitimate purpose, for example, to move the

Digging up a grave

It is forbidden to dig up a grave as long as some of the deceased's bones are believed still to be present inside it. However, exceptions to this ruling are made in the following situations: (1) When the deceased was wrapped in materials or clothing that had been taken illegally and when their owner refuses to accept their monetary value in their place. (2) When the deceased was buried on land that had been taken illegally and when its owner refuses to allow the body to stay where it is. (3) When the deceased was buried along with some money, whether intentionally or unintentionally, whether the money belongs to the deceased or to someone else, whether the amount of money is large or small (even as small as a single dirham), and whether the body of the deceased has changed or not. This ruling is agreed upon by the Shafiis, the Hanbalis and the Hanafis; for the Malikis' view, see below.[449]

---

deceased to a spot which is known to be distinguished in some way, or to be buried near a righteous man. This ruling applies provided that there is no fear that the body's odor will change during the transfer; moreover, it applies both before and after burial.

449. The Malikis hold that if money or possessions are inadvertently buried with the deceased as, for example, if a watch, a ring, or some pieces of money fell into the grave during the burial, and if the soil is then piled on top of the grave, the money or possessions concerned will either have belonged to the deceased before he died, or to someone else. If they belonged to someone else, the owner may dig up the grave and take out his money or property if no change has yet occurred in the body of the deceased. Otherwise, he will be obliged to accept an amount of money equal in value and kind out of the deceased's bequest, such as dirhams, dinars, etc., or, in the case of material objects such as clothing, their value [in some form of currency].

If the money or objects in question belonged to the deceased, the heirs must leave them in the grave once the body of the deceased has begun to change even if they are of value. However, if the body of the deceased has not yet begun to change and the objects left in the grave are of value, the heirs of the deceased may dig up the grave. Lastly, a grave may only be dug up to remove money or valuables before sufficient time has passed for there to be reason to believe that they have rotted; otherwise, the grave is not to be dug up since there would no longer be any benefit in doing so.

450. According to the Hanafis, it is undesirable to bury more than one deceased person in a single grave unless there is some need to do so, in which case it is acceptable.

* * *

According to the Malikis, several deceased persons may be buried in one grave in case of necessity, such as a situation in which the graveyard is too small to accommodate the necessary number of individual graves. It is also permissible for different deceased persons to be buried in the same grave at different times, as, for example, when a grave is reopened after the initial burial in order to bury someone

Burying more than one person in a single grave

Each of the four schools offers its own ruling on burying more than one deceased person in a single grave.[450] If more than one person is buried in the same grave, the person who was the most virtuous is placed closer to the *qiblah*, followed by the person next in virtue, and so on. When ordering the bodies in this situation, priority is to be given to adults over children, males over females, etc. It is recommended that each two bodies be separated by some soil and not only by their grave clothes. If a body disintegrates and turns to soil in its grave, the Shafiis, the Hanbalis and the Hanafis hold that it is permissible to dig up the grave and to till the land, build on it, etc.; for the Malikis' view, see below.[451]

Offering condolences

Offering condolences to the bereaved is recommended, and the time when this should be done extends from the time of the death until three days later. It is undesirable to offer condolences more than three days after the death unless the person offering the condolences or the bereaved was absent before this, in which case it is permissible to console the bereaved after this time.

There is no particular formula for such condolences; rather, each individual is to be spoken to in a manner which is appropriate to his situation; this ruling is agreed upon by the Shafiis, the Hanbalis and the Malikis. As for the Hanafis, their view may be seen below.[452] Ideally, condolences should be offered following the burial; however, if the bereaved are overcome with anguish and sorrow, it is prefer-

---

else. However, if there is no necessity involved, it is forbidden to bury different deceased people in a single grave at different times, while it is undesirable to do so at the same time.

* * *

As for the Shafiis and the Hanbalis, they hold that it is forbidden to bury more than one deceased person in a single grave unless it is required by some necessity, for example, by there being a large number of dead and the fear that they may begin to emit a stench, or due to a need, such as the need to avoid causing undue hardship for the living.

451. The Malikis hold that if the body of the deceased has decomposed and no perceptible part of it remains, it is permissible to dig up the grave in order to bury someone else there and to walk over it. However, it is not permissible to till or build on the spot because, once a spot of soil has been used as a burial site, it becomes the equivalent of a religious endowment which may not be used for anything but burials, whether the dead who were buried there previously have decomposed or not.

452. According to the Hanafis, it is desirable to say to the bereaved, "May God forgive the person you have lost, overlook his offenses and encompass him with His grace. May God grant you the patience to endure his/her loss, and reward you for [enduring] his/her death." The preferred formula in this context is the one which was used by the Messenger of God, namely, "To God belongs that which He has taken, to Him belongs what He has given, and everything has its appointed time in His sight." It is thus desirable to add these phrases to those mentioned above.

able to offer them before the burial according to the Shafiis, the Hanbalis and the Hanafis. As for the Malikis, they hold that condolences should only be offered after the burial, even if the bereaved are in great anguish and sorrow.

It is desirable for the condolences to be addressed to all the deceased's relations, both women and men, adults and children. However, young women are only to be consoled by their non-marriageable relatives in order to avoid temptation; nor are condolences to be addressed to young children who have not yet reached the age of discernment.

According to the Shafiis and the Hanbalis, it is undesirable for the bereaved to sit down to receive condolences, whether they are in their own home or elsewhere. According to the Hanafis, it is simply a departure from the ideal to receive condolences while seated; as for the Malikis, they hold that it is acceptable. As for sitting down in the middle of the road and spreading out rugs and the like as some people are in the habit of doing, this is an innovation which is prohibited.

Lastly, the Shafiis, the Hanbalis and the Hanafis hold that once condolences have been offered to the deceased's family, it is undesirable for them to be offered to them again; as for the Malikis, they hold that offering condolences to the same family twice is not undesirable.

Sacrificing animals and preparing food at funeral ceremonies

One undesirable innovation in this connection is the current practice of sacrificing animals when someone dies, either from the home or at the grave and preparing food for those who gather to offer condolences as they do at weddings and other festive occasions. If there are minors among the deceased's heirs, it is not only undesirable, but forbidden to prepare and serve food to those who come to offer condolences. Imam Aḥmad and Ibn Mājah narrate a hadith on the authority of Jarīr Ibn 'Abdullāh, who said, "We view gathering at the home of the deceased's family and their preparing food [for those thus gathered] as [tantamount to] loud weeping and wailing."[453] As for the practice of having neighbors and friends prepare food for the family of the deceased and send it to them, this is recommended based on the words of the Prophet, "Prepare food for Ja'far's family, since something has happened to preoccupy them." Moreover, the family of the deceased should be strongly encouraged to eat, since their grief might otherwise prevent them from doing so.

---

453. Since loud weeping and wailing over the deceased are forbidden, this statement is, in effect, a condemnation of the practices mentioned [t.n.].

454. According to the Hanbalis, it is not an emphatically enjoined emulation of the Sunnah to visit graves on any particular day of the week.

* * *

According to the Shafiis, it is an emphatically enjoined emulation of the Sunnah to visit graves from mid-afternoon on Thursday until sunrise on Saturday; this is a well-attested view among the Malikis as well.

A concluding note on visiting graves

It is recommended that people visit graves in order to ponder the lessons offered by death and to be mindful of the afterlife. It is an emphatically enjoined emulation of the Sunnah to visit graves on Friday as well as on Thursdays and Saturdays according to the Hanafis and the Malikis; for the views of the Hanbalis and the Shafiis, see below.[454]

When someone visits a grave, he or she should occupy himself or herself with making supplication and entreaty to God, reflecting on the lessons to be gained from those who have died, and reciting the Qur'ān to the person buried there since all of this, properly speaking, is of benefit to the deceased. One traditional prayer the visitor may recite when he or she sees a grave is as follows: "O God, Sustainer of eternal spirits and of decaying bodies, broken hair, torn skin, and disintegrating bones which have departed from this world with faith in You: Send down upon them a spirit from Yourself, and a greeting of peace from me."

Another such supplication is: "May peace be upon you, O abode of believing people. God willing, we shall be joining you."

According to the Shafiis, the Hanafis and the Malikis, the ruling on visiting graves is the same whether the graves are near or far; the Hanbalis' view is presented below.[455] It is recommended that one undertake a journey to visit the deceased, and especially to visit the graves of the righteous. As for visiting the tomb of the Prophet, this is one of the greatest acts one can perform to draw nearer to God. Moreover, just as it is recommended that men visit graves, it is likewise recommended for elderly women in whose case there is no reason to fear that they would cause others temptation provided that their visiting the graves would not lead to lamentation or loud weeping and wailing; otherwise, such women are forbidden to visit graves. As for women in whose case there is reason to fear that they might cause others temptation, their going out on such a visit is forbidden according to the Hanafis and the Malikis. As for the Hanbalis and the Shafiis, their views may be seen below.[456]

Lastly, visits to graves must be conducted in accordance with the principles of Islamic law. Hence, they must not involve circumambulation around the grave, kissing a stone, a threshold or a piece of wood, or making requests of the deceased.

---

455. The Hanbalis hold that if the graves concerned are so far away that they can only be reached by going on a journey, visiting them is permissible, but not recommended.

456. According to the Hanbalis and the Shafiis, women are forbidden to go out to visit graves under any circumstances whether they are elderly or young unless it is known for a certainty that their going out will not lead to temptation or the commission of forbidden acts.

On Fasting

On Fasting

The definition of fasting

The meaning of the term 'fasting' (*ṣiyām*, or *ṣawm*) as used in the Arabic language in general is abstention from something, whatever it happens to be. Hence, if someone abstains from speech or food such that he or she does not speak or eat, he or she may be said to be 'fasting'. An example of this use of the term is found in the Qur'anic passage which reads, "...Behold, abstinence [from speech] have I vowed unto the Most Gracious..." [*innī nadhartu lil-raḥmān ṣawman fa lan akillama al-yawma insiyyan*] (19:26).

As employed within the context of Islamic jurisprudence, the term 'fasting' is used to refer to abstention from all things which would serve to break one's fast for an entire day, that is, from true dawn until sundown, given the conditions to be explained below. This definition is agreed upon by the Hanafis and the Hanbalis; as for the Malikis and the Shafiis, they add the phrase "with intention" to the end of the above definition. The reason for this is that intention is not a pillar of fasting according to the Hanafis and the Hanbalis and, consequently, is not included in their definition. Nevertheless, intention is a necessary condition in the sense that if someone does not consciously intend to fast in the manner to be explained below, all four schools agree that his or her fast will be invalid. This being the case, it is clear that the dispute over whether intention is a condition or a pillar [of fasting] is an issue relating to Islamic jurisprudence of which those seeking knowledge in this sphere need to be aware; others, however, need only to understand that the intention to fast is necessary and that without it, fasting will not be valid.

Types of fasting

The Malikis, the Shafiis and the Hanbalis divide fasting into four types: (1) obligatory fasting (which includes fasting the month of Ramaḍān, whether during the month itself or later as a compensatory fast, expiatory fasting, and fasting in fulfillment of a vow), (2) fasting in emulation of the prophetic Sunnah, (3) forbidden fasting, and (4) undesirable fasting. Each type of fasting as understood by each of these three schools will be explained below. As for the Hanafis, they divide fasting into numerous types.[1]

---

1. The Hanafis differ in their views on fasting in fulfillment of a vow, whether the time for the fast is specified (such as the vow to fast on a particular day, like Thursday, for example) or unspecified (such as vowing to fast for a day, a month, etc., yet without designating which day or month). Some Hanafis hold that fulfilling such a vow is a 'duty', but not a full obligation. As we have seen, a 'duty' in the Hanafis' understanding is the same, in effect, as an emphatically enjoined Sunnah-based practice. As a consequence, those who do not perform a 'duty' are not punished in the Fire, although they will be denied the intercession of the chosen Prophet [on the Day of Resurrection]. The argument put forward by those who hold this

view is that the necessity of fulfilling vows is confirmed by God's saying, "...and let them fulfill the vows which they have made..." (22:29). This verse, however, does not bear an unequivocal meaning, since someone who vows to commit an act of disobedience is not under obligation to fulfill this vow, and when the verse is applied to a vow to commit disobedience, it cannot mean unequivocally that one is required to fulfill the vow.

The Hanafis also draw a distinction between performing a ritual prayer one has vowed to pray and making up a ritual prayer which is obligatory. They say, for example, that if someone has vowed to perform two *rak'ahs* in simple devotion to God, he may not perform them after the mid-afternoon prayer, whereas if someone missed the obligatory dawn prayer, for example, he may perform these two obligatory *rak'ahs* after the mid-afternoon prayer. [One will recall that it is considered undesirable, if not forbidden, to perform voluntary prayers between the mid-afternoon and sundown prayers – t.n.] What this indicates is that a vow is a 'duty' rather than a full obligation given the difference between the ruling on how [and when] a vow is to be fulfilled and how [and when] an obligation is to be made up.

Other Hanafis, however, hold that fulfillment of a vow one has made is a full obligation; hence, if someone vows to fast a day without specifying which day, he is obliged to fulfill this vow. However, the obligation to fulfill such a vow is not confirmed by the verse quoted above, namely, "...and let them fulfill the vows which they have made..." (22:29) but, rather, by the consensus of the Muslim community. This latter view is the one best attested among the Hanafis, and is shared by other imams as well.

Based on the first view [namely, that fulfilling a vow is a 'duty' rather than a full obligation], fasting is divided into the following eight types: (1) Obligatory fasting with a specified time frame, such as fasting Ramaḍān during the month of Ramaḍān itself. (2) Obligatory fasting without a specified time frame, such as fasting Ramaḍān compensatorily at a time other than the month of Ramaḍān itself. Someone who misses fasting some or all of the month of Ramaḍān is not required to make up the days missed at a particular time. The same applies to expiatory fasting which, although it is obligatory, is not required at a specified time. (3) Fasting which is a 'duty' with a specified time frame, such as a vow to fast a particular day, month, etc. (4) Fasting which is a 'duty' without a specified time frame, such as a vow to fast without designating a given day, month, etc. (5) Voluntary fasting. (6) Fasting in emulation of the prophetic Sunnah. (7) Desirable fasting. (8) Fasting which is either simply undesirable, or undesirable to the point of being forbidden.

Based on the second view [namely, that fulfilling a vow is a full obligation], fasting is divided into the following seven types: (1) Obligatory fasting with a specific time frame, such as fasting Ramaḍān during the month of Ramaḍān itself and fasting in fulfillment of a vow with a designated time frame. (2) Obligatory fasting without a specific time frame, such as making up fasting days missed during the month of Ramaḍān, and fasting in fulfillment of a vow without a specified day, month, etc. (3) Fasting which is a 'duty'. This includes all voluntary fasts once they have been commenced. If someone wishes to fast Thursday voluntarily, for example, he now has a 'duty' to fast the day to completion; hence, if he breaks his fast before the day is over, he will be guilty of a minor transgression and he should

Type one: Obligatory fasting—the fast of Ramaḍān

As we have seen, obligatory fasting includes fasting Ramaḍān during the month of Ramaḍān itself, fasting Ramaḍān compensatorily at some other time, expiatory fasting, and fasting in fulfillment of a vow. These elements of obligatory fasting are agreed upon by all four schools, although some of the Hanafis differ in their rulings on fasting in fulfillment of a vow, holding that this is a 'duty' rather than a full obligation.

What follows is an explanation of each of the types of fasting mentioned thus far:

Fasting the month of Ramaḍān and evidence in its favor

Fasting is an individual obligation for every Muslim who is held accountable under Islamic law for the performance of the various forms of worship and who is capable of fasting. Fasting was legislated as a religious requirement for Muslims on the 10th of Sha'bān, one and a half years after the Hijrah. The evidence for the obligatory nature of fasting in Islam is based on the Qur'ān, the Sunnah, and the consensus of the Muslim community. The evidence found in the Qur'ān is based on the passage which begins: "O You who have attained to faith! Fasting is ordained for you as it was ordained for those before you…" and which ends with the words, "[It was] the month of Ramaḍān in which the Qur'ān was [first] bestowed from on high…" (2:183-185). In the passage just quoted, "the month of Ramaḍān" is the predicate referring back to an unstated subject [rendered by Asad as "It was…"] which is, likewise, "the month of Ramaḍān"; in other words, the period of time during which fasting is ordained for Muslims is the month of Ramaḍān. The obligatory nature of this fast is likewise based on the phrase, found in the same passage, which reads, "Hence, whoever of you lives to see this month shall fast throughout it…."

The evidence in favor of fasting within the prophetic Sunnah may be found in the following statement of the Prophet: "Islam was founded upon five [pillars]: the testimony that 'there is no god but God, and Muḥammad is God's Messenger', the performance of ritual prayer, the payment of the purifying dues (*zakāh*), performing the greater pilgrimage to Mecca, and fasting the month of Ramaḍān."[2]

As for the consensus of the Muslim community, it likewise supports the obligatory nature of fasting. The obligatory nature of fasting within Islam is a fact which no Muslim disputes and the acknowledgment of which is a necessary aspect of the faith. In fact, anyone who does dispute it is considered an unbeliever, as are those who deny the obligatory nature of ritual prayer, *zakāh* and the greater pilgrimage.

---

make the day up later. The same ruling applies to fasting that is done while one is secluded in a mosque for prayer and devotion, but which is not in fulfillment of a vow, since this likewise is considered a 'duty'. (4) Fasting which is forbidden. (5) Fasting in emulation of the prophetic Sunnah. (6) Voluntary fasting. (7) Fasting which is undesirable.

All the aforementioned types of fasting will be explained below.

2. Narrated by al-Bukhārī and Muslim on the authority of Ibn 'Umar.

The pillars of fasting

According to the Hanafis and the Hanbalis, fasting has a single pillar, namely, abstinence from all things which would serve to break one's fast, and which will be discussed below. For the views of the Malikis and the Shafiis, see below.[3]

Conditions for fasting

The conditions for fasting are divided into three categories, namely: (a) conditions for its necessity [that which makes it obligatory], (b) conditions for its validity, and (c) conditions for its performance. However, each school offers its own detailed rulings on these conditions.[4]

---

3. The Malikis differ among themselves on this point, with some of them saying that fasting has two pillars, namely, abstinence and intention. Based on this first view, the concept of fasting is not fulfilled without both of these pillars. Other Malikis, on the other hand, hold that there is compelling evidence that intention is a condition, not a pillar, as a result of which the concept of fasting is fulfilled through abstinence alone.

* * *

According to the Shafiis, fasting has three pillars: (1) abstinence from those things that would break one's fast, (2) intention, and (3) the person fasting. Thus, they hold that the concept of fasting is only fulfilled in the presence of all three of these. As we have seen, the Hanbalis and the Hanafis hold that intention and the person fasting are conditions which are external to the concept of fasting, but that their presence is necessary.

4. The Shafiis divide the conditions for fasting into two categories, namely, conditions for its being obligatory, and conditions for its validity. As for the conditions for fasting's being obligatory, they list the following four: (1) Maturity. Hence, fasting is not obligatory for a young child. However, a child is to be instructed to fast when he reaches seven years of age if he can tolerate it, and he is to be struck for not fasting once he reaches ten years of age. This view is shared likewise by the Hanafis, whereas according to the Malikis, it is neither obligatory nor recommended that a guardian instruct a young child or even an adolescent to fast. As for the Hanbalis, they hold that the determining factors here are ability and tolerance; hence, if the child is an adolescent who is capable of tolerating fasting, his guardian must instruct him to fast and strike him if he refuses. (2) Islam. Fasting is not required of someone who is not a Muslim, at least in the sense that others should insist that he do so, even though such a person will be punished in the afterlife for not having fasted. As for someone who has left Islam, others are to insist that he fast after he returns to Islam. (3) Full possession of one's mental faculties. Fasting is not required of someone who is insane unless his insanity came about as a result of a transgression on his part, in which case he is required to fast after he becomes lucid again. The same ruling applies to someone who is inebriated due to a transgression on his own part. However, if the person's inebriation came about due to no fault of his own—as, for example, if he drank from a container which he thought contained water, only to discover after it was too late that it contained wine—he is not required to make up the time he missed on account of his inebriation. As for someone

who has fallen unconscious, he must make up whatever he missed on account of his unconsciousness regardless of the circumstances, that is, whether his loss of consciousness was due to a transgression on his part or not. (4) Ability, both physical and legal. Fasting is not required of someone who would not be able to tolerate it due to old age, illness, or some other impairing condition which is not expected to end. Nor is it required of a woman who is experiencing post-partum bleeding due to her inability to fast in the legal sense.

As for the conditions for the validity of fasting, they are as follows: (1) Being a Muslim at the time of one's fast. Fasting is not valid if the person doing so is an apostate from Islam or a non-believer who has never been a Muslim. (2) Discernment. Fasting is not valid if the person doing so lacks powers of discernment. Someone who is insane, therefore, may not validly fast even if he only loses his sanity for a moment out of the day. As for someone who is drunk or unconscious, his fasting will not be valid if the loss of discernment lasts the entire day; however, if it lasts for only part of the day, his fasting will be valid. Hence, the presence of someone's powers of discernment, if only in a legal sense, is sufficient in such a case; if, for example, someone intends to fast before dawn, after which he or she sleeps until sundown, his fasting will be valid since, legally speaking, he possesses powers of discernment. (3) In the case of a woman, she must be neither menstruating, experiencing post-partum bleeding, nor giving birth, even if the birth takes place without the mother's seeing blood. (4) The fasting must be done during a time when fasting is allowed. Hence, fasting will not be valid if it is done on the Day of Fastbreaking, on the Day of Sacrifice, or during the three days following the Day of Sacrifice, since all these are days on which fasting is not allowed. Another day on which fasting is not acceptable is the 'day of doubt' unless there is some necessity which requires one to fast, for example, because one needs to fast this day in order to make up a day of fasting missed before, because one had vowed to fast on Monday, after which Monday happened to coincide with the 'day of doubt', or because one is in the habit of fasting on Thursdays and the 'day of doubt' happened to fall on a Thursday. However, if someone deliberately intends to fast the 'day of doubt' because it is the 'day of doubt', his fasting will not be valid (as will be seen below in the discussion of fasting on this day). Similarly, one's fasting will not be valid if one has fasted part or all of the latter half of the month of Sha'bān; in fact, it is forbidden to fast during this period of time unless there is something that requires one to do so (examples of such things are given below in the discussion of the 'day of doubt'), or unless one fasted during the first half of Sha'bān and continued fasting additional, consecutive days in the latter half of the month. This exception applies even if only one day of the latter half of the month was fasted immediately after the days fasted in the first half.

These, then, are the conditions for fasting according to the Shafiis. They do not include intention since, as we have seen, the Shafiis view intention as a pillar rather than as a condition of fasting. Moreover, the Shafiis hold that one must renew one's intention to fast on every day one fasts and that one must initiate the intention the night before the day one intends to fast; one's intention to fast the following day may be initiated as early as sundown and it will be valid even if, later in the evening, something occurs which is inconsistent with fasting, since fasting takes place not at night, but during the day. If the fast concerned is obligatory, such as the fast of Ramaḍān, expiatory fasting, or fasting in fulfillment of a vow, one must initiate one's intention the night before, specifying which type of fast one intends to undertake by saying in one's heart, for example, "I intend to fast tomorrow as part of Ramaḍān," "I intend to fast tomorrow in fulfillment of a vow I have made," etc. It is an emulation of the Sunnah for one to voice one's intention as well, since this serves to strengthen one's inward resolve. One might say, for example, "I intend to fast tomorrow in fulfillment of the obligation to fast the current month of Ramaḍān for the sake of God Almighty." If, by contrast, it is a voluntary fast, a simple intention will suffice even if one initiates it during the day provided that it is initiated before noon, and provided that one's intention is not preceded by anything that would preclude fasting based on the best attested view. Eating the pre-dawn meal (*suḥūr*) does not take the place of intention in connection with any type of fasting unless, while one is eating the meal, it occurs to him or her to fast and he or she intends to do so. Similarly, if one abstains from food at sunrise for fear of breaking one's fast, this takes the place of an explicit intention.

* * *

The Hanafis divide the conditions for fasting into three categories: (a) conditions for fasting's being obligatory, (b) conditions for its performance being obligatory, and (c) conditions for the validity of its performance.

The conditions for fasting's being obligatory are as follows: (1) Islam. Hence, fasting is not obligatory for someone who is not a Muslim, since the non-Muslim is not addressed by the branches of Islamic law, as we have seen. Nor is fasting valid if performed by a non-Muslim, since intention is a condition for fasting's validity, as will be seen below, and as has been mentioned, intention is only valid if it is initiated on the part of a Muslim. Hence, Islam is necessary in order for fasting to be both obligatory and valid. (2) Full possession of one's mental faculties. Fasting is thus not required of someone who is insane as long as his insanity continues. If someone lost his sanity for half the month of Ramaḍān, then regained it for the second half, he would be required to fast what remains of the month, then make up what he had missed. However, if he did not regain his sanity until the month was over, he would not be required to make up any of the fast. The same ruling applies to someone who has lost consciousness [such as someone who has gone into a coma, for example] and someone who is afflicted by sleeping sickness before the month begins and does not regain consciousness until the month is over. (3) Maturity. Fasting is not obligatory for a young child even if he has reached the age of discernment. Nevertheless, a child should be instructed to fast when he is seven years old, and when he reaches ten years of age, he is to be struck if he is capable of fasting but neglects to do so.

There are two conditions that must be fulfilled in order for the performance of fasting to be obligatory, namely, health and residence: (1) Health. The actual performance of fasting is not required of someone who is ill, although such a person is required to make up the fast once he has recovered from his illness. (2) Residence. Those who are on a journey are not required to fast while traveling, although they are required to make up the fast after their journey is over.

As for the conditions for the validity of fasting's performance, there are two of these as well, namely, (1) purity from menstrual flow and post-partum bleeding, and (2) intention. Thus, if a woman who is menstruating or experiencing post-partum bleeding fasts, her fast will not be valid even though she is required to fast [after these conditions have ended]. Moreover, the performance of fasting will only be valid with a conscious intention by which one distinguishes between acts of worship and [mere] customs or habits. Intention is considered to be sufficient if someone knows in his heart that he is going to fast a certain day, month, etc. Moreover, it is an emulation of the Sunnah for such a person to voice his intention. The time for forming one's intention is every day from sundown until the middle of the following day, where the legal definition of a 'day' is from the time when light spreads across the Eastern horizon at dawn until sundown. This period of time is divided into two halves, and intention is to be formed during the first half such that what remains of the day before sundown is greater than what has already passed. If someone did not form the intention to fast after sunset and if such a person rises the next morning still not having formed the intention to fast, yet without having done anything which would break a fast, he or she may form his or her intention any time until before the first half of the day has passed. In addition, the Hanafis hold that one must renew one's intention to fast for every day of Ramaḍān and that eating *suḥūr* is considered tantamount to an intention to fast unless, while taking this meal, one actually intends not to fast. It is possible, even in a case where someone formed the intention to fast during the early part of the night, for the person concerned to go back on his intention before dawn, in which case his retreat from the intention to fast is considered valid for all types of fasting. The Hanafis hold that it is permissible to fast Ramaḍān, to fast in fulfillment of a vow with a specified time frame, and to fast voluntarily with a simple, unspecified intention to fast; when fasting voluntarily, one may form one's intention any time from the night before until before the first half of the following day has passed. However, it is preferable that one form the intention to fast the night before and that one specify exactly what type of fast it is to be. If, during Ramaḍān, someone intends to perform a fast which is in fulfillment of a vow or which is simply recommended, it will count as part of the Ramaḍān fast unless the person is on a journey and intends a fast which is a 'duty'; in this latter case, the fast will count as fulfilling the 'duty' concerned, since someone who is traveling is given special permission to break his fast while on his journey. However, when it comes to making up fasting days missed, expiatory fasting, and fasting in fulfillment of an unspecified vow, one must form the intention to do so the night before and specify what type of fast one intends to perform. As for fasts performed on days when fasting is not permitted, such as the Day of Fastbreaking, the Day of Sacrifice, and the three days following the Day of Sacrifice, such fasts will still be valid despite fasting's being forbidden on such days; if someone vows to fast on one of these days, the vow will be valid, but it should be fulfilled on some day other than these days. If the person concerned does fulfill his vow on one of these days, his fast will be valid, but he will be guilty of wrongdoing.

* * *

The Malikis divide the conditions for fasting into three categories: (a) conditions for fasting's being obligatory only, (b) conditions for fasting's being valid only, and (c) conditions for fasting's being both obligatory and valid.

There are two conditions for fasting's being obligatory only, namely: (1) maturity, and (2) the ability to fast. Hence, fasting is not obligatory for a child even if he is an adolescent. Similarly, it is neither obligatory nor even recommended that such a child's guardian instruct him to fast. Nor is fasting required of someone who is unable to do so.

The Malikis stipulate the following three conditions for fasting's being valid only: (1) That one be a Muslim. Hence, fasting is not valid if it is performed by a non-Muslim even though non-Muslims ought to fast and will be punished for not doing so in addition to the punishment they receive for their unbelief. (2) That it be a time during which fasting is permitted. Hence, fasting during the Day of Fastbreaking and the Day of Sacrifice will not be valid. (3) That one intend to fast (based on the best attested view). As for the rulings on these conditions, they will be presented below.

The conditions for fasting's being both obligatory and valid are as follows: (1) Full possession of one's mental faculties. Hence, fasting is neither obligatory nor valid for someone who is insane or unconscious. As for the obligation to make up a fast one missed on account of insanity or unconsciousness, there are detailed rulings on this matter which may be summarized as follows: If someone (a) loses consciousness for an entire day, from dawn to sunset, (b) loses consciousness for most of the day, whether he was awake at the time when the intention was to be formed or not, or (c) loses consciousness for half or less than half of the day but was not awake during the time when the intention was to be formed, he must make up whatever fasting he missed while unconscious. If, on the other hand, someone loses consciousness for half or less than half of the day and if this person was awake at the time when the intention was to be formed, he is not obliged to make up the fasting he missed if he formed the intention to fast before the loss of consciousness occurred. The same rulings that apply to loss of consciousness apply likewise to insanity. Someone must make up fasting that was missed in accordance with the details already presented if he or she loses his sanity or loses consciousness, even if this condition lasts for a long period of time. As for someone who is drunk, the ruling relating to making up fasting which he missed is the same as that which applies to someone who has lost consciousness, whether the drunkenness resulted from a transgression on the part of the drunk person or not. As for someone who is asleep, he is not required to make up what he missed while he was sleeping if he formed his intention to fast on the night before the first day of Ramaḍān. (2) Freedom from menstrual flow and post-partum bleeding. Fasting is neither required nor valid on the part of a woman who is menstruating or experiencing post-partum bleeding. If her condition passes before dawn, even if only a moment before, she is required to form the intention to fast; in addition, a woman who menstruates or experiences post-partum bleeding during the month of Ramaḍān is required to make up whatever fasting she missed once the condition has passed. (3) The commencement of the month of Ramaḍān. Fasting is neither obligatory nor valid before the month is confirmed to have begun.

As for intention, the Malikis hold that it is a condition for the validity of fasting according to the best attested view, where intention is defined as the intent to fast; as for the intent to draw near to God Almighty, this is recommended. Fasting is not valid, regardless of whether it is obligatory or voluntary, without intention. When forming one's intention to fast, one must specify whether the fasting one intends to perform is a voluntary fast, a compensatory fast, a fast in fulfillment of a vow, etc. If one is certain about one's intention to fast but later has doubts about whether one intended a voluntary fast, a fast in fulfillment of a vow, or a compensatory fast, it will count as a voluntary fast only. If someone has doubts about whether he intended the fast as a fulfillment of a vow or as a compensatory fast, it will count as neither of these, but rather, as a voluntary fast which one is obliged to complete. As for the time during which one is to form one's intention, it begins at sundown and ends at dawn. Hence, if someone forms the intention to fast at the very end of the night so that dawn breaks immediately afterwards, his intention will still be valid, although it is preferable that the intention be formed before the final part of the night since this is indicative of greater conscientiousness. Once the intention to fast [the following day] has been formed, there is no harm in eating, drinking, engaging in sexual relations, sleeping, etc.; however, if one loses consciousness or loses one's sanity after such an intention is formed, the intention will be nullified and it must be renewed even if the person regains consciousness or becomes lucid again before the time period for forming the intention to fast has run out. Forming one's intention during the day is not valid for any type of fasting, even if it is a voluntary fast. However, a single intention is sufficient for every fast which must be performed on consecutive days, such as the Ramaḍān fast, as well as expiatory fasting for some transgression relating to the fast of Ramaḍān and fasting in expiation for murder or *ẓihār* provided that the continuity of the fast is not interrupted. If the continuity is interrupted by illness, travel, etc., the officially recognized view holds that one must repeat one's intention every night even if one goes on fasting. [This is how the text reads, although if one goes on fasting, it would appear that the continuity in one's fast hasn't been broken, after all – t.n.] However, once the journey, illness, etc. has ended, a single intention is then sufficient for the remainder of the month. As for fasting that need not be performed on consecutive days, such as days one is making up from a past Ramaḍān and expiatory fasting for breaking a vow, one must form one's intention anew every night rather than limiting oneself to a single intention at the beginning of the fast. However, a tacit intention with legal validity is also sufficient. For example, someone may eat *suḥūr* without thinking explicitly about fasting; however, if he is asked, "Why did you eat *suḥūr*?" and he replies, "Because I'm going to fast", this is a tacit, and valid, intention.

* * *

As for the Hanbalis, they divide the conditions for fasting into three types: (1) conditions for fasting's being obligatory only, (2) conditions for fasting's being valid only, and (3) conditions for fasting's being both obligatory and valid.

The following are the conditions for fasting's being obligatory only: (1) Islam, (2) maturity, and (3) the ability to fast. Hence, fasting is not obligatory for a young child or even for an adolescent, although a child's guardian should instruct him to fast if he is able to tolerate it, and he should strike him if he refuses. Fasting is not obligatory for someone who is unable to do so due to old age or an illness for which no cure is anticipated. As for someone who is ill and for whom there is hope of a cure, he must fast when he recovers and make up whatever he missed of the fast of Ramaḍān.

As for the conditions for fasting's being valid only, they are as follows: (1) Intention. The time during which intention is to be formed lasts from sunset until dawn if the fast concerned is obligatory; if it is voluntary, however, one's intent will be valid during the day as well, including during the time after noon provided that the person concerned has done nothing contrary to fasting, such as eating, drinking, etc., since the beginning of the day. One must also specify which fast one intends to perform, such as Ramaḍān or some other fast. However, it is not necessary to specify whether the fast is obligatory or not. Lastly, one's intention must be formed every day, whether one is fasting Ramaḍān or some other fast. (2) The absence of menstrual flow and post-partum bleeding. Fasting is thus not valid if performed by a woman who is menstruating or experiencing post-partum bleeding, although she is required to make up the fast later.

As for the conditions for fasting's being both obligatory and valid, they are as follows: (1) Islam. Fasting is neither obligatory nor valid for a non-Muslim, even if he or she is an apostate from Islam. (2) Full possession of one's mental faculties. Fasting is not required of someone who is insane, nor is it valid if such a person does fast. (3) Discernment. Fasting is not valid if performed by a young child who still lacks discernment, such as a young child less than seven years of age. If someone goes insane during a day of Ramaḍān, or if someone is insane and regains his sanity during a day of Ramaḍān, he must make up this day. If, on the other hand, someone loses his sanity for an entire day or more, he is not required to make it up. As for someone who loses consciousness for a day or more, he or she will be obliged to make up the fasting missed even if he remains unconscious for a long period of time. The ruling that applies to someone who loses consciousness applies likewise to someone who is drunk or asleep; as for someone who becomes drunk, the same ruling applies whether his drunkenness is due to some transgression on his part or not.

Confirming the commencement of Ramaḍān

The commencement of the month of Ramaḍān is confirmed in one of two ways: (1) sighting of the full moon if the sky is free of clouds, smoke, dust or other obstructions to visibility, or (2) allowing thirty days for the month of Sha'bān if the sky is not free of such obstructions. This ruling is based on the words of the Prophet, "Begin fasting when you sight it,[5] conclude your fast when your sight it,[6] and if your vision is obstructed, then count Sha'bān as a full thirty days."[7]

What this statement means is that if the sky is clear, the commencement of the Ramaḍān fast is dependent on a sighting of the new moon; fasting may not begin unless the new moon has been sighted. If, on the other hand, there are clouds in the sky, we are to allow a full thirty days for the month of Sha'bān. In other words, if fewer than thirty days of the month of Sha'bān have passed, we are to allow one more day before we begin to fast whereas, if a full thirty days of Sha'bān have passed, we are to begin the fast of Ramaḍān. This rule was laid down by the Lawgiver who issued the command to fast, and who possesses the unqualified right to establish the signs which he sees fit. It is he who has told us: If the sky is clear and the new moon may be seen, then be on the lookout for it and once you have sighted it, begin to fast; otherwise, do not begin to fast. If, on the other hand, there are clouds in the sky, rely on the number of days in the month of Sha'bān and allow it to run for a full thirty days.

The ruling just presented is adopted by the Shafiis, the Hanafis and the Malikis; as for the Hanbalis, they differ with the other three schools with respect to a situation in which there are clouds in the sky based on another prophetic hadith in which he said, "Begin fasting when you sight it, conclude your fast when your sight it, and if you are unable to see it [due to cloud cover, etc.], then make [an estimated] allowance for it." The Hanbalis take the phrase, "then make [an estimated] allowance for it" to mean, "Make provision for it by fasting." The Hanbalis support this interpretation on the basis of the practice followed by Ibn 'Umar, the narrator of this hadith. Whenever twenty-nine days of the month of Sha'bān had passed, Ibn 'Umar would send someone to look for the new moon; if this person saw the new moon, the beginning of Ramaḍān was confirmed. If he did not see it and if his vision was not blocked by clouds or dust, he was not to fast the next day; if his vision was blocked, however, he was likewise to fast the following day. This day,

5. That is, at the beginning of Ramaḍān [t.n.].
6. That is, at the end of Ramaḍān [t.n.].
7. Narrated by al-Bukhārī on the authority of Abū Hurayrah.

then, is not referred to in this situation as a "day of doubt"; rather, the Hanbalis do not acknowledge any doubt unless the day is clear and people still fail to sight the new moon.[8]

As for the way in which the sighting of the new moon is to be confirmed, each school offers its own ruling in this regard.[9]

---

8. The Hanbalis hold that if the new moon is concealed behind cloud cover at sundown on the 29th of Sha'bān, there is no need to complete Sha'bān as thirty days. Rather, people are to form the intention to fast that night and to fast the following day as part of Ramaḍān whether the day belongs, in fact, to Ramaḍān or to Sha'bān. However, if it becomes apparent in the course of the following day that it is still Sha'bān, no one is obliged to fast the rest of the day.

9. The Hanafis hold that if there is nothing in the sky to inhibit visibility, the new moon must be sighted by a large group of people whose reports are considered sufficiently reliable to be a basis for certainty. As for what constitutes a 'large' group, this is to be determined by the imam or his proxy; hence, the term 'large' is not defined in terms of a set number of individuals according to the best attested view. In this case, witnesses must use the phrase, "I bear witness" in their testimonies.

If, on the other hand, the sky is not completely clear and if someone reports that he has sighted the new moon, his testimony will be taken as sufficient evidence for certainty if he is an adult Muslim in full possession of his mental faculties who is known to be of good character. In this latter case, it is not necessary for the witness to use the phrase, "I bear witness", nor is it necessary for there to be a formal legal verdict [that Ramaḍān has begun] or a decision by a judiciary council.

If there is something in the sky to prevent visibility, it is not necessary for the new moon to be sighted by a group of people due to the limited visibility at such a time. Nor is any distinction made among witnesses based on whether they are male or female, free or slaves. If the new moon is sighted by someone whose testimony is deemed valid, if this person informs someone else whose testimony is also deemed valid, and if the second person goes to the magistrate and testifies based on the testimony of the first person, the magistrate may accept this person's testimony. Properly speaking, the same credibility is to be granted in such a situation to someone who is known to be of good character (*'adl*) and to someone who has not been proven to be either of good or bad character (*mastūr al-ḥāl*).

If someone whose testimony is deemed valid sights the crescent moon in a city, he or she must testify to this before the magistrate on the same night as the sighting. If such a person is in a village, he must testify to the sighting publicly in the mosque, even if the witness is a woman who normally remains in seclusion from the outside world. Moreover, whoever sights the new moon, together with whoever believes this person's testimony, is obliged to fast [the following day] even if the magistrate has rejected the witness's testimony. If such individuals break their fast due to the magistrate's rejection of the witness's testimony, they must make up this day of fasting; however, no expiation will be required of them.

* * *

According to the Shafiis, the beginning of the month of Ramaḍān is confirmed by a sighting of the new moon by someone who is either known to be of good character, or by someone who has not been proven to be either of good or bad character. This applies whether the sky is clear or contains elements that make visibility difficult. The witness must be an adult, free male Muslim who is in full possession of his mental faculties and who is known, if even only based on appearances, to be of good character. The witness must also utter the phrase, "I bear witness" in his testimony, by saying before the magistrate, for example, "I bear witness that I have seen the new moon." However, it is not necessary for him to add, "and that tomorrow is [the first day of] Ramaḍān."

According to the Shafiis, the general public is not required to fast unless the magistrate has heard such a person's testimony and ruled that it is valid or said, "the [beginning of the] month of Ramaḍān has been confirmed to me." Anyone who has personally sighted the new moon is obliged to fast Ramaḍān even if he has not testified before the magistrate, or even if he has testified but without his testimony being recognized. Similarly, fasting Ramaḍān becomes obligatory for everyone who has heard and believed such a person's testimony. This ruling applies even if the person who sighted the new moon is a young child, a woman, a slave, a *fāsiq*, or a non-Muslim.

* * *

The Malikis hold that the Ramaḍān new moon is confirmed by its being sighted. Such a sighting, in turn, may take place in three ways: (1) The new moon may be sighted by two persons who meet the qualifications for being described as *'adl*, namely, two free male adults who are in full possession of their mental faculties and who have never committed a major sin, persisted in minor sins, or done that which would be inconsistent with the ideals of manhood and honor. (2) The new moon may be sighted by a large group of people whose reports are considered sufficiently reliable to be a basis for certainty and who one can be assured would not collude in deception. It is not necessary, however, that all individual members of the group be free males who are known to be of good character. (3) The new moon may be sighted by a single individual. However, the sighting is binding only for the person who actually saw the new moon and for whomever he has informed if the person who was informed possesses no specialized knowledge pertaining to matters of astronomy and the like. As for those who do possess such knowledge, they are not bound to fast Ramaḍān based on a single person's sighting unless they themselves have sighted the new moon. The one person who sights the new moon need not be male or free; rather, as long as this person is not known to be a liar, it is required of all who have no specialized knowledge of astronomy to fast as soon as they hear this person's report if they trust in its reliability even if the person is a woman or a slave.

When the new moon is sighted by two people who are *'adl* or by a large group of people whose reports are considered sufficiently reliable to be a basis for certainty and who one can be assured would not collude in deception, everyone who hears their testimony, as well as everyone who receives a report of their testimony, is required to fast. If the report received is based on the testimony of two people who are *'adl*, each of these two individuals' reports must be transmitted by two others who are likewise *'adl*. However, it is not necessary for more than one pair to pass on the original testimony. Thus, if two people who qualify to be described as *'adl* transmit the testimony of a sighting by one of the two persons, after which they transmit the other's testimony as well, everyone who received either of the reports is required to fast, just as fasting is required of everyone who receives such a report from a large group of people whose reports are considered sufficiently reliable to be a basis for certainty and who one can be assured would not collude in deception. However, a single person's transmission of such a report is not sufficient to be binding. Moreover, if the report is passed on by a large group of people whose reports are considered sufficiently reliable to be a basis for certainty and whom one can be assured would not collude in deception, it is not necessary that more than one member of the group qualify to be described as *'adl*. In addition, a single person's transmission of the report is sufficient if the report has to do with the ruler's declaration or ruling that the beginning of Ramaḍān has been confirmed. If the new moon is sighted by a single person who qualifies as *'adl* or by a single person who has been proved to be neither of good character nor of bad character, he must bring the matter before the ruler so that he can open the floor for further testimony since, in a case such as this, someone else might come forward and join his testimony with the first person's if the first person qualifies to be described as *'adl*, whereas in the case of someone who is not considered *'adl*, his testimony may be backed up by that of a large group of people whose reports are considered sufficiently reliable to be a basis for certainty and who one can be assured would not collude in deception. Lastly, neither the testimonies of those who are *'adl* nor those of others must include the phrase, "I bear witness."

* * *

As for the Hanbalis, they hold that a sighting of the Ramaḍān new moon must be testified to by a Muslim who is held morally accountable under Islamic law and who has been proven to be of good character both outwardly and inwardly. Hence, the beginning of Ramaḍān may not be confirmed based on a sighting of the new moon reported by a young boy who has reached the age of discernment [since he is still not held morally responsible under Islamic law – t.n.], nor by someone who has not been proven to be of either good character or bad character. However, when it comes to individuals who have been shown to be of good character, no distinction is made between male and female, free and slave. Nor is it necessary that the person's testimony include the phrase, "I bear witness." In sum, everyone who hears the report of a sighting of the new moon by someone who is of proven good character is thereby obliged to fast, even if this person's testimony has been rejected by the ruler due to insufficient knowledge of the witness's character. Lastly, it is not required of someone who has sighted the new moon to go to the magistrate or to the mosque, nor even to inform people.

If there is a confirmed sighting of the new moon in a given region

If there is a confirmed sighting of the new moon in a given region, fasting is obligatory for those living in other regions as well, whether they are nearby or distant, if the news of the sighting reaches them in a binding manner; hence, no importance is placed on their disparate locations. This is the ruling agreed upon by the Hanafis, the Hanbalis and the Malikis; for the view of the Shafiis, see below.[10]

Whether the views of astrologers should be given consideration

No consideration should be given to statements made by astrologers; hence, people are not obliged to fast based on their calculations even if they trust what they have said. The reason for this is that the Lawgiver has made fasting dependent upon an unchanging sign, namely, the sighting of the new moon or the completion of [the month of Sha'bān] as thirty days.

The statements made by astrologers may well be based on explicit rules; however, we believe them to be imprecise as evidenced by the inconsistency among their opinions on most occasions. This view is shared by the Malikis, the Hanbalis and the Hanafis; for the view of the Shafiis, see below.[11]

Rulings on looking for the new moon

It is a collective duty for Muslims to look for the new moon beginning at sunset on the 29th of Sha'bān and on the 29th of Ramaḍān in order to determine whether or not they will fast the following day. This ruling is agreed upon by all the schools except the Hanbalis, who hold that looking for the new moon on these days is not obligatory, but merely recommended. It should be clear, however, that the view held by the other schools, namely, the Shafiis, the Hanafis and the Malikis, is the most reasonable one, since fasting the month of Ramaḍān is one of the pillars of the Islamic religion, and this fast has been made to rest on whether the new moon is sighted. How, then, could it be merely recommended, rather than obligatory, that we look for the new moon?

If the new moon is sighted during the day, either before or after noon, Muslims must fast the following day if the sighting occurs at the end of the month of Sha'bān, whereas they must break their fast the following day if the sighting occurs at the end of Ramaḍān. In the view of the Malikis and the Hanafis, it is not necessary to

---

10. The Shafiis hold that if there has been a confirmed sighting of the new moon in a particular location, people residing in nearby areas in all directions must also fast based on this confirmed sighting. As for the meaning of 'nearby', it is defined as the two locations' being less than 24 parasangs [72 miles] away from each other. As for those who live in areas which are more distant, they are not required to fast based on the aforementioned sighting due to their disparate locations.

11. The Shafiis hold that an astrologer's statement may be considered valid for himself and for those who believe what he says; however, according to the best attested view, the community as a whole is not required to fast based on his statements.

begin abstaining [immediately] from whatever would break a fast if the Ramaḍān new moon is sighted during the day at the end of Sha'bān, nor is it necessary to break one's fast [immediately] if the Shawwāl new moon is sighted during the day at the end of Ramaḍān; for the views of the Shafiis and the Hanbalis, see below.[12]

Whether it is necessary for the ruler to issue a verdict in order for fasting to begin

It is not necessary for the ruler to issue a verdict in order for the sighting of the new moon to be confirmed and for people to be obliged to fast. However, if the ruler does issue a judgment that the sighting of the new moon has been confirmed based on a means of confirmation supported by his own school, fasting thereby becomes obligatory for the whole Muslim community even if his ruling conflicts with the school of jurisprudence to which some of them adhere, since the ruler's verdict overrides any such conflict. This view is agreed upon by the Hanafis, the Hanbalis and the Malikis; for the view of the Shafiis, see below.[13]

Confirming the beginning of the month of Shawwāl

The commencement of the month of Shawwāl is confirmed by a sighting of its new moon. As for the exact manner in which this confirmation is to take place, each school offers its own ruling on this matter.[14]

---

12. The Shafiis and the Hanbalis attach no significance to sighting the new moon during the day; rather, they hold that it must be sighted after sundown.

13. According to the Shafiis, the ruler must issue a verdict in order for the sighting of the new moon to be confirmed and for people to be obliged to fast. Once the ruler has issued such a verdict, the people are required to fast even if his verdict is based on the testimony of a single individual known to be of good character.

14. The Hanafis hold that if there are clouds or other impediments to visibility in the sky, the commencement of the month of Shawwāl is confirmed by the testimony of two men who are *'adl*, or that of one man and two women. If the sky is completely clear, however, the new moon must be sighted by a large group of people. Moreover, each witness must utter the phrase, "I bear witness" as part of his or her testimony.

***

According to the Malikis, the appearance of *Shawwāl*'s new moon is confirmed by its being sighted by two individuals who are of proven good character, or by a large group of people who one can be assured would not collude in deception and whose reports are considered sufficiently reliable to be a basis for certainty. It is not necessary that the members of such a group be free or male (as was mentioned in the earlier discussion of the confirmation of the beginning of Ramaḍān). Moreover, if the new moon is sighted by a single person of proven good character, this is sufficient for the person concerned to end his Ramaḍān fast. In such a case, such a person must break his fast by means of a deliberate intention not to fast. However,

If *Shawwāl*'s new moon has not been sighted, Ramaḍān must be fasted for a full thirty days. If, after a full thirty days of Ramaḍān, *Shawwāl*'s new moon is still not sighted and if the sky is clear, the fast may not be ended on that night; rather, the following day must be fasted as well and the witnesses who testified to seeing the new moon at the beginning of Ramaḍān must be judged not to have been reliable. If, on the other hand, the sky is not clear, the fast must be broken that night, and that day must be considered to belong to Shawwāl. This is the view of the Hanafis and the Malikis; for the views of the Shafiis and the Hanbalis, see below.[15]

---

he is still not allowed to eat, drink, or indulge in anything else which would break his fast even if he is certain that no one else will see him. If such a person finds himself in circumstances that would make it legitimate for him to take a journey or if he falls ill, he is permitted to eat, drink, etc. However, if he breaks his fast without a legitimate excuse to eat, etc., he is to be admonished severely if he is someone of manifest integrity; otherwise, the magistrate is to impose upon him whatever discretionary punishment he deems appropriate.

* * *

The Shafiis hold that in order to confirm the beginning of Shawwāl, the testimony of a single person of proven good character is sufficient. This situation is thus like [the confirmation of] Ramaḍān according to the best attested view, and according to all of the schools except the Malikis, the person who gives his or her testimony is to say, "I bear witness."

* * *

As for the Hanbalis, they hold that the beginning of the month of Shawwāl can only be confirmed by the testimony of two men of proven good character, and that each testimony must include the phrase, "I bear witness."

15. The Shafiis hold that if people began fasting based on the testimony of someone known to be of good character and if they have fasted Ramaḍān for a full thirty days, then properly speaking, they must bring their fast to an end after this whether the sky is clear or not.

* * *

As for the Hanbalis, they hold that if the beginning of the Ramaḍān fast was based on the testimony of two witnesses of proven good character, if a full thirty days of Ramaḍān have been fasted, and if the Shawwāl new moon is not seen on the eve of the 31st day, the fast must be ended. If, on the other hand, the beginning of the Ramaḍān fast was based on the testimony of a single witness known to be of good

Fasting on "the day of doubt"

Each of the four schools offers its own definition of the "day of doubt" and its own ruling on the practice of fasting on this day.[16]

---

character or based on an estimation that the month of Sha'bān was 29 days due to cloud cover and the like, the 31st day must be fasted as well.

16. According to the Hanafis, the 'day of doubt' is the last day of Sha'bān which might, instead, be the first day of Ramaḍān. This occurs when the Ramaḍān new moon is not seen due to cloud cover after sundown on the 29th of Sha'bān, as a result of which there is doubt concerning whether the following day belongs to Sha'bān or to Ramaḍān. Alternatively, the doubt may arise due to the magistrate's having rejected the testimony of witnesses [who reported having sighted the Ramaḍān new moon], or people's having discussed a sighting but without its being confirmed.

As for the matter of fasting the 'day of doubt', there are some situations in which it is undesirable to the point of being forbidden or merely undesirable, whereas in other situations it will be recommended, or invalid. Fasting the 'day of doubt' is undesirable to the point of being forbidden if someone intends to fast the day with the certainty that it belongs to Ramaḍān, whereas it is merely undesirable if someone intends to fast it to fulfill a vow which is a 'duty'; it is likewise merely undesirable to fast this day without one's being decisive concerning whether one is doing it as a full religious obligation or as a 'duty' (as, for example, when one says, "I intend to fast tomorrow if it is Ramaḍān; otherwise, I intend to fast it in fulfillment of some other 'duty'"), or whether one is doing it as a full religious obligation or as a voluntary fast (as, for example, when one says, "I intend to fast tomorrow as an obligation if it is Ramaḍān, and as a voluntary fast if it is Sha'bān"). Fasting the 'day of doubt' is recommended if it is done with the intention of performing a voluntary fast and if it happens to coincide with the day one is accustomed to fasting anyway; it is also acceptable to fast the 'day of doubt' with this intention even if it does not coincide with one's regular day to fast. Fasting the 'day of doubt' will be invalid if one does so while vacillating between fasting and not fasting (as, for example, when someone says, "I intend to fast tomorrow if it is Ramaḍān; otherwise, I will not fast"). Lastly, if it is confirmed that the 'day of doubt' is the first day of Ramaḍān, one's fasting will count whether one's fast is undesirable to the point of being forbidden, merely undesirable, recommended, or allowed.

* * *

According to the Shafiis, the 'day of doubt' is the 30th day of Sha'bān if people speak about sighting the Ramaḍān new moon on the night before but without anyone's testifying to this effect, or with a testimony from someone whose testimony may not be accepted (such as a woman or a young child). It is forbidden to fast on this day whether the sky was clear or cloudy at sundown on the previous day; moreover, no allowance is to be made for the opposing view offered by Imam Aḥmad [Ibn Ḥanbal] according to which this day should be fasted, since giving another viewpoint the benefit of a doubt is not desirable when the other viewpoint runs counter to an unequivocal hadith. The hadith which applies here is the one in which the Prophet said, "And if your vision is obstructed, count Sha'bān as a full thirty days." Hence, if people do not talk about sighting the Ramaḍān new moon, it must be concluded that the month of Sha'bān has not yet ended. If, on the other hand, someone of known good character testifies to having sighted the new moon, it must be concluded that Ramaḍān has begun with certainty.

Exceptions are made to the prohibition against fasting the 'day of doubt' if someone fasts it for some reason that requires him or her to fast, such as fulfillment of a vow, making up earlier fasting days missed, or custom (as, for example, if someone is accustomed to fasting every Thursday, and Thursday happens to coincide with the 'day of doubt'). In cases such as these, it is not forbidden to fast the 'day of doubt'; in fact, it is obligatory to do so if the fast involved is in fulfillment of a duty, and it is recommended when the fasting involved is voluntary. If someone starts out the 'day of doubt' without fasting, after which it becomes apparent that Ramaḍān has begun, he or she must abstain for the remainder of the day from anything which would break a fast, then make the day up immediately after the conclusion of Ramaḍān.

If someone intends to fast the 'day of doubt' in the belief that it is the first day of Ramaḍān and if it then becomes apparent that it is the last day of Sha'bān, the fast will be invalid due to the person's lack of [proper] intention. If, on the other hand, it becomes apparent that it is, in fact, the first day of Ramaḍān and if the person is fasting based on his having believed someone who gave him a report [of sighting the new moon] but whose testimony may not be accepted (such as a slave or a *fāsiq*), his fast will nevertheless be valid for Ramadān. If, however, this person's fast is not based on such a belief, it will not be valid as a Ramaḍān fast. If someone intends to fast this day with the idea that if it is in Sha'bān, it will be a voluntary fast and if it is in Ramaḍān, it will count as part of Ramaḍān and if it becomes apparent that it is still Sha'bān, it will be valid as a voluntary fast, whereas if it becomes apparent that it is Ramaḍān, it will be valid neither as an obligatory fast nor as a voluntary fast.

* * *

The Malikis provide two definitions for the 'day of doubt', the second of which is the most widely accepted among them: The 'day of doubt' is the 30th of Sha'bān if, on the night before this, someone whose testimony may not be accepted (such as a *fāsiq*, a woman, or a slave) speaks of having sighted the Ramaḍān new moon. (1) The 'day of doubt' is the 30th of Sha'bān if, on the night before this, there are clouds in the sky and the Ramaḍān moon is not sighted. (2) Fasting the 'day of doubt' voluntarily, with or without its being a result of custom (as, for example, in the case of someone who is accustomed to fasting every Thursday, after which the 'day of doubt' happens to fall on a Thursday) is recommended. If someone fasts this day in order to make up a day missed from the previous Ramaḍān, in expiation for a broken oath, or to fulfill a vow (as in the case of someone who has vowed to fast on Friday, after which Friday happens to coincide with the 'day of doubt'), his fasting will count as having fulfilled the obligation on account of which the fast was undertaken provided that it does not become apparent that Ramaḍān has begun. If it does become apparent that Ramaḍān has begun, his fast will not count as part of the present Ramaḍān due to his lack of [proper] intention; nor will it count as making up for any previous fasting missed, as expiation, or as fulfillment of a vow. The reason for this is that fasting done during the month of Ramaḍān may not be counted as anything else; hence, days missed from a previous Ramaḍān, expiatory fasting one is obliged to perform, etc., must be performed at some other time. If someone vows to fast on a particular day but fails to do so, this fast does not have to be made up later, since its time has passed. If, on the other hand, someone fasts the 'day of doubt' with the intention that if it turns out to be the first day of Ramaḍān, it will count as part of Ramaḍān whereas if it turns out not to be Ramaḍān, it will count as a voluntary fast, his fast will be deemed undesirable. If, in such a case, the day turns out to be Ramaḍān, this person's fast will not count as part of Ramaḍān and he will have to make it up later; however, he will be obliged to abstain from whatever might break his fast out of reverence for the sacredness of the month itself. It is thus recommended that one abstain from whatever might break one's fast on the 'day of doubt' until the day has progressed sufficiently to make it clear whether the day is a day of fasting or not. If it turns out to be Ramaḍān, one must continue to abstain for the rest of the day, then make up one day later; if, after it becomes clear that the day is the beginning of Ramaḍān, someone deliberately, knowingly breaks his fast, he must not only make up the day later, but perform expiation for it as well.

* * *

According to the Hanbalis, the 'day of doubt' is the 30th of Sha'bān if the Ramaḍān new moon was not sighted on the night before this despite the fact that the sky on that night was perfectly clear. It is undesirable to fast the 'day of doubt' day voluntarily unless it coincides with a day on which one is accustomed to fasting anyway, or unless one fasted two days or more prior to it, in which case there is no undesirability attached to fasting it. If it turns out that this day is the first day of Ramaḍān, one's fast will not count as part of Ramaḍān; however, one must still abstain all day from whatever would break one's fast, then make up the day later.

If someone fasts the 'day of doubt' in fulfillment of an obligation, such as making up for a day missed during the previous Ramaḍān, in fulfillment of a vow, or in expiation for some transgression, it will be valid and serve to fulfill its intended purpose if it turns out to be the last day of Sha'bān. However, if it turns out to be the first day of Ramaḍān, one's fast will count neither as part of Ramaḍān nor as any other type of fast. One must nevertheless abstain from whatever would break a fast till the end of the day, then make it up later.

Lastly, if someone intends to fast the 'day of doubt' by saying that if it turns out to be Ramaḍān, the fast will count for Ramaḍān, it will not count for Ramaḍān even if it becomes apparent that the day is, in fact, the first day of Ramaḍān; nevertheless, one must abstain throughout the day from whatever would break a fast, then make up the day later, as we have seen. If, on the other hand, the day turns out not

Fasting which is prohibited: fasting on religious holidays, and a woman's fasting without her husband's permission

The Lawgiver has prohibited fasting at particular times, such as the Day of Fastbreaking and the Day of Sacrifice, as well as the three days following the Day of Sacrifice. The Hanafis hold that fasting on these three days is undesirable to the point of being forbidden, whereas according to the Malikis, it is forbidden to fast only on the two days (rather than three days) following the Day of Sacrifice. For each school's detailed ruling on this matter, see below.[17]

In addition, a married woman is forbidden to perform a voluntary fast without her husband's permission or without knowing whether he agrees or not; this prohibition applies unless he is not in need of her—because he is absent, for example, in a state of ritual consecration, or secluding himself in the mosque for prayer and worship. This is the view held by the Shafiis and the Malikis; for the views of the Hanafis and the Hanbalis, see below.[18]

---

to be the beginning of Ramaḍān, the fast will be valid neither as a voluntary fast nor as any other kind of fast.

17. According to the Malikis, fasting on the Day of Fastbreaking, the Day of Sacrifice and the two days following the Day of Sacrifice is prohibited except in the case of someone who, before performing the *ḥajj*, first completes the *'umrah*, then remains in the sacred Meccan precinct until the days of the *ḥajj* and, while still there, reenters a state of ritual consecration for the *ḥajj*, as well as in the case of someone who performs both the *'umrah* and the *ḥajj* with a single ritual consecration. In these two cases, it is permissible to fast the two days following the Day of Sacrifice. As for fasting the third day following the Day of Sacrifice, it is deemed undesirable.

* * *

According to the Shafiis, fasting on the Day of Fastbreaking, the Day of Sacrifice, and the three days following the Day of Sacrifice is not only forbidden, but invalid as well, even when one is on the greater pilgrimage.

* * *

According to the Hanbalis, fasting is forbidden on the Day of Fastbreaking, the Day of Sacrifice, and the three days following the Day of Sacrifice except in the two cases described above in connection with the Malikis' ruling on this matter.

* * *

As for the Hanafis, they hold that fasting on the Day of Fastbreaking, the Day of Sacrifice, and the three days following the Day of Sacrifice is undesirable to the point of being forbidden unless one is on the greater pilgrimage.

18. According to the Hanafis, it is undesirable for a woman to fast without her husband's permission.

* * *

As for the Hanbalis, they hold that as long as a woman's husband is present, she may not fast without his permission even if he is in a condition which would

Fasting which is recommended: Fasting on the 9th and 10th of *Muḥarram*, the 'white days', etc.

Recommended fasts include fasting the month of *Muḥarram*, with preference given to fasting the 9th and 10th days of this month. According to the Hanafis, fasting these two days is not merely recommended, but an emulation of the Sunnah. As we have seen, the Shafiis and the Hanbalis agree with this ruling based on the fact that they make no distinction between that which is recommended and that which is an emulation of the Sunnah. The Malikis, however, do not agree with it based on the distinction which they draw, together with the Hanafis, between that which is recommended and that which is 'Sunnah.'

Recommended fasts also include fasting three days out of every month; it is likewise recommended that these be the 'white days', that is, the 13th, the 14th and the 15th of each lunar month; the Malikis, however, disagree on this point.[19]

Fasting on the Day of 'Arafah

It is recommended that one fast the 9th of Dhū al-Ḥijjah, which is known as the Day of 'Arafah. However, this fast is only recommended for those who are not performing the major pilgrimage; as for those who are performing the pilgrimage, each of the four schools offers its own ruling in this connection.[20]

---

prevent him from having sexual relations with her, such as being in a state of ritual consecration, being secluded in the mosque for prayer and worship, or illness.

19. According to the Malikis, it is undesirable to intend specifically to fast the 'white days'.

20. The Hanbalis hold that fasting the Day of 'Arafah is recommended for those pilgrims who stand at Mt. 'Arafah at night. However, if they stand there during the day, it is undesirable for them to fast the Day of 'Arafah.

* * *

According to the Hanafis, it is undesirable for a pilgrim to fast the Day of 'Arafah if this will weaken him; the same ruling applies to fasting the 'Day of Watering' on the 8th of Dhū al-Ḥijjah [so called because it was on this day that pilgrims to Mecca used to water their camels and replenish their water supplies in preparation for going to 'Arafah – t.n.].

* * *

According to the Malikis, it is undesirable for pilgrims to fast either the Day of 'Arafah or the Day of Watering.

* * *

As for the Shafiis, they hold that if a pilgrim is a resident of Mecca and goes to 'Arafah during the day, his fasting the Day of 'Arafah is a departure from the ideal, whereas if he goes to 'Arafah at night, it is permissible for him to fast. As for

Fasting on Thursdays and Mondays

Fasting on Thursdays and Mondays is recommended, and there are clear physical benefits in so doing.

Fasting six days of the month of Shawwāl

According to the Shafiis, the Hanafis and the Hanbalis, it is recommended that one fast six days of the month of Shawwāl without any conditions attached thereto; only the Malikis differ with this ruling. According to the Shafiis and the Hanbalis, it is preferable that one fast these days in uninterrupted succession; for the views of the Malikis and the Hanafis, see below.[21]

Fasting on alternate days

For those able to do so, it is recommended that they fast one day, then break their fast the next; it is stated [in a prophetic hadith] that this is the best type of recommended fasting.

Fasting Rajab, Sha'bān, and the other sacred months

According to the Shafiis, the Malikis and the Hanafis, it is recommended that one fast the months of Rajab and Sha'bān; for the view of the Hanbalis, see below.[22]

As for the four sacred months—three consecutive months, namely, Dhū al-Qa'dah, Dhū al-Ḥijjah, *Muḥarram*, and one month which stands alone, namely, Rajab—fasting them is recommended according to the Shafiis, the Malikis and the Hanbalis. For the view of the Hanafis, see below.[23]

---

pilgrims who have traveled from elsewhere to perform the pilgrimage, it is an emulation of the Sunnah for them not to fast at all.

21. According to the Malikis, fasting six days of the month of Shawwāl is undesirable given the following conditions: (1) The person who is fasting is someone whom others emulate as an example, or there is concern that he will believe that fasting these days is obligatory. (2) The days are fasted immediately after the Day of Fastbreaking. (3) The days are fasted in succession. (4) The person who fasts these days makes his fasting visible to others.

If any of these conditions is unfulfilled, it is acceptable to fast these days unless the person doing so believes that fasting them immediately following the Day of Fastbreaking is an emulation of the Sunnah. If the person fasting holds this belief, fasting these days is undesirable even if he or she does not make his or her fasting visible to others, or fasts on nonsuccessive days.

* * *

As for the Hanafis, they deem it desirable for the six days to be fasted nonsuccessively, and specifically, for one to fast two days each week.

22. The Hanbalis hold that it is undesirable to fast the month of Rajab alone unless one breaks one's fast sometime during the month.

If someone begins a voluntary fast which is then invalidated

The Shafiis and the Hanbalis hold that once someone has commenced a voluntary fast, it is an emulation of the Sunnah to complete the fast, then to make it up later if something happens to invalidate it. For the view of the Hanafis, see below.[24] The same ruling applies to fasting the days on which one has vowed to seclude oneself for the purpose of prayer and worship. One might say, for example, "I have promised God that I will seclude myself in the mosque for prayer and worship for ten days." Having said this, it is an emulation of the Sunnah for such a person to fast the ten days during which he has vowed to seclude himself. Such a fast is not obligatory according to the Shafiis and the Hanbalis; for the views of the Malikis and the Hanafis, see below.[25]

Undesirable fasting

It is deemed undesirable to fast Nayrūz[26] and 'The Festival Day'[27] by themselves, that is, without fasting days before or after them, if they do not coincide with days that one would have fasted anyway out of custom. If they do fall on days when one would have fasted out of custom, the Malikis, the Hanafis and the Hanbalis hold that fasting them is not undesirable. As for the Shafiis, they hold that it is not undesirable to fast these two days under any circumstances.

According to the Shafiis, the Hanafis and the Hanbalis, it is undesirable to fast Friday or Saturday alone; the Malikis, however, hold that it is not undesirable to fast Friday or any other day alone.

---

23. According to the Hanafis, the recommended manner of fasting the sacred months is for one to fast three days out of each month, namely, Thursday, Friday and Saturday.

24. According to the Hanafis, if someone commences a voluntary fast, then invalidates it in some manner, it is his 'duty' to make it up (bearing in mind that for the Hanafis, a 'duty' is on a par with an emphatically enjoined emulation of the prophetic Sunnah). Hence, as we saw in our discussion of the types of fasting, the Hanafis hold that invalidating a voluntary fast is undesirable to the point of being forbidden and, similarly, that not making up such a fast if it is invalidated is likewise undesirable to the point of being forbidden.

* * *

According to the Malikis, completing a voluntary fast one has begun is obligatory; it is likewise obligatory to make up such a fast if one invalidates it deliberately. An exception to this ruling is made, however, in the case of someone who began to fast voluntarily and was then commanded by one of his parents or by his sheikh to break his fast for fear that his continuing to fast would cause him harm. In such a case, it is permissible for one to break one's fast, and one is not obliged to make it up later.

25. According to the Hanafis, fasting is a condition for the validity of a period of seclusion for prayer and worship which one has vowed to take, as we have seen.

* * *

According to the Hanafis and the Hanbalis, it is undesirable to fast one or two days immediately prior to the beginning of Ramaḍān; as for the Malikis, they hold that it is not undesirable to fast at this time, whereas according to the Shafiis, it is forbidden to do so. In addition, the Shafiis hold that it is forbidden to fast the second half of Sha'bān unless one joins the days fasted during the second half of the month with days fasted during the first half of the month and unless there is something that would require one to fast at this time, such as a vow or a habitual custom.

It is also deemed undesirable to fast the 'day of doubt'. (For details concerning this matter, see the earlier discussion of the 'day of doubt'.)

There are, in addition, other undesirable practices associated with fasting, the details concerning which are presented below.[28]

As for the Malikis, they hold that fasting is an obligatory part of seclusion in a mosque for the sake of prayer and worship. However, if one makes a vow to undertake such a spiritual retreat for a number of days, it is not necessary to vow to fast during these days, and one may fulfill one's vow to go on the retreat by simply fasting voluntarily, but the retreat will not be valid if one does not fast at all, since fasting, in the view of the Malikis, is a condition for such a retreat's validity.

26. 'Nayrūz' is the Persian New Year's Day (21 March by the Christian calendar) [t.n.].

27. 'The Festival Day' (*al-mihrajān*) is the Persian 'Festival of Autumn' [t.n.].

28. The Hanafis divide undesirable fasting into two types: (a) Fasting which is undesirable to the point of being forbidden, and (b) Fasting which is merely undesirable.

The first type includes fasting the Day of Fastbreaking, the Day of Sacrifice and the three days following the Day of Sacrifice. If someone fasts these days, his fast will be valid, but he will be guilty of wrongdoing. Moreover, if someone begins to fast one of these days, then invalidates the fast in some way, he is not required to make it up later. As for the second type, namely, fasting which is merely undesirable, this includes the following: (1) fasting the 10th of the month without fasting either the 9th or the 11th as well, (2) fasting 'Nayrūz' and the 'Festival Day' alone if they do not coincide with one's customary fasting days, (3) fasting all year round, since it tends to weaken the body, (4) fasting both night and day rather than breaking one's fast after sundown, (5) engaging in the "fast of silence", i.e., fasting while abstaining from speech as well, (6) a woman's undertaking a voluntary fast without her husband's permission unless he is ill, fasting, or in a state of ritual consecration for the major or minor pilgrimage, and (7) fasting when one is on a journey if fasting is stressful under these circumstances.

* * *

The Malikis list the following as undesirable: (1) Fasting the fourth day after the Day of Sacrifice. They make an exception to this ruling, however, for people performing either *qirān* or *tamattu'*. In addition, those who are required to provide a sacrificial animal due to some action they failed to perform when on the *ḥajj* and or *'umrah* may fast this day without any undesirability attached thereto, and if they fast it voluntarily, it will be valid. If someone fasts this day, then breaks the fast deliberately, not because he realizes fasting is forbidden on this day but, rather, for

That which invalidates fasting

Those things which invalidate fasting are divided into two categories, namely: those things which require one to make up the fast later and to perform expiation, and those things which require one only to make up the fast later.

---

some other reason, he must make up the day later. If, on the other hand, someone vows to fast this day, he or she must fulfill this vow in view of its being a form of worship in and of itself. (2) Fasting days in continuous succession for those who would be weakened by this and, as a consequence, be unable to perform other actions which are superior to fasting. (3) Fasting the day on which the Prophet's birthday is commemorated, since this day is similar to the [official] religious holidays. (4) Undertaking a voluntary fast when one has obligatory fasting to do, such as obligatory fasting days which need to be made up. (5) A guest's fasting without his host's permission; as for a wife's undertaking a voluntary fast without her husband's permission, this is entirely forbidden, as we have seen. (5) Fasting night and day without breaking one's fast after sundown, which is forbidden. (6) Someone's fasting on a journey if it will cause undue hardship. Otherwise, however, fasting while on a journey is deemed superior to not fasting.

* * *

The Shafiis list the following as undesirable: (1) Fasting by someone who is ill, traveling, pregnant, nursing or elderly if there is reason to fear that fasting would cause the person concerned to suffer undue hardship; fasting may even be forbidden if there is reason to fear that not taking nourishment might cause death or damage to some bodily organ. (2) Fasting Friday, Saturday or Sunday alone if there is no other reason to fast, such as a vow or the like. If one fasts one of these days alone for a reason, however, there is no undesirability attached to doing so. Nor is fasting these days undesirable if the day concerned falls on a day when the person has been accustomed to fasting in any case, or when it falls within the framework of a longer fast. (3) Fasting all year round. (4) Undertaking a voluntary fast when one has obligatory fasting to make up, since the performance of that which is obligatory is more important than doing that which is voluntary.

* * *

That which requires making up one's fast and expiation

Each school offers its own listing of those things which require someone both to make up his or her fast and to perform expiation.[29]

As for the Hanbalis, they view the following as undesirable: (1) Fasting continuously both day and night rather than breaking one's fast at sundown, though no undesirability attaches to this practice if one eats [at least] a date or some similar food [after sunset]. (2) Fasting the month of Rajab alone.

29. According to the Hanafis, there are two types of action which require that one both make up one's fast and perform expiation: (1) taking nourishment or its equivalent (including food, drink, etc.) without a legitimate excuse when the substance taken is something that one finds desirable and which helps to satisfy hunger, and (2) fully satisfying one's sexual desires.

In order for acts included under (1) and (2) above to require expiation, the following conditions must be fulfilled: (a) The person fasting must have formed his or her intention to fast the night before, and be performing the fast of Ramadān. If he or she did not form his or her intention to fast the night before, no expiation is required. Moreover, if the person concerned formed the intention to fast the night before but is making up days missed from a previous Ramaḍān or is performing some other fast altogether, no expiation is required. (b) There must not have arisen any circumstance which would make it permissible for the person to break his or her fast, such as the commencement of a journey, falling ill, etc. It is permissible to break one's fast after becoming ill; however, if someone broke his fast before commencing a journey, expiation would still be required. (c) The person who commits an act included in (1) or (2) above must have done so willingly and of his own accord. (d) The person concerned must have committed the act deliberately. Thus, if someone breaks his or her fast out of forgetfulness or by mistake, no expiation is required.

Sexual intercourse, whether anal or vaginal, when engaged in deliberately, requires expiation for both parties given the conditions mentioned above. In addition, the party who is 'entered', as it were, must be a living human being who is sexually desirable; if this is the case, expiation is required by the mere touching of the two parties' genitals even if no ejaculation takes place. If a woman allows a young boy or an insane person to have relations with her, she must perform expiation by means of payment [to be explained later]. If a woman experiences sexual pleasure with another woman with the resulting vaginal secretions, she must make up the fast later, but no expiation is required. As for intercourse with a domestic animal, someone who is dead, or a young girl who is not sexually desirable, it requires no expiation, but if ejaculation occurs, it requires one to make up the fast later.

Actions belonging to type (1) above include smoking regular tobacco, opium, hashish and similar substances, since the desire involved is apparent in each case. Also included is swallowing one's spouse's saliva for the sake of the pleasure it brings and swallowing a grain of wheat or a sesame seed which was not originally in one's mouth since one may find pleasure in doing so, unless one chews it up so thoroughly that it dissolves and none of it reaches one's stomach. This category also includes eating "Armenian clay" or a small amount of salt, and eating deliberately after having spoken ill of someone in his absence because one thinks that by doing so, one has already broken one's fast; the reason for this is that speaking ill of someone in his absence does not break one's fast. The same ruling applies if one breaks one's fast after undergoing cupping, touching [someone of the opposite sex with one's hand], or kissing with physical desire but without ejaculation. These things do not break one's fast; hence, if one deliberately breaks one's fast after performing any of these actions, one is required to perform expiation.

Other actions will be mentioned below in the section on that which requires someone to make up his or her fast later but without expiation.

* * *

According to the Shafiis, there is only one action which requires that one both make up one's fast later and perform expiation, namely, sexual intercourse. In order for sexual intercourse to require that one both make up one's fast and perform expiation, the following fourteen conditions must be met: (1) One must have formed the intention to fast. Hence, if the person concerned abandoned his intention to fast the night before, his fasting the following day will not be valid, although he must nevertheless abstain from things which would break a fast. If someone approaches his wife sexually under these circumstances during the day, he is not required to perform expiation, since he is not truly fasting. (2) One must perform the act deliberately. Hence, if someone approaches his wife forgetting that he is fasting, his fast will not be broken, and consequently, he is required neither to make up the fast later nor to perform expiation. (3) One must do so willingly. Hence, if someone were forced to have intercourse, his fast would not be broken. (4) One must be aware that such an act is forbidden and not have a legitimate excuse for ignorance. Hence, if the person fasting is new to Islam or grew up far from Muslim scholars, his engaging in sexual relations under these circumstances will not break his fast. (5) The event must occur while one is performing the fast of Ramaḍān during Ramaḍān itself. Hence, if one engages in such an act during a voluntary fast or during a fast being performed in fulfillment of a vow, to make up for days missed in a previous Ramaḍān, or in expiation for some transgression, no expiation is required even if one engages in the act deliberately. (6) The act of engaging in sexual relations must be the only thing that has invalidated one's fast; hence, if someone were to eat while engaged in the act, he would not be required to perform expiation but rather, only to make up the fast later. (7) The person concerned must be in full possession of his mental faculties and be qualified to be held morally responsible under Islamic law; hence, if a young boy engaged in sexual relations while fasting, no expiation would be required of him. Similarly, if someone is on a journey, then forms the intention to fast and starts out the next day fasting, after which he breaks his fast during the day by engaging in sexual intercourse, no expiation is required of him due to the allowance granted to those who are traveling. (8) The person concerned must believe that his fast is still valid when he engages in the act. Thus, if someone ate out of forgetfulness and, as a consequence, thought that his fast had thereby been broken, after which he deliberately engaged in sexual intercourse, no expiation would be required of him. However, his fast would now be invalidated and he would have to make it up later. (9) The person concerned must not lose his sanity between the time he has sexual relations and the time the sun sets. If this should happen, no expiation will be required of him. (10) The person concerned must commit this act on his own initiative [the text reads "must not commit..." – t.n.]. Hence, if someone were approached by his wife sexually while he was asleep and he responded to her advances while still asleep, no expiation would be required of him unless he had enticed her to do so. (11) One must not be mistaken. In other words, if someone engaged in sexual relations, thinking that dawn had not broken or that the sun had already set, after which it became apparent that he had had sexual relations during the day, no expiation would be required of him, although he would be required to make up the fast later and to abstain from anything else that might break his fast for the rest of the day. (12) The glans of the penis, or its equivalent in the case of a penis which has been cut off, must have entered [the vagina, the anus, etc.]. Hence, if only part of the glans is inserted, his fast will not be broken. If someone has an ejaculation under these circumstances, he must simply make up the fast later without performing expiation; however, he must continue to abstain from whatever would break a fast for the rest of the day, and if he fails to do so, he will be guilty of wrongdoing. (13) The intercourse must be either vaginal or anal even if no ejaculation takes place. Hence, if it takes place through any other opening, no expiation is required. (14) The person concerned must be the actor rather than the recipient, as it were. Hence, if a male approaches a female, the expiation is required of the initiator in all cases.

Lastly, if dawn breaks while a man is having intercourse with his wife and if he withdraws immediately, his fast will be valid. However, if he continues even for a short while after this, he must make up the fast later and perform expiation as well if he realizes that dawn has broken. If he does not realize it, however, he must make up the fast later but without performing expiation.

* * *

The Hanbalis list two things that require that one both make up one's fast later and perform expiation: (1) Vaginal or anal intercourse during the day in the month of Ramaḍān. This ruling applies whether the party that was 'entered' is living or dead, in full possession of his/her mental faculties or otherwise, or even an animal. Similarly, this ruling applies whether the person who did the 'entering' did so deliberately or out of forgetfulness, knowingly or out of ignorance, willingly or under duress, or mistakenly (such as someone who had sexual intercourse while thinking that dawn had not broken yet, after which it became apparent that it was already past dawn). The basis for their position on this is that the Prophet commanded a man who had had sexual relations during the day in the month of Ramaḍān to make up his fast later and to perform expiation as well. He did not, however, ask him to explain what his circumstances had been at the time when he had intercourse. The Hanbalis hold that expiation is required in such a situation whether the person who engaged in this act was truly fasting or merely abstaining from those things that would break a fast out of 'duty'. This ruling also applies to those who did not form the intention to fast on the night before, since their fast is not valid despite their obligation to abstain from whatever would break a fast, and if they engage in intercourse in such a case, they must perform expiation as well as make up for the fast they missed. According to the Hanbalis, withdrawal of the penis is also tantamount to intercourse; hence, if someone is engaged in intercourse when dawn breaks and he withdraws, he must still make up the fast later and perform expiation. As for the person who was 'entered', their ruling is that if he or she was a willing participant, if he or she is aware of the ruling on this matter, and if he or she has not forgotten that he or she is fasting, he or she must also make up the fast and perform expiation. (2) If two women have sexual contact and one of them has the vaginal secretions associated with such an act, she must perform expiation.

Lastly, the Hanbalis hold that if, when someone engages in intercourse, he is healthy, after which he falls ill, this will not exempt him from the expiation which he owes. The same ruling applies to someone who, when he engages in intercourse, is free, after which he is imprisoned, or who is resident in a place, after which he departs on a journey. Moreover, if a woman who has been lain with is not menstruating while intercourse takes place, after which her menstrual period begins, she must still perform the required expiation.

* * *

As for the Malikis, they hold that anything that invalidates one's fast likewise requires that one make up the fast and perform expiation given specific conditions. What follows is a listing of those things which invalidate a fast and which require that one make up the fast and perform expiation. One: Sexual intercourse which would require the performance of major ablutions and which would invalidate the fast of an adult, whether he or she is the party which 'enters' or the party which is 'entered'. If an adult has intercourse with a young girl who cannot tolerate it, his fast is not invalidated unless he has an ejaculation. If a man has an emission of semen without intercourse, this necessitates the performance of expiation but without his having to make up the fast. If the emission occurs due to looking [at a woman] or erotic thoughts, this does not necessitate expiation unless the following two conditions are met: (a) One must continue looking or thinking such thoughts for a long time. Hence, if someone looks at a woman, then averts his gaze before having looked at her for a long time, and if, in spite of looking away, he has an emission of semen, no expiation is required. (b) It must be the person's habit to have a seminal emission whenever he looks [at a sexually attractive person] for a long time; if it is not customary for the person to have an emission of semen from looking for a long time, there are two views on whether expiation is required. If semen is secreted by simply looking or thinking accompanied by moderate pleasure yet without engaging in extended glances or thoughts, this requires that one make up the fast later but without making expiation; as for the secretion of pre-seminal fluid only, this likewise requires only that one make up the fast later without expiation. If a man approaches a woman sexually as she sleeps during the day in the month of Ramaḍān, he must perform expiation for this. Expiation is also required of someone who pours something deliberately down someone else's throat while the latter is sleeping during the day in the month of Ramaḍān, provided that the substance poured reaches the person's stomach. As for making up the fast later, this is required of the woman and of the person down whose throat something was poured because of the fact that fasting cannot be made up on someone else's behalf. Two: The deliberate expulsion of vomit, whether it fills one's mouth or not. If anyone vomits deliberately and without being ill, he must both make up the fast later and perform expiation. If, on the other hand, someone vomits involuntarily, his fast is not invalidated unless some of the vomit goes back down; if this occurs even involuntarily, the person's fast is invalidated. This ruling does not apply to phlegm or mucus if it goes down into one's stomach; if this occurs, the person's fast is not invalidated even if he or she would have been able to spit it out but did not do so. Three: Deliberately allowing a non-solid substance to reach one's esophagus by way of the mouth, the ear, the eye or the nose. If this occurs, one is required both to make up the fast later and to perform expiation. However, if such a substance reaches the esophagus accidentally (as, for example, when one is rinsing out one's mouth [as part of ritual ablutions] and some water goes down into one's esophagus against one's will), one is required only to make up the fast later. The same ruling applies to a substance taken in by mistake, as when someone eats during the day thinking that the sun has not risen yet or that it has already set, or wondering whether it has risen or set. If it then becomes apparent that, in fact, the person ate before sunrise or after sunset, his fast is, of course, still valid; however, it is also valid if it becomes apparent that he or she ate after sunrise or before sunset [due to the uncertainty involved – t.n.]. Those things which are classified as non-solid include the following: (a) Incense and the steam coming from a kettle if someone inhales them and they reach his esophagus. (b) Tobacco smoke if the person concerned is a smoker; its merely reaching one's throat (even without reaching the stomach) will invalidate one's fast. As for the smoke from burning firewood, this does not invalidate one's fast, and the same applies to the smell of food if one inhales it. (c) If someone applies kohl (eyeliner) during the day, then finds the taste of it in his throat, his or her fast will be invalidated and he or she will be obliged to perform expiation if this was done deliberately; however, if someone applies kohl at night and then tastes it during the day, this will not invalidate his or her fast. (d) If someone deliberately oils his or her hair without a legitimate excuse for doing so and if the oil reaches the person's throat through the pores in his or her head, his or her fast will be invalidated and he or she will be required to perform expiation. The same ruling applies to a woman who applies henna to her hair deliberately and without a valid excuse for doing so; if she later finds the taste of the henna in her mouth, her fast will be invalidated and she will be obliged to perform expiation. Four: Deliberately allowing anything to reach the stomach without a legitimate excuse for doing so, be it a non-solid or anything else. This ruling applies whether the substance or object reaches the stomach from above or from below; however, that which reaches it from below will not invalidate one's fast unless it does so through a bodily orifice such as the anus. Hence, one's fast is not invalidated by oil or some similar substance flowing from the pores to the stomach; an injection, therefore, in the arm, buttocks or elsewhere will not cause one's fast to be broken; as for an injection in the male urethra, this does not invalidate one's fast under any circumstances. If a pebble, a dirham, etc. reaches the stomach, one's fast will be broken only if it reaches it from one's mouth. Anything that reaches the stomach through the mouth will invalidate one's fast and require that one make up the fast if it takes place in the month of Ramaḍān; this ruling applies regardless of whether it reached the stomach deliberately or against one's will, out of forgetfulness or by mistake (as in the case of non-solids reaching the esophagus, as we saw above); however, some things which reach the stomach deliberately require that one perform expiation as well, as has been explained.

In sum, whoever consumes any of the substances mentioned thus far as invalidating one's fast is required to make up the fast and to perform expiation given the following conditions: (1) The breaking of one's fast must take place during the month of Ramaḍān; if it takes place during any other fast, such as a fast to make up days missed from a previous Ramaḍān, in fulfillment of a vow, in expiation, or a voluntary fast, no expiation is required. In some cases, however, one must make up the fast, details concerning which will be presented below. (2) The breaking of one's fast must be deliberate. Hence, if someone breaks his or her fast out of forgetfulness or error or due to a legitimate excuse such as illness or travel, all that is required is that he or she make up the fast later. (3) The person concerned must take the substance which breaks his or her fast voluntarily. Hence, if he or she does so under duress, no expiation is required; rather, he or she must simply make up the fast later. (4) The person concerned must be aware that the breaking of one's fast is forbidden, even if he or she is unaware of the necessity of performing expiation. However, someone who deliberately, voluntarily breaks his or her fast without knowing that breaking one's fast is forbidden, as might happen with someone who is new to Islam, is not required to perform expiation. (5) The person fasting must be indifferent to the sacredness of the month. This does not apply, however, to someone who breaks his fast based on his or her interpretation of an existing circumstance, since in this case, no expiation is required. An example of such a situation is one in which someone first breaks his or her fast out of forgetfulness or under duress; then, after remembering that he or she is fasting or after the duress has come to an end, the person thinks that it is not necessary to go on abstaining for the rest of the day from those things which would break one's fast and, as a consequence, he or she deliberately does something that would be inconsistent with fasting. If this occurs, no expiation is required, since the person concerned based his or her behavior on an event that had already taken place, namely, having first broken his or her fast out of forgetfulness or by coercion. Another example of this type of situation is one in which someone who is fasting travels a distance which is less than that required for one to be allowed to shorten prayers; then, thinking that the distance traveled was sufficient to warrant the shortening of prayers, the person believes that it is permissible for him or her to break his or fast based on the apparent meaning of the Qur'anic phrase, "...but he that is ill or on a journey [shall fast instead for the same] number of other days..." (2:185), as a result of which he or she intends from the night before not to fast the following day. In such a situation, no expiation is required. A third example of this type of situation is one in which someone sees the Shawwāl new moon during the daytime on the 30th of Ramaḍān and thinks that, as a consequence, it is the Day of Fastbreaking and that he is allowed to break his fast based on the apparent meaning of the words of the Prophet, "Begin fasting when you sight it and conclude your fast when your sight it." In this situation also, no expiation is required. As for someone who breaks his or her fast based on an occurrence that has yet to take place, he or she is required to perform expiation. An example of this type of situation is one in which someone knows that he tends to get a fever on a particular day; consequently, he forms the intention on the night before`

That which requires making up one's fast without expiation, and that which requires no action at all

Having listed those things that require one to make up one's fast and to perform expiation, it remains now for us to discuss those things that require that one make up one's fast without expiation, and those which do not invalidate one's fast to begin with. There are many things which fall into the latter category, and each school offers its own detailed listing of these.[30]

---

to break his fast the following day, thinking that this is permissible. Such a person is required to perform expiation even if he does get a fever the next day. A second example is that of a woman who is accustomed to having her menstrual period begin on a particular day; as a result, she forms the intention not to fast beginning the night before, thinking that this is permissible given the fact that her period will begin the following day; however, she is required to perform expiation even if her period does begin on the day concerned, since she formed the intention not to fast before it began. A third example is that of someone who, on a particular day of Ramaḍān, speaks ill of someone in his or her absence; then, thinking that his or her fast has been invalidated because of this, he or she deliberately does something that would be inconsistent with fasting. In such a situation, expiation is required. (6) That which reaches [the stomach] must have reached it by way of one's mouth; if it reaches it through one's ear, eye, etc., no expiation is required, although one's fast must be made up later. (7) The fast-breaking substance must reach the stomach; hence, if something reaches only the esophagus, after which the person fasting forces it out again, no expiation is required. However, one must make up the fast if some non-solid substance reaches one's esophagus.

Those things which both break one's fast and require that one make up the fast and perform expiation include the following: 1) Abandoning one's intention to fast during the day, as well as abandoning it at night if the abandonment continues until the break of dawn. 2) Allowing vomit which has been deliberately expelled to reach one's stomach whether intentionally or against one's will, but not out of forgetfulness. 3) Allowing a fragment of a moist, wooden toothpick (from which bits resembling coconut bark tend to slough off) to reach [one's stomach]; this ruling applies even if the fragment reaches one's stomach against one's will if one has deliberately set about cleaning one's teeth with a toothpick during the day in the month of Ramaḍān.

These things require expiation given the conditions mentioned above with the exception of deliberateness with respect to vomit that has gone back down into one's stomach after someone vomits deliberately, and with respect to the bits of a wooden toothpick that slough off; in these two cases, it makes no difference whether the substance reached one's stomach deliberately or against one's will. As for allowing either of these two substance to reach one's stomach out of forgetfulness, this requires only that one make up the fast later.

30. The Hanafis list three things that require one to make up one's fast without expiation: (1) Taking in something that contains no nourishment or its equivalent. (They define 'nourishment' as that which one would be naturally inclined to partake of and which would satisfy one's hunger, while the 'equivalent' of nourish-

ment refers to medicine.) (2) Taking in nourishment or medicine given a legitimate excuse for doing so, such as illness, travel, coercion or error, such as when someone rinses out his mouth carelessly, allowing some water to go down his esophagus, or as when someone treats a wound on his abdomen or head, as a result of which the medicine reaches his stomach or his brain. As for substances taken in out of forgetfulness, they do not invalidate one's fast to begin with and, as a consequence, they require one neither to make up one's fast nor to perform expiation. (3) Satisfying sexual desire incompletely.

Examples from category (1) above include eating raw rice, dough or flour if it has not been mixed with anything that is customarily eaten, such as shortening and honey; otherwise, expiation is required. Similarly, if someone eats clay other than the Armenian variety, no expiation is required. As for Armenian clay, which is known among druggists, its consumption requires that one both make up one's fast and perform expiation. If someone eats a large amount of salt all at once, no expiation is required since this is not something one would normally find palatable, nor would it satisfy a person's hunger. As for eating a small amount of salt, this calls for expiation and for making up the fast later since one would normally find it to be pleasurable. Similarly, if someone eats a date pit, a piece of leather, or a piece of fruit which is not edible before it is ripe, such as quince which has not been cooked or salted, no expiation is required. One's fast must also be made up if he or she swallows a pebble, a piece of iron, a dirham, a dinar, some soil, or the like, or if he introduces water or medicine into his stomach by means of an injection through the anus, nose, or vagina, or if he pours oil into his ear; if he pours water, however, it will not invalidate his fast, properly speaking, due to water's not flowing [as oil does]. In addition, one's fast must be made up later if rain or snow gets into one's mouth without one's swallowing it, or if someone vomits either deliberately or involuntarily, after which he deliberately swallows the vomit again (provided that, in both cases, the amount of vomit would be enough to fill one's mouth, and provided that one remembers that he is fasting). If someone has forgotten that he is fasting, however, his fast will not be broken in any of the aforementioned situations. Similarly, one's fast is not broken if the amount of vomit is less than sufficient to fill one's mouth, properly speaking. If someone eats what remains of something like a piece of fruit lodged between his teeth (if it is as large as a chickpea), his or her fast must be made up; if it is smaller than this, however, it will not break one's fast since it is too small to merit consideration. If someone swallows his saliva after it collects in his mouth, or if water remains in his mouth after he has rinsed his mouth as part of ritual ablutions and he swallows it with his saliva, this will not invalidate his fast; nevertheless, one should spit between rinsing one's mouth and swallowing one's saliva again, though it is not necessary to spit excessively.

Category (2) above includes taking in nourishment or its equivalent with a legitimate excuse. Examples of this include a situation in which a woman breaks her fast for fear that she will become ill given all the service she is performing, someone fasting who is asleep, after which someone places something that would break his fast down his throat, and someone who breaks his fast deliberately based on a judicial error—as when, for example, someone eats deliberately after having eaten out of forgetfulness, someone who has sexual relations out of forgetfulness after which he engages in sexual relations or eats deliberately, etc. Another example is that of someone who did not form the intention to fast during the night, then formed it during the following day; if such a person breaks his fast, he must perform expiation due to the ambiguity as to whether he is actually fasting or not in the Shafiis' view. If someone forms the intention to fast during the night without going back on this intention, then begins the following day on a journey, after which he intends to stay in a particular place, no expiation is required of him if he eats after this even though, properly speaking, he is forbidden to eat in this case. Similarly, if someone eats, drinks or engages in sexual relations while unsure whether dawn has broken yet, and if dawn has, in fact, broken, [no expiation is required of him] due to the ambiguity in the situation. As for breaking one's fast at the time for sundown, uncertainty is not sufficient cause for exempting someone from expiation; rather, one must have good reason to believe that the sun either has or has not set. If dawn breaks while a man is engaged in sexual relations and if he withdraws immediately, his fast will not be broken, whereas if he does not withdraw, he must both make up the fast and perform expiation.

As for Category (3) above, namely, satisfying sexual desire incompletely, this includes having a seminal emission by having intercourse with someone who is dead, with an animal, or with a young girl who is not sexually desirable, having an emission [due to touching or looking at] a thigh or an abdomen or by fondling someone's shoulder, or a woman's having sexual intercourse while she is asleep or placing drops of oil or the like inside her vagina. This category also includes a man's placing his finger, which has either water or oil on it, inside his anus and performing abstersion, as a result of which water goes inside the anus; however, that which goes inside the anus only invalidates one's fast if it goes in as far as an enema would; in addition, it must have taken place intentionally and to excess. The same ruling applies if someone inserts into his anus a rag, a piece of wood or an instrument used for administering enemas such that no part of it remains outside; however, if part of the object remains outside, his fast will not be invalidated. Similarly, if a woman inserts her finger with water or oil on it inside her vagina, or if she inserts a piece of wood used for enemas or something similar inside her vagina such that no part of it remains outside, she must make up her fast later, but without expiation.

Lastly, it should be noted that according to the Hanafis, one's fast is not broken by his pouring water or oil into his urethra as treatment for some kind of ailment. Nor it is broken by one's looking with physical desire and having an emission of semen as a result, even if he looks more than once, nor if he has an emission due to thinking about sexual contact or having a "wet dream." Nor is one's fast broken due to smelling aromatic fragrances such as those of roses, narcissus, etc., or by delaying the performance of major ablutions for the removal of major ritual impurity until after sunrise, even if one remains in a state of major ritual impurity all day. Nor does it break one's fast for dust from the road, the dust from sifting flour, flies or mosquitoes to get into one's throat despite efforts to prevent it.

* * *

The Malikis hold that if someone partakes of any of the substances or engages in any of the actions which break one's fast (and which have been listed above), and if the aforementioned conditions for the necessity of expiation are not fulfilled, the person concerned is required only to make up the fast later. This ruling applies whether the person is performing the fast of Ramaḍān or some other obligatory fast, such as a fast to make up for days missed during the previous Ramaḍān, an expiatory fast, or a fast in fulfillment of a vow but without a specified time frame. As for a fast in fulfillment of a vow in which the time frame is specified, if one breaks such a fast with a legitimate excuse, such as an existing or anticipated illness (as when, for example, someone has good reason to believe that fasting at the time specified in the vow will cause him or her to become ill, or one fears that if one fasts at this time, one will become more ill or one's recovery will be delayed), a woman's menstrual period or post-partum bleeding, a loss of consciousness or a loss of sanity, there is no obligation to make the fast up later, although if some of the fasting period remains after such a condition passes, one should fast during the time remaining. If, on the other hand, someone breaks his fast during this time period out of forgetfulness, as when someone has vowed to fast on Thursday and fasts on Wednesday instead thinking that it is Thursday, then does not fast on Thursday, he or she must make up this fast later.

Lastly, if someone performs the *'umrah* during the months designated for the *ḥajj*, then remains in the sacred Meccan precinct until the days of the *ḥajj* and, while still there, reenters a state of ritual consecration for the *ḥajj*, or if someone performs both the *'umrah* and the *ḥajj* with a single ritual consecration, he or she is obliged to fast if he or she has not found a sacrificial animal to offer; if someone in either of these situations does not fast, he must make up the fast later.

In sum: Any time someone breaks an obligatory fast, he or she must make it up later unless it is in fulfillment of a vow to fast at a particular time in accordance with the details presented above. As for voluntary fasts, they do not need to be made up if they are broken unless the person concerned broke his or her fast deliberately and by commission of a forbidden act.

As for those things which do not break one's fast and do not require that one make up one's fast later, they are as follows: (1) Vomiting involuntarily without swallowing any of the vomit. (2) Allowing road dust, flour, etc. to reach one's esophagus when engaged in labor that exposes one to such substances, as when someone is employed to grind or sift flour. The same ruling applies if a fly goes down one's throat despite efforts to prevent it. (3) If dawn breaks while one is still eating or drinking, for example, and one immediately spits out whatever is in one's mouth, one's fast will not thereby be broken. (4) An emission of semen or pre-seminal fluid on the part of someone who has such emissions by merely looking [at a sexually attractive person] or thinking [erotic thoughts]. (5) Swallowing saliva which has collected in one's mouth or swallowing bits of food lodged between one's teeth; this does no harm and one's fast remains valid even if one deliberately swallows what is between one's teeth based on the officially recognized view; however, if the amount of food is large by commonly accepted standards and one nevertheless swallows it—even if one does so despite efforts not to—one's fast will be invalidated. (6) Placing oil on a wound on one's abdomen in an area directly adjacent to one's stomach. This will not break one's fast since the oil will not reach the place where food and drink are deposited. (7) Having a "wet dream."

* * *

The Hanbalis list the following as requiring one to make up one's fast but without expiation: (1) Deliberately allowing something to reach one's stomach via one's mouth or elsewhere, whether the substance would dissolve in one's stomach, such as a bite [of food], or not, such as a piece of iron or lead. (2) If someone finds the taste of chewing gum [in his mouth] after chewing it during the day, if one swallows phlegm, mucus, etc. that has gotten into one's mouth, if one allows medicine to reach one's stomach through an injection, if the taste of eyeliner reaches one's throat, if vomit comes up into one's mouth after which one swallows it deliberately, or if one's saliva comes in contact with an impure substance after which one swallows it deliberately, one's fast will be invalidated and one must make it up later, but without expiation. (3) One's fast is broken by anything which is deliberately allowed to reach the brain, such as medicine which reaches the membrane that encloses the brain when treating a skull fracture through which medicine can flow to the brain. (4) One's fast is broken and one is obliged to make up the fast, though without expiation, if one has an emission of semen by looking repeatedly [at someone attractive] or by masturbating with one's own hand or someone else's hand. The same ruling applies if someone has an emission of pre-seminal fluid due to looking or some other cause, or if one has a seminal emission as a result of kissing, touching or sexual intercourse short of actual penetration. If any of these actions is undertaken deliberately, one's fast is invalidated and one must make it up later even if one was [originally] ignorant of this ruling. (5) One's fast is broken if one vomits involuntarily even if it is only a small amount, and one is obliged to make up the fast later but without expiation. (6) One's fast is also broken as a result of cupping; hence, anyone who deliberately undergoes cupping or performs it on someone else invalidates his or her fast if blood appears; otherwise, however, one's fast is not invalidated.

Lastly, it should be noted that none of the events mentioned here invalidates one's fast if it occurs out of forgetfulness or by coercion, even if the coercion involves introducing medicine into someone's stomach.

As for those things which require neither that one make up one's fast nor that one perform expiation, they are as follows: (1) Bloodletting (venesection), even if blood comes out. This also includes making an incision with a razor blade in lieu of cupping for purposes of medical treatment. (2) Nosebleeds with involuntary vomiting, even if the vomit contains some blood. (3) Unintentionally allowing a fly, road dust, etc. to reach someone's throat due to the impossibility of guarding against it. (4) A woman's inserting her finger or something else into her vagina, even if it is wet. (5) Having an ejaculation due to thinking [about erotic themes] or having a 'wet dream'. (6) Sprinkling henna on the bottom of one's foot, then finding the taste of henna in the back of one's mouth. (7) Rinsing out one's mouth or drawing water up one's nose in order to force it out again [as part of ritual ablutions], as a result of which one unintentionally allows water into one's stomach. This does not break one's fast even if the person goes to excess in these two actions, and even if one rinses out one's mouth as a kind of undesirable diversion. (8) Eating, drinking or engaging in sexual relations when one is uncertain whether dawn has broken or not, or when one has reason to believe that the sun has set but is not certain yet whether it has or not. In such a case, one's fast is not broken; however, if it becomes clear that dawn has broken or that the sun has not set, one must simply make up the fast later in the case of eating and drinking, whereas in the case of having sexual relations, one must both make up the fast later and perform expiation. (9) Eating or drinking at a time which one believes to be night, after which it becomes apparent that it was day, or eating out of forgetfulness, after which one believes that one's fast has been broken by eating out of forgetfulness and, as a result, one eats deliberately; in such cases, one's fast is broken and one is required to make up the fast later but without expiation.

* * *

The Shafiis list the following things as breaking one's fast and requiring that one make up the fast later, but without expiation: (1) Allowing something to reach one's stomach, be it a large or a small amount, even if it is as small as a sesame seed or a pebble, and including even a small amount of water. However, this will only invalidate one's fast given the following conditions: (a) The person must be ignorant of this ruling due to his having embraced Islam only recently. (b) The person must have allowed the substance to reach his stomach deliberately; if it reaches his stomach despite his efforts to prevent it, his fast will not be invalidated. (c) The substance must have reached the person's stomach by way of a legally recognized pathway, such as his or her nose, mouth, ears, genital orifice, urethra or anus, or through a wound which leads to the brain. (2) Taking in smoking tobacco, "Persian tobacco" (which is used in a narghile, or water pipe), snuff, and the like. The use of such substances breaks one's fast and requires that one make up the fast later but without expiation due to the fact that, as we have seen, the only thing which requires expiation in the Shafiis' view is sexual intercourse, given the aforementioned conditions. (3) Unnecessarily inserting one's finger or part thereof, even if it is dry, in one's genital opening or anus while performing abstersion; if there is a need to do so, however, one's fast is not invalidated. (4) Inserting a stick or similar object inside one's ear, since the inside of the ear is, legally speaking, considered to be part of one's 'gut' (*jawf*). Similarly, if one goes to excess when rinsing out one's mouth or drawing water up one's nostrils in order to force it out again [as part of ritual ablutions], or if one performs these actions more than three times and water goes down into one's stomach, one's fast is invalidated and one must make it up later. (5) Eating food that has remained lodged between one's teeth when one would have been able to recognize what it is and spit it out; this ruling applies even if the amount of food is less than the size of a chickpea. (6) Deliberately, knowingly vomiting, even if the amount of vomit was not sufficient to fill one's mouth. (7) A fly's going down inside one's stomach, even if one forces it out again. (8) Deliberately belching, thereby causing something to come up from one's stomach and into one's upper throat (the "upper throat" being defined as the part of the throat where one produces the letter ḥa' in Arabic). The expulsion of phlegm or mucus due to the repeated need to do so does not, by contrast, invalidate one's fast; however, if one

Actions that are undesirable for someone who is fasting

Each school offers its own detailed listing of those actions that are undesirable for someone who is fasting.[31]

---

then swallows it after it has come up into one's mouth and settled there, one's fast is invalidated. (9) Having an ejaculation due to sensual touching (though without entry), even if it is adulterous in nature, or due to kissing, touching and the like. As for an ejaculation resulting simply from looking [at a sexually attractive person] or thinking [erotic thoughts], this—like having a 'wet dream'—does not invalidate one's fast if it is not habitual.

31. The Hanafis list the following as undesirable for someone who is fasting: (1) Tasting something no part of which has dissolved and gone down into one's stomach; this ruling applies equally whether the fast being performed is obligatory or voluntary unless it is done out of necessity. It is permissible, for example, for a woman to taste the food she is cooking in order to test its saltiness if her husband is ill-tempered; the same applies to a chef. Similarly, someone purchasing something to eat or drink may taste it if he has reason to fear that he might be buying an inferior product or that it may not suit him. (2) Chewing something without a legitimate excuse. It is permissible without any undesirability attached thereto for a woman to chew up food for her infant if she can find no one who is permitted not to fast to do this for her. However, it is undsirable to chew gum even if no part of it would dissolve and reach one's stomach. (3) Kissing one's wife. This ruling applies whether the kiss is merely a 'peck', as it were, or a deep kiss; the same applies to engaging in sensual contact with her, for example, by the man's placing his genitals in contact with hers without any barrier between them. However, this is only undesirable if the man cannot ensure that he will not have an ejaculation or engage in full penetration; if he can ensure this, there is no undesirability involved. (4) Allowing saliva to collect in one's mouth, then swallowing it; this is deemed undesirable due to the dubious appearance it presents. (5) Doing anything one has good reason to believe would make one too weak to fast, such as cupping and venesection. However, if there is no good reason to believe that a given activity will weaken one so much that he cannot fast, there is no undesirability attached to it.

As for those things which it is not undesirable for a person to do while fasting, they include the following: (1) Kissing or direct genital contact if, when doing so, one can ensure that neither ejaculation nor full intercourse will take place. (2) Oiling one's moustache, since this involves nothing inconsistent with fasting. (3) Applying kohl (eyeliner) and the like, even if one finds traces of it in one's throat. (4) Cupping and the like if it will not make one too weak to fast. (5) Using a toothpick throughout the day; in fact, doing so is an emulation of the Sunnah. This applies whether the toothpick is dry or green, and whether it has been moistened with water or not. (6) Rinsing out one's mouth and drawing water up one's nostrils in order to force it out again, even if this is not done as part of ritual ablutions. (7) Performing major ablutions (*ghusl*). (8) Cooling oneself off by wrapping one's body in a wet garment and the like.

* * *

The Malikis list the following as undesirable for someone who is fasting: (1) Tasting food, even if one is preparing it. If someone does taste food, he must spit it out lest any of it reach his esophagus. If any of it does reach his esophagus despite his efforts to prevent it, he must make up the fast later if the fast being performed is obligatory, whereas if one deliberately allows some of the food to go down into his stomach, he must make up the fast later and perform expiation as well if this takes place during Ramaḍān. (2) Chewing something like dried dates or gum. If one does chew something of this nature, one must spit it out; otherwise, he must make up the fast later and perform expiation as well if this takes place during Ramaḍān. (3) Treating teeth with abscessed or otherwise unsound roots during the day unless there is reason to fear that the person concerned will suffer harm if treatment is delayed until after sundown. In the latter case, no undesirability is attached to this practice; in fact, treatment must be administered during the day if it is feared that by delaying the treatment, the person will die or suffer serious harm. (4) Spinning flax which has a taste, i.e., that which is macerated in a liquid medium, if the woman doing the spinning has no choice but to engage in this activity; otherwise, there is no undesirability attached to this practice. In either case, however, she is required to spit out the saliva which has collected in her mouth. As for flax which has no taste, i.e., that which macerates in the sea, it is not undesirable to spin it even if it is not done out of necessity. (5) Harvesting, lest any of the resulting dust should get into one's esophagus. However, if one is obliged to do the harvesting, there is no undesirability attached thereto. As for farm owners, they may oversee the harvesting during its season, since they are required to observe the state of the harvest and to protect it. (6) Sexual foreplay, including kisses, thoughts about sexual contact and looking [at a sexually desirable person], if one is certain that one can avoid an emission of semen or pre-seminal fluid. If one is uncertain as to whether one can avoid either of these occurrences, or if one is certain that he cannot avoid it, foreplay is forbidden altogether. If no emission of either semen or pre-seminal fluid occurs, one's fast will remain valid; if there is an emission of pre-seminal fluid, one must make up the fast later unless this occurs as a result of merely looking or thinking without intending to do so and without continuing in the activity. If one has an emission of pre-seminal fluid due to unintentional thoughts or glances and if, once they begin, one does not prolong them, one is not required to make up the fast later. If someone has an emission of semen, he is required to make up the fast later and to perform expiation if this takes place during the month of Ramaḍān and if the foreplay involved is forbidden—as when, for example, the person who is doing the looking knows that he will not be able to avoid having an emission, or is uncertain whether he will be able to avoid it. If, on the other hand, the foreplay concerned is merely undesirable—as when, for example, someone knows that he can avoid having an emission of either semen or pre-seminal fluid—he must simply make up the fast later unless he persists in the activity concerned until he has an ejaculation, in which case he must both make up the fast later and perform expiation. (7) Using a moist toothpick from which bits slough off; if nothing sloughs off the toothpick, it is permissble to use it throughout the day; in fact, it is recommended if it is used in connection with a legal requirement such as ritual ablutions and ritual prayer. (8) Cupping and venesection if the person fasting is ill and is uncertain whether such processes will exacerbate his or her illness to the extent that he would have to break his fast. If he is uncertain that they will not have such an effect, it is permissible for him to undergo either process. Similarly, cupping and venesection are permissible for someone who is in good health if he or she knows that they will not cause illness or harm, or is not certain that they would do so. If a person in good health knows that by undergoing cupping or venesection he will become ill, or if an ill person knows that by undergoing either of these processes he will become sicker, both processes will be forbidden.

* * *

The Hanbalis list the following as undesirable practices for those who are fasting: (1) Rinsing out one's mouth as a mere pastime or wasteful habit or due to heat or thirst, as well as diving into water for any reason other than to cool oneself off or to bathe. However, if water goes down into one's stomach in any of these cases, one's fast will not be invalidated despite the undesirability of such actions. (2) Allowing saliva to collect in one's mouth, then swallowing it. (3) Chewing something no part of which will disintegrate or dissolve; if part of it will dissolve or disintegrate, chewing it is forbidden even if one does not swallow his saliva. (4) Tasting food unnecessarily; if there is a need to do so, however, it is not undesirable. If there is no necessity which calls for one to taste food and if part of it reaches one's esophagus, one's fast will be invalidated. (5) Leaving particles of food between one's teeth. (6) Smelling anything one cannot ensure would not reach one's esophagus by itself, such as musk or camphor powder, incense such as aloewood, etc. However, if one can be assured that the substance would not be drawn by itself into one's esophagus, as in the case of roses, for example, it is not undesirable to smell it. (7) Kissing or other actions that might lead to sexual intercourse, such as embracing, touching, repeated glances, etc. if such things arouse one's physical desire; otherwise, however, they are not undesirable. If someone has good reason to believe that he might have an ejaculation, he is forbidden to kiss or do anything else that might lead to sexual intercourse. (8) Having sexual intercourse when one is uncertain whether the second dawn call to prayer has sounded; eating *suḥūr* under these same circumstances, by contrast, is not undesirable since the pre-dawn meal gives one's strength for the fast, whereas sexual intercourse does not.

* * *

According to the Shafiis, there are some things for which a person fasting may be pardoned, and others which are considered undesirable. They hold that the person fasting may be pardoned if: (1) Something reaches the person's stomach out of forgetfulness or by coercion, or due to ignorance for which the person may be excused under Islamic law. (2) If something that was lodged between one's teeth goes down into one's stomach by virtue of the flow of one's saliva and if one would not have been able to spit it out. However, if someone swallows something that was lodged between his teeth although he would have been able to spit it out, his fast will be broken. This ruling applies likewise to phlegm, mucus, and the like, coffee grounds, etc. As for dust from the road, flour particles after flour has been sifted, flies, mosquitoes, etc, the Shafiis hold that if they reach one's stomach, this will do no harm, since it would cause undue hardship to guard against them going inside one's body.

The ruling on someone whose fast was invalidated during Ramaḍān

If someone's fast is invalidated during this or that day of Ramaḍān, he must go on abstaining from whatever would break his or her fast for the rest of the day out of reverence for the sacredness of the month. If someone caresses, embraces or kisses his wife and has an emission of semen as a result, his fast will be invalidated. In this case, such a person much continue to abstain for the rest of the day [from that which would break a fast]. As for someone whose fast is broken at a time other than Ramaḍān, such as during a fast in fulfillment of a vow (regardless of whether it has a specified time frame or not), an expiatory fast, a fast to make up for days missed from a previous Ramaḍān, or a voluntary fast, he is not obliged to go on abstaining for the rest of the day according to the Shafiis, the Hanafis and the Hanbalis. For the Malikis' view, see below.[32]

Excuses which allow one to break one's fast: illness and undue hardship

There are a number of excuses which allow someone to break his or her fast. One of these is illness. Hence, if someone falls ill while fasting and fears that continuing to fast will make him more ill or delay his recovery, or if fasting causes someone undue hardship, her or she is permitted to break his or her fast according to the Shafiis, the Hanafis, and the Malikis. As for the Hanbalis, they hold that it is an emulation of the Sunnah for such a person to break his or her fast, and that it is undesirable for him or her to fast. If, on the other hand, there is good reason to believe that one might die or experience serious harm as a result of fasting, as in a

---

As for those things which are undesirable for someone who is fasting, they include the following: (1) Verbally abusing someone. (2) Delaying one's fast-breaking meal past sundown if one believes that this is a virtue; otherwise, it is not undesirable. (3) Chewing gum. (4) Chewing up food [for someone]. This does not invalidate one's fast, but it is undesirable unless it is done out of some necessity, as when someone chews up food for his baby and the like. (5) Tasting food unless it is done out of necessity, as when someone is working as a chef and the like. (6) Cupping and venesection unless they are done out of necessity. (7) Kissing if it does not arouse one's physical desires; if it does, it is forbidden. The same thing applies to embracing and direct genital contact. (8) Entering the bathroom unless it is necessary to do so, since this weakens someone who is fasting. (9) Using a toothpick after noon unless there is some reason to do so, such as a change in one's mouth due to having eaten something like an onion out of forgetfulness after noon. (10) Indulging in pleasures which appeal to the eye, the nose and the ear if they are things which are permissible to begin with. As for indulging in that which is forbidden to begin with, this is clearly prohibited both to those who are fasting and to those who are not. (11) Applying kohl which, according to the best-attested view, is a departure from the ideal.

32. According to the Malikis, it is also necessary to go on abstaining for the rest of the day if one is fasting in fulfillment of a vow with a specified time frame, whether one broke one's fast deliberately or not, due to the fact that the time for the fast was specified in the vow just as Ramaḍān is set aside specifically for fasting. With respect to fasts in fulfillment of vows without specified time frames and all

case where someone feared that fasting might cause one of his senses to cease functioning, all four schools agree that the person concerned is required to break his or her fast and is forbidden to fast.

The ruling just mentioned applies to cases in which the person fasting is actually ill already. If, on the other hand, the person is in good health and has good reason to believe that fasting would cause him a serious illness, each of the schools offers its own ruling on this situation.[33]

---

other obligatory fasts, the Malikis' ruling is that if one is required to perform such a fast in continuous succession, as is the case in a fast being performed in expiation for a transgression relating to the fast of Ramaḍān, fasting a month in fulfillment of a vow to fast an entire month in succession, etc., then if one has broken the fast deliberately, it is not necessary to go on abstaining for the rest of the day because the fast has now been invalidated and because (due to the interruption in the successive fasting days), one will have to start all over again. If someone breaks his or her fast out of forgetfulness or due to some cause outside of his or her control and if this occurred on some day other than the first day of the fast, he or she must abstain for the rest of the day, whereas if it occurred on the first day of the fast, it is recommended, but not required, that one abstain for the rest of the day.

If, on the other hand, the fasting days need not be performed in continuous succession, as is the case when one is making up days missed from a previous Ramaḍān or performing a fast in expiation for a broken oath, one is permitted, but not required, to go on abstaining for the rest of the day; this applies regardless of whether one broke the fast intentionally or unintentionally, since the time [at which one broke the fast] had not been specified as a time for fasting.

In the case of a voluntary fast, the Malikis rule that if one breaks the fast out of forgetfulness, one must go on abstaining for the rest of the day, since one is not required to make up the fast later if one has broken it out of forgetfulness. However, if one breaks a voluntary fast deliberately, abstaining for the rest of the day is not obligatory due to the fact that one is required to make up such a fast later if it was broken on purpose.

33. According to the Hanbalis, it is an emulation of the Sunnah for such a person not to fast as though he were actually ill, and it is undesirable for him to fast.

* * *

The Hanafis hold that if someone is not ill but has good reason to believe that he would become ill by fasting, he is permitted either to fast or not to fast as would be the case if he were actually ill.

* * *

According to the Malikis, the Hanafis and the Hanbalis, it is not necessary for someone who is ill consciously to intend to avail himself of the special allowance granted by the Lawgiver to those with conditions that would exempt them from fasting. As for the Shafiis, they hold that the intention to avail oneself of the divinely granted allowance not to fast is required, and that if one neglects this intention he will be guilty of wrongdoing.

Fear of harm from fasting on the part of a pregnant or nursing mother

If a woman who is pregnant or nursing fears that fasting might be harmful both to her and to her baby, harmful only to her, or harmful only to her baby, it is permissible for her to break her fast; for each school's detailed view on this matter, see below.[34]

According to the Malikis, if someone who is healthy has good reason to believe that fasting would cause him serious harm or even death, he is required not to fast as he would be if he were actually ill.

* * *

As for the Shafiis, they hold that if someone is healthy and has good reason to believe that by fasting he would become ill, he is not permitted to refrain from fasting unless he actually begins to fast and experiences harm as a result.

34. The Malikis hold that if a woman who is pregnant or nursing, whether the woman nursing is the baby's biological mother or not, fears that by fasting she will cause herself, her baby, or both herself and her baby to become ill, she may abstain from fasting. If she does so, she is obliged to make up the fast later. In the case of a nursing mother, a *fidyah*, or redemption is required of her, but none is required of a pregnant woman. If a pregnant or nursing woman fears that by fasting she would cause serious or even mortal harm to herself or her baby, she is required not to fast. In the case of a nursing mother, she is only allowed to abstain from fasting if she has no choice but to nurse her baby, as in a case where she cannot find a wet nurse for her child, or her child will not accept any other woman's breast. However, if she does find a wet nurse whom her baby will accept, she is obliged to fast and will not be permitted to abstain from doing so. Moreover, if the wet nurse whom the child has accepted is in need of remuneration and if the child owns money, the wet nurse's wages are to be taken out of this. If the child has no money, her wages are to be paid by the child's father, since they are considered to be part of the financial support the father is responsible for providing on the child's behalf if the child has no money.

* * *

The Hanafis hold that if a woman who is pregnant or nursing fears that by fasting she will cause harm to herself, to her baby, or to both herself and her baby, she may refrain from fasting, but she must make up the fast when she is able to. No redemption is required of her, nor is she required to complete the compensatory fasting days in continuous succession. Moreover, in the case of a woman who is nursing, this ruling applies equally to a biological mother and a woman who has been hired to nurse someone else's infant since, in the case of the mother, she is obliged to nurse her child as a religious duty while in the case of a wet nurse, she is obliged to nurse based on a contractual agreement; hence, in either case she has no choice but to nurse.

* * *

According to the Hanbalis, it is permissible for a woman who is pregnant or nursing to refrain from fasting if she fears that her fasting would bring harm to her and her baby, or to her only. In either case, she must make up the fast later without a redemption. If she fears that by fasting she will cause harm only to her baby, she must make up the fast later and pay a redemption as well. In the case of a woman who is nursing an infant, if the infant accepts another woman's breast and she is able to hire a wet nurse for him, or if the infant himself has money with which to hire a wet nurse, his mother should hire a wet nurse for him and not refrain from fasting. Moreover, the ruling on a woman who has been hired as a wet nurse is the same as that which applies to a nursing mother.

* * *

As for the Shafiis, they hold that if a woman who is pregnant or nursing fears that by fasting she will cause intolerable hardship for both herself and her baby, for herself alone, or for her baby alone, she is obliged not to fast. In all three situations mentioned here, the woman is obliged to make up the fast later, whereas she is only required to pay a redempton in the final situation (that is, if she fears that fasting will cause intolerable hardship for her baby alone). It makes no difference whether the woman nursing is the infant's mother, a hired wet nurse, or a wet nurse who is volunteering this service. In the case of a woman who is nursing, she is only required to refrain from fasting if she has no choice but to nurse—as will be the case, for example, if there is no other woman capable of nursing the infant who is either not fasting or who is fasting but for whom fasting causes no hardship. If the woman is not obliged to nurse, she may refrain from fasting and nurse, or fast and refrain from nursing; however, she is not required to refrain from fasting. This ruling ap-

Fast-breaking on account of travel

A traveler is permitted to break his or her fast provided that his or her journey is long enough to justify the shortening of prayers, and provided that the traveler begins his or her journey long enough before the break of dawn that he or she arrives at the place at which the shortening of prayers becomes permissible before dawn. If the journey is not long enough to justify the shortening of prayers, the traveler is not permitted to break his fast on this account. These two conditions for breaking one's fast on account of travel are agreed upon by the Shafiis, the Malikis and the Hanafis; however, the Hanbalis disagree concerning the first condition.[35] In addition, the Shafiis include a third condition for breaking one's fast on account of travel.[36] If the traveler begins his journey after dawn, he is forbidden to break his fast, and if he does break his fast, he must make it up later but without expiation according to the Malikis, the Hanafis and the Hanbalis. For the view of the Shafiis, see below.[37]

According to the Shafiis and the Hanbalis, it is permissible for a traveler who formed the intention to fast on the previous night to break his fast; if such a person does break his fast, he incurs no guilt, though he is required to make up the fast later. For the views of the Hanafis and the Malikis, see below.[38] It is recommended that a traveler fast if it does not pose undue hardship based on God's words, "…for to fast is to do good unto yourselves…" (2:184) If fasting causes undue hardship, it is preferable not to fast according to the Hanafis and the Shafiis. For the views of the Malikis and the Hanbalis, see below.[39] However, if fasting leads one to fear that one might suffer harm, damage to some bodily organ, or malfunction in such an organ, all four schools agree that one is forbidden to fast.

---

plies to a hired wet nurse if the fear [mentioned above] is recognized before she is hired; after she is hired, however, if she has good reason to believe that she needs to break her fast, she is obliged to break her fast when she fears that fasting might do her harm even if she is not obliged to nurse.

As for the relevant redemption, this consists in feeding one needy person (for every day of fasting one must make up) an amount of food equal to that which is given to a needy person when performing expiation, details concerning which will be presented below according to each of the four schools.

35. The Hanbalis hold that if someone who is fasting departs from his home on a journey during the day, even if his departure is after noon, and if the journey is a legitimate journey which is long enough to justify the shortening of prayers, he will be permitted to break his fast. However, the ideal practice is for such a person to complete this day's fast.

36. The Shafiis hold that in order to break one's fast while on a journey, the person must not be traveling all year round. If he is traveling all year round, he is forbidden to break his fast on account of this unless fasting causes him undue hardship such as the hardship that makes it permissible for a person to perform sand ablutions [rather then regular ablutions], in which case he is obliged not to fast.

37. According to the Shafiis, if someone who is fasting and who began his journey after the break of dawn does something that would require him to make up his fast later and perform expiation, he must fulfill both these obligations, whereas if he does something that would require him only to make up the fast later, he must

Fasting on the part of a woman who is menstruating or experiencing post-partum bleeding

If, while a woman is fasting, her menstrual period begins or she gives birth, she is obliged to break her fast. If she does fast during her menstrual period or before her post-partum bleeding ceases, her fast will be invalid and she will have to make up the fast later.

The ruling on someone who suffers from severe hunger or thirst

If, while someone is fasting, he suffers such severe hunger or thirst that he is unable to continue his fast, he is permitted to break his fast, in which case he must make up the fast later.

Rulings on fast-breaking due to old age

A frail, decrepit elderly person who is not able to fast during any season of the year is to refrain from fasting, and is obliged to feed one needy person as a redemption for every day that he does not fast. According to the Malikis, it is desirable, but not required, for such a person to offer a redemption for the days he does not fast. Similarly, an ill person for whom no recovery is anticipated is not required to make up the fast later due to lack of ability according to the Shafiis, the Hanafis and the Malikis; for the Hanbalis' view on this matter, see below.[40] As for someone who is unable to fast during the month of Ramaḍān but is capable of doing so at another time, he must make up the fast at this time, but without providing any redemption.

---

simply make up the fast without expiation. In either case, however, he is forbidden to break his fast.

38. According to the Malikis, if someone on a journey forms the intention to fast at night [i.e., on the night preceding the day on which he is to fast], and if he starts off the following day fasting, then breaks his fast, he must both make up the fast later and perform expiation. This ruling applies whether he breaks his fast based on his own intepretation of the situation or not.

* * *

As for the Hanafis, they hold that if a traveler forms the intention to fast at night, he is forbidden to break his fast the following day; if he does break his fast, he must make up the fast later without expiation.

39. Accordiing to the Malikis, it is preferable for a traveler to fast if it causes no undue hardship.

* * *

As for the Hanbalis, they hold that it is an emulation of the Sunnah for a traveler not to fast and that fasting for a traveler is undesirable even if fasting does not

If someone who is fasting unexpectedly loses his sanity

If, while someone is fasting, he loses his sanity, even if only for a moment, he is no longer required to fast; in fact, if he continues to fast, his fasting will not be valid. As for whether it is necessary for such a person to make up the fast later, the various schools offer their own rulings on this question.[41]

If the condition which made it permissible for someone not to fast passes during the day, as in the case where a woman's menstrual period ends, a traveler takes up residence in a place, or a young boy reaches puberty [during a fasting day], he or she must fast for the remainder of the day out of respect for the month according to the Hanafis and the Hanbalis; for the views of the Malikis and the Shafiis, see below.[42]

Desirable practices associated with fasting

The following practices are deemed desirable when fasting: (1) Taking the fast-breaking meal without delay once it is certain that the sun has set. It is recommended that one break one's fast on the following, in descending order of preference: ripe dates, dried dates, sweets, and water. It is also recommended that one eat an odd number of such foods, with three being the minimum. (2) Uttering a traditional supplication following one's fast-breaking meal. One might say, for example, "O God, for You have I fasted and on Your provisions have I broken my fast. On You do I rely and in You do I place my fiath. Thirst has departed, veins have been replenished with fluid, and the reward [of those who fast] has been confirmed. Most

---

cause him undue hardship. They base this ruling on the following words of the Prophet, "It is not [a sign of righteousness] to fast while on a journey."

40. The Hanbalis hold that someone who is unable to fast due to old age or an illness from which he is not expected to recover must provide a redemption for every day of fasting he misses. If he provides the required redempton, he need not make up the fast if he becomes capable of fasting later. If, by contrast, he does not provide the redemption and later becomes capable of fasting, he must make up the fasting he missed.

41. The Shafiis hold that if the person's loss of sanity is due to some transgression on his part, as in a case where, during the night, he deliberately took something that robbed him of his senses during the following day, he is obliged to make up whatever fasting days he missed.

* * *

The Hanbalis hold that if someone's insanity lasts for the entire day, he is not obliged to make up the fast later whether the insanity was a result of some transgression on his part or not. However, if he becomes lucid again during part of the day, he must make up the fast later.

* * *

The Hanafis hold that if the person's insanity lasts for the entire month, he is not obliged to make up the fast later whereas, if it lasts less than this, he must make up what he missed.

* * *

Gracious One, forgive me. Praise be to God, who has helped me to fast, and who has blessed me with the wherewithal to break my fast" (*Allāhumma laka ṣumtu wa 'alā rizqika aftartu wa 'alayka tawakkaltu wa bika āmant. dhahaba al-ẓama' wabtallat al-'urūq wa thabat al-ajr. yā wāsi' al-faḍl ighfir lī, al-ḥamdu lillāh alladhī a'ānanī fa ṣumtu, wa razaqanī fa afṭart*). (3) Taking a pre-dawn meal, however light, even if it consists of nothing but a sip of water. This ruling is based on the words of the Prophet, "Partake of a pre-dawn meal, for it holds a blessing." The time period during which the pre-dawn meal is to be taken commences with the beginning of the latter half of the night. The later one partakes of the pre-dawn meal, the better, such that there is no doubt concerning the break of dawn. This ruling is based on the words of the Prophet, "Abandon that which would cause you uncertainty in favor of that which does not cause you uncertainty." (4) Refraining from unnecessary speech. As for refraining from that which is forbidden, such as backbiting and slander, this is required at all times, but its necessity is stressed during Ramaḍān. (5) Giving generously of charity and engaging in many deeds of kindness and compassion toward one's relatives and toward the poor and unfortunate. (6) Occupying oneself with the pursuit of knowledge, recitation of the Qur'ān, the remembrance of God and prayers for blessings upon the Prophet whenever one is able, day or night. (7) Secluding oneself in the mosque for the sake of worship and prayer, more details concerning which will be presented below.

Making up fasting days missed during Ramaḍān

If someone is required to make up fasting days from the month of Ramaḍān due to his having broken his fast in a previous Ramaḍān either deliberately or for any of the other reasons mentioned thus far, he is to make up the days he missed during a period of time in which voluntary fasting is permitted. Hence, one's make-up fast will not be valid if it is performed during a period of time in which fasting has been prohibited, such as the Day of Fastbreaking and the Day of Sacrifice, during a time which has been set aside for an obligatory fast, such as the current Ramaḍān, or days on which one has vowed to fast, as when one vows to fast ten days from the beginning of Dhū al-Qa'dah, for example. According to the Malikis and the Shafiis, one may not make up days missed from a previous Ramaḍān during these days since they have been set aside for the fulfillment of this vow; for the views of the Hanbalis and the Hanafis, see below.[43] Similarly, one may not validly make up days missed from a previous Ramaḍān during the current Ramaḍān, since the current Ramaḍān is reserved for the initial performance of this fast; hence, no other type of fast may be performed at this time. Hence, if someone formed the intention to fast

---

As for the Malikis, they hold that if someone loses his sanity for an entire day or most of the day and if he was lucid at the beginning of the day, he must make up that day's fast. Similarly, one is obliged to make up the day's fast if he loses his sanity for half or less than half the day and if he was not lucid as the day began; otherwise, he is not obliged to make it up.

42. The Malikis hold that in this case, it is not necessary or even desirable to go on abtaining for the rest of the day unless the circumstance that made it permissible not to fast was coercion; hence, if the coercion comes to an end, the person fasting

part or all of the current Ramaḍān in order to make up fasting days missed in a previous Ramaḍān, his fast will be valid neither for the previous Ramaḍān nor for the current one. It will not be valid for the current Ramaḍān because he did not intend his fast for this purpose, nor will it be valid for the past Ramaḍān since no fast other than that of the current Ramaḍān may be performed at this time. This view is agreed upon by the Shafiis, the Malikis and the Hanbalis; for the Hanafis' view, see below.[44]

One may validly make up a previously missed fasting day on the "day of doubt", since it is permissible to perform voluntary fasting on this day. When one makes up fasting days, one is to go by the number of days, not the new moon. Hence, supposing someone missed an entire Ramaḍān which lasted for thirty days; if this person begins making up the fast on the first day of *Muḥarram*, for example, and if *Muḥarram* lasts for twenty-nine days, he must fast one additional day after the end of *Muḥarram* in order to make up the same number of days that he missed during Ramaḍān.

It is desirable for someone who has fasting days to make up to do so promptly in order to "clear his debt" quickly, as it were, and to fast the days consecutively once he has begun. If someone delays making up his fasting days, or if he fasts the days separately, his fast will still be valid even though he will have departed from that which is recommended. The Malikis and the Hanbalis hold that if the days remaining before the commencement of the coming Ramaḍān are equal to the number of days one missed from the previous Ramaḍān, one must make up these days

---

must go on abstaining for the rest of the day. Similarly, if someone eats out of forgetfulness, then remembers that he is fasting, he must go on abstaining for the rest of the day.

43. According to the Hanafis, if someone makes up fasting days missed in a previous Ramaḍān on days during which he has vowed to fast, his fasting will be valid as making up for the previous Ramaḍān, but he will have to fulfill his vow to fast these days at another time. The reason for this is that a vow is not defined by a particular time, place, dirham, etc. In other words, someone may validly fast the month of Rajab, for example, in lieu of the month of Sha'bān in fulfillment of a vow; similarly, one may validly give one dirham in charity rather than another in a place other than the one which he specified in his vow [to donate the aforementioned dirham].

* * *

As for the Hanbalis, the apparent meaning of what is stated in *Al-Iqnā'* is that if someone makes up days missed from a previous Ramaḍān on days during which he has vowed to fast, his fast will be valid [as both making up for the days missed in Ramaḍān and fulfilling the vow].

44. The Hanafis hold that if someone forms the intention to make up for fasting missed during a past Ramaḍān during the current Ramaḍān, his fast will be valid for the current Ramaḍān, but not for the past one. The reason for this is that the current Ramaḍān has been reserved for this fast in particular and no other. How-

immediately and not delay any longer; for the views of the Shafiis and the Hanafis on this point, see below.[45]

If somebody delays making up fasting days from a previous Ramaḍān until the subsequent Ramaḍān has begun, he must pay a redemption[46] in addition to making up the days missed. The redemption required in this context is to feed one needy person for every day of fasting one must make up, while the amount given to the needy person is equal to that given to someone when performing expiation. This is the view of the Shafiis, the Hanbalis and the Malikis. (As for the Hanafis, they hold that no redemption is required of someone who delays making up fasting days missed from the previous Ramaḍān until the subsequent Ramaḍān has begun, regardless of whether there was a legitimate excuse for the delay or not.) However, the redemption is only required if the person concerned was capable of making up the days missed before the subsequent Ramaḍān began but failed to do so; if he was not capable of doing so, no redemption is required of him. According to the Malikis, the Hanafis and the Hanbalis, one is only required to pay the redemption once regardless of how many years pass before one makes up the fasting days missed; as for the Shafiis, they hold that on the contrary, the redemption must be paid again for every year that passes without the fasting days being made up.

The expiation required of someone who broke his fast during Ramaḍān, and rulings on those who are unable to perform it

As we have seen, fasting may be either obligatory or non-obligatory. Additionally, obligatory fasting is divided into the following types: (1) the fast of Ramaḍān, (2) expiatory fasting, and (3) fasting in fulfillment of a vow. The fast of Ramaḍān has already been discussed; as for expiatory fasting, it is likewise divided into types, namely: (1) expiation for breaking an oath, (2) expiation for *ẓihār*, and (3) expiation for homicide. A separate discussion is devoted to each of these types of fasting in the section on *mu'āmalāt*, that is, Islamic legal rulings pertaining to people's everyday dealings and transactions. (We discuss expiation for breaking an oath in Part II of this work, and expiation for *ẓihār* in Part IV.)

One type of expiation is the expiation which is required of someone for fasting days he or she has missed during the month of Ramaḍān. This type of expiation consists in freeing a believing slave according to the Shafiis, the Malikis and the Hanbalis; as for the Hanafis, they hold that when performing expiation for missed fasting days, it is not necessary that the freed slave be a believer; rather, it is simply required that he or she be free of harmful defects such as blindness, dumbness and insanity. If the person from whom the expiation is required can find no slave to emancipate, he or she is to fast two months in continuous succession. If the person concerned fasts from the beginning of the lunar month, he is to complete this month and the succeeding month based on the new moons. If he begins somewhere in the middle of the lunar month, he should first fast what remains of this month, then fast

---

ever, there is no need to specify one's intention in this regard, as we saw in the discussion of the conditions for fasting.

the entire month which follows it based on the new moon, then fast enough days out of the third month to bring the first month to a total of thirty days. The day one fasts in order to make up for the fasting day missed does not count as part of the two months of fasting for the purpose of expiation. Moreover, the Shafiis, the Hanafis and the Malikis hold that the two months must be fasted in perfect succession such that if one day's fast is invalidated, even based on a legitimate excuse, such as travel, this day's fast will be considered a voluntary fast and he must begin the expiatory fasting all over again due to the fact that the required continuity has been broken. However, the Hanbalis hold that if one's fast is broken due to a legitimate excuse such as travel, the continuity required for expiation is not broken.

If someone is not able to fast two months in succession due to the hardship it involves or for some other reason, he or she may feed sixty needy people. According to the Shafiis, the Hanbalis and the Hanafis, this order (i.e., freeing a slave, fasting two months in succession, and feeding sixty needy people) must be preserved. For the Malikis' view on this matter, see below.[47]

The Shafiis, the Hanbalis and the Hanafis base their view on this matter on the report narrated by Muslim and al-Bukhārī on the authority of Abū Hurayrah, may God be pleased with him, according to which a man came to the Prophet and said, "There's no hope for me!" "Why is there no hope for you?" the Prophet asked him. The man replied, "I had sexual relations with my wife during [the daytime] in Ramaḍān." In response, the Prophet asked him, "Do you have the wherewithal to free a slave?" "No," he replied. "Then are you able to fast two months in suceession?" "No," he replied. "Do you have enough to feed sixty needy people?" "No," replied the man. The man who had come to seek the Prophet's counsel then sat down, and the Prophet brought a large palm-leaf basket (which held the standard amount used for purposes of expiation) of dried dates and said, "Give this away in charity." The man asked, "Shall I give it to those who are poorer than we are, O Messenger of God? I swear to God, there isn't a household among us who is more in need of this than we are!" Laughing heartily, the Prophet said, "Go and feed it to your family!"

---

45. According to the Shafiis, it is also necessary to make up missed fasting days immediately if one's fast-breaking during the previous Ramaḍān was deliberate and without a legitimate excuse.

* * *

As for the Hanafis, they hold that although one is obliged to make up whatever fasting days one missed during a previous Ramaḍān, one has wide latitude in terms of when these days must be made up, and one incurs no guilt by delaying the make-up of fasting days until the subsequent Ramaḍān begins.

46. According to the Shafiis, the redemption must be paid again for every year that passes.

47. As for the Malikis, they hold that when someone is required to perform expiation for breaking his or her fast during Ramaḍān, he or she is to be given a choice between freeing a slave, feeding sixty needy people and fasting two months in succession. The preferable means of expiation is to feed sixty needy people, the second in order of preference is to free a slave, and the third in order of preference

The provision made in this prophetic hadith for allowing the charity that has been donated for purposes of expiation to be given instead to the family of the person performing the expiation—including those family members for whose material support this person is responsible—was an allowance that was unique to this particular man, since it is a requirement of expiation that one feed sixty needy people who do not belong to one's own family. Moreover, the person performing

---

is to fast two months in succession. This choice applies to someone who is free [i.e., not a slave], competent and discerning; as for a slave, he may not validly free another slave because he has no right of guardianship [over himself, much less over another]; hence, he may perform expiation by feeding sixty needy persons if his master gives him permission to do so. He may also perform expiation through fasting. Hence, if his master does not allow him to feed sixty needy persons, he has no choice but to perform the expiation through fasting. As for someone who is mentally incompetent, his guardian is to instruct him to perform expiation through fasting; if he is unwilling or unable to do so, his guardian should instruct him either to feed sixty needy persons or to free a slave, whichever is less costly.

48. According to the Malikis, each needy person is to be given one *mudd* as this unit was measured by the Prophet, namely, the maximum amount that would fill two medium-sized, cupped hands. The food given should be the most common foodstuff consumed by the inhabitants of the country in which the person performing the expiation resides, such as wheat, etc. It is not acceptable to provide lunch or dinner as a substitute for the above according to the officially recognized view. A *mudd* by measure is equal to one-third of an Egyptian *qadaḥ* [literally, 'cup'] and by weight it is equal to one and one-third of a *raṭl* [that is, a little over half a kilo] where one *raṭl* is equal to 128 Meccan dirhams, and one dirham weighs the equivalent of 50 and one-fifth grains (*ḥabbah*) of medium-sized barley. Those to whom such charity is to be given are the poor and the needy; it is not valid to give it to those for whose material support one is responsible, such as one's father, mother, wife, or young children; as for relatives for whose support one is not responsible, such as one's brothers, sisters, and grandparents, there is nothing to prevent one from giving them some of the expiation if they are poor.

* * *

The Hanafis hold that to feed sixty needy individuals, it is sufficient to feed them two lunches or two dinners in which they eat until they are satisfied, or one pre-dawn meal and one fast-breaking meal. Alternatively, one may give each person half a *ṣā'* of wheat or its monetary equivalent, or a *ṣā'* of barley, dried dates, or raisins. A *ṣā'* is equal to 2 1/3 *qadaḥs* by the Egyptian measure. They also hold that those who receive such charity must not include individuals for whose material support one is responsible, such as one's forbears, progeny, or wife.

* * *

The Shafiis hold that the person performing expiation is to give each of the sixty needy people one *mudd* of some type of food which may validly been distributed as *zakāh* on the Day of Fastbreaking, such as wheat and barley. Such food must be the most common foodstuff consumed by the inhabitants of the country in

the expiation is to give each individual a specified amount, details concerning which differ from school to school.[48]

Expiation must be performed for each day on which an act requiring expiation took place according to the Shafiis and the Malikis; for the views of the Hanafis and the Hanbalis, see below.[49] However, if the act requiring expiation is repeated on the same day, only one expiation is required even if the second act calling for it occurs after one has performed expiation for the first. Thus, if someone has sexual intercourse several times during the same day, he is only required to perform a single expiation even if he performed this expiation by either freeing a slave or feeding sixty needy people after the first occurrence. However, he will be guilty of not having abstained for the remainder of the day as he should have done. If someone is unable to perform any of the various types of expiation, his obligation to perform it will remain in effect until he becomes capable of doing so. This view is agreed upon by the Shafiis, the Malikis and the Hanafis; for the Hanbalis' view, see below.[50]

---

which the person performing the expiation resides, whereas substances such as flour and *sawīq* are not acceptable, since they may not be distributed as *zakāh* on the Day of Fastbreaking. A *mudd*, according to the Shafiis, is equal to half an Egyptian *qadaḥ*, which is one-eighth of the Egyptian *kaylah*. Moreover, it is necessary that one place such food into these people's possession; hence, it is not sufficient simply to feed them out of this amount of food. Hence, if one were to feed it to them as lunch or dinner, this would not be sufficient. Lastly, if the person who committed some transgression relating to the fast of Ramaḍān is performing expiation for himself, the needy people who receive the food must not include any for whose material support he is responsible; however, if someone else is performing the expiation on his behalf, it is permissible for the family of the person who committed the transgression to be included among the needy who receive the food.

* * *

As for the Hanbalis, they hold that the person performing expiation is to give each needy person a *mudd* of wheat. A *mudd* is defined as 1 1/3 Iraqi *raṭls*, while an Iraqi *raṭl* is equal to 128 dirhams or 1/2 *ṣā'* of dried dates, barley, raisins, or cottage cheese. As long as one is able to provide any of these types of food, no other food will be acceptable. A *ṣā'* here is equal to four *mudds*, while a *ṣā'* by Egyptian measures is equal to two *qadaḥs*. It is permissible to distribute wheat and barley flour or their *sawīq*, namely, that which is roasted, then ground, if it equals the required amount of grain by weight, not by measure, even if it has not been sifted. It is also permissible to distribute grain from which the impurities have not yet been picked out. When performing expiation it is not permissible to feed the poor bread or to give them spoiled grain, such as wheat which is wormy, wet or so old that its taste has been altered. In addition, the needy people who are fed in performance of expiation must not include anyone who is either an ascendent or a descendent of the person performing the expiation, such as his mother or his son, even if he is not responsible for their material support; nor may they include those for whom he is financially responsible, such as his wife or a sister of his who is not being supported by anyone else. This ruling applies, moreover, whether the person is performing expiation for himself or someone else is performing expiation on his behalf.

49. According to the Hanafis, expiation need not be performed again for each time there is a repetition of the event or act which required it the first time, whether the repetition takes place on a single day or on different days, and whether it takes place during a single Ramaḍān or during Ramaḍān in different years. However, if someone does something which calls for expiation, then performs the expiation required of him, after which he again does the same thing requiring expiation and the repetition takes place in a single day, a single expiation will be sufficient, whereas if the repetition takes place on another day or on several different days, the person must perform another expiation for the event or act which followed the initial event or act. Lastly, the Hanafis appear to hold that if the expiation is required on account of sexual intercourse, it must be performed again for every repetition of the act, whereas if it is required by some other act, no additional expiations are required for repetitions of such acts.

* * *

As for the Hanbalis, they hold that if the act that requires expiation is repeated on a single day and if the person who committed the act performs expiation for it, he will have to perform a second expiation for any similar act committed after this. However, if the person has not performed expiation for the first act, a single expiation will be sufficient for all such acts committed [on a single day].

50. According to the Hanbalis, if someone is unable to perform any of the various types of expiation at the time they are required of him, the obligation is waived, even if he becomes capable of performing them at a later time.

51. According to the Hanbalis, secluding oneself in the mosque for prayer and worship is an emphatically enjoined Sunnah-based practice during the month of Ramaḍān, and even more emphatically enjoined during the last ten days of this month.

* * *

According to the Shafiis, spiritual retreats are an emphatically enjoined emulation of the Sunnah both during Ramaḍān and at other times, whereas during the last ten days of Ramaḍān, they are enjoined even more emphatically.

* * *

On Spiritual Retreats

The definition and pillars of spiritual retreats

A spiritual retreat is the act of remaining in the mosque for the specific purpose of worship. Hence, intention as such is not a pillar of spiritual retreats; otherwise, it would have been mentioned in the definition. The Hanafis and the Hanbalis hold that intention is a condition, not a pillar, of spiritual retreats; as for the Malikis and the Shafiis, they hold that it is a pillar, not a condition. However, this difference of opinion is easily resolved, since both groups agree on the necessity of intention, be it a condition or a pillar. Those who say that intention is a pillar of spiritual retreats mention it in the definition thereof by adding the phrase "with intention" at the end. As for those who do not hold that intention is a pillar of spiritual retreats, they leave out this phrase.

The pillars of spiritual retreats, then, are as follows: (1) remaining in the mosque, (2) the mosque, and (3) the person remaining in the mosque. A fourth pillar, namely, intention, is added by those who include this in the definition of spiritual retreats.

Spiritual retreats are divided into different types; in addition, there are specific conditions, events or acts which render them invalid, practices which are undesirable during a retreat, and rules of conduct associated with retreats.

Types of spiritual retreats and how long they are to last

There are two types of spiritual retreats: (1) Obligatory retreats, that is, spiritual retreats one has vowed to undertake; in other words, if someone vows to undertake a spiritual retreat, he or she is obliged to fulfill this vow. (2) Sunnah-based retreats, which include all other spiritual retreats. As for whether a given spiritual retreat is an emphatically enjoined emulation of the Sunnah at this time or that, each school offers its own ruling in this regard.[51]

According to the Hanafis, undertaking a spiritual retreat is a collective, emphatically enjoined Sunnah-based practice during the last ten days of Ramaḍān, whereas it is desirable at other times. Hence, they divide spiritual retreats into three types.

* * *

According to the ruling most widely accepted among the Malikis, engaging in spiritual retreats is a desirable practice both during Ramaḍān and at other times. During the month of Ramaḍān, it is an emphatically enjoined practice, while during the last ten days of Ramaḍān, it is enjoined even more emphatically. Hence, the Malikis divide spiritual retreats into two types, namely: (1) obligatory, i.e., those which someone has vowed to undertake, and (2) desirable, which includes all other spiritual retreats.

52. Based on the best-attested view of the Malikis, the minimum period of time for a spiritual retreat is one day and one night.

According to the Hanafis and the Hanbalis, the minimum period of time that such a retreat may last is a moment in time of unspecified duration; for the views of the Malikis and the Shafiis, see below.[52]

Conditions for spiritual retreats—a woman's going on such a retreat without her husband's permission

The conditions for engaging in a spiritual retreat are as follows: (1) One must be a Muslim. Hence, a spiritual retreat is not valid if undertaken by a non-Muslim. (2) One must possess full powers of discernment. Spiritual retreats are not valid if undertaken by someone who is insane or by a young child who has not reached the age of discernment; if a child has reached the age of discernment, however, his retreat will be valid. (3) It must take place in a mosque. Hence, a spiritual retreat will not be valid in a house or some other place. However, it will likewise not be valid in every mosque; rather, in order for a spiritual retreat to be valid in a given mosque, the mosque must fulfill certain conditions which differ from one school to another.[53] (4) Intention. A spiritual retreat will not be valid without intention. As we have seen, the Hanafis and the Hanbalis hold that intention is a condition for the

---

* * *

As for the Shafiis, they hold that a spiritual retreat must last a moment which is longer than that required to utter the phrase *subḥān Allāh.*

53. The Malikis stipulate that the mosque in which a spiritual retreat is undertaken must be open to the general public and that it must be a mosque in which Friday prayers are held for those of whom the Friday prayers are required. Hence, one may not validly undertake a spiritual retreat in a household mosque even if the person undertaking the retreat is a woman; nor it is valid in the Ka'bah or at the shrine of a Muslim saint.

* * *

According to the Hanafis, the mosque in which a spiritual retreat may be held must be a community mosque, that is, one which has an imam and a muezzin, whether all five daily prayers are performed there or not. This ruling applies if the person undertaking the retreat is a man; in the case of a woman, she may undertake a spiritual retreat in her household mosque, i.e., the spot in her house which she has prepared as a place for prayer. It is undesirable for a woman to undertake a spiritual retreat in a community mosque; in fact, she may not validly undertake a retreat anywhere other than the spot where she is accustomed to praying, whether she has set up her own mosque in her home or has simply designated a specific spot in the house as her place of prayer.

* * *

The Shafiis hold that if the person undertaking the retreat has good reason to believe that a given mosque has been set aside for the sole purpose of serving as a mosque, then either a man or a woman may validly undertake a spiritual retreat there even if the mosque is not one where the Friday congregational prayers are performed and even if it is not open to the general public.

* * *

validity of a spiritual retreat, whereas according to the Malikis and the Shafiis, intention is a pillar of spiritual retreats, not a condition for their validity. The Shafiis do not stipulate that one's intention to engage in a spiritual retreat be formed while one is settled in the mosque, even if in a purely legal sense. Hence, it [the state of being on a spiritual retreat – t.n.] may include someone who frequents the mosque, while according to the officially recognized view, an intention formed while such a person is simply passing through a mosque is sufficient. (5) One must be free of major ritual impurity, menstrual flow and post-partum bleeding according to the Shafiis and the Hanbalis. For the views of the Malikis and the Hanafis, see below.[54]

In addition to the conditions mentioned thus far, the Malikis [and the Hanafis] list further conditions as well.[55]

A woman's retreat will not be valid if she undertakes it without her husband's permission even if it is a retreat she has vowed to perform. This ruling applies whether or not she knows for certain or has good reason to believe that he needs her for [sexual] enjoyment. For the views of the Shafiis and the Malikis on this matter, see below.[56]

As for the Hanbalis, they stipulate no conditions which must be met by a mosque in order for both men and woman to undertake spiritual retreats there. However, they hold that if someone wishes to undertake a retreat during a period of time which spans obligatory prayers that must be performed in community, it will only be valid to undertake a spiritual retreat in a mosque in which communal prayers are performed, even if those performing them include no one but those on retreat.

54. According to the Hanafis, being free of major ritual impurity is a condition for the permissibility of a spiritual retreat, but not for its validity. Hence, if someone in a state of major ritual impurity undertakes a spiritual retreat, the retreat will be valid, even though it is forbidden. As for being free of menstrual flow and post-partum bleeding, this is a condition for the validity of obligatory spiritual retreats, that is, spiritual retreats one has vowed to undertake. Thus, if a woman who is menstruating or experiencing post-partum bleeding goes on an obligatory spiritual retreat, the retreat will not be valid because in order for an obligatory spiritual retreat to be valid, one must fast, and fasting is not valid when undertaken by a woman who is menstruating or experiencing post-partum bleeding. As for spiritual retreats which are emulations of the Sunnah, they are valid even if one is not free of menstrual flow or post-partum bleeding since, according to the best-attested view, fasting is not a condition for the validity of this type of retreat.

* * *

As for the Malikis, they hold that being free of major ritual impurity is not a condition for the validity of a spiritual retreat; rather, it is a condition for the permissibility of remaining in the mosque. Hence, if something happens to someone on retreat in a mosque that brings about major ritual impurity in this person, if the cause of the ritual impurity is something which does not invalidate spiritual retreats (such as having a 'wet dream'), and if there is no water in the mosque, he must leave the mosque in order to perform major ablutions elsewhere, then return immediately afterwards. If such a person delays coming back to the mosque after performing major ablutions, his retreat will be invalidated unless the delay occurs because of some necessity relating to the ablutions themselves, such as trimming one's fingernails or one's moustache. As for being free of menstrual flow and post-partum bleeding, this is a condition for the validity of all spiritual retreats, whether they are in fulfillment of a vow or not. The reason for this is that one of the conditions for the validity of a spiritual retreat is fasting, and fasting is not valid if a woman is menstruating or experiencing post-partum bleeding. Hence, if, while a woman is on a spiritual retreat, she begins to menstruate or to have post-partum bleeding, she must leave the mosque, then return after her menstrual flow or post-partum bleeding has stopped to complete the retreat she had vowed or intended to undertake when she first entered the mosque. If the retreat is one she had vowed to undertake, she should stay in the mosque for as many days as remain of the period she had vowed to seclude herself, and make up for whatever days she missed. If, on the other hand, it is a voluntary retreat, she should complete whatever days remain of the period she had originally intended to seclude herself, but without making up the days she missed on account of her menstrual flow or post-partum bleeding.

55. According to the Malikis, fasting is a condition for the validity of spiritual retreats whether they are retreats one has vowed to perform or are voluntary.

* * *

As for the Hanafis, they hold that fasting is a condition for the validity of obligatory retreats, but not voluntary ones.

56. The Shafiis hold that if a woman goes on a spiritual retreat without her husband's permission, it will be valid but she will be guilty of wrongdoing. If her husband gives her permission to do so and she is a woman with a striking appearance, her retreat will be deemed undesirable.

* * *

As for the Malikis, they hold that it is not permissible for a woman to vow or volunteer to undergo a spiritual retreat without her husband's permission if she knows or has good reason to believe that he needs her for sexual intercourse. If she does go on a retreat without his permission, the retreat will still be valid, though he has the right to invalidate it by having sexual relations with her. If her husband does invalidate her retreat in this way, she must make it up later even if it was voluntary since she committed a transgression by undertaking it without asking for his permission; however, she is not to make it up promptly unless she has his permission to do so.

57. According to the Malikis, the same ruling which applies to sexual intercourse applies to kissing on the mouth, even if the person who does the kissing does not intend to find pleasure in it, even if he, in fact, finds no pleasure in doing so, and even if he has no ejaculation. As for touching and direct genital contact, they only invalidate one's spiritual retreat on the condition that one seeks and/or finds physical pleasure in so doing; otherwise, they do not invalidate it.

58. The Malikis hold that having an emission of semen due to erotic thoughts or looking [at an attractive person] invalidates one's spiritual retreat whether it

That which invalidates a spiritual retreat

There are a number of things which will invalidate a spiritual retreat, including the following: (1) Engaging deliberately in sexual intercourse, even if it does not result in ejaculation. This ruling, which is agreed upon by all four schools, applies whether the act occurs during the night or day. As for engaging in sexual relations out of forgetfulness, this invalidates one's spiritual retreat according to the Hanafis, the Hanbalis and the Malikis; as for the Shafiis, they hold that if someone engages in sexual relations out of forgetfulness, his retreat will not be invalidated. As for acts which might lead to sexual intercourse, such as kissing with physical desire, direct genital contact and the like, they do not invalidate one's spiritual retreat unless there is ejaculation according to the Shafiis, the Hanafis and the Hanbalis. For the view of the Malikis, see below.[57] However, someone who is undertaking a spiritual retreat is forbidden to engage in such acts with physical desire. As for having an emission of semen due to erotic thoughts, looking [at a sexually attractive person] or having a 'wet dream', the Hanafis and the Hanbalis hold that this does not invalidate a spiritual retreat whether it is habitual or not; for the views of the Malikis and the Shafiis, see below.[58] (2) Leaving the mosque.[59] (3) Apostasy. If someone undertaking a spiritual retreat commits apostasy, his retreat will be invalidated. If he

---

happens by day or by night, and whether it takes place deliberately or out of forgetfulness.

* * *

As for the Shafiis, they hold that if someone is in the habit of having a seminal emission in response to erotic thoughts or looking [at someone attractive], his spiritual retreat will be invalidated by this, whereas if this is not customary for him, it will not invalidate his retreat.

59. According to the Hanafis, there are two situations in which someone on a spiritual retreat might leave the mosque: (1) when the retreat is obligatory by virtue of one's having vowed to undertake it, and (2) when the retreat is voluntary. In the first situation, i.e., where the retreat is obligatory by virtue of someone's having vowed to undertake it, one is not allowed to leave the mosque at all, whether at night or during the day, deliberately or out of forgetfulness, and if someone does leave the mosque in this situation, his retreat will be invalidated unless he leaves on the basis of a legitimate excuse. As for the excuses which allow someone on an obligatory retreat to leave the mosque, they are divided into three types: (1) 'Natural' excuses, such as the need to urinate, defecate, or perform major ablutions due to having entered a state of major ritual impurity because of a 'wet dream' (assuming there is no place in the mosque to perform such ablutions). In such a case, the person on the retreat may leave the mosque to perform major ablutions in order to purify himself from his state of major ritual impurity or to 'relieve nature', provided that he stays out only long enough to take care of the need at hand. (2) Legal

excuses, such as the need to leave in order to perform the Friday congregational prayer if the mosque in which one is undertaking one's retreat is not one where the Friday prayers are held. However, one may only leave early enough to be able to perform four *rak'ahs* before the call to prayer at the pulpit, and once the prayer is concluded, one may only stay long enough to perform four or six additional *rak'ahs*. If one stays longer than this, his spiritual retreat will not be invalidated since the second mosque to which the person has gone would also be fit as a place for spiritual retreats; however, it is undesirable for one to stay longer than this due to one's having violated what he originally had committed himself to do, namely, to undertake a spiritual retreat in the first mosque. (3) 'Necessary' excuses, such as fear for oneself or one's possessions if one remains in this mosque; similarly, if the mosque in which one is on retreat collapses, it is permissible to leave it provided that one goes to another mosque immediately with the intention of undertaking his spiritual retreat there.

As for the second situation in which one might leave the mosque, namely, one in which the retreat is voluntary, there is nothing to prevent one from leaving the mosque even without an excuse, since such a spiritual retreat has no set time period at the end of which one is to come out. If someone leaves the mosque in this situation, the days of retreat he has already completed will not be invalidated, and if he returns to the mosque again and intends to undertake a retreat there, he will receive the reward for doing so, whereas if he were to leave the mosque while on an obligatory retreat without any excuse, he would be guilty of wrongdoing and whatever days he had already spent in retreat would be invalidated.

* * *

The Malikis hold that if someone undertaking a spiritual retreat leaves the mosque to take care of some necessity, such as to buy food or drink for himself, to perform ablutions, or to urinate, for example, his retreat will not be invalidated. However, if such a person leaves the mosque for something other than a necessity, such as to visit a sick person, to perform the Friday congregational prayer due to the fact that the mosque where he is on retreat is not one where the Friday prayers are held, to give testimony, or to escort a funeral procession, even if it happens to be the funeral of his mother or his father, his retreat will be invalidated. If leaving the mosque is obligatory, such as it would be in order to attend the Friday congregational prayer, and if one stays in the mosque rather than leaving to attend the prayer, the person concerned will be guilty of wrongdoing, but his retreat will remain valid; the reason for this is that neglecting to attend a single Friday congregational prayer is not a major sin in Islam, and a spiritual retreat will only be invalidated by one's committing a major sin based on the most widely accepted view. Nor will one's spiritual retreat be invalidated by one's leaving the mosque due to an excuse such as menstrual flow or post-partum bleeding, as we have seen. Lastly, if part of one's spiritual retreat coincides with a day on which fasting is not valid, such as the Day of Fastbreaking or the Day of Sacrifice, one must remain in the mosque based on the best-attested view; then, once the holiday has passed, one should complete the remaining days of the retreat one had vowed or volunteered to undertake.

* * *

According to the Hanbalis, a spiritual retreat is invalidated by one's leaving the mosque deliberately and consciously unless it is in order to take care of an urgent necessity such as to urinate, to vomit if one has an overwhelming urge to do so, to wash a garment which one needs and which has become contaminated with ritual impurity, or to perform minor or major ritual ablutions. It is permissible to perform minor or major ritual ablutions in the mosque if this will cause no harm to the mosque or to other people. If someone on retreat leaves the mosque for any of the aforementioned reasons, he may walk at his usual pace, that is, without hurrying. He may also leave to get himself food and drink if he has no one to bring these things to him, or to attend the Friday congregational prayer if this is required of him without his retreat's being invalidated since in doing so he is performing a duty. It is also permissible for such a person to leave early for the Friday prayer and to remain in the other mosque for a long time after the prayer without any undesirability attaching to this, since the other mosque would also be a suitable place for a spiritual retreat. Nevertheless, it is desirable for him to come back promptly to the mosque where he is on retreat so as to complete his retreat there. Generally speaking, then, it does not invalidate a spiritual retreat to leave the mosque for a legitimate or 'natural' purpose.

* * *

The Shafiis hold that leaving the mosque without a legitimate excuse invalidates one's spiritual retreat. As for the excuses which make it permissible to leave the mosque, they are classified as either 'natural' excuses, such as needing to urinate or defecate, or 'necessary' excuses, such as the walls of the mosque collapsing, in which case someone undertaking a retreat there may leave the mosque where he has been staying and go to another mosque without invalidating his retreat. Moreover, one's retreat will only be invalidated if the invalidating act, as it were, is committed deliberately, willingly, and with full knowledge that it is forbidden. If someone commits such an act out of forgetfulness, under coercion, or out of ignorance which is excusable under Islamic law (such as ignorance resulting from one's being new to Islam), his retreat will not be invalidated. If someone leaves the mosque based on a legally acceptable excuse, the continuity of his retreat is not deemed to have been interrupted by the period of time he was absent, nor is he required to renew his intention to undertake the retreat upon his return. However, he must make up the time he missed on account of his absence, not including the time it took to meet his need (such as the need to defecate, for example), though the latter time period is so short in most cases that there is no need to make it up. The ruling just presented applies when the retreat concerned is an obligatory retreat in which continuity must be maintained, as when someone has vowed to fast a certain number of consecutive days. However, in the case of a retreat one has vowed to undertake either without specifying a time period, or with a time period that need not be fulfilled in continuous succession, one is permitted to leave the mosque even without an excuse. The retreat is nevertheless interrupted by one's leaving; hence, one must renew one's intention to undertake the retreat unless he has made a clear determination to return, or unless the reason for his leaving is simply to meet a need such as defecation, in which case there is no need to renew one's intention. The

returns to Islam, the Hanafis and the Malikis hold that he is not required to make up the retreat, since in this way he may be given further incentive to remain within Islam. For the views of the Shafiis and the Hanbalis on this point, see below.[60]

There are other things which invalidate a spiritual retreat, and which are listed by each school separately.[61]

---

same ruling applies to retreats that are simply recommended. As for the matter of urinating into a container in the mosque, this is forbidden, although it does not invalidate one's retreat.

60. The Hanbalis hold that if someone who committed apostasy while engaging in a spiritual retreat returns to Islam, he must make the retreat up.

* * *

As for the Shafiis, they hold that if the retreat someone has vowed to perform is limited to a period of time that must be fulfilled in uninterrupted succession, as when someone has vowed to fast ten consecutive days, and if this person commits apostasy during this retreat, then if he returns to Islam, he must start the retreat over from the beginning. If, on the other hand, he vows to undertake a retreat for a period of time that need not be completed in uninterrupted succession and if he commits apostasy during this retreat, then returns to Islam, he is not required to begin the retreat all over again; rather, he may simply build on what he had already completed thereof.

61. The Malikis list the following as also invalidating a spiritual retreat: (1) Eating or drinking deliberately during the day. If someone eats or drinks deliberately during the day, his retreat will be invalidated and he must begin it all over again. This ruling applies whether the retreat is obligatory or not. In such a case, the person may not build on what he has already done. However, if someone eats or drinks out of forgetfulness, he is not required to begin all over again; rather, he may build on what he has already done and simply make up the day on which he broke his fast, even if the retreat is a voluntary one. (2) Consuming a prohibited intoxicant by night, even if one becomes sober again before dawn. The same ruling applies to taking a narcotic if it exerts a narcotic effect on the person who takes it. If someone takes anything of this nature, his retreat will be invalidated and he must start all over again. (3) Committing a major sin that does not break one's fast, such as backbiting and slander. This is one of two widely accepted points of view; according to the opposing point of view, committing major sins does not invalidate one's retreat, as has been mentioned. (4) Insanity and loss of consciousness. If someone on a spiritual retreat loses his sanity or loses consciousness and if the person's situation meets the conditions for breaking a fast, his retreat will be invalidated as well; however, he need not begin it all over again after the condition passes. Rather, he is simply to build on whatever he has already completed of the retreat and make up the days he missed if the retreat is an obligatory one (as a woman would be required to after the cessation of her menstrual flow or post-partum bleeding). (5) Menstrual flow and post-partum bleeding (as we saw in the section on conditions for the validity of a spiritual retreat).

* * *

According to the Hanafis, a spiritual retreat is also invalidated by a loss of consciousness if it continues for days; the same applies to a loss of sanity. As for intoxication at night, this does not invalidate a retreat; nor is it invalidated by reviling others, contentiousness, and other forms of disobedience. As for menstrual flow and post-partum bleeding, we have seen that their absence is a condition for the validity of an obligatory retreat and for the permissibility of a non-obligatory retreat. Hence, if a woman undertaking an obligatory spiritual retreat begins her menstrual period or starts to have post-partum bleeding, her retreat will be invalidated. If a spiritual retreat is invalidated by someone's committing apostasy, he is not required to make it up after he returns to Islam, as we have seen; if a retreat is invalidated by something other than this and if it is a retreat one has vowed to undertake during a designated period of time (for a specific ten days, for example), the person concerned is to make up whatever days of the retreat were invalidated, but he need not start the retreat over from the beginning. If, on the other hand, the retreat is not tied to a specific period of time, one is to start it over from the beginning, since the days of the retreat which were completed before the invalidation occurred no longer count.

* * *

The Hanbalis list the following as invalidating a spiritual retreat: (1) Intoxication on the part of the person undertaking the retreat, even if it takes place at night. However, if someone drinks an intoxicant without becoming intoxicated or if he commits a major sin, his retreat will remain valid. (2) Menstrual flow and post-partum bleeding. If a woman on a spiritual retreat experiences the onset of menstrual flow or post-partum bleeding, her retreat will be invalidated; however, once the invalidating condition has passed, she may simply resume her retreat where she left off, building on what she had already completed thereof. Someone who has become intoxicated, by contrast, and whose retreat was not invalidated based on a legitimate excuse, must both resume his retreat after the intoxication passes, and begin his retreat all over again. As for a loss of consciousness, it does not invalidate a retreat. (3) Intending to discontinue one's retreat, even if one does not carry out the intention.

* * *

As for the Shafiis, they hold that a spiritual retreat is invalidated by intoxication and loss of sanity if they take place due to some transgression on the part of the person undertaking the retreat. As for menstrual flow and post-partum bleeding, they hold that these invalidate a woman's spiritual retreat if the period of time she vowed to spend on the retreat is one in which she would not expect to be interrupted by such conditions. If, for example, the retreat is no more than fifteen days long, she would not expect it to be interrupted by menstrual flow, and if it is no longer than 9 months, one would not expect it to be interrupted by post-partum bleeding. If, on the other hand, the retreat is longer than 15 days and if, consequently, one might expect it to be interrupted by menstrual flow, or if it is longer than 9 months, in which case one might expect it to be interrupted by post-partum bleeding, it will not be invalidated by either of them. Nor is a spiritual retreat invalidated by the commission of a major sin such as backbiting or slander.

Undesirable practices associated with spiritual retreats and relevant rules of conduct

As for those practices which are considered undesirable when associated with spiritual retreats and rules of etiquette relevant thereto, each school provides its own detailed listing.[62]

---

62. The Malikis list the following practices as being undesirable in connection with a spiritual retreat: (1) Making one's retreat shorter than ten days or longer than a month. (2) Eating outside the mosque but nearby, as, for example, in its inner or outer courtyard or the open space around it; as for eating far from the mosque, it will invalidate one's retreat. (2) Not bringing into the mosque all the food, drink and clothing one will need when one would have been able to do so. (3) Entering one's house when it is near the mosque in order to take care of some necessity when neither one's wife nor one's slave girl is in the house lest he be distracted by them from his retreat; if his home is far from the mosque, his retreat will be invalidated by going there. (4) Acquiring or passing on knowledge through teaching during one's retreat, since the purpose of a spiritual retreat is the training and discipline of one's soul, which tends to take place through the remembrance of God and prayer; an exception to this ruling is made, however, for knowledge relating to one's craft or livelihood, which it is not undesirable to occupy oneself with while on a retreat. (5) Occupying oneself with a great deal of writing when one is not obliged to engage in it in order to make one's living; otherwise, there is no undesirability attached to this practice. (6) Occupying oneself with activities other than ritual prayer, the remembrance of God, recitation of the Qur'ān, uttering words of praise and glorification to God, saying, *lā ilāha illā Allāh*, asking for God's forgiveness and praying for blessings upon the Prophet by, for example, visiting someone who is ill in the mosque, praying over a deceased person at his funeral, etc. (7) Ascending a minaret or going up to a roof to deliver the call to prayer. (8) Going on a retreat for which one has insufficient provisions.

As for the rules of etiquette one is encouraged to follow, they include the following: (1) Bringing along an extra garment when one enters the mosque in case one should need it. (2) Remaining in the mosque to which one has come for the retreat for the night preceding the Day of Fastbreaking or the Day of Sacrifice if the end of the person's retreat coincides with this night, since by so doing, one can come directly from the mosque to the holiday prayer site [the following day], thereby joining one act of worship with another. (3) Staying at the rear of the mosque in order to avoid people who would cause one distraction by starting conversations. (4) Undertaking one's spiritual retreat during Ramaḍān. (5) Scheduling one's spiritual retreat during the final ten days of Ramaḍān in order to wait for the "Night of Power" (*laylat al-qadr*), since it generally falls within this period of time. (6) Making certain that one's retreat lasts no fewer than ten days.

* * *

The Hanafis list the following practices as being undesirable to the point of being forbidden during a spiritual retreat: (1) Remaining silent if one believes that this is a means of drawing near to God; if one does not believe this, however, it is not undesirable. As for refraining from forms of disobedience that are committed with the tongue, this is one of the greatest expressions of worship. (2) Bringing a commodity into the mosque in order to sell it. Contracting a sale to meet one's own needs or those of one's family without bringing the commodity itself into the mosque is permissible; however, concluding business deals is not allowed.

As for rules of etiquette they encourage one to adhere to, they include the following: (1) Speaking nothing but good. (2) Choosing the best mosques, namely, the Sacred Mosque in Mecca, followed by the Prophet's Mosque in Medina, followed by Al-Aqṣā Mosque in Jerusalem if one is resident in these places, followed by the mosque in one's own community where the Friday congregational prayers are held. (3) Chanting the Qur'ān, reciting hadiths, seeking and conveying knowledge, and the like.

* * *

The Shafiis list the following practices as undesirable during a spiritual retreat: (1) Cupping and venesection if one can guarantee that they will not cause any contamination of the mosque with ritual impurity; otherwise, they are forbidden. (2) Engaging excessively in one's craft in the mosque; however, if one does only a little, such as sewing a bit or weaving a small amount of palm leaves, this is not deemed undesirable.

As for rules of etiquette they encourage one to follow, they include: (1) Engaging in acts of obedience to God Almighty, such as chanting of the Qur'ān, recitation of hadiths, engaging in the remembrance of God and [exchanging] knowledge. (2) Fasting, which is an emulation of the Sunnah. (3) Undertaking one's retreat in the mosque where the Friday congregational prayers are performed. The best of all mosques is the Sacred Mosque in Mecca, followed by the Prophet's Mosque in Medina, followed by Al-Aqṣā Mosque in Jerusalem. (3) Speaking only that which is good by not reviling others or engaging in foolish talk.

* * *

As for the Hanbalis, they hold that it is undesirable for someone on a spiritual retreat to maintain silence until nightfall and that if someone vows to do so, he should not fulfill such a vow.

As for the rules of conduct which they suggest, they are: (1) That one should spend one's time in acts of obedience to God Almighty, such as recitation of the Qur'ān, remembrance of God and ritual prayer, and (2) That one should avoid interfering in matters which are none of one's concern.

On *Zakāh*

On *Zakāh*

The definition of *zakāh*

The term *zakāh* conveys the notion of purification and growth. God Almighty says, "To a happy state shall indeed attain he who causes this [self] to grow in purity (*man zakkāhā*)..." (91:9). In other words, such a person has cleansed his or her soul of impurities. The related verb, *zakā* in Arabic, conveys the notion of growth as when one says, "The crop grew and increased" (*zakā al-zar'u*). In terms of Islamic law, the term *zakāh* refers to the act of placing a specific amount of money in the possession of someone who deserves such money given the fulfillment of certain conditions. What this means is that those who possess the minimum amount of wealth required in order for one to be obliged to pay *zakāh* must give a certain percentage of their wealth to the poor and other unfortunate people who are worthy of receiving it. (The conditions for such worthiness will be discussed below.) Moreover, they must give it in such a way that it becomes the possession of those who receive it.

The Hanbalis define *zakāh* as the right of a specified group to a certain person's money at a specified time. The Hanbalis' definition means the same as the former one except that the first definition explicitly states the necessity of placing the required amount of *zakāh* in the possession of those who deserve it, since the obligatory nature of the giving does not necessarily involve placing something in another's possession.

Rulings on *zakāh* and the evidence in support of it

Zakāh is one of the five pillars of Islam and an individual obligation for everyone who fulfills certain conditions to be outlined below. *Zakāh* was established as a legal requirement for Muslims in the year 2 A.H. Its obligatory nature is an aspect of the [Islamic] religion which must be recognized of necessity, while the evidence for its obligatory nature is found in the Qur'ān, the Sunnah, and the consensus of the Muslim community.

The evidence for *zakāh* in the Qur'ān includes the words of God Almighty, "...and spend in charity... [*wa ātū al-zakāh*]" (2:43) as well as its praise for those "in whose possessions there is a due share, acknowledged [by them], for such as ask [for help], and such as are deprived [of what is good in life]..." (70:24-25).[63]

As for the support for *zakāh* from the Sunnah, it is found in the words of the Prophet, "Islam is founded on five [pillars]," after which he mentions as one of these five pillars "the payment of *zakāh*". Other evidence from the Sunnah is found in a hadith narrated by al-Tirmidhī on the authority of Sulaym Ibn 'Āmir, who said,

---

63. This phrase is a description of "those who consciously turn towards God in prayer, and [who] incessantly persevere in their prayer...." (vv. 22-23 of the same passage) [t.n.].

"I heard Abū Umāmah say that he had heard the Messenger of God deliver his farewell address in which he said, 'Be conscious of God, pray your five [daily ritual prayers], fast your month, give the required *zakāh* out of your wealth, and obey those who have authority to give you commands, and you will enter your Lord's paradise.'" (This is a good, authentic hadith.) There are other sayings from the Sunnah which likewise support the obligatory nature of *zakāh*.

As for the consensus of the Muslim community, the [Islamic] nation is in agreement that *zakāh* is a pillar of Islam given specified conditions.

Conditions for the necessity of *zakāh*

In order for *zakāh* to be required, a number of conditions must be met: (1) Adulthood. Hence, a child who owns wealth is not required to pay *zakāh* on it. (2) Full possession of one's mental faculties. Hence, an insane person is not required to pay *zakāh*. Nevertheless, *zakāh* must be paid on the wealth owned by a minor and by someone who is insane; hence, his or her guardian is responsible for paying this according to the Shafiis, the Malikis and the Hanbalis. For the view of the Hanafis, see below.[64]

Whether *zakāh* is required of a non-Muslim

Another condition for the necessity of *zakāh* is that one be a Muslim; in other words, no *zakāh* is required of someone who is a non-Muslim, whether he was born a non-Muslim or is someone who left Islam. According to the Hanafis and the Hanbalis, someone who has renounced Islam, then returned to it is not required to

---

64. According to the Hanafis, *zakāh* need not be paid by a child or someone who is insane on the wealth that he or she owns, nor is his or her guardian required to pay it. The reason for this is that the payment of *zakāh* is considered to be a kind of pure worship, whereas children and the insane are not held accountable for such worship. However, their money must be used to pay fines and expenses since these fall under the category of rights due to other human beings; similarly, their wealth is subject to a tithe (*'ushr*) as well as the charity distributed on the Day of Fastbreaking. The reason for this is that such wealth is considered to be a type of provision and, as such, is subject to being used to fulfill others' rights. The ruling on someone who is mentally incompetent is the same as that which applies to a child; hence, no *zakāh* is due on such a person's wealth.

65. According to the Malikis, being a Muslim is a condition for the validity of one's *zakāh*, but not for its being obligatory; hence, a non-Muslim is under obligation to pay *zakāh* even though his or her *zakāh* will only be valid if he or she becomes a Muslim. If this person then becomes a Muslim, the obligation to pay *zakāh* for the period before he or she became a Muslim will be waived based on the Qur'anic statement, "Tell those who are bent on denying the truth that if they desist, all that is past shall be forgiven them…" (8:38). This ruling applies equally to those who were born non-Muslims and those who have renounced Islam.

66. According to the Shafiis, *zakāh* is required provisionally of an apostate pending his return to Islam. If he then returns to Islam, it will become apparent that *zakāh* is required of him due to his continued ownership of his wealth, and he must pay it at this time. However, even if someone were to pay his *zakāh* while still an

pay *zakāh* for the period of time during which he was apostate. For the views of the Malikis and the Shafiis, see below.[65]

Moreover, just as being a Muslim is a condition for the *zakāh*'s being obligatory, it is likewise a condition for its validity. The reason for this is that *zakāh* will only be valid if it is accompanied by intention, while intention is not valid from a non-Muslim according to the Malikis, the Hanafis and the Hanbalis. As for the Shafiis, they hold that intention is also valid on the part of someone who has renounced Islam. Consequently, they hold that *zakāh* is required provisionally of the non-Muslim, as detailed below.[66]

Whether *zakāh* must be paid on a woman's dowry

In order for *zakāh* to be required on a given sum of money, possession, etc., the person must have full ownership thereof. The question, then, is whether a woman's dowry is considered to be her full possession before she collects it. Each school offers its own ruling on this matter.[67]

---

apostate, it would be valid. Similarly, one's intention is valid even while he is an apostate, since intention is for the purpose of distinguishing one act from another, not for the purpose of worship. If, on the other hand, someone dies while still an apostate, his wealth will be considered no longer to belong to him and will be classified instead as spoils of war which were acquired without combat (*fay'*), upon which no *zakāh* is required.

67. The Hanafis hold that in order to be fully in possession of something, one must both own it and have it in one's hand, as it were. Hence, if someone owns something which he has not yet collected, he is not required to pay *zakāh* on it. This ruling applies to a woman's dowry before she collects it; hence, she is not required to pay *zakāh* on it until after she has collected it. Similarly, no *zakāh* is required of someone who has collected something which he does not own, as in the case of a debtor who has someone else's money in his possession. As for money owned by a slave who has a contract of manumission, the Hanafis rule that although this money is partially owned by him, it is nevertheless not subject to *zakāh* until he attains his freedom. As for a regular slave's money, no *zakāh* is required on it because the money is not his possession, and because he does not enjoy freedom. Nor is *zakāh* due on money which has been set aside as a religious endowment since it is, legally speaking, owned by no one; nor is it due on crops growing on publicly owned land for the same reason.

* * *

The Malikis hold that full ownership of something requires that the thing owned be at one's full disposal. Hence, no *zakāh* is required of slaves on what they own, since their ownership of it is not complete. This ruling applies likewise to a slave with a contract of manumission, since if he were to dispose of his money [by paying *zakāh* on it, for example – t.n.], this might render him unable to pay his debt of manumission, thereby causing him to revert fully to slavehood. Nor is *zakāh* required of someone who is holding something that does not belong to him, as in the case of someone who has received something in pledge or security. As for a woman's dowry, she enjoys full ownership of it; however, she is not required to pay *zakāh* on it as long as it is in the husband's possession. Rather, she must pay *zakāh* on it once a year has passed since the time she collected it. In the case of a debtor who has someone else's property (not money) in his possession, the Malikis rule that if he has enough (by way of real estate and other possessions) with which to pay back the debt, he must pay *zakāh* on the money he is holding once he has had it for an entire year. The reason for this is that by virtue of his ability to pay back the value of the debt out of his own possessions, it has become his property. If the property he is holding is tilled land or its produce, livestock or minerals, he must pay *zakāh* on it regardless of whether he has enough property of his own to repay the debt. However, *zakāh* need not be paid on publicly owned wealth, such as crops that grow unassisted on land not owned by any particular individual; in such a case, the crops are there for the taking, and no *zakāh* is due on them. As for wealth that has been set aside as a religious endowment—whether for the benefit of specified individuals or on behalf of 'the poor' without specifying particular beneficiaries—*zakāh* is due on that which is owned by the person who set the property aside as a religious endowment. The reason for this is that setting aside non-monetary property as a religious endowment does not preclude its being owned. Hence, if someone set aside an orchard as a religious endowment in order to distribute its produce among the poor in general or among a particular group of people (such as so-and-so's children), he must pay *zakāh* on this produce when it amounts to the relevant *niṣāb*. If its produce amounts to less than this, no *zakāh* is due on it unless the person who set it aside as a religious endowment has produce from another orchard which, when added to the produce of the first orchard, brings it up to the minimum for *zakāh* to be due on it; in this latter case, he must pay *zakāh* on the entire amount.

* * *

The Shafiis hold that the condition requiring wealth to be one's full possession [in order for *zakāh* to be due on it] exempts both full slaves and slaves with contracts of manumission from the obligation to pay *zakāh*; in the first case, they are not required to pay *zakāh* because they have no ownership of anything, and in the second case, they pay no *zakāh* because what they own is so little and vulnerable to depletion. Similarly, no *zakāh* is due on publicly owned wealth, such as crops which grow of their own accord in an untilled, open area, since it is no one's property. Also exempted from *zakāh* is property which has been set aside as a religious endowment for the benefit of unspecified individuals. For example, if someone sets aside an orchard as a religious endowment [whose yield would go to] benefit a mosque, a retreat center for dervishes, or non-specified groups such as the poor and the needy, no *zakāh* is due on its yield. If, on the other hand, the land is rented out and cultivated, the renter must pay *zakāh* along with the rent he pays for the use of the land; similarly, *zakāh* is due on religious endowments for the benefit of a specified individual or group of individuals. As for a woman's dowry, if the dowry is still being held by her husband, it is treated like a debt and, as we shall see below, *zakāh* is due on it; however, the *zakāh* due on the dowry is only to be paid after the woman collects it. Lastly, if someone borrows money, he must pay *zakāh* on the money he borrowed if it remains in his possession for an entire year; the reason for this is that by virtue of his having borrowed the money, it comes to be considered his full possession.

* * *

The minimum amount of property one must own in order to be liable for *zakāh* (*niṣāb*), and the passing of one year since its acquisition

In order for someone to be obliged to pay *zakāh*, the money which he owns must amount to a prescribed minimum (*niṣāb*); if one owns less than this minimum, no *zakāh* is due. In terms of Islamic law, the meaning of the term *niṣāb* is that which the Lawgiver has set up (*naṣaba*) as a sign of the necessity of paying *zakāh*, whether the property owned is in the form of gold and silver or in some other form. The exact amount of the *niṣāb* varies according to the type of wealth concerned; the *niṣāb* for each type of property will be detailed in what follows.

As for the matter of one year's passing, what this means is that no *zakāh* must be paid unless the person owns the wealth, and unless a full year has passed since he or she acquired it. The standard year employed in this context is the lunar, rather than the solar, year; the lunar year is 354 days, while the solar year differs from one year to the next, sometimes being 365 days and sometimes one day longer. For each school's ruling on the passing of one year since the acquisition of one's wealth, see below.[68]

As for the Hanbalis, they hold that complete ownership requires that no one else have any claim over what one has in one's possession and that one be completely free to dispose of it as one chooses based on one's own interests and not those of someone else. Hence, no *zakāh* is due on the debt incurred by a slave with a contract of manumission; nor is it due on wealth which has been set aside as a religious endowment for the benefit of a general group, such as 'the needy', or for the benefit of a school, a mosque, etc. As for wealth that has been aside as a religious endowment for the benefit of a specific party, *zakāh* must be paid on it. Hence, if someone sets aside some land or a tree as a religious endowment for the benefit of a particular party, he must pay *zakāh* on the yield produced by the land or the tree if it comes to a *niṣāb*, i.e., the minimum amount required for *zakāh* to be due on it. As for a woman's dowry, it is viewed as a kind of debt; the ruling on this and on money someone has borrowed from someone else will be discussed below. As for a slave, he is not required to pay any *zakāh*; this ruling will be discussed further in connection with the condition of 'freedom'.

68. According to the Hanafis, the *niṣāb* must be present in full both at the beginning and at the end of the year, whether it remains present in full throughout the year or not. Hence, if someone owns a full *niṣāb* at the beginning of the year and if the *niṣāb* remains complete until the end of the year, he must pay *zakāh* on it. Similarly, if the amount diminishes during the year but is back up to the *niṣāb* by the end of the year, *zakāh* must be paid on it. However, if the amount of wealth diminishes during the year and remains less than the *niṣāb* when the year is out, no *zakāh* is to be paid on it. If someone owns a full *niṣāb* at the beginning of the year, then acquires further wealth during the year, the newly acquired wealth is to be added to the original amount and *zakāh* is to be paid on it if the total amount equals a *niṣāb* and if the type of wealth acquired during the year is of the same type as that which the person had at the beginning of the year. Lastly, the Hanafis hold that the stipulation that a whole year must pass since one acquired one's wealth applies only to types of wealth other than cultivated land and produce; in the case of cultivated land and its produce, this stipulation does not apply.

* * *

The Malikis hold that in order for *zakāh* to be required, an entire year must pass since one's acquisition of wealth other than minerals (*ma'dan*), *rikāz* and cultivated land and its produce. As for the three types of wealth just mentioned, *zakāh* must be paid on them even if one has not had them for an entire year, as will be seen in the discussion below of each of these three types. If someone owns enough silver or gold at the beginning of the year to be liable to pay *zakāh* on it, after which the amount of gold or silver diminishes, and if he makes sufficient profit on it to bring the amount back up to the *niṣāb* by the end of the year, he must pay *zakāh* on it; the reason for this is that profit gained on a certain amount of capital is considered to have been owned for the entire year during which the original capital has been owned. Similarly, if someone owns less than the *niṣāb* at the beginning of the year, after which he trades with it and earns sufficient profit to bring it up to the *niṣāb* by the end of the year, he must pay *zakāh* on the entire amount.

* * *

The Hanbalis hold that in order for *zakāh* to be due on a given amount of wealth, one must have had it in one's possession for one year; the same ruling applies if one has had the wealth for one year minus half a day. This same condition is taken into account in connection with the *zakāh* to be paid on money collected on sales, livestock, and commercial goods. In connection with other forms of wealth, however, such as agricultural produce, minerals and buried treasure (*rikāz*), it is not necessary for one to have owned them for an entire year in order to be liable to pay *zakāh* on them. When someone owns a *niṣāb* of a given type of wealth, it is necessary for an entire year (or less than this by half a day) to pass since the time of its acquisition. If someone has less than the *niṣāb* at the beginning of the year, after which he trades with the wealth and earns enough to bring it up to the *niṣāb*, the beginning of the year which must pass before *zakāh* is required on the wealth is calculated from the time when the *niṣāb* was reached, and no *zakāh* is required until an entire year has passed since the *niṣāb* was completed. If, on the other hand, someone owns a full *niṣāb* at the beginning of the year, after which he earns more wealth of the same type by trading with what he has, these earnings are added to what he had to begin with, and he is to pay *zakāh* on the entire amount at the end of the year; the reason for this is that profit which is earned on a certain amount of capital is considered to have been owned for the entire year during which the original capital has been owned provided that the original capital amounted to a *niṣāb*.

* * *

As for the Shafiis, they hold that in order for *zakāh* to be due on one's wealth, one must have owned it for one year and no less; hence, if the year fell short even by a single moment, no *zakāh* would be due on the wealth concerned. However, the requirement that an entire year must have passed since one's acquisition of the wealth does not apply to the *zakāh* due on grains, minerals, *rikāz* and business profit, since *zakāh* on business profit is figured on the basis of the same year which passed since the acquisition of the capital on which the profit was earned provided that the original capital came to a full *niṣāb*. Hence, if someone owns less than the *niṣāb*, after which he earns enough profit to bring it up to the *niṣāb*, the beginning of the required year is calculated from the time when the *niṣāb* is complete. If, on

Freedom, and money's being free of debt

In order for someone to be liable for the payment of *zakāh*, he or she must be free; hence, no *zakāh* is required of someone who is a slave even if he holds a contract of manumission. In addition, the money which the person owns must be free of debt. Hence, if someone has a debt which would deplete the entire *niṣāb* or even merely diminish it, he is not required to pay *zakāh*.[69]

---

the other hand, the *niṣāb* is complete from the beginning of the year, after which it diminishes during the year, after which it becomes complete again [by the end of the year], no *zakāh* is due on it. In other words, the *niṣāb* must be complete from the beginning of the year to the end without interruption in order for its owner to be liable to pay *zakāh* on it.

69. According to the Shafiis, it is not necessary for one's money to be debt-free in order for one to be obliged to pay *zakāh*. Hence, one is still required to pay *zakāh* even if one is in debt, and even if one's debt is equal to the entire *niṣāb*.

* * *

The Hanafis divide debt into three types: (1) Debt which is owed solely to other human beings. (2) Debt which is owed to God Almighty but upon which someone has a claim on behalf of other human beings. An example of this is the debt of *zakāh*, where the party with a claim to it is the imam [the 'imam' here being the figure in a position of religious and political authority, such as the caliph – t.n.], and the types of wealth to which he has a claim are 'evident' wealth (*al-amwāl al-ẓāhirah*), namely, freely grazing livestock and that which grows in the ground; or the claimant might be the imam's proxy, who has a claim to 'hidden' wealth (*al-amwāl al-bāṭinah*), namely, types of wealth relating to commerce, such as gold and silver. The imam's proxy is the proprietor, because until the time of 'Uthmān, may God be pleased with him, the imam used to take this *zakāh*; after this, however, 'Uthmān turned it over to the owners of 'hidden' wealth. (3) Debt which is owed solely to God Almighty, without any claimant upon it on behalf of other human beings. Examples of this type of debt include vows, various sorts of expiation, the charity distributed on the Day of Fastbreaking, expenses relating to the major pilgrimage, etc.

The types of debt that exempt someone from the payment of *zakāh* are types (1) and (2) above. Thus, if someone who owns a *niṣāb* fails to pay *zakāh* after one year has passed since he acquired it, and if a second year then passes, he is not required to pay *zakāh* for the second year because the debt he incurred by not paying *zakāh* the first year will reduce his wealth to less than the *niṣāb*. Similarly, if someone owns wealth and is in debt to someone else, it makes no difference whether the debt is a loan, the price of a purchase, etc., or whether it is in the form of cash, something which is measured or weighed, an animal, or anything else. Moreover, the aforementioned debt exempts one from having to pay *zakāh* of all types with the exception of *zakāh* on agricultural land and on produce (the tithe, or *'ushr* and the land tax, or *kharāj*).

As for the third type of debt, it does not exempt one from the payment of *zakāh*.

* * *

Whether *zakāh* must be paid on one's residence, clothing, household furniture and costly gems

Zakāh need not be paid on one's residence, clothing, household furnishings, riding animals, weapons for daily use, or ornamental containers or utensils if they are not made of gold or silver. Nor is *zakāh* due on gems such as pearls, corundum [varieties of which include rubies and sapphires – t.n.], aquamarine (peridot) and the like if they are not owned for purposes of trade; this ruling is agreed upon by all four schools. According to the Shafiis, the Malikis and the Hanbalis, *zakāh* is not due on crafting tools of any kind, regardless of whether their marks are left on the item crafted or not; for the view of the Hanafis, see below.[70] Similarly, the Shafiis, the Malikis and the Hanbalis hold that no *zakāh* is due on books dealing with science and other branches of knowledge unless they are owned for purposes of trade. This ruling applies whether their owner is a scholar or not; for the view of the Hanafis, see below.[71]

The Malikis hold that if someone has a debt that would reduce the amount of the wealth he owns to less than the *niṣāb* and if he does not have enough money to repay the debt over and above the wealth he owes as *zakāh* (and over and above what he requires to meet his basic needs, such as paying for a place to live), he is not required to pay *zakāh* on the wealth he owns. This condition applies only to the *zakāh* due on gold and silver if they are neither 'minerals' (*ma'ādin*) nor *rikāz*. As for livestock and agricultural land and its produce, *zakāh* must be paid on them even if one is in debt; the same applies to minerals and *rikāz*.

* * *

As for the Hanbalis, *zakāh* is not due from someone who has a debt that would diminish or entirely deplete his *niṣāb*. This ruling applies even if the debt involves a kind of wealth other than that which the person owes *zakāh* on and even if it is a debt of *kharāj* (land tax), harvest, or the lease of agricultural land. The presence of a debt exempts one from having to pay *zakāh* on 'hidden' wealth (*al-amwāl al-bāṭinah*) such as cash, the value of commercial goods and minerals, or 'evident' wealth (*al-amwāl al-ẓāhirah*) such as livestock, grains, and agricultural produce. Hence, if someone owns wealth on which he owes *zakāh* and if he is in debt as well, he must first pay the debt, then pay *zakāh* on what remains if it amounts to a *niṣāb*.

70. The Hanafis hold that if the effect of crafting tools remains evident in the thing crafted, as in the case of dying, *zakāh* must be paid on them; otherwise, no *zakāh* is due on them.

71. The Hanafis hold that *zakāh* is due on such books unless their owner is a scholar.

The types of property on which *zakāh* must be paid

There are five types of property on which *zakāh* must be paid: (1) Grazing livestock, which include camels, cattle, sheep and goats. The term "grazing livestock" as used here refers only to domestic animals, as no *zakāh* is due on wild animals, namely, those which are born in the mountains. Hence, if someone owns a number of wild cows or gazelles, he is not required to pay *zakāh* on them. According to the Malikis and the Shafiis, the same exemption applies to animals that have been interbred between wild and domestic animals, whether the mother is domestic or not; for the views of the Hanafis and the Hanbalis, see below.[72] The word 'cattle' as used here includes buffaloes. However, no *zakāh* is due on any other type of animal; hence, none is due on horses, mules, donkeys, cheetahs, marked dogs and the like unless they are owned for purposes of trade, in which case the *zakāh* due on commerce is to be paid. (2) Gold and silver, even if they have not been made into coins. (3) Commercial goods. (4) Minerals and *rikāz*.[73] (5) Cultivated land and its produce.

No *zakāh* is due on anything other than these five types of property.

---

72. The Hanafis hold that in the case of wild-domestic hybrids, whether *zakāh* is due depends on the mother. If the mother is domestic, *zakāh* is due; if the mother is wild, no *zakāh* is due.

* * *

As for the Hanbalis, they hold that *zakāh* is due on both domestic animals and on those which are domestic-wild hybrids.

73. An editor's note on the term *rikāz* reads as follows: "*Rikāz* refers to pieces of gold and silver which come out of the ground and mines. The people of Ḥijāz say that *rikāz* refers to treasures from pre-Islamic times. It has also been said that *rikāz* is buried money, especially that which was hoarded by people in pre-Islamic times. Imam Shāfi'ī, may God be pleased with him, has been quoted as saying, 'I have no doubt that *rikāz* refers to [things] buried in pre-Islamic times.'" [t.n.]

Conditions for paying *zakāh* on camels, cattle, goats and sheep, and an explanation of the meaning of "freely grazing livestock"

Zakāh is due on camels, cattle, goats and sheep given the following two conditions: (1) They must be freely grazing rather than livestock which are fed. This ruling is agreed upon by the Shafiis, the Hanafis and the Hanbalis. For the view of the Malikis, see below.[74] As for the term "freely grazing" (*sā'imah*), each school offers its own ruling on its meaning.[75] (2) One must own a particular number of them, that is, a *niṣāb*. If one owns fewer than this number or if the animals are fed rather than being allowed to graze on open pastures, no *zakāh* is due on them.

---

74. The Malikis hold that it is not necessary that sheep, camels, cattle and goats graze freely in order for *zakāh* to be due on them; rather, so long as they amount to a *niṣāb*, *zakāh* must be paid on them regardless of whether they graze freely or are fed, even if they are fed all year round, and whether they perform labor or not.

75. The Hanbalis define the term 'freely grazing' (*sā'imah*) as referring to livestock that grazes on nothing but open pasture for more than half the year. They also stipulate that such livestock must be kept for the purpose of milking, breeding or fattening; hence, if the animals are used for carrying, riding or tilling, no *zakāh* is due on them. If the animals are owned for purposes of trade, the *zakāh* due on commerce must be paid. It is not necessary, however, for the animals to be sent out to pasture; thus, even if they graze of their own accord or are taken to graze by someone who acquired them illegally for the better part of the year without their owner's intending this, *zakāh* must still be paid on them.

* * *

According to the Shafiis, 'freely grazing' refers to those camels, cattle, sheep and goats which are sent out by their acknowledged owner or his proxy to graze on open pasture all year round. The same ruling applies if the pasture on which the animals graze is owned by someone but is of negligent value. In addition, it does no harm for one to feed them a modest amount which they could dispense with without suffering evident harm, such as feeding them for one or two days without intending thereby to stop having them graze freely.

If any of these conditions is unfulfilled, the animals cannot be considered 'freely grazing'. Thus, no *zakāh* will be due on the animals if: (1) they graze of their own accord or are taken out to graze by someone other than their owner or his proxy; (2) they are fed enough that they could not live without it; (3) they are fed an amount that they could live without, but not without suffering evident harm; (4) they have been fed something which, although they could live without it without suffering evident harm, has been fed to them in order to stop them from continuing to graze freely; or (5) they are inherited by someone who does not realize that their ownership has been transferred to him. Nor is *zakāh* due on animals which, although they are 'freely grazing', are kept in order to perform labor.

* * *

The Hanafis define the term 'freely grazing' as referring to camels, cattle, sheep and goats which are sent out by their owner to graze on uncultivated land for most of the year for purposes of milking, breeding, or fattening (fattening, that is, in order to strengthen the animal rather than to prepare it for slaughter). If the animals' owner sends them out to graze in order to prepare them for slaughter, to carry merchandise or riders, or to till the earth, no *zakāh* is due on them. If, on the other hand, he sends them out to graze for purposes of trade, he will be obliged to pay the *zakāh* due on commerce (details of which will be explained below). Nor is *zakāh* due on such animals if their owner feeds them for half or more than half the year, or if they graze on their own without their owner's intending them to do so.

* * *

As for the Malikis, they give no definition for the term 'freely grazing' since, as we have seen, they hold that *zakāh* is due on all such animals whether they are 'freely grazing' or not.

How much must be offered by way of *zakāh* on camels

The first *niṣāb* for camels is five. If there are five camels, the *zakāh* due on them is one sheep or goat, as will be explained further below. For each additional five camels, the *zakāh* due is one sheep or goat, up to twenty camels; hence, if one owns twenty camels, the *zakāh* due will be four goats or sheep. If the number of camels comes to twenty-five, the *zakāh* due on them is one camel between one and two years old. If the number of camels comes to 36, the *zakāh* due on them is a camel between two and three years old. If the number of camels comes to 46, the *zakāh* due is a camel between three and four years old. If the number of camels comes to 61, the *zakāh* due on them is a camel between four and five years old. The Shafiis, the Malikis and the Hanafis agree on the stipulation that the camel must not be one, two or three years old exactly but rather, *between* one and two years old, *between* two and three years old, *between* three and four years old, etc. The Hanbalis, on the other hand, stipulate simply that the animal must have reached the specified age (one year, two years, and so on). If the number of camels comes to 76, the *zakāh* due on them is two camels between two and three years old. If the number of camels comes to 91, the *zakāh* due is two camels between three and four years old. If the number of camels comes to 121, the *zakāh* due on them is three camels between two and three years old according to the Shafiis and the Hanbalis; for the views of the Malikis and the Hanafis, see below.[76]

---

76. The Malikis hold that if the number of camels is between 121 and 129, the *zakāh* collector is given a choice between taking three she-camels between two and three years old or two she-camels between three and four years old if both types are found in the owner's flocks, or if neither type is found [in which case, the *zakāh* collector may presumably insist that the owner purchase one of the two types to offer as *zakāh* – t.n.]. If only one of these two types is available, the *zakāh* must be taken from this type, and the owner of the animals is exempted from paying the *zakāh* out of the missing type if the *zakāh* collector believes this to be most appropriate.

* * *

The Hanafis hold that if the number of camels exceeds 120, the calculation of the *zakāh* must begin all over again, with the *zakāh* on this excess being figured in the same way as it was on the first *niṣāb*. Hence, for every five camels over and above the original *niṣāb*, the *zakāh* due is one sheep or goat along with the two she-camels between three and four years old; this applies up to 145 camels, at which point the *zakāh* due is two she-camels between three and four years old and one she-camel between one and two years old. If the person has 150 camels, the *zakāh* due is three she-camels between three and four years old; for every five camels over and above 150, the *zakāh* due is one sheep or goat up to 174 camels. The *zakāh* due on 175 camels is three she-camels between three and four years old and one she-camel between one and two years old; on 186 camels, the *zakāh* due is three she-camels between three and four years old and one she-camel between two and three years old. On 196 camels, the *zakāh* due is four she-camels between three and four years old up to 200 camels. When the owner has 200 camels, he is given the choice

If the number of camels comes to 130, there is a change in what is due. Specifically, for every 40 camels, the *zakāh* due is one camel between two and three years old; for every 50 camels, the *zakāh* due is one camel between three and four years old. For every 130 camels, the *zakāh* due is two camels between two and three years old and one camel between three and four years old; on 140 camels, the *zakāh* due is two camels between three and four years old and one camel between two and three years old; on 150 camels, the *zakāh* due is three camels between three and four years old. Hence, the numbers increase by increments of ten.

Moreover, between each two *niṣābs* there is a certain number which is exempted from *zakāh*; it may be seen, for example, that on five camels, the *zakāh* due is one sheep or goat, while on nine camels, the *zakāh* is likewise one sheep or goat. Hence, there is nothing due on the four camels in excess of the basic *niṣāb*.

Lastly, offering a sheep or a goat as *zakāh* on camels is only acceptable given certain detailed conditions as stipulated by the various schools.[77]

---

between paying four she-camels between three and four years old, or five she-camels between two and three years old. At this point, the calculation of the *zakāh* begins yet again just as it did at 150 camels. Hence, for every five camels over and above 200, the *zakāh* due is a sheep or goat in addition to whatever the person already owed, and this continues to apply up to 224 camels. If the person has 225 camels, the *zakāh* owed is one she-camel between one and two years old along with the four she-camels between three and four years old or the five she-camels between two and three years old. This applies up to 236 camels, at which point the *zakāh* owed is a she-camel between two and three years old together with whatever was due on the 200. This applies up to 245 camels; if someone owns 246 camels, the *zakāh* due is five she-camels between three and four years old, and this applies up to 250 camels. If the number of camels exceeds 250, the additional 50 camels are dealt with as described above, and so on.

77. According to the Hanafis, the sheep or goat which is acceptable as *zakāh* on camels must be between one and two years old. Moreover, the sheep or goat must be free of blemishes even if the camels on which *zakāh* is being paid are blemished.

* * *

According to the Hanbalis, a sheep offered as *zakāh* must be at least six months old, while a goat offered as *zakāh* must be at least one year old. Moreover, the sheep or goat must be free of blemishes that would make it unacceptable as a sacrifice. However, if the camels on which *zakāh* is being paid are ill, the value of the sheep or goat being offered as *zakāh* will be reduced in proportion to the difference in value between the camels when they are ill and the value they would have if they were healthy; for example, if someone has five camels which, on account of their illness, are worth 80 Egyptian pounds as opposed to the 100 pounds they would have been worth if they were healthy, this means that the sick camels have lost one-fifth of their original value. Hence, if the sheep or goat paid as *zakāh* on the healthy camels were worth five [pounds, dinars, etc. – t.n.], then the sheep or goat which is paid in *zakāh* on the sick camels should be a healthy animal worth only 4 [pounds, dinars, etc. – t.n.].

* * *

Zakāh on cattle

The first *niṣāb* on cattle is 30 cows; if someone owns this many, the *zakāh* due is either a bull or a cow between one and two years of age. According to the Shafiis and the Malikis, offering a cow is preferable to offering a bull. If the number of cattle comes to 40, the *zakāh* due is a cow between two and three years old. According to the Malikis, the Hanbalis and the Shafiis, only a cow (as opposed to a bull) is acceptable in this instance; for the Hanafis' view on this point, see below.[78]

If the number of cattle exceeds 40, then on every 30 the *zakāh* due is a cow or a bull between one and two years old. On every 40, the *zakāh* due is a cow between two and three years old. On 60 head of cattle, the *zakāh* due is two bulls or two cows between one and two years of age. On 70 head of cattle, the *zakāh* due is a cow between two and three years old and a bull between one and two years old. On 80 head of cattle, the *zakāh* due is two cows between two and three years of age. On 90, the *zakāh* due is three bulls between one and two years old. On 100, the *zakāh* due is a cow between two and three years old and two bulls between one and two years old. On 110, the *zakāh* due is two cows between two and three years of age and one bull between one and two years of age. On 120, the Shafiis, the Hanbalis and the Hanafis hold that the *zakāh* due is either four bulls between one and two years of age or three cows between two and three years of age; for the Malikis' view on this point, see below.[79]

According to the Shafiis, a sheep offered as *zakāh* on camels must be a full year old unless it dropped its front teeth six months after it was born, in which case it is acceptable as *zakāh* even if it is not yet one year old. As for a goat offered as *zakāh* on camels, it must be between two and three years old. Moreover, both sheep and goats offered as *zakāh* must be free of blemishes or defects even if the camels on which they are being offered as *zakāh* are defective.

* * *

As for the Malikis, they hold that the sheep or goat offered as *zakāh* must be a male or a female which is a full year old. When paying the required *zakāh* of either type, the following ruling applies: If there are more sheep in the country than there are goats, the *zakāh* offered should be a sheep, even if the person paying the *zakāh* has more goats than sheep. If, by contrast, there are more goats in the country than there are sheep, the *zakāh* offered should be a goat unless the person paying the *zakāh* volunteers to pay a sheep instead, in which case the *zakāh* collector must accept the sheep. If, on the other hand, there are equal numbers of sheep and goats in the country, the *zakāh* collector is given a choice between taking a sheep or a goat. Moreover, the sheep or goat offered must be free of defects; hence, it is not acceptable to offer a defective animal as *zakāh* unless the *zakāh* collector is of the opinion that the defective animal would be of more benefit to the poor—due to its being more fleshy, for example. Hence, it is permissible to offer such an animal as *zakāh*; however, the owner may not be forced to offer such an animal against his will.

78. According to the Hanafis, either a bull or a cow between two and three years of age may be offered as *zakāh* on 40 head of cattle.

Moreover, the Shafiis, the Malikis and the Hanbalis hold that between each two *niṣābs* there is a certain number which is exempted from *zakāh*; for the Hanafis' view, see below.[80]

Lastly, the Arabic terms rendered here as "a bull or a cow between one and two years old" (Arabic, *tabīʿ* or *tabīʿah*) and "a cow between two and three years old" (Arabic, *musinnah*) are defined in this manner by the Shafiis, the Hanbalis and the Hanafis; for the Malikis' definition of these terms, see below.[81]

Zakāh on sheep and goats

The first *niṣāb* for sheep and goats is 40; if someone owns 40 sheep and goats, the *zakāh* due on them is one sheep or one goat of the age specified above. If all the animals are sheep, the animal offered as *zakāh* must be a sheep, while if they are all goats, the animal offered as *zakāh* must be a goat. If the flock is a mixture of sheep and goats and if there are more of one kind than the other, the animal offered as *zakāh* must be of the predominant kind. If there are equal numbers of sheep and goats in the flock, such as there being 20 sheep and 20 goats, their owner is given a choice between offering a sheep or a goat. This ruling is agreed upon by the Hanafis and the Malikis; for the views of the Hanbalis and the Shafiis, see below.[82]

---

79. The Malikis hold that on 120 head of cattle, the *zakāh* due is four bulls between one and two years old or three cows between two and three years old and that the *zakāh* collector is free to take whichever of the two he chooses if they are both available; this also applies if neither type is available [in which case, the *zakāh* collector may presumably insist on the owner's purchasing one of the two types to offer as *zakāh* – t.n.]. If the owner has only one of the two, the *zakāh* collector must take the one which is available and may not force the owner to purchase the other.

80. The Hanafis hold that there is a number of cattle which are exempted from *zakāh*, but not those between 40 and 60. Rather, their ruling appears to be that *zakāh* must be offered on that which exceeds 40 in the following manner: If there are 41, the *zakāh* due is one-fourth of a tenth of a cow between two and three years old; if there are 42, the *zakāh* due is one-half of a tenth of a cow between two and three years of age, and so on up to 60.

81. The Malikis define a *tabīʿ* as a bull between two and three years old [where a *tabīʿah* would be a cow this age], while they define a *musinnah* as a cow between three and four years old.

82. According to the Shafiis, it is acceptable to offer a sheep as *zakāh* on goats, and vice-versa, so long as their value is taken into consideration. Hence, if someone has nothing but sheep and he wishes to offer a goat which has lost one or more of its front teeth as *zakāh*, this is acceptable on condition that its value is equal to that of a sheep between 8 and 9 months of age.

* * *

As for the Hanbalis, they hold that it is acceptable to offer a goat as *zakāh* on sheep provided that it is one year old; similarly, it is acceptable to offer a sheep as *zakāh* on 40 goats provided that it is no less than 6 months old, as we have seen.

Zakāh on gold and silver

Zakāh must be paid on gold and silver if they amount to a *niṣāb*, the *niṣāb* for gold and silver being 20 *mithqāls* (which is equal to 20 dinars).[83] This ruling is agreed upon by the Shafiis, the Hanafis and the Malikis; for the view of the Hanbalis, see below.[84] In Egyptian currency, the *niṣāb* for gold and silver comes to 11 Egyptian pounds plus one-half, one-fourth and one-eighth of a pound. This comes to 1187.5 Egyptian piasters; the value of this *niṣāb* in English pounds is 12 and one-eighth pounds. The value of this *niṣāb* in 'pintos' comes to 15 ['pintos'] and two-fifths of a fifth of a 'pinto'.[85] In *majars*, it comes to 25 *majars* and eight-ninths of a *majar*. In *bunduqīs*, it comes to 25 and one-half *bunduqīs*.

The person who owns a *niṣāb* of gold in one of these forms must pay one-fourth of one-tenth [2.5 %]. As for the *niṣāb* for silver, it comes to 200 dirhams. In Egyptian riyals, this comes to 26 Egyptian riyals plus nine and two-thirds piasters. In Egyptian piasters, it comes to 529 and two-thirds piasters. If someone owns a *niṣāb* of silver, he is to pay one-fourth of one-tenth of this as *zakāh*.

It makes no difference whether the gold and silver one owns are in the form of coins or not; as for ornaments and jewelry, the rulings on these are detailed below.[86]

---

83. A *mithqāl* is a unit of weight, while a dinar is a type of coin which weighs one *mithqāl*, that is, approximately 4.25 grams [t.n.].

84. According to the Hanbalis, a dinar is smaller than a *mithqāl*; hence, they hold that the *niṣāb* in dinars amounts to 25 dinars, two-sevenths of a dinar and one-ninth of a dinar.

85. I have not been able to locate a definition for this monetary unit. It should also be noted that, with the effects of inflation in virtually all countries of the world, the person wanting to determine what the *niṣāb* for payment of *zakāh* is will, in any case, need to consult local Muslim jurists for a determination of this amount [t.n.].

86. The Malikis hold that in the case of permitted forms of ornamentation, such as a woman's bracelet, the handle of a sword prepared for use in *jihād*, and a man's gold tooth or nose, no *zakāh* is due on them except in the following situations: (1) The object is broken so badly that it may only be restored to its former state by being recast. (2) The object is broken and can be restored to its former state without being recast; however, its owner does not intend to repair it. (3) The object is being kept in anticipation of unforeseen events and catastrophes, not for [daily] use. (4) The object's owner is keeping it for a future wife, a daughter, etc. (5) The object's owner is keeping it as a dowry for someone he wishes to marry, or to whom he wishes to marry his son. (6) The object's owner intends to use it for commercial purposes.

As for ornaments which are disallowed, such as [gold and silver] utensils and kohl jars, *zakāh* must be paid on them without further detail. The determining factor with regard to the *zakāh* owed on ornaments is weight rather than value.

* * *

According to the Hanafis, *zakāh* is due on all ornaments, both men's and women's, whether they are in the form of raw gold or ingots, and whether they are

Zakāh on debts

If someone has given someone else a loan which amounts to a *niṣāb*, if the loan has remained unpaid for an entire year, and if the loan meets the aforementioned conditions, each of the four schools offers its own relevant ruling concerning the payment of *zakāh* thereon.[87]

---

containers or something else. Like the Malikis, the Hanafis employ weight rather than value as their standard for determining the amount of *zakāh* due.

* * *

The Hanbalis hold that no *zakāh* is due on permitted ornaments which are being kept for [everyday] use or for lending to others who would be permitted to use them. If they are not being kept for [everyday] use, *zakāh* must be paid on them if they come to the *niṣāb* in terms of weight. If they amount to the *niṣāb* in terms of value only but not weight, no *zakāh* is due on them. As for ornaments which are forbidden, *zakāh* must be paid on them; thus, for example, *zakāh* must be paid on a gold or silver utensil if it comes to the *niṣāb* in terms of weight. If an ornament is broken and if it can be worn despite its being broken, no *zakāh* is due on it; if it may not be worn due to the break and if its repair requires that it be recast, *zakāh* must be paid on it; if, on the other hand, it does not need to be recast and the owner intends to repair it, no *zakāh* is due on it.

* * *

As for the Shafiis, they hold that no *zakāh* is due on ornaments which are permitted and whose owner has had them for an entire year with the awareness that they are in his possession. If their owner does not realize that he owns them, however, as in the case of someone who inherits some ornaments which amount to a *niṣāb* and has them for a year without knowing that they have passed into his possession, *zakāh* is due on them. As for ornaments which are forbidden, such as gold for a man, *zakāh* must be paid on them; the same applies to a woman's ornaments if they are excessive, as in the case of a woman's anklet if it weighs as much as 200 *mithqāls*. *Zakāh* must be paid on utensils made of gold and silver. *Zakāh* must also be paid on a woman's necklace if it is made from gold and silver coins and if it does not have a loop or clasp made from some other material; if it has a clasp made from some other material [the text reads, 'from the two'; I have rendered it as I have so as to harmonize the latter part of the ruling with the former – t.n.], no *zakāh* is due on it. When calculating *zakāh* on ornaments, it is figured on the basis of weight rather than value. If an ornament breaks, no *zakāh* is due on it if its owner intends to repair it and if its repair does not require it to be recast; otherwise, *zakāh* is due on it.

87. The Hanafis divide debts into three types: (1) 'strong' debts, (2) 'intermediate' debts, and (3) 'weak' debts. A 'strong' debt is a debt that results from borrowing money and from commerce if the person in debt recognizes his indebtedness, even if he is bankrupt. An 'intermediate' debt is a debt that does not result from commerce, such as the price of a residence, the price of clothing one needs if one has sold them, and other things which relate to a person's basic necessities, such as food and drink. A 'weak' debt is one which is in return for something other than money. An example of this type of debt is a dowry, since it is not in place of money

which the husband took from his wife; another example is a debt relating to *khul'*, that is, a divorce at the instance of the wife who pays a compensation to her husband. Hence, if a husband agrees to divorce his wife in return for a monetary compensation and she remains in his debt, this debt was not in return for something which he took from her. Another example of a 'weak' debt is a debt relating to a will or bequest [as, for example, when the deceased willed money to a given individual who, for one reason or another, has not yet collected what was willed to him or her – t.n.].

In the case of 'strong' debts, one is required to pay *zakāh* on them for every 40 dirhams (or their equivalent) which he or she collects of them. Every time someone collects 40 dirhams of such a debt, he or she is to pay one dirham in *zakāh* on this amount. If the sum collected amounts to less than 40 dirhams, no *zakāh* is due on it; this applies whether a smaller amount is received at first—as when someone is paid an initial installment of 30 dirhams, for example, or when someone receives an initial payment of 40 dinars, after which he is paid a smaller installment. In either case, no *zakāh* is due on anything less than a full 40 dirhams, since no *zakāh* is due on fractions of the 40. Suppose, for example, that someone lends someone else 300 dirhams, after which three years pass; after the three years have passed, the lender receives two hundred dirhams in repayment. In this case, he must pay 5 dirhams as *zakāh* for the first year. At this point, there remain 195 dirhams, which are divisible by 40 four times. Out of these four units, which equal 160 dirhams, the lender pays 4 dirhams in *zakāh* for the second year. At this point, 186 dirhams remain [the correct figure would seem to be 191—t.n.], which likewise contain four units of 40 dirhams; hence, the lender pays 4 dirhams in *zakāh* for the third year as well. Beyond this, no more is required of him. In the case of 'strong' debts, the passing of a year is calculated from the time a complete *niṣāb* is owned, not from the time the money is collected. However, there is unanimous agreement that *zakāh* must be paid upon collection. As for 'intermediate' debts, no *zakāh* is due on them unless one has collected of them what amounts to a *niṣāb*. Suppose, for example, that the debt amounts to 500 dirhams and the lender collects 200 dirhams out of the 500; in this situation, he must pay 5 dirhams in *zakāh*, whereas he would not have to pay *zakāh* on anything less than this, as we have seen. 'Intermediate' debts are similar to 'strong' debts with respect to the passing of one year; in other words, the year is calculated from the time the debt was incurred, not from the time the debt is collected, properly speaking. As for 'weak' debts, *zakāh* must be paid on them once enough of them have been collected to amount to a *niṣāb*, provided that an entire year has passed since the time they were collected.

All of the foregoing applies if the person has nothing with which to acquire a *niṣāb* other than the money he has collected of the debt. If, by contrast, the person concerned has other money which amounts to a *niṣāb*, after which he collects part of the money owed him (whether the amount collected is small or large, and regardless of whether the debt in question is 'weak', 'intermediate' or 'strong'), he must add whatever he has collected of the debt to the money he already had, then pay *zakāh* on the total amount. The reason for this is that the money he collects from the outstanding debt in this case is comparable to money he has earned during the year on a given amount of principle since, as we have seen, such money must be added to its principle.

* * *

The Hanbalis hold that *zakāh* must be paid on a debt if it has been clearly established that the debt is owed by the debtor, even if the debtor is bankrupt. However, it is not necessary to pay *zakāh* on the debt until it has been collected; when a debt, or part thereof, is collected, *zakāh* must be paid on it immediately if it amounts to a *niṣāb* either by itself or after having been added to the money which the creditor already owned. Moreover, no *zakāh* is owed on debts unless it has been clearly established that they are owed by the debtor.

* * *

According to the Malikis, if someone owns money due to inheritance, the receipt of a gift, charity, or monetary compensation from a wife who petitioned for a divorce, by having sold some type of goods he had acquired—as when someone sells an item or a piece of real estate—or having received some sort of indemnity or other compensation without having taken actual possession of it, he is not obliged to pay *zakāh* on the debt until he has collected the money and has had it in his possession for one year. For example, if a man inherits money from his father and, for one reason or another, the court appoints someone to safeguard the money for him before he collects it; if, moreover, this money continues to be owed to him for many years, he is not required to pay *zakāh* on it throughout these years even if he has deliberately postponed collecting the money in order to avoid having to pay *zakāh* on it. However, once a year has passed since the day he collected it, he must pay *zakāh* on the money for that year.

If someone has collected money which is now in his hands and he then lends the money to someone else, and if the money remains in the debtor's possession for many years, the lender must pay *zakāh* on this money for only one year unless he deliberately postpones collecting the money he owed in order to avoid having to pay *zakāh* on it. In the latter case, he must pay *zakāh* on the lent money for as many years as he deliberately postpones collecting it. The beginning of the year for which the *zakāh* on such money is to be paid is calculated from the time it came into the person's possession, or from the time when he [last] paid *zakāh* on it if he did so before lending it to someone else. Hence, if someone acquires a certain amount of money and if it remains in his possession for six months, after which he lends it to someone else who keeps it for another six months, the lender must pay *zakāh* for this year since the beginning of the year is calculated from the time when the money became his possession. If, on the other hand, the owner of the money keeps it in his possession for a year, after which he pays *zakāh* on it and lends it out, the beginning of the year is to be calculated from the time when he paid the *zakāh*.

Nevertheless, *zakāh* is only to be paid on the aforementioned debt given the following four conditions: (1) The debt's principle, i.e., that which was originally given to the debtor, must be either currency (gold or silver), or goods intended for trade by a monopolistic merchant (*tājir muḥtakir*). (A monopolistic merchant is one who neither sells nor purchases at the current price but rather, hordes commodities in the hope that prices will rise.) An example of principle consisting of currency is for someone to have 20 pounds and then lend it to someone else. An example of principle consisting of goods intended for trade by a monopolistic merchant is for such a merchant to have some garments for trade, after which he sells the garments for 20 pounds, to be paid a year or more later. If, on the other hand, the debt's principle consists of an article which is being retained for personal use and which one has no intention of selling for a profit—as in the case of someone who obtains a house in order to live in it, after which he sells it for 400 pounds to be paid a year or more later—he is not required to pay *zakāh* on the price of the item until he collects an amount which comes to a *niṣāb* or more and until an entire year has passed since he collected the sum concerned. Once these two conditions are met, the seller is to pay *zakāh* on the amount he has collected, and no more. If the debt's principle consists of goods intended for trade by a regular merchant (*tājir mudīr*) (a regular merchant being one who buys and sells at the current price), he is to pay *zakāh* every year on the unpaid price of the goods by adding it to the value of the other goods in his possession, as well as to the value of the gold and silver he has received from various sales. (Further details concerning *zakāh* on commerce will be presented below.) (2) The lender must have collected part of what is owed him; if none of the debt has been collected, no *zakāh* need be paid on it unless the money has been lend to merchants, as will be seen below. (3) That which is collected must consist of gold or silver. If that which is collected consists of goods such as clothing or wheat, no *zakāh* must be paid on them unless the person sells these goods and an entire year has passed since the time he received the price of the goods. This ruling applies if the merchant concerned is monopolistic; if he is a regular merchant, he is to pay *zakāh* every year on the value of the goods even if he has not sold them. If the owner of the goods is not a merchant but simply acquired the goods for his own use, then sold them out of necessity, he or she is to pay *zakāh* on the goods if a year has passed since the time he collected their price. (4) The money which is collected must amount to at least a *niṣāb*, even if it is not collected all at one time; if the amount collected from the debt is less than a *niṣāb*, the person must already have sufficient gold or silver which he has had for an entire year (or metals, which he may have had for less than a year) which, when placed together with the amount collected, comes to a full *niṣāb*. Thus, if someone collects enough of the debt to amount to a *niṣāb*, he is to pay *zakāh* on it all at once; he should then pay *zakāh* on whatever else he collects later, be it a large or small amount. However, the basis for calculating the year in the future differs from the basis for calculating it in the past; in other words, the year that passes after the collection of the first repayment that amounts to a full *niṣāb* is calculated from the day on which it is collected, whereas the year which passes after the collection of subsequent repayments is calculated from the time at which each of them is received. If, on the other hand, the first repayment amounts to less than a *niṣāb* and the creditor does not have enough money already in his possession to bring it up to a *niṣāb*, he is not to pay *zakāh* until he has collected enough through subsequent repayments to bring the sum up to a full *niṣāb*. Once the sum he has collected comes to a full *niṣāb*, the year on which *zakāh* is to be paid is calculated from the day on which this takes place. The person concerned is then to pay *zakāh* on whatever else he collects, be it a small or large amount, and the year on which *zakāh* is to be paid is calculated from the day of collection.

* * *

Zakāh on banknotes (paper money)

Most scholars of Islamic jurisprudence agree that *zakāh* must be paid on banknotes (i.e., paper money), since they have taken the place of gold and silver in people's financial transactions and because they can easily be exchanged for silver. It would not be reasonable for people to be permitted to own fortunes in the form of banknotes and to be able to exchange them for a *niṣāb* of silver, yet not be required to pay *zakāh* on them. Hence, the Shafiis, the Malikis and the Hanafis agree that *zakāh* must be paid on banknotes, with only the Hanbalis dissenting. For each school's ruling on this matter, see below.[88]

According to the Shafiis, *zakāh* must be paid on a debt if it has been clearly established that it is actually owed and if it is in the form of dirhams, dinars, or goods intended for trade. This ruling applies whether the debt is to be repaid immediately or has been deferred. If the debt consists of livestock or food, such as grapes and dried dates, no *zakāh* need be paid on it. Moreover, the lender is not required to pay *zakāh* on money if he is not able to collect it; once he does become able to collect the debt, he must pay *zakāh* on it for the years which have passed. Moreover, if the materials owed spoil before it becomes possible to collect them, the requirement to pay *zakāh* on them is waived.

88. According to the Shafiis, transactions made with paper money (referred to here as banknotes) are comparable to a draft, or written order of payment, by virtue of which someone owns the value stated on the banknotes in the form of a debt owed him by the bank. The bank, then, is a debtor which acknowledges its indebtedness and which is able and prepared to pay immediately. Whenever the debtor fulfills these specifications, *zakāh* on the debt must be paid immediately and, in accordance with prevailing practice, the absence of verbal affirmation and consent [referring to the agreement voiced by both parties to a contractual arrangement – t.n.] concerning the bank draft does not invalidate it. However, some Shafii imams hold that what is meant by affirmation and consent is every statement or action which conveys a sense of satisfaction, and such satisfaction is present in this situation.

* * *

According to the Hanafis, banknotes (paper money) are comparable to a 'strong' loan. However, they may be exchanged immediately for silver; hence, *zakāh* must be paid on them immediately as well.

* * *

The Malikis hold that although banknotes are promissory notes, they may nevertheless be exchanged immediately for silver. They also take the place of gold in [daily financial] transactions; hence, *zakāh* must be paid on them given the aforementioned conditions.

* * *

As for the Hanbalis, they hold that no *zakāh* is due on banknotes unless they have been exchanged for gold or silver; moreover, the aforementioned conditions relating to *zakāh* must be fulfilled as well.

Zakāh on goods intended for commercial use

Goods intended for commercial use (*'urūḍ al-tijārah*) comprise a category that excludes gold and silver; this exclusion applies regardless of whether the gold and silver have been made into money, such as pounds or riyals, or into other items, such as women's jewelry. The Shafiis, the Hanafis and the Hanbalis agree that gold and silver are never included in the category, "goods intended for commercial use"; however, the Malikis disagree with respect to gold and silver which have not been made into money. Specifically, they hold that if the gold and silver have not been made into money, they are considered goods for commercial use rather than money.

Zakāh must be paid on goods intended for commercial use, such as fabric, iron and the like; hence, anyone who owns a business must pay the required *zakāh*, which is one-fourth of one-tenth, given specific conditions and in accordance with particular details which differ from one school to another.[89]

---

89. The Shafiis hold that *zakāh* must be paid on goods intended for commercial use given the following six conditions: (1) The goods' owner must have come into possession of them through some type of exchange, such as a purchase. If someone purchases goods which he intends to use for commercial purposes, whether he purchased them with cash or on credit, and whether payment was immediate or deferred, he must pay *zakāh* on them in the manner to be described below. If, on the other hand, someone comes into possession of goods without any sort of exchange taking place—as when someone dies and bequeaths goods [originally] intended for commercial purposes to his heirs—the heirs are not required to pay *zakāh* on these goods until they actually dispose of them with the intention of engaging in some type of commerce. (2) The goods' owner must have intended to use them for commercial purposes during the exchange by which he acquired them, either by its being written into the contract or by his having made a statement to this effect during the relevant consultations. If he did not intend to use the goods for commercial purposes in either of these contexts, no *zakāh* is due on them. The intention to engage in commercial activity must be renewed with each new exchange until the capital runs out; once the capital has run out, however, the intention is no longer necessary with every new act, since the ruling applying to commerce still applies to it based on one's prior intention. (3) The owner must not intend simply to keep the money for his own personal benefit rather than trading with it. If someone forms the intention to do this, i.e., simply to keep his money for his personal benefit, calculation of the year on which he would have paid *zakāh* on the money is discontinued, and if he wishes to trade with the money after this, he must renew his intention to do so, and this intention must be accompanied by some act of monetary disposal. (4) One year must have passed since the time when the goods came into their owner's possession. If less than a year has passed since that time, no *zakāh* is due on them unless (a) the price he paid for the goods was cash paid immediately, or, (b) although the cash he paid amounted to less than a *niṣāb*, he nevertheless owns enough other cash to bring it up to the *niṣāb*. In both of these latter cases, *zakāh* must be paid on the goods once a year has passed since their principle, i.e., the cash, came into the owner's possession. (5) The wealth intended for commer-

cial purposes during the year must not have all become cash of the type in terms of which the goods are appraised (based on the explanation to be given below on the manner in which *zakāh* is to be paid on goods) if it amounts to less than a *niṣāb*. If all the wealth has become cash which amounts to less than a *niṣāb*, the year on the basis of which *zakāh* would have been paid on the wealth will be interrupted. If the owner then purchases a commodity for commercial use, its year will be calculated from the time he bought it without consideration for the time that passed prior to this. If, on the other hand, some of the wealth is turned into cash while some of it remains in the form of goods, if the owner sells all of it for a *niṣāb* of cash or for some other good, or if he sells it for a type of currency other than that in terms of which the appraisal is done at the end of the year, the year on the basis of which the *zakāh* is paid will not be interrupted. (6) The value of the goods at the end of the year must amount to a *niṣāb*; hence, the determining factor is what it amounts to at the end of the year, not throughout the entire year or at both ends of the year. If the commercial goods consist of something on which *zakāh* is due, such as freely grazing livestock and produce, the owner must look to see whether he has a *niṣāb* in terms of both the goods' substance and their value. If he does, *zakāh* must be paid on the substance of the goods without regard for their value based on the ruling which applies to freely grazing livestock and produce. If, on the other hand, the owner finds that he has a *niṣāb* in terms of the substance of the goods but not their value, or in terms of their value but not their substance, he should pay *zakāh* on whatever he has a *niṣāb* of, such as the value of his commercial goods or the substance of his freely grazing livestock and produce. The *zakāh* due on goods for commercial use must be paid again every year so long as there remains a complete *niṣāb*. As for the manner in which *zakāh* on such goods is to be paid, it consists in calculating, at the end of the year, the value of the gold and silver with which they were purchased. If the owner purchased the goods with something other than cash, the value of the goods is estimated based on the prevailing currency of the land in which the owner is living. Moreover, the end-of-year appraisal requires two trustworthy witnesses; the reason for this is that the testimony concerned pertains to something's value, and in this type of situation, more than one witness is required. As for the rate of the *zakāh*, it comes to one-fourth of one-tenth.

* * *

The Hanafis hold that *zakāh* is due on goods obtained for commercial purposes given the following four conditions: (1) The value of the goods must come to a *niṣāb* of gold or silver. If the gold and silver are in the form of money, the goods' owner may appraise their value according to whichever of the two he chooses unless, when the appraisal is done, it turns out that when it is done based on gold, it comes to a *niṣāb,* but when it is done based on silver, it falls short, or vice-versa. In this case, the appraisal must be done based on the currency in which the goods amount to a full *niṣāb*. Goods are to be assessed based on their value in the country where they are located; hence, if someone sends commercial goods to another country and if a year passes from the time they were sent abroad, they are to be assessed based on their value in the country to which they have been sent. If someone sends commercial goods to a desert area, they are to be assessed based on their value in the city located nearest the desert area of concern. Moreover, when assessing goods' value, they are to be combined with one another, even if they are of different types. (2) A full year must have passed since the owner came into possession of the goods. The determining factors in terms of whether *zakāh* is due are the beginning and the end of the year, not the time in between. Hence, if someone owns an entire *niṣāb* at the beginning of the year, after which it falls below the *niṣāb* during the year, then comes back up to the *niṣāb* at the end of the year, he must pay *zakāh* on it. If, on the other hand, the person concerned owns less than a *niṣāb* at either the beginning or the end of the year, no *zakāh* is due on it (as was seen in the discussion of conditions associated with *zakāh*). Moreover, if someone has more than a *niṣāb* at the end of the year, he is to pay *zakāh* on the entire amount. (3) The owner of the goods must intend to use them for commercial purposes, and this intention must be accompanied by concrete action consistent with the intention. Hence, if someone purchased an animal for his own use, after which he decided to use it for commercial purposes, the animal would still not be considered a commercial item until its owner had actually undertaken to sell it or hire it out. If someone receives wealth (other than gold or silver money) as a gift or bequest and if he intends to use it for commercial purposes at the time he receives it, this intention will not be valid until he actually acts on it. If someone exchanges one commodity for another which is like it, the intention to use the commodity for commercial purposes will be deemed to apply to the original item and, by extension, to the one which came to replace it as well unless the person forms the conscious intention not to use the replacement for commercial purposes, in which case it will not be considered a commercial item. (4) The property one puts to commercial use must be suited to this purpose. Hence, if someone purchases land owned by Muslims or land whose inhabitants have become Muslims (referred to as *arḍ 'ushriyah*) and cultivates it, or if he buys seeds which he plants, he must pay a tithe (one-tenth, i.e., *'ushr*) on the resulting crops rather than *zakāh*. If someone buys land which is classified as *arḍ 'ushriyah* and does not cultivate it, he must pay *zakāh* on its value. If, on the other hand, someone purchases land which was owned by non-Arabs and which was conquered by force or through a peaceful agreement, though left in the possession of its original owners on the condition that they pay a *kharāj* tax (known as *arḍ kharājiyah*), the buyer is not required to pay *zakāh* on the land even if he does not cultivate it. If someone has livestock for commercial purposes and which he has owned for less than a year, after which he abandons his intention to use them for commercial purposes and intends to let them be freely grazing livestock which he keeps for milking, breeding, etc., the year on the basis of which he would have paid *zakāh* on the livestock as commodities is interrupted, and the calculation of a new year begins from the time he makes them freely grazing livestock. When a year has passed since this transition, he must pay *zakāh* on the livestock themselves based on the aforementioned ruling pertaining to *zakāh* on freely grazing livestock, but he is not required to appraise their value.

If someone trades in gold or silver, he must pay *zakāh* on them based on the aforementioned ruling pertaining to *zakāh* on cash. However, in order for someone to be required to pay *zakāh* on gold or silver, it is not necessary that he intend to use them for commercial purposes. Lastly, if goods intended for commercial purposes remain in someone's possession for a number of years, after which he sells them, he must pay *zakāh* on them for every year that has passed, not for just one year.

* * *

According to the Malikis, *zakāh* must always be paid on goods which are intended for commercial use whether they are owned by a monopolistic merchant or by a regular merchant. *Zakāh* on such goods must be paid given the following five conditions and in a specified manner: (1) The goods in question must be of the type on whose substance no *zakāh* is due, such as clothing and books. If the substance of the goods is something on which *zakāh* is due, such as gold or silver ornaments or livestock (including camels, cattle, sheep and goats), *zakāh* must be paid on them in the manner explained above in connection with *zakāh* on grazing livestock, gold and silver if they amount to a *niṣāb*. If they do not amount to a *niṣāb*, however, *zakāh* must be paid on their value as is done with other goods. (2) The goods must have come into their owner's possession by means of an immediate exchange, such as a purchase or a rental agreement, and not by means of inheritance, a divorce at the wife's instance in which she pays her husband an indemnity, a gift, charity, etc. Suppose that someone acquires something due to such an exchange, after which he intends to put it to commercial use: If he sells it, the calculation of the year on the basis of which *zakāh* is to be paid begins on the day he collects its price, not on the day he initially acquires it. If, on the other hand, he does not sell the good, it is not to be included in the end-of-year appraisal, nor is any *zakāh* due on it even if he is a regular (non-monopolistic) merchant. (3) The owner of the goods must intend to use them for commercial purposes from the time he purchases them, whether he intends to use them for commercial purposes only or, in addition, to use them for his own personal benefit. If, for example, someone purchases a house with the intention of using it for commercial purposes in addition to the intention to rent it or to live in it until he can make a profit by selling it, he is obliged to pay *zakāh* on it in accordance with the details to be presented below on how *zakāh* should be paid on goods. If, on the other hand, someone buys something simply in order to use it and benefit from it personally, or if he purchases it without any intention at all, no *zakāh* is due on it. (4) The price of the item must be either cash or another item which the person acquired through a financial transaction; if, on the other hand, the price of the item is another item which he or she acquired as a gift or by inheritance, for example, no *zakāh* is due on it; however, *zakāh* will be due on it if he sells it after having begun a new *zakāh* year beginning on the day he collected it. (5) The item's owner must sell part or all of it in exchange for a *niṣāb* of gold or silver if he is a monopolistic merchant or, if he is a regular merchant, for any amount of gold or silver, even if no more than a dirham. If the monopolistic merchant does not sell his merchandise for a *niṣāb* of gold and silver or if the regular merchant does not sell his merchandise for any portion thereof, no *zakāh* is due unless the monopolistic merchant has sufficient gold, silver, or other wealth (such as wealth he has acquired through inheritance, for example) to bring it up to a *niṣāb*. If the wealth the monopolistic merchant already had has been in his possession for an entire year (although in the case of metals, it is not necessary for them to have been in his possession for a whole year), he must pay *zakāh* on the total amount.

As for the manner in which *zakāh* is to be paid on goods intended for commercial use, it is as follows: In the case of a monopolistic merchant, he is to pay *zakāh* on the gold and silver money which he received by selling the goods, added to whatever money he already had in his possession; however, he is only to pay *zakāh* on them for a single year, even if the goods remain in his possession for a number of years. As for debts which such a person has in his favor as a result of business transactions, he is not to pay *zakāh* on them until he actually collects them, at which point he is to pay *zakāh* on them for one year only. In the case of a regular merchant, he is to appraise his merchandise once a year, even if its market is sluggish and it has been in his possession for years; he then adds its value to whatever gold and silver money he has and pays *zakāh* on the entire amount. As for the debts which others owe the regular merchant as a result of business transactions, the Malikis rule that if they involve cash which has come due or if they were originally to be paid immediately, and if, in both cases, there is hope that they will be repaid by those who owe them, they are to be added to the foregoing. If the debt consists of goods or deferred cash and if there is hope that it will be repaid, the merchant is to appraise it and add its value to the foregoing, then pay *zakāh* on the total amount. Deferred cash is to be appraised in the following manner: It is first appraised in terms of merchandise, then in terms of the current value of this merchandise in gold and silver. For example, if someone has ten deferred Egyptian pounds he should ask: How many garments could be purchased with these ten deferred pounds? If the answer is five garments, one asks: If these five garments were sold for gold or silver at their current value, how much would the price come to? If the answer to this question is eight pounds, this eight pounds is considered to be the value of the deferred ten pounds. This value is then added to the cash which the merchant already possesses as well as to the value of the goods in his possession. If the total amounts to a *niṣāb*, he is to pay *zakāh* on it; otherwise, no *zakāh* is due. If the debt is owed by someone who is in abject poverty and there is no hope of his repaying it, no *zakāh* is due on the debt unless the creditor actually collects it from the debtor. If he does collect the money, he is to pay *zakāh* on it for one year only. The same ruling applies to a debt resulting from a loan, on which *zakāh* is to be paid for one year only after it has been collected. The beginning of the year on the basis of which *zakāh* is paid by a regular merchant is calculated from the time when he came into possession of the price which he paid for the goods intended for commercial purposes if no *zakāh* has [yet] been calculated on them. If, by contrast, *zakāh* has been calculated on the substance of the goods [as when *zakāh* is calculated, for example, on a herd of livestock – t.n.], the *zakāh* year is calculated to have begun from the time when the merchant came into possession of the principle, or from the time he paid *zakāh* thereon [by adding it to other goods in his possession] if it amounts to less than a *niṣāb*. According to the best attested view, this ruling applies even if the owner becomes a regular merchant after this takes place.

In the case of a monopolistic merchant, the beginning of his *zakāh* year is calculated from the day he comes into possession of the principle or from the day when he pays *zakāh* thereon if he has paid *zakāh* on it; there is unanimous agreement on this ruling. In the case of a regular merchant, he is not required to appraise the containers in which his merchandise is stored or the tools of his trade. If he acts in the capacity of a monopolistic merchant with respect to some goods and as a regular merchant with respect to other goods, he is to figure his *zakāh* as follows: If the amount of merchandise with respect to which he acts as a regular merchant is equal to the amount of merchandise with respect to which he acts as a monopolistic merchant, he is to pay *zakāh* on the former in accordance with the ruling on regular merchants (i.e., by appraising his goods every year), and on the latter in accordance with the ruling on monopolistic merchants (i.e., by paying *zakāh* on the price of the goods after he has collected it, and for one year only). If the owner acts as a monopolistic merchant with respect to most of his merchandise and as a regular merchant with respect to the rest, *zakāh* is to be figured on each type in accordance with the relevant ruling; that is, the goods being dealt with as by a regular merchant are to appraised every year, while *zakāh* on the goods being dealt with as by a monopolistic merchant is only to be paid after the goods are sold and their price has been collected. If, on the other hand, he deals with most of his goods as a regular merchant, all the goods are to be appraised every year. When appraising the goods, moreover, one person suffices for the job; the reason for this is that such an appraisal is not considered a type of testimony but rather, as a type of ruling, and the issuance of a ruling requires only one person.

* * *

As for the Hanbalis, they hold that *zakāh* is due on goods intended for commercial purposes that amount to a *niṣāb* if the following two conditions are met: (1) Their owner must have acquired them by means of his own action, such as a purchase; if he acquired them by some other means, such as inheritance, he is not required to pay *zakāh* on them. (2) The owner of the goods must intend to use them for commercial purposes from the time he acquires them. That is, when he comes into possession of the goods, he must intend to make a profit on them; moreover, this intention must continue to be present throughout the year.

If someone has purchased something to keep for his own benefit, after which he forms the intention to use it for commercial purposes, it will not thereby be considered a commercial item [simply by virtue of this intention] with the exception of jewelry which has been purchased in order to be worn. In other words, if someone initially purchases jewelry in order to wear it, after which he or she decides to use it for commercial purposes, it will become a commercial item merely by his intending it to be so.

Goods intended for commercial use are to be appraised at the end of the year; moreover, the appraisal is to be done in terms of their value in gold or silver depending on which would be more beneficial to the poor. This ruling applies whether it is the currency of the land or not, and whether the value of the goods comes to a *niṣāb* in both gold and silver or in just one of the two. When undertaking the appraisal, no consideration is to be given to the gold or silver with which the goods were purchased in terms of either amount or type. If the amount decreases or increases after the appraisal, this need not be taken into consideration provided that the appraisal was done at the end of the year.

If someone owns a *niṣāb* of freely grazing livestock for commercial purposes, and if he owns them for a full year while intending both to keep them as freely grazing livestock and to use them for commercial purposes, he must pay *zakāh* on

Whether *zakāh* is due on the substance of commercial goods or on their value

Zakāh is due on the value of commercial goods and on their substance, and when their appraisal is being done, the two are combined even if they are of different types, such as clothes and copper. Profit which has resulted from trade is to be added during the year to the original wealth owned (the capital), as is wealth which is acquired during the year by means other than trade. For the various schools' rulings on this matter, see below.[90]

---

them in accordance with the rulings on commercial *zakāh* rather than the rulings on *zakāh* on freely grazing livestock. If, on the other hand, he owns freely grazing livestock for commercial purposes for half a year, then abandons his intention to use them for commercial purposes, he is to begin calculating a new year from the time he abandons this intention.

If someone purchases land to cultivate for commercial purposes and if its value comes to a *niṣāb*, or if he purchases land for commercial purposes and plants it in commercial seed, he must pay *zakāh* on all of it based on its value if its value comes to a *niṣāb*.

90. The Hanafis hold that if someone owns a *niṣāb* from the beginning of the year, then makes a profit on it during the year or acquires wealth by some means other than trade, such as inheritance or gifts, both the profit and the other wealth he has acquired are to be added to the *niṣāb* for the year; the owner must then pay *zakāh* on the total amount once he has owned the original *niṣāb* for an entire year. Hence, what determines whether *zakāh* is due in the Hanafis' view is whether the *niṣāb* is present throughout the year, as we have seen.

* * *

The Malikis hold that profit, namely, the wealth that results from trade, is added to its capital, the capital being the money out of which the profit has grown during the year, even if the capital began as less than a *niṣāb*. Thus, if someone had ten dinars in the month of *Muḥarram*, after which he traded with this money until, by the month of Rajab, it had become twenty dinars; and if this amount continued to be present until *Muḥarram* of the following year, its owner would be obliged to pay *zakāh* on the total amount. The reason for this is that profit is viewed as being 'latent' within its capital; hence, it is viewed as existing by the mere fact that its capital exists and, as a consequence, it is always added thereto automatically even if the capital began as less than a *niṣāb*. As for money acquired during the year by means other than trade, such as inheritance or a gift, this is not added to the other wealth one has owned during the year, even if the original wealth owned amounts to a *niṣāb*. Rather, when someone acquires additional wealth by some means other than trade, he begins calculating a new *zakāh* year from the day he acquires it. Suppose, for example, that someone has a *niṣāb* of gold which he acquired in *Muḥarram*, after which he acquires ten dinars in the month of Rajab. When *Muḥarram* of the following year arrives, he is to pay *zakāh* on the *niṣāb* of gold; then when the following Rajab arrives, he should pay *zakāh* on the ten dinars.

With regard to *zakāh* on gold and silver, there is a difference between what is profit and what is not. With regard to *zakāh* on livestock, however, if someone has a *niṣāb* of livestock, after which he acquires more livestock through a purchase or as a gift, whether that which is acquired amounts to a *niṣāb* or not, the acquired livestock are to be added to the original livestock and *zakāh* is to be paid on the total number at the end of the year. If the livestock which is owned initially does not amount to a *niṣāb*, livestock acquired later is not to be added to it even if the latter amounts to a *niṣāb*; rather, a new *zakāh* year is calculated from the day on which the additional livestock is acquired. However, if the additional livestock results from one's animals' giving birth to offspring, the offspring are counted as part of the livestock which was owned from the beginning of the year even if the mothers amount to less than a *niṣāb*, since their offspring are considered to have been latent in their source.

* * *

According to the Shafiis, profit is added to its capital as the *zakāh* year progresses; so also is the wealth which the person owned from the beginning of the trade year, even if the capital amounts to less than a *niṣāb*. In the case of wealth acquired by means other than trade, a new *zakāh* year is calculated from the day it is acquired; this wealth is not to be added to the wealth gained through trade during the year unless it consists of fruit borne by a tree which is owned for commercial purposes or the offspring of animals owned for similar purposes, in which case it should be added to what has been owned since the beginning of the year.

* * *

As for the Hanbalis, they hold that profit is to be added to its capital during the year if the capital amounts to a *niṣāb*. If the capital comes to less than a *niṣāb*, profit is not to be added to it [based on the *zakāh* year which began with the acquisition of the capital]; rather, a new *zakāh* year is to be calculated from the time at which the total amounts to an entire *niṣāb*. As for wealth that is acquired by means other than trade, it is not to be added to the wealth that was owned earlier in the year; rather, a new *zakāh* year is calculated from the time it is acquired. However, if freely grazing livestock produce offspring, the *zakāh* year for the offspring is coterminous with the *zakāh* year for their mothers.

Zakāh on gold and silver which are mixed [with other metals]

If gold and silver are mixed with some other substance such as copper or nickel, no *zakāh* is due on them unless the amount of pure gold or silver which they contain amounts to a full *niṣāb*. According to the Shafiis and the Hanbalis, this ruling applies whether the percentage of gold or silver in the mixture is greater or smaller than that of the other material. For the views of the Hanafis and the Malikis, see below.[91]

Metals (*ma'ādin*) and *rikāz*

Each of the four schools offers its own definition of the Arabic term *ma'ādin* (rendered here as metals) as well as its own rulings thereon.[92]

---

91. The Hanafis hold that when dealing with adulterated gold and silver, the *zakāh* paid on it depends on which substance is predominant in the mixture, be it gold, silver, or some other substance. If, for example, gold is mixed with silver and the percentage of gold is greater than the percentage of silver, *zakāh* is to be paid on it as though it were all gold, whereas if the percentage of silver is greater than the percentage of gold, *zakāh* is to be paid on it as if it were pure silver; however, no *zakāh* is due on it unless it amounts to a *niṣāb*. In a case in which the greater part of the mixture is copper, the Hanafis' ruling is that if its use is as widespread as that of money and if its value amounts to a *niṣāb*, *zakāh* is to be paid on it as though it were money. Similarly, *zakāh* is to be paid on it as though it were money if the amount of pure [copper] which it contains amounts to a *niṣāb*. If its use is not as widespread as that of money and if the amount of copper it contains is less than a *niṣāb*, the Hanafis rule that if its owner intends to use it for commercial purposes, it is to be treated like goods owned for commercial purposes; in other words, it should be appraised, then *zakāh* should be paid on its value. Otherwise, no *zakāh* is due on it.

* * *

As for the Malikis, they hold that if the use of gold and silver which have been mixed with other substances is as widespread as that of unadulterated gold and silver, *zakāh* must be paid on the former just as it is on the latter. Otherwise, they rule that if the amount of pure gold or silver in the mixture amounts to a *niṣāb*, *zakāh* is to be paid on it; if it does not, however, no *zakāh* is due.

92. The Hanafis hold that minerals/metals (*al-ma'dan*) and *rikāz* refer to the same thing; in other words, they are both, legally speaking, wealth which has been found under the ground, be it naturally occurring metals (metals God Almighty has created under the ground without any human being placing them there), or a treasure which was buried by non-Muslims. However, what is paid on *ma'dan* and *rikāz* is not referred to as *zakāh*, properly speaking, because the conditions which apply to *zakāh* do not apply to these two categories.

Ma'dan is divided into three types: (1) that which becomes malleable when exposed to fire, (2) that which is liquescent, and (3) that which is neither rendered malleable by fire nor liquescent. Type (1) includes things such as gold, silver, copper, lead and iron. Type (2) includes pitch (tar), petroleum, natural gas and the like. As for Type (3), it includes limestone, gems, and precious stones such as corundum, rubies, sapphires and topaz. When what is found under the ground belongs to Type (1), one must pay one-fifth of it; this one-fifth is to be spent in the same way as the fifth of war booty mentioned in the words of God Almighty, "And know that whatever booty you acquire [in war], one-fifth thereof belongs to God and the Apostle, and the near of kin, and the orphans, and the needy, and the wayfarer..." (8:41). Whatever remains after one-fifth has been set aside belongs to the person who found the metals if they were found on land which is no one's private property, such as desert or mountain territory. Moreover, the one-fifth offering is only due if there is some sign to indicate that what was found was placed there during the pre-Islamic era; if, on the other hand, it was placed there by Muslims, it is to be treated merely as a 'find', in which case the offering of one-fifth is not required. If there is some doubt as to the find's origin, however, it is to be considered pre-Islamic. If it is found on land which is privately owned, the one-fifth offering is required, and the remainder goes to the land's owner, whereas if someone finds such *ma'dan* or *rikāz* in his own home, he is not required to offer one-fifth of it; rather, it is considered to belong the owner of the house. Moreover, when someone finds a treasure or type of *ma'dan*, it makes no difference whether the person is a man or a woman, free or a slave, an adult or a child, a Muslim or a *dhimmī*, i.e., a Christian or a Jew living under Muslim rule.

As for the types of *ma'dan* that are classified as 'liquescent', such as pitch, petroleum and salt, nothing is due on them under any circumstances; the same ruling applies to that which is neither liquescent nor rendered malleable by fire, such as limestone, gems, etc. No offering is due on these; however, the ruling on liquescent substances does not apply to mercury, upon which the one-fifth offering must be paid. 'Treasures' are also considered to include weapons, instruments, furniture, etc. which are found under the ground; hence, the one-fifth offering on them is to be paid. Lastly, nothing is due on substances extracted from the sea, such as ambergris, pearls, coral, fish, etc. unless they are to be put to commercial uses, as we have seen.

* * *

The Malikis hold that *ma'dan* is what God Almighty has created in the ground such as gold, silver, copper, lead, ochre, sulfur, etc.; the Malikis distinguish these from *rikāz*, which will be discussed below. Their ruling on *ma'dan* is that one is obliged to pay *zakāh* thereon if it consists in gold or silver given the conditions for *zakāh* listed above, namely: (1) that the person concerned be free and a Muslim, and (2) that the gold or silver come to a full *niṣāb*. The requirement that the person concerned have owned the wealth for an entire year does not apply here. As for the condition that the person concerned be free and a Muslim, there are two points of view on this [recognized by the Malikis], both of which are valid. When someone acquires a *niṣāb* of gold or silver, whether all at once or in stages, he must pay *zakāh* on it. If there is a single vein [of gold or silver], the person concerned is required to add what he came upon on the second occasion to what he came upon on the first; moreover, *zakāh* must also be paid on whatever is acquired over and above the original *niṣāb*, whether the amount is large or small. If there is more than one vein and if the second vein appears before work on the first has been completed, the two veins are to be treated as one; hence, whatever is extracted from one of them is to be added to what has been extracted from the other and if the total extracted comes to a *niṣāb*, *zakāh* is to be paid on it whereas if it amounts to less than a *niṣāb*, no *zakāh* is due. If the second vein does not appear until after work on the first has been completed, each vein is to be considered separately; hence, if a full *niṣāb* is extracted from either vein separately, *zakāh* is to be paid on it. However, if no *niṣāb* is extracted from either vein, no *zakāh* is to be paid on it even if, when added to what was extracted from the other, it would have come to a full *niṣāb*. Moreover, just as one vein is not to be added to another, neither is one type of *ma'dan* to be added to another; rather, the amount of each type extracted must amount separately to a *niṣāb* [in order for *zakāh* to be due thereon].

The amount of *zakāh* due on *ma'dan* is one-fourth of one-tenth, and it is to be distributed among the eight types of people listed in the Qur'anic verse in which God declares, "The offerings [given] for the sake of God are [meant] only for the poor and the needy, and those who are in charge thereof, and those whose hearts are to be won over, and for the freeing of human beings from bondage, and [for] those who are overburdened with debts, and [for every struggle] in God's cause, and [for] the wayfarer: [this is] an ordinance from God—and God is all-knowing, wise" (9:60).

An exception to this ruling is made for what is referred to as a 'rarity' (*nudrah*), namely, a piece of pure gold or silver which is easily removed from the soil. On this, an offering of one-fifth is required and it is to be spent in the same manner as spoils of war, i.e., to serve the general benefit of the Muslim community. This [one-fifth offering] is not designated specifically for the eight categories listed in the Qur'anic passage quoted, whether what is extracted amounts to a *niṣāb* or not. The one-fifth offering is only required on a 'rarity' if the person who extracted it from the ground did not have to bear major expenses or engage in a great deal of labor in order to extract it; if he did, only one-fourth of one-tenth is required rather than a full fifth. This one-fourth of one-tenth is to be spent in the same manner as *zakāh* offerings even if the 'rarity' did not amount to a *niṣāb* and even if the person who extracted it from the ground is a slave or a non-Muslim.

As for metals other than gold and silver, such as copper and tin, no *zakāh* is due on them unless they are treated as goods intended for commercial purposes, in which case the detailed rulings on *zakāh* on commercial goods are to be adhered to.

As for *rikāz*, it refers to gold, silver or other substances which were buried in the ground in pre-Islamic times, then found (and which are known to date back to pre-Islamic times by some sign associated with the materials themselves). If there is some uncertainty as to whether the materials were buried during pre-Islamic times or not, it is to be assumed that they were buried in pre-Islamic times. When *rikāz* is found, one-fifth of it is due as an offering; this ruling applies whether it consists of gold, silver or something else, and whether it was found by a Muslim or a non-Muslim, a free person or a slave. The one-fifth offering from the *rikāz* is to be treated in the same way as spoils of war—i.e., it is to be spent on the public welfare—unless it required a great deal of work or major expense to obtain the *rikāz*, in which case the offering required is only one-fourth of one-tenth rather than one-fifth. Lastly, this offering is to be spent in the same way as *zakāh* offerings are.

In neither case described above [that is, whether the offering is one-fifth or one-fourth of one-tenth of the *rikāz*], the *rikāz* must amount to an entire *niṣāb*. After the required amount has been set aside, the remainder of the *rikāz* goes to the owner of the land on which it was found if he acquired the land by inheritance or by virtue of having revitalized it. If the land's current owner acquired the land through a purchase or as a gift, for example, the remainder goes to its original owner, that is, the person who sold it to him or, if the land is no one's property, the remainder goes to the person who found it.

As for *rikāz* which was buried by Muslims or by *ahl al-dhimmah* (Christians and/or Jews living under Muslim rule), it will belong to its owner or his heirs once they have been identified. If its rightful owner is not identified, the *rikāz* is to be treated like a mere 'find' which is considered to be public property. In this latter case, it goes to the person who found it unless there is evidence to indicate that it was buried so long ago that its original owners and their heirs can no longer be identified. In a situation such as this, the buried materials are considered the property of owners who are unknown; hence, they are to be placed in the public treasury and spent on the public welfare.

The same ruling that applies to materials buried in pre-Islamic times applies likewise to wealth which dates back to pre-Islamic times and which is found on top of the ground or on the seashore. One-fifth of such materials are to be offered up, while the rest belongs to the person who found them. As for materials which come out of the sea, such as ambergris, pearls, coral, and *yusr* [I was unable to find a meaning for this term that bore any relation to the present context – t.n.], no offering is due on them; rather, they go to whoever found them unless it is discovered that they belonged previously to someone in pre-Islamic times or to someone else. If such a discovery is made, the materials found in the sea will be treated either as *rikāz* or as a 'find' based on the guidelines presented above.

* * *

According to the Hanbalis, the term *ma'dan* includes everything which has been produced by the earth and which is, nevertheless, distinct from it. Such a substance might be solid, such as gold, silver, crystal, agate, copper, antimony, etc., or liquescent, such as arsenic, petroleum, etc. Whoever extracts such materials from the ground and takes possession of them must pay one-tenth of what he has acquired given the following two conditions: (1) In the case of gold or silver, it must amount to a *niṣāb* after having been purified and cast; if it is something other than gold and silver, its value must amount to a *niṣāb*. (2) The person who extracted the material must be someone from whom *zakāh* is due; in other words, he or she must not be a Christian or a Jew living under Muslim rule, some other non-Muslim, or someone in debt.

If the *ma'dan* is solid or if it has been extracted from land which is privately owned, it goes to the land's proprietor even if was extracted by someone else, since ownership of the *ma'dan* goes automatically to the land's proprietor by virtue of his ownership of the land on which it was found. However, he is not required to pay *zakāh* on it unless it actually comes into his possession. It is not permissible to add one type of *ma'dan* to another in order to bring the total amount up to a *niṣāb* unless the two types concerned are gold and silver, in which case it is permissible to add them together in order to come out with a complete *niṣāb*.

If the land on which *ma'dan* is found is not privately owned, it becomes the property of whoever extracted it. In such a case, the person who extracted it must pay *zakāh* on it (one-fourth of one-tenth) whether it is gold, silver, a weapon, clothing, or anything else belonging to this category. However, if someone finds musk or civet, or if he extracts pearls, coral, fish, etc. from the sea, he is not required to pay *zakāh* on it even if it comes to a *niṣāb*.

As for *rikāz*, it refers to materials which were buried during the pre-Islamic era or by non-Muslims. This category also includes materials which are found on top of the ground and which bear some sign that they were placed or left there by non-Muslims. If, on the other hand, they bear some sign that they were placed or left there by Muslims, or if they bear signs which indicate that they may have come from either Muslims or non-Muslims, they are to be considered a 'find' and dealt with based on the rulings that apply thereto. When someone finds *rikāz*, he is to pay one-fifth of it to the public treasury, after which the religious and political ruler or his proxy is to spend it on that which serves the public welfare. As for the remainder of the *rikāz*, it belongs to the person who found it if it was found on publicly owned land or on his own land. If someone finds *rikāz* on someone else's land, it likewise belongs to him if the land's proprietor puts forward no claim to it. If the land's proprietor makes a claim to the *rikāz* without providing evidence or a description, it still goes to him if he takes an oath to the effect that it is his. If the person who finds the *rikāz* does so while trespassing on the land, it belongs to those who own the land; however, if he entered the land and worked there by its owner's permission, he is considered to be more entitled to the *rikāz* than the land's proprietor.

* * *

As for the Shafiis, they define *ma'dan* as that which is extracted from a place where God Almighty created it; specifically, it refers here to gold and silver. As for other metals, such as iron, copper, lead, and others, no *zakāh* is due on them if they are thus extracted. In this respect, no distinction is made among different *ma'dan*-like materials based on whether they are solid, liquescent, rendered malleable by fire, or otherwise. One-fourth of one-tenth is the *zakāh* due on gold and silver, except that it is not necessary that one own them for an entire year before doing so in this case [i.e., in cases where they are extracted from the ground]. One other condition which applies here, however, is that the *ma'dan* must be found on land which either belongs to the person or the use of which has been granted to him; otherwise, no *zakāh* is due on it unless it was found on land which has been set aside as a religious endowment for the benefit of a specified individual or group and was found there after the religious endowment went into effect; in this latter situation, *zakāh* must be paid on it. It is not necessary that *ma'dan* which has been extracted come to a *niṣāb* all at once; rather, if it only comes to a *niṣāb* after several separate extractions, each one is to be added to what preceded it, after which *zakāh* is to be paid on the total amount even if one no longer owns what he extracted at the beginning. This ruling applies provided that all the *ma'dan* concerned is of a single type and that the extraction work is ongoing (or, if it is not ongoing, that it have been interrupted for a legitimate reason, such as illness). No *zakāh* is due on what was first extracted if it does not come to a *niṣāb*; however, it is to be added to what

Zakāh on agricultural produce and fruits

The obligation to pay *zakāh* on agricultural produce and fruits has been established not only on the basis of general evidence but, in addition, on the basis of specific texts from the Qur'ān and the Sunnah. God Almighty says, "Eat of their fruit when it comes to fruition, and give [unto the poor] their due on harvest day" (6:141). The Prophet stated, "That which has been watered by the heavens [i.e., that which has grown without irrigation – t.n.], one-tenth thereof is due. As for that which has been watered by means of a pail or a waterwheel, one-half of one-tenth thereof is due." This prophetic hadith provides a more specific explanation of what is stated in general terms by the Qur'anic verse just quoted.

As for the conditions associated with these offerings, they are the same as those associated with *zakāh* in general, and which have been listed previously. In addition, however, the offerings on agricultural produce and fruits have other conditions associated with them as well as specific rulings relating thereto.[93]

---

was extracted second. If the total amount then comes to a *niṣāb*, *zakāh* is due on the second only and is to be paid when the *ma'dan* has been extracted and purified; if its owner pays the *zakāh* before it has been purified, it will have no validity.

As for *rikāz*, it refers to things which were buried during the pre-Islamic era. One-fifth of such materials are to be offered immediately based on the same conditions which apply to *zakāh*. The only condition which does not apply here is that the owner have had the materials in his possession for an entire year from the time when they came to a *niṣāb*; this exception applies even if he adds the *rikāz* to wealth he already owns, and even if this includes [gold and silver which have] not been made into money.

If someone finds something on top of the ground, it is not classified as *rikāz* but rather, as a 'find'. Moreover, if there is evidence that these materials do not belong to the pre-Islamic era but rather, to Muslims, or if it is not possible to determine whether they are pre- or post-Islamic, they must be restored to their owner or to his heir if his heir can be identified; if such identification is not possible, they are to be considered a 'find'.

Lastly, if *rikāz* is found on privately owned land, it goes to the owner of the land if he puts forward a claim to it. If he makes no such claim, it goes to whichever previous owners [of the land] can be identified.

93. The Hanafis note that the general conditions for the payment of *zakāh* include being in full possession of one's mental faculties, and maturity. Hence, no *zakāh* is due on the wealth owned by a young boy or by someone who is insane. However, these two conditions do not apply to *zakāh* paid on agricultural produce and fruits; as a result, *zakāh* must be paid on these even if they belong to a child or to someone who is not in his right mind. Further conditions associated with *zakāh* on agricultural produce and fruits are as follows: (1) The land concerned must be *'ushriyah*; hence, no *zakāh* is due on the produce of land which is classified as *kharājiyah*. (2) The produce must be a result of cultivation the purpose of which is to make use of and enrich the land. Hence, no *zakāh* is due on things such as firewood, grass, Persian cane, and palm leaves or branches, since the planting of these

does not enrich the land; on other contrary, it depletes it. If, on the other hand, someone cuts such plants and sells them to make a profit, he must pay *zakāh* on their value if they come to a *niṣāb*. It bears noting here that unlike the *kharāj* tax, *zakāh* is due on land only if it is actually cultivated. When a plot of land is arable and when its owner is capable of cultivating it but does not do so, no *zakāh* will be due thereon; however, *kharāj* will be due on the land based on an estimation of its 'enrichment' (*numuw*). In sum, the basis for the imposition of *zakāh* on land is that it is actually being enriched by the crops being produced thereon, whereas *kharāj* is due based either on the land's enrichment or on an estimation thereof.

The ruling on the *zakāh* due on agricultural produce and fruits is that if they are produced by land which has been watered by rainfall or by run-off from drains, ditches and the like, one-tenth of them are due, whereas if they are produced by land which has been watered by means of pails and the like, one-half of one-tenth of them is due. *Zakāh* must be offered on all of the following: wheat, barley, millet, rice, the various types of grains and legumes, sweet basil, roses, sugar cane, watermelon, "Egyptian cucumber", cucumber, eggplant, safflower, figs, grapes, etc. whether they bear fruit all year round or not and whether the amount is large or small. In order for *zakāh* to be due on such produce, it is not necessary that it come to a *niṣāb* or that it have been in one's possession for an entire year.

Zakāh is due on flax and flaxseed, as well as on walnuts, almonds, cumin, coriander, and on the fruits which have been gathered from trees which are not privately owned (such as trees that grow in the mountains). However, no *zakāh* is due on seeds which are only good for planting, such as watermelon seeds, henna seeds, fenugreek seeds, eggplant seeds, etc., nor is it due on that which makes up part of the land, such as date palms and other trees, nor on that which is extracted from trees, such as resin and tar, nor on dried cotton plant stalks used for fuel and the like, nor on bananas. Whatever expenses are entailed by cultivation are to be borne by the farmer; hence, *zakāh* is due on all produce without cultivation-related expenses being deducted therefrom. If a farmer sells his crop before it is ready to be harvested, its *zakāh* must be paid by the purchaser; if it is sold after it has become ready for harvest, it must be paid by the seller. *Zakāh* comes due on produce at the time when the fruits appear and one can be assured that they will not spoil; the *zakāh* is then calculated and paid when they are picked.

As for *zakāh* on grains, it is due after the grains have been measured and their impurities removed. If produce spoils or is destroyed by some act or event for which its owner is not responsible, he is exempted from paying *zakāh* on it. If some portion of the produce is destroyed by some cause for which he is not responsible, the amount of *zakāh* from which he is exempted is proportionate to the amount which was destroyed; the same ruling applies if the owner consumes some of the produce out of necessity.

* * *

The Shafiis list, over and above those which have already been mentioned, three conditions which must be met in order for *zakāh* to be due on agricultural produce and fruits: (1) They must be substances which one would consume voluntarily for nourishment, such as wheat, barley, rice, corn, lentils, chickpeas, broad beans and millet; if they are not suitable for consumption, such as fenugreek, caraway, coriander, and flax, no *zakāh* is due on them, and the same ruling applies to substances which are only consumed when one has no other choice, such as lupine [seeds], etc. (2) They must be owned by a specific individual; no *zakāh* is due on that which has been set aside as a religious endowment for the benefit of mosques, properly speaking, since it has no particular owner. Similarly, no *zakāh* is due on date palms in the open desert, since they are not owned by anyone in particular. (3) They must amount to a full *niṣāb* or more.

The only fruits on which *zakāh* is due are grapes and ripe dates. No *zakāh* is due on plums, apricots, walnuts, almonds or figs. When the color of grapes and ripe dates appears, when their skins become tender and they are ready to eat, or when grains and agricultural produce appear to be ready for harvesting, their owner is not permitted to do anything with them (including giving some of them away as charity) until he has paid the *zakāh* due on them. Similarly, he is forbidden to eat green broad beans or crushed wheat or to pay harvesters their wages (even if this is a form of charity) before he has paid the *zakāh* due. (This is the officially recognized view among the Shafiis.)

Moreover, no *zakāh* is due on agricultural produce and fruits unless they amount to a *niṣāb*, a *niṣāb* being equal to five *wasqs*. No *zakāh* is due an any amount less than this; as for that which exceeds it, *zakāh* is figured on it proportionately. One *wasq* is equal to sixty *ṣā'ṣ*, one *ṣā'* is equal to four *mudds*, and one *mudd* is equal to one and one-third *raṭls* by Baghdad measurements; by Egyptian measurements, a *niṣāb* comes to four *irdabbs* and two *kaylahs*. This ruling applies if the grain is free of flour and dirt and has been hulled; if it is the type which is stored in its hull, such as rice barley, or if it contains impurities such as flour and dirt, only that which is pure is counted in the calculation of the *niṣāb*. Moreover, the *niṣāb* must consist of one type only; hence, wheat may not be added to barley in order to reach a *niṣāb*, nor may other disparate types be added together for this purpose. Nor may the agricultural produce or fruits from the current year be added to the previous year's produce in order to reach a *niṣāb*. However, if there is more than one harvest in the same year, as happens with summer corn and "Nile corn", the two harvests may be added together since less than an entire year (i.e., 12 lunar months) has intervened between them. The determining factor [in whether *zakāh* has become due] for grains is the harvest, while for fruits, it is their appearance. Similarly in the case of grapes, those which come out early in the year may be added to those which come out later. As for dates which come out more than once during the same year, as when a date palm bears fruit twice in one year, *zakāh* is paid on the first date harvest if it amounts to a *niṣāb*. However, if the first date harvest does not amount to a *niṣāb*, it is not to be added to the second.

As for the amount of *zakāh* which is due, this depends not on the number of waterings but rather, on how long the crop has been alive and growing. Hence, if agricultural crops or fruits have been watered by means of rainfall or from a river without the use of machinery, or if they have soaked up water through their roots as in the case of unirrigated crops, the *zakāh* due on them is one-tenth; if they are watered by means of a waterwheel or a shadoof (a sweep) or with purchased water, the *zakāh* due on them is one-half of one-tenth due to the intensive use of resources involved in their care. If, on the other hand, they have been watered by a combination of both methods, as when half the land has been watered by rainfall while the other half has been watered by means of a waterwheel, the *zakāh* due is three-fourths of one-tenth, even if the number of waterings [given to the respective halves of the land] differed. The reason for this is that the determining factor is not the number of waterings but rather, how long the crops have been alive and growing.

* * *

The Hanbalis hold that *zakāh* is due on agricultural produce and fruits given two conditions (over and above those listed previously): (1) They must be fit for storage. (2) They must amount to a *niṣāb* at the time when *zakāh* is due.

A *niṣāb* in this situation amounts to five *wasqs* after the grain has been hulled or its chaff has been removed, and after dates and leaves have been dried. Five *wasqs* amount to 300 *ṣa'*s, which are equal to 1,428 4/7 Egyptian *raṭls*. Hence, no distinction is made—with respect to what substances *zakāh* is due on—between grains and non-grains, edible and non-edible substances, such as wheat, broad beans, peppergrass seed, radish seed, mustard seed, thyme, potash, and tree leaves which are sought out for specific purposes, such as the leaves of the lotus jujube (Christ's thorn), myrtle, and such as dried dates, raisins, almonds, peanuts, pistachios and hazelnuts. As for jujube and olives, no *zakāh* is due on them; nor is it due on coconut, figs, mulberries and other fruits, sugar cane, turnips, cabbage, onions, radishes, *wars*, indigo, henna, oranges, cotton, flax, saffron or safflower, since these items do not meet condition (1) above. As for *'alas* (a type of wheat which has two or three grains in a single husk) and rice, both of which are stored in their husks, experience has shown that their *niṣāb* while in their husks equals ten *wasqs*. However, it is not permissible to estimate the amounts of other grains while still in their husks, nor is it permissible to pay *zakāh* on them until their impurities have been removed. The standard relied upon in these measures is that which is medium-weight, namely, lentils and wheat. Hence, *zakāh* is due on a light substance which comes to a *niṣāb* by measure if it approaches this weight [i.e., the weight of lentils and wheat] even if it falls somewhat short of it since, in terms of measure, it is like that which is heavy. However, no *zakāh* is due on a heavy substance which comes to a *niṣāb* by weight, but not by measure.

Different batches of a particular type of crop or fruit may be added together in order to bring them up to a *niṣāb* if they were produced during the same year; the same ruling applies to dried dates if they are produced by a tree that bears twice a year.

As for *zakāh* due on agricultural produce and fruits, it comes to one-tenth if the land has been watered by rainfall alone, while it comes to one-half of one-tenth if the land has been watered by mechanical means. If half the land has been watered by means of rainfall while the other half has been watered by mechanical means, the *zakāh* due is three-fourths of one-tenth of its yield. If more than half the land has been watered by means of rainfall while less than half has been watered mechanically, the ruling on the amount of *zakāh* depends on which of the two types of watering was more beneficial to the crops. Lastly, if the proportions of the land which were watered by the respective methods are not known, the amount of *zakāh* due is set at one-tenth to be on the safe side, as it were.

Zakāh on grains is due at the time when they are fit to be harvested and stored, while *zakāh* on fruits is due at the time when they have come out and taken on a pleasant taste. [By paying *zakāh* at this time], their owner ensures that if he destroys or sells them after this, he will have given the poor their due. If the crops are destroyed due to some cause for which their owner bears no responsibility, he is exempted from the obligation to pay *zakāh* so long as they have not been placed on the threshing floor. If they spoil or are destroyed after being placed there, the poor will still have received the *zakāh* due them.

* * *

As for the Malikis, they hold that *zakāh* is due on agricultural produce and fruits when they reach the point where they taste good. Mālik, may God be pleased with him, stated, "When the date palms bloom, when the [fruit on the] grapevines takes on a pleasant flavor, when the olives turn black, or almost so, and when the grains are ready to be rubbed to rid them of their husks and can do without further water, *zakāh* is due on them." Moreover, given that *zakāh* becomes mandatory on crops and fruits when they reach the point where they have a good flavor, then whatever grains are eaten after they have been husked, whatever unripe dates are eaten when they are in the desired state of unripeness, and whatever grapes are eaten after their sweetness has become detectable, are counted, and *zakāh* thereon is to be calculated. Hence, if someone pays the *zakāh* due on such foodstuffs at this time, it will be acceptable. That which is counted as being subject to *zakāh* also includes whatever is blown away by the wind but which, nevertheless, can be gathered again and benefited from or which one might give away, feed to his riding animals, or use as wages for his harvesters or others. As for that which is not counted as being subject to *zakāh*, it includes that which is eaten by birds or locusts, and that which spoils or is otherwise ruined due to heat, cold or some cataclysmic act of God. Nor is any account taken of what is eaten by an animal as it threshes the grain.

In order for *zakāh* to be due on produce, it must amount to a *niṣāb*, i.e. five *wasqs*. This is based on the words of the Prophet, "No charity need be set aside from grains or dates unless they amount to five *wasqs*." The Prophet estimated the *wasq* at sixty *ṣā'*s based on the *ṣā'* which was used in the city of Medina at that time. A *ṣā'* is equal to five and one-third Iraqi *raṭls*; by measure, it is equal to four *mudds* based on the *mudd* used by the Prophet, that is, one-third of a *qadaḥ* by Egyptian standards. Hence, a *ṣā'* comes to one and one-third *qadaḥs*. By Egyptian standards, he estimated the *niṣāb* at four *irdabbs* and one *waybah*. If the *wasqs* concerned are not actually dry, their dry weight is estimated; moreover, inferior quality dates are not counted as part of the *niṣāb*. In the case of crops which are stored without their husks (as in the case of the outer husks of broad beans), *zakāh* is figured on them when they are free of their husks. As for crops that are stored along with their husks, such as whole broad beans [with the inner husks], *zakāh* is figured on them along with their husks.

Zakāh is only due on grains and fruits if they have been planted deliberately; this ruling applies whether the land is *kharājiyah* or not. As for crops which have come up by themselves in the mountains or on publicly owned land, no *zakāh* is due on them, and whoever picks them first has the right of ownership over them.

Zakāh is due on the following types: (1) wheat, (2) barley, (3) *sult* (a type of huskless barley), (4) *'alas* (a type of wheat that has two grains in a single husk, and which is eaten by the inhabitants of Sanaa, Yemen), (5) rice, (6) millet, (7) corn, (8) the seven types of grain which are stored at home and cooked, namely: a) broad beans, b) black-eyed peas or snap beans (*lūbiyā*), c) chickpeas, d) lentils, e) lupine, f) peas, and g) chickling vetch, (9) the four "oil sources", namely: a) olives, b) sesame seeds, c) safflower, and d) red radish seeds, and (10) two types of fruits, namely: a) dates and b) raisins.

No *zakāh* is due on anything other than these unless it has been acquired for commercial purposes, in which case *zakāh* is paid on its value.

The amount of *zakāh* due comes to one-half of one-tenth of grains or dates, or the oil contained by that which contains oil, when the grain comes to a *niṣāb* even if the oil itself does not amount to a *niṣāb*. One-half of one-tenth is due if the crop was watered by means of machinery, whereas if it was watered by means of rainfall or run-off water, one-tenth is due thereon even if the owner bought rainwater from someone else on whose land it fell or spent money in order to bring the water to his land without the use of a lifting device. If the crop was watered both mechanically and by other means, its owner is to take the period of time into consideration; if the time which each of the two types of watering lasted is equal or nearly so, the owner is to pay one-tenth on one-half of the crop, and one-half of one-tenth on the other half, the result being that he pays three-fourths of one-tenth on the total. If one-third (or thereabouts) of the time was taken up by one of the two types of watering, one point of view holds that the amount of *zakāh* due is figured on the basis of the type of watering which was used the majority of the time. According to another point of view, each of the periods of time is to be considered separately. The latter point of view holds that if the crop was watered by means of rainfall during two-thirds of the total time and by mechanical means for the remaining one-third, the owner should pay one-tenth on two-thirds of the crop and one-half of one-tenth on the remaining third of the crop. Based on the former point of view, by contrast, the owner should pay one-tenth on the entire crop.

Different types may be added together in the following manner: The seven types of grain which are stored at home and cooked [and which are listed above] are considered a single type in relation to *zakāh*; hence, they may be added together, and if the total amount comes to a *niṣāb* or more, *zakāh* is due on the entire amount and their owner is to pay *zakāh* on each type in proportion to the amount which he has of the type concerned. Wheat, barley, and *sult* are likewise classified as a single type in relation to *zakāh*; hence, if they come to a *niṣāb* when added together, *zakāh* is due on the total amount, with *zakāh* due on each type in proportion to the amount present of said type. As for the conditions which must be met when adding together the aforementioned types, they are as follows: (1) In order for two types to be added together, the type which is added must have been planted before the type to which it is added is ready to be harvested. (2) The owner of the crops must keep enough grain from the first harvest until the time when *zakāh* is due on the second harvest to ensure a complete *niṣāb* when the two are added together.

As for those items which may not be added together, they include everything remaining of the twenty listed above, such as rice, corn, *'alas*, dried dates and raisins. Each of these types must be treated separately. Hence, if it comes to a *niṣāb* by itself, *zakāh* is due on it; otherwise, it is not. Rice may not be added to corn, for example, nor dried dates to raisins, nor broad beans to wheat, nor lentils to barley. As for items which belong to the same category, such as dates of differing levels of quality, they may be added together; for example, if someone has some dates of good quality and some of poor quality and if the two, when added together, come to a *niṣāb*, he is to pay *zakāh* on the total, paying the amount of *zakāh* which is appropriate to the quantity he has of each type of dates. If someone has a *niṣāb* of dates consisting of high, medium and low quality dates, he should pay his *zakāh* out of the medium quality dates, although it is preferable to pay it out of the superior ones; however, it is not acceptable to pay it out of the poor quality ones either on his own behalf or on behalf of anyone else. If, for example, unripe dates (*balaḥ*) appear ready for consumption based on their yellow or red hue or if grapes appear ready for consumption based on their sweetness, and if their owner needs to eat some of them, sell them or give them away, he should first estimate, with the assistance of a knowledgeable, trustworthy person, the quantity of grapes and dates on the vines and trees if they have both dried enough that the unripe dates have turned into dried dates (*tamr*) and the grapes have turned into raisins. The estimate is to be done one tree at a time, after which he may dispose of his crop however he wishes. If the amount of raisins or dried dates comes to a *niṣāb*, *zakāh* is to be paid on them if they are both of the type that tends to dry out and become hard. Otherwise, the owner should pay the *zakāh* based on their price if he sells them or, if he does not sell them, based on their value. In this latter case, he should pay either one-tenth, or one-half of one-tenth of the price or the value based on the conditions described earlier if, based on the estimate that was done, the [amount of] crop comes to a *niṣāb* (even if it does not come to a *niṣāb* in terms of either its price or its value). The same ruling applies to every type of crop or fruit which tends not to dry up. If the owner does not need to sell or eat any of the crop, he is to pay *zakāh* based on its price if he sells it, or based on its value if he does not sell it. Examples of items to which this ruling applies include *misqāwī* broad beans, the ripe dates and grapes of Egypt, and olives which contain no oil; *zakāh* is to be paid on them based on their price or their value if their quantity comes to a *niṣāb*.

How *zakāh* is to be spent

Zakāh is to be distributed among the eight groups of people who are mentioned in the words of God Almighty, "The offerings [given] for the sake of God are [meant] only for the poor and the needy, and those who are in charge thereof, and those whose hearts are to be won over, and for the freeing of human beings from bondage, and [for] those who are overburdened with debts, and [for every struggle] in God's cause, and [for] the wayfarer: [this is] an ordinance from God—and God is all-knowing, wise" (9:60). Each of the four schools offers its own definition for each of these eight groups, as well as detailed rulings thereon.[94]

---

94. According to the Hanafis, 'the poor' are those who own less than a *niṣāb*, or who own a *niṣāb* which is incomplete because it is depleted by meeting their immediate needs; the same definition applies to those who own numerous *niṣābs* which are incomplete for this reason. Hence, one's ownership of such a *niṣāb* (or such *niṣābs*) does not exclude him from the category of 'the poor' to whom it is permissible to distribute *zakāh*. It is considered preferable, nevertheless, to distribute *zakāh* to those who, though they are poor, are educated as well. As for 'the needy', they are those who have nothing to begin with; hence, they need to beg in order to obtain their daily sustenance and to acquire enough with which to clothe themselves. As a consequence, it is permissible for the needy, unlike the poor, to engage in begging, since the poor have enough for their daily sustenance as well as clothing for their bodies. The third group listed in this Qur'anic verse, namely, "those who are in charge thereof", are those who have been appointed by the imam to collect charity and tithes and who receive according to the amount of work they have performed. Those who are referred to in the verse as being in bondage and in need of being freed are slaves with contracts of manumission. As for the phrase, "those who are overburdened with debts", this refers to people who have debts to pay and who, after repaying their debt, no longer own an entire *niṣāb*. It is considered better to give people in this group the money they need to repay their debts than to give to the poor. The phrase, "every struggle in God's cause" refers to the poor who are cut off [from financial income] due to their going out on expeditions on behalf of God's cause, properly speaking. "The wayfarer" is the stranger who has no access to his own wealth, in whose case it is permissible to distribute *zakāh* to him only to the extent that he needs it. It is preferable, however, for such a person to borrow money in such a situation. As for "those whose hearts are to be won over", they were forbidden to receive *zakāh* during the caliphate of [Abū Bakr] the Righteous.

In order for the payment of *zakāh* to be valid, it must be accompanied by an intention, and this intention must coincide with the act of setting aside that which is due. Someone who owns a *niṣāb* is permitted to distribute *zakāh* to all the types of people mentioned in the verse above, or to only some of them, even down to a single type. If the amount being distributed is less than a *niṣāb*, it is preferable that the owner give it to one type only; if he gives an entire *niṣāb* or more to a single type of person, his *zakāh* will be valid, but he will have done something which is considered undesirable unless the person who merits the *zakāh* is in debt, in which case it is permissible for the money's owner to repay this person's debt through *zakāh* even if the amount required in order to do so comes to more than a *niṣāb*. Similarly, if the person to receive the *zakāh* has a family dependent on him, it is permissible for the owner to give him more than a *niṣāb* in *zakāh*. However, the amount given to such a head of household should be such that when he distributes it among his dependents, each of them receives less than a *niṣāb*. Moreover, in order for the practice of repaying someone's debt with *zakāh* to be valid, the person who is entitled to the *zakāh* must have given instructions for this to be done. Thus, if the owner of some money repays a debt on behalf of someone who is entitled to *zakāh* without instructions to this effect from the latter, his *zakāh* will be invalid, though the debt of the person who received it will be voided.

It is not permissible for someone to give *zakāh* to either an ascendant, such as his father, his grandfather, his great-grandfather, etc., or to a descendent, such as his son, his grandson, his great-grandson, etc. A husband is not permitted to give *zakāh* to his wife even if she has been irrevocably divorced and is in her waiting period following the divorce; nor may a wife give *zakāh* to her husband according to Abū Ḥanīfah. Rather, it is preferable to distribute one's *zakāh* among one's other relatives instead, and to do so based on the following order of preference: brothers, sisters, one's brothers' and sisters' children; maternal uncles, maternal aunts, and their children; followed by one's remaining relatives. It is also permissible for someone to give *zakāh* to those for whose financial support he is responsible provided that he count it [the *zakāh*] as part of this support.

One is not permitted to spend one's *zakāh* on the construction of a mosque or a school, the pilgrimage to Mecca, *jihād* [armed struggle in defense of Islam], road repair, the provision of drinking or irrigation water, [building] an archway, providing grave clothes for a deceased person, or anything which does not involve placing something in the possession of those who qualify to receive *zakāh*. As we have seen, one of the pillars of *zakāh* is that what is given as *zakāh* must be placed in the possession of its recipient.

It is permissible to give *zakāh* to someone who owns less than a *niṣāb* even if he or she is in good health and is earning an income. As for those who own a *niṣāb* consisting of any type of wealth over and above their basic needs, that is, their residence, their furniture, their clothing, their servants, their means of transportation, and their weapon, it is not permissible to give them *zakāh*. It is permissible to give *zakāh* to the older son of a rich man if he is poor; as for his younger son, it is not permissible to give him *zakāh*. *Zakāh* may also be given to the poor wife of a rich man and to an impoverished father even if he has a well-to-do son.

It is deemed undesirable to move *zakāh* from one country to another unless this is done in order to give it to one's relatives or to people who are in greater need of it than the people of one's own country. If *zakāh* is transferred to people other than these two groups, it will still be valid, but the practice is undesirable. However, moving *zakāh* from one location to another is only undesirable if one sets it aside at the time when it is due; if one sets it aside earlier than this, however, it is not undesirable. As for the locale to which *zakāh* is said to belong, it is the place where the wealth itself is, even if the wealth is in one place and its owner is in another. *Zakāh* is to be calculated and set aside in the place where the wealth is located, and if its owner intends to consider what he gives his relatives' children or what he gives to people who have brought him welcome news and the like to be his *zakāh*, it will be valid. Similarly, one's *zakāh* is valid if it consists of what one gives to indigent men and women during the holiday seasons; it is also permissible to give charity other than *zakāh* to a *dhimmī*. *Zakāh* may not be given to descendents of Banū Hāshim, although they may be given other types of voluntary charity and religious bequests.

* * *

The Malikis define as 'poor' someone who owns less wealth than he needs for the year; hence, he may be given *zakāh* even if he owns a *niṣāb* and is required to pay *zakāh* himself on this *niṣāb*. The category 'poor' does not include those for whose financial support someone else is responsible when the responsible person is wealthy enough to provide this support. Hence, it is not permissible for someone to give *zakāh* to his poor father even if he has not actually given him [the father] support, since the father would be able to obtain the support from him by making a legal appeal to the ruler. If, on the other hand, someone is voluntarily providing financial assistance to someone for whom he is not responsible financially [under Islamic law], it is permissible for the person providing such assistance to give *zakāh* to the person receiving it. If someone has a trade or craft by means of which he earns enough to meet his needs, or if he receives a salary, he may not receive *zakāh*. If, on the other hand, his salary is insufficient to meet his needs, he may be given enough *zakāh* to meet the needs which are as yet unmet.

The 'needy' are defined here as those who own nothing at all and who, consequently, are in greater need than the 'poor'. Moreover, there are three conditions which must be met by both the poor and the needy in order for them to be qualified to receive *zakāh*: (1) They must be free, (2) They must be Muslims, and (3) They must not be descendents of Hāshim Ibn 'Abd Manāf and have received what they need from the public treasury; if they have not, they may receive *zakāh* in order that their poverty not cause them harm. As for the descendents of al-Muṭṭalib, Hāshim's brother, they are not considered to be descendents of the Prophet and, as a consequence, they may be given *zakāh*. As for voluntary charity other than *zakāh*, it may be given to the descendents of both Hāshim and others.

The Malikis define "those whose hearts are to be won over" as non-Muslims who are given *zakāh* as a means of attracting them to Islam, even if they are descendents of Hāshim. Some say that this term refers to recent converts to Islam who are given *zakāh* in order to strengthen their faith. Based on the second point of view, the ruling pertaining to this group is still in effect and has not been superceded. As for those who adhere to the former point of view [according to which "those whose hearts are to be won over" are non-Muslims], there is disagreement among them as to whether this ruling still applies or not, and the criterion by which it is decided whether non-Muslims are to be given *zakāh* is that in order for them to qualify for *zakāh*, there must be a need for Muslims to form an alliance with them.

As for "those who are in charge thereof", this phrase refers to people such as *zakāh* collectors, clerks, those who calculate and set aside the amount of *zakāh* due, and those who gather livestock owners in order to receive *zakāh* from them. People who work in capacities such as these are given *zakāh* even if they are wealthy, since they qualify for it not by being poor, but by having worked for it. If they are poor as well, they thus qualify for *zakāh* on two counts, though in order to receive *zakāh* by virtue of their poverty, they must be free, Muslims and non-descendents of Hāshim. Moreover, in order for someone to be appointed to this type of work, he must be known for his integrity and trustworthiness and be well-versed in the rulings pertaining to *zakāh*; hence, neither a non-Muslim, a Muslim not meeting the legal requirements of righteousness, nor someone ignorant of the relevant rulings may be appointed in such a capacity. If the ruler appoints to such a job someone who is a slave or a descendent of the line of Hāshim, his appointment will stand; however, he must be paid not with *zakāh*, but out of the public treasury.

As for the phrase, "for the freeing of human beings from bondage", it refers to the freeing of Muslim slaves by buying them with *zakāh* out of bondage and [as a result of which], the freed slave's allegiance will be to the Muslims. "Those who are overburdened with debts" are those who do not possess sufficient wealth to repay their debts. As a consequence, the debt may be repaid with *zakāh* money even after such a person's death. As stated above, the conditions for such a person's being qualified to receive *zakāh* are that he be (1) free, (2) a Muslim, and (3) not a Hashemite. In addition, the person must not have borrowed money in order to engage in any sort of corruption, such as imbibing in liquor, in which case, the person is not to be given *zakāh* unless he repents. It is also stipulated that the debt be to another human being; if it is a debt to God, such as an obligation to perform some type of expiation, the person may not be given *zakāh* in order to make good on the expiation.

As for someone struggling in the way of God, he is to be given *zakāh* if he is free, a Muslim, and not a Hashemite. If he meets these three conditions, however, he qualifies for *zakāh* even if he is wealthy. Also included in this category is the spy [who works on behalf of the Muslims in war time], even if he is not a Muslim. If the spy is a Muslim, he must be free and a non-Hashemite in order to qualify for *zakāh* whereas if he is a non-Muslim, the only condition is that he be free. It is also permissible to use *zakāh* money to purchase a weapon or a horse for the sake of *jihād*, whereas the horse's expenses are to be taken from the public treasury.

The 'wayfarer' is a foreigner who needs someone to help him return to his homeland and who is a free Muslim and a non-Hashemite who has not undertaken his journey in order to commit some disobedience (as in the case of a highway robber). If the foreigner meets these conditions and if he has not been able to find anyone from whom to borrow what he needs for his journey, he is to be given *zakāh* in order to help him reach home even if he is wealthy in his homeland. If the foreigner fails to meet any of these conditions, however, he is not to be given *zakāh*.

In order for *zakāh* to be valid, the person offering it must intend that this particular amount of his wealth being given away is to be *zakāh*. If this intention is not formed while the wealth is being set aside, it should accompany its distribution. If someone forms this intention while setting aside a given amount of his wealth, this is sufficient. However, if he fails to form any intention at all, the *zakāh* will not be valid.

It is not necessary that one announce that the wealth being received is *zakāh*; in fact, this is undesirable because this could be humiliating to the poor. As for distribution of *zakāh*, this should take place in or near the same location where the *zakāh* is due; it is not permissible to transport the *zakāh* a distance equal to or greater than the distance one must travel in order to be allowed to shorten ritual prayers unless the inhabitants of the location to which the *zakāh* is being transported are in greater need of it than the inhabitants of the location where the *zakāh* came due, in which case one is required to transport most of the *zakāh* to those in greater need and to distribute the lesser amount to local inhabitants. As for the expenses involved in transporting the *zakāh*, they should be taken out of the Muslims' public treasury. If they have no public treasury, the goods which were to be transported should be sold and similar goods then purchased in the locale to which they would have been taken; or, the money for which the original goods were sold may be distributed directly in the other locale based on the public interest.

If the *zakāh* is to be taken out of agricultural produce and fruits, the place where the *zakāh* is due is the place where the produce and fruits were grown and harvested, even if they are not in the country where their owner resides. As for *zakāh* to be paid on livestock, it is due in the place where the livestock are located if there is a *zakāh* collector available; otherwise, it is due wherever their owner is located. Lastly, it is not necessary to distribute *zakāh* among all eight of the groups mentioned in the Qur'anic verse above; rather, it is permissible to give all of it to someone belonging to a single group. However, one may not pay all of the *zakāh* to the person employed in overseeing and distributing the *zakāh* if this exceeds the wages he merits based on the work he has performed.

* * *

The Hanbalis define the 'poor' as someone who either has nothing, or who has less than half of what he needs. They define the 'needy' as someone who has half, or more than half, of what he needs. Both these types are to be given sufficient *zakāh* to meet their needs, along with those of their dependent families, for the period of one year.

The phrase "those who are in charge thereof" refers to all those whose services are required for the collection of *zakāh*, and who are given out of the *zakāh* that which suffices to cover their wages even if they are wealthy. As for "those whose hearts are to be won over", they include chiefs who command obedience in their clans and whose conversion to Islam is hoped for, individuals concerning whom there is reason to fear that they might do others harm, those in whose case it is hoped that their Islamic faith will grow stronger, someone the conversion of whose counterpart [in another clan, for example] is hoped for, or someone whose services are needed in collecting *zakāh* from those who do not pay it. People belonging to this group are to be given *zakāh* in the hope of achieving one of the goals indicated in the aforementioned situations.

The Hanbalis identify those who are to be freed from bondage through *zakāh* as slaves who have contracts of manumission, even before any of the debt resulting from such a contract has come due, and who are to be given sufficient *zakāh* to repay their debts of manumission.

As for "those who are overburdened with debts", the Hanbalis divide them into two groups: (1) Those who have borrowed money in order to bring about a reconciliation among people, and (2) those who have borrowed money in order to assist themselves either in accomplishing a legitimate aim, or in achieving an illegitimate aim of which they have repented. Both groups are to be given enough *zakāh* to repay their debts.

Those struggling "in God's cause" are identified as those who have gone on expeditions [with the aim of *jihād*] if there is no government fund from which to meet their expenses. Such people are to be given whatever they need by way of weapons, horses, food or drink, as well as whatever they need in order to return home. As for the 'wayfarer', the Hanbalis define him as a foreigner who, while traveling in a foreign country—either for a legitimate purpose, or for an illegitimate purpose of which he has repented—has run out of money. Such a person is to be given sufficient *zakāh* to pay his way home even if he has found someone who could lend him the money, and whether he is poor or wealthy.

It is sufficient to pay *zakāh* to just one of the groups mentioned in the Qur'anic verse above. Moreover, it is permissible for a single person to pay *zakāh* to a group of people, or for a group of people to pay *zakāh* to a single individual. However, it is not permissible to distribute *zakāh* in the form of the [monetary] value of what is owed [rather than its substance, such as crops, for example]. It is not permissible to pay *zakāh* to a non-Muslim, to a slave, to someone who is wealthy by virtue of wealth [he has inherited, received as a gift] or money he has earned, or to someone for whose financial support the person paying the *zakāh* is responsible unless the recipient is employed [in connection with the calculation and collection of *zakāh*], is on a military expedition for purposes of *jihād*, belongs to the category of those "whose hearts are to be won over", is a slave with a contract of manumission, is a 'wayfarer' as defined above, or is someone who is in debt due to having borrowed money to bring about reconciliation among people. A wife is not allowed to pay *zakāh* to her husband, nor a husband to his wife, nor is one permitted to pay *zakāh* to a Hashemite. If someone unknowingly gives *zakāh* to someone who is not qualified to receive it, after which he discovers that the recipient was not qualified to receive *zakāh*, the *zakāh* thus paid will not be valid and the person who paid it must take it back. If someone gives *zakāh* to someone whom he has good reason to believe is poor, the *zakāh* will be valid; it will likewise be valid if the giver distributes it among relatives for whose financial support he is not responsible, although it is preferable to distribute all of it among those who are poor. It is permissible to transport *zakāh* away from the place where the wealth is located by a distance less than that which one must travel in order to be allowed to shorten ritual prayers, although it is preferable to distribute it all among the poor of one's own locale; as for transporting the *zakāh* a distance which is equal to [or greater than] that which one must travel in order to shorten ritual prayers, it is forbidden, although the *zakāh* will still be valid.

* * *

The Shafiis define the 'poor' as someone who has no wealth at all and no legitimate source of income, or who has wealth or a legitimate source of income which is less than half of what he needs and who has no one who is financially responsible for him who provides him with all he needs (such as a husband with respect to his wife). Moreover, 'sufficiency' is measured in terms of average life span, namely, 62 years of age unless he has wealth with which to engage in trade. If he does, his profit for each day is considered separately; if his profit every day is less than half of what he needs for that day, he is deemed poor. Similarly if someone exceeds the average life span, the determining factor is each day considered separately. If someone who exceeds this age has wealth or earned income which is insufficient for him for half of the day, he is poor.

The 'needy' is defined by the Shafiis as someone who is able to acquire wealth or a legitimate source of income equal to half or more of what he needs at the age mentioned above. Hence, having a suitable dwelling and clothing (including even garments which are merely for adornment) does not prevent one from being poor and needy. Similarly, a woman may be poor and needy despite the fact that she has jewelry which she customarily needs for adornment. It is possible to be deemed poor and needy despite the fact that one has scholarly books which one needs for purposes of study or reference. Similarly, someone might have an illegitimate source of income, wealth which is two or more *marḥalahs* [64 miles] away, or a debt someone has agreed to repay on a deferred basis, yet still be qualified to receive *zakāh* on the basis of poverty or need.

"Those who are in charge thereof" [i.e., of *zakāh*] are identified by the Shafiis as those who earn an income by engaging in tasks relating to *zakāh*, such as the *zakāh* collector, the person who guards the *zakāh*, and the clerk. However, such workers only receive some of the *zakāh* if the religious and political ruler has distributed it but has allotted them no set wage, in which case they are to be given the same wage as others performing the same task.

As for "those whose hearts are to be won over", they are divided into four groups: (1) newly converted Muslims whose faith is weak and who are given *zakāh* in order to strengthen their faith, (2) Muslim converts who hold positions of honor among their people such that, by giving them *zakāh*, it is hoped that other non-Muslims will embrace Islam as well, (3) Muslims whose faith is strong and who, if they receive *zakāh*, it is hoped will protect the Muslim community from harm by non-Muslims who are under their influence, and (4) those who can protect the Muslim community from the harm that might be done to them by those who prevent others from paying *zakāh*.

Human beings who are to be freed from bondage include slaves with contracts of manumission who are given enough *zakāh* to enable them to pay the installments entailed by their debts of manumission so as to free themselves from slavery. However, such persons are only to receive *zakāh* given the following conditions: (1) The contract of manumission must be valid. (2) The slave must be a Muslim. (3) He must not have enough money to repay his debt. (4) The slave's debt of manumission must not be owed to the person giving the *zakāh*.

As for "those who are overburdened with debt", the Shafiis divide them into the following three groups: (1) Those who have gone into debt in order to bring about reconciliation among parties in dispute, and who are to be given *zakāh* even if they themselves are wealthy. (2) Those who went into debt for their own personal benefit, in order to spend the money either on some legitimate pursuit, or on an illegitimate pursuit of which they have repented. (3) Those who are in debt due to having underwritten someone else with the latter's permission and who, together with the underwritten party, are impoverished. If the person in debt underwrote someone else without the latter's permission, he is to be given *zakāh* when he himself is impoverished, even if the underwritten party is in good financial condition. Those belonging to categories (2) and (3) above are to be given sufficient *zakāh* to repay whatever debt they are unable to repay, whereas those in category (1) are to receive *zakāh* even if they are wealthy.

Those who are struggling in God's cause are identified as those who have volunteered to go out on a *jihād*-related expedition and who receive no share of the allotments set aside for fighters by the government office. Even if they are wealthy, such fighters are to be provided with living quarters and with whatever they need in order to make the journey to and from the battlefield. They are also to be given what they need to cover the expenses of those they support, clothing, and the value of a weapon and a horse; in addition, they are to be provided with something on which to carry their personal articles and their provisions for the journey if they are not accustomed to carrying such things themselves.

As for the wayfarer, he is identified as someone who is traveling out of or passing through the country where the *zakāh* concerned is being distributed. Such a person is to be given sufficient *zakāh* to enable him to reach either his destination or his wealth, if he owns wealth, provided that: (1) he is in need at the time of his departure or at the time when he passes through, (2) he is not being disobedient by traveling, and (3) he is making the journey for some legitimate purpose.

In order for *zakāh* to be given to these eight groups, the following five conditions (over and above the conditions already mentioned in connection with each group separately) must be fulfilled: (1) They must be Muslims. (2) They must be either entirely free or slaves with contracts of manumission. (3) They must not be descendents of Hāshim or al-Muṭṭalib or have been freed from slavery by anyone belonging to either of these two groups. This condition applies even if the people concerned have been denied their right to assistance from the public treasury. However, exceptions are made for those who work as *zakāh* transporters or guards, and who may receive *zakāh* even if they are non-Muslims, slaves, or descendents of the Prophet, since what they receive is considered a wage for the work they have performed. (4) The person distributing the *zakāh* to the group must not be responsible for their financial support. (5) The person who directly receives the *zakāh* must be an adult who conducts himself well and who is in full possession of his mental faculties.

If all eight groups of people mentioned in the Qur'anic verse above are present, all of them should be included in the distribution of *zakāh*, whether the distribution is undertaken by the political and religious authority or by the owner of the money from which the *zakāh* has been taken. However, in the case of the owner, he is not required to include all eight groups unless all of them are present in the country in which he is located, and unless there is sufficient wealth to go around among them. Otherwise, he is to give *zakāh* to three individuals out of each group. If some groups are not present, *zakāh* is to be distributed among the groups that are present, and the owner is to choose a group to which it is permissible to give *zakāh*, even if it is *zakāh* on wealth belonging to a single person. The conscious intention to pay *zakāh* must accompany either the act of giving it to the imam [the religious and political authority] or those who are qualified to receive it, or the act of setting it aside. The

Fast-breaking charity (*ṣadaqat al-fiṭr*)

Fast-breaking charity (that is, the distribution of charity on the Day of Fastbreaking) is obligatory for every free Muslim who is capable of doing so. We were commanded to do so by the Prophet during the same year in which he legislated the fast of Ramaḍān, and before he legislated *zakāh*. He gave instructions to distribute such charity while delivering an address prior to the Day of Fastbreaking. 'Abd al-Razzāq narrates with a sound chain of transmission on the authority of 'Abd Ibn Tha'labah that the Messenger of God delivered a sermon one or two days before the Day of Fastbreaking in which he said, "Bring forth one *ṣā'* of wheat, dried dates or barley for every free person or slave, young or old." For more details on the various schools' rulings on this hadith as well as specific measures, see below.[95]

---

owner of the wealth concerned is not permitted to transport his *zakāh* from one country to another, even if it is nearby, so long as there is someone in the original country who is qualified to receive it. As for the imam, he may transport *zakāh* from one country to another. As for the meaning of "country of origin" where *zakāh* is concerned, it is the country in which the wealth concerned was located throughout the year.

The foregoing applies to types of wealth on which *zakāh* must be paid only if they have been owned for an entire year, such as gold. As for other types of wealth, such as agricultural produce, their *zakāh*'s country of origin is the one in which the *zakāh* came due on the wealth concerned.

95. According to the Hanafis, fast-breaking charity is a 'duty', though not a full religious obligation, given three conditions. Specifically, the giver must: (1) be free, (2) be a Muslim, and (3) own a *niṣāb* which exceeds his or her basic necessities. Unlike *zakāh*, it is not necessary for the *niṣāb* to grow or remain; thus, if someone acquires a *niṣāb* after the time at which the fast-breaking charity is due, then dies before offering it, the obligation to do so is not thereby waived as it would be with *zakāh*. Nor is the fast-breaking charity obligatory only for adults and those in full possession of their mental faculties; rather, it is required also of children and the insane, and if the guardian of a child or an insane person does not pay *zakāh* out of the latter's wealth, he will be guilty of wrongdoing. As for adults and those in full possession of their mental faculties, they must pay the fast-breaking dues to the poor at the time they are due, that is, from dawn on the Day of Fastbreaking. However, if someone pays the fast-breaking charity before or after this time, it will be valid, since the time for doing so is one's entire lifetime; hence, whenever one happens to offer it, it will be 'on time' rather than a compensatory performance of a religious duty that should have been performed at an earlier time. In this respect, payment of fast-breaking charity is similar to all other religious obligations in which there is latitude in terms of when they may be performed. Nevertheless, it is desirable to pay the fast-breaking charity before one has gone out to the site of the holiday prayers on the Day of Fastbreaking. This is based on the saying of the Prophet, "Spare them the necessity of begging on this day."

Whoever is obliged to pay fast-breaking charity must offer it on his own behalf and on behalf of his young sons who are poor, his servants, and his older sons if they are not in full possession of their mental faculties. If an adult son is in full possession of his mental faculties, his father is not obliged to pay the fast-breaking charity on his behalf even if the son is poor; however, he may volunteer to do so. A husband is not obliged to pay fast-breaking charity on behalf of his wife, although if he does so voluntarily, it will be valid even if he does so without her permission.

Fast-breaking charity is offered out of four substances: (1) wheat, (2) barley, (3) dried dates and (4) raisins. In the case of wheat (*ḥinṭah*) the amount due is one-half *ṣā'* per person, where a *ṣā'* equals four *mudds*, a *mudd* equals two *raṭls*, and a *raṭl* is equal to 130 dirhams. By Egyptian measurements, the *ṣā'* is estimated at 2 1/3 *qadaḥs*. The amount of fast-breaking charity due on wheat (*qamḥ*) is 1 1/6 *qadaḥs* per person. One Egyptian measure (*kaylah*) is a sufficient offering on behalf of seven persons if 1/6 *qadaḥ* is added to it. In the case of dried dates, barley and raisins, one full *ṣā'* is due per person. One Egyptian measure (*kaylah*) of these foods is a sufficient offering on behalf of three persons, with one Egyptian *qadaḥ* remaining. It is also permissible to calculate the amount of *zakāh* due based on the substance's value and to offer its value in money instead; in fact, this is viewed as preferable since it is of more benefit to the poor. It is permissible to pay the *zakāh* due on behalf of a group to a single needy person, or to pay the *zakāh* due on behalf of a single person to a number of needy people.

Lastly, fast-breaking charity is to be spent in the same way as general *zakāh* is, namely, by distributing it among the groups of people listed in the verse which reads, "The offerings [given] for the sake of God are [meant] only for the poor and the needy, and those who are in charge thereof, and those whose hearts are to be won over, and for the freeing of human beings from bondage, and [for] those who are overburdened with debts, and [for every struggle] in God's cause, and [for] the wayfarer: [this is] an ordinance from God—and God is all-knowing, wise" (9:60).

* * *

According to the Hanbalis, the fast-breaking *zakāh* becomes obligatory at sundown on the day before the Day of Fastbreaking for every Muslim who has more than enough to meet his own needs and those of his dependent family at this time and throughout the Day of Fastbreaking. In this context, the person's 'needs' include things such as his dwelling, his servants, his mount, his clothing, and his scholarly books. Such a person must pay the fast-breaking charity on behalf of himself and on behalf of all other Muslims for whose sustenance he is responsible. If he does not have enough to pay on behalf of all of them, he should begin with himself, then do so for his wife, his companion, his mother, his father, his children, and so on in the same order that applies to inheritance rights. It is an emulation of the Sunnah to pay the fast-breaking *zakāh* on behalf of an unborn infant as well.

It is considered preferable to pay the fast-breaking *zakāh* on the Day of Fastbreaking itself, before the holiday prayer; it is deemed undesirable to pay it after this. It is forbidden to delay this *zakāh* past the Day of Fastbreaking if the person concerned would have been able to pay it on the very day, and he or she must make it up later. It is acceptable to pay this *zakāh* up to two days before the Day of Fastbreaking, but not before this. When someone is obliged to pay his or her fast-breaking *zakāh*, he or she should pay it in the same place where he or she broke his or her fast on the last day of Ramaḍān; the same applies to someone who was obliged to break his fast in this place.

As for the amounts which are due, they are as follows: Each person is to offer one *ṣāʻ* of wheat, barley, dried dates, raisins or *iqṭ*. It is also acceptable to offer flour if it equals grains in weight; if none of these things is available, one may pay in the form of a foodstuff that would serve as a substitute, such as corn, rice, lentils, and the like. It is permissible for a group to give their fast-breaking *zakāh* to a single person. However, it is not permissible for someone to buy back what he offered as *zakāh*, even if he buys it from someone other than the person who received it from him. Lastly, fast-breaking *zakāh* is to be distributed in the same manner as the obligatory *zakāh*.

* * *

According to the Shafiis, the fast-breaking *zakāh* is obligatory for every Muslim; it is also obligatory for the non-Muslim to distribute fast-breaking *zakāh* on behalf of his Muslim servants and relatives if he is able to provide for his own sustenance and that of his family on the Day of Fastbreaking and the day before after spending whatever he is accustomed to at that time. In other words, he is obliged to pay the fast-breaking *zakāh* if he has enough for himself and his family on these two days over and above the customary items prepared and consumed for the Day of Fastbreaking, such as fish as the like, as well as suitable clothing for himself and his dependents, a suitable dwelling and servants, as well as utensils and books even if he has numerous items of a single type, as well as mounts or other modes of transport which are suitable for himself and his dependents. The fast-breaking *zakāh* is obligatory even if someone is in debt, and the person concerned must pay it on behalf of himself and those for whose financial support he is responsible at the time when it is due.

Those for whom such a person is responsible financially are divided into four groups: (1) One's wife (provided she is not refractory), even if she is well-to-do, revocably divorced, or irrevocably divorced and pregnant if she has no support being allotted to her; the same applies to one's slaves and servants. (2) One's ascendants [such as one's father, grandfather, great-father, etc.]. (3) One's descendants [such as one's sons, daughters, grandchildren, etc.], be they male or female, young or old. However, one is not obliged to pay *zakāh* on behalf of one's ascendants and descendants unless they are poor or needy, even if their poverty is due to their being engaged in the pursuit of knowledge. As for an older descendant who is not engaged in the pursuit of knowledge, he must be incapable of earning a living [in order for *zakāh* to be paid on his behalf]. (4) Those who are 'owned', such as slaves, even if they are fugitives or captives.

The time when this *zakāh* is due is the last part of Ramaḍān and the first part of Shawwāl. It is an emulation of the Sunnah to distribute it on the Day of Fastbreaking between the dawn prayer and the holiday prayer, and it is undesirable to distribute it between the holiday prayer and sundown unless one has a legitimate excuse for doing so, such as needing to wait for the arrival of a poor relative or the like. It is forbidden to distribute it after sundown on the Day of Fastbreaking unless one has a legitimate excuse, such as the absence of those who are qualified to receive it; however, it is not an acceptable excuse in such a case to have to wait for the arrival of a relative or the like. It is also permissible to distribute fast-breaking *zakāh* on any day one chooses after the beginning of Ramaḍān. If one did not distribute it during the month of Ramaḍān in one's own country, one must distribute it in the country in which the sun set during the final days of Ramaḍān. [This presumably means, "in the country where one spent the final days of Ramaḍān." – t.n.]

The amount that must be paid on behalf of each individual is one *ṣā'* (or two *qadaḥs* by Egyptian measures) of the food which is the primary staple of the person on whose behalf it is being distributed. The preferred foodstuffs, in descending order of preference, are: wheat, *sult* ("the Prophet's barley"), barley, corn, rice, chickpeas, lentils, broad beans, dried dates, raisins, *iqt*, milk and cheese. Foods found higher on this list may validly be offered even if they are not more frequently consumed in the country than those found lower on the list, and even if the item lower on the list is the most frequently consumed of all the foods listed. It is not permissible to offer *zakāh* half of which consists of one type of food and half of which consists of some other type, even if the food most commonly consumed is itself a mixture. Nor is it permissible to offer the food's value [in the form of money]. As for someone who is obliged to pay *zakāh* on behalf of an entire group but does not have enough to pay on behalf of every one in the group, he should begin with himself, then pay on behalf of his wife, then his wife's servant, then his younger son, then his father, then his mother, then his older son, then his companion. If some members of the group are equal in status, such as young children, he may choose whichever of them he wishes and pay the *zakāh* on his behalf.

* * *

The Malikis hold that the fast-breaking *zakāh* is obligatory for every free Muslim who is capable of offering it at the time when it is due, whether he actually has the wealth in his possession or is capable of borrowing it. This is because someone who is capable of obtaining a loan is considered capable of paying *zakāh* if he wishes to fulfill this obligation. However, the available wealth must exceed that which he needs for his basic necessities and for those dependent on him for financial support on the Day of Fastbreaking. If he needs the wealth in order to provide the required financial support, he is not obliged to pay the *zakāh*. As for those on whose behalf one is required to pay *zakāh*, they are as follows: oneself and all relatives for whose financial support one is responsible, namely, one's poor parents, one's male children who have no wealth of their own until they reach maturity and become capable of earning an income, as well as one's female children who are poor until they marry or agree to a marriage proposal (provided that they are old enough to tolerate sexual relations), one's male and female slaves, and one's wife or wives, even if they have wealth of their own, as well as one's father's wife if the father is poor.

The amount of *zakāh* due on behalf of every individual is one *ṣā'*, namely, 1 1/3 *qadaḥs* by Egyptian measures. One measure (*kaylah*) is sufficient on behalf of six people. One *ṣā'* must be offered by everyone capable of doing so; however, if someone is able to offer only part of this amount, this is all that is required of him. Out of the nine foods listed below, the *zakāh* must be offered out of the food most widely consumed in the country in which the person making the offering resides. The nine foods referred to here are as follows; (1) wheat, (2) barley, (3) *sult*, (4) corn, (5) millet, (6) rice, (7) dried dates, (8) raisins, and (9) *iqṭ* ([defined here as] dried milk from which the butter has been removed). If the inhabitants of the country concerned eat two of these types of food and if neither is consumed more widely than the other, the person offering the *zakāh* may offer either of the two he prefers. It is not permissible to offer *zakāh* out of some food which is not widely consumed unless it is superior, as in a situation where the people of the land eat barley most of the time, whereas the person offering the *zakāh* gives wheat. As for foods not listed above, such as broad beans and lentils, it is not valid to offer *zakāh* out of them unless the inhabitants of the country eat only these to the exclusion of the nine foods listed above, in which case it is required that one pay one's *zakāh* out of the food actually eaten by the population. If the food concerned is the one most commonly consumed in the country, *zakāh* should be offered out of this, whereas if two foods are consumed with equal frequency, such as broad beans and lentils, *zakāh* may be offered out of either of the two. If *zakāh* is offered in the form of meat, one should consider how much it would take to satisfy the hunger of the person who eats it; if, for example, one *ṣā'* of wheat would satisfy two people after being made into bread, one should offer enough meat to satisfy the same two people. In order for *zakāh* to be offered to one of the groups of people listed in the Qur'anic verse quoted above, the recipient must be poor or needy, and a free Muslim who is not descended from Hāshim. Hence, if someone finds a 'wayfarer' who is neither poor nor needy, *zakāh* is not to be given to him, and so on. It is permissible to give each poor or needy person one *ṣā'* or more or less, though it is preferable to give him or her exactly one *ṣā'*.

Lastly, the following relevant points are to be noted: (1) If the food from which one intends to offer *zakāh* is not clean, the impurities must be removed from it if they represent one-third or more of the total volume; otherwise, it is recommended that it be sifted. (2) It is recommended that *zakāh* be distributed on the Day of Fastbreaking between dawn and the time at which one attends the holiday prayer. It may also be distributed one or two days prior to the Day of Fastbreaking, but not earlier than this based on the officially recognized point of view. (3) If someone is obliged to offer *zakāh* on behalf of several people but is unable to offer it on behalf of all of them, he should begin by offering it on his own behalf, then on behalf of his wife, then his parents, then his children. (4) It is forbidden to postpone one's offering of the fast-breaking *zakāh* past the Day of Fastbreaking itself; however, the obligation to offer it is not waived with the passing of this day. Rather, it continues to be an unfulfilled obligation until the person concerned has offered it on behalf of himself and everyone for whose financial support he is responsible if he was in a comfortable financial condition on the eve of the Day of Fastbreaking. (5) If someone is unable to offer the fast-breaking *zakāh* at the time when it is due and if he becomes able to do so before the Day of Fastbreaking has ended, he is not obliged to offer it, but it is recommended that he do so. (6) If someone is obliged to offer the fast-breaking *zakāh* while on a journey, it is recommended that he offer it on his own behalf. However, he is not obliged to do so if his family is accustomed to offering it on his behalf, or if he has given them instructions to do so. If, on the other hand, his family is not accustomed to offering the fast-breaking *zakāh* on his behalf and/or he has not instructed them to do so, he must offer it on his own behalf. (7) If someone is accustomed to eating a type of food which is lower on the list of preferences presented above rather than what is eaten by the majority of the country's population (for example, if he is accustomed to eating barley rather than wheat), and if he usually eats this food due to his poverty, he may offer his *zakāh* out of this same food on behalf of himself and those for whose support he is responsible and it will be valid. However, if he eats, for example, barley rather than wheat simply because the latter is in short supply or for some other reason, it is not acceptable for him to offer his *zakāh* from barley rather than wheat; instead, he must offer it out of the food that is highest on the aforementioned list of preferences. (8) It is permissible to offer one's fast-breaking *zakāh* in the form of flour or *sawīq* by measure, that is, 1 1/3 *qadaḥs*, and in the form of bread by weight, estimated at two *raṭls* by Egyptian measures.

On the *Ḥajj*

On the *Ḥajj,* or Greater Pilgrimage

Its definition

The word rendered here as "greater pilgrimage" (*ḥajj*) is defined, in terms of ordinary language use, as a journey toward something which is highly venerated. As used in the realm of Islamic jurisprudence, the word *ḥajj* refers to specific actions which are performed at a particular time and place and in a specified manner.

Rulings on the *ḥajj* and the evidence in its support

The *ḥajj* is obligatory once in a lifetime for every individual Muslim, male and female, given the conditions to be explained below. The necessity of the performance of the *ḥajj* has been established based on the Qur'ān, the Sunnah, and the consensus of the Muslim community. The evidence supporting it in the Qur'ān consists in the words of God Almighty, "Hence, pilgrimage unto the Temple is a duty owed to God by all people who are able to undertake it…" (3:97). As for evidence for the *ḥajj* in the Sunnah, it is found in the words of the Prophet, "Islam was founded on five 'pillars'…." quoted above. The obligation to perform this rite is also agreed upon by the Muslim community as a whole, or *ummah*. Hence, whoever denies the necessity of performing the *ḥajj* is deemed an unbeliever. As for the necessity of performing the *ḥajj* once in a lifetime, it is evidenced by the words of the Prophet, "O people, the *ḥajj* has been made obligatory for you, so make the pilgrimage." In response, a man asked, "Are we to make the pilgrimage every year, O Messenger of God?" He remained silent until the man had asked the question a second time and a third time. Then he said, "If I said, 'Yes', it would become obligatory for you, but you would not be able to do it."

God has imposed the duty of the *ḥajj* on Muslims for numerous reasons, all of which embody the divine wisdom. One of these reasons is that by means of the *ḥajj*, the Muslims come together on a single plane, worshipping a single Deity in sincere devotion to the precious religion which is the foundation of prosperity and success both in this life and in the life to come. One of the principles of this religion is that its adherents are brothers and sisters who are bound to cooperate in righteousness and the consciousness of God. Hence, each of them should labor to offer support and assistance to his or her companions, even if they are separated by geographical distances and even if their homes are scattered abroad. When in this situation, they should remember that they are in the presence of their supreme, all-powerful Sustainer who created them and granted them favor over many of His other creatures; they are to remember that they will die and stand in God's presence on a Day on which nothing will be of any benefit to anyone but the righteous deeds he or she has performed and his or her having clung to what God commands in all of life's affairs.

When the *ḥajj* is to be performed

The *ḥajj* is an obligation that must be performed without delay; hence, whoever fulfills the conditions for its being obligatory but postpones its performance past the first year during which he would have been able to do so is guilty of wrongdoing according to the Malikis, the Hanafis and the Hanbalis; for the view of the Shafiis, see below.[96]

The *ḥajj* will be discussed in what follows under a number of relevant headings, including the conditions which must be fulfilled in order for it to be obligatory, the conditions for its validity, its pillars, its associated duties and Sunnah-based practices, practices which are recommended and others which are undesirable in connection with the *ḥajj*, actions or events which invalidate the *ḥajj*, and actions which are forbidden during the *ḥajj* but which do not render it invalid.

Conditions for its necessity

According to the Shafiis, the Hanafis and the Hanbalis, one condition which must be fulfilled in order for the *ḥajj* to be obligatory is that the person concerned be a Muslim; for the Malikis' view, see below.[97] Hence, the *ḥajj* is not required of someone who was born a non-Muslim; as for someone who has renounced Islam, the Hanafis and the Hanbalis hold that he is not obliged to perform the *ḥajj*, whereas the Malikis hold, as we have seen, that being a Muslim is a condition for the *ḥajj*'s validity, but not for its being obligatory. For the view of the Shafiis, see below.[98]

---

96. According to the Shafiis, the *ḥajj* is an obligation which does not have to be performed immediately; hence, if someone delays it past the first year in which he would have been capable of performing it, he will not be deemed disobedient on account of this delay given the following two conditions: (1) He must have no reason to fear that on account of this delay, he will miss the opportunity to perform the *ḥajj*, due, for example, to old age, the inability to reach his destination, or a loss of his wealth. If the person concerned has reason to fear that he might miss the opportunity to perform the *ḥajj* altogether, he is obliged to perform it promptly, and he will be guilty of disobedience if he delays. (2) He must be determined to perform it later; if this determination is absent, he will be guilty of wrongdoing.

97. According to the Malikis, being a Muslim is a condition for the validity of the *ḥajj*, but not for its being obligatory; in other words, the non-Muslim is under obligation to perform the *ḥajj*, but his performance of it will not be valid unless he becomes a Muslim.

98. According to the Shafiis, the *ḥajj* is not required of someone who was born a non-Muslim. As for someone who has renounced Islam and is capable of performing it, he is under obligation to perform the *ḥajj*, but it will only have validity if he reenters Islam. If such a person becomes a Muslim again, then dies before performing the *ḥajj*, someone else should perform it on his behalf and finance the journey with the deceased's bequest.

Conditions for the necessity of the *ḥajj*: adulthood, sanity, and freedom

In order for the *ḥajj* to be required of someone, he or she must be an adult. Hence, it is not required of a child who has not reached puberty based on the words of the Prophet, "If a child were to perform the *ḥajj* ten times, after which he reached puberty, he would still be required to perform the *ḥajj* of Islam." If a child performing the *ḥajj* has reached the age of discernment with the result that he understands what its various rites mean, his *ḥajj* will be valid; however, he will still be required to perform it after he reaches maturity. If, on the other hand, a child who has not yet reached the age of discernment comes on the *ḥajj*, his guardian is required to perform the various *ḥajj* rites on the child's behalf, as will be seen in the discussion of the conditions for the validity of the *ḥajj*.

In addition, the *ḥajj* is only required of someone who is in full possession of his mental faculties. Hence, the *ḥajj* is not required of someone who is insane, nor is it valid if such a person performs it since, mentally speaking, he is deemed to be like a young child who has not reached the age of discernment.

One must also be free in order to be required to perform the *ḥajj*; hence, it is not required of a slave.

The aforementioned conditions are agreed upon by all four schools.

Ability, and rulings on the performance of the *ḥajj* by women and the blind

Another condition which must be met in order for someone to be required to perform the *ḥajj* is ability; hence, all four schools agree that it is not required of someone who would not be capable of performing it based on the words of God Almighty, "Hence, pilgrimage unto the Temple is a duty owed to God by all people who are able to undertake it..." (3:97). However, the schools differ over the meaning of the term 'ability' in general and, in particular, over what this term means with respect to a woman and someone who is blind.[99]

---

99. According to the Hanafis, 'ability' (*al-istiṭā'ah*) refers to the ability to obtain the necessary provisions for the journey and a riding camel, provided that both of these are in addition to one's basic necessities, such as whatever debts one owes, one's dwelling, one's clothing, the livestock one requires, the tools of one's trade, and one's weapon; they must also be in addition to the financial support such a person would be required to provide for those for whose support he is responsible during his absence. Consideration must also be given to what is most fitting for the traveler based on his or her habits and what is customary for a person of his or her social class and other circumstances. For example, a man who is unable to ride a she-ass or to straddle a camel's hump and who is also unable to rent a sedan chair is not required to perform the *ḥajj* since, in this situation, he is considered incapable of doing so. The same ruling applies to someone who is not able to hire a mount he can ride alone; thus, for example, if someone is able to obtain a riding camel with a partner with whom he can take turns such that each of them alternately rides and walks, he is not considered capable of performing the *ḥajj* and, as a consequence, it is not required of him.

The aforementioned ruling applies to someone who is three days' journey or more away from Mecca. As for those who are closer to Mecca than this, they are required to undertake the *ḥajj* even if they are not able to obtain a riding camel, provided that they are capable of walking and of securing provisions beyond the basic necessities detailed above.

One condition for the *ḥajj*'s being obligatory is that if the person concerned is not in a Muslim country, he must be aware that the *ḥajj* is an obligation required of Muslims. If someone was raised outside of any Muslim country and if he or she was not informed about the obligatory nature of the *ḥajj* by either two men or one man and two women, he or she is not required to perform the *ḥajj*. However, if the person concerned is in a Muslim country, he or she is required to perform the *ḥajj* even if he or she has never learned that it is obligatory, and whether he or she was raised as a Muslim or not.

These, then, are the conditions for the *ḥajj*'s being obligatory according to the Hanafis; in addition to these, the Hanafis list what they refer to as "conditions of performance", since the Hanafis draw a distinction between the obligation to perform a rite and the performance itself as we saw in the section on ritual prayer above. There are four conditions of performance: (1) Soundness of body. Hence, the *ḥajj* is not required of an invalid, a hemiplegic, an elderly person who is unable to remain seated on a riding camel, etc. Nor should people such as these appoint anyone else to undertake the *ḥajj* on their behalf. This category of people also includes those who are in prison and those who are fearful of a ruler who forbids people to undertake the *ḥajj*. As for someone who is blind but who is able to obtain both provisions for the journey and a riding camel, the ruling is that if he cannot find a guide, he is not required to undertake the *ḥajj* either by himself or with anyone else. If he does find a guide, he is required to appoint someone else to perform the *ḥajj* on his behalf. (2) Safe passage. In other words, the way leading from the point of origin to Mecca, be it land or sea, must be predominantly safe. (3) The presence of a husband or *maḥram* for a woman. This condition applies whether the woman is young or old if she is a three days' journey or more away from Mecca. If she is closer than this, however, she is obliged to undertake the *ḥajj* even if she has no husband or *maḥram* to accompany her. The *maḥram* who escorts the woman must be trustworthy, in full possession of his mental faculties, and an adult; however, it is not necessary that he be a Muslim. (4) The woman concerned must not be in a post-marriage waiting period (*'iddah*), whether the marriage ended through divorce or through the husband's death.

* * *

The Malikis define 'ability' as the material possibility of reaching Mecca and the sites at which the *ḥajj* rites are performed, whether they can be reached by walking or riding, and whether what the person rides is his own possession or hired. However, the journey must not be so arduous as to cause the person undue hardship; hence, if someone would only be able to reach Mecca by enduring severe hardship, he is not considered 'able' and he is not required to undertake the *ḥajj*. However, if he takes it upon himself to endure the hardship, the *ḥajj* will be valid for him, and it will count in fulfillment of his obligation in this regard. Similarly, if someone would only be able to reach Mecca by some out-of-the-ordinary means, such as flying, he is not considered 'able', and he is not required to do so; however, if he does so, his performance of the *ḥajj* will be valid. When determining ability to undertake the *ḥajj*, consideration is also given to whether the person can ensure the safety of his person and possessions; hence, someone who cannot ensure his personal safety is not required to perform the *ḥajj*, nor is someone who cannot guarantee that his wealth will be safe from some wrongdoer unless the wrongdoer is just one person, unless the wrongdoer has not taken enough to do harm to the person from whom it was taken, and unless he has not returned to take more. In this latter situation, the wrongdoer's presence and his taking what he has taken do not prevent the person from whom the wealth was taken from being considered able to undertake the *ḥajj*. 'Ability' also includes the ability to secure the needed provisions for the journey and a riding camel. Moreover, provisions for the journey may be replaced by a trade or craft [by which the pilgrim can finance the purchase of such provisions] provided that the craft or trade in question causes the person no dishonor, and provided that he knows, or has good reason to believe, that the trade will thrive throughout the journey. As for the riding camel, this condition may be fulfilled by the ability to walk; hence, if someone is capable of walking, he is obliged to perform the *ḥajj* even if he is separated from Mecca by a distance which is equal to or greater than that which one must travel in order to shorten ritual prayers. In the case of someone who is blind, he is obliged to perform the *ḥajj* if he is able to walk, if he has enough money with him to complete the journey, and if he either has someone to guide him or is able to find his way on his own. Ability to perform the *ḥajj* is not precluded by someone's not leaving anything for those for whose financial support he is responsible, such as his son, for example; nor is it precluded by the person's fear that by undertaking the journey, he might be stricken by poverty later unless he has reason to fear that he or his dependents might perish, in which case he is not required to perform the *ḥajj*.

If the person has nothing but that which may be sold on behalf of someone who is bankrupt, such as real estate, livestock, clothing for mere adornment, scholarly books, and tools of his trade, he is considered able to undertake the *ḥajj* and is, therefore, obliged to do so. Moreover, ability is considered only in terms of the trip to Mecca, and not the return trip, if the person concerned would be able to live in Mecca. If not, however, ability is defined also in terms of the return journey from Mecca to a place where the person would be able to live, even if this is not his original home. In short, the pilgrim must have sufficient resources to reach Mecca, then return to a place where he is able to live, or have a profitable craft or trade by which to obtain such resources, as we have seen.

With respect to the ability to make the journey, no distinction is made between traveling by sea or by land provided that safety is sufficiently guaranteed. Otherwise, the person concerned is not required to perform the *ḥajj* if the only way to travel is by sea. All the aforementioned factors in relation to 'ability' are taken into consideration with respect to both men and women; in a woman's case, however, it is also necessary that she travel with a husband or *maḥram*, or with a trustworthy group of [female] companions. If none of these is available, she is not required to perform the *ḥajj*.

In the case of a woman, it is also necessary that she have a comfortable way to ride if she must travel a great distance. Distance here is not measured solely in terms of whether it is more or less than the distance one must travel in order to shorten ritual prayers; rather, the distance is considered too great if it is farther than she would be able to walk without suffering undue hardship. This distance, of course, will differ from one woman to another. Hence, if walking would pose too much hardship for the woman concerned and if it would not be possible for her to ride, she is not required to perform the *ḥajj*. Nor is she required to do so if she would have to travel in a boat which is so small that she would not be able to maintain the proper modesty; as for large ships in which there are places where a woman can seclude herself, she is not exempted from the *ḥajj* and she must travel in one of these if it is necessary to travel by sea.

Lastly, if a woman is in her waiting period following a divorce or the death of her spouse, she must remain at home, and she is not permitted to enter a state of ritual consecration for the *ḥajj* since this would necessitate her leaving home at a time when she is not allowed to do so. However, if she does perform the *ḥajj*, her *iḥrām* will be valid even though she will be guilty of wrongdoing; hence, she is to proceed with the *ḥajj* rather than remaining at home as would normally be required during the *'iddah*.

* * *

According to the Hanbalis, 'ability' refers to the ability to obtain the provisions needed for the *ḥajj* as well as a riding camel suited to the person concerned. The provisions and the camel must be in addition to the person's basic necessities, including scholarly books, his dwelling, his servants, and what he needs in order to provide without interruption for those for whose support he is responsible.

In order for the *ḥajj* to be required of someone, the way to Mecca must be safe, meaning that the person concerned has no reason to fear for his own safety or for that of his wealth, his honor, etc. As for the woman, she is not required to perform the *ḥajj* unless she has with her her husband or a *maḥram*, such as a brother, a son, a paternal uncle, a father, or some other male relative who would not be permitted to marry her. In addition, the *ḥajj* is only required if the person concerned is sighted; if he is blind, he is not required to perform the *ḥajj* unless he finds a guide to lead him. If he finds no guide, he is not required to perform the *ḥajj* either by himself or with anyone else. If someone is unable to perform the *ḥajj* alone due to old age or an illness which he has no hope of recovering from, or if he is unable to ride without suffering severe hardship, he must appoint someone to perform the *ḥajj* in his place, as will be seen in the section below on performing the *ḥajj* on someone else's behalf.

* * *

As for the Shafiis, they divide 'ability' into two types: the ability to perform the *ḥajj* by oneself, and the ability to perform it through someone else. The first type of ability exists given the following conditions: (1) The ability to obtain the provisions one needs and to provide for hiring a guard or escort, etc. when going to Mecca, as well as the expenses involved in staying in Mecca after one's arrival and returning home if one does not intend to remain there. If one intends to remain in Mecca, however, there is no need to provide for the journey back. (2) The availability of a riding camel. In the case of a woman, this condition applies regardless of whether the distance is long or short. In the case of a man, the availability of the riding camel is only necessary if the distance is long, where 'long' is defined as two or more *marḥalahs* [48 miles]. If the distance is short and the person concerned is capable of walking without suffering hardship that would normally be intolerable, he is obliged to perform the *ḥajj* [even] if he has no riding camel; otherwise, however, he is not obliged to do so. As for what is meant by a riding camel here (*rāḥilah*), it refers to whatever camel one is able to reach Mecca on, whether it belongs to a single person or is shared and the person concerned can find someone to ride with him. If he finds no one to ride with him and if he is not able to ride alone, he is not obliged to perform the *ḥajj*. In addition, the riding camel must be provided with what it needs for the journey, such as a tent that can be pitched over it to protect it from severe heat or cold; one is not required to perform the *ḥajj* if, without such provisions, the journey will entail intolerable hardship. In the case of the woman, these provisions are not negotiable even if she would not actually be harmed by their absence, since she is required to have whatever is necessary to maintain the required modesty and privacy. Moreover, the provisions and riding camel mentioned must be available in addition to whatever the person needs to repay debts he may owe, even if they are deferred, and to pay the expenses of those for whose financial support he is responsible until he returns, as well as a suitable dwelling if he cannot do without such (otherwise, he is to sell his dwelling and undertake the *ḥajj* with the proceeds), agricultural livestock, a horse and necessary weapons in the case of a soldier, as well as the tools of one's trade, one's books on jurisprudence, and the like. (3) Safe passage (even if this is only based on good evidence for believing the way to be safe) for oneself, one's spouse and one's money, even if one has little. If there are animals of prey, highway robbers and the like along the way and if there is no alternative route, one is not required to perform the *ḥajj*. (4) The availability of water, provisions and fodder for one's riding animal as need for them arises along the way, and for prices comparable to those one would pay elsewhere based on prevailing market conditions. (5) Accompaniment of a woman by her husband, a *maḥram*, or two or more trustworthy women. If she finds only one other woman to accompany her, she is not required to go on the *ḥajj*, though it is permissible for her to perform the obligatory *ḥajj* with her; in fact, it is permissible for her to go out alone to perform the obligatory *ḥajj* provided that the way is safe. If it is a voluntary performance of the *ḥajj*, however, she is not permitted to go out even with a large group of women. If the woman concerned only finds a *maḥram* or a husband to accompany her in return for pay, she must pay the required amount if she is able to afford it. In the case of someone who is blind, he is not obliged to perform the *ḥajj* unless he finds a guide, even if he must hire him, provided that he is able to afford the cost. If he finds no guide, or if he finds a guide but cannot afford to hire him, he is not required to perform the *ḥajj* even if he is a resident of Mecca and is adept at walking with a cane. (6) The ability to remain seated on the mount without experiencing severe harm. (7) That sufficient time remain of the *ḥajj* season for the person concerned to perform the *ḥajj* after becoming able to do so. The *ḥajj* season lasts from the beginning of the month of Shawwāl until 10 Dhū al-Ḥijjah. If someone was able to perform the *ḥajj* before this season began, after which he lost his ability to do, the *ḥajj* is not required of him.

As for the second type of ability, namely, the ability to perform the *ḥajj* through someone else, it will be discussed below under the heading, "Performing the *ḥajj* on someone else's behalf."

Conditions for the validity of the *ḥajj*, the *ḥajj* performed by a child who has reached the age of discernment and by others, the *ḥajj* season, etc.

In order for the *ḥajj* to be valid, the person who performs it must meet the following conditions: (1) He must be a Muslim, whether he performs the *ḥajj* by himself or whether someone else performs it on his behalf, since the *ḥajj* is not valid if performed by a non-Muslim, nor is it valid if it is performed on a non-Muslim's behalf. (2) He must have reached the age of discernment. If the *ḥajj* rites are performed by a child who has reached the age of discernment, they will be valid, as in the case of ritual prayer, according to the Shafiis, the Hanafis and the Hanbalis; as for the Malikis, they hold that discernment is a condition for the validity of one's entering a state of ritual consecration (*iḥrām*), but not for the validity of the *ḥajj*. However, this difference is easily resolved based on the fact that in either case, discernment is required [since without entering a state of ritual consecration, one's *ḥajj* will not be valid]. As for a child who has not reached the age of discernment or someone who is insane, his or her performance of the *ḥajj* will not be valid, nor will his or her *iḥrām*. However, such a person's guardian must enter into a state of ritual consecration on his or her behalf, bring him/her to the sites where the various *ḥajj* rites are performed, take him/her to 'Arafah, etc. (3) He must perform the *ḥajj* during its specified season; if the *ḥajj* rites are performed at some other time, they will not be valid. However, the various schools differ concerning exactly when the *ḥajj* season is.[100]

---

100. The Hanafis hold that the time during which the *ḥajj* must be performed in order for it to be valid is the time of the circumambulation of visitation (*ṭawāf al-ziyārah*) [also known as *ṭawāf al-ifāḍah*] and the time at which pilgrims stand on Mt. 'Arafah. The time at which pilgrims stand on Mt. 'Arafah extends from noon on the Day of 'Arafah [9 Dhū al-Ḥijjah] until dawn on the Day of Sacrifice [10 Dhū al-Ḥijjah], while the time for the circumambulation of visitation extends from dawn on the Day of Sacrifice until the end of one's lifetime; hence, this circumambulation will be valid at any time after one has stood on Mt. 'Arafah during the time period specified above. If someone does not stand on Mt. 'Arafah at its specified time before performing the circumambulation of visitation, his circumambulation will not be valid. If the *ḥajj* rites are performed before the period extending from the beginning of Shawwāl through Dhū al-Qa'dah and up to 10 Dhū al-Ḥijjah, they will not be valid; however, an exception to this ruling is made for the *iḥrām*, or act of entering a state of ritual consecration, which can be validly undertaken before the *ḥajj* season, though it is undesirable to do so. The Hanafis list additional conditions for the validity of the *ḥajj* as well, namely, (1) the proper place, which is the land of 'Arafāt for standing [on Mt. 'Arafah], and the Sacred Mosque for the circumambulation of visitation, and (2) being in a state of ritual consecration. Hence, they list a total of only three conditions for the validity of the *ḥajj*: (1) being in a state of ritual consecration, (2) the proper time, and (3) the proper place. Being a Muslim is a condition for both the necessity and the validity of the *ḥajj*. As for discernment, the Hanafis do not list it among the conditions for the *ḥajj*'s validity; however, implicitly speaking, it is included among them, since someone who has not reached the age of discernment may not validly enter a state of ritual consecration.

* * *

According to the Malikis, the time during which the rites of the *ḥajj* must be performed in order for them to be valid includes some time periods beyond which the *ḥajj* will be invalid, and other time periods beyond which the *ḥajj* will not be invalid. These periods of time are divided into the following types: (1) the time for entering a state of ritual consecration for the *ḥajj*, (2) the time for standing on Mt. ʻArafah, (3) the time for the circumambulation of the Kaʻbah which is a pillar of the *ḥajj*, i.e., the circumambulation of visitation, and (4) the time for the remaining *ḥajj* rites, such as throwing pebbles, shaving, slaughtering, and walking at a brisk place between al-Ṣafā and al-Marwah.

The time for entering a state of ritual consecration extends from the beginning of Shawwāl until sufficient time remains before the break of dawn on the Day of Sacrifice to allow one to enter a state of ritual consecration and stand on Mt. ʻArafah. However, entering a state of ritual consecration after this period of time has begun is not a condition for the validity of the *ḥajj*; rather, one may enter a state of ritual consecration before this time period begins provided that one remains in this state until after it has begun, although this practice is undesirable. If one enters a state of ritual consecration after this time period has ended, it will only be valid for the following year because once the time for standing on Mt. ʻArafah has passed, it is no longer possible to perform the *ḥajj* until the next year.

The time for standing on Mt. ʻArafah as a pillar of the *ḥajj* extends from sundown on the Day of ʻArafah until the break of dawn on the Day of Sacrifice. However, standing [on Mt. ʻArafah] for a moment between noon on the Day of ʻArafah and sundown on the same day is an obligation the omission of which requires that one offer a sacrificial animal (*hady*).

The time for the circumambulation of visitation extends from the Day of Sacrifice [10 Dhū al-Ḥijjah] until the end of Dhū al-Ḥijjah. If someone postpones this circumambulation until after this period has ended, he must offer an animal sacrifice, but the circumambulation will be valid despite the delay. The standing on Mt. ʻArafah which is a pillar of the *ḥajj*, by contrast, may not be performed either before or after its appointed time.

As for the times for the remaining *ḥajj* rites, they will be discussed separately and in detail below. The brisk walk between al-Ṣafā and al-Marwah, for example, must be performed after the circumambulation of visitation if it was not performed prior to this after the circumambulation of arrival. The throwing of pebbles has specified days on which it is to be performed, namely, the Day of Sacrifice and the three days subsequent to it. The *ḥajj* season during which all of its rites are performed extends from the beginning of Shawwāl through the month of Dhū al-Qaʻdah and until the end of the month of Dhū al-Ḥijjah. As for the designated place, it is the land of ʻArafah for the standing on Mt. ʻArafah. However, this place is neither a pillar in and of itself, nor is it a condition; rather, it is part of the concept of the 'pillar', namely, standing on Mt. ʻArafah. Similarly, the sacred mosque with respect to circumambulation is not a condition for the validity of the *ḥajj*; rather, it is a condition for the validity of the circumambulation. As for discernment, the Malikis do not list it among the conditions for the *ḥajj*. However, the ritual consecration of someone who has not reached the age of discernment is not valid, since a condition of the validity of one's ritual consecration is intention, and since intention is not valid on the part of someone who has not reached the age of discernment. Hence, the Malikis' only condition for the validity of the *ḥajj* is that one be a Muslim.

* * *

According to the Shafiis, the time during which the *ḥajj* must be performed in order to be valid extends from the first day of Shawwāl until dawn on the Day of Sacrifice. If someone enters a state of ritual consecration for the *ḥajj* before the beginning of this time period or after it ends, it will not be valid for the *ḥajj* (i.e., the greater pilgrimage); however, it will be valid for the *'umrah*. As for standing on Mt. 'Arafah, the circumambulation of visitation, the brisk walk between al-Ṣafā and al-Marwah, and other *ḥajj* rites, each of these has a specified time which will be defined in the discussion of the rite itself. In sum, then, the Shafiis only specify three conditions for the validity of the *ḥajj*, namely: (1) Islam, (2) discernment, and (3) the specified time.

* * *

As for the Hanbalis, they divide the time during which the *ḥajj* must be performed in order to be valid into four categories, namely: (1) the time for entering into a state of ritual consecration, (2) the time for standing on Mt. 'Arafah, (3) the time for the circumambulation of visitation, and (4) the time for the remaining *ḥajj* rites such as the brisk walk between al-Ṣafā and al-Marwah. The time for entering into a state of ritual consecration extends from the first day of Shawwāl until shortly before dawn on the Day of Sacrifice, provided that sufficient time remains both to enter into a state of ritual consecration and to stand on Mt. 'Arafah. It is an emulation of the Sunnah to enter into a state of ritual consecration during this period of time; it is undesirable to do so outside of this time period, but if one does so, it will still be valid. As for standing on Mr. 'Arafah and other rites of the *ḥajj*, the times for their performance will be mentioned in the discussion of each one.

The pillars of the *ḥajj*

According to the Shafiis, the Malikis and the Hanbalis, the *ḥajj* is comprised of four pillars, all of which must be present in order for one's pilgrimage to be valid: (1) entering into a state of ritual consecration, (2) the circumambulation of visitation, (3) walking at a brisk pace between al-Ṣafā and al-Marwah, and (4) standing on Mt. 'Arafah. As for the Hanafis, they hold that the *ḥajj* consists of only two pillars.[101]

Each of the pillars of the *ḥajj* will be discussed in the sections to follow.

---

101. According to the Hanafis, the *ḥajj* consists of only two pillars, namely: (1) standing on Mt. 'Arafah, and (2) most of the circumambulation of visitation, i.e., four out of the seven courses around the Ka'bah, whereas the three remaining courses are viewed as a 'duty', as will be seen. As for *iḥrām*, it is a condition for the *ḥajj*'s validity, as we have seen, while the brisk walk between al-Ṣafā and al-Marwah is likewise a 'duty' rather than a pillar.

* * *

As for the Shafiis, they hold that the *ḥajj* consists of six pillars, namely, the four listed in the main text above in addition to the following two: (1) removal of hair, provided that one remove three hairs, some or all of which must be from one's head, and (2) removal of the hair after one has stood on Mt. 'Arafah and after midnight on the Day of Sacrifice. The Shafiis specify that in terms of temporal order: (1) one must enter a state of ritual consecration before the *ḥajj* proper; (2) standing on Mt. 'Arafah must precede the circumambulation of visitation and shaving; and (3) the circumambulation [of visitation] must precede the brisk walk between al-Ṣafā and al-Marwah if the latter was not performed immediately after the circumambulation of arrival.

The first pillar: *Iḥrām*

Within the context of Islamic jurisprudence, the term *iḥrām* means the intention to enter upon the greater or lesser pilgrimage (i.e., the *ḥajj* or the *'umrah*). In order for this intention to be formed, it is not necessary for one to utter the *talbiyah*, i.e., the phrase, "Here am I at Your service, O God, here am I at Your service. Here am I at Your service; You have no partner, here am I at Your service. Praise, blessing, and dominion are Yours, and You have no partner!" (*labbayka Allāhumma, labbayk, labbayka, lā sharīka laka, labbayk. Inna al-ḥamda wal-ni'mata laka wal-mulk, lā sharīka lak*). Nor, according to the Shafiis and the Hanbalis, does it need to be accompanied by the presentation of a sacrificial camel or the like. For the views of the Malikis and the Hanafis, see below.[102] However, it is an emulation of the Sunnah to accompany one's *iḥrām* with the *talbiyah* alone, that is, by forming the intention to undertake the *ḥajj* or the *'umrah*, then immediatedly uttering the *talbiyah*.

---

102. The Hanafis define *iḥrām* as observance of specified prohibitions and sacred rites; it is fulfilled by means of two conditions: (1) intention, and (2) the intention's being accompanied by the *talbiyah*. However, the *talbiyah* may be replaced by the utterance of words and phrases of divine remembrance or the act of placing a collar around the neck of one's sacrificial camel or cow and leading it forward. If someone simply forms an intention without uttering the *talbiyah* or engaging in acts that would serve to take its place, or if he utters the *talbiyah* without intention, he is not considered to have completed the *iḥrām*. Similarly, if someone marks his sacrificial animal by wounding its left hump (an act which pertains specifically to camels), places a saddle on it, or lets it loose, and if he is performing only the *ḥajj* [rather than the *'umrah* and the *ḥajj* combined], after which he decides to perform the *'umrah* yet without having joined this intention initially with his intention to perform the *ḥajj*, or if he places a collar around the neck of a sheep or goat [instead of a camel], he is not considered to be in a state of *iḥrām*.

* * *

As for the Malikis, they define *iḥrām* as entering into the prohibitions and sacred rites associated with the *ḥajj*. According to the officially recognized view, *iḥrām* is realized by means of intention alone, although it is an emulation of the Sunnah to accompany it with the recitation of something like the *talbiyah* or the phrase, *lā ilāha illā Allāh* or some action connected with the *ḥajj* such as heading toward Mecca and placing a collar around the neck of one's sacrificial camel or cow.

The places which a pilgrim may not pass through on his way to Mecca without *iḥrām* (referred to as *mawāqīt*, singular, *mīqāt*)

As used in the everyday language, the Arabic term *mīqāt* refers to the place where a pilgrim is to enter into a state of ritual consecration. This definition is consistent with the word's meaning as it is used in connection with Islamic jurisprudence, since *iḥrām*, or the act of entering a state of ritual consecration, has both a time and a place associated with it. The time associated with *iḥrām* was discussed above in the section on "when the *ḥajj* is to be performed." As for the place associated with *iḥrām*, this differs according to the direction from which the pilgrim is traveling to Mecca. For the people of Egypt, Syria, North Africa and those coming from beyond them from Andulusia, Byzantium and Takrūr, the place at which they are to enter a state of ritual consecration is al-Juḥfah, which is a village (now a ruin) between Mecca and Medina; al-Juḥfah is located near the well-known village known as Rābigh, from which a pilgrim may enter a state of ritual consecration without any undesirability attached thereto. When pilgrims traveling to Mecca by sea reach the point parallel to this village, they are to enter a state of ritual consecration, since the meaning of *mīqāt* is not restricted only to passing through the place in question by land; rather, the criterion by which it is decided whether one is to enter a state of ritual consecration is the person's either passing through the place on land or passing alongside it, even if this is by sea. As for the people of Iraq and all other inhabitants of the East, the point at which they are to enter a state of ritual consecration is Dhāt 'Irq, a village located two *marḥalahs* [48 miles] from Mecca. (The village is called by this name because there is a mountain there by the name of 'Irq, which overlooks a valley by the name of Wādī al-'Aqīq.) As for the inhabitants of Medina (which was illumined with the light of the Prophet), they are to enter a state of ritual consecration at Dhū al-Ḥalīfah, which is a watering site for Banū Jushm less than five miles from Medina. However, it is farther from Mecca than all the other points at which pilgrims are required to enter a state of ritual consecration, being nine *marḥalahs*, that is, nine days' journey, from Mecca. The *mīqāt* for the inhabitants of Yemen and India is Lamlam, one of the mountains of Tihāmah located two *marḥalahs* from Mecca. For the inhabitants of Najd, their *mīqāt* is a place known as Qarn al-Manāzil, which is a mountain that overlooks 'Arafāt.

These sites for *iḥrām* are for the inhabitants of the regions mentioned. However, everyone who passes through them or parallel to them, even if he or she is not a resident of the region from which he or she is traveling, must perform *iḥrām* at these points if his or her intention is to engage in the acts of worship involved in the pilgrimage to Mecca. If such a person passes beyond one of these points without engaging in *iḥrām*, he must return there and do so if the way leading back is safe and if there is sufficient time to do so without his or her missing the *ḥajj* as a result. If the person does not return, he or she is required to offer a sacrificial animal for having passed his or her *mīqāt* without entering a state of ritual consecration. This ruling applies also if the person could not have returned (due, for example, to fear of danger or lack of time); however, in the event that the person could have returned, he or she incurs guilt for not having done so. Moreover, this ruling applies whether there are other *mīqāts* on the way to Mecca or not. The aforementioned ruling is agreed upon by the Shafiis and the Hanbalis; for the views of the Hanafis and the Malikis, see below.[103]

As for someone who is already in Mecca, whether he is an inhabitant of the city or not, his *mīqāt* is Mecca itself; hence, even if the person is not from Mecca, he is not required to go out to the *mīqāt* for the region from which he originates in order to engage in *iḥrām* there even if there would be sufficient time for him to do so. As for someone who lives somewhere between Mecca and the nearest *mīqāt*, he is to engage in *iḥrām* in his home according to the Shafiis, the Hanbalis and the Hanafis; for the view of the Malikis, see below.[104]

What is required of someone intending to enter the state of *iḥrām*

When someone wishes to enter a state of *iḥrām*, certain actions are expected of him or her, some of which are in emulation of the Sunnah, and some of which are simply recommended. For a listing of such actions according to each school, see below.[105]

---

103. According to the Hanafis, if a pilgrim passes beyond the *mīqāt* without entering a state of ritual consecration, he has committed a forbidden act and, as a consequence, he is required to offer a sacrificial animal if there is no other *mīqāt* between the one he passed and Mecca. If there is another *mīqāt* along the way to Mecca, it is preferable for him or her to enter a state of ritual consecration at the first *mīqāt* if there is no danger that, before reaching Mecca, he or she will commit some act which is incompatible with the state of *iḥrām*. If there is danger of this happening, it is preferable to delay *iḥrām* until one reaches the last *mīqāt* he or she will pass through before reaching Mecca.

* * *

As for the Malikis, they hold that when a pilgrim passes a *mīqāt*, he is obliged to enter a state of ritual consecration there; if he passes beyond it without doing so, he will have committed a forbidden act and he will be required to offer a sacrificial animal unless the *mīqāt* for the region of which he is an inhabitant is still ahead of him. If it is, it is recommended [though not required] that he enter a state of ritual consecration at the first *mīqāt*; hence, if he does not do so, he will incur no guilt and he need not offer a sacrificial animal. Rather, he will simply have departed from what is recommended.

104. The Malikis hold that in the case of someone who is in Mecca but is not a resident of the city and who wishes to enter a state of ritual consecration for the *ḥajj*, he may do so while in Mecca without incurring guilt. However, it is recommended that he go to the site which is his own *mīqāt* and enter a state of *iḥrām* there if there is sufficient time for him to do so and if he can ensure that neither his person nor his possessions will be endangered by his leaving Mecca. Otherwise, it is not recommended that he leave the city in order to enter *iḥrām* from his regular *mīqāt*.

105. The Hanafis list the following actions as being either emulations of the Sunnah or desirable on the part of someone who wishes to enter a state of ritual consecration: (1) Performance of major ablutions. This is an emphatically enjoined emulation of the Sunnah. The Sunnah is also emulated by performance of minor ritual ablutions; however, major ablutions are preferable. This bath is for purposes

of hygiene, not ritual purity; hence, it is expected of a woman who is menstruating or experiencing post-partum bleeding. If no water is available, this requirement is dropped, but it is not legitimate to perform sand ablutions in its place, since sand ablutions do not serve the purpose of hygiene. (2) Trimming one's fingernails and toenails and shaving off hair the removal of which is permitted, such as the hair on one's head and one's moustache if one is accustomed to shaving it off. Otherwise, it is desirable to let it hang loose. This is to be done prior to major ablutions. (3) Having sexual relations with one's wife if there is no reason on her part for this not to be possible or permitted. The reason for this practice is to prevent the time of his abstinence from being so long that something occurs to invalidate his *iḥrām*. (4) Putting on an *izār*, i.e., a garment which covers the body from the navel to the knee, and a *ridā'*, which is a garment that covers the back, the chest and the shoulders. This practice is deemed desirable. If one buttons or ties the *izār*, this is an offense, but one is not required to offer a sacrificial animal on this account. It is also desirable for the *izār* and the *ridā'* to be white and new, or at least washed and ritually pure. (5) Perfuming one's body and garments with a perfume whose substance does not remain after *iḥrām*, even though its fragrance may linger. This practice is desirable if one has perfume on hand; otherwise, it is not. (6) Praying two voluntary *rak'ahs* after the foregoing if it is not a time at which it would be undesirable to do so. This pair of *rak'ahs*, properly speaking, is an emulation of the Sunnah. During the first *rak'ah*, it is preferable to recite the *Fātiḥah* and Surah 109, and during the second, it is preferable to recite the *Fātiḥah* and Surah 112. These two *rak'ahs* may be replaced by a regular obligatory prayer if one entered a state of ritual consecration after performing them. (7) Uttering words that express what is in one's heart, such as, for example, "O God, I wish to undertake the *ḥajj*. I ask Your assistance in completing this rite, and I ask You to accept it from me." Such words are to be followed by the *talbiyah* which, as we have seen, consists of the words, "Here am I at Your service, O God, here am I at Your service. Here am I at Your service. You have no partner, here am I at Your service. Praise, blessing, and dominion are Yours, and You have no partner" (*labbayka, Allāhumma, labbayk, labbayka, lā sharīka laka, labbayk, inna al-ḥamda wal-ni'mata laka wal-mulk, lā sharīka lak.*) After completing the *talbiyah*, one is to pray for blessings upon the Prophet in a low voice. In addition, one is to repeat the *talbiyah* as many times as possible following each obligatory prayer, as well as every time one meets a company of riders, every time one reaches higher ground, and every time one descends into a valley. One should also repeat the *talbiyah* as much as one can during the hours preceding daybreak, when one wakes from sleep, and when mounting and dismounting. Moreover, it is desirable, whenever one recites the *talbiyah*, to raise one's voice but without straining it.

* * *

The Malikis list the following as desirable actions for someone who wishes to enter a state of ritual consecration: (1) It is an emulation of the Sunnah to perform major ablutions even if one is menstruating or experiencing post-partum bleeding since this is required of everyone who wishes to enter a state of ritual consecration. However, the Sunnah is not fulfilled unless the ablutions are performed immediately prior to one's *iḥrām*; hence, if someone bathes, then waits what would commonly be agreed to be a long time without entering *iḥrām*, he must repeat his bath. It is recommended that one's major ablutions be performed in Medina if one wishes to enter *iḥrām* from Dhū al-Ḥalīfah. Moreover, if no water is available, it is not legitimate to perform sand ablutions in place of major ablutions. (2) It is also an emulation of the Sunnah to hang a collar around the neck of one's sacrificial animal if one has it, then to mark it. The purpose of hanging the collar around the animal's neck is to allow the needy to recognize it as a sacrificial animal and to take comfort from this recognition. As for marking, this refers to the act of placing a one or two fingertip-long incision on the left side of the animal's hump, beginning from the front and moving toward its rump. Only camels and cows are to have collars hung around their necks; as for the marking, it applies only to camels and to cows with humps. As for sheep and goats, they are neither to have collars hung around their necks nor are they to be marked. (3) It is recommended that one wear an *izār*, a *ridā'*, and sandals. The *izār* is a garment by means of which one conceals the private area between the navel and the knee, while the *ridā'* is a garment which is thrown over the shoulders. If someone wears something other than these two garments which contains no stitching and which does not wrap all the way around the body, no harm is done, although this is a departure from the recommended practice. (4) It is an emulation of the Sunnah to enter a state of ritual consecration after a ritual prayer; it is recommended that the prayer consist of a two-*rak'ah* voluntary prayer if it is at a time when voluntary prayers are allowed. Otherwise, one is to wait until a time when voluntary prayers are allowed. The ideal practice is for someone who is riding to undertake *iḥrām* after he has seated himself on the back of his mount, and for someone walking to do so after he has begun walking. It is also an emulation of the Sunnah to combine one's *iḥrām* with the utterance of the *talbiyah*, as we have seen. The *talbiyah* in itself is obligatory, and it is recommended that one repeat it whenever one's situation changes in some form or another, as, for example, when one ascends to higher ground or descends into a valley, when one encounters travel companions, and after one has performed a ritual prayer. The pilgrim is to continue repeating the *talbiyah* until he enters Mecca, then stop until he circumambulates the Ka'bah and performs the brisk walk between al-Ṣafā and al-Marwah (that is, if he wishes to perform this rite after the circumambulation of arrival). He or she should then resume repeating the *talbiyah* until the sun sets on the Day of 'Arafah and until he reaches its prayer site, at which point he or she is to stop uttering it again. If the pilgrim does not resume uttering the *talbiyah* after this, he or she will have neglected a duty and will, as a consequence, be obliged to offer a sacrificial animal. However, it is recommended that one observe moderation in the *talbiyah* by not uttering it so frequently that one grows weary and bored. It is likewise recommended that one observe moderation in the pitch of one's voice; in other words, one should utter it neither too softly nor too loudly. Lastly, one should restrict oneself to the wording of the *talbiyah* which was passed down from the Prophet, namely, *Labbayka Allāhumma, labbayk, labbayka, lā sharīka laka, labbayk, inna al-ḥamda wal-ni'mata laka wal-mulk, lā sharīka lak.*

* * *

The Hanbalis list the following actions as being emulations of the Sunnah for someone who wishes to enter a state of ritual consecration. (1) Performing major ablutions before entering *iḥrām* even if one is menstruating or experiencing post-partum bleeding. If no water is available or if one is unable to use water due to illness or some other cause, it is an emulation of the Sunnah to perform sand ablutions. Moreover, it does no harm if one has an occurrence of major or minor ritual impurity between the time one performs major ablutions and the time of one's *iḥrām*. (2) Attending to one's personal hygiene by the removal of hair, trimming one's fingernails and toenails, and removal of any unpleasant odors. (3) Perfuming one's body; however, it is undesirable to perform one's clothing. If one perfumes one's clothing and if one goes on wearing the same garments, no harm is done provided that one does not take them off; however, if one takes them off, one is not permitted to put them on again before washing them. (4) For a male to put on sandals and an *izār* and a *ridā'* which are white, clean and new after taking off anything which contains stitching. (5) Entering *iḥrām* after the performance of a ritual prayer, be it obligatory or voluntary, provided that the voluntary prayer was not performed at a time when voluntary prayers are disallowed, and provided that one does not lack [*ṭahūr*] water and soil. (6) Specifying verbally that one intends to perform the rites of the pilgrimage and specifying, further, whether one intends to perform the *ḥajj*, the *'umrah*, or both. In this connection, it is an emulation of the Sunnah to utter the words, "O God, I wish to perform the rites of such-and-such a pilgrimage. I ask You to assist me in doing so and to accept it from me. If some detainer should detain me, I will be released from the state of ritual consecration wherever You have detained me." If, in fact, the person is detained by illness, an enemy, etc., he is freed from the obligation to fulfill his stated intention, and no expiation or compensation is required of him.

* * *

As for the Shafiis, they list the following as Sunnah-practices associated with *iḥrām*: (1) Performance of major ablutions beforehand, even if one is menstruating. When doing so, one should intend to perform the major ablutions associated with *iḥrām* (*ghusl al-iḥrām*). It is undesirable to omit this practice without a legitimate excuse; hence, if one is unable to perform major ablutions due to a lack of water or due to the inability to use water, one should perform sand ablutions instead. (2) Removal of underarm hair and pubic hair, trimming one's moustache, fingernails and toenails, and shaving one's head for those whose head hair is a type of adornment; otherwise, one should keep such hair and mat it down with something viscous. This ruling applies if one is determined not to offer an animal sacrifice; otherwise, one should delay these actions until after the sacrifice has been offered. It is an emulation of the Sunnah to perform these actions before doing major ablutions if one is not in a state of major ritual impurity. As for someone who is in such a state, he emulates the Sunnah by doing major ablutions first. (3) Perfuming the body after performing major ablutions. This does not apply, however, to someone who is fasting, for whom this practice is undesirable, whereas in the case of a woman who is mourning the death of a husband, it is forbidden to do so. It is also acceptable for the fragrance to linger after the person has entered a state of ritual consecration, and for his or her clothing to take on the fragrance as well. (4) Having sexual relations [with one's spouse] before entering *iḥrām*. (5) For a woman to dye her hands up to the wrists, but without inscriptions, and for her to daub her face with some dye as well. (6) In the case of a man, for him to put on sandals and an *izār* and a *ridā'* which are new and white (or, at the least, washed). It is undesirable to wear something which has been dyed. (7) Performing two *rak'ahs* as a Sunnah-based practice preceding one's *iḥrām*, provided that the time at which this is done is not one during which voluntary prayers are forbidden. As for someone who is within the Meccan precincts, he may perform these two *rak'ahs* no matter what time it is. Moreover, these two *rak'ahs* may be replaced by any ritual prayer the person performs, be it obligatory or voluntary, and when performing the prayer, the worshiper should do the Qur'anic recitations silently even if he is praying at night. (8) Facing the *qiblah* as one commences one's *iḥrām* and saying, "O God, to You I devote my hair, my skin, my flesh and my blood." (9) Uttering the *talbiyah*, and doing so in a calm, solemn manner as a means of keeping God in remembrance. It is an emulation of the Sunnah to utter the *talbiyah* aloud so long as one is in a state of ritual consecration; otherwise, the Sunnah-based practice is to utter it silently. Moreover, the Sunnah-based practice for the woman is to utter it silently whether she is in a state of ritual consecration or not, while it is undesirable for her to utter it aloud in the presence of strangers. The same ruling that applies to the woman applies to the hermaphrodite. Following the *talbiyah* one is to pray for blessings upon the Prophet. It is an emphatically enjoined Sunnah-based practice to utter the *talbiyah* three times whenever one's situation changes, as, for example, when one goes from stillness to motion, when one ascends or descends a slope, when one joins companions, and when morning breaks or night falls. Lastly, one may follow the *talbiyah* with whatever supplications one wishes, although traditional supplications are preferable.

Actions which are forbidden to someone once he or she has entered the state of *iḥrām*: Sexual intercourse, hunting and the use of perfume

The lawgiver has forbidden those who are in a state of ritual consecration to do certain things, some of which are not permissible at all, and some of which are undesirable. The following is a list of such forbidden actions: (1) Concluding a marriage contract. According to the Shafiis, the Malikis and the Hanbalis, such a contract will be null and void if it is concluded while one is in a state of ritual consecration. For the Hanafis' view, see below.[106] (2) Sexual relations and actions which might lead up to it, such as kissing and direct genital contact. (3) Disobeying God by performing any forbidden act. For although certain actions are forbidden at all times, the prohibition against them is all the more emphatic during the time of the *ḥajj*. (4) Being argumentative and contentious with companions, servants and others. This prohibition is based on the words of God Almighty, "And whoever undertakes the pilgrimage in those [months] shall, while on pilgrimage, abstain from lewd speech, from all wicked conduct, and from quarrelling..." (2:197). (5) Killing or slaughtering game animals, pointing to them if they are visible, or making reference to them if they are not visible, such as referring to their eggs which have rotted inside their shells. However, it is only forbidden to hunt a game animal if it is wild and edible; if it is not edible, it may be hunted according to the Shafiis and the Hanbalis. As for the Hanafis and the Malikis, they hold that it is forbidden to kill any wild terrestrial game whatsoever, whether it is edible or not. As for aquatic game, it is permissible to hunt it based on the words of God Almighty, "Lawful to you is all water-game, and what the sea brings forth, as a provision for you [who are settled] as well as for travelers, although you are forbidden to hunt on land while you are in the state of pilgrimage" (5:96). The term 'terrestrial' (*barrī*) is defined as that which procreates on land, even if it lives in water, while 'aquatic' (*baḥrī*) is defined as the opposite of 'terrestrial' by the Malikis, the Hanafis and the Hanbalis; for the Shafiis' view, see below.[107] (6) Using perfume, such as musk, for example, on one's clothing or body. (7) Trimming one's fingernails and toenails. (8) Wearing something which is stitched or which extends all the way around part or all of one's body, such as a shirt, trousers, a turban or a *jubbah* (a long outer garment); this prohibition applies only to men. Men are likewise forbidden to wear regular shoes unless they are unable to find any sandals to wear, in which case they are permitted to wear regular shoes after cutting them out under the upper rim. (9)

---

106. The Hanafis hold that it is permissible for someone who is in a state of ritual consecration to formalize a marriage contract since the state of *iḥrām* does not prevent the woman from being eligible to marry; rather, it only precludes sexual relations. Hence, like menstruation, post-partum bleeding and the practice of *ẓihār* before the person guilty of doing so has offered the required expiation, being in a state of *iḥrām* precludes sexual relations, but not the validity of the marriage contract.

107. The Shafiis define 'terrestrial' as that which lives on land alone, or which lives on land and in the water, such as sea turtles; as for 'aquatic', they define this term as referring to that which lives nowhere but in the water.

Concealing one's head and face, fully or partially, with any sort of a cover. This is forbidden according to the Hanafis and the Malikis; as for the Shafiis and the Hanbalis, they hold that the man is not forbidden to cover his face.

The required covering for the face and head of a woman in the state of *iḥrām*

A woman in a state of ritual consecration is permitted to cover her face and her hands if, by so doing, her intention is to conceal herself from strange men. However, the Hanafis and the Shafiis hold that her veil must not touch her face; for the views of the Hanbalis and the Malikis, see below.[108]

Wearing a robe dyed with a fragrant substance, and removal of hair

A pilgrim is forbidden to wear a garment which has been dyed with a substance that has a pleasant fragrance.[109]

---

108. The Hanbalis hold that a woman may cover her face if there is a need to do so, as, for example, in order to conceal herself from strange men passing near her. Moreover, no harm is done if her veil comes in contact with her face. This ruling offers latitude which spares the woman undue hardship.

* * *

As for the Malikis, they hold that if the woman's intention in covering her hands or face is to conceal herself from people's gazes, she may do so if she is certain that there is someone actually looking at her, or if she is so stunningly beautiful that there is good reason to believe that men will look at her while she is in a state of ritual consecration. However, the veil with which she covers herself must contain no stitching or knots; otherwise, it is forbidden. In addition, a woman in a state of ritual consecration must pay a *fidyah* for covering her face. If these two conditions are not met [that is, if her veil contains stitching or knots, and/or if she does not pay a *fidyah*], she is forbidden to cover her face and her hands with something that would enclose them, such as gloves (a garment made to fit the hands and protect them from the cold). She is likewise forbidden to cover her hands with something that contains stitching or knots. As for placing her hands inside her tunic, this is permitted. She is also permitted to conceal part of her face as a result of covering her head and her hair.

109. According to the Hanafis, a pilgrim is forbidden to wear anything which has been dyed with safflower, *wars*, saffron, or any other type of fragrance unless the garment has been washed sufficiently that its fragrance is no longer detectable.

* * *

According to the Malikis, a pilgrim is forbidden to wear anything which has been dyed with a fragrant substance such as *wars* or saffron. As for things dyed with safflower, the ruling is that if the dye is well-set, as when something has been dyed repeatedly, the garment may not be worn until after it has been washed. If, on the other hand, the dye is faint, or if it is bright and well set but has been washed, it is not forbidden to wear it. However, it is undesirable for it to be worn by someone

Smelling or carrying perfume while in the state of *iḥrām*

All four schools agree that it is undesirable for a pilgrim to smell or to carry perfume or perfume-like fragrances. As for staying in a place where there is a perfume-like scent, the Malikis and the Hanafis hold that it is undesirable whether the person intends to smell it or not; for the views of the Hanbalis and the Shafiis, see below.[110]

The removal of hair from the head and elsewhere in the state of *iḥrām*

When in a state of ritual consecration, one is not allowed to remove hair from his or her head by shaving, cutting, etc. Nor may one remove other hair, even if it is growing in one's eye. An exception to this ruling is made if the person concerned would be harmed by the hair's not being removed; in this latter case, it is permissible to remove the hair, although the person who does so must pay a redemption on this account. If a hair is in the person's eye and if it would cause the person harm not to remove it, no redemption is required according to the Shafiis, the Hanafis and the Hanbalis; for the Malikis' view, see below.[111]

---

who is an example to others lest his behavior encourage uninformed lay people to wear what is forbidden, i.e., that which has a fragrance.

* * *

According to the Shafiis, it is forbidden to wear something which has been dyed with a substance that is used for the sake of its fragrance, such as saffron or *wars* unless the fragrance has completely disappeared. As for a garment which has been dyed with a substance that is used for the sake of its color rather than its fragrance, such as safflower or henna, it is permissible to wear it.

* * *

As for the Hanbalis, they hold that a pilgrim may not wear anything dyed with *wars* or saffron; however, it is permissible for him or her to wear something dyed with safflower regardless of whether the dye is faint or bright.

110. The Hanbalis and the Shafiis hold that if someone intends to smell a fragrance, as when one places a rose to his nose in order to sniff it, this action is prohibited whether the substance smelled is with the pilgrim or in a place where the pilgrim happens to be. However, if there is no intention to smell the fragrance, this prohibition does not apply.

111. The Malikis hold that removal of any and all hair is prohibited for a pilgrim to Mecca, whether the hair is in one's eye or elsewhere, unless there is a legitimate excuse which requires its removal. Given such an excuse, however, one must pay a *fidyah* even if the hair removed was in one's eye.

The use of henna while in the state of *iḥrām*

According to the Malikis and the Hanafis, those who are in a state of ritual consecration, whether they are men or women, are not permitted to dye their hands, their heads or any other part of their bodies with henna, since henna is a type of perfume, and the pilgrim is not allowed to perfume himself or herself. For the views of the Shafiis and the Hanbalis, see below.[112]

Whether someone in the state of *iḥrām* is permitted to eat or drink anything containing perfume

According to the Shafiis, the Hanafis and the Hanbalis, someone who is in a state of ritual consecration is forbidden to eat or drink perfume or anything mixed with it, whether the amount is large or small, unless the perfume has been consumed to the extent that neither its taste nor its smell remains; for the views of the Malikis, see below.[113] All four schools agree that if the perfume's taste or smell remains, it is forbidden to those in a state of ritual consecration. According the Shafiis, the Hanbalis and the Malikis, this ruling applies whether the substance to which the perfume has been added is cooked or not; for the view of the Hanafis, see below.[114]

---

112. The Shafiis hold that it is undesirable for a woman to use henna while she is in a state of ritual consecration, and that if she is in her waiting period following the death of a husband, she is forbidden entirely to use it. She is also forbidden to apply henna to her body in the form of inscriptions even if she is not in her waiting period following a husband's death. As for the man in a state of *iḥrām*, he may use henna anywhere on his body except his hands and feet. As for the use of henna on a man's hands and feet, it is forbidden unless there is a need to do so; nor is he allowed to cover his head with thick henna.

* * *

As for the Hanbalis, they hold that both men and women in a state of ritual consecration may use henna anywhere on their bodies, the only exception being the man's head.

113. The Malikis hold that in order for perfume to be consumed in food, its substance must have disappeared through cooking. When this occurs, it is not forbidden to eat it even if its fragrance remains, as in the case of musk, or even if its color remains, as in the case of saffron. However, if perfume is combined with something without its being cooked, it may not be eaten by someone in a state of ritual consecration. Some Malikis hold the view that if perfume has been cooked in food, it is permissible to eat it even if the substance of the perfume remains.

114. The Hanafis hold that if the perfume has been altered through the cooking, there is nothing wrong with its being eaten by someone in a state of ritual consecration whether he can detect its fragrance or not. If the perfume is mixed with something edible without its being cooked and if the perfume is less than half the total volume, there is nothing wrong with eating it; however, it is undesirable to do so if its fragrance remains. If the perfume makes up more than half the volume, the person who eats it must offer 'compensation' (*jazā'*). The aforementioned ruling applies if perfume has been mixed with something edible. If the perfume is mixed

The use of kohl (antimony) containing perfume and applying oil to one's hair and body

Those who are in a state of ritual consecration are not permitted to apply kohl (antimony) to their eyes if it contains perfume, and if someone does so, he or she must offer compensation (*jazā'*) to be detailed below. As for the use of kohl which contains no perfume, this is permitted according to the Shafiis, the Hanafis and the Hanbalis; for the view of the Malikis, see below.[115]

Those in a state of ritual consecration are forbidden to cause their hair to fall out, and if they do so, they must offer a compensation to be detailed below. Nor is someone in a state of ritual consecration permitted to oil his hair or his body, though each school offers its own detailed ruling on this matter.[116]

---

with a drink and if the perfume makes up more than half the volume, the person who drinks it must offer an animal sacrifice for doing so; if the perfume makes up less than half the drink's volume, the person who drinks it must offer charity unless he has drunk of it numerous times, in which case he must offer an animal sacrifice as he would if the perfume represented more than half the volume of the mixture. If someone eats a large amount of the substance of the perfume itself, he or she must offer an animal sacrifice, whereas if it was a small amount, nothing is required of him or her.

115. According to the Malikis, a person in a state of ritual consecration is forbidden to use kohl unnecessarily whether it contains perfume or not; if there is a need to do so, however, it is permissible. If one uses kohl containing perfume out of necessity, he must offer a *fidyah*, whereas if he uses kohl which is free of perfume out of necessity, none is required.

116. The Malikis hold that those in a state of ritual consecration are forbidden to oil either their hair or their bodies, in whole or in part, with any kind of substance, even if it contains no perfume. If someone does so, he must pay a *fidyah* as will be seen below, unless the substance is scentless and unless some illness requires it, in which case no *fidyah* is required. This ruling applies whether the illness concerned is on one's palms, one's feet, or elsewhere. If the illness is elsewhere, there is disagreement among the Malikis as to whether a *fidyah* is required or not.

* * *

The Hanafis divide the things that may be used on one's body into three types: (1) Perfumes prepared specifically to be applied as a fragrance, such as musk, camphor, ambergris, etc. No one in a state of *iḥrām* may use this type to oil his hair or body or for any other purpose. (2) Substances such as grease (suet) which are not perfume, which are not considered to be perfume, and which cannot become perfume. This type may be used by someone in a state of ritual consecration for oiling [his body or hair] and the like, and no compensation or redemption is required as a result. (3) Substances such as oil which are not perfumes themselves, but which serve as a base for perfumes. This type of substance is used sometimes for purposes of perfuming and oiling [the body and hair], and sometimes for medicinal purposes. If it is used for perfuming and oiling, it is subject to the ruling on perfume itself; in other words, its use is forbidden to those in a state of ritual consecration.

The ruling on cutting grass and trees within the sacred precincts

No one in a state of ritual consecration—or anyone else—may cut down, uproot or damage the trees inside the Meccan precinct or the branches thereof. This prohibition applies even if the branches reach outside the precinct.[117] If the trees have their roots outside the precinct, they may be cut, uprooted and benefited from if they are not someone else's private property, even if their branches reach inside the precinct. The same ruling that applies to trees applies to the grass inside the sacred precinct with the exception of *idhkhir*, a well-known plant with a fragrant aroma, and *al-sanā* (also known as *al-sanāmakī*), which may be cut, etc. Regarding the trees and grass inside the Meccan precinct, each school offers its own detailed ruling.[118]

If, however, it is used for medicinal purposes, those in a state of ritual consecration are permitted to apply it to their bodies and hair and to eat it as well.

* * *

According to the Shafiis, no one in a state of ritual consecration is permitted to oil [his or her body or hair] with anything that contains a pleasant fragrance; if the substance contains no such fragrance, it is permissible to oil one's entire body with it except for the hair on one's head and face, in which case it is permitted only if there is a need to do so.

* * *

As for the Hanbalis, they hold that no one in a state of ritual consecration may apply a substance which has a pleasant fragrance to any part of his body; however, if it contains no such fragrance, as is the case with [some] oil, one may oil any part of one's body with it, including even the hair on one's head and face.

117. The boundaries of the sacred Meccan precinct extend 3 miles in the direction of Medina, 7 miles in the direction of Iraq, 10 miles in the direction of Ṭā'if, 10 miles in the direction of Jedda, 9 miles in the direction of al-Ji'rānah, and 7 miles in the direction of Yemen [t.n.].

118. The Shafiis hold that, with the exception of the plants mentioned above, it is forbidden to cut, uproot or damage the green trees and green grass within the Meccan precincts even if they are owned by the person who wishes to do so. However, it is permissible to cut thorns. Moreover, one is only forbidden to cut or uproot the grass and trees inside the sacred precincts if it is done for some purpose other than to restore them, as when one trims trees to help them grow. As for dry trees, it is permissible to cut them down or uproot them. It is likewise permissible to cut dry grass; as for uprooting it, it is completely forbidden unless its roots have rotted. Moreover, the ruling on trees is the same whether they grow up by themselves, as in the case of the *safaṭ* tree, or have been planted by someone, as in the case of a date palm; it is forbidden to cut down, uproot or damage either type. As for grass, grains, and the like, it is only forbidden to cut or uproot them if they grew up by themselves; if they were planted, however, it is permissible to cut them and the like whether the people who do so are in a state of ritual consecration or not.

The aforementioned prohibitions are subject to the following exceptions: (1) One may take palm branches and tree leaves without striking the tree in a way that is harmful to it; otherwise, however, this is forbidden. (2) One may take the fruit of a tree, as well as sticks to use as toothpicks from the *siwāk* tree, provided that a similar fruit will take its place within a year's time. (3) One may allow domestic animals to graze on trees. (4) One may take plants to use them for medicinal purposes, as is done with colocynth and *al-sanāmakī*.

* * *

The Hanbalis hold that it is forbidden to uproot green trees and grass inside the Meccan precincts if they contain something harmful such as thorns. The same ruling applies to the *siwāk* tree and to green leaves. As for trees and grass which are dry, they may be cut or uprooted because they are considered to be dead; one may also cut *idhkhir*, truffles and fruit even if they are moist. It is likewise permissible to cut or uproot trees or grass which have been planted by human beings since such plants are private property, to graze one's animals on the grass in the Meccan precincts, and to make use of fallen tree leaves and plants which have come uprooted on their own or which have been broken without any action on the part of a human being, yet without becoming separated from their source. As for that which has been cut off by a human being, neither the person who cut if off nor anyone else is allowed to make use of it.

* * *

As for the Hanafis, they note, first of all, that what grows inside the Meccan precinct will be dry, broken, or in some other condition. That which is dry and broken is not counted as being part of the greenery inside the Meccan precincts since it is firewood; *idhkhir* grass is also excluded from the category of 'greenery'. As for that which is not dry, that is, plants which are still growing, it will either have grown up by itself or not. That which has grown up by itself may either be a type of plant which people cultivate (such as agricultural crops) or not (such as the tree known as "Umm Ghīlān"). Plants which have grown up by themselves and which are not the type which people cultivate may not be cut at all, whether they are owned by someone or not. If their owner does cut them, he will have committed a forbidden act but he will not be required to offer any compensation; if they are cut by someone other than their owner, the person who cut them will be required to offer compensation (to be detailed below) as well as their value. However, an exception to this ruling is made for what is cut off as a result of setting up a tent, digging a site for an oven, or its being trampled by riding animals, since in cases such as these, it could not have been avoided. As for plants which are cultivated by people or which grow up by themselves but also belong to a type which may be cultivated by people, it is permissible to cut them and to make use of them if they are not owned by someone else; if they are someone else's property, their value must be paid to their owner.

* * *

As for the Malikis, they hold that it is forbidden to cut trees and plants which tend to grow by themselves, such as wild herbs and tamarisk trees (even if they have been planted), and whether they are green or dry. However, exceptions to this ruling are made for the following:

(1) *Idhkhir*, which is a sweet-smelling plant similar to esparto.

(2) *Sanā*, known as *sanāmakī*, which is required for some medical treatments.

(3) *'Aṣā*. [This might possibly refer to *'asā al-rā'ī* (knotgrass), *'aṣā hirmis* (mercury) or *'aṣā ya'qūb* (rampion) (*Al-Mawrid*, Beirut: Dar al-'Ilm lil-Malāyin, Munir Ba'albaki, 1983) – t.n.]

Actions which are permitted to someone in a state of *iḥrām*: Venesection, cupping, and scratching the skin and hair

According to the Shafiis, the Hanafis and the Hanbalis, someone who is in a state of ritual consecration may perform venesection and cupping without shaving the hair; for the view of the Malikis, see below.[119] According to the Malikis, the Hanafis and the Hanbalis, such a person is also allowed to scratch his skin and hair provided that this does not cause his hair to fall out or remove vermin from his skin or hair. As for the Shafiis, they hold that it is undesirable for someone in a state of ritual consecration to scratch his skin and hair if this does not cause hair to fall out, and if it does cause this, it is forbidden.

Washing the head and the body, and seeking protection from the sun

The Shafiis and the Hanbalis hold that someone in a state of ritual consecration is allowed to wash his or her head and body with water in order to remove dirt provided that he or she does not wash with anything that would kill vermin; hence, it is permissible to bathe with soap and other cleansing agents that do not kill vermin, even if they have a fragrance; for the views of the Malikis and the Hanafis, see below.[120]

It is also permissible for someone in a state of ritual consecration to seek protection from the sun under a tree or an umbrella or inside a tent, a house or a sedan chair. However, none of these things should touch his head and his face, since it is

---

(4) The *siwāk* tree [the twigs of which are used to clean the gums and teeth – t.n.].

(5) Cutting down trees for construction and making a dwelling on the same site, or for the repair of orchards.

(6) Cutting off tree leaves with the use of a *mijann*, a type of curved stick. The *mijann* is placed on the branch and shaken, as a result of which the leaves fall without being struck. However, beating a stick against a tree in order to make its leaves fall is forbidden.

As for trees or plants which tend to be cultivated by human beings, such as lettuce, wheat, watermelon and pomegranate, they may be cut within the Meccan precincts even if they have come up by themselves.

119. The Malikis hold that it is undesirable for someone in a state of ritual consecration to perform venesection and cupping unless there is a need to do so; if such a need exists, however, these practices are permitted. If the person places a bandage over the site of the cupping or venesection, he must pay a redemption; otherwise, however, he is not required to do so.

120. The Malikis hold that it is not permissible for someone in a state of ritual consecration to remove dirt by washing; however, they make an exception for the hands, which may be washed with soap or something similar which removes dirt provided that it has no scent. As for washing with a scented substance the fragrance of which remains on one's hands, this is forbidden.

* * *

As for the Hanafis, they hold that it is permissible for someone in a state of ritual consecration to bathe with something that removes dirt but which does not kill vermin (in agreement with the Shafiis and the Hanbalis); however, it is not permissible to wash with something that has a perfume-like fragrance.

obligatory to keep them exposed according to the Malikis and the Hanafis; for the views of the Shafiis and the Hanbalis, see below.[121]

What is required of someone in the state of *iḥrām* in order to enter Mecca

It is an emulation of the Sunnah for the pilgrim to bathe before entering Mecca. This bath is for the sake of cleanliness only, not for the sake of the circumambulation of arrival according to the Shafiis, the Hanafis and the Hanbalis; hence, it is also required of women who are menstruating or experiencing post-partum bleeding. For the Malikis' view, see below.[122]

It is considered desirable to enter Mecca during the day and to enter it from its upper side, that is, from its gate known as Bāb al-Mu'allā, in order for the pilgrim to be facing the Ka'bah as a means of showing the proper veneration. Once inside Mecca, the pilgrim should first secure his or her belongings, then go to the Sacred Mosque. It is recommended that one enter the Sacred Mosque through the door known as Bāb al-Salām during the day, uttering the *talbiyah* with an attitude of humility and reverence. Upon sighting the Ka'bah one should raise one's hands and say, *Allāhu akbar* and *lā ilāha illā Allāh*, then: "O God, increase this house in honor, glory, veneration, dignity and righteousness. And grant that its grandeur and its nobility may cause those who come to it in pilgrimage to themselves increase in veneration, respect, honor, solemnity and righteousness." The foregoing is agreed upon; however, the Hanafis hold that it is undesirable to raise one's hands while uttering the supplication, the traditional wording of which is as follows: "O God, You are peace and from You does peace come. So, our Lord, greet us with peace." After uttering these words, the pilgrim may offer any other supplication he wishes.

---

121. The Shafiis hold that it is permissible to seek shade from the sun by all of the means mentioned above, even if they come in contact with one's head or face. However, if someone places on his head some object which is customarily used for concealment, such as an outer cloak and if his purpose is, in fact, to conceal himself, he will have committed a forbidden act; otherwise, such an action is not forbidden.

* * *

The Hanbalis hold that it is forbidden for someone to seek protection from the sun by means of something which remains with him the majority of the time, such as his sedan chair. This ruling applies whether the person concerned is riding or walking. However, it is permissible to seek protection from the sun by means of something that does not remain with the person concerned, such as a tree or a tent.

122. According to the Malikis, the bath taken before one enters Mecca is recommended, but not an emulation of the Sunnah; moreover, they hold that it is not for the sake of cleanliness, but for the sake of performing the circumambulation of arrival. Hence, it is not to be taken by women who are menstruating or experiencing post-partum bleeding since they would be forbidden to perform this circumambulation due to the fact that ritual purity is a condition for its validity, as will be seen. It is also recommended that one enter Mecca between dawn and noon; if someone arrives at night, he should spend the night in a place known as Dhū Tawā and postpone his entry until the following day. Moreover, the Malikis do not stipulate that one should utter a supplication when one sees the Sacred Mosque, be it a specific prayer or a general one.

Following the aforementioned supplications, the pilgrim may perform the circumambulation of arrival (*ṭawāf al-qudūm*). However, this circumambulation is only an emulation of the Sunnah given the following two conditions: (1) that the pilgrim be coming from outside Mecca (which is why it is referred to as "the circumambulation of arrival"); and (2) that there be sufficient time for it; if the pilgrim has good reason to believe that by performing the circumambulation of arrival, he will miss being able to stand on Mt. 'Arafah [during its specified time period], he should omit the circumambulation and go directly to Mt. 'Arafah.

The second pillar of the *ḥajj*: *ṭawāf al-ifāḍah*

There are three types of circumambulation: (1) One which is a pillar of the *ḥajj* such that if it is not performed, one's *ḥajj* will not be valid. This is referred to as *ṭawāf al-ifāḍah* or *ṭawāf al-ziyārah*, i.e., the circumambulation of visitation. (2) One which is a 'duty'; this circumambulation is referred to sometimes as *ṭawāf al-ziyārah* and sometimes as *ṭawāf al-ṣadr*. (3) One which is an emulation of the Sunnah; this refers to the circumambulation of arrival referred to above.

The definition of *ṭawāf al-ifāḍah*

All four schools agree that the circumambulation referred to sometimes as *ṭawāf al-ifāḍah*, and sometimes as *ṭawāf al-ziyārah*, is one of the four pillars of the *ḥajj*. Hence, if the pilgrim fails to perform this circumambulation, his *ḥajj* will not be valid. This circumambulation consists of seven circuits around the Ka'bah, which are performed in a specified manner to be explained shortly. According to the Hanafis, the circumambulation which is a pillar of the *ḥajj* consists of only four circuits around the Ka'bah; hence, once the pilgrim has completed four circuits, he has performed this pillar. As for the remaining three circuits, they are a 'duty', not a pillar; the reason for this is that performance of four circuits represents more than half of the total pillar, and anything over 'half' is treated, in terms of Islamic law, as if it were the whole.

The time for *ṭawāf al-ifāḍah*

The various schools offer different rulings on the time for *ṭawāf al-ifāḍah.*[123]

---

123. According to the Hanafis, the time for the performance of *ṭawāf al-ifāḍah* begins at dawn on the Day of Sacrifice and extends until the end of one's lifetime once one has stood on Mt. 'Arafah. Once the pilgrim has stood on Mt. 'Arafah, he is required to perform the *ṭawāf al-ifāḍah*; if he does not stand on Mt. 'Arafah at the time specified for this pillar, his performance of *ṭawāf al-ifāḍah* will be invalid, and so will his entire *ḥajj*. It is also necessary that one perform *ṭawāf al-ifāḍah* during the months designated for the *ḥajj*, namely, Shawwāl, Dhū al-Qa'dah, and Dhū al-Ḥijjah. If someone stands on Mt. 'Arafah during the month of Dhū al-Ḥijjah but does not perform *ṭawāf al-ifāḍah* before the month is out, he must perform it during the *ḥajj* months of some other year.

* * *

According to the Malikis, the time for *ṭawāf al-ifāḍah* extends from the Day of Sacrifice until the end of the month of Dhū al-Ḥijjah; if the pilgrim delays it until after this time, he must offer an animal sacrifice, but his *ḥajj* will be valid. *Ṭawāf al-ifāḍah* will not be valid before the Day of Sacrifice; as for standing on Mt. 'Arafah, it will not be valid either before or after the time specified for it, as will be seen below in the discussion of this pillar.

* * *

According to the Shafiis, the time for *ṭawāf al-ifāḍah* (or *ṭawāf al-ziyārah)*, which is a pillar of the *ḥajj*, begins after midnight on the eve of the Day of Sacrifice. The preferred time for *ṭawāf al-ifāḍah* is the Day of Sacrifice. There is no end to the time during which it may be performed; rather, one may postpone it for as long as one wishes. However, the pilgrim will not be permitted to have sexual relations until he has performed the circumambulation; until he does so, then, it is as if he were in a state of ritual consecration, but once he performs the circumambulation, he is released from this state. Once this occurs, the only requirement left is the pebble throwing to be performed during the days of *tashrīq* and spending the night at Minā, which are duties required of the pilgrim after he is released from the state of ritual consecration as a continuation of the *ḥajj* rites.

* * *

As for the Hanbalis, they hold that the time for *ṭawāf al-ifāḍah* which is a pillar of the *ḥajj* begins at midnight on the eve of the Day of Sacrifice for those pilgrims who have stood on Mt. 'Arafah; like the Hanafis, the Hanbalis hold that if someone performs this circumambulation before standing on Mt. 'Arafah, his *ḥajj* will be invalidated. However, there is no end to the time during which one may perform it; rather, one may perform it at any time for the rest of his life. The Hanbalis thus agree with the Hanafis on all points except the specification of the time period for this pillar.

Conditions for circumambulation

Circumambulation of the Ka'bah, of whatever type, has specific conditions which must be fulfilled in order for it to be valid.[124]

---

124. The Shafiis list the following eight conditions for the circumambulation of the Ka'bah: (1) Concealment of those private parts which must be concealed during ritual prayer. (2) Being free of both *ḥadath* and *khabath*, as in the case of ritual prayer. (3) Beginning one's circumambulation of the Ka'bah with part or all of one's body opposite the Black Stone from one's left side. In other words, no part of one's body should be ahead of any part of the stone. If one begins the circumambulation of the Ka'bah at any other point, the distance covered before one reaches the Black Stone will not count. Once one has come around again to the Black Stone, one begins a new circuit, at which point it is necessary to be opposite the Black Stone again in the manner described above. (4) Keeping the Ka'bah to one's left throughout the circumambulation and facing forward. The pilgrim must keep his or her entire body away from the wall of the Ka'bah, the *shādharwān*, and from the *ḥijr*. If someone steps on the *shādharwān* or touches the wall while passing by, or if he steps inside the *ḥijr* from one end and exits through the other, his *ḥajj* will be invalid. Similarly, one's circumambulation will be invalid if one faces the Ka'bah directly, faces directly away from it, performs the circumambulation with the Ka'bah to his right, or walks around backwards with the Ka'bah to his left. (5) Being certain that one has performed seven complete circuits of the Ka'bah; if any of the seven is omitted, one's circumambulation will be invalid. (6) Being in the Sacred Mosque or its immediate environs. Hence, one's circumambulation will be valid so long as one is inside the Sacred Mosque, in the air surrounding it or on its roof; this applies even if one is elevated above the Ka'bah, and even if there is a barrier of sorts between the Ka'bah and the person performing the circumambulation. (7) Not interrupting one's circumambulation in order to do something else; if one does so, the circumambulation will be invalidated. (8) Intending to perform the circumambulation. This is only a condition for a circumambulation which is neither a pillar of the *ḥajj* nor the circumambulation of arrival; in these two situations, by contrast, no intention is required since the intention to perform the major or minor pilgrimage to Mecca is sufficient. The intention to perform the circumambulation must coincide with one's being opposite the Black Stone; if someone forms this intention after passing the Black Stone, his circumambulation will only be counted from the time he passes it again. However, if one returns to a position opposite the Black Stone after forming this intention, the circumambulation will count from that point onward. (9) Performing the circumambulation before standing on Mt. 'Arafah; the circumambulation is not required of someone who enters Mecca after having stood on Mt. 'Arafah or after midnight.

There are also 'duties' associated with the circumambulation. These include: (1) refraining from any kind of transgression during the time the circumambulation is being performed; (2) not allowing oneself to despise anyone one sees, (3) being courteous, and (4) restraining one's hands and one's eyes from any disobedience.

* * *

According to the Malikis, there are seven conditions for the validity of *ṭawāf*, or circumambulation: (1) The performance of seven entire circuits. If someone performs fewer than seven circuits, his circumambulation will not be valid; nor is it sufficient to offer an animal sacrifice in such a case if the circumambulation in question is a pillar of the *ḥajj*. If one has doubts about how many circuits one has performed, one should build on whatever number one is certain to have performed until a total of seven circuits have been completed. If one performs more than seven, however, no harm is done, since anything extra is void and not taken into account. (2) Freedom from minor and major ritual impurity, as well as from impurities on one's body and clothing. If someone has an occurrence of ritual impurity while performing the circumambulation, or if he realizes that there is some impurity on his body or clothing, it will be invalidated. If one has an occurrence of ritual impurity after completing the circumambulation and before performing the two *rak'ahs* associated with it, he must repeat the circumambulation, since these two *rak'ahs* are considered part thereof. However, if the person concerned has already left Mecca and would face undue hardship by trying to go back, the circumambulation already performed must suffice and all he or she is required to do is to perform the two *rak'ahs*, then send an animal sacrifice back to Mecca. The ruling on these two *rak'ahs* is that they are a 'duty' after the circumambulation of visitation (*ṭawāf al-ifāḍah*) and the circumambulation of arrival (*ṭawāf al-qudūm*). Following the circumambulation of farewell (*ṭawāf al-wadā'*), there are some who hold that they are a 'duty' and others who hold that they are an emulation of the Sunnah; however, both views are valid. It is recommended that one recite Surah 109 after the *Fātiḥah* in the first *rak'ah*, and Surah 112 following the *Fātiḥah* in the second *rak'ah*. It is likewise recommended that one perform these two *rak'ahs* behind the Station of Abraham and that one utter supplications following them in the *Multazam*, i.e., the area between the Black Stone and the door of the Ka'bah. In the case of those who performed the circumambulation after the mid-afternoon prayer, it is recommended that they perform these two *rak'ahs* between the obligatory sundown prayer and the two Sunnah-based *rak'ahs* which follow it. (3) Concealing the same private parts that must be concealed during ritual prayer. (4) Keeping the Ka'bah to one's left. (5) Keeping one's entire body outside the *ḥijr* and away from the *shādharwān*. (6) Continuity. If one waits too long between one and another of the circuits, the circumambulation will be invalidated. However, a slight delay between them is excusable. (7) Being inside the Sacred Mosque. The circumambulation will not be valid on its roof or outside it. Moreover, one must begin the circumambulation from the Black Stone. If one begins before it, one must still end the final circuit at the Black Stone; if one does not complete the circumambulation and if there is a long delay before one's completion of it, or if one's ritual ablutions are invalidated while performing it, one must repeat it unless one has already come home [from Mecca], in which case one is only required to send an animal sacrifice.

* * *

The Hanbalis list the following conditions for the validity of the circumambulation: (1) Intention. (2) The beginning of the specified time period. This condition applies to the circumambulation of visitation, and the time period referred to begins at midnight on the eve of the Day of Sacrifice for those who have already stood on

Mt. 'Arafah; it will not be valid before one has stood on Mt. 'Arafah, but there is no end to the time period during which the circumambulation may be performed. (3) Concealing one's private parts as in ritual prayer. (4) Freedom from impurities on one's body and clothing, as in ritual prayer. (5) Freedom from major and minor ritual impurity unless the pilgrim is a child who has not reached the age of discernment, in whose case the circumambulation will be valid even if he has had an occurrence of ritual impurity and has impurities on his body or clothing. (6) Performance of seven circuits which were begun at the Black Stone. If the pilgrim begins a circuit at any other point, it will not be counted. (7) Walking for those who are able to do so. (8) Continuity among the circuits. If someone has an occurrence of ritual impurity during the circumambulation, it will be invalidated and he must start all over again. However, if the time for one of the five daily prayers arrives and if it will be led by the regular imam, the pilgrim may pray with the imam, then build later on the circuits he has already completed; when doing so, he should begin again from the Black Stone. The same ruling applies if a funeral procession arrives; in other words, he may interrupt his circumambulation to pray over the deceased. (8) Being inside the Sacred Mosque. The circumambulation will not be valid outside it; however, it will be valid on its roof. (9) Keeping the Ka'bah on one's left and keeping one's entire body away from the *ḥijr* and the *shādharwān*.

As for 'duties', the Hanbalis list none in connection with the circumambulation.

* * *

The Hanafis list the following conditions for the validity of the circumambulation: (1) One must remain inside the Sacred Mosque. One may perform the circumambulation from beyond the Well of Zamzam or from beyond the pillars inside the mosque. However, if it is performed from outside the mosque, it will not be valid. (2) One must begin the circumambulation of visitation after the break of dawn on the Day of Sacrifice, but there is no deadline for its performance as was seen above. As for the circumambulation of arrival, one is to begin it from the time one enters Mecca, while the latest it may be performed is the time before one stands on Mt. 'Arafah; hence, once someone has stood on Mt. 'Arafah, it is too late to perform the circumambulation of arrival. For someone who has not stood on Mt. 'Arafah, the time period for the circumambulation of arrival ends with the break of dawn on the Day of Sacrifice.

Sunnah-based practices and duties associated with circumambulation

Each of the schools lists a number of Sunnah-based practices and duties associated with circumambulation.[125]

---

125. The Shafiis list eight Sunnah-based practices in connection with circumambulation of the Ka'bah: (1) To face the Ka'bah in the beginning of the circumambulation and to stop beside the Black Stone in the direction of the Yemeni corner such that the entire Stone is to one's right and one's right shoulder is parallel with its edge. One then forms the intention to perform the circumambulation, after which one faces the Stone as one moves toward the door of the Ka'bah. Once one has passed the door, one is to face ahead so that the Ka'bah is to one's left. This applies only to the first circuit. (2) To walk (rather than ride) if one is capable of doing so. This applies even to women, since riding during circumambulation is a departure from the ideal unless one has a legitimate excuse for doing so. If one does have such an excuse, there is no harm in riding provided that one rides on something other than an animal; the reason for this ruling is to protect the Sacred Mosque from [the impurities that would result from the presence of] animals. It is deemed preferable to perform the circumambulation barefoot if one will not be harmed by doing so. It is recommended that one keep one's steps short in order to increase the reward one earns for the circumambulation, and that one touch the Black Stone with one's hand at the beginning and kiss it lightly. It is not an emulation of the Sunnah for the woman to do so unless the area is empty, whether during the day or at night; as for the man, it is desirable for him to place his forehead on the Black Stone and for him to touch it with his hand and kiss it three times. If he is unable to touch it with his hand, he should do so with a stick or the like, then kiss whatever part of the stick came in contact with the Stone. If he is unable to do this, either, he is to point toward it with his hand or with whatever he is holding in his hand, preferably the right. (3) To utter the traditional supplication. When one touches the Black Stone at the beginning of each circuit, one is to raise one's hands as at the beginning of a ritual prayer and say, "In the name of God. God is greatest. O God, [I perform this rite] based on faith in You and belief in Your Book, in loyalty to Your covenant, and in emulation of the example of Your Prophet, our master Muḥammad" (*bismillāhi wa Allāhu akbar. Allāhumma, īmānan bika wa taṣdīqan bi kitābika wa wafā'an bi 'ahdika wa ittibā'an li sunnat nabiyyik, sayyidinā Muḥammadin ṣallā Allāhu 'alayhi wa sallam*). This supplication is a more emphatically enjoined emulation of the Sunnah during the first circuit than it is in subsequent circuits. (4) For males to walk quickly, yet without breaking into a run. There is no jumping in the first three circuits, and in the remaining four, males are to walk at a leisurely pace. As for women, they are to walk at their regular pace. (5) For the male, whether he is an adult or a boy, to wear his *ridā'* in such a way that its mid-section passes under his right arm while its ends are draped over his left shoulder. (6) For men and boys to remain close to the Ka'bah if the area is not too crowded and if it causes no harm or disturbance; as for women, however, it is an emulation of the Sunnah for them not to walk close to the Ka'bah, since this is an expression of greater modesty. (7) To maintain continuity throughout one's circumambulation. Hence, if someone has

an occurrence of ritual impurity while circumambulating the Ka'bah, even if it takes place deliberately, he may repeat his ritual ablutions and continue the circumambulation where he left off; however, it is preferable to begin all over again. Similarly, if one of the five ritual prayers is begun during one's circumambulation, one may perform the prayer, then complete one's circumambulation afterwards, but it is considered preferable to start again from the beginning. (8) To perform two *rak'ahs* after the circumambulation; it is sufficient to perform an obligatory prayer, or a voluntary prayer other than this. It is recommended that these two *rak'ahs* be performed directly after the circumambulation and that one touch the Black Stone immediately after the two *rak'ahs*. After touching the Black Stone, it is recommended that one perform the *sa'ī*, that is, the brisk walk between al-Ṣafā and al-Marwah, if this is required of the person concerned. It is preferable to perform these two *rak'ahs* behind the Station of Abraham; [if this is not possible], then inside the *ḥijr*, and [if this is not possible], then as close as possible to the Ka'bah. This is a Sunnah-based practice which remains desirable even if one delays it till some time after the circumambulation.

It is undesirable: (1) to discontinue the circumambulation without reason, (2) to spit without a legitimate excuse even if one does so in a garment, (3) to place one's hands behind one's back or on one's mouth for any reason other than to conceal a yawn, (4) to crack one's knuckles, or (5) to perform the circumambulation while attempting to suppress the need to urinate, defecate, pass gas, etc.

* * *

The Malikis list two duties associated with circumambulation: (1) performance of two *rak'ahs* afterwards, as we have seen, and (2) walking for those who are able to do so.

As for Sunnah-based practices associated with circumambulation, they list the following: (1) Kissing the Black Stone during the first circuit while uttering the words *Allāhu akbar*. If one is not able to kiss the Stone, one should touch it with his hand; if he is unable to touch it with his hand, he is to touch it with an object, such as a cane, for example, then place his hand or the cane on his mouth while uttering the words *Allāhu akbar*. If the pilgrim is unable to do any of the foregoing, he is to say *Allāhu akbar* while passing parallel to the Stone. (2) Touching the Yemeni corner with one's hand during the first circuit, then placing one's hand on one's mouth. (3) Uttering whatever supplications one wishes while performing the circumambulation. (4) Walking faster than normal during the first three circuits; however, this is an emulation of the Sunnah for men only, and during circumambulations other than the circumambulation of visitation (*ṭawāf al-ifāḍah*); as for walking faster then usual during the circumambulation of visitation, it is recommended, but not an emulation of the Sunnah. Specifically, it is recommended that the man walk faster than usual during the first three circuits of the circumambulation of visitation if he did not perform the circumambulation of arrival, and that he kiss the Black Stone and touch the Yemeni Corner with his hand during the first circuit. (5) For men to remain close to the Ka'bah; as for women, it is an emulation of the Sunnah for them to circumambulate behind the men, as in ritual prayer.

* * *

The Hanbalis list the following Sunnah-based practices in connection with circumambulation: (1) Touching the Yemeni Corner with one's right hand during every circuit. (2) Touching and kissing the Black Stone during every circuit or, if this is not possible, pointing to it with one's hand. (3) Wearing the *ridā'* in such a way that its mid-section passes under one's right arm and its ends pass over one's left shoulder. (4) Walking faster than one's normal pace while taking short steps (referred to as *ramal*). However, this is only an emulation of the Sunnah during the first three circuits of the circumambulation of arrival for male pilgrims who are not riding and who have no legitimate excuse for not walking in this fashion, and for those who entered a state of ritual consecration either in or near Mecca. As for women and others who do not meet the aforementioned descriptions, it is not an emulation of the Sunnah for them to engage in *ramal*; nor is *ramal* an emulation of the Sunnah in the circumambulation of visitation or in any circumambulation other than the circumambulation of arrival. (5) Supplication. (6) Uttering words and phrases of divine remembrance. (7) Remaining close to the Ka'bah. (8) Performing two *rak'ahs* after the circumambulation.

* * *

As for the Hanafis, they list a number of 'duties' and Sunnah-based practices associated with circumambulation. The 'duties' are as follows: (1) To begin one's circumambulation from the Black Stone; if one fails to do this, one must repeat the circumambulation provided that one is still in Mecca, and if one returns home from Mecca without repeating it, one must offer an animal sacrifice. It is preferable that one stop with one's entire body across from the Black Stone, with the Stone on one's right and one's right shoulder parallel to it. (2) To perform the circumambulation to the right of the Ka'bah, beginning with its door to one's left. The reason for this is that the Ka'bah is to the pilgrim as the imam is to the worshiper, and a worshiper who is praying alone is to stand to the right of his imam. Hence, if someone reverses the circumambulation by moving around the Ka'bah with the Ka'bah to his right, he must either repeat the circumambulation or offer an animal sacrifice. (As for the ritual purity of one's clothing, one's body and the place, this is an emphatically enjoined emulation of the Sunnah. Hence, if someone performs the circumambulation wearing clothes which are contaminated with impurities, he will not be required to offer compensation (*jazā'*), but he will have neglected the Sunnah.) (3) To conceal those private parts which must be concealed during ritual prayer. If one-fourth of a private part that must be concealed during ritual prayer is exposed while one is performing the circumambulation, one will have neglected a 'duty' and one must either repeat the circumambulation or offer an animal sacrifice. Moreover, it should be noted that concealment of one's private parts is, in and of itself, a full religious obligation (*farḍ*); hence, when we say here that it is a 'duty' (*wājib*), what we mean is that one's circumambulation will not be invalidated if one fails to do this but rather, that it will be valid even though the person who performed it will be guilty of wrongdoing and, as a result, he will be required either to repeat it or offer *jazā'*. If, on the other hand, less than one-fourth of what must be concealed is exposed, no harm is done; this ruling applies equally to ritual prayer and to circumambulation. (4) To walk if one is able. If someone performs the circumambulation riding, crawling or being carried without a legitimate excuse, he or she must either repeat it or offer an animal sacrifice. If there is a legitimate excuse for such a practice, however, it involves no consequences. (5) To circumambulate outside the *ḥijr*, since part of it belongs to the Ka'bah proper. (6) To complete seven circuits of the Ka'bah, each of which must begin and end at the Black Stone. These seven circuits are all a 'duty' in the circumambulation of arrival and the circumambulation of farewell. If someone omits most of the circuits of the circumambulation of farewell (four circuits, that is), he will be required to offer an animal sacrifice, whereas someone who omits fewer than this will be required to offer charity for each circuit missed. In the case of the circumambulation of arrival, by contrast, all one is required to do if one omits more than or fewer than half of its circuits is to repent, since this circumambulation is an emulation of the Sunnah which only becomes a 'duty' once one has begun to perform it (as in the case of voluntary prayers); as a consequence, the ruling that applies to the circumambulation of arrival differs from the ruling that applies to rites which are 'duties'. As for the obligatory circumambulation of visitation, it is a pillar [of the *ḥajj*] to perform more than half of its circuits. Hence, if one omitted four circuits of the circumambulation of visitation, it would be invalidated. As for the remaining three circuits, they are a 'duty', as we have seen. However, one is not considered to have neglected a 'duty' by omitting them until one actually leaves Mecca. Moreover, one is not allowed to let someone else perform the circumambulation on one's behalf without a legitimate excuse. (7) To perform two *rak'ahs* after every seven circuits of one's circumambulation, whether the circumambulation was obligatory, a 'duty', an emulation of the Sunnah or voluntary. It is preferable that one maintain continuity by praying these two *rak'ahs* immediately after one's circumambulation unless one performed the circumambulation during a time when prayer is undesirable. One's not performing these two *rak'ahs* immediately does not exempt one from the obligation to do so later; rather, one is free to do so at any time one wishes, even after one returns home from Mecca, though it is considered undesirable to do so. It is preferable to perform the post-circumambulation *rak'ahs* in the following places, in descending order of preference: 1. behind the Station of Abraham, 2. in the Ka'bah, 3. in the *ḥijr* under the waterspout, 4. any spot within the *ḥijr* which is close to the Ka'bah, 5. [elsewhere] in the Sacred Mosque, 6. in the Meccan precincts. If one performs them outside the Meccan precincts, one commits an offense. Lastly, one is to recite Surah 109 during the first *rak'ah*, and Surah 112 during the second.

As for the Sunnah-based practices associated with circumambulation, the Hanafis list the following: (1) Before commencing the circumambulation, to pass one end of one's *ridā'* under one's right arm and to place the other end over one's left shoulder; one is to do this during each circumambulation which is followed by *sa'ī,* such as the circumambulation of arrival. (2) To walk quickly, keeping one's steps short and shaking one's shoulders (referred to as *ramal*). This is only to be done during the first three circuits; if the pilgrim encounters something that would hinder him, he is to pause until he is able to resume his *ramal*. (3) To touch and kiss the Black Stone at the end of every circuit. (Moreover, it is an emphatically enjoined emulation of the Sunnah to form a conscious intention to perform circumambulation during the first and last circuits.) If someone is unable to touch the Stone with

The third pillar of the *ḥajj*: *sa'ī*, that is, walking at a brisk pace between al-Ṣafā and al-Marwah

Walking briskly (*al-sa'ī*) between al-Ṣafā and al-Marwah is a pillar of the *ḥajj*; hence, if someone does not do this, his or her *ḥajj* will be invalidated according to the Shafiis, the Malikis and the Hanbalis. As for the Hanafis, they hold that *al-sa'ī* is not a pillar, but a 'duty', which means that if someone omits it, his or her *ḥajj* will not be invalidated, but he must pay a redemption.

Conditions for *al-sa'ī* between al-Ṣafā and al-Marwah, how it is done, and Sunnah-based practices associated with it

The conditions and Sunnah-based practices associated with *al-sa'ī* are listed in detail by each school.[126]

---

his hand, he should touch it with something like a cane if possible, then kiss whatever he touched it with. If he is unable to do this, either, he should face the Stone and raise his hands with his palms toward it saying, *Allāhu akbar*, *lā ilāha illā Allāh* and *al-ḥamdu lillāh*, then pray for blessings upon the Prophet. This action is desirable; it is likewise desirable to touch the Yemeni Corner, though it is not an emulation of the Sunnah.

Other desirable actions in this connection include the following: (1) After performing the two *rak'ahs* of circumambulation behind the Station of Abraham, to utter supplications for whatever one needs in this life and in the life to come. (2) Between performing the two *rak'ahs* of circumambulation and going out to al-Ṣafā, to come to the Well of Zamzam, drink as much as one can, then pour what remains back into the well, saying, "O God, I ask You to provide me generous sustenance, beneficial knowledge, and healing from every ailment" (*Allāhumma, as'aluka rizqan wāsi'an wa 'ilman nāfi'an wa shifā'an min kulli dā'*). (3) To come to the *multazam* before going out to al-Ṣafā.

126. The Hanafis list duties, Sunnah-based practices, and one condition associated with *sa'ī*. The duties are as follows: (1) To delay *sa'ī* until after one's circumambulation. (2) To make seven circuits, each circuit of which is itself a 'duty'. (3) To walk during *sa'ī*. Hence, if someone performs the *sa'ī* riding without a legitimate excuse, he must either repeat it or offer a sacrificial animal. (3) To begin *sa'ī* from al-Ṣafā and end it at al-Marwah; this is considered to be one circuit. If someone begins at al-Marwah and ends at al-Ṣafā, the circuit will not be counted.

The following are the Sunnah-based practices listed by the Hanafis in connection with *al-sa'ī*: (1) To maintain continuity between one's circumambulation and one's *sa'ī*. If someone pauses between them, whether for a short time or a long time, he will have neglected the Sunnah, but he will not be required to offer any compensation. (2) To be free of major and minor ritual impurity. Hence, *sa'ī* performed by a woman who is menstruating or experiencing post-partum bleeding will still be valid and have no undesirability attached to it if she performs it while in this state with a legitimate excuse. (3) To ascend both al-Ṣafā and al-Marwah in one's *sa'ī* and to perform the *sa'ī* between the two green pillars, one of which is beneath Minārat Bāb 'Alī (the minaret situated at 'Alī's gate) and the other of which is across from Ribāṭ al-'Abbās. (4) To hasten between these two pillars. (5) To utter the words *Allāhu akbar* and *lā ilāha illā Allāh*, to pray for blessings upon the Prophet, to utter supplications for whatever one wishes, and to face the Ka'bah from atop al-Ṣafā and al-Marwah. (5) To touch the Black Stone with one's hand before going to perform the *sa'ī*. If one is unable to do this, one should perform the alternative actions described in the section above on "Sunnah-based practices associated with circumambulation." It is preferable that one come out through the Ṣafā Door, that is, the Banū Makhzūm Door, and that one put one's left foot forward when doing so.

It is recommended that one lift one's hands toward heaven when uttering supplications on al-Ṣafā and al-Marwah. If one of the five daily ritual prayers begins while one is performing a circumambulation or *sa'ī*, one should perform the prayer, then resume where he left off.

It is undesirable for one to engage in discussions of buying and selling and similar matters during one's *sa'ī* or circumambulation.

As for the condition listed by the Hanafis in connection with *sa'ī*, it is that it be performed after the circumambulation; if someone performs the *sa'ī* first, then the circumambulation, his or her *sa'ī* will not count, and as long as he is able to do so, he must repeat it.

* * *

According to the Malikis, the *sa'ī* between al-Ṣafā and al-Marwah is a pillar of the *ḥajj* which has associated conditions for its validity, Sunnah-based practices, recommended practices, and one duty. The conditions for its validity are as follows: (1) That one perform seven circuits. If someone performs fewer than seven circuits, his *sa'ī* will be invalid and he will be obliged to continue until he has performed a full seven unless what would commonly be considered a 'long' time has passed since the last circuit performed, in which case he should start all over again. (2) That one begin at al-Ṣafā. If someone begins at al-Marwah, this circuit will not be counted. Going from al-Ṣafā to al-Marwah is considered to be one circuit, while the return from al-Marwah to al-Ṣafā is another circuit. (3) That one maintain continuity among the various circuits. If one pauses for a long time between them, one must begin again, though a short pause is excusable, as, for example, if someone interrupts his *sa'ī* to perform a funeral prayer, or to make a sale or a purchase which does not take what would be commonly be considered a 'long' time. (4) That it be performed after a circumambulation, whether the circumambulation was a pillar of the *ḥajj* or not. If the *sa'ī* is not performed after a circumambulation, it will not be valid. One will not be required to repeat the *sa'ī* if the circumambulation which preceded it was a pillar of the *ḥajj*, namely, the circumambulation of visitation, or a 'duty', such as the circumambulation of arrival. However, if the *sa'ī* is performed after a recommended circumambulation, such as the circumambulation of mosque greeting (*ṭawāf taḥiyyat al-masjid*), the pilgrim must repeat the *sa'ī* after the circumambulation of arrival if he has not yet stood on Mt. 'Arafah; if the pilgrim has already stood on Mr. 'Arafah, he must repeat the *sa'ī* after the circumambulation of visitation, since the circumambulation of arrival may no longer be performed after one has stood on Mt. 'Arafah. The repetition of the *sa'ī* is to be done in the manner just described if the pilgrim is still in Mecca or has not yet traveled far on his return journey, in which case he is to return to do the repetition. Similarly, one is to repeat the *sa'ī* as described here if it was performed after the circumambulation of visitation, which is a pillar of the *ḥajj*, without believing that it was a pillar and without intending it as such, or after the circumambulation of arrival, which is a 'duty', without believing that it was a duty or intending it as such.

The Sunnah-based practices associated with the *sa'ī* are as follows: (1) Kissing the Black Stone and praying two *rak'ahs* between performing the circumambulation and going out to perform the *sa'ī*. (2) Performing the *sa'ī* as promptly as possible after one's circumambulation and the two *rak'ahs* that follow it. (3) Ascending both al-Ṣafā and al-Marwah during every circuit. One must not neglect to stop on each hill for a good period of time. However, ascending the two hills is only an emulation of the Sunnah for men, and for women if there is no crowd of men there; if there are many men on the hills, women are not to ascend them. (4) Making supplications however one wishes while on the two hills. (5) For men: Walking between the two green pillars (one of which is under Minārat Bāb 'Alī, while the other is across from Ribāt al-'Abbās) at a pace which is faster than the *ramal* described above in connection with circumambulation. This fast walk is to be done only when going from al-Ṣafā to al-Marwah, whereas upon returning to al-Ṣafā one is not to hurry according to the best-attested point of view.

As for the recommended actions associated with *sa'ī*, the Malikis list the following: (1) That one be free of major and minor ritual purity and from impure substances on one's body and clothing, and (2) That one fulfill all remaining conditions which apply to ritual prayer if possible; as for those which cannot be fulfilled, such as facing the *qiblah*, they are not recommended.

As for duties associated with *sa'ī*, the Malikis list only one, namely, that one perform it on foot if one is able.

* * *

The Hanbalis list the following seven conditions for the *sa'ī* between al-Ṣafā and al-Marwah: (1) Intention. (2) Full possession of one's mental faculties. (3) Continuity between the various parts of the *sa'ī*. (4) Walking for those able to walk. (5) Performance of the *sa'ī* after a circumambulation, even if it is a circumambulation which is simply recommended [rather than obligatory or a 'duty']. (6) Performance of seven full circuits; traversing the distance from al-Ṣafā to al-Marwah is considered to be one circuit, while returning from al-Marwah is another circuit. (7) Traversing the entire distance between al-Ṣafā and al-Marwah by placing one's heel at the bottom of al-Ṣafā, walking to al-Marwah until one has placed one's toes on it, then placing one's heel at the bottom of al-Marwah and returning to al-Ṣafā until one places one's toes at the bottom of al-Ṣafā, and so on. One is to begin at al-Ṣafā and end at al-Marwah; hence, if one begins at al-Marwah, it will not be counted.

As for Sunnah-based practices relating to *sa'ī*, the Hanbalis list the following: (1) That one be free of minor and major ritual impurity, as well as from the presence of impure substances on one's body or clothing, (1) That one have all one's private parts concealed, and (3) That one maintain continuity between one's *sa'ī* and one's circumambulation.

* * *

The Shafiis list the following conditions for *sa'ī*: (1) That one begin at al-Ṣafā and end at al-Marwah. Going from al-Ṣafā to al-Marwah is considered to be one circuit, while returning from al-Marwah to al-Ṣafā is another circuit. (2) That one be certain to have completed seven circuits. If someone has a doubt concerning the number of circuits he has performed, he should build on the lesser number, because he can be certain to have completed this number. It is also necessary to traverse the entire distance in each circuit, and not to intend by means of his *sa'ī* anything other than to perform an act of worship entailed by the *ḥajj*; if one intends simply to traverse the distance, one's *sa'ī* will not be valid. (3) That one's *sa'ī* be performed after the circumambulation of visitation or the circumambulation of arrival, provided that one does not stop on Mt. 'Arafah between one's *sa'ī* and one's circumambulation. If someone performs the circumambulation of arrival, then stops on Mt. 'Arafah, he should not perform the *sa'ī* at this time but rather, delay it until after he has performed the circumambulation of visitation.

The Shafiis list the following actions as recommended in connection with *sa'ī*: (1) That one go out to perform the *sa'ī* through the Ṣafā door, which is one of the doors of the Sacred Mosque. (2) That men ascend al-Ṣafā until they can see the Ka'bah; as for women, they are not to do so unless the place is free of strange men. (3) That one utter the words of divine remembrance peculiar to each site. When one faces the Ka'bah, whether one has gone to the top of al-Ṣafā or not, one is to say *Allāhu akbar* three times, then: "To God belongs all praise. May God be exalted for the guidance He has granted us, and praised for what He has entrusted to us. There is no god but God, and He has no partner. To Him belongs dominion and praise. He causes to live and He causes to die. In His hand is all goodness, and He is capable of all things. There is no god but God alone, and He has no partner. He has fulfilled His promise, granted victory to His servant and has alone defeated the confederates. There is no god but God, and we worship none but Him, 'sincere in our faith in Him alone, however hateful this may be to those who deny the Truth' (40:14)." Having said this, the pilgrim may utter any other prayers of supplication he wishes, after which he is to repeat the same words of divine remembrance and the prayer of supplication mentioned here two more times. (4) That one be free of major and minor ritual impurity and impurities on one's body and clothing, and that one have one's private parts concealed. (5) That one not ride unless one has a legitimate excuse for doing so. (6) That men hasten during the middle of the distance between al-Ṣafā and al-Marwah, both going and coming back; at the beginning and at the end, however, they are to walk normally. As for women, they are not to hasten at any point along the way. (7) That one say during one's *sa'ī*, "My Lord, forgive and have mercy, overlooking what You know. Indeed, You are the most Powerful, the most Munificent" (*rabbi ighfir wa arḥam wa tajāwaz 'ammā ta'lam, innaka al-a'azz al-akram*). (8) That one perform the *sa'ī* immediately after one's circumambulation, that one perform the circuits in close succession, and that one perform two *rak'ahs* after the *sa'ī* with the intention of emulating the Sunnah in this manner. (It is undesirable to stop during the *sa'ī* without a legitimate excuse for doing so, or to perform the *sa'ī* more than once.)

The fourth pillar of the ḥajj: Coming to ʻArafah and how one is to stand there

The fourth pillar of the *ḥajj* is for the pilgrim to come to ʻArafah in whatever state he or she happens to be: awake or asleep, sitting or standing, standing still or walking. This is agreed upon by all four schools. Moreover, each school gives a detailed listing of the conditions and Sunnah-based practices associated with coming to ʻArafah.[127]

---

127. The Shafiis list the following conditions for coming to ʻArafah. (1) That one do so during the time specified for it, namely, between noon on 9 Dhū al-Ḥijjah and dawn on the Day of Sacrifice [10 Dhū al-Ḥijjah]. Out of this time period, it is sufficient to come to ʻArafah for as little as a single moment. (2) That the pilgrim be qualified to engage in acts of worship by not being insane or so inebriated that he has lost the proper use of his mental faculties. If the person is insane or inebriated to the degree described here, his coming to ʻArafah will not fulfill his obligation in this regard. As for someone who is in a coma or a swoon, he is considered to be like someone who is insane if there is no hope that he will regain consciousness; otherwise, he is to remain in a state of ritual consecration until he does regain consciousness.

As for Sunnah-based practices associated with coming to ʻArafah, the Shafiis list the following: (1) That men stop in the place where the Prophet used to do so, namely, at the large boulders at the foot of Mt. Mercy (Jabal al-Raḥmah) if this poses no difficulty; otherwise, they should stand as close to the site as possible. As for women, it is recommended that they sit along the outer edges of the site unless they have sedan chairs or something similar, in which case it is preferable for them to ride in these. (2) That one engage in frequent supplication, remembrance of God, and utterance of the words *lā ilāha illā Allāh*. One might say, for example, "There is no god but God alone, who has no partner. To Him belongs dominion and praise, and He is capable of all things. O God, place light in my heart and in my eyes. O God, open my breast and facilitate my endeavors. O God, You merit all the praise we utter, and more than what we can utter." It is also recommended that one recite other known supplications as well; one should repeat each supplication three times, opening by praising and glorifying God and praying for blessings upon the Prophet, and closing in the same way with an utterance of, "Amen." One should also weep profusely and keep reciting Surah 59. (3) That one take care to eat only foods which are permitted under Islamic law, keep one's intention pure, and cultivate an attitude of humble reverence and brokenness. (4) That one lift one's hands, though not above one's head, that one remain exposed to the sun unless one has a legitimate excuse to do otherwise, that one free one's mind of distractions and preoccupations before the time for stopping at Mt. ʻArafah begins, and that one avoid stopping in the road. (5) That one be free of major or minor ritual impurity and of impurities on one's body and clothing, keep one's private parts concealed, face the *qiblah*, ride [rather than walk] if possible, not turn away beggars or despise any human being, and refrain from arguing, cursing and name-calling. (6) That one stop on Mt. ʻArafah until sundown in order to be present there at the time when day and night converge.

* * *

The Hanafis list one condition, one duty, and several Sunnah-based practices in connection with coming to 'Arafah.

The condition is that one must come to 'Arafah at the time specified for this in Islamic law, namely, from noon on 9 Dhū al-Ḥijjah until dawn on the Day of Sacrifice (10 Dhū al-Ḥijjah). However, it is not necessary that one form a conscious intention, that one have knowledge concerning what one is doing, or that one be in full possession of one's mental faculties. Rather, if a pilgrim comes to 'Arafah during this time period, his *ḥajj* will be valid regardless of whether he intends to do so or not, whether he knows that he is at 'Arafah or not, whether he is sane or not, and whether he is unconscious, asleep, or awake.

It is a duty to remain on Mt. 'Arafah until sundown if one arrived there during the day; if one arrives during the day and comes down from 'Arafah before sundown, one must offer an animal sacrifice. However, if one arrives there at night, there is no further duty to fulfill.

As for the Sunnah-based practices associated with stopping on Mt. 'Arafah, they are as follows: (1) That the pilgrim perform major ablutions. (2) That the imam deliver two sermons. (3) That the pilgrim combine the noon and mid-afternoon prayers given the conditions listed above in the section on ritual prayer, and that he stop on Mt. 'Arafah as soon thereafter as possible. (4) That one not be fasting. (5) That one be in a state of ritual purity. (6) That one maintain a relaxed posture. (7) That one be behind the imam, but as close to him as possible. (8) That one be fully attentive in one's heart and free of thoughts that would distract one from one's supplications. (9) That one stop at the black boulders, which is where the Prophet used to stop; if it is not possible to stop at the boulders themselves, one should do one's best to be as near as possible to them. (10) That one raise one's hands with palms open. (11) That one utter supplications after praising God, uttering the words, *lā ilāha illā Allāh* and *Allāhu akbar* and praying for blessings upon the Prophet, and that one utter the *talbiyah* while stopping at the black boulders. (12) That one utter many supplications for forgiveness for oneself, one's parents, and for believers both men and women, that one continue uttering the *talbiyah*, the words *lā ilāha illā Allāh* and *subḥān Allāh*, that one praise God in reverence, submissiveness and sincerity, that one pray for blessings upon the Prophet, and that one ask God to meet one's various needs until sundown. There is no set formula for such supplications. Rather, one may pray as one wishes, though it is deemed preferable for most of one's supplications to consist of words such as, "There is no god but God alone, Who has no partner. To Him belongs dominion and praise. He causes to live and He causes to die, and He himself is the Ever-Living who does not die. In His hand lies all goodness, and He is capable of all things. We worship none but Him, and we recognize no other sovereign. O God, place light in my heart, my ears and my eyes. O God, open my breast and facilitate my endeavors. O God, this is the place of one who seeks refuge and protection from the fire. Grant me protection from the fire by Your pardon, and usher me into Paradise by Your mercy, O Most Merciful of the merciful. O God, now that You have led me to Islam, take it not from me, nor me from it, so that when You take my spirit, I will be a Muslim still." (13) That one lower one's voice when uttering supplications.

* * *

The Hanbalis list several conditions, one duty and a number of Sunnah-based practices associated with stopping on Mt. ʻArafah.

The conditions are as follows: (1) That one's coming to ʻArafah be voluntary; it will not be valid if the person has been coerced into coming. (2) That the person be qualified to engage in acts of worship; hence, it will not be valid if the person is insane, inebriated, or unconscious. (3) That one come at the time specified in Islamic law, which extends from dawn on 9 Dhū al-Ḥijjah until dawn on 10 Dhū al-Ḥijjah, which is the Day of Sacrifice. One's stopping on Mt. ʻArafah will be valid even if one does not know that the place in which he is stopping is part of ʻArafah, and even if he does not know that the time at which he stops there is the time for doing so. Rather, even if someone just happens to stop on Mt. ʻArafah at the right time, his stopping there will be valid as a part of the *ḥajj*.

The duty listed by the Hanbalis in this connection is that one must stop on ʻArafah for part of the night if he arrived during the day. However, if one arrives there at night, it is sufficient for him simply to have come during the specified time period.

As for Sunnah-based practices associated with stopping on ʻArafah, the Hanbalis list the following: (1) That one stop on his mount. (2) That one face the *qiblah*. (3) That one be at the boulders [where the Prophet used to stop] and at Mt. Mercy, yet without seeking to ascend it. (4) That one raise one's hands when uttering supplications. (5) That one utter many supplications and pleas for divine forgiveness, beseeching God for an answer and revealing one's weakness and neediness. One should also be earnest in one's request, and not expect God's answer to be delayed. (6) That one repeat each supplication three times, and that one repeat the following words as much as possible: "There is no god but God alone, Who has no partner. To Him belongs dominion and praise. He causes to live and He causes to die, and He himself is the Ever-Living who does not die. In His hand lies all goodness, and He is capable of all things. O God, place light in my heart, light in my sight, and light in my hearing, and facilitate my endeavors."

* * *

The Malikis hold that one of the pillars of the *ḥajj* is to come to any part of ʻArafah and in any state in which one happens to be, whether one remains there for a period of time or simply passes through. If the person merely passes through it, two conditions apply: (1) One must know that the place through which one is passing is Mt. ʻArafah; if one passes through the place without knowing where one is, it will not be valid as a pillar of the *ḥajj*. (2) One must intend, by passing through the area, to be present there as a pillar of the *ḥajj*; if one passes through the site without this intention, it will not count. As for those who do not merely pass through, but who stay on ʻArafah for a period of time, these two conditions do not apply to them; rather, it is sufficient for them to stay on Mt. ʻArafah, even if they are asleep or unconscious when they do so. Moreover, as we have seen, in order to perform this pillar, one must be present on Mt. ʻArafah for at least one moment between sundown on 9 Dhū al-Ḥijjah and dawn of the following day.

As for the duties associated with this pillar of the *ḥajj*, they are as follows: (1) That one adopt an unhurried posture during one's presence on Mt. ʻArafah; if one fails to do so, one will be obliged to offer an animal sacrifice. (2) That one stop at

'Arafah during the day on 9 Dhū al-Ḥijjah between noon and sunset; if one fails to do so without a legitimate excuse, one will be obliged to offer a sacrificial animal.

There are thus two types of stopping on 'Arafah: (1) one which is a pillar the neglect of which will cause one's *ḥajj* to be invalidated, and (2) one which is a duty the neglect of which obliges one to offer an animal sacrifice. In order to perform (1) above, i.e., the pillar, one must stop on 'Arafah for at least one moment between sundown on the Day of 'Arafah (9 Dhū al-Ḥijjah) and dawn on the Day of Sacrifice (10 Dhū al-Ḥijjah); in order to perform (2) above, i.e., the duty, one must stop on 'Arafah sometime between noon and sundown on the Day of 'Arafah. As has been stated, one may stop on any part of 'Arafah; however, it is deemed preferable to stop at the same site at which the Prophet used to stop, namely, at the huge, sprawling boulders at the foot of Mt. Mercy.

As for actions which are recommended in connection with coming to 'Arafah, the Malikis list the following: (1) That one set out for 'Arafah after sunrise on 9 Dhū al-Ḥijjah and, once has arrived there, that one stop at a place known as al-Namirah. (2) That one perform major ablutions in preparation for this rite. (3) That one utter supplications to God, beseeching Him in earnestness and humility. (4) That one rid oneself of ritual impurity. (5) That one ride, and that one stand up if one is a man unless one has a legitimate excuse not to do so. It is not recommended that women stand up.

It is an emulation of the Sunnah to do the following according to the Malikis: (1) To combine the noon and mid-afternoon prayers at 'Arafah during the time period for the noon prayer. (2) For the imam to preach two sermons in which he informs the people of what will be done on 'Arafah until the end of the *ḥajj*. These two sermons are to be delivered after noon on 9 Dhū al-Ḥijjah; after the sermons, the imam issues the *adhān* and the *iqāmah* for the noon prayer while still on the pulpit, after which he comes down and leads the people in the noon prayer. He then issues the *adhān* and the *iqāmah* for the mid-afternoon prayer and leads the people in this prayer as well. (The noon and mid-afternoon prayers are to be joined on 'Arafah even if it is a Friday; hence, there is no Friday congregational prayer on the Day of 'Arafah.) The people then depart after the prayers to stop on 'Arafah until sundown; once the sun has set and night has begun, they will have completed both this pillar of the *ḥajj* and its associated duty by coming to 'Arafah during the day.

Duties of the *ḥajj*: Casting stones, spending the night at Minā, and being present at Muzdalifah

As we have seen, each of the pillars of the *ḥajj* has conditions, duties and Sunnah-based practices associated with it, and we have presented each school's listing of these. There are, in addition, general duties [of the *ḥajj*] which are not connected with any particular pillar. Such general duties include: (1) throwing pebbles at the three pillars in Minā, (2) Staying the night in Minā, (3) Being present at Muzdalifah, and (4) Shaving and shortening [of the hair]. For each school's listing of these, and other, duties associated with the *ḥajj*, see below.[128]

---

128. The Shafiis list five general duties associated with the *ḥajj*: (1) To enter a state of ritual consecration from the appropriate *mīqāt* as explained earlier. (2) To be present at Muzdalifah, if even for only a moment, provided that this takes place during the second half of the night after one's having stopped at 'Arafah. It is not necessary that one remain there for a period of time; rather, it is sufficient simply to pass through, whether one knows that the place one is passing through is Muzdalifah or not. (3) To throw pebbles at the three pillars in Minā. One is to throw pebbles at the 'Aqabah Pillar on the Day of Sacrifice, and at all three pillars on each of the three subsequent days (referred to as *ayyām al-tashrīq*, i.e., the days of meat drying). The time for the throwing begins at midnight on the eve of the Day of Sacrifice provided that one has already stood on Mt. 'Arafah, and it extends until the last of the "days of meat drying", i.e., the fourth day after the Day of Sacrifice. Moreover, it is necessary for the actual act of throwing to take place; hence, if someone simply places a stone in the place where it is to be thrown, this will not count. It is also necessary that one intend to hit the mark with the stone thrown; hence, it will not count simply to throw it in the air, even if it happens to hit its mark. In addition, the throwing will only count if one hits the mark. A legitimate throw is one which is done with one's hand, not with a bow or some other instrument, which may only be used if one has a legitimate excuse for doing so. As for what may be thrown, it includes only stones; as for pearls, salt, baked brick, etc, they are not acceptable. In addition, the thrower must be certain that he has thrown seven stones at each of the three pillars. As we have seen, the throwing must be done on the three days following the Day of Sacrifice in addition to the throwing of seven stones at the 'Aqabah Pillar on the Day of Sacrifice itself. If one has doubts about how many stones he has thrown, he should keep throwing until he is certain that he has thrown seven. It is also necessary that one throw each of the seven stones separately; if more than one stone is thrown at one time, only one of them will be counted. Lastly, one must observe the correct order among the three pillars at which stones are to be thrown on the "days of meat drying"; specifically, one is first to throw stones at the Khayf Mosque Pillar, then the Middle Pillar, then the 'Aqabah Pillar; one is not permitted to depart from this order. (4) To spend the night at Minā. Someone who is not in a hurry should stay most of the three nights preceding the three "days of meat drying." As for those who wish to depart in haste from Minā to Mecca on the second "day of meat drying" (which is two days after the Day of Sacrifice), they are exempted from staying the night at Minā on the eve of the final "day of meat drying" and throwing stones on that day. This is based on the words of God Almighty,

"...but he who hurries away in two days shall incur no sin, and he who tarries longer shall incur no sin, provided that he is conscious of God. Hence, remain conscious of God, and know that unto Him you shall be gathered" (2:203). This ruling applies if the pilgrim leaves Minā before sundown on the second "day of meat drying"; if the sun goes down on this day before the pilgrim has left Minā, he must stay the third night and throw stones there unless his departure was delayed due to a legitimate excuse. In order for one to leave Minā early, the following conditions must be met: (a) One's departure must be accompanied by a simultaneous intention to do so. If one leaves Minā early without a conscious intention to do so, he must return. (b) When departing Minā, one must not do so with a determination to return. If someone leaves Minā with a determination to return, he must return, and his intention to leave will count for nothing. Hence, unless one has a legitimate excuse for not doing so, one must spend three nights in Minā, i.e., the three nights preceding the three days of stone throwing. As for those who have a legitimate excuse for not spending these nights in Minā, such as camel herders and those responsible for providing water and food for pilgrims either in Mecca or along the way, and those who have reason to fear for their safety or for that of their money if they stay the night in Minā, they are to be given special permission not to spend the night there; however, they are not exempted from the requirement to perform the stone throwing. (5) To abstain from the aforementioned prohibited actions while one is in a state of ritual consecration.

As for Sunnah-based practices associated with throwing stones at the three pillars, the Shafiis list the following, the neglect of which is deemed undesirable: (1) Performing major ablutions for every day that one engages in the throwing. (2) Performing the stone throwing during the "days of meat drying" before the noon prayer. (3) Maintaining continuity among throws, and among the three pillars. (4) Throwing with one's right hand unless it is difficult to do so. (5) Washing the stones if there is any impurity on them. (6) Throwing only stones which are smaller than the size of a fingertip. (7) Replacing the *talbiyah* with *takbīr*, that is, the words, *Allāhu akbar* as one throws the first stone. (8) Throwing while riding if one rode from Minā. (9) Throwing stones that no one else has thrown before.

* * *

The Hanafis list five basic duties of the *ḥajj*: (1) Performing the brisk walk between al-Ṣafā and al-Marwah. (2) Coming to Muzdalifah, even if one only arrives one hour before dawn. If someone neglects to come to Muzdalifah before the break of dawn, he must offer a sacrificial animal unless he has some illness or other ailment, in which case nothing is required of him. (3) Throwing stones for every pilgrim. The throwing is to be done as follows: On the Day of Sacrifice, the pilgrim is to throw approximately seven stones (or anything that one would be permitted to use for sand ablutions; one might, for example, throw a handful of dirt, which is deemed equal to one stone) at the 'Aqabah Pillar from inside the valley. It is not permissible to throw such things as wood, ambergris, pearls, gold, silver, jewels, dung, etc, since they are not considered to be of the same substance as the earth. It is undesirable to take stones away from the pillar or to scatter them; it is also undesirable to throw more than seven stones. It is an emulation of the Sunnah for the thrower to leave a distance of five cubits [about 8 feet] between himself and the pillar at which he is throwing the stones, and to hold each stone with his fingertips. If someone throws a stone and it lands on a man or on a camel and if it falls by itself near the pillar, it will count as a throw; if, on the other hand, it falls far from the pillar ('far' being defined as three or more cubits [i.e., about 5 feet] from the pillar), it will not count, and the person will be obliged to throw another stone. It is also an emulation of the Sunnah for the pilgrim to utter the words *bismillāh, Allāhu akbar* every time he throws a stone, and to discontinue uttering the *talbiyah* for the first throw. It is undesirable to take one larger stone and to break it into smaller ones in order to throw them. The time during which stones are to be thrown at the 'Aqabah Pillar extends from dawn on the Day of Sacrifice until dawn of the following day. If one throws stones at the 'Aqabah Pillar before this, it will not count, and if someone delays it until after this, he will be required to offer a sacrificial animal. It is deemed desirable for this throwing to be performed between sunrise and noon, although it is permissible to do so between noon and sunset, and it is undesirable to perform it at night. It is also undesirable to perform it between dawn and sunrise on the Day of Sacrifice. On the day after the Day of Sacrifice one is to throw stones at all three pillars, and it is an emulation of the Sunnah to begin with the Khayf Mosque Pillar, then go to the Middle Pillar, and end with the 'Aqabah Pillar, throwing seven stones at each pillar in the manner described above. If someone reverses this order by, for example, throwing stones at the Middle Pillar before the Khayf Mosque Pillar, it is an emulation of the Sunnah to repeat the throwing. It is also an emulation of the Sunnah for the pilgrim to stop for as long as it would take to recite three-fourths of one part (*juz'*) of the Qur'ān (about 20 minutes) after every throwing other than the final one. The time during which stone throwing is to be performed on the two days after the Day of Sacrifice extends from noon to sundown; it is deemed undesirable to perform it at night up until dawn, and if it is done before noon, it will not count, while if it is done after dawn on the second day, one must offer a sacrificial animal due to the delay. [When performing the throwing], one may offer whatever prayers of supplication he wishes for himself and for others, raising his hands toward the *qiblah* or skyward. Throwing is likewise to be performed on the third day following the Day of Sacrifice, and on the following day as well if the pilgrim remains there. It is permissible for the pilgrim to perform the throwing while walking or riding, though it is deemed preferable to be walking when throwing stones at the first and second pillars, and to be riding when one throws at the 'Aqabah Pillar. (4) Shaving and shortening [of hair]. (5) Performing the circumambulation of farewell (sometimes referred to as *ṭawāf al-ṣadr*).

As for whatever other duties remain, they will be connected either to one of these basic duties, or to some particular condition or pillar. We have now presented the duties associated with circumambulation, the brisk walk between al-Ṣafā and al-Marwah, and stopping on Mt. 'Arafah. The duties which remain are: (1) maintaining the correct order between stone throwing and shaving, (2) slaughtering on the Day of Sacrifice, and (3) the proper time and location for shaving. As for the criterion by which one can distinguish which actions are 'duties', one may say that a 'duty' is any action the neglect of which requires the pilgrim to offer a sacrificial animal.

* * *

The Hanbalis list the following seven duties associated with the *ḥajj*: (1) Entering a state of ritual consecration in one's legally prescribed *mīqāt*. (2) Stopping on Mt. 'Arafah until sundown if one arrived there during the day. (3) Staying the night at Muzdalifah on the eve of the Day of Sacrifice for those who are not engaged in supplying water and food to pilgrims or tending livestock. This duty is fulfilled by being present at Muzdalifah at any moment of the second half of the night. (4) Staying at Minā during the nights which precede the "days of meat drying" for those who are not engaged in supplying water and food to pilgrims or tending livestock. (5) Throwing stones at the three pillars in Minā in the proper order, the proper order being: first, the Khayf Mosque Pillar, second, the Middle Pillar and third, the 'Aqabah Pillar. It is not acceptable for one to throw stones that are either very small or very large, or to throw something that has already been thrown by someone else. Nor will this duty be fulfilled if one throws something other than stones, such as jewels, gold, and the like. It is also necessary that one actually throw the stones rather than simply placing them on the site at which they are to be thrown, and to make one throw after another until a full seven throws have been performed. Thus, if someone throws more than one stone at a time, they will be counted as just one. In addition, the person throwing must know with certainty that the stones have reached their mark. If someone throws a stone and it falls outside the mark, then rolls until it falls inside it, the throw will count; similarly, if someone throws a stone which first lands on someone's clothes, after which it falls onto the mark, it will count, even if it reaches the mark by someone else's pushing it there. The time for stone throwing begins at midnight on the eve of the Day of Sacrifice for those who have stopped on Mt. 'Arafah. Lastly, one's stone throwing during the "days of meat drying" will only be valid if it is performed after noon. (6) Shaving or shortening [one's hair]. (7) Performing the circumambulation of farewell (*ṭawāf al-wadā'*).

* * *

The Malikis list the following as nonspecific duties that do not pertain to any particular pillar of the *ḥajj*: (1) Stopping at Muzdalifah at night (while on one's way to Minā after coming down from Mt. 'Arafah) for as long as it takes to halt unless one has an excuse for not doing so, in which case one is not obliged to stop there. (2) Throwing stones at the 'Aqabah Pillar on 10 Dhū al-Ḥijjah before shaving or performing the circumambulation of visitation; if someone shaves or performs the circumambulation before the stone throwing, he or she must offer a sacrificial animal. As for performing the stone throwing before slaughtering one's sacrificial animal, slaughtering before shaving, and shaving before performing the circumambulation of visitation, this is recommended. There are thus four things one is expected to do on the Day of Sacrifice: (a) throw stones at the 'Aqabah Pillar, (b) slaughter one's sacrificial animal (*hady*), (c) shave, and (d) perform the circumambulation of visitation, in this order. Throwing stones at the 'Aqabah Pillar is, in and of itself, a 'duty', the time for which extends from the break of dawn on the Day of Sacrifice. It is recommended that one perform this rite between sunrise and noon, and it is undesirable to delay it past this time. (3) Returning to spend the night at Minā after performing the circumambulation. It is a 'duty' to spend three nights—that is, the eve of the 11th, the 12th, and the 13th of Dhū al-Ḥijjah—at Minā if the pilgrim is not in a hurry. If he or she has some reason for haste, it is sufficient to spend only the first two nights there, and the pilgrim is exempted from staying at Minā the third night and performing the stone throwing the following day provided that he or she passes the 'Aqabah Pillar before sundown on 12 Dhū al-Ḥijjah. If this condition is not fulfilled, the pilgrim is obliged to stay the third night in Minā as well and to perform the stone throwing there the following day. (4) Throwing stones at the three pillars at Minā on the three days following the Day of Sacrifice (the "days of meat drying"). Specifically, one is to throw seven stones at each of the three pillars on each of these three days. The time for the stone throwing on each day extends from noon until sundown. If a pilgrim performs the stone throwing before noon, it will not be valid and he or she must offer a sacrificial animal unless he or she repeats the throwing after noon. Similarly, if a pilgrim delays the stone throwing until after sundown or until the following day, he or she must offer a sacrificial animal. Lastly, it is recommended that one perform the stone throwing on each of these days before performing the noon prayer.

The Malikis stipulate the following conditions for the validity of stone throwing. *First*: That one begin with the largest pillar, namely, the one located near the Minā Mosque [also referred to as the Khayf Mosque], followed by the Middle Pillar which is in the market, and ending with the 'Aqabah Pillar. As we have seen, the only pillar at which stones are to be thrown on the Day of Sacrifice itself is the 'Aqabah Pillar. *Second*: That the object thrown be a type of rock. If one were to throw clay, for example, it would not be valid. *Third*: That the stones thrown be very small, the size of a grain of wheat. In fact, they should be the size of the pebbles that young boys pelt each other with when they are at play. One may place the stone between the forefinger and thumb of one's left hand, then lob it with one's right forefinger. If someone throws an excessively small stone, it will not be valid, whereas if one throws a stone which is excessively large, it will be valid, but undesirable. Lastly, it is not necessary that the stones thrown be ritually pure; hence, if one were to throw a stone which was contaminated with some impurity, the throw would be valid, but it would be recommended that one repeat the throw with something ritually pure. (5) Throwing the stones with one's hand. If one were to kick them, this would not be valid; it is also recommended that the throwing be done with one's right hand if one is able to throw well with this hand. (6) Shaving. If a pilgrim neglects to shave, he must offer a sacrificial animal; he is also obliged to offer a sacrificial animal if he postpones shaving until he returns home from Mecca or if he delays it beyond the "days of meat drying" and does not do so in Mecca. If, on the other hand, one shaves while in Mecca, even if one has delayed it until after the "days of meat drying", one is not obliged to offer a sacrificial animal. Rather than shaving, it is also acceptable for a man to shorten his hair, even though merely shortening it is a departure from the Sunnah. As for the woman, what is required is that she shorten her hair rather than shave. The manner in which she is to shorten her hair is for her to take a fingertip's length of hair off the ends, whereas in the case of the man, he is to take the hair from near its roots. If a man takes hair from the ends as the woman does, the shortening will still be valid, but he will have committed an offense. (7) Offering redemption (*fidyah*). (8) Offering a sacrificial animal (*hady*) if one's *ḥajj* has been invalidated. (9) Offering a sacrificial animal when one is engaging in *qirān*, that is, joining the *'umrah* and the *ḥajj* during the *ḥajj* season based on a single act of *iḥrām*, or when one is engaging in *tamattu'*, that is, performing the *'umrah* during the *ḥajj* season based on one act of *iḥrām*, being released from the state of *iḥrām*, then reentering it and performing the *ḥajj*.

Sunnah-based practices associated with the *ḥajj*

As for the Sunnah-based practices associated with the *ḥajj*, these include practices connected with the following: (1) *Iḥrām*; these were discussed above in the section dealing with actions which should be performed before entering a state of ritual consecration. (2) Circumambulation. (3) The brisk walk between al-Ṣafā and al-Marwah. (4) Stopping on Mt. 'Arafah.

All the aforementioned types of Sunnah-based practices associated with the *ḥajj* have been discussed in earlier sections. In addition, each school offers its own detailed listing of other *ḥajj*-related practices by which one may emulate the Sunnah.[129]

---

129. The Hanafis list the following Sunnah-based practices in connection with the *ḥajj*: (1) Staying the night at Muzdalifah after leaving 'Arafah on the eve of the Day of Sacrifice. (2) Going from Muzdalifah to Minā before sunrise. (3) Spending the night at Minā on the eve of the 11th, the 12th, and the 13th of Dhū al-Ḥijjah. [I have changed the order of these three practices in conformity with their temporal order – t.n.] (4) Maintaining the proper order among the three pillars in Minā at which stones are thrown. As we have seen, the throwing of stones at these three pillars is, in its origin, a 'duty'.

The Hanafis also list a number of rules of etiquette associated with the *ḥajj*. Specifically, they hold that a pilgrim should: (1) Repay his debts before going on the *ḥajj*. (2) Consult someone whose opinion he can trust concerning whether to travel in the year in which he intends to perform the *ḥajj*. (3) Seek guidance from God Almighty [concerning whether to make the *ḥajj* in a given year]. The Sunnah-based practice in this respect is for one to perform two *rak'ahs* in which one recites the *Fātiḥah* followed by Surah 112, after which one recites the traditional prayer for seeking guidance (*ṣalāt al-istikhārah*). In addition, one should begin by repenting of any sins of which one is guilty, purifying one's intention, and making reparations for any wrongs one may have committed against others. (4) Seek forgiveness from one's opponents and all those one has had dealings with. (5) Make up any required acts of worship one has neglected to perform. (6) Rid oneself of hypocrisy, concern for reputation, and boastful pride. (7) Make a diligent effort to obtain the money one needs for the journey by honest means, since there will be no reward from God for those who perform the *ḥajj* with money that has been dishonestly acquired (although the performance of the *ḥajj* will fulfill one's obligation even if it was financed by illicit gain). (8) Take along a righteous companion who will remind him if he forgets, shore up his endurance if he becomes anxious or impatient, and assist him if he grows weak. (9) Leave on the *ḥajj* on a Thursday or, if not a Thursday, then on a Monday at the beginning of the day and at the beginning of the month. (10) Bid farewell to his family, seeking their forgiveness, asking for their prayers and going to where they are for this purpose. As for the family of someone who is about to perform the *ḥajj*, it is an emulation of the Sunnah for them to visit him upon his return. (11) Perform two *rak'ahs* before leaving home, and again after returning home. Following the prayers when one departs one is to say, "O God, to You do I direct myself, in You have I sought protection, and upon You have I relied.

O God, You are my trust and You are my hope. O God, protect me both from those things that cause me concern and anxiety, and from those things for which I feel no concern, as well as those things of which You know better than I. Those who seek Your protection will be strengthened, and there is no god but You. O God, enable me to be conscious of You, forgive my sins, and direct me toward that which is good wherever I go. O God, I seek refuge in You from the hardships of the journey, from a gloomy fate, from want after plenty, and from having to see harm befall my wealth or my kin." As one departs, one is to say, "In the name of God. There is no power or strength in aught but God the Almighty, the Sublime. I rely upon God. O God, grant me success in that which is pleasing and acceptable to You, and protect me from the accursed Satan." The pilgrim should then recite the Throne Verse (2:255) and Surahs 112, 113 and 114. When he mounts his riding animal he is to say, "In the name of God. Praise be to God Who has led us to Islam, Who has taught us the Qur'ān, and Who has graciously bestowed upon us Muḥammad, may blessings and peace be upon him. Praise be to God, Who has made me a member of 'the best nation that has been brought forth for [the good of] mankind' (3:110) and, 'Limitless in His glory is He Who has made [all] this subservient to our use, since [but for Him], we would not have been able to attain to it. Hence, verily it is unto Him that we must always turn' (43:13). Praise be to God, Lord of the worlds."

* * *

The Shafiis list the following Sunnah-based practices associated with the *ḥajj*: (1) Staying the night at Minā on the eve of the Day of 'Arafah [9 Dhū al-Ḥijjah]. This practice is simply an emulation of the Sunnah since the purpose behind it is to allow the pilgrim to rest, whereas staying the night at Minā on the eve of the 11th, the 12th and 13th of Dhū al-Ḥijjah is a 'duty', as we have seen. (2) Walking at a hurried pace when passing through the Muḥassar Valley. The Muḥassar Valley, located between Muzdalifah and Minā, was so named because this is the place where the elephants with which Abrahah hoped to destroy the Ka'bah were caused to grow weary (*ḥussira*). This incident is mentioned in Surah 105. (3) Delivering the four Sunnah-based sermons during the *ḥajj*, namely: (a) The sermon delivered on 7 Dhū al-Ḥijjah, which is a single sermon delivered by the imam or his proxy, such as the official responsible for the *ḥajj*, after the noon prayer in the Sacred Mosque. This sermon is to be opened with the words *Allāhu akbar* if the person delivering it is not in a state of ritual consecration and, if he is in a state of ritual consecration, with the *talbiyah*. It is preferable, however, for the speaker to be in a state of ritual consecration. (b) The double sermon delivered at al-Namirah before the noon prayer on the Day of 'Arafah. (c) The single sermon delivered at Minā after the noon prayer on the Day of Sacrifice. (d) The single sermon delivered at Minā after the noon prayer on the first day following the Day of Sacrifice. In each of the aforementioned sermons, the speaker is to inform the congregation of the *ḥajj* rites which will follow the sermon. (4) Shaving for men, and shortening [of the hair] for females. (5) Stopping at *al-Mash'ar al-Ḥarām*, that is, Mt. Quzaḥ, while facing the *qiblah* and uttering phrases of divine remembrance and supplications until daylight. (6) Not rushing away from Minā but rather, staying there every night throughout the "days of meat drying." (7) Uttering the Sunnah-based phrases of divine remembrance. This includes uttering the phrases mentioned earlier upon seeing the

Ka'bah, as well as the phrases mentioned earlier for when one begins the circumambulation. In addition, it is an emulation of the Sunnah to say the following when one is across from the Ka'bah: "O God, the Ka'bah is Yours, the holy precincts are Yours, security is Yours to grant, and this is the place where those seeking refuge with You from the fire are to stand." While the pilgrim is between the two Yemeni corners of the Ka'bah, he or she is to say: "O our Sustainer! Grant us good in this world and good in the life to come, and keep us safe from suffering through the fire" (2:201). While throwing stones at the three pillars at Minā, one is to say, "O God, [I ask You to grant me] a valid, blessed pilgrimage, forgiveness for my transgressions, and labor worthy of praise and reward." While performing the brisk walk between al-Ṣafā and al-Marwah, one is to say, "My Lord, forgive and have mercy, overlooking what You know. Indeed, You are the most Powerful, the most Munificent." (8) Repaying one's debts before performing the *ḥajj*. (9) Making peace with one's adversaries, repenting of all acts of disobedience, learning how to perform the *ḥajj*, and seeking forgiveness from all people with whom one has had dealings of any sort. (10) Writing a will before departing on the *ḥajj* and testifying to its validity. One should, in addition, seek out a righteous, suitable, willing companion to accompany one on the journey and gather ample provisions and money for the expedition in order to be able to assist those in need. (11) Taking the opportunity to perform ritual prayer, circumambulation, and seclusion for the purpose of worship and divine remembrance in the Sacred Mosque whenever one enters it. (12) Entering the Ka'bah and performing ritual prayer there, even if it is only a voluntary prayer. (13) Drinking as much as one can from the Well of Zamzam. As one drinks, one should face the *qiblah* and say, "O God, Your Prophet Muḥammad said, 'The water of Zamzam is for whatever one drinks it for.' I am drinking it for the sake of happiness in this life and in the life to come. So, O God, please grant this to me." The pilgrim is then to utter the *basmalah*, drink, and take three breaths. It is an emulation of the Sunnah to go in to the well and to look into it, then to dip some water out with a pail, moisten one's face, head and chest, then stock up on its water when one is ready to make one's return journey.

* * *

The Malikis list Sunnah-based practices and recommended practices associated with the *ḥajj*. As for the Sunnah-based practices, they are as follows: (1) Delivery of the two sermons after noon in the 'Arafah Mosque, as we have seen. (2) Combining the noon and mid-afternoon prayers at the 'Arafah Mosque during the time period for the noon prayer, as we have seen. (3) Shortening the noon and mid-afternoon prayers mentioned above for those who are not residents of 'Arafah; as for those who reside in 'Arafah, they are not to shorten these two prayers. (4) Combining the sundown and evening prayers during the time period for the evening prayer at Muzdalifah after coming down from 'Arafah. However, this is only an emulation of the Sunnah for those who stood at 'Arafah with the imam, then came to Muzdalifah with the people or did not come with them even though they would have been able to do so. Those who did not stop at 'Arafah with the imam are not to combine these two prayers; rather, they are to perform each prayer during its own time period. As for those who did not come down from 'Arafah with the people due to their inability to do so, they should delay the sundown prayer and combine it with the evening prayer wherever they wish. (5) Shortening the evening prayer for those who are not residents of Muzdalifah. The joining of prayers in 'Arafah and Muzdalifah is an emulation of the Sunnah for every pilgrim even if he or she is a resident of these two places, whereas shortening of prayers is only an emulation of the Sunnah for those who are not residents. (6) Placing a collar around the neck of one's sacrificial animal. (7) Marking one's sacrificial animal by making an incision on the left side of its hump. (There was a discussion earlier of which sacrificial animals are to be collared and which are to be marked.) (8) Other Sunnah-based practices associated with the *ḥajj* are listed in the earlier discussion of the pillars of the *ḥajj*.

As for recommended *ḥajj*-related practices, the Malikis list the following: (1) Staying at Dhū Ṭawā for those who arrive in Mecca at night so that they can enter Mecca during the mid-morning hours. (2) Performing major ablutions for those who have entered Mecca and who are neither menstruating nor experiencing post-partum bleeding. As for women who are in one of these states, it is not recommended that they do so, since these ablutions are to be performed in preparation for circumambulation, and circumambulation is not valid for women in either of these conditions. (3) Offering prayers of supplication after completing the circumambulation. (4) Drinking as much as one can of the water of Zamzam with a good intention; this is based on the prophetic saying, "The water of Zamzam is for whatever one drinks it for." It is also recommended that pilgrims take Zamzam water away with them. (5) Stopping with the people on Mt. 'Arafah till sundown, offering prayers of supplication and beseeching God to respond. (6) Staying the night at Muzdalifah on the eve of the Day of Sacrifice, then departing for Minā between the dawn prayer and daylight. (7) Stopping at *al-Mash'ar al-Ḥarām* [Mt. Quzaḥ] while facing the *qiblah*, making supplication to God Almighty and uttering His praises until daylight. (8) Moving at a brisk pace as one passes through the Muḥassar Valley, which is a valley between Muzdalifah and Minā and a stone's throw away [from Muzdalifah]. The valley was so named because it was here that "the army of the Elephant" about which we read in Surah 105 grew weary and it was here that chastisement was visited upon them. However, hurrying through this valley is not recommended for women unless they are riding. (9) Throwing stones at the 'Aqabah Pillar when one arrives in Minā and after sunrise, as we have seen. (10) Walking [rather than riding] when throwing stones at the first and second pillars (the third being the 'Aqabah Pillar). (11) Uttering the words *Allāhu akbar* with every stone one throws. (12) Throwing all seven stones in close succession rather than pausing between any two of them. (13) Picking up the stones one is going to throw by oneself. (14) Slaughtering [one's sacrificial animal] and shaving [one's head] before noon on the Day of Sacrifice. (15) Postponing shaving until after slaughtering. (16) Performing the circumambulation of visitation wearing both of one's *iḥrām* robes and after shaving. (17) Pausing after throwing stones at the first and second pillars to utter prayers of supplication, with one's back to the first pillar. (18) For those who are not in a hurry, stopping at al-Muḥaṣṣab, a valley which contains a large number of small stones and which is located in the direction of the Mecca cemetery at Kadā'. When the pilgrim returns from Minā to Mecca after performing the fourth day of stone-throwing, it is recommended that he stop in this place be-

That which the pilgrim is forbidden to do

Some of the things a pilgrim is forbidden to do are forbidden in such a way that if he does them, his *ḥajj* will be invalidated. Such acts include those on account of which the pilgrim must offer a sacrificial animal (a camel, a cow, a sheep or a goat), which will be discussed further below. Other acts belonging to this category are those on account of which one must offer a 'redemption' (*fidyah*) consisting of food, charity, etc.

That which invalidates the *ḥajj*

All four schools agree that one's *ḥajj* will be invalidated if one neglects to stop on Mt. 'Arafah at the time specified for this rite, or if one omits any of the pillars of the *ḥajj*. It is also agreed upon by all four schools that the *ḥajj* will be invalidated by one's engaging in sexual intercourse; however, they differ concerning the time at which the *ḥajj* will be invalidated by such an act and the conditions which apply to such a situation.[130]

---

fore stopping in Mecca. When he or she stops at al-Muḥaṣṣab, he is to stay there long enough to perform four ritual prayers, namely, the noon, mid-afternoon, sundown and evening prayers; hence, he should postpone the noon prayer until after his arrival there if he has no reason to fear that by doing so, he will miss the noon prayer's 'elective' time phase. However, it is not desirable for someone to stop at al-Muḥaṣṣab if his return from Minā falls on a Friday; if it does fall on a Friday, the pilgrim should simply go straight to Mecca. Nor is it desirable to stop in al-Muḥaṣṣab for someone who is in a hurry and who, as a result, left Minā after the third day of stone-throwing. (19) Performing the circumambulation of farewell for those who wish to leave Mecca.

Other recommended actions were listed earlier in the discussion of the pillars of the *ḥajj*.

* * *

The Hanbalis list, among others, the following four recommended actions associated with the *ḥajj*: (1) Staying the night at Minā on the eve of the Day of 'Arafah (9 Dhū al-Ḥijjah). (2) The imam's delivering a sermon to the pilgrims on 8 Dhū al-Ḥijjah in the Sacred Mosque, on 9 Dhū al-Ḥijjah (The Day of 'Arafah) in the same place, and on 10 Dhū al-Ḥijjah (The Day of Sacrifice) in Minā. (3) Continuing to utter the *talbiyah* until one throws stones at the 'Aqabah Pillar. (4) Facing the *qiblah* while throwing stones at the three pillars at Minā.

130. The Malikis hold that the *ḥajj* is invalidated by sexual intercourse, which they define as the glans of the penis (or the equivalent thereof in the absence of the glans) disappearing inside a human (or non-human) vagina or anus, whether the male is a child or an adult and whether the female is able to tolerate intercourse or not. If a man performing the *ḥajj* is married to a child who is performing the *ḥajj* with him and if he engages in such an action with her, both his and her *ḥajj* will be invalidated; how much more, then, would the *ḥajj* of an adult wife be invalidated in such a situation. Moreover, one's *ḥajj* will be invalidated by virtue of such an act whether the person who commits it remembers [that he is on the *ḥajj*] or has forgotten, and even if he commits the act out of ignorance. A man's *ḥajj* will likewise be

invalidated if he has a seminal emission as a result of kissing, direct genital contact, looking [at a woman], thinking [erotic thoughts], etc.; however, in order for his *ḥajj* to be invalidated by a seminal discharge resulting from looking or thinking, he must have looked [at a sexual stimulus] or thought [erotic thoughts] for an extended period of time, whereas a seminal discharge resulting from simply looking at a sexual stimulus or thinking erotic thoughts for a brief period of time will not invalidate one's *ḥajj*. As for a seminal emission resulting from a kiss, it will invalidate one's *ḥajj* even if the act is not repeated; hence, if a man is accompanied on the *ḥajj* by a wife, he must avoid caressing or kissing her during the time when the Lawgiver has forbidden him to have sexual contact with a woman. However, a man's *ḥajj* will only be invalidated by sexual intercourse or by a seminal discharge resulting from one of the aforementioned causes if it takes place before he has thrown stones at the 'Aqabah Pillar. The time at which stones are to be thrown at this pillar is the Day of Sacrifice before the circumambulation of visitation and before the Day of Sacrifice is over. One's *ḥajj* will be invalidated by sexual intercourse or a seminal emission resulting from the causes mentioned above if it occurs before the aforementioned throwing of stones at the 'Aqabah Pillar regardless of whether it occurs before or after one's stopping at Mt. 'Arafah. If someone has sexual relations or a discharge of semen for one of the aforementioned causes: (a) after throwing stones at the 'Aqabah Pillar, (b) after performing the circumambulation of visitation, or (c) after the Day of Sacrifice has passed but before throwing stones at the 'Aqabah Pillar or performing the circumambulation, his or her *ḥajj* will not be invalidated; however, he will be required to slaughter a 'ransom' (*fidā'*). After throwing stones at the 'Aqabah Pillar, sexual intercourse, sexual foreplay and the finalization of marriage contracts are forbidden; if someone commits any of these acts at this time, his *ḥajj* will not be invalidated, but he will have done something which is not permitted and he will, as a consequence, be obliged to offer a 'ransom'. If, by contrast, a pilgrim engages in such an act after performing the circumambulation of visitation but before shaving, he will have performed that which is permitted, but he will still be required to offer an animal sacrifice (*hady*). If he does so after shaving, he will likewise have done that which is permitted, without anything being required of him as a result. A pilgrim is also required to offer an animal sacrifice if he has an emission of semen (*manī*) or preseminal fluid (*madhī*) due to looking briefly [at a sexually attractive object] or engaging briefly in erotic thoughts. Someone whose *ḥajj* is invalidated must still complete all of the *ḥajj* rites; if someone fails to complete the entire *ḥajj* due to the belief that he is no longer in a state of ritual consecration, he will nevertheless still be in such a state and if he enters a state of ritual consecration again the following year, the new *iḥrām* will be null and void and he will, instead, simply continue in the state of ritual consecration which he had violated the year before.

Lastly, someone whose *ḥajj* is invalidated by sexual intercourse or for any other reason must do the following: (1) complete the *ḥajj* rites which he has not yet performed even though his *ḥajj* has been invalidated, (2) make up the *ḥajj* which was invalidated at the earliest opportunity (since if he delays making it up, he will be guilty of wrongdoing), (3) slaughter an animal sacrifice due to the invalidation of his *ḥajj*, and (4) postpone slaughtering the animal sacrifice until the time at which he performs the compensatory *ḥajj*.

* * *

The Hanafis hold that a pilgrim's *ḥajj* is invalidated by sexual intercourse if it takes place before he has stopped on Mt. 'Arafah. If a pilgrim has intercourse with his wife after stopping on Mt. 'Arafah and before performing the second pillar, namely, the circumambulation of visitation, his *ḥajj* will not be invalidated since in the view of the Hanafis, one's *ḥajj* may not be invalidated once one has stood on Mt. 'Arafah. When someone's *ḥajj* is invalidated by sexual intercourse, it makes no difference whether the person concerned had sexual relations out of forgetfulness or deliberately, whether he was asleep or awake, or whether he did so voluntarily or under duress. If a man has intercourse with his wife while either he or she is asleep, both his and her *ḥajj* will be invalidated. However, sexual intercourse will only invalidate the *ḥajj* of someone who is an adult and in full possession of his or her mental faculties; hence, if a boy or an insane man had intercourse with an adult woman in full possession of her mental faculties, only the woman's *ḥajj* would be invalidated. Similarly, if an adult man had intercourse with a young girl or an insane woman, only his *ḥajj* would be invalidated. Moreover, sexual intercourse will invalidate one's *ḥajj* even if no ejaculation takes place; rather, one's *ḥajj* will be invalidated by the mere disappearance of the glans inside the vagina or the anus, whether there is an ejaculation or not. Moreover, the Hanafis agree with the Malikis that when someone's *ḥajj* is invalidated, he must continue to perform the *ḥajj* rites to completion even though they are no longer valid, make up the invalidated *ḥajj* in a subsequent year, and slaughter a sheep or a goat as a sacrifice. If intercourse takes place more than once and if the various instances occur in a single session, a single sacrificial animal will suffice; however, if they occur during different sessions, then for every such session the person must offer another sacrificial animal.

* * *

The Shafiis hold that one's *ḥajj* is invalidated by sexual intercourse given the following conditions: (1) The glans of the penis (or its equivalent if there is no glans) was inserted in a vagina or an anus, be it human or animal; the insertion of the glans counts even if there is a barrier between the penis and the opening into which it is inserted. (2) The penetration occured before one's first 'release' (*taḥallul*) from the state of ritual consecration. The first release from *iḥrām* occurs once the pilgrim has performed two of the following three actions: a) throwing stones at the three pillars at Minā, b) shaving, and c) the circumambulation of visitation. Thus, if one has thrown stones at the three pillars at Minā and shaved, he has gone through the first release, after which his *ḥajj* will not be invalidated by sexual intercourse. Similarly, if the pilgrim has performed the circumambulation of visitation and shaved [his head], or shaved and thrown stones at the three pillars at Minā, his *ḥajj* will not be invalidated by sexual intercourse. Hence, it is not necessary to follow any particular order among such actions, although it is preferable to order them as follows: 1. stone throwing, 2. shaving, 3. circumambulation. Nevertheless, even though one's *ḥajj* will not be invalidated by sexual relations between the first and second release, it is still forbidden during this time period to engage in sexual relations or in sexual foreplay, including kissing and direct genital contact accompanied by erotic desire. This ruling applies whether ejaculation occurs or not, and it requires that the pilgrim offer a *fidyah*, since the condition for such acts' being forbidden is that one experience sexual pleasure, and such pleasure is obtained by looking and touching.

Bringing about a seminal discharge by manual stimulation is also forbidden; however, it does not require a *fidyah* if no ejaculation takes place. Similarly, desirous looking and touching with the presence of a barrier such as clothing, etc. is forbidden, but it does not require a *fidyah* whether there is an ejaculation or not; the reason for this is that whereas the condition for such acts' being forbidden is that they bring about sexual pleasure, which is obtained through the aforementioned looking and touching, the condition for a *fidyah* being required is direct contact with erotic desire, which in such a case has not taken place.

If someone's *ḥajj* is invalidated by sexual intercourse, he must still perform all of the *ḥajj* rites to completion; he must also avoid all actions which he would have been required to avoid if his *ḥajj* were still valid, and if he commits some forbidden act after this, he must offer a *fidyah* if the act concerned is one which requires such. In addition, the person must make up the invalidated *ḥajj* immediately, that is, in the following year. This ruling applies even if the *ḥajj* thus invalidated was voluntary. One must also offer the expiation (*kaffārah*) required for sexual intercourse which invalidates the *ḥajj*, i.e., a she-camel or a he-camel, provided that the camel offered fulfills all the conditions required of a sacrificial animal to be slaughtered on the Day of Sacrifice (to be discussed below under the heading, "On animal sacrifice"). If the pilgrim is unable to offer such a camel, he must offer a cow which would be fit for slaughter on the Day of Sacrifice; if he cannot offer a cow that meets these specifications, he must offer seven sheep or goats fit for slaughter on the Day of Sacrifice. If he cannot offer these, either, an appraisal of their value must be done based on the prevailing prices in Mecca and the pilgrim must distribute their value as charity in the form of food (not cash) to three or more poor and needy within the Meccan precincts. As for the food distributed, it must consist of the types of food that may be distributed as fastbreaking *zakāh*, which was discussed above in the section on fasting. If the pilgrim is unable to do this, either, he must fast one day for every *mudd* of food based on the aforementioned appraisal with the intention of making the required expiation. He might say, for example, "I intend to fast tomorrow in expiation for performing sexual intercourse [before being released from a state of ritual consecration]."

The aforementioned rulings apply to a man whose *ḥajj* is invalidated by sexual intercourse; as for the woman, she is not required to offer expiation in such a situation, although her *ḥajj* is also invalidated and although she incurs guilt if she engaged in sexual relations with the realization of what she was doing, willingly and deliberately, and with the knowledge that it was forbidden. Otherwise, she incurs no guilt, nor is her *ḥajj* invalidated.

* * *

According to the Hanbalis, one's *ḥajj* is invalidated by penetration of the vagina or anus of a human being or an animal if it takes place before one's first release from the state of ritual consecration. If someone has sexual intercourse after the first release, his *ḥajj* will not be invalidated, which is the same view as that held by the Shafiis. According to the Hanbalis, there are three actions by which a pilgrim is released from the state of ritual consecration: a) throwing stones at the three pillars at Minā, b) circumambulation, and c) shaving. In agreement with the Shafiis, the

That which requires a 'redemption' (*fidyah*) for a missed or incorrectly performed religious rite, with an explanation of the meaning of 'release' (*taḥallul*)

As we have seen, there are some forbidden acts which, if committed by a pilgrim, invalidate his *ḥajj* altogether, while others require him to offer a *fidyah* or redemption, while still others require him to offer food. As for those acts the commission of which requires the pilgrim to offer a *fidyah*, detailed rulings concerning these are offered by each of the four schools.[131]

Hanbalis hold that the first release takes place by performing two of these three acts; hence, if a pilgrim throws stones at the 'Aqabah Pillar and shaves, after which he has sexual relations before performing the circumambulation, his *ḥajj* will not be invalidated, but he must sacrifice a slaughter camel. (The state of ritual consecration is invalidated by nothing but sexual intercourse.) If someone's *ḥajj* has been invalidated, he or she must continue performing the *ḥajj* rites to completion, and if one commits a forbidden act after this, one must offer a *fidyah*; in addition, both parties who took part in the sexual act must make up the invalidated *ḥajj* during the following year.

131. The Hanbalis divide acts the commission of which requires a pilgrim to offer a *fidyah* into two categories: (a) those which allow the pilgrim a choice among various types of *fidyah*, and (b) those which require one out of several types of *fidyah* based on a descending order of priority.

Category (a) above includes the following acts: (1) wearing something which is stitched or which encloses the body all the way around, (2) using perfume, (3) covering the head for a man and, for a woman, covering the face, and (4) removing more than two hairs from one's body or more than two fingernails or toenails.

The commission of any of the four actions mentioned here requires that one offer one of the following three types of *fidyah*: a) Slaughtering a sheep which is at least six months old or a goat which is a year old, b) fasting three days, or c) feeding six needy people, each of whom is to receive one *mudd* of wheat or one-half *ṣā'* (two *mudds*) of dried dates, raisins, barley or cottage cheese.

Another action the commission of which allows a choice among more than one type of *fidyah* is hunting a game animal. If a game animal is killed inside the Meccan precincts, it will either have an equivalent among domestic animals offered for sacrifice, or it will not. If it does have an equivalent, the person who killed the animal is to be given a choice among the following three types of *fidyah*: (1) Slaughtering an equivalent domestic animal and giving its meat to the poor of the Meccan precincts at any time he wishes. (2) Appraising the value of the game animal's equivalent in the place where the game animal died. The appraisal is to be done in terms of dirhams, with which the pilgrim is to purchase food of the types mentioned above and give each needy person one *mudd* of wheat or two *mudds* of other foods, as we have seen. (3) Fasting a number of days equivalent to the number of *mudds* of food which the game animal was estimated to equal. Hence, each day of fasting takes the place of the food that would have been given to one needy person.

If the appraisal includes a fraction of a *mudd* [as, for example, if it comes to 8 2/3 *mudds* – t.n.], the pilgrim must fast an entire day in its place.

If the game animal which died has no equivalent among domestic animals, the pilgrim is to be given a choice between (2) and (3) above, namely, feeding the needy an amount of food equal to the appraised value of the game animal, and fasting.

Forbidden acts the commission of which requires one of several types of *fidyah* based on a descending order of priority are as follows: (1) Sexual intercourse before the first release from the state of ritual consecration. The first release occurs by performing two of the following three actions: a) throwing stones at the 'Aqabah Pillar, b) shaving or shortening one's hair, and c) the circumambulation of visitation. This also includes having an ejaculation due to having looked repeatedly [at a sexual stimulus], direct physical contact somewhere other than the genitals, kissing, or touching with erotic desire before the first release. If either sexual intercourse or ejaculation takes place in any of the ways mentioned here, the pilgrim must slaughter a five-year-old camel. If such a camel is not available, he should fast ten days: three days before completing the *ḥajj* rites and seven days after this. If the woman participated willingly in the sexual act, she is required to offer the same *fidyah* as the man. As for direct physical contact which results in no ejaculation, this calls for a *fidyah*, with the pilgrim being given a choice among the three types of *fidyah* mentioned above, namely, a) slaughtering a sheep or a goat, b) feeding six needy persons, and c) fasting three days.

This type also includes having an emission of semen without looking repeatedly [at someone attractive], and having sexual relations after the first release from the state of ritual consecration. (2) Passing one's *mīqāt* on the way to Mecca for the *ḥajj* without entering a state of ritual consecration. (3) Omitting some duty of the *ḥajj*, such as throwing stones at the three pillars at Minā. If one omits such a duty, one must choose between the following types of *fidyah*: (a) slaughtering a sheep or a goat, or, if this is not possible, (b) fasting ten days, three of them before completing the *ḥajj* and seven afterwards, as we have seen.

The forbidden acts whose commission requires that one feed the needy include: (1) cutting up to two fingernails or toenails, and (2) removing up to two hairs. One needy person must be fed one *mudd* of wheat or two *mudds* (one-half *ṣā'*) of some other food for every fingernail or part thereof which is cut and for every hair or part thereof which is removed. For every two fingernails or toenails cut, and for every two hairs removed, two needy persons must be fed the aforementioned amount.

Those acts which require that one offer an appraised value include: (1) breaking the egg of a game bird, and (2) killing locusts. If someone breaks the egg of a game bird or kills a locust, he must give as charity the value of the egg or the locust in the place where it was broken or killed, respectively.

As for those acts which do not require anything, they include the killing of lice and concluding a marriage contract.

As mentioned above, a person in a state of ritual consecration is forbidden to cut down the trees that grow within the Meccan precincts or to cut the grass therein except for stated exceptions. If a pilgrim cuts down what would be considered a small tree by commonly accepted standards, he is to slaughter a sheep or a goat, whereas if he cuts down a medium-sized or large tree, he must slaughter a cow; if he cuts grass or leaves, he is to donate their value to the needy.

* * *

According to the Malikis, a *fidyah* is required for any forbidden action that results in luxury or ease for the pilgrim, or which causes him to become less unkempt or unclean, such as bathing in a bathroom. If a pilgrim sits in a bathroom until he perspires, then pours hot water over his body, even if he does not scrub himself, he must offer a *fidyah* for having done so, since such an action is likely to remove dirt from the body. The same ruling applies to touching something with which one might perfume oneself, trimming one's moustache, putting on regular clothing, covering one's head (for the man) or covering one's face or one's hands with gloves (for the woman) for reasons other than concealing oneself from view, trimming one's fingernails or toenails, plucking out one's underarm hair, dying one's body with henna, etc. However, a *fidyah* is only required for wearing clothing and the like if one benefits from doing so by protecting oneself from heat or cold, whereas if one puts on a garment and immediately takes it off again before deriving any benefit from it, no *fidyah* is required. As for perfume and other things from which one benefits by merely touching them, one must offer a *fidyah* for putting them on even if one removes them immediately.

There are three types of *fidyah* from which a pilgrim may choose: a) Feeding two *mudds* (by the Prophet's measure) of the most prevalent food staple to six needy persons. Instead of the two *mudds*, one might also provide lunch or dinner if they amount to two *mudds*, although placing the food in the needy person's possession is preferable. b) Fasting three days. c) Slaughtering a sheep or a goat or something larger, such as a cow or a camel, with the same age considerations as those that apply to a *hady*. There is no specified time or place for the slaughter of such an animal; rather, the pilgrim may slaughter it wherever and whenever he wishes unless he intends it as a *hady*, in which case he must slaughter it in Minā or in Mecca.

Those actions which require one to offer a handful of food are as follows: (1) Trimming one fingernail or toenail without intending to remove dirt, such as someone's trimming a toenail or a fingernail in order to treat an ulcer beneath it, because he considers it ugly when it is long, or just to pass the time. If, on the other hand, one trims a toenail or a fingernail in order to remove dirt, one must offer a *fidyah*. (2) Removing up to twelve hairs. (3) Removing ticks from one's camel or killing them; either action requires one handful of food even if one has removed or killed numerous ticks.

If someone commits more than one action requiring a *fidyah* or a handful of food, more than one *fidyah* or handful of food is required as well. For example, if someone puts on [regular] clothing and applies perfume, he must offer two *fidyah*s: one for the clothing and one for the use of the perfume. If someone trims one toenail or fingernail and removes one hair, he must offer two handfuls of food. However, the following situations are exceptions to this ruling, in which the commission of more than one act requiring a redemption or a handful of food does not require that one offer more than one redemption or handful of food: (1) When someone believes that the act he has committed is permissible due to his *ḥajj*'s having been invalidated, due to his rejecting the prohibition of the act, or due to his believing mistakenly that he has performed a given part of the *ḥajj* correctly. For example, if someone performs the circumambulation of visitation in the belief that it is valid, then commits several acts requiring a redemption or a handful of food, after which it becomes apparent to him that his circumambulation was not valid, he will not be required to offer multiple expiations (redemptions or handfuls of food) for the various acts committed. (2) When someone commits several such acts without any pause between them. (3) When someone, while performing the first of such a series of actions, intends to repeat it and perform other such actions as well. An example of this would be for someone to put on a garment and, at the same time, intend to apply perfume also; if such a person puts on the garment and applies perfume, he must offer only one redemption provided that he does not offer a redemption for the first action before committing the second. However, if the person offers a redemption for the first action before committing the second, he must offer a second redemption as well. (4) When someone first performs an action which yields a more comprehensive benefit, as when someone puts on a robe first, then a pair of trousers, in which case he is required to offer only one redemption.

* * *

The Hanafis define the term 'redemption' (*fidyah*) as the slaughtering of a goat, a sheep, etc. A redemption is required by the following: (1) Engaging in sexual foreplay such as embracing, direct genital contact, kissing, and touching with sensual desire, whether there is an ejaculation or not. This also includes a man's looking at a woman's genitals or having erotic thoughts and having an ejaculation as a result, or his penetrating the vagina of an animal and having an ejaculation; however, if he penetrates an animal without having an ejaculation, nothing is required of him. A blood sacrifice is also required if he places his penis on someone's abdomen or between her thighs, whether he has an ejaculation or not. (2) Removing at least one-fourth of one's head hair or beard. If one removes less than one-fourth of either or both of these, however, no blood sacrifice is required. A blood sacrifice is likewise required of someone who removes the hair from his neck, his underarms, or either of these, or if he removes his pubic hair. However, a blood sacrifice is required for the removal of hair only if it is done without a legitimate excuse. If it is done with a legitimate excuse, as when there are vermin attached to it and causing the person harm, the person concerned is given a choice among the following three actions: a) slaughtering a goat or a sheep, b) fasting three days, and c) feeding six needy persons, each of whom is to receive one-half *ṣā'*. God Almighty declares, "...but he from among you who is ill or suffers from an ailment of the head shall redeem himself by fasting, or alms, or [any other] act of worship" (2:196). (3) A man's wearing something that contains stitching; as for the woman, she may wear whatever she wishes as long as she does not conceal her face with something that comes in direct contact with her face, as we have seen. What is forbidden, specifically, is the wearing of regular clothing; thus, if a man simply wraps something stitched around himself, or if he places it on his body in other than the usual way, no redemption is required of him. This ruling applies if the man wears such clothing without a legitimate excuse; for cases in which he does so with a legitimate excuse, however, see the details on this presented above. (4) A man's covering his head for an entire day; for details concerning the usual types of head coverings, see above. (5) Applying any of the aforementioned types of perfume to an entire larger member of the body, such as the thigh, the calf, the arm, the face, the head or the neck. However, no redemption is required for applying perfume to one's clothing unless one wears the perfumed garment for an entire day and unless either the amount of perfume used is large, or is small and covers an area of one's garment equal to one square *shibr*. Henna is considered to be a type of perfume; if someone applies henna to his head and if it is too thin to conceal what is beneath it, the person concerned must offer one blood sacrifice, while if it is thick enough to conceal what is beneath it, he must offer two blood sacrifices since in this case, he will have both applied perfume and covered his head. Perfume also includes safflower and saffron, as we have seen. If someone uses perfume for a legitimate reason, the relevant ruling presented above applies. If someone applies olive or sesame oil to an entire member of the body without a legitimate excuse, this is subject to the same ruling as that which applies to the use of perfume without a legitimate excuse; however, if it is done for a legitimate reason, such as medical treatment, no redemption is required. (6) Trimming the fingernails on one hand or the toenails on one foot; the same ruling applies if someone trims the toenails and fingernails of both hands and feet in a single session. However, if someone trims them over several sessions, he must offer four blood sacrifices: one for each hand and each foot. (7) Omitting the circumambulation of arrival or the circumambulation of farewell, omitting one circuit of the [circumbulation for the] *'umrah*, or omitting any of the aforementioned duties.

* * *

The Shafiis define a 'redemption' as one of the following: a) the slaughter of a goat or a sheep which meets the specifications that must be met by animals slaughtered on the Day of Sacrifice (and which will be listed below under the heading, "On Animal Sacrifice"), b) feeding six needy persons, or c) fasting three days.

A redemption is required for the following actions: (1) The use of perfume. If someone applies perfume during the *ḥajj*, he must slaughter a goat or a sheep whose meat he then distributes as charity. (2) Wearing a tunic, trousers, boots, a turban, or some other item which contains stitching or which wraps all the way around one's body. However, a redemption is only required for wearing such items given the following conditions: a) One must be aware that the act one has committed is forbidden. If one commits it out of ignorance, no redemption is required. b) One must have committed the act before the first release from the state of ritual consecration (the meaning of which was explained above). c) The person who committed the act must be discerning, and must have committed it voluntarily. d) The person who committed the act must be a male. As for women, they are not to remove their regular clothing, and the only part of their bodies they are required to reveal is the face. If a woman conceals her face with a covering that touches her face directly, she is required to offer a *fidyah*. However, she may conceal her face with something that does not come in direct contact with it. For example, she may place a large comb on her head that protrudes beyond her face, then attach a veil to the comb in order to conceal her face without touching it; it is also acceptable for her to cover that portion of her face which she has no choice but to conceal as a result of covering her hair. A woman is also required to offer a *fidyah* if she covers her hands with gloves or some such thing. (3) Shaving off one's hair or trimming one's toenails or fingernails. Whoever does any of these things must offer a *fidyah*. Moreover, there is no difference in connection with hair removal between shaving it off, shortening it with scissors, using a razor blade, plucking it, or burning it off, whether one removes all of it or part of it, provided that what is removed amounts to part or all of three or more hairs. Nor does it make any difference whether one removes one's own hair or has someone else remove it. However, in order for a redemption to be required, the following three conditions must be met: (a) The act must have been carried out voluntarily. Thus, if someone's hair was removed while he was asleep and without his consent, or if he rubbed up against something unknowingly, causing some of his hair to come out, nothing is required of him. (b) The hair must have been removed needlessly. If, on the other hand, someone removed the hair out of necessity, as when one's eyebrows have grown so long that they cause harm and one removes the harmful portion, no redemption is required. Nor is it necessary for the hair to have been removed from one's head; rather, if someone removes three hairs from any part of his body unnecessarily and by his own volition, he is required to offer a redemption. (c) The removal of the hair must have been deliberate. Hence, if someone scrapes off skin on which hair was growing, no redemption is required of him. For example, if there is a sore on some part of one's body, if there is hair on the sore and if he removes the sore with the result that the hair is removed as well, no redemption is required. (As we have seen before, there is nothing wrong with the use of kohl [antimony], entering the bathroom, venesection, cupping, or arranging one's hair.) (4) Actions involved in sexual foreplay, such as kissing and skin-to-skin contact with a woman of the sort that invalidates one's ritual ablutions. Such actions are forbidden to a pilgrim until his final release from the state of ritual consecration, and if he engages in any of them prior to this, he must offer a redemption. As for looking with sensual desire or kissing with a barrier [between the two people], this requires no redemption. (5) Bringing about an ejaculation through manual stimulation, which is forbidden and requires a redemption. (6) Rubbing one's head hair, beard, or other facial hair with any sort of fat, be it oil, animal fat, or anything else, and whether it is mixed with a pleasant fragrance or not. However, a redemption is only required in such a situation given the following conditions: (a) The bodily member which has been oiled must be one on which hair grows. No redemption is required of someone whose head grows no hair, or of a bald person whose hair has fallen out completely, in whose case it is permissible to oil the bald spot. The same exception applies to a young man who still has no beard, in whose case it is permissible to oil his chin and the rest of his face. In addition, someone who has a head wound is permitted to oil the inside of the wound. (b) One must engage in the act deliberately. If someone oils some part of his body out of forgetfulness, no redemption is required of him. (c) The person concerned must be aware of the prohibition against oiling; hence, no redemption is required of someone who is ignorant of this prohibition. (d) One must have done the oiling of his own volition; hence, no redemption is required of someone who did so against his will.

The punishment for someone who hunts an animal before being released from the state of *iḥrām*

A pilgrim is not permitted to hunt an animal before being released from the state of ritual consecration. We have seen what the various schools say about the actions a pilgrim must perform in order to be released from the state of ritual consecration; as for the compensation (*jazā'*) due from a person who hunts an animal in this situation, each school offers its own detailed ruling concerning how such compensation is to be determined.[132]

---

132. The Shafiis hold that if a pilgrim hunts a wild terrestrial animal such as a gazelle, a wild cow, etc. or shows a hunter where to find such an animal, or if he has such an animal under his power and harms it or causes it to become ill, he must offer the compensation to be explained below if: (a) the animal concerned has done no harm to the pilgrim's person or wealth, as might occur with a hyena, for example, and (b) the animal has caused no harm by contaminating the pilgrim's belongings with ritual impurity, eating his food, or blocking his path, as could be done by massive numbers of locusts. If someone kills an animal in this situation, he is not required to offer a *fidyah* or guarantee.

If a *jazā'* (compensation) is required and if the game animal has an equivalent among domestic animals, as is the case with doves, pigeons and turtledoves, one must offer a goat or a sheep for each bird; for a male or female ostrich, the *jazā'* is a camel; for a wild cow or a wild ass, the *jazā'* due is a domestic cow; for a male antelope, the *jazā'* required is a billy goat while for a female antelope, the *jazā'* required is a she-goat. For a gazelle, the *jazā'* is a young goat; for a rabbit, a young female goat after it has grown stronger but before it has reached a year of age; for a jerboa or a hyrax, a four-month-old she-goat; for a hyena, a ram; and for a fox, a goat or a sheep.

All the aforementioned animals have rulings concerning which we have an authentic saying from the Lawgiver. Otherwise, a ruling is to be given by two trustworthy individuals who have experience with what would be their rough equivalents in terms of appearance and other characteristics. Hence, if the game animal was large, the animal sacrificed must likewise be large, if the game animal was small, the animal judged to be its equivalent must be small as well, if the game animal was healthy, its equivalent must be healthy, and if the game animal was defective, its equivalent must be defective as well provided that it is the same type of defect, such as both animals being one-eyed. If the two animals have different defects, they may not be considered equivalents; the same ruling applies to traits such as fatness, thinness and pregnancy. However, if the domestic equivalent is pregnant, it is not to be slaughtered but rather, its value is to be appraised, after which the person owing the *jazā'* is either to donate its value as charity in the form of food, or fast one day for each *mudd* of food based on said appraisal. If there is no saying [on the part of the Lawgiver] concerning the situation and if no ruling has been issued by two trustworthy persons concerning which animal would serve as the game animal's equivalent, the person must offer the game animal's value based on the appraisal of two trustworthy persons, and the *fidyah* owed will consist of one of the following three options: (a) slaughtering the game animal's domestic equivalent and donating it as charity to the poor within the Meccan precincts, (b) purchasing food equal to the animal's appraised value [the food being of the types which are acceptable as fastbreaking charity] and donating it as charity to the poor within the Meccan precincts, or (c) fasting one day for each *mudd* of food that would have been donated as charity. The foregoing applies to situations in which the game animal has a domestic equivalent; in the case of game that has no domestic equivalent, such as locusts and game birds other than doves and the like, the person who harmed or killed it may choose between the following two options: (a) donating food equal in value to the game animal to the poor within the Meccan precincts, or (b) fasting one day for each *mudd* of food that would have been donated. No distinction is made in such situations between game animals inside and outside the Meccan precincts so long as the person who harmed or killed them is in a state of ritual consecration; otherwise, these rulings apply only to game which is inside the Meccan precincts. Moreover, they apply to any person who has harmed or killed a game animal and who has reached the age of discernment, whether he did so out of forgetfulness or ignorance, by mistake, or under duress. It is forbidden—though it does not invalidate one's *ḥajj*—to cut the grass and trees inside the Meccan precincts in accordance with the details presented in the earlier discussion of this topic; specifically, if someone cuts down a large tree, he must offer a cow, while if he cuts down a relatively small tree, he must offer a goat or a sheep; as for cutting down a very small tree, this requires that one offer the value of the tree cut down. Moreover, as in the situations described above, the pilgrim is given a choice between slaughtering the sacrificial animal and donating its meat as charity, purchasing food equal in value to the animal and donating it as charity, or fasting one day for each *mudd* of the food that would have been donated. As for grass inside the Meccan precincts, one must offer its value if what was cut will not grow back; if it will grow back, the person who cut it need offer neither a guarantee nor a redemption.

The following persons must slaughter a sacrificial animal which meets the criteria for an animal slaughtered on the Day of Sacrifice (*uḍḥiyah*); or, if they are not able to do this, they must fast three days during the *ḥajj* and seven days after they return home: (1) The pilgrim intending to perform the *'umrah*, then the *ḥajj* on separate *iḥrāms* because in so doing, he has failed to perform the *ḥajj* before the *'umrah*. (2) The pilgrim who sets out to perform the *'umrah*, then the *ḥajj* based on a single *iḥrām* because in so doing he has failed to perform the *ḥajj* separately. (3) The pilgrim who fails to throw at least three stones at the three pillars at Minā. (4) The pilgrim who neglected to spend the nights preceding the three "days of meat drying" at Minā. (5) The pilgrim who neglected to spend the night at Muzdalifah without a legitimate excuse. (6) The pilgrim who failed to enter a state of ritual consecration at the legally prescribed *mīqāt* without a legitimate excuse. (7) The pilgrim who failed to perform the circumambulation of farewell without a legitimate excuse. (8) The pilgrim who failed to perform an act which he had vowed to perform, such as walking, riding or shaving during the *ḥajj*, or performing the *ḥajj* separately. (9) The pilgrim who missed stopping on Mt. 'Arafah even though there had been nothing to prevent him from doing so, meaning that dawn broke on the Day of Sacrifice before he had appeared on Mt. 'Arafah or some part of its environs. Such a person must offer a blood sacrifice if he is in a state of ritual consecration for the *ḥajj* alone or for the *'umrah* and the *ḥajj* together (*qirān*). Someone who has thus missed stopping on Mt. 'Arafah must achieve release from the state of ritual consecration as if he were only performing the *'umrah*. He does this by performing all remaining rites involved in the *ḥajj* with the exception of stopping on Mt. 'Arafah; the person is exempted from staying the night at Muzdalifah and Minā and throwing stones at the three pillars at Minā. However, he must perform the circumambulation and the brisk walk between al-Ṣafā and al-Marwah if he has not already done so, and shave with the intention of being released from the state of ritual consecration. He must also make up the *ḥajj* as soon as possible (i.e., in the following year) even if he missed it for a legitimate reason, even if the original *ḥajj* was a voluntary one, and whether or not he is able to afford it. It is not permissible, however, for him to slaughter during the year in which he missed [stopping on Mt. 'Arafah]; rather, he must performing the slaughtering in the year in which he makes up the *ḥajj*. As for someone who missed stopping on Mt. 'Arafah due to some occurrence which prevented him from doing so, the ruling on this situation will be discussed below.

* * *

The Hanafis hold that if someone hunts a terrestrial animal, he must offer its value given the aforementioned restrictions pertaining to hunting game within the Meccan precincts; the same ruling applies to someone who cuts the grass within the Meccan precincts. If someone in a state of ritual consecration hunts something which he is not permitted to hunt, the animal, bird, etc. will be appraised in the place where it was hunted or in a place nearby based on the knowledge of two trustworthy persons. If the value of the animal hunted comes to the price of an animal sacrifice (*hady*), the pilgrim will be allowed to choose among the following three options: (a) purchasing, with the appraised value of the animal hunted, a *hady* and slaughtering it within the Meccan precincts; (b) purchasing food equal in value to the hunted animal and donating it as charity to the poor in any place he wishes, with each person receiving one-half a *ṣā'* of food; and (c) fasting one day for every one-half *ṣā'* of food which would have been donated. (Such fasting does not have to be completed in uninterrupted succession.) If the appraised value of the animal hunted does not come to the price of a *hady*, the pilgrim is to be given a choice between the last two options only, namely, donating food and fasting. No distinction is made in this regard between an animal which was hunted deliberately and one which was harmed or killed by mistake; nor is it necessary for the pilgrim to offer an equivalent to what he hunted. Rather, it is sufficient for him to offer its value. As for deliberate intention and equivalency as mentioned in the following Qur'anic verse, deliberate intention is mentioned here since in most cases, such an action is performed deliberately, whereas the equivalency referred to is symbolic in nature. God Almighty declares, "O you who have attained to faith! Kill no game while you are in the state of pilgrimage. And whoever of you kills it intentionally [shall make] amends in cattle equivalent to what he has killed—with two persons of probity giving their judgment thereon—to be brought as an offering to the Ka'bah; or else he may atone for his sin by feeding the needy, or by the equivalent thereof in fasting: [this,] in order that he taste the full gravity of his deed, [while] God shall have effaced the past. But whoever does it again, God will inflict His retribution on him: for God is almighty, an avenger of evil" (5:95).

The aforementioned applies if the game animal does not belong to anyone; if it belongs to someone else, however, one must offer two equivalents, one of which is the *jazā'* explained above, and the other of which is to be offered to the animal's owner. Hunting within the Meccan precincts is forbidden under all circumstances even if the person who does the hunting is not in a state of ritual consecration. If someone hunts game within the Meccan precincts and slaughters it, it may not be eaten and is to be treated as though it had died on its own; in fact, it is preferable in cases of necessity to eat an animal which died on its own rather than to eat an animal hunted within the Meccan precincts. Moreover, if someone destroys a member of the animal's body, plucks its feathers, etc., he must offer the value of what he destroyed or removed. Nothing is required of someone who kills 'vermin' such as ticks, turtles, wasps, butterflies, flies, ants, porcupines, snakes, scorpions, mice, crows, and mordacious dogs, and if someone cuts the grass within the Meccan precincts, he must offer the value of what he cut, as we have seen.

The Hanafis hold that charity of one-half *ṣā'* of wheat or the value thereof must be offered for any of the following: (1) Perfuming less than one member of one's body. (2) Wearing a tunic or a perfumed robe for less than a day. (3) Covering one's head. (4) Shaving less than one-fourth of one's head or beard, or shaving one's calf or upper arm. (5) Cutting one or two toenails or fingernails. (6) Performing the circumambulation of arrival or farewell while in a state of minor ritual impurity. (7) Omitting one, or part of one, circuit of the circumambulation of farewell. (8) Shaving someone else's head, even if the person whose head was shaved is not in a state of ritual consecration.

As for those actions which require that one offer charity of less than one-half *ṣā'*, these include killing a locust. Someone who kills a single locust may offer whatever he wishes in the way of charity; if someone kills two or three locusts, he must offer charity in the amount of one handful of food, and if someone kills more than three, he must offer one-half a *ṣā'*.

* * *

The Malikis hold that if someone hunts an animal inside the Meccan precincts, he must offer the compensation (*jazā'*) to be described below; the same ruling applies if one causes the animal to die, as in a situation in which the game animal sees the person, starts with fright, falls down and dies, or if the person inserts a spear in the ground, after which a game animal injures itself on it and dies. This is the officially recognized point of view within the Maliki school, though some Malikis say that no *jazā'* is required in this type of situation, since no pilgrim would intend to hunt a game animal, and that no compensation is required of someone in a state of ritual consecration who shows someone else where a game animal is. It is not permissible to eat game hunted by someone in a state of ritual consecration under any circumstances, as is the case with animals which died by themselves; the same ruling which applies to game animals' meat applies likewise to their eggs in this respect. Compensation is required of someone who kills a game animal or harms it in some way, as when one plucks its feathers with the result that it is placed in mortal danger; the same ruling applies if one injures an animal or drives it out of the

Meccan precincts as a result of which it is hunted by someone outside or dies before coming back in. There are three kinds of compensation (*jazā'*) which are required for hunting game within the Meccan precincts, of which the pilgrim may choose one: (1) Offering a livestock animal which is equivalent to the game animal, i.e., one which resembles it in appearance and size. If there is no domestic animal available which resembles the game animal in appearance, it is sufficient for it to resemble it in size. The only animals which may be offered as compensation (*jazā'*) are those which are acceptable as offerings on the Day of Sacrifice, namely, a sheep or a goat which is one year old, a cow which is three years old, or a camel which is five years old, as we saw in our discussion of *hady*. (2) Offering the game animal's value in the form of food. The animal's value is to be appraised on the day on which it died, and in the place where it died. If it has no value in the place where it died, it is to be appraised as near as possible to this place; the animal's value is then to be given to the needy in the place where the animal died, with each person receiving one *mudd* by the Prophet's standards. (3) Fasting a number of days equal to the number of *mudds* of food which the game animal was estimated to equal. One is also to fast an entire day for part of a *mudd*, since fasting days are not subject to division. Moreover, the compensation is not to be offered until after a ruling has been issued by two trustworthy individuals who are well-versed in the Islamic legal rulings pertaining to game animals, since such expertise is required in order to determine which animal would serve as an equivalent or what the game animal's value would come to. Since the number of days fasted must equal the number of *mudds* that correspond to the value of the game animal, the appraisal of the game animal's value is also necessary before one fasts. Game animals and birds which are exceptions to the equivalency ruling include doves and pigeons in Mecca and within the wider Meccan precincts, either of which requires that one sacrifice a sheep or goat without any ruling being issued beforehand. If the pilgrim is unable to offer a sheep or a goat, he must fast ten days. Moreover, the compensation due for each animal is determined on the basis of the characteristics of the animal itself. Thus, if someone wishes to offer an equivalent of the game animal hunted, the equivalent of an ostrich is a male or female camel, since a camel resembles an ostrich in terms of size and overall appearance; the equivalent of an elephant is a two-humped camel; the equivalent of a wild ass or a wild cow is a cow, while the equivalent of a hyena or a fox is a sheep or a goat. The aforementioned compensation will be based on a ruling issued by two trustworthy persons who are well-versed in the Islamic legal rulings pertaining to game animals, either on the appropriate equivalent or value or the number of days to be fasted. In the case of a tailed lizard, a rabbit, a jerboa, or any of the birds inside or outside the Meccan precincts other than doves and pigeons, the ruling will either be an assessment of the animal's or bird's value at the time it was destroyed, or a ruling to fast ten days; hence, in the case of these animals or birds, the compensation will consist of either an offering of the animal's or bird's value in the form of food, or fasting as explained above.

* * *

The Hanbalis hold that if someone destroys a game animal inside the Meccan precincts either by his own direct act or by causing it to die indirectly and if the animal was owned by someone else, the person who destroyed it must provide two things: (1) a compensation for the animal hunted which he is to distribute among the needy of the Meccan precincts, and (2) a guarantee to the animal's owner. Provision of such a guarantee involves appraising the value of the game animal destroyed if it has no domestic equivalent, or purchasing its equivalent and giving it to the animal's owner. If, on the other hand, the game animal did not belong to anyone, the person who hunted it is obliged only to offer a compensation.

The Hanbalis divide game animals into two types. Class One includes game animals which have an equivalent among domestic animals, such as the wild ass, the mountain goat, and the like. The rulings on this type are divided, in turn, into two categories: (a) rulings concerning which we have a written text passed down on the authority of the Companions of the Prophet, and (b) rulings concerning which we have no written text of this sort. Type (a) includes animals such as the following: (1) Ostriches. If someone hunts an ostrich inside the Meccan precincts, he must slaughter a male or female camel. This is based on the ruling passed down from 'Umar, 'Uthmān, 'Alī and others. (2) Wild asses and mountain goats. If someone hunts one of these, he must slaughter a cow and distribute it as charity among the needy inside the Meccan precincts. (3) The hyena, the compensation for which is a ram. (4) The gazelle, the compensation for which is a she-goat, which is likewise to be slaughtered and distributed among the needy within the Meccan precincts. As for the hunting of a fox, it requires no compensation. (5) The tailed lizard, the compensation for which is a six-month-old he-goat. (6) Rabbits. If someone hunts a rabbit, the compensation required of him is that he slaughter a young she-goat less than four months old. (7) The hyrax, which is a black animal smaller than a cat the compensation for which is the slaughter of a six-month-old he-goat. (8) Pigeons. This category includes all birds which make a cooing sound and which drink by placing their beaks in the water and sipping the way a sheep or goat does. This manner of drinking, which is similar to lapping, characterizes chickens, sparrows, turtledoves and the like. Whoever hunts any of these birds inside the Meccan precincts owes a compensation which consists of a sheep or a goat which is to be slaughtered and distributed among the needy.

As for Type (b) above, namely, those animals concerning which we have no written text from the Companions, the ruling is that if someone hunts any of these inside the Meccan precincts, the animal's value is to be appraised by two trustworthy arbiters. It is permissible for one or both of the arbiters to have killed the animal in question if they were not aware of the prohibition against killing it, if they killed it accidentally, or if they killed it out of necessity (as in a case where there was no other food available). Moreover, if there is a guarantee to be paid in the form of an equivalent, consideration must be given to smallness and largeness, health and sickliness, soundness and defectiveness, etc.

As for Class Two, namely, those game animals which have no equivalents among domestic animals, the ruling on them is that if they are hunted, the person who hunted them must offer their value. These animals include all birds other than the ones mentioned above, including water birds such as geese and others. If someone plucks a game animal's or bird's feathers, fur or down, he is not required to offer anything provided that what he harmed grows back or that the wound he caused heals over. However, if he causes the animal or bird to be permanently disabled, he must offer the difference between the animal's or bird's original value and its value after the damage which he did to it.

On the *'umrah*, or the lesser pilgrimage

As used generally in the Arabic language, the word *'umrah* means 'visit'; hence, one might say in Arabic, *a'marahu* to mean "he visited him." As used in the context of Islamic law, the word *'umrah* refers to a visit to the Sacred Mosque undertaken in a specified manner to be explained below.

The ruling on the *'umrah* and the evidence in its support

The *'umrah*, like the *ḥajj*, is an individual obligation to be fulfilled once in the person's lifetime; moreover, the details presented above regarding whether the *ḥajj* must be performed as soon as one becomes able to do so or whether it may be performed at any time thereafter apply likewise to the *'umrah*. This is the view of the Shafiis and the Hanbalis; for the views of the Malikis and the Hanafis, see below.[133]

The evidence for viewing the *'umrah* as obligatory is found in the words of God Almighty, "And perform the pilgrimage [the *ḥajj*] and the pious visit [the *'umrah*] [to Mecca] in honor of God…" (2:196). What this verse means is: Perform these two rites to completion, fulfilling all their conditions and executing all their pillars. Further evidence in favor of viewing the *'umrah* as obligatory is found in the hadith passed down on the authority of 'Āishah, who said, "O Messenger of God, are women required to participate in *jihād*?" He replied, "Yes, they are re-

---

133. According to the Malikis and the Hanafis, the *'umrah* is an emphatically enjoined emulation of the Sunnah to be performed once in a lifetime, but not an obligation. This is based on the words of the Prophet, "The *ḥajj* is obligatory, while the *'umrah* is voluntary." (This saying is narrated by Ibn Mājah.) As for the words of God Almighty, "And perform the pilgrimage [the *ḥajj*] and the pious visit [the *'umrah*] [to Mecca] in honor of God…" (2:196), it is a command to perform these pilgrimages to completion once they have been commenced. As we have seen, it is obligatory to perform an act of worship to completion once one has commenced it, even if it was voluntary to begin with; hence, the statements quoted above do not serve as evidence that the *'umrah* is obligatory. Similarly, the prophetic statement, "They [women] are required to participate in *jihād* which involves no combat, namely, the *ḥajj* and the *'umrah*" does not serve as evidence that the *'umrah* is obligatory, since the phrase "they [women] are required to participate in…" may include both obligations and voluntary actions. In this case, the *ḥajj* is an obligation, whereas the *'umrah* is voluntary based on the evidence provided by the hadith quoted above, namely, "The *ḥajj* (the greater pilgrimage) is obligatory, while the *'umrah* (the lesser pilgrimage) is voluntary." As for the obligatory nature of the *ḥajj*, it is supported definitively by the words of God Almighty, "Hence, pilgrimage to the Temple [the *ḥajj*] is a duty owed to God by all people who are able to undertake it…" (3:97), as well as by other textual evidence cited at the beginning of our discussion of the *ḥajj*.

quired to participate in *jihād* which involves no combat, that is, the *ḥajj* and the *'umrah*."[134] However, anything over a single *'umrah* is voluntary.

Conditions of the *'umrah*

The same conditions which apply to the *ḥajj*, which have been detailed above, apply likewise to the *'umrah*.

The pillars of the *'umrah*

According to the Malikis and the Hanbalis, the *'umrah* consists of three pillars: (1) *iḥrām*, (2) circumambulation of the Ka'bah, and (3) the brisk walk between al-Ṣafā and al-Marwah. The Shafiis include two pillars in addition to these three, while the Hanafis recognize only one.[135]

The time for performance of the *'umrah*, and those places through which a pilgrim must not pass on his way to perform the *'umrah* without entering a state of ritual consecration

The *'umrah* may be performed all year round; hence, one may validly enter a state of ritual consecration (*iḥrām*) for the *'umrah* without any undesirability attached thereto at any time of the year except in particular situations, details of which are ruled on by each of the schools.[136]

---

134. Narrated by Imām Aḥmad [Ibn Ḥanbal] and Ibn Mājah with reliable transmitters. It has been narrated on the authority of Abū Razīn al-'Uqaylī that he once came to the Prophet and said, "My father is an elderly man who is not able to undertake the *ḥajj*, the *'umrah*, or even an ordinary journey." The Prophet replied, saying, "Perform both the *ḥajj* and the *'umrah* on your father's behalf." (This is narrated by al-Bukhārī, Muslim, Abū Dāwūd, al-Nasā'ī, and Ibn Mājah, while al-Tirmidhī also classifies it as an authentic hadith.)

135. The pillars of the *'umrah* listed by the Shafiis are as follows: (1) *iḥrām*, (2) circumambulation, (3) the brisk walk between al-Ṣafā and al-Marwah, (4) removal of hair, and (5) maintenance of the proper order among these pillars.

* * *

As for the Hanafis, they hold that the *'umrah*'s only pillar is the performance of most of the circumambulation (four circuits); as for *iḥrām*, they classify it as a condition for the *'umrah*'s validity, whereas they view the brisk walk between al-Ṣafā and al-Marwah as a 'duty' as we saw earlier in our discussion of the *ḥajj*. They classify shaving or shortening of the hair likewise as a 'duty' only, not as a pillar.

136. The Hanafis hold that it is undesirable to the point of being forbidden to enter a state of ritual consecration for the *'umrah* while one is on Mt. 'Arafah, whether before noon or after noon, based on the best attested view. It is also undesirable to do so on the Day of Sacrifice and the three days subsequent to it or to do so during the *ḥajj* months for inhabitants of Mecca, be they permanent or temporary residents, if they wish to perform the *ḥajj* during the same year.

If someone enters a state of ritual consecration for the *'umrah* during any of the aforementioned times and if he has already commenced its rites, he is obliged to perform them to completion even though it is undesirable to the point of being forbidden to do so [at this time]. Hence, the person concerned should refrain from performing the *'umrah* in order not to become guilty of wrongdoing, then make it up at a later time. Even so, one must offer a sacrificial animal for having refrained from completing the *'umrah*. Similarly, if the pilgrim does not refrain from completing the *'umrah* under such circumstances, his *'umrah* will be valid, but he will have committed wrongdoing and must, as a consequence, offer a sacrificial animal. In addition, it is undesirable to the point of being forbidden to combine two states of ritual consecration for two *'umrahs*; hence, if someone enters a state of ritual consecration for one *'umrah* and performs one circuit of the circumambulation, the entire circumambulation, or no circumambulation for this *'umrah*, and if he then enters *iḥrām* again for another *'umrah*, the second *'umrah* will be void even if the pilgrim has not formed the intention not to complete it. In such a case, he must make up the second *'umrah* later and offer a sacrificial animal on this account. If someone performs the circumambulation and the *sa'ī* for the first *'umrah* such that all that remains for him to do is the shaving, and if he then enters *iḥrām* for another *'umrah*, he must complete the other *'umrah* as well rather than refraining from completing it; however, he must offer a sacrificial animal for combining two *iḥrāms*. If the pilgrim shaves for the first *'umrah* before completing the rites for the second, he must offer still another sacrificial animal; however, if he shaves after completing the second *'umrah*, no additional blood sacrifice is required of him.

If a pilgrim enters *iḥrām* for the *ḥajj*, then does so again for the *'umrah* before performing the circumambulation of arrival, he will be obliged to perform them both and will, in so doing, become *qārin*, [i.e., someone who engages in *qirān*]. However, he will also have committed an offense, since the *'umrah* will not have been performed in the proper order with respect to the *ḥajj*. The Sunnah-based practice in a case of *qirān* is for the pilgrim to enter a state of ritual consecration for the *ḥajj* and the *'umrah* together, or to enter *iḥrām* for the *'umrah* before doing so for the *ḥajj*. It is not recommended that such a person renounce the *'umrah*, but he is required to offer an animal sacrifice of thanksgiving (*dam shukr*). This *'umrah* of his will be invalidated by stopping on Mt. 'Arafah for the *ḥajj* before performing its [other] rites; if, on the other hand, the pilgrim enters *iḥrām* for the *'umrah* after performing the circumambulation of arrival for the *ḥajj*, it is recommended that he renounce the *'umrah*; he must also offer an animal sacrifice on this account and make up the *'umrah* later. If he does not renounce the *'umrah* but, rather, completes both the *ḥajj* and the *'umrah*, he must offer an animal sacrifice of completion (*dam jabr*), and he will have departed from what is recommended.

* * *

According to the Malikis, one may validly enter a state of ritual consecration for the *'umrah* at any time of the year unless one is already in a state of ritual consecration for a *ḥajj* or another *'umrah*, in which case one may only enter *iḥrām* for a new *'umrah* after completing the rites for the *ḥajj* or the first *'umrah*. One completes the rites for the *ḥajj* by stopping on Mt. 'Arafah, circumambulating the Ka'bah, performing the *sa'ī* and either throwing stones at the three pillars in Minā on the third day after the Day of Sacrifice or waiting until the passage of the time it would have taken to perform the stone throwing after high noon on the third day following the Day of Sacrifice if one did not throw stones on this day. It is recommended that one delay entering *iḥrām* for the *'umrah* until sundown on the third day after the Day of Sacrifice; if a pilgrim enters *iḥrām* for the *'umrah* after the time for stone throwing on this day and before sundown of the same day, his *iḥrām* will be valid, although to do so is deemed undesirable. Nevertheless, one is not to commence the rites for this *'umrah* until sundown, and if someone does perform any of these rites, such as circumambulating the Ka'bah or performing the *sa'ī* before sundown, it will not count and he must repeat it after sundown. It is not undesirable to enter *iḥrām* for the *'umrah* on the Day of 'Arafah, nor during the "days of meat drying" or any other day. If someone enters *iḥrām* for two *ḥajjs* or two *'umrahs*, the second of the two will be null and void; moreover, if someone enters *iḥrām* for the *ḥajj*, then incorporates a *'umrah* into it, the *'umrah* will have no validity.

* * *

The Hanbalis hold that the *'umrah* is valid all year round, and that it is not undesirable to perform it during the "days of meat drying" or at any other time. However, if someone enters *iḥrām* for the *ḥajj*, then introduces the *'umrah* into it, his *iḥrām* for the *'umrah* will be null and void. As a consequence, he will not be classified as *qārin*, and he will not be obliged to do anything as a result of his second *iḥrām*. If someone enters *iḥrām* for two *'umrahs*, his *iḥrām* for the first *'umrah* will be valid, while the second will not; the same applies to a situation in which one enters *iḥrām* for two *ḥajjs*.

* * *

As for the Shafiis, they hold that the *'umrah* is valid at any time of the year without any undesirability attached to it unless one has already entered a state of ritual consecration for the *ḥajj*; if someone who has already entered *iḥrām* for the *ḥajj*, it will not be valid for the *'umrah*. Similarly, if someone enters *iḥrām* for two *ḥajjs* or for two *'umrahs*, one of the two will be valid, while the other will be void.

As for the place in which the pilgrim must enter a state of ritual consecration for the *'umrah*, the same rulings which apply to this matter in connection with the *ḥajj* apply likewise with respect to the *'umrah* except in the case of those who are in Mecca, whether they are permanent residents of the city or simply staying there for a period of time. Those who are in Mecca itself must enter *iḥrām* for the *'umrah* outside the Meccan precincts, that is, beyond the area in which hunting is forbidden. The Malikis and the Shafiis hold that the best place outside the Meccan precincts in which to enter *iḥrām* for the *'umrah* is al-Ji'rānah (located between Mecca and al-Ṭā'if), followed by al-Tan'īm, which is now called Masājid Ā'ishah, whereas the Hanafis and the Hanbalis hold that the best location for this is al-Tan'īm, followed by al-Ji'rānah.

Someone in Mecca who wishes to undertake the *'umrah* must go out to a place near where the Meccan precincts end, then enter a state of ritual consecration, whereas someone in Mecca who wishes to undertake the *ḥajj* must enter a state of ritual consecration from within the Meccan precincts. The Shafiis, the Hanafis and the Hanbalis hold that if someone from Mecca enters *iḥrām* for the *'umrah* from inside the Meccan precincts, his *iḥrām* will still be valid, but he will be obliged to offer an animal sacrifice for neglecting to enter a state of ritual consecration from the proper place; for the Malikis' view, see below.[137] If the pilgrim leaves the Meccan precincts and enters *iḥrām* from outside before circumambulating the Ka'bah and performing the brisk walk between al-Ṣafā and al-Marwah, nothing is required of him.

It is recommended that one perform the *'umrah* as many times as one can. Moreover, the Shafiis, the Hanbalis and the Hanafis hold that it is an emphatically enjoined emulation of the Sunnah during the month of Ramaḍān; for the view of the Malikis, see below.[138]

---

137. The Malikis hold that if someone from Mecca enters a state of ritual consecration for the *'umrah* from within the Meccan precincts, he is not required to offer an animal sacrifice; however, he must leave the Meccan precincts before performing the circumambulation and the *sa'ī*, since every *iḥrām* must include some time outside the Meccan precincts as well as some time inside. If someone performs the circumambulation and the *sa'ī* for the *'umrah* before leaving the Meccan precincts, they will not count, and he must repeat them after leaving the Meccan precincts and coming back inside.

138. According to the Malikis, it is undesirable to repeat the *'umrah* twice in the same year except for someone who is already in Mecca before the *ḥajj* months begin and who has been forbidden to pass beyond his [legally prescribed] *mīqāt* after being released from his *iḥrām*. Rather, such a person is to enter *iḥrām* for the *'umrah* when he enters Mecca even if he already performed the *'umrah* earlier in the same year, since it is not undesirable for such a person to repeat the *'umrah* twice in one year. If such a person wishes to enter Mecca during the *ḥajj* months, he should enter with the intention of performing the *ḥajj* rather than the *'umrah* since in this situation, it is not undesirable to enter a state of ritual consecration for the *ḥajj* (whereas it is undesirable to do so before the *ḥajj* months). As for performing the *'umrah* again in another year, this is recommended; moreover, when doing so, one should intend to perform the *'umrah* during the *ḥajj* season in order for it to

Duties and Sunnah-based practices associated with the *'umrah* and that which renders the *'umrah* invalid

Whatever is required with respect to the *ḥajj* is likewise required with respect to the *'umrah*; similarly, whatever represents an emulation of the Sunnah in connection with the *ḥajj* is an emulation of the Sunnah in connection with the *'umrah* as well. In sum, the *'umrah* is identical to the *ḥajj* with respect to entering a state of ritual consecration, rites, duties, Sunnah-based practices, prohibitions, undesirable acts, the rulings which apply if someone is prevented by some circumstance from completing the pilgrimage after entering a state of ritual consecration, and that which invalidates one's pilgrimage. As for what invalidates the *ḥajj* and the *'umrah*, the Malikis differ from the other schools on this point.[139]

However, the *'umrah* also differs from the *ḥajj* in the following respects: (1) The *'umrah*, unlike the *ḥajj*, has no specified season. (2) The *'umrah* includes neither stopping on Mt. 'Arafah nor spending the night at Muzdalifah. (3) The *'umrah* does not include the rite of throwing stones at the three pillars in Minā. (4) According to the Malikis, the Hanafis and the Hanbalis, prayers are to be combined during the *ḥajj* only, but not during the *'umrah*. As for the Shafiis, they hold that neither the *ḥajj* nor the *'umrah* is the basis for the combining of prayers but rather, the fact that the pilgrim is on a journey. (5) The *'umrah* includes neither a circumambulation of arrival nor a sermon. (6) All pilgrims undertaking the *'umrah* are to enter a state of ritual consecration outside the Meccan precincts, whereas in the case of the *ḥajj*, those already inside Mecca are to do so within the Meccan precincts as we saw earlier in our discussion of *iḥrām*. (7) According to the Malikis and the Hanafis, the

---

fulfill a collective emulation of the Sunnah on behalf of the Muslim community. This is because the *'umrah* is a collective Sunnah-based practice every year with respect to the Muslim community as a whole, and [marks] the beginning of the year with respect to the *'umrah* performed by someone [already] in a state of ritual consecration. Lastly, the Malikis draw no distinction between Ramaḍān and other months in this regard; in other words, they hold that the *'umrah* is not more emphatically enjoined during Ramaḍān than it is at any other time of the year.

139. According to the Malikis, the *'umrah* and the *ḥajj* are invalidated by the same acts, such as intercourse and the like; however, sexual intercourse does not invalidate the *'umrah* unless it takes place before it has been completed with the *sa'ī*. If the *'umrah* is invalidated, the pilgrim must nevertheless perform all its rites to completion, then make it up immediately and slaughter a sacrificial animal (*hady*) on account of the first *'umrah*'s invalidation. As in the case of a *ḥajj* which has been invalidated, however, the slaughter of the *hady* on account of the *'umrah*'s invalidation must be postponed until the time at which it is made up. If, on the other hand, intercourse (or some other act which invalidates the *'umrah*) takes place after the pilgrim has performed the *sa'ī* and before shaving, it will not be invalidated, though the pilgrim must still offer a *hady* just as one is obliged to do (in connection with both the *'umrah* and the *ḥajj*) if one has had an emission of preseminal fluid and the like.

'umrah is an emphatically enjoined emulation of the Sunnah rather than an obligation.

In addition to the differences cited above, the Hanafis list two other distinctions between the *'umrah* and the *ḥajj*.[140]

A discussion of the practices referred to as *qirān*, *tamattu'*, and *ifrād*

When someone wishes to perform the *ḥajj* and the *'umrah*, he may enter the required *iḥrām* in one of the following three ways: (1) *Ifrād*, in which one enters *iḥrām* for the *ḥajj* alone; once the pilgrim has completed the rites for the *ḥajj*, he may enter *iḥrām* again for the *'umrah* and perform the circumambulation and the brisk walk between al-Ṣafā and al-Marwah in accordance with the details presented above in our discussion of the *'umrah*. (2) *Qirān*, in which one joins the *ḥajj* and the *'umrah* based on the same *iḥrām*, whether in actual fact or in a legal sense. (3) *Tamattu'*, in which one performs the *'umrah* first, then the *ḥajj* during the same year.

Each of the four schools presents its own detailed rulings on these three practices.[141]

---

140. The Hanafis further distinguish between the *'umrah* and the *ḥajj* by holding that: (1) As distinct from the *ḥajj*, invalidation of the *'umrah* does not call for the sacrifice of a camel or a cow, nor does the [missing of] the circumambulation for the *'umrah*; rather, these require only a sheep or a goat. (2) The *'umrah* includes no circumambulation of farewell.

141. The Shafiis list the following three ways in which the *ḥajj* and the *'umrah* may be performed: (1) *Ifrād*, in which the pilgrim enters *iḥrām* for the *ḥajj* during the *ḥajj* months from his own homeland's *mīqāt*; then, after completing all of the *ḥajj* rites, the pilgrim enters *iḥrām* for the *'umrah*. (2) *Tamattu'*, in which the pilgrim enters *iḥrām* for the *'umrah* during the *ḥajj* months from whatever *mīqāt* he passes through on his way to Mecca, even if it is not the *mīqāt* specified for his own homeland. The pilgrim then performs the rites for the *'umrah* and after completing them, he enters *iḥrām* for the *ḥajj* either (a) in Mecca, (b) in the same *mīqāt* in which he entered *iḥrām* for the *'umrah*, (c) in a place located the same distance [as the *mīqāt*] from Mecca, or (d) in a *mīqāt* which is closer to Mecca. If the pilgrim enters *iḥrām* for the *'umrah* after passing through the *mīqāt*, and if he then enters *iḥrām* for the *ḥajj* after completing the *'umrah*, he is likewise considered to have performed *tammatu'*, since the pilgrim concerned has abided by the prohibitions associated with *iḥrām* [during the interval] between the *'umrah* and the *ḥajj*. (3) *Qirān*, which is to enter *iḥrām* for the *ḥajj* and the *'umrah* together in the *mīqāt* for the *ḥajj*, whether it is the legally prescribed *mīqāt* for the pilgrim's own homeland or simply the *mīqāt* through which he passes on his way to Mecca. If the pilgrim starts out in Mecca and enters *iḥrām* from there for both the *ḥajj* and the *'umrah*, he is considered to be performing *qirān*. In such a case, the pilgrim is not required to leave the Meccan precincts for the sake of [his *iḥrām* for] the *'umrah*, since it is included within the *ḥajj*. Another way of performing *qirān* is to enter *iḥrām* first for the *'umrah*, whether this is done during or prior to the *ḥajj* months, then to introduce the *ḥajj* into the *'umrah* during the *ḥajj* months before commencing the circu-

mambulation for the *'umrah*. (The practice of introducing the *ḥajj* into the *'umrah* involves intending to perform the *ḥajj* before beginning the circumambulation for the *'umrah*, as we have seen; as for introducing the *'umrah* into the *ḥajj*, this is not valid.)

Of these three approaches, the Shafiis consider *ifrād* to be the most preferable, followed by *tamattu'*, then *qirān*. However, *ifrād* is only considered superior if the pilgrim performs the *'umrah* during the same year in which he performed the *ḥajj*; if the *'umrah* is delayed past the year in which the person performed the *ḥajj*, his *ifrād* will be inferior, since it is deemed undesirable to delay the *'umrah* past the year in which one undertook the *ḥajj*.

The pilgrim who is performing *qirān* is required only to perform the *ḥajj*; hence, it is sufficient for him to perform one circumambulation and one *sa'ī* for both the *ḥajj* and the *'umrah* based on the words of the Prophet, "If someone enters *iḥrām* for the *ḥajj* and the *'umrah*, it will suffice him to perform one circumambulation and one *sa'ī* for both of them." (Al-Tirmidhī classifies this as an authentic hadith.) Both those pilgrims performing *tamattu'* and those performing *qirān* are required to offer a *hady*. The obligation of those performing *tamattu'* to offer such a sacrifice is based on the words of God Almighty, "... then he who takes advantage of a pious visit [*tamatta'a bil-'umrah*] before the [time of pilgrimage] shall give whatever offering he can easily afford; whereas he who cannot afford it shall fast for three days during the pilgrimage and for seven days after your return: that is, ten full days" (2:196). As for the obligation of someone performing *qirān* to offer an animal sacrifice, it is based on the hadith narrated by Muslim and al-Bukhārī on the authority of 'Ā'ishah, may God be pleased with her, who stated that the Prophet slaughtered cows on the Day of Sacrifice on behalf of his wives, who were performing *qirān*.

However, the *hady* is only required of those performing *tamattu'* and *qirān* given the following conditions: (1) They must "not live near the Inviolable House of Worship [the Sacred Mosque]" (2:196). Specifically, they must not have a dwelling within a radius of two *marḥalahs* [48 miles] of the Sacred Mosque; if they do, they are not obliged to offer a *hady*. (2) The *'umrah* of the pilgrim performing *tamattu'* must fall within the *ḥajj* months; if he enters *iḥrām* for the *'umrah* before the *ḥajj* months begin (whether he completes the *'umrah* before the *ḥajj* months begin or after they have begun), no *hady* is required of him, since in this case, he will not have combined the *'umrah* and the *ḥajj* during the *ḥajj* season and, as a consequence, he is similar to someone who has practiced *ifrād*. (3) The person performing *tamattu'* or *qirān* must perform the *ḥajj* during the same year; if someone performs the *'umrah* during the *ḥajj* season, then performs the *ḥajj* during another year or does not perform it at all, no animal sacrifice is required of him. (4) After completing the *'umrah*, the pilgrim performing *tamattu'* must not return to the *mīqāt* where he first entered *iḥrām* or to any other *mīqāt* in order to enter *iḥrām* for the *ḥajj*. As for the person performing *qirān*, he must not return to his *mīqāt* between entering Mecca and commencing some rite of the *ḥajj* such as stopping on Mt. 'Arafah and the circumambulation of arrival. If the person performing *tamattu'* returns to his *mīqāt* in order to enter *iḥrām* for the *ḥajj*, no animal sacrifice is required of him; similarly, if the person performing *qirān* returns to any *mīqāt* after having entered *iḥrām* for the *'umrah* and the *ḥajj* together, or after having introduced the *ḥajj* into the *'umrah* based on the above definition of *qirān*, no animal sacrifice is required of him.

The person performing *tamattu'* becomes obliged to offer his animal sacrifice when he enters *iḥrām* for the *ḥajj*, although properly speaking, he is permitted to slaughter his sacrifice before this time once he has completed his *'umrah*. The preferred time for offering one's *hady* is the Day of Sacrifice; however, there is no final deadline for offering it, as is the case with other animal sacrifices of completion. If a pilgrim is unable to offer a *hady* within the Meccan precincts—whether on account of its not being available, because he cannot afford its price, because he has found it being sold at a price higher than other, comparable animals, or because he is in need of the money he would have paid for the animal—he must fast ten days instead: three days during the *ḥajj* and seven after he returns home. The first three days must be fasted after the pilgrim has entered *iḥrām* for the *ḥajj*. If the person performing *tamattu'* fasts these three days before entering *iḥrām* for the *ḥajj*, they will not be valid. However, it is an emulation of the Sunnah to fast them before the Day of 'Arafah, since it is also an emulation of the Sunnah not to fast on this day; if someone postpones these three fasting days past the "days of meat drying", he will be guilty of wrongdoing and his fasting of them will be compensatory, but he will not be required to offer an animal sacrifice on account of the delay. As for the seven remaining days, the pilgrim is to fast them after returning to his homeland or to any country in which he wishes to settle, whereas if someone settles in Mecca following his pilgrimage, he is to fast these seven days in Mecca. However, the fasting of these seven days in one's homeland will only be valid if one has completed all pilgrimage rites; hence, if someone were to return to his homeland before performing the required circumambulation or *sa'ī*, his fast would be invalid. If, on the other hand, the only rite which he has not yet performed is shaving, the pilgrim may fast these days in his homeland after having shaved.

* * *

The Malikis hold that when someone wishes to perform both the *ḥajj* and the *'umrah*, there are three ways in which this may be done: (1) *Ifrād*, in which the pilgrim enters *iḥrām* for the *ḥajj* alone, then performs the *'umrah* after completing the *ḥajj*. (2) *Tamattu'*, in which the pilgrim enters *iḥrām* for the *'umrah* first and performs one or more of its rites during the *ḥajj* season, then performs the *ḥajj* during the same year. The *ḥajj* season begins at sundown on the last day of Ramaḍān. If a pilgrim enters *iḥrām* for the *'umrah* on the last day of Ramaḍān and completes its rites on the night before the Day of Sacrifice, he is considered to have performed *tamattu'* if he performs the *ḥajj* during the same year. If, on the other hand, he completes the rites for the *'umrah* before sundown [on the last day of Ramaḍān], then performs the *ḥajj* during the same year, he may not be considered to have performed *tamattu'* because he did not perform any of the pillars of the *'umrah* during the *ḥajj* season. (3) *Qirān*, which may be performed in one of the following two ways: (a) by entering *iḥrām* for the *ḥajj* and the *'umrah* together, or (b) by entering *iḥrām* for the *'umrah* first, then introducing the *ḥajj* into the *'umrah* before performing the two *rak'ahs* of ritual prayer following the circumambulation for the *'umrah*. The introduction of the *ḥajj* into the *'umrah* may take place before one begins the circumambulation for the *'umrah*, after beginning the circumambulation and before completing it, or after completing the circumambulation and before performing the two *rak'ahs* of ritual prayer associated with it; in all these three cases, the pilgrim is considered to have performed *qirān*. However, it is considered undesirable to introduce the *ḥajj* into the *'umrah* after completing the circumambulation for the *'umrah* and before performing the two *rak'ahs* which follow it; hence, if someone introduces the *ḥajj* into the *'umrah* after commencing the *'umrah*'s circumambulation, he should complete the circumambulation as a voluntary act, in which case the circumambulation required for the *'umrah* will be incorporated into the circumambulation required for the *ḥajj*, since a pilgrim performing *qirān* is only required to perform one circumambulation and one *sa'ī*, as we will see. If someone introduces the *ḥajj* into the *'umrah* after the *'umrah*'s circumambulation and before performing the two *rak'ahs* which follow it, his *iḥrām* for the *ḥajj* will turn into a voluntary act; if, on the other hand, he introduces the *ḥajj* into the *'umrah* after performing the two *rak'ahs* which follow the circumambulation for the *'umrah*, his *iḥrām* for the *ḥajj* will be invalid. Similarly, one's *iḥrām* for the *ḥajj* will be nullified if the *'umrah* into which it is introduced has been invalidated; even so, one is required to complete the invalidated *'umrah*, then make it up immediately as we saw earlier in our discussion of the *'umrah*.

It is only valid to introduce the *ḥajj* into the *'umrah* given the following two conditions: (1) The introduction of the *ḥajj* into the *'umrah* must take place before one has performed the two *rak'ahs* which follow the circumambulation for the *'umrah*. (2) The *'umrah* into which the *ḥajj* is introduced must be valid. If either of these two conditions is unfulfilled, the introduction of the *ḥajj* into the *'umrah* will be invalid, and one's *iḥrām* for the *ḥajj* will be invalid as well. As for introducing the *'umrah* into the *ḥajj* by one's entering *iḥrām* for the *ḥajj* first, then introducing the *'umrah* into the *ḥajj* one has already begun, this is not valid, since that which is 'weak' cannot be introduced into that which is 'strong'.

Of the three approaches to entering *iḥrām* for the *ḥajj* and the *'umrah*, *ifrād* is deemed the most desirable, followed in preference by *qirān*, then *tamattu'*. Only one thing is required of the pilgrim who is performing *qirān*, namely, the performance of the *ḥajj* itself, since it suffices him to perform a single circumambulation and a single *sa'ī*, and to shave a single time for both the *ḥajj* and the *'umrah*.

In addition, both those performing *qirān* and those performing *tamattu'* are required to offer an animal sacrifice (*hady*). God Almighty declares, "... then he who takes advantage of a pious visit [*tamatta'a bil-'umrah*] before the [time of pilgrimage] shall give whatever offering he can easily afford ..." (2:196), while the prophetic Sunnah supports the view that offering a *hady* is obligatory for those performing *qirān* as well.

However, in order for the offering of an animal sacrifice to be required of those performing *tamattu'* and *qirān*, the following two conditions must be met: (1) The pilgrim must not be a permanent resident of Mecca or of an area considered to be part thereof at the time when he engages in *qirān* or *tamattu'*, i.e., at the time when he enters *iḥrām* for the *ḥajj* and the *'umrah* together in the first of the two aforementioned forms of *qirān*, at the time when he enters *iḥrām* for the *'umrah* in the second, or at the time he enters *iḥrām* for the performance of *tamattu'*. As for the area which is considered, legally speaking, to be part of Mecca, it is that area beyond which one must travel [when departing from Mecca] in order to be permitted to shorten one's ritual prayers. If the pilgrim is a permanent resident of Mecca or the area considered legally to be part thereof at the time when he performs the *ḥajj* and the *'umrah*, no animal sacrifice is required of him because he was not required to perform either of the journeys on account of which an animal sacrifice is required for those performing *qirān* and *tamattu'*. God Almighty declares that this sacrifice is required of those who do "not live near the Inviolable House of Worship [the Sacred Mosque]" (2:196), while the Malikis interpret the phrase "near the Inviolable House of Worship" to refer to Mecca and the area which would legally be considered to be a part of it. (2) The pilgrim must perform the *ḥajj* during the same year. If he is prevented from doing so during the same year by an enemy or some other cause after he has begun to perform *qirān* or *tamattu'*, and if he is released from his *iḥrām* due to the aforementioned restraint, he is not required to offer any animal sacrifice.

There is also a third condition which applies only to a pilgrim who is performing *tamattu'*, namely, that he must not return to his homeland or to some other place which is an equal distance away [from Mecca] between completing the rites for the *'umrah* and entering *iḥrām* for the *ḥajj*.

In addition, the *hady* required of someone performing *tamattu'* is not due until the pilgrim has entered *iḥrām* for the *ḥajj*; the reason for this is that the state of performing *tamattu'* is only realized once the pilgrim has entered *iḥrām* for the *ḥajj*. Wide latitude is allowed the pilgrim performing *tamattu'* with respect to when he fulfills the obligation to offer the *hady*; however, such latitude is reduced by someone's throwing stones at the 'Aqabah Pillar on the Day of Sacrifice. If such a pilgrim were to die after throwing stones at the 'Aqabah Pillar, his heirs would be required to offer a *hady* on the deceased's behalf out of his capital; however, if he were to die before this, his heirs would not be required to offer a *hady* on his behalf either out of all his capital or out of one-third thereof. It is valid to offer the *hady* required of those performing *tamattu'* after they have entered *iḥrām* for the *'umrah* and before they have entered *iḥrām* for the *ḥajj*. As for those who are unable to offer a *hady*, they must fast ten days instead: three days during the *ḥajj* and seven days after they return to their homeland following the *ḥajj*; as God Almighty states, "...whereas he who cannot afford it shall fast for three days during the pilgrimage and for seven days after your return..." (2:196). The circumstances which prevent someone from being able to offer a *hady* include: (a) the unavailability of an animal to sacrifice, (b) the unavailability of the money needed to purchase the animal, (c) the unavailability of someone who could lend the pilgrim the money required, and (d) the pilgrim's needing the money which he would have used to purchase the *hady* for his personal expenses.

As for the period of time during which the first three days of fasting may be performed, it begins when the pilgrim enters *iḥrām* for the *ḥajj*, and it continues until the Day of Sacrifice. If the pilgrim does not fast these three days before the Day of Sacrifice, he will be required to fast the three days subsequent to it, namely, the "days of meat drying"; however, it is undesirable to postpone this fast until the days of meat drying without a legitimate excuse for doing so. If one postpones these fasting days until after the "days of meat drying," he may fast them at any time he wishes, whether he fasts them continuously with the remaining seven days or not. As for the seven remaining days, one is to fast them after completing the *ḥajj* rites, that is, after completing the throwing of stones at the three pillars in Minā, whether one has returned to his homeland or not. Hence, what is meant by the words "after your return" in the phrase, "and for seven days after your return..." is the completion of the rites of the *ḥajj*, though it is recommended that one postpone the remaining seven days of fasting until one has actually returned to one's family. As for fasting them before completing the rites of the *ḥajj*, this will not be valid whether it takes place before or after one stops on Mt. 'Arafah.

In the case of someone who is required to offer a *hady* due to some omission from the *ḥajj* or the *'umrah* (as when someone neglects some duty associated with *iḥrām*, such as failing to enter *iḥrām* at his legally prescribed *mīqāt*, having an emission of preseminal fluid, or doing anything else which calls for a *hady*) and who is unable to offer a *hady* for some reason, he, too, must fast ten days in accordance with the details presented above. Such a person must fast the first three days before the "days of meat drying", or during these days if the event calling for the *hady* occurred before his stopping on Mt. 'Arafah; if, on the other hand, the event calling for the *hady* occurs on or after the Day of 'Arafah, the pilgrim concerned should not fast the first three days until after the "days of meat drying."

Lastly, if someone becomes able to offer a *hady* while fasting the first three days, it is recommended that he finish fasting whatever day it is, then offer the *hady*. If, on the other hand, he becomes able to offer the *hady* after completing the first three days of fasting, it is not recommended that he offer the *hady*, although if he does so, it will be valid, and he will not be required to fast any more since the original provision in such a situation is for the person to offer a *hady*.

* * *

The Hanbalis hold that if someone wishes to enter *iḥrām*, he has the choice of doing so in one of three ways: *tamattu'*, *ifrād* and *qirān*, with the most preferred approach being *tamattu'*, followed by *ifrād*, followed by *qirān*. In *tamattu'*, the pilgrim enters *iḥrām* for the *'umrah* during the *ḥajj* season, completes its rites and is released from *iḥrām*. If the pilgrim does not enter *iḥrām* for the *'umrah* during the *ḥajj* season, he will not be eligible for *tamattu'*. In order to perform *tamattu'*, the pilgrim must also perform the *ḥajj* during the same year in which he performed the *'umrah*. This condition is based on the words of God Almighty, "... then he who takes advantage of a pious visit [*tamatta'a bil-'umrah*'] before the [time of pilgrimage] shall give whatever offering he can easily afford; whereas he who cannot afford it shall fast for three days during the pilgrimage and for seven days after your return: that is, ten full days" (2:196), the apparent meaning of which requires continuity between the *'umrah* and the *ḥajj*. In *ifrād*, the pilgrim enters *iḥrām* for the *ḥajj* alone; then, after completing the rites for the *ḥajj*, he performs the *'umrah* required of him if he has not yet done so. In *qirān*, the pilgrim either enters *iḥrām* for the *ḥajj* and the *'umrah* together or first enters *iḥrām* for the *'umrah* only, then introduces the *ḥajj* into it before commencing the circumambulation for the *'umrah* unless he has a *hady* with him, in which case he may validly introduce the *ḥajj* into the *'umrah* even after the *sa'ī*. It is valid to introduce the *ḥajj* into the *'umrah* even if the person concerned is in a state of ritual consecration for the *ḥajj* outside of the *ḥajj* season. If, on the other hand, the pilgrim enters *iḥrām* for the *ḥajj*, then introduces the *'umrah* into the *ḥajj*, his *iḥrām* for the *'umrah* will not be valid nor will he be considered to be practicing *qirān*. As we have seen, the person practicing *qirān* is not required to do anything over and above what is required of someone performing the *ḥajj* alone; rather, he is simply to perform one circumambulation, one *sa'ī*, and so forth.

Someone performing *tamattu'* is required to offer a *hady* based on the words of God Almighty, "... then he who takes advantage of a pious visit [*tamatta'a bil-'umrah*] before the [time of pilgrimage] shall give whatever offering he can easily afford..." (2:196). This is an animal sacrifice offered as a means of worship, not as a means of completion. However, a *hady* is only required given the following seven conditions: (1) The pilgrim performing *tamattu'* must not be a permanent resident of Mecca or the Meccan precincts; at the same time, however, the pilgrim must be no further from the Sacred Mosque than the minimum distance one must travel in order to be permitted to shorten ritual prayers. (2) The pilgrim must perform the *'umrah* during the *ḥajj* season. (3) The pilgrim must perform the *ḥajj* during the same year. (4) The pilgrim must not travel a distance equal to or greater than the distance once must travel in order to shorten ritual prayers between the *'umrah* and the *ḥajj*; if he does so, then enters *iḥrām* for the *ḥajj*, no *hady* will be required of him. (5) The pilgrim must be released from his *iḥrām* for the *'umrah* before entering *iḥrām* again for the *ḥajj*; if he enters *iḥrām* for the *ḥajj* before being released from his *iḥrām* for the *'umrah*, he will not be performing *tamattu'*, but rather, *qirān*, and he will be required to offer the *hady* associated with *qirān*. (6) The pilgrim must enter *iḥrām* for the *'umrah* at the legally prescribed *mīqāt* for pilgrims coming from his homeland, or in a place which is separated from Mecca by at least the distance one must travel in order to shorten ritual prayers. If he enters *iḥrām* in a place closer to Mecca than this, he will either be considered a permanent resident of Mecca or of the area legally considered to be a part thereof, or he will owe a *hady* due to having passed beyond his legally prescribed *mīqāt* without entering *iḥrām*. (7) The pilgrim must consciously intend to perform *tamattu'* either at the beginning of the *'umrah* or while it is in progress.

The offering of the *hady* associated with *tamattu'* and *qirān* is required after dawn on the Day of Sacrifice. The performance of *qirān* also requires the offering of a *hady* as an act of worship if the pilgrim is not a permanent resident of Mecca or the area legally considered to be part thereof. Moreover, the requirement of offering a *hady* in association with *tammatu'* and *qirān* is not waived due to their having been invalidated or due to one's missing the *ḥajj*; hence, if someone makes up a *qirān* which was invalidated, he must offer two such animal sacrifices: one for his first *qirān*, and one for the second, compensatory, *qirān*. If someone performing *tamattu'* is leading a *hady*, he may not be released from his *iḥrām* for the *'umrah*; rather, he should enter *iḥrām* for the *ḥajj* once he has performed the circumambulation and the *sa'ī* for the *'umrah* before being released from his *iḥrām* by shaving. If he then sacrifices the *hady* on the Day of Sacrifice, he will be released from his *iḥrām* for both the *ḥajj* and the *'umrah* together. The pilgrim performing the *'umrah* is released from his *iḥrām* once he has completed the rites of the *'umrah* whether he performed them during the *ḥajj* season or at some other time; this ruling applies whether he has a *hady* with him or not. If, by contrast, a pilgrim performing *tamattu'* has a *hady* with him, he is to slaughter it at al-Marwah, although it is permissible for him to slaughter it anywhere within the Meccan precincts. If someone is unable to offer a *hady*—either because none is available for sale, or because the pilgrim cannot afford to pay for it—he must fast ten days: three days during the *ḥajj* season and seven after he returns to his family. The preferable practice is for the last of the initial three fasting days to fall on the Day of 'Arafah. If the pilgrim does not fast these three days before the Day of Sacrifice, he is to fast the "days of Minā", namely, the "days of meat drying", in which case no *hady* is required of him. If the pilgrim does not fast the three "days of meat drying", he is to fast ten entire days [after the *ḥajj* season has ended], in which case he is required to offer a *hady* due to having delayed one of the duties of the *ḥajj* beyond its specified time. It is permissible for a pilgrim to fast the first three days after entering *iḥrām* for the *'umrah* and before entering *iḥrām* for the *ḥajj*; as for fasting these days before one enters *iḥrām* for the *'umrah*, this is not allowed. And as for the time at which the fasting of these three days is obligatory, it is the same time at which the *hady* is obligatory, namely, the break of dawn on the Day of Sacrifice. One may not validly fast the seven remaining days between the time when one enters *iḥrām* for the *ḥajj* and the time when one completes the *ḥajj*; nor is it valid to fast them during the "days of meat drying", nor between the conclusion of the "days of meat drying" and one's circumambulation of visitation. However, if one fasts these days after performing the circumambulation of visitation and the *sa'ī*, one's fast will be valid. Lastly, it is not necessary to fast either the first three days or the remaining seven days in immediate succession; nor it is necessary to fast them separately. If, after someone becomes required to fast, he obtains a *hady*, he is not obliged to abandon fasting in favor of offering the *hady* even if he has not begun fasting yet; rather, he is free either to offer the *hady* rather than fasting or to fast rather than offering the *hady*.

* * *

The Hanafis hold that someone who wishes to enter *iḥrām* may choose between *ifrād*, *qirān* and *tamattu'*, although they deem *qirān* to be superior to both *tamattu'* and *ifrād*, and *tamattu'* to be superior to *ifrād*. However, *qirān* is only superior if the pilgrim has no reason to fear that as a result of performing *qirān*, he will commit some act which is forbidden to those in a state of ritual consecration due to the extended length of time throughout which he is required to remain in this state. If the pilgrim concerned fears that he might fall into the commission of such forbidden acts while engaging in *qirān*, it is preferable for him to perform *tamattu'* instead of *qirān* since *tamattu'* requires the pilgrim to remain in a state of ritual consecration for a shorter period of time and, as a consequence, requires less self-control. The Hanafis define *ifrād* as entering *iḥrām* for the *ḥajj* alone. As for *qirān*, the meaning of this term in everyday language is the joining of two different things, while its meaning within the context of Islamic law is the act of entering *iḥrām* for the *ḥajj* and the *'umrah* together, either in actual fact or merely in the legal sense. Joining the *ḥajj* and the *'umrah* in actual fact involves performing both of them simultaneously based on a single *iḥrām*, while joining them merely in the legal sense involves postponing one's entry into *iḥrām* for the *ḥajj* until after one has entered *iḥrām* for the *'umrah*, then combining their respective rites. Specifically, the pilgrim enters *iḥrām* for the *'umrah* first; then, before performing four circuits of the circumambulation for the *'umrah*, he enters *iḥrām* for the *ḥajj*. If the pilgrim enters *iḥrām* for the *ḥajj* after performing four circuits of the circumambulation for the *'umrah*, he will not be considered to be performing *qirān*, but rather, *tamattu'* based on the fact that his circumambulation for the *'umrah* was performed during the *ḥajj* season; if his circumambulation for the *'umrah* takes place at a time other than the *ḥajj* season, the pilgrim will have performed neither *qirān* nor *tamattu'*. If, on the other hand, someone enters *iḥrām* for the *ḥajj* first, then intends to perform the *'umrah* before the circumambulation of arrival [for the *ḥajj*], he will be performing *qirān* but he will have committed an offense, and he will be obliged to offer a *hady* after the circumambulation of arrival as we saw in our earlier discussion of the *'umrah*. Someone performing *qirān* may validly enter *iḥrām* either at his legally prescribed *mīqāt* or before reaching it; however, if he passes beyond his *mīqāt* without entering *iḥrām*, he will be obliged to offer a *hady* unless he then returns to the *mīqāt* while in a state of ritual consecration. Such a pilgrim may validly enter *iḥrām* either before or after the *ḥajj* season begins; however, it is deemed undesirable to enter *iḥrām* before the *ḥajj* season has begun. As for the rites of the *ḥajj* and the *'umrah*, the pilgrim performing *qirān* is required to perform them during the *ḥajj* season; specifically, he must perform all or most of the circumambulation for the *'umrah* during the *ḥajj* season, as well as the entire *sa'ī* for both the *ḥajj* and the *'umrah*. Moreover, it is an emulation of the Sunnah for the pilgrim undertaking *qirān* to utter the following words, "O God, I wish to perform the *'umrah* and the *ḥajj*, so facilitate them for me and receive them from me."

It is desirable for the pilgrim to mention the *'umrah* before mentioning the *ḥajj*, and to perform the *'umrah* before the *ḥajj* as well. The reason for this is that the *ḥajj* will not suffice for the performance of the *'umrah*; hence, the pilgrim must first perform seven circuits of the circumambulation for the *'umrah*, performing *ramal* (that is, walking rapidly while shaking one's shoulders) during the first three of these circuits, provided that most or all of this circumambulation is performed during the *ḥajj* months, as we saw earlier. If, when performing the circumambulation for the *'umrah*, the pilgrim intends the circumambulation to be for the *ḥajj*, it will count for the *'umrah* rather than for the [*ḥajj*], since a circumambulation performed during the time period for the *'umrah* will count for the *'umrah* whether one intends this or not. The pilgrim must then perform the *sa'ī* for the *'umrah*, thereby completing the *'umrah* rites. However, he may not be released from his *iḥrām* for the *'umrah* due to the fact that he is still in a state of *iḥrām* for the *ḥajj*; hence, his release from his *iḥrām* depends on his completing the rites for the *ḥajj* as well, and if such a pilgrim were to shave, he would be required to offer two blood sacrifices for having violated two states of ritual consecration. After completing the rites for the *'umrah*, the pilgrim proceeds to complete the rites for the *ḥajj*, as we have seen. If, for example, someone performed only a circumambulation, after which he performed a circumambulation for the *ḥajj*, then performed the *sa'ī* for the *'umrah*, followed by the *sa'ī* for the *ḥajj*, all these rites would be valid, but the person concerned would have committed an offense, though without being required on this account to offer an animal sacrifice.

In order for a pilgrim's *qirān* to be valid, he must: (1) Enter a state of ritual consecration for the *ḥajj* before performing most or all of the circumambulation for the *'umrah*. If a pilgrim enters *iḥrām* for the *ḥajj* after performing most of the circumambulation for the *'umrah*, he will not be considered to be performing *qirān*. (2) Enter *iḥrām* for the *ḥajj* before doing anything to invalidate his *'umrah*. (3) Perform most or all of the circumambulation for the *'umrah* before stopping on Mt. 'Arafah. If the pilgrim does not perform the circumambulation for the *'umrah* until he has stopped on 'Arafah after noon, his *'umrah* will be invalidated, as will his *qirān*, and he will be exempted from the *hady* associated with the *'umrah*. If, by contrast, the pilgrim performs most of the circumambulation for the *'umrah*, then stops at Mt. 'Arafah, he is to complete the remainder of the circumambulation for the *'umrah* before the circumambulation of visitation. (4) Guard against anything which would invalidate the *ḥajj* or the *'umrah*. For example, if a pilgrim engages in sexual intercourse before stopping on Mt. 'Arafah and before performing most of the circumambulation for the *'umrah*, his *qirān* will be invalidated and he will be exempted from the requirement to offer a *hady*. (5) Perform most or all of the circumambulation for the *'umrah* during the *ḥajj* months. If the pilgrim performs most of the circumambulation for the *'umrah* before the *ḥajj* months begin, he will not be considered to be performing *qirān*. (6) Not be a resident of Mecca. The *qirān* of someone who is a resident of Mecca will not be valid unless he leaves Mecca for some other location before the *ḥajj* months begin. (7) Not miss the *ḥajj*. If a pilgrim misses the *ḥajj*, he will not be considered to have performed *qirān*, and he will be exempted from the associated *hady*.

However, it is not necessary for the validity of his *qirān* for the pilgrim to refrain from being reunited with his family; rather, if someone performs the circumambulation for the *'umrah*, then returns to his homeland after this but without being released from his *iḥrām*, his *qirān* will still be valid.

As for the performance of *tamattu'* in the legal sense, this involves first entering *iḥrām* for the *'umrah* during or before the *ḥajj* months, provided that the pilgrim performs most of the circuits of the circumambulation during the *ḥajj* months. After this, the pilgrim is to enter *iḥrām* for the *ḥajj* on a single journey, whether in fact or in a merely legal sense. In other words, he must either not return to his homeland at all after the *'umrah*, or he must return there with the obligation to return after this to Mecca for two reasons, namely: (1) because he has led a *hady* along with him, since a *hady* will prevent him from being released from his *iḥrām* before the Day of Sacrifice, and (2) because he has come home before shaving, since in this case, his return to the Meccan precincts will be obligatory for him due to the necessity of shaving there. This type of return to one's homeland is referred to as an "invalid reunion with one's family." Hence, if someone performs the *'umrah* without leading a sacrificial animal along with him, after which he returns to his homeland before shaving, he will thereby remain in a state of ritual consecration; if this person then resumes his *ḥajj* before shaving in his homeland, he will be considered to be performing *tamattu'* since his reunion with his family was not valid. If, on the other hand, the pilgrim only shaves in his homeland, his *tamattu'* will be invalidated. If the pilgrim performs the *'umrah* while leading a *hady* along with him and he postpones slaughtering it until the Day of Sacrifice, his *tamattu'* will be valid, and all he will be required to offer is this particular *hady* regardless of whether he returns to his family or not. If the pilgrim slaughters his *hady* before the Day of Sacrifice and returns to his family, nothing will be required of him whether he performs the *ḥajj* during the same year or not, but his *tamattu'* will be invalidated, whereas if he neither returns to his family nor performs the *ḥajj* during the same year, he is likewise not required to offer anything. If, on the other hand, he does perform the *ḥajj* during the same year, he must offer two blood sacrifices: one for his *tamattu'*, and one for being released early from his *iḥrām*.

In order for a pilgrim's *tamattu'* to be valid, he must: (1) Perform all or most of the circumambulation for the *'umrah* during the *ḥajj* season. (2) Enter *iḥrām* for the *'umrah* before the *ḥajj*. (3) Perform all or most of the circumambulation for the *'umrah* before entering *iḥrām* for the *ḥajj*. (4) Not do anything which would invalidate his *'umrah*. (5) Not do anything which would invalidate his *ḥajj*. (6) Not have a valid reunion with his family. (7) Perform the *'umrah* and the *ḥajj* during the same year; if a pilgrim performs the circumambulation for the *'umrah* during the *ḥajj* season of one year, then performs the *ḥajj* in a subsequent year, he will not be considered to have performed *tamattu'* even if he does not return to his family or remains in a state of ritual consecration until the following year. (8) Not settle permanently in Mecca; if someone performs the *'umrah*, then decides to remain permanently in Mecca, he will not be considered to have performed *tamattu'*. (9) Not be released from his *iḥrām* and still be in Mecca when the *ḥajj* months begin, since in this case he, like the permanent residents of Mecca, will be ineligible to be considered to have performed *tamattu'*. (10) Not still be in a state of ritual consecration when the *ḥajj* months begin if he performed most of the circumambulation for the *'umrah* at a time other than the *ḥajj* months.

After completing the rites for the *'umrah*, the pilgrim performing *tamattu'* may be released from his *iḥrām* if he wishes by shaving or shortening his hair. Then he should remain in this state until he enters *iḥrām* again for the *ḥajj* on 8 Dhū al-Ḥijjah (also known as the Day of Watering), since this is the day on which the residents of Mecca enter *iḥrām*. One may also postpone one's *iḥrām* until 9 Dhū al-Ḥijjah, that is, the Day of 'Arafah, if one can stand on Mt. 'Arafah during the time specified for this rite. Both pilgrims undertaking *tamattu'* and those undertaking *qirān* are required to offer a *hady*, which is to be slaughtered on the Day of Sacrifice after throwing stones at the 'Aqabah Pillar. As God Almighty declares, "... then he who takes advantage of a pious visit [*tamatta'a bil-'umrah*] before the [time of pilgrimage] shall give whatever offering he can easily afford; whereas he who cannot afford it shall fast for three days during the pilgrimage and for seven days after your return..." (2:196).

As for *qirān*, it is similar to *tamattu'* in meaning; hence, it requires the offering of a *hady* if one is available just as this is required by *tamattu'*. If the pilgrim is unable to provide a *hady*, he is required to fast three days, even if they are not fasted in immediate succession (though fasting them in immediate succession is preferable). These three days are to be fasted during the *ḥajj* season if one has already entered *iḥrām* for the *'umrah*; however, it is not valid to fast three days before entering *iḥrām* for the *'umrah*. In addition, one must fast seven days after completing the rites for the *ḥajj*, and it is preferable to fast these seven days in immediate succession as well. It is also deemed preferable to postpone the beginning of one's fast until just three days before the Day of Sacrifice in the hope that one might be able to provide a *hady* by this time. As for the

A discussion of *hady*, or the animal sacrifice required of the pilgrim

The Arabic term rendered here as 'animal sacrifice', namely, *hady*, refers to the livestock (camels, cattle, sheep and goats) which are presented as gifts to the sacred Meccan precincts. The order of preference is: (1) camels, (2) cattle, and (3) sheep and goats. The only camels acceptable as sacrifices are those which have completed five years of age and entered their sixth year, while the only cattle which are acceptable as sacrifices are those which have completed two years of age and entered their third year; however, the Malikis differ with the other schools on this point.[142] As for sheep and goats which may be offered as sacrifices, each school offers its own detailed rulings on this point.[143]

---

seven remaining days, one may fast them at any time after completing the rites for the *ḥajj* (with the exception of days on which fasting is forbidden, such as the "days of meat drying", during which one's fast will not be valid). If the pilgrim does not fast the first three days until the Day of Sacrifice, only the *hady* will suffice; if he is not able to provide the *hady*, he is to be released from his *iḥrām*. In this latter case, the pilgrim will owe two such animal sacrifices: one for his *qirān* or *tamattu'*, and the other for being released from his *iḥrām* before slaughtering the required *hady*. If the pilgrim becomes able to provide the *hady* before being released from his *iḥrām* for the *ḥajj* by shaving or shortening his hair, his fast will be invalidated and he will again be required to offer the *hady*.

As we have seen, neither *qirān* nor *tamattu'* will be valid on the part of someone who starts out inside the Meccan precincts. As God Almighty declares, *qirān* and *tamattu'* are for people whose families do "not live near the Inviolable House of Worship [the Sacred Mosque]" (2:196). In other words, they must not be permanent residents of the Meccan precincts, that is, those who live either in Mecca or between Mecca and the sites from which pilgrims must enter *iḥrām* on their way to Mecca.

142. According to the Malikis, the only cows acceptable as sacrifices are those that are three years old and have entered somewhat into their fourth year, even if by only one day.

143. According to the Shafiis, a sheep offered as a sacrifice must be a full year old, properly speaking, although it is also acceptable at the age of six months if its front teeth have dropped; as for goats, they must be two years old.

* * *

According to the Malikis, sheep must be a full year old and have entered their second year somewhat, if even by just one day, whereas goats must be one year old and have entered their second year by a month or thereabouts.

* * *

The Hanbalis hold that sheep must be six months old, while goats must be one year old.

* * *

As for the Hanafis, they hold that both sheep and goats offered as sacrifices must be a full year old; however, if a sheep which is more than six months old is sufficiently plump that it cannot be distinguished from a sheep which is a full year old, it is acceptable as well.

Types of animal sacrifice

Animal sacrifices classified as *hady* are divided into three types: (1) Those which are required due to one's performance of the *ḥajj* or the *'umrah*, such as the *hady* required by someone undertaking *tamattu'* or *qirān*. This type, which is referred to by the Hanafis as "a blood sacrifice of thanksgiving", also includes animal sacrifices which are required on account of a pilgrim's having omitted some duty associated with the *ḥajj* or the *'umrah*. (2) Those which are required because of a vow one has made. (3) Those which are voluntary, i.e., those which are freely donated by the pilgrim.

The time and place for slaughtering an animal sacrifice

Each school offers its own details concerning the time and place for slaughtering one's *hady*.[144]

---

144. The Hanbalis hold that the time for slaughtering one's *hady*, regardless of which type it is, begins on the Day of Sacrifice after the holiday prayer even if the sermon has not been delivered yet, although it is preferable to do so after the sermon. This time period extends up to the end of the second of the "days of meat drying", which is the third day after the Day of Sacrifice. Hence, there are three sacrifice days: the Day of Sacrifice itself, and the two subsequent days. It is undesirable to slaughter one's *hady* on the nights before the second and third sacrifice days, while it is deemed preferable to do so on the first day. If someone slaughters his *hady* before the sacrifice days have begun, it will not count and he must sacrifice another animal in its place. If someone misses the specified time period and if the *hady* was a voluntary sacrifice, one's obligation to slaughter it is waived, whereas if it was obligatory, it must be slaughtered late compensatorily. As for the place where the *hady* is to be slaughtered, it is anywhere within the Meccan precincts; however, it is preferable for someone performing the *'umrah* to slaughter his *hady* at al-Marwah, and for someone performing the *ḥajj* to slaughter at Minā. It is not valid to slaughter one's *hady* anywhere outside the Meccan precincts unless the animal is injured or dies before reaching Mecca, in which case the pilgrim is to slaughter the animal in the place where the injury or death took place.

* * *

The Hanafis hold that a *hady* being offered by someone undertaking *tamattu'* or *qirān* should be slaughtered on the Day of Sacrifice or one of the two days which follow it. The slaughter is to take place after one has thrown stones at the 'Aqabah Pillar, as we have seen; if someone slaughters his *hady* before the days set aside for this, it will not count, and if he slaughters it after they have passed, the sacrifice will count, but he must offer an additional *hady* for delaying the slaughter until after the days specified for this rite. As for animal sacrifices other than the *hady* due on the part of those undertaking *qirān* and *tamattu'*, they may be slaughtered at any time.

Slaughtering should take place within the Meccan precincts. If the slaughtering is done during the three days specified for this rite, it is an emulation of the Sunnah for it to be done in Minā. If the slaughtering is done at some other time, Mecca is the preferred site for it except in the case of a camel one has vowed to sacrifice, in which case the slaughter may be done anywhere.

* * *

As for the Shafiis, they hold that the time for slaughtering a *hady* which is due in fulfillment of a vow or a *hady* which is simply recommended begins once sufficient time for the holiday prayer plus two medium-length sermons has passed since sunrise on the Day of Sacrifice. The time during which the slaughtering may be done extends up to sundown on the last of the "days of meat drying." It is permissible to slaughter one's *hady* during the night or day during this period of time, although it is deemed undesirable to do so at night unless there is some need for this, as, for example, in a case where people who need to eat part of the sacrifice come at night [to the place where the pilgrim concerned is staying]. If the time specified for slaughtering the *hady* passes, the pilgrim must slaughter it compensatorily if it was due in fulfillment of a vow; otherwise, it will be too late to do so, and if the person does slaughter the animal, it will be nothing but ordinary meat rather than a *hady*. As for a *hady* which is required due to the pilgrim's having committed a forbidden act during the *ḥajj*, the time for slaughtering it is any time after the commission of the act in question; however, this does not apply to a sacrifice due on account of someone's having missed the *ḥajj* entirely, which must be slaughtered at the time of one's compensatory *ḥajj*. And as for the *hady* required of someone who is undertaking *tamattu'*, the time for slaughtering it is the time at which he enters *iḥrām* for the *ḥajj*. Once a pilgrim has completed the rites for the *'umrah*, he may slaughter his *hady* before entering *iḥrām* for the *ḥajj*. There is no end to the time during which the slaughtering may be done, although it is deemed preferable to slaughter one's *hady* on the Day of Sacrifice.

As for the place in which a *hady* is to be slaughtered, it is within the Meccan precincts; it is not permissible to slaughter a *hady* anywhere else, but anywhere one slaughters one's *hady* inside the Meccan precincts is acceptable. It is an emulation of the Sunnah for someone undertaking the *'umrah* to slaughter his *hady* in Mecca, since it is in Mecca that he will be released from his *iḥrām*; moreover, it is most preferable to do so at al-Marwah. As for someone who has been prevented from completing the *ḥajj* or the *'umrah*, he is to slaughter his *hady* in the place in which he was detained, although it is considered preferable to send the animal on to the Sacred Mosque. Lastly, it is an emulation of the Sunnah for someone performing the *ḥajj* to slaughter his *hady* in Minā, since it is in Minā that pilgrims performing the *ḥajj* are released from the state of *iḥrām*.

* * *

According to the Malikis, the time for slaughtering one's *hady* begins on the Day of Sacrifice, and it is recommended that it be done after throwing stones at the 'Aqabah Pillar. The time for throwing stones begins at dawn on the Day of Sacrifice, but it is recommended that the stone-throwing be postponed until the sun is up as was pointed out above in the section on recommended practices associated with the *ḥajj*. The time for slaughtering one's *hady* lasts until the end of the third day of the holiday, since the days set aside for slaughtering are three: the Day of Sacrifice and the two days which follow it. Even if these days have passed, however, one is to slaughter's one's *hady*.

On eating of one's animal sacrifice, and the like

It is permissible for the person who is offering a blood sacrifice to eat of the animal given differences in detail among the various schools.[145]

The slaughtering should be done in Minā if: (1) The pilgrim brought the animal along when entering *iḥrām* for the *ḥajj*. (2) The pilgrim stood on Mt. 'Arafah with the *hady* during part of the night before the Day of Sacrifice or stopped the animal elsewhere outside the Meccan precincts, such as in al-Tan'īm, for example. Moreover, it is permissible for the pilgrim to appoint a proxy to stand with the animal in one of these places. (3) The pilgrim intended to slaughter the animal either on the Day of Sacrifice or on one of the two following days. If any of these three conditions is unfulfilled—as in a situation where the animal was brought along when entering *iḥrām* for the *'umrah*, the pilgrim purchased the animal from Mecca rather than bringing it from elsewhere, neither the pilgrim himself nor his proxy stopped the animal on Mt. 'Arafah on the eve of the Day of Sacrifice, or the pilgrim wishes to slaughter the animal after the three days specified for this rite have passed—the animal is to be slaughtered in Mecca, and if it is slaughtered anywhere else, the sacrifice will not be valid. The slaughtering in such cases may be done validly anywhere inside the Meccan precincts; however, it is deemed preferable for it to be done at al-Marwah. Moreover, if someone slaughters an animal in Mecca in a situation in which all of the three aforementioned conditions are fulfilled, the sacrifice will be valid, but the pilgrim concerned will be guilty of wrongdoing for having neglected a duty, namely, that of slaughtering the animal in Minā.

145. According to the Hanafis, it is recommended that the pilgrim eat of a sacrifice which has been offered for the sake of performing *qirān* and *tamattu'*—referred to as a "sacrifice of thanksgiving" (*hady shukr*). It is likewise recommended that the pilgrim eat of a sacrifice which he has offered voluntarily unless it is injured or dies along the way and he slaughters it before it reaches its destination; in this latter situation, the pilgrim is required to leave the slaughtered animal where it is after spattering its blood on its collar in order to let the poor know that it was a voluntary sacrifice. As for a *hady* which is being offered in fulfillment of a vow, the pilgrim is not permitted to eat of it because it is a form of charity and, as such, belongs by right to the poor; if the pilgrim offering such a sacrifice eats of it, he must guarantee its value [to the poor]. The same ruling applies to: (a) a *hady* being offered in expiation (*hady al-kaffārāt*), which is obligatory in order to make up for some omission in one's pilgrimage, and (b) a *hady* being offered by someone who has been prevented from completing the pilgrimage and/or reaching Mecca. In those cases in which it is permissible to eat of one's sacrifice, it is considered desirable to divide it into three parts, then for the pilgrim to eat one-third, to give away one-third as charity, and to offer one-third to the Sacred Mosque as one does in the case of an *uḍḥiyah*, i.e., an animal slaughtered on the Day of Sacrifice. The pilgrim who is offering charity is likewise to donate the animals' packsaddles, their bones and their skins. A pilgrim offering a *hady* is not permitted to pay the butcher his wages out of the animal's meat, nor is he permitted to make use of the animal's milk, and if he does so, he must guarantee the value of the milk to the poor.

* * *

As for the Malikis, they hold that with respect to sacrificial animals which are slaughtered during the *ḥajj* or the *'umrah*, including those which are offered as compensatory equivalents for animals which have been hunted [while one is in a state of *iḥrām*] and animals which are slaughtered as a 'redemption' for some harm one has caused, in some cases the person offering the sacrifice is permitted to eat of it, while in others he is not permitted to do so. Such sacrifices are classified on this basis into four categories: (1) Those which may not be eaten under any circumstances, i.e., whether the animal reaches the customary slaughter site (Minā or Mecca) in sound condition and is slaughtered after this, or whether it is harmed or damaged before this and is slaughtered along the way. This category includes three types: (a) A specific animal which one has vowed to sacrifice and to donate to the needy, either by a spoken vow or by an inward intention. One might say, for example, "This animal have I vowed to present to God on behalf of the needy." Or one might simply say, "This animal have I vowed to present to God" accompanied by the inward intention of donating it to the needy. (b) A voluntary *hady* that one has decided to donate to the needy. (c) An animal offered as a redemption for some harm done if the person offering it has not consciously formed the intention to offer it as a *hady*. Those offering any of these three types of sacrifice are forbidden to eat of them under any circumstances. Someone offering an animal he has set aside specifically through a vow for the benefit of the needy is forbidden to eat of the animal because, due to this conscious specification, he would not be required to offer a substitute if the animal were damaged or harmed before reaching the slaughter site. Consequently, the pilgrim may eat of the animal if it is damaged or harmed before reaching the slaughter site, whereas he may not eat of it if it reaches the slaughter site in sound condition, since it has been set aside for the needy. Similarly, one is unconditionally forbidden to eat of a voluntary *hady* in view of the fact that it has been earmarked for the needy. As for a redemption one owes for causing some sort of harm and which one has not declared to be a *hady*, it is due as a compensation for some luxury or ease which was afforded to the pilgrim by, for example, causing him to be less unkempt. Consequently, one is not permitted to eat of this type, either. (2) Those which may be eaten if they undergo harm or damage before reaching the slaughter site, but which may not be eaten if they reach the slaughter site in sound condition. This category includes the following three types: (a) An animal offered in fulfillment of an unspecified vow to offer a blood sacrifice and to donate it to the needy. One might say, for example, "I have vowed to offer God a *hady* for the sake of the needy." (b) A redemption for having caused some harm if one consciously intends it to be a *hady*. (c) An animal which is slaughtered as the compensatory equivalent of an animal which has been hunted. In each of these three cases, the person offering the sacrifice may eat of the animal if it undergoes harm or damage before reaching the slaughter site. In the case of the unspecified vow, it is permissible to eat of it along the way because if this takes place, he may offer a substitute; if, on the other hand, the animal reaches the slaughter site in sound condition, its owner may not eat of it because it now belongs by right to the needy. In the case of a redemption for harm done, one may not eat of it if it arrives in sound condition because it serves as a compensation for the luxury or ease one has allowed oneself. And in the case of an animal being sacrificed as compensation for an animal that was hunted, it may not be eaten if it arrives in sound condition since the person offering it owes its value in return for the animal he hunted. (3) Those which may not be eaten before they reach the slaughter site, but which may be eaten after this. This type includes animals which are being sacrificed voluntarily and which are being offered in fulfillment of a vow to offer a specific animal but which have not been earmarked for the needy. These animals may not be eaten before they reach the slaughter site because the pilgrim would not be required to provide a substitute for them [if they did not reach their destination in sound condition]. Moreover, if the pilgrim were allowed to eat such an animal along the way, he would be accused of having himself caused it to be damaged before its arrival at the slaughtering site so as to be able to eat it. After the animal has reached its destination, however, the pilgrim may eat of the animal since it has not been earmarked for the needy. (4) Those animals which may be eaten both before and after they reach the slaughtering site. This category includes all types of sacrifices not included in categories (1), (2) and (3) above, such as: (a) a *hady* which is required of the pilgrim for omitting some duty of the *ḥajj*, (b) a *hady* which is required in order to fulfill a vow to sacrifice an unspecified animal and which has not been set aside for the needy, (c) a *hady* which is due as part of one's *qirān* or *tamattu'*. All of the types listed here may be eaten both before and after the animal has reached its destination.

When it is permissible to eat of an animal, it is likewise permissible for the pilgrim to stock up on provisions and to feed both rich and poor. If someone who is offering a *hady* eats that which he is forbidden to eat, he is to guarantee a substitute for what he ate in the form of an entire *hady* unless what he ate was an animal which he had vowed specifically to sacrifice and to donate to the needy, in which case he is required to guarantee only the amount which he ate based on the officially recognized point of view. Moreover, the same ruling that applies to the animal's meat applies likewise to its bridle and packsaddle; in other words, if it is not permissible to eat an animal's meat, it is likewise not permissible to take its bridle and its packsaddle. Rather, the pilgrim must leave them for the poor just as he does its meat; if the pilgrim takes any of these things, he must restore them to the poor if any of them remain; otherwise, he must guarantee them their value.

In the case of an animal whose meat the pilgrim is allowed to eat, he is also allowed to take its bridle and its packsaddle. It is deemed undesirable to make use of the milk of a *hady* after a collar has been placed around its neck or after it has been marked by placing an incision in its left hump since, in so doing, one has designated the animal as a means of drawing near to God Almighty. If one's use of the milk does no harm to the animal's young, it is merely undesirable to use it; if, however, it does harm to the mother's young, it is forbidden. It is likewise undesirable to ride a *hady* or to use it to carry loads unless necessary.

* * *

According to the Hanbalis, it is recommended that the pilgrim eat of a *hady* being offered voluntarily, and that he give some to others as well; specifically, it is recommended that he eat one-third, that he give his family one-third, and that he give one-third to the needy as is done with an *uḍḥiyah*, i.e., an animal slaughtered on the Day of Sacrifice. If he eats the entire animal himself, he must guarantee one-

If someone is prevented from performing the *ḥajj* (*iḥṣār*), or if he misses it by failing to stop at Mt. ‘Arafah (*fawāt*)

As used in the context of Islamic law, the term *iḥṣār* refers to the prevention of someone who has entered a state of ritual consecration from completing the rites of the pilgrimage (be it the *‘umrah* or the *ḥajj*). As for the term *fawāt*, it refers to a pilgrim's missing the opportunity to stand on Mt. ‘Arafah. As for rulings on these two situations, they differ from one school to another.[146]

---

third of it [or the equivalent value thereof – t.n.] to the needy. As for a *hady* which is obligatory, it is not permissible to eat it regardless of whether it is required in fulfillment of a vow or because one has specified that one will sacrifice a particular animal by saying, for example, "This [animal] is a *hady*", by placing a collar around its neck or by making an incision in its left hump. An exception to this ruling is made for the *hady* which is required of someone performing *qirān* or *tamattu‘*, which may be eaten even though it is obligatory. If a pilgrim eats of a sacrificial animal which he is not permitted to eat of, he is to guarantee an equivalent amount of meat to the needy. Someone offering a *hady* is forbidden to sell the animal's skin or packsaddle; however, he is permitted to make use of them himself. A pilgrim is likewise forbidden to give the butcher his wages out of the sacrificial animal's skin or packsaddle. Lastly, a pilgrim is permitted to make use of a sacrificial animal's milk provided that it is surplus, i.e., over and above what the animal's young require; if the milk is needed by the animal's young, one is forbidden to drink it and if one does so, one must guarantee the same amount of milk or its equivalent value to the needy.

* * *

As for the Shafiis, they hold that a pilgrim offering an animal sacrifice is not permitted to sell any part thereof regardless of whether it is obligatory or voluntary. In the case of a *hady* which is obligatory, the person offering it is required to offer the entire animal in charity, including its skin; hence, he is not permitted to take any part of it for himself. If the *hady* is voluntary, on the other hand, the person offering it may make use of its skin and save its fat and some of its meat to eat and to give away; in addition, he must donate some of the meat as charity, even if it is a small amount, provided that it would not be judged to be of little value by commonly accepted standards and provided that it is raw. In sum, then, the pilgrim offering a voluntary *hady* may eat of it, while he may not eat of a *hady* which is obligatory.

146. The Hanafis divide the reasons for which one might be prevented from performing the pilgrimage rites into two categories, namely, 'legal' and 'concrete'. Reasons which are classified as 'legal' include, for example, (a) a woman's losing her husband through divorce or death, or her *maḥram*, after she enters *iḥrām*, (b) a woman's being forbidden by her husband to perform a voluntary pilgrimage, (c) the pilgrim's losing the money with which he was going to pay his expenses for the journey when he would not be able to walk inside of ride, etc. As for reasons which are classified as 'concrete', they include, for example, (a) the presence of a human or non-human enemy who is preventing the pilgrim from proceeding forward in the performance of the pilgrimage, (b) the pilgrim's falling ill, (c) the pilgrim's being imprisoned, etc.

The ruling on such situations is that the pilgrim concerned is to send his *hady*, or its price, on to Mecca for the animal to be slaughtered in the Meccan precincts on his behalf and/or for an animal to purchased with the money sent, then slaughtered in Mecca. Such a pilgrim may not be released from his *iḥrām* until his *hady* has actually been slaughtered; hence, he must agree [with someone] on a particular day on which the animal is to be slaughtered so that he can know on which day this has occurred rather than prolonging his *iḥrām*. If the pilgrim who has been prevented from completing the pilgrimage rites commits any act which is forbidden to those in a state of *iḥrām* before his *hady* has been slaughtered, he must bear the same consequences for this act as someone who is likewise in a state of *iḥrām* but who has not been thus prevented. Moreover, if such a pilgrim is released from his *iḥrām* on the day on which his *hady* was to be slaughtered, thinking that it has been slaughtered, after which it becomes apparent that it has not, in fact, been slaughtered, he will still be in a state of *iḥrām*, and he must offer a blood sacrifice for having released himself from his *iḥrām* before it was the proper time to do so. If, on the other hand, the *hady* is slaughtered before the agreed upon day, this is acceptable. When being released from *iḥrām* under these circumstances, it is not necessary that one shave, but if one shaves, this is acceptable. Moreover, if a pilgrim who has been prevented from completing the pilgrimage rites is released from his *iḥrām* by means of the slaughter of a *hady* and if he is performing the *ḥajj* alone (*ifrād*), he must perform a compensatory *ḥajj* and a compensatory *'umrah* the following year if the hindering circumstances do not end until it is too late to perform the *ḥajj* during the current year; if he is performing the *'umrah* alone, he must perform a compensatory *'umrah*; and if he is undertaking *qirān*, he may only be released from his *iḥrām* by slaughtering two sacrificial animals as well as performing two compensatory *'umrahs* and one compensatory *ḥajj*.

The aforementioned rulings apply to someone who has been released from *iḥrām* by means of a *hady*; as for someone who has been released from his *iḥrām* by means of a *'umrah* and who is undertaking *ifrād*, all he is required to do is to make up the *ḥajj* alone, whereas if he is undertaking *qirān*, he must perform a compensatory *ḥajj* and a compensatory *'umrah*. In a situation in which the circumstances that were preventing the pilgrim from completing the pilgrimage come to an end after he has sent his *hady* on ahead to Mecca, one of the following will be true of him: (1) that he is capable of both performing the rites for which he first entered *iḥrām* and of offering the *hady*, (2) that he is capable of doing one of these two things, or (3) that he is incapable of doing either. In case (1), the pilgrim must proceed to complete his pilgrimage, whereas he is free to do whatever he wishes with his *hady*. In case (2), if he is only capable of offering the *hady*, he is not required to complete his pilgrimage due to having missed the opportunity to do what he had intended; rather, he may be released from his *iḥrām* by performing a *'umrah*. If, on the other hand, he is only capable of performing the intended pilgrimage rites, he may either complete the pilgrimage or be released from his *iḥrām*. In case (3), the pilgrim is to be released from his *iḥrām* and, if he wishes, he may do so by performing a *'umrah*. As for someone who missed the *ḥajj* by virtue of the fact that he stood on Mt. 'Arafah at other than the specified time for this rite, he must perform a circumambulation and a *sa'ī*, be released from *iḥrām* and perform a compensatory *ḥajj* the following year; however, no blood sacrifice is required of him.

* * *

The Hanbalis hold that if dawn breaks on the Day of Sacrifice for someone who has entered *iḥrām* for the *ḥajj* and who did not stand on Mt. 'Arafah at the time specified for this rite, whether or not he had a legitimate excuse for failing to do so, he will have missed the *ḥajj* for the year in question and his *iḥrām* will be transformed from *iḥrām* for the *ḥajj* to *iḥrām* for the *'umrah* unless he chooses to remain in the same state of *iḥrām* and to perform the *ḥajj* the following year on the same *iḥrām*. As for the *'umrah* to which such a pilgrim's *iḥrām* is shifted in circumstances such as these, it will not take the place of the *'umrah* which is required of every Muslim. If someone has missed the *ḥajj*, he must make up the *ḥajj* which he missed even if it was a voluntary one; in addition, he must offer a *hady* for having missed the *ḥajj*, but he must postpone slaughtering it until the time when he makes up the *ḥajj* the following year. If no *hady* is available at the time when it is required, i.e., at the break of dawn on the Day of Sacrifice, the pilgrim concerned is to fast as someone performing *tamattu'* fasts. Someone who is prevented from reaching the Sacred Mosque (referred to as *muḥṣar*), whether before or after he stands on Mt. 'Arafah must slaughter a *hady* with the intention of being released from his *iḥrām*. This ruling also applies to someone who is prevented from proceeding to the Sacred Mosque after entering *iḥrām* for the *'umrah*. If such a person is unable to obtain a *hady*, he is to fast ten days with the intention of being released from his *iḥrām*, after which he will, in fact, be released therefrom. It is also permissible to seek release from a state of *iḥrām* due to a particular need, as, for example, when someone needs to pay a considerable sum of money to either a Muslim or a non-Muslim, or for the sake of combat, or even to pay a small sum to a non-Muslim. If someone is released from his *iḥrām* before missing the *ḥajj* [that is, before having missed standing on Mt. 'Arafah – t.n.], he is not required to make up the *ḥajj* concerned; nor is a compensatory *ḥajj* required of someone who loses his sanity or falls unconscious. If, on the other hand, a pilgrim is not released from his *iḥrām* until after he has been deemed to have missed the *ḥajj* [i.e., after he has missed standing on Mt. 'Arafah – t.n.], he must make it up. As for someone who has been prevented from performing the circumambulation of visitation but who has stood on Mt. 'Arafah, thrown stones at the three pillars at Minā and shaved, he may not be released from his *iḥrām* until after he has performed the circumambulation of visitation and the *sa'ī* (if he has not already done so). A pilgrim may not be released from his *iḥrām* if he has been prevented only from performing the *sa'ī*; the reason for this is that Islamic law provides for one to be released from a complete *iḥrām*, i.e., one which renders unlawful all acts forbidden by a state of ritual consecration, whereas this only forbids one to approach women. Similarly, someone who has been prevented from performing a duty of the pilgrimage or throwing stones at the three pillars at Minā may not be released from his *iḥrām*; such a person must also offer a blood sacrifice for the omission of a duty as though he had omitted it deliberately. If someone is in a state of *iḥrām* for the *ḥajj* but is unable to stand on Mt. 'Arafah or is able to reach Mecca [but is unable to complete the pilgrimage rites – t.n.], he may be released from his *iḥrām* by performing a *'umrah*, and nothing else will be required of him. If someone who missed the opportunity to stand on Mt. 'Arafah and who was unable to reach the Sacred Mosque performed the circumambulation of visitation and the *sa'ī* before this, he must be released from his *iḥrām* by another circumambulation and another *sa'ī*. As for someone who was prevented from reaching the Sacred Mosque due to illness, due to having lost the money he would need to pay his expenses, or by losing his way, he is to remain in a state of *iḥrām* until he is able to reach the Sacred Mosque, since he will gain nothing by being released from *iḥrām*. If a pilgrim misses the *ḥajj*, he may be released from his *iḥrām* by performing a *'umrah*, but he is not to slaughter a *hady* which is with him anywhere but in the sacred Meccan precincts. Hence, such a pilgrim is not like someone who was prevented from reaching the Sacred Mosque by an enemy. All of the aforementioned rulings apply to children just as they do to adults. If someone states when he first enters *iḥrām*, "I intend to enter a state of ritual consecration for such-and-such a pilgrimage, so facilitate it for me and accept it from me [O Lord], and if I am detained by one who detains, I will be released from my state of ritual consecration in the place where I was detained," he may be released from his *iḥrām* without any of the aforementioned rulings applying to him, and he will not be required to make up the pilgrimage which he missed.

* * *

According to the Shafiis, if dawn breaks on the Day of Sacrifice before the pilgrim has stood on some portion of 'Arafah, he will miss the *ḥajj* and, as a consequence, he must offer a blood sacrifice if he was in a state of *iḥrām* for the *ḥajj* alone or if he was engaging in *qirān*. If a pilgrim misses standing on 'Arafah, he must be released from his *iḥrām* by performing a *'umrah*, i.e., by completing whatever rites of the *ḥajj* remain other than the standing on Mt. 'Arafah with the intention of being released from *iḥrām*. Such a pilgrim must also perform the circumambulation [of visitation] and the *sa'ī* if he has not already done so. If someone has missed the *ḥajj*, he is exempted from the need to spend the night at Minā and Muzdalifah and throw stones at the three pillars in Minā; such a pilgrim is to shave with the intention to perform the *'umrah*. This *'umrah* will not take the place of the *'umrah* which is required of every Muslim, however, and the pilgrim concerned must make it up the following year even if he missed it due to a legitimate excuse, even if the original *ḥajj* was voluntary, even if he cannot [presently] afford it, and even if he is two *marḥalahs* [48 miles] or more away from Mecca. In addition to making up the *ḥajj* which he missed, the pilgrim must offer a blood sacrifice like that required by someone engaging in *tamattu'*. Moreover, he may not validly slaughter the animal during the year in which he missed the *ḥajj*, but must do so in the year in which he makes it up. If the pilgrim was engaging in *qirān* and missed the standing on Mt. 'Arafah, he must offer three blood sacrifices: one for missing the *ḥajj*, one for his *qirān*, and one for the compensatory *ḥajj*; this ruling applies even if he engages in *ifrād* when making up the *ḥajj* he missed, because in so doing, he will have violated his original commitment to engage in *qirān*. Someone may have failed to complete the *ḥajj* or the *'umrah* because he was prevented from doing so by an enemy, because he was unjustly incarcerated by a ruler or the like, or due to a debt he cannot repay and without having evidence with which to prove his insolvency. If such a person does not have good reason to believe that his deterring circumstances will pass soon enough for him to complete the *ḥajj* (if he is performing the *ḥajj*), or within three days (if he is performing the *'umrah*) and if he wishes to be released from his *iḥrām*, he may do so by slaughtering a sacrificial animal and shaving with the intention of being released from *iḥrām* by means of these two acts if a sacrificial animal is available. If no sacrificial animal is available or he can find no food due to insolvency or for some other reason, he may simply shave with the intention of being released from his *iḥrām*.

In the case of someone who is prevented from completing the *'umrah*, it is deemed preferable that he wait before he seeks release from his *iḥrām*; similarly in the case of someone who is prevented from completing the *ḥajj*, it is preferable that he wait before seeking release from his *iḥrām* if time permits. Otherwise, it is advisable that one act promptly to be released from one's *iḥrām* lest one miss the pilgrimage [i.e., lest one miss the chance to stand on Mt. 'Arafah – t.n.]. A pilgrim may not be released from his *iḥrām* if he is performing the *ḥajj* and has good reason to believe that the situation preventing him from completing the *ḥajj* will pass soon enough that he will still have time afterwards to complete it; nor may a pilgrim be released from his *iḥrām* if he is performing the *'umrah* and is certain that the circumstances preventing him from completing it will pass within three days.

The following are legitimate excuses for being released from one's *iḥrām*: (1) Illness, if the person concerned stipulated when first entering *iḥrām* that if he falls ill, he will thereby be released from his *iḥrām*. If, when forming the intention to enter the state of ritual consecration, someone says, "If I fall ill, I will be free from my state of *iḥrām*," and if he does fall ill while in the state of ritual consecration, he will automatically be released from it. If, on the other hand, one says, "If I fall ill, I will seek release from my *iḥrām*," and if the person concerned has stipulated that in order to be released from his *iḥrām* he must offer a *hady*, he must be released from *iḥrām* by slaughtering a sacrificial animal, then shaving with the intention of being released from his *iḥrām* by means of these two acts. If, on the other hand, the pilgrim did not stipulate that in order to be released from his *iḥrām* he must offer a *hady*, he may be released from it by shaving only. (2) Losing one's way. (3) Running out of money for travel expenses.

When a pilgrim is prevented by some circumstance from completing his pilgrimage, he is either to slaughter a sacrificial animal at whatever point he was detained, even if he has not reached the Meccan precincts yet, or send his sacrificial animal to the Meccan precincts to be slaughtered there. However, he may not be released from his *iḥrām* until he knows that the animal has been slaughtered; nor is he allowed to send the animal anywhere other than the Meccan precincts. If the pilgrim is detained inside the Meccan precincts, he must slaughter his animal there. Moreover, if the pilgrimage which he was to perform was voluntary, he is not required to make it up, whereas if it was obligatory, it will continue to be required of him in the form in which he originally intended to perform it. If the pilgrim is prevented from reaching 'Arafah but not Mecca, he must enter Mecca and be released from his *iḥrām* by performing a *'umrah*; if, on the other hand, he is prevented from reaching Mecca but not 'Arafah, he is to stand on Mt. 'Arafah, then be released from his *iḥrām*. In both cases, the apparent sense of this school's rulings indicates that the pilgrim is exempted from having to make up the pilgrimage. When a pilgrim is thus prevented from completing the pilgrimage rites, he is required to sacrifice a sheep or a goat which meets the specifications for an *uḍḥiyah*. If the pilgrim is unable, for reasons either legal or concrete, to offer such a sacrifice, he must donate food equal in value to such a goat or sheep, provided that the food is of the type which is acceptable as fastbreaking *zakāh*, and distribute it among the needy of the same location. If the pilgrim is unable to provide the food either, he must fast one day for every *mudd* of food that would have been donated and distributed; as for a redemption (*fidyah*), he is not required to offer this due to his not having committed any transgression.

* * *

As for the Malikis, they hold that the term *ihṣār* refers to someone's being prevented from performing the pilgrimage, be it the *'umrah* or the *ḥajj*. For example, someone performing the *'umrah* might be prevented from entering Mecca as was the Prophet in the Year of Ḥudaybiyah when the polytheists drove him back, thus preventing him from entering Mecca after he had entered *iḥrām* for the *'umrah*. Another example of this would be for someone performing the *ḥajj* to be prevented from performing the circumambulation, the *sa'ī*, standing on Mt. 'Arafah, or all of the above; this ruling applies whether the person has been prevented unjustly, as when unbelievers prevent Muslims from reaching Mecca, or due to a conflict amongst the Muslims in which the rebellious faction is victorious and prevents people from reaching the holy land (i.e., Mecca and the sites surrounding it where the pilgrimage rites are performed) or justly, as when a pilgrim who has been in debt puts off repaying what he owes even though he is capable of doing so and as a result of which he is imprisoned in order to oblige him to pay what he owes.

As for the term *fawāt*, the Malikis define it to mean someone's not performing the *ḥajj* due to his not having been able to reach 'Arafah on account of an illness which prevented him from standing there, or due to an error on the part of the pilgrims as a group; an example of the latter would be a situation in which the pilgrims stand on Mt. 'Arafah on 8 Dhū al-Ḥijjah [rather than 9 Dhū al-Ḥijjah] and only realize their error after the end of the time period specified for standing on Mt. 'Arafah (i.e., the eve of 10 Dhū al-Ḥijjah) has passed. It is not possible to miss the *ḥajj* in any other way; the reason for this is that when the pilgrim stands on Mt. 'Arafah, he has, in effect, completed the *ḥajj*, whereas the rites which remain after one has stood on Mt. 'Arafah, namely, the circumambulation and the *sa'ī*, may validly be performed at any time.

If someone is performing the *'umrah* and is prevented from reaching the sites where the pilgrimage rites are performed, or if someone has entered *iḥrām* for the *ḥajj* and is prevented unjustly from reaching both the Sacred Mosque and 'Arafah, it is preferable for him to be released from his *iḥrām* by forming the intention to do so. Once this intention has been formed, he is automatically released from his *iḥrām*; as a result, he is no longer forbidden to have sexual contact with a woman, to hunt, to use perfume, or to engage in any other acts which are forbidden to someone in a state of *iḥrām*. When being released from his state of ritual consecration, it is an emulation of the Sunnah for the pilgrim to shave and, if he has a *hady* with him, for him to slaughter it wherever he happens to be if he would find it difficult to send it to Mecca. Otherwise, he is to send the *hady* to Mecca. If the pilgrim has no *hady* with him, he is not required to provide one. As for the words of God Almighty, "and if you are held back [*in uḥṣirtum*], give instead whatever offering you can easily afford" (2:196), they are understood to apply to a situation in which the person who was prevented from completing the pilgrimage already had a sacrificial animal with him, as, for example, in the case of someone who had brought an animal to sacrifice voluntarily.

However, such a pilgrim may only be released from his *iḥrām* given the following three conditions: (1) The pilgrim must not have been aware of the restraining circumstance before his *iḥrām*; thus, if he entered *iḥrām* with the knowledge that, for example, an enemy would accost him and prevent him from performing the *ḥajj* or the *'umrah*, he may not be released from his *iḥrām* once he is prevented from completing the pilgrimage rites. Rather, he must remain in a state of ritual consecration until he has completed the pilgrimage on account of which he originally set out, even if this means remaining in a state of *iḥrām* until the following year. (2) The pilgrim must have no hope that the preventing circumstance will pass before the time period specified for performing the pilgrimage has come to an end. Specifically, he must know, or have good reason to believe, that the restraining circumstance will not pass before the end of the time period specified for standing on Mt. 'Arafah. If the pilgrim has some hope that the preventing circumstance will pass before this time, he must wait to see whether this occurs or not. (3) When the pilgrim enters *iḥrām*, there must be enough time to perform the *ḥajj* to completion within the time specified for this rite barring unforeseen circumstances. If, on the other hand, he would not be able to stand on Mt. 'Arafah during its specified time period even on the assumption that nothing would happen to prevent him from doing so, after which something does, in fact, occur to prevent him from doing so, he may not be released from the state of *iḥrām* because in this case, he has committed himself, in essence, to remaining in this state until the following year. Moreover, if the pilgrim is prevented from completing the *ḥajj* by some just cause, as when someone is incarcerated for being in debt when he is capable of repaying the debt, he may not be released from his *iḥrām* since he has the ability to rid himself of the restraining circumstance and proceed with his pilgrimage; hence, if he fails to do so, he must remain in a state of *iḥrām* indefinitely. If, on the other hand, he is unable to repay the debt, he will be like someone who has been detained unjustly, in whose case it is preferable for him to be released from his *iḥrām* by forming the intention to do so; hence, he may remain in a state of *iḥrām* if he wishes, though it is a departure from the ideal.

If a pilgrim stands on Mt. 'Arafah and is prevented from reaching the Sacred Mosque as well as the subsequent sites for the performance of pilgrimage rites, such as Muzdalifah, Minā, and the place where the brisk walk is performed between al-Ṣafā and al-Marwah, his *ḥajj* will now be completed; however, he may not be released from his *iḥrām* until he has performed the circumambulation of visitation followed by the *sa'ī* if he did not perform the *sa'ī* after the circumambulation of arrival. If a pilgrim continues to be detained until he has missed the opportunity to stop at Muzdalifah, throw stones at the three pillars in Minā and spend the night in Minā on the eves of the days of stone throwing, he must offer only one *hady* due to having missed all these rites even though each of them is a 'duty' in and of itself. Moreover, this ruling applies whether one has been detained by incarceration or due to some other cause, and whether the incarceration was just or unjust. Such a pilgrim is to remain in a state of ritual consecration until he has completed his *ḥajj*, even if this means remaining in a state of ritual consecration for years. As for someone who was prevented from reaching 'Arafah by some cause but who is capable of reaching the Sacred Mosque, he may either be released from his *iḥrām* or remain in this state until the following year, though it is deemed preferable for him to be released from his *iḥrām* if he is far from Mecca, since remaining in a state of ritual consecration is a departure from the ideal. Similarly, if the pilgrim is near Mecca or has entered it, it is undesirable for him to remain in a state of *iḥrām*. Moreover, being released from *iḥrām* under these circumstances will entail performing a *'umrah* if one is not far from Mecca; if one is far from Mecca, one may be released from one's *iḥrām* simply by the intention to do so, and without being required to perform the *'umrah*. If a pilgrim is released from *iḥrām* by performing a *'umrah* and if he first entered *iḥrām* for the *ḥajj* from within the Meccan precincts, he must leave the Meccan precincts immediately after entering *iḥrām* for the *'umrah*, since every entry into *iḥrām* must involve some time inside the Meccan precincts and some time outside.

Moreover, if a pilgrim is prevented from completing the *ḥajj* or the *'umrah*, this does not exempt him from the requirement to perform the *ḥajj* and the *'umrah* required of every Muslim. Hence, if someone is prevented by some circumstance from completing the *ḥajj* or the *'umrah*, after which he is released from his state of ritual consecration, he must make up the *ḥajj* missed as a religious obligation, and the *'umrah* which was missed as an emulation of the Sunnah. In addition, he must offer a *hady* for having missed the pilgrimage, but he is not to slaughter it until the time at which he makes it up. Nor is a pilgrim exempted from the obligation to fulfill a vow he has made if it was not a vow to perform the *ḥajj* or the *'umrah* at a specified time; if someone makes a vow to perform the pilgrimage at a specific time and is then prevented from performing it, he is exempted from the obligation to make it up since its specified time has now passed. If, at the time when he enters *iḥrām* for the *ḥajj* or the *'umrah*, a pilgrim forms the intention that if something occurs to prevent him for completing the pilgrimage, he will be released from his *iḥrām*—if he says, for example, "O God, I will be released from the state of ritual consecration wherever You cause me to be detained," this will do him no good; rather, if something happens to detain him and thereby prevents him from completing the pilgrimage, he must be released from his *iḥrām* either by means of a new intention or by performing a *'umrah* based on the details presented above. If someone demands money of the pilgrim in return for allowing him passage, it is permissible for the pilgrim to pay him even if the person demanding the money is a non-Muslim, since the disgrace of being prevented from performing the *ḥajj* is more grievous than the disgrace of having to pay such money.

When someone who has entered *iḥrām* for the *ḥajj* and has been prevented from completing the pilgrimage throws stones at the 'Aqabah Pillar on the Day of Sacrifice, it becomes permissible for him to engage in all acts which are forbidden to those in a state of ritual consecration with the exception of approaching a woman

Performing the *ḥajj* on someone else's behalf

Acts of worship in Islam are divided into three categories: (1) Those which are strictly physical, such as ritual prayer and fasting. These are classified as 'physical' because the purpose of such acts of worship is to cause the worshiper to bring his or her whole person before God, may He be glorified and exalted, in humble submission and reverence, and because they bear no connection with money or wealth. (2) Those which are strictly monetary, such as *zakāh* and charity, since the purpose of these acts of worship is to bring monetary benefit to their recipients. (3) Those which are a combination of physical and monetary, such as the *ḥajj*, which involves both a demonstration of one's humble submission to God Almighty through the performance of the circumambulation, the brisk walk between al-Safā and al-Marwah, and the other pilgrimage rites, and the expenditure of money toward this end.

The first category above precludes anyone's performing any act of worship on someone else's behalf; hence, no one is permitted to assign someone else to pray or fast on his behalf, and if he did so, it would bring him no benefit. The second category, by contrast, does allow for one person to perform a given act of worship on someone else's behalf. Hence, someone who owns wealth may authorize someone else to distribute the *zakāh* due on his wealth or to donate charity on his behalf. As for the third category, which includes only the *ḥajj*, the various schools differ over whether or not one is allowed to perform this on someone else's behalf.[147]

---

sexually and hunting, both of which remain forbidden. As for the use of perfume, it remains undesirable during this phase, which is referred to as "the lesser release" (*al-taḥallul al-aṣghar*). As for "the greater release" (*al-taḥallul al-akbar*) by virtue of which all acts forbidden to someone in a state of ritual consecration become permitted, including sexual contact with a woman and hunting, this occurs once the pilgrim has performed the circumambulation of visitation if he performed the *sa'ī* following the circumambulation of arrival. Otherwise, the pilgrim may not be released from his *iḥrām* until after he has performed the circumambulation of visitation followed by the *sa'ī*; once he has performed these two rites in this order, all acts which were forbidden to him while in a state of ritual consecration become permissible again if: (a) the pilgrim has shaved and (b) either he has thrown stones at the 'Aqabah Pillar or the time specified for this rite, i.e., the Day of Sacrifice, has passed. If the pilgrim has sexual intercourse before shaving or throwing stones at the 'Aqabah Pillar, he must offer a blood sacrifice, whereas if he hunts or engages in any other act that would be forbidden in a state of ritual consecration before having shaved or thrown stones at the 'Aqabah Pillar, nothing is required of him.

147. The Malikis hold that even though the *ḥajj* is a combination of physical and monetary, it is nevertheless more physical than it is monetary in nature and, as a consequence, one person may not perform it on someone else's behalf. If someone has yet to perform the *ḥajj* which is required of all Muslims, he is not permitted to appoint someone else to perform this rite on his behalf, whether he is healthy or afflicted with an illness which he is expected to recover from. If such a person hires someone else to perform the obligatory *ḥajj* on his behalf, the hiring agreement will

be invalid, and if the person thus hired performs the *ḥajj* to completion, he will receive the same wages which would be received by someone else in a similar position; if, on the other hand, the person hired does not complete the *ḥajj* because the ruler nullified the hiring agreement upon being apprised of it, he is not entitled to any wages whatsoever. If someone hires someone else to perform the *ḥajj* on his behalf in a voluntary capacity, such as someone who is afflicted with an illness which he is not expected to recover from or someone who has already performed the obligatory *ḥajj*, the hiring agreement is undesirable, but it is nevertheless valid. The same ruling applies to someone who hires someone else to undertake the *'umrah* on his behalf in a voluntary capacity; in other words, the hiring agreement will be undesirable but nevertheless valid, since the *'umrah* is not obligatory, but an emulation of the Sunnah. In the case of someone who is unable to perform the *ḥajj* on his own and who will not be able to do so during any year of his life, the obligation to perform the *ḥajj* is waived in its entirety; as a consequence, he is not required to hire someone else to perform the *ḥajj* on his behalf even if he would be able to afford to pay such a person's wages. Moreover, if such a person hires someone else to perform the *ḥajj* on his behalf, whether he is healthy or ill and whether the *ḥajj* which he has hired the other person to perform is obligatory or voluntary, it will not be counted to his credit; rather, the *ḥajj* will be counted as having been performed voluntarily by the person who was hired, whereas the person who hired him will simply receive the reward due to him for having helped the person hired to perform the *ḥajj* as well as the blessing resulting from the supplications offered by the person he hired.

If, before dying, someone leaves instructions to the effect that someone should perform the *ḥajj* on his behalf, and if someone does perform the *ḥajj* on his behalf after his death, or if the heirs of the deceased perform it on his behalf without his having left them instructions to do so by hiring someone to perform the *ḥajj* for him after his death, this will, likewise, not be counted to the deceased's credit either as an obligation or as a voluntary act of worship. Hence, his obligation to have performed the *ḥajj* during his lifetime, if he did not actually do so when he was capable of such, will not be waived; rather, the deceased will simply receive the reward due to him for having helped the person thus hired to perform the *ḥajj*, as we have seen. It is undesirable for someone to leave instructions for the *ḥajj* to be performed on his behalf after he dies; nevertheless, the heirs of a deceased person who has left such instructions are obliged to perform the *ḥajj* on his behalf out of one-third of his bequest provided that doing so does not preclude the execution of some other instruction to which no undesirability is attached, such as someone's leaving instructions to give money to the poor and the needy. If, however, the deceased's instructions to have someone perform the *ḥajj* on his behalf after his death do preclude the implementation of other instructions to which no undesirability is attached, such as in a case where one-third of his bequest will only be sufficient to cover the costs of carrying out one of the two directives, priority is to be given to carrying out the other of the two directives while the directive to have someone perform the *ḥajj* on the deceased's behalf is to be canceled. If, for example, someone leaves instructions that the *ḥajj* is to be performed on his behalf after his death and that 50 Egyptian pounds are to be distributed among the poor; and if, moreover, the wages of the person to perform the *ḥajj* on his behalf amount to 50 Egyptian pounds while one-third of his bequest likewise amounts to 50 Egyptian pounds, then one-third of his bequest will only be sufficient to cover the cost of one of the deceased's two directives—either distributing 50 pounds among the poor, or performing the *ḥajj* on his behalf. In such a case, one-third of the deceased's bequest should be distributed among the poor, while the directive to have someone perform the *ḥajj* on his behalf should be annulled. Based on the best-attested view, this ruling applies regardless of whether or not the *ḥajj* to be performed on behalf of the deceased is the *ḥajj* which he would have been obliged to perform as a Muslim during his lifetime. Moreover, if the directive to have someone perform the *ḥajj* on the deceased's behalf does not come into conflict with some other directive, then the directive to have someone perform the *ḥajj* on the deceased's behalf is to be carried out, as we have seen; in such a case, those responsible for carrying out the deceased's instructions are to hire someone to perform the *ḥajj* on his behalf from the town in which he died unless the deceased specified that the person should perform the *ḥajj* from somewhere else. If the deceased specified that the person performing the *ḥajj* for him should do so from some other place, as, for example, by his saying, "Perform the *ḥajj* for me from Mecca", then his condition is to be fulfilled by hiring for him someone who can perform the *ḥajj* on his behalf from Mecca rather than from the town in which he died.

If one-third of the deceased's bequest is insufficient to cover the cost of the *ḥajj* from the place he specified, or from his own town in the event that he did not specify any other place, and if the amount of money available would be sufficient to finance the *ḥajj* from some other location, the *ḥajj* should be performed on his behalf from wherever is financially feasible. Similarly, if the deceased specified a particular sum of money, such as 30 Egyptian pounds, and if it would not be possible for someone to perform the *ḥajj* with this amount of money either from the town in which the deceased died or from the location he specified in his instructions, the *ḥajj* should performed on his behalf from any town from which it is possible to hire someone with this sum of money. Moreover, if one-third of the bequest, or the sum which the deceased specified for the *ḥajj* on his behalf, is sufficient to cover the cost of more than one *ḥajj*, the *ḥajj* should be performed on his behalf once, while the remainder of the money allotted for the *ḥajj* should be treated as inheritance money unless the deceased said, "Perform the *ḥajj* on my behalf with one-third of my bequest, or with this sum", such as one hundred Egyptian pounds, in which case his heirs must hire several people, each of whom is to perform the *ḥajj* once on the deceased's behalf until all of the one-third or the sum set aside for the *ḥajj* has been used up. If the amount of money in question is sufficient to cover the costs of two performances of the *ḥajj*, the heirs are to hire two people, each of whom will perform the *ḥajj* on behalf of the deceased. According to the best attested view, both of these pilgrimages are to be performed in the same year. If, after the two pilgrimages have been performed on behalf of the deceased, the money which remains is not sufficient to fund a third one, it is to be treated as inheritance money. The same ruling applies if one-third of the bequest or the sum set aside for the pilgrimage is sufficient to fund three pilgrimages or more.

* * *

The Hanafis hold that the *ḥajj* is a rite that one person may validly perform on someone else's behalf. Hence, if someone is unable to perform it himself, he is obliged to appoint someone else to perform the *ḥajj* on his behalf given the following conditions: (1) The person's inability to perform the *ḥajj* on his own must be due to a condition which is likely to continue his entire life, such as an illness from which he is not expected to recover, blindness, or a permanent disability. If someone does not expect to be able to perform the *ḥajj* before he dies, and if this person then appoints someone else to perform the *ḥajj* on his behalf and the proxy does, in fact, perform the *ḥajj* for him, he is thereby released from the obligation to perform the *ḥajj* himself; this ruling applies even if, after this, the person's debilitating condition passes. As for someone who suffers from an illness from which he expects to recover or someone who is in prison, he may appoint someone else to perform the *ḥajj* on his behalf. However, if this person does, in fact, perform the *ḥajj* for him after which his debilitating condition passes, he will no longer be exempted from the obligation to perform it himself. (2) The person performing the *ḥajj* on another's behalf must consciously intend to perform it for this other person's sake. He might say, for example, "I have entered a state of ritual consecration on behalf of so-and-so, and I have uttered the *talbiyah* on behalf of so-and-so." However, it is sufficient for the intention to be present in his heart. If, on the other hand, the proxy intends the *ḥajj* which he is performing to be on his own behalf, it will not count for the person on whose behalf he was assigned to perform it. (3) Most of the money to cover the costs of the *ḥajj* should come from the person on whose behalf it is being performed. Hence, if someone volunteers to perform the *ḥajj* on behalf of someone else at his own expense, it will not count for the other person if he left instructions for someone else to perform the *ḥajj* on his behalf; if, on the other hand, a deceased person left no instructions for the *ḥajj* to be performed on his behalf and if one of his heirs or someone else volunteers to perform it on his behalf and at his own expense, it is to be hoped that the *ḥajj* performed by this person will be acceptable to God Almighty on the deceased's behalf. Moreover, if someone combines his own money with that of the person on whose behalf he is performing the *ḥajj*, it will still count in favor of the person for whose sake it is being performed. Lastly, if the money which has been paid to the person performing the *ḥajj* falls short of his expenses for the journey, the difference must be made up by the person who assigned him to perform the *ḥajj*. (4) The person on whose behalf the *ḥajj* is to be performed must not stipulate a specific wage for his proxy; rather, he is to commit himself to covering the proxy's expenses in an amount equal to what some other person in the same position would need in the way of expenses. If the person on whose behalf the *ḥajj* is to be performed pays his proxy a certain amount of money for him to spend in the course of the journey, and if, after he has completed the *ḥajj*, some of this amount remains, the proxy must return it to the person on whose behalf he performed the *ḥajj* unless the latter has chosen to forego it voluntarily or unless his heirs have chosen to do so. (However, the heirs must be qualified to forego it voluntarily, meaning that they must be of full legal age.) However, the person on whose behalf the *ḥajj* is to be performed is not permitted to stipulate the proxy's wages by saying, for example, "I will hire you to perform the *ḥajj* on my behalf in return for such-and-such a sum," nor will this *ḥajj* count to the credit of the person doing the hiring. In such a case, the agreement by which the proxy was hired will be null and void, as are the agreements by which proxies are hired to engage in any other act of obedience to God. Exceptions to this rule are made only out of necessity, for example, in connection with the impartation of scholarly learning and teaching someone how to deliver the *adhān* or serve as an imam. (5) The proxy must not violate any condition set down by the person on whose behalf he is to perform the *ḥajj*. Hence, if the person on whose behalf the *ḥajj* is to be performed stipulates that his proxy is to engage in *ifrād*, and if the proxy performs the *ḥajj* by engaging in *qirān* or *tamattu'* instead, the *ḥajj* in this instance will not count in favor of the person who hired the proxy, and he will be obliged to return whatever expenses were provided for him. If, on the other hand, the person on whose behalf the *ḥajj* is to be performed instructs his proxy to perform the *'umrah* for him, and if the proxy performs the *'umrah* on the other person's behalf followed by the *ḥajj* on his own behalf, or if the person on whose behalf the *ḥajj* is to be performed instructs his proxy to perform the *ḥajj* on his behalf, after which the proxy performs the *ḥajj* on the other's behalf followed by the *'umrah* on his own behalf, this is acceptable. In the first case described here, the *'umrah* performed counts in favor of the person who instructed the proxy to perform it; similarly, in the second, the *ḥajj* performed counts in favor of the person who instructed the proxy to perform it. However, the expenses entailed by the proxy's performance of the *ḥajj* on his own behalf in the first case and the *'umrah* on his own behalf in the second must be borne by the proxy himself. Once the proxy has completed the rites he has chosen to perform on his own behalf, he may once again spend money out of that provided by the person who has taken him into his service. However, if the proxy performs the rites he wishes to perform on his own behalf before performing those which he has been assigned to perform on the other person's behalf—as when, for example, someone assigns a proxy to perform the *ḥajj* on his behalf but, instead of first performing the *ḥajj*, the proxy first performs the *'umrah* on his own behalf followed by the *ḥajj* on the other person's behalf—this will not be valid, and as a result, the proxy will be required to provide for all expenses himself. (6) The proxy must enter *iḥrām* for only one performance of the *ḥajj*; if he were to enter *iḥrām* once to perform the *ḥajj* for the person who has assigned him to perform it on his behalf, then again to perform the *ḥajj* on his own behalf, this would not be valid. In fact, even the *ḥajj* the proxy performs on the other person's behalf will not be valid in such a situation unless he refrains from performing the *ḥajj* on his own behalf. Similarly, if two other men assigned the proxy to perform the *ḥajj* on their behalf and if he then entered *iḥrām* for both performances of the *ḥajj*, this would likewise not be valid, and he would have to bear the expenses for both of them. (7) Both the proxy and the person on whose behalf he is to perform the *ḥajj* must be Muslims and in full possession of their mental faculties. It is thus not valid for a proxy to perform the *ḥajj* on behalf of a non-Muslim or someone who is insane unless the person's insanity came upon him suddenly after he had become obliged to perform the *ḥajj*. (8) The proxy must have reached the age of discernment; hence, a young boy who has not yet reached the age of discernment may not perform the *ḥajj* on someone else's behalf. A teenager, however, could perform the *ḥajj* on someone else's behalf, as could a woman, a slave, or someone who has not yet performed the obligatory *ḥajj* on his or her own behalf.

The aforementioned conditions apply to the performance of the *ḥajj* on someone else's behalf if it is obligatory; as for performing the *ḥajj* on someone else's behalf as a voluntary act, the only conditions which must be fulfilled for its validity are: (1) that both the proxy and the person for whose sake he is to perform the *ḥajj* must be Muslims and in full possession of their mental faculties, (2) that the proxy must have reached the age of discernment, and (3) that it must not involve hiring.

If the proxy commits some act that would invalidate the *ḥajj* he is performing and if this occurs before he has stood on Mt. 'Arafah, he must return whatever money he has received from the person who charged him with performing the *ḥajj* on his behalf. If it occurs after he has stood on Mt. 'Arafah, however, he is not obliged to return any money, since by this time he has performed the central pillar of the *ḥajj*, namely, standing on Mt. 'Arafah. Any and all expiations required due to some transgression committed during the *ḥajj* must be borne by the proxy, since he is the one who has caused them to be required; as for the *hady* required of someone who has been detained and thereby prevented from completing the *ḥajj*, its cost is to be borne by the person on whose behalf the proxy is performing the *ḥajj*, since he is not responsible for having thus been detained. When someone has left instructions to the effect that someone is to perform the *ḥajj* on his behalf after he dies, and when the deceased has specified a particular sum of money to cover the cost of the *ḥajj* as well as the place from which the person performing the *ḥajj* is to set out, his instructions are to be followed with respect to these details. If the deceased has not specified the amount of money to be allocated for the *ḥajj* or the place from which the person performing the *ḥajj* is to set out, he or she is to set out from the deceased's own hometown if one-third of his or her bequest will suffice to cover the cost of the journey from this point; if one-third of the bequest will not suffice given a departure from the deceased's hometown, the *ḥajj* must be performed from whatever point from which it will suffice. If one-third of the bequest will not suffice to cover the costs of the *ḥajj* from any point, the deceased's directive to have someone perform the *ḥajj* on his or her behalf is to be considered invalid. If, on the other hand, the bequest will suffice to cover the costs of more than one performance of the *ḥajj* on the deceased's behalf and if the deceased stipulated that only one *ḥajj* should be performed on his behalf, whatever money is left over after this one *ḥajj* should go to his or her heirs; otherwise, the *ḥajj* should be performed as many times in a single year as are required to deplete the money allotted thereto, as this is considered preferable to performing it several times over a period of several years.

* * *

The Shafiis hold that the *ḥajj* is among the acts of worship which one person can perform on someone else's behalf. Hence, if someone is unable to perform the *ḥajj*, he or she must assign someone else to perform it on his or her behalf, either by hiring him to do so or by paying his expenses. The person's inability to perform the *ḥajj* must be due either to a handicap, old age, or an illness from which he does not expect to recover based on the stated opinions of two trustworthy physicians or based on the person's own knowledge provided that he is knowledgeable in medical matters. 'Inability' is defined here as the person's being in a condition which renders him incapable of remaining seated on his camel without suffering hardship so severe that it would normally be deemed intolerable; moreover, the person concerned must have despaired of recovering the ability to ride without exposing himself to such hardship.

In some situations one will be obliged to assign a proxy to perform the *ḥajj* on one's behalf immediately, for example, when one loses the ability to perform the *ḥajj* after having become accountable for its performance and after having become able to afford to do so. In other situations, one will be granted leeway as to when one must assign a proxy to perform the *ḥajj* on one's behalf, for example, when one loses the ability to perform the *ḥajj* either before, simultaneously with, or after becoming accountable for performance of the *ḥajj*, yet without being able to afford to do so.

It is also necessary that someone who is unable to perform the *ḥajj* be at least two *marḥalahs* away from Mecca; if he is closer to Mecca than this or if he is in Mecca itself, he will not be permitted to appoint a proxy to perform the *ḥajj* on his behalf. Rather, he must perform the pilgrimage himself since, under these circumstances, he will be able to bear the hardship involved. If the person is unable to undertake the pilgrimage on his own even under these circumstances, someone else is to perform the *ḥajj* on his behalf after his death, and finance it from his bequest. However, if the person's strength has been so depleted by illness that he has become immobile, he is permitted to appoint someone to perform the *ḥajj* on his behalf during his lifetime.

Another condition of relevance here is that the proxy must have already performed the obligatory *ḥajj*, since it is not permissible to appoint as a proxy someone who has not yet done so. The proxy must also be a trustworthy, reliable person of good repute. As for the contract on the basis of which the proxy is hired, its validity requires that the contracting parties have a good knowledge of the rites of the *ḥajj*, both as an obligatory act of worship and as a voluntary one, such that if the proxy were to omit any of the Sunnah-based practices associated with the *ḥajj*, his compensation for undertaking the *ḥajj* on the other's behalf would be reduced accordingly. In order for the hiring arrangement to be valid, the person hired must be capable of commencing the *ḥajj* [at the time at which he is hired – t.n.], since it is not permissible to hire someone who would not be able to commence the *ḥajj* due to some excuse.

It is not necessary that a particular *miqāt* be specified. Nevertheless, the person hired must go out to the *miqāt* of the person on whose behalf he is performing the *ḥajj*, or to a location which is an equal distance from Mecca if they have specified a particular *miqāt* from which he is to enter *iḥrām*. If no *miqāt* has been specified, the person hired to perform the *ḥajj* may enter *iḥrām* from a *miqāt* other than that of the person on whose behalf the *ḥajj* is being performed even if it is a shorter distance from Mecca than the original *miqāt*. Nor is it necessary that the *ḥajj* be performed with the knowledge of the person on whose behalf it is being performed; however, the proxy must consciously intend to do so for the person on whose behalf he is performing it.

If someone who was unable to perform the *ḥajj* recovers from the illness which was preventing him from doing so after the proxy has completed the *ḥajj* on his behalf, he must perform the *ḥajj* on his own behalf after his recovery since, under such circumstances, the agreement on the basis of which the proxy was hired will have been shown to be invalid. In such a situation, the *ḥajj* performed will count in favor of the proxy but he will no longer be entitled to any wages; in fact, whatever wages he had received are to be recovered from him. Moreover, just as a proxy may be appointed to perform the *ḥajj* on behalf of someone who is living, a proxy may likewise be appointed to perform it on behalf of someone who is deceased. In this situation the deceased's trustee, his heir, or the ruler (in this order of priority) must appoint a proxy to perform the *ḥajj* on the deceased's behalf, to be financed with the deceased's bequest, and to be performed immediately. If the deceased left no bequest, no proxy need be appointed; however, it is an emulation of the Sunnah for the deceased's heir or an outsider—even if he has not been granted permission by the heir—to perform the *ḥajj* on behalf of the deceased either on his own or by being appointed as a proxy. In order for the *ḥajj* to be performed on the deceased's behalf, he must not have been an apostate and he must have owed a performance of the *ḥajj* and the *'umrah*, even if only due to a vow taken; otherwise, it is not permissible for anyone to perform the *ḥajj* on his behalf out of his bequest. Nevertheless, it is permissible for someone else to perform the *ḥajj*, or to appoint a proxy to do so, on his behalf [at his or her own expense – t.n.] even if he or she would not have been held accountable for doing so during the deceased's lifetime.

All of the foregoing applies to someone who has not performed the *ḥajj* before; however, if someone has performed the *ḥajj* which is required of every Muslim and if someone else wishes to perform the *ḥajj* on his behalf as a voluntary act of worship, it is not permissible to perform the *ḥajj* or the *'umrah* on his behalf unless he has left explicit instructions to this effect. If, under such circumstances, the proxy invalidates the *ḥajj*, he must make it up on his own behalf, in which case the compensatory *ḥajj* will count on his own behalf and he must either: (a) return whatever money he received from the person who hired him, (b) perform the *ḥajj* on behalf of the person for whom he was performing it originally during another year, that is, during a year other than the year in which he made up the *ḥajj* on his own behalf, or (c) appoint someone else to perform the *ḥajj* in his place in that same year.

* * *

The Hanbalis hold that both the *ḥajj* and the *'umrah* are acts of worship which one person may perform on another's behalf. Hence, if someone who has an unfulfilled obligation to perform the *ḥajj* and the *'umrah* is unable to do so, he is required to appoint someone else to perform them on his behalf without delay. As for the possible causes of one's inability to perform these rites, they include: (1) old age, (2) a physical handicap, (3) an illness from which one is not expected to recover, (4) overweightness which is so extreme that it prevents the person from being able to ride a camel without having to endure severe hardship, and (5) such extreme emaciation that the person cannot remain seated firmly on his camel without facing hardship that would normally be considered intolerable.

It is not necessary for the proxy to be a man; rather, it is permissible to appoint a woman as one's proxy as well. If the person who has been unable to perform the *ḥajj* or the *'umrah* recovers from his disability and becomes able once again to perform them on his own, he need not perform them again, regardless of whether he recovered his ability to do so after the proxy had completed the rites for both pilgrimages, or after he had begun them and before he had completed them. If, on the other hand, the person who has been unable to perform the *'umrah* or the *ḥajj* recovers his ability to do so before the proxy has entered *iḥrām* for these two pilgrimages, he must perform them on his own behalf and if the proxy does perform them in his place, they will not count in his favor. Similarly, if someone suffers from a disabling condition from which he is expected to recover, he may not appoint a proxy to perform the *ḥajj* or the *'umrah* in his place, and once his disabling condition has passed, he must perform them on his own. Moreover, if someone who is not able to perform the *ḥajj* and the *'umrah* is able to cover the expenses incurred by a proxy but is unable to find someone to appoint as his proxy, he is released from the obligation to perform the *ḥajj*; if he does find a proxy after this, he is only required to appoint him as a proxy if he is able to afford it.

If someone dies before performing the *ḥajj* required of him, whether his failure to do so was due to a legitimate excuse or not, sufficient money must be aside out of his total wealth to finance one performance of the *ḥajj* and one performance of the *'umrah*, even if the deceased did not leave explicit instructions for this to be done. Someone must then perform the *ḥajj* on the deceased's behalf from the same place from which the deceased would have been obliged to depart, not from the place where he died; moreover, it is permissible for someone to perform the *ḥajj* on behalf of the deceased from some place other than the deceased's home town if the distance between the two locations is less than the distance one must travel in order to begin shortening ritual prayers; if the distance is greater than this, however, this is not allowed, and the proxy's *ḥajj* will not count on the deceased's behalf. The obligation to perform the *ḥajj* is waived on behalf of the deceased if a non-relative performs the *ḥajj* on his behalf even if he does so without receiving permission from the deceased's trustee. However, the proxy must not himself owe a performance of the *ḥajj*, either because he has not yet performed the *ḥajj* which is required of every Muslim, because he has a *ḥajj* to make up, or because he vowed to perform a *ḥajj* which he has not yet performed. If someone assigns a proxy to perform the *ḥajj* on his behalf when the latter still owes a performance of the *ḥajj* for any of the aforementioned reasons, the *ḥajj* which he performs in this situation will not count on behalf of the deceased, and the proxy must return to the person who assigned him to the task of performing the *ḥajj* whatever money the latter had given him in return for doing so. Moreover, the same ruling which applies to the *ḥajj* in this regard applies to the *'umrah* as well; hence, it is not permissible for someone to perform the *'umrah* on behalf of someone else if the proxy has not already performed on his own behalf the *'umrah* required of every Muslim, if he still owes a performance of the *'umrah* due to a vow he has made, or because he has a *'umrah* to make up. Nevertheless, it is permissible to assign a proxy to perform the *ḥajj* on one's behalf even if the proxy has not yet performed the *'umrah* on his own behalf (provided that he has performed the *ḥajj* for himself); and, conversely, it is permissible to assign a proxy to perform the *'umrah* on one's behalf even if the proxy has not yet performed the *ḥajj* on his own behalf (provided that he has performed the *'umrah* for himself). Lastly, the proxy must carry out what the person assigning him has instructed him to do. Thus, for example, if the person assigning him has instructed him to perform the *ḥajj* but he performs the *'umrah* instead, or vice-versa, this is not acceptable, and the rite performed by the proxy will not count on behalf of the person who assigned him; in addition, the proxy must return to the person who assigned him whatever money the latter gave him to finance the pilgrimage he had assigned him to perform.

The foregoing applies to the performance of the *ḥajj* and the *'umrah* on behalf of someone who is living; as for performing them on behalf of someone who is deceased, the Hanbalis' ruling is that whatever is performed by the proxy, be it the *ḥajj* or the *'umrah*, will count in favor of the deceased, whether or not permission has been granted by the deceased's heir. It is sufficient for the proxy to form a conscious intention to perform the pilgrimage—the *ḥajj* or the *'umrah*—on behalf of the person for whom he is performing it; hence, it is not necessary to utter the name of the person on whose behalf he is performing it. Moreover, the proxy is entitled to receive the financial support that would be due to others in a similar situation in accordance with prevailing practice, and whatever is left over upon his completion of the pilgrimage, he is to return. The proxy is also entitled to the money he requires for his return trip from Mecca even if he remains there for a long time. However, if he decides to take up residence there, if even for as short a time as a single hour, he is not entitled to the expenses entailed in his return trip from Mecca. If the proxy invalidates his *ḥajj*, he must make it up and return whatever money he received from the person on whose behalf he was performing it since, in this case, the *ḥajj* will not have counted on his behalf. Similarly, if the proxy fails to complete the *ḥajj* due to his own negligence, he is not due to be paid his expenses; however, if there was no neglect on his part, he is entitled to them. If the proxy falls ill on his way to Mecca, he is entitled to the money required for his return journey. As for animal sacrifices required of those engaging in *qirān* and *tamattu'*, they are to be provided by the person on whose behalf the proxy is performing the pilgrimage if he has given the proxy permission to engage in one or the other of these; otherwise, they must be provided by the proxy himself. Lastly, any expiation required due to the commission of some transgression during the pilgrimage must be provided by the proxy.

Visiting the tomb of the Prophet

Visiting the tomb of the Chosen One, may peace and blessings be upon him, is undoubtedly one of the greatest, most sublime means of drawing near to God. After all, a spot [of ground] which once embraced the best and noblest of God's messengers will inevitably be endowed with a special significance, indeed, a uniqueness which surpasses the ability of the written word to describe. Nevertheless, the actual purpose for visiting tombs is to help the visitor to remember the afterlife. This may be seen in the authentic hadith which grants us permission to visit tombs for the sake of receiving wise admonition and recalling the life after death. When such a visit is undertaken for a valid reason which is approved by the originator of the Islamic law, it will be praiseworthy in all respects. Moreover, it may be clearly perceived that visiting the tomb of the Chosen One will have a more profound influence on "the hearts of those endowed with insight"[148] than any other act of worship. Those who stand at the tomb of the Chosen One, bringing to mind what he suffered in order to call others to God and bring people out of the darkness of polytheism and into the light of true guidance, the virtuous morals he spread throughout the world, the ubiquitous corruption he eradicated, and the law he brought—a law founded upon serving the interests of human society and protecting it from corruption—are bound to find their hearts filled with love for this Messenger who "strove hard in God's cause with all the striving that is due to Him."[149] Not only so, but they will be stirred by such love to act on all the teachings he brought and to shy away from disobeying God and His Messenger. Indeed, such is "a triumph supreme."[150]

Visiting the tomb of the Chosen One, looking upon the place where the divine revelation descended and visiting those who labored so earnestly in defense of the religion of God Almighty—sacrificing their lives and their wealth in the way of God alone without being dissuaded by the satisfaction of power and authority and without allowing their souls to be captivated by the lust for "the passing enjoyment of life in this world, and…its embellishment"[151] but rather, leaving behind their abundant wealth and their vast enjoyments in order to strive in the way of God and for God's sake and in so doing, to uphold the religion of God—are most assuredly practices worthy of pursuing for the sake of drawing near to the Divine. After all, such practices convey eloquent wisdom to visitors' souls, inspiring them to emulate the deceased whose tombs they are visiting in both word and deed. If the Muslims clung truly to what those dwelling in these tombs clung to—bearing in mind that they defeated the Persians and the Byzantines at the height of their power despite the fact that the Muslims' material strength at that time was hardly worth mentioning by comparison with that of their foes—their present condition would be other than what it is, and they would have been overpowered by no one. Hence, visiting the tomb of the Chosen One and the tombs of his companions who labored

---

148. An allusion to Surah 2:179 [t.n.].
149. An allusion to Surah 22:78 [t.n.].
150. An allusion to Surah 4:13 [t.n.].
151. Surah 28:60 [t.n.].

with him is one of the most sublime, potent means of drawing near to God in its effect on the souls of those sincere laborers who worship God alone, who obey His Messenger's commands to them, and who shun what he has forbidden. Indeed, it is they who will triumph.

Hence, if visiting the tomb of the Chosen One offered nothing but this wise admonition and this uplifting effect, this alone would be sufficient to render it one of the most majestic of the righteous acts which the true faith urges us to perform. Not only so, but if a believing Muslim is capable of performing the pilgrimage to the Sacred Mosque and of visiting the Chosen One, how can his heart be at peace if he fails to take the initiative to do so? How is it possible for a believer to be capable of coming to Mecca and being in such close proximity to Medina, the site of the divine revelation's descent, without experiencing a heartfelt yearning to visit both the city and the Chosen One?

After all, the basis for the supplication uttered by our lord Abraham, may God's blessings be upon him, may be seen in the people of Medina as well. God Almighty speaks to us of Abraham having said, "O our Sustainer! Behold, I have settled some of my offspring in a valley in which there is no arable land, close to Thy sanctified Temple, so that, O our Sustainer, they might devote themselves to prayer: cause Thou, therefore, people's hearts to incline towards them, and grant them fruitful sustenance, so that they might have cause to be grateful."[152] Medina was the city where the glory and power of Islam witnessed their inception and where the true faith was founded upon [the example of] the Helpers who originated from Medina and the sincere believers who emigrated there. Hence, the inhabitants of Medina likewise stand in need of visits by those who can exchange benefits with them, contribute to the city's upbuilding, and perform good works for their sake. The exchange of benefits in Medina is among the most sacred and significant acts in which one can engage. Who is it, then, who would be able to reach Mecca without likewise visiting Medina, the wellspring of the true faith, and enjoying the sight of the places in which the divine revelation descended?

As for the authentic prophetic hadiths that deal with visiting the Prophet's tomb, it may be said that whether their chains of transmission are reliable or not, the fact of the matter is that we have no need for them now that we have expounded the benefits and virtues of visiting the Prophet's tomb and its consistency with the overall principles of the religion.

Scholars of Islamic jurisprudence have the following things to say about the rules of etiquette associated with visiting the Prophet's tomb, as well as other mosques. To wit, they say that when someone sets out to visit the tomb of the Chosen One, he should pray frequently for blessings and peace upon the Prophet throughout the journey; he should also, if possible, perform ritual prayers in the twenty mosques which he passes while on his way from Mecca to Medina. When the traveler comes within view of the walls of Medina, he is to pray for blessings and peace upon the Prophet and say, "O God, this is Your Prophet's sacred city. Grant that it might protect me from the fire and keep me safe from torment and an evil reckoning." If possible, one should perform major ablutions before and after

152. Surah 14:37 [t.n.].

entering the city, apply perfume and put on one's best clothes. The visitor should enter the city in a spirit of humility, tranquility and earnestness. Once the visitor has entered Medina, he is to say, "O God, Lord of the heavens and that which they canopy, Lord of the earth and that which it upholds, Lord of the winds and that which they scatter: I ask you to grant me the best this city has to offer, the best its people have to offer, and the best of all it contains. I seek refuge in You from its evil, the evil of that which resides therein, and the evil of its inhabitants. O God, this is Your Prophet's Sacred Mosque; hence, please grant that my entering it might protect me from the fire and keep me safe from torment and an evil reckoning."

When the visitor enters the Prophet's mosque, he should follow rules of etiquette which apply to entering mosques in general, including stepping inside with his right foot. He should then say, "O God, send down blessings upon Muhammad and his descendents. O God, forgive me my sins and open before me the portals of Your mercy. O God, cause me this day to be among the most worthy of those who turn their faces toward You, the most intimate of those who draw near to You, and the most successful of those who provide sustenance for those in their care and seek Your good pleasure."

The visitor is to perform two *rak'ahs* at the Prophet's pulpit and stand between the honorable tomb and the pulpit in such a way that the pulpit's pillar is opposite his right shoulder, which is where the Prophet used to stand. He should then perform a prostration of thanksgiving to God Almighty for the success He has granted him and offer whatever supplications he wishes, then rise and proceed in the direction of the tomb. The visitor should stand at his honorable head, facing the qiblah, then come up to a distance of three or four cubits [between one and two yards] (but no more than this) from the tomb. The visitor should not place his hand on the dirt wall; rather, he should stand as he would during ritual prayer while contemplating his radiant, noble visage as if he were merely sleeping in his grave and as if he were conscious and able to hear what the visitor is saying. The visitor should then say, "Peace be upon you, O Prophet of God, and God's mercy and blessings. I testify that you are the Messenger of God, for you delivered the message, you carried out the mission entrusted to you, you offered wise counsel to the Muslim nation, and you struggled in God's cause until God took your spirit, praiseworthy and meritorious. May God grant you the best of rewards on behalf of our young and our old, may He grant you the greatest and the sweetest of His blessings, and may He greet you with the fullest and most perfect of greetings. O God, cause our Prophet on the Day of Resurrection to be the closest of all prophets to You. Give us to drink from his cup, sustain us through his intercession, and cause us to be among his companions on the Day of Resurrection. O God, let this not be our last opportunity to visit the tomb of our Prophet, upon him be peace; rather, grant that we may return to this place, O You who are 'full of majesty and glory.'"[153]

When thus praying, the visitor should speak neither very loudly nor very softly. He should deliver to the Prophet the greetings of whoever has charged him to do so, saying, for example, "Peace be upon you, O Messenger of God, from so-and-so, son of so-and-so, who seeks your intercession with your Lord. Hence, make inter-

153. An allusion to Surah 55:27 [t.n.].

cession for him and for all Muslims." The visitor is then to stand opposite the Prophet's face, facing the *qiblah*, pray for blessings upon him however he wishes, then shift by one cubit until he is opposite the head of [Abū Bakr] the Righteous, may God be pleased with him, and say, "Peace be upon you, O Caliph of God's Messenger. Peace be upon you, O companion of God's Messenger in the cave. Peace be upon you, O you who accompanied him on his journeys. Peace be upon you, O faithful preserver of his secrets. May God grant you, on our behalf, the finest reward He has ever bestowed upon any imam on behalf of His Prophet's people. You were the best possible successor to him, you trod his path and followed his example in the best possible manner, and you waged war on the fomenters of apostasy and [illegitimate] innovation. You put Islam's affairs in order, you took care to preserve your ties with your blood relations, and you never ceased to stand up for the truth, granting succor and aid to the people of truth until the certain reality [i.e., death] came upon you. May peace be upon you, and God's mercy and blessings. O God, cause us to die still loving him and do not thwart our striving to visit him by Your mercy, O Beneficent One."

The visitor should then turn again until he is facing the tomb of 'Umar, may God be pleased with him, and say, "Peace be upon you, O Commander of the Faithful. Peace be upon you, O you who raised high the banner of Islam. Peace be upon you, O you who broke the idols. May God grant you the best of all rewards on our behalf, and may God be pleased with him who appointed you as his successor. You upheld Islam and the Muslims both in life and in death, you took the orphans under your care, you preserved your ties with your kin, and through you Islam grew strong. You were to the Muslims an able imam and a well-guided leader; you reunited them when they were scattered, you enriched their poor, and you restored those among them who were broken. Peace be upon you, and God's mercy and blessings."

The visitor should then step back half a cubit [9 inches] and say, "Peace be upon both of you, O you who were the bedfellows of the Messenger of God, his companions, his ministers, his advisors, those who assisted him in upholding the religion and who, after his departure, undertook to serve the Muslims' best interests. May God grant you the best of rewards." He should then offer supplications for himself, for his parents, for whoever may have asked him to pray for them, and for all Muslims. He should then stand once again at the Prophet's noble head and say, "O God, you spoke truly when You said, 'If, then, after having sinned against themselves, they would but come round to thee and ask God to forgive them—with the Apostle, too, praying that they be forgiven—they would assuredly find that God is an acceptor of repentance, a dispenser of grace.'[154] We have come to You, giving heed to Your words, obeying Your commands, and seeking the intercession of Your Prophet: O our Lord, forgive us and our brothers and sisters who preceded us in the faith, and let no ill-will enter our hearts against those who have believed. O our Lord, You are indeed compassionate, a dispenser of grace. 'O our Sustainer! Grant us good in this world and good in the life to come, and keep us safe from suffering through the fire'.[155] 'Limitless in His glory is thy Sustainer, the Lord of almighti-

154. Surah 4:64 [t.n.].
155. Surah 2:201 [t.n.].

ness, [exalted] above all that men may devise by way of definition! And peace be upon all His message-bearers! Praise is due to God alone, the Sustainer of all the worlds.'"[156]

The visitor should follow this with whatever supplications he has memorized. Following this, he should come to Abū Lubābah's pillar (the pillar located between the Prophet's tomb and the pulpit to which Abū Lubābah bound himself until God had accepted his repentance), pray two *rak'ahs*, repent to God, and utter whatever supplications he wishes. After this he should come to the *Rawḍah*, which is like a square basin, and perform ritual prayers there and offer supplications. The visitor should spend a good deal of time praising and glorifying God Almighty and seeking His forgiveness, then come to the pulpit and place his hand on the pomegranate upon which the Prophet used to rest his hand while he preached, thereby seeking the Prophet's blessing for himself. While in this spot, the visitor should pray for blessings upon the Prophet, offer whatever supplications he wishes, and seek refuge in God's mercy from His wrath and displeasure. Following this the worshiper should come to the "tenderhearted pillar", i.e., the pillar that contains the remains of the tree trunk that wept in longing for the Prophet when he left it and preached from the pulpit instead. It is desirable after visiting the Prophet for the worshiper to go out to the Baqī' Cemetery and see the saints' tombs and shrines. This includes visits to al-'Abbās,[157] al-Ḥasan Ibn 'Ali, Zayn al-'Ābidīn, his son Muḥammad al-Bāqir and his son Ja'far al-Ṣādiq. One should also visit the Commander of the Faithful, 'Uthmān, the tomb of Ibrāhim, the Prophet's son, and a number of the Prophet's wives, his paternal aunt Ṣafiyah, and many of the Companions and Followers, especially our master Mālik and our master Nāfi'. It is also desirable to visit those who died as martyrs in the Battle of Uḥud on Thursday, especially the tomb of the chief martyr, our master Ḥamzah, saying, "'Peace be upon you, for you persevered! How excellent, then, this fulfillment in the hereafter!'[158] Peace be upon you, O abode of a believing people. We, God willing, will be coming to join you."

The visitor should then recite the Throne Verse and Surah 112. It is also desirable to come to the Qubā' Mosque on Saturday and to utter the following supplication, "O You who respond to those who cry out to You for help, O You who come to the aid of those who cry out for assistance, O You who relieve the distress of the afflicted, O You who answer the supplications of those who are in distress! Grant Your blessings to Muḥammad and his descendents, and dispel my sorrow and anguish as You did for Your Messenger when he stood in this place. O Tenderhearted, Munificent One who is bountiful in His favors and constant in His kindness, O Most Merciful of the merciful!"

It is desirable for the visitor to perform all prayers in the Prophet's Mosque as long as he is in Medina, and if he wishes to return to his hometown, it is desirable for him to bid farewell to the mosque by performing two *rak'ahs*, to offer whatever supplications he wishes, then come to the tomb of the Messenger of God and offer whatever other supplications he wishes. And God is the One who answers supplication.

---

156. Surah 37:180-182.

157. Namely, al-' Abbās Ibn 'Abd al-Muṭṭalib, the Messenger of God's paternal uncle, whom the Prophet honored and revered, as did the rightly guided caliphs after him. Al-'Abbās died on 1 Ramaḍān, 32 AH. [editor's note].

158. Surah 13:24 [t.n.].

On Animals Slaughtered For the Day of Sacrifice (*uḍḥiyah*)

The definition of *uḍḥiyah*

The Arabic term *uḍḥiyah* [which is the nominal form of the verb *ḍaḥḥā*, meaning to sacrifice – t.n.] refers to the camels, cattle, sheep and goats which are slaughtered as a means of drawing near to God on the days set aside for such slaughtering. According to the Hanafis, the Hanbalis and the Shafiis, the *uḍḥiyah* is required of both those who are performing the *ḥajj* and those who are not, whereas the Malikis hold that it is not required of those performing the *ḥajj*.

The evidence in its favor

The practice of offering an *uḍḥiyah* was legislated in the year 2 AH, as were the Day of Sacrifice and the Day of Fastbreaking, the practice of paying *zakāh* on one's wealth, and the fastbreaking *zakāh*. The legitimacy of the practice of offering the *uḍḥiyah* is supported definitively by the Qur'ān, the Sunnah and the consensus of the Muslim community. God Almighty declares, "...pray unto thy Sustainer [alone], and sacrifice [unto Him alone]" (8:2).

Muslim narrates the following hadith on the authority of Anas, may God be pleased with him. He states, "The Prophet sacrificed two pure white rams with straight horns, and he slaughtered them with his own hands. (Some say that the word rendered here as "pure white" (*amlaḥ*) means, "having more white in their hides than black.") When he did so, he uttered the words *bismillāh al-rahmān al-rahīm* and *Allāhu akbar*, and he placed his foot on their sides." Other hadiths likewise support the practice of offering an *uḍḥiyah*, and the Muslim community agrees unanimously on its legitimacy.

The ruling on the offering of an *uḍḥiyah*

The ruling on the offering of an *uḍḥiyah* is that it is an emphatically enjoined individual emulation of the Sunnah, adherence to which merits a reward but omission of which does not merit punishment. This much is agreed upon among the four schools; however, the Hanafis hold that if someone omits this practice, he will not be punished through the torment of the fire, but will be deprived of the Prophet's intercession on his behalf on the Day of Resurrection. This type of a practice is referred to by the Hanafis as a 'duty', as we have seen. According to the Shafiis, the offering of an *uḍḥiyah* is an individual Sunnah-based practice for each single person, but not for the members of a given household, as one may see below.[159]

---

159. According to the Shafiis, the offering of an *uḍḥiyah* is both an individual Sunnah-based practice for a single person and a collective Sunnah-based practice for the members of a single household or several households for whose financial support one person is responsible. In other words, if an *uḍḥiyah* is slaughtered by the person who is financially responsible for the members of a given household or

Conditions associated with the *uḍḥiyah*

The conditions associated with the offering of an *uḍḥiyah* are divided into two categories: (a) conditions for its being an emulation of the Sunnah, and (b) conditions for its validity.

The conditions for its being an emulation of the Sunnah are as follows: (1) That one be capable of doing so; hence, offering an *uḍḥiyah* is not an emulation of the Sunnah for someone who is unable to do so. As for the definition of 'ability' in this context, each school offers its own ruling on this point.[160] (2) Freedom; hence, it is not an emulation of the Sunnah for a slave to offer an *uḍḥiyah*. (3) In addition to these two conditions, the Malikis stipulate that in order for the offering of an *uḍḥiyah* to be an emulation of the Sunnah, the person concerned must not be performing the

---

a number of given household(s), the members of this household, or these households, will be exempted from the requirement to offer an *uḍḥiyah* even though it would be an emulation of the Sunnah for each of them separately.

160. According to the Hanafis, one is capable of offering an *uḍḥiyah* if he owns two hundred dirhams (as was mentioned above in the discussion of *zakāh*), or if he owns merchandise which equals one hundred dirhams over and above his dwelling, his clothing, and whatever other material articles he has need of. If the person has real estate from which he benefits financially, he is required to offer an *uḍḥiyah* if he receives his yearly sustenance through it and if, in addition, he owns the aforementioned *niṣāb*. Some hold that one is required to offer an *uḍḥiyah* if he receives even as little as one month's income from such real estate. If the real estate has been set aside as a religious endowment, one must offer an *uḍḥiyah* if the income he has received from it equals the value of a *niṣāb* at the time the *uḍḥiyah* is due.

* * *

According to the Hanbalis, someone is able to offer an *uḍḥiyah* if he is capable of obtaining the money with which to purchase one, even if he has to purchase it on credit, provided that he is able to pay back the debt.

* * *

The Malikis hold that someone is able to offer an *uḍḥiyah* if he will not need the money required to purchase the animal within the current year for any sort of necessity. If he will need the money during the current year, it is not an emulation of the Sunnah for him to offer an *uḍḥiyah*, whereas if he is able to borrow the money, he should (although some hold that one should not).

* * *

As for the Shafiis, they hold that someone is able to offer an *uḍḥiyah* if, on the Day of Sacrifice and the "days of meat drying", he owns the money required to purchase the animal over and above his basic needs and the needs of those for whom he provides financial support. 'Needs' in this context include items which are customarily purchased [on the Day of Sacrifice] such as holiday cakes, fish, pastries, transport costs, and the like.

ḥajj, even if he is a resident of Mecca, as we have seen.[161] As for someone who is on a journey for some purpose other than the *ḥajj*, it is an emulation of the Sunnah for him to offer an *uḍḥiyah*. As for being of legal age, it is not a condition for the offering of an *uḍḥiyah* to be an emulation of the Sunnah; hence, it is an emulation of the Sunnah for a young boy to offer such a sacrifice if he is able to do so, and his guardian may sacrifice on his behalf even if the child is an orphan according to the Malikis and the Hanbalis; for the views of the Hanafis and the Shafiis, see below.[162]

As for the conditions for the validity of one's *uḍḥiyah*, they are as follows: (1) The animal must be free of defects. Hence, it is not valid to sacrifice an animal that suffers from the any of the defects listed below.[163] (2) The slaughtering must be done at the time specified for this rite. Hence, the *uḍḥiyah* will not be valid if it is slaughtered before or after this time.[164]

---

161. The Hanafis also stipulate that in order for the offering of an *uḍḥiyah* to be an emulation of the Sunnah, the person concerned must be resident in one place; hence, offering an *uḍḥiyah* is not an emulation of the Sunnah for someone who is on a journey. If someone who is on a journey offers an *uḍḥiyah* voluntarily, however, it will be acceptable. If someone purchases a sheep or a goat in order to sacrifice it, then embarks on a journey before the time when the *uḍḥiyah* is due, he is to sell it and he is not required to offer it as a sacrifice. Similarly, if such a person embarks on a journey after the beginning of the time period during which the *uḍḥiyah* is due but before he has actually slaughtered it, he is not required to sacrifice it. Lastly, someone who is performing the *ḥajj* must offer an *uḍḥiyah* if he is not on a journey, that is, if he is a resident of Mecca.

162. The Hanafis hold that being of legal age is not necessary for the offering of an *uḍḥiyah* to be required; hence, it is required of a young child, and his guardian is to sacrifice with the child's money if he has money. Hence, a father is not to sacrifice in place of his young child. Muḥammad [Ibn al-Ḥasan al-Shaybāni], by contrast, holds that it is necessary for one to be of legal age in order for the *uḍḥiyah* to be required; in his view, then, one is not required to offer an *uḍḥiyah* with a child's money. [The question then arises:] Is the father required to sacrifice on his child's behalf, or not? Some answer this question in the affirmative, and others in the negative; however, both views are valid. Moreover, the same ruling which applies to a child applies likewise to someone who is insane.

* * *

As for the Shafiis, they hold that the offering of an *uḍḥiyah* is not an emulation of the Sunnah for a child; hence, being of legal age is a condition for its being an emulation of the Sunnah. Moreover, they apply the same ruling to one's being in full possession of one's mental faculties.

163. The Hanafis hold that one may not validly offer as an *uḍḥiyah* an animal which is blind, one-eyed, or so thin that its bones contain no marrow. One is likewise forbidden to sacrifice an animal which is lame in the sense that it is unable to walk to the slaughter site; as for an animal which walks on three legs and places the fourth on the ground to help propel itself forward, it may be offered. One may not offer an animal if more than one-third of its ear, tail or buttocks is missing; if two-thirds of it are left, however, it may be offered. One may not offer an animal whose

front teeth are missing unless most of its teeth are left. One may not offer an animal which was born without ears, whose teats are missing, whose milk has stopped flowing, which was born without a buttocks, or which was grazing on [substances contaminated by] human excrement before it was confined and fed ritually pure substances. It is permissible to offer an animal which was born without horns and an animal part of whose horn is gone; however, if the break in the horn reaches into the marrow, it may not be offered. It is also permissible to offer an animal which is mad if its madness does not prevent it from grazing; if it prevents the animal from grazing, however, it may not be offered as an *uḍḥiyah.* One may also offer an animal which suffers from scabies if it is fat; if it has grown emaciated due to the scabies, however, it may not be offered. Nor it is permissible to offer a sheep or goat that is less than one year old unless it is fat and has a large body, in which case it is permissible to offer it if it is at least six months old and if, when placed together with animals which are a full one year old, it cannot be distinguished from the older animals. Goats may not be offered unless they are a year old and have entered significantly into their second year. As for cows and buffaloes, they may not be offered unless they are two years old and have entered significantly into their third year. Young camels are those which are less than five years old; hence, camels may not be offered unless they are five years old and have entered significantly into their sixth year. One sheep or goat may be offered on behalf of one person, while a single she-camel or cow may be offered on behalf of seven people provided that each person is given one-seventh of the animal. If any of the seven people has a share of less than one-seventh, it will not count for him.

* * *

According to the Malikis, it is not permissible to offer as an *uḍḥiyah* an animal which is blind or one-eyed, with the criterion for blindness and one-eyedness being that one or both eyes are sightless, even though the eye's appearance is normal. One may not offer an animal which is sick in the sense that it does not behave like an animal which is healthy. If, on the other hand, the illness is minor, no harm is done. One may not sacrifice an animal which has scabies if the scabies are visible, or an animal which has eaten to the point of surfeit provided that there is no diarrhea; if there is diarrhea, however, it may be sacrificed. One may not sacrifice an animal which has gone permanently mad; as for temporary madness, this does no harm.

It is permissible to sacrifice an animal which twirls about in place out of madness and which does not follow the other sheep and goats. However, one may not sacrifice an animal which is clearly emaciated, that is, one which has no marrow in its bones, an animal with a visible limp which prevents it from keeping up with other animals of its kind, nor an animal which is missing a body part, such as a front or back leg, whether the body part concerned has been missing from birth or was lost later on, and whether the body part is 'extra' or not. However, no harm is done if an animal is missing a testicle; hence, one may sacrifice an animal which has been castrated, since its meat is still of benefit; no distinction is made between an animal which was born castrated and one which was castrated later. One may not offer an animal which has very small ears, an animal which has no tail (whether it was born without a tail or lost it later), nor an animal which is mute, unless the animal lost its voice due to an ordinary event, such as a she-camel which has been pregnant for several months, since it is normal for a she-camel to lose her voice under these circumstances. It is not permissible to sacrifice an animal which has bad breath unless it was born with this condition, which happens in the case of some camels. Nor may one sacrifice an animal with dry udders or with a slit ear if the slit extends through more than one-third of the ear; however, if the slit is no longer than one-third the length of the animal's ear, it may be sacrificed based on the most widely accepted point of view. Nor may one sacrifice an animal with two or more broken teeth; as for an animal which has one broken tooth, it may be sacrificed; similarly, an animal may be sacrificed if it has lost its teeth due to old age or change. One may not sacrifice an animal which has lost one-third of its tail; as for an animal which has lost one-third of its ear, it may be sacrificed. Nor may one sacrifice an animal which is a hybrid between a wild animal and a domestic animal; if, for example, the father was a sheep or a goat and the mother was a gazelle, or vice-versa, none of their offspring may be offered as an *uḍḥiyah*, properly speaking. One may sacrifice an animal which was born without horns; however, if its horns have been removed, there is disagreement as to whether it may be sacrificed or not. This situation applies if the stumps are not bloody; if they are, there is unanimous agreement that the animal may be not be offered as an *uḍḥiyah*. It is permissible to sacrifice an animal which is unable to stand up due to obesity rather than due to illness. It is also permissible to sacrifice a sheep which is one lunar year old, the sign of which is that the wool on its back lies down rather than standing straight up as it does on a younger sheep. One may also sacrifice a cow which is three years old or a camel which is five years old. In determining such animals' ages, the lunar year is relied upon even if it is missing some of its months.

* * *

The Shafiis hold that it is not permissible to sacrifice an animal with a defect that has resulted in a reduction in the animal's flesh, fat, or some other edible part of its body. It is not permissible to sacrifice an animal which is one-eyed or blind, where the criterion for one-eyedness or blindness is that there is no sight in one or both eyes; nor may one sacrifice an animal which has a white film over one of its eyes if there is a great deal of it; otherwise, no harm is done. Nor is any harm done by the animal's being bleary-eyed, that is, having weak sight and, in most cases, a flow of tears. One may not sacrifice an animal which limps visibly, that is, one which falls behind other animals of its kind on their way to the pasture; this ruling applies even if the limp only occurs at the time of slaughter, or at the time when the trachea and the esophagus are being cut. Nor may one sacrifice an animal which is visibly ill and, as a result of which, it has become emaciated and its flesh has gone bad; if the animal's illness is not severe, however, no harm is done. One may not sacrifice an animal which is so thin that there is no marrow in its bones, nor an animal which goes around the pasture but only grazes sparsely, thereby becoming too thin. Nor may one sacrifice an animal afflicted with scabies, even if the scabies are mild, since this condition ruins the animal's meat. Nor may one sacrifice an animal which has lost part or all of its ear or its buttocks. However, one may sacrifice an animal the end of whose buttocks was cut off when it was young, since this loss can be made up for by the animal's fatness. As for an animal which was born without a tail, it is acceptable as an *uḍḥiyah*, as is an animal which was born without teats or a buttocks. An animal that was born without an ear is not acceptable and may not be offered as an *uḍḥiyah*. One may, however, sacrifice an animal which has a slit or perforated ear provided that some of the ear still remains. One may sacrifice an animal which has been castrated, although in order for castration to be permissible, the following three conditions must be met: (1) The animal must be one whose flesh is edible. (2) It must be done while the animal is young. (3) It must be done during a moderate time [of the year]. Otherwise, it is forbidden. It is permissible to sacrifice an animal which has a broken horn even if the site of the break is bloody, provided that this causes no reduction in the animal's flesh. One may also sacrifice an animal which has had no horns from birth, although an animal with horns is preferable. One may sacrifice an animal that was born without teeth, but not one that was born with teeth but then lost them. Nor may one sacrifice an animal some of whose teeth are gone if this has an effect on its feeding; if it has no effect, however, it may be offered as an *uḍḥiyah*. A sheep may be sacrificed if it is a full year old or has dropped its front teeth, provided that this occurred after it was six months old. One may sacrifice a goat which is a two full years old, a cow or a buffalo which is two full years old, and a camel which is five full years old. However, one may not sacrifice an animal which is a wild-domestic hybrid.

* * *

As for the Hanbalis, they hold that it is not permissible to sacrifice an animal which is blind, that is, one which can no longer see, even if its eyes still look normal, nor an animal which is one-eyed, that is, one who has a sunken eye. If the animal has a white film over its eye while still being able to see, it may be sacrificed. One may not sacrifice an animal which is so thin that there is no marrow in its bones, nor an animal which is unable to walk with other animals of its kind to pasture. Nor may one sacrifice an animal which is broken or one which is afflicted with an illness which ruins its meat, such as scabies. One may not sacrifice an animal which has lost more than half of its ear or horn; as for one whose ear or horn has been perforated or slit or half or less of which is missing, it may be sacrificed although it is undesirable to do so. One may not sacrifice an animal with dry udders or an animal which has lost its central incisor teeth. Nor may one sacrifice an animal the outer casing of whose horn has been broken or one which has lost more than half its buttocks; if only half or less of it is gone, however, it may be sacrificed. One may also sacrifice an animal which was born without horns, one which has very small ears, and one which was born without ears; one may also sacrifice an animal which has had no tail since birth or whose tail has been cut off. One may also sacrifice an animal that has been castrated; as for an animal whose penis and testicles have all been removed, it may not be offered as an *uḍḥiyah*. As for an animal which is pregnant, it is subject to the same rulings as other animals of its kind. One may not sacrifice a wild animal or a wild-domestic hybrid. One may sacrifice a sheep which is six months old, and one may determine that an animal has reached the age of six months by the fact that the wool lies down on its back. In the case of a goat, it may be sacrificed once it has reached one full year of age; in the case of cattle, they may be sacrificed once they have reached two full years of age; as for camels, they may be sacrificed once they have reached five full years of age and entered their sixth year.

164. According to the Hanafis, the time for offering one's *uḍḥiyah* begins at the break of dawn on the Day of Sacrifice and it continues until immediately before sundown on the third day after this. This time period applies equally to city dwellers and village dwellers. However, in order for the *uḍḥiyah* to be valid for someone living in a city, the slaughtering must be done after the holiday prayer, even if it is done before the sermon, although it is preferable to delay the slaughtering until after the sermon. If someone living in a city slaughters his *uḍḥiyah* before the holiday prayer, it will not be valid and he must eat it as regular meat. If the holiday prayer is not performed, he must wait with his *uḍḥiyah* until the time for the prayer has passed (the time for the holiday prayer extending from the time when the sun has risen in the sky until high noon), then slaughter it after this. As for someone living in a village, the aforementioned condition does not apply to him; rather, he may slaughter his sacrificial animal any time after the break of dawn on the Day of Sacrifice. If people are mistaken concerning which day the Day of Sacrifice falls on and, as a consequence, they perform the holiday prayer and slaughter their sacrificial animals only to discover after this that they did so on the Day of 'Arafah, both their prayer and their sacrifices will still be valid. As for someone who fails to slaughter his sacrificial animal until after the time for doing so has passed, he must donate it live as charity.

* * *

According to the Malikis, the time for slaughtering one's *uḍḥiyah* for people other than the imam begins on the Day of Sacrifice after the imam has slaughtered his. The time for doing so for the imam himself begins after he has completed his sermon following the holiday prayer, or after sufficient time for the imam to have slaughtered his *uḍḥiyah* has passed if he does not, in fact, slaughter an *uḍḥiyah*. The time for slaughtering then continues until sundown on the third day after the Day of Sacrifice. If someone wishes to slaughter his *uḍḥiyah* on the second day, he is not required to wait until sufficient time has passed for the imam to have prayed; rather, he may slaughter his sacrificial animal as soon as the sun has begun to rise in the sky, and if he slaughters his animal after dawn, it will be valid. If someone deliberately slaughters his sacrificial animal before the imam slaughters his, his sacrifice will be invalid and he must slaughter another one. If, on the other hand, such a person does not deliberately slaughter his sacrificial animal before the imam—as in a case where, for example, he seeks out the nearest imam, who happens not to have brought out his *uḍḥiyah*, as a result of which he thinks that the imam has already slaughtered when, in fact, he has not, after which it becomes apparent that he slaughtered before the imam did—his sacrifice will be valid. If the imam delays slaughtering his animal for a legitimate reason, others are to wait for him until there is just enough time remaining before high noon to slaughter, then slaughter their own animals, even if the imam has not slaughtered his.

* * *

The Hanbalis hold that the time for slaughtering one's *uḍḥiyah* begins on the Day of Sacrifice after the holiday prayer. It is permissible to slaughter after the holiday prayer and before the sermon, although it is preferable to do so after both the prayer and the sermon. However, it is not necessary for one to wait until the holiday prayer has been completed in all the places where it is being performed if it is being performed in several different places; rather, if one slaughters one's sacrificial animal before the prayer has been completed in just some places, it will still be valid. In the case of someone in a location where the holiday prayer is not performed, such as a desert area or in an encampment where there is no holiday celebration, the time for slaughtering one's *uḍḥiyah* begins once sufficient time for the performance of the holiday prayer has passed. If the holiday prayer is missed by the arrival of high noon, one is to sacrifice at noon. The end of the time period for slaughtering one's *uḍḥiyah* is the second of the three "days of meat drying" (since the days set aside for slaughtering according to the Hanbalis are three: the Day of Sacrifice and the two days thereafter). It is permissible to slaughter one's sacrifice on the eve of either the second or the third day set aside for slaughtering; however, it is preferable to slaughter during the day.

* * *

As for the Shafiis, they hold that the time for slaughtering one's *uḍḥiyah* begins when sufficient time has passed since sunrise on the Day of Sacrifice for one to have performed two *rak'ahs* and delivered two sermons, even if the sun has not risen a spear's length in the sky; however, it is preferable to delay one's slaughtering until the sun has risen this much. The time for slaughtering lasts until the end of the three "days of meat drying." Once the time period set aside for slaughtering has begun, it is permissible to slaughter both at night and during the day; nevertheless, it is undesirable to slaughter at night unless there is a need to do so, as in a case where the person concerned is occupied during the day with tasks which prevent him from slaughtering at this time, or due to an overriding interest, as in a case where the poor can come more easily at night.

Some of the schools list other conditions as well, as may be seen below.[165] According to the Hanafis, the Hanbalis and the Shafiis, it is permissible to share with others in a single *uḍḥiyah*, whether this involves sharing in its price or in the reward due for offering it; for the view of the Malikis, see below.[166] It is permissible to share with others in an *uḍḥiyah* if it is a camel or a cow. Hence, if seven people share in a single cow or she-camel, this is acceptable provided that no person's share is less than one-seventh of the animal. It is not permissible for more than seven people to share in a single *uḍḥiyah*; however, if the number of people sharing in the *uḍḥiyah* is fewer than seven, it is acceptable.

The only animals which may be offered as an *uḍḥiyah* are camels, cattle, buffaloes, sheep and goats; as for which of these is preferable, each of the four schools offers its own rulings on this matter.[167]

---

165. The Malikis stipulate the following: (1) That the slaughtering must be done during the day; if it is done at night, the *uḍḥiyah* will not be valid. This condition as it pertains to the Day of Sacrifice itself is agreed upon unanimously among the Malikis; as it pertains to other days, however, there is a difference of opinion among them as to whether slaughtering at night is valid or not, but the most widely accepted view is that it is not. (2) The person who does the slaughtering must be a Muslim; if the animal is slaughtered by a Christian or a Jew, the *uḍḥiyah* will not be valid, although its meat may be eaten. (3) The person who does the slaughtering must not share with anyone else therein; in other words, it is permissible for those whose financial support he is responsible to share with him the reward due for the slaughtering, but in not the price of the animal, if they are living with him in a single household. However, if they are not living with him in the same household, they may share neither in the price of the animal nor in the reward due for the slaughtering. This is the most widely held point of view among the Malikis.

* * *

The Hanafis stipulate that the slaughtering must be done during the daytime on the Day of Sacrifice itself or the fourth day thereafter. If someone slaughters on the evening of the Day of Sacrifice or the evening of the fourth day, it will be invalid; however, slaughtering on the evening of the second day or third day is simply undesirable.

166. According to the Malikis, it is not permissible to share with others in the price of an *uḍḥiyah*, but it is permissible to share in the reward due for offering the *uḍḥiyah* given the aforementioned conditions.

167. The Hanafis hold that a sheep or a goat is preferable to one-seventh of a cow or a camel if the two are equal in terms of their meat and their monetary value. Similarly, they hold that a ram is preferable to a ewe if they are equal in terms of their price and value. They hold that a female goat is preferable to a male goat if they are equal in value, while a female camel is preferable to a male and a cow is preferable to a bull if they are equal in value.

* * *

If someone fails to utter the *basmalah* when slaughtering an *uḍḥiyah*

According to the Malikis, the Hanafis and the Hanbalis, the utterance of the *basmalah* (referred to in this context as *tasmiyah*) is a condition which must be fulfilled in order for it to be permissible to eat of any animal sacrifice whether it is an *uḍḥiyah* or not; for the view of the Shafiis, see below.[168]

If the person slaughtering an animal sacrifice omits the *tasmiyah* deliberately, it may not be eaten, whereas if he omits its unintentionally, it may be eaten, as will be seen below in the discussion of *dhabḥ*. Similarly, if someone invokes a name other than God's when slaughtering an animal, it may not be eaten. Specifically, the invocation of a name other than God's refers here to the practice of shouting out the name of an idol or the like when slaughtering as a means of currying favor with such a 'being'; this was the custom of the polytheists when they offered animal sacrifices to their idols.

According to the Shafiis, the most preferable *uḍḥiyah* is seven sheep or goats on behalf of one person, followed in order of preference by a camel or a cow; as for perfection, it has no upper limit.

* * *

According to the Hanbalis, the best *uḍḥiyah* is a camel, followed by a cow if it is offered whole rather than shared in by more than one person. These are followed in order of preference by a sheep or a goat, then by a she-camel or a male camel which is shared in by seven people, then a cow which is shared in [by seven people]. In all of these cases, the animal most preferred is the fattest, then the most expensive; however, no preference is assigned to males over females or the reverse.

* * *

The Malikis hold that the most preferable *uḍḥiyah* is a sheep, followed by a goat, followed by a cow; the apparent sense of the Malikis' ruling is that they give preference to cattle over camels. It is recommended that one sacrifice a non-castrated male unless the castrated male available is fatter; hence, a castrated male is preferable to a non-castrated one if the former is fatter than the latter.

168. According to the Shafiis, utterance of the *tasmiyah* is not required in order for it to be permissible to eat of an animal sacrifice. Rather, they hold that it is permissible to eat of an animal sacrifice even if someone omits the *tasmiyah* deliberately, although it is undesirable to do so. The only animal sacrifice which a Muslim would be forbidden to eat is one over which the name of some being other than God has been pronounced, such as the animal sacrifices which used to be offered to idols.

Recommended and undesirable practices associated with the *uḍḥiyah*

Each of the four schools details those practices which are recommended and those which are undesirable in connection with the offering of an *uḍḥiyah*.[169]

---

169. The Malikis hold that the following practices are recommended: (1) That one display his *uḍḥiyah* publicly; however, not doing so is undesirable only for the imam. (2) That one sacrifice an animal of the highest quality and that it be purchased with money which has been honestly acquired. (3) That the animal be free even of those defects which are acceptable in an *uḍḥiyah*. (4) That the animal not have a circular perforation in its ear. (5) That the animal not have a slit ear and that its ear not be cut off either from the front or from the back. (6) That the animal be fat and that, based on the best attested view, that it be urged to eat in order for it to grow fatter. (7) That it be a white male with two horns. (8) That the animal be an uncastrated male unless an available castrated male is fatter. (9) That the animal be a sheep, followed in order of preference by a goat, and so on down the aforementioned scale of preferences. (10) That the person who wishes to sacrifice an animal leave off shaving and trimming his fingernails and toenails on 10 Dhū al-Hijjah until after he has sacrificed. (11) That one slaughter one's *uḍḥiyah* with one's own hands. (12) That the heir of someone who has left instructions to sacrifice an *uḍḥiyah* on his behalf carry out the latter's instructions by offering the *uḍḥiyah* if the deceased specified it before his death so long as it was not a vow; otherwise, it is not merely recommended, but obligatory that such instructions be carried out. (13) That the person who has sacrificed an *uḍḥiyah* eat part of the animal, give part of it away as charity, and give some away as a gift; the proportions by which one is to do so are not specified, however. Rather, one may divide the portions as one wishes.

The Malikis also specify that if an animal to be sacrificed gives birth before being slaughtered (whether by *dhabḥ* or by *naḥr*, to be explained below), it is an emulation of the Sunnah to slaughter the offspring in the same manner provided that it was born alive and is viable; if the offspring is fully formed and has hair growing on it, it may be eaten. If the offspring comes out of the mother after she has been slaughtered and if it is viable, its slaughter is not merely recommended, but obligatory.

Lastly, the Malikis hold that is it undesirable to shear the wool of an animal before it is slaughtered given the following two conditions: (a) That the person slaughtering the animal not have intended to shear it at the time when he purchased it. If he intended to shear it in order to make legitimate use of the wool, it is permissible for him to shear it without any undesirability attached thereto. However, if he intends to sell the wool, it is undesirable to shear it. (b) That no wool have grown in to fully or partially replace the wool sheared before the animal is slaughtered; if new wool does grow in before the animal is slaughtered, it is not undesirable to shear it. In the case of an animal to be slaughtered in fulfillment of a vow, shearing its wool is not allowed under any circumstances; however, some hold that an animal to be slaughtered in fulfillment of a vow is subject to the same ruling as other animal sacrifices in this regard.

* * *

The Hanafis list the following as recommended actions in connection with the offering of an *uḍḥiyah*: (1) That the person offering the *uḍḥiyah* eat some of its meat, save some, and give some away as charity. It is preferable to give away one-third as charity, to save one-third, and to take one-third to one's relatives and friends. However, if one were to take the entire animal for oneself, this would be permissible, since one draws near to God by the mere act of shedding blood. This ruling applies if the person concerned has not vowed to offer a particular sacrificial animal; if he has made such a vow, he will not be permitted to eat of the animal at all; rather, he must give the entire animal away as charity. The same applies to a sacrificial animal which one is required to give away in its entirety as charity after the days of slaughtering are over. If someone purchases an animal in order to offer it as an *uḍḥiyah*, after which he confines it until after the days of slaughter have passed, he must give it away as charity while it is still alive, and he is forbidden to eat any of it. Similarly, one is forbidden to eat of the offspring borne to a sacrificial animal before it is slaughtered; if the sacrificial animal gives birth to a baby before it is slaughtered, the baby must be slaughtered with its mother, and both of them must be given away as charity; it is forbidden to eat either of them, and if one eats any of their meat, he must give away its value in charity. Moreover, it is deemed desirable to give it away as charity while it is still alive. As for a baby which is stillborn, the difference of opinion concerning whether it is to be slaughtered will be discussed below in the section on *dhakāh*. It is forbidden to eat of an *uḍḥiyah* which was sacrificed on behalf on a deceased person based on his instructions, as well as to eat of an animal which is being shared in by seven different people, one of whom has formed the intention to use his share of the animal in order to make up for something he omitted in the past, since animal sacrifices of this nature are to be donated in their entirety as charity. (2) That someone who has children refrain from giving any of a sacrificial animal away in charity, since in this way he will provide more generously for his own family. (3) That one slaughter one's sacrificial animal by one's own hand if one knows how to do so; otherwise, one should witness the slaughtering personally and give instructions in this regard to someone else.

The Hanafis list the following actions as undesirable in association with the offering of an *uḍḥiyah*: (1) It is undesirable for a Christian or a Jew to do the slaughtering, while it is forbidden to eat of a sacrifice which was slaughtered by a Magian or a worshiper of idols. (2) It is undesirable to sell the animal's skin or to trade it for something which is perishable, such as meat, cheese, vinegar, and the like; as for trading it for a sieve, a pail or some other long-lasting item, this is permissible. One may also use the skin in order to make such items; that is, one might make a sieve, a water skin, or a mat on which to spread food from the animal's hide. There are some, however, who hold that selling a sacrificial animal's skin is not only undesirable, but results in an invalid transaction as well. (3) It is undesirable to shear the wool of a sacrificial animal before it is slaughtered in order to make use of it, and if someone does so, he must give the wool away as charity. (4) It is undesirable to ride or rent out an animal intended for slaughter as a sacrifice, and if one does rent it out, one must give away in charity the rent one collects as a result. 5) It is undesirable to make use of such an animal's milk before it is slaughtered. (6) It is undesirable to pay the butcher's wages with some part of the animal. (7) It is undesirable to slaughter at night on the evening of the Day of Sacrifice and on the evening of the fourth day thereafter; as for slaughtering at night on the second and third days, it is invalid. (8) It is undesirable to sell the sacrificial animal's wool. (9) It is undesirable to drink its milk or feed a non-Muslim its meat, be he a Jew, a Christian, or a Magian, by sending some of it to his home. If, however, a non-Muslim receives the person who offered the sacrifice in his home, or if one is visited by a non-Muslim while one is eating at home, it is not undesirable to feed the non-Muslim some of the animal based on the best attested view. (10) It is undesirable to purchase a sacrificial animal for an inflated price or to purchase a large number of animals if, in doing so, one fears that one is being ostentatious. However, if one's intention in purchasing a more expensive animal or a larger number of animals is to receive a greater reward from God, it is recommended. (11) It is undesirable to offer an *uḍḥiyah* on behalf of someone who is deceased if he did not stipulate in a religious endowment in his name that this should be done. Otherwise, one is obliged to offer the *uḍḥiyah* on his behalf and, in so doing, one must adhere to the conditions he has laid down, whether such conditions are desirable or undesirable. Moreover, if someone specified before his death that an *uḍḥiyah* should be offered on his behalf, it is recommended that this be done. (12) It is undesirable to follow the practice known as *'atirah*, that is, slaughtering a sheep or goat during the month of Rajab as polytheists did during the pre-Islamic era on behalf of their idols. This practice was permitted in the beginning of the Islamic era, after which it was superceded by the *uḍḥiyah*. (13) It is undesirable to replace one's sacrificial animal with one of lesser or equal value if the particular animal in question has not been set aside based on someone's vow; if it has been, this practice is not only undesirable, but forbidden.

As for practices which are emulations of the Sunnah in association with the offering of an *uḍḥiyah*, the Hanafis list the following: (1) Having the sacrificial animal face the *qiblah*. (2) Following the practices which are recommended in connection with other animals for slaughter, including sharpening one's knife and not causing the animal undue suffering.

* * *

The Shafiis list the following as emulations of the Sunnah in connection with the offering of an *uḍḥiyah*: (1) That the animal be fat, whether its fatness is its own doing or that of someone else. (2) That the animal not have a broken or lost horn. (3) That the animal be slaughtered after the holiday prayer. (4) That the person who does the slaughtering be a Muslim. (5) That the slaughtering be done during the day; it is undesirable to slaughter at night unless it is done out of some necessity. (6) That the person doing the slaughtering seek out a soft place on which the animal can lie. (7) That the animal be caused to face the *qiblah* upon being slaughtered, and that the person slaughtering it face the *qiblah* as well. (8) That the person slaughtering invoke the name of God; as we have seen, it is undesirable to omit this invocation deliberately. (9) That the person slaughtering pray for blessings upon the Prophet, utter the words *Allāhu akbar* three times after invoking the name of God, and then say, "O God, this is from You and for You, so please accept it from me." (10) That goats, sheep and cattle be slaughtered by means of *dhabḥ*, that camels be slaughtered by means of *naḥr*, and that the animal's head not be severed. (11) That one cut the two jugular veins. (12) That when a camel is being slaughtered, it be standing up with its left hind leg tied. (13) That when a sheep, a goat or a cow is slaughtered, it be lying on its left side. (14) That the person doing the slaughtering sharpen his knife beforehand. However, it is undesirable to sharpen one's knife while the sacrificial animal is looking on; it is likewise undesirable to slaughter one animal while another is looking on.

* * *

The Hanbalis hold that it is an emulation of the Sunnah to eat one-third of one's *uḍḥiyah*, to give one-third away, even if one gives it to someone who is wealthy, and to give away one-third of it as charity to the poor. This ruling applies equally to a sacrificial animal which is to be sacrificed in fulfillment of a vow, an animal one has specified as the one will offer as an *uḍḥiyah*, and others. However, it is not permissible to give a non-Muslim any of an animal one has designated as the animal one will offer as an *uḍḥiyah*, or of one which is to be sacrificed in fulfillment of a vow. As for an *uḍḥiyah* which is being offered voluntarily, one may give some of it to a non-Muslim; moreover, it is desirable to give away the best part of it as charity, to give away the medium-quality part as a gift, and to eat the most inferior part. If the *uḍḥiyah* is being offered on behalf of an orphan, his or her guardian is not permitted to donate any of the animal as charity on the orphan's behalf or to give any of it away as a gift; rather, he must save it for the orphan himself or herself. One may drink of the animal's milk unless it has young, in which case it is forbidden to drink so much that it would detract from the amount required by the animal's nursing young, and if someone does so, he must provide the value of what he drank. As for milk which is left over after the animal's young has nursed, this may be drunk. It is likewise permissible to shear the wool of a sacrificial animal if it offers some benefit toward helping the animal become fatter; however, if it helps toward the animal's survival, by protecting it, for example, from heat and cold, shearing is not permissible. One may not give the butcher his wages out of the animal he has slaughtered; however, one may give him some of the animal as charity or as a gift. One is forbidden to sell a sacrificial animal's skin, packsaddle or blanket, or to sell any part of the animal, for that matter. However, one may make use of the animal's skin, packsaddle or blanket, by praying on it, for example, using it as a sieve, etc. One may also donate such items as charity. If a sacrificial animal which has been designated as an *uḍḥiyah* gives birth, her young must be slaughtered with her, whether the designation occurred before or after she became pregnant. It is recommended that one slaughter a fetus which emerges lifeless from its mother's womb, or one which exhibits movements like those of an animal which has been slaughtered; as for one which is born alive and viable, slaughtering it is obligatory. The ritual slaughter of a fetus is thus included in the slaughter of its mother, whether hair has begun growing on its body or not. It is recommended that a camel be slaughtered while it is standing up and with its left hind leg tied; in addition, it is recommended that in one's treatment of the *uḍḥiyah*, one adhere to the practices detailed below in the section dealing with the proper manner of slaughtering a sacrificial animal.

The manner in which the slaughter of an *uḍḥiyah* (termed *dhakāh*) is to be undertaken

The term *dhakāh* refers to the slaughter of an animal whose flesh one is permitted to eat in one of three different ways: (1) *dhabḥ*, (2) *naḥr*, or (3) *'aqr* in accordance with conditions which are detailed below by each of the four schools.[170]

---

170. The Hanafis divide *dhakāh* which is in accordance with Islamic law into two categories; (a) obligatory *dhakāh*, and (b) optional *dhakāh*.

Obligatory *dhakāh* (*dhakāt al-ḍarūrah*) refers to a wound which is inflicted on any part of the animal's body, provided that it is not a tame animal. Hence, if a sheep, a goat, a cow or a camel goes wild and it is impossible to slaughter it in the usual manner and if, after this, someone shoots it with an arrow, thereby wounding it in some part of its body, drawing blood and killing it, its flesh may be eaten. Similarly, if a camel bolts and its owner is unable to overtake it without assistance from a group of people, he may shoot it; if, in this situation, the animal is wounded, bleeds and dies of this wound, its flesh may be eaten. Another applicable situation is one in which an animal attacks someone, as a result of which the person shoots it in self-defense and kills it; in such a case, the animal's flesh may be eaten if the person who shot it wounded it and caused it to bleed. Similarly, if an animal falls into a well with the result that it is impossible to slaughter it, and if someone shoots it and wounds it and knows that it died as a result of the wound, its flesh may be eaten; moreover, even if it is not known whether the animal died of the wound or from some other cause, its flesh may be eaten. However, if it is known that the animal died from some cause other than the wound, its flesh may not be eaten. Similarly, if a cow has a difficult delivery and a man places his hand inside her womb and slaughters her young, its flesh may be eaten. If he is not able to slaughter the young and simply injures it, its flesh may still be eaten, whereas if he is able neither to slaughter it nor to injure it, its flesh may not be eaten even if its mother is slaughtered, since the slaughter of the mother does not necessarily include the slaughter of her young according to Abū Ḥanīfah. Abū Yūsuf and Muḥammad hold that if the young was fully formed, it may be eaten if its mother was slaughtered based on the hadith that states, "the slaughter (*dhakāh*) of a fetus is included in the slaughter of its mother." As for Imam Abū Ḥanīfah, he understood this hadith to be a simile meaning simply that the slaughter of the fetus is like the slaughter of its mother.

As for optional *dhakāh* (*dhakāt al-ikhtiyār*) it refers to the act of slaughtering (*dhabḥ*) an animal by making a slit which extends from the top of the throat to the top of the chest. Specifically, it involves cutting the two jugular veins, which are two large veins located along either side of the front of the neck, as well as the trachea and the esophagus. In order for the operation to be complete, three of the above must be cut, since most of an entity is subject to the same ruling as the entity in its entirety. Hence, it is necessary to cut the trachea or the esophagus along with the two jugular veins, or to cut one jugular vein along with the trachea and the esophagus. Moreover, some hold that it is necessary to cut both the trachea and the esophagus along with one of the jugular veins. When cutting has been done in the aforementioned manner, the act of performing *dhabḥ* is legally acceptable and the flesh of the animal thus slaughtered may be eaten regardless of whether the slaughtering was done above or below the Adam's apple.

In addition, the Hanafis stipulate the following three conditions for the validity of *dhakāh*: (1) The person who does the slaughtering must be a Muslim, a Jew or a Christian, whether he is a foreigner or not. Christians are considered to include Sabeans, since the Sabeans recognize Jesus, may peace be upon him, while Jews are considered to include Samaritans, since the Samaritans recognize the law of Moses, may peace be upon him. Hence, the flesh of animals slaughtered by all these groups may be eaten. However, sacrificial animals slaughtered by anyone else, including idol-worshipers, Magians and apostates from Islam, may not be eaten. Nor may a Muslim eat the flesh of an animal slaughtered by a Druze, since the Druzes do not acknowledge any divinely inspired book of revelation. Lastly, if a Christian invokes the name of Christ over his sacrificial animal, a Muslim will not be permitted to eat of it. (2) The animal slaughtered must not be a game animal hunted within the Meccan precincts, since the flesh of such an animal may not be eaten even if the person who slaughtered it was not in a state of ritual consecration. (3) The person who does the slaughtering must not have deliberately neglected to invoke the name of God over the animal as he slaughtered it; if the omission was unintentional, however, the flesh of the animal may still be eaten.

The following conditions must be met in connection with the *tasmiyah*: (a) The *tasmiyah* must be in the form of a pure invocation of God; for example, one might mention any of the names of God Almighty, whether accompanied by a descriptive phrase, such as "God, the Most Gracious", or accompanied by expressions of praise or glorification. As for mentioning God's name in conjunction with a supplication, for example, by one's saying, "O God, forgive me", this will render the sacrifice invalid and it may not be eaten. It is deemed desirable to say, "In the name of God, God is greatest" (*bismillāh, Allāhu akbar*). (b) The *tasmiyah* must be uttered by the same person who is undertaking the slaughter as he slaughters, by the person shooting the game as he shoots, or by the person sending out the hunting dog as he sends it out. If the *tasmiyah* is uttered by someone other than the person responsible for killing the animal, its flesh may not be eaten. (c) The slaughter must take place following the *tasmiyah* and before a transition to another situation. Hence, if someone utters the *tasmiyah*, then occupies himself with eating or drinking, and if the time which elapses between the *tasmiyah* and the slaughter is prolonged, the slaughtering will not be valid; otherwise, however, it will be valid. As for the criterion for what constitutes a 'long' time, it is whatever period of time is perceived as 'long' by an observer. (d) The person doing the slaughtering must not intend the *tasmiyah* for some other purpose, such as seeking a blessing, as he commences the act of slaughtering. If he does so, or if he intends something else altogether other than slaughtering, the animal slaughtered may not be eaten. If, on the other hand, the person doing the slaughtering has no conscious intention to begin with, the *tasmiyah* will render valid the sacrifice of a young boy who knows how to utter the *tasmiyah* even if he does not know that it is a condition for the validity of the sacrifice, properly speaking. The same ruling applies to someone who is drunk but who has sufficient presence of mind to utter the *tasmiyah*, and to someone who is insane. In sum, if any of these persons (a young child, a drunk person, or an insane person) properly performs the act of slaughtering and mentions the name of God, the flesh of his sacrifice may be eaten.

The flesh of an animal slaughtered by someone who is mute or uncircumcised may be eaten without any undesirability attached thereto. Moreover, it is permissible to slaughter with anything that will cut through the veins that have to be cut through and which will cause the blood to flow; hence, one may slaughter with a knife, with blue cane bark, with a piece of millepore (a type of coral), flint, etc., but not with a tooth or a claw, neither of which may be used if they are still attached; if they are detached, however, they may be used, although it is undesirable to do so because of the torment which they could cause to the animal, such as slaughtering with a dull knife which does not cut properly. If someone slaughters an animal (by means of *naḥr*) for a dignitary as a means of currying favor with him, the animal's flesh may not be eaten because the person concerned devoted it to someone other than God; if, by contrast, someone slaughters an animal for a guest as a way of honoring him, this is acceptable, even if the host offers the guest something other than the slaughtered animal at the actual meal.

* * *

The Malikis define *dhakāh* which is consistent with Islamic law as that which renders it permissible to eat voluntarily of the flesh of a terrestrial animal. They divide *dhakāh* into four types: (1) *dhabḥ*, (2) *naḥr*, (3) *'aqr*, and (4) any act by virtue of which an animal loses its life, and by any means.

The first type of slaughtering, namely, *dhabḥ*, is to be practiced on cattle, buffaloes, sheep, goats, birds, wild animals, and animals which may be physically overcome or hunted with the exception of the giraffe, which is to be slaughtered by means of *naḥr*. The type of slaughtering referred to as *dhabḥ* is defined by the Malikis as cutting the trachea and the two jugular veins from the front with a sharp instrument and with a conscious intention. It is not necessary when performing *dhabḥ* to cut the esophagus. However, it is necessary that the person doing the slaughtering be a Muslim who has reached the age of discernment, or a Jew or a Christian. The person doing the slaughtering must not deliberately keep his hand raised for a long time before completing the act of slaughtering.

In order for it to be permissible to eat of the animal slaughtered by a Christian or a Jew, the following conditions must be met: (1) The person must slaughter an animal which it is permissible for him to eat based on our law. (2) He must not invoke a name other than God's when performing the slaughter (a topic which was discussed above in the section on what occurs if a Jew or a Christian slaughters an *uḍḥiyah*). (3) The slaughtering must be done in the presence of a Muslim who has reached the age of discernment and who is knowledgeable concerning the rulings pertaining to *dhakāh* if the Jew or the Christian is among those who consider it permissible to eat an animal which has died on its own. Moreover, it is not permissible to eat the flesh of a creature that does not have separate toes—such as a camel, a duck, a goose or a giraffe—and which has been slaughtered by a Jew, since the Jews are forbidden to consume such creatures, and it is confirmed in our own law that this is forbidden to them. Hence, if a Jew slaughters an animal or a bird belonging to this class, it may not be eaten; as for those creatures which they are permitted to eat by their own law, such as doves, pigeons, chickens, etc., they may be eaten by Muslims if they are slaughtered by a Jew.

The second type of ritual slaughtering, namely, *naḥr*, is to be used with camels, giraffes, and elephants. Its use is undesirable in connection with cows and buffaloes, horses, mules and wild donkeys. The act of *naḥr* is defined as a piercing of the upper chest, without raising one's hand for a long time before completing the act; *naḥr* must be performed with conscious intention by a Muslim who has reached the age of discernment or by a Jew or a Christian.

The third type of ritual slaughter, namely, *'aqr*, is to be used when slaughtering a wild animal which can only be overpowered with difficulty, whether it is a bird or some other type of creature. *'Aqr* is defined as the wounding of either a wild animal or a marked game animal with a sharp instrument by a Muslim who has reached the age of discernment; *'aqr* must be accompanied by conscious intention and by the utterance of the *tasmiyah*. *'Aqr* is not valid if it is performed by a non-Muslim, although some hold that it may validly be performed by a Jew or a Christian as in the case of *dhabḥ*. Nor may *'aqr* may be performed by a young child or someone who is insane or drunk. It is not permissible to kill a domestic animal by means of *'aqr* if it breaks loose; hence, if a cow, a sheep, a goat or a camel bolts, it may not be killed by means of *'aqr*. Similarly, if an animal falls into a well and it can only be slaughtered by means of *'aqr*, and if it is slaughtered by this means, it may not be eaten. Nor is it permissible to perform *'aqr* with a stick or an unpointed rock, although it may be done with a bullet, since a bullet is more effective than a sharp instrument.

As for type (4) above, namely, any act by means of which an animal is caused to die, this method is employed for bloodless creatures such as locusts, worms, etc., since such creatures are ritually slaughtered by putting them to death by any means available, such as fire, cutting with teeth, striking with a stick, etc.; the *dhakāh* of such creatures must also be accompanied by a conscious intention. Lastly, all four types of *dhakāh* must be accompanied by the mention of the name of God Almighty by a mindful, capable Muslim; however, if someone forgets to utter the *tasmiyah* or is incapable of doing so, as in the case of someone who is mute, his sacrifice may still be eaten.

* * *

The Shafiis define *dhakāh* which is in conformity with Islamic law as cutting through both the trachea and the esophagus; if either of them remains intact, the animal slaughtered may not be eaten. The animal must be fully alive before it is slaughtered if there is some cause to which its death might be attributed; otherwise, it is not necessary that the animal be fully alive before being slaughtered. Hence, if an animal which is ill without there being some other cause to which its death might be attributed is slaughtered when it is breathing its last, it will be permissible to eat of its flesh even if the blood does not gush out when it is slaughtered and even if it does not make violent jerking motions. The term 'fully alive' is used to describe an animal that exhibits voluntary movement as well as other signs which would indicate that life is present. One such sign is that if the animal's trachea and esophagus are cut, the blood gushes out or the animal makes violent movements. It makes no difference whether the trachea and the esophagus are cut from above or below the Adam's apple provided that (once the cutting has been performed), there is a complete ring above and a complete ring below; otherwise, it will not be permissible to eat the slaughtered animal since, in this latter case, the animal would be deemed to have been killed by tearing rather than slaughtering. The cutting of the two jugular veins is an emulation of the Sunnah, and if the entire head is cut off, this is also sufficient.

As for an animal which is not tame, such as a sheep, a goat or a cow which has gone wild, a camel that has bolted, a gazelle in the desert and a beast that has fallen into a well and cannot be reached so as to be slaughtered, it is to be killed by means of *'aqr* in any part of its body with something commonly associated with the taking of life. Hence, *'aqr* cannot be carried out with a hoof or a shoe or by lightly scratching the animal.

In order for it to be permissible to eat of the flesh of a slaughtered animal, the following conditions must be met: (1) The person who does the slaughtering must have intended to kill an individual or a particular species. Hence, if someone shoots something, thinking that it is a stone or an inedible animal, after which it becomes apparent that it is an animal which may be eaten, it is permissible to eat of it because the person who killed it was intending to strike a particular individual. Similarly, if someone shot at a flock of gazelles and struck one gazelle, or if he intended to strike one gazelle and instead struck another, it would be permissible to eat of the flesh of the gazelle which was struck because it belonged to the same species which the hunter had intended. If, on the other hand, the person intends to strike neither a particular individual nor a species, the animal struck may not be eaten. Hence, if a knife falls out of someone's hand and strikes an animal, causing it to die, or if an animal strikes up against a knife and dies as a result, or if someone swings with his sword and strikes the site where an animal is being slaughtered, it will not be permissible to eat of the flesh of the animal slaughtered due to the lack of intention. Moreover, the process by which the animal is put to death should be restricted solely to a rapid cutting of its trachea and its esophagus; hence, if one person set about cutting the trachea and the esophagus while someone else set about removing its entrails while a third was piercing its side, the animal's flesh could not be eaten. (2) The animal must be fully alive before being slaughtered when there is some other cause to which its death could be attributed. Hence, if an animal has been wounded, a roof has fallen on top of it, etc., and if it is still fully alive and is then slaughtered, it will be permissible to eat of the animal's flesh. Evidence that the animal was fully live before being slaughtered is found in the fact that, when the slaughter takes place, the animal makes violent movements and its blood gushes out; moreover, the animal may be said to have been fully alive before being slaughtered even if it is certain that, one hour after the slaughter, it would have died. Otherwise, it is not permissible to eat of its flesh due to the presence of some other cause to which its death could be attributed, namely, the wound the animal had sustained or the roof that had fallen on top of it. Nevertheless, it is not necessary for there to be absolute certainty that at the time of slaughter, the animal was fully alive; rather, it is sufficient for there to be good reason to believe that it was. If, before the animal was slaughtered, it had reached a state in which it had lost its vision and the ability to engage in voluntary movement due to an illness or hunger, it will still be permissible to eat its flesh even if, when it was slaughtered, its blood did not gush out and it did not make violent movements. If, by contrast, an animal has surfeited itself so badly that it is about to die, it will not be permissible to eat of its flesh based on the officially recognized view if, when it is slaughtered, its blood does not gush out and it makes no violent movements. (3) The animal slaughtered must be one whose flesh it is permissible to eat; thus, it is not permissible to slaughter an animal whose flesh may not be eaten even if it was killed to put it out of its misery for one reason or another. (4) The slaughtering must be done with a sharp instrument, even if it happens to be made of reed, wood, gold or silver; however, slaughtering may not be done with teeth, claws, hooves and other [types of] bones. If an animal is killed with something that is not sharp, as in a case where it is beaten with a rifle or with a pointless arrow or is strangled to death with a net, its flesh may not be eaten. (5) The cutting must be done at one fell swoop; hence, if someone cuts the trachea and then pauses, and if the pause between the first and second blows would be agreed based on commonly accepted standards to be 'long', the animal must be fully alive at the time of the second blow. However, if the first and second blows would be considered by commonly accepted standards not to be separate, it is not necessary for the animal to be fully alive when the second blow is begun. An example of such a situation is one in which the person doing the slaughtering raises the knife and lowers it again immediately, or in which he throws the knife down because it is dull, then immediately takes up another one, or in which he drops the knife, then immediately picks it up again or quickly picks up a different one, or turns the knife over before cutting what remains; all such situations are acceptable since they involve no separation between the first and second blows. (6) The person who does the slaughtering must not be in a state of *iḥrām* if the animal slaughtered is a wild, terrestrial game animal; otherwise, the animal's flesh may not be eaten. (7) The person who does the slaughtering must be a Muslim, a Christian or a Jew, not a Magian, an idol-worshiper or an apostate. Thus, *dhakāh* performed by a Christian or a Jew is valid just as it would be if performed by a Muslim. Based on the best attested view, *dhakāh* is also valid [the text reads in the negative here, but the context suggests that the affirmative is intended – t.n.] if performed by someone who is insane or drunk or someone who has not reached the age of discernment, even if the animal is one which may not be overcome, although it is undesirable. It is also undesirable for *dhakāh* to be performed by someone who is blind. It is not necessary when performing *dhakāh* to utter the *tasmiyah*, but it is an emulation of the Sunnah, and if the name of God is mentioned in conjunction with some other name (as in a case where someone says, "In the name of God and the name of Muḥammad") with the intention of associating the other entity with God, he will be guilty of unbelief and it will not be permissible to eat of the sacrifice. If no such association is intended, the flesh of the sacrifice may be eaten, although it is undesirable to do so if the person's intention was to seek a blessing for himself [through the entity invoked]. It is likewise forbidden to eat of the sacrifice if the person, when mentioning the name of the other entity, did not specify whether his intention was association of other entities with the Divine (*shirk*) or the seeking of a blessing.

* * *

The Hanbalis hold that *dhakāh* as carried out in accordance with Islamic law is the slaughtering (*dhabḥ*) of an animal which can be overtaken, whose flesh may be lawfully eaten, and which lives on land or the like, with the exception of locusts and other similar creatures which are not slaughtered (either by *dhabḥ* or by *naḥr*). The act of *dhakāh* is performed by cutting through the trachea and the esophagus, whereas *naḥr* takes place by cutting through the upper chest, specifically, the depression located between the neck and the chest. It is not necessary to cut through the jugular veins, i.e., the two veins which flank the trachea, although it is preferable to do so. If it is impossible to slaughter an animal by means of either *dhabḥ* or *naḥr*, it is be killed by means of *ʻaqr*, that is, by shooting it with an arrow or the like anywhere in its body such that it is wounded and dies. In such a case the flesh of the animal may be eaten as game. If a camel bolts and cannot be overcome, or if an animal whose flesh may lawfully be eaten falls into a well such that it is impossible to slaughter it by means of *dhabḥ*, and if it is killed by means of *ʻaqr* instead, its flesh may be eaten provided that it dies of the wound caused by the act of *ʻaqr*. If the animal dies of some other cause, its flesh may not be eaten even if the wound was serious enough to have killed it. Moreover, it is necessary for the person who shot the animal to fulfill the same conditions that must be fulfilled by someone who slaughters an animal. Hence, if the shooting is done by a Magian, for example, the animal may not be eaten.

In order for it to be lawful to eat of a slaughtered animal, the following four conditions must be fulfilled: (1) One must say *bismillāh* when moving one's hand in order to perform the act of *dhabḥ*, *naḥr* or *ʻaqr*. No other phrase will take the place of the *tasmiyah*; hence, if someone were to utter the phrase, *subḥān Allāh*, this would not be acceptable. However, it is permissible to utter the *tasmiyah* in a language other than Arabic even if the person doing the slaughtering is capable of speaking Arabic. It is an emulation of the Sunnah to utter the words *Allāhu akbar*, by saying, for example, *bismillāh wa Allāhu akbar*. If the person doing the slaughtering is mute, he is to gesture with his head toward the sky and give a signal to indicate the *tasmiyah* such that others will understand that this is what he intends, and this will suffice to render it permissible to eat of the animal's flesh. If the *tasmiyah* is omitted deliberately or out of ignorance, the flesh of the animal slaughtered may not be eaten based on the words of God Almighty, "Hence, eat not of that over which God's name has not been pronounced" (6:121). However, if it is omitted unintentionally, the animal's flesh may be eaten based on the hadith passed down on the authority of Shaddād Ibn Saʻd on the authority of the Prophet, who said, "An animal sacrificed by a Muslim may lawfully be eaten even if he did not utter the *tasmiyah*, provided that he did not omit it deliberately." It is also necessary that one intend the *tasmiyah* to apply to the same animal one is slaughtering; hence, if someone utters the *tasmiyah* over a sheep or a goat, then slaughters some other animal in association with the same *tasmiyah*, it will not be permissible to eat of the animal slaughtered. It does no harm, however, for there to be a slight pause between the *tasmiyah* and the *dhabḥ*. Hence, someone may utter the *tasmiyah*, then speak, then slaughter the animal. Similarly, if someone lays a sheep or a goat down in order to slaughter it and utters the *tasmiyah*, then casts down his knife and picks up another one, returns someone's greeting of peace or drinks some water before performing the slaughter, the animal's flesh may still be eaten. Moreover, these rulings apply equally to Muslims, Christians and Jews. However, if a Christian invokes the name of Christ when slaughtering, the slaughtered animal may not be eaten. Lastly, if it is not known whether the person slaughtering uttered the *tasmiyah* or not, or whether he invoked the name of God or some other name, the flesh of the animal slaughtered may still be eaten. (2) The person who performs the slaughter, be it *dhabḥ*, *naḥr* or *'aqr*, must be legally competent. In other words, he must be in full possession of his mental faculties or have the conscious intention of performing *dhakāh*. Hence, if the knife falls on the throat of a sheep or a goat and slaughters it, it will not be permissible to eat of its flesh due to the absence of the intention to perform *dhakāh*. In addition, the person doing the slaughtering must be a Muslim, a Christian or a Jew, even if he is a citizen of a non-Muslim state which is at war with Muslims, and even if he is a Christian of the tribe of Banū Taghlib. It makes no difference whether the person who does the slaughtering is a male or a female, free or a slave; moreover, he or she can be in a state of major ritual impurity, menstruating, experiencing post-partum bleeding, blind, or a *fāsiq*. The flesh of an animal slaughtered by someone who is insane or drunk, or by a young child who has not reached the age of discernment may not be lawfully eaten since such persons are not capable of conscious intention; however, an animal slaughtered by a child who has reached the age of discernment will be acceptable even if he or she is under ten years of age. It is not permissible to eat of an animal slaughtered by a Magian, an apostate, an idol-worshiper, an atheist [*zindīq*, a term used variously to refer to a hypocrite, and/or to a Zoroastrian – t.n.], a Druze, or anyone who acknowledges no divinely revealed scripture based on the words of God Almighty, "And the food of those who have been vouchsafed revelation aforetime is lawful to you" (5:5); this Qur'anic verse is thus taken to mean that the food of anyone else is forbidden to Muslims. (3) The animal must be slaughtered with a sharpened instrument which cuts through or pierces with its edge rather than by virtue of its weight. Such an instrument may be made of iron, such as a knife, a sword, an arrowhead or a spearhead, or of stone, wood, or bone. As for a tooth, a claw or a nail, one may not validly perform *dhakāh* with these, whether they are attached or detached. (4) Both the trachea and the esophagus must be cut through. If a Christian or a Jew slaughters something which he is forbidden to eat according to his own law and if it is confirmed in our law that it is forbidden to him, it may not be eaten [the text reads, "may be eaten" – t.n.]; the same applies if a Jew slaughters a creature that does not have separate toes such as a camel, an ostrich or a duck, since God Almighty declares that He has prohibited such creatures to the Jews. The ruling applies if a Jew slaughters some animal which he claims is forbidden to him but which our own law does not confirm as being forbidden to him, or if he slaughters an animal whose lungs are attached to its ribs, since they claim that they are forbidden to eat the lung.

It is an emulation of the Sunnah to slaughter camels by means of *naḥr* according to the Shafiis, the Hanafis and the Hanbalis; for the view of the Malikis, see below.[171] It is likewise an emulation of the Sunnah to employ *naḥr* in the slaughter of long-necked creatures, whereas everything else—including cattle, sheep and goats—is to be slaughtered by means of *dhabḥ*.

It is an emulation of the Sunnah to sharpen one's knife first, and to do so far away from the animal to be slaughtered. One also emulates the Sunnah by not slaughtering one animal while another looks on and by having the animal to be slaughtered lie down on its left side if it is a goat, a sheep or a cow. Then, before slaughtering the animal, one emulates the Sunnah by saying, "O God, this is from You and for You. 'Behold, unto Him who brought into being the heavens and the earth have I turned my face, having turned away from all that is false; and I am not of those who ascribe divinity to aught beside Him' (6:79). 'Behold, my prayer, and [all] my acts of worship, and my living and my dying are for God [alone], the Sustainer of all the worlds' (6:162)."

It is undesirable to break the animal's neck before the life has gone completely out of it and it has become still. It is likewise undesirable to skin it, cut any member off of it or pluck its feathers before it is completely dead. It is also undesirable to face in any direction other than the *qiblah* or to cause the animal any needless suffering.

We have thus fully explicated the aforementioned topics. As for what may and may not lawfully be eaten and what may and may not lawfully be worn, we shall discuss these matters in the second volume of this work; hence, whoever wishes to learn more about these questions may refer to the second volume if he so desires.[172] And God is the Source of all success.

---

171. The Malikis hold that it is obligatory to slaughter camels, giraffes and elephants by means of *naḥr*, since they are edible, and that if they are slaughtered by means of *dhabḥ*, they may not be eaten. As for other livestock, wild animals and birds, they must be slaughtered by means of *dhabḥ*, and if they are slaughtered by means of *naḥr*, it is not permissible to eat them. Nevertheless, both means are permissible, though *dhabḥ* is preferable in connection with cattle, buffaloes, horses, mules, and wild donkeys. The aforementioned rulings apply to situations in which one has a choice concerning which method of slaughtering one will use. However, when sheer necessity reigns, as in a situation in which there is no instrument with which to slaughter the animal, or in which the animal has fallen into a hole such that it is not possible to slaughter it by means of either *dhabḥ* or *naḥr*, it is possible to reverse the above ruling, that is, by slaughtering by means of *dhabḥ* that which would normally be slaughtered by means of *naḥr*, and vice-versa [or slaughtering by means of *'aqr* that which would otherwise have been slaughtered by means of *dhabḥ* or *naḥr*], out of necessity. And God knows best. May God's blessings and peace be upon the one who brought the divinely revealed law, our master Muḥammad, and upon his descendents and companions.

172. 'Abdulraḥmān al-Jazirī's entire work entitled, *Al-Fiqh 'alā al-Madhāhib al-Arba'ah* consists of five volumes, of which this book represents Volume I [t.n.].

Glossary of Terms

Abstersion: See *istinjā'*.

Adhān: The call to prayer issued by a muezzin.

'Adl: A term used to describe someone who is known to be reliable and of good character.

al-'Aṣr : The mid-afternoon prayer, and the third of the five obligatory daily prayers.

Āmīn: "Amen!"

'Aqr: A form of ritual slaughter, *'aqr* refers to the wounding of an animal with a sharp instrument; it is to be used when slaughtering a wild animal that can only be overpowered with difficulty, and in situations in which neither *dhabḥ* nor *naḥr* may be used.

A'ūdhu billāhi min al-shayṭān al-rajīm: "I seek refuge in God from the accursed Satan."

Basmalah: Utterance of the words *bismillāh al-raḥmān al-raḥīm* ("in the name of God, the Most Gracious, the Most Merciful").

Bunduqī: I was not able to determine the value of a *bunduqī*; however, the term refers to a type of gold attributed to the city of Venice (Arabic, *al-Bunduqiyah*).

Compensation: See *jazā'*.

Cubit: See *dhirā'*.

Cupping: See *ḥijāmah*.

Dhabḥ: The act of slaughtering an animal by cutting through the trachea and the two jugular veins. The various schools of jurisprudence differ over some details pertaining to this definition. *Dhabḥ* is defined by the Malikis, for example, as cutting the trachea and the two jugular veins from the front with a sharp instrument and with a conscious intention.

Dhakāh: Generally speaking, *dhakāh* refers to ritual slaughter that renders it permissible under Islamic law to eat of the flesh of a terrestrial animal, with the exact components of *dhakāh* differing from one school to another. The Shafiis, for example, stipulate that *dhakāh* must entail cutting through both the trachea and the esophagus; if either of them remains intact, the animal slaughtered may not be eaten.

Optional *dhakāh* (*dhakāt al-ikhtiyār*) refers to the act of slaughtering (*dhabḥ*) an animal by making a slit which extends from the top of the throat to the top of the chest. Specifically, it involves cutting the two jugular veins as well as the trachea and the esophagus. According to the Hanafis, three of the above must be cut, since the greater part of an entity is subject to the same ruling as the entity in its entirety. Hence, it is necessary to cut the trachea or the esophagus along with the two jugular veins, or to cut one jugular vein along with the trachea and the esophagus. Moreover, some hold that it is necessary to cut both the trachea and the esophagus along with one of the jugular veins. As for obligatory *dhakāh* (*dhakāt al-ḍarūrah*), it refers to a wound inflicted on any part of the body of an animal that is not tame (for example, a sheep, a goat, a cow or a camel that goes wild and cannot be slaughtered in the usual manner). The wound must cause blood to flow and kill the animal in order for it to be permissible to eat its flesh. (Obligatory *dhakāh* is thus similar to the concept of *'aqr*, particularly as described by the Hanbalis.)

Dhikr (plural, *adhkār*): Literally, 'mentioning' or 'remembering', the term *dhikr* refers to the utterance of words and phrases which are repeated as a means of praising God and holding Him in remembrance.

Dhimmī: A Christian or a Jew living under Muslim rule.

Dhirā': A measure of length and/or area equal to approximately 47 centimeters, or 18.5 inches. (In his *Mu'jam Lughat al-Fuqahā', English-Arabic-French*, Muḥammad Rawwas al-Qal'aji (Dar al-Nafaés, 1996) gives two equivalents for the cubit: 62 cm and 47 cm. For the purposes of this translation I have adopted the smaller of the two, since it appears to be more consistent with the lengths and areas being referred to in the book's various discussions.)

Dirham: A unit of weight equal to approximately 3.12 grams. The term *dirham* can also refer to a silver coin which weighs 2.812 grams.

Du'ā' al-iftitāḥ (prayer of commencement): A prayer the utterance of which following *takbīrat al-iḥrām* as ritual prayer is begun is viewed by the Shafiis as an emulation of the Sunnah. The Shafii version is as follows: "I turn my face with a pure heart and in full surrender toward the One who created the heavens and the earth, and I am not among those who associate created beings with the Divine. My prayer, my devotion, my life and my death belong to God, the Sustainer of the worlds, who has no partner. Thus have I been commanded, and I am among those who surrender themselves to God." (*Wajjahtu wajhī lilladhī faṭara al-samawāti wal-arḍa ḥanīfan musliman, wa mā anā min al-mushrikīn. Inna ṣalāti wa naskī wa maḥyāyā wa mamātī lillāhi rabb al-'ālamīn, lā sharīka lah, wa bi dhalika umirtu wa anā min al-muslimīn.*) According to the Hanafis, the wording to be used for this prayer is as follows: "Glory be to You, O God, and praise! May Your name be blessed and Your majesty exalted! There is no god but You!" (*subḥānuk Allāhumma wa biḥamdika, wa tabāraka ismuk wa ta'āla jadduk wa lā ilāha ghayruk*).

Du'ā' al-qunūt (prayer of obedience): "O God, guide me with those You have guided, grant me wholeness with those to whom You have granted wholeness, watch over me with those You have watched over, bless me in that which You have given, and protect me from the evil of what You have decreed, for You alone are the One who decrees and disposes. No one to whom You grant your succor will be disgraced, nor will anyone whom You oppose enjoy honor and glory. Blessed are You, O Lord, and exalted!" (*Allāhumma ihdinī fī man hadayt, wa 'āfinī fī man 'āfayt, wa tawwalanī fī man tawwallayt, wa bārik lī fī mā a'ṭayt, wa qinī sharra mā qaḍayt. Fa'innak taqḍī wa lā yuqḍā 'alayka, wa innahu lā yudhallu man wālayt, wa lā ya'izzu man 'ādayt. Tabārakta rabbanā wa ta'ālayt.*) Another version, passed down by Imām Mālik, is as follows: "O God, we seek Your aid and Your forgiveness, placing in You our faith and full confidence. We submit ourselves to You and refuse to follow those who deny Your truth. O God, You alone do we worship. To You do we pray and before You do we prostrate ourselves. It is You for whose sake we strive and We make haste to do Your bidding. We hope to receive Your mercy and we fear Your grievous chastisement; indeed, Your chastisement will overtake those who deny Your truth" (*Allāhumma innā nasta'īnuk wa nastaghfiruk wa nu'minu bika wa natawakkalu 'alayka and nakhḍa'u laka wa nakhla'u, wa natruku man yakfuruk. Allāhumma iyyāka na'budu wa laka nuṣallī wa nasjud, wa ilayka nas'ā wa naḥfud. Narjū raḥmataka wa nakhāfu 'adhābaka al-jidd. Inna 'adhābaka bil-kāfirīna mulḥiq.*)

Al-ḍuḥā (mid-morning prayer): A voluntary prayer consisting of two *rak'ahs* performed between the dawn prayer (*al-ṣubḥ*) and the noon prayer (*al-ẓuhr*).

Farḍ (obligation): A term used to refer to any act which, under Islamic law, one merits reward for performing and punishment for neglecting.

Fāsiq: A Muslim who commits actions which are classified as major sins under Islamic law, or who habitually engages in minor sins.

The *Fātiḥah*: The first chapter of the Qur'ān.

Fidyah (redemption): A payment made to compensate for having departed from the required or ideal practice in certain situations, such as a woman's covering her face while in a state of ritual consecration (*iḥrām*), or someone's not having fasted certain days of Ramaḍān.

The final testimony: See *al-tashahhud al-akhīr*.

Ghusl: Major ritual ablutions, which are required by major ritual impurity (*al-ḥadath al-akbar*). *Ghusl* involves, first, the performance of *wuḍū'*, or minor ritual ablutions, followed by the act of covering one's entire body with water in a specified manner.

Ḥadath: A state of ritual impurity attributed by the Lawgiver to someone's entire body when there has been sexual discharge (referred to as *al-ḥadath al-akbar*), or to some members of the body when something has occurred to invalidate one's ablutions such as passing wind, stool, urine and the like (referred to as *al-ḥadath al-aṣghar*, or minor ritual impurity); the term *ḥadath* may also refer to the occurrence of something that brings about such a state of ritual impurity, such as the secretion of urine or stool, passing gas, etc.

Al-ḥadath al-akbar: A state of major ritual impurity.

Al-ḥadath al-aṣghar: A state of minor ritual impurity.

Ḥadīth: A Prophetic Tradition, that is, a report of words uttered by the Prophet or actions performed by him.

Hady: An animal to be offered for sacrifice within the sacred Meccan precincts.

Ḥajj: The major rite of pilgrimage to Mecca required of every Muslim able to undertake it once in his or her lifetime.

Al-ḥamdu lillāh: "Praise be to God!"

Ḥanūṭ: A mixture of perfumes used especially for embalming.

Ḥijamah: Cupping, which is the process of drawing blood from the body by making superficial incisions in the skin and the application of a cupping glass.

Al-ḥijr: Also referred to as "Ishmael's precinct", the *ḥijr* is the space between the wall of the Ka'bah that extends from the Iraqi corner to the Syrian corner (the northern wall) and the short, semi-circular wall located six cubits out from it.

'Iddah: The legally prescribed waiting period for a Muslim woman who has been divorced or widowed before she may remarry.

Ifrād: The act of entering *iḥrām* for the *ḥajj* alone, completing the rites for the *ḥajj*, then entering *iḥrām* again for performance of the *'umrah*.

Iḥrām: The state of ritual consecration into which one enters by intending to enter upon the greater or lesser pilgrimage (i.e., the *ḥajj* or the *'umrah*).

Imāmah: The act of serving as a prayer leader.

Irdabb: A unit of measure equal to 150 kilos; it is also equal to 24 *ṣā's*.

Iqṭ: A kind of cheese made from camel's buttermilk.

Al-Istidhkār: An exhaustive commentary on the contents of *al-Muwaṭṭa'* by Imām Mālik.

Al-i'tidāl : The act of moving to a fully upright position after bowing in ritual prayer; the act of holding still for a moment or two between rising to a standing position after bowing and going down into a prostration; returning to the position one was in before bowing (that is, returning to a standing position) or prostrating (that is, to a seated position).

Iqāmah: The announcement of ritual prayer's having commenced in the mosque.

Al-'Ishā': The evening prayer, and the last of the five obligatory daily ritual prayers.

Istibrā': The act of expelling all the urine or stool one possibly can in order to make certain that nothing more remains to be eliminated.

Istiḥāḍah: Chronic vaginal bleeding.

Istijmār: The act of cleaning off bodily orifices with small stones or some other suitable material rather than water.

Istinjā' (abstersion): The act of cleaning an orifice (the vagina, the urethra or the anus) from which a ritually impure substance has been secreted, as well as the surrounding area.

Istiyāk: The act of cleaning one's gums and teeth with the use of a *miswāk*, a small stick from the *arāk* tree.

Izār: A garment, sometimes referred to as a wrapper or a loincloth, that is tied at the waist and covers the lower half of the body. The type of *izār* used for wrapping a deceased person, however, may extend all the way from the crown of the head to one's feet.

Janābah: The state of major ritual impurity resulting from sexual intercourse and/or the secretions resulting therefrom.

Jazā' (compensation): A type of payment required of someone who has failed to perform an obligation in the required manner.

Junub: In a state of major ritual impurity as a result of sexual intercourse and/or the secretions resulting therefrom.

Kaylah: A measure of weight equivalent to 2.536 kilos.

Khabath: A ritually impure substance found on one's body or clothing which renders one unable to perform actions that require one to be in a state of ritual purity. The term *khabath* may also refer to the state of ritual impurity resulting from the presence of concrete impurities, such as urine, fecal matter, and the like, on one's body or clothing.

Kharājiyah: A term referring to land which was owned by non-Arabs and which was conquered by force or through a peaceful agreement, though left in the possession of its original owners on the condition that they pay a *kharāj*, or land tax.

Laḥd: An opening at the bottom of a grave's *qiblah*-oriented wall which is spacious enough to hold the body of the deceased.

Lā ilāha illā Allāh: "There is no god but God."

Lā ḥawla wa lā quwwata illā billāh: "There is no power save in God."

Lams: The act of touching someone either with the hand or with some other part of the body.

Ma'ādin ('minerals'): Valuables extracted from under the ground such as iron, copper and the like.

Madhī: Pre-seminal fluid, discharged prior to a man's ejaculation during foreplay and the like.

al-Maghrib: The sundown prayer, and the fourth of the five obligatory daily prayers.

Maḥram (plural, *maḥārim*): A near relative whom one would not be allowed to marry under Islamic law.

Majar: A *majar* is a gold standard or measure. So named because of its attribution to the country of Hungary (*al-Majar*), the use of the *majar* was once widespread in the appraisal of women's jewelry and its value was set at 18 carats.

Marḥalah: Defined as one day's journey on a loaded camel, a *marḥalah* is equal to 8 parasangs, or 24 miles.

Mass: The act of touching someone with one's hand.

Mid-morning prayer: See *al-Ḍuḥā*.

Miḥrāb: A recess in one of the walls of a mosque indicating the *qiblah*, or direction of prayer.

Mīqāt (plural, *mawāqīt*): The place(s) along the route to Mecca for the *ḥajj* or *'umrah* at which a pilgrim must enter into a state of ritual consecration (*iḥrām*) before proceeding further.

Mithqāl: A unit of weight equal to approximately 4.24 grams for gold, and 4 grams for other things.

Monopolistic merchant: See *tājir muḥtakir*.

Mosque greeting: See *taḥiyyat al-masjid.*

Muballigh: Someone who repeats the imam's words in a loud voice during communal prayer in order to make certain that the other worshippers heard what he said.

Mudd: A measure of weigh equal to 815 grams according to the Hanafis, and 543 grams according to the Shafiis, the Hanbalis and the Malikis.

Al-multazam: The area between the door of the Ka'bah and the corner containing the Black Stone.

Muwālāh ('continuity'): The requirement that someone performing ritual ablutions wash each relevant part of the body before the part which was washed immediately previous to it has dried.

Naḥr: A form of ritual slaughter, *naḥr* is the act of piercing the upper chest, specifically, the depression located between the neck and the chest. The Malikis specify that *naḥr* is the method of slaughter to be used with camels, giraffes, and elephants.

Najāsah: Ritual impurity.

Najis: Ritually impure.

Naṣb al-Rāyah: This book, whose full title is *Naṣb al-Rāyah li Aḥādīth al-Hidāyah* ("Raising the Banner of the Hadiths of True Guidance"), contains a thorough study of all the hadiths cited in the book entitled, *al-Hidāyah* ("True Guidance") by 'Alī Ibn Abī Bakr al-Murghaynānī (d. 593 AH). *Naṣb al-Rāyah* is considered to be the most significant abridged presentation of Hanafi jurisprudence.

Niṣāb: The minimum amount of wealth one must have possessed for an entire year in order to be held accountable for paying *zakāh*.

Parasang: A unit of distance equal to approximately three miles.

Prayer for guidance: See *ṣalāt al-istikhārah.*

Prayer of commencement: See *du'ā' al-iftitāḥ*.

The prayer of fear: See *ṣalāt al-khawf.*

Prayer of obedience: See *du'ā' al-qunūt*.

Prayer of praise. See *al-thanā'*.

Problematic hemaphrodite (*khanthā mushkil*): Someone who has neither male nor female genitalia.

Prostration of forgetfulness: See *sujūd al-sahw.*

Qaraẓ: A species of sant tree (Acacia nilotica).

Qiblah: A term referring to the direction in which the Ka‘bah is located, or to the Ka‘bah itself. The term *qiblah* is also used more generally to refer to the direction in which one is required to turn when performing ritual prayer.

Qirān: The act of joining the *‘umrah* and the *ḥajj* during the *ḥajj* season based on a single act of *iḥrām*.

Qullatān (literally, ‘two pitchers full’): A *qullah* has been defined as a jar or pitcher which, if filled with water, will come to the maximum that a medium-sized individual could carry. The Shafiis estimate ‘two pitchers full’ as the equivalent of 160 liters.

Raghībah: The term used by the Maliki school to refer to the two voluntary *rak‘ahs* performed before the dawn prayer.

Rak‘ah: A unit of ritual prayer which begins with recitation and ends with prostration, and which consists of one bow and two prostrations with certain formulaic recitations associated with specific postures.

Ramal: The practice of walking with short steps and faster than one’s normal pace while circumambulating the Ka‘bah or performing the *sa‘ī*.

Ratībah (plural, *rawātib*): A Sunnah-based voluntary prayer associated with one of the five daily obligatory prayers.

Raṭl: A unit of weight equal to 384.24 grams, and alternatively, 408 grams.

Rawḍah: The spot in the Prophet’s Mosque in Medina between the Prophet’s tomb and the pulpit from which he used to preach.

Redemption: See *fidyah*.

Regular merchant: See *tājir mudīr*.

Ridā’: A garment that covers the back, the chest and the shoulders.

Rikāz: Treasure which has been buried in the ground and whose owner is unknown.

Rukn (pillar): An element of an act of worship which the Lawgiver has commanded us to perform, and without which this act of worship will be incomplete.

Ṣā‘: A measure of weight. The Hanafis define the *ṣā‘* as equivalent to approximately 3.3 kilos, while the other three schools define it as the equivalent of approximately 2.2 kilos.

Ṣadaqa Allāh al-‘aẓīm: “Truly has God spoken.”

Al-Sa‘ī: The brisk walk between al-Ṣafā and al-Marwah which is a pillar of the major pilgrimage, or *ḥajj*.

Sand ablutions. See *tayammum*.

Al-ṣalāh: Ritual prayer.

Ṣalāt al-istikhārah (prayer for guidance): Before performing two *rak‘ahs*, one says, “O God, I seek sound guidance through reliance on Your knowledge, I ask You for strength through reliance on Your power, and I request Your great bounty. For You are capable while I am not, You know while I know not, and You are fully aware of all that is hidden from human perception. O God, if You know that this undertaking would be beneficial for my spiritual condition, my earthly existence and my life in the hereafter, then give me the ability to pursue it, facilitate it for me, and bless me in it. However, if You know that it would be harmful to my spiritual condition, my earthly existence and my life in the hereafter, then put it away from me, help me to pursue that which is good wherever it may lie, and enable me to find contentment therein." (*Allāhumma, innī astakhīruka bi 'ilmika wa astaqdiruka bi qudratika, wa as'aluka min faḍlika al-'aẓīm, fa innaka taqdir wa lā aqdiru, wa ta'lamu wa lā a'lam, wa anta 'allām al-ghuyūb. Allāhumma, in kunta ta'lamu anna hādha al-amra khayrun lī fī dīnī wa ma'āshī wa 'āqibati amrī, fa aqdirhu lī wa yassirhu lī, thumma bārik lī fīhi. wa'in kunta ta'lam anna hādha al-amra sharrun lī fī dīnī wa ma'āshī wa 'āqibati amrī, faṣrifhu 'annī waṣrifnī 'anhu, wa aqdir lī al-khayra ḥaythu kāna, thumma arḍinī fīhi.*)

Ṣalāt al-khawf (the prayer of fear): A prayer consisting of two *rak'ahs* performed in a time of war first by one regiment, then by another, for fear that they would not be able to fend off an attack by the enemy if they were all praying at the same time. Another definition of the prayer of fear is a recommended, two-*rak'ah* prayer performed when one feels fearful on account of earthquakes, lightning bolts, extreme darkness, strong winds, plague, or the like.

Sami'a Allāhu li man ḥamidah: "God hears those who praise Him." This phrase is uttered during ritual prayer as the worshiper comes up from the bowing position (*al-rukū'*).

Sawīq: A kind of mush made of crushed wheat and barley.

Shādharwān: The ledge that extends two-thirds of a cubit out from the foundation of the Ka'bah; it is found on only three sides of the Ka'bah: the southwest, the southeast, and the northwest. There has been disagreement among Muslim scholars as to whether it is to be considered a part of the Ka'bah or not.

Shaf': Meaning 'an even number', the term *shaf'* refers to a voluntary prayer consisting of an even number of *rak'ahs*.

Shibr, or hand span: A unit of length or area equal to 23.32 centimeters, or 9 inches.

Al-ṣubh: The dawn prayer, and the first of the five obligatory daily prayers.

Subḥān Allāh: "Glory be to God!"

Suḥūr: The pre-dawn meal eaten during the month of Ramaḍān.

Sujūd al-sahw (prostration of forgetfulness): A set of two prostrations performed at the conclusion of a ritual prayer if the person praying forgot a certain part of the prayer concerned or is uncertain if some part thereof was not performed in the correct manner.

Sult: A wheat-like type of thin-husked or huskless barley.

Surah: A chapter of the Qur'ān.

Sutrah: Literally, a shield or screen, the term *sutrah* refers to something the worshipper places in front of him – be it a chair, a stick, a wall, a line in the ground, etc. – in order to prevent anyone from passing in front of him as he prays.

Al-tablīgh: The term *tablīgh* (literally, 'notification') as used in this context refers to one of two practices: (1) the imam's raising his voice so that he can be heard by those being led in prayer, or (2) the repetition of the imam's *takbīrat al-iḥrām* in a loud voice by one of the worshippers being led in prayer in order to ensure that the others have heard it.

Ṭahārah: Ritual purity.

Taḥiyyat al-masjid: A two-*rak'ah* prayer which one is encouraged to perform when first entering a mosque.

Ṭāhir: Ritually pure.

Ṭahūr: Possessing the capacity to render objects or persons ritually pure. Water that meets certain specified conditions may thus be described as *ṭahūr*.

Tājir mudīr (regular merchant): A merchant who buys and sells at the current price.

Takbīrat al-iḥrām: The utterance of the words *Allāhu akbar* by means of which one enters into the sanctity of ritual prayer. By uttering *takbīrat al-iḥrām*, one commits oneself to continue praying until the prayer is complete rather than interrupting it for any but the most compelling of reasons.

Takbīr al-tashrīq: The practice of uttering a formula including the phrase *Allāhu akbar* following the five daily prayers during the days subsequent to the Day of Sacrifice. One version of the formula is as follows: *Allāhu akbar Allāhu akbar, lā ilāha illā Allāh, wa Allāhu akbar Allāhu akbar, wa lillāhi al-ḥamd.*

Tājir muḥtakir (monopolistic merchant): A merchant who neither sells nor purchases at the current price but rather, hordes commodities in the hope that prices will rise.

Talbiyah: Utterance of the phrase, "Here am I at Your service, O God, here am I at Your service. Here am I at Your service; You have no partner, here am I at Your service. Praise, blessing, and dominion are Yours, and You have no partner!" (*labbayka Allāhumma, labbayk, labbayka, lā sharīka laka, labbayk. Inna al-ḥamda wal-ni'mata laka wal-mulk, lā sharīka lak*).

Tamattu': The act of performing the *'umrah* during the *ḥajj* season based on one act of *iḥrām*, being released from the state of *iḥrām*, then reentering it and performing the *ḥajj*.

Al-tarāwīḥ: A Sunnah-based set of voluntary prayers performed daily during Ramaḍān after the evening prayer. The *tarāwīḥ* prayers are performed communally and consist of a mininum of eight and a maximum of twenty *rak'ahs* performed in sets of two, and followed by the *witr*.

Tarjī': Literally, 'repetition', the term *tarjī'* is used to refer to the practice of uttering the two confessions of faith twice in a low, but audible voice, then another two times in a loud voice when issuing the *adhān*, or call to prayer.

Al-tashahhud al-akhīr (final testimony of faith): A formulaic prayer of supplication which includes a Muslim's statement of faith, and which is uttered at the conclusion of the ritual prayer from a seated position. One version of the testimony is as follows: "Greetings to God, prayers, and good things! May peace be upon you, O Prophet, and God's mercy and blessings. May peace be upon us, and upon God's righteous servants. I bear witness that there is no god but God alone, who has no partner, and I bear witness that Muḥammad is God's Servant and Messenger" (*al-taḥiyyāt lillāh wal-ṣalawāt wal-ṭayyibāt. Al-salāmu 'alayka ayyuhā al-nabī wa raḥmat Allāhi wa barakātuhu. Al-salāmu 'alaynā wa 'alā 'ibād Allāhi al-ṣāliḥīn. Ashhadu an lā ilāha illā Allāh, wa ashhadu anna Muḥammadan 'abduhu wa rasūluhu.*) (This is the version received through 'Abdullah Ibn Mas'ūd.) The testimony is generally, though not always, concluded with a prayer for blessings upon the Prophet referred to as *al-ṣalāt al-ibrāhīmiyah.*

Tasmiyah: Utterance of the words *bismillāh al-raḥmān al-raḥīm* (hence, it is the equivalent of the *basmalah*).

Ṭawāf: The act of circumambulating the Ka'bah.

Tayammum (sand ablutions): The act of wiping one's face, hands and arms in a prescribed manner in place of regular ritual ablutions when no water is available or when, for one reason or another, one is unable to use water.

Al-Thanā' (prayer of praise): See *du'ā' al-iftitāḥ.*

Al-Ṭuma'nīnah: The act of pausing and allowing one's limbs to remain still momentarily between the performance of the various actions involved in prayer. *Al-ṭuma'nīnah* is defined by the Hanafis as "a quieting of the limbs until the joints are relaxed and each part of the body 'settles' into position."

'Two pitchers full': See *qullatān.*

Uḍḥiyah: An animal slaughtered on the Day of Sacrifice (10 Dhū al-Ḥijjah).

'Umrah: The lesser rite of pilgrimage to Mecca.

'Ushriyah: A term used to refer to land owned by Muslims or land whose inhabitants have become Muslims, and on whose produce a tithe (*'ushr*) is to be paid.

Wadi: A white, viscous substance secreted by a man following urination.

Wājib ('duty'): A term used by the Hanafi school to refer to an act that is more binding than a Sunnah-based practice and less binding than a full obligation (*farḍ*). Hence, they hold that omitting a 'duty', although it does not subject us to punishment in the afterlife as would the neglect of a full obligation, nevertheless deprives us of the intercession of the Prophet.

Wars: A plant grown in Yemen that yields a yellow dye.

Wasq: A camel load. One *wasq* equals a volume of 165 liters.

Waybah: A measure equaling five and one-half *ṣā's*, which comes to somewhere between 15 and 18 liters.

Witr: A voluntary prayer consisting of an odd number of *rak'ahs*, with a minimum of one *rak'ah* (through three is preferable) and a maximum of eleven. It is preferred that one utter the concluding greeting of peace after each pair of *rak'ahs*, as well as after the final *rak'ah*. The time for the *witr* is between the evening prayer and daybreak.

Wrapper (*lifāfah*): A large robe used to wrap the dead which is tied below the feet and over the head, and which encloses the *izār* and the tunic.

Wuḍū': Minor ritual ablutions, which consist of stating one's intention, then washing the hands, rinsing out the mouth and nose, then rinsing one's face and the arms up to the elbows, passing a wet hand over the top of the head, back over the neck and ears, and rinsing the feet. Each school prescribes a particular manner in which *wuḍū'* is to be performed.

Zawiyah: A center devoted to spiritual retreats, worship, *dhikr*, etc.

Ẓihār: "Injurious assimilation", i.e., a man's declaring his wife to be forbidden to him sexually based on his likening her to his mother or to one of his non-marriageable female relatives.

Al-ẓuhr: The noon prayer, and the second of the five obligatory daily prayers.

* * *

* Sources from which definitions have been taken include, in addition to the text of the present work, *Al-Mawsū'ah al-'Arabiyah al-'Ālamiyah* (Mu'assasat A'māl al-Mawsū'ah lil-Nashr wal-Tawzī', Riyadh, 1996), Muḥammad Rawwās al-Qal'aji, *Mu'jam Lughat al-Fuqahā' (Dictionary of Islamic Legal Terminology), Arabic-English-French* (Beirut: Dar An-Nafaés, 1996), Ashraf Ṭaha Abū al-Dhahab, *al-Mu'jam al-Islāmī: al-Jawānib al-Dīniyah wal-Siyāsiyah wal-Iqtiṣādiyah* (Cairo: Dār al-Shurūq, 2002), and Deeb al-Khudrawi, *A Dictionary of Islamic Terms* (Damascus; Beirut: Al-Yamamah Press, 1995).

Biographies of Translator and Contributors

Nancy Roberts, a native of Wichita, Kansas, has translated works in the areas of modern Arabic literature, current events, Islamic law, Islamic thought and history, and Muslim-Christian relations. Previous translations include *The Subtle Blessings in the Saintly Lives of Abū al-'Abbās al-Mursī and his Master, Abū al-Ḥasan, by Ibn 'Ata' Allah al-Iskandari* (Louisville, KY: Fons Vitae, 2005), *Imam al-Shatibi's Theory of the Higher Objectives and Intents of Islamic Law* by Ahmad al-Raysuni (London and Washington: The International Institute of International Thought, 2005), *There Shall Be No Compulsion in Matters of Faith: The Islamic View of Apostasy and Apostates From the Dawn of Islam to the Present Day* by Dr. Taha Jabir al-'Alwani (London: The International Institute of Islamic Thought, forthcoming), *The Mirage* by Naghib Mahfouz (Cairo: The American University in Cairo Press, forthcoming), and *The Man from Bashmour* by Salwa Bakr (Cairo: AUC Press, 2007), for which she won a commendation by the panel of judges for the 2008 Saif Ghobash-Banipal Prize for Arabic Literary Translation. She has also published a number of articles on Muslim-Christian relations. Nancy lives with her husband and two daughters, Batoul and Salaam, in Amman, Jordan.

Sherman A. Jackson is presently Arthur F. Thurnau professor of Arabic and Islamic Studies, Visiting Professor of Law and Professor of Afro-American Studies at the University of Michigan. He is author of *Islamic Law and the State: The Constitutional Jurisprudence of Shihāb al-Dīn al-Qarāfī* (Brill, 1996), *On the Boundaries of Theological Tolerance in Islam: Abū Hāmid al-Ghazālī's Faysal al-Tafriqa* (Oxford, 2002), *Islam and the Blackamerican: Looking Towards the Third Resurrection* (Oxford, 2005) and *Islam and the Problem of Black Suffering* (Oxford, 2009). He has also authored numerous articles on various aspects of Islamic law, theology, history and Islam and Muslims in modern America.

Frank E. Vogel is an independent scholar and consultant on Islamic law and the laws and legal systems of the Muslim world. He taught Islamic law at Harvard Law School from 1987 to 2006, retiring in 2007. He held the Custodian of the Two Holy Mosques Chair for Islamic Legal Studies from 1993 to 2007, and founded the School's Islamic Legal Studies Program, serving as its Director from 1991 to 2006. Major publications include *Islamic Law and Legal System: Studies of Saudi Arabia* (a study of past and present applications of Islamic law through case-studies of Saudi Arabia); *Islamic Law and Finance: Religion, Risk, and Return* (with Prof. Samuel Hayes of the Harvard Business School) (an analysis of Islamic finance law and practice as an application of Islamic law); and the 150-page entry "The Contract Law of Islam and of the Arab Middle East," in *The International Encyclopedia of Comparative Law*. He has offered courses of varying lengths on Islamic law and legal systems, contemporary Islamic legal thought, Islamic contract and commercial law, Islam and human rights, comparative adjudication, Islamic constitutional history, and US contract law. He conducted research in Saudi Arabia for five years and in Egypt for one year, and has traveled and lectured widely throughout the Muslim world. His education was at Harvard College (AB 1972), Washington College of Law at American University (JD magna cum laude 1975), and Harvard University (PhD in Law and Middle Eastern Studies 1993).